W9-BCV-852

THE ENLIGHTENMENT AND ENGLISH LITERATURE

THE ENLIGHTENMENT AND ENGLISH LITERATURE

Prose and Poetry of the Eighteenth Century

With Selected Modern Critical Essays

Edited, with introductions and notes by

JOHN L. MAHONEY

Boston College

D. C. HEATH AND COMPANY

Lexington, Massachusetts Toronto

Published simultaneously in Canada.

Printed in the United States of America.

International Standard Book Number: 0-669-02321-3

Library of Congress Catalog Card Number: 79-84250

This book is dedicated to

JOHN L. MAHONEY SR. AND WILLIAM J. DOWD,

humble men whose lives were their greatest achievements.

Preface

The Enlightenment and English Literature, like its companion volume *The English Romantics,* is an introductory collection that focuses on the principal figures of a major era in the history of English literature and offers generous selections that are, as often as possible, complete works. At the same time it includes editorial apparatus that supplies the necessary historical and philosophical background for understanding the writers and illuminates, wherever possible, special textual problems. Some relatively minor but nevertheless important poets and prose writers are also included; no attempt, however, has been made to be comprehensive. The eighteenth-century writers represented have given strength and grace to a great epoch in English literary history and also have a continuing vitality for twentieth-century readers, since many of the ideas that dominate our own age originated then.

The format of this volume is like that of *The English Romantics.* A general introduction describes the spirit of the age and its literature, while special essays focus on major figures like Pope, Swift, Burke, and Johnson. Short essays, which provide an overview of the poetry and critical prose, precede the selections from the minor poets and prose writers. All of the introductions include a listing of and commentary on the most important secondary source material. The final section of the book contains some of the best modern critical essays on the period and its writers. It is the editor's hope that these essays, which present varying points of view, will stimulate further reflections on the literature and trigger fruitful classroom discussion and critical writing. They are reprinted in order to aid both students and teachers in securing hard-to-find materials in libraries and to spare them the expense of obtaining companion volumes of secondary sources.

I have sought to provide the best texts available, intruding only to modernize spelling and punctuation when it seemed necessary in order to assist students in their reading. Unless otherwise indicated, the publication date (or dates) of each text is printed below the particular text. I have quite deliberately kept editorial machinery to a minimum, injecting comment and explanation only when it seemed absolutely necessary. In this regard, I cannot help but offer thanks to the many editors of these materials, who have preceded me. They have obviously influenced me greatly, and if I cannot praise them individually, it is only because their influence has by this time become so much a part of my thinking that it is difficult to sort out the different strands.

The chronology of this book was a calculated decision. In the past, most anthologies have used 1660 and perhaps Dryden as the point of departure, ending with a late-century figure like Blake. These anthologies, while providing an abundance of material, contained too many writers and too many short excerpts. What has been most sadly lacking is a truly clear vision of the uniqueness of eighteenth-century England and its distinctive literary achievement. Surely the Restoration period deserves its own book, while the inclusion of any extensive samples from a figure like Blake is clearly within the province of Romanticism.

A final word of clarification. Any editor of an anthology like this one must face the problem of how many major genres to present and must recognize that there are simply no easy answers to the difficult question: What do I include, excerpt, omit? After considerable thought and consultation with respected and valued colleagues in the field, I decided to exclude the novel and the drama in order to keep the book to a reasonable length: the spectacle of a 2,000-page volume would weary me and certainly trouble my publisher. Moreover, fiction of the era like *Gulliver's Travels, Pamela, Tom Jones* and the more famous drama are easily available in inexpensive paperback editions. At the same time, however, I have not always been completely resolute and have included the complete *Rasselas* of Samuel Johnson and fairly strategic selections from great prose monuments like Boswell's *Life of Johnson* and Swift's *A Tale of A Tub,* hoping to whet the appetite of the beginning reader for a more intensive study of these works.

J. L. M.

Acknowledgments

I am grateful for the advice and practical assistance of many colleagues and friends who are teachers, students, or simply lovers of the art of the age. As I prepared the materials and wrote the introductions, I felt the continuing presence of the late Edward Hirsh of Boston College, my first teacher of eighteenth-century English literature, whose remarkable feeling for the period first drew me to Pope, Swift, and Johnson. My other and continuing debt is to W. J. Bate of Harvard University, inspiration of my graduate and post-graduate years, who generously advised me about special difficulties that I brought to him in the preparation of this volume.

Special thanks are due Maurice Quinlan, William Youngren, Daniel McCue, Richard Hughes, and John Fitzgerald of Boston College; David Anderson of the College of St. Olaf and Ronald Wendeln of Dyke College; Stephen Fix of Williams College; James Engell of Harvard University; and Bonnie Stevens of the College of Wooster. Ellen Castle, Patricia Mahoney, John L. Mahoney, III, and William D. Mahoney provided special help in the preparation of the manuscript. Alice Bourneuf, Teddi King, and Irene Kral provided inspiration.

I am grateful for the continuing help provided by Boston College administrators, specifically Rev. Charles F. Donovan, S.J., Dean of Faculties; Donald J. White, Dean of the Graduate School and Associate Dean of Faculties; Rev. Thomas P. O'Malley, S.J., Dean of the College of Arts and Sciences; and Professor Robert E. Reiter, Chairman of the Department of English. All of them took time to encourage and support my scholarship and teaching.

For their many courtesies and services I once again offer thanks to the staffs of the Boston College Library, Tufts University Library, and the Cary Memorial Library of Lexington.

And again, I must pay tribute to my extraordinary editor, Holt Johnson of D. C. Heath and Company, a flawless guide, a firm but supportive co-worker in this entire enterprise, and above all, a humanist *par excellence*. Unlike Bartelby, he always preferred to be of service.

My wife Ann, who has the rare gift of knowing when and when not to take me seriously, is, of course, my greatest source of strength. She is Wordsworth's "perfect woman nobly planned / To warn, to comfort, and command."

Contents

Jonathan Swift

Samuel Johnson • James Boswell

Edmund Burke

A Selection of Key Eighteenth-Century Minor Poetry

A Selection of Critical and Philosophical Prose

Selected Modern Critical Essays

THE ENLIGHTENMENT AND ENGLISH LITERATURE

General Introduction

Whether one argues over a proper descriptive terminology for the age—"Enlightenment," "Neoclassic," "Augustan," or simply "Eighteenth-Century England"—or calls it, as some have, "an age of prose and reason," or as others have, "the nearest approach to earthly felicity ever known to man"—the literature of eighteenth-century England remains, like the age that produced it, one of enormous strength, originality, and variety, a body of writing that in so many ways serves to usher in the modern world through its attitudes, themes, genres, and techniques. An age that produced the flawless poetry of Pope, the ringing and prophetic satire of Swift, the wonderfully insightful moral and literary criticism of Johnson would be notable enough to command the attention of the student of literature. When that same age offers the reader the urbane and lucid periodical essays of Addison and Steele, the stately prose of Burke and Gibbon, the grand biographical ventures of a Boswell, the stunning poetic achievements of writers as different as Gray, Goldsmith, Thomson, and Cowper, and an explosion of varied forms of the novel in Richardson, Fielding, and Sterne, the reader, like Coleridge's Wedding Guest, "cannot choose but hear."

Yet the age and its artistic accomplishments have not of late, perhaps for reasons peculiar to our own culture and to our own time, held the fascination for students that the Renaissance, the Romantic, or even the Modern period seem to command. No period has been more susceptible to stereotyping or labeling—the "Age of Reason" comes to mind most immediately. Because the Enlightenment follows an age dominated by figures like Spenser, Shakespeare, the Metaphysical poets, and Milton, there is the attitude that it represents a major falling-off in literary achievement. High art, some feel, precludes an undue concern with philosophy, critical theory, satire of all kinds, and the literature of the mundane. How often one hears the Enlightenment described as the calm, measured, elegant, but ultimately unexciting era that must be dealt with before the rich Romantic rewards of Blake, Wordsworth, Coleridge, and Keats are savored.

Engaging in analyses of these responses or, even worse, claiming for eighteenth-century writers accomplishments like those of a Shakespeare, Milton, or Wordsworth would, of course, be the height of critical folly. It is always well to remember Dryden's brilliant reminder that the genius of every age is different and that the beginning of a wise and illuminating criticism is not a process of playing off one writer against another, but rather of accepting and trying to understand the spirit of a different era with its dominant ideals and trends, of allowing writers with different purposes and techniques to speak for themselves and, in so doing, to find ways of coming to terms with their special achievements. Or if Dryden's injunction will not do, there may be merit in the present editor's strong sense that one kind of artistic excellence, of a particular time and place, should not unduly prejudice or intimidate; that art, like life itself, is an unfolding process with inexhaustible possibilities; and that in these possibilities are continuing sources of pleasure and wisdom.

Needless to say, this editor begins with certain prejudices (he would like to call them enthusiasms) of his own—a great admiration for a remarkable group of writers of wide-ranging genius; his sense that, for all the challenges that can be brought against it, "Enlightenment" is a useful way to describe the spirit of the eighteenth century and its major writers. There is also his confidence that it is possible, indeed necessary, to reckon with a certain unity that underlies the variety of the literature and a certain basic direction in the ideas and ideals of the age. It is his strong hope that these prejudices will as often as possible illuminate rather than darken the great works represented in this anthology.

THE SETTING AND BACKGROUNDS

Modern readers are understandably inclined to marvel at the pace of change that has characterized our own age: the remarkable developments in every area of human endeavor, from space exploration to scientific phenomena to the media; the upheavals and innovations in religion, politics, philosophy, the arts, manners and morals that they have witnessed in a single lifetime. Often underlying this wonderment is a sense that the further civilization progresses, the more rapid and penetrating the degree of change. Yet who can study seventeenth-century England, from almost any cultural standpoint, and not be aware of the turbulence of those years, which, on the one hand, saw new earthly and celestial worlds coming into view and, on the other, witnessed the splintering of the monarchy and Parliament, the killing of King Charles I, Civil War from 1642 until 1649, the shattering of the Established Church, and remarkable developments like the Baroque and the Metaphysical in the arts. Still, these phenomena were only a beginning. As the century progresses, there is the Restoration of Charles II, with its promise of a new stability, and yet its failure to reconcile conflicting political and religious principles and interests—principles and interests that ultimately triggered the Glorious Revolution of 1688, in which Parliament demonstrated its prerogatives and power by removing the Roman Catholic James II and crowning his Dutch son-in-law, William of Orange, as new monarch. The famous Revolution Settlement, with its religious tests, the collaboration of Whigs and Tories, the development of a cabinet system of government, the emergence of wealthy and powerful families with interests to be served, the Stock Market boom of 1714 with the collapse in 1720—these and other events suggest years of tremendous vitality as well as older political and religious ideals that were to give way to new and drastically different ones.

Is it any wonder that as early as the Restoration of 1660, but especially after the Revolution of 1688, concerned Englishmen yearned for a new beginning after the chaos of decades, that they sought freedom from fanaticism of all kinds, from the superstitions of religion to the dangerously abstract theorizing of philosophy, and that they vigorously tried to work out a more common-sense, reality-oriented approach to life than the plain speaking and emotionalism of the previous years had provided? What they sought was Enlightenment in all phases of human endeavor, from political reform, to religious worship, to the social milieu, and, especially for our purposes, to the arts. The reestablishment of the Church of England was, of course, an event of major importance, but many others rivalled its impact. The Royal Society had been founded in 1662, and, in reading Thomas Sprat's celebrated history of that organization, one can understand vividly its quest for a scientific, rationalistic approach to life, as it turned away from Christian Revelation and Aristotelian deduction. Unlike the Puritans, who regarded philosophy as an illegitimate science and the Bible as the source of individual illumination, the new intellectuals scorned speculation about the supernatural, which for them could bring only more civil war and social disorder.

The roots of this new scientific rationalism run deep; Bacon is perhaps the early and great harbinger. A religious man, to be sure, his words in the preface to his *Great Instauration* of 1620 clearly suggest the dawning of a new era and a new spirit: "That the state of knowledge is not prosperous nor greatly advancing: and that a way must be opened for the understanding entirely different from any hitherto known, and other helps provided, in order that the mind may exercise over the nature of things the authority which properly belongs to it." So do the personal prayers of this great promulgator of the need for the advancement of learning: "This likewise I humbly pray, that things human may not interfere with things divine, and that from the opening of the ways of sense and the increase of natural light there may arise in our minds no incredulity or darkness with regard to the divine mysteries; but rather that the understanding being thereby purified and purged of fancies and vanity, and yet not the less subject and entirely submissive to the divine oracles, may give to faith what is faith's." In these sentiments one finds not so much a militant antagonism toward faith and the supernatural but rather a polite and earnest attempt to reconcile them with reason or to relegate them to a special realm of experience beyond scientific observation. And, certainly, in France there is the force of Descartes' influential thinking as he approaches the whole question of the relationship of mind and matter and advances his revolutionary epistemology. Marveling at the diversity of nature in his *Discours de la méthode* of 1637, he "... believed it to be impossible for the human mind to distinguish the forms or species of bodies that are upon the earth, from an infinity of others which might have been, if it had pleased God to place them there, or consequently to apply them to our use, unless we rise to causes through their effects, and avail ourselves of many particular experiments."

Newtonian physics provided not so much a poetic view of the universe as a mathematically ordered vision where everything has its proper place and explanation and from which human beings may draw sustenance, confidence, even exhilaration. The call for Enlightenment, however, as well as the philosophy that was to define and support it, came from two noted English empirical philosophers, Thomas Hobbes and John Locke. Their political views—more importantly, their psychological theories—provided the basis for a new rationalism that was rooted in the experience of human beings and was free from the vagaries of poetic fancy. In Hobbes' sternly materialistic and enormously influential *Leviathan* of 1651, but even more so in Locke's thoroughly empirical *An Essay Concerning Human Understanding* of 1690, one finds an almost manifesto-like spirit that would liberate the mind from vain imaginings, keep it open to human action, and build knowledge on the bedrock of human experience. For Locke, knowledge is not the product of innate ideas or imaginative ingenuity, but of sensation and reflection, both mechanical processes rooted in the real world of everyday experience. As he puts it, "The senses at first let in *particular* ideas, and furnish the yet empty cabinet, and the mind by degrees growing familiar with some of them, they are lodged in the memory, and names got to them. Afterwards, the mind proceeding further, abstracts them, and by degrees learns the use of general names. In this manner the mind comes to be furnished with ideas and language, the *materials* about which to exercise its discursive faculty. And the use of reason becomes daily more visible, as these materials that give it employment increase." There is indeed nothing in the mind that was not first in the senses. Clear and distinct ideas, with the brightness of the sun as their controlling symbol, are the goal of the human mind.

Indeed, in these two great ideals—nature as the created order of the universe, with human nature as the microcosm seen in the light of its great laws, and reason as a common-sense secular approach to knowledge—the eighteenth century found its credo. A sublime trust in the critical examination of all phenomena; a reverence for the achievement of the Ancients of Greece and Rome, and a desire to imitate their example rather than to venture forth on the dangerous seas of originality and individualism; a desire to build a stable commonwealth rooted in a reasonable balance of varied interests; a concern for social reform of all kinds—these became great goals of an age that hoped it had seen the end of revolution and looked to a new Peace of Augustus. While France offered the greatest example of the new Enlightenment spirit and, as Peter Gay has argued, gave the age its dominant intellectual type in the philosophe, "a man of and in the world, a lucid and persuasive writer, and an adept in the new sciences," England had its unique counterpart, less secular to be sure, clearly among Roman Catholic writers like Pope and Protestant writers like Johnson, who also "... ridiculed superstition, deplored fanaticism, extolled humanitarianism, admired science. The philosophes, in other words, were in no way alienated from their culture; they shared many of its presuppositions and enjoyed the unwilling and unwitting support of many respectable people. That is why the name Enlightenment stands ultimately for something broader than a great movement. It is appropriately the name for an age."

In spite of the failure of Charles II to fulfill the dream of a new Caesar Augustus, in spite of the turmoil created by the 1688 revolution, the dissatisfaction with the Revolution Settlement, and the undistinguished rule of the Georges, there was, at least on the surface, a sense of calm among the upper classes as well as a sense of a reasonable and practical approach to the business of society. The years of the late seventeenth and early eighteenth century were a period of great growth. The population of London increased from 500,000 to 900,000 in roughly one hundred years, and with this growth came an expanding economy, a burgeoning group of businessmen who represented a special class with special interests, new developments in agriculture, the enclosure of common lands, and the expansion of technology. In a word, the Industrial Revolution was a reality. Meanwhile a great colonial empire existed overseas in America, Canada, India, and Australia. England developed into a great conservative power. The cabinet system of government that had matured under William grew stronger under Anne and the Georges, especially under Walpole's long reign as Prime Minister from 1721–1742. Granted the many problems that lay beneath the surface—the gulf between rich and poor, learned and ignorant, so brilliantly sketched in the paintings of William Hogarth, and the corruption associated with Walpole's heavy-handed use of patronage in the administration of the court system—there was the sense of a new beginning, in which reason and order would ultimately prevail—the sense, as A. R. Humphreys puts it, that even problems and weaknesses existed "... within a general acceptance of the rule of law and the autonomy of judges."

Again one notes that the Enlightenment in England, while different from more stridently mechanistic and antireligious manifestations in Europe, did offer a rationalistic paradigm of the world and of man in the world. It was this world, rather than any supernatural realm, that commanded the attention of intelligent men. It was the city, with its full range of human activity, where man might most fully flourish, not the wild countryside. The order of the natural world, created by a benevolent, if somewhat remote, Deity and best understood when emotion and imagination were guided by calm reason, was the great source of wisdom and happiness. While the English may not have had their philosophes, they clearly had their intellectual elite, often found developing a consensus of ideas and ideals in the great gathering places like Will's Coffee House, Button's, or the Turk's Head, or in the legendary clubs of Scriblerus or Johnson. These clubs conveyed the image of eminently intelligent and civilized men, freed from cant and bolstered by the wisdom of the classical forefathers and their modern counterparts. The opinion of the group became more and more a standard of belief and action.

THE ENLIGHTENMENT AND ITS LITERARY IDEALS

The impact of this spirit of Enlightenment in literature and literary theory was enormous, and while students should quite properly resist the image of a monolithic age, certain dominant trends do stand out sharply, especially in the major writers. In criticism the impact of a rigid Neoclassic theory, long popular in Italy and France, was strong—a theory that was prevalent in the works of Ben Johnson and Sidney and was only gradually relaxed in those of Dryden and Pope. The spirit of a certain common-sense rationalism, of reverence for models; the didactic emphasis that blurred the distinction between poetry and rhetoric; the great concern with a very narrow norm of probability; the wariness of the workings of imagination—these and many other guidelines emerged. They represent a most constricting literary theory and can be seen in documents like Sir William Davenant's preface to *Gondibert*, Hobbes' preface to his translation of the *Odyssey*, Thomas Rymer's *Short View of Tragedy*, and in influential French works like Boileau's *Art of Poetry* and Corneille's *Examens* and *Discours*.

The supreme achievement of major eighteenth-century writers like Pope, Swift, and Johnson was their ability to retain the essence of the classical tradition, with its emphasis on the uses of literature, on form, on clarity of language, and yet to bring to these ideals a flexibility and grace that were to mark them as true models of Augustan writing. Yet no amount of rationalization can make of these writers what they are not—writers who transcend their age, pre-Romantics, or what you will. They illustrate—and many others in our anthology do to a greater degree—the amazing versatility and vitality of poets and prose writers who, while revealing certain common ideals, nevertheless bring their unique responses, interests, and techniques to the expression of these ideals. A. R. Humphreys is a perceptive observer as he writes: "Indeed, the essence of Augustan literature is that it is integrated with social life, and treats, in their natural idiom, the interests of men in society. In so far as the idiom is modified by some other fashion—for classical or Miltonic diction, for Spenserian or Shakespearian imitation—and in so far as its substance is not the interested acknowledgement of social life, it is the less Augustan."

Eighteenth-century English literature is indeed a literature of the human situation, one which seeks not the spontaneous expression of individual feeling, but rather the clear and elegant expression of general and representative truth, of the order revealed in the operations of the universe and the affairs of humankind. It seeks to measure the individual example, the local idiosyncracy, against a higher standard and to criticize or satirize or praise accordingly. Humphreys sees it as "... the utterance of intelligent men concerned to make the most of human nature, and facing always new problems which compel continual evolution of idea." Pope's "True Wit is Nature to advantage dress'd, / What oft was thought, but ne'er so well express'd" is a terse and vivid expression of this artistic goal.

One effect of this literary ideal is the dominance of certain genres; one might describe them as those which are, to a great extent, closely tied to the real situation of human beings. There is, of course, the dominance of prose. In the periodical essay of Addison and Steele, *The Rambler* of Johnson, the "Citizen of the

World" essays of Goldsmith, one finds the sensible, urbane expression of ideas that touch not man's supernatural longings, but his real-life delights, struggles, and hopes. In the notable biographies—Boswell's *Life of Johnson,* Johnson's *Lives of the Poets*—or the major political and philosophical writings—Burke's *Reflections on the Revolution in France,* Gibbon's *Decline and Fall of the Roman Empire*—there is emphasis on the individual life and the example it holds for readers or on the sources and implications of the great political events in which nations and men find themselves involved. In the satire—Pope's *Rape of the Lock* and *The Dunciad;* Swift's *Gulliver's Travels* and *The Tale of a Tub;* Mandeville's *The Fable of the Bees;* Johnson's *The Vanity of Human Wishes*—there is witty or biting exposure of man's inhumanity to man, of the perversion of human intelligence, of the vanity of earthly striving. In the glorious emergence of the novel—Defoe's *Robinson Crusoe,* Richardson's *Pamela,* Fielding's *Tom Jones*—the emphasis is on the real, on the social, on characters as they behave comically or tragically in believable human predicaments.

The poetry vividly captures the spirit of the age; at its best that poetry frequently seems to have a quite overt purpose, seems eager to provide a sense of the real, to utilize all the resources of language to convey its analysis of life and character. Witness the restraint in the use of verse forms in the major poets, with the iambic pentameter couplet by far the most dominant. With its ability to shape clearly and sharply a single observation or a specific step in an argument, its facility in providing a sense of continuity by its process of pairing, its smoothness of movement uninterrupted by long stanzaic pauses, it seemed the perfect vehicle of expression. Witness also the strong emphasis on the sacredness of the word, on a rich, denotative diction that would articulate ideas gracefully and with a minimum of ambiguity, on the predominance of the simile, with its greater control of the points of comparison, in contrast to the complexity of the metaphor, with its tendency to confuse or upset the mind in search of truth. It was truly a more rhetorical poetry that sought to provide for its readers a vivid awareness of what was implanted in the mind. As Edward Hirsh has stated, the best eighteenth-century poetry tends to move toward the evolution of a general conclusion, using as its basis the actual, the life of the world around us. It sees the poet keenly aware of an audience and of his work as a kind of social record; further, it sees certain areas of agreement between poet and audience that it would exploit. Its goal is not amazement, or "sudden wonder" as Johnson describes it, but tranquillity, not the enlargement, but the fuller recognition and understanding of experience. Clearly great poems like Pope's *Essay on Criticism* and *The Rape of the Lock,* Gray's *Elegy Written in a Country Churchyard,* Goldsmith's *The Deserted Village,* Johnson's *The Vanity of Human Wishes* are stunning cases in point.

Pope's brilliant rehearsal of the Neoclassic ideal is carried forward with a power of language and a sense of rhythm that seem in perfect balance:

> First follow Nature, and your judgment frame
> By her just standard, which is still the same:
> Unerring Nature, still divinely bright,
> One clear, unchang'd, and universal light,

Life, force, and beauty, must to all impart,
At once the source, and end, and test of Art.

His remarkable insight into the foibles of proud human beings in his portrait of Belinda in *The Rape of the Lock* is enhanced by the superb mock-heroic effect with its subtle deflation of the heroine, its perfect choice of language and image, its strategic use of rhyme:

And now, unveil'd the Toilet stands display'd,
Each Silver Vase in mystic Order laid.
First, rob'd in White, the Nymph intent adores,
With Head uncover'd, the Cosmetic Pow'rs.
A heaven'ly image in the Glass appears,
To that she bends, to that her eyes she rears;
Th' inferior Priestess, at her Altar's side,
Trembling begins the sacred rites of Pride.
Unnumber'd Treasures ope at once, and here
The various Off'rings of the World appear;
From each she nicely culls with curious Toil,
And decks the Goddess with the glitt'ring Spoil.

. . .

Here Files of Pins extend their shining Rows,
Puffs, Powders, Patches, Bibles, Billet-doux.
Now awful Beauty puts on all its Arms;
The Fair each moment rises in her Charms,
Repairs her Smiles, awakens ev'ry Grace,
And calls forth all the Wonders of her Face;
Sees by Degrees a purer Blush arise,
And keener Lightnings quicken in her eyes.

Johnson's memorable reflections on the limitations of human hope, the capacity for self-deception in all of us, are enhanced by the public voice, keenly aware of instructing his audience. They are elevated by the almost perfect intermingling of sound and sense in the organ tones of *The Vanity of Human Wishes:*

Let observation with extensive view,
Survey mankind, from China to Peru;
Remark each anxious toil, each eager strife,
And watch the busy scenes of crowded life;
Then say how hope and fear, desire and hate,
O'erspread with snares the clouded maze of fate,
Where wav'ring man, betray'd by vent'rous pride,
To tread the dreary paths without a guide,
As treach'rous phantoms in the mist delude,
Shuns fancied ills, or chases airy good;
How rarely reason guides the stubborn choice,
Rules the bold hand, or prompts the suppliant voice.

INNOVATION AND NEW DEVELOPMENTS IN THE ENLIGHTENMENT

As has already been suggested, the Enlightenment was never an era of complete harmony. Great minds in any age, however committed they may be to certain common beliefs, must be themselves and must criticize the prevailing spirit where it is found incomplete or wanting or must modify prevailing ideas and forms of expression to cater to the needs and demands of their special genius. This tendency is nowhere more obvious than in the political arena, even in the early eighteenth century, where major figures like Pope and Swift were strongly critical of the costs involved in Walpole's authoritarianism and his widespread use of patronage to achieve political stability. Who can forget the stinging irony of Swift's *Modest Proposal* and its savage indictment of the exploitation of the Irish people for the furtherance of English and Irish ambition alike? Similarly, there is the scathing criticism of the gradual erosion of the Church of England's power and perquisites, the perversion of true religion in general in Swift's *Argument Against Abolishing Christianity, The Tale of a Tub,* and *Gulliver's Travels.* The misdirection of human intelligence, the silly practices of education, the abuses of pedantry are brilliantly satirized in works like Pope's *Dunciad* and Swift's *The Battle of the Books.*

Later in the century figures like Burke and Johnson were equally critical. Both staunchly conservative and loyal to the constancy and dignity of the monarchy, they yearned for the stability and sense of tradition that they felt was slipping away due to the increasing power of the Whigs, the further concentration of power in families of great wealth, the dangerous alliances of Whigs and wealthy merchants, the new and growing individualism that saw the loss of America, the revolution in France and its implications for England, and the inertia at home under the Georges. The optimism of the age, so notably seen in its confidence in science and in the new rationalism and so strikingly expressed in Pope's *Essay on Man,* is matched by the stark picture of man's degeneration in Book IV of *Gulliver's Travels,* in the tragic portraits of great figures like Wolsey and Charles XII of Sweden in Johnson's moving poem *The Vanity of Human Wishes,* and in his superb and remarkably modern analysis of the hunger of imagination and the treachery of the human heart in his *Rambler* papers. In short, one sees dramatic evidence of human greed and ambition, of intellectual pride, of a full range of human folly in the new so-called Peace of Augustus. Yet what persists is a massive commitment to the dignity of human nature, defined in its uniquely human circumstances—a faith in an accumulated wisdom rooted in real experience and ultimately seen as civilization itself, a commitment that stands strongly against the growing violence, greed, and stupidity of the times.

The variety of the age and its many new approaches to issues and problems within an overall set of governing principles is graphically seen in the literature. While there will be occasion to discuss individual writers in more detail in the separate sections of this anthology, some brief observations seem appropriate at this point. As the eighteenth century progresses, one senses in much of the literature a growing emotion and spiritual intensity. There is an awareness and revelation of the power of feeling and imagination in the individual human being, a more immediate and stronger response to the concrete beauties of external nature, now seen less as an abstraction than as the rich panorama of sea, sky, mountain, and forest that can exert a moral force on those who are dedicated to those beauties. These reverberations are all the more fascinating for the sensitive reader and more frustrating for the simplistic student who would regard them immediately as Romantic, for they often are present in the prevailing genres, forms, and modes of expression of the day. Ironically, Locke's philosophy, which had been a foundation stone for so much eighteenth-century rationalism, began to stir among poets and critics, almost through its warnings, an interest in the creative and associative powers of the mind. The concept of imagination is thus ever so gradually widened. Joseph Addison's remarkable papers on "The Pleasures of the Imagination" in *The Spectator* are stunning examples of Locke's influence. Likewise Anthony Ashley Cooper, the Third Earl of Shaftesbury, and a kind of English Rousseau, became the apostle of a new gospel of benevolence and philanthropy with his philosophy, expressed strongly in his *Characteristics*, of a God of feeling rather than of strict justice, a God whose benevolence becomes an attribute for his creatures to emulate. For Shaftesbury, reason in a narrow sense is no longer seen as man's most distinctive faculty; indeed, he argues strongly for a moral, intuitive sense that, if properly cultivated, can lead one to morality and beauty. Throughout his writing there is a shift toward the idea of the freedom and the individuality of man and the need to give expression to the full range of human faculties.

One interesting manifestation of freedom and innovation can be seen in the loco-descriptive, meditative blank verse poem. Without effecting a revolution in any way, this poetry clearly expanded the subject matter and techniques of the medium, offering a stronger and more spontaneous expression of the artist's emotions, a more relaxed, natural mode of writing, a concern with a more detailed examination of the natural world and its people and with the reader's response to such an examination. James Thomson's *The Seasons* is such a poem. It attempts to capture the epic Miltonic sound, expressing wonder at the beauties of nature in the changing seasons, and adds a strong dose of social and humanitarian comment, bringing new effects without rejecting the sense of control—the end-stopped line, the abstraction and allegory, the didacticism—that stand out in the poetry of the age. Joseph Warton's *The Enthusiast, or, The Lover of the Nature* reveals a certain restlessness with well-ordered landscape and a strong interest in the sublime, in rugged settings in nature that evoke intense emotions in the viewer. Thomas Warton's *The Pleasures of Melancholy,* Edward Young's *The Complaint, or Night Thoughts,* Robert Blair's *The Grave* dramatize a new sense of pleasure in isolation, in the eerie and remote outposts of nature free from the corruptions of civilization. The imagination gradually becomes unshackled from the restraints of reason and the limits of the couplet framework, and a new kind of descriptive ode is born, one which seeks a certain compression of thought and feeling within a new and venturesome, but still somewhat contained lyric form. Fine examples of this lyric form are Mark Akenside's *The Pleasures of Imagination,* William Collins' *Ode on the Poetical Character* and *Ode on the Popular*

Superstitions of the Scottish Highlands, and Thomas Gray's *The Bard: A Pindaric Ode.* Another phenomenon of the age, often loosely termed "antiquarianism" but actually much more complex than that, is the search for some authority, however remote, to justify new feelings and attitudes in poets and readers. Such a phenomenon can be found in many epochs and areas of the world. Bishop Thomas Percy sought it in his *Reliques of Ancient English Poetry* in the wonder and mystery of the Middle Ages. In his famous house at Strawberry Hill and in his popular novel *The Castle of Otranto,* Horace Walpole sought it in the Gothic. Thomas Gray admired the heroic, primitive qualities of Norse and Icelandic literature. James Macpherson, an overnight sensation in spite of his exposure as a literary fraud by Samuel Johnson, sought to capture an era of bravery and heroism in his *Ossian* poems set in the distant past in the Scottish Highlands. Robert Burns, in a sense anticipating Wordsworth, scorned the rules and produced a song-like poetry and a bellicose satire that captured the dialect and feelings of his native Scotland and brought to literature a remarkable compassion for the joys and sorrows of humble and rustic life. The lilting beauty of *A Red, Red Rose* or *John Anderson My Jo,* the powerful satire of *A Cotter's Saturday Night,* seem to move very close to the Romantic spirit. And, of course, the strong influence of Methodism in the latter part of the century, with its emphasis on feeling the presence of God and on personal witness and testimony, its concern with the struggle of the individual soul for supernatural grace, was to occasion great religious and autobiographical poems like *Olney Hymns* and *The Castaway* of William Cowper.

A brief word should be said about the kind of freshness and experimentation that characterizes the novel, as it moves from a strict, almost journalistic realism to the epistolary, autobiographical techniques of Richardson's *Pamela* to the lively and vital world of Fielding's *Tom Jones* to the self-conscious narrative innovations of Sterne's *Tristram Shandy.* These developments in fiction point up a shift from external to internal, from city to countryside, from the realistic detail of daily life to the rapturous beauties of nature. The novel develops remarkably indeed.

Even literary criticism, in spite of the awesome influence of an earlier Dryden and Pope and a later Johnson, reveals a variety of interests and approaches that caught the attention of both artists and general readers. It began to look beyond literature as a mimetic and pragmatic vehicle, beyond an elegant, functional, and denotative language and imagery, to explore new and added sources of aesthetic pleasure. As early as 1712 Addison's *Spectator* is praising the so-called secondary pleasures of imagination, those that come not simply from the mere viewing of reality, but from the activity of mind that compares the original in nature and its artistic imitation. As will be shown later, the impact of Addison on poets like Akenside was enormous. Edward Young's *Conjectures on Original Composition* deplores slavish imitation of ancient models and praises the kind of spontaneity that captures the spirit of a great genius rather than the letter of his book. Two influential and intriguing mid-century documents, Joseph Warton's *Essay on the Genius and Writings of Pope* and Thomas Warton's *Observations on Spenser's Faerie Queene,* seem to begin a trend of reexamining established poetic reputations—a trend that distinguishes between a poetry of polish and control and one of passion and intensity and in the process sets a higher value on Spenser and Shakespeare than on Pope and other contemporaries without doing any disservice to those modern writers. Burke's influential *Philosophical Enquiry Into the Origin Of Our Ideas Of the Sublime and Beautiful* sharply distinguishes the two psychological effects, and reserves higher praise for the sublime with its power to stir the soul, to gather its strength not from order and form, but from the dark, the rugged, the turbulent aspects of nature. Richard Hurd's *Letters on Chivalry and Romance* is a carefully reasoned, indeed Neoclassic, defense of the Gothic as a valid source of literary pleasure. Reynolds' *Discourses on Art,* delivered to the faculty and students of the Royal Academy, stands as a superb example in aesthetics and criticism of a marvelous eighteenth-century balance of tradition and originality.

A summary of the kind usually found in an introduction like this one is never completely fair to the large body of material represented nor to the reader looking for complexity and nuance. There is simply no substitute for confronting the literature itself, for reading, rereading, discussing, arguing—for continued savoring of the poetry and prose. The editor earnestly hopes an insight into that literature will be provided by the rich selections from major figures like Pope, Swift, Burke, and Johnson, accompanied by full general introductions, together with as generous a miscellany as possible of lesser figures. As suggested at the beginning of this introduction, he will be satisfied if the brilliance and variety of the Enlightenment in England is revealed in its intellectual strength and emotional warmth, and in its attempt to see life clearly and to develop a method for criticizing it. He will be pleased if the artistry of its writers and critics reveals an era whose principles were constantly tested with a lively flexibility and surrounded by a sparkling variety and experimentation. He will feel that his efforts have been amply justified if readers are drawn to a greater understanding of and delight in the wealth of poetry, satire, biography, criticism, moral and political philosophy produced by some of England's greatest writers.

Suggestions for Further Reading

There is such a wealth of material on the Enlightenment and eighteenth-century English literature that it is difficult to know where to begin. Perhaps all we can do is to point to some of the more famous and valuable general studies and to suggest ways in which they might be useful for the student who wants to move beyond primary texts and to develop special interests. The current paperback *Restoration and Eighteenth Century, 1660–1789,* with up-to-date bibliographies by Donald F. Bond, has been issued by Appleton-Century-Crofts as Part III of the respected *Literary History of England,* ed. Albert C. Baugh (1948). A most helpful bibliography of criticism, covering the period 1926–1960, is *English Literature 1660–1800, A Bibliography of Modern Studies Compiled for Philological Quarterly,* eds. Louis A. Landa, R. S. Crane, Louis I. Bredvold, et al. (1950–1962). This descriptive bibliography continues work done since 1960 in the annual July issue of *Philological Quarterly.* The annual bibliography of the *Publications of the Modern Language Association* of America is another important tool.

General Background Reading

Three volumes of the great *Oxford History of England* are strongly recommended: Sir George Clark, *The Later Stuarts 1660–1714* (1956); Basil Williams, *The Whig Supremacy 1714–1760*, revised by C. H. Stuart (1961); J. Steven Watson, *The Reign of George III 1760–1815* (1960). G. M. Trevelyan is, as always, most helpful for the student interested in historical backgrounds, and his *England Under the Stuarts* (1904), *England Under Queen Anne*, 3 vols. (1930–1934), and *English History* (1942), will be useful in studying this period. Also recommended are A. S. Turberville, *Johnson's England: An Account of the Life and Manners of His Age*, 2 vols. (1933), and *English Men and Manners in the Eighteenth Century* (1926), and J. H. Plumb, *The Growth of Political Stability in England 1675–1725* (1967).

Philosophical and Literary Backgrounds

Despite its date of publication (1876), students of the period still find Leslie Stephens *History of English Thought in the Eighteenth Century*, 2 vols., quite valuable for its treatment of intellectual history. Basil Willey, *The Eighteenth Century Background* (1940) is also helpful in this area of study as is Bonamy Dobrée, *English Literature in the Early Eighteenth Century 1700–1740* (1950), *part of the Oxford History of English Literature*. W. J. Bate, *From Classic to Romantic* (1946), and M. H. Abrams, *The Mirror and the Lamp* (1953), continue to be invaluable in setting the context and considering the major themes of the literature and criticism. Peter Gay, *The Enlightenment*, 2 vols. (1966–1969), is a magisterial study of the spirit of this great age.

More specialized studies of the prose and poetry are James Sutherland, *A Preface to Eighteenth-Century Poetry* (1948); Samuel Holt Monk, *The Sublime* (1935); Ian Jack, *Augustan Satire* (1952); Marjorie Hope Nicolson, *Newton Demands the Muse* (1946); Paul Fussell, *The Rhetorical World of Augustan Humanism* (1965); Earl Wasserman, *The Subtler Language* (1959); Ian Watt, *The Rise of the Novel* (1957); Ronald Paulson, *Satire and the Novel in Eighteenth-Century England* (1967); Patricia Spacks, *The Poetry of Vision* (1967); John Loftis, *Comedy and Society from Congreve to Fielding* (1959).

Two extremely helpful collections of modern essays on the period are James Clifford, ed., *Eighteenth-Century English Literature: Modern Essays in Criticism* (1959), and F. W. Hilles and Harold Bloom, eds., *From Sensibility to Romanticism* (1965).

Alexander Pope

1688–1744

If there be such a figure as the eighteenth-century English man-of-letters *par excellence,* Alexander Pope must certainly hold that distinction. While very much a child of the Enlightenment and a formulator and devotee of the ideals of Neoclassicism, he nevertheless brings to those ideals a breadth, a flexibility, and a warmth of spirit that make labels seem flimsy and force the student to confront directly a major figure in English literary history. He is a writer who achieved distinction in a remarkable variety of literary genres—satire, literary criticism, elegy, translation, philosophical, pastoral, and moral poetry. He is also one of the first poets for whom writing was truly a profession. Perhaps Samuel Johnson said it best in his famous observation: "After all this, it is surely superfluous to answer the question that has once been asked, Whether Pope was a Poet? otherwise than by asking in return, If Pope be not a poet, where is poetry to be found?"

Born in London on May 21, 1688, of a not terribly distinguished Roman Catholic family (his father Alexander was a linen merchant), he knew the slings and arrows of ill fortune from the beginning. Both of his parents were past forty-five when he was born, a factor at least in part responsible for his continuing physical problems. Pope suffered from a crippling curvature of the spine (in maturity he was only four feet, six inches in height), a severe asthmatic condition, and chronic headaches that must have made daily living an ordeal in itself and makes his famous description of "this long disease, my life" strangely apt. Furthermore, to be a Catholic in his day, especially after the Glorious Revolution and the inauguration of certain somewhat stringent religious tests, was at best disconcerting. Legally Catholics could not practice their religion openly (it has always been interesting to note how little evidence of Pope's religion one can garner from his work), could not earn degrees at public schools or universities, could not enter several of the professions or hold office or sit in Parliament. They were also subject to double taxation and, significantly for Pope's career, were restricted in purchasing land and in living within ten miles of London. Such discrimination helps to explain the family's move to a small home in idyllic Binfield near Windsor Forest and his attendance at Catholic schools in the area for a time. It may also, in combination with his chronically painful physical condition, help us to understand his sense of being somewhat of an outsider and his determination—indeed, as time went by, his fierce commitment—to make his way in the world by following a career of letters.

At Binfield he was literally self-educated, mapping out a plan of study, reading voraciously in classical literature and steeping himself in the great native tradition of Shakespeare, Milton, and Dryden. He had studied Latin at school, but he taught himself Greek, and learned Italian and French in London. The adolescent Pope was a virtual prodigy, composing a tragedy and epic, now lost, clearly setting for himself the vocation of poetry. By the time he was seventeen, he was known to the "Wits" of London literary circles—among others, to William Wycherley, the great dramatist, and to William Walsh, the critic, whose urging that he should become England's first correct poet had such a marked influence on the direction of his career. In Joseph Spence's priceless *Anecdotes*, Pope, looking back, recalls that encouragement strikingly: "About fifteen I got acquainted with Mr. Walsh: he used to encourage me much, and used to tell me that there was one way left of excelling; for though we had several great poets, we never had any one great poet that was correct; and he desired me to make that my study and aim." This same young Pope, physically frail, intellectually and artistically precocious, and socially somewhat reclusive, was not, however, at least in his imaginings, unresponsive to the delights of a young woman's companionship in settings of lush natural beauty. More than one biographer has given us the image of the awkward young man seeking the company of Martha Blount or, later, of Lady Mary Wortley Montagu. This romantic side of his nature is sometimes buried in the mass of popular material that would have us see him as a remote and unfeeling human being and poet.

Interestingly enough, Pope's first efforts were very much in what might loosely be called a romantic vein; Ian Watt, the noted critic of eighteenth-century literature, actually writes of two separate phases of Pope's career. His *Pastorals*, published in 1709, were by any standard remarkable efforts for a teenager once it is seen, as Pope clearly outlines in his essay on pastoral poetry, that they are not so much poems of humble and rustic life as imitations of Virgil and other classical poets. Even the modern reader is engaged by the polish and artistry, the command of language, the lilting music despite the old conventions of pale, longing shepherds wooing or mourning the loss of their lovely ladies amid the beauties of an ideal nature. Listen to the shepherds lamenting the death of the lovely Daphne and notice the ability of the young poet to evoke the elegiac mood:

> No more the mounting larks, while Daphne sings,
> Shall, listening in mid-air, suspend their wings;
> No more the birds shall imitate her lays,
> Or hush'd with wonder, hearken from the sprays:
> No more the streams their murmurs shall forbear,
> A sweeter music than their own to hear;
> But tell the reeds, and tell the vocal shore,
> Fair Daphne's dead, and music is no more!

Nature is also a vital force in *Windsor Forest,* although there the other side of Pope's poetic bent can be seen. The loveliness of the forest and its surroundings are vividly sketched, to be sure; but there is a strong sense of how a more civilized age has taken "A dreary desert, and a gloomy waste" and brought order to it: "Not chaos-like together crush'd and bruised, / But, as the world harmoniously confused: / Where order in variety we see, / And where, though all things differ, all agree." The flawless beauty of the setting, the control of essentially lawless forces by a directing human intelligence point to strong political forces at work, forces with larger ramifications for every area of English society. As the poet concludes one of his perfectly chiselled verse paragraphs: "Rich Industry sits smiling on the plains, / And peace and plenty tell a STUART reigns."

The same romantic strain, now accompanied by a certain melancholic and even tragic spirit, can be seen in two other rather early poems, the *Elegy to the Memory of an Unfortunate Lady* and *Eloisa to Abelard,* both written before 1717. The *Elegy* is a singularly disarming Pope poem. Debates about its sad heroine's identity (Martha Blount and Lady Mary Wortley Montagu have been advanced) are futile and really irrelevant. The intensity of the speaker's voice, the metaphysical and Gothic qualities of language, setting and mood, the striking portrait of the woman as a creature who defied narrow and hypocritical societal rules to love even to death—all of these point to a poem beyond convention, revealing the young artist's already notable ability to imagine and compress strong emotion within taut and polished iambic pentameter couplets. Sections like the following seem superior to the more celebrated *Eloisa* and leave the student with the puzzling question of how, in another time and other circumstances, Pope's career might have moved in dramatically different directions:

> Why bade ye else, ye powers! her soul aspire
> Above the vulgar flight of low desire?
> Ambition first sprung from your blest abodes,
> The glorious fault of angels and of gods:
> Thence to these images on earth it flows,
> And in the breast of kings and heroes glows.
> Most souls, 'tis true, but peep out once an age,
> Dull, sullen prisoner's in the body's cage:

Dim lights of life, that burn a length of years,
Useless, unseen, as lamps in sepulchres.

While the *Elegy* is a quite unconventional poem, with a passionate woman very much a creature of the poet's creative powers, *Eloisa* is a poem with a long tradition behind it. The medieval story of the two lovers separated and living in religious houses, the fervent letters exchanged between them, the many versions and translations of the story (Pope knew the 1717 translation of John Hughes best) had become an important part of the experience of many readers. Consequently, although there are sections of the poem that ring with both the tenderness and intensity of a hopeless love, the lovers are not as graphically realized as the Lady or even the speaker of the *Elegy*. Pope saw in the story of Eloisa and Abelard the opportunity to explore the central human conflicts of passion and honor, of nature and grace, and he brought a kind of heroic romanticism to lines like the following:

Relentless walls! whose darksome round contains
Repentant sighs, and voluntary pains:
Ye rugged rocks! which holy knees have worn;
Ye grots and caverns shagg'd with horrid thorn!
Shrines! where their vigils pale-eyed virgins keep,
And pitying saints, whose statues learn to weep!
Though cold like you, unmoved and silent grown,
I have not yet forgot myself to stone.
All is not Heaven's while Abelard has part,
Still rebel nature holds out half my heart;
Nor prayers nor fasts its stubborn pulse restrain,
Nor tears for ages taught to flow in vain.

As early as 1712 Pope had published his famous *Essay on Criticism* (he was later to do a hilarious poetics-in-reverse titled *The Art of Sinking in Poetry* in 1727), a didactic poem in which the reader sees the young man's attempt, in the fashion of Horace's ancient *Ars Poetica* or of many such contemporary treatises, not just to set down advice or critical guidelines for the would-be poet or critic, but to develop a sustained outline of the basic values and standards of the Neoclassic theory of literature. The *Essay* is notable not only for its message but for its medium of communication—its concentration of couplets, its rich diction, its functional imagery. Its three carefully worked-out sections, offering general and specific rules for criticism and a portrait of the ideal critic, urge the need for a degree of objectivity rooted in Nature and Reason, a respect for ancient models, and yet they reveal a consistent liberal strain that leaves room for the "grace beyond the reach of art." They further, and most succinctly, offer a theory of wit and language that seems just as vital today. Language and imagery must be vehicles of thought, not mere adornment or demonstrations of individual virtuosity. The end or purpose of the work of art must be the critic's basic concern; he or she must explore the total effect, not merely the brilliance of individual parts. The memorable couplet, often misunderstood when taken out of context, says it best: "True wit is Nature to advantage dress'd; / What oft was thought, but ne'er so well express'd; / Something, whose truth convinced at sight we find, / That gives us back the image of our mind." Apart from the age of its author, *An Essay on Criticism* is a remarkable document of the first phase of Pope's career.

Clearly the great work of Pope's earlier years is *The Rape of the Lock,* in many ways a turning point in which we see a blend of the early Pope's sense of romance and a new concern (to be discussed at some length later) with the disarming and debunking of human folly and vice. There are, it should be remembered, two versions: the first, a short, comic piece, and the later, the magnificent, full-blown mock-epic of 1713 with its elaborate Rosicrucian machinery of sylphs, gnomes, nymphs, and salamanders. The story at the root of the poem is well known and needs little retelling. Pope's friend John Caryll first told him the stirring saga of human pride, the enmity that developed between the families of Lady Arabella Fermor and Lord Petre because of the young man's exuberant cutting of a lock of the lady's hair as a memento. However, Pope, always the wide-ranging observer, saw the event and its consequences in larger terms—as a metaphor of human vanity and hypocrisy, of the concern with respectability rather than true virtue, of the lack of good sense and good humor that isolate otherwise civilized and potentially happy human beings, of the need for human warmth and sociability if life's potential darkness is to be illuminated. Clarissa, so often cited as the poet's voice, delivers the great homily after the cutting of the lock, climaxing the mock-heroism and deflating the characters after having brilliantly elevated them to epic proportions:

> "But since, alas! frail beauty must decay,
> Curl'd or uncurl'd, since locks will turn to grey;
> Since painted, or not painted, all shall fade,
> And she who scorns a man must die a maid;
> What then remains, but well our power to use,
> And keep good-humour still whate'er we lose?
> And trust me, dear, good-humour can prevail,
> When airs, and flights, and screams, and scolding fail.
> Beauties in vain their pretty eyes may roll;
> Charm strikes the sight, but merit wins the soul."

A great speech, a wise speech—perhaps the best example of the complexity and nuance of Pope's and of all great satire, of the satirist's special genius in steering a middle course between mere burlesque and angry indignation to make us laugh or sneer, but always to come to terms with the vice and folly of human nature. In an age of Enlightenment, where social rather than religious standards prevailed, satire became a powerful sanction. Ian Jack seems to capture this strategy perfectly as he speaks of a certain sadness in Pope's optimism, ". . . a sombre diminishing of man's estate reminiscent rather of medieval *contemptus mundi* than of the thought of the more shallow among the thinkers of the Enlightenment. Hazlitt was right when on reading *The Rape of the Lock* he did not know whether to laugh or cry. Pope often reminds one of Mozart: there is in his work the same depth of emotion, perfectly restrained by the strict patterning of art."

In 1714 the legendary Scriblerus Club of Tory wits was formed, a club dedicated to assaulting all pedantry and literary dullness, and Pope, along with literary figures like Swift, John Arbuthnot, Francis Atterbury, Thomas Parnell, John Gay, and the two government ministers Robert Harley, Earl of Oxford, and Henry St. John, Viscount Bolingbroke, was a leading light, although the association ended when the Tory strength faded with the death of Queen Anne and the coming to power of the Hanoverian Whigs. Pope was courted more and more now, even by the Whiggish Addison and Steele. In 1718 his growing reputation prompted a move to Twickenham, a charming village on the Thames, still pleasant to visit today, beyond the ten-mile limit set for Catholics. Here he transformed a small house, at least a part of which may still be seen, into a classical villa, with picturesque landscaping and lovely walks within view of the great river, and here he lived until his death.

The years 1715–1720 saw Pope at work on his famed translation of the *Iliad* while the 1720s were relatively quiet, as he worked on an edition of Shakespeare and collaborated on a translation of the *Odyssey*. The later years of the decade, however, saw the emergence of his major works. Bolingbroke's return from exile in 1725, Swift's visits to Twickenham, the gatherings at Pope's home of both Tory and Whig opponents of Walpole and his repressive politics, the growing public image of Pope as a figure admired and feared—all of these seemed to kindle the creative spark. It was not, however, the spark of satire pure and simple but rather a satire of darkening vision and stern prophecy in the *Satires*, the *Dunciad*, the *Moral Essays*. And how appropriate this satiric vein seems in an England that was plagued by political corruption, personal and public avarice, and the general decline of literary ideals—and how appropriate in the larger context of the Enlightenment, with its strong emphasis on the centrality of Reason, a body of civilized standards, and the need to expose any perversion of these standards. Pope writes basically in the more informal manner of Horace, with its superb use of precepts and examples and its fascinatingly shifting *persona*, although there are more than a few sections in which the bitterness and indignation of Juvenal ring out sharply. His own words in a letter to Swift are most instructive: "I have not the courage to be such a satirist as you, but I would be as much, or more, a philosopher. You call your satires libels. I would rather call my satires epistles. They will consist more of morality than of wit, and grow graver, which you call duller."

Pope's justification of his satire is always abundantly clear. Pestered by bad writers and sycophants, surrounded by dilettantes and malicious critics, he sees humane learning as seriously threatened. The keen observer of dishonesty in public and private life, he sees the sound values of beauty, virtue, and truth undermined by the unscrupulous. He would become the defender of manners and morals, at times indeed the angry opponent and exposer of foolish and evil human beings—an opponent whose greatest weapon is his satiric strength. "Not Fortune's worshipper, nor Fashion's fool, / Not Lucre's madman, nor Ambition's tool," he thinks, ". . . a lie in verse or prose the same." To all who question his anger and his satiric barbs, his reply is consistently an admirable *apologia* of his profession, a defense of virtue, a statement of moral purpose:

Ask you what provocation I have had?
The strong antipathy of good to bad.
When truth or virtue an affront endures,
The affront is mine, my friend, and should be yours.
Mine, as a foe profess'd to false pretence,
Who think a coxcomb's honour like his sense;
Mine as a friend to every worthy mind;
And mine as man, who feel for all mankind.

His satire is also effective as he moves from general ridicule to the telling portraits that pervade both the *Satires* and the *Moral Essays*. The sharpness of characterization, the vigor of phrasing, the brilliant use of dialogue, the subtle use of rhythm and rhyme for strategic effect—these and other techniques contribute to some of his most memorable insights. Perhaps his greatest success stems from his uncanny talent for seeing the general truth in the individual sketch. Who can forget the timeliness of Pope's expression of the struggle of the true poet in the midst of the patronage and faddishness of Augustus (George II), the vulgarity and extravagance of Timon (the Duke of Chandos), the moral and physical ugliness of Sporus (Lord Hervey), the scathing horror of the wealthy and powerful, but loveless Atossa (Sarah Hennings, Duchess of Marlborough)? Certainly one of his most famous and oft-quoted portraits is that of the vain, jealous, and priggish Atticus (Joseph Addison), with its powerful use of almost every device of sound, its gathering intensity, its shattering exposure:

Should such a man, too fond to rule alone,
Bear, like the Turk, no brother near the throne,
View him with scornful, yet with jealous eyes,
And hate for arts that caused himself to rise;
Damn with faint praise, assent with civil leer,
And, without sneering, teach the rest to sneer;
Willing to wound, and yet afraid, to strike,
Just hint a fault and hesitate dislike;
Alike reserved to blame, or to commend,
A timorous foe and a suspicious friend;
Dreading e'en fools, by flatterers beseiged,
And so obliging that he ne'er obliged;
Like Cato, give his little senate laws,
And sit attentive to his own applause;
While wits and templars every sentence raise,
And wonder with a foolish face of praise—
Who but must laugh, if such a man there be?
Who would not weep, if Atticus were he?

The great keystone of Pope's literary and moral philosophy, *An Essay on Man,* was published in 1734. Written over a number of years, at times a seeming blend of ideas from thinkers like Shaftesbury, Bolingbroke, and Leibnitz, it is indeed a grand scheme. It is Pope's plan for describing the universe and its order, for vindicating God's ways to man, for positioning human beings in the nature of things, for offering an answer to the problem of evil. It is Pope's counsel for achieving happiness in the golden mean between self-love and social concern, between pride and deference. *An Essay on Man* is very much a document of natural theology, urging readers to look through nature to its creator and placing little or no emphasis on a personal, loving God. The poem is filled with eminently quotable passages as the speaker urges man: "Cease then, nor order imperfection name: / Our proper bliss depends on what we blame. / Know thy own point: this kind, this due degree / Of blindness, weakness, Heaven bestows on thee," reassuring him of the ultimate rightness of things in the famous couplets of sublime optimism: "All discord, harmony not understood; / All partial evil, universal good: / And, spite of pride, in erring reason's spite, / One truth is clear, Whatever is, is right."

The history of Pope's last great poem, *The Dunciad,* is complex. Passing through several versions from 1728 to its final publication in 1743, changing mock-heroes from the pedant Lewis Theobald to the foolish laureate Colley Cibber, it is a relentless satire of all sham in literature and learning. A mock-heroic in four books, it lacks the delicate artistry of *The Rape of the Lock,* yet its ruggedness of tone, its uncompromising commitment to truth, and its hatred of pretension are powerful. It is, without doubt, too long and too digressive, especially in the sections poking fun at the conventions of invocation, sacrifice, the games, and the like, but the fourth book rings with power, as it ominously foretells the overthrow of true learning by the dark cloud of human folly. We see a frightening picture, a cosmic yawn of the goddess of Dullness, a climactic prophecy, "Thy hand, great Anarch! lets the curtain fall, / And universal darkness buries all." It is a picture that speaks just as powerfully today about the dangers of misdirected schemes of learning, the supervision of education by a ruling class of dullards and human engineers, the total loss of meaning in language and literature. On May 30, 1744, shortly after its publication, Alexander Pope was dead.

Pope's literary reputation has changed considerably through the years. Although not without enemies, who scorned him, he was, as already suggested, the object of considerable praise, admiration, and even awe during his lifetime. Johnson's memorable tribute in his *Life of Pope* is typical. Yet even in the eighteenth century the impact of remarks like those of Joseph Warton, in his *Essay on the Genius and Writings of Pope,* suggesting that although a master of the witty and didactic, Pope was a writer of the second order, began to take its toll. The Romantics of the next century were generally critical of his artificiality and lack of imaginative power while the Victorians probably brought his reputation to an all-time low. Matthew Arnold's famous discussion set the tone of a great deal of Pope criticism through the early twentieth century. In Arnold's view, Pope, like Dryden, was a poet of polish and elegance; both poets, however, ". . . are not classics of our poetry, they are classics of our prose."

In the 1920s and 1930s T. S. Eliot's book on John Dryden, Edith Sitwell's extravagant biography of Pope, and a most influential essay by F. R. Leavis revived an interest in the period in general and in Pope in particular. It was for this editor, however, the work of Geoffrey Tillotson, especially his 1939 book called *On the Poetry of Pope,* that led the way to a fresh revaluation and appreciation for Pope as an artist in his own right, not Romantic or Modern to be sure, but one whose sense of the human situation, whose mastery of language, and whose power of satire transcend an age and have a perennial power for readers. A feast of critics followed—George Sherburn, Maynard Mack, Reuben Brower, William Wimsatt, Ian Jack, G. Wilson Knight, Patricia Spacks, and Thomas Edwards, to name a few—and today there is a firmly established interest in his work.

The best criticism of Pope is that which begins by taking up the poetry in its own terms, not in relation to the lyrical and metaphysical qualities of Renaissance and seventeenth-century poetry on the one hand or the romantic self-expression of nineteenth-century poetry on the other. Pope's is a special genius. As a writer he sees himself and his art as having a certain public, social, and didactic quality; he seems keenly aware of an audience. Beyond the romantic excursions in the *Pastorals,* the *Elegy to the Memory of an Unfortunate Lady,* and *Eloisa to Abelard,* his work is increasingly concerned with manners and morals, with the quest for an enlightened view of man and his sphere of activity, and with the criticism of those forces, internal and external, which pervert that view. He was intimidated, as W. J. Bate observes, by the burden of the past—by the necessity of writing in an era dominated by such towering figures as Milton, Shakespeare, Virgil, and Homer. He turned, therefore, to didactic poetry—to the critical injunctions of *An Essay on Criticism,* the gentle but profoundly moralizing satire of *The Rape of the Lock,* the powerful critiques of the *Satires* and *Moral Essays,* the philosophical ruminations of *An Essay on Man.*

How clearly Pope's sense of mission is seen as the student moves through the poetry. To the young poet-critic he is the sage advisor:

> You then whose judgment the right course would steer,
> Know well each Ancient's proper character:
> His fable, subject, scope in every page;
> Religion, country, genius of his age:
> Without all these at once before your eyes
> Cavil you may, but never criticize.
> Be Homer's works your study and delight,
> Read them by day, and meditate by night.

To the vain Belinda, still mourning unreasonably the loss of her all-too-conspicuous lock of hair, he counsels in mock-heroic fashion the larger view of beauty as a gift to be shared and savored rather than selfishly guarded:

> Then cease, bright nymph! to mourn thy ravish'd hair,
> Which adds new glory to the shining sphere!
> Not all the tresses that fair head can boast

Shall draw such envy as the lock you lost.
For, after all the murders of your eye,
When, after millions slain, yourself shall die;
When those fair suns shall set, as set they must,
And all the tresses shall be laid to dust;
This lock, the Muse shall consecrate to fame,
And midst the stars inscribe Belinda's name.

To the perceptive listener he extends an invitation to the unnecessary and vain lavishness of Timon's villa so that both may share a sense of the pride of humankind:

At Timon's villa let us pass a day,
Where all cry out, "What sums are thrown away!"
So proud, so grand: of that stupendous air,
Soft and agreeable come never there.
Greatness, with Timon, dwells in such a draught
As brings all Brobdingnag before your thought.
To compass this, his building is a town,
His pond an ocean, his parterre a down:
Who but must laugh, the master when he sees,
A puny insect, shivering at a breeze!

Pope's vision is, as we have already noted, rooted in the cosmology of *An Essay on Man,* an ordered universe in which everything has its place if only human beings as creatures of Reason can subdue the great demon Pride and recognize that, dwelling "on this isthmus of a middle state," apparent evil and frustration are part of a larger universal good. As Martin Price puts it, man is "... part of a vital organism, always in movement, held together by infinite relatedness. His moral end comes in recognizing the claim of that organic harmony and contributing freely and voluntarily to its order. In this way man becomes an artist himself as well as a contributor to the larger order of art."

While many readers can appreciate, indeed even delight in, Pope's critical injunctions or satiric barbs, they are less inclined to do so with his style and technique. Keats's "Pegasus on a rocking horse" typifies the kind of gentle put-down of the care and regularity that characterize the rhythm and movement of his verse. The familiar charge that he is "too abstract and general" is another negative reaction. Such views seem to be rooted in a Romantic love of spontaneous self-expression, of abrupt shifts in the mode of poetic expression. Lest we forget, Pope, although certainly a poet of care and correctness, was no robot-like, slow-moving artist working long and laboriously over his verse. His remark recorded in Spence's *Anecdotes* is a telling one. "The things," he says, "that I have written fastest, have always pleased the most. I wrote the *Essay on Criticism* fast, for I had digested all the matter, in prose before I began upon it in verse. The *Rape of the Lock* was written fast: all the machinery was added afterwards; and the making that, and what was published before, fit so well together, is, I think, one of the greatest proofs of judgment of anything I ever did." The enormous amount of creative work produced in a relatively short career is further strong evidence.

Wit and Judgment—the happy balance of the two great Neoclassical ideals of spontaneity and discrimination—are the keystones of Pope's artistry. His, as William Empson has said, is that rare gift of seeing the general truth in fresh ways and of discovering the most nearly perfect vehicle of expression to embody and express that truth. The virtue is propriety, a bond of intimacy between word and idea. Far from resorting to the lifeless abstraction to emphasize the truth of an observation, Pope seeks out the apt and fertile word to exemplify vividly that observation. To quote William Youngren, whose past and present work on generality in Restoration and eighteenth-century poetry is of great importance, "... we might say that Pope is sketching in the relevant background in the way that will best 'set off' the image or figure of Wit, or set it 'strongly and beautifully' before our inner eye."

Believing strongly in rhythm as a key element in the rhetorical power of poetry, he relied heavily on the iambic pentameter couplet, used it, as Martin Price puts it, "... as the module with which to build a world." So devoted was he to the couplet that we find the number of variations—triplets, Alexandrines, run-on lines, hypermeter—very few indeed. Whatever the genre, Pope used the couplet wisely to suit his purpose. Consider the moving lines of Eloisa to her beloved Abelard, the somber movement of the rhythm, the strategic effects of the rhymes:

> Canst thou forget that sad, that solemn day,
> When victims at yon altar's foot we lay?
> Canst thou forget what tears that moment fell,
> When warm in youth I bade the world farewell.

or the biting words, and the power of their sound, addressed to still another group of bad poets in *The Dunciad*:

> "Silence, ye wolves! while Ralph to Cynthia howls,
> And makes night hideous—Answer him, ye owls!
> "Sense, speech, and measure, living tongues and dead,
> Let all give way, and Morris may be read.
> Flow, Welsted, flow! like thine inspirer, beer,
> Though stale, not ripe; though thin, yet never clear;
> So sweetly mawkish and so smoothly dull;
> Heady, not strong; o'erflowing, though not full."

One can observe, upon examination, a certain constraint in the pattern of twenty syllables rather sharply divided into a pair of five-stress lines. Punctuation occurring regularly at the end of the line gives that line a decided emphasis. Sense and sound are subtly blended. Indeed, as Pope developed, his couplets took their place in the development of an argument in larger verse paragraphs. Some of the more memorable sections of *An Essay on Man* employ this verse paragraph most effectively; notice the structure of Pope's argument for the order of things:

All are but parts of one stupendous whole,
Whose body Nature is, and God the soul;
That, changed through all, and yet in all the same;
Great in the sun, as in the ethereal frame;
Warms in the sun, refreshes in the breeze,
Glows in the stars, and blossoms in the trees;
Lives through all life, extends through all extent;
Spreads undivided, operates unspent!

Needless to say, if Pope had produced only order and regularity, his poetry would hardly be memorable. What he managed to achieve was a variety of effects within an overall framework of order so that it is possible for us to speak of a uniquely Popean couplet. His rhyming sounds rarely recur quickly; they are quite generally monosyllabic for maximum effect. By regularly using a verb for at least one of the rhyming words, a special kind of strength and energy is achieved. He is a master of the caesura, or poetic pause, shifting it regularly to avoid the monotony of a predictable mid-line pause and to gain the pleasure of an expected kind of musical effect. In his *Sixth Epistle of the First Book of Horace,* the melody gained from this variation is especially evident, as the caesura shifts in each line, following respectively the fourth, fifth, sixth, fifth, fourth, and sixth syllables:

For Virtue's self may too much zeal be had;
The worst of madmen is a saint run mad.
Go then, and if you can, admire the state
Of beaming diamonds, and reflected plate;
Procure a taste to double the surprise,
And gaze on Parian charms with learned eyes.

The skillful use of sound effects like alliteration and assonance further contributes to the variety and melodic pleasure of reading Pope. The section on representative meter in *An Essay on Criticism* is justly famous for practicing what it preaches. Gently mocking the practice of much contemporary verse and advising, "The sound must seem an echo to the sense," he proceeds:

Soft is the strain when Zephyr gently blows,
And the smooth stream in smoother number flows;
But when loud surges lash the sounding shore,
The hoarse, rough verse should like the torrent roar.
When Ajax strives some rock's vast weight to throw,
The line too labours, and the words move slow:
Not so, when swift Camilla scours the plain,
Flies o'er the unbending corn, and skims along the main.

More often he suggests rather than imitates exactly, as in the lines from *The Dunciad,* "Lo! where Maeotis sleeps and hardly flows / The freezing Tanais through a waste of snows," in which the long vowels and the predominance of *s* and *z* sounds suggest the slow, soporific quality which the meaning of the lines conveys. Another brilliant example can be found in the lines spoken by Thyrsis in the pastoral *Winter*:

> But see, Orion sheds unwholesome dews;
> Arise, the pines a noxious shade diffuse;
> Sharp Boreas blows, and Nature feels decay,
> Time conquers all, and we must time obey.

How effectively the dews are suggested by the *s* sounds of the first two lines and the intensity of the wind conveyed by the alliterative *b* and the recurring *o* of "Boreas blows." How the long vowels of the last line heighten the awe and solemnity of the message.

Pope's mastery of the art of balance and antithesis is almost flawless. As Tillotson has perceptively suggested, while the Pope line is complete in itself, we are on occasion drawn to the significance of the half-line, to the balance of two halves with four key words arranged in pairs to compare or contrast, to communicate the full force of the poet's meaning. Whether setting up the subtle reverberations of Belinda's virtue and delicate China jars:

> Whether the nymph shall break Diana's law,
> Or some frail China-jar receive a flaw;
> Or stain her honor or her new brocade;
> Forget her prayers, or miss a masquerade;
> Or lose her heart, or necklace, at a ball;
> Or whether Heaven has doom'd that Shock must fall,

or acidly analyzing the sinister tactics of Atticus:

> Damn with faint praise, assent with civil leer,
> And, without sneering, teach the rest to sneer;
> Willing to wound, and yet afraid to strike.
> Just hint a fault, and hesitate dislike,

or warning about the spitefulness of Atossa, "Offend her, and she knows not to forgive; / Oblige her, and she'll hate you while you live," Pope leaves us with a sense of wonder at the resources at his command.

While not a poet of great theatricality, of deeply confessional verse, of idiosyncratic language and imagery, Alexander Pope is the great artist of the Enlightenment in England, the sharp and sensitive observer, the critic and satirist of the human drama. Invariably he moves beyond the particular person or individual incident to see things in more general and representative terms, to express in a new way the consensus of reasonable and enlightened human beings. He is truly a poet who loves variety but within a context of order, who has a sense of the tragic dimension of life but not without an enormous capacity for compassion and laughter. Above all, he is the poet of the word, the one, to use his own phrase, "That gives us back the image of our mind."

Suggestions for Further Reading

Students of Pope are now fortunate in having the complete Twickenham Edition of the *Poems of Alexander Pope,* 10 vols, gen. ed. John Butt (1939–1969). Most of this great edition, including a great deal of its invaluable annotation, is available in a convenient and relatively inexpensive one-volume paperback, *The Poems of Alexander Pope,* ed. John Butt (1963). Two other useful paperback collections are *The Poetry and Prose of Alexander Pope,* ed. Aubrey Williams (1967), and *The Selected Poetry of Pope,* ed. Martin Price (1970).

We still await the definitive biography of the great poet. Samuel Johnson's *Life of Pope* (printed in this anthology), although written in 1781, is still a treasure of insight and analysis. George Sherburn's *Early Career of Alexander Pope* (1956) is a splendid study taking us to 1727, and W. J. Courthope's *Life of Pope* (*Volume* 5 of the famous Elwin-Courthope edition) covers the years until Pope's death. Edith Sitwell's *Alexander Pope* (1930) is an appreciative biography, and Peter Quennell's *Alexander Pope: The Education of Genius* (1968) is an interesting first volume of a life of Pope, still to be completed.

Two classic early studies of Pope's poetry are Samuel Johnson's *Life of Pope,* already mentioned, and Matthew Arnold's observations on Dryden, Pope, and their age in "The Study of Poetry," *Essays on Criticism,* 1st and 2nd series (1880).

Strongly recommended for further and more specialized study are Austin Warren, *Alexander Pope as Critic and Humanist* (1929); the provocative and insightful essay on Pope in F. R. Leavis', *Revaluation: Tradition and Development in English Poetry* (1936); Geoffrey Tillotson's pioneering and stunning books *On the Poetry of Pope* (1938) and *Pope and Human Nature* (1958); Reuben Brower's brilliant close reading of the poems in *Alexander Pope: The Poetry of Allusion* (1959); G. Wilson Knight, *The Poetry of Alexander Pope: Laureate of Peace* (1965); Marjorie Hope Nicolson and G. S. Rousseau, *"This Long Disease, My Life": Alexander Pope and the Sciences* (1968); and Patricia Spacks, *An Argument of Images: The Poetry of Alexander Pope* (1971).

Splendid essays on Pope's poetry and on the poetry of the Neoclassical period in general are William Wimsatt's incisive and comprehensive introduction to his Alexander Pope: *Selected Poetry and Prose* (1951); Maynard Mack's, "Wit and Poetry and Pope" in James Clifford's rich collection, *Eighteenth-Century English Literature: Modern Essays in Criticism* (1959); and William Youngren's, "Generality in Augustan Satire" in *In Defense of Reading* (1962), and the same writer's "Generality, Science and Poetic Language in the Restoration," *Journal of English Literary History,* 35, no. 2 (1968).

Maynard Mack, in his *Essential Articles for the Study of Pope* (1964), has done a fine job of collecting the best articles on almost every facet of Pope's work. All students will find it a valuable resource.

FROM

Pastorals

AUTUMN: THE THIRD PASTORAL, OR HYLAS AND ÆGON

Beneath the shade a spreading beech displays,
Hylas and Ægon sung their rural lays:
This mourn'd a faithless, that an absent, Love;
And Delia's name and Doris' fill'd the grove.
Ye Mantuan nymphs, your sacred succour bring;
Hylas and Ægon's rural lays I sing.
Thou, whom the Nine with Plautus' wit inspire,
The art of Terence, and Menander's fire;
Whose sense instructs us, and whose humour charms,
Whose judgment sways us, and whose spirit warms!
Oh, skill'd in Nature! see the hearts of swains,
Their artless passions, and their tender pains.
Now setting Phœbus shone serenely bright,
And fleecy clouds were streak'd with purple light:
When tuneful Hylas with melodious moan,
Taught rocks to weep, and made the mountains groan.
Go, gentle gales, and bear my sighs away!
To Delia's ear the tender notes convey.
As some sad turtle his lost love deplores,
And with deep murmurs fills the sounding shores;
Thus, far from Delia, to the winds I mourn,
Alike unheard, unpitied, and forlorn.
Go, gentle gales, and bear my sighs away!
For her, the feather'd quires neglect their song:
For her, the lines their pleasing shades deny;
For her, the lilies hang their heads and die.
Ye flowers that droop, forsaken by the spring,
Ye birds that, left by summer, cease to sing,
Ye trees that fade when autumn-heats remove,
Say, is not absence death to those who love?
Go, gentle gales, and bear my sighs away!
Cursed be the fields that cause my Delia's stay;
Fade every blossom, winter every tree,
Die every flower, and perish all, but she.
What have I said? where'er my Delia flies,
Let spring attend, and sudden flowers arise;
Let opening roses knotted oaks adorn,
And liquid amber drop from every thorn.
Go, gentle gales, and bear my sighs along!
The birds shall cease to tune their evening song,
The winds to breathe, the waving woods to move,
And streams to murmur, ere I cease to love.
Not bubbling fountains to the thirsty swain,
Not balmy sleep to labourers faint with pain,
Not showers to larks, or sunshine to the bee,
Are half so charming as thy sight to me.
Go, gentle gales, and bear my sighs away!
Come, Delia, come; ah, why this long delay?
Through rocks and cave the name of Delia sounds,
Delia, each cave and echoing rock rebounds.
Ye powers, what pleasing frenzy soothes my mind!
Do lovers dream, or is my Delia kind?
She comes, my Delia comes!—Now cease my lay,
And cease, ye gales, to bear my sighs away!
Next Ægon sung, while Windsor groves admired;
Rehearse, ye Muses, what yourselves inspired.
Resound, ye hills, resound my mournful strain!
Of perjured Doris, dying I complain:
Here where the mountains, lessening as they rise,
Lose the low vales, and steal into the skies;
While labouring oxen, spent with toil and heat,
In their loose traces from the field retreat;
While curling smokes from Village-tops are seen,
And the fleet shades glide o'er the dusky green.
Resound, ye hills, resound my mournful lay!
Beneath yon' poplar oft we pass'd the day:
Oft on the rind I carved her amorous vows,
While she with garlands hung the bending boughs.
The garlands fade, the vows are worn away;
So dies her love, and so my hopes decay.
Resound, ye hills, resound my mournful strain!
Now bright Arcturus glads the teeming grain,
Now golden fruits on loaded branches shine,
And grateful clusters swell with floods of wine;

AUTUMN: THE THIRD PASTORAL, OR HYLAS AND ÆGON. **5. Mantuan:** from Mantua, a city in Northern Italy. The great Roman epic poet Virgil was born near Mantua. **7. Nine:** the Muses, sources of inspiration in history, the arts, astronomy. **7–8. Plautus . . . Menander:** Plautus, Terence, and Menander were masters of classical Roman comedy. **13. Phœbus:** Apollo, god of the sun.

72. Arcturus: the brightest star in the constellation Boötes.

Now blushing berries paint the yellow grove;
Just Gods! shall all things yield returns but love?
  Resound, ye hills, resound my mournful lay!
The shepherds cry, "Thy flocks are left a prey."—
Ah! what avails it me, the flocks to keep,
Who lost my heart while I preserved my sheep?
Pan came, and ask'd, what magic caused my smart,
Or what ill eyes malignant glances dart?
What eyes but hers, alas, have power to move?
And is there magic but what dwells in love?
  Resound, ye hills, resound my mournful strains!
I'll fly from shepherds, flocks, and flowery plains.
From shepherds, flocks, and plains, I may remove,
Forsake mankind, and all the world—but Love!
I know thee, Love! on foreign mountains bred,
Wolves gave thee suck, and savage tigers fed.
Thou wert from Ætna's burning entrails torn,
Got by fierce whirlwinds, and in thunder born!
  Resound, ye hills, resound my mournful lay!
Farewell, ye woods, adieu the light of day!
One leap from yonder cliff shall end my pains;
No more, ye hills, no more resound my strains!
  Thus sung the shepherds till th' approach of night,
The skies yet blushing with departing light,
When falling dews with spangles deck'd the glade,
And the low sun had lengthen'd every shade.

(1709)

WINDSOR FOREST

TO THE RIGHT HONOURABLE GEORGE LORD LANSDOWNE*

Thy forest, Windsor! and thy green retreats,
At once the Monarch's and the Muse's seats,
Invite my lays. Be present, sylvan maids!
Unlock your springs, and open all your shades.
GRANVILLE commands; your aid, O Muses, bring!
What Muse for GRANVILLE can refuse to sing?
  The groves of Eden, vanish'd now so long,
Live in description, and look green in song:
These, were my breast inspired with equal flame,
Like them in beauty, should be like in fame.
Here hills and vales, the woodland and the plain,
Here earth and water seem to strive again;
Not chaos-like together crush'd and bruised,
But, as the world harmoniously confused:
Where order in variety we see,
And where, though all things differ, all agree.
Here waving groves a chequer'd scene display,
And part admit, and part exclude the day;
As some coy nymph her lover's warm address
Not quite indulges, nor can quite repress.
There, interspersed in lawns and opening glades,
Thin trees arise that shun each other's shades.
Here in full light the russet plains extend:
There, wrapt in clouds the bluish hills ascend.
Even the wild heath displays her purple dyes,
And 'midst the desert, fruitful fields arise,
That crown'd with tufted trees and springing corn,
Like verdant isles the sable waste adorn.
Let India boast her plants, nor envy we
The weeping amber, or the balmy tree,
While by our oaks the precious loads are borne,
And realms commanded which those trees adorn.
Not proud Olympus yields a nobler sight,
Though gods assembled grace his towering height,
Than what more humble mountains offer here,
Where, in their blessings, all those gods appear.
See Pan with flocks, with fruits Pomona crown'd,
Here blushing Flora paints th' enamell'd ground,
Here Ceres' gifts in waving prospect stand,
And nodding tempt the joyful reaper's hand;
Rich Industry sits smiling on the plains,
And peace and plenty tell, a STUART reigns.
  Not thus the land appear'd in ages past,
A dreary desert, and a gloomy waste,
To savage beasts and savage laws a prey,
And kings more furious and severe than they;
Who claim'd the skies, dispeopled air and floods,
The lonely lords of empty wilds and woods:
Cities laid waste, they storm'd the dens and caves
(For wiser brutes were backward to be slaves).

81. Pan: god of fields, forests, animals, shepherds, etc.

* George Granville, Lord Lansdowne (1667–1735), a great admirer of Pope's poetry, was part of the Tory government that effected the Treaty of Utrecht in 1713. Pope praises the peace that ensued in this poem.

WINDSOR FOREST. **37. Pomona:** goddess of fruit. **38. Flora:** goddess of flowers. **39. Ceres:** goddess of agriculture. Her "gifts" are wheat. **42. Stuart:** Queen Anne, who reigned from 1702 to 1714, was the last of the Stuart line. Pope sees her reign as one of calm in the body politic and of great beauty in the landscape.

What could be free, when lawless beasts obey'd,
And even the elements a tyrant sway'd?
In vain kind seasons swell'd the teeming grain,
Soft showers distill'd, and suns grew warm in vain;
The swain with tears his frustrate labour yields,
And famish'd dies amidst his ripen'd fields.
What wonder then, a beast or subject slain
Were equal crimes in a despotic reign?
Both doom'd alike for sportive tyrants bled,
But while the subject starv'd, the beast was fed.
Proud Nimrod first the bloody chase began,
A mighty hunter and his prey was man;
Our haughty Norman boasts that barbarous name,
And makes his trembling slaves the royal game.
The fields are ravish'd from th' industrious swains,
From men their cities, and from gods their fanes:
The levell'd towns with weeds lie cover'd o'er;
The hollow winds through naked temples roar;
Round broken columns clasping ivy twined;
O'er heaps of ruin stalk'd the stately hind;
The fox obscene to gaping tombs retires,
And savage howlings fill the sacred quires.
Awed by his Nobles, by his Commons cursed,
Th' oppressor ruled tyrannic where he durst,
Stretch'd o'er the poor and Church his iron rod,
And served alike his vassals and his God.
Whom even the Saxon spared, and bloody Dane,
The wanton victims of his sport remain.
But see, the man who spacious regions gave
A waste for beasts, himself denied a grave!
Stretch'd on the lawn his second hope survey,
At once the chaser, and at once the prey:
Lo Rufus, tugging at the deadly dart,
Bleeds in the forest like a wounded hart.
Succeeding monarchs heard the subjects' cries,
Nor saw displeased the peaceful cottage rise.
Then gathering flocks on unknown mountains fed,
O'er sandy wilds were yellow harvests spread.
The forests wonder'd at th' unusual grain,
And sacred transport touch'd the conscious swain.
Fair Liberty, Britannia's goddess, rears
Her cheerful head, and leads the golden years.

Ye vigorous swains! while youth ferments your blood,
And purer spirits swell the sprightly flood,
Now range the hills, the gameful woods beset,
Wind the shrill horn, or spread the waving net.
When milder autumn summer's heat succeeds,
And in the new-shorn field the partridge feeds,
Before his lord the ready spaniel bounds,
Panting with hope, he tries the furrow'd grounds;
But when the tainted gales the game betray,
Couch'd close he lies, and meditates the prey:
Secure thy trust th' unfaithful field beset,
Till hovering o'er them sweeps the swelling net.
Thus (if small things we may with great compare)
When Albion sends her eager sons to war,
Some thoughtless town, with ease and plenty blest,
Near, and more near, the closing lines invest;
Sudden they seize th' amazed, defenceless prize,
And high in air Britannia's standard flies.
See! from the brake the whirring pheasant springs,
And mounts exulting on triumphant wings:
Short is his joy; he feels the fiery wound,
Flutters in blood, and panting beats the ground,
Ah! what avail his glossy, varying dyes,
His purple crest, and scarlet-circled eyes,
The vivid green his shining plumes unfold,
His painted wings and breast that flames with gold?

Nor yet, when moist Arcturus clouds the sky
The woods and fields their pleasing toils deny.
To plains with well-breath'd beagles we repair,
And trace the mazes of the circling hare:
(Beasts, urged by us, their fellow beast pursue,
And learn of man each other to undo)
With slaughtering guns the unwearied fowler roves,
When frosts have whiten'd all the naked groves;
Where doves in flocks the leafless trees o'ershade,
And lonely woodcocks haunt the watery glade.
He lifts the tube, and levels with his eye;
Straight a short thunder breaks the frozen sky:

61. Nimrod: a cruel and powerful hunter (see Genesis 10:8–9). **63. Norman:** the famous William I, the Conqueror. The destruction described in the lines that follow refers to the barbarism of William, who created the New Forest by leveling towns, buildings, etc. **80.** Pope tells us that William's burial place in Normandy was claimed by someone else. His son had to repurchase it. **83. Rufus:** William II, killed in the New Forest.

106. Albion: Great Britain. **111. brake:** a clump of brush or branches.

Oft, as in airy rings they skim the heath,
The clamorous lapwings feel the leaden death:
Oft, as the mounting larks their notes prepare,
They fall, and leave their little lives in air.
In genial spring, beneath the quivering shade,
Where cooling vapours breathe along the mead,
The patient fisher takes his silent stand,
Intent, his angle trembling in his hand:
With looks unmoved, he hopes the scaly breed,
And eyes the dancing cork, and bending reed.
Our plenteous streams a various race supply,
The bright-eyed perch with fins of Tyrian dye,
The silver eel, in shining volumes roll'd,
The yellow carp, in scales bedroop'd with gold,
Swift trouts, diversified with crimson stains,
And pikes, the tyrants of the watery plains.
Now Cancer glows with Phœbus' fiery car:
The youth rush eager to the sylvan war,
Swarm o'er the lawns, the forest walks surround,
Rouse the fleet hart, and cheer the opening hound.
The impatient courser pants in every vein,
And pawing, seems to beat the distant plain:
Hills, vales, and floods appear already cross'd,
And ere he starts, a thousand steps are lost.
See the bold youth strain up the threat'ning steep,
Rush through the thickets, down the valleys sweep,
Hang o'er their coursers' heads with eager speed,
And earth rolls back beneath the flying steed.
Let old Arcadia boast her ample plain,
The immortal huntress, and her virgin train;
Nor envy, Windsor! since thy shades have seen
As bright a goddess, and as chaste a QUEEN;
Whose care, like hers, protects the sylvan reign,
The earth's fair light, and empress of the main.
Here too, 'tis sung, of old Diana stray'd,
And Cynthus' top forsook for Windsor shade!
Here was she seen o'er airy wastes to rove,
Seek the clear spring, or haunt the pathless grove;
Here arm'd with silver bows, in early dawn,
Her buskin'd virgins traced the dewy lawn.
Above the rest a rural nymph was famed,
Thy offspring, Thames! the fair Lodona named:
(Lodona's fate, in long oblivion cast,
The Muse shall sing, and what she sings shall last.)
Scarce could the goddess from her nymph be known,
But by the crescent, and the golden zone.
She scorn'd the praise of beauty, and the care;
A belt her waist, a fillet binds her hair;
A painted quiver on her shoulder sounds,
And with her dart the flying deer she wounds.
It chanced, as eager of the chase, the maid
Beyond the forest's verdant limits stray'd,
Pan saw and loved, and, burning with desire,
Pursued her flight, her flight increased his fire.
Not half so swift the trembling doves can fly,
When the fierce eagle cleaves the liquid sky;
Not half so swiftly the fierce eagle moves,
When through the clouds he drives the trembling doves;
As from the god she flew with furious pace,
Or as the god, more furious, urged the chase.
Now fainting, sinking, pale, the nymph appears;
Now close behind, his sounding steps she hears;
And now his shadow reach'd her as she run,
His shadow lengthen'd by the setting sun;
And now his shorter breath, with sultry air,
Pants on her neck, and fans her parting hair.
In vain on Father Thames she calls for aid,
Nor could Diana help her injured maid.
Faint, breathless, thus she pray'd, nor pray'd in vain:
"Ah, Cynthia! ah—though banish'd from thy train,
Let me, O let me, to the shades repair,
My native shades—there weep, and murmur there."
She said, and melting as in tears she lay,
In a soft silver stream dissolved away.
The silver stream her virgin coldness keeps,
For ever murmurs, and for ever weeps;
Still bears the name the hapless virgin bore,
And bathes the forest where she ranged before.
In her chaste current oft the goddess laves,
And with celestial tears augments the waves.

142. Tyrian: purple. **147.** the beginning of summer. Phoebus, the sun, enters the constellation of Cancer on June 21 or 22. **165. Diana:** goddess of the moon, the hunt, virginity. Pope is comparing Queen Anne to Diana. **166. Cynthus:** Diana's birthplace, a mountain on the island of Delos.

172. Lodona: one of Diana's retinue of virgins who escapes the advances of the lusty Pan by becoming the river Loddon. **200. Cynthia:** another name for Diana. **207. the name:** Loddon.

Oft in her glass the musing shepherd spies
The headlong mountain and the downward skies,
The watery landskip of the pendant woods,
And absent trees that tremble in the floods;
In the clear azure gleam the flocks are seen,
And floating forests paint the waves with green,
Through the fair scene roll slow the ling'ring streams,
Then foaming pour along, and rush into the Thames.
Thou, too, great father of the British floods!
With joyful pride survey'st our lofty woods;
Where towering oaks their growing honours rear
And future navies on thy shores appear.
Not Neptune's self from all her streams receives
A wealthier tribute, than to thine he gives.
No seas so rich, so gay no banks appear.
No lake so gentle, and no spring so clear.
Nor Po so swells the fabling poet's lays,
While led along the skies his current strays,
As thine, which visits Windsor's famed abodes,
To grace the mansion of our earthly gods:
Nor all his stars above a lustre show,
Like the bright beauties on thy banks below;
Where Jove, subdued by mortal passion still,
Might change Olympus for a nobler hill.
Happy the man whom this bright court approves,
His sovereign favours, and his country loves;
Happy next him, who to these shades retires,
Whom Nature charms, and whom the Muse inspires;
Whom humbler joys of home-felt quiet please,
Successive study, exercise, and ease.
He gathers health from herbs the forest yields,
And of their fragrant physic spoils the fields:
With chemic art exalts the mineral powers,
And draws the aromatic souls of flowers:
Now marks the course of rolling orbs on high;
O'er figured worlds now travels with his eye;
Of ancient writ unlocks the learned store,
Consults the dead, and lives past ages o'er:
Or wandering thoughtful in the silent wood,
Attends the duties of the wise and good,
To observe a mean, be to himself a friend,
To follow Nature, and regard his end;
Or looks on heaven with more than mortal eyes,
Bids his free soul expatiate in the skies,
Amid her kindred stars familiar roam,
Survey the region, and confess her home!
Such was the life great Scipio once admired,
Thus Atticus, and TRUMBULL thus retired.
Ye sacred Nine! that all my soul possess,
Whose raptures fire me, and whose visions bless,
Bear me, oh bear me to sequester'd scenes,
The bowery mazes, and surrounding greens:
To Thames's banks which fragrant breezes fill,
Or where ye Muses sport on COOPER'S HILL.
(On COOPER'S HILL eternal wreaths shall grow,
While lasts the mountain, or while Thames shall flow.)
I seem through consecrated walks to rove,
I hear soft music die along the grove:
Led by the sound, I roam from shade to shade,
By godlike poets venerable made:
Here his first lays majestic DENHAM sung;
There the last numbers flow'd from COWLEY'S tongue.
O early lost! what tears the river shed,
When the sad pomp along his banks was led!
His drooping swans on every note expire,
And on his willows hung each Muse's lyre.
Since fate relentless stopp'd their heavenly voice,
No more the forests ring, or groves rejoice;
Who now shall charm the shades, where COWLEY strung
His living harp, and lofty DENHAM sung?
But hark! the groves rejoice, the forest rings!
Are these revived? or is it GRANVILLE sings?
'Tis yours, my lord, to bless our soft retreats,
And call the Muses to their ancient seats;
To paint anew the flowery sylvan scenes,
To crown the forests with immortal greens,
Make Windsor hills in lofty numbers rise,
And lift her turrets nearer to the skies;
To sing those honours you deserve to wear,

219. great father: the Thames River.

257. Scipio: The ancient Roman general, leader of the great victory over Carthage in the Second Punic War, quietly retired to his country estate south of Rome. **258. Atticus:** Cicero's friend who left Rome in 88 B.C., with civil war imminent, to lead a life of studious leisure and writing in Athens. **Trumbull:** Sir William Trumbull, regarded by some as the one who suggested the writing of *Windsor Forest*, was a friend of Pope who retired to a house near the forest in 1700. ***264. Cooper's Hill:*** the setting and title of the great topographical poem by Sir John Denham (1615–1669). **272. Cowley:** Abraham Cowley (1618–1667), the Metaphysical poet.

And add new lustre to her silver star.
Here noble SURREY felt the sacred rage,
SURREY, the GRANVILLE of a former age:
Matchless his pen, victorious was his lance,
Bold in the lists, and graceful in the dance:
In the same shades the Cupids tuned his lyre,
To the same notes, of love and soft desire:
Fair Geraldine, bright object of his vow,
Then fill'd the groves, as heavenly Mira now.
Oh would'st thou sing what heroes Windsor bore,
What kings first breathed upon her winding shore,
Or raise old warriors, whose adored remains
In weeping vaults her hallow'd earth contains!
With Edward's acts adorn the shining page,
Stretch his long triumphs down through every age,
Draw monarchs chain'd, and Cressy's glorious field,
The lilies blazing on the regal shield;
Then, from her roofs when Verrio's colours fall,
And leave inanimate the naked wall,
Still in thy song should vanquish'd France appear,
And bleed for ever under Britain's spear.
Let softer strains ill-fated Henry mourn,
And palms eternal flourish round his urn.
Here o'er the martyr-king the marble weeps,
And, fast beside him, once-fear'd Edward sleeps:
Whom not th' extended Albion could contain,
From old Belerium to the northern main,
The grave unites; where e'en the great find rest,
And blended lie th' oppressor and th' oppress'd!
Make sacred Charles's tomb for ever known,
(Obscure the place, and uninscribed the stone)
O fact accursed! what tears has Albion shed,
Heavens, what new wounds! and how her old have bled!
She saw her sons with purple deaths expire,
Her sacred domes involved in rolling fire,
A dreadful series of intestine wars,
Inglorious triumphs and dishonest scars.
At length great Anna said: "Let discord cease!"
She said, the world obey'd, and all was peace!
In that blest moment from his oozy bed
Old Father Thames advanced his reverend head;
His tresses dropp'd with dews, and o'er the stream
His shining horns diffused a golden gleam:
Graved on his urn appear'd the moon, that guides
His swelling waters, and alternate tides;
The figured streams in waves of silver roll'd,
And on her banks Augusta rose in gold;
Around his throne the sea-born brothers stood,
Who swell with tributary urns his flood:
First the famed authors of his ancient name,
The winding Isis, and the fruitful Thame:
The Kennet swift, for silver eels renown'd;
The Loddon slow, with verdant alders crown'd;
Cole, whose dark streams his flowery islands lave;
And chalky Wey, that rolls a milky wave;
The blue, transparent Vandalis appears;
The gulphy Lee his sedgy tresses rears;
And sullen Mole, that hides his diving flood;
And silent Darent, stain'd with Danish blood.
High in the midst, upon his urn reclined,
(His sea-green mantle waving with the wind,)
The god appear'd: he turn'd his azure eyes
Where Windsor-domes and pompous turrets rise;
Then bow'd and spoke; the winds forgot to roar,
And the hush'd waves glide softly to the shore.
Hail, sacred peace! hail, long expected days,
That Thames's glory to the stars shall raise!
Though Tiber's streams immortal Rome behold,
Though foaming Hermus swells with tides of gold,
From Heaven itself though sevenfold Nilus flows,
And harvests on a hundred realms bestows;
These now no more shall be the Muse's themes,
Lost in my fame, as in the sea their streams.
Let Volga's banks with iron squadrons shine,
And groves of lances glitter on the Rhine,
Let barbarous Ganges arm a servile train;
Be mine the blessings of a peaceful reign.

291. Surrey: Henry Howard, Earl of Surrey (1517–1547), the great Renaissance lyric poet. "Geraldine" was the lady of his love poetry; "Mira," the beloved of Granville's verse. **303.** King Edward III. He defeated the French soundly at Crècy in France on August 26, 1346. **307. Verrio's colours:** Antonio Verrio (1639–1709), the Italian painter engaged by Charles II to adorn Windsor Castle with paintings celebrating Charles' victory over France. **311. ill-fated Henry:** Henvy VI, killed during the War of the Roses. **314. once-fear'd Edward:** Edward IV overthrew Henry VI in 1461. **316. Belerium:** Land's End, in Cornwall. **323. purple deaths:** the Great Plague of 1665.

324. rolling fire: the Great London fire of 1666. **336. Augusta:** London. **339–348.** a catalogue of rivers seen imaginatively by poets as creating the great Thames.

No more my sons shall dye with British blood
Red Iber's sands, or Ister's foaming flood:
Safe on my shore each unmolested swain
Shall tend the flocks, or reap the bearded grain;
The shady empire shall retain no trace
Of war or blood, but in the sylvan chase;
The trumpet sleep, whilst cheerful horns are blown,
And arms employ'd on birds and beasts alone.
Behold! th' ascending villas on my side
Project long shadows o'er the crystal tide.
Behold! Augusta's glittering spires increase,
And temples rise, the beauteous works of Peace,
I see, I see, where two fair cities bend
Their ample bow, a new Whitehall ascend!
There mighty nations shall inquire their doom,
The world's great oracle in times to come;
There kings shall sue, and suppliant states be seen
Once more to bend a British queen.
  Thy trees, fair Windsor! now shall leave their woods,
And half thy forest rush into thy floods,
Bear Britain's thunder, and her cross display,
To the bright regions of the rising day:
Tempt icy seas, where scarce the waters roll,
Where clearer flames glow round the frozen pole;
Or under southern skies exalt their sails,
Led by new stars, and borne by spicy gales!
For me the balm shall bleed, and amber flow,
The coral redden, and the ruby glow,
The pearly shell its lucid globe infold,
And Phœbus warm the ripening ore to gold,
The time shall come, when free as seas or wind
Unbounded Thames shall flow for all mankind,
Whole nations enter with each swelling tide,
And seas but join the regions they divide;
Earth's distant ends our glory shall behold,
And the new world launch forth to seek the old.
Then ships of uncouth form shall stem the tide,
And feather'd people crowd my wealthy side,
And naked youths and painted chiefs admire
Our speech, our colour, and our strange attire!
O stretch thy reign, fair Peace! from shore to shore,
Till conquest cease, and slavery be no more;
Till the freed Indians in their native groves
Reap their own fruits, and woo their sable loves,
Peru once more a race of kings behold,
And other Mexicos be roof'd with gold.
Exiled by thee from earth to deepest hell,
In brazen bonds, shall barbarous Discord dwell:
Gigantic Pride, pale Terror, gloomy Care,
And mad Ambition shall attend her there:
There purple Vengeance bathed in gore retires,
Her weapons blunted, and extinct her fires:
There hateful Envy her own snakes shall feel,
And Persecution mourn her broken wheel:
There Faction roar, Rebellion bite her chain,
And gasping Furies thirst for blood in vain.
  Here cease thy fight, nor with unhallow'd lays
Touch the fair fame of Albion's golden days:
The thoughts of gods let Granville's verse recite,
And bring the scenes of opening fate to light:
My humble Muse, in unambitious strains,
Paints the green forests and the flowery plains.
Where Peace descending bids her olives spring,
And scatters blessings from her dove-like wing.
Even I more sweetly pass my careless days,
Pleased in the silent shade with empty praise;
Enough for me, that to the listening swains
First in the fields I sung the sylvan strains.

(1713)

379. two fair cities: London and Westminster. **380. new Whitehall:** the royal palace, burned completely in 1698. Many plans for a new palace were being advanced.

AN ESSAY ON CRITICISM

I

'Tis hard to say, if greater want of skill
Appear in writing or in judging ill;
But, of the two, less dangerous is the offence
To tire our patience, then mislead our sense.
Some few in that, but numbers err in this,
Ten censure wrong for one who writes amiss;
A fool might once himself alone expose,
Now one in verse makes many more in prose.
  'Tis with our judgments as our watches, none
Go just alike, yet each believes his own.
In poets as true genius is but rare,
True taste as seldom is the critic's share,
Both must alike from Heaven derive their light,

These born to judge, as well as those to write.
Let such teach others who themselves excel,
And censure freely who have written well.
Authors are partial to their wit, 'tis true,
But are not critics to their judgment too?
Yet, if we look more closely, we shall find
Most have the seeds of judgment in their mind
Nature affords at least a glimmering light;
The lines, though touch'd but faintly, are drawn right.
But as the slightest sketch, if justly traced,
Is by ill colouring but the more disgraced,
So by false learning is good sense defaced;
Some are bewilder'd in the maze of schools,
And some made coxcombs Nature meant but fools.
In search of wit these lose their common sense,
And then turn critics in their own defence:
Each burns alike, who can, or cannot write,
Or with a rival's, or an eunuch's spite.
All fools have still an itching to deride,
And fain would be upon the laughing side.
If Mævius scribble in Apollo's spite,
There are who judge still worse than he can write.
Some have at first for wits, then poets pass'd,
Turn'd critics next, and proved plain fools at last.
Some neither can for wits nor critics pass,
As heavy mules are neither horse nor ass.
Those half-learn'd witlings, numerous in our isle,
As half-form'd insects on the banks of Nile;
Unfinish'd things, one knows not what to call,
Their generation's so equivocal:
To tell them would a hundred tongues require,
Or one vain wit's, that might a hundred tire.
But you who seek to give and merit fame,
And justly bear a critic's noble name,
Be sure yourself and your own reach to know,
How far your genius, taste, and learning go;
Launch not beyond your depth, but be discreet,
And mark that point where sense and dulness meet.
Nature to all things fix'd the limits fit,
And wisely curb'd proud man's pretending wit.
As on the land while here the ocean gains,
In other parts it leaves wide sandy plains;
Thus in the soul while memory prevails,
The solid power of understanding fails;
Where beams of warm imagination play,
The memory's soft figures melt away.
One science only will one genius fit:
So vast is art, so narrow human wit:
Not only bounded to peculiar arts,
But oft in those confined to single parts.
Like kings we lose the conquests gain'd before,
By vain ambition still to make them more:
Each might his servile province well command,
Would all but stoop to what they understand.
First follow Nature, and your judgment frame
By her just standard, which is still the same:
Unerring Nature, still divinely bright,
One clear, unchanged, and universal light,
Life, force, and beauty, must to all impart,
At once the source, and end, and test of Art.
Art from that fund each just supply provides;
Works without show, and without pomp presides:
In some fair body thus th' informing soul
With spirits feeds, with vigour fills the whole,
Each motion guides, and every nerve sustains;
Itself unseen, but in th' effects remains.
Some, to whom Heaven in wit has been profuse,
Want as much more to turn it to its use;
For wit and judgment often are at strife,
Though meant each other's aid, like man and wife.
'Tis more to guide, than spur the Muse's steed;
Restrain his fury, than provoke his speed:
The winged courser, like a generous horse,
Shows most true mettle when you check his course.
Those rules of old discover'd, not devised,
Are Nature still, but Nature methodised:
Nature, like liberty, is but restrain'd
By the same laws which first herself ordain'd.
Hear how learn'd Greece her useful rules indites,
When to repress, and when indulge our flights:
High on Parnassus' top her sons she show'd,
And pointed out those arduous paths they trod;
Held from afar, aloft, the immortal prize,
And urged the rest by equal steps to rise.
Just precepts thus from great examples given,
She drew from them what they derive from Heaven.

AN ESSAY ON CRITICISM. **34. Mævius:** a bad poet of ancient Rome. Pope is fond of using such names to characterize types of bad poets and critics.

80. wit: creativity, genius. **82. judgment:** discrimination, restraint. **94. Parnassus:** the mountain in southern Greece, dwelling place of Apollo and the Muses, sources of poetic inspiration.

The generous critic fann'd the poet's fire,
And taught the world with reason to admire.
Then criticism the Muse's handmaid proved,
To dress her charms, and make her more beloved:
But following wits from that intention stray'd,
Who could not win the mistress, woo'd the maid;
Against the poets their own arms they turn'd,
Sure to hate most the men from whom they learn'd.
So modern 'pothecaries, taught the art
By doctor's bills to play the doctor's part,
Bold in the practice of mistaken rules,
Prescribe, apply, and call their masters fools.
Some on the leaves of ancient authors prey,
Nor time nor moths e'er spoil'd so much as they:
Some drily plain, without invention's aid,
Write dull receipts how poems may be made.
These leave the sense, their learning to display,
And those explain the meaning quite away.

You then whose judgment the right course would steer,
Know well each Ancient's proper character:
His fable, subject, scope in every page;
Religion, country, genius of his age:
Without all these at once before your eyes,
Cavil you may, but never criticise.
Be Homer's works your study and delight,
Read them by day, and meditate by night;
Thence form your judgment, thence your maxims bring,
And trace the Muses upward to their spring.
Still with itself compared, his text peruse;
And let your comment be the Mantuan Muse.

When first young Maro in his boundless mind
A work to outlast immortal Rome design'd,
Perhaps he seem'd above the critic's law,
And but from Nature's fountains scorn'd to draw:
But when to examine every part he came,
Nature and Homer were, he found, the same.
Convinced, amazed, he checks the bold design;
And rules as strict his labour'd work confine,
As if the Stagyrite o'erlook'd each line.
Learn hence for ancient rules a just esteem;
To copy Nature is to copy them.

Some beauties yet no precepts can declare,
For there's a happiness as well as care.
Music resembles poetry, in each
Are nameless graces which no methods teach,
And which a master-hand alone can reach.
If, where the rules not far enough extend,
(Since rules were made but to promote their end)
Some lucky licence answer to the full
The intent proposed, that licence is a rule.
Thus Pegasus, a nearer way to take,
May boldly deviate from the common track.
Great wits sometimes may gloriously offend,
And rise to faults true critics dare not mend;
From vulgar bounds with brave disorder part,
And snatch a grace beyond the reach of art,
Which, without passing through the judgment, gains
The heart, and all its end at once attains.
In prospects thus, some objects please our eyes,
Which out of Nature's common order rise,
The shapeless rock, or hanging precipice.
But though the ancients thus their rules invade,
(As kings dispense with laws themselves have made)
Moderns, beware! or if you must offend
Against the precept, ne'er transgress its end;
Let it be seldom, and compell'd by need;
And have, at least, their precedent to plead.
The critic else proceeds without remorse,
Seizes your fame, and puts his laws in force.

I know there are, to whose presumptuous thoughts
Those freer beauties, even in them, seem faults.
Some figures monstrous and misshaped appear,
Consider'd singly, or beheld too near,
Which, but proportion'd to their light, or place,
Due distance reconciles to form and grace.
A prudent chief not always must display
His powers, in equal ranks, and fair array,
But with the occasion and the place comply,
Conceal his force, nay seem sometimes to fly.
Those oft are stratagems which errors seem,
Nor is it Homer nods, but we that dream.

Still green with bays each ancient altar stands,
Above the reach of sacrilegious hands;
Secure from flames, from envy's fiercer rage,
Destructive war, and all-involving age.

115. receipts: prescriptions, rules. **120. fable:** story, myth. **129. Mantuan Muse:** Virgil, born near Mantua. **130. Maro:** Virgil. **138. Stagyrite:** Aristotle, born in Stagyra in Greece.

150. Pegasus: poetic inspiration. **181. bays:** a wreath of laurel leaves.

See from each clime the learn'd their incense bring!
Hear in all tongues consenting pæans ring!
In praise so just let every voice be join'd,
And fill the general chorus of mankind.
Hail, bards triumphant! born in happier days;
Immortal heirs of universal praise!
Whose honours with increase of ages grow,
As streams roll down, enlarging as they flow;
Nations unborn your mighty names shall sound,
And worlds applaud that must not yet be found!
O may some spark of your celestial fire,
The last, the meanest of your sons inspire,
(That on weak wings, from far, pursues your flights;
Glows while he reads, but trembles as he writes)
To teach vain wits a science little known,
To admire superior sense, and doubt their own!

II

Of all the causes which conspire to blind
Man's erring judgment, and misguide the mind,
What the weak head with strongest bias rules,
Is PRIDE, the never-failing voice of fools.
Whatever Nature has in worth denied,
She gives in large recruits of needful pride;
For as in bodies, thus in souls we find
What wants in blood and spirits, swell'd with wind:
Pride, where wit fails, steps in to our defence,
And fills up all the mighty void of sense.
If once right reason drives that cloud away,
Truth breaks upon us with resistless day.
Trust not yourself; but your defects to know,
Make use of every friend—and every foe.
A little learning is a dangerous thing;
Drink deep, or taste not the Pierian spring:
There shallow draughts intoxicate the brain,
And drinking largely sobers us again.
Fired at first sight with what the Muse imparts,
In fearless youth we tempt the heights of arts,
While from the bounded level of our mind,
Short views we take, nor see the lengths behind;
But more advanced, behold with strange surprise
New distant scenes of endless science rise!
So pleased at first the towering Alps we try,
Mount o'er the vales, and seem to tread the sky,
The eternal snows appear already passed,
And the first clouds and mountains seem the last:
But, those attain'd, we tremble to survey
The growing labours of the lengthen'd way,
The increasing prospect tires our wandering eyes,
Hills peep o'er hills, and Alps on Alps arise!
A perfect judge will read each work of wit
With the same spirit that its author writ:
Survey the WHOLE, nor seeks slight faults to find
Where Nature moves, and rapture warms the mind,
Nor lose, for that malignant dull delight,
The generous pleasure to be charm'd with wit.
But in such lays as neither ebb nor flow,
Correctly cold, and regularly low,
That shunning faults, one quiet tenor keep;
We cannot blame indeed—but we may sleep.
In wit, as Nature, what affects our hearts
Is not th' exactness of peculiar parts;
'Tis not a lip, or eye, we beauty call,
But the joint force and full result of all.
Thus when we view some well-proportion'd dome,
(The world's just wonder, and ev'n thine, O Rome!)
No single parts unequally surprise,
All comes united to th' admiring eyes;
No monstrous height, or breadth or length appear;
The whole at once is bold and regular.
Whoever thinks a faultless piece to see,
Thinks what ne'er was, nor is, nor e'er shall be,
In every work regard the writer's end,
Since none can compass more than they intend;
And if the means be just, the conduct true,
Applause, in spite of trivial faults, is due.
As men of breeding, sometimes men of wit,
To avoid great errors, must the less commit:
Neglect the rules each verbal critic lays,
For not to know some trifles, is a praise.
Most critics, fond of some subservient art,
Still make the whole depend upon a part:
They talk of principles, but notions prize,
And all to one loved folly sacrifice.
Once on a time, La Mancha's knight, they say,

216. Pierian spring: Hippocrene, the fountain on Mt. Helicon sacred to the Muses and a source of poetic inspiration.

267. La Mancha's knight: Don Quixote. Lines 267–284 recall the episode in a sequel to Cervantes' novel, in which Quixote meets two scholars, one of whom had written a play. The scholar, eager to follow Aristotle's rules, asks for the Knight's advice, and Quixote promptly urges him to include an exciting battle scene, even if such a scene involves taking liberties with ancient rules.

A certain bard encountering on the way,
Discoursed in terms as just, with looks as sage,
As e'er could Dennis, of the Grecian stage;
Concluding all were desperate sots and fools,
Who durst depart from Aristotle's rules.
Our author, happy in a judge so nice,
Produced his play, and begg'd the knight's advice;
Made him observe the subject and the plot,
The manners, passions, unities; what not?
All which, exact to rule, were brought about,
Were but a combat in the lists left out.
"What! leave the combat out?" exclaims the knight;
Yes, or we must renounce the Stagyrite.
"Not so, by heaven, (he answers in a rage)
"Knights, squires, and steeds, must enter on the stage."
So vast a throng the stage can ne'er contain.
"Then build a new, or act it in a plain."
Thus critics of less judgment than caprice,
Curious, not knowing, not exact but nice,
Form short ideas; and offend in arts
(As most in manners) by a love to parts.
Some to Conceit alone their taste confine,
And glittering thoughts struck out at every line;
Pleased with a work where nothing's just or fit;
One glaring chaos and wild heap of wit.
Poets, like painters, thus, unskill'd to trace
The naked Nature and the living grace,
With gold and jewels cover every part,
And hide with ornaments their want of art.
True wit is Nature to advantage dress'd;
What oft was thought, but ne'er so well express'd;
Something, whose truth convinced at sight we find,
That gives us back the image of our mind.
As shades more sweetly recommend the light,
So modest plainness sets off sprightly wit.
For works may have more wit than does 'em good,
As bodies perish through excess of blood.
Others for Language all their care express,
And value books, as women men, for dress:
Their praise is still,—The style is excellent;
The sense, they humbly take upon content.
Words are like leaves; and where they most abound,
Much fruit of sense beneath is rarely found.
False eloquence, like the prismatic glass,
Its gaudy colours spreads on every place;
The face of Nature we no more survey,
All glares alike, without distinction gay:
But true expression, like th' unchanging sun,
Clears and improves whate'er it shines upon,
It gilds all objects, but it alters none.
Expression is the dress of thought, and still
Appears more decent, as more suitable;
A vile conceit in pompous words express'd
Is like a clown in regal purple dress'd:
For different styles with different subjects sort,
As several garbs, with country, town, and court.
Some by old words to fame have made pretence,
Ancients in phrase, mere moderns in their sense;
Such labour'd nothings, in so strange a style,
Amaze the unlearn'd, and make the learned smile.
Unlucky as Fungoso in the play,
These sparks with awkward vanity display
What the fine gentleman wore yesterday;
And but so mimic ancient wits at best,
As apes our grandsires, in their doublets dress'd.
In words, as fashions, the same rule will hold;
Alike fantastic, if too new, or old:
Be not the first by whom the new are tried,
Nor yet the last to lay the old aside.
But most by numbers judge a poet's song:
And smooth or rough, with them, is right or wrong:
In the bright muse, though thousand charms conspire,
Her voice is all these tuneful fools admire
Who haunt Parnassus but to please their ear,
Not mend their minds; as some to church repair,
Not for the doctrine, but the music there.
These equal syllables alone require,
Though oft the ear the open vowels tire;
While expletives their feeble aid do join;
And ten low words oft creep in one dull line:
While they ring round the same unvaried chimes,
With sure returns of still expected rhymes;
Where'er you find "the cooling western breeze,"
In the next line, it "whispers through the trees":

270. Dennis: John Dennis (1657–1734), regarded by many as a highly conservative critic, although his works reveal a strong interest in matters like passion and sublimity in art. **289. Conceit:** elaborate imagery. **308. take upon content:** accept at face value.

328. Fungoso: a student in Ben Jonson's play, *Every Man Out of His Humour*; one who seems a bit behind the style of the day. **344–83.** In these lines the medium is the message as Pope uses concrete examples, good and bad, of various techniques of meter, rhyme, language, etc.

If crystal streams "with pleasing murmurs creep":
The reader's threaten'd (not in vain) with "sleep."
Then, at the last and only couplet fraught
With some unmeaning thing they call a thought,
A needless Alexandrine ends the song,
That, like a wounded snake, drags its slow length along.
Leave such to tune their own dull rhymes, and know
What's roundly smooth, or languishingly slow;
And praise the easy vigour of a line,
Where Denham's strength, and Waller's sweetness join.
True ease in writing comes from art, not chance,
As those move easiest who have learn'd to dance.
'Tis not enough no harshness gives offence,
The sound must seem an echo to the sense:
Soft is the strain when Zephyr gently blows,
And the smooth stream in smoother numbers flows;
But when loud surges lash the sounding shore,
The hoarse, rough verse should like the torrent roar.
When Ajax strives some rock's vast weight to throw,
The line too labours, and the words move slow:
Not so, when swift Camilla scours the plain,
Flies o'er the unbending corn, and skims along the main.
Hear how Timotheus' varied lays surprise,
And bid alternate passions fall and rise!
While, at each change, the son of Libyan Jove
Now burns with glory, and then melts with love;
Now his fierce eyes with sparkling fury glow,
Now sighs steal out, and tears begin to flow:
Persians and Greeks like turns of Nature found,
And the world's victor stood subdued by sound!
The power of music all our hearts allow,
And what Timotheus was, is DRYDEN now.
  Avoid extremes; and shun the fault of such,
Who still are pleased too little or too much.
At every trifle scorn to take offence,
That always shows great pride, or little sense;
Those heads, as stomachs, are not sure the best,
Which nauseate all, and nothing can digest.
Yet let not each gay turn thy rapture move;
For fools admire, but men of sense approve:
As things seem large which we through mists descry,
Dulness is ever apt to magnify.
  Some foreign writers, some our own despise;
The ancients only, or the moderns prize.
Thus wit, like faith, by each man is applied
To one small sect, and all are damn'd beside.
Meanly they seek the blessing to confine,
And force that sun but on a part to shine,
Which not alone the southern wit sublimes,
But ripens spirits in cold northern climes;
Which from the first has shone on ages past,
Enlights the present, and shall warm the last;
Though each may feel increases and decays,
And see now clearer and now darker days.
Regard not then if wit be old or new,
But blame the false, and value still the true.
  Some ne'er advance a judgment of their own,
But catch the spreading notion of the town;
They reason and conclude by precedent,
And own stale nonsense which they ne'er invent.
Some judge of authors' names, not works, and then
Nor praise nor blame the writings, but the men.
Of all this servile herd, the worst is he
That in proud dulness joins with quality,
A constant critic at the great man's board,
To fetch and carry nonsense for my lord.
What woful stuff this madrigal would be,
In some starved hackney sonnetteer, or me?
But let a lord once own the happy lines,
How the wit brightens! how the style refines!
Before his sacred name flies every fault,
And each exalted stanza teems with thought!
  The vulgar thus through imitation err;
As oft the learn'd by being singular;
So much they scorn the crowd, that if the throng
By chance go right, they purposely go wrong:
So schismatics the plain believers quit,
And are but damn'd for having too much wit.
Some praise at morning what they blame at night;
But always think the last opinion right.
A Muse by these is like a mistress used,

356. Alexandrine: an iambic hexameter line thought to be an unnecessary variation from the standard pentameter. The next line is in fact an Alexandrine. **361. Denham . . . Waller:** John Denham (1615–1669) and Edmund Waller (1606–1687) were regarded as the great masters of the iambic pentameter couplet. **370. Ajax:** one of the Greek heroes of the *Iliad.* **372. Camilla:** a legendary Volscian maiden, described by Virgil in the *Aeneid* as a woman of remarkable speed. **374. Timotheus:** the noted ancient poet and musician of Miletus. He claimed to have revolutionized music. **376. son:** Alexander the Great.

This hour she's idolized, the next abused;
While their weak heads, like towns unfortified,
'Twixt sense and nonsense daily change their side.
Ask them the cause; they're wiser still, they say;
And still to-morrow's wiser than to-day.
We think our fathers fools, so wise we grow;
Our wiser sons, no doubt, will think us so.
Once school-divines this zealous isle o'erspread;
Who knew most sentences, was deepest read:
Faith, Gospel, all seem'd made to be disputed,
And none had sense enough to be confuted:
Scotists and Thomists, now in peace remain,
Amidst their kindred cobwebs in Duck-lane.
If Faith itself has different dresses worn,
What wonder modes in wit should take their turn?
Oft leaving what is natural and fit,
The current folly proves the ready wit;
And authors think their reputation safe,
Which lives as long as fools are pleased to laugh.
  Some valuing those of their own side or mind,
Still make themselves the measure of mankind:
Fondly we think we honour merit then,
When we but praise ourselves in other men.
Parties in wit attend on those of state,
And public faction doubles private hate.
Pride, malice, folly, against Dryden rose,
In various shapes of parsons, critics, beaus;
But sense survived when merry jests were past;
For rising merit will buoy up at last.
Might he return, and bless once more our eyes,
New Blackmores and new Milbourns must arise:
Nay, should great Homer lift his awful head,
Zoilus again would start up from the dead.
Envy will merit, as its shade, pursue;
But like a shadow, proves the substance true:
For envied wit, like Sol eclipsed, makes known
The opposing body's grossness, not its own.
When first that sun too powerful beams displays,
It draws up vapours which obscure its rays;
But even those clouds at last adorn its way,
Reflect new glories, and augment the day.
  Be thou the first true merit to befriend;
His praise is lost, who stays till all commend.
Short is the date, alas! of modern rhymes,
And 'tis but just to let them live betimes.
No longer now that golden age appears,
When patriarch-wits survived a thousand years:
Now length of fame (our second life) is lost,
And bare threescore is all even that can boast;
Our sons their fathers' failing language see,
And such as Chaucer is, shall Dryden be.
So when the faithful pencil has design'd
Some bright idea of the master's mind,
Where a new word leaps out at his command,
And ready Nature waits upon his hand;
When the ripe colours soften and unite,
And sweetly melt into just shade and light;
When mellow years their full perfection give,
And each bold figure just begins to live,
The treacherous colours the fair art betray,
And all the bright creation fades away!
  Unhappy wit, like most mistaken things,
Atones not for that envy which it brings.
In youth alone its empty praise we boast,
But soon the short-lived vanity is lost:
Like some fair flower the early spring supplies,
That gaily blooms, but even in blooming dies.
What is this wit, which must our cares employ?
The owner's wife, that other men enjoy;
Then most our trouble still when most admired,
And still the more we give, the more required;
Whose fame with pains we guard, but lose with ease,
Sure some to vex, but never all to please;
'Tis what the vicious fear, the virtuous shun,
By fools 'tis hated, and by knaves undone!
  If wit so much from ignorance undergo,
Ah, let not learning too commence its foe!
Of old, those met rewards who could excel,
And such were praised who but endeavour'd well:
Though triumphs were to generals only due,
Crowns were reserved to grace the soldiers too.
Now, they who reach Parnassus' lofty crown,

444. Scotists and Thomists: disciples of Duns Scotus and Thomas Aquinas, the two great medieval philosophers at odds with each other on many issues. **445. Duck-lane:** Pope notes: "A place where old and second-hand books were sold formerly, near Smithfield." **463. Blackmore . . . Milbourn:** a reference to Sir Richard Blackmore (1654–1729) and the Reverend Luke Milbourn (1649–1720), two of the critics and clergymen who attacked Dryden's work. **465. Zoilus:** the ancient critic who attacked Homer. His became a type name for the bad critic.

477. betimes: until their time has come.

Employ their pains to spurn some others down;
And while self-love each jealous writer rules,
Contending wits become the sport of fools:
But still the worst with most regret commend,
For each ill author is as bad a friend.
To what base ends, and by what abject ways,
Are mortals urged though sacred lust of praise!
Ah ne'er so dire a thirst of glory boast,
Nor in the critic let the man be lost.
Good nature and good sense must ever join;
To err is human, to forgive, divine.
  But if in noble minds some dregs remain,
Not yet purged off, of spleen and sour disdain;
Discharge that rage on more provoking crimes,
Nor fear a dearth in these flagitious times.
No pardon vile obscenity should find,
Though wit and art conspire to move your mind;
But dulness with obscenity must prove
As shameful sure as impotence in love.
In the fat age of pleasure, wealth, and ease,
Sprung the rank weed, and thrived with large
    increase:
When love was all an easy monarch's care;
Seldom at council, never in a war:
Jilts ruled the state, and statesmen farces writ;
Nay wits had pensions, and young lords had wit:
The fair sat panting at a courtier's play,
And not a mask went unimproved away:
The modest fan was lifted up no more,
And virgins smiled at what they blush'd before.
The following licence of a foreign reign
Did all the dregs of bold Socinus drain;
Then unbelieving priests reform'd the nation,
And taught more pleasant methods of salvation;
Where Heaven's free subjects might their rights
    dispute,
Lest God Himself should seem too absolute:
Pulpits their sacred satire learn'd to spare,
And vice admired to find a flatterer there!
Encouraged thus, Wit's Titans braved the skies,
And the press groan'd with licensed blasphemies.
These monsters, critics! with your darts engage,
Here point your thunder, and exhaust your rage!
Yet shun their fault, who, scandalously nice,
Will needs mistake an author into vice;
All seems infected that th' infected spy,
As all looks yellow to the jaundiced eye.

III

  Learn then what morals critics ought to
    show,
For 'tis but half a judge's task, to know.
'Tis not enough, taste, judgment, learning, join;
In all you speak, let truth and candour shine:
That not alone what to your sense is due
All may allow; but seek your friendship too.
  Be silent always, when you doubt your sense;
And speak, though sure, with seeming diffidence:
Some positive, persisting fops we know,
Who, if once wrong, will needs be always so;
But you, with pleasure own your errors past,
And make each day a critique on the last.
  'Tis not enough your counsel still be true;
Blunt truths more mischief than nice falsehoods do;
Men must be taught as if you taught them not,
And things unknown proposed as things forgot.
Without good-breeding, truth is disapproved;
That only makes superior sense beloved.
  Be niggards of advice on no pretence;
For the worst avarice is that of sense.
With mean complaisance ne'er betray your
    trust,
Nor be so civil as to prove unjust.
Fear not the anger of the wise to raise;
Those best can bear reproof who merit praise.
  'Twere well might critics still this freedom take,
But Appius reddens at each word you speak,
And stares, tremendous, with a threatening eye,
Like some fierce tyrant in old tapestry.
Fear most to tax an Honourable fool,
Whose right it is, uncensured, to be dull;
Such, without wit, are poets when they
    please,
As without learning they can take degrees.
Leave dangerous truths to unsuccessful satires,
And flattery to fulsome dedicators,
Whom, when they praise, the world believes no
    more,
Than when they promise to give scribbling o'er.

527. spleen: The spleen was formerly regarded as being the source of such hostile emotions. **529. flagitious:** wicked. **536.** The reference is to Charles II. **545. Socinus:** Faustus Socinus (1539–1604), Italian religious reformer and propounder of several heresies.

585. Appius: a reference to John Dennis (1657–1734), dramatist, critic, author of the unsuccessful play, *Appius and Virginia.*

'Tis best sometimes your censure to restrain,
And charitably let the dull be vain:
Your silence there is better than your spite,
For who can rail so long as they can write?
Still humming on, their drowsy course they keep,
And lash'd so long, like tops, are lash'd asleep.
False steps but help them to renew the race,
As, after stumbling, jades will mend their pace.
What crowds of these, impenitently bold,
In sounds and jingling syllables grown old,
Still run on poets in a raging vein,
Even to the dregs and squeezings of the brain,
Strain out the last dull dropping of their sense,
And rhyme with all the rage of impotence!
Such shameless bards we have; and yet 'tis true,
There are as mad, abandon'd critics too.
The bookful blockhead, ignorantly read,
With loads of learned lumber in his head,
With his own tongue still edifies his ears,
And always listening to himself appears.
All books he reads, and all he reads assails,
From Dryden's Fables down to D'Urfey's Tales:
With him, most authors steal their works, or buy;
Garth did not write his own Dispensary.
Name a new play, and he's the poet's friend,
Nay show'd his faults—but when would poets mend?
No place so sacred from such fops is barr'd,
Nor is Paul's church more safe than Paul's church-yard:
Nay, fly to altars; there they'll talk you dead;
For fools rush in where angels fear to tread,
Distrustful sense with modest caution speaks,
It still looks home, and short excursions makes;
But rattling nonsense in full volleys breaks,
And never shock'd, and never turn'd aside,
Bursts out, resistless, with a thundering tide.
But where's the man who counsel can bestow,
Still pleased to teach, and yet not proud to know?
Unbiass'd, or by favour, or by spite;
Not dully prepossess'd, nor blindly right;
Though learn'd, well-bred; and though well-bred, sincere;
Modestly bold, and humanly severe:
Who to a friend his faults can freely show,
And gladly praise the merit of a foe?
Bless'd with a taste exact, yet unconfined;
A knowledge both of books and human kind;
Generous converse; a soul exempt from pride;
And love to praise, with reason on his side?
Such once were critics; such the happy few,
Athens and Rome in better ages knew.
The mighty Stagyrite first left the shore,
Spread all his sails, and durst the deeps explore;
He steer'd securely, and discover'd far,
Led by the light of the Mæonian star.
Poets, a race long unconfined, and free,
Still fond and proud of savage liberty,
Received his laws; and stood convinced 'twas fit,
Who conquer'd Nature, should preside o'er Wit.
Horace still charms with graceful negligence,
And without method talks us into sense,
Will, like a friend, familiarly convey
The truest notions in the easiest way.
He, who supreme in judgment, as in wit,
Might boldly censure, as he boldly writ,
Yet judged with coolness, though he sung with fire;
His precepts teach but what his works inspire.
Our critics take a contrary extreme,
They judge with fury, but they write with phlegm:
Nor suffers Horace more in wrong translations
By wits, than critics in as wrong quotations.
See Dionysius Homer's thoughts refine,
And call new beauties forth from every line!
Fancy and art in gay Petronius please,
The scholar's learning with the courtier's ease.
In grave Quintilian's copious work, we find
The justest rules and clearest method join'd:
Thus useful arms in magazines we place,
All ranged in order, and disposed with grace,
But less to please the eye, than arm the hand,
Still fit for use, and ready at command.

603. jades: worn-out horses. **617.** A reference to John Dryden's *Fables Ancient and Modern* (1700) and to *Tales Tragical and Comical* (1704) by Thomas Durfey (1653–1723), a popular and versatile writer of the day. **619.** A reference to Samuel Garth (1661–1719) and to his great satire on apothecaries, *The Dispensary*, published in 1699.

648. Mæonian star: Homer was, according to one legend, born in Maeonia, the ancient name for Lydia. **662. with phlegm:** sluggishly. **665. Dionysius:** Dionysius of Halicarnassus, a critic from ancient Rome. **667. Petronius:** Still another critic from ancient Rome, Petronius Arbiter is supposedly the author of the *Satyricon*. **669. Quintilian:** a reference to the great Roman critic and rhetorician, author of the influential *Institutio Oratoria*.

Thee, bold Longinus! all the Nine inspire,
And bless their critic with a poet's fire.
An ardent judge, who, zealous in his trust,
With warmth gives sentence, yet is always just:
Whose own example strengthens all his laws:
And is himself that great sublime he draws.
Thus long succeeding critics justly reign'd,
Licence repress'd, and useful laws ordain'd.
Learning and Rome alike in empire grew;
And arts still follow'd where her eagles flew;
From the same foes, at last, both felt their doom,
And the same age saw Learning fall, and Rome.
With Tyranny, then Superstition join'd,
As that the body, this enslaved the mind;
Much was believed, but little understood,
And to be dull was construed to be good;
A second deluge learning thus o'errun,
And the monks finish'd what the Goths begun.
At length Erasmus, that great injured name,
(The glory of the priesthood, and the shame!)
Stemm'd the wild torrent of a barbarous age,
And drove those holy Vandals off the stage.
But see! each Muse, in Leo's golden days,
Starts from her trance, and trims her wither'd bays;
Rome's ancient Genius, o'er its ruins spread,
Shakes off the dust, and rears his reverend head.
Then Sculpture and her sister-arts revive;
Stones leaped to form, and rocks began to live;
With sweeter notes each rising temple rung;
A Raphael painted, and a Vida sung.
Immortal Vida: on whose honour'd brow
The poet's bays and critic's ivy grow:
Cremona now shall ever boast thy name,
As next in place to Mantua, next in fame!
But soon by impious arms from Latium chased,
Their ancient bounds the banish'd Muses pass'd;
Thence Arts o'er all the northern world advance,
But critic-learning flourish'd most in France;
The rules a nation, born to serve, obeys;
And Boileau still in right of Horace sways.
But we, brave Britons, foreign laws despised,
And kept unconquer'd, and uncivilised;
Fierce for the liberties of wit and bold,
We still defined the Romans, as of old.
Yet some there were, among the sounder few
Of those who less presumed, and better knew,
Who durst assert the juster ancient cause,
And here restored Wit's fundamental laws.
Such was the Muse, whose rules and practice tell,
"Nature's chief Masterpiece is writing well,"
Such was Roscommon, not more learn'd than good,
With manners generous as his noble blood;
To him the wit of Greece and Rome was known,
And every author's merit, but his own.
Such late was Walsh—the Muse's judge and friend,
Who justly knew to blame or to commend:
To failings mild, but zealous for desert;
The clearest head, and the sincerest heart.
This humble praise, lamented shade! receive,
This praise at least a grateful Muse may give:
The Muse, whose early voice you taught to sing,
Prescribed her heights, and pruned her tender wing,
(Her guide now lost) no more attempts to rise,
But in low numbers short excursions tries:
Content, if hence the unlearn'd their wants may view,
The learn'd reflect on what before they knew;
Careless of censure, nor too fond of fame;
Still pleased to praise, yet not afraid to blame;
Averse alike to flatter, or offend;
Not free from faults, nor yet too vain to mend.

(1711)

675. Longinus: a Greek rhetorician, reputedly the author of the famous treatise *On the Sublime,* a document widely admired in the eighteenth century. **693. Erasmus:** Erasmus (1466?–1536), the gifted Dutch humanist and author of the *Praise of Folly.* An influential figure in the Renaissance. **697. Leo:** The reference is to Pope Leo X, patron of the arts. **704. Vida:** Marco Sirolamo Vida (ca. 1485–1566), Italian humanist and author of the important *Art of Poetry.* He was born in Cremona. **709. Latium:** The reference here is to ancient Italy. **714. Boileau:** Nicolas Boileau (1636–1711), French critic and author of still another *Art of Poetry.* **724.** Pope attributes the quotation to the Duke of Buckingham's *Essay on Poetry.* **725. Roscommon:** Wentworth Dillon (ca. 1630–1685), Fourth Earl of Roscommon, translator of Horace's *Art of Poetry.* **729. Walsh:** William Walsh (1663–1708), friend and advisor of Pope. See p. 16.

The Rape of the Lock

AN HEROI-COMICAL POEM

*Dedication to Mrs. Arabella Fermor**

MADAM,—It will be in vain to deny that I have some regard for this piece, since I dedicate it to you. Yet you may bear me witness, it was intended only to divert a few young ladies, who have good sense and good humour enough to laugh not only at their sex's little unguarded follies, but at their own. But as it was communicated with the air of a secret, it soon found its way into the world. An imperfect copy having been offered to a bookseller, you had the good-nature for my sake to consent to the publication of one more correct: this I was forced to before I had executed half my design, for the machinery was entirely wanting to complete it.

The machinery, Madam, is a term invented by the critics to signify that part which the Deities, Angels, or Dæmons are made to act in a Poem: for the ancient Poets are in one respect like many modern ladies: let an action be never so trivial in itself, they always make it appear of the utmost importance. These machines I determined to raise on a very new and odd foundation, the Rosicrucian** doctrine of Spirits.

I know how disagreeable it is to make use of hard words before a lady; but 'tis so much the concern of a Poet to have his works understood, and particularly by your sex, that you must give me leave to explain two or three difficult terms.

The Rosicrucians are a people I must bring you acquainted with. The best account I know of them is in a French book called *Le Comte de Gabalis*, which, both in its title and size, is so like a novel that many of the fair sex have read it for one by mistake. According to these gentlemen, the four elements are inhabited by Spirits which they call Sylphs, Gnomes, Nymphs and Salamanders. The Gnomes, or Dæmons of Earth, delight in mischief; but the Sylphs, whose habitation is in the air, are the best-conditioned creatures imaginable. For they say any mortals may enjoy the most intimate familiarities with these gentle Spirits, upon a condition very easy to all true adepts, an inviolate preservation of chasity.

As to the following Cantos, all the passages of them are as fabulous as the vision at the beginning, or the transformation at the end (except the loss of your hair, which I always mention with reverence). The human persons are as fictitious as the airy ones; and the character of Belinda, as it is now managed, resembles you in nothing but in beauty.

If this Poem had as many graces as there are in your person, or in your mind, yet I could never hope it should pass through the world half so uncensured as you have done. But let its fortune be what it will, mine is happy enough, to have given me this occasion of assuring you that I am, with the truest esteem, Madam, your most obedient, humble Servant,

A. POPE.

Nolueram, Belinda, tuos violare capillos;
Sed juvat, hoc precibus me tribuisse tuis.
—MART.***

CANTO I

What dire offence from amorous causes springs,
What mighty contests rise from trivial things,
I sing—This verse to CARYLL, Muse! is due:
This, even Belinda may vouchsafe to view;
Slight is the subject, but not so the praise,
If she inspire, and he approve my lays.
Say what strange motive, goddess! could compel
A well-bred lord to assault a gentle belle?
O say what stranger cause, yet unexplored,
Could make a gentle belle reject a lord?
In tasks so bold, can little men engage,
And in soft bosoms dwells such mighty rage?
Sol through white curtains shot a tim'rous ray,
And oped those eyes that must eclipse the day:
Now lap-dogs gave themselves the rousing shake,
And sleepless lovers, just at twelve awake:
Thrice rung the bell, the slipper knock'd the ground,
And the press'd watch return'd a silver sound.
Belinda still her downy pillow press'd,
Her guardian sylph prolong'd the balmy rest:

* A young beauty, daughter in a Catholic family known to Pope through his friend John Caryll. Caryll told Pope of the incident in which Robert Lord Petre cut a lock of Arabella's hair as a memento and thereby caused a deep enmity between the two families. Caryll hoped that Pope would treat the event lightly and effect some sort of reconciliation. The rest is literary history.

** The Rosicrucians were members of a secret cult in the seventeenth and eighteenth centuries who claimed various kinds of mysterious knowledge and power.

*** **Nolueram . . . tuis**: "I did not want to violate your locks, but I am pleased to have offered that much to your prayers." The quotation is from Martial, *Epigrams*, XII, 84.

'Twas he had summon'd to her silent bed
The morning-dream that hover'd o'er her head;
A youth more glittering than a birth-night beau,
(That ev'n in slumber caused her cheek to glow)
Seem'd to her ear his winning lips to lay,
And thus in whispers said, or seem'd to say:
"Fairest of mortals, thou distinguish'd care
Of thousand bright inhabitants of air!
If e'er one vision touch thy infant thought,
Of all the nurse and all the priest have taught;
Of airy elves by moonlight shadows seen,
The silver token, and the circled green,
Or virgins visited by angel powers,
With golden crowns and wreaths of heavenly
flowers;
Hear and believe! thy own importance know,
Nor bound thy narrow views to things below.
Some secret truths, from learned pride conceal'd,
To maids alone and children are reveal'd:
What, though no credit doubting wits may give?
The fair and innocent shall still believe.
Know, then, unnumbered spirits round thee fly,
The light militia of the lower sky:
These, though unseen, are ever on the wing,
Hang o'er the box, and hover round the ring.
Think what an equipage thou hast in air,
And view with scorn two pages and a chair.
As now your own, our beings were of old,
And once inclosed in woman's beauteous mould;
Thence, by a soft transition, we repair
From earthly vehicles to these of air.
Think not, when woman's transient breath is fled,
That all her vanities at once are dead;
Succeeding vanities she still regards,
And though she plays no more, o'erlooks the cards.
Her joy in gilden chariots, when alive,
And love of ombre, after death survive.
For when the fair in all their pride expire,
To their first elements their souls retire:
The sprites of fiery termagants in flame
Mount up, and take a Salamander's name.

THE RAPE OF THE LOCK. CANTO I. **23. birth-night beau:** young man celebrating his birthday at night. **44. box . . . ring:** The box is a section of a theatre, and the ring was a circular drive in Hyde Park. Both were places where young men and women might meet. **45. equipage:** retinue. **56. ombre:** a popular card game of the time and part of Pope's mock-heroic machinery in the poem. There are references to the various cards throughout the poem. **59. termagants:** shrews.

Soft yielding minds to water glide away,
And sip, with nymphs, their elemental tea.
The graver prude sinks downward to a gnome,
In search of mischief still on earth to roam.
The light coquettes in sylphs aloft repair,
And sport and flutter in the fields of air.
"Know further yet; whoever fair and chaste
Rejects mankind, is by some sylph embraced:
For spirits, freed from mortal laws, with ease
Assume what sexes and what shapes they
please.
What guards the purity of melting maids,
In courtly balls, and midnight masquerades,
Safe from the treach'rous friend, the daring spark,
The glance by day, the whisper in the dark,
When kind occasion prompts their warm desires,
When music softens, and when dancing fires?
'Tis but their sylph, the wise celestials know,
Though honour is the word with men below.
"Some nymphs there are, too conscious of their
face,
For life predestined to the gnome's embrace.
These swell their prospects and exalt their pride,
When offers are disdain'd and love denied:
Then gay ideas crowd the vacant brain,
While peers, and dukes, and all their sweeping
train,
And garters, stars, and coronets appear,
And in soft sounds, 'Your Grace' salutes their ear.
'Tis these that early taint the female soul,
Instruct the eyes of young coquettes to roll,
Teach infant cheeks a bidden blush to know,
And little hearts to flutter at a beau.
"Oft when the world imagine women stray,
The sylphs through mystic mazes guide their way,
Through all the giddy circle they pursue,
And old impertinence expel by new.
What tender maid but must a victim fall
To one man's treat, but for another's ball?
When Florio speaks, what virgin could withstand,
If gentle Damon did not squeeze her hand?
With varying vanities, from ev'ry part,
They shift the moving toy-shop of their
heart;
Where wigs with wigs, with sword-knots sword-
knots strive,
Beaux banish beaux, and coaches coaches drive.
This erring mortals levity may call,
Oh, blind to truth! the sylphs contrive it all.
"Of these am I, who thy protection claim,

A watchful sprite, and Ariel is my name.
Late, as I ranged the crystal wilds of air,
In the clear mirror of thy ruling star
I saw, alas! some dread event impend,
Ere to the main this morning sun descend;
But heaven reveals not what, or how, or where:
Warn'd by the sylph, oh, pious maid, beware!
This to disclose is all thy guardian can:
Beware of all, but most beware of man!"
He said; when Shock, who thought she slept too long,
Leap'd up, and waked his mistress with his tongue.
'Twas then, Belinda, if report say true,
Thy eyes first open'd on a billet-doux;
Wounds, charms, and ardours, were no sooner read,
But all the vision vanish'd from thy head.
And now, unveil'd, the toilet stands display'd,
Each silver vase in mystic order laid.
First, robed in white, the nymph intent adores,
With head uncover'd, the cosmetic powers.
A heav'nly image in the glass appears,
To that she bends, to that her eye she rears;
Th' inferior priestess, at her altar's side,
Trembling, begins the sacred rites of pride.
Unnumber'd treasures ope at once, and here
The various offerings of the world appear;
From each she nicely culls with curious toil,
And decks the goddess with the glitt'ring spoil.
This casket India's glowing gems unlocks,
And all Arabia breathes from yonder box.
The tortoise here and elephant unite,
Transform'd to combs, the speckled and the white.
Here files of pins extend their shining rows,
Puffs, powders, patches, Bibles, billet-doux.
Now awful beauty puts on all its arms;
The fair each moment rises in her charms,
Repairs her smiles, awakens every grace,
And calls forth all the wonders of her face:
Sees by degrees a purer blush arise,
And keener lightnings quicken in her eyes.
The busy sylphs surround their darling care,
These set the head, and those divide the hair,
Some fold the sleeve, while others plait the gown;
And Betty's praised for labours not her own.

115. Shock: Belinda's lapdog. **127. inferior priestess:** Belinda's maid, Betty.

CANTO II

Not with more glories, in th' ethereal plain,
The sun first rises o'er the purpled main,
Than, issuing forth, the rival of his beams
Launch'd on the bosom of the silver Thames.
Fair nymphs and well-dress'd youths around her shone,
But every eye was fix'd on her alone.
On her white breast a sparkling cross she wore,
Which Jews might kiss, and infidels adore.
Her lively looks a sprightly mind disclose,
Quick as her eyes, and as unfix'd as those:
Favours to none, to all she smiles extends;
Oft she rejects, but never once offends.
Bright as the sun, her eyes the gazers strike,
And, like the sun, they shine on all alike.
Yet graceful ease, and sweetness void of pride,
Might hide her faults, if belles had faults to hide:
If to her share some female errors fall,
Look on her face, and you'll forget them all.
This nymph, to the destruction of mankind,
Nourish'd two locks, which graceful hung behind
In equal curls, and well conspired to deck
With shining ringlets the smooth ivory neck.
Love in these labyrinths his slaves detains,
And mighty hearts are held in slender chains.
With hairy springes we the birds betray,
Slight lines of hair surprise the finny prey,
Fair tresses man's imperial race insnare,
And beauty draws us with a single hair.
Th' adventurous baron the bright locks admired;
He saw, he wish'd, and to the prize aspired.
Resolved to win, he meditates the way,
By force to ravish, or by fraud betray;
For when success a lover's toils attends,
Few ask, if fraud or force attain'd his ends.
For this, ere Phœbus rose, he had implored
Propitious Heaven, and every power adored:
But chiefly Love—to Love an altar built,
Of twelve vast French romances, neatly gilt.
There lay three garters, half a pair of gloves;
And all the trophies of his former loves:
With tender billet-doux he lights the pyre,
And breathes three amorous sighs to raise the fire.
Then prostrate falls, and begs with ardent eyes
Soon to obtain, and long possess the prize:

CANTO II. **25. springes:** traps.

The powers gave ear, and granted half his prayer,
The rest, the winds dispersed in empty air.
But now secure the painted vessel glides,
The sun-beams trembling on the floating tides;
While melting music steals upon the sky,
And soften'd sounds along the waters die;
Smooth flow the waves, the zephyrs gently play,
Belinda smiled, and all the world was gay.
All but the sylph—with careful thoughts oppress'd,
Th' impending woe sat heavy on his breast.
He summons straight his denizens of air;
The lucid squadrons round the sails repair:
Soft o'er the shrouds aërial whispers breathe,
That seem'd but zephyrs to the twain beneath.
Some to the sun their insect-wings unfold,
Waft on the breeze, or sink in clouds of gold;
Transparent forms, too fine for mortal sight,
Their fluid bodies half dissolved in light.
Loose to the wind their airy garments flew,
Thin glittering textures of the filmy dew,
Dipp'd in the richest tincture of the skies,
Where light disports in ever-mingling dyes;
While ev'ry beam new transient colours flings,
Colours that change whene'er they wave their wings.
Amid the circle on the gilded mast,
Superior by the head, was Ariel placed;
His purple pinions op'ning to the sun,
He raised his azure wand, and thus begun:
"Ye sylphs and sylphids, to your chief give ear;
Fays, fairies, genii, elves, and dæmons, hear:
Ye know the spheres, and various tasks assign'd
By laws eternal to the aërial kind.
Some in the fields of purest ether play,
And bask and whiten in the blaze of day.
Some guide the course of wand'ring orbs on high,
Or roll the planets through the boundless sky.
Some less refined beneath the moon's pale light
Pursue the stars that shoot athwart the night,
Or suck the mists in grosser air below,
Or dip their pinions in the painted bow,
Or brew fierce tempests on the wintry main,
Or o'er the glebe distil the kindly rain.
Others on earth o'er human race preside,
Watch all their ways, and all their actions guide:
Of these the chief the care of nations own,
And guard with arms divine the British throne.
"Our humbler province is to tend the fair,
Not a less pleasing, though less glorious care;
To save the powder from too rude a gale,
Nor let the imprison'd essences exhale;
To draw fresh colours from the vernal flowers;
To steal from rainbows, ere they drop in showers,
A brighter wash; to curl their waving hairs,
Assist their blushes and inspire their airs;
Nay, oft, in dreams, invention we bestow,
To change a flounce, or add a furbelow.
"This day, black omens threat the brightest fair
That e'er deserved a watchful spirit's care;
Some dire disaster, or by force, or flight;
But what, or where, the Fates have wrapp'd in night.
Whether the nymph shall break Diana's law,
Or some frail china-jar receive a flaw;
Or stain her honour or her new brocade;
Forget her prayers, or miss a masquerade;
Or lose her heart, or necklace, at a ball;
Or whether Heaven has doom'd that Shock must fall.
Haste, then, ye spirits! to your charge repair:
The flutt'ring fan be Zephyretta's care;
The drops to thee, Brillante, we consign;
And, Momentilla, let the watch be thine;
Do thou, Crispissa, tend her fav'rite lock;
Ariel himself shall be the guard of Shock.
"To fifty chosen sylphs, of special note,
We trust th' important charge, the petticoat:
Oft have we known that seven-fold fence to fail,
Though stiff with hoops, and arm'd with ribs of whale;
Form a strong line about the silver bound,
And guard the wide circumference around.
"Whatever spirit, careless of his charge,
His post neglects, or leaves the fair at large,
Shall feel sharp vengeance soon o'ertake his sins,
Be stopp'd in vials, or transfix'd with pins;
Or plunged in lakes of bitter washes lie,
Or wedged whole ages in a bodkin's eye:
Gums and pomatums shall his flight restrain,
While clogg'd he beats his silken wings in vain:
Or alum styptics with contracting power
Shrink his thin essence like a shrivell'd flower:
Or, as Ixion fix'd, the wretch shall feel
The giddy motion of the whirling mill,

100. flounce . . . furbelow: a ruffle, a trimming. **105. Diana's law:** chastity. **128. bodkin's:** A bodkin is a needle. **129. pomatums:** ointments. **133. Ixion:** the character in Greek mythology punished by being bound on a perpetually revolving wheel. Ixion had been guilty of crimes, the chief of which was his attempt to win the wife of Zeus.

In fumes of burning chocolate shall glow,
And tremble at the sea that froths below!"
He spoke; the spirits from the sails descend;
Some, orb in orb, around the nymph extend;
Some thrid the mazy ringlets of her hair;
Some hang upon the pendants of her ear:
With beating hearts the dire event they wait,
Anxious and trembling for the birth of Fate.

CANTO III

Close by those meads, for ever crown'd with flowers,
Where Thames with pride surveys his rising towers,
There stands a structure of majestic frame,
Which from the neighb'ring Hampton takes its name.
Here Britain's statesmen oft the fall foredoom
Of foreign tyrants, and of nymphs at home;
Here thou, great ANNA! whom three realms obey,
Dost sometimes counsel take—and sometimes tea.
Hither the heroes and the nymphs resort,
To taste a while the pleasures of a court;
In various talk th' instructive hours they pass'd,
Who gave the ball, or paid the visit last;
One speaks the glory of the British Queen,
And one describes a charming Indian screen;
A third interprets motions, looks, and eyes;
At every word a reputation dies.
Snuff, or the fan, supply each pause of chat,
With singing, laughing, ogling, *and all that*.
Meanwhile, declining from the noon of day,
The sun obliquely shoots his burning ray;
The hungry judges soon the sentence sign,
And wretches hang that jurymen may dine;
The merchant from th' exchange returns in peace,
And the long labours of the toilet cease.
Belinda now, whom thirst of fame invites,
Burns to encounter two adventurous knights,
At ombre singly to decide their doom;
And swells her breast with conquests yet to come.
Straight the three bands prepare in arms to join,
Each band the number of the sacred nine.
Soon as she spreads her hand, th' aërial guard
Descend, and sit on each important card:
First Ariel perch'd upon a Matadore,
Then each according to the rank he bore;
For sylphs, yet mindful of their ancient race,
Are, as when women, wondrous fond of place.
Behold, four Kings in majesty revered,
With hoary whiskers and a forky beard;
And four fair Queens, whose hands sustain a flower,
Th' expressive emblem of their softer power;
Four knaves in garbs succinct, a trusty band;
Caps on their heads, and halberts in their hand;
And party-colour'd troops, a shining train,
Drawn forth to combat on the velvet plain.
The skilful nymph reviews her force with care:
"Let Spades be trumps!" she said, and trumps they were.
Now move to war her sable Matadores,
In show like leaders of the swarthy Moors.
Spadillio first, unconquerable lord!
Led off two captive trumps, and swept the board.
As many more Manillio forced to yield,
And march'd a victor from the verdant field.
Him Basto follow'd; but his fate more hard
Gain'd but one trump, and one plebeian card.
With his broad sabre next, a chief in years,
The hoary Majesty of Spades appears,
Puts forth one manly leg, to sight reveal'd,
The rest, his many-colour'd robe conceal'd.
The rebel Knave, who dares his prince engage,
Proves the just victim of his royal rage.
Ev'n mighty Pam, that kings and queens o'erthrew,
And mow'd down armies in the fights of Lu,
Sad chance of war! now destitute of aid,
Falls undistinguish'd by the victor Spade!
Thus far both armies to Belinda yield;
Now to the baron fate inclines the field.
His warlike Amazon her host invades,
Th' imperial consort of the crown of Spades.
The Club's black tyrant first her victim dyed,
Spite of his haughty mien, and barb'rous pride:
What boots the regal circle on his head,
His giant limbs, in state unwieldy spread;
That long behind he trails his pompous robe,
And, of all monarchs, only grasps the globe?
The baron now his Diamonds pours apace;
Th' embroider'd King who shows but half his face,
And his refulgent Queen, with powers combined
Of broken troops an easy conquest find.

CANTO III. **4.** Hampton Court was on occasion used by Queen Anne. It was a favorite gathering place for the elite of the day. **27. ombre:** the card game raised to the level of an epic battle of the sexes. The following lines follow the course of the game with its special cards, moves, trumps, victories, defeats.

Clubs, Diamonds, Hearts, in wild disorder seen,
With throngs promiscuous strow the level
green.
Thus when dispersed a routed army runs,
Of Asia's troops, and Afric's sable sons,
With like confusion different nations fly,
Of various habit, and of various dye,
The pierced battalions disunited fall,
In heaps on heaps; one fate o'erwhelms them all.
The Knave of Diamonds tries his wily arts,
And wins (oh shameful chance!) the Queen of
Hearts.
At this, the blood the virgin's cheek forsook,
A livid paleness spreads o'er all her look;
She sees, and trembles at th' approaching ill,
Just in the jaws of ruin, and Codille.
And now (as oft in some distemper'd state)
On one nice trick depends the gen'ral fate,
An Ace of Hearts steps forth: the King unseen
Lurk'd in her hand, and mourn'd his captive
Queen:
He springs to vengeance with an eager pace,
And falls like thunder on the prostrate Ace.
The nymph exulting fills with shouts the sky;
The walls, the woods, and long canals reply.
O thoughtless mortals! ever blind to fate,
Too soon dejected, and too soon elate.
Sudden, these honours shall be snatch'd away,
And cursed for ever this victorious day.
For lo! the board with cups and spoons is
crown'd,
The berries crackle, and the mill turns round:
On shining altars of Japan they raise
The silver lamp; the fiery spirits blaze:
From silver spouts the grateful liquors glide,
While China's earth receives the smoking
tide:
At once they gratify their scent and taste,
And frequent cups prolong the rich repast.
Straight hover round the fair her airy band;
Some, as she sipp'd the fuming liquor fann'd,
Some o'er her lap their careful plumes display'd,
Trembling, and conscious of the rich brocade.
Coffee (which makes the politician wise,
And see through all things with his half-shut eyes)
Sent up in vapours to the baron's brain
New stratagems, the radiant lock to gain.
Ah cease, rash youth! desist ere 'tis too late,
Fear the just gods, and think of Scylla's fate!
Changed to a bird, and sent to flit in air,
She dearly pays for Nisus' injured hair!
But when to mischief mortals bend their will,
How soon they find fit instruments of ill!
Just then, Clarissa drew with tempting grace
A two-edged weapon from her shining case:
So ladies, in romance, assist their knight,
Present the spear, and arm him for the fight.
He takes the gift with reverence and extends
The little engine on his fingers' ends;
This just behind Belinda's neck he spread,
As o'er the fragrant steams she bends her head.
Swift to the lock a thousand sprites repair,
A thousand wings, by turns, blow back the hair;
And thrice they twitch'd the diamond in her ear;
Thrice she look'd back, and thrice the foe drew
near.
Just in that instant, anxious Ariel sought
The close recesses of the virgin's thought:
As on the nosegay in her breast reclin'd,
He watch'd th' ideas rising in her mind,
Sudden he view'd, in spite of all her art,
An earthly lover lurking at her heart.
Amazed, confused, he found his power expired,
Resign'd to fate, and with a sigh retired.
The peer now spreads the glitt'ring forfex wide,
T' inclose the lock; now joins it, to divide.
Ev'n then, before the fatal engine closed,
A wretched sylph too fondly interposed;
Fate urged the shears, and cut the sylph in twain,
(But airy substance soon unites again)
The meeting points the sacred hair dissever
From the fair head, for ever, and for ever!
Then flash'd the living lightning from her eyes,
And screams of horror rend th' affrighted skies.
Not louder shrieks to pitying Heaven are cast,
When husbands or when lap-dogs breathe their
last;

92. Codille: in ombre Codille means loss of the game, one's opponent having won the greater number of tricks. **106. berries:** coffee beans. Coffee time becomes an epic feast in the lines that follow.

122. The ancient story of Scylla is recalled here. She was the daughter of Nisus, king of Megara, the security of whose land depended on a purple lock of his hair. Scylla fell in love with Minos of Crete, who was attacking Megara, and she cut the lock of her father's hair and offered it to him. Her lover was shocked by her act, however, and after his victory, both father and daughter were changed to birds.

Or when rich China vessels, fall'n from high,
In glitt'ring dust and painted fragments lie;
"Let wreaths of triumph now my temples twine,
(The victor cried) the glorious prize is mine!
While fish in streams, or birds delight in air,
Or in a coach and six the British fair,
As long as *Atalantis* shall be read,
Or the small pillow grace a lady's bed,
While visits shall be paid on solemn days,
When numerous wax-lights in bright order blaze,
While nymphs take treats, or assignations give,
So long my honour, name, and praise shall live!"
What Time would spare, from steel receives its date,
And monuments, like men, submit to fate!
Steel could the labour of the gods destroy,
And strike to dust th' imperial towers of Troy;
Steel could the works of mortal pride confound,
And hew triumphal arches to the ground.
What wonder then, fair nymph! thy hairs should feel
The conquering force of unresisted steel?

CANTO IV

But anxious cares the pensive nymph oppress'd,
And secret passions labour'd in her breast.
Not youthful kings in battle seized alive,
Not scornful virgins who their charms survive,
Not ardent lovers robb'd of all their bliss,
Not ancient ladies when refused a kiss,
Not tyrants fierce that unrepenting die,
Not Cynthia when her manteau's pinn'd awry,
E'er felt such rage, resentment, and despair,
As thou, sad virgin! for thy ravish'd hair.
For, that sad moment, when the sylphs withdrew,
And Ariel weeping from Belinda flew,
Umbriel, a dusky, melancholy sprite,
As ever sullied the fair face of light,
Down to the central earth, his proper scene,
Repair'd to search the gloomy Cave of Spleen.
Swift on his sooty pinions flits the gnome,
And in a vapour reach'd the dismal dome.
No cheerful breeze this sullen region knows,
The dreaded east is all the wind that blows.
Here in a grotto, shelter'd close from air,
And screen'd in shades from day's detested glare,
She sighs for ever on her pensive bed,
Pain at her side, and Megrim at her head.
Two handmaids wait the throne: alike in place,
But diff'ring far in figure and in face.
Here stood Ill-nature like an ancient maid,
Her wrinkled form in black and white array'd;
With store of prayers, for mornings, nights, and noons,
Her hand is fill'd; her bosom with lampoons.
There Affectation, with a sickly mien,
Shows in her cheek the roses of eighteen,
Practised to lisp, and hang the head aside,
Faints into airs, and languishes with pride,
On the rich quilt sinks with becoming woe,
Wrapp'd in a gown, for sickness, and for show.
The fair ones feel such maladies as these,
When each new night-dress gives a new disease.
A constant vapour o'er the palace flies;
Strange phantoms rising as the mists arise;
Dreadful, as hermits' dreams in haunted shades,
Or bright, as visions of expiring maids.
Now glaring fiends, and snakes on rolling spires,
Pale spectres, gaping tombs, and purple fires:
Now lakes of liquid gold, Elysian scenes,
And crystal domes, and angels in machines.
Unnumber'd throngs on every side are seen
Of bodies changed to various forms by Spleen.
Here living tea-pots stand, one arm held out,
One bent; the handle this, and that the spout:
A pipkin there, like Homer's tripod walks;
Here sighs a jar, and there a goose-pie talks:
Men prove with child, as powerful fancy works,
And maids turn'd bottles call aloud for corks.
Safe pass'd the gnome through this fantastic band,
A branch of healing spleen-wort in his hand.
Then thus address'd the power: "Hail, wayward Queen!
Who rule the sex to fifty from fifteen;

165. *Atalantis:* a shocking, gossipy novel by Mary Manley (1672–1724).

CANTO IV. **16. Cave of Spleen:** a takeoff on the descent to the underworld in epic poetry. The spleen is associted with irritability, melancholy.

24. Megrim: a severe headache, migraine. **45. Elysian:** heavenly. **48–54.** a series of fantasies experienced in the Cave of Spleen. **51. pipkin:** a small earthenware jar. **56. spleen-wort:** an antidote to the power of spleen.

Parent of vapours, and of female wit,
Who give th' hysteric or poetic fit;
On various tempers act by various ways,
Make some take physic, others scribble plays;
Who cause the proud their visits to delay,
And send the godly in a pet to pray;
A nymph there is, that all thy power disdains,
And thousands more in equal mirth maintains.
But oh! if e'er thy gnome could spoil a grace,
Or raise a pimple on a beauteous face,
Like citron waters matrons' cheeks inflame,
Or change complexions at a losing game;
If e'er with airy horns I planted heads,
Or rumpled petticoats, or tumbled beds,
Or caused suspicion when no soul was rude,
Or discomposed the head-dress of a prude,
Or e'er to costive lap-dog gave disease,
Which not the tears of brightest eyes could ease;
Hear me, and touch Belinda with chagrin,
That single act gives half the world the spleen."
The Goddess with a discontented air
Seems to reject him, though she grants his
prayer.
A wondrous bag with both her hands she binds,
Like that where once Ulysses held the winds;
There she collects the force of female lungs,
Sighs, sobs, and passions, and the war of tongues.
A vial next she fills with fainting fears,
Soft sorrows, melting griefs, and flowing tears.
The gnome rejoicing bears her gifts away,
Spreads his black wings, and slowly mounts to day.
Sunk in Thalestris' arms the nymph he found,
Her eyes dejected, and her hair unbound.
Full o'er their heads the swelling bag he rent,
And all the furies issued at the vent.
Belinda burns with more than mortal ire,
And fierce Thalestris fans the rising fire;
"O wretched maid!" she spreads her hands, and
cried,
(While Hampton's echoes, "Wretched maid!"
replied)
"Was it for this you took such constant care
The bodkin, comb, and essence to prepare?
For this your locks in paper durance bound?
For this with torturing irons wreathed
around?
For this with fillets strain'd your tender head,
And bravely bore the double loads of lead?
Gods! shall the ravisher display your hair,
While the fops envy and the ladies stare?
Honour forbid! at whose unrivall'd shrine
Ease, pleasure, virtue, all our sex resign.
Methinks already I your tears survey,
Already hear the horrid things they say,
Already see you a degraded toast,
And all your honour in a whisper lost!
How shall I then your helpless fame defend?
'Twill then be infamy to seem your friend!
And shall this prize, th' inestimable prize,
Exposed through crystal to the gazing eyes,
And heighten'd by the diamond's circling rays,
On that rapacious hand for ever blaze?
Sooner shall grass in Hyde Park Circus grow,
And wits take lodgings in the sound of Bow;
Sooner let earth, air, sea, to Chaos fall,
Men, monkeys, lap-dogs, parrots, perish all!"
She said; then raging to Sir Plume repairs,
And bids her beau demand the precious hairs:
(Sir Plume of amber snuff-box justly vain,
And the nice conduct of a clouded cane)
With earnest eyes, and round, unthinking face,
He first the snuff-box open'd, then the case,
And then broke out—"My Lord, why, what the
devil!
Z—ds! damn the lock! 'fore Gad, you must be civil!
Plague on't! 'tis past a jest—nay prithee, pox!
Give her the hair"—he spoke, and rapp'd his
box.
"It grieves me much (replied the peer again)
Who speaks so well should ever speak in vain,
But by this lock, this sacred lock, I swear,
(Which never more shall join its parted hair;
Which never more its honours shall renew,
Clipp'd from the lovely head where late it grew)
That while my nostrils draw the vital air,
This hand, which won it, shall for ever wear."
He spoke, and speaking, in proud triumph spread
The long-contended honours of her head.
But Umbriel, hateful gnome! forbears not so;

69. citron waters: the juice of a lemon-like fruit. **75. costive:** constipated. **82. winds:** After the Trojan War Aeolus (Book X of the *Odyssey*) gave Odysseus a bag filled with winds unfavorable to his safe return home to Ithaca. **89. Thalestris:** Queen of the Amazons; here, the defender of Belinda, probably a relative.

118. sound of Bow: within the bell sounds of the church of St. Mary-le-Bow. **121. Sir Plume:** Thalestris' lord. Some editors believe that Sir Plume is Sir George Brown and that Thalestris is his sister, Mrs. Morley.

He breaks the vial whence the sorrows flow.
Then see! the nymph in beauteous grief appears,
Her eyes half-languishing, half-drowned in tears;
On her heaved bosom hung her drooping head,
Which, with a sigh, she raised; and thus she said:
"For ever cursed be this detested day,
Which snatch'd my best, my fav'rite curl away!
Happy! ay ten times happy had I been,
If Hampton Court these eyes had never seen!
Yet am I not the first mistaken maid,
By love of courts to numerous ills betray'd,
Oh had I rather unadmired remain'd
In some lone isle, or distant northern land;
Where the gilt chariot never marks the way,
Where none learn ombre, none e'er taste bohea!
There kept my charms conceal'd from mortal eye,
Like roses that in deserts bloom and die.
What moved my mind with youthful lords to roam?
Oh had I stayed, and said my prayers at home!
'Twas this the morning omens seem'd to tell:
Thrice from my trembling hand the patch-box fell;
The tott'ring china shook without a wind;
Nay, Poll sat mute, and Shock was most unkind!
A sylph too warn'd me of the threats of Fate,
In mystic visions, now believed too late!
See the poor remnants of these slighted hairs!
My hands shall rend what e'en thy rapine spares:
These in two sable ringlets taught to break,
Once gave new beauties to the snowy neck;
The sister-lock now sits uncouth, alone,
And in its fellow's fate foresees its own;
Uncurl'd it hangs, the fatal shears demands,
And tempts, once more, thy sacrilegious hands.
Oh hadst thou, cruel! been content to seize
Hairs less in sight, or any hairs but these!"

CANTO V

She said: the pitying audience melt in tears;
But Fate and Love had stopp'd the baron's ears.
In vain Thalestris with reproach assails,
For who can move when fair Belinda fails?
Not half so fix'd the Trojan could remain,
While Anna begg'd and Dido raged in vain.
Then grave Clarissa graceful waved her fan;
Silence ensued, and thus the nymph began:
"Say, why are beauties praised and honoured most,
The wise man's passion, and the vain man's toast?
Why deck'd with all that land and sea afford?
Why angels call'd, and angel-like adored?
Why round our coaches crowd the white-gloved beaux?
Why bows the side-box from its inmost rows?
How vain are all these glories, all our pains,
Unless good sense preserve what beauty gains;
That men may say, when we the front-box grace,
'Behold the first in virtue as in face!'
Oh! if to dance all night, and dress all day,
Charm'd the small-pox, or chased old age away;
Who would not scorn what housewife's cares produce,
Or who would learn one earthly thing of use?
To patch, nay, ogle, might become a saint,
Nor could it sure be such a sin to paint.
But since, alas! frail beauty must decay,
Curl'd or uncurl'd, since locks will turn to grey;
Since painted, or not painted, all shall fade,
And she who scorns a man must die a maid;
What then remains, but well our power to use,
And keep good-humour still, whate'er we lose?
And trust me, dear, good-humour can prevail,
When airs, and flights, and screams, and scolding fail.
Beauties in vain their pretty eyes may roll;
Charms strike the sight, but merit wins the soul."
So spoke the dame, but no applause ensued;
Belinda frown'd, Thalestris call'd her prude.
"To arms, to arms!" the fierce virago cries,
And swift as lightning to the combat flies.
All side in parties, and begin th' attack:
Fans clap, silks rustle, and tough whalebones crack;
Heroes' and heroines' shouts confusedly rise,
And bass and treble voices strike the skies.

---

156. bohea: tea.

CANTO V. **5–6.** The lines refer to that section of the *Aeneid* of Virgil in which Aeneas determines to leave Carthage to found Rome. He left his beloved Dido, Queen of Carthage, in spite of her pleading and that of her sister Anna. **7. Clarissa:** clearly the poet's spokesman. Pope notes that Clarissa's function is to articulate the moral of the poem. **37. virago:** a strong, aggressive woman.

No common weapons in their hands are found,
Like Gods they fight, nor dread a mortal wound.
So when bold Homer makes the Gods engage,
And heavenly breasts with human passions rage;
'Gainst Pallas, Mars; Latona, Hermes arms;
And all Olympus rings with loud alarms;
Jove's thunder roars, Heaven trembles all around,
Blue Neptune storms, the bellowing deeps resound:
Earth shakes her nodding towers, the ground gives way,
And the pale ghosts start at the flash of day!
Triumphant Umbriel on a sconce's height
Clapp'd his glad wings, and sate to view the fight:
Propp'd on their bodkin spears, the sprites survey
The growing combat, or assist the fray.
While through the press enraged Thalestris flies,
And scatters death around from both her eyes,
A beau and witling perish'd in the throng,
One died in metaphor, and one in song.
"O cruel nymph! a living death I bear,"
Cried Dapperwit, and sunk beside his chair.
A mournful glance Sir Fopling upwards cast,
"Those eyes are made so killing,"—was his last.
Thus on Mæander's flowery margin lies
Th' expiring swan, and as he sings he dies.
When bold Sir Plume had drawn Clarissa down,
Chloe stepp'd in, and kill'd him with a frown;
She smiled to see the doughty hero slain,
But, at her smile, the beau revived again.
Now Jove suspends his golden scales in air,
Weighs the men's wits against the lady's hair:
The doubtful beam long nods from side to side;
At length the wits mount up, the hairs subside.
See fierce Belinda on the baron flies,
With more than usual lightning in her eyes:
Nor fear'd the chief th' unequal fiight to try,
Who sought no more than on his foe to die.
But this bold lord with manly strength endued,
She with one finger and a thumb subdued:
Just where the breath of life his nostrils drew,
A charge of snuff the wily virgin threw;
The gnomes direct, to every atom just,
The pungent grains of titillating dust.
Sudden, with starting tears each eye o'erflows,
And the high dome re-echoes to his nose.
"Now meet thy fate," incensed Belinda cried,
And drew a deadly bodkin from her side.
(The same, his ancient personage to deck,
Her great-great-grandsire wore about his neck,
In three seal rings; which after, melted down,
Form'd a vast buckle for his widow's gown:
Her infant grandame's whistle next it grew,
The bells she jingled, and the whistle blew;
Then in a bodkin graced her mother's hairs,
Which long she wore, and now Belinda wears.)
"Boast not my fall, (he cried) insulting foe!
Thou by some other shalt be laid as low.
Nor think, to die dejects my lofty mind:
All that I dread is leaving you behind!
Rather than so, ah let me still survive,
And burn in Cupid's flames—but burn alive."
"Restore the lock!" she cries; and all around
"Restore the lock!" the vaulted roofs rebound.
Not fierce Othello in so loud a strain
Roar'd for the handkerchief that caused his pain.
But see how oft ambitious aims are cross'd,
And chiefs contend till all the prize is lost!
The lock, obtain'd with guilt, and kept with pain,
In every place is sought, but sought in vain:
With such a prize no mortal must be blest,
So Heaven decrees! with Heaven who can contest?
Some thought it mounted to the lunar sphere,
Since all things lost on earth are treasured there.
There heroes' wits are kept in pond'rous vases,
And beaux' in snuff-boxes and tweezer-cases.
There broken vows, and death-bed alms are found,
And lovers' hearts with ends of riband bound,
The courtier's promises, and sick man's prayers,
The smiles of harlots, and the tears of heirs,
Cages for gnats, and chains to yoke a flea,
Dried butterflies, and tomes of casuistry.
But trust the Muse—she saw it upward rise,
Though mark'd by none but quick, poetic eyes:
(So Rome's great founder to the heavens withdrew,
To Proculus alone confess'd in view)
A sudden star it shot through liquid air,
And drew behind a radiant trail of hair.

53. sconce: a candle holder. **65. Mæander:** the famous winding river in Asia.

125–26. The reference here is to Romulus, founder of Rome, who, according to legend, came down from heaven at the request of Proculus Julius to predict that Rome would become the capital of the world and then returned to heaven.

Not Berenice's lock first rose so bright,
The heavens bespangling with dishevell'd
light.
The sylphs behold it kindling as it flies,
And pleased pursue its progress through the skies.
This the beau-monde shall from the Mall survey,
And hail with music its propitious ray.
This the blest lover shall for Venus take,
And send up vows from Rosamonda's lake.
This Partridge soon shall view in cloudless skies,
When next he looks through Galileo's eyes;
And hence th' egregious wizard shall foredoom
The fate of Louis, and the fall of Rome.
Then cease, bright nymph! to mourn thy
ravish'd hair,
Which adds new glory to the shining sphere!
Not all the tresses that fair head can boast
Shall draw such envy as the lock you lost.
For, after all the murders of your eye,
When, after millions slain, yourself shall die;
When those fair suns shall set, as set they must,
And all those tresses shall be laid in dust;
This lock, the Muse shall consecrate to fame,
And 'midst the stars inscribe Belinda's name.

(1712–1714)

ELEGY

TO THE MEMORY OF AN UNFORTUNATE LADY

What beckoning ghost along the moonlight shade
Invites my steps, and points to yonder glade?
'Tis she!—but why that bleeding bosom gored,
Why dimly gleams the visionary sword?
Oh, ever beauteous, ever friendly! tell,
Is it, in heaven, a crime to love too well?
To bear too tender or too firm a heart,
To act a lover's or a Roman's part?
Is there no bright reversion in the sky
For those who greatly think, or bravely die?
Why bade ye else, ye powers! her soul aspire
Above the vulgar flight of low desire?
Ambition first sprung from your blest abodes,
The glorious fault of angels and of gods:
Thence to their images on earth it flows,
And in the breast of kings and heroes glows.
Most souls, 'tis true, but peep out once an age,
Dull, sullen prisoners in the body's cage:
Dim lights of life, that burn a length of years,
Useless, unseen, as lamps in sepulchres;
Like Eastern kings a lazy state they keep,
And, close confined to their own palace, sleep.
From these perhaps (ere Nature bade her die)
Fate snatched her early to the pitying sky.
As into air the purer spirits flow,
And separate from their kindred dregs below;
So flew the soul to its congenial place,
Nor left one virtue to redeem her race.
But thou, false guardian of a charge too good,
Thou, mean deserter of thy brother's blood!
See on these ruby lips the trembling breath,
These cheeks now fading at the blast of death;
Cold is that breast which warm'd the world before,
And those love-darting eyes must roll no more.
Thus, if eternal justice rules the ball,
Thus shall your wives, and thus your children fall:
On all the line a sudden vengeance waits,
And frequent hearses shall besiege your gates;
There passengers shall stand, and pointing say,
(While the long funerals blacken all the way,)
"Lo! these were they, whose souls the Furies
steel'd,
And cursed with hearts unknowing how to yield."
Thus unlamented pass the proud away,
The gaze of fools, and pageant of a day!
So perish all, whose breast ne'er learn'd to glow
For others' good, or melt at others' woe.
What can atone (oh ever-injured shade!)
Thy fate unpitied, and thy rites unpaid?
No friend's complaint, no kind domestic tear
Pleased thy pale ghost, or graced thy mournful
bier.
By foreign hands thy dying eyes were closed,
By foreign hands thy decent limbs composed,

129. **Berenice's lock:** Berenice, wife of Ptolemy III, dedicated a lock of her hair for the safety of her husband when he went to war. The lock was supposedly transformed into a constellation. 133. **Mall:** the great walk in St. James's park. The **beau monde** refers to the world of the elite, the fashionable. 136. **Rosamonda's lake:** a pond in the same park. 137. John Partridge was a somewhat suspect astrologer who predicted great public events.

UNFORTUNATE LADY. 8. **a Roman's part:** to commit suicide.

41. **Furies:** the avenging female spirits of Greek mythology.

By foreign hands thy humble grave adorn'd,
By strangers honour'd, and by strangers mourn'd!
What, though no friends in sable weeds appear,
Grieve for an hour, perhaps then mourn a year,
And bear about the mockery of woe
To midnight dances, and the public show?
What, though no weeping loves thy ashes grace,
Nor polish'd marble emulate thy face?
What, though no sacred earth allow thee room,
Nor hallow'd dirge be mutter'd o'er thy tomb?
Yet shall thy grave with rising flowers be dress'd,
And the green turf lie lightly on thy breast:
There shall the morn her earliest tears bestow,
There the first roses of the year shall blow;
While angels with their silver wings o'ershade
The ground now sacred by thy reliques made.
So peaceful rests, without a stone, a name,
What once had beauty, titles, wealth, and fame.
How loved, how honour'd once, avails thee not,
To whom related, or by whom begot;
A heap of dust alone remains of thee,
'Tis all thou art, and all the proud shall be!
Poets themselves must fall, like those they sung,
Deaf the praised ear, and mute the tuneful tongue.
Even he, whose soul now melts in mournful lays,
Shall shortly want the generous tear he pays;
Then from his closing eyes thy form shall part,
And the last pang shall tear thee from his heart,
Life's idle business at one gasp be o'er,
The Muse forgot, and thou beloved no more!

(1717)

ELOISA TO ABELARD

In these deep solitudes and awful cells,
Where heavenly-pensive Contemplation dwells,
And ever-musing Melancholy reigns,
What means this tumult in a Vestal's veins?
Why rove my thoughts beyond this last retreat?
Why feels my heart its long-forgotten heat?
Yet, yet I love! From Abelard it came,
And Eloisa yet must kiss the name.
Dear fatal name! rest ever unreveal'd,
Nor pass these lips in holy silence seal'd:

61. sacred earth: Christians who committed suicide were denied burial in consecrated ground.

Hide it, my heart, within that close disguise,
Where, mix'd with God's, his loved idea lies:
Oh, write it not, my hand—the name appears
Already written—wash it out, my tears!
In vain lost Eloisa weeps and prays,
Her heart still dictates, and her hand obeys.
Relentless walls! whose darksome round contains
Repentant sighs, and voluntary pains:
Ye rugged rocks! which holy knees have worn;
Ye grots and caverns shagg'd with horrid thorn!
Shrines! where their vigils pale-eyed virgins keep,
And pitying saints, whose statues learn to weep!
Though cold like you, unmoved and silent grown,
I have not yet forgot myself to stone.
All is not Heaven's while Abelard has part,
Still rebel nature holds out half my heart;
Nor prayers nor fasts its stubborn pulse restrain,
Nor tears for ages taught to flow in vain.
Soon as thy letters trembling I unclose,
That well-known name awakens all my woes.
Oh name for ever sad! for ever dear!
Still breathed in sighs, still usher'd with a tear.
I tremble too, where'er my own I find,
Some dire misfortune follows close behind.
Line after line my gushing eyes o'erflow,
Led through a sad variety of woe;
Now warm in love, now with'ring in my bloom,
Lost in a convent's solitary gloom!
There stern religion quench'd th' unwilling flame,
There died the best of passions, Love and Fame.
Yet write, oh write me all, that I may join
Griefs to thy grief, and echo sighs to thine.
Nor foes nor fortune take this power away;
And is my Abelard less kind than they?
Tears still are mine, and those I need not spare,
Love but demands what else were shed in prayer;
No happier task these faded eyes pursue;
To read and weep is all they now can do.
Then share thy pain, allow that sad relief;
Ah, more than share it, give me all thy grief.
Heaven first taught letters for some wretch's aid,
Some banish'd lover, or some captive maid:
They live, they speak, they breathe what love inspires,
Warm from the soul, and faithful to its fires;
The virgin's wish without her fears impart,
Excuse the blush, and pour out all the heart;
Speed the soft intercourse from soul to soul,

And waft a sigh from Indus to the pole.
  Thou know'st how guiltless first I met thy flame,
When love approach'd me under friendship's
    name;
My fancy form'd thee of angelic kind,
Some emanation of th' all-beauteous mind.
Those smiling eyes, attemp'ring every ray,
Shone sweetly lambent with celestial day.
Guiltless I gazed; Heaven listen'd while you sung;
And truths divine came mended from that tongue.
From lips like those what precepts fail to move?
Too soon they taught me 'twas no sin to love:
Back through the paths of pleasing sense I ran,
Nor wish'd an angel whom I loved a man.
Dim and remote the joys of saints I see;
Nor envy them that Heaven I lose for thee.
  How oft, when press'd to marriage, have I said,
Curse on all laws but those which Love has made!
Love, free as air, at sight of human ties,
Spreads his light wings, and in a moment flies.
Let wealth, let honour, wait the wedded dame,
August her deed, and sacred be her fame;
Before true passion all those views remove;
Fame, wealth, and honour! what are you to
    love?
The jealous God, when we profane his fires,
Those restless passions in revenge inspires,
And bids them make mistaken mortals groan,
Who seek in love for aught but love alone.
Should at my feet the world's great master fall,
Himself, his throne, his world, I'd scorn them all:
Not Cæsar's empress would I deign to prove;
No, make me mistress to the man I love;
If there be yet another name more free,
More fond than mistress, make me that to
    thee!
Oh, happy state! when souls each other draw,
When love is liberty, and Nature law:
All then is full, possessing, and possessed,
No craving void left aching in the breast:
Even thought meets thought ere from the lips it
    part,
And each warm wish springs mutual from the
    heart.
This sure is bliss, if bliss on earth there be,
And once the lot of Abelard and me.
  Alas, how changed! what sudden horrors rise!
A naked lover bound and bleeding lies!
Where, where was Eloise? her voice, her hand,
Her poniard had opposed the dire command.
Barbarian, stay! that bloody stroke restrain;
The crime was common, common be the pain.
I can no more, by shame, by rage suppress'd,
Let tears, and burning blushes speak the rest.
  Canst thou forget that sad, that solemn day,
When victims at yon altar's foot we lay?
Canst thou forget what tears that moment fell,
When warm in youth I bade the world
    farewell?
As with cold lips I kiss'd the sacred veil,
The shrines all trembled, and the lamps grew pale:
Heaven scarce believed the conquest it survey'd,
And saints with wonder heard the vows I made.
Yet then, to those dread altars as I drew,
Not on the cross my eyes were fix'd, but you:
Not grace, or zeal, love only was my call;
And if I lose thy love, I lose my all.
Come! with thy looks, thy words, relieve my woe;
Those still at least are left thee to bestow.
Still on that breast enamour'd let me lie,
Still drink delicious poison from thy eye,
Pant on thy lip, and to thy heart be press'd;
Give all thou canst—and let me dream the rest.
Ah no! instruct me other joys to prize,
With other beauties charm my partial eyes;
Full in my view set all the bright abode,
And make my soul quit Abelard for God.
  Ah, think at least thy flock deserves thy care,
Plants of thy hand, and children of thy
    prayer.
From the false world in early youth they fled,
By thee to mountains, wilds, and deserts led.
You raised these hallow'd walls; the desert smiled,
And Paradise was open'd in the wild.
No weeping orphan saw his father's stores
Our shrines irradiate, or emblaze the floors;
No silver saints by dying misers given,
Here bribed the rage of ill-requited Heaven:
But such plain roofs at Piety could raise,
And only vocal with the Maker's praise.
In these lone walls, (their day's eternal bound)
These moss-grown domes with spiry turrets
    crown'd,

ELOISA TO ABELARD. **58. Indus:** the great river that flows from northwestern India to the Arabian Sea. **64. lambent:** radiant.

102. poniard: a dagger. **103.** Abelard was castrated at the command of Eloisa's uncle.

Where awful arches make a noon-day night,
And the dim windows shed a solemn light;
Thy eyes diffused a reconciling ray,
And gleams of glory brighten'd all the day.
But now no face divine contentment wears,
'Tis all blank sadness, or continual tears.
See how the force of others' pray'rs I try,
(O pious fraud of amorous charity!)
But why should I on others' prayers depend?
Come thou, my father, brother, husband, friend!
Ah, let thy handmaid, sister, daughter move,
And all those tender names in one, thy love!
The darksome pines that o'er yon rocks reclined
Wave high, and murmur to the hollow wind,
The wand'ring streams that shine between the hills,
The grots that echo to the tinkling rills,
The dying gales that pant upon the trees,
The lakes that quiver to the curling breeze;
No more these scenes my meditation aid,
Or lull to rest the visionary maid.
But o'er the twilight groves and dusky caves,
Long-sounding aisles, and intermingled graves,
Black Melancholy sits, and round her throws
A death-like silence, and a dread repose:
Her gloomy presence saddens all the scene,
Shades ev'ry flow'r, and darkens ev'ry green,
Deepens the murmur of the falling floods,
And breathes a browner horror on the woods.
  Yet here for ever, ever must I stay;
Sad proof how well a lover can obey!
Death, only death, can break the lasting chain;
And here, ev'n then, shall my cold dust remain,
Here all its frailties, all its flames resign,
And wait till 'tis no sin to mix with thine.
  Ah, wretch! believed the spouse of God in vain,
Confess'd within the slave of love and man.
Assist me, Heaven! but whence arose that prayer?
Sprung it from piety, or from despair?
Ev'n here, where frozen chastity retires,
Love finds an altar for forbidden fires.
I ought to grieve, but cannot what I ought;
I mourn the lover, not lament the fault;
I view my crime, but kindle at the view,
Repent old pleasures, and solicit new:
Now turn'd to Heaven, I weep my past offence,
Now think of thee, and curse my innocence.
Of all affliction taught a lover yet,
'Tis sure the hardest science to forget!
How shall I lose the sin, yet keep the sense,
And love the offender, yet detest th' offence?
How the dear object from the crime remove,
Or how distinguish penitence from love?
Unequal task! a passion to resign,
For hearts so touch'd, so pierced, so lost as mine.
Ere such a soul regains its peaceful state,
How often must it love, how often hate!
How often hope, despair, resent, regret,
Conceal, disdain,—do all things but forget!
But let Heaven seize it, all at once 'tis fired;
Not touch'd, but rapt; not weaken'd, but inspired!
Oh come! oh teach me nature to subdue,
Renounce my love, my life, myself—and you.
Fill my fond heart with God alone, for He
Alone can rival, can succeed to thee.
  How happy is the blameless Vestal's lot!
The world forgetting, by the world forgot:
Eternal sunshine of the spotless mind!
Each prayer accepted, and each wish resign'd;
Labour and rest that equal periods keep;
"Obedient slumbers that can wake and weep";
Desires composed, affections ever even;
Tears that delight, and sighs that waft to Heaven.
Grace shines around her with serenest beams,
And whisp'ring angels prompt her golden dreams.
For her th' unfading rose of Eden blooms,
And wings of seraphs shed divine perfumes;
For her the spouse prepares the bridal ring,
For her white virgins hymeneals sing;
To sounds of heavenly harps she dies away,
And melts in visions of eternal day.
  Far other dreams my erring soul employ,
Far other raptures, of unholy joy:
When at the close of each sad, sorrowing day,
Fancy restores what vengeance snatch'd away,
Then conscience sleeps, and leaving Nature free,
All my loose soul unbounded springs to thee.
O cursed, dear horrors of all-conscious night!
How glowing guilt exalts the keen delight!
Provoking demons all restraint remove,
And stir within me ev'ry source of love.
I hear thee, view thee, gaze o'er all thy charms,
And round thy phantom glue my clasping arms.
I wake:—no more I hear, no more I view,
The phantom flies me, as unkind as you.

212. Pope tells us his source for this line, the seventeenth-century poet Richard Crashaw (1612–1649). The line is quoted from Crashaw's *Description of a Religious House.* **220. hymeneals:** wedding hymns.

I call aloud; it hears not what I say:
I stretch my empty arms; it glides away.
To dream once more I close my willing eyes;
Ye soft illusions, dear deceits, arise!
Alas, no more! methinks we wand'ring go
Through dreary wastes, and weep each other's woe,
Where round some mould'ring tower pale ivy creeps,
And low-brow'd rocks hang nodding o'er the deeps.
Sudden you mount, you beckon from the skies;
Clouds interpose, waves roar, and winds arise.
I shriek, start up, the same sad prospect find,
And wake to all the griefs I left behind.
For thee the Fates, severely kind, ordain
A cool suspense from pleasure and from pain;
Thy life a long dead calm of fix'd repose;
No pulse that riots, and no blood that glows.
Still as the sea, ere winds were taught to blow,
Or moving spirit bade the waters flow;
Soft as the slumbers of a saint forgiven,
And mild as opening gleams of promised Heaven.
Come, Abelard! for what hast thou to dread?
The torch of Venus burns not for the dead.
Nature stands check'd; religion disapproves:
Ev'n thou art cold—yet Eloisa loves.
Ah hopeless, lasting flames! like those that burn
To light the dead, and warm th' unfruitful urn.
What scenes appear where'er I turn my view?
The dear ideas, where I fly, pursue,
Rise in the grove, before the altar rise,
Stain all my soul, and wanton in my eyes.
I waste the matin lamp in sighs for thee,
Thy image steals between my God and me,
Thy voice I seem in ev'ry hymn to hear,
With ev'ry bead I drop too soft a tear.
When from the censer clouds of fragrance roll,
And swelling organs lift the rising soul,
One thought of thee puts all the pomp to flight,
Priests, tapers, temples, swim before my sight:
In seas of flame my plunging soul is drowned,
While altars blaze, and angels tremble round.
While prostrate here in humble grief I lie,
Kind, virtuous drops just gath'ring in my eye,
While praying, trembling, in the dust I roll,
And dawning grace is opening on my soul:
Come, if thou dar'st, all charming as thou art!
Oppose thyself to Heaven; dispute my heart;
Come, with one glance of those deluding eyes
Blot out each bright idea of the skies;
Take back that grace, those sorrows, and those tears;
Take back my fruitless penitence and prayers;
Snatch me, just mounting, from the bless'd abode;
Assist the fiends and tear me from my God!
No, fly me, fly me, far as pole from pole;
Rise Alps between us! and whole oceans roll!
Ah, come not, write not, think not once of me,
Nor share one pang of all I felt for thee,
Thy oaths I quit, thy memory resign;
Forget, renounce me, hate whate'er was mine.
Fair eyes, and tempting looks, (which yet I view!)
Long loved, adored ideas, all adieu!
O Grace serene! O Virtue heavenly fair!
Divine oblivion of low-thoughted care!
Fresh blooming Hope, gay daughter of the sky!
And Faith, our early immortality!
Enter, each mild, each amicable guest:
Receive, and wrap me in eternal rest!
See in her cell sad Eloisa spread,
Propped on some tomb, a neighbour of the dead.
In each low wind methinks a spirit calls,
And more than echoes talk along the walls.
Here, as I watch'd the dying lamps around,
From yonder shrine I heard a hollow sound.
"Come, sister, come! (it said, or seem'd to say,)
Thy place is here, sad sister, come away!
Once, like thyself, I trembled, wept, and prayed,
Love's victim then, though now a sainted maid:
But all is calm in this eternal sleep;
Here Grief forgets to groan, and Love to weep,
Ev'n Superstition loses ev'ry fear:
For God, not man, absolves our frailties here."
I come, I come! prepare your roseate bowers,
Celestial palms, and ever-blooming flowers.
Thither, where sinners may have rest, I go,
Where flames refined in breasts seraphic glow:
Thou, Abelard! the last sad office pay,
And smooth my passage to the realms of day;
See my lips tremble, and my eye-balls roll,
Suck my last breath, and catch my flying soul!
Ah no—in sacred vestments may'st thou stand,
The hallow'd taper trembling in thy hand,
Present the cross before my lifted eye,
Teach me at once, and learn of me to die.
Ah then, thy once-loved Eloisa see!
It will be then no crime to gaze on me.
See from my cheek the transient roses fly!
See the last sparkle languish in my eye!

Till ev'ry motion, pulse, and breath be o'er,
And ev'n my Abelard be lov'd no more.
O Death all-eloquent! you only prove
What dust we dote on, when 'tis man we love.
  Then too, when fate shall thy fair frame destroy,
(That cause of all my guilt, and all my joy,)
In trance ecstatic may thy pangs be drowned,
Bright clouds descend, and angels watch thee
    round;
From opening skies may streaming glories shine,
And saints embrace thee with a love like mine.
  May one kind grave unite each hapless name,
And graft my love immortal on thy fame!
Then, ages hence, when all my woes are o'er,
When this rebellious heart shall beat no more;
If ever chance two wand'ring lovers brings
To Paraclete's white walls and silver springs,
O'er the pale marble shall they join their heads,
And drink the falling tears each other sheds;
Then sadly say, with mutual pity moved,
"Oh may we never love as these have loved!"
From the full choir when loud Hosannas rise,
And swell the pomp of dreadful sacrifice,
Amid that scene, if some relenting eye
Glance on the stone where our cold relics lie,
Devotion's self shall steal a thought from Heaven,
One human tear shall drop, and be forgiven.
And sure, if Fate some future bard shall join,
In sad similitude of griefs to mine,
Condemn'd whole years in absence to deplore,
And image charms he must behold no more;
Such if there be, who love so long, so well,
Let him our sad, our tender story tell;
The well-sung woes will soothe my pensive ghost;
He best can paint them who shall feel them most.

(1717)

343–50. Pope's own words are helpful for the reader here: "Abelard and Eloisa were interred in the same grave, or in monuments adjoining in the monastery of the Paraclete: he died in the year 1142, she, in 1163."

Essay on Man

IN FOUR EPISTLES
TO H. ST. JOHN, LORD BOLINBROKE*

EPISTLE I

Argument

of the Nature and State of Man With Respect to the Universe

Of man in the abstract.—I. That we can judge only with regard to our own system, being ignorant of the relation of systems and things, ver. 17, etc. II. That man is not to be deemed imperfect, but a being suited to his place and rank in the creation, agreeable to the general order of things, and conformable to ends and relations to him unknown, ver. 35, etc. III. That it is partly upon his ignorance of future events, and partly upon the hope of a future state, that all his happiness in the present depends, ver. 77, etc. IV. The pride of aiming at more knowledge, and pretending to more perfection, the cause of man's error and misery. The impiety of putting himself in the place of God, and judging of the fitness or unfitness, perfection or imperfection, justice or injustice, of his dispensations, ver. 113, etc. V. The absurdity of conceiting himself the final cause of the creation, or expecting that perfection in the moral world which is not in the natural, ver. 131, etc. VI. The unreasonableness of his complaints against Providence, while on the one hand he demands the perfections of the angels and on the other the bodily qualifications of the brutes; though to possess any of the sensitive faculties in a higher degree would render him miserable, ver. 173, etc. VII. That throughout the whole visible world an universal order and gradation in the sensual and mental faculties is observed, which causes a subordination of creature to creature, and of all creatures to Man. The gradations of sense, instinct, thought, reflection, reason; that reason alone countervails all the other faculties, ver. 207. VIII. How much farther this order and subordination of living creatures may extend above and below us; were any part of which broken, not that part only, but the whole connected creation, must be destroyed, ver. 233. IX. The extravagance, madness, and pride of such a desire, ver. 259. X. The consequence of all the absolute submission due to

* Henry St. John Bolingbroke (1678–1751), supporter of the Tory Party, became Secretary of State in 1710, Viscount Bolingbroke in 1712. He was in charge of the negotiations that led to the Treaty of Utrecht in 1713.

Providence, both as to our present and future state, ver. 281, etc., to the end.

Awake, my St. John! leave all meaner things
To low ambition and the pride of kings.
Let us (since life can little more supply
Than just to look about us, and to die)
Expatiate free o'er all this scene of man;
A mighty maze! but not without a plan:
A wild, where weeds and flowers promiscuous shoot;
Or garden, tempting with forbidden fruit.
Together let us beat this ample field,
Try what the open, what the covert yield!
The latent tracts, the giddy heights explore
Of all who blindly creep, or sightless soar;
Eye Nature's walks, shoot folly as it flies,
And catch the manners living as they rise:
Laugh where we must, be candid where we can;
But vindicate the ways of God to man.
I. Say first, of God above, or man below,
What can we reason, but from what we know?
Of man, what see we but his station here,
From which to reason, or to which refer?
Through worlds unnumbered, though the God be known,
'Tis ours to trace him only in our own.
He, who through vast immensity can pierce,
See worlds on worlds compose one universe,
Observe how system into system runs,
What other planets circle other suns,
What varied being peoples every star,
May tell why Heaven has made us as we are.
But of this frame the bearings and the ties,
The strong connections, nice dependencies,
Gradations just, has thy pervading soul
Look'd through? or can a part contain the whole?
Is the great chain, that draws all to agree,
And drawn, supports, upheld by God or thee?
II. Presumptuous man! the reason wouldst thou find,
Why form'd so weak, so little, and so blind?
First, if thou canst, the harder reason guess,
Why form'd no weaker, blinder, and no less?
Ask of thy mother earth, why oaks are made
Taller and stronger than the weeds they shade?
Or ask of yonder argent fields above,
Why Jove's satellites are less than Jove?
Of systems possible, if 'tis confess'd,
That Wisdom infinite must form the best,
Where all must fall, or not coherent be,
And all that rises, rise in due degree;
Then in the scale of reas'ning life, 'tis plain,
There must be, somewhere, such a rank as man:
And all the question (wrangle e'er so long)
Is only this, if God has placed him wrong?
Respecting man, whatever wrong we call,
May, must be right, as relative to all.
In human works, though labour'd on with pain,
A thousand movements scarce one purpose gain;
In God's, one single can its end produce;
Yet serves to second too, some other use.
So man, who here seems principal alone,
Perhaps acts second to some sphere unknown,
Touches some wheel, or verges to some goal;
'Tis but a part we see, and not a whole.
When the proud steed shall know why man restrains
His fiery course, or drives him o'er the plains;
When the dull ox, why now he breaks the clod,
Is now a victim, and now Egypt's god:
Then shall man's pride and dulness comprehend
His actions', passions', being's use and end;
Why doing, suff'ring, check'd, impell'd; and why
This hour a slave, the next a deity.
Then say not man's imperfect, Heaven in fault;
Say rather, man's as perfect as he ought:
His knowledge measured to his state and place;
His time a moment, and a point his space.
If to be perfect in a certain sphere,
What matter, soon or late, or here or there?
The blest to-day is as completely so,
As who began a thousand years ago.
III. Heaven from all creatures hides the book of Fate,
All but the page prescribed, their present state:
From brutes what men, from men what spirits know:
Or who could suffer being here below?
The lamb thy riot dooms to bleed to-day,

ESSAY ON MAN. EPISTLE I. **33. chain:** a reference to the so-called Great Chain of Being, in which all creation is organized from the lowest form of being to the angels. The chain ultimately reaches up to God.

41. argent: silver.

Had he thy reason, would he skip and play?
Pleased to the last, he crops the flowery food,
And licks the hand just raised to shed his blood.
Oh blindness to the future! kindly given,
That each may fill the circle mark'd by Heaven:
Who sees with equal eye, as God of all,
A hero perish, or a sparrow fall,
Atoms or systems into ruin hurl'd,
And now a bubble burst, and now a world.
Hope humbly then; with trembling pinions soar;
Wait the great teacher, Death; and God adore.
What future bliss, He gives not thee to know,
But gives that hope to be thy blessing now.
Hope springs eternal in the human breast:
Man never Is, but always To be blest.
The soul, uneasy, and confined from home,
Rests and expatiates in a life to come.
Lo, the poor Indian! whose untutor'd mind
Sees God in clouds, or hears Him in the wind;
His soul, proud Science never taught to stray
Far as the solar-walk, or milky-way;
Yet simple Nature to his hope has given,
Behind the cloud-topp'd hill, and humbler Heaven,
Some safer world in depth of woods embraced,
Some happier island in the watery waste,
Where slaves once more their native land behold,
No fiends torment, no Christians thirst for gold.
To Be, contents his natural desire,
He asks no angel's wings, no seraph's fire;
But thinks, admitted to that equal sky,
His faithful dog shall bear him company.
IV. Go, wiser thou! and in thy scale of sense,
Weigh thy opinion against Providence;
Call imperfection what thou fanciest such,
Say, here He gives too little, there too much:
Destroy all creatures for thy sport or gust,
Yet cry, If man's unhappy, God's unjust;
If man alone engross not Heaven's high care,
Alone made perfect here, immortal there:
Snatch from his hand the balance and the rod,
Re-judge his justice, be the god of God.
In pride, in reas'ning pride, our error lies;
All quit their sphere, and rush into the skies.
Pride still is aiming at the blest abodes,
Men would be angels, angels would be gods.
Aspiring to be gods, if angels fell,
Aspiring to be angels, men rebel:
And who but wishes to invert the laws
Of Order, sins against the Eternal Cause.
V. Ask for what end the Heavenly bodies shine—
Earth for whose use? Pride answers, " 'Tis for mine:
For me kind Nature wakes her genial power,
Suckles each herb, and spreads out ev'ry flower;
Annual for me, the grape, the rose renew,
The juice nectareous, and the balmy dew;
For me, the mine a thousand treasures brings;
For me, health gushes from a thousand springs;
Seas roll to waft me, suns to light me rise;
My footstool earth, my canopy the skies."
But errs not Nature from this gracious end,
From burning suns when livid deaths descend,
When earthquakes swallow, or when tempests sweep
Towns to one grave, whole nations to the deep?
"No, ('tis replied) the first Almighty Cause
Acts not by partial, but by gen'ral laws;
The exceptions few: some change since all began:
And what created perfect?"—Why then man?
If the great end be human happiness,
Then Nature deviates; and can man do less?
As much that end a constant course requires
Of showers and sunshine, as of man's desires;
As much eternal springs and cloudless skies,
As men for ever temperate, calm, and wise.
If plagues or earthquakes break not Heaven's design,
Why then a Borgia, or a Catiline?
Who knows but He, whose hand the lightning forms,
Who heaves old Ocean, and who wings the storms;
Pours fierce ambition in a Cæsar's mind,
Or turns young Ammon loose to scourge mankind?
From pride, from pride, our very reas'ning springs;
Account for moral as for natural things:
Why charge we Heaven in those, in these acquit?
In both, to reason right, is to submit.
Better for us, perhaps, it might appear,
Were there all harmony, all virtue here;

156. Borgia . . . Cataline: The Borgias were the awesome and powerful Italian Renaissance family known for their scandalous public and private escapades. Catiline, the object of some of the Roman Cicero's greatest oratory, plotted revolution against the state, died in 62 B.C. **160. Ammon:** Alexander the Great, who had visited the sacred priest of the Egyptian god Ammon and was celebrated as the son of the god.

That never air or ocean felt the wind,
That never passion discomposed the mind.
But all subsists by elemental strife;
And passions are the elements of life.
The general order, since the whole began,
Is kept by Nature, and is kept in man.
VI. What would this man? Now upward will he soar,
And little less than angel, would be more;
Now looking downwards, just as grieved appears,
To want the strength of bulls, the fur of bears.
Made for his use all creatures if he call,
Say what their use, had he the powers of all?
Nature to these, without profusion, kind,
The proper organs, proper powers assign'd;
Each seeming what compensated of course,
Here with degrees of swiftness, there of force;
All in exact proportion to the state;
Nothing to add, and nothing to abate.
Each beast, each insect, happy in its own:
Is Heaven unkind to man, and man alone?
Shall he alone, whom rational we call,
Be pleased with nothing, if not blest with all?
The bliss of man (could pride that blessing find)
Is not to act or think beyond mankind;
No powers of body or of soul to share,
But what his Nature and his state can bear.
Why has not man a microscopic eye?
For this plain reason, man is not a fly.
Say what the use, were finer optics given,
To inspect a mite, not comprehend the heaven?
Or touch, if trembling alive all o'er.
To smart and agonise at every pore?
Or quick effluvia darting through the brain,
Die of a rose in aromatic pain?
If Nature thunder'd in his opening ears,
And stunn'd him with the music of the spheres,
How would he wish that Heaven had left him still
The whisp'ring zephyr, and the purling rill?
Who finds not Providence all good and wise,
Alike in what it gives and what denies?
VII. Far as creation's ample range extends,
The scale of sensual, mental powers ascends:

199. effluvia: Epicurus, the Greek philosopher, argued that smells reached the brain in a wave of invisible particles. **202. music of the spheres:** a reference to the belief, a favorite in Elizabethan times, that the orderly movement of the heavenly bodies produced a music heard only by the angels.

Mark how it mounts to man's imperial race,
From the green myriads in the peopled grass:
What modes of sight betwixt each wide extreme,
The mole's dim curtain, and the lynx's beam:
Of smell, the headlong lioness between,
And hound sagacious on the tainted green:
Of hearing, from the life that fills the flood,
To that which warbles through the vernal wood?
The spider's touch, how exquisitely fine!
Feels at each thread, and lives along the line:
In the nice bee, what sense so subtly true
From poisonous herbs extract the healing dew?
How instinct varies in the grov'ling swine,
Compared, half-reasoning elephant, with thine!
'Twixt that, and reason, what a nice barrier?
For ever separate, yet for ever near!
Remembrance and reflection, how allied;
What thin partitions sense from thought divide;
And middle natures, how they long to join,
Yet never pass the insuperable line!
Without this just gradation could they be
Subjected, these to those, or all to thee?
The powers of all subdued by thee alone,
Is not thy reason all these powers in one?
VIII. See, through this air, this ocean, and this earth,
All matter quick, and bursting into birth.
Above, how high, progressive life may go!
Around, how wide! how deep extend below!
Vast chain of being! which from God began,
Natures ethereal, human, angel, man,
Beast, bird, fish, insect, what no eye can see,
No glass can reach; from infinite to thee,
From thee to nothing.—On superior powers
Were we to press, inferior might on ours;
Or in the full creation leave a void,
Where, one step broken, the great scale's destroy'd:
From Nature's chain whatever link you strike,
Tenth, or tenth thousandth, breaks the chain alike.
And, if each system in gradation roll
Alike essential to the amazing whole,
The least confusion but in one, not all
That system only, but the whole must fall.
Let earth, unbalanced, from her orbit fly,
Planets and suns run lawless through the sky;
Let ruling angels from their spheres be hurl'd,
Being on being wreck'd, and world on world;
Heaven's whole foundations to their centre nod,
And Nature trembles to the throne of God.

All this dread order break—for whom? for thee?
Vile worm!—oh madness! pride! impiety!
IX. What if the foot, ordain'd the dust to tread,
Or hand, to toil, aspired to be the head?
What if the head, the eye, or ear repined
To serve mere engines to the ruling mind?
Just as absurd for any part to claim
To be another, in this general frame;
Just as absurd, to mourn the tasks or pains
The great Directing Mind of all ordains.
All are but parts of one stupendous whole,
Whose body Nature is, and God the soul;
That, changed through all, and yet in all the same;
Great in the earth, as in the ethereal frame;
Warms in the sun, refreshes in the breeze,
Glows in the stars, and blossoms in the trees;
Lives through all life, extends through all extent;
Spreads undivided, operates unspent!
Breathes in our soul, informs our mortal part,
As full, as perfect, in a hair as heart:
As full, as perfect in vile man that mourns,
As the rapt seraph that adores and burns:
To him no high, no low, no great, no small;
He fills, He bounds, connects, and equals all.
X. Cease then, nor order imperfection name:
Our proper bliss depends on what we blame.
Know thy own point: this kind, this due degree
Of blindness, weakness, Heaven bestows on thee.
Submit, in this, or any other sphere,
Secure to be as blest as thou canst bear:
Safe in the hand of one Disposing Power,
Or in the natal, or the mortal hour.
All Nature is but art, unknown to thee
All chance, direction, which thou canst not
see;
All discord, harmony not understood;
All partial evil, universal good:
And, spite of pride, in erring reason's spite,
One truth is clear, Whatever is, is right.

EPISTLE II

Argument

of the Nature and State of Man With Respect to Himself as an Individual

I. The business of Man not to pry into God, but to study himself. His middle nature: his powers and frailties, ver. 1 to 19. The limits of his capacity, ver. 19, etc. II. The two principles of man, self-love and reason, both necessary, ver. 53, etc. Self-love the stronger, and why, ver. 67, etc. Their end the same, ver. 81, etc. III. The passions, and their use, ver. 93 to 130. The predominant passion, and its force, ver. 132 to 160. Its necessity in directing men to different purposes, ver. 165, etc. Its providential use, in fixing our principle and ascertaining our virtue, ver. 177. IV. Virtue and vice joined in our mixed nature; the limits near, yet the things separate and evident: what is the office of reason, ver. 202 to 216. V. How odious vice in itself, and how we deceive ourselves into it, ver. 217. VI. That, however, the ends of Providence and general good are answered in our passions and imperfections, ver. 238, etc. How usefully these are distributed to all orders of men, ver. 241. How useful they are to society, ver. 251. And to individuals, ver. 263. In every state, and every age of life, ver. 273, etc.

Know then thyself, presume not God to scan,
The proper study of mankind is man.
Placed on this isthmus of a middle state,
A being darkly wise, and rudely great:
With too much knowledge for the sceptic side,
With too much weakness for the stoic's pride,
He hangs between; in doubt to act, or rest;
In doubt to deem himself a god, or beast;
In doubt his mind or body to prefer;
Born but to die, and reasoning but to err;
Alike in ignorance, his reason such,
Whether he thinks too little, or too much:
Chaos of Thought and Passion, all confused;
Still by himself abused or disabused;
Created half to rise, and half to fall;
Great lord of all things, yet a prey to all;
Sole judge of truth, in endless error hurl'd:
The glory, jest, and riddle of the world!
Go, wondrous creature! mount where Science
guides,
Go, measure earth, weigh air, and state the
tides;
Instruct the planets in what orbs to run,
Correct old Time, and regulate the sun;
Go, soar with Plato to th' empyreal sphere,
To the first good, first perfect, and first fair;
Or tread the mazy round his followers trod,
And quitting sense call imitating God;
As Eastern priests in giddy circles run,
And turn their heads to imitate the sun.
Go, teach Eternal Wisdom how to rule—
Then drop into thyself, and be a fool!
Superior beings, when of late they saw

261. repined: desired.

A mortal man unfold all Nature's law,
Admired such wisdom in an earthly shape,
And show'd a Newton as we show an ape.
Could he, whose rules the rapid comet bind,
Describe or fix one movement of his mind?
Who saw its fires here rise, and there descend,
Explain his own beginning, or his end?
Alas what wonder! Man's superior part
Uncheck'd may rise, and climb from art to art;
But when his own great work is but begun,
What reason weaves, by passion is undone.
Trace Science then, with modesty thy guide;
First strip off all her equipage of pride;
Deduct but what is vanity or dress,
Or learning's luxury, or idleness;
Or tricks to show the stretch of human brain,
Mere curious pleasure, or ingenious pain;
Expunge the whole, or lop the excrescent parts
Of all our vices have created arts;
Then see how little the remaining sum,
Which served the past, and must the times to come!
II. Two principles in human nature reign;
Self-love, to urge, and Reason, to restrain;
Nor this a good, nor that a bad we call,
Each works its end, to move or govern all:
And to their proper operation still,
Ascribe all good; to their improper, ill.
Self-love, the spring of motion, acts the soul;
Reason's comparing balance rules the whole.
Man, but for that, no action could attend,
And, but for this, were active to no end:
Fix'd like a plant on his peculiar spot,
To draw nutrition, propagate, and rot:
Or, meteor-like, flame lawless through the void,
Destroying others, by himself destroy'd.
Most strength the moving principles requires;
Active its task, it prompts, impels, inspires.
Sedate and quiet the comparing lies,
Form'd but to check, deliberate, and advise.
Self-love, still stronger, as its objects nigh;
Reason's at distance, and in prospect lie:
That sees immediate good by present sense;
Reason, the future and the consequence.
Thicker than arguments, temptations throng,
At best more watchful this, but that more strong.
The action of the stronger to suspend
Reason still use, to reason still attend.
Attention, habit, and experience gains;
Each strengthens reason, and self-love restrains.
Let subtle schoolmen teach these friends to fight,
More studious to divide than to unite;
And grace and virtue, sense and reason split,
With all the rash dexterity of wit.
Wits, just like fools, at war about a name,
Have full as oft no meaning, or the same.
Self-love and reason to one end aspire,
Pain their aversion, pleasure their desire;
But greedy that its object would devour,
This taste the honey, and not wound the flower:
Pleasure, or wrong or rightly understood,
Our greatest evil, or our greatest good.
III. Modes of self-love the passions we may call:
'Tis real good, or seeming, moves them all:
But since not every good we can divide,
And reason bids us for our own provide;
Passions, though selfish, if their means be fair,
'List under reason, and deserve her care:
Those that imparted court a nobler aim,
Exalt their kind, and take some virtue's name.
In lazy apathy let Stoics boast
Their virtue fix'd; 'tis fix'd as in a frost;
Contracted all, retiring to the breast;
But strength of mind is exercise, not rest:
The rising tempest puts in act the soul,
Parts it may ravage, but preserves the whole.
On life's vast ocean diversely we sail,
Reason the card, but passion is the gale;
Nor God alone in the still calm we find,
He mounts the storm, and walks upon the wind.
Passions, like elements, though born to fight,
Yet, mix'd and soften'd, in his work unite:
These 'tis enough to temper and employ;
But what composes man, can man destroy?
Suffice that reason keep to Nature's road,
Subject, compound them, follow her and God.
Love, hope, and joy, fair pleasure's smiling train,
Hate, fear, and grief, the family of pain,
These mix'd with art, and to due bounds confined,
Make and maintain the balance of the mind:
The lights and shades, whose well-accorded strife
Gives all the strength and colour of our life.
Pleasures are ever in our hands or eyes;
And when in act, they cease; in prospect, rise:
Present to grasp, and future still to find,
The whole employ of body and of mind.
All spread their charms, but charm not all alike;

EPISTLE II. **108. card:** the face of the sailor's compass.

On different senses, different objects strike;
Hence different passions more or less inflame,
As strong or weak, the organs of the frame;
And hence one master passion in the breast,
Like Aaron's serpent, swallows up the rest.
As man, perhaps, the moment of his breath
Receives the lurking principle of death;
The young disease, that must subdue at length,
Grows with his growth, and strengthens with his strength;
So, cast and mingled with his very frame,
The mind's disease, its ruling passion came;
Each vital humour which should feed the whole,
Soon flows to this, in body and in soul:
Whatever warms the heart, or fills the head,
As the mind opens, and its functions spread,
Imagination plies her dangerous art,
And pours it all upon the peccant part.
Nature its mother, habit is its nurse;
Wit, spirit, faculties, but make it worse;
Reason itself but gives it edge and power;
As Heaven's blest beam turns vinegar more sour.
We, wretched subjects though to lawful sway,
In this weak queen some favourite still obey:
Ah! if she lend not arms as well as rules,
What can she more than tell us we are fools?
Teach us to mourn our nature, not to mend,
A sharp accuser, but a helpless friend!
Or from a judge turn pleader, to persuade
The choice we make, or justify it made;
Proud of an easy conquest all along,
She but removes weak passions for the strong:
So, when small humours gather to a gout,
The doctor fancies he has driven them out.
Yes, Nature's road must ever be preferr'd;
Reason is here no guide, but still a guard;
'Tis hers to rectify, not overthrow,
And treat this passion more as friend than foe;
A mightier power the strong direction sends,
And several men impels to several ends:
Like varying winds, by other passions toss'd,
This drives them constant to a certain coast.
Let power or knowledge, gold or glory please,
Or (oft more strong than all) the love of ease;
Through life 'tis follow'd, even at life's expense;
The merchant's toil, the sage's indolence,
The monk's humility, the hero's pride,
All, all alike find reason on their side.
The eternal art educing good from ill,
Grafts on this passion our best principle:
'Tis thus the mercury of man is fix'd,
Strong grows the virtue with his nature mix'd;
The dross cements what else were too refined,
And in one interest body acts with mind.
As fruits, ungrateful to the planter's care,
On savage stocks inserted learn to bear;
The surest virtues thus from passions shoot,
Wild Nature's vigour working at the root.
What crops of wit and honesty appear
From spleen, from obstinacy, hate, or fear!
See anger, zeal and fortitude supply;
Even av'rice, prudence; sloth, philosophy;
Lust, through some certain strainers well refined,
Is gentle love, and charms all womankind;
Envy, to which the ignoble mind's a slave,
Is emulation in the learn'd or brave;
Nor virtue, male or female, can we name,
But what will grow on pride, or grow on shame.
Thus Nature gives us (let it check our pride)
The virtue nearest to our vice allied:
Reason the bias turns to good from ill,
And Nero reigns a Titus, if he will.
The fiery soul abhorr'd in Catiline,
In Decius charms, in Curtius is divine:
The same ambition can destroy or save,
And makes a patriot as it makes a knave.
IV. This light and darkness in our chaos join'd,
What shall divide? The God within the mind.
Extremes in Nature equal ends produce,
In man they join to some mysterious use;
Though each by turns the other's bounds invade,
As, in some well-wrought picture, light and shade,
And oft so mix, the difference is too nice
Where ends the virtue or begins the vice.
Fools! who from hence into the notion fall
That vice or virtue there is none at all.
If white and black blend, soften, and unite

132. Aaron's serpent: The story is told in Exodus 7:10–12. Aaron transforms his rod into a serpent that swallows other serpents that have also been transformed from rods by the magicians of Pharaoh. **144. peccant:** erring.

198–200. The concrete examples exemplify the general philosophical point just made, that strong emotions can be useful when controlled by Reason. Titus, the Roman emperor, had just as sensual a nature as Nero, yet he checked his cruelty and sensuality when he assumed leadership and thus was a good ruler. Decius and Curtius were impetuous, yet performed brave deeds in noble causes.

A thousand ways, is there no black or white?
Ask your own heart, and nothing is so plain;
'Tis to mistake them, costs the time and pain.
V. Vice is a monster of so frightful mien,
As, to be hated, needs but to be seen;
Yet seen too oft, familiar with her face,
We first endure, then pity, then embrace.
But where the extreme of vice, was ne'er agreed:
Ask where's the north? at York, 'tis on the Tweed;
In Scotland, at the Orcades; and there,
At Greenland, Zembla, or the Lord knows where.
No creature owns it in the first degree,
But thinks his neighbour farther gone than he:
Even those who dwell beneath its very zone,
Or never feel the rage, or never own;
What happier natures shrink at with affright,
The hard inhabitant contends is right.
Virtuous and vicious every man must be,
Few in the extreme, but all in the degree;
The rogue and fool by fits is fair and wise;
And even the best by fits what they despise.
'Tis but by parts we follow good or ill;
For, vice or virtue, self directs it still;
Each individual seeks a several goal;
But Heaven's great view is one, and that the whole,
That counter-works each folly and caprice
That disappoints the effect of every vice;
That, happy frailties to all ranks applied:
Shame to the virgin, to the matron pride,
Fear to the statesman, rashness to the chief;
To kings presumption, and to crowds belief:
That, virtue's ends from vanity can raise,
Which seeks no interest, no reward but praise;
And build on wants, and on defects of mind,
The joy, the peace, the glory of mankind.
Heaven forming each on other to depend,
A master, or a servant, or a friend,
Bids each on other for assistance call,
Till one man's weakness grows the strength of all.
Wants, frailties, passions, closer still ally
The common interest, or endear the tie.
To these we owe true friendship, love sincere,
Each homefelt joy that life inherits here;
Yet from the same we learn, in its decline,
Those joys, those loves, those interests to resign;
Taught half by reason, half by mere decay,
To welcome death, and calmly pass away.
Whate'er the passion, knowledge, fame, or pelf,
Not one will change his neighbour with himself.
The learn'd is happy Nature to explore,
The fool is happy that he knows no more;
The rich is happy in the plenty given,
The poor contents him with the care of Heaven.
See the blind beggar dance, the cripple sing,
The sot a hero, lunatic a king;
The starving chemist in his golden views
Supremely blest, the poet in his muse.
See some strange comfort every state attend,
And pride bestow'd on all, a common friend:
See some fit passion every age supply,
Hope travels through, nor quits us when we die.
Behold the child, by Nature's kindly law,
Pleased with a rattle, tickled with a straw:
Some livelier plaything gives his youth delight,
A little louder, but as empty quite:
Scarfs, garters, gold, amuse his riper stage,
And beads and prayer-books are the toys of age:
Pleased with this bauble still, as that before;
Till tired he sleeps, and life's poor play is o'er.
Meanwhile opinion gilds with varying rays
Those painted clouds that beautify our days;
Each want of happiness by hope supplied,
And each vacuity of sense by pride:
These build as fast as knowledge can destroy;
In folly's cup still laughs the bubble, joy;
One prospect lost, another still we gain;
And not a vanity is given in vain;
Even mean self-love becomes, by force divine,
The scale to measure others' wants by thine.
See! and confess, one comfort still must rise;
'Tis this,—though man's a fool, yet God is wise.

261. pelf: wealth.

EPISTLE III

Argument

of the Nature and State of Man With Respect to Society

I. The whole universe one system of society, ver. 7, etc. Nothing made wholly for itself, nor yet wholly for another, ver. 27. The happiness of animals mutual, ver. 49. II. Reason or instinct operate alike to the good of each individual, ver. 79. Reason or instinct operate also to society in all animals, ver. 109. III. How far society carried by instinct, ver. 115. How much farther by reason, ver. 128. IV.

Of that which is called the state of nature, ver. 144. Reason instructed by instinct in the invention of arts, ver. 166, and in the forms of society, ver. 176. V. Origin of political societies, ver. 196. Origin of monarchy, ver. 207. Patriarchal government, ver. 212. VI. Origin of true religion and government, from the same principle of love, ver. 231, etc. Origin of superstition and tyranny, from the same principle of fear, ver. 237, etc. The influence of self-love operating to the social and public good, ver. 266. Restoration of true religion and government on their first principle, ver. 285. Mixed government, ver. 288. Various forms of each, and the true end of all, ver. 300, etc.

Here then we rest: "The Universal Cause
Acts to one end, but acts by various laws."
In all the madness of superfluous health,
The train of pride, the impudence of wealth,
Let this great truth be present night and day;
But most be present if we preach or pray.
  Look round our world; behold the chain of love
Combining all below and all above.
See plastic Nature working to this end,
The single atoms each to other tend,
Attract, attracted to, the next in place
Form'd and impell'd its neighbour to embrace.
See Matter next, with various life endued,
Press to one centre still, the general good.
See dying vegetables life sustain,
See life dissolving vegetate again:
All forms that perish other forms supply;
(By turns we catch the vital breath, and die)
Like bubbles on the sea of Matter borne,
They rise, they break, and to that sea return.
Nothing is foreign: parts relate to whole;
One all-extending, all-preserving soul
Connects each being, greatest with the least;
Made beast in aid of man, and man of beast;
All served, all serving: nothing stands alone:
The chain holds on, and where it ends, unknown.
  Has God, thou fool! work'd solely for thy good,
Thy joy, thy pastime, thy attire, thy food?
Who for thy table feeds the wanton fawn,
For him as kindly spread the flowery lawn:
Is it for thee the lark ascends and sings?
Joy tunes his voice, joy elevates his wings.
Is it for thee the linnet pours his throat?
Loves of his own and raptures swell the note.
The bounding steed you pompously bestride
Shares with his lord the pleasure and the pride.
Is thine alone the seed that strews the plain?
The birds of heaven shall vindicate their grain.
Thine the full harvest of the golden year?
Part pays, and justly, the deserving steer:
The hog, that ploughs not, nor obeys thy call,
Lives on the labours of this lord of all.
  Know, Nature's children shall divide her care;
The fur that warms a monarch warm'd a bear.
While man exclaims, "See all things for my use!"
"See man for mine!" replies a pamper'd goose:
And just as short of reason he must fall,
Who thinks all made for one, not one for all.
  Grant that the powerful still the weak control;
Be man the wit and tyrant of the whole:
Nature that tyrant checks; he only knows,
And helps, another creature's wants and woes.
Say, will the falcon, stooping from above,
Smit with her varying plumage, spare the dove?
Admires the jay the insect's gilded wings?
Or hears the hawk when Philomela sings?
Man cares for all: to birds he gives his woods,
To beasts his pastures, and to fish his floods;
For some his interest prompts him to provide,
For more his pleasure, yet for more his pride:
All feed on one vain patron, and enjoy
The extensive blessing of his luxury.
That very life his learned hunger craves,
He saves from famine, from the savage saves:
Nay, feasts the animal he dooms his feast,
And, till he tends the being, makes it bless'd;
Which sees no more the stroke, or feels the pain.
Than favour'd man by touch ethereal slain.
The creature had his feast of life before;
Thou too must perish when thy feast is o'er!
  To each unthinking being, Heaven, a friend.
Gives not the useless knowledge of its end:
To man imparts it; but with such a view
As, while he dreads it, makes him hope it too:
The hour conceal'd, and so remote the fear,
Death still draws nearer, never seeming near.
Great standing miracle! that Heaven assign'd
Its only thinking thing this turn of mind.

EPISTLE III. **9. plastic**: shaping, organizing, unifying.

56. Philomela: the nightingale. **68.** Pope notes that many of the Ancients and many of the Orientals of the day regarded those struck by lightning as sacred persons and favorites of heaven.

II. Whether with reason or with instinct blest,
Know, all enjoy that power which suits them best;
To bliss alike by that direction tend,
And find the means proportion'd to their end.
Say, where full instinct is the unerring guide,
What pope or council can they need beside?
Reason, however able, cool at best,
Cares not for service, or but serves when press'd,
Stays till we call, and then not often near;
But honest instinct comes a volunteer,
Sure never to o'ershoot, but just to hit;
While still too wide or short is human wit;
Sure by quick nature happiness to gain,
Which heavier reason labours at in vain.
This too serves always, reason never long;
One must go right, the other may go wrong.
See then the acting and comparing powers
One in their nature, which are two in ours;
And reason raise o'er instinct as you can,
In this 'tis God directs, in that 'tis man.
Who taught the nations of the field and wood
To shun their poison, and to choose their food?
Prescient, the tides or tempests to withstand,
Build on the wave, or arch beneath the sand?
Who made the spider parallels design,
Sure as De Moivre, without rule or line?
Who bade the stork, Columbus-like, explore
Heavens not his own, and worlds unknown before?
Who calls the council, states the certain day,
Who forms the phalanx, and who points the way?
III. God, in the nature of each being, founds
Its proper bliss, and sets its proper bounds:
But as he framed a whole, the whole to bless,
On mutual wants build mutual happiness:
So from the first eternal Order ran,
And creature link'd to creature, man to man.
Whate'er of life all-quick'ning ether keeps,
Or breathes through air, or shoots beneath the deeps,
Or pours profuse on earth, one nature feeds
The vital flame, and swells the genial seeds.
Not man alone, but all that roam the wood,
Or wing the sky, or roll along the flood,
Each loves itself, but not itself alone,
Each sex desires alike, till two are one.
Nor ends the pleasure with the fierce embrace;
They love themselves, a third time, in their race.
Thus beast and bird their common charge attend,
The mothers nurse it, and the sires defend;
The young dismiss'd to wander earth or air,
There stops the instinct, and there ends the care;
The link dissolves, each seeks a fresh embrace,
Another love succeeds, another race.
A longer care man's helpless kind demands;
That longer care contracts more lasting bands:
Reflection, reason, still the ties improve,
At once extend the interest, and the love:
With choice we fix, with sympathy we burn;
Each virtue in each passion takes its turn;
And still new needs, new helps, new habits rise,
That graft benevolence on charities.
Still as one brood, and as another rose,
These natural love maintain'd, habitual those:
The last, scarce ripen'd into perfect man,
Saw helpless him from whom their life began:
Memory and forecast just returns engage,
That pointed back to youth, this on to age;
While pleasure, gratitude, and hope combined,
Still spread the interest and preserved the kind.
IV. Nor think, in Nature's state they blindly trod;
The state of Nature was the reign of God:
Self-love and social at her birth began,
Union the bond of all things, and of man.
Pride then was not; nor arts, that pride to aid;
Man walk'd with beast, joint tenant of the shade;
The same his table, and the same his bed;
No murder clothed him, and no murder fed.
In the same temple, the resounding wood,
All vocal beings hymn'd their equal God:
The shrine with gore unstain'd, with gold undress'd,
Unbribed, unbloody, stood the blameless priest:
Heaven's attribute was universal care,
And man's prerogative, to rule, but spare.
Ah! how unlike the man of time to come!
Of half that live the butcher and the tomb;
Who, foe to Nature, hears the general groan,
Murders their species, and betrays his own.
But just disease to luxury succeeds,
And every death its own avenger breeds;
The fury-passions from that blood began,

101. prescient: knowing the future. **104. De Moivre:** Abraham de Moivre (1667–1754), celebrated French mathematician, member of the Royal Society, friend of Sir Isaac Newton.

And turn'd on man, a fiercer savage, man.
See him from Nature rising slow to Art!
To copy instinct then was reason's part;
Thus then to man the voice of Nature spake:
"Go, from the creatures thy instructions take:
Learn from the birds what food the thickets yield;
Learn from the beasts the physic of the field;
Thy arts of building from the bee receive;
Learn of the mole to plough, the worm to weave;
Learn of the little nautilus to sail,
Spread the thin oar, and catch the driving gale.
Here too all forms of social union find,
And hence let reason, late, instruct mankind:
Here subterranean works and cities see;
There towns aerial on the waving tree.
Learn each small people's genius, policies,
The ants' republic, and the realm of bees;
How those in common all their wealth bestow,
And anarchy without confusion know;
And these for ever, though a monarch reign,
Their separate cells and properties maintain.
Mark what unvaried laws preserve each state,
Laws wise as Nature, and as fix'd as fate.
In vain thy reason finer webs shall draw,
Entangle Justice in her net of law,
And right, too rigid, harden into wrong;
Still for the strong too weak, the weak too strong.
Yet go! and thus o'er all the creatures sway,
Thus let the wiser make the rest obey:
And for those arts mere instinct could afford,
Be crown'd as monarchs, or as gods adored."
V. Great Nature spoke; observant man obey'd;
Cities were built, societies were made:
Here rose one little state; another near
Grew by like means, and join'd, through love or fear.
Did here the trees with ruddier burdens bend,
And there the streams in purer rills descend?
What war could ravish, commerce could bestow,
And he return'd a friend, who came a foe.
Converse and love mankind might strongly draw,
When love was liberty, and nature law.
Thus states were form'd; the name of king unknown,
Till common interest placed the sway in one.
'Twas virtue only (or in arts or arms,
Diffusing blessings, or averting harms),
The same which in a sire the sons obey'd.
A prince the father of a people made.
VI. Till then, by Nature crown'd, each patriarch sate,
King, priest, and parent of his growing state;
On him, their second Providence, they hung,
Their law his eye, their oracle his tongue.
He from the wondering furrow call'd the food,
Taught to command the fire, control the flood,
Draw forth the monsters of the abyss profound,
Or fetch the aerial eagle to the ground.
Till drooping, sickening, dying, they began
Whom they revered as God to mourn as man:
Then, looking up from sire to sire, explored
One great first Father, and that first adored.
Or plain tradition that this all begun,
Convey'd unbroken faith from sire to son;
The worker from the work distinct was known,
And simple reason never sought but one:
Ere wit oblique had broke that steady light,
Man, like his Maker, saw that all was right;
To virtue, in the paths of pleasure trod,
And own'd a Father when he own'd a God.
Love, all the faith and all the allegiance then;
For Nature knew no right divine in men,
No ill could fear in God; and understood
A sovereign Being, but a sovereign good:
True faith, true policy, united ran,
That was but love of God, and this of man.
Who first taught souls enslaved, and realms undone,
The enormous faith of many made for one;
That proud exception to all Nature's laws,
To invert the world, and counter-work its cause?
Force first made conquest, and that conquest, law;
Till Superstition taught the tyrant awe,
Then shared the tyranny, then lent it aid,
And gods of conquerors, slaves of subjects made:
She midst the lightning's blaze, and thunder's sound,
When rock'd the mountains, and when groan'd the ground,
She taught the weak to bend, the proud to pray,
To power unseen, and mightier far than they:
She, from the rending earth and bursting skies,
Saw gods descend, and fiends infernal rise:
Here fix'd the dreadful, there the blest abodes:
Fear made her devils, and weak hope her gods;

174. physic: medicinal herbs.

Gods partial, changeful, passionate, unjust,
Whose attributes were rage, revenge, or lust;
Such as the souls of cowards might conceive,
And, form'd like tyrants, tyrants would believe.
Zeal then, not charity, became the guide;
And hell was built on spite, and heaven on pride.
Then sacred seem'd the ethereal vault no more;
Altars grew marble then, and reek'd with gore:
Then first the flamen tasted living food;
Next his grim idol smear'd with human blood;
With Heaven's own thunders shook the world below,
And play'd the god an engine on his foe.
So drives self-love through just and through unjust,
To one man's power, ambition, lucre, lust:
The same self-love, in all, becomes the cause
Of what restrains him, government and laws.
For, what one likes, if others like as well,
What serves one will, when many wills rebel?
How shall he keep, what, sleeping or awake,
A weaker may surprise, a stronger take?
His safety must his liberty restrain:
All join to guard what each desires to gain.
Forced into virtue thus, by self-defence,
Even kings learn'd justice and benevolence:
Self-love forsook the path it first pursued,
And found the private in the public good.
'Twas then the studious head or generous mind,
Follower of God, or friend of human kind,
Poet or patriot, rose but to restore
The faith and moral Nature gave before;
Relumed her ancient light, not kindled new,
If not God's image, yet his shadow drew;
Taught power's due use to people and to kings,
Taught nor to slack, nor strain its tender strings,
The less, or greater, set so justly true,
That touching one must strike the other too:
Till jarring interests of themselves create
The according music of a well-mix'd state.
Such is the world's great harmony, that springs
From order, union, full consent of things:
Where small and great, where weak and mighty, made
To serve, not suffer—strengthen, not invade;
More powerful each as needful to the rest,
And, in proportion as it blesses, blest;
Draw to one point, and to one centre bring
Beast, man, or angel, servant, lord, or king.
For forms of government let fools contest:
Whate'er is best administer'd is best:
For modes of faith, let graceless zealots fight;
His can't be wrong whose life is in the right;
In faith and hope the world will disagree,
But all mankind's concern is charity:
All must be false that thwart this one great end:
And all of God that bless mankind or mend.
Man, like the generous vine, supported lives:
The strength he gains is from the embrace he gives.
On their own axis as the planets run,
Yet make at once their circle round the sun;
So two consistent motions act the soul;
And one regards itself, and one the whole.
Thus God and Nature link'd the general frame,
And bade self-love and social be the same.

265. flamen: a priest of ancient Rome. **287. relumed:** rekindled.

EPISTLE IV

Argument

of the Nature and State of Man With Respect to Happiness

I. False notions of happiness, philosophical and popular, answered from ver. 19 to 27. II. It is the end of all men, and attainable by all, ver. 29. God intends happiness to be equal; and to be so it must be social, since all particular happiness depends on general, and since he governs by general, not particular, laws, ver. 35. As it is necessary for order, and the peace and welfare of society, that external goods should be unequal, happiness is not made to consist in these, ver. 51. But notwithstanding that inequality, the balance of happiness among mankind is kept even by Providence by the two passions of hope and fear, ver. 70. III. What the happiness of individuals is, as far as is consistent with the constitution of this world; and that the good man has here the advantage, ver. 77. The error of imputing to virtue what are only the calamities of Nature or of Fortune, ver. 94. IV. The folly of expecting that God should alter his general laws in favour of particulars, ver. 121. V. That we are not judges who are good; but that, whoever they are, they must be happiest, ver. 131, etc. VI. That external goods are not the proper rewards, but often inconsistent with, or destructive of virtue, ver. 167. That even these can make no man happy without virtue: instanced in riches, ver. 185. Honours, ver. 193. Nobility, ver. 205. Greatness, ver. 217. Fame, ver. 237. Superior talents, ver. 259, etc. With pictures of human infelicity in men possessed of them all, ver. 269, etc. VII. That virtue only constitutes a happiness whose object is universal, and whose prospect eternal, ver. 309. That the perfection of virtue and happiness consists in a conformity to the order of Providence here, and a resignation to it here and hereafter, ver. 326, etc.

Oh Happiness! our being's end and aim!
Good, pleasure, ease, content! whate'er thy name:
That something still which prompts the eternal sigh,
For which we bear to live, or dare to die,
Which still so near us, yet beyond us lies,
O'erlook'd, seen double, by the fool and wise.
Plant of celestial seed! if dropp'd below,
Say, in what mortal soil thou deign'st to grow?
Fair opening to some court's propitious shine,
Or deep with diamonds in the flaming mine?
Twined with the wreaths Parnassian laurels yield,
Or reap'd in iron harvests of the field?
Where grows? where grows it not? If vain our toil,
We ought to blame the culture, not the soil:
Fix'd to no spot is happiness sincere,
'Tis nowhere to be found, or everywhere:
'Tis never to be bought, but always free,
And, fled from monarchs, St. John! dwells with thee.
  Ask of the learn'd the way? the learn'd are blind;
This bids to serve, and that to shun, mankind;
Some place the bliss in action, some in ease,
Those call it pleasure, and contentment these;
Some, sunk to beasts, find pleasure end in pain;
Some, swell'd to gods, confess even virtue vain;
Or, indolent, to each extreme they fall,
To trust in everything, or doubt of all.
  Who thus define it, say they more or less
Than this, that happiness is happiness?
  II. Take Nature's path, and mad opinions leave;
All states can reach it, and all heads conceive;
Obvious her goods, in no extreme they dwell;
There needs but thinking right, and meaning well;
And, mourn our various portions as we please,
Equal is common sense and common ease.
  Remember, man, "The Universal Cause
Acts not by partial, but by general laws";
And makes what happiness we justly call
Subsist, not in the good of one, but all.
There's not a blessing individuals find,
But some way leans and hearkens to the kind:
No bandit fierce, no tyrant mad with pride,
No cavern'd hermit, rests self-satisfied:
Who most to shun or hate mankind pretend,
Seek an admirer, or would fix a friend:
Abstract what others feel, what others think,
All pleasures sicken, and all glories sink;
Each has his share; and who would more obtain,
Shall find the pleasure pays not half the pain.
  Order is Heaven's first law; and, this confess'd,
Some are, and must be, greater than the rest,
More rich, more wise; but who infers from hence
That such are happier, shocks all common sense.
Heaven to mankind impartial we confess,
If all are equal in their happiness:
But mutual wants this happiness increase;
All nature's difference keeps all nature's peace.
Condition, circumstance, is not the thing;
Bliss is the same in subject or in king,
In who obtain defence, or who defend,
In him who is, or him who finds a friend:
Heaven breathes through every member of the whole
One common blessing, as one common soul.
But fortune's gifts, if each alike possess'd,
And each were equal, must not all contest?
If then to all men happiness was meant,
God in externals could not place content.
  Fortune her gifts may variously dispose,
And these be happy call'd, unhappy those;
But Heaven's just balance equal will appear,
While those are placed in hope, and these in fear:
Not present good or ill, the joy or curse,
But future views of better or of worse.
  Oh sons of earth! attempt ye still to rise,
By mountains piled on mountains, to the skies?
Heaven still with laughter the vain toil surveys,
And buries madmen in the heaps they raise.
  III. Know, all the good that individuals find,
Or God and Nature meant to mere mankind,
Reason's whole pleasure, all the joys of sense,

Lie in three words—health, peace, and
competence.
But health consists with temperance alone;
And peace, O Virtue! peace is all thy own.
The good or bad the gifts of fortune gain;
But these less taste them as they worse obtain.
Say, in pursuit of profit or delight,
Who risk the most, that take wrong means, or
right?
Of vice or virtue, whether blest or curst,
Which meets contempt, or which compassion first?
Count all the advantage prosperous vice attains,
'Tis but what virtue flies from and disdains:
And grant the bad what happiness they would,
One they must want, which is, to pass for good.
Oh blind to truth, and God's whole scheme below,
Who fancy bliss to vice, to virtue woe!
Who sees and follows that great scheme the best,
Best knows the blessing, and will most be blest.
But fools, the good alone unhappy call,
For ills or accidents that chance to all.
See Falkland dies, the virtuous and the just!
See godlike Turenne prostrate on the dust!
See Sidney bleeds amid the martial strife!
Was this their virtue, or contempt of life?
Say, was it virtue, more though Heaven ne'er gave,
Lamented Digby? sunk thee to the grave?
Tell me, if virtue made the son expire,
Why, full of days and honour, lives the sire?
Why drew Marseilles' good bishop purer breath,
When nature sicken'd, and each gale was death?
Or why so long (in life if long can be)
Lent Heaven a parent to the poor and me?
What makes all physical or moral ill?
There deviates nature, and here wanders will.
God sends not ill, if rightly understood;
Or partial ill is universal good,
Or change admits, or nature lets it fall,
Short, and but rare, 'till man improved it all.
We just as wisely might of Heaven complain
That righteous Abel was destroy'd by Cain,
As that the virtuous son is ill at ease
When his lewd father gave the dire disease.
IV. Think we, like some weak prince, the
Eternal Cause
Prone for his favourites to reverse his laws?
Shall burning Ætna, if a sage requires,
Forget to thunder, and recall her fires?
On air or sea new motions be impress'd,
Oh blameless Bethel! to relieve thy breast?
When the loose mountain trembles from on high,
Shall gravitation cease if you go by?
Or some old temple, nodding to its fall,
For Chartres' head reserve the hanging wall?
V. But still this world (so fitted for the knave)
Contents us not. A better shall we have?
A kingdom of the just then let it be:
But first consider how those just agree.
The good must merit God's peculiar care!
But who but God can tell us who they are?
One thinks on Calvin Heaven's own spirit fell;
Another deems him instrument of hell;
If Calvin feel Heaven's blessing, or its rod,
This cries, There is, and that, There is no
God.
What shocks one part will edify the rest,
Nor with one system can they all be blest.
The very best will variously incline,
And what rewards your virtue, punish mine.
Whatever is, is right.—This world, 'tis true,
Was made for Cæsar—but for Titus too;
And which more blest? who chain'd his country,
say,
Or he whose virtue sigh'd to lose a day?

EPISTLE IV. **99. Falkland:** Lucius Cary, Lord Falkland (1610–1643), a brilliant and devoted royalist, died fighting for Charles I at the Battle of Newbury. He deplored the extremism of the English Civil War. **100. Turenne:** Henry, Viscount of Turenne (1611–1675), was killed in battle at Sassbach in Baden. **101. Sidney:** Sir Philip Sidney (1554–1586), poet, soldier, Renaissance man *par excellence,* was wounded in battle at Zutphen, the Netherlands, and died shortly thereafter, barely thirty years of age. **104. Digby:** Robert Digby (1686–1726), friend of Pope. **107. Marseilles' good bishop:** Henri F. de Belsunce (1671–1755) put his own life in danger by ministering to the sick during the plague of 1720–1721. **110.** a reference to Pope's mother who died in 1733 at the age of ninety-one, shortly before this epistle was written.

123. a reference to the story of the Empedocles, the Greek philosopher of the fifth century B.C., who supposedly perished in an eruption of Mount Etna, when he came too close to a crater while attempting to demonstrate his power. **126–28. Bethel:** a reference to Pope's friend Hugh Bethel who had complained about his physical ailments while travelling in Italy. **130. Chartres:** Francis Charteris (1675–1732) described by Pope as a notorious gambler and lecher. **137. John Calvin:** French theologian (1509–1564), famous for his doctrines of original sin and predestination.

"But sometimes virtue starves, while vice is
fed."
What then? is the reward of virtue bread?
That, vice may merit, 'tis the price of toil;
The knave deserves it, when he tills the soil,
The knave deserves it, when he tempts the main,
Where folly fights for kings, or dives for gain.
The good man may be weak, be indolent;
Nor is his claim to plenty, but content.
But grant him riches, your demand is o'er?
"No—shall the good want health, the good want
power?"
Add health and power, and every earthly thing,
"Why bounded power? why private? why no
king?"
Nay, why external for internal given?
Why is not man a god, and earth a heaven?
Who ask and reason thus will scarce conceive
God gives enough while he has more to give;
Immense the power, immense were the demand;
Say, at what part of nature will they stand?
VI. What nothing earthly gives, or can destroy,
The soul's calm sunshine, and the heartfelt joy,
Is virtue's prize: a better would you fix?
Then give humility a coach and six,
Justice a conqueror's sword, or truth a gown,
Or public spirit its great cure, a crown.
Weak, foolish man! will Heaven reward us there
With the same trash mad mortals wish for here?
The boy and man an individual makes,
Yet sigh'st thou now for apples and for cakes?
Go, like the Indian, in another life
Expect thy dog, thy bottle, and thy wife;
As well as dream such trifles are assign'd,
As toys and empires, for a godlike mind.
Rewards, that either would to virtue bring
No joy, or be destructive of the thing:
How oft by these at sixty are undone
The virtues of a saint at tweny-one!
To whom can riches give repute, or trust,
Content, or pleasure, but the good and just?
Judges and senates have been bought for gold,
Esteem and love were never to be sold.
O fool! to think God hates the worthy mind,
The lover and the love of human kind,
Whose life is healthful, and whose conscience
clear,
Because he wants a thousand pounds a year.
Honour and shame from no condition rise:
Act well your part; there all the honour lies.
Fortune in men has some small difference made,
One flaunts in rags, one flutters in brocade;
The cobbler apron'd, and the parson gown'd,
The friar hooded, and the monarch crown'd.
"What differ more (you cry) than crown and
cowl?"
I'll tell you, friend! a wise man and a fool.
You'll find, if once the monarch acts the monk,
Or, cobbler-like, the parson will be drunk,
Worth makes the man, and want of it the fellow:
The rest is all but leather or prunella.
Stuck o'er with titles and hung round with
strings,
That thou may'st be by kings or whores of kings,
Boast the pure blood of an illustrious race,
In quiet flow from Lucrece to Lucrece:
But by your father's worth if yours you rate,
Count me those only who were good and
great.
Go! if your ancient but ignoble blood
Has crept through scoundrels ever since the flood,
Go! and pretend your family is young;
Nor own your fathers have been fools so long.
What can ennoble sots, or slaves, or cowards?
Alas! not all the blood of all the Howards.
Look next on greatness; say where greatness
lies.
Where, but among the heroes and the wise?
Heroes are much the same, the point's agreed,
From Macedonia's madman to the Swede;
The whole strange purpose of their lives to find
Or make an enemy of all mankind!
Not one looks backward, onward still he goes,
Yet ne'er looks forward farther than his nose.
No less alike the politic and wise;
All sly slow things, with circumspective eyes:
Men in their loose unguarded hours they take,
Not that themselves are wise, but others weak.
But grant that those can conquer, these can cheat;
'Tis phrase absurd to call a villain great:
Who wickedly is wise, or madly brave,

204. leather . . . prunella: The cobbler's apron is made of leather; the parson's robe is made of prunella, a strong woolen cloth. Pope's point is, of course, that clothes do not make the man. **208. Lucrece:** the Roman matron who was raped by Sextus Tarquinius. She called in her husband and father, asked for their promise of revenge, and then proceeded to stab herself. **216. Howards:** the most distinguished of English families. **220. Macedonia's madman:** Alexander the Great; **the Swede:** King Charles XII of Sweden, a rash warrior.

Is but the more a fool, the more a knave.
Who noble ends by noble means obtains,
Or failing, smiles in exile or in chains,
Like good Aurelius let him reign, or bleed
Like Socrates, that man is great indeed.
  What's fame? A fancied life in others' breath,
A thing beyond us, even before our death.
Just what you hear, you have, and what's unknown
The same (my lord) if Tully's, or your own.
All that we feel of it begins and ends
In the small circle of our foes or friends;
To all beside as much an empty shade
An Eugene living, as a Cæsar dead;
Alike or when, or where, they shone, or shine,
Or on the Rubicon, or on the Rhine.
A wit's a feather, and a chief's a rod;
An honest man's the noblest work of God.
Fame but from death a villain's name can save,
As Justice tears his body from the grave!
When what to oblivion better were resign'd
Is hung on high to poison half mankind.
All fame is foreign, but of true desert;
Plays round the head, but comes not to the heart:
One self-approving hour whole years outweighs
Of stupid starers, and of loud huzzas;
And more true joy Marcellus exiled feels,
Than Cæsar with a senate at his heels.
  In parts superior what advantage lies?
Tell (for you can) what is it to be wise?
'Tis but to know how little can be known;
To see all others' faults and feel our own:
Condemn'd in business or in arts to drudge,
Without a second or without a judge:
Truths would you teach, or save a sinking land?
All fear, none aid you, and few understand.
Painful pre-eminence! yourself to view
Above life's weakness, and its comforts too.
  Bring then these blessings to a strict account;
Make fair deductions; see to what they mount:
How much of other each is sure to cost;
How each for other oft is wholly lost;
How inconsistent greater goods with these;
How sometimes life is risk'd, and always ease:
Think, and if still the things thy envy call,
Say, wouldst thou be the man to whom they fall?
To sigh for ribands if thou art so silly,
Mark how they grace Lord Umbra or Sir Billy.
Is yellow dirt the passion of thy life?
Look but on Gripus or on Gripus' wife.
If parts allure thee, think how Bacon shined,
The wisest, brightest, meanest of mankind:
Or, ravish'd with the whistling of a name,
See Cromwell, damn'd to everlasting fame!
If all, united, thy ambition call,
From ancient story, learn to scorn them all.
There, in the rich, the honour'd, famed, and great,
See the false scale of happiness complete!
In hearts of kings, or arms of queens, who lay,
How happy those to ruin, these betray.
Mark by what wretched steps their glory grows,
From dirt and sea-weed as proud Venice rose;
In each how guilt and greatness equal ran,
And all that raised the hero sunk the man:
Now Europe's laurels on their brows behold,
But stain'd with blood, or ill exchanged for gold:
Then see them broke with toils, or sunk in ease,
Or infamous for plunder'd provinces.
Oh wealth ill-fated! which no act of fame
E'er taught to shine, or sanctified from shame!
What greater bliss attends their close of life?
Some greedy minion, or imperious wife,
The trophied arches, storied halls invade,
And haunt their slumbers in the pompous shade.
Alas! not dazzled with their noontide ray,
Compute the morn and evening to the day:
The whole amount of that enormous fame,
A tale that blends their glory with their shame!
  VII. Know then this truth (enough for man to know),
"Virtue alone is happiness below."
The only point where human bliss stands still,
And tastes the good without the fall to ill;

235. Aurelius: the Roman emperor Marcus Aurelius, known for his greatness of mind and spirit. **240. Tully:** Cicero. **244. Eugene:** Prince Eugene of Savoy (1663–1736), Austrian military commander who collaborated with the Duke of Marlborough in the great victory at Blenheim in 1704. **257. Marcellus:** Marcus Marcellus, an ally of Pompey against Julius Caesar, retired to a life of studious leisure after the famous Battle of Pharsalia in 48 B.C.

278. Lord Umbra . . . Sir Billy: showy characters of no moral worth. **279. yellow dirt:** gold. **280.** The reference here is to Vanbrugh's Restoration comedy, *The Confederacy,* in which Gripus' wife spends all his money. (Gripus was a miser.)

Where only merit constant pay receives,
Is blest in what it takes and what it gives;
The joy unequall'd, if its end it gain,
And if it lose, attended with no pain:
Without satiety, though e'er so bless'd,
And but more relish'd as the more distress'd:
The broadest mirth unfeeling folly wears,
Less pleasing far than virtue's very tears:
Good, from each object, from each place acquired,
For ever exercised, yet never tired;
Never elated while one man's oppress'd;
Never dejected while another's bless'd;
And where no wants, no wishes can remain,
Since but to wish more virtue, is to gain.
  See the sole bliss Heaven could on all bestow;
Which who but feels can taste, but thinks can
  know.
Yet poor with fortune, and with learning blind,
The bad must miss, the good, untaught, will
  find;
Slave to no sect, who takes no private road,
But looks through Nature up to Nature's God:
Pursues that chain which links the immense
  design,
Joins Heaven and earth, and mortal and divine;
Sees that no being any bliss can know,
But touches some above, and some below;
Learns, from this union of the rising whole,
The first, last purpose of the human soul;
And knows where faith, law, morals, all began,
All end, in love of God, and love of man.
For him alone, hope leads from goal to goal,
And opens still, and opens on his soul;
Till lengthen'd on to faith, and unconfined,
It pours the bliss that fills up all the mind.
He sees why nature plants in man alone
Hope of known bliss, and faith in bliss unknown:
(Nature, whose dictates to no other kind
Are given in vain, but what they seek they find;)
Wise is her present; she connects in this
His greatest virtue with his greatest bliss;
At once his own bright prospect to be blest,
And strongest motive to assist the rest.
  Self-love thus push'd to social, to divine,
Gives thee to make thy neighbour's blessing thine.
Is this too little for the boundless heart?
Extend it, let thy enemies have part:
Grasp the whole worlds of reason, life, and sense,
In one close system of benevolence:
Happier as kinder, in whate'er degree,
And height of bliss but height of charity.
  God loves from whole to parts: but human soul
Must rise from individual to the whole.
Self-love but serves the virtuous mind to wake,
As the small pebble stirs the peaceful lake;
The centre moved, a circle straight succeeds,
Another still, and still another spreads;
Friend, parent, neighbour, first it will embrace;
His country next; and next all human race;
Wide and more wide, the o'erflowings of the mind
Take every creature in, of every kind;
Earth smiles around, with boundless bounty blest,
And Heaven beholds its image in his breast.
  Come, then, my friend! my genius! come along;
Oh master of the poet and the song!
And while the Muse now stoops, or now ascends,
To man's low passions, or their glorious ends,
Teach me, like thee, in various nature wise,
To fall with dignity, with temper rise;
Form'd by thy converse happily to steer
From grave to gay, from lively to severe;
Correct, with spirit; eloquent, with ease;
Intent to reason, or polite to please.
Oh! while along the stream of time thy name
Expanded flies, and gathers all its fame;
Say, shall my little bark attendant sail,
Pursue the triumph, and partake the gale?
When statesmen, heroes, kings, in dust repose,
Whose sons shall blush their fathers were thy foes,
Shall then this verse to future age pretend
Thou wert my guide, philosopher, and
  friend?
That, urged by thee, I turn'd the tuneful art
From sounds to things, from fancy to the heart;
For Wit's false mirror held up Nature's light;
Show'd erring Pride,—Whatever is, is right!
That reason, passion, answer one great aim;
That true self-love and social are the same;
That virtue only makes our bliss below;
And all our knowledge is,—Ourselves to know.

(1733–1734)

FROM

Moral Essays

EPISTLE II

TO A LADY*

Argument

*of the Characters of Women***

The author being very sensible how particular a tenderness is due to the female sex, and, at the same time, how little they show to each other, declares, upon his honour, that no one character is drawn from the life in this Epistle. It would otherwise be most improperly inscribed to a lady who, of all the women he knows, is the last that would be entertained at the expense of another.

Nothing so true as what you once let fall:
"Most women have no characters at all."
Matter too soft a lasting mark to bear,
And best distinguish'd by black, brown, or fair.
  How many pictures of one nymph we view,
All how unlike each other, all how true!
Arcadia's Countess, here, in ermin'd pride,
Is there, Pastora by a fountain side.
Here Fannia, leering on her own good man,
And there, a naked Leda with a swan.
Let then the fair one beautifully cry
In Magdalen's loose hair and lifted eye,
Or dress'd in smiles of sweet Cecilia shine,
With simpering angels, palms, and harps divine;
Whether the charmer sinner it, or saint it,
If folly grow romantic, I must paint it.
  Come, then, the colours and the ground
    prepare!
Dip in the rainbow, trick her off in air;
Choose a firm cloud before it fall, and in it
Catch, ere she change, the Cynthia of this
    minute.
  Rufa, whose eye quick glancing o'er the park
Attracts each light gay meteor of a spark,
Agrees as ill with Rufa studying Locke,
As Sappho's diamonds with her dirty smock;
Or Sappho at her toilet's greasy task,
With Sappho fragrant at an evening mask:
So morning insects, that in muck begun,
Shine, buzz, and fly-blow in the setting sun.
  How soft is Silia! fearful to offend;
The frail one's advocate, the weak one's
    friend.
To her, Calista proved her conduct nice;
And good Simplicius asks of her advice.
Sudden, she storms! she raves! You tip the wink,
But spare your censure—Silia does not drink.
All eyes may see from what the change arose,
All eyes may see—a pimple on her nose.
  Papillia, wedded to her amorous spark,
Sighs for the shades—"How charming is a park!"
A park is purchased, but the fair he sees
All bathed in tears—"Oh odious, odious
    trees!"
  Ladies, like variegated tulips, show,
'Tis to their changes half their charms we owe;
Fine by defect, and delicately weak,
Their happy spots the nice admirer take.
'Twas thus Calypso once each heart alarm'd,
Awed without virtue, without beauty charm'd;
Her tongue bewitch'd as oddly as her eyes,
Less wit than mimic, more wit than wise;
Strange graces still, and stranger flights she had,
Was just not ugly, and was just not mad;
Yet ne'er so sure our passion to create,
As when she touch'd the brink of all we hate.
  Narcissa's nature, tolerably mild,

* Regarded by many critics and editors as Martha Blount, one of Pope's closest female friends.

** The characters of Philomedé, Atossa, and Chloe were added in a later edition that Pope had prepared for the press with the help of Warburton. As a result, the epistle was extended from 200 to 292 lines.

MORAL ESSAYS. EPISTLE II. **7. Arcadia's Countess:** The general reference is to the sister of Sir Philip Sidney, the Countess of Pembroke, to whom the poet dedicated his great pastoral romance *Arcadia.* Pope may be referring specifically to Mary Howe. **8. Pastora:** a stock heroine of pastoral romance. **9. Fannia:** possibly a reference to a woman of ancient Rome convicted of adultery. **10. Leda:** In Greek mythology Leda is a Spartan queen, mother by Zeus (who visited her in the form of a swan) of Helen of Troy. She is seen frequently in Renaissance paintings.

13. Cecilia: a reference to St. Cecilia, patroness of music. **21. Rufa:** feminine for Rufus. A number of fictional names follow. **45. Calypso:** the beautiful nymph in the *Odyssey,* who detains Odysseus on his long journey home.

To make a wash would hardly stew a child;
Has e'en been proved to grant a lover's prayer,
And paid a tradesman once, to make him stare;
Gave alms at Easter, in a Christian trim,
And made a widow happy for a whim.
Why then declare good-nature is her scorn,
When 'tis by that alone she can be borne?
Why pique all mortals, yet affect a name?
A fool to pleasure, yet a slave to fame:
Now deep in Taylor and the Book of Martyrs,
Now drinking citron with his grace and Chartres:
Now conscience chills her, and now passion burns;
And atheism and religion take their turns;
A very heathen in the carnal part,
Yet still a sad, good Christian at her heart.
See Sin in state, majestically drunk;
Proud as a peeress, prouder as a punk;
Chaste to her husband, frank to all beside,
A teeming mistress, but a barren bride.
What then? let blood and body bear the fault,
Her head's untouch'd, that noble seat of thought:
Such this day's doctrine—in another fit
She sins with poets through pure love of wit.
What has not fired her bosom or her brain?
Cæsar and Tall-boy, Charles and Charlemagne.
As Helluo, late dictator of the feast,
The nose of *haut-goût* and the tip of taste,
Critiqued your wine, and analysed your meat,
Yet on plain pudding deign'd at home to eat:
So Philomedé, lecturing all mankind
On the soft passion, and the taste refined,
The address, the delicacy—stoops at once,
And makes her hearty meal upon a dunce.
Flavia's a wit, has too much sense to pray;
To toast our wants and wishes is her way;
Nor asks of God, but of her stars, to give
The mighty blessing, "While we live, to live."
Then all for death, that opiate of the soul!
Lucretia's dagger, Rosamonda's bowl.
Say, what can cause such impotence of mind?
A spark too fickle, or a spouse too kind.
Wise wretch! with pleasures too refined to please;
With too much spirit to be e'er at ease;
With too much quickness ever to be taught;
With too much thinking to have common thought;
You purchase pain with all that joy can give,
And die of nothing but a rage to live.
Turn then from wits; and look on Simo's mate,
No ass so meek, no ass so obstinate.
Or her that owns her faults, but never mends,
Because she's honest, and the best of friends.
Or her whose life the church and scandal share,
For ever in a passion or a prayer.
Or her who laughs at hell, but (like her grace)
Cries, "Ah! how charming if there's no such place!"
Or who in sweet vicissitude appears
Of mirth and opium, ratafia and tears,
The daily anodyne, and nightly draught,
To kill those foes to fair ones, time and thought.
Woman and fool are two hard things to hit;
For true no-meaning puzzles more than wit.
But what are these to great Atossa's mind?
Scarce once herself, by turns all womankind!
Who, with herself, or others, from her birth
Finds all her life one warfare upon earth:
Shines in exposing knaves and painting fools,
Yet is whate'er she hates and ridicules.
No thought advances, but her eddy brain
Whisks it about, and down it goes again.
Full sixty years the world has been her trade,
The wisest fool much time has ever made.
From loveless youth to unrespected age,
No passion gratified, except her rage,
So much the fury still outran the wit,
The pleasure miss'd her, and the scandal hit.
Who breaks with her, provokes revenge from hell,
But he's a bolder man who dares be well.
Her every turn with violence pursued,
No more a storm her hate than gratitude:
To that each passion turns, or soon or late;
Love, if it makes her yield, must make her hate.
Superior? death! and equals? what a curse!

57. trim: dress. **63. Taylor . . . Book of Martyrs:** references to Jeremy Taylor (1613–1667) and to a work of John Foxe (1517–1587). Both Taylor and Foxe were religious writers. **64. Chartres:** the great gambler and lecher described in a note to the *Essay on Man.* **78. Tall-boy:** a foolish lover in a popular comedy called *The Jovial Crew;* **Charles:** a commoner. **79. Helluo:** Latin for glutton. **80. *haut-goût:*** nearly over-ripe food. **92. Lucretia . . . Rosamonda:** a reference to the suicides of Lucrece after being raped by Tarquinius and of Rosamonda, mistress of Henry II.

110. ratafia: a liqueur. **111. anodyne:** pain-killer. **115. Atossa:** again a fictional name for a type of character. Atossa was the daughter of Cyrus the Great, King of Persia. Most commentators have seen Sarah, Duchess of Marlborough, as the chief source for this great Popean satiric portrait. **121. eddy:** whirling.

But an inferior not dependant? worse!
Offend her, and she knows not to forgive;
Oblige her, and she'll hate you while you live:
But die, and she'll adore you—then the bust
And temple rise—then fall again to dust.
Last night, her lord was all that's good and great;
A knave this morning, and his will a cheat.
Strange! by the means defeated of the ends,
By spirit robbed of power, by warmth of friends,
By wealth of followers! without one distress,
Sick of herself, through very selfishness!
Atossa, cursed with every granted prayer,
Childless with all her children, wants an heir.
To heirs unknown descends the unguarded store,
Or wanders, heaven-directed, to the poor.
  Pictures like these, dear Madam, to design,
Ask no firm hand, and no unerring line;
Some wandering touches, some reflected light,
Some flying stroke alone can hit them right:
For how should equal colours do the knack?
Cameleons who can paint in white and black?
  "Yet Chloe sure was form'd without a spot."—
Nature in her then err'd not, but forgot.
"With every pleasing, every prudent part,
Say, what can Chloe want?"—She wants a heart.
She speaks, behaves, and acts, just as she ought,
But never, never reached one generous thought.
Virtue she finds too painful an endeavour,
Content to dwell in decencies for ever.
So very reasonable, so unmoved,
As never yet to love, or to be loved.
She, while her lover pants upon her breast,
Can mark the figures on an Indian chest;
And when she sees her friend in deep despair,
Observes how much a chintz exceeds mohair!
Forbid it, Heaven, a favour or a debt
She e'er should cancel—but she may forget.
Safe is your secret still in Chloe's ear;
But none of Chloe's shall you ever hear.
Of all her dears she never slander'd one,
But cares not if a thousand are undone.
Would Chloe know if you're alive or dead?
She bids her footman put it in her head.
Chloe is prudent—would you too be wise?
Then never break your heart when Chloe dies.

157. Chloe: again a type of character. Some commentators have seen in Chloe Mrs. Howard, Countess of Suffolk. **170. chintz:** a cheap printed cotton fabric.

  One certain portrait may (I grant) be seen,
Which Heaven has varnish'd out, and made a queen:
The same for ever! and described by all
With truth and goodness, as with crown and ball.
Poets heap virtues, painters gems, at will,
And show their zeal, and hide their want of skill.
'Tis well—but artists! who can paint or write,
To draw the naked is your true delight.
That robe of quality so struts and swells,
None see what parts of nature it conceals:
The exactest traits of body or of mind,
We owe to models of an humble kind.
If Queensberry to strip there's no compelling,
'Tis from a handmaid we must take a Helen.
From peer to bishop 'tis no easy thing
To draw the man who loves his God or king:
Alas! I copy (or my draught would fail)
From honest Mahomet, or plain Parson Hale.
  But grant, in public, men sometimes are shown,
A woman's seen in private life alone:
Our bolder talents in full light display'd;
Your virtues open fairest in the shade.
Bred to disguise, in public 'tis you hide;
There, none distinguish 'twixt your shame or pride,
Weakness or delicacy; all so nice,
That each may seem a virtue or a vice.
  In men we various ruling passions find;
In women, two almost divide the kind;
Those, only fix'd, they first or last obey,
The love of pleasure, and the love of sway.
  That, Nature gives; and where the lesson taught
Is but to please, can pleasure seem a fault?
Experience, this; by man's oppression cursed,
They seek the second not to lose the first.
  Men, some to business, some to pleasure take;
But every woman is at heart a rake:
Men, some to quiet, some to public strife;
But every lady would be queen for life.
  Yet mark the fate of a whole sex of queens!
Power all their end, but beauty all the means:
In youth they conquer with so wild a rage,

193. Queensberry: Catherine Hyde, Duchess of Queensberry (1700–1777), a dazzling beauty. **198. Mahomet . . . Hale:** Pope notes that Mahomet was servant to ". . . the late King, said to be the son of a Turkish Bassa, whom he took at the siege of Buda, and constantly kept about his person." Parson Hale is Stephen Hales, a friend of Pope, a scientist and a model of virtue.

As leaves them scarce a subject in their age:
For foreign glory, foreign joy, they roam;
Not thought of peace or happiness at home.
But wisdom's triumph is well-timed retreat,
As hard a science to the fair as great!
Beauties, like tyrants, old and friendless grown,
Yet hate repose, and dread to be alone.
Worn out in public, weary every eye,
Nor leave one sigh behind them when they die.
  Pleasures the sex, as children birds, pursue,
Still out of reach, yet never out of view;
Sure, if they catch, to spoil the toy at most,
To covet flying, and regret when lost:
At last, to follies youth could scarce defend,
It grows their age's prudence to pretend;
Ashamed to own they gave delight before,
Reduced to feign it, when they give no more:
As hags hold sabbaths, less for joy than spite,
So these their merry, miserable night;
Still round and round the ghosts of beauty glide,
And haunt the places where their honour died.
  See how the world its veterans rewards!
A youth of frolics, an old age of cards;
Fair to no purpose, artful to no end,
Young without lovers, old without a friend;
A fop their passion, but their prize a sot,
Alive, ridiculous, and dead, forgot!
  Ah, friend! to dazzle let the vain design;
To raise the thought and touch the heart be thine!
That charm shall grow, while what fatigues the ring,
Flaunts and goes down, an unregarded thing:
So when the sun's broad beam has tired the sight,
All mild ascends the moon's more sober light,
Serene in virgin modesty she shines,
And unobserved the glaring orb declines.
  Oh! bless'd with temper, whose unclouded ray
Can make to-morrow cheerful as to-day;
She who can love a sister's charms, or hear
Sighs for a daughter with unwounded ear;
She who ne'er answers till a husband cools,
Or, if she rules him, never shows she rules;
Charms by accepting, by submitting sways,
Yet has her humour most when she obeys;
Let fops or fortune fly which way they will,
Disdains all loss of tickets, or codille;
Spleen, vapours, or small-pox, above them all,
And mistress of herself, though China fall.
  And yet, believe me, good as well as ill,
Woman's at best a contradiction still.
Heaven, when it strives to polish all it can
Its last best work, but forms a softer man;
Picks from each sex, to make the favourite blest,
Your love of pleasure, our desire of rest:
Blends, in exception to all general rules,
Your taste of follies, with our scorn of fools:
Reserve with frankness, art with truth allied,
Courage with softness, modesty with pride;
Fix'd principles, with fancy ever new;
Shakes all together, and produces—you!
  Be this a woman's fame; with this unblest,
Toasts live a scorn, and queens may die a jest.
This Phœbus promised (I forget the year)
When those blue eyes first open'd on the sphere;
Ascendant Phœbus watch'd that hour with care,
Averted half your parents' simple prayer;
And gave you beauty, but denied the pelf
That buys your sex a tyrant o'er itself.
The generous god, who wit and gold refines,
And ripens spirits as he ripens mines,
Kept dross for duchesses, the world shall know it,
To you gave sense, good humour, and a poet.

(1735)

239. **sabbaths:** midnight devil-meetings. 251. **ring:** an elegant drive in Hyde Park.

266. **tickets . . . codille:** a reference to lottery tickets. Codille, as noted in *The Rape of the Lock* textual commentary, is the loser in the game of ombre.

EPISTLE IV

TO RICHARD BOYLE, EARL OF BURLINGTON *

Argument

of the Use of Riches

The vanity of expense in people of wealth and quality. The abuse of the word taste, ver. 13. That the first principle and foundation in this, as in everything else, is good sense, ver. 39. The chief

* Burlington (1695–1753) studied architecture in Italy, designed buildings himself in a Roman classic style. He spared no expense.

proof of it is to follow Nature, even in works of mere luxury and elegance. Instanced in architecture and gardening, where all must be adapted to the genius and use of the place, and the beauties not forced into it, but resulting from it, ver. 47. How men are disappointed in their most expensive undertakings for want of this true foundation, without which nothing can please long, if at all; and the best examples and rules will be but perverted into something burdensome or ridiculous, ver. 65, etc., to 98. A description of the false taste of magnificence; the first grand error of which is to imagine that greatness consists in the size and dimensions, instead of the proportion and harmony of the whole, ver. 99; and the second, either in joining together parts incoherent, or too minutely resembling, or in the repetition of the same too frequently, ver. 105, etc. A word or two of false taste in books, in music, in painting, even in preaching and prayer, and lastly in entertainments, ver. 133, etc. Yet Providence is justified in giving wealth to be squandered in this manner, since it is dispersed to the poor and laborious part of mankind, ver. 169 (recurring to what is laid down in the *Essay on Man*, Epistle II., and in the epistle preceding, ver. 159, etc.). What are the proper objects of magnificence, and a proper field for the expense of great men, ver. 177, etc.; and finally, the great and public works which become a prince, ver. 191 to the end.

'Tis strange, the miser should his cares employ
To gain those riches he can ne'er enjoy:
Is it less strange, the prodigal should waste
His wealth to purchase what he ne'er can taste?
Not for himself he sees, or hears, or eats;
Artists must choose his pictures, music, meats:
He buys for Topham drawings and designs,
For Pembroke statues, dirty gods, and coins;
Rare monkish manuscripts for Hearne alone,
And books for Mead, and butterflies for
Sloane.
Think we all these are for himself? no more
Than his fine wife, alas! or finer whore.
For what has Virro painted, built, and planted?
Only to show how many tastes he wanted.
What brought Sir Visto's ill-got wealth to waste?
Some demon whisper'd, "Visto! have a taste."
Heaven visits with a taste the wealthy fool,
And needs no rod but Ripley with a rule.
See! sportive Fate, to punish awkward pride,
Bids Bubo build, and sends him such a guide:
A standing sermon, at each year's expense,
That never coxcomb reach'd magnificence!
You show us Rome was glorious, not profuse,
And pompous buildings once were things of use.
Yet shall (my lord) your just, your noble rules
Fill half the land with imitating fools;
Who random drawings from your sheets shall take,
And of one beauty many blunders make;
Load some vain church with old theatric state,
Turn acts of triumph to a garden-gate;
Reverse your ornaments, and hang them all
On some patch'd dog-hole eked with ends of wall;
Then clap four slices of pilaster on 't,
That, laced with bits of rustic, makes a front.
Shall call the winds through long arcades to roar,
Proud to catch cold at a Venetian door;
Conscious they act a true Palladian part,
And, if they starve, they starve by rules of art.
Oft have you hinted to your brother peer
A certain truth, which many buy too dear:
Something there is more needful than expense,
And something previous even to taste—'tis sense:
Good sense, which only is the gift of Heaven,
And, though no science, fairly worth the seven:
A light, which in yourself you must perceive;
Jones and Le Nôtre have it not to give.
To build, to plant, whatever you intend,
To rear the column, or the arch to bend,
To swell the terrace, or to sink the grot,
In all, let Nature never be forgot,
But treat the goddess like a modest fair,
Nor over-dress, nor leave her wholly bare;
Let not each beauty everywhere be spied,

EPISTLE IV. **7. Topham:** Pope identified him as a man famous for his collection of drawings. **8. Pembroke:** Thomas Herbert, Earl of Pembroke. **9. Hearne:** Thomas Hearne (1678–1735) was a distinguished medievalist. **10. Mead . . . Sloane:** Pope notes of Meade and Sloane: "Two eminent physicians; the one had an excellent library, the other the finest collection in Europe of natural curiosities; both men of great learning and humanity."

18. Ripley: an undistinguished architect, but a political favorite of Sir Robert Walpole. **20. Bubo:** Bubb Dodington, politician and patron of the day, who was extravagant in his tastes. **23. You:** Burlington. He was at the time publishing the *Designs* of Inigo Jones and the *Antiquities of Rome* by the great Italian architect Andrea Palladio. **33. pilaster:** rectangular architectural column. **46. Jones . . . Le Nôtre:** Inigo Jones, the great English Renaissance architect; Le Nôtre, the distinguished designer of formal gardens, especially those at Versailles.

Where half the skill is decently to hide.
He gains all points, who pleasingly confounds,
Surprises, varies, and conceals the bounds.
Consult the genius of the place in all:
That tells the waters or to rise or fall;
Or helps the ambitious hill the heavens to scale,
Or scoops in circling theatres the vale;
Calls in the country, catches opening glades,
Joins willing woods, and varies shades from shades;
Now breaks, or now directs, the intending lines;
Paints, as you plant, and, as you work, designs.
Still follow sense, of every art the soul,
Parts answering parts shall slide into a whole,
Spontaneous beauties all around advance,
Start ev'n from difficulty, strike from chance,
Nature shall join you; Time shall make it grow
A work to wonder at—perhaps a Stowe.
Without it, proud Versailles! thy glory falls;
And Nero's terraces desert their walls:
The vast parterres a thousand hands shall make,
Lo! Cobham comes, and floats them with a lake:
Or cut wide views through mountains to the plain,
You'll wish your hill or shelter'd seat again.
Even in an ornament its place remark,
Nor in an hermitage set Dr. Clarke.
Behold Villario's ten years' toil complete;
His quincunx darkens, his espaliers meet;
The wood supports the plain, the parts unite,
And strength of shade contends with strength of light;
A waving glow the bloomy beds display,
Blushing in bright diversities of day,
With silver-quivering rills meander'd o'er—
Enjoy them, you! Villario can no more:
Tired of the scene parterres and fountains yield,
He finds at last he better likes a field.
Through his young woods how pleased Sabinus stray'd,
Or sate delighted in the thickening shade,
With annual joy the reddening shoots to greet,
Or see the stretching branches long to meet!
His son's fine taste an opener vista loves,
Foe to the Dryads of his father's groves;
One boundless green, or flourish'd carpet views,
With all the mournful family of yews:
The thriving plants, ignoble broomsticks made,
Now sweep those alleys they were born to shade.
At Timon's villa let us pass a day,
Where all cry out, "What sums are thrown away!"
So proud, so grand: of that stupendous air,
Soft and agreeable come never there.
Greatness, with Timon, dwells in such a draught
As brings all Brobdignag before your thought.
To compass this, his building is a town,
His pond an ocean, his parterre a down:
Who but must laugh, the master when he sees,
A puny insect, shivering at a breeze!
Lo, what huge heaps of littleness around!
The whole, a labour'd quarry above ground,
Two cupids squirt before: a lake behind
Improves the keenness of the northern wind.
His gardens next your admiration call,
On every side you look, behold the wall!
No pleasing intricacies intervene,
No artful wildness to perplex the scene:
Grove nods at grove, each alley has a brother,
And half the platform just reflects the other.
The suffering eye inverted Nature sees,
Trees cut to statues, statues thick as trees;
With here a fountain, never to be play'd;
And there a summer-house, that knows no shade:
Here Amphitrite sails through myrtle bowers;
There gladiators fight, or die in flowers;
Unwater'd see the drooping sea-horse mourn,
And swallows roost in Nilus' dusty urn.
My Lord advances with majestic mien,
Smit with the mighty pleasure to be seen:
But soft—by regular approach—not yet—
First through the length of yon hot terrace sweat;
And when up ten steep slopes you've dragg'd your thighs,

57. genius of the place: the protecting spirit. **70. Stowe:** the house and gardens of Lord Cobham in Buckinghamshire. **73. parterres:** ornamental gardens. **78. Dr. Clarke:** Samuel Clarke (1675–1729), philosopher and theologian in the liberal, rationalistic tradition. Queen Caroline (1683–1757), consort of George II, placed a bust of Clarke in the artificial hermitage she had constructed in Richmond Park. **80. quincunx:** an arrangement of five trees, one in the center of a square formed by the four others; **espaliers:** fruit trees that grow flat against a garden wall.

94. Dryads: wood nymphs. **99.** The Timon portrait is thought to be a satire on James Brydges, Duke of Chandos, who built an extravagant house, called Canons, near Edgware. **106. down:** an open expanse of elevated land. **123. Amphitrite:** a sea goddess, wife of Poseidon. **126. Nilus' dusty urn:** statue of the river god.

Just at his study-door he'll bless your eyes.
His study! with what authors is it stored?
In books, not authors, curious is my Lord;
To all their dated backs he turns you round;
These Aldus printed, those Du Sueïl has bound.
Lo, some are vellum, and the rest as good
For all his Lordship knows, but they are wood.
For Locke or Milton 'tis in vain to look,
These shelves admit not any modern book.
And now the chapel's silver bell you hear,
That summons you to all the pride of prayer:
Light quirks of music, broken and uneven,
Make the soul dance upon a jig to Heaven.
On painted ceilings you devoutly stare,
Where sprawl the saints of Verrio or Laguerre,
Or gilded clouds in fair expansion lie,
And bring all Paradise before your eye.
To rest, the cushion and soft dean invite,
Who never mentions Hell to ears polite.
But hark! the chiming clocks to dinner call;
A hundred footsteps scrape the marble hall:
The rich buffet well-coloured serpents grace,
And gaping Tritons spew to wash your face.
Is this a dinner? this a genial room?
No, 'tis a temple, and a hecatomb.
A solemn sacrifice, perform'd in state,
You drink by measure, and to minutes eat.
So quick retires each flying course, you'd swear
Sancho's dread doctor and his wand were there.
Between each act the trembling salvers ring,
From soup to sweet-wine, and God bless the king.
In plenty starving, tantalised in state,
And complaisantly help'd to all I hate,
Treated, caress'd, and tired, I take my leave,
Sick of his civil pride from morn to eve;
I curse such lavish cost, and little skill,
And swear no day was ever pass'd so ill.
Yet hence the poor are clothed, the hungry fed;
Health to himself, and to his infants bread,
The labourer bears: what his hard heart denies,
His charitable vanity supplies.
Another age shall see the golden ear
Imbrown the slope, and nod on the parterre,
Deep harvest bury all his pride has plann'd,
And laughing Ceres reassume the land.
Who then shall grace, or who improve the soil?—
Who plants like Bathurst, or who builds like Boyle.
'Tis use alone that sanctifies expense,
And splendour borrows all her rays from sense.
His father's acres who enjoys in peace,
Or makes his neighbours glad, if he increase:
Whose cheerful tenants bless their yearly toil,
Yet to their lord owe more than to the soil;
Whose ample lawns are not ashamed to feed
The milky heifer and deserving steed;
Whose rising forests, not for pride or show,
But future buildings, future navies grow:
Let his plantations stretch from down to down,
First shade a country, and then raise a town.
You too proceed! make falling arts your care,
Erect new wonders, and the old repair;
Jones and Palladio to themselves restore,
And be whate'er Vitruvius was before:
'Till kings call forth the ideas of your mind
(Proud to accomplish what such hands design'd),
Bid harbours open, public ways extend,
Bid temples, worthier of the god, ascend;
Bid the broad arch the dangerous flood contain,
The mole projected break the roaring main;
Back to his bounds their subject sea command,
And roll obedient rivers through the land;
These honours Peace to happy Britain brings,
These are imperial works, and worthy kings.

(1731)

136. Aldus . . . Du Seuïl: Aldus was the famous Renaissance Venetian printer; Du Sueïl was a well-known Parisian binder. **146. Verrio . . . Laguerre:** Verrio and Laguerre were popular court painters. **150.** Pope notes an actual Dean of Peterborough Cathedral, who, while preaching at court, threatened the sinner with punishment in "a place which he thought it not decent to name in so polite an assembly." **154. Tritons:** sea gods with a human form in the upper part of the body and that of a fish in the lower. **160.** a reference to *Don Quixote* (Part II, Ch. 47), in which Sancho Panza's doctor uses a magic wand to make all kinds of succulent dishes disappear just as Sancho is about to devour them. **161. salvers:** trays.

176. Ceres: goddess of the harvest. **178. Bathurst . . . Boyle:** Allen, Lord Bathurst was a friend of Pope and a great gardener. Pope devoted one of his *Epistles to Several Persons* to him. Richard Boyle, Earl of Burlington, is the person to whom this poem is dedicated. **194. Vitruvius:** Roman author of a celebrated work on architecture.

FROM

Satires

EPISTLE TO DR. ARBUTHNOT*

OR, PROLOGUE TO THE SATIRES

Neque sermonibus vulgi dederis te, nec in præmiis humanis spem posueris rerum tuarum; suis te oportet illecebris ipsa virtus trahat ad verum decus. Quid de te alii loquantur, ipsi videant, sed loquentur tamen.

—CICERO.

[*And do not yield yourself up to the speeches of the vulgar, nor in your affairs place hope in human rewards: virtue ought to draw you to true glory by its own allurements. Why should others speak of you? Let them study themselves—yet they will speak.*]

Advertisement

This paper is a sort of bill of complaint, begun many years since, and drawn up by snatches, as the several occasions offered. I had no thoughts of publishing it, till it pleased some persons of rank and fortune (the authors of *Verses to the Imitator of Horace,* and of an *Epistle to a Doctor of Divinity from a Nobleman at Hampton Court*) to attack, in a very extraordinary manner, not only my writings (of which, being public, the public is judge), but my person, morals, and family, whereof, to those who know me not, a truer information may be requisite. Being divided between the necessity to say something of myself and my own laziness to undertake so awkward a task, I thought it the shortest way to put the last hand to this Epistle. If it have anything pleasing, it will be that by which I am most desirous to please, the truth and the sentiment; and if anything offensive, it will be only to those I am least sorry to offend, the vicious or the ungenerous.

Many will know their own pictures in it, there being not a circumstance but what is true; but I have for the most part spared their names, and they may escape being laughed at if they please.

I would have some of them know it was owing to the request of the learned and candid friend to whom it is inscribed that I make not as free use of theirs as they have done of mine. However, I shall have this advantage and honour on my side, that whereas, by their proceeding, any abuse may be directed at any man, no injury can possibly be done by mine, since a nameless character can never be found out but by its truth and likeness.

P. Shut, shut the door, good John! fatigued, I said;
Tie up the knocker, say I'm sick, I'm dead.
The Dog-star rages! nay 'tis past a doubt,
All Bedlam, or Parnassus, is let out:
Fire in each eye, and papers in each hand,
They rave, recite, and madden round the land.
What walls can guard me, or what shades can hide?
They pierce my thickets, through my grot they glide,
By land, by water, they renew the charge,
They stop the chariot, and they board the barge.
No place is sacred, not the church is free,
Ev'n Sunday shines no Sabbath-day to me:
Then from the Mint walks forth the man of rhyme,
Happy! to catch me, just at dinner-time.
Is there a parson, much bemused in beer,
A maudlin poetess, a rhyming peer,
A clerk, foredoom'd his father's soul to cross,
Who pens a stanza, when he should engross?
Is there, who, lock'd from ink and paper, scrawls
With desperate charcoal round his darken'd walls?
All fly to Twit'nam, and in humble strain
Apply to me, to keep them mad or vain.
Arthur, whose giddy son neglects the laws,
Imputes to me and my damn'd works the cause:
Poor Cornus sees his frantic wife elope,
And curses wit, and poetry, and Pope.
Friend to my life! (which did not you prolong,
The world had wanted many an idle song)

* John Arbuthnot (1667–1735), physician to Queen Anne, friend of Pope and Swift.

SATIRES. EPISTLE TO DR. ARBUTHNOT. **1. John:** John Serle, Pope's old and trusted servant. **3. Dog-star:** Sirius. It reappears in late summer, a time for reading bad epic poems that occasioned the satiric furor of the great Roman writer Juvenal. **8. grot:** grotto, picturesque cavern. **13. Mint:** a sanctuary for debtors in Southwark. Sunday, however, was a day when they could go about free from the threat of arrest. **18. engross:** record a legal document. **21. Twit'nam:** Twickenham, where Pope lived. **23. Arthur:** Arthur Moore, father of the dull poet, James Moore Smythe.

What drop or nostrum can this plague remove?
Or which must end me, a fool's wrath or love?
A dire dilemma! either way I'm sped,
If foes, they write, if friends, they read me dead.
Seized and tied down to judge, how wretched I!
Who can't be silent, and who will not lie:
To laugh, were want of goodness and of grace,
And to be grave, exceeds all power of face.
I sit with sad civility, I read
With honest anguish, and an aching head;
And drop at last, but in unwilling ears,
This saving counsel,—"Keep your piece nine
years."
"Nine years!" cries he, who, high in Drury Lane,
Lull'd by soft zephyrs through the broken pane,
Rhymes ere he wakes, and prints before Term
ends,
Obliged by hunger, and request of friends:
"The piece, you think, is incorrect? why take it,
I'm all submission; what you'd have it, make it."
Three things another's modest wishes bound,
My friendship, and a prologue, and ten pound.
Pitholeon sends to me: "You know his grace,
I want a patron; ask him for a place."
Pitholeon libell'd me—"But here's a letter
Informs you, Sir, 'twas when he knew no better.
Dare you refuse him? Curll invites to dine,
He'll write a journal, or he'll turn divine."
Bless me! a packet. " 'Tis a stranger sues,
A virgin tragedy, an orphan Muse."
If I dislike it, "Furies, death and rage!"
If I approve, "Commend it to the stage."
There (thank my stars) my whole commission
ends,
The players and I are, luckily, no friends;
Fired that the house reject him, " 'Sdeath! I'll
print it,
And shame the fools—Your interest, Sir, with
Lintot."
Lintot, dull rogue! will think your price too much:
"Not, Sir, if you revise it, and retouch."
All my demurs but double his attacks:
And last he whispers, "Do; and we go snacks."
Glad of a quarrel, straight I clap the door:
Sir, let me see your works and you no more.
'Tis sung, when Midas' ears began to spring
(Midas, a sacred person and a king),
His very minister who spied them first
(Some say his queen) was forced to speak or
burst:
And is not mine, my friend, a sorer case,
When every coxcomb perks them in my face?
A. Good friend, forbear! you deal in dangerous
things,
I'd never name queens, ministers, or kings:
Keep close to ears, and those let asses prick,
'Tis nothing—— *P.* Nothing? if they bite and kick?
Out with it, DUNCIAD! let the secret pass,
That secret to each fool, that he's an ass:
The truth once told (and wherefore should we lie?)
The Queen of Midas slept, and so may I.
You think this cruel? Take it for a rule,
No creature smarts so little as a fool.
Let peals of laughter, Codrus! round thee break,
Thou unconcerned canst hear the mighty crack:
Pit, box, and gallery in convulsions hurl'd,
Thou stand'st unshook amidst a bursting world.
Who shames a scribbler? break one cobweb
through,
He spins the slight, self-pleasing thread anew:
Destroy his fib or sophistry, in vain,
The creature's at his dirty work again,
Throned in the centre of his thin designs,
Proud of a vast extent of flimsy lines!
Whom have I hurt? has poet yet, or peer,
Lost the arch'd eyebrow, or Parnassian sneer?
And has not Colley still his lord, and whore?
His butchers Henley, his Freemasons Moore?
Does not one table Bavius still admit?
Still to one bishop Philips seem a wit?
Still Sappho—— *A.* Hold! for God's sake—you'll
offend:
No names—be calm—learn prudence of a friend.
I too could write, and I am twice as tall;

40. A marvelous *double-entendre.* Horace gives the advice straightforwardly in his *Art of Poetry.* Pope puns on "piece" to suggest that the bad poet keep quiet. **43. Term:** the legal court season that corresponds to the publishing season. **53. Curll:** Edmund Curll, an unscrupulous bookseller. **62. Lintot:** Bernard Lintot was the publisher of Pope's *Homer.*

66. we go snacks: we split the profits. **69–72.** The old story of King Midas, who was given the ears of an ass, because he preferred the music of the inferior Pan. His queen whispered the secret into a hole in the ground and covered the place, but the reeds that grew in that area communicated the story in the wind. **97–100. Colley . . . Philips:** more examples of contemporary dunces.

But foes like these—— *P.* One flatterer's worse than all.
Of all mad creatures, if the learn'd are right,
It is the slaver kills, and not the bite.
A fool quite angry is quite innocent:
Alas! 'tis ten times worse when they repent.
  One dedicates in high heroic prose,
And ridicules beyond a hundred foes:
One from all Grub Street will my fame defend,
And, more abusive, calls himself my friend.
This prints my letters, that expects a bribe,
And others roar aloud, "Subscribe, subscribe!"
  There are, who to my person pay their court:
I cough like Horace, and, though lean, am short.
Ammon's great son one shoulder had too high—
Such Ovid's nose,—and, "Sir! you have an eye."
Go on, obliging creatures, make me see
All that disgraced my betters met in me.
Say, for my comfort, languishing in bed,
"Just so immortal Maro held his head";
And, when I die, be sure you let me know
Great Homer died three thousand years ago.
Why did I write? what sin to me unknown
Dipp'd me in ink, my parents', or my own?
As yet a child, nor yet a fool to fame,
I lisp'd in numbers, for the numbers came.
I left no calling for this idle trade,
No duty broke, no father disobey'd:
The Muse but served to ease some friend, not wife,
To help me through this long disease, my life;
To second, ARBUTHNOT! thy art and care,
And teach the being you preserved to bear.
  But why then publish? Granville the polite,
And knowing Walsh, would tell me I could write;
Well-natured Garth inflamed with early praise,
And Congreve loved, and Swift endured my lays;
The courtly Talbot, Somers, Sheffield read,
Even mitred Rochester would nod the head,
And St. John's self (great Dryden's friend before)
With open arms received one poet more.
Happy my studies, when by these approved!
Happier their author, when by these beloved!
From these the world will judge of men and books,
Not from the Burnets, Oldmixons, and Cookes.
  Soft were my numbers; who could take offence
While pure description held the place of sense?
Like gentle Fanny's was my flowery theme,
A painted mistress, or a purling stream.
Yet then did Gildon draw his venal quill;
I wish'd the man a dinner, and sate still.
Yet then did Dennis rave in furious fret;
I never answer'd—I was not in debt.
If want provoked, or madness made them print,
I waged no war with Bedlam or the Mint.
  Did some more sober critic come abroad—
If wrong, I smiled; if right, I kiss'd the rod.
Pains, reading, study, are their just pretence,
And all they want is spirit, taste, and sense.
Commas and points they set exactly right,
And 'twere a sin to rob them of their mite;
Yet ne'er one sprig of laurel graced these ribalds,
From slashing Bentley down to piddling Tibbalds:
Each wight, who reads not, and but scans and spells,
Each word-catcher, that lives on syllables,
Even such small critics, some regard may claim,
Preserved in Milton's or in Shakespeare's name.
Pretty! in amber to observe the forms
Of hairs, or straws, or dirt, or grubs, or worms!
The things we know are neither rich nor rare,
But wonder how the devil they got there.
  Were others angry—I excused them too;
Well might they rage, I gave them but their due.
A man's true merit 'tis not hard to find;
But each man's secret standard in his mind,
That casting-weight pride adds to emptiness,
This, who can gratify, for who can guess?
The bard whom pilfer'd Pastorals renown,
Who turns a Persian tale for half-a-crown,
Just writes to make his barrenness appear,
And strains from hard-bound brains, eight lines a-year;
He, who still wanting, though he lives on theft,
Steals much, spends little, yet has nothing left:
And he, who now to sense, now nonsense leaning,
Means not, but blunders round about a meaning:
And he, whose fustian's so sublimely bad,
It is not poetry, but prose run mad:
All these, my modest satire bade translate,
And own'd that nine such poets made a Tate.
How did they fume, and stamp, and roar, and chafe!

146. Burnets . . . Cookes: In contrast to the good critics, who encouraged Pope's literary career, are those hacks like Burnet, Oldmixon, and Cooke, who attacked him.

149. gentle Fanny: some dilettantish poet. **179. bard:** a reference to the poet Ambrose Philips.

all these critics

And swear, not Addison himself was safe.
  Peace to all such! but were there one whose fires
True genius kindles, and fair fame inspires;
Blest with each talent, and each art to please,
And born to write, converse, and live with ease;
Should such a man, too fond to rule alone,
Bear, like the Turk, no brother near the throne,
View him with scornful, yet with jealous eyes,
And hate for arts that caused himself to rise;
Damn with faint praise, assent with civil leer,
And, without sneering, teach the rest to sneer;
Willing to wound, and yet afraid to strike,
Just hint a fault, and hesitate dislike;
Alike reserved to blame, or to commend,
A timorous foe, and a suspicious friend;
Dreading e'en fools, by flatterers besieged,
And so obliging, that he ne'er obliged;
Like Cato, give his little senate laws,
And sit attentive to his own applause;
While wits and Templars every sentence raise,
And wonder with a foolish face of praise—
Who but must laugh, if such a man there be?
Who would not weep, if Atticus were he?
  What though my name stood rubric on the walls,
Or plaster'd posts, with claps, in capitals?
Or smoking forth, a hundred hawkers load,
On wings of winds came flying all abroad?
I sought no homage from the race that write;
I kept, like Asian monarchs, from their sight:
Poems I heeded (now be-rhym'd so long)
No more than thou, great George! a birthday song.
I ne'er with wits or witlings pass'd my days,
To spread about the itch of verse and praise;
Nor like a puppy, daggled through the town,
To fetch and carry, sing-song up and down;
Nor at rehearsals sweat, and mouth'd, and cried,
With handkerchief and orange at my side;
But sick of fops, and poetry, and prate,
To Bufo left the whole Castalian state.
  Proud as Apollo on his forked hill,
Sate full-blown Bufo, puff'd by every quill;
Fed with soft dedication all day long,
Horace and he went hand in hand in song.
His library (where busts of poets dead
And a true Pindar stood without a head)
Received of wits an undistinguish'd race,
Who first his judgment asked, and then a place:
Much they extoll'd his pictures, much his seat,
And flatter'd every day, and some days eat:
Till grown more frugal in his riper days,
He paid some bards with port, and some with
    praise,
To some a dry rehearsal was assign'd,
And others (harder still) he paid in kind.
Dryden alone (what wonder?) came not nigh,
Dryden alone escaped this judging eye:
But still the great have kindness in reserve,
He help'd to bury whom he help'd to starve.
  May some choice patron bless each grey goose
    quill!
May every Bavius have his Bufo still!
So when a statesman wants a day's defence,
Or Envy holds a whole week's war with Sense,
Or simple pride for flattery makes demands,
May dunce by dunce be whistled off my hands!
Bless'd be the great! for those they take away,
And those they left me—for they left me GAY;
Left me to see neglected Genius bloom,
Neglected die, and tell it on his tomb:
Of all thy blameless life the sole return
My verse, and QUEENSBERRY weeping o'er thy
    urn!
  Oh let me live my own, and die so too!
(To live and die is all I have to do:)
Maintain a poet's dignity and ease,
And see what friends, and read what books I
    please:
Above a patron, though I condescend
Sometimes to call a minister my friend.
I was not born for courts or great affairs:
I pay my debts, believe, and say my prayers;
Can sleep without a poem in my head,
Nor know if Dennis be alive or dead.
  Why am I ask'd what next shall see the light?
Heavens! was I born for nothing but to write?
Has life no joys for me? or (to be grave)

192. Addison: There is no doubt that the brilliant satiric portrait that follows is not so much a type as it is Joseph Addison himself. **216. claps:** clasps of some kind. **225. daggled:** sauntered. **230. Castalian state:** poetry. The reference is to the sacred spring on Mount Parnassus, source of inspiration.

248. Pope notes: "Mr. Dryden, after having lived in exigencies, had a magnificent Funeral bestowed upon him by the contribution of several persons of quality." **256. Gay:** John Gay (1685–1732), poet, dramatist—author of *The Beggar's Opera*—friend of Pope, and fellow-member of the famous Scriblerus Club. The Duke and Duchess of Queensberry were patrons.

Have I no friend to serve, no soul to save?
"I found him close with Swift—Indeed? no doubt
(Cries prating Balbus) something will come out."
'Tis all in vain, deny it as I will:
"No, such a genius never can lie still";
And then for mine obligingly mistakes
The first lampoon Sir Will or Bubo makes.
Poor guiltless I! and can I choose but smile,
When every coxcomb knows me by my style?
  Cursed be the verse, how well soe'er it flow,
That tends to make one worthy man my foe,
Give Virtue scandal, Innocence a fear,
Or from the soft-eyed virgin steal a tear!
But he who hurts a harmless neighbour's peace,
Insults fall'n worth, or beauty in distress,
Who loves a lie, lame slander helps about,
Who writes a libel, or who copies out;
That fop, whose pride affects a patron's name,
Yet absent, wounds an author's honest fame;
Who can your merit selfishly approve,
And show the sense of it without the love;
Who has the vanity to call you friend,
Yet wants the honour, injured, to defend;
Who tells whate'er you think, whate'er you say,
And if he lie not, must at least betray;
Who to the dean and silver bell can swear,
And sees at Canons what was never there;
Who reads, but with a lust to misapply,
Makes satire a lampoon, and fiction lie;
A lash like mine no honest man shall dread,
But all such babbling blockheads in his stead.
  Let Sporus tremble —— *A.* What? that thing of silk,
Sporus, that mere white curd of ass's milk?
Satire or sense, alas! can Sporus feel,
Who breaks a butterfly upon a wheel?
  P. Yet let me flap this bug with gilded wings,
This painted child of dirt, that stinks and stings;
Whose buzz the witty and the fair annoys,
Yet wit ne'er tastes, and beauty ne'er enjoys:
So well-bred spaniels civilly delight
In mumbling of the game they dare not bite.
Eternal smiles his emptiness betray,
As shallow streams run dimpling all the way.
Whether in florid impotence he speaks,
And, as the prompter breathes, the puppet squeaks;
Or at the ear of Eve, familiar toad!
Half froth, half venom, spits himself abroad,
In puns, or politics, or tales, or lies,
Or spite, or smut, or rhymes, or blasphemies.
His wit all see-saw, between that and this,
Now high, now low, now master up, now miss,
And he himself one vile antithesis.
Amphibious thing! that acting either part,
The trifling head, or the corrupted heart;
Fop at the toilet, flatterer at the board,
Now trips a lady, and now struts a lord.
Eve's tempter thus the Rabbins have express'd,
A cherub's face, a reptile all the rest.
Beauty that shocks you, parts that none will trust,
Wit that can creep, and pride that licks the dust.
  Not Fortune's worshipper, nor Fashion's fool,
Not Lucre's madman, nor Ambition's tool,
Not proud, nor servile; be one poet's praise,
That, if he pleased, he pleased by manly ways:
That flattery, even to kings, he held a shame,
And thought a lie in verse or prose the same;
That not in Fancy's maze he wander'd long,
But stoop'd to Truth, and moralised his song:
That not for Fame, but Virtue's better end,
He stood the furious foe, the timid friend,
The damning critic, half-approving wit,
The coxcomb hit, or fearing to be hit;
Laughed at the loss of friends he never had,
The dull, the proud, the wicked, and the mad;
The distant threats of vengeance on his head,
The blow unfelt, the tear he never shed;
The tale revived, the lie so oft o'erthrown,
The imputed trash, and dulness not his own;
The morals blacken'd when the writings 'scape,
The libell'd person, and the pictured shape;
Abuse, on all he loved, or loved him, spread,
A friend in exile, or a father dead;
The whisper, that to greatness still too near,
Perhaps yet vibrates on his sovereign's ear—
Welcome for thee, fair Virtue! all the past:
For thee, fair Virtue! welcome even the last!

299–300. Warburton's editorial note is helpful: "Meaning the man who would have persuaded the Duke of Chandos that Mr. P. meant him in those circumstances ridiculed in the Epistle on *Taste*. See Mr. Pope's Letter to the Earl of Burlington concerning this matter." **305. Sporus:** Like Atticus, Sporus seems directed more against a specific individual than a general type. The individual is Lord Hervey, a figure about the court of George II, an enemy of Pope, a ridiculer of Pope's works. Sporus was a homosexual in the court of Nero.

A. But why insult the poor, affront the great?
P. A knave's a knave, to me, in every state;
Alike my scorn, if he succeed or fail,
Sporus at court, or Japhet in a jail,
A hireling scribbler, or a hireling peer,
Knight of the post corrupt, or of the shire;
If on a pillory, or near a throne,
He gain his prince's ear, or lose his own.
Yet soft by nature, more a dupe than wit,
Sappho can tell you how this man was bit:
This dreaded satirist Dennis will confess
Foe to his pride, but friend to his distress:
So humble, he has knocked at Tibbald's door,
Has drunk with Cibber, nay has rhymed for Moore.
Full ten years slander'd, did he once reply?
Three thousand suns went down on Welsted's lie;
To please a mistress one aspersed his life;
He lash'd him not, but let her be his wife:
Let Budgell charge low Grub Street on his quill
And write whate'er he pleased, except his will;
Let the two Curlls of town and court abuse
His father, mother, body, soul, and Muse.
Yet why? that father held it for a rule,
It was a sin to call our neighbour fool:
That harmless mother thought no wife a whore:
Hear this, and spare his family, James Moore!
Unspotted names, and memorable long!
If there be force in virtue, or in song.
Of gentle blood (part shed in honour's cause,
While yet in Britain honour had applause)
Each parent sprung— *A.* What fortune, pray?—
P. Their own,
And better got, than Bestia's from the throne.
Born to no pride, inheriting no strife,
Nor marrying discord in a noble wife,
Stranger to civil and religious rage,
The good man walk'd innoxious through his age.
No courts he saw, no suits would ever try,
Nor dared an oath, nor hazarded a lie.
Unlearn'd, he knew no schoolman's subtle art,
No language, but the language of the heart.
By nature honest, by experience wise,
Healthy by temperance, and by exercise,
His life, though long, to sickness pass'd unknown,
His death was instant, and without a groan.
O grant me thus to live, and thus to die!
Who sprung from kings shall know less joy than I.
O friend! may each domestic bliss be thine!
Be no unpleasing melancholy mine:
Me, let the tender office long engage,
To rock the cradle of reposing age,
With lenient arts extend a mother' breath,
Make languor smile, and smooth the bed of death.
Explore the thought, explain the asking eye,
And keep awhile one parent from the sky!
On cares like these if length of days attend,
May Heaven, to bless those days, preserve my friend,
Preserve him social, cheerful, and serene,
And just as rich as when he served a queen.
A. Whether that blessing be denied or given,
Thus far was right, the rest belongs to Heaven.

(1735)

363. Japhet: Japhet Crook, a well-known forger. **365. Knight of the post:** a man who earns a living from giving false testimony. **369. Sappho:** most probably Lady Mary Wortley Montagu, once Pope's friend. There had been a break between them, however, and she joined Hervey's attack on Pope. **375. Welsted's lie:** Welsted had told several lies, most notably that Pope had caused a lady's death. **378–79. Budgell . . . will:** Budgell had abused Pope in a pamphlet titled *The Bee.* He had also forged a will to make himself an heir. **380. two Curlls:** Edmund Curll, the unscrupulous bookseller, and Lord Hervey. Both had attacked Pope personally and professionally. **391. Bestia:** a Roman consul bribed into collaborating in a dishonorable peace.

406. friend: Arbuthnot.

THE FIRST EPISTLE OF THE FIRST BOOK OF HORACE

TO LORD BOLINGBROKE

St. John, whose love indulged my labours past,
Matures my present, and shall bound my last!
Why will you break the Sabbath of my days?
Now sick alike of envy and of praise.
Public too long, ah, let me hide my age!
See modest Cibber now has left the stage:
Our generals now, retired to their estates,
Hang their old trophies o'er the garden gates;
In life's cool evening satiate of applause,
Nor fond of bleeding, even in Brunswick's cause.

FIRST HORACE. **6. Cibber:** Colley Cibber (1671–1757), a much satirized dramatist. Pope made him the hero of the final version of *The Dunciad.* **10.** Brunswick was a dukedom of George II.

A voice there is, that whispers in my ear
('Tis Reason's voice, which sometimes one can hear),
"Friend Pope! be prudent, let your Muse take breath,
And never gallop Pegasus to death;
Lest stiff, and stately, void of fire or force,
You limp, like Blackmore on a Lord Mayor's horse."
Farewell, then, verse, and love, and every toy.
The rhymes and rattles of the man or boy;
What right, what true, what fit we justly call,
Let this be all my care, for this is all:
To lay this harvest up, and hoard with haste,
What every day will want, and most, the last.
But ask not, to what doctors I apply?
Sworn to no master, of no sect am I:
As drives the storm, at any door I knock:
And house with Montaigne now, or now with Locke;
Sometimes a patriot, active in debate,
Mix with the world, and battle for the state,
Free as young Lyttelton, her cause pursue,
Still true to virtue, and as warm as true;
Sometimes with Aristippus, or St. Paul,
Indulge my candour, and grow all to all;
Back to my native moderation slide,
And win my way by yielding to the tide.
Long, as to him who works for debt, the day,
Long as the night to her whose love's away,
Long as the year's dull circle seems to run,
When the brisk minor pants for twenty-one;
So slow the unprofitable moments roll,
That lock up all the functions of my soul;
That keep me from myself; and still delay
Life's instant business to a future day:
That task, which as we follow or despise,
The eldest is a fool, the youngest wise:
Which done, the poorest can no wants endure;
And which, not done, the richest must be poor.
Late as it is, I put myself to school,
And feel some comfort not to be a fool.
Weak though I am of limb, and short of sight,
Far from a lynx, and not a giant quite;
I'll do what Mead and Cheselden advise,
To keep these limbs, and to preserve these eyes.
Not to go back, is somewhat to advance,
And men must walk at least before they dance.
Say, does thy blood rebel, thy bosom move
With wretched avarice, or as wretched love?
Know, there are words, and spells, which can control
Between the fits this fever of the soul:
Know, there are rhymes, which, fresh and fresh applied,
Will cure the arrant'st puppy of his pride.
Be furious, envious, slothful, mad or drunk,
Slave to a wife, or vassal to a punk,
A Switz, a High-Dutch, or a Low-Dutch bear;
All that we ask is but a patient ear.
'Tis the first virtue, vices to abhor:
And the first wisdom, to be fool no more.
But to the world no bugbear is so great,
As want of figure, and a small estate.
To either India see the merchant fly,
Scared at the spectre of pale poverty!
See him, with pains of body, pangs of soul,
Burn through the tropic, freeze beneath the pole!
Wilt thou do nothing for a nobler end,
Nothing, to make philosophy thy friend?
To stop thy foolish views, thy long desires,
And ease thy heart of all that it admires?
Here Wisdom calls: "Seek Virtue first, be bold!
As gold to silver, virtue is to gold."
There, London's voice: "Get money, money still!
And then let Virtue follow, if she will."
This, this the saving doctrine, preach'd to all,
From low St. James's up to high St. Paul!
From him whose quill stands quiver'd at his ear,
To him who notches sticks at Westminster.
Barnard in spirit, sense, and truth abounds;

16. Blackmore: Richard Blackmore (d. 1729), physician to Queen Anne, mediocre poet, author of the bombastic epic *The Creation*. His versification is here described as stiff and dull, like the animal used to carry the Lord Mayor. Strangely enough, he had a sound literary reputation in London at the time. **29. Lyttelton:** literary patron, friend of Pope, leader of the Whig opposition in Parliament from 1735 to 1756. **31. Aristippus:** a Greek thinker who taught that immediate pleasure is the goal of life.

51. Mead . . . Cheselden: Richard Mead, the physician; William Cheselden, the surgeon. Cheselden was a personal friend of Pope and attended him in his final illness. **60. arrant'st:** most erring. **62. punk:** prostitute. **82. low . . . high:** a reference to Low and High Church of England; to Whig and Tory politics. **84. notches sticks:** a reference to one who kept a record of debts at the Royal Exchequer. **85. Barnard:** Sir John Barnard, Member of Parliament for London, Lord Mayor in 1737, an opponent of Walpole, a man of virtue.

"Pray, then, what wants he?" Fourscore thousand pounds;
A pension, or such harness for a slave
As Bug now has, and Dorimant would have.
Barnard, thou art a cit, with all thy worth;
But Bug and D*l, their honours, and so forth.
Yet every child another song will sing,
"Virtue, brave boys! 'tis virtue makes a king."
True, conscious honour is to feel no sin,
He's arm'd without that's innocent within;
Be this thy screen, and this thy wall of brass;
Compared to this a minister's an ass.
And say, to which shall our applause belong,
This new Court-jargon, or the good old song?
The modern language of corrupted peers,
Or what was spoke at Cressy or Poitiers?
Who counsels best? who whispers, "Be but great,
With praise or infamy leave that to fate;
Get place and wealth—if possible with grace;
If not, by any means get wealth and place."
For what? to have a box where eunuchs sing,
And foremost in the circle eye a king.
Or he, who bids thee face with steady view
Proud fortune, and look shallow greatness through:
And, while he bids thee, sets the example too?
If such a doctrine, in St. James's air,
Should chance to make the well-dressed rabble stare;
If honest S*z take scandal at a spark,
That less admires the palace than the park:
Faith, I shall give the answer Reynard gave:
"I cannot like, dread sir, your royal cave:
Because I see, by all the tracks about,
Full many a beast goes in, but none comes out."
Adieu to Virtue, if you're once a slave:
Send her to Court, you send her to her grave.
Well, if a king's a lion, at the least
The people are a many-headed beast:
Can they direct what measures to pursue,
Who know themselves so little what to do?
Alike in nothing but one lust of gold,
Just half the land would buy, and half be sold:
Their country's wealth our mightier misers drain,
Or cross, to plunder provinces, the main;
The rest, some farm the poor-box, some the pews;
Some keep assemblies, and would keep the stews;
Some with fat bucks on childless dotards fawn;
Some win rich widows by their chine and brawn;
While with the silent growth of ten per cent.,
In dirt and darkness, hundreds stink content.
Of all these ways, if each pursues his own,
Satire, be kind, and let the wretch alone:
But show me one who has it in his power
To act consistent with himself an hour.
Sir Job sail'd forth, the evening bright and still,
"No place on earth (he cried) like Greenwich hill!"
Up starts a palace, lo, the obedient base
Slopes at its foot, the woods its sides embrace,
The silver Thames reflects its marble face.
Now let some whimsy, or that devil within
Which guides all those who know not what they mean,
But give the knight (or give his lady) spleen;
"Away, away! take all your scaffolds down,
For snug's the word: My dear! we'll live in town."
At amorous Flavio is the stocking thrown?
That very night he longs to lie alone.
The fool whose wife elopes some thrice a quarter,
For matrimonial solace dies a martyr.
Did ever Proteus, Merlin, any witch,
Transform themselves so strangely as the rich?
Well, but the poor—the poor have the same itch;
They change their weekly barber, weekly news,
Prefer a new japanner to their shoes.
Discharge their garrets, move their beds, and run
(They know not whither) in a chaise and one;
They hire their sculler, and, when once aboard,
Grow sick, and damn the climate—like a lord.
You laugh, half beau, half sloven if I stand,
My wig all powder, and all snuff my band;
You laugh, if coat and breeches strangely vary,
White gloves, and linen worthy Lady Mary!

89. cit: Barnard is called a city man. The other characters in this section are undesirables. **100. Cressy or Poitiers:** scenes of great English victories over the French. **112. S*z:** Augustus Schutz, Keeper of the Privy Purse under George II, a man noted for his seriousness. **114. Reynard:** the reply of the fox to the lion in the fifteenth-century fable *Reynard the Fox.*

130. fat bucks: attractive lovers; **dotards:** foolish persons. **131. chine:** strength. **152. Merlin:** the magician in King Arthur's Court. **156. japanner:** shoe shiner. **159. sculler:** someone to row their boat. **164. Lady Mary:** a reference to the often unkempt Lady Mary Wortley Montagu.

But, when no prelate's lawn with hair-shirt lined
Is half so incoherent as my mind;
When (each opinion with the next at strife,
One ebb and flow of follies all my life)
I plant, root up; I build, and then confound;
Turn round to square, and square again to
round;
You never change one muscle of your face,
You think this madness but a common case,
Nor once to Chancery, nor to Hale apply;
Yet hang your lip, to see a seam awry!
Careless how ill I with myself agree,
Kind to my dress, my figure, not to me.
Is this my guide, philosopher, and friend?
This he who loves me, and who ought to mend;
Who ought to make me (what he can, or none),
That man divine whom wisdom calls her
own;
Great without title, without fortune bless'd;
Rich, e'en when plunder'd, honour'd while
oppress'd;
Loved without youth, and follow'd without power;
At home, though exiled—free, though in the
Tower;
In short, that reasoning, high, immortal thing,
Just less than Jove, and much above a king,
Nay, half in Heaven—except (what's mighty odd)
A fit of vapours clouds this demi-god.

(1738)

THE FIRST EPISTLE OF THE SECOND BOOK OF HORACE

Advertisement

The reflections of Horace, and the judgments passed in his Epistle to Augustus, seemed so seasonable to the present times, that I could not help applying them to the use of my own country. The author thought them considerable enough to address them to his prince,* whom he paints with all the great and good qualities of a monarch upon whom the Romans depended for the increase of an absolute empire. But to make the poem entirely English, I was willing to add one or two of those which contribute to the happiness of a free people, and are more consistent with the welfare of our neighbours.

This Epistle will show the learned world to have fallen into two mistakes: one, that Augustus was a patron of poets in general, whereas he not only prohibited all but the best writers to name him, but recommended that care even to the civil magistrate: *Admonebat Prætores, ne paterentur Nomen suum obsolefieri*, etc. The other, that this piece was only a general discourse of poetry, whereas it was an apology for the poets, in order to render Augustus more their patron. Horace here pleads the cause of his contemporaries, first, against the taste of the town, whose humour it was to magnify the authors of the preceding age; secondly, against the court and nobility, who encouraged only the writers for the theatre; and lastly, against the emperor himself, who had conceived them of little use to the government. He shows (by a view of the progress of learning and the change of taste among the Romans) that the introduction of the polite arts of Greece had given the writers of his time great advantages over their predecessors; that their morals were much improved, and the licence of those ancient poets restrained: that satire and comedy were become more just and useful; that whatever extravagances were left on the stage were owing to the ill-taste of the nobility; that poets, under due regulations, were in many respects useful to the State; and concludes that it was upon them the emperor himself must depend for his fame with posterity.

We may further learn from this Epistle, that Horace made his court to this great prince by writing with a decent freedom toward him, with a just contempt of his low flatterers, and with a manly regard to his own character.

TO AUGUSTUS

While you, great patron of mankind! sustain
The balanced world, and open all the main;
Your country, chief, in arms abroad defend,
At home, with morals, arts, and laws amend;
How shall the Muse from such a monarch steal
An hour, and not defraud the public weal?

173. Chancery: the judicial court of the Lord Chancellor of England; **Hale:** a doctor dealing with cases of insanity at Bedlam. **181–88.** One should remember in reading these lines that although Bolingbroke had lost his title and estates and was virtually exiled to France, he continued to oppose Walpole, even when he returned home. **184. Tower:** He escaped the infamous Tower of London in his flight to France. **188. vapours:** melancholy.

* George II, christened Augustus, was during his reign, however, absolutely unconcerned about the state of literature in England.

Edward and Henry, now the boast of fame,
And virtuous Alfred, a more sacred name,
After a life of gen'rous toils endured,
The Gaul subdued, or property secured,
Ambition humbled, mighty cities storm'd,
Or laws establish'd, and the world reform'd;
Closed their long glories with a sigh, to find
The unwilling gratitude of base mankind!
All human virtue, to its latest breath,
Finds envy never conquer'd, but by death.
The great Alcides, every labour pass'd,
Had still this monster to subdue at last.
Sure fate of all, beneath whose rising ray
Each star of meaner merit fades away!
Oppress'd we feel the beam directly beat,
Those suns of glory please not till they set.
  To thee, the world its present homage pays,
The harvest early, but mature the praise:
Great friend of liberty! in kings a name
Above all Greek, above all Roman fame:
Whose word is truth, as sacred and revered,
As Heaven's own oracles from altars heard.
Wonder of kings! like whom, to mortal eyes
None e'er has risen, and none e'er shall rise.
  Just in one instance, be it yet confess'd
Your people, sir, are partial in the rest:
Foes to all living worth except your own,
And advocates for folly dead and gone.
Authors, like coins, grow dear as they grow old;
It is the rust we value, not the gold.
Chaucer's worst ribaldry is learn'd by rote,
And beastly Skelton heads of houses quote:
One likes no language but the *Faery Queen;*
A Scot will fight for Christ's Kirk o' the Green:
And each true Briton is to Ben so civil,
He swears the Muses met him at the Devil.
  Though justly Greece her eldest sons admires,
Why should not we be wiser than our sires?
In every public virtue we excel;
We build, we paint, we sing, we dance as well;
And learned Athens to our art must stoop,
Could she behold us tumbling through a hoop.
  If time improve our wits as well as wine,
Say at what age a poet grows divine?
Shall we, or shall we not, account him so,
Who died, perhaps, an hundred years ago?
End all dispute; and fix the year precise
When British bards begin to immortalise?
  "Who lasts a century can have no flaw,
I hold that wit a classic, good in law."
  Suppose he wants a year, will you compound?
And shall we deem him ancient, right and sound,
Or damn to all eternity at once,
At ninety-nine, a modern and a dunce?
  "We shall not quarrel for a year or two;
By courtesy of England, he may do."
  Then, by the rule that made the horse-tail bare,
I pluck out year by year, as hair by hair,
And melt down ancients like a heap of snow:
While you, to measure merits, look in Stowe,
And estimating authors by the year,
Bestow a garland only on a bier.
  Shakespeare (whom you and every play-house bill
Style the divine, the matchless, what you will),
For gain, not glory, wing'd his roving flight,
And grew immortal in his own despite.
Ben, old and poor, as little seem'd to heed
The life to come, in every poet's creed.
Who now reads Cowley? if he pleases yet,
His moral pleases, not his pointed wit;
Forgot his epic, nay Pindaric art,
But still I love the language of his heart.
  "Yet surely, surely, these were famous men!
What boy but hears the sayings of old Ben?
In all debates where critics bear a part,
Not one but nods, and talks of Jonson's art,
Of Shakespeare's nature, and of Cowley's wit;
How Beaumont's judgment check'd what Fletcher writ;
How Shadwell hasty, Wycherley was slow;
But, for the passions, Southern sure and Rowe.
These, only these, support the crowded stage,
From eldest Heywood down to Cibber's age."

SECOND HORACE. **17. Alcides:** the powerful Hercules. **38. Skelton:** (1460?–1529), Henry VIII's Poet Laureate. **40.** The reference here is to a ballad by James I of Scotland. **42. Devil:** the Devil Tavern, where Ben Jonson held meetings of his Poetical Club.

66. A reference to Stowe's *Summarie of Englyshe Chronicles,* published in 1580. **86. Southern . . . Rowe:** Thomas Southern (1659–1746), friend of Dryden, dramatist whose most famous works are his tragedies *The Fatal Marriage* and *Oroonoko.* Nicholas Rowe (1674–1718), acquaintance of Pope, became Poet Laureate in 1715. He was chiefly known for his dramas (e.g., *The Ambitious Stepmother, Tamerlane, The Fair Penitent*). **88. Heywood:** John Heywood (1497?–1580?), famous for his dramatic interludes like *The Four P's* and *The Play of the Wether.*

All this may be; the people's voice is odd,
It is, and it is not, the voice of God.
To *Gammer Gurton* if it give the bays,
And yet deny the *Careless Husband* praise,
Or say our fathers never broke a rule;
Why then, I say, the public is a fool.
But let them own, that greater faults than we
They had, and greater virtues, I'll agree.
Spenser himself affects the obsolete,
And Sidney's verse halts ill on Roman feet:
Milton's strong pinion now not Heaven can bound,
Now serpent-like, in prose he sweeps the
ground;
In quibbles, angel and archangel join,
And God the Father turns a school-divine.
Not that I'd lop the beauties from his book,
Like slashing Bentley with his desperate hook,
Or damn all Shakespeare, like the affected fool
At Court, who hates whate'er he read at school.
But for the wits of either Charles's days,
The mob of gentlemen who wrote with ease;
Sprat, Carew, Sedley, and a hundred more,
(Like twinkling stars the *Miscellanies* o'er)
One simile, that solitary shines
In the dry desert of a thousand lines,
Or lengthen'd thought that gleams through many
a page,
Has sanctified whole poems for an age.
I lose my patience, and I own it too,
When works are censured, not as bad but new;
While if our elders break all reason's laws,
These fools demand not pardon, but applause.
On Avon's bank, where flowers eternal blow,
If I but ask, if any weed can grow;
One tragic sentence if I dare deride,
Which Betterton's grave action dignified,
Or well-mouth'd Booth with emphasis proclaims
(Though but, perhaps, a muster-roll of names),
How will our fathers rise up in a rage,
And swear, all shame is lost in George's age!
You'd think no fools disgraced the former reign,
Did not some examples yet remain,
Who scorn a lad should teach his father skill,
And, having once been wrong, will be so
still.
He, who to seem more deep than you or I,
Extols old bards, or Merlin's prophecy,
Mistake him not; he envies, not admires,
And to debase the sons, exalts the sires.
Had ancient times conspired to disallow
What then was new, what had been ancient now?
Or what remain'd, so worthy to be read
By learned critics, of the mighty dead?
In days of ease, when now the weary sword
Was sheath'd, and luxury with Charles
restored;
In every taste of foreign courts improved,
"All, by the king's example, lived and loved."
Then peers grew proud in horsemanship to excel,
Newmarket's glory rose, as Britain's fell;
The soldier breathed the gallantries of France,
And every flowery courtier writ romance.
Then marble, soften'd into life, grew warm,
And yielding metal flow'd to human form:
Lely on animated canvas stole
The sleepy eye, that spoke the melting soul.
No wonder then, when all was love and sport,
The willing Muses were debauch'd at Court:
On each enervate string they taught the note
To pant, or tremble through an eunuch's throat.
But Britain, changeful as a child at play,
Now calls in princes, and now turns away.
Now Whig, now Tory, what we loved we hate;
Now all for pleasure, now for Church and State;
Now for prerogative, and now for laws;
Effects unhappy! from a noble cause.
Time was, a sober Englishman would knock
His servants up, and rise by five o'clock;
Instruct his family in every rule,
And send his wife to church, his son to school.
To worship like his fathers was his care;
To teach their frugal virtues to his heir:
To prove that luxury could never hold;

91. *Gammer Gurton:* reference to *Gammer Gurton's Needle,* one of the first printed plays in English. **92. *Careless Husband:*** a play by Colley Cibber. **109. Sprat, Carew, Sedley**: Restoration poets. **122–23. Betterton . . . Booth:** Thomas Betterton (1635?–1710) and Barton Booth (1681–1733) were noted actors of the day.

142. Pope notes: "A verse of Lord Landsdowne." **143–46.** Pope notes: "The Duke of Newcastle's book of Horsemanship: the Romance of *Parthenissa,* by the Earl of Orrery; and most of the French Romances translated by *Persons of Quality.*" **149. Lely**: Sir Peter Lely (1618–1680), a Dutch portrait painter who came to England and gained some reputation. **153. enervate**: tender, delicate. **153–54.** a reference, according to Pope, to Sir William Davenant's *The Siege of Rhodes,* the first opera sung in England.

And place, on good security, his gold.
Now times are changed, and one poetic itch
Has seized the court and city, poor and rich:
Sons, sires, and grandsires, all will wear the bays,
Our wives read Milton, and our daughters plays,
To theatres, and to rehearsals throng,
And all our grace at table is a song.
I, who so oft renounce the Muses, lie,
Not —'s self e'er tells more fibs than I;
When sick of Muse, our follies we deplore,
And promise our best friends to rhyme no more;
We wake next morning in a raging fit
And call for pen and ink to show our wit.
He served a 'prenticeship, who sets up shop;
Ward tried on puppies, and the poor, his drop;
E'en Radcliffe's doctors travel first to France,
Nor dare to practise till they've learn'd to dance.
Who builds a bridge that never drove a pile?
(Should Ripley venture, all the world would smile)
But those who cannot write, and those who can,
All rhyme, and scrawl, and scribble, to a man.
Yet, sir, reflect, the mischief is not great;
These madmen never hurt the Church or
State;
Sometimes the folly benefits mankind;
And rarely avarice taints the tuneful mind.
Allow him but his plaything of a pen,
He ne'er rebels, or plots, like other men;
Flight of cashiers, or mobs, he'll never mind;
And knows no losses while the Muse is kind.
To cheat a friend, or ward, he leaves to Peter;
The good man heaps up nothing but mere metre,
Enjoys his garden and his book in quiet;
And then—a perfect hermit in his diet.
Of little use the man you may suppose,
Who says in verse what others say in prose;

182. Ward: Pope notes: "A famous Empiric, whose Pill and Drop had several surprising effects, and were one of the principal subjects of writing and conversation at this time." **183. Radcliffe:** John Radcliffe (1650–1714), a good physician often called to minister to royalty. He had taken care of Pope when the poet was younger. Radcliffe was also a philanthropist who left a good deal of money for the support of science and medicine at Oxford. **186. Ripley:** Thomas Ripley, a carpenter who quickly became an architect thanks to the political influence of Walpole. **195.** Pope is referring to Robert Knight, cashier of the ill-fated South Sea Company, who fled to France after being found guilty of improprieties by the House of Lords. **197. Peter:** Peter Walter was a famous moneylender.

Yet let me show a poet's of some weight,
And (though no soldier) useful to the State.
What will a child learn sooner than a song?
What better teach a foreigner the tongue?
What's long or short, each accent where to place,
And speak in public with some sort of grace.
I scarce can think him such a worthless thing,
Unless he praise some monster of a king;
Or virtue or religion turn to sport,
To please a lewd or unbelieving court.
Unhappy Dryden!—in all Charles's days,
Roscommon only boasts unspotted bays;
And in our own (excuse from courtly stains)
No whiter page than Addison remains.
He from the taste obscene reclaims our youth,
And sets the passions on the side of truth,
Forms the soft bosom with the gentlest art,
And pours each human virtue in the heart.
Let Ireland tell, how wit upheld her cause,
Her trade supported, and supplied her laws;
And leave on Swift this grateful verse engraved,
"The rights a court attack'd, a poet saved."
Behold the hand that wrought a nation's cure,
Stretch'd to relieve the idiot and the poor,
Proud vice to brand, or injured worth adorn,
And stretch the ray to ages yet unborn.
Not but there are, who merit other palms;
Hopkins and Sternhold glad the heart with
psalms:
The boys and girls whom charity maintains,
Implore your help in these pathetic strains:
How could devotion touch the country pews,
Unless the gods bestow'd a proper Muse?
Verse cheers their leisure, verse assists their work,
Verse prays for peace, or sings down Pope and
Turk.
The silenced preacher yields to potent strain,
And feels that grace his prayer besought in vain;
The blessing thrills through all the labouring
throng,
And Heaven is won by violence of song.
Our rural ancestors, with little blest,
Patient of labour when the end was rest,
Indulged the day that housed their annual grain,
With feasts and offerings, and a thankful strain:

224. Swift was a fierce literary fighter for the rights of Ireland. **230. Hopkins . . . Sternhold:** John Hopkins (d. 1570) and Thomas Sternhold (d. 1549), joint versifiers of the Psalms.

The joy their wives, their sons, and servants share,
Ease of their toil, and partners of their care:
The laugh, the jest, attendants on the bowl,
Smooth'd every brow, and open'd every soul:
With growing years the pleasing licence grew,
And taunts alternate innocently flew.
But times corrupt, and Nature ill-inclined,
Produced the point that left a sting behind;
Till friend with friend, and families at strife,
Triumphant malice raged through private life.
Who felt the wrong, or fear'd it, took the alarm,
Appeal'd to law, and justice lent her arm.
At length, by wholesome dread of statutes bound,
The poets learn'd to please, and not to wound:
Most warp'd to flattery's side; but some, more nice,
Preserved the freedom, and forbore the vice.
Hence satire rose, that just the medium hit,
And heals with morals, what it hurts with wit.
  We conquer'd France, but felt our captive's charms;
Her arts victorious triumph'd o'er our arms:
Britain to soft refinements less a foe,
Wit grew polite, and numbers learn'd to flow.
Waller was smooth; but Dryden taught to join
The varying verse, the full-resounding line,
The long majestic march and energy divine.
Though still some traces of our rustic vein
And splayfoot verse remain'd, and will remain.
Late, very late, correctness grew our care,
When the tired nation breathed from civil war.
Exact Racine, and Corneille's noble fire,
Show'd us that France had something to admire.
No but the tragic spirit was our own,
And full in Shakespeare, fair in Otway shone:
But Otway fail'd to polish or refine,
And fluent Shakespeare scarce effaced a line.
Even copious Dryden wanted, or forgot,
The last and greatest art, the art to blot.
Some doubt, if equal pains, or equal fire,
The humbler Muse of comedy require.
  But in known images of life, I guess
The labour greater, as the indulgence less.
Observe how seldom even the best succeed:
Tell me if Congreve's fools are fools indeed?
What pert low dialogue has Farquhar writ!
How Van wants grace, who never wanted wit!
The stage how loosely does Astræa tread,
Who fairly puts all characters to bed!
And idle Cibber, how he breaks the laws,
To make poor Pinky eat with vast applause!
But fill their purse, our poets' work is done,
Alike to them, by pathos or by pun.
  O you! whom Vanity's light bark conveys
On Fame's mad voyage by the wind of praise,
With what a shifting gale your course you ply,
For ever sunk too low, or borne too high!
Who pants for glory finds but short repose,
A breath revives him, or a breath o'erthrows.
Farewell the stage! if just as thrives the play,
The silly bard grows fat, or falls away.
  There still remains, to mortify a wit,
The many-headed monster of the pit;
A senseless, worthless, and unhonour'd crowd;
Who, to disturb their betters mighty proud,
Clattering their sticks before ten lines are spoke,
Call for the farce, the bear, or the black-joke.
What dear delight to Britons farce affords!
Ever the taste of mobs, but now of lords
(Taste, that eternal wanderer, which flies
From heads to ears, and now from ears to eyes).
The play stands still; damn action and discourse,
Back fly the scenes, and enter foot and horse;
Pageants on pageants, in long order drawn,
Peers, heralds, bishops, ermine, gold and lawn;
The champion, too! and to complete the jest,
Old Edward's armour beams on Cibber's breast.
With laughter sure Democritus had died,
Had he beheld an audience gape so wide.
Let bear or elephant be e'er so white,
The people, sure, the people are the sight!
Ah, luckless poet! stretch thy lungs and roar,

271. splayfoot verse: clumsily formed verse. **277. Otway:** Thomas Otway (1652–1685), the dramatist, author of *Venice Preserved.* **287. Congreve:** William Congreve (1670–1729), popular Restoration dramatist, author of *Love for Love* and *The Way of the World.*

288. Farquhar: George Farquhar (1678–1707), dramatist, author of *The Recruiting Officer* and *The Beaux Stratagem.* **289. Van:** Sir John Vanbrugh (1664–1726), still another Restoration comic dramatist, author of *The Confederacy.* **290. Astræa:** In Greek mythology the daughter of Zeus and Themis. Pope notes: "A Name taken by Mrs. Afra Behn, Authoress of several obscene plays." **293. Pinky:** William Penkethman, a comic actor of the day. **309. black-joke:** a sausage made of blood and suet. **319. Old Edward . . . breast:** The reference is to the competition among playhouses in representing the coronation of Henry VIII and Anne Boleyn. In the competition the armor of one of the Kings of England was borrowed from the Tower to dress the hero.

That bear or elephant shall heed thee more;
While all its throats the gallery extends,
And all the thunder of the pit ascends!
Loud as the wolves, on Orcas' stormy steep,
Howl to the roarings of the Northern deep.
Such is the shout, the long-applauding note,
At Quin's high plume, or Oldfield's petticoat;
Or when from Court a birthday suit bestow'd,
Sinks the lost actor in the tawdry load.
Booth enters—hark! the universal peal!
"But has he spoken?" Not a syllable.
What shook the stage, and made the people stare?
Cato's long wig, flower'd gown, and lacquer'd
chair.
Yet lest you think I rally more than teach,
Or praise malignly arts I cannot reach,
Let me for once presume to instruct the
times,
To know the poet from the man of rhymes:
'Tis he who gives my breast a thousand pains,
Can make me feel each passion that he feigns;
Enrage, compose, with more than magic art,
With pity, and with terror, tear my heart;
And snatch me, o'er the earth, or through the air,
To Thebes, to Athens, when he will, and where.
But not this part of the poetic state
Alone, deserves the favour of the great:
Think of those authors, sir, who would rely
More on a reader's sense, than gazer's eye.
Or who shall wander where the Muses sing?
Who climb their mountain, or who taste their
spring?
How shall we fill a library with wit,
When Merlin's cave is half unfurnish'd yet?
My liege! why writers little claim your thought
I guess; and, with their leave, will tell the fault:
We poets are (upon a poet's word)
Of all mankind, the creatures most absurd:
The season, when to come, and when to go,
To sing, or cease to sing, we never know;
And if we will recite nine hours in ten,
You lose your patience just like other men.
Then, too, we hurt ourselves, when to defend
A single verse, we quarrel with a friend;
Repeat unask'd; lament, the wit's too fine
For vulgar eyes, and point out every line.
But most, when straining with too weak a wing,
We needs will write epistles to the king;
And from the moment we oblige the town,
Expect a place, or pension from the Crown;
Or dubb'd historians by express command,
To enrol your triumphs o'er the seas and land,
Be call'd to Court to plan some work divine,
As once for Louis, Boileau and Racine.
Yet think, great sir! (so many virtues shown)
Ah think, what poet best may make them known?
Or choose, at least, some minister of grace,
Fit to bestow the laureate's weighty place.
Charles, to late times to be transmitted
fair,
Assign'd his figure to Bernini's care;
And great Nassau to Kneller's hand decreed
To fix him graceful on the bounding steed;
So well in paint and stone they judged of merit;
But kings in wit may want discerning spirit.
The hero William, and the martyr Charles,
One knighted Blackmore, and one pension'd
Quarles;
Which made old Ben and surly Dennis swear,
"No Lord's anointed, but a Russian bear."
Not with such majesty, such bold relief,
The forms august of king, or conqu'ring chief,
E'er swell'd on marble, as in verse have shined
(In polish'd verse) the manners and the mind.
Oh! could I mount on the Mæonian wing,
Your arms, your actions, your repose to sing!
What seas you traversed, and what field you
fought!
Your country's peace, how oft, how dearly bought!
How barb'rous rage subsided at your word,
And nations wonder'd, while they dropp'd the
sword!
How, when you nodded, o'er the land and
deep,
Peace stole her wing, and wrapp'd the world in
sleep;

328. Orcas: Pope notes: "The farthest Northern Promontory of Scotland, opposite to the Orcades." **331. Quin . . . Oldfield:** James Quin (1693–1766) and Anne Oldfield (1683–1730), a popular actor and actress of the day. **354.** Pope notes: "The Palatine Library then building by Augustus." **355.** Pope notes: "A Building in the Royal Gardens of Richmond, where is a small, but choice collection of books."

381. Bernini: the architect who designed the colonnade of St. Peter's. He had done a bust of Charles I. **382. Kneller:** the painter who did the portrait of William III on William's return to England after signing the Peace of Ryswick in 1697. **394. Mæonian:** Homeric.

Till earth's extremes your mediation own,
And Asia's tyrants tremble at your throne.
But verse, alas! your Majesty disdains;
And I'm not used to panegyric strains:
The zeal of fools offends at any time,
But most of all the zeal of fools in rhyme.
Besides, a fate attends on all I write,
That when I aim at praise, they say I bite.
A vile encomium doubly ridicules:
There's nothing blackens like the ink of fools.
If true, a woeful likeness; and if lies,
"Praise undeserved is scandal in disguise":
Well may he blush who gives it, or receives;
And when I flatter, let my dirty leaves
(Like journals, odes, and such forgotten things
As Eusden, Philips, Settle, writ of kings)
Clothe spice, line trunks, or flutt'ring in a row,
Befringe the rails of Bedlam and Soho.

(1737)

FROM

The Dunciad

TO DR. JONATHAN SWIFT

BOOK THE FIRST

Argument

The proposition, the invocation, and the inscription. Then the original of the great empire of Dulness, and cause of the continuance thereof. The college of the goddess in the city, with her private academy for poets in particular; the governors of it, and the four cardinal virtues. Then the poem hastes into the midst of things, presenting her on the evening of a Lord Mayor's day, revolving the long succession of her sons, and the glories past and to come. She fixes her eyes on Bays to be the instrument of that great event which is the subject of the poem. He is described pensive among his books, giving up the cause, and apprehending the period of her empire: after debating whether to betake himself to the church, or to gaming, or to party-writing, he raises an altar of proper books, and (making first his solemn prayer and declaration) purposes thereon to sacrifice all his unsuccessful writings. As the pile is kindled, the goddess, beholding the flame from her seat, flies and puts it out by casting upon it the poem of Thule. She forthwith reveals herself to him, transports him to her temple, unfolds her arts, and initiates him into her mysteries; then announcing the death of Eusden, the Poet Laureate, anoints him, carries him to court, and proclaims him successor.

The mighty mother, and her son, who brings
The Smithfield muses to the ear of kings,
I sing. Say you, her instruments, the great!
Call'd to this work by Dulness, Jove, and Fate;
You by whose care, in vain decried, and curst,
Still Dunce the second reigns like Dunce the first;
Say, how the goddess bade Britannia sleep,
And pour'd her spirit o'er the land and deep.
In eldest time, ere mortals writ or read,
Ere Pallas issued from the Thunderer's head,
Dulness o'er all possess'd her ancient right,
Daughter of Chaos and eternal Night:
Fate in their dotage this fair idiot gave,
Gross as her sire, and as her mother grave,
Laborious, heavy, busy, bold, and blind,
She ruled, in native anarchy, the mind.
Still her old empire to restore she tries,
For, born a goddess, Dulness never dies.
O thou! whatever title please thine ear,
Dean, Drapier, Bickerstaff, or Gulliver!
Whether thou choose Cervantes' serious air,
Or laugh and shake in Rabelais' easy chair,
Or praise the court, or magnify mankind,
Or thy grieved country's copper chains unbind;
From thy Bœotia though her pow'r retires,
Mourn not, my Swift, at aught our realm acquires.
Here pleased behold her mighty wings outspread
To hatch a new Saturnian age of lead.

417. **Eusden . . . Settle:** Laurence Eusden, Ambrose Philips, Elkanah Settle, not especially memorable poets.

THE DUNCIAD. BOOK I. **1. son:** Colley Cibber (1671–1757), the Poet-Laureate, became the hero of the final version of *The Dunciad*, replacing Lewis Theobald. **2. Smithfield:** the place where Bartholomew Fair with all of its entertainments was held. Pope notes that the mock-epic hero of this poem has brought these entertainments, formerly suitable only for the lower classes, to the great centers of the court and city. **10. Pallas:** In Greek mythology Pallas Athene was born full-grown from the head of Zeus. **20. Dean . . . Gulliver:** names associated with Jonathan Swift and his works. **25. Bœotia:** Greece. **28.** Pope notes: "The ancient golden age is by poets styled Saturnian; but in the chemical language Saturn is lead."

Close to those walls where Folly holds her throne,
And laughs to think Monro would take her down,
Where o'er the gates, by his famed father's hand,
Great Cibber's brazen, brainless brothers stand;
One cell there is, conceal'd from vulgar eye,
The cave of Poverty and Poetry.
Keen, hollow winds howl through the bleak recess,
Emblem of music caused by emptiness.
Hence bards, like Proteus long in vain tied down,
Escape in monsters, and amaze the town.
Hence miscellanies spring, the weekly boast
Of Curll's chaste press, and Lintot's rubric post:
Hence hymning Tyburn's elegiac lines,
Hence journals, medleys, merc'ries, magazines:
Sepulchral lies, our holy walls to grace,
And new-year odes, and all the Grub Street race.
In clouded majesty here Dulness shone;
Four guardian virtues, round, support her throne:
Fierce champion Fortitude, that knows no fears
Of hisses, blows, or want, or loss of ears:
Calm Temperance, whose blessings those partake
Who hunger and who thirst for scribbling sake:
Prudence, whose glass presents th' approaching jail:
Poetic justice, with her lifted scale,
Where, in nice balance, truth with gold she weighs,
And solid pudding against empty praise.
Here she beholds the chaos dark and deep,
Where nameless somethings in their causes sleep,
Till Genial Jacob, or a warm third day,
Call forth each mass, a poem, or a play:
How hints, like spawn, scarce quick in embryo lie,
How new-born nonsense first is taught to cry,
Maggots half-form'd in rhyme exactly meet,
And learn to crawl upon poetic feet.
Here one poor word an hundred clenches makes,
And ductile Dulness new meanders takes;
There motley images her fancy strike,
Figures ill-pair'd, and similes unlike.
She sees a mob of metaphors advance,
Pleased with the madness of the mazy dance!
How tragedy and comedy embrace;
How farce and epic get a jumbled race;
How Time himself stands still at her command,
Realms shift their place, and ocean turns to land.
Here gay Description Egypt glads with show'rs,
Or gives to Zembla fruits, to Barca flow'rs;
Glitt'ring with ice here hoary hills are seen,
There painted valleys of eternal green.
In cold December fragrant chaplets blow,
And heavy harvests nod beneath the snow.
And these, and more, the cloud-compelling queen
Beholds through fogs, that magnify the scene.
She, tinsell'd o'er in robes of varying hues,
With self-applause her wild creation views;
Sees momentary monsters rise and fall,
And with her own fool's-colours gilds them all.
'Twas on the day, when Thorold rich and grave,
Like Cimon, triumph'd both on land and wave:
(Pomps without guilt, of bloodless swords and maces
Glad chains, warm furs, broad banners, and broad faces)
Now night descending, the proud scene was o'er,
But lived, in Settle's numbers, one day more.
Now mayors and shrieves all hush'd and satiate lay,
Yet eat, in dreams, the custard of the day;

29. A reference to Rag Fair, a London market for used goods. **30. Monro:** physician to Bedlam Hospital for the insane. **32. Cibber:** Pope notes: "Mr. Caius Gabriel Cibber, father of the Poet Laureate. The two Statues of the Lunatics over the gates of Bedlam Hospital were done by him, and (as the son justly says of them) are no ill monuments of his fame as an Artist." **37. Proteus:** a sea deity who could assume a multitude of different forms to elude men. **40. Curll . . . Lintot:** two booksellers of the time. Curll was fined for publishing obscene books. Lintot adorned his shop with titles printed in red letters. **41. Tyburn:** the place where the gallows were located. At the time of hanging criminals often sang hymns, which were published. **44. Grub Street:** Grub Street was the center of hack writing.

57. Jacob: a reference to Jacob Jonson, the publisher. **warm third day:** It was customary for the proceeds of a third performance to go to the playwright. **63. clenches:** tortured phrases, puns. **64. ductile:** watery. **74. Zembla:** Nova Zembla, near the Arctic Circle. **Barca:** the desert of Libya. **85. Thorold:** Sir George Thorold was Lord Mayor of London in 1720. His annual procession to Westminster had just taken place and is compared to that of Cimon, the great Athenian general. **90. Settle:** Elkanah Settle, last official poet of the city of London, who composed eulogies to the Lord Mayor.

While pensive poets painful vigils keep,
Sleepless themselves to give their readers sleep.
Much to the mindful queen the feast recalls
What city swans once sung within the walls;
Much she revolves their arts, their ancient praise,
And sure succession down from Heywood's days.
She saw, with joy, the line immortal run,
Each sire impress'd and glaring in his son:
So watchful Bruin forms, with plastic care,
Each growing lump, and brings it to a bear.
She saw old Pryn in restless Daniel shine,
And Eusden eke out Blackmore's endless line,
She saw slow Philips creep like Tate's poor page,
And all the mighty mad in Dennis rage.
In each she marks her image full express'd,
But chief in Bay's monster-breeding breast;
Bays, form'd by Nature stage and town to bless,
And act, and be, a coxcomb with success.
Dulness with transport eyes the lively dunce,
Remembr'ring she herself was Pertness once.
Now (shame to Fortune!) an ill run at play
Blank'd his bold visage, and a thin third day:
Swearing and supperless the hero sate,
Blasphemed his gods, the dice, and damn'd his fate.
Then gnaw'd his pen, then dash'd it on the ground,
Sinking from thought to thought, a vast profound!
Plunged for his sense, but found no bottom there,
Yet wrote and flounder'd on, in mere despair.
Round him much embryo, much abortion lay,
Much future ode, and abdicated play;
Nonsense precipitate, like running lead,
That slipp'd through cracks and zig-zags of the head;
All that on Folly Frenzy could beget,
Fruits of dull heat, and sooterkins of wit.
Next, o'er his books his eyes began to roll,
In pleasing memory of all he stole,
How here he sipped, how there he plundered snug,
And sucked all o'er, like an industrious bug.
Here lay poor Fletcher's half-eat scenes, and here
The frippery of crucified Molière;
There hapless Shakespeare, yet of Tibbald sore,
Wished he had blotted for himself before.
The rest on outside merit but presume,
Or serve (like other fools) to fill a room;
Such with their shelves as due proportion hold,
Or their fond parents dressed in red and gold;
Or where the pictures for the page atone,
And Quarles is saved by beauties not his own.
Here swells the shelf with Ogilby the great;
There, stamped with arms, Newcastle shines complete:
Here all his suff'ring brotherhood retire,
And 'scape the martyrdom of jakes and fire:
A Gothic library! of Greece and Rome
Well purged, and worthy Settle, Banks, and Broome.
But, high above, more solid learning shone,
The classics of an age that heard of none;
There Caxton slept, with Wynkyn at his side,
One clasped in wood, and one in strong cow-hide.
There saved by spice, like mummies, many a year,
Dry bodies of divinity appear;
De Lyra there a dreadful front extends,
And here the groaning shelves Philemon bends.
Of these, twelve volumes, twelve of amplest size,
Redeemed from tapers and defrauded pies,
Inspired he seizes; these an altar raise;
An hecatomb of pure unsullied lays
That altar crowns; a folio common-place
Founds the whole pile, of all his works the base;
Quartos, octavos, shape the less'ning pyre;
A twisted birthday ode completes the spire.

98. John Heywood, the great writer of interludes in the age of Henry VIII. **101–106. Bruin ... Dennis:** a catalogue of bad poets. **106. Dennis:** John Dennis, critic, lover of the sublime, object of Pope's wrath. **108. Bays:** The general reference here is to the hapless Laureate, Colley Cibber. Specifically *bays* refers to the laurel crown of poets. **126. sooterkins:** a kind of false birth, fabled to be produced by Dutch women from sitting over their stoves; figuratively, abortive schemes.

133. Tibbald: Lewis Theobald, earlier King of the Dunces, was a furious editor and emender of Shakespeare's text. **135–46.** Still another catalogue of writers noted not so much for their own distinction as for their borrowings from others or for the sheer quantity of their work. **149. Caxton ... Wynkyn:** William Caxton and Wynkyn de Worde were printers before the great heyday of the English Renaissance. **153–54. De Lyra ... Philemon:** De Lyra was an unstoppable fourteenth-century commentator. Philemon Holland was a similarly prolific Elizabethan translator.

Then he: "Great tamer of all human art!
First in my care, and ever at my heart;
Dulness! whose good old cause I yet defend,
With whom my muse began, with whom shall end,
E'er since Sir Fopling's periwig was praise,
To the last honours of the Butt and Bays;
O thou! of bus'ness the directing soul!
To this our head like bias to the bowl,
Which, as more pond'rous, made its aim more true,
Obliquely waddling to the mark in view:
O! ever gracious to perplexed mankind,
Still spread a healing mist before the mind;
And, lest we err by wit's wild dancing light,
Secure us kindly in our native night.
Or, if to wit a coxcomb make pretence,
Guard the sure barrier between that and sense;
Or quite unravel all the reas'ning thread,
And hang some curious cobweb in its stead!
As, forced from wind-guns, lead itself can fly,
And pond'rous slugs cut swiftly through the sky;
As clocks to weight their nimble motion owe,
The wheels above urged by the load below:
Me emptiness and dulness could inspire,
And were my elasticity and fire.
Some demon stole my pen (forgive the offence)
And once betrayed me into common sense:
Else all my prose and verse were much the same;
This prose on stilts, that poetry fall'n lame.
Did on the stage my fops appear confined?
My life gave ampler lessons to mankind.
Did the dead letter unsuccessful prove?
The brisk example never failed to move.
Yet sure had Heav'n decreed to save the state,
Heav'n had decreed these works a longer date.
Could Troy be saved by any single hand,
This grey-goose weapon must have made her stand.
What can I now? my Fletcher cast aside,
Take up the Bible, once my better guide?
Or tread the path by vent'rous heroes trod,
This box my thunder, this right hand my God?
Or chaired at White's amidst the doctors sit,
Teach oaths to gamesters, and to nobles wit?
Or bidst thou rather party to embrace?
(A friend to party thou, and all her race;
'Tis the same rope at different ends they twist;
To dulness Ridpath is as dear as Mist.)
Shall I, like Curtius, desp'rate in my zeal,
O'er head and ears plunge for the commonweal?
Or rob Rome's ancient geese of all their glories,
And cackling save the monarchy of Tories?
Hold—to the minister I more incline;
To serve his cause, O queen! is serving thine.
And see! thy very gazetteers give o'er,
Even Ralph repents, and Henley writes no more.
What then remains? Ourself. Still, still remain
Cibberian forehead, and Cibberian brain.
This brazen brightness, to the squire so dear;
This polished hardness, that reflects the peer:
This arch absurd, that wit and fool delights;
This mess, tossed up of Hockley-hole and White's;
Where dukes and butchers join to wreathe my crown,
At once the bear and fiddle of the town.
"O born in sin, and forth in folly brought!
Works damned, or to be damned! (your father's fault)
Go, purified by flames ascend the sky,
My better and more Christian progeny!
Unstained, untouched, and yet in maiden sheets;
While all your smutty sisters walk the streets.
Ye shall not beg, like gratis-given Bland,
Sent with a pass, and vagrant through the land;
Not sail with Ward, to ape-and-monkey climes,
Where vile Mundungus trucks for viler rhymes:
Not sulphur-tipt, emblaze an ale-house fire;
Not wrap up oranges, to pelt your sire!
O! pass more innocent, in infant state,

167. Sir Fopling's periwig: the elaborate wig worn by Cibber in his first play, *The Fool of Fashion*. **168. Butt:** The Laureate received a butt of wine annually. **181. wind-guns:** air rifles. **203. White's:** a gambling club.

208. Ridpath . . . Mist: one, a writer for a Whig journal; the other, for a Tory. **209. Curtius:** the mythological hero who jumped into a chasm to save Rome. **211. Rome's ancient geese:** Geese warned the Romans of the approach of the Gauls. **215. gazetteers:** hack political writers. **216. Ralph . . . Henley:** Ralph and Henley were writers controlled by Sir Robert Walpole. **222. Hockley-hole:** a famous site for bear-baiting. **231. gratis-given Bland:** Bland was still another Walpole hack writer whose pamphlets were sent post-free all over England. **233. Ward:** Edward Ward, whose works were sold in the colonies. **234. Mundungus:** tobacco of poor quality.

To the mild limbo of our father Tate:
Or peaceably forgot, at one be blest
In Shadwell's bosom with eternal rest!
Soon to that mass of nonsense to return,
Where things destroyed are swept to things
unborn."
With that, a tear (portentous sign of grace!)
Stole from the master of the seven-fold face;
And thrice he lifted the birthday brand,
And thrice he dropt it from his quiv'ring hand;
Then lights the structure, with averted eyes:
The rolling smoke involves the sacrifice.
The opening clouds disclose each work by turns;
Now flames the Cid, and now Perolla burns,
Great Cæsar roars, and hisses in the fires;
King John in silence modestly expires;
No merit now the dear Nonjuror claims,
Molière's old stubble in a moment flames.
Tears gushed again, as from pale Priam's eyes
When the last blaze sent Ilion to the skies.
Roused by the light, old Dulness heaved the
head,
Then snatched a sheet of Thule from her bed;
Sudden she flies, and whelms it o'er the pyre;
Down sink the flames, and with a hiss
expire.
Her ample presence fills up all the place;
A veil of fogs dilates her awful face:
Great in her charms! as when on shrieves and
may'rs
She looks, and breathes herself into their airs.
She bids him wait her to her sacred dome:
Well pleased he entered, and confessed his home.
So spirits ending their terrestrial race
Ascend, and recognize their native place.
This the great mother dearer held than all
The clubs of Quidnuncs, or her own
Guildhall:
Here stood her opium, here she nursed her owls,
And here she planned th' imperial seat of fools.
Here to her chosen all her works she shows;
Prose swelled to verse, verse loit'ring into prose:
How random thoughts now meaning chance to
find,
Now leave all memory of sense behind;
How prologues into prefaces decay,
And these to notes are frittered quite away.
How index-learning turns no student pale,
Yet holds the eel of science by the tail:
How, with less reading than makes felons scape,
Less human genius than God gives an ape,
Small thanks to France, and none to Rome or
Greece,
A vast, vamped, future, old, revived, new piece,
'Twixt Plautus, Fletcher, Shakespeare, and
Corneille,
Can make a Cibber, Tibbald, or Ozell.
The Goddess then, o'er his anointed head,
With mystic words, the sacred opium shed.
And lo! her bird (a monster of a fowl,
Something betwixt a Heideggre and owl)
Perched on his crown. "All hail! and hail again,
My son: the promised land expects thy reign.
Know, Eusden thirsts no more for sack or praise;
He sleeps among the dull of ancient days;
Safe, where no critics damn, no duns molest,
Where wretched Withers, Ward, and Gildon
rest,
And high-born Howard, more majestic sire,
With "Fool of Quality" completes the quire.
Thou, Cibber! thou, his laurel shalt support,
Folly, my son, has still a friend at court.
Lift up your gates, ye princes, see him come!
Sound, sound, ye viols; be the cat-call dumb!
Bring, bring the madding bay, the drunken
vine;
The creeping dirty, courtly ivy join.
And thou! his aide-de-camp, lead on my sons,
Light-armed with points, antitheses, and puns.

238–40. Tate . . . Shadwell: Nahum Tate and Thomas Shadwell were former Poet Laureates. **250–54.** scenes from some of Cibber's tragedies. **258. Thule:** poem by Ambrose Philips. Pope's note is interesting: "It is an unusual method of putting out a fire, to cast wet sheets upon it. Some critics have been of the opinion that this sheet was of the nature of the asbestos, which cannot be consumed by fire: But I rather think it an allegorical allusion to the coldness and heaviness of the writing." **270. Quidnuncs:** (Latin for "what news?"), gossipy members of political clubs. **Guildhall:** the celebrated meeting hall in London.

286. Tibbald: Theobald's name as pronounced; **Ozell:** John Ozell, a translator of French plays, and, like Theobald and Cibber, a ready borrower from the works of others. **290. Heideggre:** John James Heidegger, a Swiss manager of the opera house in the Haymarket and Master of Revels under George II. He was noted for his ugliness. **293–99.** Still another Popean catalogue of bad poets. **295. duns:** bill collectors.

Let Bawdry, Billingsgate, my daughters dear,
Support his front, and oaths bring up the rear:
And under his, and under Archer's wing,
Gaming and Grub Street skulk behind the
king.
"O! when shall rise a monarch all our own,
And I, a nursing-mother, rock the throne;
'Twixt prince and people close the curtain draw,
Shade him from light, and cover him from law;
Fatten the courtier, starve the learned band,
And suckle armies, and dry-nurse the land:
Till senates nod to lullabies divine,
And all be sleep, as at an ode of thine."
She ceased. Then swells the chapel-royal throat:
"God save King Cibber!" mounts in every
note.
Familiar White's, "God save King Colley!" cries;
"God save King Colley!" Drury Lane replies:
To Needham's quick the voice triumphal rode,
But pious Needham dropt the name of God:
Back to the Devil the last echoes roll,
And "Coll!" each butcher roars at Hockley Hole.
So when Jove's block descended from on high
(As sings thy great forefather Ogilby)
Loud thunder to its bottom shook the bog,
And the hoarse nation croaked, "God save
King Log!"

(1743)

307. Billingsgate: the name of one of the gates of London and of the fish market set up there. It was a place where foul language was frequently heard. Foul language thus came to be called Billingsgate. **309. Archer:** Thomas Archer presided over court-gambling. **310.** Pope notes: "When the Statute against Gaming was drawn up, it was represented, that the King, by ancient custom, plays at Hazard one night in the year; and therefore a clause was inserted, with an exception as to that particular. Under this pretence, the groom-porter had a room appropriated to gaming all the summer the Court was at Kensington, which His Majesty accidentally being acquainted of, with a just indignation prohibited. It is reported the same practice is yet continued wherever the Court resides, and the Hazard table there open to all the professed Gamesters in town." **322. Drury Lane:** a seedy section of London in the eighteenth century; a favorite spot for prostitutes. **324. Needham:** Mother Needham, who ran a well-known house of prostitution, hoped to become affluent enough to abandon her work and make her peace with God. She died in the pillory. **325. Devil:** the Devil Tavern where these poems were practiced. **328. Ogilby:** Ogilby was a translator of *Aesop's Fables.* The frogs prayed to Zeus for a king, but he gave them a log.

BOOK THE FOURTH

Argument

The poet being, in this book, to declare the completion of the prophecies mentioned at the end of the former, makes a new invocation; as the greater poets are wont, when some high and worthy matter is to be sung. He shows the goddess coming in her majesty to destroy order and science, and to substitute the kingdom of the dull upon earth. How she leads captive the sciences and silenceth the muses, and what they be who succeed in their stead. All her children, by a wonderful attraction, are drawn about her, and bear along with them divers others, who promote her empire by connivance, weak resistance, or discouragement of arts; such as half-wits, tasteless admirers, vain pretenders, the flatterers of dunces, or the patrons of them. All these crowd round her; one of them offering to approach her is driven back by a rival; but she commends and encourages both. The first who speak in form are the geniuses of the schools, who assure her of their care to advance her cause, by confining youth to words, and keeping them out of the way of real knowledge. Their address, and her gracious answer; with her charge to them and the universities. The universities appear by their proper deputies, and assure her that the same method is observed in the progress of education. The speech of Aristarchus on this subject. They are drawn off by a band of young gentlemen returned from travel with their tutors; one of them delivers to the goddess, in a polite oration, an account of the whole conduct and fruits of their travels: presenting to her at the same time a young nobleman perfectly accomplished. She receives him graciously, and endues him with the happy quality of want of shame. She sees loitering about her a number of indolent persons abandoning all business and duty, and dying with laziness. To these approaches the antiquary Annius, entreating her to make them Virtuosos, and assign them over to him; but Mummius, another antiquary, complaining of his fraudulent proceeding, she finds a method to reconcile their difference. Then enter a troop of people fantastically adorned, offering her strange and exotic presents. Amongst them one stands forth and demands justice on another, who had deprived him of one of the greatest curiosities in nature; but he justifies himself so well that the goddess gives them both her approbation. She recommends to them to find proper employment for the indolents before mentioned, in the study of butterflies, shells, birds' nests, moss, etc., but with particular caution not to proceed beyond trifles, to any useful or extensive views of nature, or of the Author of Nature. Against the last of these apprehensions she is secured by a hearty address from the minute philosophers and freethinkers, one of whom speaks in the name of the rest. The youth, thus instructed and principled, are delivered to her in a body by the hands of Silenus, and then admitted to taste the cup of the Magus, her high priest, which causes a total oblivion of all obligations, divine, civil, moral, or rational. To these her adepts she sends priests, attendants, and comforters of various kinds; confers on them orders and degrees, and then dismissing them with a speech confirming to each his privileges, and telling what she expects from each, concludes with a yawn of extraordinary virtue: the progress and effects whereof on all orders of men, and the consummation of all in the restoration of night and chaos, conclude the poem.

Yet, yet a moment, one dim ray of light
Indulge, dread Chaos, and eternal Night!
Of darkness visible so much be lent,
As half to show, half veil, the deep intent.
Ye pow'rs! whose mysteries restored I sing,
To whom Time bears me on his rapid wing,
Suspend a while your force inertly strong,
Then take at once the poet and the song.
  Now flamed the dog-star's unpropitious ray,
Smote ev'ry brain, and withered ev'ry bay;
Sick was the sun, the owl forsook his bower,
The moon-struck prophet felt the madding hour:
Then rose the seed of Chaos, and of Night,
To blot out order, and extinguish light,
Of dull and venal a new world to mould,
And bring Saturnian days of lead and gold.
  She mounts the throne: her head a cloud
    concealed,
In broad effulgence all below revealed;
('Tis thus aspiring Dulness ever shines)
Soft on her lap her laureate son reclines.
  Beneath her footstool, Science groans in chains,
And Wit dreads exile, penalties, and pains,
There foamed rebellious Logic, gagged and
    bound,
There, stripped, fair Rhet'ric languished on the
    ground;
His blunted arms by Sophistry are borne,
And shameless Billingsgate her robes adorn.
Morality, by her false guardians drawn,
(Chicane in furs, and Casuistry in lawn,)
Gasps, as they straiten at each end the cord,
And dies when Dulness gives her Page the
    word.
Mad Máthesis alone was unconfined,
Too mad for mere material chains to bind,
Now to pure space lifts her ecstatic stare,
Now running round the circle finds it square.
But held in tenfold bonds the Muses lie,
Watched both by Envy's and by Flattery's eye:
There to her heart sad Tragedy addrest
The dagger wont to pierce the tyrant's breast;
But sober History restrained her rage,
And promised vengeance on a barb'rous age.
There sunk Thalia, nerveless, cold, and dead,
Had not her sister Satire held her head;
Nor couldst thou, Chesterfield! a tear refuse,
Thou wep'st, and with thee wept each gentle
    Muse.
  When lo! a harlot form soft sliding by,
With mincing step, small voice, and languid eye:
Foreign her air, her robe's discordant pride
In patch-work flutt'ring, and her head aside:
By singing peers upheld on either hand,
She tipped and laughed, too pretty much to
    stand;
Cast on the prostrate Nine a scornful look,
Then thus in quaint recitativo spoke.
  "O Cara! Cara! silence all that train:
Joy to great Chaos! let division reign:
Chromatic tortures soon shall drive them hence,
Break all their nerves and fritter all their sense:
One trill shall harmonise joy, grief, and rage,
Wake the dull church, and lull the ranting stage;
To the same notes thy sons shall hum, or snore,
And all thy yawning daughters cry, "Encore."
Another Phœbus, thy own Phœbus, reigns,
Joys in my jigs, and dances in my chains.
But soon, ah soon, rebellion will commence,
If music meanly borrows aid from sense.
Strong in new arms, lo! Giant Handel stands,
Like bold Briareus, with a hundred hands;
To stir, to rouse, to shake the soul he comes,
And Jove's own thunders follow Mars's Drums.
Arrest him, empress; or you sleep no more——"

BOOK IV. **30. Page:** quite possibly a pun on the famous "hanging judge," Sir Francis Page. **31. Máthesis:** purely theoretical mathematics. **41. Thalia:** the Muse of Comedy, severely limited by the Licensing Act of 1737 against which Chesterfield fought so strongly. **45. harlot form:** a reference to the growing popularity of opera.

She heard, and drove him to the Hibernian
shore.
And now had Fame's posterior trumpet blown,
And all the nations summoned to the throne.
The young, the old, who feel her inward sway,
One instinct seizes, and transports away.
None need a guide, by sure attraction led,
And strong impulsive gravity of head;
None want a place, for all their centre found,
Hung to the goddess and cohered around.
Not closer, orb in orb, conglobed are seen
The buzzing bees about their dusky queen.
The gath'ring number as it moves along,
Involves a vast involuntary throng,
Who gently drawn, and struggling less and less,
Roll in her vortex, and her power confess.
Not those alone who passive own her laws,
But who, weak rebels, more advance her cause.
Whate'er of dunce in college or in town
Sneers at another in toupee or gown;
Whate'er of mongrel no one class admits,
A wit with dunces, and a dunce with wits.
Nor absent they, no members of her state,
Who pay her homage in her sons, the great;
Who, false to Phœbus, bow the knee to Baal;
Or, impious, preach his word without a call.
Patrons, who sneak from living worth to dead,
Withhold the pension, and set up the head;
Or vest dull flatt'ry in the sacred gown;
Or give from fool to fool the laurel crown.
And (last and worst) with all the cant of wit,
Without the soul, the Muse's hypocrite.
There marched the bard and blockhead, side
by side,
Who rhymed for hire, and patronised for pride.
Narcissus, praised with all a person's power,
Looked a white lily sunk beneath a shower.
There moved Montalto with superior air;
His stretched-out arm displayed a volume fair;
Courtiers and patriots in two ranks divide,
Through both he passed, and bowed from side
to side;
But as in graceful act, with awful eye
Composed he stood, bold Benson thrust
him by:
On two unequal crutches propped he came,
Milton's on this, on that one Johnston's name.
The decent knight retired with sober rage,
Withdrew his hand, and closed the pompous page.
But (happy for him as the times went then)
Appeared Apollo's mayor and aldermen,
On whom three hundred gold-capped youths
await,
To lug the pond'rous volume off in state.
When Dulness, smiling—"Thus revive the wits!
But murder first, and mince them all to bits;
As erst Medea (cruel so to save!)
A new edition of old Æson gave;
Let standard authors, thus, like trophies borne,
Appear more glorious as more hacked and torn.
And you, my critics! in the chequered shade,
Admire new light through holes yourselves have
made.
Leave not a foot or verse, a foot of stone,
A page, a grave, that they can call their own;
But spread, my sons, your glory thin or thick,
On passive paper, or on solid brick.
So by each bard an alderman shall sit,
A heavy lord shall hang at ev'ry wit,
And while on fame's triumphal car they ride,
Some slave of mine be pinioned to their side."
Now crowds on crowds around the goddess
press,
Each eager to present their first address.
Dunce scorning dunce beholds the next advance,
But fop shows fop superior complaisance.
When lo! a spectre rose, whose index-hand
Held forth the virtue of the dreadful wand;
His beavered brow a birchen garland wears,
Dropping with infant's blood, and mother's tears.
O'er every vein a shuddering horror runs;
Eton and Winton shake through all their sons.

93. Baal: a false god, probably of luxury. **103. Narcissus:** Lord Hervey, who had a very pale face. **105. Montalto:** Sir Thomas Hanmer, a pompous man, who brought out an extravagant edition of Shakespeare at his own expense.

110. Benson: a reference to William Benson, who replaced Sir Christopher Wren as Royal Architect because of political ties. He was a great builder of lavish statues and monuments. He also published Arthur Johnston's Latin version of the Psalms. **116.** A reference to officials at Oxford, where Hanmer's edition of Shakespeare was published. **139. spectre:** the ghost of Dr. Busby, celebrated headmaster of Westminster School. The "dreadful wand" is the cane he used to discipline students. Busby's students could be found at Eton and Winton schools.

All flesh is humbled, Westminster's bold race
Shrink, and confess the genius of the place:
The pale boy-senator yet tingling stands,
And holds his breeches close with both his hands.
Then thus: "Since man from beast by words is known,
Words are man's province, words we teach alone.
When reason doubtful, like the Samian letter,
Points him two ways; the narrower is the better.
Placed at the door of learning, youth to guide,
We never suffer it to stand too wide.
To ask, to guess, to know, as they commence,
As fancy opens the quick springs of sense,
We ply the memory, we load the brain,
Bind rebel wit, and double chain on chain;
Confine the thought, to exercise the breath;
And keep them in the pale words till death.
Whate'er the talents, or howe'er designed,
We hang one jingling padlock on the mind:
A poet the first day he dips his quill;
And what the last? A very poet still.
Pity! the charm works only in our wall,
Lost, lost too soon in yonder house or hall.
There truant Wyndham ev'ry muse gave o'er,
There Talbot sunk, and was a wit no more!
How sweet an Ovid, Murray, was our boast!
How many Martials were in Pulteney lost!
Else sure some bard, to our eternal praise,
In twice ten thousand rhyming nights and days,
Had reached the work, the All that mortal can;
And South beheld that masterpiece of man.
"Oh" (cried the goddess) "for some pedant reign!
Some gentle James, to bless the land again;
To stick the doctor's chair into the throne,
Give law to words, or war with words alone,
Senates and courts with Greek and Latin rule,
And turn the council to a grammar school!
For sure, if Dulness sees a grateful day,
'Tis in the shade of arbitrary sway.
O! if my sons may learn one earthly thing,
Teach but that one, sufficient for a king;
That which my priests, and mine alone, maintain,
Which as it dies, or lives, we fall, or reign:
May you, may Cam and Isis, preach it long!
The Right Divine of kings to govern wrong."
Prompt at the call, around the goddess roll
Broad hats, and hoods, and caps, a sable shoal:
Thick and more thick the black blockade extends,
A hundred head of Aristotle's friends.
Nor went thou, Isis! wanting to the day,
[Though Christchurch long kept prudishly away].
Each staunch Polemic, stubborn as a rock.
Each fierce Logician, still expelling Locke;
Came whip and spur, and dashed through thin and thick
On German Crousaz, and Dutch Burgersdyck.
As many quit the streams that murmuring fall
To lull the sons of Margaret and Clare Hall,
Where Bentley late tempestuous wont to sport
In troubled waters, but now sleeps in port.
Before them marched that awful Aristarch;
Ploughed was his front with many a deep remark:
His hat, which never vailed to human pride,
Walker with reverence took and laid aside.
Low bowed the rest: he, kingly, did but nod;
So upright Quakers please both man and God.
"Mistress! dismiss that rabble from your throne:
Avaunt——is Aristarchus yet unknown?

151. Samian letter: the letter used by Pythagoras to symbolize the different roads to Virtue and Vice. **166. house or hall:** Pope's note: "Westminster Hall and the House of Commons." **167. Wyndham:** Sir William Wyndham, great English statesman, firm opponent of Walpole. **168. Talbot:** an outstanding member of Parliament. **169. Murray:** Earl of Mansfield, Chancellor of Great Britain. **170. Pulteney:** a gifted poet who became a political writer and opponent of Walpole. Martial was, of course, the great Roman writer of epigrams. **174.** Pope and Warburton note: "Dr. South declared a perfect epigram as difficult a performance as an epic poem, and the critics say, 'an epic poem is the greatest work human nature is capable of.' " **176. James:** James I, known for his pedantry. It was he who established the Divine Right of Kings.

187. Cam and Isis: Cambridge and Oxford Universities. **196.** In 1703, at a meeting of the heads of Oxford, Locke's *Essay Concerning Human Understanding* was censured, and members of the university were forbidden to read it. **198. Crousaz . . . Burgersdyck:** philosophers. Crousaz wrote a famous attack on the religious and philosophical views of Pope's *Essay on Man*. **200. Margaret and Clare Hall:** St. John's and Clare College in Cambridge. **201. Bentley:** Richard Bentley (1662–1742), the great textual critic had quarrelled with his Fellows while he was Master of Trinity College, Cambridge. **203. Aristarch:** a famous commentator on Homer. Here, the name is given to Bentley. **206. Walker:** John Walker was Vice-Master of Trinity College and Bentley's good friend.

Thy mighty scholiast, whose unwearied pains
Made Horace dull, and humbled Milton's strains.
Turn what they will to verse, their toil is vain,
Critics like me shall make it prose again.
Roman and Greek grammarians! know your
better:
Author of something yet more great than letter;
While towering o'er your alphabet, like Saul,
Stands our Digamma, and o'ertops them all.
'Tis true, on words is still our whole debate,
Disputes of *me* or *te*, of *aut* or *at*,
To sound or sink in *cano*, O or A,
Or give up Cicero to C or K.
Let Freind affect to speak as Terence spoke,
And Alsop never but like Horace joke:
For me, what Virgil, Pliny may deny,
Manilius or Solinus shall supply:
For Attic phrase in Plato let them seek,
I poach in Suidas for unlicensed Greek.
In ancient sense if any needs will deal,
Be sure I give them fragments, not a meal;
What Gellius or Stobæus hashed before,
Or chewed by blind old scholiasts o'er and o'er.
The critic eye, that microscope of wit,
Sees hairs and pores, examines bit by bit:
How parts relate to parts, or they to whole,
The body's harmony, the beaming soul,
Are things which Kuster, Burman, Wasse shall see
When man's whole frame is obvious to a flea.
"Ah, think not, mistress! more true dulness lies
In folly's cap, than wisdom's grave disguise.
Like buoys that never sink into the flood,
On learning's surface we but lie and nod.
Thine is the genuine head of many a house.
And much divinity without a νοῦς.
Nor could a Barrow work on every block,
Nor has one Atterbury spoiled the flock.

218. Digamma: a letter reinstituted by Bentley in his planned edition of Homer. **220–22. Disputes . . . K:** disputes over choice of words, correct pronunciation, in which meaning became less important than pedantic battles. **223–24. Freind . . . Alsop:** Freind and Alsop were scholars who, in Pope's judgment, caught the true spirit of the Ancients. **226. Manilius . . . Solinus:** Manilius and Solinus are minor Latin authors. Bentley is more interested in words than in literary quality. **228–38.** Again, a Popean collection of pedantic critics and scholars. **244. νοῦς:** mind. **245. Barrow:** Isaac Barrow (1630–1677), Master of Trinity College, great preacher, excellent mathematician. **246. Atterbury:** Francis Atterbury (1662–1732), celebrated preacher, classical scholar, political writer.

See! still thy own, the heavy cannon roll,
And metaphysic smokes involve the pole.
For thee we dim the eyes and stuff the head
With all such readings as was never read:
For thee explain a thing till all men doubt it,
And write about it, goddess, and about it:
So spins the silk-worm small its slender store,
And labours till it clouds itself all o'er.
"What though we let some better sort of fool.
Thrid ev'ry science, run through ev'ry school?
Never by tumbler through the hoops was shown
Such skill in passing all, and touching none;
He may indeed (if sober all this time)
Plague with dispute, be persecute with
rhyme.
We only furnish what he cannot use,
Or wed to what he must divorce, a Muse:
Full in the midst of Euclid dip at once,
And petrify a genius to a dunce;
Or set on metaphysic ground to prance
Show all his paces, not a step advance.
With the same cement, ever sure to bind,
We bring to one dead level ev'ry mind.
Then take him to develop, if you can,
And hew the block off, and get out the man.
But wherefore waste I words? I see advance
W——, pupil, and laced governor from
France.
Walker! our hat——nor more he deigned to
say,
But, stern as Ajax's spectre, strode away.
In flowed at once a gay embroidered race,
And tittering pushed the pedants off the place:
Some would have spoken, but the voice was
drowned
By the French horn, or by the opening hound.
The first came forwards, with as easy mien,
As if he saw St. James's and the queen.
When thus th' attendant orator begun,
"Receive, great empress! thy accomplished son:
Thine from the birth, and sacred from the rod,
A dauntless infant! never scared with God.
The sire saw, one by one, his virtues wake:
The mother begged the blessing of a rake.
Thou gavest that ripeness, which so soon began,
And ceased so soon, he ne'er was boy, nor man.

256. Thrid: thread. **270.** The old philosophical idea that there is in every block of stone a potential statue, which the artist discovers. **280. St. James's:** the palace.

Through school and college, thy kind cloud
o'ercast,
Safe and unseen the young Æneas past:
Thence bursting glorious, all at once let down,
Stunned with his giddy larum half the town.
Intrepid then, o'er seas and lands he flew:
Europe he saw, and Europe saw him too.
There all thy gifts and graces we display,
Thou, only thou, directing all our way!
To where the Seine, obsequious as she runs,
Pours at Great Bourbon's feet her silken sons;
Or Tiber, now no longer Roman, rolls,
Vain of Italian arts, Italian souls:
To happy convents, bosomed deep in vines,
Where slumber abbots, purple as their wines:
To isles of fragrance, lily-silvered vales,
Diffusing languor in the panting gales:
To lands of singing, or of dancing slaves,
Love-whisp'ring woods, and lute-resounding
waves.
But chief her shrine where naked Venus keeps,
And Cupids ride the lion of the deeps;
Where, eased of fleets, the Adriatic main
Wafts the smooth eunuch and enamoured
swain.
Led by my hand, he sauntered Europe round,
And gathered ev'ry vice on Christian ground;
Saw ev'ry court, heard ev'ry king declare
His royal sense of operas or the fair;
The stews and palace equally explored,
Intrigued with glory, and with spirit whored:
Tried all *hors-d'œuvres,* all *liqueurs* defined,
Judicious drank, and greatly-daring dined;
Dropped the dull lumber of the Latin store,
Spoiled his own language, and acquired no
more;
All classic learning lost on classic ground;
And last turned air, the echo of a sound!
See now, half-cured, and perfectly well-bred,
With nothing but a solo in his head;
As much estate, and principle, and wit,
As Jansen, Fleetwood, Cibber shall think fit;
Stolen from a duel, followed by a nun,
And, if a borough choose him not, undone;
See, to my country happy I restore
This glorious youth, and add one Venus
more.
Her too receive, (for her my soul adores)
So may the sons of sons of sons of whores
Prop thine, O empress! like each neighbour
throne,
And make a long posterity thy own."
Pleased, she accepts the hero, and the dame
Wraps in her veil, and frees from sense of shame.
Then looked, and saw a lazy, lolling sort,
Unseen at church, at senate, or at court,
Of ever-listless loit'rers, that attend
No cause, no trust, no duty, and no friend.
Thee too, my Paridel! she marked thee there,
Stretched on the rack of a too easy chair,
And heard thy everlasting yawn confess
The pains and penalties of idleness.
She pitied! but her pity only shed
Benigner influence on thy nodding head.
But Annius, crafty seer, with ebon wand,
And well-dissembled em'rald on his hand,
False as his gems, and cankered as his coins,
Came, crammed with capon, from where Pollio
dines.
Soft, as the wily fox is seen to creep,
Where bask on sunny banks the simple sheep,
Walk round and round, now prying here, now
there,
So he; but pious, whispered first his prayer.
"Grant, gracious goddess; grant me still to
cheat,
O may thy cloud still cover the deceit!
Thy choicer mists on this assembly shed,
But pour them thickest on the noble head.
So shall each youth, assisted by our eyes,
See other Cæsars, other Homers rise;
Through twilight ages hunt th' Athenian fowl,

292. larum: alarm, noise. **298.** The Bourbon monarchy in France was associated with loose living. **308. lion of the deeps:** emblem of Venice, seen here as a den of iniquity. **315. stews:** brothels. **326. Jansen, Fleetwood, Cibber:** All three were associated with the theater, with young people. All three were also great gamblers.

327. stolen: escaped. **328.** The reference here is to the fact that Members of Parliament could not be arrested for debt. **341. Paridel:** a wandering courtly squire in the poetry of Edmund Spenser. **347. Annius:** name taken from Annius the Monk of Viterbo, a famous forger of old manuscripts. **350. Pollio:** a prototype of the patron. Pollio was a Roman patron. **361. Athenian fowl:** The owl was stamped on the back of Athenian coins.

Which Chalcis, gods, and mortals call an owl,
Now see an Attys, now a Cecrops clear,
Nay, Mahomet! the pigeon at thine ear;
Be rich in ancient brass, though not in gold,
And keep his lares, though his house be sold;
To headless Phœbe his fair bride postpone,
Honour a Syrian prince above his own;
Lord of an Otho, if I vouch it true;
Blest in one Niger, till he knows of two."
  Mummius o'erheard him; Mummius, fool-renowned,
Who like his Cheops stinks above the ground,
Fierce as a startled adder, swelled, and said,
Rattling an ancient sistrum at his head:
  "Speakest thou of Syrian princes? traitor base!
Mine, goddess! mine is all the hornèd race.
True, he had wit, to make their value rise;
From foolish Greeks to steal them, was as wise;
More glorious yet, from barb'rous hands to keep,
When Sallee rovers chased him on the deep.
Then taught by Hermes, and divinely bold,
Down his own throat he risked the Grecian gold,
Received each demi-god, with pious care,
Deep in his entrails—I revered them there,
I bought them, shrouded in that living shrine,
And, at their second birth, they issue mine."
  "Witness, great Ammon! by whose horns I swore,"
(Replied soft Annius) "this our paunch before
Still bears them, faithful; and that thus I eat,
Is to refund the medals with the meat.
To prove me, goddess! clear of all design,
Bid me with Pollio sup, as well as dine:

362. Chalcis: The city was a trade center of Hellenistic Greece, but was involved in the Macedonian and Syrian wars against Rome. **363. Attys . . . Cecrops:** ancient kings of Athens, probably forged on coins. Mahomet had actually forbidden all images of himself to be inscribed. **366. lares:** statues of household gods. **369–70. Otho . . . Niger:** coins of Roman emperors who ruled for very short periods. Such coins would, of course, be extremely rare. **371. Mummius:** probably the Roman general who burned Corinth and sought out all the valuable antiquities for sale. **372. Cheops:** a king of Egypt, buried alone in his pyramid. **374. sistrum:** a musical instrument. **381. Hermes:** a Greek god with several roles; here, Hermes is seen as a god of thieves. **387. Ammon:** Pope notes: "Jupiter Ammon is called to witness, as the father of Alexander, to whom those kings succeeded, and whose horns they wore on their medals."

There all the learned shall at the labour stand,
And Douglas lend his soft, obstetric hand."
  The goddess smiling seemed to give consent;
So back to Pollio, hand in hand, they went.
  Then thick as locusts black'ning all the ground,
A tribe, with weeds and shells fantastic crowned,
Each with some wondrous gift approached the power,
A nest, a toad, a fungus, or a flower.
But far the foremost, two, with earnest zeal
And aspect ardent to the throne appeal.
  The first thus opened: "Hear thy suppliant's call,
Great queen, and common mother of us all!
Fair from its humble bed I reared this flower,
Suckled, and cheered, with air, and sun, and shower,
Soft on the paper ruff its leaves I spread,
Bright with the gilded button tipped its head;
Then throned in glass, and named it Caroline:
Each maid cried, Charming? and each youth, Divine!
Did Nature's pencil ever blend such rays,
Such varied light in one promiscuous blaze?
Now prostrate! dead! behold that Caroline:
No maid cries, Charming! and no youth, Divine!
And lo, the wretch! whose vile, whose insect lust
Laid this gay daughter of the spring in dust.
Oh, punish him, or to th' Elysian shades
Dismiss my soul, where no carnation fades!"
He ceased, and wept. With innocence of mien,
Th' accused stood forth, and thus addressed the queen:
  "Of all the enamelled race, whose silv'ry wing
Waves to the tepid zephyrs of the spring,
Or swims along the fluid atmosphere,
Once brightest shined this child of heat and air.
I saw, and started from its vernal bow'r,
The rising game, and chased from flow'r to flow'r
It fled, I followed; now in hope, now pain;
It stopt, I stopt; it moved, I moved again.
At last it fixed, 'twas on what plant it pleased,
And where it fixed, the beauteous bird I seized:
Rose or carnation was below my care;
I meddle, goddess! only in my sphere.

394. Douglas: James Douglas (1675–1742), a famous obstetrician and collector of materials related to Horace. **409. Caroline:** the Queen.

I tell the naked fact without disguise,
And, to excuse it, need but show the prize;
Whose spoils this paper offers to your eye,
Fair even in death! this peerless butterfly."
"My sons!" (she answered) "both have done your parts:
Live happy both, and long promote our arts.
But hear a mother, when she recommends
To your fraternal care our sleeping friends.
The common soul, of Heav'n's more frugal make,
Serves but to keep fools pert, and knaves awake:
A drowsy watchman, that just gives a knock,
And breaks our rest, to tell us what's o'clock.
Yet by some object ev'ry brain is stirred;
The dull may waken to a humming bird;
The most recluse, discreetly opened, find
Congenial matter in the cockle-kind;
The mind, in metaphysics at a loss,
May wander in a wilderness of moss;
The head that turns at super-lunar things,
Poised with a tail, may steer on Wilkins' wings.
"O! would the sons of men once think their eyes
And reason giv'n them but to study flies!
See Nature in some partial narrow shape,
And let the Author of the whole escape:
Learn but to trifle, or, who most observe,
To wonder at their Maker, not to serve!"
"Be that my task" (replies a gloomy clerk,
Sworn foe to mystery, yet divinely dark;
Whose pious hope aspires to see the day
When moral evidence shall quite decay,
And damns implicit faith, and holy lies,
Prompt to impose, and fond to dogmatise:)
"Let others creep by timid steps, and slow,
On plain experience lay foundations low,
By common sense to common knowledge bred,
And last, to Nature's cause through Nature led.
All-seeing in thy mists, we want no guide,
Mother of arrogance, and source of pride!
We nobly take the high Priori Road,
And reason downward, till we doubt of God;
Make Nature still encroach upon His plan;
And shove Him off as far as e'er we can:
Thrust some mechanic cause into His place;
Or bind in matter, or diffuse in space.
Or, at one bound o'erleaping all His laws,
Make God man's image, man the final cause,
Find virtue local, all relation scorn,
See all in self, and but for self be born:
Of nought so certain as our reason still,
Of nought so doubtful as of soul and will.
Oh hide the God still more! and make us see
Such as Lucretius drew, a God like thee:
Wrapped up in self, a God without a thought,
Regardless of our merit or default.
Or that bright image to our fancy draw,
Which Theocles in raptured vision saw,
While through poetic scenes the Genius roves,
Or wanders wild in academic groves;
That Nature our society adores,
Where Tindal dictates, and Silenus snores.
Roused at his name, up rose the bousy sire,
And shook from out his pipe the seeds of fire;
Then snapped his box, and stroked his belly down,
Rosy and rev'rend, though without a gown.
Bland and familiar to the throne he came,
Led up the youth, and called the Goddess dame:
Then thus: "From priest-craft happily set free,
Lo! ev'ry finished son returns to thee:
First slave to words, then vassal to a name,
Then dupe to party; child and man the same;
Bounded by Nature, narrowed still by art,
A trifling head, and a contracted heart.

452. Wilkins: John Wilkins, another Enlightenment project-director, who sought to fly to the moon, and who commissioned wings to be made for that purpose. **471. high Priori:** Pope's note is helpful: "Those who, from the effects in this Visible world, deduce the Eternal Power and Godhead of the First Cause, though they cannot attain to an adequate idea of the Deity, yet discover so much of him, as enables them to see the End of their Creation, and the Means of their Happiness: whereas they who take this high Priori road (such as Hobbes, Spinoza, Descartes, and some better Reasoners) for one that goes right, ten lose themselves in Mists, or ramble after Visions, which deprive them of all sight of their End, and mislead them in the choice of wrong means."

484. Lucretius, the great Roman poet, whose philosophical poem *De Rerum Natura* offers a totally rationalistic, materialistic theory of nature. **488. Theocles:** the enthusiastic character in the Third Earl of Shaftesbury's work called *The Moralists*. Theocles saw God in nature and expressed his delight in florid prose. **492. Tindal . . . Silenus:** Tindal, the celebrated Deist and freethinker; Silenus, the gross, drunken companion of the Greek god Dionysius. Silenus here is associated with Thomas Gordon, a political hack who was made Commissioner of Wine Licenses by Walpole. **493. bousy:** boozy. **494. seeds of fire:** the atoms of Epicurus. **495. box:** snuff-box.

Thus bred, thus taught, how many have I seen,
Smiling on all, and smiled on by a queen?
Marked out for honours, honoured for their birth,
To thee the most rebellious things on earth:
Now to thy gentle shadow all are shrunk,
All melted down, in pension, or in punk!
So K* so B** sneaked into the grave,
A monarch's half, and half a harlot's slave.
Poor W** nipped in folly's broadest bloom,
Who praises now? his chaplain on his tomb.
Then take them all, oh take them to thy breast!
Thy Magus, Goddess! shall perform the rest."
  With that, a wizard old his cup extends;
Which whoso tastes, forgets his former friends,
Sire, ancestors, himself. One casts his eyes
Up to a star, and like Endymion dies:
A feather, shooting from another's head,
Extracts his brain; and principle is fled;
Lost is his God, his country, ev'rything;
And nothing left but homage to a king!
The vulgar herd turn off to roll with hogs,
To run with horses, or to hunt with dogs,
But, sad example! never to escape
Their infamy, still keep the human shape.
But she, good Goddess, sent to ev'ry child
Firm impudence, or stupefaction mild;
And straight succeeded, leaving shame no room,
Cibberian forehead, or Cimmerian gloom.
  Kind self-conceit to some her glass applies,
Which no one looks in with another's eyes:
But as the flatt'rer or dependant paint,
Beholds himself a patriot, chief, or saint.
  On others Int'rest her gay liv'ry flings,
Int'rest that waves on party-coloured wings:
Turned to the sun, she casts a thousand dyes,
And, as she turns, the colours fall or rise.
  Others the siren sisters warble round,
And empty heads console with empty sound.
No more, alas! the voice of fame they hear,
The balm of dulness trickling in their ear.
Great C**, H**, P**, R**, K*,
Why all your toils? your sons have learned to sing.
How quick ambition hastes to ridicule!
The sire is made a peer, the son a fool.
  On some, a priest succinct in amice white
Attends; all flesh is nothing in his sight!
Beeves, at his touch, at once to jelly turn,
And the huge boar is shrunk into an urn:
The board with specious miracles he loads,
Turns hares to larks, and pigeons into toads.
Another (for in all what one can shine?)
Explains the *sève* and *verdeur* of the vine.
What cannot copious sacrifice atone?
Thy truffles, Perigord! thy hams, Bayonne!
With French libation, and Italian strain,
Wash Bladen white, and expiate Hays's
    stain.
Knight lifts the head, for what are crowds undone,
To three essential partridges in one?
Gone every blush, and silent all reproach,
Contending princes mount them in their coach.
  Next, bidding all draw near on bended knees,
The queen confers her titles and degrees.
Her children first of more distinguished sort,
Who study Shakespeare at the Inns of Court,
Impale a glow-worm, or vertù profess,
Shine in the dignity of F.R.S.
Some, deep Freemasons, join the silent race
Worthy to fill Pythagoras's place:
Some botanists, or florists at the least,
Or issue members of an annual feast.
Nor past the meanest unregarded, one
Rose a Gregorian, one a Gormogon.
The last, not least in honour or applause,
Isis and Cam made doctors of her laws.

510. punk: a prostitute. **511.** Several editors have speculated that K* is Henry de Grey, Duke of Kent (1671–1740) and B** is James, Third Earl of Berkley (1680–1736), First Lord of the Admiralty under George I. **516. Magus:** a magician. **520. Endymion:** Beloved by Cynthia, the Moon, he was cast into an everlasting sleep and was visited by her each night. **532. Cimmerian:** a reference to the land of darkness in Homer. **545.** Nobles who seek preferment for their families.

549. amice: a priestly vestment worn over the shoulders. **556. *sève and verdeur:*** flavorful and brisk, qualities associated with wine. **558. Perigord . . . Bayonne:** luxurious districts of France. **560–61. Bladen . . . Knight:** Bladen and Hays were two famous gamblers, who lived lavishly in France. Robert Knight was cashier of the ill-fated South Sea Company, who fled to France and lived the good life. **569. vertù:** dilettantism. **570. F.R.S.:** Fellow of the Royal Society, not always a title awarded to the most deserving. **571–72. Freemasons:** The Pope-Warburton note is helpful: Freemasons were part of society "where taciturnity is the *only* essential qualification, as it was the *chief* of the disciples of Protagoras." The brotherhood of Pythagoras was a strongly disciplined ascetic group devoted to the study of mathematical and religious mysteries in Italy during the period 600–450 B.C. **576. Gregorian . . . Gormogon:** anti-Freemason societies.

Then, blessing all, "Go, children of my care!
To practice now from theory repair.
All my commands are easy, short, and full:
My sons! be proud, be selfish, and be dull.
Guard my prerogative, assert my throne:
This nod confirms each privilege your own.
The cap and switch be sacred to his grace;
With staff and pumps the marquis lead the race;
From stage to stage the licensed earl may run,
Paired with his fellow-charioteer, the sun;
The learned baron butterflies design,
Or draw to silk Arachne's subtle line;
The judge to dance his brother sergeant call;
The senator at cricket urge the ball;
The bishop stow (pontific luxury!)
An hundred souls to turkeys in a pie;
The sturdy squire to Gallic masters stoop,
And drown his lands and manors in a soupe.
Others import yet nobler arts from France,
Teach kings to fiddle, and make senates dance.
Perhaps more high some daring son may soar,
Proud to my list to add one monarch more!
And nobly conscious, princes are but things
Born for first ministers, as slaves for kings.
Tyrant supreme! shall three estates command,
And make one mighty Dunciad of the land!"
More she had spoke, but yawned—All Nature nods:
What mortal can resist the yawn of Gods?
Churches and chapels instantly it reached;
(St. James's first, for leaden G— preached)
Then catched the schools; the hall scarce kept awake;
The convocation gaped, but could not speak:
Lost was the nation's sense, nor could be found,
While the long solemn unison went round:
Wide, and more wide, it spread o'er all the realm;
Even Palinurus nodded at the helm:
The vapour mild o'er each committee crept;
Unfinished treaties in each office slept;
And chiefless armies dozed out the campaign;
And navies yawned for orders on the main.
O Muse; relate, (for you can tell alone
Wits have short memories, and dunces none,)
Relate, who first, who last resigned to rest;
Whose heads she partly, whose completely, blest;
What charms could faction, what ambition lull,
The venal quiet, and entrance the dull;
Till drowned was sense, and shame, and right, and wrong—
O sing, and hush the nations with thy song!

. . .

In vain, in vain—the all-composing hour
Resistless falls: the Muse obeys the pow'r.
She comes! she comes! the sable throne behold
Of Night primeval and of Chaos old!
Before her, fancy's gilded clouds decay,
And all its varying rainbows die away.
Wit shoots in vain its momentary fires,
The meteor drops, and in a flash expires.
As one by one, at dread Medea's strain,
The sick'ning stars fade off th' ethereal plain;
As Argus' eyes by Hermes' wand oppress,
Closed one by one to everlasting rest;
Thus at her felt approach, and secret might,
Art after art goes out, and all is night,
See skulking Truth to her old cavern fled,
Mountains of casuistry heaped o'er her head!
Philosophy, that leaned on Heaven before,
Shrinks to her second cause, and is no more.
Physic of metaphysic begs defence,
And metaphysic calls for aid on sense!
See mystery to mathematics fly!
In vain! they gaze, turn giddy, rave, and die.
Religion blushing veils her sacred fires,
And unawares morality expires.
For public flame, nor private, dares to shine,
Nor human spark is left, nor glimpse divine!
Lo! thy dread empire, Chaos! is restored;
Light dies before thy uncreating word;
Thy hand, great Anarch! lets the curtain fall,
And universal darkness buries all.

(1742)

590. The Pope-Warburton note is useful: "This is one of the most ingenious employments assigned, and therefore recommended only to peers of Learning. Of weaving stockings of the webs of spiders, see the *Philosophical Transactions.*" **608. G—:** Dr. John Gilbert, Archbishop of York. He had attacked Dr. King of Oxford, a man respected by Pope. **614. Palinurus:** The pilot of Aeneas' ship in the *Aeneid*. Here the reference to Walpole is clear.

637. Argus: In mythology the creature who had countless eyes so that some would always be open and observant.

Jonathan Swift

1667–1745

"Drown the World, I am not content with despising it, but I would anger it if I could with safety," wrote Jonathan Swift to his friend Alexander Pope on November 26, 1725, and in this and similar statements one perhaps can find a way of coming to terms with that strange, erratic, at times even mad, figure who dominated and angered not only his own age, but who continues to puzzle and frustrate modern readers of his legendary *Gulliver's Travels* and even of lesser works like *A Tale of a Tub, The Battle of the Books,* and *A Modest Proposal.* Edward Rosenheim's statement remains a salutary and constructive one, as he warns readers that it is ". . . a mistake to regard Swift's satire as the eccentric expression of a recluse—just as it is wrong to urge, as some have done, that his sentiments should be viewed as typical of his period. . . . The satirist rarely strives for literary immortality; he carries out his attack in the arena of contemporary opinion. Swift's satire was addressed to an informed, influential, thoroughly human audience of readers, and we are not so different from that audience that we cannot join it." We certainly can, because for many, Swift is the master satirist not simply of English but of world literature, whose artistic sword was directed not simply at the fools and knaves of the Enlightenment but at the perennial vices and follies of mankind in general.

In many ways Swift and his writings would seem to provide a field day for psychoanalytic criticism. His background, family relationships, political disappointments, and love life are filled with possibilities, and indeed such an approach has had and can continue to have its values where it avoids the simplistic and reductionistic dimension that offers a view of Swift as a kind of inspired madman, an artist in spite of himself. The aim of this editor is to keep the text central, while using biography, history, politics, and psychology as aids to further understanding of a great mind and talent.

From the beginning, the life of Swift offers a particular image that is fruitful for speculation. Strange creature indeed, we are tempted quite rightly to say. The image is, to use the currently fashionable but in this case appropriate expression, that of alienation. Swift always seems to have been an outsider looking in, wanting very much to belong to a particular social, political, and literary milieu, and yet never quite becoming a full-fledged part of it. Still, the very denial of admission triggered an imaginative response, the response of an alienated, but now more enlightened man who sees the world and its people more clearly as he, like Lemuel Gulliver and other of his heroes or anti-heroes, moves through it; whose creatures, through their cast of mind and behavior, communicate the roots of the world's ills; who in his anger uses his position as outsider to lash out at the forces that undermine the sweetness and light of the good society. But more critical commentary will follow a little later in this introduction.

Swift was born in Ireland on November 30, 1667, of English parents—Abigaile Erick Swift and, posthumously, Jonathan Swift. His father was one of those Englishmen who found himself in a no-win situation at the time of the Restoration of 1660: his own father was an Anglican who suffered under the Puritans, and his wife's father was a Puritan who knew the wrath of the Anglicans. Swift's family consequently settled in Ireland, with the resulting sense of being expatriates. Ireland, of course, looms large in Swift's life and work, as he alternately pitied and hated the people for their exploitation by the English and yet for their acquiescence in their subservient state.

Born after his father's death, he suffered the further trauma of being carried off to Whitehaven as an infant by a well-meaning but foolish nurse and kept from his mother for three years. When his mother some three years later went to live with her sister at Leicester, the young boy was left as a virtual ward with relatives, especially a niggardly uncle, who barely supported him and certainly contributed to a growing negative feeling toward Ireland and the Irish. After attending the Kilkenny Grammar School until 1681, Swift went to Trinity College, Dublin, proceeded through the formal curriculum with no notable success, and was awarded a degree in February of 1686. He was a young man of keen intellect, but also a proud, arrogant, and sensitive one who proved fitful in his studies and generally unhappy with the college.

The year 1689 proved a momentous one in the young Swift's life. James II, ousted in the Glorious Revolution and succeeded by William and Mary, looked to Catholic Dublin as a stronghold, and, with Trinity College permitting a general evacuation, Swift headed for Leicester and a reunion with his mother, whom he had not seen for many years. As more than one biographer has observed, the pattern of displacement was firmly fixed in Swift's psyche very early, and it was to continue. He left his mother's household in June of 1689 and joined that of Sir William Temple at Moor Park near London. Temple was a politician and literary patron, and even though he was not the warmest of superiors, Swift became his secretary and found the world of writers and other intellectuals congenial. Most important, he seemed to discover what one might call a sense of home; it was here that he met the legendary Esther Johnson, daughter of the housekeeper, a child of eight who touched him deeply and became the Stella of the mysterious relationship that continued for years until her death in 1728 and is chronicled in the strange language of his *Journal to Stella*.

Swift's trip to Ireland to support King William against James II did not bring the favor expected, and he was back in the Temple household shortly, remaining there until May of 1694. In July of 1692 he received the M.A. from Oxford, apparently as a step toward ordination to the ministry; and, much to Temple's displeasure, his restlessness and ambition took him to Dublin in search of still another career. In October of 1694 he was ordained in the Anglican Church in Dublin and served in the unpromising vicarage of Kilroot, near Belfast. The work was disappointing, and his state of mind was even further depressed by his unsuccessful wooing of Jane "Varina" Waring, daughter of the Archdeacon of Dromore. Resigning the post, he returned to Moor Park in May of 1696 and remained there until Temple's death in January 1699. These were the years during which the great minor satires like *Tale of a Tub* and *The Battle of the Books* were written, although they were not published until considerably later. Temple's death was obviously still another blow to Swift's quest for worldly success. With a legacy of a hundred pounds, but with no career to speak of, he headed for Ireland again in 1699, this time as chaplain to Lord Berkeley, who was about to become Chief Justice. While there, he held clerical posts at Laracor and St. Patrick's and received the D.D. degree at Trinity on February 16, 1701.

For all intents and purposes Swift pursued his clerical career in Ireland from 1701 to 1707. He settled Stella and her companion, Mrs. Dingley, in Dublin. *A Tale of a Tub, The Battle of the Books*, and *A Discourse Concerning the Mechanical Operation of the Spirit* were published in 1704 and clearly did little to further his ambitions or gain him an audience. For the better part of 1707 to 1709, he was in England on the famous "first fruits" mission to seek remission of taxes on Irish clerical incomes. During this period he also wrote *The Partridge-Bickerstaff Papers* and the great *Argument Against Abolishing Christianity*. He returned to Laracor in 1709 and remained there until the momentous events of September 10, 1710, of which the *Journal to Stella* is such a marvelous record, brought him back to England, full of promise.

The Whig government fell in 1710, and Swift wholeheartedly threw himself into the Tory cause, which was to prevail until the death of Queen Anne in 1714. He defended staunchly the supremacy of the Church of England, and was editor and a key contributor to the Tory paper *The Examiner* under the conservative Harley-Bolingbroke ministry (his great pamphlet, *The Conduct of the Allies*, contributing strongly to the Treaty of Utrecht, which ended the Whig-supported War of the Spanish Succession). He was also named Dean of St. Patrick's Cathedral in Dublin on June 13, 1713, a good appointment, although he hoped for even better (perhaps St. Paul's in London). The residue of resentment in high places concerning his religious satire was to plague him consistently.

In September of 1713 Swift returned to London, joining with several of the Tory wits and politicians to form the great Scriblerus Club dedicated to the debunking of all cant and pedantry wherever it might be found. *Gulliver's Travels* and Pope's comic *The Art of Sinking in Poetry* are but two of the outstanding literary endeavors inspired by the group. Even though separated from Whigs like Addison and Steele, he was clearly a man of enormous power and influence at this time; but after the death of Anne and the collapse of the Tory government in 1714, he was immediately under suspicion, an undesirable character, and he returned to Ireland to take up permanent residence in September of 1714. He was unquestionably a man broken in spirit, and as one follows the rest of his life story, there is a marked tragic dimension. In addition to political alienation, there was the conflict of his strange and continuing love for Stella and the added pursuit of him by Esther van Homrigh (the celebrated Vanessa), whom he rejected, and then the death of both women. These were the years of Swift, the Irish champion, the years in which *Gulliver's Travels* was probably begun. In 1720 the *Proposal for the Universal Use of Irish Manufacture* appeared, and 1724 and 1725 saw the publication of the *Drapier's Letters,* documents defending Irish political and economic interests and arguing specifically against Wood's scandalous copper coinage, which was still another device for economic exploitation of the Irish. There were brief trips to England in 1726 and 1727 to visit, among others, his kindred spirit, Alexander Pope, and then the great flurry of publication: *Gulliver's Travels* on October 28, 1726; *A Modest Proposal* in October of 1729; and the continuing *Miscellanies* (1727–1736), produced by him and Pope.

The 1730s were wretched years. Great poems like *Verses on the Death of Dr. Swift, D.S.P.D.,* appeared; but the loneliness occasioned by Stella's death, his political isolation, his declining physical and mental conditions took their toll. He was declared of unsound mind in 1742, and guardians were officially appointed by Chancery to care for his affairs. He died on October 19, 1745, and was buried next to his Stella in St. Patrick's with the celebrated epitaph, "Savage indignation can no longer tear the heart."

Although Swift did write poetry of considerable quality and interest, and produced the fascinatingly autobiographical *Journal to Stella,* it is primarily as a satirist that he commands our attention and criticism. Like his close friend and fellow Scriblerian, Pope, he committed himself to the unmasking of hypocrisy and pretension, the exposure of injustice, and the mockery of pedantry and shallowness in learning. As the words "Savage indignation" from his epitaph suggest, however, his was an angrier, more Juvenalian satire—one that, while it addresses specific causes like the plight of the Irish poor, the state of the established church, the direction of contemporary criticism and learning, seems to have a certain cosmic quality not always present in Pope. And yet angry though his work can be, he is not always the complete misanthropist, the mad, didactic preacher haranguing the world. His keen and comic sense of the ridiculous, of the vital difference between appearance and reality; his mastery of the fine art of irony, of developing a number of masks that reveal the object of his wrath while keeping himself as artist quite detached; his rare gift of manipulating the small and the large, the ugly and the dignified in such a way that the mind of the reader is constantly kept active and at times even delighted—these and many other techniques, as John Bullitt has so well demonstrated, become marvelous strategies for using the comic to at least soften and make more effective the gloom of the essential vision. Swift skillfully uses the pleasant, bland, complacent storyteller who, in the midst of a seemingly innocent tale, shocks us into the realization of something deeper about human activities, of something that cries out for our attention and meditation. His double vision, so to speak, is a key to his art.

Swift's masterpiece *Gulliver's Travels,* while delightful in its introduction of the little folk as a basis for portraying English politics in Lilliput and in its uproarious sketches of activities at the Academy of Lagado as a way of ridiculing the Royal Society, brings its initially placid, docile hero through an increasingly tragic journey. The travels culminate in his apocalyptic visit to the land of the Houyhnhnms*, where human beings have become ugly brutes ruled by a race of gentle, rational horses, a land where the vision becomes so bleak that Gulliver seems to go out of his mind, happy only with the bloodless perfection of the animals and revolted by even his own family after his return to England. While all of his personal and professional frustrations must have fueled much of his anger, what is more striking in the satire is his keen sense of the human arena and its creatures, of the power of mind these creatures possess to see clearly and act accordingly. No "Whatever is, is right" advocate, he is haunted by the worm within mankind, the original sin that has left us wounded, the clouding of the brightness of the mind that keeps us satisfied with the superficial and makes us neglect the essential. This sense of the worm within underlies Swift's hatred of injustice, tyranny, abstract rationalizing, and deceit of all kinds; it takes him at times beyond the border, even beyond the hope of mankind's redemption and reform.

Swift's letters are a remarkable source of his states of mind. Returning to Dublin, he writes to Pope on September 29, 1725, describing his work on *Gulliver's Travels* and associating the book with the general purpose of all his work, ". . . to vex the world rather than divert it"; then he launches into the famous homily that reveals the nuances of his feelings so well:

> I have ever hated all nations, professions, and communities, and all my love is toward individuals: for instance, I hate the tribe of lawyers, but I love Counsellor Such-a-one, and Judge Such-a-one: so with physicians —I will not speak of my own trade—soldiers, English, Scotch, French, and the rest. But principally I hate and detest that animal called man, although I heartily love John, Peter, Thomas, and so forth. This is the system upon which I have governed myself many years, but do not tell, and so I shall go on till I have done with them. I have got materials toward a treatise, proving the falsity of that definition *animal rationale,* and to show it would be only *rationis capax.* Upon this great foundation of misanthropy, though not in Timon's manner, the whole building of my Travels is erected; and I never will have peace of mind till all honest men are of my opinion.

---

* **Houyhnhnms:** pronounced "whimms" or "whinhims"—a name coined by Swift in imitation of the whinny of a horse.

Here is a key distinction for Swift: *rationis capax*—"capable of reason"; not *animal rationale*—a "rational animal." Man has sold out his birthright, but is not totally damned; he is capable of reason and hence of reform. The great digression on madness in *A Tale of a Tub* is a chilling analysis not just of politicians or clergymen or writers, but of mankind in general. Madness is, to use Swift's favorite words, zeal or enthusiasm; it is a vapor of the brain, ". . . the Parent of all those mighty Revolutions, that have happened in *Empire*, in Philosophy, and in Religion." How clear its roots are: "But when a Man's Fancy gets *astride* on his Reason, when Imagination is at Cuffs with the Senses, and common Understanding, as well as common Sense, is Kickt out of Doors; the first Proselyte he makes, is Himself, and when that is once compass'd, the Difficulty is not so great in bringing over others. . . . For, if we take an Examination of what is generally understood by *Happiness*, as it has Respect, either to the Understanding or the Senses, we shall find all its Properties and Adjuncts will herd under this short Definition: That, *it is a perpetual possession of being well Deceived*."

Again, how graphic is his continuing analysis of human satisfaction with the external, with clothes rather than the person within, and his citation of recent experiments: "Last Week I saw a Woman *flay'd*, and you will hardly believe, how much it altered her Person for the worse. Yesterday I ordered the carcass of a *Beau* to be stript in my Presence; when we were all amazed to find so many unsuspected Faults under one Suit of Cloaths: Then I laid open his *Brain*, his *Heart*, and his *Spleen*; But, I plainly perceived at every Operation, that the farther we proceeded, we found the Defects encrease upon us in Number and Bulk."

No mere satirist, then, of particular human vices and follies, Swift the surgeon cuts to the core of the human heart for his analysis and finds a disease to be cured, a reason to be recrowned, a goodness to be restored. Hence his ultimate purpose, like Pope's, is moral in the broadest sense—the preservation through right reason of those standards that contribute to humaneness. Right reason proclaims that human beings should worship God with honesty and love, that they should take the Word given them, preserve it, and live by it. Yet, as the wonderful allegory of *A Tale of a Tub* unfolds, Peter, Jack, and Martin take the tradition, the coats bequeathed them by their father, and go off to the city to lead the good life. Adorning his coat with every fancy frill, Peter, the Roman Catholic, assumes the authoritarian role of the oldest brother and causes family friction over the interpretation of the father's will until at length: "In the midst of all this Clutter and Revolution, in comes Peter with a File of Dragoons at his Heels, and gathering from all hands what was in the Wind, He and his Gang, after several Millions of Scurrilities and Curses, not very important here to repeat, by main Force, fairly kicks them both out of Doors, and would never let them come under his Roof from that Day to this." As much as Swift ridicules Peter and the entire Roman Catholic emphasis on rites, vestments, rituals, hierarchy, and the like, he seems more good-natured than when he takes on brother Jack, the Calvinist, the radical Protestant, the Aeolist whose zeal and anti-intellectual enthusiasm is translated into ugly images of wind and belching. Jack and his fellow Aeolists are the real perverters of the father's will, as they begin a new and more dangerous rupture after living for a time under the subjection of Peter. Like the true Anglican, Martin (clearly Swift's favorite) more cautiously removes all those frivolous adornments that do not seriously damage the father's coat: "Resolving therefore to rid his Coat of a huge Quantity of *Gold Lace;* he pickt up the Stitches with much Caution, and gleaned out all the loose Threads as he went, which proved to be a Work of Time." He proceeds carefully with the restoration of the coat, "... resolving in No case whatsoever, that the substance of the Stuff should suffer Injury; which he thought the best Method for serving the true intent and meaning of his Father's Will." Brimful of wild fervor, Jack, "... being Clumsy by Nature, and of Temper, Impatient; withal, beholding Millions of Stitches, that required the nicest Hand, and sedatest Constitution, to extricate, in a great Rage, he tore off the whole Piece, Cloth and all, and flung it into the Kennel, and furiously thus continuing his Career; *Ah, Good Brother* Martin, said he, *do as I do, for the Love of God; Strip, Tear, Pull, Rent, Flay off all, that we may appear as unlike the Rogue* Peter, *as it is possible.*" Hence Jack (John Calvin) leads the Aeolists who "... maintain the Original Cause of all things to be *Wind,*" and who argue "... the Gift of BELCHING, to be the noblest act of a rational creature," and at "... certain Seasons of the Year, you might behold the Priests amongst them in vast Numbers, with their *Mouths gaping wide against a Storm.*"

An Argument Against Abolishing Christianity, a briefer but in many ways more artistically subtle treatment of the current state of Christianity, relies on the ironic mask technique as the speaker becomes the very mentality being satirized—the nominal Christian who, when confronted with the prospect of abolishing Christianity, can offer only the most pragmatic and materialistic arguments for keeping it. Why not preserve what we have, he argues. It will provide the smart young wits of the town with objects of scorn and keep the heat from the politicians. It will not rob the community of one day a week because the day is already being nicely used for everything from business to gossip. It cannot possibly unify the factions of Protestantism. The clear fact of the matter is that it does not oblige people to believe in anything at all: "I hope no Reader imagines me so weak to stand up in Defence of real Christianity, such as used in primitive Times (if we may believe the Authors of those Ages) to have an Influence upon Men's Belief and Actions; To offer at the restoring of that, would indeed be a wild Project, it would be to dig up Foundations; to destroy at one Blow all the Wit, and half the Learning of the Kingdom; to break the entire frame and Constitution of Things." Indeed, our wide-eyed speaker knows that all his serious Readers "... will easily understand my Discourse to be intended only in Defense of nominal Christianity, the other having been for some time wholly laid aside by General Consent, as utterly inconsistent with all our present Schemes of Wealth and Power."

The misapplication of intelligence and learning, the foolishness of pedantic scholarship and education similarly occupy his attention, and again Enlightenment is the key metaphor. The mind has its uses; learning should lift the darkness of ignorance; the great tradition should free, not intimidate; modern writers should value the achievements of the past and avoid the faddish. The digressions, dedications, and prefaces of *A Tale of a Tub* are delightful takeoffs on the abuses of scholarly writing. *The Battle of the Books,* ostensibly a straightforward satire defending Sir William Temple's *Essay Upon Ancient and Modern Learning* against the attacks of the scholars William Wotton and Richard Bentley, becomes in the hands of Swift a lively mock-heroic, *A Full and True Account of the Battle Fought last Friday, Between the Ancient and the Modern Books in St. James's Library.* Temple had taken the side of the Ancients in the great debate, but unfortunately had used spurious documents to defend his position against the modern gospel of progress. Wotton and Bentley, great textual critics, had quite rightly criticized the use of such documents, but Swift is much more interested in dealing with the profound question of the humanist and the pedant, polite learning and scholarship. The great question posed in the fable of the spider and the bee is a central point in the document: "*Whether is the nobler Being of the two, That which by a lazy Contemplation of four inches round; by an over-weening Pride, which feeding and engendering on itself, turns all into excrement and venom; producing nothing at all, but Fly-bane and a Cobweb: Or That, which, by an universal Range, with long Search, much Study, true Judgment, and Distinction of Things, brings home Honey and Wax.*"

As has already been suggested in this introduction, Swift's greatest political satire was produced during Queen Anne's reign for *The Examiner,* and, more impressively, during the 1720s when he was a fighter for the Irish against the injustice and inhumanity under which they were living, sometimes much too quietly. In *The Drapier's Letters* he is M.B., a linen drapier, arguing against the cheap coinage of William Wood. In his masterpiece of irony, the still vital *A Modest Proposal,* he is the social engineer of the Enlightenment, the mild-mannered, reasonable, scheme-oriented consultant offering the best theoretical plan for making the Irish less a burden to the English. The modest proposal is cannibalism, which would effectively reduce the population of Ireland and provide rare culinary delicacies and fine boots and gloves, thereby verifying the thesis that the people are the real wealth of the country. With hardly a touch of real Swiftian anger breaking through the sustained web of irony, a calm, satisfied, patriotic speaker, reminiscent of so many contemporaries who advanced clever welfare plans, outlines the scheme to use year-old infants for food and other needs, hoping that the plan "... will not be liable to the least Objection," and assuring the reader "... that I have not the least personal Interest, in endeavoring to promote this necessary Work, having no other Motive than the *publick Good of my Country, by advancing our trade, providing for Infants, relieving the Poor, and giving some Pleasure to the Rich.* I have no Children by which I can propose to get a single Penny, the youngest being nine Years Old and my wife past Child-Bearing."

Gulliver's Travels might very well be described as Swift's essay on mankind. Unlike Pope, he is, however, more disillusioned with man's achievement and situation. He launches his calm, docile, pliable hero on his journey, first to Lilliput, a land of little people where he is a giant, a land which apparently reminds him of happier days in Queen Anne's court. The antics of the rope dancers, the leaping and creeping of ministers to secure the Emperor's favor, the contrast of High Heels (Tories) and Low Heels (Whigs), of Big-Endians (Roman Catholics) and Little Endians (Protestants) amuse him. Yet the intensity of the narrative heightens as he is captured, impeached, and exiled because of his refusal, after singlehandedly defeating an invasion of the Blefuscudians, to level the enemy completely. A more sober Gulliver records the imperialistic request of his captors:

> His Majesty desired I would take some other opportunity of bringing all the rest of his enemy's ships into his ports. And so unmeasurable is the ambition of princes, that he seemed to think of nothing less than reducing the whole empire of Blefuscu into a province, and governing it by a viceroy; of destroying the Big-Endian exiles, and compelling that people to break the smaller end of their eggs, by which he would remain the sole monarch of the whole world. But I endeavoured to divert him from this design, by many arguments drawn from the topics of policy as well as justice; and I plainly protested, that I would never be an instrument of bringing a free and brave people into slavery. And when the matter was debated, the wisest part of the ministry were of my opinion.

Things are never the same in Lilliput, and it is only a matter of time before his life is in danger and he is on a new journey with those memorable words ringing in our ears: "Of so little weight are the greatest services to princes, when put into the balance with a refusal to gratify their passions."

From Lilliput our hero moves to Brobdingnag, where the scale is reversed most effectively, where Gulliver is now the pigmy among giants who, although physically repulsive, are much more humane. Their moral values are deeper; their farmers are industrious and reliable; their education and government are rooted in great concern for wisdom and justice; the affection of the nurse Glumdalclitch for Gulliver is genuine. At first Gulliver, so accustomed to the agile, bright, but petty and superficial Lilliputians, cannot find his bearings and is puzzled, especially by the noble and virtuous King "... who lives wholly secluded from the rest of the world, and must therefore be altogether unacquainted with the manners and customs that prevail in other nations: the want of which knowledge will ever produce many *prejudices,* and a certain *narrowness of thinking;* from which we and the politer countries of Europe are wholly exempted. And it would be hard indeed, if so remote a prince's notions of virtue and vice were to be offered as a standard for all mankind." Yet Gulliver widens his awareness a bit, learning however slowly to value the King and, as Swift's ingenious relative scale does its work, to recognize that true values are independent of size. All of his boasting about his beloved England and his outrageous proposal to share the secret powers of gunpowder are wonderfully debunked in that grotesque but potent image of Gulliver as dwarf standing in the palm of the King's hand and in the King's bemused reactions and final angry summary, praising Gulliver but adding that "... by what I have gathered from your own relation, and the answers I have with much pains wringed and extorted from you, I cannot but conclude the bulk of your natives to be the most pernicious race of little odious vermin that nature ever suffered to crawl upon the surface of the earth."

After the departure from Brobdingnag Gulliver continues to enlarge his experience and goes on the strange journey to Laputa, Balnibarbi, Luggnag, Glubbdubdrib, and Japan, recorded in a bulky, uneven, digressive third book that is nevertheless fascinating. Here the spirit of the Scriblerus Club, of Pope's *The Dunciad,* is everywhere in evidence, as the traveler beholds a wonderful assortment of quackery, project-making, and dilettantism. On the flying island of Laputa, he sees absent-minded and totally impractical mathematicians, who "... are so taken up with intense speculations, that they neither can speak, nor attend to the discourses of others, without being roused by some external taction upon the organs of speech and hearing; for which reason those persons who are able to afford it always keep a flapper (the original is *climenole*) in their family, as one of their domestics, nor ever walk abroad or make visits without him." In Balnibarbi, while the city is virtually in ruins for want of practical activity, the eerily modern Academy of Lagado proceeds merrily with its schemes and projects, one of them the extraction and sealing of sunbeams from cucumbers for later use in warming the raw, damp summers. In Glubbdubdrib, the spirits of Homer and Aristotle arise to denounce the stupidity of their commentators, and the recent dead return to unfold the lies and hypocrisy of history. Perhaps the most moving visit is that to the immortal Struldbrugs of Luggnag, with its somber meditation on the folly of seeking eternal life and on the ugliness and sorrow of prolonged existence and old age.

The fourth and final voyage to the land of the Houyhnhnms is, as earlier noted, the most terrifying and puzzling one, as Swift returns in a more macabre way to the technique of diminution employed in the first two books. Now man has become Yahoo, a repulsive animal in a land of rational but utterly unimaginative horses. Gulliver, increasingly unsettled and seemingly more and more like his creator, is captivated by these remarkable horses with their goodness and sense of order, and repelled by the Yahoos. Although regarded as a high-grade Yahoo, he must, of course, leave Houyhnhnm-land, and, although edified by their example and impressed by the goodness of the Portuguese sea captain on his journey home, he returns at least half-mad, horrified by the spectacle of human beings, unable even to eat with his own family. In J. Middleton Murry's words, the Yahoos "... make visible the judgment of the King of Brobdingnag on the human race; but the judgment is now passed with an added intensity of moral aversion." W. A. Eddy's summation, "Man that is born in sin is born a Yahoo, and, unless he be born again, will live and die a Yahoo," brings a note of religious tragedy to this powerful conclusion of Swift's greatest masterpiece.

The career of Jonathan Swift is one for any student of literature to ponder. His work is a ringing reminder of essential humanity and of how far that humanity has fallen short of its rich possibilities. Although Swift is often, and perhaps justifiably, seen as the complete misanthrope, there is for many readers a note of hope in his work, a sense that he laughs and sneers to avoid crying, that he must purge the world so that it can be made whole again. Interestingly enough, he once wrote that he would burn *Gulliver's Travels* if he could find a dozen men of the caliber of John Arbuthnot. In spite of so much satire of the Enlightenment and especially its aberrations, he is, however, very much of his age in his devotion to common sense, his distrust of vain speculation, his social, political, and religious conservatism, his pronounced didactic tendencies. To be sure, he is the pessimist, angry with the pride and evil of men, but always the artist eager to show us, sometimes comically, sometimes frighteningly, the image of ourselves. Perhaps we can take to heart the striking lines he would have his reader speak in his superb *Verses on the Death of Dr. Swift, D.S.P.D.*

"Perhaps I may allow, the Dean
Had too much Satyr in his Vein;
And seem'd determin'd not to starve it,
Because no Age could more deserve it.
Yet, Malice never was his Aim;
He lash'd the Vice but spar'd the Name.
No Individual could resent
Where thousands equally were meant.
His Satyr points at no Defect,
But what all Mortals may correct."

Suggestions for Further Reading

Sir Henry Craik's *Life of Jonathan Swift* (1882), Leslie Stephens' *Swift* (1882), and J. Middleton Murry's *Jonathan Swift, a Critical Biography* (1954) are good biographies of Swift, although we now have two volumes (1962–1968) of a projected three, which will surely be the definitive biography — Irvin Ehrenpreis' *Swift: The Man, His Works, and the Age.* Ehrenpreis' *The Personality of Jonathan Swift* (1958) is also extremely helpful.

Recommended for further study of Swift's themes and techniques are: W. A. Eddy, *Gulliver's Travels: A Critical Study* (1923); Ricardo Quintana, *The Mind and Art of Jonathan Swift* (1936) and *Swift: An Introduction* (1955); Herbert Davis, *The Satire of Jonathan Swift* (1947); Maurice Johnson, *The Sin of Wit: Jonathan Swift as a Poet* (1950); John Bullitt, *Jonathan Swift and the Anatomy of Satire* (1953); Martin Price, *Swift's Rhetorical Art* (1953) and *To the Palace of Wisdom* (1964); Louis A. Landa, *Swift and the Church of Ireland* (1954); Kathleen Williams, *Jonathan Swift and the Age of Compromise* (1958); Edward W. Rosenheim, *Swift and the Satirist's Art* (1963); and Denis Donoghue, *Jonathan Swift: A Critical Introduction* (1969).

FROM

A Tale of a Tub

SECTION II

Once upon a time, there was a man who had three sons by one wife,[a] and all at a birth, neither could the midwife tell certainly which was the eldest. Their father died while they were young, and upon his deathbed, calling the lads to him, spoke thus:

"Sons, because I have purchased no estate, nor was born to any, I have long considered of some good legacies to bequeath you; and at last, with much care as well as expense, have provided each of you (here they are) a new coat.[b] Now, you are to understand, that these coats have two virtues contained in them: one is, that with good wearing,

[a] By these three sons, Peter, Martin, and Jack, Popery, the Church of England, and our Protestant dissenters are designed. W. Wotton.

[b] By his coats which he gave his sons, the garments of the Israelites. W. Wotton.

An error (with submission) of the learned commentator; for by the coats are meant the doctrine and faith of

[Throughout this section the lettered footnotes and the various marginal notes are Swift's own. The editor of this anthology has numbered his own footnotes consecutively in each of Swift's satires. Footnotes for the poetry are handled in the same manner employed in documenting other poetry.]

they will last you fresh and sound as long as you live; the other is, that they will grow in the same proportion with your bodies, lengthening and widening of themselves, so as to be always fit. Here, let me see them on you before I die. So, very well; pray children, wear them clean, and brush them often. You will find in my will [c] (here it is) full instructions in every particular concerning the wearing and management of your coats; wherein you must be very exact, to avoid the penalties I have appointed for every transgression or neglect, upon which your future fortunes will entirely depend. I have also commanded in my will, that you should live together in one house like brethren and friends, for then you will be sure to thrive, and not otherwise."

Here the story says, this good father died, and the three sons went all together to seek their fortunes.

I shall not trouble you with recounting what adventures they met for the first seven years, any farther than by taking notice, that they carefully observed their father's will, and kept their coats in very good order; that they travelled through several countries, encountered a reasonable quantity of giants, and slew certain dragons.

Being now arrived at the proper age for producing themselves, they came up to town, and fell in love with the ladies, but especially three, who about that time were in chief reputation: the Duchess d'Argent, Madame de Grands Titres, and the Countess d'Orgueil.[d] On their first appearance, our three adventurers met with a very bad reception; and soon with great sagacity guessing out the reason, they quickly began to improve in the good qualities of the town: they writ, and rallied, and rhymed, and sung, and said, and said nothing: they drank, and fought, and whored, and slept, and swore, and took snuff: they went to new plays on the first night, haunted the chocolate-houses, beat the watch, lay on bulks, and got claps: they bilked hackney-coachmen, ran in debt with shopkeepers, and lay with their wives: they killed bailiffs, kicked fiddlers down stairs, ate at Locket's, loitered at Will's: they talked of the drawing-room, and never came there: dined with lords they never saw: whispered a duchess, and spoke never a word: exposed the scrawls of their laundress for billet-doux of quality: came ever just from court, and were never seen in it: attended the Levee *sub dio:*[2] got a list of peers by heart in one company, and with great familiarity retailed them in another. Above all, they constantly attended those Committees of Senators who are silent in the House, and loud in the coffee-house, where they nightly adjourn to chew the cud of politics, and are encompassed with a ring of disciples, who lie in wait to catch up their droppings. The three brothers had acquired forty other qualifications of the like stamp, too tedious to recount, and by consequence were justly reckoned the most accomplished persons in the town. But all would not suffice, and the ladies aforesaid continued still inflexible. To clear up which difficulty I must, with the reader's good leave and patience, have recourse to some points of weight, which the authors of that age have not sufficiently illustrated.

For about this time it happened a sect arose,[e] whose tenets obtained and spread very far, especially in the *grand monde*, and among everybody of good fashion. They worshipped a sort of idol,[f] who, as their doctrine delivered, did daily create men by a kind of manufactory operation. This idol they placed in the highest parts of the house, on an altar erected about three foot: he was shown in

Christianity, by the wisdom of the Divine Founder fitted to all times, places and circumstances. LAMBIN.[1]

[c] The New Testament.

[d] Their mistresses are the Duchess d'Argent, Mademoiselle de Grands Titres, and the Countess d'Orgueil, i.e., covetousness, ambition, and pride, which were the three great vices that the ancient Fathers inveighed against as the first corruptions of Christianity. W. WOTTON.

[e] This is an occasional satire upon dress and fashion, in order to introduce what follows.

[f] By this idol is meant a tailor.

A TALE OF A TUB. SECTION II. **1.** Swift is having great fun with the pretentiousness of critical commentary. Francis Lambin was a prominent French scholar of the sixteenth century who, despite his death long before *A Tale of a Tub* was written, is seen here as taking issue with Wotton, one of Swift's favorite targets.

2. Levee *sub dio:* an afternoon party outdoors.

the posture of a Persian emperor, sitting on a superficies,[3] with his legs interwoven under him. This god had a goose[4] for his ensign; whence it is, that some learned men pretend to deduce his original from Jupiter Capitolinus.[5] At his left hand, beneath the altar, Hell seemed to open, and catch at the animals the idol was creating; to prevent which, certain of his priests hourly flung in pieces of the uninformed mass, or substance, and sometimes whole limbs already enlivened, which that horrid gulf insatiably swallowed, terrible to behold. The goose was also held a subaltern divinity or *deus minorum gentium,* before whose shrine was sacrificed that creature, whose hourly food is human gore, and who is in so great renown abroad, for being the delight and favourite of the Ægyptian Cercopithecus.[g] Millions of these animals were cruelly slaughtered every day, to appease the hunger of that consuming deity. The chief idol was also worshipped as the inventor of the yard and the needle; whether as the god of seamen, or on account of certain other mystical attributes, hath not been sufficiently cleared.

The worshippers of this deity had also a system of their belief, which seemed to turn upon the following fundamental. They held the universe to be a large suit of clothes, which invests everything: that the earth is invested by the air; the air is invested by the stars; and the stars are invested by the *primum mobile.* Look on this globe of earth, you will find it to be a very complete and fashionable dress. What is that which some call land, but a fine coat faced with green? or the sea, but a waistcoat of water-tabby? [6] Proceed to the particular works of the creation, you will find how curious Journeyman Nature hath been, to trim up the vegetable beaux; observe how sparkish a periwig adorns the head of a beech, and what a fine doublet of white satin is worn by the birch. To conclude from all, what is man himself but a microcoat,[h] or rather a complete suit of clothes with all its trimmings? As to his body, there can be no dispute; but examine even the acquirements of his mind, you will find them all contribute in their order towards furnishing out an exact dress. To instance no more: is not religion a cloak; honesty a pair of shoes worn out in the dirt; self-love a surtout; vanity a shirt; and conscience a pair of breeches, which, though a cover for lewdness as well as nastiness, is easily slipt down for the service of both?

These *postulata* being admitted, it will follow in due course of reasoning, that those beings which the world calls improperly suits of clothes, are in reality the most refined species of animals, or to proceed higher, that they are rational creatures, or men. For is it not manifest that they live, and move, and talk, and perform all other offices of human life? Are not beauty, and wit, and mien, and breeding, their inseparable properties? In short, we see nothing but them, hear nothing but them. Is it not they who walk the streets, fill up parliament-, coffee-, play-, bawdy-houses? 'Tis true indeed, that these animals, which are vulgarly called suits of clothes, or dresses, do according to certain compositions receive different appellations. If one of them be trimmed up with a gold chain, and a red gown, and a white rod, and a great horse, it is called a Lord-Mayor; if certain ermines and furs be placed in a certain position, we style them a Judge; and so an apt conjunction of lawn and black satin we entitle a Bishop.

Others of these professors, though agreeing in the main system, were yet more refined upon certain branches of it; and held that man was an animal compounded of two dresses, the natural and the celestial suit, which were the body and the soul: that the soul was the outward, and the body the inward clothing; that the latter was *ex traduce,*[7] but the former of daily creation and circumfusion. This last they proved by scripture, because in them we live, and move, and have our being; as likewise by philosophy, because they are all in all, and all in every part. Besides, said they, separate these

[g] The Ægyptians worshipped a monkey, which animal is very fond of eating lice, styled here creatures that feed on human gore.

[h] Alluding to the word microcosm, or a little world, as man hath been called by philosophers.

3. **superficies:** surface. 4. **goose:** a tailor's handiron. 5. The great god Jupiter had his hill saved from the attack of the Gauls by the sounds of geese, which awakened the soldiers. 6. **water-tabby:** a silk fabric.

7. ***ex traduce:*** inherited.

two, and you will find the body to be only a senseless unsavoury carcass. By all which it is manifest, that the outward dress must needs be the soul.

To this system of religion were tagged several subaltern doctrines, which were entertained with great vogue: as particularly, the faculties of the mind were deduced by the learned among them in this manner: embroidery was sheer wit; gold fringe was agreeable conversation; gold lace was repartee; a huge long periwig was humor; and a coat full of powder was very good raillery: all which required abundance of *finesse* and *delicatesse* to manage with advantage, as well as a strict observance after times and fashions.

I have with much pains and reading, collected out of ancient authors, this short summary of a body of philosophy and divinity, which seems to have been composed by a vein and race of thinking, very different from any other systems, either ancient or modern. And it was not merely to entertain or satisfy the reader's curiosity, but rather to give him light into several circumstances of the following story, that knowing the state of dispositions and opinions in an age so remote, he may better comprehend those great events which were the issue of them. I advise therefore the courteous reader to peruse with a world of application, again and again, whatever I have written upon this matter. And so leaving these broken ends, I carefully gather up the chief thread of my story and proceed.[i]

These opinions therefore were so universal, as well as the practices of them, among the refined part of court and town, that our three brother-adventurers, as their circumstances then stood, were strangely at a loss. For, on the one side, the three ladies they addressed themselves to (whom we have named already) were ever at the very top of the fashion, and abhorred all that were below it but the breadth of a hair. On the other side, their father's will was very precise, and it was the main precept in it, with the greatest penalties annexed, not to add to, or diminish from their coats one thread, without a positive command in the will. Now, the coats their father had left them were, 'tis true, of very good cloth, and besides, so neatly sewn, you would swear they were all of a piece; but at the same time very plain, and with little or no ornament; and it happened, that before they were a month in town, great shoulder-knots[j] came up; straight all the world was shoulder-knots; no approaching the ladies' *ruelles*[8] without the *quota* of shoulder-knots. That fellow, cries one, has no soul; where is his shoulder-knot? Our three brethren soon discovered their want by sad experience, meeting in their walks with forty mortifications and indignities. If they went to the play-house, the door-keeper showed them into a twelve-penny gallery. If they called a boat, says a waterman, I am a first sculler. If they stepped to the Rose to take a bottle, the drawer would cry, Friend, we sell no ale. If they went to visit a lady, a footman met them at the door with, Pray send up your message. In this unhappy case, they went immediately to consult their father's will, read it over and over, but not a word of the shoulder-knot. What should they do? What temper should they find? Obedience was absolutely necessary, and yet shoulder-knots appeared extremely requisite. After much thought, one of the brothers who happened to be more book-learned than the other two, said, he had found an expedient. " 'Tis true," said he, "there is nothing here in this will, *totidem verbis*,[k] making mention of shoulder-knots, but I dare conjecture we may

[i] The first part of the *Tale* is the history of Peter; thereby Popery is exposed; everybody knows the Papists have made great additions to Christianity; that indeed is the great exception which the Church of England makes against them; accordingly Peter begins his pranks with adding a shoulder-knot to his coat. W. WOTTON.

His description of the cloth of which the coat was made, has a farther meaning than the words may seem to import: "The coats their father had left them were of very good cloth, and besides so neatly sewn, you would swear it had been all of a piece, but at the same time very plain with little or no ornament." This is the distinguishing character of the Christian religion. *Christiana religio absoluta et simplex,* was Ammianus Marcellinus's description of it, who was himself a heathen. W. WOTTON.

[j] By this is understood the first introducing of pageantry, and unnecessary ornaments in the Church, such as were neither for convenience nor edification, as a shoulder-knot, in which there is neither symmetry nor use.

[k] When the Papists cannot find any thing which they want in Scripture, they go to oral tradition: thus Peter is introduced satisfied with the tedious way of looking for all the letters of any word, which he has occasion for in the Will, when neither the constituent syllables, nor much less the whole word, were there *in terminis.* W. WOTTON.

8. ***ruelles:*** bedsides.

find them *inclusive,* or *totidem syllabis.*"[9] This distinction was immediately approved by all; and so they fell again to examine the will. But their evil star had so directed the matter, that the first syllable was not to be found in the whole writing. Upon which disappointment, he, who found the former evasion, took heart and said, "Brothers, there is yet hopes; for though we cannot find them *totidem verbis,* nor *totidem syllabis,* I dare engage we shall make them out, *tertio modo,* or *totidem literis.*"[10] This discovery was also highly commended, upon which they fell once more to the scrutiny, and soon picked out S,H,O,U,L,D,E,R; when the same planet, enemy to their repose, had wonderfully contrived, that a K was not to be found. Here was a weighty difficulty! But the distinguishing brother (for whom we shall hereafter find a name) now his hand was in, proved by a very good argument, that K was a modern illegitimate letter, unknown to the learned ages, nor anywhere to be found in ancient manuscripts. "'Tis true," said he, "the word *Calendæ* hath in *Q.V.C.*[o] been sometimes writ with a K, but erroneously, for in the best copies it has been ever spelt with a C. And by consequence it was a gross mistake in our language to spell Knot with a K, but that from henceforward he would take care it should be writ with a C." Upon this all farther difficulty vanished; shoulder-knots were made clearly out to be *jure paterno,*[11] and our three gentlemen swaggered with as large and as flaunting ones as the best.

[o] *Quibusdam veteribus codicibus.*

But, as human happiness is of a very short duration, so in those days were human fashions, upon which it entirely depends. Shoulder-knots had their time, and we must now imagine them in their decline; for a certain lord came just from Paris, with fifty yards of gold lace upon his coat, exactly trimmed after the court fashion of that month. In two days all mankind appeared closed up in bars of gold lace:[l] whoever durst peep abroad without his complement of gold lace, was as scandalous as a——, and as ill received among the women. What should our three knights do in this momentous affair? They had sufficiently strained a point already in the affair of shoulder-knots. Upon recourse to the will, nothing appeared there but *altum silentium.*[12] That of the shoulder-knots was a loose, flying, circumstantial point; but this of gold lace seemed too considerable an alteration without better warrant. It did *aliquo modo essentiæ adhærere,*[13] and therefore required a positive precept. But about this time it fell out, that the learned brother aforesaid had read *Aristotelis Dialectica,* and especially that wonderful piece *de Interpretatione,* which has the faculty of teaching its readers to find out a meaning in everything but itself, like commentators on the Revelations, who proceed prophets without understanding a syllable of the text. "Brothers," said he, "you are to be informed,[m] that of wills *duo sunt genera,*[14] nuncupatory[n] and scriptory; that in the scriptory will here before us, there is no precept or mention about gold lace, *conceditur:* but, *si idem affirmetur de nuncupatorio, negatur.*[15] For brothers, if you remember, we heard a fellow say when we were boys, that he heard my father's man say, that he heard my father say, that he would advise his sons to get gold lace on their coats, as soon as ever they could procure money to buy it." "By G—, that is very true," cries the other; "I remember it perfectly well," said the third. And so without more ado they got the largest gold lace in the parish, and walked about as fine as lords.

A while after there came up all in fashion a pretty sort of flame-coloured satin[o] for linings, and

[l] I cannot tell whether the author means any new innovation by this word, or whether it be only to introduce the new methods of forcing and perverting Scripture.

[m] The next subject of our author's wit is the glosses and interpretations of Scripture, very many absurd ones of which are allowed in the most authentic books of the Church of Rome. W. Wotton.

[n] By this is meant tradition, allowed to have equal authority with the scripture, or rather greater.

[o] This is purgatory, whereof he speaks more particularly hereafter, but here only to show how Scripture was perverted to prove it, which was done by giving equal au-

---

9. ***totidem verbis . . . totidem syllabis:*** "in so many words . . . in so many syllables." **10.** ***tertio modo . . . totidem literis:*** "in a third way . . . in so many letters." **11.** ***jure paterno:*** "in accordance with the father's law."

12. ***altum silentium:*** deep silence. **13.** ***aliquo . . . adhærere:*** "in some way adhere to the essence [of the will]." **14.** ***duo sunt genera:*** "there are two kinds." **15.** Swift seems here to be parodying Scholastic logic. The Latin can be translated as follows: no precept or mention about gold lace, "granted," but "if the same idea were asserted about tradition, it must be denied."

the mercer brought a pattern of it immediately to our three gentlemen, "An please your worships," said he,[p] my Lord C—and Sir J. W. had linings out of this very piece last night; it takes wonderfully, and I shall not have a remnant left enough to make my wife a pin-cushion by to-morrow morning at ten o'clock." Upon this, they fell again to rummage the will, because the present case also required a positive precept, the lining being held by orthodox writers to be of the essence of the coat. After long search, they could fix upon nothing to the matter in hand, except a short advice of their father's in the will, to take care of fire, and put out their candles before they went to sleep.[q] This though a good deal for the purpose, and helping very far towards self-conviction, yet not seeming wholly of force to establish a command; and being resolved to avoid farther scruple, as well as future occasion for scandal, says he that was the scholar. "I remember to have read in wills of a codicil annexed, which is indeed a part of the will, and what it contains hath equal authority with the rest. Now, I have been considering of this same will here before us, and I cannot reckon it to be complete for want of such a codicil. I will therefore fasten one in its proper place very dexterously; I have had it by me some time; it was written by a dog-keeper of my grandfather's,[r] and talks a great deal (as good luck would have it) of this very flame-coloured satin." The project was immediately approved by the other two; an old parchment scroll was tagged on according to art, in the form of a codicil annexed, and the satin bought and worn.

Next winter, a player, hired for the purpose by the corporation of fringe-makers, acted his part in a new comedy, all covered with silver fringe,[s] and according to the laudable custom gave rise to that fashion. Upon which, the brothers consulting their father's will, to their great astonishment found these words; "*Item,* I charge and command my said three sons to wear no sort of silver fringe upon or about their said coats," etc., with a penalty in case of disobedience, too long here to insert. However, after some pause the brother so often mentioned for his erudition, who was well skilled in criticisms, had found in a certain author, which he said should be nameless, that the same word which in the will is called fringe, does also signify a broom-stick, and doubtless ought to have the same interpretation in this paragraph. This, another of the brothers disliked, because of that epithet silver, which could not, he humbly conceived, in propriety of speech be reasonably applied to a broom-stick; but it was replied upon him, that this epithet was understood in a mythological and allegorical sense. However, he objected again, why their father should forbid them to wear a broom-stick on their coats, a caution that seemed unnatural and impertinent; upon which he was taken up short, as one that spoke irreverently of a mystery, which doubtless was very useful and significant, but ought not to be over-curiously pried into, or nicely reasoned upon. And in short, their father's authority being now considerably sunk, this expedient was allowed to serve as a lawful dispensation for wearing their full proportion of silver fringe.

A while after was revived an old fashion, long antiquated, of embroidery with Indian figures of men, women, and children.[t] Here they had no occasion to examine the will. They remembered but too well how their father had always abhorred this fashion, that he made several paragraphs on purpose, importing his utter detestation of it, and bestowing his everlasting curse to his sons whenever

---

thority with the Canon to Apocrypha, called here a codicil annexed.

It is likely the author, in every one of these changes in the brothers' dresses, refers to some particular error in the Church of Rome, though it is not easy I think to apply them all, but by this of flame-coloured satin, is manifestly intended purgatory; by gold lace may perhaps be understood the lofty ornaments and plate in the churches; the shoulder-knots and silver fringe are not so obvious, at least to me; but the Indian figures of men, women and children plainly relate to the pictures in the Romish churches, of God like an old man, of the Virgin Mary, and our Saviour as a child.

[p] This shows the time the author writ, it being about fourteen years since those two persons were reckoned the fine gentlemen of the town.

[q] That is, to take care of hell, and, in order to do that, to subdue and extinguish their lusts.

[r] I believe this refers to that part of the Apocrypha where mention is made of Tobit and his dog.

[s] This is certainly the farther introducing the pomps of habit and ornament.

[t] The images of saints, the blessed Virgin, and our Saviour an infant.

Ibid. Images in the Church of Rome give him but too fair a handle. The brothers remembered, &c. The allegory here is direct. W. WOTTON.

they should wear it. For all this, in a few days they appeared higher in the fashion than anybody else in the town. But they solved the matter by saying, that these figures were not at all the same with those that were formerly worn, and were meant in the will. Besides, they did not wear them in that sense, as forbidden by their father, but as they were a commendable custom, and of great use to the public. That these rigorous clauses in the will did therefore require some allowance, and a favourable interpretation, and ought to be understood *cum grano salis.*

But fashions perpetually altering in that age, the scholastic brother grew weary of searching farther evasions, and solving everlasting contradictions. Resolved therefore at all hazards to comply with the modes of the world, they concerted matters together, and agreed unanimously to lock up their father's will in a storage box,[u] brought out of Greece or Italy (I have forgot which) and trouble themselves no farther to examine it, but only refer to its authority whenever they thought fit. In consequence whereof, a while after it grew a general mode to wear an infinite number of points, most of them tagged with silver: upon which the scholar pronounced *ex cathedra,*[v] that points were absolutely *jure paterno,* as they might very well remember. 'Tis true, indeed, the fashion prescribed somewhat more than were directly named in the will; however, that they, as heirs-general of their father, had power to make and add certain clauses for public emolument, though not deducible, *totidem verbis,* from the letter of the will, or else *multa absurda sequerentur.*[16] This was understood for canonical, and therefore on the following Sunday they came to church all covered with points.

The learned brother so often mentioned was reckoned the best scholar in all that, or the next street to it; insomuch as, having run something behind-hand with the world, he obtained the favour from a certain lord,[w] to receive him into his house, and to teach his children. A while after the lord died, and he, by long practice of his father's will, found the way of contriving a deed of conveyance of that house to himself and his heirs; upon which he took possession, turned the young squires out, and received his brothers in their stead.

SECTION III

A DIGRESSION CONCERNING CRITICS

Though I have been hitherto as cautious as I could, upon all occasions, most nicely to follow the rules and methods of writing laid down by the example of our illustrious Moderns; yet has the unhappy shortness of my memory led me into an error, from which I must immediately extricate myself, before I can decently pursue my principal subject. I confess with shame, it was an unpardonable omission to proceed so far as I have already done, before I had performed the due discourses, expostulatory, supplicatory, or deprecatory, with my good lords the critics. Towards some atonement of this grievous neglect, I do here make humbly bold to present them with a short account of themselves and their art, by looking into the original and pedigree of the word, as it is generally understood among us, and very briefly considering the ancient and present state thereof.

By the word critic, at this day so frequent in all conversations, there have sometimes been distinguished three very different species of mortal men, according as I have read in ancient books and pamphlets. For first, by this term was understood

[u] The Papists formerly forbade the people the use of scripture in a vulgar tongue; Peter therefore locks up his father's will in a strong box, brought out of Greece or Italy. Those countries are named because the New Testament is written in Greek; and the vulgar Latin, which is the authentic edition of the Bible in the Church of Rome, is in the language of old Italy. W. WOTTON.

[v] The popes in their decretals and bulls have given their sanction to very many gainful doctrines which are now received in the Church of Rome that are not mentioned in scripture, and are unknown to the primitive church; Peter accordingly pronounces *ex cathedra,* that points tagged with silver were absolutely *jure paterno,* and so they wore them in great numbers. W. WOTTON.

[w] This was Constantine the Great, from whom the popes pretend a donation of St. Peter's patrimony, which they have been never able to produce.

Ibid. The bishops of Rome enjoyed their privileges in Rome at first by the favour of emperors, whom at last they shut out of their own capital city, and then forged a donation from Constantine the Great, the better to justify what they did. In imitation of this, Peter having run something behind-hand in the world, obtained leave of a certain lord, &c. W. WOTTON.

16. ***multa . . . sequerentur:*** "many absurd things would follow."

such persons as invented or drew up rules for themselves and the world, by observing which, a careful reader might be able to pronounce upon the productions of the learned, form his taste to a true relish of the sublime and the admirable, and divide every beauty of matter or of style from the corruption that apes it. In their common perusal of books, singling out the errors and defects, the nauseous, the fulsome, the dull, and the impertinent, with the caution of a man that walks through Edinburgh streets in a morning, who is indeed as careful as he can to watch diligently, and spy out the filth in his way; not that he is curious to observe the colour and complexion of the ordure, or take its dimensions, much less to be paddling in, or tasting it; but only with a design to come out as cleanly as he may. These men seem, though very erroneously, to have understood the appellation of critic in a literal sense; that one principal part of his office was to praise and acquit; and that a critic, who sets up to read only for an occasion of censure and reproof, is a creature as barbarous as a judge, who should take up a resolution to hang all men that came before him upon a trial.

Again, by the word critic have been meant the restorers of ancient learning from the worms, and graves, and dust of manuscripts.

Now, the races of these two have been for some ages utterly extinct; and besides, to discourse any farther of them would not be at all to my purpose.

The third, and noblest sort, is that of the TRUE CRITIC, whose original is the most ancient of all. Every true critic is a hero born, descending in a direct line from a celestial stem by Momus and Hybris, who begat Zoilus, who begat Tigellius, who begat Etcætera the Elder; who begat Bentley, and Rymer, and Wotton, and Perrault, and Dennis, who begat Etcætera the Younger.[1]

And these are the critics from whom the commonwealth of learning has in all ages received such immense benefits, that the gratitude of their admirers placed their origin in Heaven, among those of Hercules, Theseus, Perseus, and other great deservers of mankind. But heroic virtue itself hath not been exempt from the obloquy of evil tongues. For it hath been objected, that those ancient heroes, famous for their combating so many giants, and dragons, and robbers, were in their own persons a greater nuisance to mankind, than any of those monsters they subdued; and therefore to render their obligations more complete, when all other vermin were destroyed, should in conscience have concluded with the same justice upon themselves as Hercules[2] most generously did, and hath upon that score procured to himself more temples and votaries than the best of his fellows. For these reasons, I suppose it is, why some have conceived it would be very expedient for the public good of learning that every true critic, as soon as he had finished his task assigned, should immediately deliver himself up to ratsbane, or hemp, or from some convenient altitude; and that no man's pretensions to so illustrious a character should by any means be received, before that operation were performed.

Now, from this heavenly descent of criticism, and the close analogy it bears to heroic virtue, 'tis easy to assign the proper employment of a true ancient genuine critic; which is, to travel through this vast world of writings; to pursue and hunt those monstrous faults bred within them; to drag out the lurking errors like Cacus from his den; to multiply them like Hydra's heads; and rake them together like Augeas's dung. Or else drive away a sort of dangerous fowl, who have a perverse inclination to plunder the best branches of the tree of knowledge, like those Stymphalian birds that ate up the fruit.[3]

These reasonings will furnish us with an adequate definition of a true critic: that he is a discoverer and collector of writers' faults. Which may be farther put beyond dispute by the following demonstration: that whoever will examine the writings in all kinds, wherewith this ancient sect has hon-

SECTION III. **1.** A satiric genealogy of the true critic, the Modern—beginning with Momus (Night) and Hybris (Pride), who give birth to Zoilus and Tigellius, who become types of the worst Ancient critics, who beget some of the worst of the Moderns, Bentley, Rymer, Wotton, Perrault, and Dennis.

2. When he suffered unbearable wounds, Hercules had himself set on a pyre and burned to death. **3.** The references in this paragraph are to the so-called labors of Hercules and to the cast of characters involved. Hercules had to destroy the Stymphalian birds. Cacus was the monster who stole cattle from Hercules. Hydra was the many-headed monster. Aegeas was the king who possessed vast herds of animals, whose stables Hercules had to clean.

oured the world, shall immediately find, from the whole thread and tenor of them, that the ideas of the authors have been altogether conversant and taken up with the faults and blemishes, and oversights, and mistakes of other writers; and let the subject treated on be whatever it will, their imaginations are so entirely possessed and replete with the defects of other pens, that the very quintessence of what is bad does of necessity distil into their own, by which means the whole appears to be nothing else but an abstract of the criticisms themselves have made.

Having thus briefly considered the original and office of a critic, as the word is understood in its most noble and universal acceptation, I proceed to refute the objections of those who argue from the silence and pretermission of authors; by which they pretend to prove, that the very art of criticism, as now exercised, and by me explained, is wholly Modern; and consequently, that the critics of Great Britain and France have no title to an original so ancient and illustrious as I have deduced. Now, if I can clearly make out on the contrary, that the most ancient writers have particularly described both the person and the office of a true critic, agreeable to the definition laid down by me, their grand objection, from the silence of authors, will fall to the ground.

I confess to have for a long time borne a part in this general error; from which I should never have acquitted myself, but through the assistance of our noble Moderns; whose most edifying volumes I turn indefatigably over night and day, for the improvement of my mind, and the good of my country. These have with unwearied pains made many useful searches into the weak sides of the ancients, and given us a comprehensive list of them.° Besides, they have proved beyond contradiction, that the very finest things delivered of old, have been long since invented, and brought to light by much later pens; and that the noblest discoveries those ancients ever made, of art or of nature, have all been produced by the transcending genius of the present age. Which clearly shows, how little merit those Ancients can justly pretend to; and takes off that blind admiration paid them by men in a corner, who have the unhappiness of conversing too little with present things. Reflecting maturely upon all this, and taking in the whole compass of human nature, I easily concluded, that these Ancients, highly sensible of their many imperfections, must needs have endeavoured from some passages in their works, to obviate, soften, or divert the censorious reader, by satire, or panegyric upon the true critics, in imitation of their masters, the Moderns. Now, in the commonplaces of both these,° I was plentifully instructed, by a long course of useful study in prefaces and prologues; and therefore immediately resolved to try what I could discover of either, by a diligent perusal of the most ancient writers, and especially those who treated of the earliest times. Here I found to my great surprise, that although they all entered, upon occasion, into particular descriptions of the true critic, according as they were governed by their fears or their hopes; yet whatever they touched of that kind, was with abundance of caution, adventuring no farther than mythology and hieroglyphic. This, I suppose, gave ground to superficial readers, for urging the silence of authors, against the antiquity of the true critic, though the types are so apposite, and the applications so necessary and natural, that it is not easy to conceive how any reader of a modern eye and taste could overlook them. I shall venture from a great number to produce a few, which I am very confident will put this question beyond dispute.

° *See Wotton,* Of Ancient and Modern Learning.

° *Satire and panegyric upon critics.*

It well deserves considering, that these ancient writers in treating enigmatically upon the subject, have generally fixed upon the very same hieroglyph, varying only the story according to their affections or their wit. For first, Pausanias is of opinion, that the perfection of writing correct was entirely owing to the institution of critics; and that he can possibly mean no other than the true critic, is, I think, manifest enough from the following description. He says, they were a race of men, who delighted to nibble at the superfluities, and excrescencies of books; which the learned at length observing, took warning of their own accord, to lop the luxuriant, the rotten, the dead, the sapless, and the overgrown branches from their works. But now, all this he cunningly shades under the following allegory; that the Nauplians in Argia° learned the art of pruning their vines, by observing, that when an ASS had browsed upon one of them, it thrived the better, and bore fairer fruit. But Heorodotus° holding the very same hieroglyph, speaks much

° *Lib. —.*

° *Lib. 4.*

plainer, and almost *in terminis*. He hath been so bold as to tax the true critics of ignorance and malice; telling us openly, for I think nothing can be plainer, that in the western part of Libya, there were ASSES with HORNS: upon which relations Ctesias° [4] yet refines, mentioning the very same animal about India, adding, that whereas all other ASSES wanted a gall, these horned ones were so redundant in that part, that their flesh was not to be eaten because of its extreme bitterness.

° *Vide excerpta ex eo apud photium.*

Now, the reason why those ancient writers treated this subject only by types and figures, was, because they durst not make open attacks against a party so potent and so terrible, as the critics of those ages were, whose very voice was so dreadful, that a legion of authors would tremble, and drop their pens at the sound; for so Herodotus tells us expressly in another place,° how a vast army of Scythians was put to flight in a panic terror, by the braying of an ASS. From hence it is conjectured by certain profound philologers, that the great awe and reverence paid to a true critic, by the writers of Britain, have been derived to us from those our Scythian ancestors. In short, this dread was so universal, that in process of time, those authors who had a mind to publish their sentiments more freely, in describing the true critics of their several ages, were forced to leave off the use of the former hieroglyph, as too nearly approaching the prototype, and invented other terms instead thereof that were more cautious and mystical; so Diodorus,° speaking to the same purpose, ventures no farther than to say, that in the mountains of Helicon, there grows a certain weed, which bears a flower of so damned a scent, as to poison those who offer to smell it. Lucretius gives exactly the same relation:

° *Lib. 4*

° *Lib.*

> Est etiam in magnis Heliconis montibus arbos,
> Floris odore hominem retro consueta necare.[a]
> Lib. 6.

[a] Near Helicon, and round the learned hill,
Grow trees, whose blossoms with their odour kill.

But Ctesias, whom we lately quoted, hath been a great deal bolder; he had been used with much severity by the true critics of his own age, and therefore could not forbear to leave behind him at least one deep mark of his vengeance against the whole tribe. His meaning is so near the surface, that I wonder how it possibly came to be overlooked by those who deny the antiquity of the true critics. For pretending to make a description of many strange animals about India, he hath set down these remarkable words: "Amongst the rest," says he, "there is a serpent that wants teeth, and consequently cannot bite; but if its vomit (to which it is much addicted) happens to fall upon anything, a certain rottenness or corruption ensues. These serpents are generally found among the mountains where jewels grow, and they frequently emit a poisonous juice whereof whoever drinks, that person's brains fly out of his nostrils."

There was also among the Ancients a sort of critic, not distinguished in species from the former, but in growth or degree, who seem to have been only the tyros or junior scholars; yet, because of their differing employments, they are frequently mentioned as a sect by themselves. The usual exercise of these younger students, was to attend constantly at theatres, and learn to spy out the worst parts of the play, whereof they were obliged carefully to take note, and render a rational account to their tutors. Fleshed at these smaller sports, like young wolves, they grew up in time to be nimble and strong enough for hunting down large game. For it hath been observed both among Ancients and Moderns, that a true critic hath one quality in common with a whore and an alderman, never to change his title or his nature; that a gray critic has been certainly a green one, the perfections and acquirements of his age being only the improved talents of his youth; like hemp, which some naturalists inform us, is bad for suffocations though taken out in the seed. I esteem the invention, or at least the refinement of prologues, to have been owing to these younger proficients, of whom Terence[5] makes frequent and honourable mention, under the name of *malevoli*.

Now, 'tis certain, the institution of the true critics was of absolute necessity to the commonwealth of

---

4. Ctesias, a Roman doctor of the fourth century B.C., wrote a lengthy history of Persia. Photius, a critic of the ninth century A.D., wrote accounts of a huge number of prose works, one of them being that of Ctesias.

5. Terence: the famed Roman writer of comedy (195–159 B.C.).

learning. For all human actions seem to be divided like Themistocles and his company; one man can fiddle, and another can make a small town a great city; and he that cannot do either one or the other, deserves to be kicked out of the creation. The avoiding of which penalty has doubtless given the first birth to the nation of critics, and withal, an occasion for their secret detractors to report, that a true critic is a sort of mechanic, set up with a stock and tools for his trade, at as little expense as a tailor; and that there is much analogy between the utensils and abilities of both: that the tailor's hell[6] is the type of a critic's common-place book, and his wit and learning held forth by the goose; that it requires at least as many of these to the making up of one scholar, as of the others to the composition of a man; that the valour of both is equal, and their weapons near of a size. Much may be said in answer to those invidious reflections; and I can positively affirm the first to be a falsehood: for, on the contrary, nothing is more certain, than that it requires greater layings out, to be free of the critic's company, than of any other you can name. For, as to a true beggar, it will cost the richest candidate every groat he is worth; so, before one can commence a true critic, it will cost a man all the good qualities of his mind; which, perhaps, for a less purchase, would be thought but an indifferent bargain.

Having thus amply proved the antiquity of criticism, and described the primitive state of it, I shall now examine the present condition of this empire, and show how well it agrees with its ancient self. A certain author,[b] whose works have many ages since been entirely lost, does in his fifth book and eighth chapter, say of critics, that their writings are the mirrors of learning. This I understand in a literal sense, and suppose our author must mean, that whoever designs to be a perfect writer, must inspect into the books of critics, and correct his invention there as in a mirror. Now, whoever considers, that the mirrors of the Ancients were made of brass, and *sine mercurio,* may presently apply the two principal qualifications of a true Modern critic, and consequently must needs conclude, that these have always been, and must be for ever the same. For brass is an emblem of duration, and when it is skilfully burnished, will cast reflections from its own superficies, without any assistance of mercury from behind. All the other talents of a critic will not require a particular mention, being included, or easily deducible to these. However, I shall conclude with three maxims, which may serve both as characteristics to distinguish a true modern critic from a pretender, and will be also of admirable use to those worthy spirits, who engage in so useful and honourable an art.

The first is, that criticism, contrary to all other faculties of the intellect, is ever held the truest and best, when it is the very first result of the critic's mind; as fowlers reckon the first aim for the surest, and seldom fail of missing the mark, if they stay not for a second.

Secondly, the true critics are known by their talent of swarming about the noblest writers, to which they are carried merely by instinct, as a rat to the best cheese, or a wasp to the fairest fruit. So when the king is a horse-back, he is sure to be the dirtiest person of the company, and they that make their court best, are such as bespatter him most.

Lastly, a true critic, in the perusal of a book, is like a dog at a feast, whose thoughts and stomach are wholly set upon what the guests fling away, and consequently is apt to snarl most when there are the fewest bones.

Thus much, I think, is sufficient to serve by way of address to my patrons, the true Modern critics, and may very well atone for my past silence, as well as that which I am like to observe for the future. I hope I have deserved so well of their whole body, as to meet with generous and tender usage at their hands. Supported by which expectation, I go on boldly to pursue those adventures already so happily begun.

SECTION IV

A TALE OF A TUB

I have now with much pains and study conducted the reader to a period, where he must expect to hear of great revolutions. For no sooner had our learned brother, so often mentioned, got a warm house of his own over his head, than he began to

[b] A quotation after the manner of a great author. *Vide* Bentley's *Dissertation, &c.*

---

6. tailor's hell: the bin into which the tailor throws his scraps.

look big, and to take mightily upon him; insomuch, that unless the gentle reader out of his great candour will please a little to exalt his idea, I am afraid he will henceforth hardly know the hero of the play, when he happens to meet him, his part, his dress, and his mien being so much altered.

He told his brothers, he would have them to know that he was their elder, and consequently his father's sole heir, nay, a while after, he would not allow them to call him brother, but Mr. PETER; and then he must be styled *Father* PETER; and sometimes, *My Lord* PETER. To support this grandeur, which he soon began to consider could not be maintained without a better *fonde*[1] than what he was born to, after much thought, he cast about at last to turn projector and virtuoso, wherein he so well succeeded, that many famous discoveries, projects, and machines, which bear great vogue and practice at present in the world, are owing entirely to Lord Peter's invention. I will deduce the best account I have been able to collect of the chief amongst them, without considering much the order they came out in, because, I think, authors are not well agreed as to that point.

I hope, when this treatise of mine shall be translated into foreign languages (as I may without vanity affirm, that the labour of collecting, the faithfulness in recounting, and the great usefulness of the matter to the public, will amply deserve that justice) that the worthy members of the several academies abroad, especially those of France and Italy, will favourably accept these humble offers, for the advancement of universal knowledge. I do also advertise the most reverend fathers, the Eastern Missionaries, that I have, purely for their sakes, made use of such words and phrases, as will best admit an easy turn into any of the oriental languages, especially the Chinese. And so I proceed with great content of mind, upon reflecting, how much emolument this whole globe of Earth is like to reap by my labours.

The first undertaking of Lord Peter, was to purchase a large continent,[c] lately said to have been discovered in *Terra Australis Incognita*. This tract of land he bought at a very great pennyworth from the discoverers themselves (though some pretend to doubt whether they had ever been there) and then retailed it into several cantons to certain dealers, who carried over colonies, but were all shipwrecked in the voyage. Upon which Lord Peter sold the said continent to other customers again, and again, and again, and again, with the same success.

The second project I shall mention, was his sovereign remedy for the worms,[d] especially those in the spleen.[e] The patient was to eat nothing after supper for three nights: as soon as he went to bed, he was carefully to lie on one side, and when he grew weary, to turn upon the other. He must also duly confine his two eyes to the same object; and by no means break wind at both ends together, without manifest occasion. These prescriptions diligently observed, the worms would void insensibly by perspiration, ascending through the brain.

A third invention was the erecting of a whispering-office,[f] for the public good and ease of all such as are hypochondriacal, or troubled with the colic; as likewise of all eaves-droppers, physicians, midwives, small politicians, friends fallen out, repeating poets, lovers happy or in despair, bawds, privy-counsellors, pages, parasites and buffoons: in short, of all such as are in danger of bursting with too much wind. An ass's head was placed so conveniently, that the party affected might easily with his mouth accost either of the animal's ears; which he was to apply close for a certain space, and by a fugitive faculty, peculiar to the ears of that animal, receive immediate benefit, either by eructation, or expiration, or environment.

Another very beneficial project of Lord Peter's was an office of insurance[g] for tobacco-pipes, martyrs of the modern zeal, volumes of poetry, shadows,——and rivers: that these, nor any of these

[c] That is, Purgatory.

[d] Penance and absolution are played upon under the notion of a sovereign remedy for the worms, especially in the spleen, which by observing Peter's prescription would void sensibly by perspiration, ascending through the brain, &c. W. WOTTON.

[e] Here the author ridicules the penances of the Church of Rome, which may be made as easy to the sinner as he pleases, provided he will pay for them accordingly.

[f] By his whispering-office, for the relief of eaves-droppers, physicians, bawds, and privy-counsellors, he ridicules auricular confession, and the priest who takes it, is described by the ass's head. W. WOTTON.

[g] This I take to be the office of indulgences, the gross abuses whereof first gave occasion for the Reformation.

SECTION IV. 1. *fonde:* foundation.

shall receive damage by fire. From whence our friendly societies may plainly find themselves to be only transcribers from this original; though the one and the other have been of great benefit to the undertakers, as well as of equal to the public.

Lord Peter was also held the original author of puppets and raree-shows,[h] the great usefulness whereof being so generally known, I shall not enlarge farther upon this particular.

But another discovery for which he was much renowned was his famous universal pickle.[i] For having remarked how your common pickle[j] in use among housewives, was of no farther benefit than to preserve dead flesh, and certain kinds of vegetables, Peter, with great cost as well as art, had contrived a pickle proper for houses, gardens, towns, men, women, children, and cattle; wherein he could preserve them as sound as insects in amber. Now, this pickle to the taste, the smell, and the sight, appeared exactly the same with what is in common service for beef, and butter, and herring (and has been often that way applied with great success) but for its many sovereign virtues was a quite different thing.) For Peter would put in a certain quantity of his powder *pimperlim pimp*,[k] after which it never failed of success. The operation was performed by spargefaction[2] in a proper time of the moon. The patient who was to be pickled, if it were a house, would infallibly be preserved from all spiders, rats, and weasels; if the party affected were a dog, he should be exempt from mange, and madness, and hunger. It also infallibly took away all scabs and lice, and scalled heads from children, never hindering the patient from any duty, either at bed or board.

[h] I believe are the monkeries and ridiculous processions, &c. among the papists.
[i] Holy water, he calls an universal pickle, to preserve houses, gardens, towns, men, women, children, and cattle, wherein he could preserve them as sound as insects in amber. W. WOTTON.
[j] This is easily understood to be holy water, composed of the same ingredients with many other pickles.
[k] And because holy water differs only in consecration from common water, therefore he tells us that his pickle by the powder of *pimperlimpimp* receives new virtues, though it differs not in sight nor smell from the common pickles, which preserve beef, and butter, and herrings. W. WOTTON.

2. the sprinkling of holy water for a blessing.

But of all Peter's rarities, he most valued a certain set of bulls,[l] whose race was by great fortune preserved in a lineal descent from those that guarded the golden fleece.[3] Though some who pretended to observe them curiously, doubted the breed had not been kept entirely chaste; because they had degenerated from their ancestors in some qualities, and had acquired others very extraordinary, but a foreign mixture. The bulls of Colchos are recorded to have brazen feet; but whether it happened by ill pasture and running, by an allay from intervention of other parents, from stolen intrigues; whether a weakness in their progenitors had impaired the seminal virtue, or by a decline necessary through a long course of time, the originals of nature being depraved in these latter sinful ages of the world; whatever was the cause, 'tis certain that Lord Peter's bulls were extremely vitiated by the rest of time in the metal of their feet, which was now sunk into common lead. However, the terrible roaring, peculiar to their lineage was preserved; as likewise that faculty of breathing out fire from their nostrils; which notwithstanding many of their detractors took to be a feat of art; and to be nothing so terrible as it appeared; proceeding only from their usual course of diet, which was of squibs and crackers.[m][4] However they had two peculiar marks which extremely distinguished them from the bulls of Jason, and which I have not met together in the description of any other monster, beside that in Horace:

Varias inducere plumas;
and
Atrum desinit in piscem.[5]

For these had fishes' tails, yet upon occasion could outfly any bird in the air. Peter put these

[l] The papal bulls are ridiculed by name, so that here we are at no loss for the author's meaning. W. WOTTON.
Ibid. Here the author has kept the name, and means the pope's bulls, or rather his fulminations and excommunications of heretical princes, all signed with lead and the seal of the fisherman.
[m] These are the fulminations of the pope threatening hell and damnation to those princes who offend him.

3. In Greek mythology Jason, husband of Medea, sought the celebrated Golden Fleece of a ram. He searched for it in Colchis. 4. **crackers:** fireworks. 5. Phrases from the famous opening of Horace's *Art of Poetry,* which mocks incongruous combinations in a work of art: "to spread many-colored feathers"; "ends below in a black fish."

bulls upon several employs. Sometimes he would set them a-roaring to fright naughty boys,[n] and make them quiet. Sometimes he would send them out upon errands of great importance; where it is wonderful to recount, and perhaps the cautious reader may think much to believe it, an *appetitus sensibilis*, deriving itself through the whole family from their noble ancestors, guardians of the golden fleece, they continued so extremely fond of gold, that if Peter sent them abroad, though it were only upon a compliment, they would roar, and spit, and belch, and piss, and fart, and snivel out fire, and keep a perpetual coil, till you flung them a bit of gold; but then, *pulveris exigui jactu*,[6] they would grow calm and quiet as lambs. In short, whether by secret connivance, or encouragement from their master, or out of their own liquorish affection to gold, or both, it is certain they were no better than a sort of sturdy, swaggering beggars; and where they could not prevail to get an alms, would make women miscarry, and children fall into fits, who to this very day, usually call sprites and hobgoblins by the name of bull-beggars. They grew at last so very troublesome to the neighbourhood, that some gentlemen of the north-west got a parcel of right English bull-frogs, and baited them so terribly, that they felt it ever after.

I must needs mention one more of Lord Peter's projects, which was very extraordinary, and discovered him to be master of a high reach, and profound invention. Whenever it happened that any rogue of Newgate was condemned to be hanged, Peter would offer him a pardon for a certain sum of money which when the poor caitiff had made all shifts to scrape up and send, his lordship would return a piece of paper in this form.[o]

TO all mayors, sheriffs, jailors, constables, bailiffs, hangmen, &c. Whereas we are informed that A. B. remains in the hands of you, or any of you, under the sentence of death. We will and command you upon sight hereof, to let the said prisoner depart to his own habitation, whether he stands condemned for murder, sodomy, rape, sacrilege, incest, treason, blasphemy, &c., for which this shall be your sufficient warrant: and if you fail hereof, G—d—mn you and yours to all eternity. And so we bid you heartily farewell.

Your most humble
man's man,
Emperor PETER.

[n] That is, kings who incur his displeasure.

[o] This is a copy of a general pardon, signed *Servus Servorum*.[7]
Ibid. Absolution in *articulo mortis;* and the tax *cameræ apostolicæ*, are jested upon in Emperor Peter's letter. W. WOTTON.

6. ***pulveris . . . jactu:*** "by throwing them a bit of dust."
7. ***Servus Servorum:*** "Servant of the servants of God." A familiar Papal title.

The wretches trusting to this lost their lives and money too.

I desire of those, whom the learned among posterity will appoint for commentators upon this elaborate treatise, that they will proceed with great caution upon certain dark points, wherein all who are not *verè adepti*,[8] may be in danger to form rash and hasty conclusions, especially in some mysterious paragraphs, where certain *arcana* are joined for brevity sake, which in the operation must be divided. And I am certain, that future sons of art will return large thanks to my memory, for so grateful, so useful an *innuendo*.

It will be no difficult part to persuade the reader that so many worthy discoveries met with great success in the world; though I may justly assure him that I have related much the smallest number; my design having been only to single out such as will be of most benefit for public imitation, or which best served to give some idea of the reach and wit of the inventor. And therefore it need not be wondered, if by this time, Lord Peter was become exceeding rich. But alas, he had kept his brain so long and so violently upon the rack, that at last it shook itself, and began to turn round for a little ease. In short, what with pride, projects, and knavery, poor Peter was grown distracted, and conceived the strangest imaginations in the world. In the height of his fits (as it is usual with those who run mad out of pride) he would call himself God Almighty,[p] and sometimes monarch of the universe. I have seen him (says my author) take three old high-crowned hats,[q] and clap them all on his head three story high, with a huge bunch

[p] The Pope is not only allowed to be the vicar of Christ, but by several divines is called God upon earth, and other blasphemous titles.

[q] The triple crown.

8. ***verè adepti:*** true members of the club.

of keys at his girdle,[r] and an angling rod in his hand. In which guise, whoever went to take him by the hand in the way of salutation, Peter with much grace, like a well-educated spaniel, would present them with his foot,[s] and if they refused his civility, then he would raise it as high as their chops, and give them a damned kick on the mouth, which hath ever since been called a salute. Whoever walked by without paying him their compliments, having a wonderful strong breath, he would blow their hats off into the dirt. Meantime, his affairs at home went upside down; and his two brothers had a wretched time; where his first *boutade*[t] was, to kick both their wives one morning out of doors, and his own too,[u] and in their stead, gave orders to pick up the first three strollers could be met with in the streets. A while after he nailed up the cellar-door, and would not allow his brothers a drop of drink to their victuals.[v] Dining one day at an alderman's in the city, Peter observed him expatiating after the manner of his brethren, in the praises of his sirloin of beef. Beef, said the sage magistrate, is the king of meat; beef comprehends in it the quintessence of partridge, and quail, and venison, and pheasants, and plum-pudding, and custard. When Peter came home, he would needs take the fancy of cooking up this doctrine into use, and apply the precept in default of a sirloin, to his brown loaf: "Bread," says he, "dear brothers, is the staff of life; in which bread is contained, inclusive, the quintessence of beef, mutton, veal, venison, partridge, plum-pudding, and custard: and to render all complete, there is intermingled a due quantity of water, whose crudities are also corrected by yeast or barm, through which means it becomes a wholesome fermented liquor diffused through the mass of the bread." Upon the strength of these conclusions, next day at dinner was the brown loaf served up in all the formality of a city feast. "Come brothers," said Peter, "fall to, and spare not; here is excellent good mutton,[w] or hold, now my hand is in, I'll help you." At which word, in much ceremony, with fork and knife, he carves out two good slices of a loaf, and presents each on a plate to his brothers. The elder of the two not suddenly entering into Lord Peter's conceit, began with very civil language to examine the mystery. "My lord," said he, "I doubt, with great submission, there may be some mistake." "What," says Peter, "you are pleasant; come then, let us hear this jest your head is so big with." "None in the world, my lord; but unless I am very much deceived, your lordship was pleased a while ago to let fall a word about mutton, and I would be glad to see it with all my heart." "How," said Peter, appearing in great surprise, "I do not comprehend this at all."—Upon which, the younger interposing to set the business right, "My lord," said he, "my brother, I suppose, is hungry, and longs for the mutton your lordship hath promised us to dinner." "Pray," said Peter, "take me along with you; either you are both mad, or disposed to be merrier than I approve of; if you there do not like your piece, I will carve you another, though I should take that to be the choice bit of the whole shoulder." "What then, my lord," replied the first, "it seems this is a shoulder of mutton all this while." "Pray, sir," says Peter, "eat your victuals and leave off your impertinence, if you please, for I am not disposed to relish it at present." But the other could not forbear, being over-provoked at the affected seriousness of Peter's countenance. "By G—, my lord," said he, "I can only say, that to my eyes, and fingers, and teeth, and nose, it seems to be nothing but a crust of bread." Upon which the second put in his word: "I never saw a piece of mutton in my life so nearly resembling a slice from a twelve-penny loaf." "Look ye, gentlemen," cries Peter in a rage, "to convince you what a couple of blind, positive, ignorant, wilful puppies you are, I will use but this plain argument; by G—, it is true, good, natural mutton as any in Leadenhall market; and G— confound you both eternally, if you offer to believe otherwise." Such a thundering

[r] The keys of the church.
Ibid. The Pope's universal monarchy, and his triple crown and fisher's ring. W. WOTTON.

[s] Neither does his arrogant way of requiring men to kiss his slipper escape reflection. W. WOTTON.

[t] This word properly signifies a sudden jerk, or lash of a horse, when you do not expect it.

[u] The celibacy of the Romish clergy is struck at in Peter's beating his own and brothers' wives out of doors. W. WOTTON.

[v] The Popes' refusing the cup to the laity, persuading them that the blood is contained in the bread, and that the bread is the real and entire body of Christ.

[w] Transubstantiation. Peter turns his bread into mutton, and according to the popish doctrine of concomitants, his wine too, which in his way he calls palming his damned crusts upon the brothers for mutton. W. WOTTON.

proof as this left no farther room for objection: the two unbelievers began to gather and pocket up their mistake as hastily as they could. "Why, truly," said the first, "upon more mature consideration"—"Ay," says the other, interrupting him, "now I have thought better on the thing, your lordship seems to have a great deal of reason." "Very well," said Peter. "Here boy, fill me a beer-glass of claret. Here's to you both with all my heart." The two brethren much delighted to see him so readily appeased returned their most humble thanks, and said they would be glad to pledge his lordship. "That you shall," said Peter, "I am not a person to refuse you anything that is reasonable; wine moderately taken is a cordial; here is a glass a-piece for you; 'tis true natural juice from the grape; none of your damned vintners brewings." Having spoke thus, he presented to each of them another large dry crust, bidding them drink it off, and not be bashful, for it would do them no hurt. The two brothers, after having performed the usual office in such delicate conjunctures, of staring a sufficient period at Lord Peter and each other, and finding how matters were like to go, resolved not to enter on a new dispute, but let him carry the point as he pleased; for he was now got into one of his mad fits, and to argue or expostulate further, would only serve to render him a hundred times more untractable.

I have chosen to relate this worthy matter in all its circumstances, because it gave a principal occasion to that great and famous rupture,[x] which happened about the same time among these brethren, and never afterwards made up. But of that I shall treat at large in another section.

However, it is certain, that Lord Peter, even in his lucid intervals, was very lewdly given in his common conversation, extreme wilful and positive, and would at any time rather argue to the death, than allow himself to be once in an error. Besides, he had an abominable faculty of telling huge palpable lies upon all occasions; and swearing, not only to the truth, but cursing the whole company to hell, if they pretended to make the least scruple of believing him. One time he swore he had a cow[y] at home, which gave as much milk at a meal, as would fill three thousand churches; and what was yet more extraordinary, would never turn sour. Another time he was telling of an old sign-post[z] that belonged to his father, with nails and timber enough on it to build sixteen large men-of-war. Talking one day of Chinese waggons, which were made so light as to sail over mountains: "Z—nds," said Peter, "where's the wonder of that? By G—, I saw a large house of lime and stone[a] travel over sea and land (granting that it stopped sometimes to bait) above two thousand German leagues." And that which was the good of it, he would swear desperately all the while, that he never told a lie in his life; and at every word: "By G—, gentlemen, I tell you nothing but the truth; and the D— l broil them eternally that will not believe me."

In short, Peter grew so scandalous that all the neighbourhood began in plain words to say, he was no better than a knave. And his two brothers, long weary of his ill usage, resolved at last to leave him; but first they humbly desired a copy of their father's will, which had now lain by neglected time out of mind. Instead of granting this request, he called them damned sons of whores, rogues, traitors, and the rest of the vile names he could muster up. However, while he was abroad one day upon his projects, the two youngsters watched their opportunity, made a shift to come at the will,[b] and took a *copia vera*,[9] by which they presently saw how grossly they had been abused; their father having left them equal heirs, and strictly commanded, that whatever they got should lie in common among them all. Pursuant to which, their next enterprise was to break open the cellar-door and get a little good drink[c] to spirit and comfort their hearts. In

[x] By this rupture is meant the Reformation.

[y] The ridiculous multiplying of the Virgin Mary's milk among the papists, under the allegory of a cow, which gave as much milk at a meal as would fill three thousand churches. W. Wotton.

[z] By this sign-post is meant the cross of our Blessed Saviour.

[a] The chapel of Loretto. He falls here only upon the ridiculous inventions of popery: the Church of Rome intended by these things to gull silly, superstitious people, and rook them of their money; that the world had been too long in slavery, our ancestors gloriously redeemed us from that yoke. The Church of Rome therefore ought to be exposed, and he deserves well of mankind that does expose it. W. Wotton.

Ibid. The chapel of Loretto, which travelled from the Holy Land to Italy.

[b] Translated the scriptures into the vulgar tongues.

[c] Administered the cup to the laity at the communion.

9. ***copia vera:*** true copy.

copying the will, they had met another precept against whoring, divorce, and separate maintenance; upon which their next work[d] was to discard their concubines, and send for their wives. Whilst all this was in agitation, there enters a solicitor from Newgate, desiring Lord Peter would please to procure a pardon for a thief that was to be hanged to-morrow. But the two brothers told him, he was a coxcomb to seek pardons from a fellow who deserved to be hanged much better than his client; and discovered all the method of that imposture, in the same form I delivered it a while ago, advising the solicitor to put his friend upon obtaining a pardon from the king.[e] In the midst of all this clutter and revolution, in comes Peter with a file of dragoons[f] at his heels, and gathering from all hands what was in the wind, he and his gang, after several millions of scurrilities and curses, not very important here to repeat, by main force very fairly kicks them both out of doors[g] and would never let them come under his roof from that day to this.

. . .

SECTION VI

A TALE OF A TUB

We left Lord Peter in open rupture with his two brethren; both for ever discarded from his house, and resigned to the wide world, with little or nothing to trust to. Which are circumstances that render them proper subjects for the charity of a writer's pen to work on, scenes of misery ever affording the fairest harvest for great adventures. And in this the world may perceive the difference between the integrity of a generous author and that of a common friend. The latter is observed to adhere close in prosperity, but on the decline of fortune to drop suddenly off. Whereas the generous author, just on the contrary, finds his hero on the dunghill, from thence by gradual steps raises him to a throne, and then immediately withdraws, expecting not so much as thanks for his pains, in imitation of which example, I have placed Lord Peter in a noble house, given him a title to wear, and money to spend. There I shall leave him for some time, returning where common charity directs me, to the assistance of his brothers, at their lowest ebb. However, I shall by no means forget my character of an historian to follow the truth step by step, whatever happens, or wherever it may lead me.

The two exiles, so nearly united in fortune and interest, took a lodging together, where, at their first leisure, they began to reflect on the numberless misfortunes and vexations of their life past, and could not tell on the sudden, to what failure in their conduct they ought to impute them, when, after some recollection, they called to mind the copy of their father's will, which they had so happily recovered. This was immediately produced, and a firm resolution taken between them, to alter whatever was already amiss and reduce all their future measures to the strictest obedience prescribed therein. The main body of the will (as the reader cannot easily have forgot) consisted in certain admirable rules about the wearing of their coats, in the perusal whereof, the two brothers at every period duly comparing the doctrine with the practice, there was never seen a wider difference between two things, horrible downright transgressions of every point. Upon which they both resolved, without further delay, to fall immediately upon reducing the whole, exactly after their father's model.

But here it is good to stop the hasty reader, ever impatient to see the end of an adventure, before we writers can duly prepare him for it. I am to record, that these two brothers began to be distinguished at this time by certain names. One of them desired to be called MARTIN,[a] and the other took the appellation of JACK.[b] These two had lived in much friendship and agreement under the tyranny of their brother Peter, as it is the talent of fellow-sufferers to do; men in misfortune being like men in the dark, to whom all colours are the same. But when they came forward into the world, and began to display themselves to each other, and to the light, their complexions appeared extremely differ-

[d] Allowed the marriages of priests.

[e] Directed penitents not to trust to pardons and absolutions procured for money, but sent them to implore the mercy of God, from whence alone remission is to be obtained.

[f] By Peter's dragoons is meant the civil power which those princes who were bigoted to the Romish superstition, employed against the reformers.

[g] The Pope shuts all who dissent from him out of the Church.

[a] Martin Luther.

[b] John Calvin.

ent, which the present posture of their affairs gave them sudden opportunity to discover.

But here the severe reader may justly tax me as a writer of short memory, a deficiency to which a true Modern cannot but of necessity be a little subject: because, memory being an employment of the mind upon things past, is a faculty for which the learned in our illustrious age have no manner of occasion, who deal entirely with invention, and strike all things out of themselves, or at least by collision from each other, upon which account, we think it highly reasonable to produce our great forgetfulness, as an argument unanswerable for our great wit. I ought in method to have informed the reader about fifty pages ago of a fancy Lord Peter took, and infused into his brothers, to wear on their coats whatever trimmings came up in fashion; never pulling off any, as they went out of the mode, but keeping on all together, which amounted in time to a medley the most antic you can possibly conceive, and this to a degree, that upon the time of their falling out there was hardly a thread of the original coat to be seen, but an infinite quantity of lace, and ribbons, and fringe, and embroidery, and points (I mean only those tagged with silver,[c] for the rest fell off). Now this material circumstance having been forgot in due place, as good fortune hath ordered, comes in very properly here, when the two brothers are just going to reform their vestures into the primitive state, prescribed by their father's will.

They both unanimously entered upon this great work, looking sometimes on their coats, and sometimes on the will. Martin laid the first hand; at one twitch brought off a large handful of points; and with a second pull, stripped away ten dozen yards of fringe. But when he had gone thus far, he demurred a while: he knew very well there yet remained a great deal more to be done; however, the first heat being over, his violence began to cool, and he resolved to proceed more moderately in the rest of the work; having already very narrowly escaped a swinging rent in pulling off the points, which being tagged with silver (as we have observed before) the judicious workman had with much sagacity double sewn, to preserve them from falling. Resolving therefore to rid his coat of a huge quantity of gold lace, he picked up the stitches with much caution, and diligently gleaned out all the loose threads as he went, which proved to be a work of time. Then he fell about the embroidered Indian figures of men, women, and children, against which, as you have heard in its due place, their father's testament was extremely exact and severe: these, with much dexterity and application, were after a while quite eradicated, or utterly defaced. For the rest, where he observed the embroidery to be worked so close, as not to be got away without damaging the cloth, or where it served to hide or strengthen any flaw in the body of the coat, contracted by the perpetual tampering of workmen upon it; he concluded the wisest course was to let it remain, resolving in no case whatsoever, that the substance of the stuff should suffer injury, which he thought the best method of serving the true intent and meaning of his father's will. And this is the nearest account I have been able to collect of Martin's proceedings upon this great revolution.

But his brother Jack, whose adventures will be so extraordinary, as to furnish a great part in the remainder of this discourse, entered upon the matter with other thoughts, and a quite different spirit. For the memory of Lord Peter's injuries produced a degree of hatred and spite, which had a much greater share of inciting him than any regards after his father's commands, since these appeared at best only secondary and subservient to the other. However, for this medley of humor, he made a shift to find a very plausible name, honoring it with the title of zeal; which is perhaps the most significant word that hath been ever yet produced in any language; as, I think, I have fully proved in my excellent analytical discourse upon that subject; wherein I have deduced a histori-theo-physi-logical account of zeal, showing how it first proceeded from a notion into a word, and from thence in a hot summer ripened into a tangible substance. This work, containing three large volumes in folio, I design very shortly to publish by the Modern way of subscription, not doubting but the nobility and gentry of the land will give me all possible encouragement, having already had such a taste of what I am able to perform.

I record, therefore, that brother Jack, brimful of this miraculous compound, reflecting with indigna-

[c] Points tagged with silver are those doctrines that promote the greatness and wealth of the church, which have been therefore woven deepest in the body of Popery.

tion upon Peter's tyranny, and farther provoked by the despondency of Martin, prefaced his resolutions to this purpose. "What," said he, "a rogue that locked up his drink, turned away our wives, cheated us of our fortunes, palmed his damned crusts upon us for mutton, and at last kicked us out of doors; must we be in his fashions, with a pox? A rascal, besides, that all the street cries out against." Having thus kindled and inflamed himself as high as possible, and by consequence, in a delicate temper for beginning a reformation, he set about the work immediately, and in three minutes made more dispatch than Martin had done in as many hours. For (courteous reader) you are given to understand, that zeal is never so highly obliged, as when you set it a-tearing; and Jack, who doated on that quality in himself, allowed it at this time its full swing. Thus it happened, that stripping down a parcel of gold lace a little too hastily, he rent the main body of his coat from top to bottom; and whereas his talent was not of the happiest in taking up a stitch, he knew no better way than to darn it again with packthread and a skewer. But the matter was yet infinitely worse (I record it with tears) when he proceeded to the embroidery: for, being clumsy by nature, and of temper impatient; withal, beholding millions of stitches that required the nicest hand, and sedatest constitutions, to extricate; in a great rage he tore off the whole piece, cloth and all, and flung it into the kennel, and furiously thus continuing his career: "Ah, good brother Martin," said he, "do as I do, for the love of God; strip, tear, pull, rend, flay off all, that we may appear as unlike the rogue Peter as it is possible. I would not for a hundred pounds carry the least mark about me, that might give occasion to the neighbours of suspecting I was related to such a rascal." But Martin, who at this time happened to be extremely phlegmatic and sedate, begged his brother, of all love, not to damage his coat by any means; for he never would get such another: desired him to consider, that it was not their business to form their actions by any reflection upon Peter's, but by observing the rules prescribed in their father's will. That he should remember, Peter was still their brother, whatever faults or injuries he had committed; and therefore they should by all means avoid such a thought as that of taking measures for good and evil, from no other rule than of opposition to him. That it was true, the testament of their good father was very exact in what related to the wearing of their coats; yet was it no less penal and strict in prescribing agreement, and friendship, and affection between them. And therefore, if straining a point were at all dispensible, it would certainly be so rather to the advance of unity than increase of contradiction.

Martin had still proceeded as gravely as he began, and doubtless would have delivered an admirable lecture of morality, which might have exceedingly contributed to my reader's repose, both of body and mind (the true ultimate end of ethics); but Jack was already gone a flight-shot beyond his patience. And as in scholastic disputes, nothing serves to rouse the spleen of him that opposes, so much as a kind of pedantic affected calmness in the respondent; disputants being for the most part like unequal scales, where the gravity of one side advances the lightness of the other, and causes it to fly up and kick the beam; so it happened here that the weight of Martin's argument exalted Jack's levity, and made him fly out and spurn against his brother's moderation. In short, Martin's patience put Jack in a rage; but that which most afflicted him was, to observe his brother's coat so well reduced into the state of innocence; while his own was either wholly rent to his shirt, or those places which had escaped his cruel clutches, were still in Peter's livery. So that he looked like a drunken beau, half rifled by bullies; or like a fresh tenant of Newgate,[1] when he has refused the payment of garnish,[2] or like a discovered shoplifter, left to the mercy of Exchange women; or like a bawd in her old velvet petticoat, resigned into the secular hands of the mobile. Like any or like all of these, a medley of rags, and lace, and rents, and fringes, unfortunately Jack did now appear: he would have been extremely glad to see his coat in the condition of Martin's, but infinitely gladder to find that of Martin's in the same predicament with his. However, since neither of these was likely to come to pass, he thought fit to lend the whole business another turn, and to dress up necessity into a virtue. Therefore, after as many of the fox's arguments as he could muster up, for bringing Martin to reason, as he called it; or, as he meant it, into his own ragged, bobtailed condition; and observing he said

SECTION VI. **1.** the prison. **2.** a payoff by the new prisoner to the jail-master.

all to little purpose; what, alas, was left for the forlorn Jack to do, but after a million of scurrilities against his brother, to run mad with spleen, and spite, and contradiction. To be short, here began a mortal breach between these two. Jack went immediately to new lodgings, and in a few days it was for certain reported, that he had run out of his wits. In a short time after he appeared abroad, and confirmed the report by falling into the oddest whimseys that ever a sick brain conceived.

And now the little boys in the streets began to salute him with several names. Sometimes they would call him Jack the Bald;[d] sometimes, Jack with a lantern;[e] sometimes, Dutch Jack;[f] sometimes, French Hugh;[g] sometimes, Tom the beggar;[h] and sometimes, Knocking Jack of the north.[i] And it was under one, or some, or all of these appellations (which I leave the learned reader to determine) that he hath given rise to the most illustrious and epidemic sect of Æolists; who with honourable commemoration, do still acknowledge the renowned JACK for their author and founder. Of whose original, as well as principles, I am now advancing to gratify the world with a very particular account.

——Mellæo contingens cuncta lepore.[3]

SECTION VII

A DIGRESSION IN PRAISE OF DIGRESSIONS

I have sometimes heard of an *Iliad* in a nutshell; but it hath been my fortune to have much oftener seen a nutshell in an *Iliad*. There is no doubt that human life has received most wonderful advantages from both; but to which of the two the world is chiefly indebted, I shall leave among the curious, as a problem worthy of their utmost inquiry. For the invention of the latter, I think the commonwealth of learning is chiefly obliged to the great Modern improvement of digressions: the late refinements in knowledge, running parallel to those of diet in our nation, which among men of a judicious taste are dressed up in various compounds, consisting in soups and olios,[1] fricassees, and ragouts.

'Tis true, there is a sort of morose, detracting, ill-bred people, who pretend utterly to disrelish these polite innovations; and as to the similitude from diet, they allow the parallel, but are so bold to pronounce the example itself, a corruption and degeneracy of taste. They tell us that the fashion of jumbling fifty things together in a dish, was at first introduced in compliance to a depraved and debauched appetite, as well as to a crazy constitution: and to see a man hunting through an olio, after the head and brains of a goose, a widgeon, or a woodcock, is a sign he wants a stomach and digestion for more substantial victuals. Farther, they affirm, that digressions in a book are like foreign troops in a state, which argue the nation to want a heart and hands of its own, and often either subdue the natives, or drive them into the most unfruitful corners.

But, after all that can be objected by these supercilious censors, 'tis manifest, the society of writers would quickly be reduced to a very inconsiderable number, if men were put upon making books, with the fatal confinement of delivering nothing beyond what is to the purpose. 'Tis acknowledged, that were the case the same among us, as with the Greeks and Romans, when learning was in its cradle, to be reared and fed, and clothed by invention, it would be an easy task to fill up volumes upon particular occasions, without farther expatiating from the subject than by moderate excursions, helping to advance or clear the main design. But with knowledge it has fared as with a numerous army, encamped in a fruitful country, which for a few days maintains itself by the product of the soil it is on; till provisions being spent, they send to forage many a mile, among friends or enemies, it matters not. Meanwhile, the neighbouring fields, trampled and beaten down, become barren and dry, affording no sustenance but clouds of dust.

The whole course of things being thus entirely changed between us and the Ancients, and the

[d] That is, Calvin, from *calvus*, bald.
[e] All those who pretend to inward light.
[f] Jack of Leyden, who gave rise to the Anabaptists.
[g] The Huguenots.
[h] The Gueuses, by which name some Protestants in Flanders were called.
[i] John Knox, the reformer of Scotland.

3. **Mellæo . . . lepore:** "Treating everything with sweet wit."

SECTION VII. 1. **olios:** stews.

Moderns wisely sensible of it, we of this age have discovered a shorter, and more prudent method, to become scholars and wits, without the fatigue of reading or of thinking. The most accomplished way of using books at present is two-fold: either first, to serve them as some men do lords, learn their titles exactly, and then brag of their acquaintance. Or secondly, which is indeed the choicer, the profounder, and politer method, to get a thorough insight into the index, by which the whole book is governed and turned, like fishes by the tail. For, to enter the palace of learning at the great gate, requires an expense of time and forms; therefore men of much haste and little ceremony are content to get in by the back door. For the arts are all in a flying march, and therefore more easily subdued by attacking them in the rear. Thus physicians discover the state of the whole body, by consulting only what comes from behind. Thus men catch knowledge by throwing their wit on the posteriors of a book, as boys do sparrows with flinging salt upon their tails. Thus human life is best understood by the wise man's rule of regarding the end. Thus are the sciences found like Hercules's oxen, by tracing them backwards. Thus are old sciences unravelled like old stockings, by beginning at the foot.

Besides all this, the army of the sciences hath been of late, with a world of martial discipline, drawn into its close order, so that a view or a muster may be taken of it with abundance of expedition. For this great blessing we are wholly indebted to systems and abstracts, in which the modern fathers of learning, like prudent usurers, spent their sweat for the ease of us their children. For labor is the seed of idleness, and it is the peculiar happiness of our noble age to gather the fruit.

Now the method of growing wise, learned, and sublime, having become so regular an affair, and so established in all its forms, the numbers of writers must needs have increased accordingly, and to a pitch that has made it of absolute necessity for them to interfere continually with each other. Besides, it is reckoned, that there is not at this present, a sufficient quantity of new matter left in nature, to furnish and adorn any one particular subject to the extent of a volume. This I am told by a very skilful computer, who hath given a full demonstration of it from rules of arithmetic.

This, perhaps, may be objected against by those who maintain the infinity of matter, and therefore will not allow that any species of it can be exhausted. For answer to which, let us examine the noblest branch of Modern wit or invention, planted and cultivated by the present age, and which, of all others, hath borne the most and the fairest fruit. For though some remains of it were left us by the Ancients, yet have not any of those, as I remember, been translated or compiled into systems for Modern use. Therefore we may affirm, to our own honor, that it has in some sort, been both invented and brought to a perfection by the same hands. What I mean is, that highly celebrated talent among the Modern wits, of deducing similitudes, allusions, and applications, very surprising, agreeable, and apposite, from the *pudenda*[2] of either sex, together with their proper uses. And truly, having observed how little invention bears any vogue, besides what is derived into these channels, I have sometimes had a thought, that the happy genius of our age and country was prophetically held forth by that Ancient typical description of the Indian pigmies,° whose stature did not exceed above two foot; *sed quorum pudenda crassa, & ad talos usque pertingentia.*[3] Now, I have been very curious to inspect the late productions, wherein the beauties of this kind have most prominently appeared. And although this vein hath bled so freely, and all endeavours have been used in the power of human breath to dilate, extend, and keep it open; like the Scythians,° who had a custom, and an instrument, to blow up the privities of their mares, that they might yield the more milk; yet I am under an apprehension it is near growing dry, and past all recovery; and that either some new *fonde* of wit should, if possible, be provided, or else that we must e'en be content with repetition here, as well as upon other occasions.

° *Ctesiæ fragm. apud Photium.*

° *Herodot. L. 4.*

This will stand as an uncontestable argument, that our Modern wits are not to reckon upon the infinity of matter for a constant supply. What remains therefore, but that our last recourse must be had to large indexes, and little compendiums; quo-

2. ***pudenda:*** genitals. 3. ***sed . . . pertingentia:*** "but whose genitals are thick and go all the way down to their ankles."

tations must be plentifully gathered, and booked in alphabet; to this end, though authors need be little consulted, yet critics, and commentators, and lexicons carefully must. But above all, those judicious collectors of bright parts, and flowers, and observandas, are to be nicely dwelt on, by some called the sieves and boulters of learning, though it is left undetermined, whether they dealt in pearls or meal; and consequently, whether we are more to value that which passed through, or what stayed behind.

By these methods, in a few weeks, there starts up many a writer, capable of managing the profoundest and most universal subjects. For, what though his head be empty, provided his commonplace book be full; and if you will bate him but the circumstances of method, and style, and grammar, and invention; allow him but the common privileges of transcribing from others, and digressing from himself, as often as he shall see occasion; he will desire no more ingredients towards fitting up a treatise, that shall make a very comely figure on a bookseller's shelf; there to be preserved neat and clean for a long eternity, adorned with the heraldry of its title fairly inscribed on a label; never to be thumbed or greased by students, nor bound to everlasting chains of darkness in a library: but when the fulness of time is come, shall happily undergo the trial of purgatory, in order to ascend the sky.

Without these allowances, how is it possible we Modern wits should ever have an opportunity to introduce our collections, listed under so many thousand heads of a different nature? for want of which, the learned world would be deprived of infinite delight, as well as instruction, and we ourselves buried beyond redress in an inglorious and undistinguished oblivion.

From such elements as these, I am alive to behold the day, wherein the corporation of authors can outvie all its brethren in the field. A happiness derived to us with a great many others from our Scythian ancestors, among whom the number of pens was so infinite, that the Grecian° eloquence had no other way of expressing it, than by saying, that in the regions, far to the north, it was hardly possible for a man to travel, the very air was so replete with feathers.

° *Herodot. L. 4.*

The necessity of this digression will easily excuse the length; and I have chosen for it as proper a place as I could readily find. If the judicious reader can assign a fitter, I do here empower him to remove it into any other corner he pleases. And so I return with great alacrity to pursue a more important concern.

SECTION VIII

A TALE OF A TUB

The learned Æolists[a] maintain the original cause of all things to be wind, from which principle this whole universe was at first produced, and into which it must at last be resolved; that the same breath which had kindled, and blew *up* the flame of nature, should one day blow it *out:*

> Quod procul a nobis flectat Fortuna
> gubernans.[1]

This is what the *adepti* understand by their *anima mundi;* that is to say, the spirit, or breath, or wind of the world; or examine the whole system by the particulars of nature, and you will find it not to be disputed. For whether you please to call the *forma informans* of man, by the name of *spiritus, animus, afflatus,* or *anima;* what are all these but several appellations for wind, which is the ruling element in every compound, and into which they all resolve upon their corruption? Farther, what is life itself, but as it is commonly called, the breath of our nostrils? Whence it is very justly observed by naturalists, that wind still continues of great emolument in certain mysteries not to be named, giving occasion for those happy epithets of *turgidus* and *inflatus,* applied either to the *emittent* or *recipient* organs.

By what I have gathered out of ancient records, I find the compass of their doctrine took in two-and-thirty points, wherein it would be tedious to be very particular. However, a few of their most important precepts, deducible from it, are by no means to be omitted; among which the following maxim was of much weight: that since wind had the master share, as well as operation in every compound, by consequence, those beings must be of

[a] All pretenders to inspiration whatsoever.

SECTION VIII. **1. Quod . . . gubernans:** "Which wind may the pilot Fortune steer away from us."

chief excellence, wherein that *primordium*[2] appears most prominently to abound, and therefore man is in highest perfection of all created things, as having by the great bounty of philosophers, been endued with three distinct *animas* or winds, to which the sage Æolists, with much liberality, have added a fourth of equal necessity as well as ornament with the other three, by this *quartum principium,* taking in the four corners of the world; which gave occasion to that renowned cabalist, Bumbastus,[b] of placing the body of a man in due position to the four cardinal points.

In consequence of this, their next principle was, that man brings with him into the world a peculiar portion or grain of wind, which may be called a *quinta essentia,* extracted from the other four. This quintessence is of a catholic use upon all emergencies of life, is improvable into all arts and sciences, and may be wonderfully refined, as well as enlarged by certain methods in education. This, when blown up to its perfection, ought not to be covetously hoarded up, stifled, or hid under a bushel, but freely communicated to mankind. Upon these reasons, and others of equal weight, the wise Æolists affirm the gift of BELCHING to be the noblest act of a rational creature. To cultivate which art, and render it more serviceable to mankind, they made use of several methods. At certain seasons of the year, you might behold the priests amongst them, in vast numbers, with their mouths[c] gaping wide against a storm. At other times were to be seen several hundreds linked together in a circular chain, with every man a pair of bellows applied to his neighbour's breech, by which they blew up each other to the shape and size of a tun; and for that reason, with great propriety of speech, did usually call their bodies, their vessels. When, by these and the like performances, they were grown sufficiently replete, they would immediately depart, and disembogue[3] for the public good a plentiful share of their acquirements, into their disciples' chaps. For we must here observe, that all learning was esteemed among them to be compounded from the same principle. Because, first, it is generally affirmed, or confessed that learning puffeth men up; and, secondly, they proved it by the following syllogism: Words are but wind; and learning is nothing but words; *ergo,* learning is nothing but wind. For this reason, the philosophers among them did, in their schools, deliver to their pupils, all their doctrines and opinions, by eructation,[4] wherein they had acquired a wonderful eloquence, and of incredible variety. But the great characteristic, by which their chief sages were best distinguished, was a certain position of countenance, which gave undoubted intelligence to what degree or proportion the spirit agitated the inward mass. For, after certain gripings, the wind and vapours issuing forth, having first, by their turbulence and convulsions within, caused an earthquake in man's little world, distorted the mouth, bloated the cheeks, and gave the eyes a terrible kind of *relievo.* At which junctures all their belches were received for sacred, the sourer the better, and swallowed with infinite consolation by their meagre devotees. And to render these yet more complete, because the breath of man's life is in his nostrils, therefore the choicest, most edifying, and most enlivening belches, were very wisely conveyed through that vehicle, to give them a tincture as they passed.

Their gods were the four winds, whom they worshipped, as the spirits that pervade and enliven the universe, and as those from whom alone all inspiration can properly be said to proceed. However, the chief of these, to whom they performed the adoration of *latria,*[5] was the *Almighty North,* an ancient deity, whom the inhabitants of Megalopolis in Greece had likewise in highest reverence. *Omnium deorum Boream maxime celebrant.*°[6] This god, though endued with ubiquity, was yet supposed by the profounder Æolists, to possess one peculiar habitation, or (to speak in form) a *cœlum empyrœum,* wherein he was more intimately present. This was situated in a certain region, well known to the ancient Greeks by them called Σκοτία, or the Land of Darkness. And although many controversies have arisen upon that matter; yet so much is undisputed, that from a region of the like denom-

° *Pausan. L. 8.*

[b] This is one of the names of Paracelsus; he was called Christophorus, Theophrastus, Paracelsus, Bumbastus.

[c] This is meant of those seditious preachers, who blow up the seeds of rebellion, &c.

2. ***primordium:*** the beginning. 3. **disembogue:** let flow from the mouth.

4. **eructation:** belching. 5. ***latria:*** sacred worship. 6. ***Omnium . . . celebrant:*** "Of all the gods they offer the greatest celebration to the North Wind."

ination, the most refined Æolists have borrowed their original, from whence, in every age, the zealous among their priesthood have brought over their choicest inspiration, fetching it with their own hands from the fountain head in certain bladders, and disploding it among the sectaries in all nations, who did, and do, and ever will, daily gasp and pant after it.

Now, their mysteries and rites were performed in this manner. 'Tis well known among the learned, that the virtuosos of former ages had a contrivance for carrying and preserving winds in casks or barrels, which was of great assistance upon long sea voyages; and the loss of so useful an art at present is very much to be lamented, though, I know not how, with great negligence omitted by Pancirollus.[d] It was an invention ascribed to Æolus himself, from whom this sect is denominated; and who in honour of their founder's memory have to this day preserved great numbers of those barrels, whereof they fix one in each of their temples, first beating out the top. Into this barrel, upon solemn days, the priest enters, where, having before duly prepared himself by the methods already described, a secret funnel is also conveyed from his posteriors to the bottom of the barrel, which admits new supplies of inspiration from a northern chink or cranny. Whereupon, you behold him swell immediately to the shape and size of his vessel. In this posture he disembogues whole tempests upon his auditory, as the spirit from beneath gives him utterance, which, issuing *ex adytis* and *penetralibus*[7] is not performed without much pain and gripings. And the wind in breaking forth deals with his face[e] as it does with that of the sea, first blackening, then wrinkling, and at last bursting it into a foam. It is in this guise the sacred Æolist delivers his oracular belches to his panting disciples; of whom some are greedily gaping after the sanctified breath, others are all the while hymning out the praises of the winds; and, gently wafted to and fro by their own humming, do thus represent the soft breezes of their deities appeased.

[d] An author who writ *De Artibus perditis,* &c., Of Arts lost, and of Arts invented.

[e] This is an exact description of the changes made in the face by enthusiastic preachers.

7. *ex adytis . . . penetralibus:* "from the deepest caverns of the temple."

It is from this custom of the priests, that some authors maintain these Æolists to have been very ancient in the world. Because, the delivery of their mysteries, which I have just now mentioned, appears exactly the same with that of other ancient oracles, whose inspirations were owing to certain subterraneous effluviums of wind, delivered with the same pain to the priest, and much about the same influence on the people. It is true indeed, that these were frequently managed and directed by female officers, whose organs were understood to be better disposed for the admission of those oracular gusts, as entering and passing up through a receptacle of greater capacity, and causing also a pruriency by the way, such as with due management hath been refined from a carnal into a spiritual ecstasy. And to strengthen this profound conjecture, it is farther insisted, that this custom of female priests[f] is kept up still in certain refined colleges of our modern Æolists, who are agreed to receive their inspiration, derived through the receptacle aforesaid, like their ancestors, the Sybils.[8]

And whereas the mind of Man, when he gives the spur and bridle to his thoughts, doth never stop, but naturally sallies out into both extremes of high and low, of good and evil; his first flight of fancy commonly transports him to ideas of what is most perfect, finished, and exalted; till having soared out of his own reach and sight, not well perceiving how near the frontiers of height and depth border upon each other; with the same course and wing, he falls down plumb into the lowest bottom of things, like one who travels the east into the west, or like a straight line drawn by its own length into a circle. Whether a tincture of malice in our natures makes us fond of furnishing every bright idea with its reverse; or whether reason, reflecting upon the sum of things, can, like the sun, serve only to enlighten one half of the globe, leaving the other half, by necessity, under shade and darkness; or, whether fancy, flying up to the imagination of what is highest and best, becomes over-shot, and spent, and weary, and suddenly falls like a dead bird of paradise to the ground. Or whether after all these metaphysical conjectures, I

[f] Quakers who suffer their women to preach and pray.

8. Sybils: ancient prophetesses.

have not entirely missed the true reason, the proposition, however, which has stood me in so much circumstance, is altogether true; that, as the most uncivilized parts of mankind have some way or other climbed up into the conception of a God, or Supreme Power, so they have seldom forgot to provide their fears with certain ghastly notions, which, instead of better, have served them pretty tolerably for a devil. And this proceeding seems to be natural enough; for it is with men, whose imaginations are lifted up very high, after the same rate as with those whose bodies are so; that, as they are delighted with the advantage of a nearer contemplation upwards, so they are equally terrified with the dismal prospect of the precipice below. Thus, in the choice of a devil, it hath been the usual method of mankind, to single out some being, either in act or in vision, which was in most antipathy to the god they had framed. Thus also the sect of Æolists possessed themselves with a dread, and horror, and hatred of two malignant natures, betwixt whom, and the deities they adored, perpetual enmity was established. The first of these was the chameleon,[g] sworn foe to inspiration, who in scorn devoured large influences of their god, without refunding the smallest blast by eructation. The other was a huge terrible monster, called Moulinavent, who, with four strong arms, waged eternal battle with all their divinities, dexterously turning to avoid their blows, and repay them with interest.

Thus furnished, and set out with gods, as well as devils, was the renowned sect of Æolists, which makes at this day so illustrious a figure in the world, and whereof that polite nation of Laplanders are, beyond all doubt, a most authentic branch; of whom I therefore cannot, without injustice, here omit to make honourable mention, since they appear to be so closely allied in point of interest, as well as inclinations, with their brother Æolists among us, as not only to buy their winds by wholesale from the same merchants, but also to retail them after the same rate and method, and to customers much alike.

Now, whether this system here delivered was wholly compiled by Jack, or, as some writers believe, rather copied from the original at Delphos, with certain additions and emendations, suited to times and circumstances, I shall not absolutely determine. This I may affirm, that Jack gave it at least a new turn, and formed it into the same dress and model as it lies deduced by me.

I have long sought after this opportunity of doing justice to a society of men for whom I have a peculiar honour, and whose opinions, as well as practices, have been extremely misrepresented and traduced by the malice or ignorance of their adversaries. For I think it one of the greatest and best of human actions, to remove prejudices, and place things in their truest and fairest light: which I therefore boldly undertake, without any regards of my own, beside the conscience, the honour, and the thanks.

SECTION IX

A DIGRESSION CONCERNING THE ORIGINAL, THE USE, AND IMPROVEMENT OF MADNESS IN A COMMONWEALTH

Nor shall it any ways detract from the just reputation of this famous sect, that its rise and institution are owing to such an author as I have described Jack to be; a person whose intellectuals were overturned, and his brain shaken out of its natural position; which we commonly suppose to be a distemper, and call by the name of madness or phrenzy. For, if we take a survey of the greatest actions that have been performed in the world, under the influence of single men, which are the establishment of new empires by conquest, the advance and progress of new schemes in philosophy, and the contriving, as well as the propagating, of new religions, we shall find the authors of them all to have been persons whose natural reason had admitted great revolutions from their diet, their education, the prevalency of some certain temper, together with the particular influence of air and climate. Besides, there is something individual in human minds, that easily kindles at the accidental approach and collision of certain circumstances, which, though of paltry and mean appearance, do often flame out into the greatest emergencies of life. For great turns are not always given by strong hands, but by lucky adaption, and at proper seasons; and it is of no import where the fire was kindled, if the vapour

[g] I do not well understand what the Author aims at here, any more than by the terrible Monster, mentioned in the following lines, called *Moulinavent*, which is the French word for a windmill.

has once got up into the brain. For the upper region of man is furnished like the middle region of the air; the materials are formed from causes of the widest difference, yet produce at last the same substance and effect. Mists arise from the earth, steams from dunghills, exhalations from the sea, and smoke from fire; yet all clouds are the same in composition as well as consequences, and the fumes issuing from a jakes will furnish as comely and useful a vapour as incense from an altar. Thus far, I suppose, will easily be granted me; and then it will follow, that as the face of nature never produces rain but when it is overcast and disturbed, so human understanding, seated in the brain, must be troubled and overspread by vapours, ascending from the lower faculties to water the invention and render it fruitful. Now, although these vapours (as it hath been already said) are of as various original as those of the skies, yet the crop they produce differs both in kind and degree, merely according to the soil. I will produce two instances to prove and explain what I am now advancing.

A certain great prince[a] raised a mighty army, filled his coffers with infinite treasures, provided an invincible fleet, and all this without giving the least part of his design to his greatest ministers or his nearest favourites. Immediately the whole world was alarmed; the neighbouring crowns in trembling expectations towards what point the storm would burst; the small politicians everywhere forming profound conjectures. Some believed he had laid a scheme for universal monarchy; others, after much insight, determined the matter to be a project for pulling down the pope, and setting up the reformed religion, which had once been his own. Some, again, of a deeper sagacity, sent him into Asia to subdue the Turk, and recover Palestine. In the midst of all these projects and preparations, a certain state-surgeon,[b] gathering the nature of the disease by these symptoms, attempted the cure, at one blow performed the operation, broke the bag, and out flew the vapour; nor did anything want to render it a complete remedy, only that the prince unfortunately happened to die in the performance. Now, is the reader exceeding curious to learn from whence this vapour took its rise, which had so long set the nations at a gaze? What secret wheel, what hidden spring could put into motion so wonderful an engine? It was afterwards discovered that the movement of this whole machine had been directed by an absent female, whose eyes had raised a protuberancy, and before emission, she was removed into an enemy's country. What should an unhappy prince do in such ticklish circumstances as these? He tried in vain the poet's never-failing receipt of *corpora quæque*[1]; for

> Idque petit corpus mens unde est saucia
> amore;
> Unde feritur, eo tendit, gestitq; coire.
> —LUCR.[2]

Having to no purpose used all peaceable endeavours, the collected part of the semen, raised and inflamed, became a dust, converted to choler, turned head upon the spinal duct, and ascended to the brain. The very same principle that influences a bully to break the windows of a whore who has jilted him, naturally stirs up a great prince to raise mighty armies, and dream of nothing but sieges, battles, and victories.

> ——Teterrima belli
> Causa——[3]

The other instance[c] is what I have read somewhere in a very ancient author, of a mighty king, who, for the space of above thirty years, amused himself to take and lose towns; beat armies, and be beaten; drive princes out of their dominions; fright children from their bread and butter; burn, lay waste, plunder, dragoon, massacre subject and stranger, friend and foe, male and female. 'Tis recorded, that the philosophers of each country were in grave dispute upon causes natural, moral, and political, to find out where they should assign an original solution of this phenomenon. At last the

[a] This was Harry the Great of France.

[b] Ravillac, who stabbed Henry the Great in his coach.

[c] This is meant of the present French king.

SECTION IX. **1. *corpora quæque*:** see Lucretius, *On the Nature of Things*, IV, 1065. The complete line, of which these two words are a part, speaks of shedding fluid "upon any other body." **2. Idque . . . coire:** again, Lucretius, IV, 1048, 1055: "And the body seeks that by which the mind has been stricken by love. / Where it came from, there it tends, and it seeks to unite." **3. Teterrima . . . causa:** "The most hateful cause of war." See Horace, *Satires*, I, iii, 107.

vapour or spirit, which animated the hero's brain, being in perpetual circulation, seized upon that region of the human body, so renowned for furnishing the *zibeta occidentalis*,[d] and gathering there into a tumor, left the rest of the world for that time in peace. Of such mighty consequence it is where those exhalations fix, and of so little from whence they proceed. The same spirits which, in their superior progress would conquer a kingdom, descending upon the anus, conclude in a fistula.

Let us next examine the great introducers of new schemes in philosophy, and search till we can find from what faculty of the soul the disposition arises in mortal man, of taking it into his head to advance new systems with such an eager zeal, in things agreed on all hands impossible to be known; from what seeds this disposition springs, and to what quality of human nature these grand innovators have been indebted for their number of disciples. Because, it is plain, that several of the chief among them, both Ancient and Modern, were usually mistaken by their adversaries, and indeed by all except their own followers, to have been persons crazed, or out of their wits, having generally proceeded in the common course of their words and actions by a method very different from the vulgar dictates of unrefined reason; agreeing for the most part in their several models, with their present undoubted successors in the academy of modern Bedlam (whose merits and principles I shall farther examine in due place). Of this kind were *Epicurus, Diogenes, Appollonius, Lucretius, Paracelsus, Descartes,* and others; who, if they were now in the world, tied fast, and separate from their followers, would, in this our undistinguishing age, incur manifest danger of phlebotomy,[4] and whips, and chains, and dark chambers, and straw. For what man in the natural state or course of thinking, did ever conceive it in his power to reduce the notions of all mankind exactly to the same length, and breadth, and height of his own? Yet this is the first humble and civil design of all innovators in the empire of reason. Epicurus modestly hoped, that one time or other, a certain fortuitous concourse of all men's opinions, after perpetual justlings, the sharp with the smooth, the light and the heavy, the round and the square, would by certain *clinamina*[5] unite in the notions of atoms and void, as these did in the originals of all things. Cartesius reckoned to see before he died the sentiments of all philosophers, like so many lesser stars in his romantic system, wrapped and drawn within his own vortex. Now, I would gladly be informed, how it is possible to account for such imaginations as these in particular men, without recourse to my phenomenon of vapours, ascending from the lower faculties to overshadow the brain, and there distilling into conceptions, for which the narrowness of our mother-tongue has not yet assigned any other name besides that of madness or phrenzy. Let us therefore now conjecture how it comes to pass, that none of these great prescribers do ever fail providing themselves and their notions with a number of implicit disciples. And, I think, the reason is easy to be assigned: for there is a peculiar string in the harmony of human understanding, which in several individuals is exactly of the same tuning. This, if you can dexterously screw up to its right key, and then strike gently upon it, whenever you have the good fortune to light among those of the same pitch, they will, by a secret necessary sympathy, strike exactly at the same time. And in this one circumstance lies all the skill or luck of the matter; for if you chance to jar the string among those who are either above or below your own height, instead of subscribing to your doctrine, they will tie you fast, call you mad, and feed you with bread and water. It is therefore a point of the nicest conduct to distinguish and adapt this noble talent, with respect to the differences of persons and of times. Cicero understood this very well, when writing to a friend in England, with a caution, among other matters, to beware of being cheated by our hackney-coachmen (who, it seems, in those days were as arrant rascals as they are now) has these remarkable words: *Est quod gaudeas te in ista loca*

[d] Paracelsus, who was so famous for chemistry, tried an experiment upon human excrement, to make a perfume of it, which when he had brought to perfection, he called *zibeta occidentalis,* or western-civet, the back parts of man (according to his division mentioned by the author being the west).

---

4. phlebotomy: drawing blood for medical purposes.

5. ***clinamina:*** word originally used by Lucretius to explain the phenomenon in the systems of both Epicurus and Lucretius of deviations of atoms from straight lines that supposedly accounted for their coming together.

venisse, ubi aliquid sapere viderere.°[6] For, to speak a bold truth, it is a fatal miscarriage so ill to order affairs, as to pass for a fool in one company, when in another you might be treated as a philosopher. Which I desire some certain gentlemen of my acquaintance to lay up in their hearts, as a very seasonable innuendo.

° *Epist. ad. Fam. Trebatio.*

This, indeed, was the fatal mistake of that worthy gentleman, my most ingenious friend, Mr. Wotton: a person, in appearance ordained for great designs, as well as performances; whether you will consider his notions or his looks. Surely no man ever advanced into the public with fitter qualifications of body and mind, for the propagation of a new religion. Oh, had those happy talents misapplied to vain philosophy been turned into their proper channels of dreams and visions, where distortion of mind and countenance are of such sovereign use; the base detracting world would not then have dared to report that something is amiss, this his brain hath undergone an unlucky shake; which even his brother Modernists themselves, like ungrates, do whisper so loud, that it reaches up to the very garret I am now writing in.

Lastly, whosoever pleases to look into the fountains of Enthusiasm, from whence, in all ages, have eternally proceeded such fattening streams, will find the springhead to have been as troubled and muddy as the current. Of such great emolument is a tincture of this vapour, which the world calls madness, that without its help, the world would not only be deprived of those two great blessings, conquests and systems, but even all mankind would unhappily be reduced to the same belief in things invisible. Now, the former *postulatum* being held, that it is of no import from what originals this vapour proceeds, but either in what angles it strikes and spreads over the understanding, or upon what species of brain it ascends; it will be a very delicate point to cut the feather, and divide the several reasons to a nice and curious reader, how this numerical difference in the brain can produce effects of so vast a difference from the same vapour, as to be the sole point of individuation between Alexander the Great, Jack of Leyden,[7] and Monsieur Des Cartes. The present argument is the most abstracted that ever I engaged in; it strains my faculties to their highest stretch; and I desire the reader to attend with utmost perpensity, for I now proceed to unravel this knotty point.

There is in mankind a certain[e] * * *
* * * * * * * * *
* * * * * *
* * * * * *
* * * * * *
* * * And this I take to be a clear solution of the matter.

Hic multa desiderantur[8]

Having therefore so narrowly passed through this intricate difficulty, the reader will, I am sure, agree with me in the conclusion, that if the Moderns mean by madness, only a disturbance or transposition of the brain, by force of certain vapours issuing up from the lower faculties, then has this madness been the parent of all those mighty revolutions that have happened in empire, in philosophy, and in religion. For the brain, in its natural position and state of serenity, disposeth its owner to pass his life in the common forms, without any thought of subduing multitudes to his own power, his reasons, or his visions; and the more he shapes his understanding by the pattern of human learning, the less he is inclined to form parties after his particular notions, because that instructs him in his private infirmities, as well as in the stubborn ignorance of the people. But when a man's fancy gets astride on his reason, when imagination is at cuffs with the senses, and common understanding, as well as common sense, is kicked out of doors, the first proselyte he makes is himself; and when that is once compassed, the difficulty is not so great in bringing over others; a strong delusion always operating from without as vigorously as from within. For, cant and vision are to the ear and the eye, the same that tickling is to the touch. Those entertainments and pleasures we most value in life, are such

[e] Here is another defect in the manuscript, but I think the author did wisely, and that the matter which thus strained his faculties, was not worth a solution; and it were well if all metaphysical cobweb problems were no otherwise answered.

6. ***Est . . . viderere:*** "You should rejoice to have come into those places where you may be seen as a man of wisdom." **7. Jack of Leyden:** Johann Bockholdt, a Dutch tailor, a fanatical Anabaptist.

8. ***Hic . . . desiderantur:*** "Here many things are missing." (Another of Swift's takeoffs on textual emendation.)

as dupe and play the wag with the senses. For, if we take an examination of what is generally understood by happiness, as it has respect either to the understanding or the senses, we shall find all its properties and adjuncts will herd under this short definition: that it is a perpetual possession of being well deceived. And first, with relation to the mind or understanding, 'tis manifest what mighty advantages fiction has over truth; and the reason is just at our elbow; because imagination can build nobler scenes, and produce more wonderful revolutions than fortune or nature will be at expense to furnish. Nor is mankind so much to blame in his choice thus determining him, if we consider that the debate merely lies between things past and things conceived; and so the question is only this: whether things that have place in the imagination, may not as properly be said to exist, as those that are seated in the memory; which may be justly held in the affirmative, and very much to the advantage of the former, since this is acknowledged to be the womb of things, and the other allowed to be no more than the grave. Again, if we take this definition of happiness, and examine it with reference to the senses, it will be acknowledged wonderfully adapt. How fading and insipid do all objects accost us, that are not conveyed in the vehicle of delusion? How shrunk is everything, as it appears in the glass of nature? So that if it were not for the assistance of artificial mediums, false lights, refracted angles, varnish, and tinsel, there would be a mighty level in the felicity and enjoyments of mortal men. If this were seriously considered by the world, as I have a certain reason to suspect it hardly will, men would no longer reckon among their high points of wisdom, the art of exposing weak sides, and publishing infirmities; an employment, in my opinion, neither better nor worse than that of unmasking, which I think has never been allowed fair usage, either in the world or the playhouse.

In the proportion that credulity is a more peaceful possession of the mind than curiosity, so far preferable is that wisdom, which converses about the surface, to that pretended philosophy which enters into the depth of things, and then comes gravely back with informations and discoveries, that in the inside they are good for nothing. The two senses, to which all objects first address themselves, are the sight and the touch; these never examine farther than the colour, the shape, the size, and whatever other qualities dwell, or are drawn by art upon the outward of bodies; and then comes reason officiously with tools for cutting, and opening, and mangling, and piercing, offering to demonstrate, that they are not of the same consistence quite through. Now, I take all this to be the last degree of perverting nature; one of whose eternal laws it is, to put her best furniture forward. And therefore, in order to save the charges of all such expensive anatomy for the time to come, I do here think fit to inform the reader, that in such conclusions as these, reason is certainly in the right, and that in most corporeal beings, which have fallen under my cognizance, the outside hath been infinitely preferable to the in; whereof I have been farther convinced from some late experiments. Last week I saw a woman flayed, and you will hardly believe how much it altered her person for the worse. Yesterday I ordered the carcass of a beau to be stripped in my presence, when we were all amazed to find so many unsuspected faults under one suit of clothes. Then I laid open his brain, his heart, and his spleen; but I plainly perceived at every operation, that the farther we proceeded, we found the defects increase upon us in number and bulk: from all which, I justly formed this conclusion to myself; that whatever philosopher or projector can find out an art to sodder and patch up the flaws and imperfections of nature, will deserve much better of mankind, and teach us a more useful science, than that so much in present esteem, of widening and exposing them (like him who held anatomy to be the ultimate end of physic). And he, whose fortunes and dispositions have placed him in a convenient station to enjoy the fruits of this noble art; he that can with Epicurus content his ideas with the films and images that fly off upon his senses from the superficies of things; such a man truly wise, creams off nature, leaving the sour and the dregs for philosophy and reason to lap up. This is the sublime and refined point of felicity, called, the possession of being well deceived; the serene peaceful state of being a fool among knaves.

But to return to madness. It is certain, that according to the system I have above deduced, every species thereof proceeds from a redundancy of vapours; therefore, as some kinds of phrenzy give double strength to the sinews, so there are of other species, which add vigor, and life, and spirit to the brain. Now, it usually happens, that these active spirits, getting possession of the brain, resemble those that haunt other waste and empty dwellings, which for want of business, either vanish, and carry away a piece of the house, or else stay at home and fling it all out of the windows. By which are mystically displayed the two principal branches of madness, and which some philosophers not considering so well as I, have mistook to be different in their causes, over-hastily assigning the first to deficiency, and the other to redundance.

I think it therefore manifest, from what I have here advanced, that the main point of skill and address is to furnish employment for this redundancy of vapour, and prudently to adjust the season of it; by which means it may certainly become of cardinal and catholic emolument in a commonwealth. Thus one man, choosing a proper juncture, leaps into a gulf, from whence proceeds a hero, and is called the saver of his country; another achieves the same enterprise, but unluckily timing it, has left the brand of madness fixed as a reproach upon his memory; upon so nice a distinction are we taught to repeat the name of Curtius with reverence and love, that of Empedocles with hatred and contempt. Thus also it is usually conceived, that the elder Brutus only personated the fool and madman for the good of the public; but this was nothing else than a redundancy of the same vapour, long misapplied, called by the Latins, *ingenium par negotiis;*° or (to translate it as nearly as I can) a sort of phrenzy, never in its right element, till you take it up in business of the state.

° *Tacit.*

Upon all which, and many other reasons of equal weight, though not equally curious, I do here gladly embrace an opportunity I have long sought for, of recommending it as a very noble undertaking to Sir Edward Seymour, Sir Christopher Musgrave, Sir John Bowls, John How, Esq.,[9] and other patriots concerned, that they would move for leave to bring in a bill for appointing commissioners to inspect into Bedlam, and the parts adjacent; who shall be empowered to send for persons, papers, and records: to examine into the merits and qualifications of every student and professor; to observe with utmost exactness their several dispositions and behaviour, by which means, duly distinguishing and adapting their talents, they might produce admirable instruments for the several offices in a state, * * * * * [f] civil, and military, proceeding in such methods as I shall here humbly propose. And I hope the gentle reader will give some allowance to my great solicitudes in this important affair, upon account of that high esteem I have ever borne that honourable society, whereof I had some time the happiness to be an unworthy member.

Is any student tearing his straw in piece-meal, swearing and blaspheming, biting his grate, foaming at the mouth, and emptying his piss-pot in the spectators' faces? Let the right worshipful, the commissioners of inspection, give him a regiment of dragoons, and send him into Flanders among the rest. Is another eternally talking, sputtering, gaping, bawling, in a sound without period or article? What wonderful talents are here mislaid! Let him be furnished immediately with a green bag and papers, and threepence in his pocket,° and away with him to Westminster Hall. You will find a third gravely taking the dimensions of his kennel, a person of foresight and insight, though kept quite in the dark; for why, like Moses, *ecce cornuta*[g] *erat ejus facies.* He walks duly in one pace, entreats your penny with due gravity and ceremony, talks much of hard times, and taxes, and the whore of Babylon,[10] bars up the wooden window of his cell constantly at eight o'clock, dreams of fire, and shoplifters, and court-customers, and privileged places. Now, what a figure would all these acquirements amount to, if the owner were sent into the city among his brethren! Behold a fourth, in much and deep conversation with himself, biting his thumbs at proper junctures, his countenance checkered with business and design, sometimes walking very fast, with his eyes nailed to a paper that he holds in his hands; a great saver of time, somewhat thick of hearing, very short of sight, but more of

° *A lawyer's coach-hire.*

[f] Ecclesiastical.

[g] Cornutus is either horned or shining, and by this term, Moses is described in the vulgar Latin of the Bible.

9. A catalogue of some of the notable Tories in Parliament.

10. whore of Babylon: The woman in Revelation 17:5, who had inscribed on her forehead, "Mystery, Babylon the Great, the Mother of Harlots and Abominations of the Earth," an allusion to the Roman Catholic Church.

memory; a man ever in haste, a great hatcher and breeder of business, and excellent at the famous art of whispering nothing; a huge idolator of monosyllables and procrastination, so ready to give his word to everybody, that he never keeps it; one that has forgot the common meaning of words, but an admirable retainer of the sound; extremely subject to the looseness, for his occasions are perpetually calling him away. If you approach his grate in his familiar intervals, "Sir," says he, "give me a penny, and I'll sing you a song; but give me the penny first." (Hence comes the common saying, and commoner practice of parting with money for a song.) What a complete system of court skill is here described in every branch of it, and all utterly lost with wrong application. Accost the hole of another kennel, first stopping your nose; you will behold a surly, gloomy, nasty, slovenly mortal, raking in his own dung, and dabbling in his urine. The best part of his diet is the reversion of his own ordure, which expiring into steams, whirls perpetually about, and at last re-infunds. His complexion is of a dirty yellow, with a thin scattered beard, exactly agreeable to that of his diet upon its first declination, like other insects, who having their birth and education in an excrement, from thence borrow their colour and their smell. The student of this apartment is very sparing of his words, but somewhat over-liberal of his breath; he holds his hand out ready to receive your penny, and immediately upon receipt withdraws to his former occupations. Now, is it not amazing to think, the society of Warwick-lane[11] should have no more concern for the recovery of so useful a member, who, if one may judge from these appearances, would become the greatest ornament to that illustrious body? Another student struts up fiercely to your teeth, puffing with his lips, half squeezing out his eyes, and very graciously holds you out his hand to kiss. The keeper desires you not to be afraid of this professor, for he will do you no hurt; to him alone is allowed the liberty of the antechamber, and the orator of the place gives you to understand, that this solemn person is a tailor run mad with pride. This considerable student is adorned with many other qualities, upon which, at present, I shall not farther enlarge.................*Hark in your ear*[h]............. I am strangely mistaken, if all his address, his motions, and his airs, would not then be very natural, and in their proper element.

I shall not descend so minutely, as to insist upon the vast number of beaux, fiddlers, poets, and politicians, that the world might recover by such a reformation; but what is more material, besides the clear gain redounding to the commonwealth, by so large an acquisition of persons to employ, whose talents and acquirements, if I may be so bold as to affirm it, are now buried, or at least misapplied; it would be a mighty advantage accruing to the public from this inquiry, that all these would very much excel, and arrive at great perfection in their several kinds; which, I think, is manifest from what I have already shown, and shall enforce by this one plain instance, that even I myself, the author of these momentous truths, am a person, whose imaginations are hard-mouthed, and exceedingly disposed to run away with his reason, which I have observed from long experience to be a very light rider, and easily shook off, upon which account, my friends will never trust me alone, without a solemn promise to vent my speculations in this, or the like manner, for the universal benefit of human kind; which perhaps the gentle, courteous, and candid reader, brimful of that Modern charity and tenderness usually annexed to his office, will be very hardly persuaded to believe.

. . .

SECTION XI

A TALE OF A TUB

After so wide a compass as I have wandered, I do now gladly overtake, and close in with my subject, and shall henceforth hold on with it an even pace to the end of my journey, except some beautiful prospect appears within sight of my way, whereof though at present I have neither warning nor expectation, yet upon such an accident, come when it will, I shall beg my reader's favour and company, allowing me to conduct him through it along with myself. For in writing, it is as in travelling: if a man is in haste to be at home (which I acknowledge to

11. the society of Warwick-lane: the Royal College of Physicians.

[h] I cannot conjecture what the author means here, or how this chasm could be filled, tho' it is capable of more than one interpretation.

be none of my case, having never so little business as when I am there), if his horse be tired with long riding and ill ways, or be naturally a jade, I advise him clearly to make the straightest and the commonest road, be it ever so dirty. But then surely we must own such a man to be a scurvy companion at best; he spatters himself and his fellow-travellers at every step: all their thoughts, and wishes, and conversation, turn entirely upon the subject of their journey's end; and at every splash, and plunge, and stumble, they heartily wish one another at the devil.

On the other side, when a traveller and his horse are in heart and plight, when his purse is full, and the day before him, he takes the road only where it is clean or convenient; entertains his company there as agreeably as he can; but upon the first occasion, carries them along with him to every delightful scene in view, whether of art, of nature, or of both; and if they chance to refuse out of stupidity or weariness, let them jog on by themselves and be d—n'd; he'll overtake them at the next town, at which arriving, he rides furiously through; the men, women, and children run out to gaze; a hundred noisy curs[a] run barking after him, of which, if he honors the boldest with a lash of his whip, it is rather out of sport than revenge; but should some sourer mongrel dare too near an approach, he receives a salute on the chaps by an accidental stroke from the courser's heels (nor is any ground lost by the blow), which sends him yelping and limping home.

I now proceed to sum up the singular adventures of my renowned Jack, the state of whose dispositions and fortunes the careful reader does, no doubt, most exactly remember, as I last parted with them in the conclusion of a former section. Therefore, his next care must be from two of the foregoing to extract a scheme of notions, that may best fit his understanding for a true relish of what is to ensue.

Jack had not only calculated the first revolution of his brain so prudently, as to give rise to that epidemic sect of Æolists, but succeeding also into a new and strange variety of conceptions, the fruitfulness of his imagination led him into certain notions, which, although in appearance very unaccountable, were not without their mysteries and their meanings, nor wanted followers to countenance and improve them. I shall therefore be extremely careful and exact in recounting such material passages of this nature as I have been able to collect, either from undoubted tradition, or indefatigable reading; and shall describe them as graphically as it is possible, and as far as notions of that height and latitude can be brought within the compass of a pen. Nor do I at all question, but they will furnish plenty of noble matter for such, whose converting imaginations dispose them to reduce all things into types; who can make shadows, no thanks to the sun, and then mould them into substances, no thanks to philosophy; whose peculiar talent lies in fixing tropes and allegories to the letter, and refining what is literal into figure and mystery.

Jack had provided a fair copy of his father's will, engrossed in form upon a large skin of parchment; and resolving to act the part of a most dutiful son, he became the fondest creature of it imaginable. For although, as I have often told the reader, it consisted wholly in certain plain, easy directions about the management and wearing of their coats, with legacies and penalties, in case of obedience or neglect, yet he began to entertain a fancy that the matter was deeper and darker, and therefore must needs have a great deal more of mystery at the bottom. "Gentlemen," said he, "I will prove this very skin of parchment to be meat, drink, and cloth, to be the philosopher's stone, and the universal medicine." [b] In consequence of which raptures, he resolved to make use of it in the most necessary, as well as the most paltry, occasions of life. He had a way of working it into any shape he pleased; so that it served him for a nightcap when he went to bed, and for an umbrella in rainy weather. He would lap a piece of it about a sore toe, or when he had fits, burn two inches under his nose; or if anything lay heavy on his stomach, scrape off, and swallow as much of the powder as would lie on a silver penny; they were all infallible remedies. With analogy to these refinements, his common talk and conversation ran wholly in the phrase

[a] By these are meant what the author calls the true critics.

[b] The author here lashes those pretenders to purity, who place so much merit in using Scripture phrases on all occasions.

of his will,[c] and he circumscribed the utmost of his eloquence within that compass, not daring to let slip a syllable without authority from thence. Once at a strange house, he was suddenly taken short upon an urgent juncture, whereon it may not be allowed too particularly to dilate; and being not able to call to mind, with that suddenness the occasion required, an authentic phrase for demanding the way to the backside; he chose rather as the more prudent course to incur the penalty in such cases usually annexed. Neither was it possible for the united rhetoric of mankind to prevail with him to make himself clean again; because having consulted the will upon this emergency, he met with a passage[d] near the bottom (whether foisted in by the transcriber, is not known) which seemed to forbid it.

He made it a part of his religion, never to say grace to his meat,[e] nor could all the world persuade him, as the common phrase is, to eat his victuals like a Christian.[f]

He bore a strange kind of appetite to snap-dragon,[g] and to the livid snuffs of a burning candle, which he would catch and swallow with an agility wonderful to conceive; and by this procedure, maintained a perpetual flame in his belly, which issuing in a glowing steam from both his eyes, as well as his nostrils and his mouth, made his head appear in a dark night, like the skull of an ass, wherein a roguish boy had conveyed a farthing candle, to the terror of his Majesty's liege subjects. Therefore, he made use of no other expedient to light himself home, but was wont to say, that a wise man was his own lanthorn.

[c] The Protestant dissenters use Scripture phrases in their serious discourses and composures more than the Church of England men; accordingly Jack is introduced making his common talk and conversation to run wholly in the phrase of his will. W. WOTTON.

[d] I cannot guess the author's meaning here, which I would be very glad to know, because it seems to be of importance.

[e] The slovenly way of receiving the sacrament among the fanatics.

[f] This is a common phrase to express eating cleanlily, and is meant for an invective against that undecent manner among some people in receiving the sacrament, so in the lines before, which is to be understood of the Dissenters refusing to kneel at the sacrament.

[g] I cannot well find the author's meaning here, unless it be the hot, untimely, blind zeal of enthusiasts.

He would shut his eyes as he walked along the streets, and if he happened to bounce his head against a post, or fall into the kennel (as he seldom missed either to do one or both), he would tell the gibing prentices, who looked on, that he submitted with entire resignation, as to a trip, or a blow of fate, with whom he found, by long experience, how vain it was either to wrestle or to cuff; and whoever durst undertake to do either, would be sure to come off with a swinging fall, or a bloody nose. "It was ordained," said he, "some few days before the creation, that my nose and this very post should have a rencounter; and, therefore, providence thought fit to send us both into the world in the same age, and to make us countrymen and fellow-citizens. Now, had my eyes been open, it is very likely the business might have been a great deal worse; for how many a confounded slip is daily got by man with all his foresight about him? Besides, the eyes of the understanding see best, when those of the senses are out of the way; and therefore, blind men are observed to tread their steps with much more caution, and conduct, and judgment, than those who rely with too much confidence upon the virtue of the visual nerve, which every little accident shakes out of order, and a drop, or a film, can wholly disconcert; like a lanthorn among a pack of roaring bullies when they scour the streets, exposing its owner and itself to outward kicks and buffets, which both might have escaped, if the vanity of appearing would have suffered them to walk in the dark. But farther, if we examine the conduct of these boasted lights, it will prove yet a great deal worse than their fortune. 'Tis true, I have broke my nose against this post, because providence either forgot, or did not think it convenient to twitch me by the elbow, and give me notice to avoid it. But let not this encourage either the present age or posterity to trust their noses into the keeping of their eyes, which may prove the fairest way of losing them for good and all. For, O ye eyes, ye blind guides, miserable guardians are ye of our frail noses; ye, I say, who fasten upon the first precipice in view, and then tow our wretched willing bodies after you, to the very brink of destruction; but, alas, that brink is rotten, our feet slip, and we tumble down prone into a gulf, without one hospitable shrub in the way to break the fall; a fall, to which not any nose of mortal make is equal, except that of the giant Laurcalco,° who was lord of the silver bridge. Most properly therefore, O eyes, and with great justice, may you be compared to those foolish lights, which conduct men through dirt and darkness, till they fall into a deep pit or a noisome bog."

° *Vide* Don Quixote.

This I have produced as a scantling of Jack's great eloquence, and the force of his reasoning upon such abstruse matters.

He was, besides, a person of great design and improvement in affairs of devotion, having introduced a new deity, who hath since met with a vast number of worshippers, by some called Babel, by others Chaos; who had an ancient temple of Gothic structure[1] upon Salisbury plain, famous for its shrine, and celebration by pilgrims.

When he had some roguish trick to play,[h] he would down with his knees, up with his eyes, and fall to prayers, though in the midst of the kennel. Then it was that those who understood his pranks, would be sure to get far enough out of his way; and whenever curiosity attracted strangers to laugh, or to listen, he would of a sudden with one hand out with his gear, and piss full in their eyes, and with the other, all to bespatter them with mud.

In winter he went always loose and unbuttoned,[i] and clad as thin as possible, to let *in* the ambient heat; and in summer lapped himself close and thick to keep it *out*.

In all revolutions of government,[j] he would make his court for the office of hangman general; and in the exercise of that dignity, wherein he was very dextrous, would make use of no other vizard [k 2] than a long prayer.

He had a tongue so musculous and subtile, that he could twist it up into his nose, and deliver a strange kind of speech from thence. He was also the first in these kingdoms, who began to improve the Spanish accomplishment of braying; and having large ears, perpetually exposed and arrect, he carried his art to such a perfection, that it was a point of great difficulty to distinguish either by the view or the sound between the original and the copy.

He was troubled with a disease, reverse to that called the stinging of the tarantula; and would run dog-mad at the noise of music,[l] especially a pair of bagpipes. But he would cure himself again, by taking two or three turns in Westminster Hall, or Billingsgate, or in a boarding-school, or the Royal-Exchange, or a state coffee-house.

He was a person that feared no colours,[m] but mortally hated all, and upon that account bore a cruel aversion to painters; insomuch, that in his paroxysms, as he walked the streets, he would have his pockets loaden with stones to pelt at the signs.

Having from this manner of living, frequent occasion to wash himself, he would often leap over head and ears into the water, though it were in the midst of the winter, but was always observed to come out again much dirtier, if possible, than he went in.

He was the first that ever found out the secret of contriving a soporiferous medicine to be conveyed in at the ears;[n] it was a compound of sulphur and balm of Gilead, with a little pilgrim's salve.

He wore a large plaister of artificial caustics on his stomach, with the fervor of which, he could set himself a-groaning, like the famous board upon application of a red-hot iron.

He would stand in the turning of a street, and, calling to those who passed by, would cry to one, "Worthy sir, do me the honour of a good slap in the chaps";[o] to another, "Honest friend, pray favour me with a handsome kick on the arse"; "Madam, shall I entreat a small box on the ear from your ladyship's fair hands?" "Noble captain, lend a reason-

[h] The villainies and cruelties committed by enthusiasts and fanatics among us were all performed under the disguise of religion and long prayers.

[i] They affect differences in habit and behaviour.

[j] They are severe persecutors, and all in a form of cant and devotion.

[k] Cromwell and his confederates went, as they called it, to seek God, when they resolved to murder the king.

[l] This is to expose our Dissenters' aversion to instrumental music in churches. W. WOTTON.

[m] They quarrel at the most innocent decency and ornament, and defaced the statues and paintings on all the churches in England.

[n] Fanatic preaching, composed either of hell and damnation, or a fulsome description of the joys of heaven; both in such a dirty, nauseous style, as to be well resembled to pilgrim's salve.

[o] The fanatics have always had a way of affecting to run into persecution, and count vast merit upon every little hardship they suffer.

SECTION XI. **1. Gothic structure**: Stonehenge. **2. vizard**: a mask for protection.

able thwack, for the love of God, with that cane of yours over these poor shoulders." And when he had by such earnest solicitations made a shift to procure a basting sufficient to swell up his fancy and his sides, he would return home extremely comforted, and full of terrible accounts of what he had undergone for the public good. "Observe this stroke," (said he, showing his bare shoulders) "a plaguy janissary[3] gave it me this very morning at seven o'clock, as, with much ado, I was driving off the great Turk. Neighbours mine, this broken head deserves a plaister; had poor Jack been tender of his noddle, you would have seen the Pope and the French king, long before this time of day, among your wives and your warehouses. Dear Christians, the great Mogul was come as far as White-chapel, and you may thank these poor sides that he hath not (God bless us) already swallowed up man, woman, and child."

It was highly worth observing the singular effects of that aversion,[p] or antipathy, which Jack and his brother Peter seemed, even to an affectation, to bear toward each other. Peter had lately done some rogueries, that forced him to abscond; and he seldom ventured to stir out before night, for fear of bailiffs. Their lodgings were at the two most distant parts of the town from each other; and whenever their occasions or humours called them abroad, they would make choice of the oddest unlikely times and most uncouth rounds they could invent, that they might be sure to avoid one another: yet, after all this, it was their perpetual fortune to meet. The reason of which is easy enough to apprehend; for, the phrenzy and the spleen of both having the same foundation, we may look upon them as two pair of compasses, equally extended, and the fixed foot of each remaining in the same center; which, though moving contrary ways at first, will be sure to encounter somewhere or other in the circumference. Besides, it was among the great misfortunes of Jack, to bear a huge personal resemblance with his brother Peter. Their humour and dispositions were not only the same, but there was a close analogy in their shape and size, and their mien. Insomuch as nothing was more frequent than for a bailiff to seize Jack by the shoulders, and cry, "Mr. Peter, you are the king's prisoner." Or, at other times, for one of Peter's nearest friends to accost Jack with open arms, "Dear Peter, I am glad to see thee, pray send me one of your best medicines for the worms." This we may suppose was a mortifying return of those pains and proceedings Jack had laboured in so long; and finding how directly opposite all his endeavours had answered to the sole end and intention which he had proposed to himself, how could it avoid having terrible effects upon a head and heart so furnished as his? However, the poor remainders of his coat bore all the punishment; the orient sun never entered upon his diurnal progress, without missing a piece of it. He hired a tailor to stitch up the collar so close, that it was ready to choke him, and squeezed out his eyes at such a rate, as one could see nothing but the white. What little was left of the main substance of the coat, he rubbed every day for two hours against a rough-cast wall, in order to grind away the remnants of lace and embroidery, but at the same time went on with so much violence, that he proceeded a heathen philosopher. Yet after all he could do of this kind, the success continued still to disappoint his expectation. For, as it is the nature of rags to bear a kind of mock resemblance to finery, there being a sort of fluttering appearance in both, which is not to be distinguished at a distance, in the dark, or by short-sighted eyes; so, in those junctures, it fared with Jack and his tatters, that they offered to the first view a ridiculous flaunting, which assisting the resemblance in person and air, thwarted all his projects of separation, and left so near a similitude between them, as frequently deceived the very disciples and followers of both.

* * * * * * * * * *
* * * * * * * * * *
* * * * * * * *Desunt*
* * * * * * * *nonnulla.*[4]
* * * * * * * * * *
* * * * * * * * * *

[p] The papists and fanatics, tho' they appear the most averse to each other, yet bear a near resemblance in many things, as has been observed by learned men. *Ibid.* The agreement of our dissenters and the papists in that which Bishop Stillingfleet called the fanaticism of the Church of Rome, is ludicrously described for several pages together by Jack's likeness to Peter, and their being often mistaken for each other, and their frequent meeting when they least intended it. W. Wotton.

3. janissary: soldier.

4. *Desunt nonnulla:* "Several parts are missing."

The old Sclavonian proverb said well, that it is with men as with asses; whoever would keep them fast, must find a very good hold at their ears. Yet I think we may affirm, that it hath been verified by repeated experience, that,

Effugiet tamen hæc sceleratus vincula Proteus.[5]

It is good, therefore, to read the maxims of our ancestors, with great allowances to times and persons; for if we look into primitive records, we shall find, that no revolutions have been so great, or so frequent, as those of human ears. In former days, there was a curious invention to catch and keep them; which, I think, we may justly reckon among the *artes perditæ;*[6] and how can it be otherwise, when in these latter centuries the very species is not only diminished to a very lamentable degree, but the poor remainder is also degenerated so far as to mock our skilfullest tenure? For, if the only slitting of one ear in a stag hath been found sufficient to propagate the defect through a whole forest, why should we wonder at the greatest consequences, from so many loppings and mutilations, to which the ears of our fathers, and our own, have been of late so much exposed? 'Tis true, indeed, that while this island of ours was under the dominion of grace, many endeavours were made to improve the growth of ears once more among us. The proportion of largeness was not only looked upon as an ornament of the outward man, but as a type of grace in the inward. Besides, it is held by naturalists, that if there be a protuberancy of parts in the superiour region of the body, as in the ears and nose, there must be a parity also in the inferior; and therefore in that truly pious age, the males in every assembly, according as they were gifted, appeared very forward in exposing their ears to view, and the regions about them; because Hippocrates tells us,° that when the vein behind the ear happens to be cut, a man becomes a eunuch: and the females were nothing backwarder in beholding and edifying by them; whereof those who had already used the means, looked about them with great concern, in hopes of conceiving a suitable offspring by such a prospect; others, who stood candidates for benevolence, found there a plentiful choice, and were sure to fix upon such as discovered the largest ears, that the breed might not dwindle between them. Lastly, the devouter sisters, who looked upon all extraordinary dilatations of that member as protrusions of zeal, or spiritual excrescencies, were sure to honor every head they sat upon, as if they had been marks of grace; but especially that of the preacher, whose ears were usually of the prime magnitude; which upon that account, he was very frequent and exact in exposing with all advantages to the people: in his rhetorical paroxysms turning sometimes to hold forth the one, and sometimes to hold forth the other; from which custom, the whole operation of preaching is to this very day, among their professors, styled by the phrase of *holding forth.*

° Lib. de aëre locis & aquis.

Such was the progress of the saints for advancing the size of that member; and it is thought the success would have been every way answerable, if in process of time a cruel king[q] had not arose, who raised a bloody persecution against all ears above a certain standard; upon which some were glad to hide their flourishing sprouts in a black border, others crept wholly under a periwig; some were slit, others cropped, and a great number sliced off to the stumps. But of this more hereafter in my general *History of Ears,* which I design very speedily to bestow upon the public.

From this brief survey of the falling state of ears in the last age, and the small care had to advance their ancient growth in the present, it is manifest, how little reason we can have to rely upon a hold so short, so weak, and so slippery; and that whoever desires to catch mankind fast, must have recourse to some other methods. Now, he that will examine human nature with circumspection enough, may discover several handles whereof the six° senses afford one apiece, beside a great number that are screwed to the passions, and some few riveted to the intellect. Among these last, curiosity is one, and of all others affords the firmest grasp: curi-

° *Including Scaliger's.*

5. **Effugiet . . . Proteus:** "Nevertheless, the cunning Proteus will escape from all your chains." 6. ***artes perditæ:*** lost arts.

[q] This was King Charles the Second, who at his restoration turned out all the dissenting teachers that would not conform.

osity, that spur in the side, that bridle in the mouth, that ring in the nose, of a lazy and impatient, and a grunting reader. By this handle it is, that an author should seize upon his readers; which as soon as he has once compassed, all resistance and struggling are in vain, and they become his prisoners as close as he pleases, till weariness or dullness force him to let go his grip.

And therefore, I, the author of this miraculous treatise, having hitherto, beyond expectation, maintained by the aforesaid handle a firm hold upon my gentle reader, it is with great reluctance, that I am at length compelled to remit my grasp, leaving them in the perusal of what remains to that natural oscitancy[7] inherent in the tribe. I can only assure thee, courteous reader, for both our comforts, that my concern is altogether equal to thine, for my unhappiness in losing, or mislaying among my papers the remaining part of these memoirs; which consisted of accidents, turns, and adventures, both new, agreeable, and surprising; and therefore calculated, in all due points, to the delicate taste of this our noble age. But, alas, with my utmost endeavours, I have been able only to retain a few of the heads. Under which, there was a full account, how Peter got a protection out of the King's Bench; and of a reconcilement[r] between Jack and him upon a design they had in a certain rainy night, to trepan[8] brother Martin into a spunging-house,[9] and there strip him to the skin. How Martin, with much ado, showed them both a fair pair of heels. How a new warrant came out against Peter; upon which, how Jack left him in the lurch, stole his protection, and made use of it himself. How Jack's tatters came into fashion in court and city; how he got upon a great horse,[s] and eat custard.[t] But the particulars of all these, with several others, which have now slid out of my memory, are lost beyond all hopes of recovery. For which misfortune, leaving my readers to condole with each other, as far as they shall find it to agree with their several constitutions; but conjuring them by all the friendship that hath passed between us, from the title-page to this, not to proceed so far as to injure their healths for an accident past remedy; I now go on to the ceremonial part of an accomplished writer, and therefore, by a courtly Modern, least of all others to be omitted.

THE CONCLUSION

Going too long is a cause of abortion as effectual, though not so frequent, as going too short; and holds true especially in the labors of the brain. Well fare the heart of that noble Jesuit,° who first adventured to confess in print, that books must be suited to their several seasons, like dress, and diet, and diversions; and better fare our noble nation, for refining upon this among other French modes. I am living fast to see the time, when a book that misses its tide, shall be neglected, as the moon by day, or like mackerel a week after the season. No man hath more nicely observed our climate, than the bookseller who bought the copy of this work; he knows to a tittle what subjects will best go off in a dry year, and which it is proper to expose foremost, when the weather-glass is fallen to much rain. When he had seen this treatise, and consulted his almanack upon it, he gave me to understand, that he had maturely considered the two principal things, which were the bulk and the subject; and found it would never take but after a long vacation, and then only in case it should happen to be a hard year for turnips. Upon which I desired to know, considering my urgent necessities, what he thought might be acceptable this month. He looked westward, and said, "I doubt we shall have a fit of bad weather; however, if you could prepare some pretty little banter (but not in verse) or a small

° *Père d'Orleans.*

[r] In the reign of King James the Second, the Presbyterians by the king's invitation, joined with the Papists, against the Church of England, and addressed him for repeal of the penal laws and test. The king by his dispensing power gave liberty of conscience, which both Papists and Presbyterians made use of, but upon the Revolution, the Papists being down of course, the Presbyterians freely continued their assemblies, by virtue of King James's indulgence, before they had a toleration by law; this I believe the author means by Jack's stealing Peter's protection, and making use of it himself.

[s] Sir Humphry Edwyn, a Presbyterian, was some years ago Lord Mayor of London, and had the insolence to go in his formalities to a conventicle, with the ensigns of his office.

[t] Custard is a famous dish at a Lord Mayor's feast.

7. oscitancy: dullness, stupor. **8. trepan:** lure. **9. spunging-house:** debtor's prison.

treatise upon the —— it would run like wildfire. But, if it hold up, I have already hired an author to write something against Dr. Bentley, which, I am sure, will turn to account."

At length we agreed upon this expedient; that when a customer comes for one of these, and desires in confidence to know the author, he will tell him very privately, as a friend, naming whichever of the wits shall happen to be that week in the vogue; and if Durfey's last play should be in course, I had as lieve he may be the person as Congreve. This I mention, because I am wonderfully well acquainted with the present relish of courteous readers; and have often observed, with singular pleasure, that a fly, driven from a honey-pot, will immediately, with very good appetite alight and finish his meal on an excrement.

I have one word to say upon the subject of profound writers, who are grown very numerous of late; and I know very well, the judicious world is resolved to list me in that number. I conceive therefore, as to the business of being profound, that it is with writers as with wells; a person with good eyes may see to the bottom of the deepest, provided any water be there; and that often, when there is nothing in the world at the bottom, besides dryness and dirt, though it be but a yard and half under ground, it shall pass, however, for wondrous deep, upon no wiser a reason than because it is wondrous dark.

I am now trying an experiment very frequent among Modern authors; which is to write upon *Nothing;* when the subject is utterly exhausted, to let the pen still move on; by some called the ghost of wit, delighting to walk after the death of its body. And to say the truth, there seems to be no part of knowledge in fewer hands, than that of discerning when to have done. By the time that an author has writ out a book, he and his readers are become old acquaintants, and grow very loth to part; so that I have sometimes known it to be in writing, as in visiting, where the ceremony of taking leave has employed more time than the whole conversation before. The conclusion of a treatise resembles the conclusion of human life, which hath sometimes been compared to the end of a feast; where few are satisfied to depart, *ut plenus vitæ conviva:*[1] for men will sit down after the fullest meal, though it be only to doze, or to sleep out the rest of the day. But, in this latter, I differ extremely from other writers, and shall be too proud, if by all my labours, I can have any ways contributed to the repose of mankind in times[a] so turbulent and unquiet as these. Neither do I think such an employment so very alien from the office of a wit as some would suppose. For among a very polite nation in Greece,° there were the same temples built and consecrated to Sleep and the Muses, between which two deities they believed the strictest friendship was established.

° *Trezenii. Pausan. l.* 2.

I have one concluding favour to request of my reader; that he will not expect to be equally diverted and informed by every line or every page of this discourse; but give some allowance to the author's spleen, and short fits or intervals of dullness, as well as his own; and lay it seriously to his conscience, whether, if he were walking the streets, in dirty weather or a rainy day, he would allow it fair dealing in folks at their ease from a window to critic his gait, and ridicule his dress at such a juncture.

In my disposure of employments of the brain, I have thought fit to make invention the master, and give method and reason the office of its lackeys. The cause of this distribution was, from observing it my peculiar case, to be often under a temptation of being witty, upon occasion, where I could be neither wise nor sound, nor anything to the matter in hand. And I am too much a servant of the Modern way to neglect any such opportunities, whatever pains or improprieties I may be at, to introduce them. For I have observed, that from a laborious collection of seven hundred thirty-eight flowers and shining hints of the best Modern authors, digested with great reading into my book of commonplaces, I have not been able after five years to draw, hook, or force, into common conversation, any more than a dozen. Of which dozen, the one moiety failed of success, by being dropped among unsuitable company; and the other cost me so many strains, and traps, and ambages[2] to introduce, that I at length resolved to give it over. Now, this disappointment (to discover a secret) I must own,

[a] This was writ before the peace of Ryswick.

CONCLUSION. **1.** ***ut plenus vitæ conviva:*** "like a diner full of life."

2. ambages: digressions.

gave me the first hint of setting up for an author; and I have since found, among some particular friends, that it is become a very general complaint, and has produced the same effects upon many others. For I have remarked many a towardly word to be wholly neglected or despised in discourse, which has passed very smoothly, with some consideration and esteem, after its preferment and sanction in print. But now, since by the liberty and encouragement of the press, I am grown absolute master of the occasions and opportunities to expose the talents I have acquired, I already discover, that the issues of my *observanda* begin to grow too large for the receipts. Therefore, I shall here pause a while, till I find, by feeling the world's pulse and my own, that it will be of absolute necessity for us both, to resume my pen.

FINIS

(1704)

A Full and True Account of the Battel Fought last Friday Between the Antient and the Modern Books in St. James's Library

THE BOOKSELLER TO THE READER

The following Discourse, as it is unquestionably of the same author, so it seems to have been written about the same time with the former, I mean the year 1697, when the famous dispute was on foot about Ancient and Modern learning. The controversy took its rise from an essay of Sir William Temple's upon that subject, which was answered by W. Wotton, B.D., with an Appendix by Dr. Bentley, endeavouring to destroy the credit of Æsop and Phalaris for authors, whom Sir William Temple had, in the essay before-mentioned, highly commended. In that appendix, the doctor falls hard upon a new edition of Phalaris, put out by the Honourable Charles Boyle (now Earl of Orrery) to which Mr. Boyle replied at large, with great learning and wit; and the doctor voluminously rejoined. In this dispute, the town highly resented to see a person of Sir William Temple's character and methods roughly used by the two reverend gentlemen aforesaid, and without any manner of provocation. At length, there appearing no end of the quarrel, our author tells us, that the Books in St. James's Library, looking upon themselves as parties principally concerned, took up the controversy, and came to a decisive battle; but the manuscript, by the injury of fortune or weather, being in several places imperfect, we cannot learn to which side the victory fell.[1]

I must warn the reader to beware of applying to persons what is here meant only of books in the most literal sense. So, when Virgil is mentioned, we are not to understand the person of a famous poet called by that name, but only certain sheets of paper, bound up in leather, containing in print the works of the said poet, and so of the rest.

THE PREFACE OF THE AUTHOR

Satire is a sort of *glass*, wherein beholders do generally discover everybody's face but their own; which is the chief reason for that kind of reception it meets in the world, and that so very few are offended with it. But if it should happen otherwise, the danger is not great; and I have learned from long experience never to apprehend mischief from those understandings I have been able to provoke; for anger and fury, though they add strength to the *sinews* of the *body*, yet are found to relax those of the *mind*, and to render all its efforts feeble and impotent.

There is a *brain* that will endure but one *scumming*; let the owner gather it with discretion, and manage his little stock with husbandry; but of all things, let him beware of bringing it under the *lash* of his *betters*, because that will make it all bubble up into impertinence, and he will find no new supply: wit, without knowledge, being a sort of *cream*, which gathers in a night to the top, and, by a skilful hand, may be soon *whipped* into *froth;* but once scummed away, what appears underneath will be fit for nothing but to be thrown to the hogs.

THE BATTLE OF THE BOOKS. 1. See the general introduction to Swift for details of the controversy surrounding this satire. Names of authors and books are clarified there.

A FULL AND TRUE ACCOUNT OF THE BATTLE FOUGHT LAST FRIDAY, &c.

Whoever examines with due circumspection into the *Annual Records of Time*[a] will find it remarked, that war is the child of pride, and pride the daughter of riches. The former of which assertions may be soon granted, but one cannot so easily subscribe to the latter; for pride is nearly related to beggary and want, either by father or mother, and sometimes by both; and to speak naturally, it very seldom happens among men to fall out when all have enough; invasions usually travelling from north to south, that is to say from poverty upon plenty. The most ancient and natural grounds of quarrels are lust and avarice; which, though we may allow to be brethren or collateral branches of pride, are certainly the issues of want. For, to speak in the phrase of writers upon the politics, we may observe in the Republic of Dogs (which in its original seems to be an institution of the many) that the whole state is ever in the profoundest peace after a full meal; and that civil broils arise among them when it happens for one great bone to be seized on by some leading dog, who either divides it among the few, and then it falls to an oligarchy, or keeps it to himself, and then it runs up to a tyranny. The same reasoning also holds place among them in those dissensions we behold upon a turgescency in any of their females. For the right of possession lying in common (it being impossible to establish a property in so delicate a case) jealousies and suspicions do so abound, that the whole commonwealth of that street is reduced to a manifest state of war, of every citizen against every citizen, till some one of more courage, conduct, or fortune than the rest, seizes and enjoys the prize; upon which naturally arises plenty of heart-burning, and envy, and snarling against the happy dog. Again, if we look upon any of these republics engaged in a foreign war, either of invasion or defence, we shall find the same reasoning will serve as to the grounds and occasions of each; and that poverty or want in some degree or other (whether real or in opinion, which makes no alteration in the case) has a great share, as well as pride, on the part of the aggressor.

Now, whoever will please to take this scheme, and either reduce or adapt it to an intellectual state, or commonwealth of learning, will soon discover the first ground of disagreement between the two great parties at this time in arms, and may form just conclusions upon the merits of either cause. But the issue or events of this war are not so easy to conjecture at; for the present quarrel is so inflamed by the warm heads of either faction, and the pretensions somewhere or other so exorbitant, as not to admit the least overtures of accommodation. This quarrel first began (as I have heard it affirmed by an old dweller in the neighbourhood) about a small spot of ground, lying and being upon one of the two tops of the hill Parnassus; the highest and largest of which had, it seems, been time out of mind in quiet possession of certain tenants, called the Ancients, and the other was held by the Moderns. But these disliking their present station, sent certain ambassadors to the Ancients, complaining of a great nuisance; how the height of that part of Parnassus quite spoiled the prospect of theirs, especially towards the *East;* and therefore, to avoid a war, offered them the choice of this alternative; either that the Ancients would please to remove themselves and their effects down to the lower summity, which the Moderns would graciously surrender to them, and advance in their place; or else that the said Ancients will give leave to the Moderns to come with shovels and mattocks, and level the said hill as low as they shall think it convenient. To which the Ancients made answer: how little they expected such a message as this from a colony whom they had admitted out of their own free grace, to so near a neighbourhood. That, as to their own seat, they were aborigines of it, and therefore to talk with them of a removal or surrender, was a language they did not understand. That if the height of the hill on their side shortened the prospect of the Moderns, it was a disadvantage they could not help, but desired them to consider, whether that injury (if it be any) were not largely recompensed by the shade and shelter it afforded them. That, as to levelling or digging down, it was either folly or ignorance to propose it, if they did, or did not know, how that side of the hill was an entire rock, which would break their tools and hearts, without

[a] Riches produces pride; pride is war's ground, &c. *Vide Ephem. de Mary Clarke;* opt. edit.

any damage to itself. That they would therefore advise the Moderns rather to raise their own side of the hill, than dream of pulling down that of the Ancients, to the former of which they would not only give licence, but also largely contribute. All this was rejected by the Moderns with much indignation, who still insisted upon one of the two expedients; and so this difference broke out into a long and obstinate war, maintained on the one part by resolution, and by the courage of certain leaders and allies; but on the other, by the greatness of their number, upon all defeats, affording continual recruits. In this quarrel whole rivulets of ink have been exhausted, and the virulence of both parties enormously augmented. Now, it must here be understood, that ink is the great missive weapon in all battles of the learned, which conveyed through a sort of engine called a quill, infinite numbers of these are darted at the enemy, by the valiant on each side, with equal skill and violence, as if it were an engagement of porcupines. This malignant liquor was compounded by the engineer who invented it of two ingredients, which are gall and copperas, by its bitterness and venom to suit in some degree, as well as to foment, the genius of the combatants. And as the Grecians, after an engagement, when they could not agree about the victory, were wont to set up trophies on both sides, the beaten party being content to be at the same expense, to keep itself in countenance (a laudable and ancient custom, happily revived of late, in the art of war) so the learned, after a sharp and bloody dispute, do on both sides hang out their trophies too, whichever comes by the worse. These trophies have largely inscribed on them the merits of the cause, a full impartial account of such a battle, and how the victory fell clearly to the party that set them up. They are known to the world under several names; as disputes, arguments, rejoinders, brief considerations, answers, replies, remarks, reflections, objections, confutations. For a very few days they are fixed up in all public places, either by themselves or their representatives,° for passengers to gaze at; from whence the chiefest and largest are removed to certain magazines they call libraries, there to remain in a quarter purposely assigned them, and from thenceforth begin to be called Books of Controversy.

° *Their title-pages.*

In these books is wonderfully instilled and preserved the spirit of each warrior, while he is alive; and after his death his soul transmigrates there to inform[2] them. This, at least, is the more common opinion; but I believe it is with libraries as with other cemeteries, where some philosophers affirm that a certain spirit, which they call *brutum hominis,*[3] hovers over the monument till the body is corrupted and turns to dust or to worms, but then vanishes or dissolves. So, we may say, a restless spirit haunts over every book, till dust or worms have seized upon it, which to some may happen in a few days, but to others later; and therefore, books of controversy being, of all others, haunted by the most disorderly spirits, have always been confined in a separate lodge from the rest; and for fear of mutual violence against each other, it was thought prudent by our ancestors to bind them to the peace with strong iron chains. Of which invention the original occasion was this: when the works of Scotus first came out, they were carried to a certain great library and had lodgings appointed them; but this author was no sooner settled than he went to visit his master Aristotle, and there both concerted together to seize Plato by main force, and turn him out from his ancient station among the divines, where he had peaceably dwelt near eight hundred years. The attempt succeeded, and the two usurpers have reigned ever since in his stead; but to maintain quiet for the future, it was decreed, that all polemics of the larger size should be held fast with a chain.

By this expedient, the public peace of libraries might certainly have been preserved, if a new species of controversial books had not arose of late years, instinct with a most malignant spirit, from the war above-mentioned between the learned, about the higher summit of Parnassus.

When these books were first admitted into the public libraries, I remember to have said upon occasion, to several persons concerned, how I was sure they would create broils wherever they came, unless a world of care were taken; and therefore I advised that the champions of each side should be coupled together, or otherwise mixed, that like the blending of contrary poisons their malignity might be employed among themselves. And it seems I was neither an ill prophet nor an ill counsellor; for

2. inform: give life to. **3. *brutum hominis:*** the stupidity of man.

it was nothing else but the neglect of this caution which gave occasion to the terrible fight that happened on Friday last between the Ancient and Modern books in the King's Library. Now, because the talk of this battle is so fresh in everybody's mouth, and the expectation of the town so great to be informed in the particulars, I, being possessed of all qualifications requisite in an historian, and retained by neither party, have resolved to comply with the urgent importunity of my friends, by writing down a full impartial account thereof.

The guardian of the regal library, a person of great valor, but chiefly renowned for his humanity,[b] had been a fierce champion for the Moderns; and, in an engagement upon Parnassus, had vowed, with his own hands, to knock down two of the Ancient chiefs, who guarded a small pass on the superior rock, but, endeavouring to climb up, was cruelly obstructed by his own unhappy weight, and tendency towards his center, a quality to which those of the Modern party are extreme subject; for, being light-headed, they have in speculation a wonderful agility, and conceive nothing too high for them to mount, but in reducing to practice discover a mighty pressure about their posteriors and their heels. Having thus failed in his design, the disappointed champion bore a cruel rancour to the Ancients, which he resolved to gratify by showing all marks of his favour to the books of their adversaries, and lodging them in the fairest apartments; when at the same time, whatever book had the boldness to own itself for an advocate of the Ancients, was buried alive in some obscure corner, and threatened, upon the least displeasure, to be turned out of doors. Besides, it so happened, that about this time there was a strange confusion of place among all the books in the library; for which several reasons were assigned. Some imputed it to a great heap of learned dust, which a perverse wind blew off from a shelf of Moderns into the keeper's eyes. Others affirmed he had a humour to pick the worms out of the schoolmen, and swallow them fresh and fasting; whereof some fell upon his spleen, and some climbed up into his head, to the great perturbation of both. And lastly, others maintained that by walking much in the dark about the library, he had quite lost the situation of it out of his head; and therefore in replacing his books he was apt to mistake, and clap Descartes next to Aristotle; poor Plato had got between Hobbes and the Seven Wise Masters, and Virgil was hemmed in with Dryden on one side and Wither[5] on the other.

[b] The Honourable Mr. Boyle, in the preface to his edition of Phalaris, says he was refused a manuscript by the library keeper, *pro solita humanitate suâ*.[4]

Meanwhile those books that were advocates for the Moderns chose out one from among them to make a progress through the whole library, examine the number and strength of their party, and concert their affairs. This messenger performed all things very industriously, and brought back with him a list of their forces, in all fifty thousand, consisting chiefly of light-horse, heavy-armed foot, and mercenaries; whereof the foot were in general but sorrily armed, and worse clad; their horses large, but extremely out of case and heart; however, some few by trading among the Ancients had furnished themselves tolerably enough.

While things were in this ferment, discord grew extremely high, hot words passed on both sides, and ill blood was plentifully bred. Here a solitary Ancient, squeezed up among a whole shelf of Moderns, offered fairly to dispute the case, and to prove by manifest reasons, that the priority was due to them, from long possession, and in regard of their prudence, antiquity, and, above all, their great merits towards the Moderns. But these denied the premises, and seemed very much to wonder how the Ancients could pretend to insist upon their antiquity, when it was so plain (if they went to that) that the Moderns were much the more ancient° of the two. As for any obligations they owed to the Ancients, they renounced them all. " 'Tis true," said they, "we are informed, some few of our party have been so mean to borrow their subsistence from you; but the rest, infinitely the greater number (and especially we French and English) were so far from stooping to so base an example, that there never passed, till this very hour, six words between us. For our horses are of our own breed-

° *According to the modern paradox.*

4. ***pro . . . suâ:*** "with his customary humaneness." The general reference in this section is to Richard Bentley, Royal Librarian, and his rudeness to Robert Boyle.

5. Wither: George Wither (1588–1667). Another Swiftian example of the bad poet.

ing, our arms of our own forging, and our clothes of our own cutting out and sewing." Plato was by chance upon the next shelf, and observing those that spoke to be in the ragged plight mentioned a while ago, their jades lean and foundered, their weapons of rotten wood, their armour rusty, and nothing but rags underneath, he laughed aloud, and in his pleasant way swore, by G— he believed them.

Now, the Moderns had not proceeded in their late negotiation with secrecy enough to escape the notice of the enemy. For those advocates, who had begun the quarrel by setting first on foot the dispute of precedency, talked so loud of coming to a battle, that Temple happened to overhear them, and gave immediate intelligence to the Ancients, who thereupon drew up their scattered troops together, resolving to act upon the defensive; upon which several of the Moderns fled over to their party, and among the rest Temple himself. This Temple, having been educated and long conversed among the Ancients, was, of all the Moderns, their greatest favorite, and became their greatest champion.

Things were at this crisis, when a material accident fell out. For, upon the highest corner of a large window, there dwelt a certain spider, swollen up to the first magnitude by the destruction of infinite numbers of flies, whose spoils lay scattered before the gates of his palace, like human bones before the cave of some giant. The avenues to his castle were guarded with turnpikes and palisadoes, all after the Modern way of fortification. After you had passed several courts, you came to the center, wherein you might behold the constable himself in his own lodgings, which had windows fronting to each avenue, and ports to sally out upon all occasions of prey or defence. In this mansion he had for some time dwelt in peace and plenty, without danger to his person by swallows from above, or to his palace by brooms from below: when it was the pleasure of fortune to conduct thither a wandering bee, to whose curiosity a broken pane in the glass had discovered itself, and in he went; where expatiating a while, he at last happened to alight upon one of the outward walls of the spider's citadel; which, yielding to the unequal weight, sunk down to the very foundation. Thrice he endeavoured to force his passage, and thrice the center shook. The spider within, feeling the terrible convulsion, supposed at first that nature was approaching to her final dissolution; or else that Beelzebub,[6] with all his legions, was come to revenge the death of many thousands of his subjects, whom his enemy had slain and devoured. However, he at length valiantly resolved to issue forth, and meet his fate. Meanwhile the bee had acquitted himself of his toils, and posted securely at some distance, was employed in cleansing his wings, and disengaging them from the ragged remnants of the cobweb. By this time the spider was adventured out, when beholding the chasms, and ruins, and dilapidations of his fortress, he was very near at his wit's end; he stormed and swore like a madman, and swelled till he was ready to burst. At length, casting his eye upon the bee, and wisely gathering causes from events (for they knew each other by sight), "A plague split you," said he, "for a giddy son of a whore. Is it you, with a vengeance, that have made this litter here? Could you not look before you, and be d—nd? Do you think I have nothing else to do (in the devil's name) but to mend and repair after your arse?" "Good words, friend," said the bee (having now pruned himself, and being disposed to be droll) "I'll give you my hand and word to come near your kennel no more; I was never in such a confounded pickle since I was born." "Sirrah," replied the spider, "if it were not for breaking an old custom in our family, never to stir abroad against an enemy, I should come and teach you better manners." "I pray have patience," said the bee, "or you will spend your substance, and for aught I see, you may stand in need of it all, towards the repair of your house." "Rogue, rogue," replied the spider, "yet methinks you should have more respect to a person, whom all the world allows to be so much your betters." "By my troth," said the bee, "the comparison will amount to a very good jest, and you will do me a favour to let me know the reasons that all the world is pleased to use in so hopeful a dispute." At this the spider, having swelled himself into the size and posture of a disputant, began his argument in the true spirit of controversy, with a resolution to be heartily scurrilous and angry, to urge on his own reasons, without the least regard to the answers or objections of his opposite, and

6. **Beelzebub:** the devil, often regarded as the "lord of the flies."

fully predetermined in his mind against all conviction.

"Not to disparage myself," said he, "by the comparison with such a rascal, what art thou but a vagabond without house or home, without stock or inheritance, born to no possession of your own, but a pair of wings and a drone-pipe? Your livelihood is an universal plunder upon nature; a freebooter over fields and gardens; and for the sake of stealing will rob a nettle as easily as a violet. Whereas I am a domestic animal, furnished with a native stock within myself. This large castle (to show my improvements in the mathematics) is all built with my own hands, and the materials extracted altogether out of my own person."

"I am glad," answered the bee, "to hear you grant at least that I am come honestly by my wings and my voice; for then, it seems, I am obliged to Heaven alone for my flights and my music; and Providence would never have bestowed me two such gifts, without designing them for the noblest ends. I visit indeed all the flowers and blossoms of the field and the garden; but whatever I collect from thence enriches myself, without the least injury to their beauty, their smell, or their taste. Now, for you and your skill in architecture and other mathematics, I have little to say: in that building of yours there might, for aught I know, have been labor and method enough, but by woful experience for us both, 'tis too plain, the materials are naught, and I hope you will henceforth take warning, and consider duration and matter as well as method and art. You boast, indeed, of being obliged to no other creature, but of drawing and spinning out all from yourself; that is to say, if we may judge of the liquor in the vessel by what issues out, you possess a good plentiful store of dirt and poison in your breast; and, though I would by no means lessen or disparage your genuine stock of either, yet I doubt you are somewhat obliged for an increase of both, to a little foreign assistance. Your inherent portion of dirt does not fail of acquisitions, by sweepings exhaled from below; and one insect furnishes you with a share of poison to destroy another. So that in short, the question comes all to this; which is the nobler being of the two, that which by a lazy contemplation of four inches round, by an overweening pride, feeding and engendering on itself, turns all into excrement and venom, producing nothing at last, but flybane and a cobweb; or that which, by an universal range, with long search, much study, true judgment, and distinction of things, brings home honey and wax."

This dispute was managed with such eagerness, clamor, and warmth, that the two parties of books in arms below stood silent a while, waiting in suspense what would be the issue, which was not long undetermined, for the bee grown impatient at so much loss of time, fled straight away to a bed of roses, without looking for a reply, and left the spider like an orator, collected in himself and just prepared to burst out.

It happened upon this emergency, that Æsop broke silence first. He had been of late most barbarously treated by a strange effect of the regent's humanity, who had tore off his title-page, sorely defaced one half of his leaves, and chained him fast among a shelf of Moderns. Where soon discovering how high the quarrel was like to proceed, he tried all his arts, and turned himself to a thousand forms. At length in the borrowed shape of an ass, the regent mistook him for a Modern; by which means he had time and opportunity to escape to the Ancients, just when the spider and the bee were entering into their contest, to which he gave his attention with a world of pleasure; and when it was ended, swore in the loudest key, that in all his life he had never known two cases so parallel and adapt to each other, as that in the window, and this upon the shelves. "The disputants," said he, "have admirably managed the dispute between them, have taken in the full strength of all that is to be said on both sides, and exhausted the substance of every argument *pro* and *con*. It is but to adjust the reasonings of both to the present quarrel, then to compare and apply the labors and fruits of each as the bee has learnedly deduced them; and we shall find the conclusions fall plain and close upon the Moderns and us. For pray gentlemen, was ever anything so modern as the spider in his air, his turns, and his paradoxes? He argues in the behalf of you his brethren and himself, with many boastings of his native stock and great genius, that he spins and spits wholly from himself, and scorns to own any obligation or assistance from without. Then he displays to you his great skill in architecture, and improvement in the mathematics. To all this the bee, as an advocate retained by us the Ancients, thinks fit to answer; that if one may judge of the great genius or inventions of the Moderns by what they have produced, you will hardly have countenance to bear you out in boasting of either. Erect your schemes with as much method and skill as you please; yet if the materials be nothing but dirt, spun out of your own entrails (the guts of modern brains) the edifice will conclude at last in a cobweb, the duration of which, like that of other spiders' webs, may be imputed to their being forgotten, or neglected, or hid in a corner. For anything else of genuine that the Moderns may pretend to, I cannot recollect, unless it be a large vein of wrangling and satire, much of a nature and substance with the spider's poison; which, however they pretend to spit wholly out of themselves, is improved by the same arts, by feeding upon the insects and vermin of the age. As for us the Ancients, we are content with the bee to pretend to nothing of our own, beyond our wings and our voice, that is to say, our flights and our language. For the rest, whatever we have got, has been by infinite labor and search, and ranging through every corner of nature; the difference is, that instead of dirt and poison, we have rather chose to fill our hives with honey and wax, thus furnishing mankind with the two noblest of things, which are sweetness and light."

'Tis wonderful to conceive the tumult arisen among the books, upon the close of this long descant of Æsop; both parties took the hint, and heightened their animosities so on a sudden, that they resolved it should come to a battle. Immediately the two main bodies withdrew under their several ensigns, to the farther parts of the library, and there entered into cabals and consults upon the present emergency. The Moderns were in very warm debates upon the choice of their leaders; and nothing less than the fear impending from their enemies could have kept them from mutinies upon this occasion.[7] The difference was greatest among the horse, where every private trooper pretended to the chief command, from Tasso[8] and Milton to Dryden and Withers. The light-horse were commanded by Cowley and Despréaux.[9] There came the bowmen under their valiant leaders, Descartes, Gassendi,[10] and Hobbes, whose strength was such that they could shoot their arrows beyond the atmosphere, never to fall down again, but turn like that of Evander,[11] into meteors, or like the cannonball, into stars. Paracelsus brought a squadron of stink-pot-flingers from the snowy mountains of Rhætia. There came a vast body of dragoons, of different nations, under the leading of Harvey,[12] their great aga, part armed with scythes, the weapons of death; part with lances and long knives, all steeped in poison; part shot bullets of a most malignant nature, and used white powder which infallibly killed without report. There came several bodies of heavy-armed foot, all mercenaries, under the ensigns of Guicciardini, Davila, Polydore Virgil, Buchanan, Mariana, Camden, and others.[13] The engineers were commanded by Regiomontanus and Wilkins.[14] The rest were a confused multitude, led by Scotus, Aquinas, and Bellarmine,[15] of mighty bulk and stature, but without either arms, courage, or discipline. In the last place, came infinite swarms of calones,[16] a disorderly rout led by L'Estrange, rogues and ragamuffins, that follow the camp for nothing but the plunder, all without coats to cover them.

The army of the Ancients was much fewer in number; Homer led the horse, and Pindar the light-horse; Euclid was chief engineer; Plato and Aristotle commanded the bowmen; Herodotus and Livy the foot; Hippocrates the dragoons. The allies, led by Vossius[17] and Temple, brought up the rear.

7. Swift organizes the forces of the Moderns as follows: the *horsemen* are the poets; the *bowmen*, the philosophers; the *hired troops*, the historians; the *engineers*, the scientists. **8. Tasso:** Torquato Tasso (1544–1595), the Italian epic poet, author of *Jerusalem Delivered.*

9. Despréaux: Nicholas Boileau-Despréaux, better known as Boileau (1636–1711), author of the pioneering critical document, *The Art of Poetry.* **10. Gassendi:** Pierre Gassendi (1592–1655). Philosopher and mathematician, critic of Aristotle. **11. Evander:** Swift nodded here: it was the arrow of Alcestis he is thinking of. See *Aeneid* V, 525–528. **12.** Sir William Harvey (1578–1657), the discoverer of the circulation of the blood. **13.** A catalogue of modern European historians. **14. Regiomontanus and Wilkins:** Regiomontanus was Johann Müller (1436–1476), the Prussian mathematician. John Wilkins (1614–1672) was one of the founding fathers of the Royal Society, also a mathematician. **15. Bellarmine:** St. Robert Bellarmine (1542–1621), Catholic theologian. **16. calones:** the mercenary soldiers, hack writers. **17. Vossius:** Isaac Vossius (1618–1688), a Dutch theological scholar.

All things violently tending to a decisive battle, Fame, who much frequented, and had a large apartment formerly assigned her in the regal library, fled up straight to Jupiter, to whom she delivered a faithful account of all that passed between the two parties below. (For, among the gods, she always tells truth.) Jove, in great concern, convokes a council in the Milky Way. The senate assembled, he declares the occasion of convening them; a bloody battle just impendent between two mighty armies of Ancient and Modern creatures, called books, wherein the celestial interest was but too deeply concerned. Momus,[18] the patron of the Moderns, made an excellent speech in their favor, which was answered by Pallas, the protectress of the Ancients. The assembly was divided in their affections; when Jupiter commanded the book of fate to be laid before him. Immediately were brought by Mercury three large volumes in folio, containing memoirs of all things past, present, and to come. The clasps were of silver, double gilt; the covers of celestial turkey leather; and the paper such as here on earth might almost pass for vellum. Jupiter, having silently read the decree, would communicate the import to none, but presently shut up the book.

Without the doors of this assembly, there attended a vast number of light, nimble gods, menial servants to Jupiter: these are his ministering instruments in all affairs below. They travel in a caravan, more or less together, and are fastened to each other like a link of galley-slaves, by a light chain, which passes from them to Jupiter's great toe; and yet in receiving or delivering a message, they may never approach above the lowest step of his throne, where he and they whisper to each other through a long hollow trunk. These deities are called by mortal men accidents or events; but the gods call them second causes. Jupiter having delivered his message to a certain number of these divinities, they flew immediately down to the pinnacle of the regal library, and, consulting a few minutes, entered unseen and disposed the parties according to their orders.

Meanwhile Momus, fearing the worst, and calling to mind an ancient prophecy, which bore no very good face to his children the Moderns, bent his flight to the region of a malignant deity, called Criticism. She dwelt on the top of a snowy mountain in Nova Zembla; there Momus found her extended in her den, upon the spoils of numberless volumes half devoured. At her right hand sat Ignorance, her father and husband, blind with age; at her left, Pride, her mother, dressing her up in the scraps of paper herself had torn. There was Opinion, her sister, light of foot, hoodwinked, and headstrong, yet giddy and perpetually turning. About her played her children, Noise and Impudence, Dulness and Vanity, Positiveness, Pedantry, and Ill-Manners. The goddess herself had claws like a cat; her head, and ears, and voice resembled those of an ass; her teeth fallen out before, her eyes turned inward, as if she looked only upon herself; her diet was the overflowing of her own gall; her spleen was so large, as to stand prominent like a dug of the first rate; nor wanted excrescencies in form of teats, at which a crew of ugly monsters were greedily sucking; and, what is wonderful to conceive, the bulk of spleen increased faster than the sucking could diminish it. "Goddess," said Momus, "can you sit idly here while our devout worshippers, the Moderns, are this minute entering into a cruel battle, and perhaps now lying under the swords of their enemies? Who then hereafter will ever sacrifice or build altars to our divinities? Haste therefore to the British Isle, and, if possible, prevent their destruction, while I make factions among the gods, and gain them over to our party."

Momus, having thus delivered himself, stayed not for an answer, but left the goddess to her own resentment. Up she rose in a rage, and as it is the form upon such occasions, began a soliloquy: " 'Tis I" (said she) "who give wisdom to infants and idiots; by me, children grow wiser than their parents. By me, beaux become politicians, and schoolboys judges of philosophy. By me, sophisters debate, and conclude upon the depths of knowledge; and coffeehouse wits, instinct by me, can correct an author's style and display his minutest errors, without understanding a syllable of his matter or his language. By me, striplings spend their judgment, as they do their estate, before it comes into their hands. 'Tis I who have deposed wit and knowledge from their empire over poetry, and advanced myself in their stead. And shall a few upstart Ancients dare oppose me?—But come, my aged parents and you, my children dear, and thou

18. Momus: type name for the obscure, pedantic critic.

my beauteous sister; let us ascend my chariot, and haste to assist our devout Moderns, who are now sacrificing to us a hecatomb, as I perceive by that grateful smell, which from thence reaches my nostrils."

The goddess and her train having mounted the chariot, which was drawn by tame geese, flew over infinite regions, shedding her influence in due places, till at length she arrived at her beloved island of Britain; but in hovering over its metropolis, what blessings did she not let fall upon her seminaries of Gresham and Covent Garden? And now she reached the fatal plain of St. James's Library, at what time the two armies were upon the point to engage; where entering with all her caravan unseen, and landing upon a case of shelves, now desert, but once inhabited by a colony of virtuosos, she stayed a while to observe the posture of both armies.

But here the tender cares of a mother began to fill her thoughts, and move in her breast. For, at the head of a troop of Modern Bowmen, she cast her eyes upon her son W–tt–n; to whom the fates had assigned a very short thread. W–tt–n, a young hero, whom an unknown father of mortal race begot by stolen embraces with this goddess. He was the darling of his mother above all her children, and she resolved to go and comfort him. But first, according to the good old custom of deities, she cast about to change her shape, for fear the divinity of her countenance might dazzle his mortal sight, and overcharge the rest of his senses. She therefore gathered up her person into an octavo compass; her body grew white and arid, and split in pieces with dryness; the thick turned into pasteboard, and the thin into paper, upon which her parents and children artfully strewed a black juice, or decoction of gall and soot, in form of letters; her head, and voice, and spleen, kept their primitive form, and that which before was a cover of skin, did still continue so. In which guise she marched on towards the Moderns, undistinguishable in shape and dress from the divine B–ntl–y, W–tt–n's dearest friend. "Brave W–tt–n," said the goddess, "why do our troops stand idle here, to spend their present vigour, and opportunity of this day? Away, let us haste to the generals, and advise to give the onset immediately." Having spoke thus, she took the ugliest of her monsters, full glutted from her spleen, and flung it invisibly into his mouth, which, flying straight up into his head, squeezed out his eye-balls, gave him a distorted look, and half overturned his brain. Then she privately ordered two of her beloved children, Dulness and Ill-Manners, closely to attend his person in all encounters. Having thus accoutred him, she vanished in a mist, and the hero perceived it was the goddess his mother.

The destined hour of fate being now arrived, the fight began; whereof, before I dare adventure to make a particular description, I must, after the example of other authors, petition for a hundred tongues, and mouths, and hands, and pens, which would all be too little to perform so immense a work. Say, goddess, that presidest over History, who it was that first advanced in the field of battle. Paracelsus, at the head of his dragoons, observing Galen[19] in the adverse wing, darted his javelin with a mighty force, which the brave Ancient received upon his shield, the point breaking in the second fold. * * * * *

* * * * * * * *Hic pauca desunt.*[20]

* * * * * * * * *

They bore the wounded aga on their shields to his chariot * * * * * *

* * * * * * * *Desunt nonnula.*[21]

* * * * * * * * *

Then Aristotle, observing Bacon advance with a furious mien, drew his bow to the head, and let fly his arrow, which missed the valiant Modern, and went hizzing over his head. But Descartes it hit; the steel point quickly found a defect in his head-piece; it pierced the leather and the pasteboard, and went in at his right eye. The torture of the pain whirled the valiant bowman round, till death, like a star of superior influence, drew him into his own *vortex*. * * * * *

Ingens hiatus hic in MS.[22]

19. Galen: the noted Ancient Greek physician. He is seen as the leader of the Ancient men of medicine and the Modern followers of Paracelsus. **20. *Hic . . . desunt:*** "Here, something is missing." **21. *Desunt nonnula:*** "some lines missing." **22. *Ingens . . . MS:*** "Here is a major gap in the text."

when Homer appeared at the head of the cavalry, mounted on a furious horse, with difficulty managed by the rider himself, but which no other mortal durst approach; he rode among the enemy's ranks, and bore down all before him. Say, goddess, whom he slew first, and whom he slew last. First, Gondibert[23] advanced against him, clad in heavy armour, and mounted on a staid sober gelding, not so famed for his speed as his docility in kneeling, whenever his rider would mount or alight. He had made a vow to Pallas that he would never leave the field till he had spoiled Homer ° of his armor; madman, who had never once seen the wearer, nor understood his strength.

° *Vid. Homer.*

Him Homer overthrew, horse and man to the ground, there to be trampled and choked in the dirt. Then, with a long spear, he slew Denham,† a stout Modern, who from his father's side derived his lineage from Apollo, but his mother was of mortal race. He fell, and bit the earth. The celestial part Apollo took, and made it a star, but the terrestrial lay wallowing upon the ground. Then Homer slew W–sl–y[24] with a kick of his horse's heel; he took Perrault by mighty force out of his saddle, then hurled him at Fontenelle,[25] with the same blow dashing out both their brains.

On the left wing of the horse, Virgil appeared in shining armor, completely fitted to his body; he was mounted on a dapple-gray steed, the slowness of whose pace was an effect of the highest mettle and vigour. He cast his eye on the adverse wing, with a desire to find an object worthy of his valour, when behold, upon a sorrel gelding of a monstrous size, appeared a foe, issuing from among the thickest of the enemy's squadrons; but his speed was less than his noise; for his horse, old and lean, spent the dregs of his strength in a high trot, which though it made slow advances, yet caused a loud clashing of his armor, terrible to hear. The two cavaliers had now approached within the throw of a lance, when the stranger desired a parley, and lifting up the vizor of his helmet, a face hardly appeared from within, which after a pause was known for that of the renowned Dryden. The brave Ancient suddenly started, as one possessed with surprise and disappointment together; for the helmet was nine times too large for the head, which appeared situate far in the hinder part, even like the lady in a lobster, or like a mouse under a canopy of state, or like a shrivelled beau from within the penthouse of a modern periwig; and the voice was suited to the visage, sounding weak and remote. Dryden in a long harangue soothed up the good Ancient, called him father, and by a large deduction of genealogies, made it plainly appear that they were nearly related. Then he humbly proposed an exchange of armor, as a lasting mark of hospitality between them. Virgil consented (for the goddess Diffidence came unseen, and cast a mist before his eyes) though his was of gold,° and cost a hundred beeves, the other's but of rusty iron. However, this glittering armor became the Modern yet worse than his own. Then they agreed to exchange horses; but when it came to the trial, Dryden was afraid, and utterly unable to mount. * * * *

° *Vid. Homer.*

* * * * * * * * *

* * * * * *

* * * * * * *Alter hiatus in MS.*[26]

* * * Lucan[27] appeared upon a fiery horse of admirable shape, but headstrong, bearing the rider where he list, over the field; he made a mighty slaughter among the enemy's horse; which destruction to stop, Blackmore, a famous Modern (but one of the mercenaries) strenuously opposed himself, and darted a javelin with a strong hand, which falling short of its mark, struck deep in the earth. Then Lucan threw a lance; but Æsculpaius[28] came unseen, and turned off the point. "Brave Modern," said Lucan, "I perceive some god protects you, for never did my arm so deceive me before; but what mortal can contend with a god? Therefore, let us fight no longer, but present gifts

† Sir John Denham's poems are very unequal, extremely good, and very indifferent; so that his detractors said he was not the real author of *Cooper's Hill.*

---

23. **Gondibert**: the dull epic by Sir William Davenant, a true hero of the Moderns. 24. **W-sl-y**: a reference to Samuel Wesley (1662–1735), still another bad poet, author of a poem *The Life of Christ.* 25. **Perrault . . . Fontenelle**: notable French exemplars of the Modern cause.

26. ***Alter . . . MS.***: "Another gap in the manuscript." Swift continues to have fun with Modern editorial commentary. 27. **Lucan**: Roman epic writer, author of *Pharsalia.* 28. **Æsculpaius**: god of medicine in Greek mythology.

to each other." Lucan then bestowed the Modern a pair of spurs, and Blackmore gave Lucan a bridle. * * * * * * *
* * * * * * * *
* * * * * * *Pauca desunt.*[29]
* * * * * *

Creech;[30] but the goddess Dulness took a cloud, formed into the shape of Horace, armed and mounted, and placed it in a flying posture before him. Glad was the cavalier to begin a combat with a flying foe, and pursued the image, threatening loud, till at last it led him to the peaceful bower of his father Ogleby,[31] by whom he was disarmed, and assigned to his repose.

Then Pindar slew ——, and ——, and Oldham,[32] and ——, and Afra the Amazon,[33] light of foot; never advancing in a direct line, but wheeling with incredible agility and force, he made a terrible slaughter among the enemy's light horse. Him when Cowley observed, his generous heart burnt within him, and he advanced against the fierce Ancient, imitating his address, and pace, and career, as well as the vigour of his horse and his own skill would allow. When the two cavaliers had approached within the length of three javelins, first Cowley threw a lance, which missed Pindar, and passing into the enemy's ranks, fell ineffectual to the ground. Then Pindar darted a javelin so large and weighty that scarce a dozen cavaliers, as cavaliers are in our degenerate days, could raise it from the ground; yet he threw it with ease, and it went by an unerring hand singing through the air; nor could the Modern have avoided present death, if he had not luckily opposed the shield that had been given him by Venus. And now both heroes drew their swords, but the Modern was so aghast and disordered, that he knew not where he was; his shield dropped from his hands; thrice he fled, and thrice he could not escape; at last he turned, and lifting up his hands in the posture of a suppliant: "Godlike Pindar," said he, "spare my life, and possess my horse with these arms, besides the ransom which my friends will give when they hear I am alive, and your prisoner." "Dog," said Pindar, "let your ransom stay with your friends; but your carcass shall be left for the fowls of the air and the beasts of the field." With that he raised his sword, and with a mighty stroke cleft the wretched Modern in twain, the sword pursuing the blow; and one half lay panting on the ground, to be trod in pieces by the horses' feet, the other half was borne by the frighted steed through the field. This Venus took, washed it seven times in ambrosia, then struck it thrice with a sprig of amaranth; upon which the leather grew round and soft, the leaves turned into feathers, and being gilded before, continued gilded still; so it became a dove, and she harnessed it to her chariot. * *
* * * * * * * *
* * * * * *
* * * * * * *Hiatus valdè deflendus* in
* * * * * *
* * * * * * *MS.*[34]

Day being far spent, and the numerous forces of the Moderns half inclining to a retreat, there issued forth from a squadron of their heavy-armed foot, a captain, whose name was B–ntl–y,[c] in person the most deformed of all the Moderns, tall, but without shape or comeliness; large but without strength or proportion. His armor was patched up of a thousand incoherent pieces, and the sound of it, as he marched, was loud and dry, like that made by the fall of a sheet of lead, which an Etesian wind[35] blows suddenly down from the roof of some steeple. His helmet was of old rusty iron, but the vizor was brass, which, tainted by his breath, corrupted into copperas, nor wanted gall from the same fountain; so that, whenever provoked by anger or labour, an atramentous[36] quality, of most malignant nature, was seen to distil from his lips. In his right hand[d] he grasped

The Episode of B-ntl-y and W-tt-n.

[c] I do not approve the author's judgment in this, for I think Cowley's *Pindarics* are much preferable to his *Mistress*.

[d] The person here spoken of is famous for letting fly at everybody without distinction, and using mean and foul scurrilities.

29. ***Pauca desunt:*** "A bit missing." **30. Creech:** Thomas Creech (1659–1700), translator of Horace and Lucretius. **31. Ogleby:** John Ogleby (1600–1676), translator of Homer and Virgil. **32. Oldham:** John Oldham, translator and poet. Dryden wrote a superb poem in his memory. **33. Afra the Amazon:** Aphra Behn (1640–1689), novelist and also the writer of some Pindaric odes.

34. ***Hiatus . . . MS.:*** "A very serious gap in the manuscript." **35. Etesian wind:** a northwest wind. **36. atramentous:** black.

a flail, and (that he might never be unprovided of an offensive weapon) a vessel full of ordure in his left: thus completely armed, he advanced with a slow and heavy pace where the Modern chiefs were holding consult upon the sum of things; who, as he came onwards, laughed to behold his crooked leg and hump shoulder, which his boot and armor, vainly endeavouring to hide, were forced to comply with and expose. The generals made use of him for his talent of railing, which, kept within government, proved frequently of great service to their cause, but at other times did more mischief than good; for at the least touch of offence, and often without any at all, he would, like a wounded elephant, convert it against his leaders. Such, at this juncture, was the disposition of B–ntl–y; grieved to see the enemy prevail, and dissatisfied with everybody's conduct but his own. He humbly gave the Modern generals to understand, that he conceived, with great submission, they were all a pack of rogues, and fools, and sons of whores, and d–mnd cowards, and confounded loggerheads, and illiterate whelps, and nonsensical scoundrels; that if himself had been constituted general, those presumptuous dogs,[d] the Ancients, would long before this have been beaten out of the field. "You," said he, "sit here idle; but when I, or any other valiant Modern, kill an enemy, you are sure to seize the spoil. But I will not march one foot against the foe till you all swear to me, that, whomever I take or kill, his arms I shall quietly possess." B–ntl–y having spoken thus, Scaliger,[37] bestowing him a sour look: "Miscreant prater," said he, "eloquent only in thine own eyes, thou railest without wit, or truth, or discretion; the malignity of thy temper perverteth nature; thy learning makes thee more barbarous, thy study of humanity more inhuman; thy converse amongst poets, more grovelling, miry, and dull. All arts of civilizing others render thee rude and untractable; courts have taught thee ill manners, and polite conversation has finished thee a pedant. Besides, a greater coward burdeneth not the army. But never despond; I pass my word, whatever spoil thou takest shall certainly be thy own, though, I hope, that vile carcass will first become a prey to kites and worms."

[d] Vid. *Homer, de Thersite.*

37. Scaliger: probably Joseph Scaliger (1540–1609), the classical scholar and son of the famous scholar-critic Julius Caesar Scaliger.

B–ntl–y durst not reply, but half choked with spleen and rage, withdrew, in full resolution of performing some great achievement. With him, for his aid and companion, he took his beloved W–tt–n; resolving by policy or surprise, to attempt some neglected quarter of the Ancients' army. They began their march over carcasses of their slaughtered friends; then to the right of their own forces; then wheeled northward, till they came to Aldrovandus's[38] tomb, which they passed on the side of the declining sun. And now they arrived with fear towards the enemy's outguards; looking about, if haply they might spy the quarters of the wounded, or some straggling sleepers, unarmed and remote from the rest. As when two mongrel curs, whom native greediness and domestic want provoke and join in partnership, though fearful, nightly to invade the folds of some rich grazier, they, with tails depressed, and lolling tongues, creep soft and slow; meanwhile, the conscious moon, now in her zenith, on their guilty heads darts perpendicular rays; nor dare they bark, though much provoked at her refulgent visage, whether seen in puddle by reflection, or in sphere direct; but one surveys the region round, while t'other scouts the plain, if haply to discover at distance from the flock, some carcass half devoured, the refuse of gorged wolves, or ominous ravens. So marched this lovely, loving pair of friends, nor with less fear and circumspection; when, at distance, they might perceive two shining suits of armor hanging upon an oak, and the owners not far off in a profound sleep. The two friends drew lots, and the pursuing of this adventure fell to B–ntl–y; on he went, and in his van Confusion and Amaze, while Horror and Affright brought up the rear. As he came near, behold two heroes of the Ancients' army, Phalaris and Æsop, lay fast asleep: B–ntl–y would fain have dispatched them both, and stealing close, aimed his flail at Phalaris's breast. But then the goddess Affright interposing, caught the Modern in her icy arms, and dragged him from the danger she foresaw; for both the dormant heroes happened to turn at the same instant, though soundly sleeping, and busy in a dream. For Phalaris[e] was just that minute

[e] This is according to Homer, who tells the dreams of those who were killed in their sleep.

38. Aldrovandus: a reference to Ulisse Aldrovandi (1522–1605), an Italian naturalist.

dreaming how a most vile poetaster had lampooned him, and how he had got him roaring in his bull. And Æsop dreamed, that as he and the Ancient chiefs were lying on the ground, a wild ass broke loose, ran about trampling and kicking, and dunging in their faces. B–ntl–y, leaving the two heroes asleep, seized on both their armors, and withdrew in quest of his darling W–tt–n.

He, in the mean time, had wandered long in search of some enterprise, till at length he arrived at a small rivulet, that issued from a fountain hard by, called in the language of mortal men, Helicon.[39] Here he stopped, and, parched with thirst, resolved to allay it in this limpid stream. Thrice with profane hands he essayed to raise the water to his lips, and thrice it slipped all through his fingers. Then he stooped prone on his breast, but ere his mouth had kissed the liquid crystal, Apollo came, and in the channel held his shield betwixt the Modern and the fountain, so that he drew up nothing but mud. For, although no fountain on earth can compare with the clearness of Helicon, yet there lies at bottom a thick sediment of slime and mud; for so Apollo begged of Jupiter, as a punishment to those who durst attempt to taste it with unhallowed lips, and for a lesson to all not to draw too deep or far from the spring.

At the fountain-head W–tt–n discerned two heroes; the one he could not distinguish, but the other was soon known for Temple, general of the allies to the Ancients. His back was turned, and he was employed in drinking large draughts in his helmet from the fountain, where he had withdrawn himself to rest from the toils of the war. W–tt–n, observing him, with quaking knees, and trembling hands, spoke thus to himself: "Oh that I could kill this destroyer of our army, what renown should I purchase among the chiefs! But to issue out against him,° man for man, shield against shield, and lance against lance, what Modern of us dare? For he fights like a god, and Pallas or Apollo are ever at his elbow. But, Oh mother! if what Fame reports be true, that I am the son of so great a goddess, grant me to hit Temple with this lance, that the stroke may send him to hell, and that I may return in safety and triumph, laden with his spoils." The first part of his prayer, the gods granted at the intercession of his mother and of Momus; but the rest by a perverse wind sent from Fate was scattered in the air. Then W–tt–n grasped his lance, and brandishing it thrice over his head, darted it with all his might, the goddess, his mother, at the same time, adding strength to his arm. Away the lance went hissing, and reached even to the belt of the averted Ancient, upon which lightly grazing, it fell to the ground. Temple neither felt the weapon touch him, nor heard it fall; and W–tt–n might have escaped to his army, with the honor of having remitted his lance against so great a leader, unrevenged; but Apollo, enraged that a javelin, flung by the assistance of so foul a goddess, should pollute his fountain, put on the shape of ——, and softly came to young Boyle, who then accompanied Temple. He pointed first to the lance, then to the distant Modern that flung it, and commanded the young hero to take immediate revenge. Boyle, clad in a suit of armor, which had been given him by all the gods, immediately advanced against the trembling foe, who now fled before him. As a young lion in the Libyan plains or Araby desert, sent by his aged sire to hunt for prey, or health, or exercise, he scours along, wishing to meet some tiger from the mountains, or a furious boar; if chance, a wild ass, with brayings importune, affronts his ear, the generous beast, though loathing to distain his claws with blood so vile, yet much provoked at the offensive noise, which Echo, foolish nymph, like her ill-judging sex, repeats much louder, and with more delight than Philomela's song, he vindicates the honor of the forest, and hunts the noisy, long-eared animal. So W–tt–n fled, so Boyle pursued. But W–tt–n, heavy-armed and slow of foot, began to slack his course, when his lover B–ntl–y appeared, returning laden with the spoils of the two sleeping Ancients. Boyle observed him well, and soon discovering the helmet and shield of Phalaris, his friend, both which he had lately with his own hands new polished and gilded, rage sparkled in his eyes, and, leaving his pursuit after W–tt–n, he furiously rushed on against this new approacher. Fain would he be revenged on both; but both now fled different ways; and as a woman° [f] in a little house that gets a painful livelihood by spinning, if

° Vid. *Homer.*

° Vid. *Homer.*

39. **Helicon:** the mountain sacred to the inspired Muses.

[f] This is also after the manner of Homer; the woman's getting a painful livelihood by spinning, has nothing to do with the similitude, nor would be excusable without such an authority.

chance her geese be scattered o'er the common, she courses round the plain from side to side, compelling here and there the stragglers to the flock; they cackle loud, and flutter o'er the champaign. So Boyle pursued, so fled this pair of friends: finding at length their flight was vain, they bravely joined, and drew themselves in phalanx. First B–ntl–y threw a spear with all his force, hoping to pierce the enemy's breast; but Pallas came unseen, and in the air took off the point, and clapped on one of lead, which after a dead bang against the enemy's shield, fell blunted to the ground. Then Boyle observing well his time, took a lance of wondrous length and sharpness; and as this pair of friends compacted stood close side to side, he wheeled him to the right, and with unusual force, darted the weapon. B–ntl–y saw his fate approach, and flanking down his arms close to his ribs, hoping to save his body, in went the point, passing through arm and side, nor stopped or spent its force, till it had also pierced the valiant W–tt–n who, going to sustain his dying friend, shared his fate. As when a skilful cook has trussed a brace of woodcocks, he, with iron skewer, pierces the tender sides of both, their legs and wings close pinioned to their ribs; so was this pair of friends transfixed, till down they fell, joined in their lives, joined in their deaths, so closely joined that Charon would mistake them both for one, and waft them over Styx for half his fare.[40] Farewell, beloved loving pair; few equals have you left behind: and happy and immortal shall you be, if all my wit and eloquence can make you.

And, now * * * * * *
* * * * * * * * *
* * * * * * * * *
* * *Desunt cætera.*[41]

FINIS

(1704)

40. In Greek mythology Charon was the boatman who transported the dead souls across the river Styx to Hades. **41.** ***Desunt cætera:*** "The rest is missing."

An Argument to Prove that the Abolishing of Christianity in England

MAY, AS THINGS NOW STAND, BE ATTENDED WITH SOME INCONVENIENCES, AND PERHAPS NOT PRODUCE THOSE MANY GOOD EFFECTS PROPOSED THEREBY

Written in the Year 1708

I am very sensible what a weakness and presumption it is to reason against the general humour and disposition of the world. I remember it was with great justice, and a due regard to the freedom both of the public and the press, forbidden upon severe penalties to write, or discourse, or lay wagers against the *Union*,[1] even before it was confirmed by parliament, because that was looked upon as a design to oppose the current of the people, which, besides the folly of it, is a manifest breach of the fundamental law that makes this majority of opinion the voice of God. In like manner, and for the very same reasons, it may perhaps be neither safe nor prudent to argue against the abolishing of Christianity at a juncture when all parties appear so unanimously determined upon the point, as we cannot but allow from their actions, their discourses, and their writings. However, I know not how, whether from the affectation of singularity or the perverseness of human nature, but so it unhappily falls out that I cannot be entirely of this opinion. Nay, although I were sure an order were issued out for my immediate prosecution by the Attorney-General, I should still confess that in the present posture of our affairs at home or abroad, I do not yet see the absolute necessity of extirpating the Christian religion from among us.

AN ARGUMENT AGAINST ABOLISHING CHRISTIANITY. **1.** A reference to the Act of Union (joining England and Scotland) of 1707. Swift on a very serious level is, like many of his contemporaries, fearful that the Test Act of 1672 requiring officeholders to take communion in the Church of England will be repealed. He is clearly a Church of England man, devoted to the cause of true religion and angry with political influences on the Church.

This perhaps may appear too great a paradox even for our wise and paradoxical age to endure; therefore I shall handle it with all tenderness, and with the utmost deference to that great and profound majority which is of another sentiment.

And yet the curious may please to observe, how much the genius of a nation is liable to alter in half an age. I have heard it affirmed for certain by some very old people, that the contrary opinion was even in their memories as much in vogue as the other is now; and, that a project for the abolishing of Christianity would then have appeared as singular, and been thought as absurd, as it would be at this time to write or discourse in its defence.

Therefore I freely own that all appearances are against me. The system of the Gospel, after the fate of other systems, is generally antiquated and exploded; and the mass or body of the common people, among whom it seems to have had its latest credit, are now grown as much ashamed of it as their betters; opinions, like fashions, always descending from those of quality to the middle sort, and thence to the vulgar, where at length they are dropped and vanish.

But here I would not be mistaken, and must therefore be so bold as to borrow a distinction from the writers on the other side when they make a difference between nominal and real Trinitarians. I hope no reader imagines me so weak to stand up in the defence of *real* Christianity, such as used in primitive times (if we may believe the authors of those ages) to have an influence upon men's belief and actions: to offer at the restoring of that would indeed be a wild project; it would be to dig up foundations; to destroy at one blow *all* the wit and *half* the learning of the kingdom; to break the entire frame and constitution of things; to ruin trade, extinguish arts and sciences with the professors of them; in short, to turn our courts, exchanges, and shops into deserts; and would be full as absurd as the proposal of Horace, where he advises the Romans all in a body to leave their city and seek a new seat in some remote part of the world by way of cure for the corruption of their manners.

Therefore I think this caution was in itself altogether unnecessary, (which I have inserted only to prevent all possibility of cavilling) since every candid reader will easily understand my discourse to be intended only in defence of *nominal* Christianity; the other having been for some time wholly laid aside by general consent, as utterly inconsistent with our present schemes of wealth and power.

But why we should therefore cast off the name and title of Christians, although the general opinion and resolution be so violent for it, I confess I cannot (with submission) apprehend the consequence necessary. However, since the undertakers propose such wonderful advantages to the nation by this project, and advance many plausible objections against the system of Christianity, I shall briefly consider the strength of both, fairly allow them their greatest weight, and offer such answers as I think most reasonable. After which I will beg leave to show what inconvenience may possibly happen by such an innovation in the present posture of our affairs.

First, one great advantage proposed by the abolishing of Christianity is, that it would very much enlarge and establish liberty of conscience, that great bulwark of our nation, and of the *Protestant* Religion, which is still too much limited by *priestcraft* notwithstanding all the good intentions of the legislature, as we have lately found by a severe instance. For it is confidently reported that two young gentlemen of great hopes, bright wit, and profound judgment, who upon a thorough examination of causes and effects, and by the mere force of natural abilities, without the least tincture of learning, having made a discovery that there was no God, and generously communicating their thoughts for the good of the public, were some time ago, by an unparalleled severity, and upon I know not what *obsolete* law, broke *only* for blasphemy. And as it hath been wisely observed, if persecution once begins, no man alive knows how far it may reach, or where it will end.

In answer to all which, with deference to wiser judgments, I think this rather shows the necessity of a *nominal* religion among us. Great wits love to be free with the highest objects; and if they cannot be allowed a *God* to revile or renounce, they will *speak evil of dignities,* abuse the government, and reflect upon the ministry; which I am sure few will deny to be of much more pernicious consequence, according to the saying of Tiberius, *Deorum offensa diis curæ.*[2] As to the particular fact related,

2. ***Deorum . . . curæ:*** "Offenses against the gods are their own business." The source is not Tiberius, but Tacitus, *Annals,* I, 73.

I think it is not fair to argue from one instance, perhaps another cannot be produced; yet (to the comfort of all those who may be apprehensive of persecution) blasphemy we know is freely spoke a million of times in every coffeehouse and tavern, or wherever else *good company* meet. It must be allowed indeed, that to break an English free-born officer only for blasphemy, was, to speak the gentlest of such an action, a very high strain of absolute power. Little can be said in excuse for the general; perhaps he was afraid it might give offence to the allies,[3] among whom, for aught I know, it may be the custom of the country to believe a God. But if he argued, as some have done, upon a mistaken principle, that an officer who is guilty of speaking blasphemy, may some time or other proceed so far as to raise a mutiny, the consequence is by no means to be admitted; for surely the commander of an English army is likely to be but ill obeyed, whose soldiers fear and reverence him as little as they do a deity.

It is further objected against the Gospel System, that it obliges men to the belief of things too difficult for freethinkers, and such who have shaken off the prejudices that usually cling to a confined education. To which I answer, that men should be cautious how they raise objections which reflect upon the wisdom of the nation. Is not every body freely allowed to believe whatever he pleases, and to publish his belief to the world whenever he thinks fit, especially if it serve to strengthen the party which is in the right? Would any indifferent foreigner, who should read the trumpery lately written by Asgill, Tindal, Toland, Coward,[4] and forty more, imagine the Gospel to be our rule of faith, and confirmed by parliaments? Does any man either believe, or say he believes, or desire to have it thought that he says he believes one syllable of the matter? And is any man worse received upon that score, or does he find his want of *nominal* faith a disadvantage to him in the pursuit of any civil or military employment? What if there be an old dormant statute or two against him? Are they not now obsolete, to a degree, that Empson and Dudley[5] themselves if they were now alive, would find it impossible to put them in execution?

It is likewise urged that there are, by computation, in this kingdom above ten thousand parsons, whose revenues added to those of my lords the bishops would suffice to maintain at least two hundred young gentlemen of wit and pleasure, and freethinking, enemies to priestcraft, narrow principles, pedantry, and prejudices; who might be an ornament to the Court and Town: and then, again, so great a number of able (bodied) divines might be a recruit to our fleet and armies. This indeed appears to be a consideration of some weight: but then, on the other side, several things deserve to be considered likewise: as, first, whether it may not be thought necessary that in certain tracts of country, like what we call parishes, there should be *one* man at least of abilities to read and write. Then it seems a wrong computation that the revenues of the Church throughout this island would be large enough to maintain two hundred young gentlemen, or even half that number, after the present refined way of living; that is, to allow each of them such a rent, as in the modern form of speech, would make them *easy*. But still there is in this project a greater mischief behind; and we ought to beware of the woman's folly who killed the hen that every morning laid her a golden egg. For, pray what would become of the race of men in the next age, if we had nothing to trust to besides the scrofulous, consumptive productions, furnished by our men of wit and pleasure, when having squandered away their vigour, health and estates, they are forced by some disagreeable marriage to piece up their broken fortunes, and entail rottenness and politeness on their posterity? Now, here are ten thousand persons[6] reduced by the wise regulations of Henry the Eighth, to the necessity of a low diet, and moderate exercise, who are the only great restorers of our breed, without which the nation would in an age or two become but one great hospital.

Another advantage proposed by the abolishing of Christianity is the clean gain of one day in seven, which is now entirely lost, and consequently the

3. **allies:** Austria, Holland, Spain, and Saxony were England's allies against France in the War of the Spanish Succession. 4. **Asgill . . . Coward:** a catalogue of English Deists and freethinkers opposed to any consideration of the supernatural in religion.

5. **Empson . . . Dudley:** Empson and Dudley were infamous agents and tax collectors for King Henry VII. 6. Probably a reference to clergy of the Church of England, whose income was determined by Henry VIII at the time of the Reformation and the break with Rome.

kingdom one seventh less considerable in trade, business, and pleasure; beside the loss to the public of so many stately structures now in the hands of the Clergy, which might be converted into theatres, exchanges, market-houses, common dormitories, and other public edifices.

I hope I shall be forgiven a hard word, if I call this a perfect cavil. I readily own there has been an old custom time out of mind for people to assemble in the churches every Sunday, and that shops are still frequently shut, in order as it is conceived, to preserve the memory of that ancient practice, but how this can prove a hindrance to business or pleasure is hard to imagine. What if the men of pleasure are forced one day in the week to game at home instead of the chocolate-house? Are not the taverns and coffeehouses open? Can there be a more convenient season for taking a dose of physic? Are fewer claps got upon Sundays than other days? Is not that the chief day for traders to sum up the accounts of the week, and for lawyers to prepare their briefs? But I would fain know how it can be pretended that the churches are misapplied? Where are more appointments and rendezvouzes of gallantry? Where more care to appear in the foremost box with greater advantage of dress? Where more meetings for business? Where more bargains driven of all sorts? And where so many conveniences or enticements to sleep?

There is one advantage greater than any of the foregoing, proposed by the abolishing of Christianity: that it will utterly extinguish parties among us, by removing those factious distinctions of High and Low Church, of Whig and Tory, Presbyterian and Church of England, which are now so many grievous clogs upon public proceedings, and dispose men to prefer the gratifying themselves, or depressing their adversaries, before the most important interest of the state.

I confess, if it were certain that so great an advantage would redound to the nation by this expedient, I would submit and be silent: but will any man say, that if the words *whoring, drinking, cheating, lying, stealing,* were by act of parliament ejected out of the English tongue and dictionaries, we should all awake next morning chaste and temperate, honest and just, and lovers of truth. Is this a fair consequence? Or, if the physicians would forbid us to pronounce the words *pox, gout, rheumatism* and *stone,* would that expedient serve like so many talismans to destroy the diseases themselves? Are party and faction rooted in men's hearts no deeper than phrases borrowed from religion, or founded upon no firmer principles? And is our language so poor that we cannot find other terms to express them? Are *envy, pride, avarice* and *ambition* such ill nomenclators, that they cannot furnish appelations for their owners? Will not *heydukes* and *mamalukes, mandarins* and *potshaws,* or any other words formed at pleasure, serve to distinguish those who are in the ministry from others who *would be in* it *if they could?* What, for instance, is easier than to vary the form of speech, and instead of the word church, make it a question in politics, whether the Monument be in danger? Because religion was nearest at hand to furnish a few convenient phrases, is our invention so barren, we can find no other? Suppose, for argument sake, that the Tories favoured Margarita, the Whigs Mrs. Tofts, and the Trimmers[7] Valentini,[a] would not *Margaritians, Toftians* and *Valentinians* be very tolerable marks of distinction? The *Prasini* and *Veneti,* two most virulent factions in Italy, began (if I remember right) by a distinction of colours in ribbons, which we might do with as good a grace about the dignity of the blue and the green, and would serve as properly to divide the Court, the Parliament, and the Kingdom between them, as any terms of art whatsoever borrowed from religion. Therefore, I think, there is little force in this objection against Christianity, or prospect of so great an advantage as is proposed in the abolishing of it.

It is again objected, as a very absurd ridiculous custom, that a set of men should be suffered, much less employed and hired, to bawl one day in seven against the lawfulness of those methods most in use towards the pursuit of greatness, riches and pleasure, which are the constant practice of all men alive on the other six. But this objection is, I think, a little unworthy so refined an age as ours. Let us argue this matter calmly. I appeal to the breast of any polite freethinker, whether in the pursuit of gratifying a predominant passion, he hath not al-

[a] Italian singers then in vogue.

7. **Trimmers:** compromisers, who move from party to party, as their interests are served.

ways felt a wonderful incitement by reflecting it was a thing forbidden; and therefore we see, in order to cultivate this taste, the wisdom of the nation hath taken special care that the ladies should be furnished with prohibited silks, and the men with prohibited wine: and indeed it were to be wished that some other prohibitions were promoted, in order to improve the pleasures of the town which for want of such expedients begin already, as I am told, to flag and grow languid, giving way daily to cruel inroads from the spleen.

It is likewise proposed as a great advantage to the public, that if we once discard the system of the Gospel, all religion will of course be banished for ever; and consequently, along with it, those grievous prejudices of education, which under the names of virtue, conscience, honour, justice, and the like, are so apt to disturb the peace of human minds, and the notions whereof are so hard to be eradicated by right reason or freethinking, sometimes during the whole course of our lives.

Here, first, I observe how difficult it is to get rid of a phrase which the world is once grown fond of, although the occasion that first produced it be entirely taken away. For several years past if a man had but an ill-favoured nose, the deep-thinkers of the age would some way or other contrive to impute the cause to the prejudice of his education. From this fountain are said to be derived all our foolish notions of justice, piety, love of our country, all our opinions of God, or a future state, Heaven, Hell, and the like: and there might formerly, perhaps, have been some pretence for this charge. But so effectual care has been since taken to remove those prejudices, by an entire change in the methods of education, that (with honour I mention it to our polite innovators) the young gentlemen who are now on the scene seem to have not the least tincture left of those infusions, or string of those weeds; and, by consequence, the reason for abolishing nominal Christianity upon that pretext is wholly ceased.

For the rest, it may perhaps admit a controversy, whether the banishing all notions of religion whatsoever, would be convenient for the vulgar. Not that I am in the least of opinion with those who hold religion to have been the invention of politicians to keep the lower part of the world in awe by the fear of invisible powers; unless mankind were then very different from what it is now: for I look upon the mass or body of our people here in England to be as freethinkers, that is to say as staunch unbelievers, as any of the highest rank. But I conceive some scattered notions about a superior power to be of singular use for the common people, as furnishing excellent materials to keep children quiet when they grow peevish, and providing topics of amusement in a tedious winter-night.

Lastly, it is proposed as a singular advantage, that the abolishing of Christianity will very much contribute to the uniting of Protestants, by enlarging the terms of communion so as to take in all sorts of dissenters, who are now shut out of the pale upon account of a few ceremonies, which all sides confess to be things indifferent: that this alone will effectually answer the great ends of a scheme for comprehension, by opening a large noble gate at which all bodies may enter; whereas the chaffering[8] with dissenters, and dodging about this or the other ceremony, is but like opening a few wickets, and leaving them at jar, by which no more than one can get in at a time, and that not without stooping, and sideling, and squeezing his body.

To all this I answer, that there is one darling inclination of mankind, which usually affects to be a retainer to religion, although she be neither its parent, its godmother, or its friend; I mean the spirit of opposition, that lived long before Christianity, and can easily subsist without it. Let us, for instance, examine wherein the opposition of sectaries among us consists; we shall find Christianity to have no share in it at all. Does the Gospel anywhere prescribe a starched, squeezed countenance, a stiff, formal gait, a singularity of manners and habit, or any affected modes of speech different from the reasonable part of mankind? Yet, if Christianity did not lend its name to stand in the gap, and to employ or divert these humours, they must of necessity be spent in contraventions to the laws of the land, and disturbance of the public peace. There is a portion of enthusiasm assigned to every nation which, if it hath not proper objects to work on, will burst out and set all into a flame. If the quiet of a state can be bought by only flinging men a few ceremonies to devour, it is a purchase no wise man would refuse. Let the mastiffs amuse themselves about a sheep's skin stuffed with hay, provided it will keep them from worrying the flock.

8. **chaffering:** disputing.

The institution of convents abroad seems in one point a strain of great wisdom, there being few irregularities in human passions, that may not have recourse to vent themselves in some of those orders, which are so many retreats for the speculative, the melancholy, the proud, the silent, the politic and the morose, to spend themselves, and evaporate the noxious particles; for each of whom we in this island are forced to provide a several sect of religion to keep them quiet. And whenever Christianity shall be abolished, the legislature must find some other expedient to employ and entertain them. For what imports it how large a gate you open, if there will be always left a number who place a pride and a merit in refusing to enter?

Having thus considered the most important objections against Christianity, and the chief advantages proposed by the abolishing thereof, I shall now with equal deference and submission to wiser judgments as before, proceed to mention a few inconveniences that may happen, if the Gospel should be repealed; which perhaps the projectors may not have sufficiently considered.

And first, I am very sensible how much the gentlemen of wit and pleasure are apt to murmur, and be shocked at the sight of so many daggled-tail parsons, who happen to fall in their way, and offend their eyes: but at the same time, these wise reformers do not consider what an advantage and felicity it is for great wits to be always provided with objects of scorn and contempt, in order to exercise and improve their talents, and divert their spleen from falling on each other or on themselves; especially when all this may be done without the least imaginable *danger to their persons.*

And to urge another argument of a parallel nature: if Christianity were once abolished, how could the freethinkers, the strong reasoners, and the men of profound learning, be able to find another subject so calculated in all points whereon to display their abilities? What wonderful productions of wit should we be deprived of, from those whose genius by continual practice hath been wholly turned upon raillery and invectives against religion, and would therefore never be able to shine or distinguish themselves upon any other subject. We are daily complaining of the great decline of wit among us, and would we take away the greatest, perhaps the only topic we have left? Who would ever have suspected Asgill for a wit, or Toland for a philosopher, if the inexhaustible stock of Christianity had not been at hand to provide them with materials? What other subject, through all art or nature, could have produced Tindal for a profound author, or furnished him with readers? It is the wise choice of the subject that alone adorns and distinguishes the writer. For, had an hundred such pens as these been employed on the side of religion, they would have immediately sunk into silence and oblivion.

Nor do I think it wholly groundless, or my fears altogether imaginary, that the abolishing of Christianity may perhaps bring the Church in danger, or at least put the senate to the trouble of another securing vote. I desire I may not be mistaken; I am far from presuming to affirm or think that the Church is in danger at present, or as things now stand; but we know not how soon it may be so when the Christian religion is repealed. As plausible as this project seems, there may a dangerous design lurk under it. Nothing can be more notorious, than that the Atheists, Deists, Socinians, Antitrinitarians, and other subdivisions of freethinkers, are persons of little zeal for the present ecclesiastical establishment: Their declared opinion is for repealing the Sacramental Test;[9] they are very indifferent with regard to ceremonies; nor do they hold the *jus divinum*[10] of Episcopacy.[11] Therefore this may be intended as one politic step towards altering the constitution of the Church established, and setting up Presbytery[12] in the stead, which I leave to be further considered by those at the helm.

In the last place, I think nothing can be more plain, than that by this expedient, we shall run into the evil we chiefly pretend to avoid; and that the abolishment of the Christian religion will be the readiest course we can take to introduce popery. And I am the more inclined to this opinion, because we know it has been the constant practice of the Jesuits to send over emissaries, with instructions to personate themselves members of the several prevailing sects among us. So it is recorded, that they have at sundry times appeared in the guise of Presbyterians, Anabaptists, Independents

9. See Note 1. **10.** ***jus divinum:*** divine right. **11. Episcopacy:** the governance of the Church by a hierarchy of bishops. The radicals and Dissenters opposed such governance. **12. Presbytery:** governance not by bishops, but by lay elders.

and Quakers, according as any of these were most in credit; so since the fashion hath been taken up of exploding religion, the popish missionaries have not been wanting to mix with the freethinkers; among whom, Toland, the great oracle of the Anti-Christians is an Irish priest, the son of an Irish priest; and the most learned and ingenious author of a book called *The Rights of the Christian Church,* was in a proper juncture reconciled to the Romish faith, whose true son, as appears by an hundred passages in his treatise, he still continues. Perhaps I could add some others to the number; but the fact is beyond dispute, and the reasoning they proceed by is right: for, supposing Christianity to be extinguished, the people will never be at ease till they find out some other method of worship; which will as infallibly produce superstition, as this will end in popery.

And therefore, if notwithstanding all I have said, it shall still be thought necessary to have a bill brought in for repealing Christianity, I would humbly offer an amendment; that instead of the word *Christianity,* may be put *Religion* in general; which I conceive will much better answer all the good ends proposed by the projectors of it. For, as long as we leave in being a God and his providence, with all the necessary consequences which curious and inquisitive men will be apt to draw from such premises, we do not strike at the root of the evil although we should ever so effectually annihilate the present scheme of the Gospel. For, of what use is freedom of thought, if it will not produce freedom of action, which is the sole end, how remote soever in appearance, of all objections against Christianity? And therefore, the freethinkers consider it as a sort of edifice, wherein all the parts have such a mutual dependence on each other, that if you happen to pull out one single nail, the whole fabric must fall to the ground. This was happily expressed by him who had heard of a text brought for proof of the Trinity, which in an ancient manuscript was differently read; he thereupon immediately took the hint, and by a sudden deduction of a long *sorites,*[13] most logically concluded; Why, if it be as you say, I may safely whore and drink on, and defy the parson. From which, and many the like instances easy to be produced, I think nothing can be more manifest, than that the quarrel is not against any particular points of hard digestion in the Christian system, but against religion in general; which, by laying restraints on human nature, is supposed the great enemy to the freedom of thought and action.

Upon the whole, if it shall still be thought for the benefit of Church and State, that Christianity be abolished, I conceive however, it may be more convenient to defer the execution to a time of peace, and not venture in this conjuncture to disoblige our allies, who, as it falls out, are all Christians, and many of them, by the prejudices of their education, so bigoted as to place a sort of pride in the appellation. If upon being rejected by them, we are to trust to an alliance with the Turk, we shall find ourselves much deceived: for, as he is too remote, and generally engaged in war with the Persian emperor, so his people would be more scandalized at our infidelity than our Christian neighbours. Because the Turks are not only strict observers of religious worship, but what is worse, believe a God; which is more than is required of us even while we preserve the name of Christians.

To conclude: whatever some may think of the great advantages to trade by this favourite scheme, I do very much apprehend that in six months' time after the act is passed for the extirpation of the Gospel, the Bank and East-India Stock may fall at least one *percent.* And since that is fifty times more than ever the wisdom of our age thought fit to venture for the *preservation* of Christianity, there is no reason we should be at so great a loss, merely for the sake of *destroying* it.

(1710)

13. *sorites:* a method of rhetorical argument.

A MODEST PROPOSAL

FOR PREVENTING THE CHILDREN OF POOR PEOPLE IN IRELAND FROM BEING A BURDEN TO THEIR PARENTS OR COUNTRY, AND FOR MAKING THEM BENEFICIAL TO THE PUBLIC

It is a melancholy object to those who walk through this great town, or travel in the country, when they see the streets, the roads and cabin-doors crowded with beggars of the female sex, followed by three, four, or six children, all in rags, and importuning every passenger for an alms. These mothers, instead of being able to work for their honest livelihood, are forced to employ all their time in strolling, to beg sustenance for their helpless infants, who, as they grow up, either turn thieves for want of work, or leave their dear native country to fight for the Pretender in Spain, or sell themselves to the Barbadoes.

I think it is agreed by all parties that prodigious number of children, in the arms, or on the backs, or at the heels of their mothers, and frequently of their fathers, is in the present deplorable state of the kingdom a very great additional grievance; and therefore whoever could find out a fair, cheap, and easy method of making these children sound and useful members of the commonwealth would serve so well of the public as to have his statue set up for a preserver of the nation.

But my intention is very far from being confined to provide only for the children of professed beggars; it is of a much greater extent, and shall take in the whole number of infants at a certain age who are born of parents in effect as little able to support them as those who demand our charity in the streets.

As to my own part, having turned my thoughts for many years upon this important subject, and maturely weighed the several schemes of other projectors, I have always found them grossly mistaken in their computation. It is true a child just dropped from its dam may be supported by her milk for a solar year with little other nourishment, at most not above the value of two shillings, which the mother may certainly get, or the value in scraps, by her lawful occupation of begging, and it is exactly at one year old that I propose to provide for them, in such a manner as, instead of being a charge upon their parents, or the parish, or wanting food and raiment for the rest of their lives, they shall, on the contrary, contribute to the feeding and partly to the clothing of many thousands.

There is likewise another great advantage in my scheme, that it will prevent those voluntary abortions, and that horrid practice of women murdering their bastard children, alas, too frequent among us, sacrificing the poor innocent babes, I doubt, more to avoid the expense than the shame, which would move tears and pity in the most savage and inhuman breast.

The number of souls in Ireland being usually reckoned one million and a half, of these I calculate there may be about two hundred thousand couples whose wives are breeders, from which number I subtract thirty thousand couples who are able to maintain their own children, although I apprehend there cannot be so many under the present distresses of the kingdom, but this being granted, there will remain an hundred and seventy thousand breeders. I again subtract fifty thousand for those women who miscarry, or whose children die by accident or disease within the year. There only remain an hundred and twenty thousand children of poor parents annually born: the question therefore is, how this number shall be reared, and provided for, which, as I have already said, under the present situation of affairs is utterly impossible by all the methods hitherto proposed, for we can neither employ them in handicraft or agriculture; we neither build houses (I mean in the country), nor cultivate land: they can very seldom pick up a livelihood by stealing until they arrive at six years old, except where they are of towardly parts although I confess they learn the rudiments much earlier, during which time they can however be properly looked upon only as probationers, as I have been informed by a principal gentleman in the County of Cavan, who protested to me that he never knew above one or two instances under the age of six, even in a part of the kingdom so renowned for the quickest proficiency in that art.

I am assured by our merchants that a boy or a girl before twelve years old, is no saleable commodity, and even when they come to this age, they will not yield above three pounds, or three pounds and half-a-crown at most on the Exchange, which cannot turn to account either to the parents or the kingdom, the charge of nutriment and rags having been at least four times that value.

I shall now therefore humbly propose my own thoughts, which I hope will not be liable to the least objection.

I have been assured by a very knowing American of my acquaintance in London, that a young healthy child well nursed is at a year old a most delicious, nourishing and wholesome food, whether stewed, roasted, baked, or boiled, and I make no doubt that it will equally serve in a fricassee, or a ragout.

I do therefore humbly offer it to public consideration, that of the hundred and twenty thousand children, already computed, twenty thousand may be reserved for breed, whereof only one fourth part to be males, which is more than we allow to sheep, black-cattle, or swine, and my reason is that these children are seldom the fruits of marriage, a circumstance not much regarded by our savages, therefore one male will be sufficient to serve four females. That the remaining hundred thousand may at a year old be offered in sale to the persons of quality, and fortune, through the kingdom, always advising the mother to let them suck plentifully in the last month, so as to render them plump, and fat for a good table. A child will make two dishes at an entertainment for friends, and when the family dines alone, the fore or hind quarter will make a reasonable dish, and seasoned with a little pepper or salt will be very good boiled on the fourth day, especially in winter.

I have reckoned upon a medium, that a child just born will weigh twelve pounds, and in a solar year if tolerably nursed increaseth to twenty-eight pounds.

I grant this food will be somewhat dear, and therefore very proper for landlords, who, as they have already devoured most of the parents, seem to have the best title to the children.

Infant's flesh will be in season throughout the year, but more plentiful in March, and a little before and after, for we are told by a grave[a] author, an eminent French physician, that fish being a prolific diet, there are more children born in Roman Catholic countries about nine months after Lent than at any other season; therefore reckoning a year after Lent, the markets will be more glutted than usual, because the number of Popish infants is at least three to one in this kingdom, and therefore it will have one other collateral advantage by lessening the number of Papists among us.

I have already computed the charge of nursing a beggar's child (in which list I reckon all cottagers, labourers, and four-fifths of the farmers) to be about two shillings *per annum*, rags included, and I believe no gentleman would repine to give ten shillings for the carcass of a good fat child, which, as I have said, will make four dishes of excellent nutritive meat, when he hath only some particular friend or his own family to dine with him. Thus the Squire will learn to be a good landlord and grow popular among his tenants, the mother will have eight shillings net profit, and be fit for work until she produces another child.

[a] Rabelais.

Those who are more thrifty (as I must confess the times require) may flay the carcass; the skin of which artificially dressed, will make admirable gloves for ladies, and summer boots for fine gentlemen.

As to our city of Dublin, shambles[1] may be appointed for this purpose, in the most convenient parts of it, and butchers we may be assured will not be wanting, although I rather recommend buying the children alive, and dressing them hot from the knife, as we do roasting pigs.

A very worthy person, a true lover of his country, and whose virtues I highly esteem, was lately pleased, in discoursing on this matter to offer a refinement upon my scheme. He said that many gentlemen of this kingdom, having of late destroyed their deer, he conceived that the want of venison might be well supplied by the bodies of young lads and maidens, not exceeding fourteen years of age, nor under twelve, so great a number of both sexes in every county being now ready to starve, for want of work and service: and these to be disposed of by their parents if alive, or otherwise by their nearest relations. But with due deference to so excellent a friend, and so deserving a patriot, I cannot be altogether in his sentiments. For as to the males, my American acquaintance assured me from frequent experience that their flesh was generally tough and lean, like that of our schoolboys, by continual exercise, and their taste disagreeable, and to fatten them would not answer the charge. Then as to the females, it would, I think with humble submission, be a loss to the public, because they soon would become breeders themselves: and besides, it is not improbable that some scrupulous people might be apt to censure such a practice (although indeed very unjustly) as a little bordering upon cruelty, which I confess, hath always been with me the strongest objection against any project, howsoever well intended.

But in order to justify my friend, he confessed that this expedient was put into his head by the famous Psalmanazar,[2] a native of the island For-

A MODEST PROPOSAL. **1. shambles:** slaughterhouses. **2. Psalmanazar:** a reference to a celebrated literary impostor of the day, George Psalmanazar.

mosa, who came from thence to London, above twenty years ago, and in conversation told my friend that in his country when any young person happened to be put to death, the executioner sold the carcass to persons of quality, as a prime dainty, and that, in his time, the body of a plump girl of fifteen, who was crucified for an attempt to poison the emperor, was sold to his Imperial Majesty's Prime Minister of State, and other great Mandarins of the Court, in joints from the gibbet, at four hundred crowns. Neither indeed can I deny that if the same use were made of several plump young girls in this town who, without one single groat to their fortunes, cannot stir abroad without a chair, and appear at the playhouse and assemblies in foreign fineries, which they never will pay for, the kingdom would not be the worse.

Some persons of a desponding spirit are in great concern about the vast number of poor people, who are aged, diseased, or maimed, and I have been desired to employ my thoughts what course may be taken to ease the nation of so grievous an encumbrance. But I am not in the least pain upon that matter, because it is very well known that they are every day dying, and rotting, by cold, and famine, and filth, and vermin, as fast as can be reasonably expected. And as to the younger labourers they are now in almost as hopeful a condition. They cannot get work, and consequently pine away from want of nourishment, to a degree that if at any time they are accidentally hired to common labour, they have not strength to perform it; and thus the country and themselves are in a fair way of being soon delivered from the evils to come.

I have too long digressed, and therefore shall return to my subject. I think the advantages by the proposal which I have made are obvious and many, as well as of the highest importance.

For first, as I have already observed, it would greatly lessen the number of Papists, with whom we are yearly over-run being the principal breeders of the nation, as well as our most dangerous enemies, and who stay at home on purpose with a design to deliver the kingdom to the Pretender, hoping to take their advantage by the absence of so many good Protestants, who have chosen rather to leave their country than stay at home and pay tithes against their conscience to an idolatrous Episcopal curate.

Secondly, the poorer tenants will have something valuable of their own, which by law may be made liable to distress,[3] and help to pay their landlord's rent, their corn and cattle being already seized, and money a thing unknown.

Thirdly, whereas the maintenance of an hundred thousand children, from two years old, and upwards, cannot be computed at less than ten shillings a piece *per annum*, the nation's stock will be thereby increased fifty thousand pounds *per annum*, besides the profit of a new dish, introduced to the tables of all gentlemen of fortune in the kingdom, who have any refinement in taste, and the money will circulate among ourselves, the goods being entirely of our own growth and manufacture.

Fourthly, the constant breeders, besides the gain of eight shillings sterling *per annum*, by the sale of their children, will be rid of the charge of maintaining them after the first year.

Fifthly, this food would likewise bring great custom to taverns, where the vintners will certainly be so prudent as to procure the best receipts for dressing it to perfection, and consequently have their houses frequented by all the fine gentlemen, who justly value themselves upon their knowledge in good eating; and a skilful cook, who understands how to oblige his guests, will contrive to make it as expensive as they please.

Sixthly, this would be a great inducement to marriage, which all wise nations have either encouraged by rewards, or enforced by laws and penalties. It would increase the care and tenderness of mothers towards their children, when they were sure of a settlement for life, to the poor babes, provided in some sort by the public to their annual profit instead of expense. We should soon see an honest emulation among the married women, which of them could bring the fattest child to the market. Men would become as fond of their wives, during the time of their pregnancy, as they are now of their mares in foal, their cows in calf, or sows when they are ready to farrow, nor offer to beat or trick them (as it is too frequent a practice) for fear of a miscarriage.

Many other advantages might be enumerated.

3. **liable to distress:** Swift's high irony revolves around the legal point that a debtor's assets could be lawfully appropriated by his creditors.

For instance, the addition of some thousand carcasses in our exportation of barrelled beef; the propagation of swine's flesh, and improvement in the art of making good bacon, so much wanted among us by the great destruction of pigs, too frequent at our tables, are no way comparable in taste or magnificence to a well-grown, fat yearling child, which roasted whole will make a considerable figure at a Lord Mayor's feast, or any other public entertainment. But this and many others I omit, being studious of brevity.

Supposing that one thousand families in this city would be constant customers for infants flesh, besides others who might have it at merry meetings, particularly weddings and christenings; I compute that Dublin would take off annually about twenty thousand carcasses, and the rest of the kingdom (where probably they will be sold somewhat cheaper) the remaining eighty thousand.

I can think of no one objection that will possibly be raised against this proposal, unless it should be urged that the number of people will be thereby much lessened in the kingdom. This I freely own, and it was indeed one principal design in offering it to the world. I desire the reader will observe, that I calculate my remedy *for this one individual Kingdom* of Ireland, *and for no other that ever was, is, or, I think, ever can be upon earth.* Therefore let no man talk to me of other expedients: *Of taxing our absentees at five shillings a pound: Of using neither clothes, nor household furniture, except what is of our own growth and manufacture: Of utterly rejecting the materials and instruments that promote foreign luxury: Of curing the expensiveness of pride, vanity, idleness, and gaming in our women: Of introducing a vein of parsimony, prudence, and temperance: Of learning to love our country, wherein we differ even from* Laplanders, *and the inhabitants of* Topinamboo.[4] *Of quitting our animosities and factions, nor act any longer like the* Jews, *who were murdering one another at the very moment their city was taken: Of being a little cautious not to sell our country and consciences for nothing: Of teaching landlords to have at least one degree of mercy towards their tenants.* Lastly, *of putting a spirit of honesty, industry, and skill into our shopkeepers, who, if a resolution could now be taken to buy only our native goods, would immediately unite to cheat and exact upon us in the price, the measure and the goodness, nor could ever yet be brought to make one fair proposal of just dealing, though often and earnestly invited to it.*

Therefore I repeat, let no man talk to me of these and the like expedients, till he hath at least a glimpse of hope that there will ever be some hearty and sincere attempt to put them in practice.

But as to myself, having been wearied out for many years with offering vain, idle, visionary thoughts, and at length utterly despairing of success, I fortunately fell upon this proposal, which as it is wholly new, so it hath something solid and real, of no expense and little trouble, full in our own power, and whereby we can incur no danger in disobliging England. For this kind of commodity will not bear exportation, the flesh being of too tender a consistence to admit a long continuance in salt, *although perhaps I could name a country which would be glad to eat up our whole nation without it.*

After all I am not so violently bent upon my own opinion as to reject any offer, proposed by wise men, which shall be found equally innocent, cheap, easy and effectual. But before some thing of that kind shall be advanced in contradiction to my scheme, and offering a better, I desire the author, or authors, will be pleased maturely to consider two points. First, as things now stand, how they will be able to find food and raiment for a hundred thousand useless mouths and backs? And secondly, there being a round million of creatures in human figure, throughout this kingdom, whose whole subsistence put into a common stock would leave them in debt two millions of pounds sterling; adding those who are beggars by profession, to the bulk of farmers, cottagers, and labourers with their wives and children, who are beggars in effect; I desire those politicians who dislike my overture, and may perhaps be so bold to attempt an answer, that they will first ask the parents of these mortals whether they would not at this day think it a great happiness to have been sold for food at a year old, in the manner I prescribed, and thereby have avoided such a perpetual scene of misfortunes as they have since gone through, by

4. Topinamboo: a district of Brazil.

the oppression of landlords, the impossibility of paying rent without money or trade, the want of common sustenance, with neither house nor clothes to cover them from the inclemencies of weather, and the most inevitable prospect of entailing the like, or greater miseries upon their breed for ever.

I profess in the sincerity of my heart that I have not the least personal interest in endeavouring to promote this necessary work, having no other motive than the *public good of my country, by advancing our trade, providing for infants, relieving the poor, and giving some pleasure to the rich.* I have no children by which I can propose to get a single penny; the youngest being nine years old, and my wife past child-bearing.

(1729)

FROM

Swift's Poetry

A DESCRIPTION OF THE MORNING

Now hardly here and there an hackney-coach
Appearing, show'd the ruddy morn's approach.
Now Betty from her master's bed had flown,
And softly stole to discompose her own.
The slipshod prentice from his master's door,
Had par'd the dirt, and sprinkled round the floor.
Now Moll had whirl'd her mop with dext'rous airs,
Prepar'd to scrub the entry and the stairs.
The youth with broomy stumps began to trace
The kennel-edge, where wheels had worn the place.
The small-coal man was heard with cadence deep,
'Till drown'd in shriller notes of chimney-sweep,
Duns at his lordship's gate began to meet,
And brickdust Moll had scream'd through half the street.
The turnkey now his flock returning sees,
Duly let out a-nights to steal for fees:
The watchful bailiffs take their silent stands;
And school-boys lag with satchels in their hands.

(1709)

A DESCRIPTION OF A CITY SHOWER

[IN IMITATION OF VIRGIL'S GEORGICS]

Careful observers may foretell the hour
(By sure prognostics) when to dread a show'r:
While rain depends, the pensive cat gives o'er
Her frolics, and pursues her tail no more.
Returning home at night, you'll find the sink
Strike your offended sense with double stink.
If you be wise, then go not far to dine,
You'll spend in coach-hire more than save in wine.
A coming show'r your shooting corns presage,
Old aches throb, your hollow tooth will rage.
Sauntring in coffee-house is Dulman seen;
He damns the climate, and complains of spleen.

Meanwhile the South rising with dabbled wings,
A sable cloud a-thwart the welkin flings,
That swill'd more liquor than it could contain,
And like a drunkard gives it up again.
Brisk Susan whips her linen from the rope,
While the first drizzling show'r is borne aslope,
Such is that sprinkling which some careless quean
Flirts on you from her mop, but not so clean.
You fly, invoke the gods; then turning, stop
To rail; she singing, still whirls on her mop.
Not yet, the dust had shunn'd th' unequal strife,
But aided by the wind, fought still for life;
And wafted with its foe by violent gust,
'Twas doubtful which was rain, and which was dust.
Ah! where must needy poet seek for aid,
When dust and rain at once his coat invade;
His only coat! where dust confus'd with rain,
Roughen the nap, and leave a mingled stain.

Now in contiguous drops the flood comes down,
Threat'ning with deluge this *devoted* town.
To shops in crowds the daggled females fly,
Pretend to cheapen goods, but nothing buy.
The Templar spruce, while ev'ry spout's a-broach,
Stays till 'tis fair, yet seems to call a coach.
The tuck'd-up sempstress walks with hasty strides,
While streams run down her oil'd umbrella's sides.

A DESCRIPTION OF A CITY SHOWER. **3. depends:** threatens. **14. welkin:** sky. **19. quean:** an unmannered woman. **33. daggled:** rained-on. **35. Templar:** lawyer.

Here various kinds by various fortunes led,
Commence acquaintance underneath a shed.
Triumphant Tories, and desponding Whigs,
Forget their feuds, and join to save their wigs.
Box'd in a chair the beau impatient sits,
While spouts run clatt'ring o'er the roof by fits;
And ever and anon with frightful din
The leather sounds, he trembles from within.
So when Troy chair-men bore the wooden steed,
Pregnant with Greeks impatient to be freed,
(Those bully Greeks, who, as the moderns do,
Instead of paying chair-men, run them thro.)
Laocoon struck the outside with his spear,
And each imprison'd hero quaked for fear.

Now from all parts the swelling kennels flow,
And bear their trophies with them as they go:
Filth of all hues and odours seem to tell
What street they sail'd from, by their sight and
smell.
They, as each torrent drives, with rapid force
From Smithfield, or St. Pulchre's shape their
course,
And in huge confluent join at Snow-hill ridge,
Fall from the conduit prone to
Holborn-bridge.
Sweepings from butchers' stalls, dung, guts, and
blood,
Drown'd puppies, stinking sprats, all drench'd in
mud,
Dead cats and turnip-tops come tumbling down
the flood.

(1710)

43. chair: a means of transportation carried by two porters. **51. Laocoon:** priest of the Trojans, who threw his spear boldly at the deadly gift of a wooden horse presented by the Greeks. **62. sprats:** small European fishes of the herring family.

VERSES ON THE DEATH OF DR. SWIFT, D.S.P.D.*

OCCASIONED BY READING A MAXIM IN ROCHEFOUCAULT **

bit of comfort in grief of a friend

Dans l'adversité de nos meilleurs amis nous trouvons quelque chose, qui ne nous deplaist pas.

In the adversity of our best friends, we find something that doth not displease us.

Written by Himself, November 1731

As Rochefoucault his maxims drew
From nature, I believe 'em true:
They argue no corrupted mind
In him; the fault is in mankind.

This maxim more than all the rest
Is thought too base for human breast;
"In all distresses of our friends
We first consult our private ends,
While nature kindly bent to ease us,
Points out some circumstance to please us."

If this perhaps your patience move
Let reason and experience prove.

We all behold with envious eyes,
Our *equal* rais'd above our *size;*
Who wou'd not at a crowded show
Stand high himself, keep others low?
I love my friend as well as you,
But would not have him stop my view;
Then let me have the higher post;
I ask but for an inch at most.

If in a battle you should find,
One, whom you love of all mankind,
Had some heroic action done,
A champion kill'd or trophy won;
Rather than thus be over-topt,
Would you not wish his laurels cropt?

Dear honest Ned is in the gout,
Lies rackt with pain, and you without:
How patiently you hear him groan!
How glad the case is not your own!

---

* Dean of St. Patrick's, Dublin.

** François de la Rochefoucauld (1613–1680), author of the famous *Maxims,* which offer a deeply cynical view of life and humankind.

What poet would not grieve to see,
His brethren write as well as he?
But rather than they should excel,
He'd wish his rivals all in hell.

Her end when emulation misses,
She turns to envy, stings and hisses:
The strongest friendship yields to pride,
Unless the odds be on our side.

Vain human kind! Fantastic race!
Thy various follies, who can trace?
Self-love, ambition, envy, pride,
Their empire in our hearts divide:
Give others riches, power, and station,
'Tis all on me an usurpation.
I have no title to aspire;
Yet, when you sink, I seem the higher.
In Pope, I cannot read a line,
But with a sigh, I wish it mine:
When he can in one couplet fix
More sense than I can do in six:
It gives me such a jealous fit,
I cry, pox take him, and his wit.

Why must I be outdone by Gay,
In my own hum'rous biting way?

Arbuthnot is no more my friend,
Who dares to irony pretend;
Which I was born to introduce,
Refin'd it first, and shew'd its use.

St. John, as well as Pultney knows,
That I had some repute for prose;
And till they drove me out of date,
Could maul a minister of state:
If they have mortify'd my pride,
And made me throw my pen aside;
If with such talents heav'n hath blest 'em
Have I not reason to detest 'em?

To all my foes, dear fortune, send
Thy gifts, but never to my friend:
I tamely can endure the first,
But, this with envy makes me burst.

Thus much may serve by way of proem,
Proceed we therefore to our poem.

The time is not remote, when I
Must by the course of nature die:
When I foresee my special friends,
Will try to find their private ends:
Tho' it is hardly understood,
Which way my death can do them good,
Yet, thus methinks, I hear 'em speak;
"See, how the Dean begins to break:
Poor gentleman, he droops apace,
You plainly find it in his face:
That old vertigo in his head,
Will never leave him, till he's dead:
Besides, his memory decays,
He recollects not what he says;
He cannot call his friends to mind;
Forgets the place where last he din'd:
Plyes you with stories o'er and o'er,
He told them fifty times before.
How does he fancy we can sit,
To hear his out-of-fashion'd wit?
But he takes up with younger fokes,
Who for his wine will bear his jokes:
Faith, he must make his stories shorter,
Or change his comrades once a quarter:
In half the time, he talks them round;
There must another set be found.

"For poetry, he's past his prime,
He takes an hour to find a rhime:
His fire is out, his wit decay'd,
His fancy sunk, his muse a jade.
I'd have him throw away his pen;
But there's no talking to some men."

And, then their tenderness appears
By adding largely to my years:
"He's older than he would be reckon'd
And well remembers Charles the Second.

"He hardly drinks a pint of wine;
And that, I doubt, is no good sign.
His stomach too begins to fail:
Last year we thought him strong and hale;
But now, he's quite another thing;
I wish he may hold out till spring."

Then hug themselves, and reason thus;
"It is not yet so bad with us."

In such a case they talk in tropes,
And, by their fears express their hopes,
Some great misfortune to portend,

DEATH OF DR. SWIFT. **59. Pultney:** William Pultney (1684–1764), Earl of Bath, one of the disaffected Whigs who joined with Bolingbroke in opposing Walpole.

No enemy can match a friend.
With all the kindness they profess,
The merit of a lucky guess
(When daily howd'y's come of course,
And servants answer; worse and worse)
Wou'd please 'em better than to tell,
That, God prais'd, the Dean is well.
Then he who prophecy'd the best,
Approves his foresight to the rest:
"You know, I always fear'd the worst,
And often told you so at first":
He'd rather chuse, that I should die,
Than his prediction prove a lie.
Not one foretells I shall recover;
But, all agree, to give me over.

Yet shou'd some neighbour feel a pain,
Just in the parts, where I complain;
How many a message would he send?
What hearty prayers that I should mend?
Enquire what regimen I kept;
What gave me ease, and how I slept?
And more lament, when I was dead,
Than all the sniv'llers round my bed.

My good companions, never fear,
For though you may a mistake a year;
Though your prognostics run too fast,
They must be verify'd at last.

Behold the fatal day arrive!
"How is the Dean? He's just alive.
Now the departing prayer is read:
He hardly breathes. The Dean is dead."
Before the passing-bell begun,
The news thro' half the town has run.
"O, may we all for death prepare!
What has he left? And who's his heir?
I know no more than what the news is,
'Tis all bequeath'd to public uses.
To public use! A perfect whim!
What had the public done for him!
Mere envy, avarice, and pride!
He gave it all:—But first he dy'd.
And had the Dean, in all the nation,
No worthy friend, no poor relation?
So ready to do strangers good,
Forgetting his own flesh and blood?"

Now Grub-street wits are all employ'd,
With elegies, the town is cloy'd:
Some paragraph in ev'ry paper,
To curse the Dean or bless the Drapier.

The doctors tender of their fame,
Wisely on me lay all the blame:
"We must confess his case was nice:
But he would never take advice:
Had he been rul'd, for ought appears,
He might have liv'd these twenty years:
For when we open'd him we found,
That all his vital parts were sound."

From Dublin soon to London spread,
'Tis told at Court, the Dean is dead.
Kind Lady Suffolk in the spleen,
Runs laughing up to tell the Queen,
The Queen so gracious, mild, and good,
Cries, "Is he gone? 'Tis time he shou'd.
He's dead you say; Why, let him rot;
I'm glad the medals were forgot.
I promis'd him, I own, but when?
I only was a Princess then;
But now as consort of a king
You know 'tis quite a different thing."

Now, Chartres at Sir Robert's levee,
Tells, with a sneer, the tidings heavy:
"Why, is he dead without his shoes?"
(Cries Bob) "I'm sorry for the news;

168. Drapier: The author supposes that the scriblers of the prevailing party, which he always opposed, will libel him after his death; but that others who remember the service he had done to Ireland, under the name of M. B. Drapier, by utterly defeating the destructive project of Wood's half-pence, in five Letters to the People of Ireland, at the time read universally, and convincing every reader, will remember him with gratitude. (Swift.) **178.** The Dean supposeth himself to dye in Ireland. (Swift.) **179. Lady Suffolk:** Mrs. Howard, afterwards Countess of Suffolk, then of the Bedchamber to the Queen, professed much favour for the Dean. The Queen then Princess, sent a dozen times to the Dean (then in London) with her command to attend her; which at last he did, by advice of all his friends. She often sent for him afterwards, and always treated him very graciously. He taxed her with a present worth ten pounds, which she promised before he should return to Ireland, but on his taking leave, the medals were not ready. (Swift.) **184. medals . . . forgot:** The medals were to be sent to the Dean in four months, but she forgot, or thought them too dear. The Dean being in Ireland sent Mrs. Howard a piece of plaid made in that kingdom, which the Queen seeing took it from her and wore it herself, and sent to the Dean for as much as would clothe herself and children—desiring he would send the

Oh, were the wretch but living still,
And, in his place my good friend Will;
Or, had a mitre on his head
Provided Bolingbroke were dead."

Now, Curl his shop from rubbish drains;
Three genuine tomes of *Swift's Remains.*
And then, to make them pass the glibber,
Revis'd by Tibbalds, Moore, and Cibber.
He'll treat me as he does my betters.
Publish my will, my life, my letters.
Revive the libels born to die;
Which Pope must bear, as well as I.

Here shift the scene, to represent
How those I love, my death lament.
Poor Pope will grieve a month; and Gay
A week; and Arbuthnot a day.

St. John himself will scarce forbear,
To bite his pen, and drop a tear.
The rest will give a shrug, and cry,
I'm sorry; but we all must die.
Indifference clad in wisdom's guise,
All fortitude of mind supplies:
For how can stony bowels melt,
In those who never pity felt;
When *We* are lash'd, *They* kiss the rod;
Resigning to the will of God.

The fools, my juniors by a year,
Are tortur'd with suspence and fear.
Who wisely thought my age a screen,
When death approach'd, to stand between:
The screen remov'd, their hearts are trembling,
They mourn for me without dissembling.

My female friends, whose tender hearts,
Have better learn'd to act their parts,
Receive the news in doleful dumps,
"The Dean is dead, (and what is trumps?)
Then Lord have mercy on his soul.
(Ladies I'll venture for the vole.)
Six deans they say must bear the pall.
(I wish I knew what king to call.)
Madam, your husband will attend
The funeral of so good a friend.
No madam, 'tis a shocking sight,
And he's engag'd to-morrow night!
My Lady Club wou'd take it ill,
If he shou'd fail her at quadrill.
He lov'd the Dean. (I led a heart.)
But dearest friends, they say, must part.
His time was come, he ran his race;
We hope he's in a better place."

---

charge of it. He did the former; it cost 35l. but he said he would have nothing except the medals: he went next summer to England and was treated as usual, and she being then Queen, the Dean was promised a settlement in England but return'd as he went, and instead of receiving of her intended favours or the medals hath been ever since under her Majesty's displeasure. (Swift.) **189. Chartres:** Chartres is a most infamous, vile scoundrel, grown from a foot-boy, or worse, to a prodigious fortune both in England and Scotland: he had a way of insinuating himself into all Ministers under every change, either as pimp, flatterer, or informer. He was tried at seventy for a rape, and came off by sacrificing a great part of his fortune (he is since dead, but this poem still preserves the scene and time it was writ in.) (Swift.) **192. Bob:** Sir Robert Walpole, Chief Minister of State, treated the Dean in 1726, with great distinction, invited him to dinner at Chelsea, with the Dean's friends chosen on purpose; appointed an hour to talk with him of Ireland, to which kingdom and people the Dean found him no great friend; for he defended Wood's project of half-pence, &c. The Dean would see him no more; and upon his next year's return to England, Sir Robert on an accidental meeting, only made a civil compliment, and never invited him again. (Swift.) **194. Will:** Mr. William Pultney, from being Mr. Walpole's intimate friend, detesting his administration, became his mortal enemy, and joyned with my Lord Bolingbroke, to expose him in an excellent paper, called the *Craftsman,* still continued. (Swift.) **196. Bolingbroke:** Henry St. John, Lord Viscount Bolingbroke, Secretary of State to Queen Anne of blessed memory. He is reckoned the most universal genius in Europe; Walpole dreading his abilities, treated him most injuriously, working with King George who forgot his promise of restoring the said lord, upon the restless importunity of Sir Robert Walpole. (Swift.) **197. Curl:** Curl hath been the most infamous bookseller of any age or country; his character in part may be found in Mr. Pope's *Dunciad.* He published three volumes all charged on the Dean, who never writ three pages of them; he hath used many of the Dean's friends in almost as vile a manner. (Swift.) **200. Tibbalds . . . Cibber:** Three stupid verse writers in London, the last to the shame of the Court, and the highest disgrace to wit and learning, was made Laureat. Moore, commonly called Jemmy Moore, son of Arthur Moore, whose father was jaylor of Monaghan in Ireland. See the character of Jemmy Moore, and Tibbalds, Theobald in the *Dunciad.* (Swift.) **201. He'll treat . . . betters:** Curl is notoriously infamous for publishing the Lives, Letters, and Last Wills and Testaments of the nobility and Ministers of State, as well as of all the rogues, who

Why do we grieve that friends should die?
No loss more easy to supply.
One year is past; a different scene;
No further mention of the Dean;
Who now, alas, no more is missed,
Than if he never did exist.
Where's now this fav'rite of Apollo?
Departed; and his words must follow:
Must undergo the common fate;
His kind of wit is out of date.
Some country Squire to Lintot goes,
Enquires for SWIFT in Verse and Prose:
Says Lintot, "I have heard the name:
He dy'd a year ago." The same.
He searches all his shop in vain;
"Sir you may find them in Duck-Lane:
I sent them with a load of books,
Last Monday, to the pastry-cooks.
To fancy they cou'd live a year!
I find you're but a stranger here.
The Dean was famous in his time;
And had a kind of knack at rhyme:
His way of writing now is past;
The town hath got a better taste:
I keep no antiquated stuff;
But, spick and span I have enough.
Pray, do but give me leave to shew'em,
Here's Colley Cibber's Birth-day poem.
This ode you never yet have seen,
By Stephen Duck, upon the Queen.
Then, here's a Letter finely penn'd
Against the Craftsman and his friend;
It clearly shews that all reflection
On ministers, is disaffection.
Next, here's a Sir Robert's *Vindication,*
And Mr. Henly's last Oration:
The hawkers have not got 'em yet,
Your Honour please to buy a set?

"Here's Woolston's tracts, the twelfth edition;
'Tis read by ev'ry politician:
The country members, when in town,
To all their boroughs send them down:
You never met a thing so smart;
The courtiers have them all by heart:
Those Maids of Honour (who can read)
Are taught to use them for their creed.
The rev'rend author's good intention,
Hath been rewarded with a pension:
He doth an honour to his gown,
By bravely running priest-craft down:
He shews as sure as God's in *Gloc'ster,*
That Jesus was a grand impostor:
That all his miracles were cheats,
Perform'd as jugglers do their feats:
The Church had never such a writer:
A shame, he hath not got a mitre!"

Suppose me dead; and then suppose
A club assembled at the Rose;
Where from discourse of this and that,
I grow the subject of their chat:
And, while they toss my name about,
With favour some, and some without;
One quite indiff'rent in the cause,
My character impartial draws.

"The Dean, if we believe report,
Was never ill receiv'd at Court.
As for his Works in Verse and Prose,
I own my self no judge of those:
Nor, can I tell what critics thought 'em;
But, this I know, all people bought 'em;

---

are hanged at Tyburn. He hath been in custody of the House of Lords for publishing or forging the letters of many peers; which made the Lords enter a resolution in their Journal Book, that no life or writings of any lord should be published without the consent of the next heir at law, or licence from their House. (Swift.) **230. vole:** winning all the tricks in one of the current fashionable card games like quadrille. **253. Lintot:** Bernard Lintot, a bookseller in London, *Vide* Mr. Pope's *Dunciad.* (Swift.) **258. Duck-Lane:** A place where old books are sold in London. (Swift.) **272. Stephen Duck:** the so-called Thresher Poet (1705–1756) was in fact a farmer-turned-poet, who was a court favorite. **277. Vindication:** Walpole hath a set of party scriblers, who do nothing else but write in his defence. (Swift.)

278. Henley's . . . Oration: Henly is a clergyman who wanting both merit and luck to get preferment, or even to keep his curacy in the Established Church, formed a new conventicle, which he calls an Oratory. There, at set times, he delivereth strange speeches compiled by himself and his associates, who share the profit with him; every hearer pays a shilling each day for admittance. He is an absolute dunce, but generally reputed crazy. (Swift.) **281. Woolston's tracts:** Woolston was a clergyman, but for want of bread, hath in several treatises, in the most blasphemous manner, attempted to turn Our Savior and his miracles into ridicule. He is much caressed by many great courtiers and by all the infidels, and his books read generally by the court ladies. (Swift.) **300. Rose:** a famous tavern of the time.

As with a moral view design'd
To cure the vices of mankind;
His vein, ironically grave,
Expos'd the fool, and lash'd the knave:
To steal a hint was never known,
But what he writ, was all his own.

"He never thought an honour done him,
Because a duke was proud to own him:
Would rather slip aside, and chuse
To talk with wits in dirty shoes:
Despis'd the fools with Stars and Garters,
So often seen caressing Chartres:
He never courted men in station,
Nor persons had in admiration;
Of no man's greatness was afraid,
Because he sought for no man's aid.
Though trusted long in great affairs,
He gave himself no haughty airs:
Without regarding private ends,
Spent all his credit for his friends:
And only chose the wise and good;
No flatt'rers; no allies in blood;
But succour'd virtue in distress,
And seldom fail'd of good success;
As numbers in their hearts must own,
Who, but for him, had been unknown.

"With princes kept a due decorum,
But never stood in awe before 'em:
He follow'd David's lesson just,
In Princes never put thy Trust.
And, would you make him truly sour;
Provoke him with a slave in power:
The Irish Senate, if you nam'd,
With what impatience he declaim'd!
Fair LIBERTY was all his cry;
For her he stood prepar'd to die;
For her he boldly stood alone;
For her he oft expos'd his own.
Two kingdoms, just as faction led,
Had set a price upon his head;
But, not a traitor cou'd be found.
To sell him for six hundred pound.

"Had he but spar'd his tongue and pen,
He might have rose like other men:
But, power was never in his thought;
And, wealth he valu'd not a groat:
Ingratitude he often found,
And pity'd those who meant the wound:
But, kept the tenor of his mind,
To merit well of human kind:
Nor made a sacrifice of those
Who still were true, to please his foes.
He labour'd many a fruitless hour
To reconcile his friends in power;
Saw mischief by a faction brewing,
While they pursu'd each others ruin.
But, finding vain was all his care,
He left the court in mere despair.

"And, oh! how short are human schemes!
Here ended all our golden dreams.
What St. John's skill in state affairs,
What Ormond's valour, Oxford's cares,
To save their sinking country lent,
Was all destroy'd by one event.
Too soon that precious life was ended,
On which alone, our weal depended.

---

324. Chartres: See the notes before on Chartres. (Swift.) **352. Had set . . . head:** In the Year 1713, the late Queen was prevailed with by an Address of the House of Lords in England, to publish a Proclamation, promising three hundred pounds to whatever person would discover the author of a pamphlet called *The Publick Spirit of the Whiggs;* and in Ireland, in the year 1724, my Lord Carteret at his first coming into the Government, was prevailed on to issue a Proclamation for promising the like reward of three hundred pounds, to any person who could discover the author of a pamphlet called, *The Drapier's Fourth Letter,* &c. writ against that destructive project of coining half-pence for Ireland; but in neither kingdoms was the Dean discovered. (Swift.) **358. groat:** an obsolete English coin; a trifle. **366. To reconcile . . . power:** Queen Anne's Ministry fell to variance from the first year after their Ministry began: Harcourt the Chancellor, and Lord Bolingbroke the Secretary, were discontented with the Treasurer Oxford, for his too much mildness to the Whig Party; this quarrel grew higher every day till the Queen's death: the Dean, who was the only person that endeavoured to reconcile them, found it impossible; and thereupon retired to the country about ten weeks before that fatal event: upon which he returned to his Deanry in Dublin, where for many years he was worryed by the new people in power, and had hundreds of libels writ against him in England. (Swift.) **374. Ormond:** James Butler, second Duke of Ormond (1665–1746), English military commander-in-chief against France and Spain. **Oxford:** Robert Harley, Earl of Oxford (1661–1724), a Tory statesman. With the death of Queen Anne, the Tory government fell, and men like Bolingbroke, Ormond, and Oxford lost their positions of power. **377. Too soon . . . ended:** In the height of the quarrel between the Ministers, the Queen died. (Swift.)

"When up a dangerous faction starts,
With wrath and vengeance in their hearts;
By solemn League and Cov'nant bound,
To ruin, slaughter, and confound;
To turn religion to a fable,
And make the Government a Babel:
Pervert the law, disgrace the gown,
Corrupt the senate, rob the crown;
To sacrifice old England's glory,
And make her infamous in story.
When such a tempest shook the land,
How could unguarded virtue stand?

"With horror, grief, despair the Dean
Beheld the dire destructive scene:
His friends in exile, or the Tower,
Himself within the frown of power;
Pursu'd by base envenom'd pens,
Far to the land of slaves and fens;
A servile race in folly nurs'd,
Who truckle most, when treated worst.

"By innocence and resolution,
He bore continual persecution;
While numbers to preferment rose;
Whose merits were, to be his foes.
When, ev'n his own familiar friends
Intent upon their private ends;
Like renegadoes now he feels,
Against him lifting up their heels.

"The Dean did by his pen defeat
An infamous destructive cheat.
Taught fools their int'rest how to know;
And gave them arms to ward the blow.
Envy hath own'd it was his doing,
To save that helpless land from ruin;
While they who at the steerage stood,
And reapt the profit, sought his blood.

"To save them from their evil fate,
In him was held a crime of state.
A wicked monster on the bench,
Whose fury blood could never quench;
As vile and profligate a villain,
As modern Scroggs, or old Tressilian;
Who long all justice had discarded,
Nor fear'd he God, nor man regarded;
Vow'd on the Dean his rage to vent,
And make him of his zeal repent;
But Heav'n his innocence defends,
The grateful people stand his friends:
Nor strains of law, nor judges frown,
Nor topics brought to please the crown,
Nor witness hir'd, nor jury pick'd,
Prevail to bring him in convict.

"In exile with a steady heart,
He spent his life's declining part;
Where folly, pride, and faction sway,
Remote from St. John, Pope, and Gay.

379. dangerous . . . starts: Upon Queen Anne's death the Whig faction was restored to power, which they exercised with the utmost rage and revenge; impeached and banished the chief leaders of the Church party, and stripped all their adherents of what employments they had, after which England was never known to make so mean a figure in Europe: the greatest preferments in the Church in both kingdoms were given to the most ignorant men. Fanatics were publicly caressed; Ireland utterly ruined and enslaved; only great Ministers heaping up millions; and so affairs continued to this 3rd. of May 1732, and are likely to remain so. (Swift.) **394. Himself . . . power:** Upon the Queen's death, the Dean returned to live in Dublin, at his Deanry-house: numberless libels were writ against him in England, as a Jacobite; he was insulted in the street, and at nights he was forced to be attended by his servants armed. (Swift.) **396. land . . . fens:** The Land of slaves and fens, is Ireland. (Swift.) **398. truckle:** submit cowardly. **408. infamous . . . cheat:** One Wood, a hardware-man from England, had a patent for coining copper halfpence in Ireland, to the sum of £108,000 which in the consequence, must leave that kingdom without gold or silver. (Swift.) **417. wicked . . . bench:** One Whitshed was then Chief Justice: he had some years before prosecuted a printer for a pamphlet writ by the Dean, to perswade the people of Ireland to wear their own manufactures. Whitshed sent the jury down eleven times, and kept them nine hours until they were forced to bring in a special verdict. He sat as judge afterwards on the tryal of the printer of the *Drapier's Fourth Letter;* but the jury, against all he could say or swear, threw out the bill: all the kingdom took the Drapier's part, except the courtiers, or those who expected places. The Drapier was celebrated in many poems and pamphlets: his sign was set up in most streets in Dublin (where many of them still continue) and in several country towns. (Swift.) **420. Scroggs . . . Tressilian:** Scroggs was Chief Justice under King Charles the Second: his judgment always varied in state tryals, according to directions from Court. Tressilian was a wicked judge, hanged above three hundred years ago. (Swift.) **431. exile:** In Ireland, which he had reason to call a place of exile; to which country nothing could have driven him, but the Queen's death, who had determined to fix him in England, in Spight of the Dutchess of Somerset, &c. (Swift.) **434. St. John:** Henry St. John, Lord Viscount Bolingbroke, mentioned

"His friendship there to few confin'd,
Were always of the midling kind:
No fools of rank, a mungril breed,
Who fain would pass for Lords indeed;
Where titles give no right or power,
And peerage is a wither'd flower,
He would have held it a disgrace,
If such a wretch had known his face.
On rural squires, that kingdom's bane,
He vented oft his wrath in vain:
Biennial squires, to market brought;
Who sell their souls and votes for naught;
The nation stripp'd go joyful back,
To rob the Church, their tenants rack,
Go snacks with rogues and rapparees
And, keep the peace, to pick up fees:
In every job to have a share,
A jail or barrack to repair;
And turn the tax for public roads
Commodious to their own abodes.

"Perhaps I may allow, the Dean
Had too much satire in his vein;
And seem'd determin'd not to starve it,
Because no age could more deserve it.
Yet, malice never was his aim;
He lash'd the vice, but spar'd the name.
No individual could resent,
Where thousands equally were meant.
His satire points at no defect,
But what all mortals may correct:
For he abhorr'd that senseless tribe,
Who call it humour when they jibe:
He spar'd a hump, or crooked nose,
Whose owners set not up for beaux.
True genuine dullness mov'd his pity,
Unless it offer'd to be witty.
Those, who their ignorance confess'd,
He ne'er offended with a jest;
But laugh'd to hear an idiot quote,
A verse from Horace, learn'd by rote.

"He knew an hundred pleasant stories,
With all the turns of Whigs and Tories:
Was cheerful to his dying day,
And friends would let him have his way.

"He gave the little wealth he had,
To build a house for fools and mad:
And shew'd by one satiric touch,
No nation wanted it so much:
That kingdom he hath left his debtor,
I wish it soon may have a better."

(1731)

before. (Swift.) **435. friendship . . . confin'd:** In Ireland the Dean was not acquainted with one single Lord Spiritual or Temporal. He only conversed with private gentlemen of the clergy or laity, and but a small number of either. (Swift.) **440. wither'd flower:** The peers of Ireland lost their jurisdiction by one single Act, and tamely submitted to the infamous mark of slavery without the least resentment or remonstrance. (Swift.) **445. Biennial . . . brought:** The Parliament, as they call it, in Ireland meet but once in two years, and after having given five times more than they can afford return home to reimburse themselves by all country jobs and oppressions of which some few only are mentioned. (Swift.) **449. Go . . . rapparees:** The highwaymen in Ireland, are, since the late wars there, usually called Rapparees, which was a name given to those Irish soldiers who in small parties used at that time to plunder Protestants. (Swift.) **452. A jail . . . repair:** The army in Ireland are lodged in barracks, the building and repairing whereof and other charges have cost a prodigious sum to that unhappy kingdom. (Swift.)

483. kingdom: Meaning Ireland, where he now lives, and probably may dye. (Swift.)

Samuel Johnson · James Boswell

1709–1784 1740–1795

Few English writers have fared so well with their biographers as has Samuel Johnson. In spite of the Victorian image, fostered in large part by Macaulay, of an awkward, unseemly, and strange man whose conversation would outlive his literary efforts, the great tradition of James Boswell's *Life of Samuel Johnson* has continued in our own century with superior works like James Clifford's *Young Sam Johnson,* Joseph Wood Krutch's *Samuel Johnson,* Bertrand Bronson's *Johnson Agonistes,* John Wain's *Samuel Johnson,* and the recently published and Pulitzer Prize-winning biography by W.J. Bate. Indeed, more than one critic has favorably compared Bate's wonderfully comprehensive and warmly sympathetic study to Boswell's. There is, then, no reason why the student should have any difficulty in seeing the main outlines and details of Johnson's long and full life. The challenge is interpretation, an understanding of and sensitivity to the rhythms of this life, a concern with dominant themes and patterns, a search for some sort of middle ground—a middle ground between Johnson, the great mind ranging over manners and morals in a remarkable variety of genres, and Johnson, the emotionally troubled, erratic, prejudiced, at times even cruel individual who is continually searching for a sense of tranquillity in his life and work. Very early in his endeavor, Boswell reminds his readers that man is a creature of "contradictory qualities" and that reckoning with these qualities is important in any attempt to understand the essential Johnson. He contends in his great biography, "In proportion to the native vigour of the mind, the contradictory qualities will be the more prominent, and more difficult to be adjusted; and, therefore, we are not to wonder, that Johnson exhibited an eminent example of this remark which

I have made upon human nature." This observation is indeed most helpful, as we proceed to examine the great man's life.

Samuel Johnson was born in Lichfield on September 18, 1709, into a family that had always known the ravages of poverty. His father, Michael, was a large somber bookseller and his mother, Sarah, a woman of some background and intelligence. Both were approaching middle age when their two sons were born. While intellectually precocious, proud, and rebellious, Johnson was plagued with physical ailments at an early age—afflictions that haunted him throughout his life and were subtly mirrored in his work. From the time of his birth until he was six, he had an aggravated running sore on his left arm. In addition, he was disfigured and his sight was impaired by the scrofula he had contracted from his wet nurse. Compulsive nervous twitches, which grew worse as he became older, called further attention to his appearance. How difficult it was for the brilliant and proud spirit living within this scarred body to function in the ordinary world. At the local schools in Lichfield and Stourbridge he was but an average student. His strongest early education was thus in the midst of his father's books, and he read voraciously in Latin and Greek, in philosophy and literature, as well as in the kind of escapist romance that stirred a youthful and vigorous imagination.

On October 31, 1728, Johnson entered Pembroke College, Oxford, where he pursued studies with no great inspiration or plan. He left without a degree, the victim of an emotional breakdown, a broken man seemingly without hope of making a career for himself. One notable event at Oxford, however, was his reading of William Law's *Serious Call to a Devout and Holy Life,* a work which engaged him deeply and which did much to draw him away from excessive self-absorption toward the Christianity of the Church of England. This religious dimension will be discussed in some detail later; but it should be stated now that Law's book played an important role in shaping Johnson's strong self-criticism, his sense of the dangers of excessive imagination and emotion, and his belief in the need for activity to release the great potential of human beings who are searching for some measure of human happiness.

Johnson's father died in December, 1731. Returning to his hometown of Lichfield, Johnson became involved in the world outside of himself. He showed an interest in a legal career, but did not possess the financial resources for pursuing it. He also made various attempts at becoming a teacher, but seemed to lack those special talents needed for such a demanding profession. In the midst of these disappointments, Johnson, twenty-six years old and with only a translation of Father Lobo's *Voyage to Abyssinia* behind him, shocked his friends by marrying Mrs. Elizabeth Porter, a buxom, not especially attractive widow some twenty years his senior. "Tetty," as he fondly called her, was clearly not the answer to all of his prayers, but she was certainly a tower of strength. She was a woman who saw in him the "most sensible" person she had ever known and who then and throughout the marriage gave him a sense of his own dignity and, most important, an awareness of responsibility and of his potential as a writer. With her help he tried to organize a small school at Edial in Staffordshire, but could enroll only six or eight pupils, one of whom, David Garrick, was to become an important person in his life.

In March of 1737, throwing caution to the wind, Johnson and Garrick went to London in order to try the literary life; later in the year Elizabeth joined them. Thus began a long period of hack work so vividly recounted in Boswell's *Life of Johnson* and in an extraordinary recent book by Paul Fussell, *Samuel Johnson and the Life of Writing*. Indeed, no one can read Johnson's own biography, *An Account of the Life of Mr. Richard Savage,* without developing a strong feeling for the kind of poverty and struggle he experienced in these desperate years. Observing graphically the varieties of human behavior while trudging the streets of London with the down-and-out Savage, a young Grub Street hack writer, Johnson worked at every conceivable menial assignment for Edward Cave, editor of *The Gentleman's Magazine*. He even reported the Parliamentary debates, no small feat, considering that he attended very few of them and depended to a great extent on hearsay and imagination.

His professional fortunes took a slight turn for the better with the appearance of a favorable critical response to his first important creative work in 1738, *London, a Poem, in Imitation of the Third Satire of Juvenal,* a poem that reflects vividly the noise and turbulence of the great city. In 1744 he produced his memorable biography of Savage, mentioned above. Some regard it as one of the best short novels in the language; others, as almost an autobiography. In this brilliant work, Johnson captures the misery of Grub Street, revealing a remarkable sympathy for Savage, the abandoned illegitimate child of royalty who lived in abject poverty, his hopes marred by bad luck, until his death in a debtor's prison. Although Savage was a scoundrel in many ways, Johnson was clearly attracted to this tragic figure, perhaps because he saw a good deal of his own life in Savage's. As Bertrand Bronson contends, "It is evident what motivates Johnson in his account is not merely the spirit of Christian charity and forgiveness. He had a deep and ever-present consciousness of this mortal state. It was not only that none can foretell the events of tomorrow, but that we cannot be sure of the steadiness of our own purposes, nor be confident that today's resolve may not be subverted by tomorrow's emotional impulse."

During the ten years that followed, Johnson seemed truly to come into his own. Indeed, his name became famous with an astonishing release of creative effort that made for a golden decade. His first signed work, *The Vanity of Human Wishes, The Tenth Satire of Juvenal Imitated by Samuel Johnson,* appeared in January of 1749; it was followed by Garrick's production of his play *Irene* a month later; the writing and publication of the vast majority of the essays in *The Rambler* from March 20, 1750, to March 14, 1752; essays for *The Adventurer* in 1753 and 1754; the still monumental achievement of his great *Dictionary of the English Language* in 1755; the *Proposals for Printing the Dramatick Works of William Shakespeare,* the plays appearing in October of 1765; the writing and publication of most of *The Idler* essays between April 25, 1758, and April 5, 1760; and the publication of his philosophical novel *Rasselas* in April of 1759. As Boswell puts it, "In 1750 he came forth in the character for which he was eminently qualified, a majestick teacher of moral and religious wisdom." Two events, however, marred his happiness during these years—the death of his beloved wife, who had meant so much to his personal and professional rejuvenation, on March 28, 1752, and the passing of his mother, whom he had not visited for twenty years and for whose funeral expenses he hastily wrote *Rasselas*, in January of 1759.

In 1762 Johnson, now recognized as a major English literary figure, was awarded an annual pension of £300 for life. In 1764 he and Sir Joshua Reynolds founded the celebrated Literary Club, certainly by any standard one of the greatest galaxies of intellectuals and artists ever assembled—Edmund Burke, Oliver Goldsmith, David Garrick, Thomas Percy, Richard Sheridan, and the man who now enters Johnson's story, James Boswell. One can only delight in the image of a gathering of these and others and of the great conversations and debates that took place. Trinity College, Dublin, honored Johnson with a Doctorate in Civil Law in 1765, and even though he disliked titles, he nevertheless became from that time forward "Doctor Johnson."

What must be regarded as one of the major encounters in literary history took place in May of 1763, when James Boswell met the now famous Johnson at the bookshop of Thomas Davies. Although many modern critics have debunked the caricature of Boswell as the snooping reporter who never let Johnson out of his sight, he did observe keenly and perceptively and noted vividly the life and words of the great man until his death. We know a great deal about Johnson and about his famous biographer today due to the remarkable manuscript discoveries since the 1920s. Indeed, the phenomenal discovery of 1,300 pages from the original manuscript of *The Life of Johnson* in a deserted cowbarn in Malahide, Ireland, and the subsequent acquisition and publication of these materials by Yale University has shed new light on the two men as individuals and on the relationship that existed between them.

Although he was a free-spirited Scotsman, who devoted his life to pleasure, James Boswell was nevertheless drawn to Johnson, as Johnson was to him. He felt, it would seem, a kind of hero worship of Johnson, and yet that designation will not quite do. Given Boswell's own unhappy young life, his isolation from his father, Johnson became a kind of surrogate parent, critical of his indiscretions to be sure, but always there, ready to lend advice and comfort. And Boswell responded with the special gifts of a great biographer—a fidelity to fact and a creative power to bring a subject to life by a certain sympathy, by an ability to stage a scene, capture the humor or pathos of a situation without any rhapsodical flights of fancy. His account of the first meeting of the two moves from the solemn to the comic, as he describes the anticipation and first encounters in splendid fashion. First, "1763. This is to me a memorable year; for in it I had the happiness to obtain the acquaintance of that extraordinary man whose memoirs I am now writing; an acquaintance which I shall ever esteem as one of the most fortunate circumstances in my life. Though then but two-and-twenty, I had for several years read his works with delight and instruction, and had the highest reverence for their authour, which had grown up in my fancy into a kind of mysterious veneration, by figuring to myself a state of solemn elevated abstraction, in which I supposed him to live in the immense metropolis of London." Then Boswell's wonderful first view of his subject: "At last, on Monday the 16th of May, when I was sitting in Mr. Davies's back-parlour, after having drunk tea with him and Mrs. Davies, Johnson unexpectedly came into the shop; and Mr. Davies having perceived him through the glass-door in the room in which we were sitting, advancing towards us,—he announced his awful approach to me, somewhat in the manner of an actor in the part of Horatio, when he addresses Hamlet on the appearance of his father's ghost, 'Look, my Lord, it comes.'" And still later, the introduction by the fun-loving Davies with its reference to Boswell's origins: "I was much agitated; and recollecting his prejudice against the Scotch, of which I had heard much, I said to Davies, 'Don't tell where I come from.'—'From Scotland,' cried Davies, roguishly. 'Mr. Johnson, (said I) I do indeed come from Scotland, but I cannot help it.'" Then there is Johnson's witty response, "That, Sir, I find, is what a very great many of your countrymen cannot help," followed by his put-down of Boswell for assuming too much familiarity in commenting on one of Johnson's observations on David Garrick. This exchange is concluded by the great moment of triumph, as Davies assures Boswell, "I can see he likes you very well." Boswell's re-creation of a visit to Johnson shortly afterwards is deeply touching and reveals a wealth of insight into his subject:

> He received me very courteously: but, it must be confessed, that his apartment, and furniture, and morning dress, were sufficiently uncouth. His brown suit of cloaths looked very rusty: he had on a little old shrivelled unpowdered wig, which was too small for his head; his shirt-neck and knees of his breeches were loose; his black worsted stockings ill drawn up; and he had a pair of unbuckled shoes by way of slippers. But all these slovenly particularities were forgotten the moment he began to talk. Some gentlemen, whom I do not recollect, were sitting with him; and when they went away, I also rose; but he said to me, "Nay, don't go."—"Sir, (said I), I am afraid that I intrude upon you. It is benevolent to allow me to sit and hear you." He seemed pleased with this compliment, which I sincerely paid him, and answered, "Sir, I am obliged to any man who visits me."

Maynard Mack is most perceptive in paying tribute to Boswell, who "... manages to convey with incomparable vividness the very habit of Johnson's conversation; its pursuit of underlying principles, its characteristic thrust toward the positions that command the area of debate and its sinewy athletic challenge." Boswell's biography, unlike Bate's, may focus heavily on the years after the 1763 meeting, but it still stands as a masterpiece of its kind.

Biographers have been quick to point to a second serious emotional disorder after 1750, when, for the better part of five years, Johnson was extremely distressed, fearful, as he had been before, of insanity, anxious about aging, death, and the state of his soul. How striking are his *Prayers and Meditations* of these years, as the man of reason and control realizes the need for some supernatural help and prays fervently for it. Certainly the hospitality afforded him by Henry and Hester Thrale in taking him into their home at Streatham in 1765, brought a measure of security and peace, and Mrs. Thrale's memoirs are rich with insights into Johnson at this time. He also responded well to the memorable trip to Scotland and the Hebrides, which he and Boswell took in 1773, and which is vividly recorded in his *Journey to the Western Islands of Scotland* in 1775 and Boswell's *Journal of a Tour to the Hebrides* in 1785. A second Doctor in Civil Law degree, this time from Oxford, also brought him great pleasure.

Johnson's last major, and indeed magisterial, work, *The Lives of the English Poets,* was begun when he was nearly seventy years of age and occupied him from 1778 to 1781. His final years were ones of physical and mental deterioration. A paralytic stroke in 1783, the virtual loss of speech in a man for whom words were life, dropsy, and heart disease—all weakened him irrevocably. Equally powerful too were his fear of death and his sense of guilt for what he felt was his continuing irresponsibility. The prayer in his letter of June 19, 1783, to Mrs. Thrale reveals these emotions: "O God! give me comfort and confidence in Thee: forgive my sins; and if it be Thy good pleasure, relieve my diseases for Jesus Christ's sake. Amen." Johnson died on December 13, 1784.

Any critic or editor of Johnson's varied work looks for a focus, and this writer is no exception. He turns to the moral writing first and finds there certain key points of reference from which to move to larger generalizations about Johnson's themes and techniques. Strange and paradoxical as the language may seem, Johnson had a passion for the rational, for that which is rooted in the experience of real men in real life situations. Indeed, what human beings in many eras and many contexts have found to be true becomes a kind of cumulative wisdom, a test against which we can measure moral actions and works of art. Civilization is a precious treasure one does not tamper with or alter lightly, whether to produce the drama of radical change or to display the brilliance of individual virtuosity. Coming to terms with life, keeping the lines of communication open between the human heart and concrete experience is the root of wisdom and of moral health. To Goldsmith on the question of whether war can be justified on moral grounds, Johnson replies, "Nay, Sir, if you will not take the universal opinion of mankind, I have nothing to say." To Boswell he remarks, thinking of the developing philosophies of natural goodness in his time, "We can have no dependence upon that instinctive, that constitutional goodness which is not founded upon principle." When discussing the freedom of the human will, he observes that while all theory argues against it, all practical experience argues for it.

At the same time Johnson, like his contemporaries Pope and Swift, is impatient with easy schemes for the improvement of life and with facile optimism about human progress. He insists on the importance of realizing that life is a situation in which there is much to be endured and little to be enjoyed. He is very quick to associate the trust in an orderly universe found in Soame Jenyns' *A Free Inquiry Into the Nature and Origin of Evil* with "... many of the books which now croud the world," and which "... may be justly suspected to be written for the sake of some invisible order of beings, for they surely are of no use to any of the corporeal inhabitants of the world."

While stressing the centrality of experience, Johnson points to the snares and clouds, to borrow a few of his familiar images, that draw one away from the bedrock of truth. Life, he contends, is an arena in which pain and sorrow and frustration play vital roles; to ignore this fact is to indulge a fatal fancy. The sonorous, measured prose in *Rambler 184* develops his general point aptly.

> Since life itself is uncertain, nothing which has life for its basis, can boast much stability. Yet this is but a small part of our perplexity. We set out on a tempestuous sea, in quest of some port, where we expect to find rest, but where we are not sure of admission; we are not only in danger of sinking in the way, but of being misled by meteors mistaken for stars, of being driven from our course by the changes of the wind, and of losing it by unskillful steerage; yet it sometimes happens, that cross winds blow us to a safer coast, that meteors draw us aside from whirlpools, and that negligence or error contributes to our escape from mischiefs to which a direct course would have exposed us.

Similarly, in human beings themselves are forces that war with common sense, with a firm grasp of the present reality. There is a fundamental restlessness, a fascination with memories that may help us forget or with hopes that may lift us beyond our current predicament. This restlessness is the result in Johnsonian terms of "... that hunger of imagination which preys incessantly upon life, and must always be appeased by some employment." Imagination is the villain, especially imagination that is out of control and unable to measure its creations against the test of reality. Johnson is not a bloodless human being—indeed, his own personal life is filled with examples of the power of imagination and emotion—he simply believes that all forms of intellectual activity must be rooted in and subservient to the direct confrontation of reality.

The second great subverter of the quest for knowledge and understanding is human pride, the avoidance of reality and the need for self-justification at any cost. With a sense of Shakespeare's "With what I most enjoy contented least," Johnson penetratingly describes fear, anxiety, envy, and the treachery of the heart. All of these emotions shut out reality, build up fantasies and imagined adversaries that make life a constant strife, and prevent the outlets for activity that are essential for some measure of health and happiness. *Rambler 76* is a masterpiece of psychological insight, as it analyzes this special problem: "The sentence most dreaded is that of reason and conscience, which they would engage in their side at any price but the labours of duty, and the sorrows of repentance. For this purpose every seducement and fallacy is sought, the hopes still rest upon some new experiment till life is at an end; and the last hour steals on unperceived, while the faculties are engaged in resisting reason, and repressing the sense of disapprobation." W. J. Bate's succinct sentence on this dimension of Johnson's thought is almost perfect. "Freedom," he says, "is the harmony of the inner life with truth."

Johnson's *The History of Rasselas,* whether we regard it as a novel or as a contemporary version of an Eastern tale, is in a very real sense a parable dramatizing his moral theory and setting forth some of his most quotable reflections. A simple story—in fact one with very little action—it records the adventures of Rasselas, Prince of Abyssinia, who plots an escape from an inaccessible Happy

Valley of satiety because he feels a restlessness, a need for a change of setting, a new kind of life. Along with his sister and her companion and with Imlac, a philosopher, as his guide (who serves as the vehicle for Johnson's ideas), he manages to escape and to wander in the great world outside, convinced that he will find new pleasures and happiness. He is repelled and disappointed, however, by the hedonism of Cairo and gradually realizes the folly of his romanticized dreams through observation of the lives of a philosopher, a hermit, and an astronomer. Even the wonders of the pyramids—indeed, of the Great Pyramid itself—fail to satisfy him, especially in view of Imlac's startling analysis:

> It seems to have been erected only in compliance with that hunger of imagination which preys incessantly upon life, and must always be appeased by some employment. Those who have already all that they can enjoy, must enlarge their desires. He that has built for use, till use is supplied, must begin to build for vanity, and extend his plan to the utmost power of human performance, that he may not be soon reduced to form another wish.

The title of the book's last chapter—"The Conclusion, In Which Nothing is Concluded"—is strangely appropriate. The group are confined to their house in Cairo by the yearly inundation of the Nile, and they thus have time to review the different lives that they have observed and to compare the various schemes for happiness that they have contemplated. So many of Imlac's final comments ring loudly; their spirit seems so similar to that of Pope and Swift in their critique of delusion and their suggestion of the spirit of true Enlightenment. Two, in particular, stand out: "Such . . . are the effects of visionary schemes: when we first form them we know them to be absurd, but familiarise them by degrees, and in time lose sight of their folly." Then: "It seems to me . . . that while you are making the choice of life, you neglect to live." Each member of the group proceeds to describe a plan for achieving personal happiness. Rasselas wants a kingdom ". . . in which he might administer justice in his own person, and see all the parts of government with his own eyes; but he could never fix the limits of his dominion, and was always adding to the number of his subjects." The return to the Happy Valley thus seems inevitable; they know that their wishes are unattainable, and the reader is drawn back to the opening of the tale with its warning about the vanity of human wishes.

It is interesting and instructive to note how Johnson's massive body of literary criticism moves from the same pivotal premises as his moral theory. He is truly the last great figure in the classical tradition, firmly grounded in the pioneering endeavors of Aristotle and Horace, in Neoclassic codifiers like Sidney, Jonson, and Rymer, in the more flexible theory of Dryden and Pope, and yet keenly attuned to that staggering body of new critical and psychological theories that are so vibrant in the eighteenth century—Addison on the pleasures of the imagination, Burke on the sublime, Young on original genius, and a host of others.

Following the logic used in his moral essays, Johnson turns to objective experience—life as lived is the great criterion of success in a work of art. "General nature," the "grandeur of generality" are key terms in his praise of the writer who eschews fad and fashion, outlives his age, and offers the nourishment of truth to succeeding ages. "The irregular combinations of fanciful invention," he writes in the majestic *Preface to Shakespeare*, "may delight a-while, by that novelty of which the common satiety of life sends us all in quest; but the pleasures of sudden wonder are soon exhausted, and the mind can only repose on the stability of truth." Shakespeare is the great exemplar of this power, and Johnson, in spite of other reservations, praises him mightily for it. His drama "... holds up to his readers a faithful mirrour of manners and of life." His characters "... are the genuine progeny of common humanity, such as the world will always supply, and observation will always find." Gray's *Elegy Written in a Country Churchyard* "... abounds with images which find a mirrour in every mind, and with sentiments to which every bosom returns an echo." *The Rape of the Lock*, a poem filled with artificial machinery and elaborate imagery, nevertheless appeals to Johnson: "To the praises which have been accumulated on *The Rape of the Lock*," he argues, "from the critick to the waiting maid, it is difficult to make any addition." In the great Popean mock-heroic, "New things are made familiar, and familiar things are made new."

Given Johnson's central critical premise, it is relatively easy to understand his impatience with gimmickry or novelty, with whatever distorts the general to call attention to the particular or transitory. A work of art must have rhetorical strength; language, imagery, and versification must possess those qualities that serve to enhance and vivify the truth of poetry. A clear, rich, denotative diction; a controlled, functional imagery; an ordered rhythmic pattern of verse—these are some of Johnson's key values. Perhaps his most notable objection is to the conceits of Metaphysical poetry, especially that of Abraham Cowley and John Donne, even though he admires the learning and intellectuality of these writers. "What they wanted however of the sublime," he contends in the *Life of Cowley*, "they endeavoured to supply by hyperbole; their amplification had no limits; they left not only reason but fancy behind them; and produced combinations of confused magnificence, that not only could not be credited, but could not be imagined." Even in Shakespeare's great drama, "... the equality of words to things is very often neglected, and trivial sentiments and vulgar ideas disappoint the attention, to which they are recommended by sonorous epithets and swelling figures."

Although impatient with Milton for extra-literary reasons, he nevertheless grants him the greatness of the heroic poet. Yet in his *Life of Milton* he expresses grave reservations about the pastoral motif of *Lycidas*, its equation of Milton and Edward King with shepherds driving their flocks together, its strange and at times grotesque manner of expression, its harsh diction, its inappropriate rhymes, its jarring versification. In a strongly critical passage he seems to bring together his several criteria as he writes, "In this poem there is no nature, for there is no truth; there is no art, for there is nothing new. Its form is that of a pastoral, easy, vulgar, and therefore disgusting; whatever images it can supply, are long ago exhausted; and its inherent improbability always forces dissatisfaction on the mind." Pope, of course, is Johnson's great hero, not content to satisfy, but to excel. "He examined lines and words with minute and punctilious observation, and retouched every part with indefatigable diligence, till he had left nothing to be forgiven." Pope's great sense of life and delicate care for rhetorical effect "... enabled him to condense his sentiments, to multiply his images, and to accumulate all that study might produce, or chance might supply. If the flights of Dryden therefore are higher, Pope continues longer on the wing. If of Dryden's fire the blaze is brighter, of Pope's the heat is more regular and constant. Dryden often surpasses expectation, and Pope never falls below it. Dryden is read with frequent astonishment, and Pope with perpetual delight."

Johnson the artist is sometimes neglected in the midst of the praise of his moral theory and literary criticism, and this neglect is, of course, a serious mistake. The great compiler of *A Dictionary of the English Language* was ever a master of words, of a pure, vigorous, and elevated prose style that strikes that happy balance between the ordinary and the artificial; of a balanced, periodic sentence structure; of a rhythm and sound that bring dignity and grandeur to whatever he writes. His best poems, especially *The Vanity of Human Wishes* and the *Ode on the Death of Dr. Robert Levet,* are, while in the tradition of the illumination rather than the enlargement of experience, a fine blend of theme and technique. How brilliantly *The Vanity,* with its metaphors of snares and clouds and noise and its deep but controlled emotion, moves from its general theme about the futility of human ambition to the particular roots of that ambition. How striking are the more particular examples of its destructive force on figures like Alexander the Great, Cardinal Wolsey, Charles XII of Sweden, and others. How typically Johnsonian is the solemn movement to the closing lines of resignation:

> Yet when the sense of sacred presence fires,
> And strong devotion to the skies aspires,
> Pour forth thy fervours for a healthful mind,
> Obedient passions, and a will resign'd;
> For love, which scarce collective man can fill;
> For patience sov'reign o'er transmuted ill;
> For faith, that panting for a happier seat,
> Counts death kind Nature's signal of retreat:
> These goods for man the laws of heav'n ordain,
> These goods he grants, who grants the pow'r to gain;
> With these celestial wisdom calms the mind,
> And makes the happiness she does not find.

W. J. Bate's is a stunning tribute to *The Vanity of Human Wishes*: "Certainly English poetry, from the beginning of the seventeenth century down to the present, contains nothing else quite like the style... in which the complexity of the thought is gripped and compressed into a strangely powerful, abbreviated generality."

And how wonderfully exemplary is the shorter poem on Robert Levet, the poor physician befriended, housed, and cared for by Johnson, ever a reminder of the single talent well used to the brilliant Johnson, who was so often guilt-ridden by the sense of his own sloth. The familiar image of the illusory mine of human hope opens the first quatrain:

Condemn'd to hope's delusive mine,
  As on we toil from day to day,
By sudden blasts, or slow decline,
  Our social comforts drop away.

Yet Levet somehow faced life and dealt with it in his daily rounds:

In misery's darkest cavern known,
  His useful care was ever nigh,
Where hopeless anguish pour'd his groan,
  And lonely want retir'd to die.

. . .

His virtues walk'd their narrow round,
  Nor made a pause, nor left a void;
And sure th' Eternal Master found
  The single talent well employ'd.

Johnson's ability to convey deep feeling in direct, vibrant, almost Donne-like language and imagery can be seen in his compelling final stanza on Levet's death in his eightieth year:

Then with no throbbing fiery pain,
  No cold gradations of decay,
Death broke at once the vital chain,
  And free'd his soul the nearest way.

In his *Lives of the Poets,* Johnson, continuing to write in a variety of styles, virtually invented a new kind of critical biography, one that seems to be flourishing today. Skillfully he uses a technique of interweaving biography and criticism so that each illuminates and strengthens the other. His intense response to Savage, his incisive comparison of Dryden and Pope—these and other biographical approaches anticipate a kind of scholarship we now associate with Richard Ellmann's great work on Joyce and W. J. Bate's on Keats and on Johnson himself.

Critic, moralist, biographer, dictionary-maker, essayist, poet—any one or two of these titles might have made Johnson a major figure of the eighteenth century. Yet he was all and more—a man of a rich and flawed humanity, brilliant and erratic, talented and indolent, religious and remorseful—perhaps a representative of the whole range of human possibility. In his compassion, his love of life in all of its forms and his persistence in the midst of despair, he seemed to transcend most mortals. Indeed, he seemed profoundly modern in his constant urging that life is not something to be rationalized but to be lived, that talents are not to be hoarded but to be put to use, that human beings truly grow only when they are constantly widening the range of their awareness.

Toward the end of *The Life of Johnson* Boswell quotes the moving tribute paid to Johnson by William Gerard Hamilton: "He has made a chasm, which not only nothing can fill up, but which nothing has a tendency to fill up.—Johnson is dead.—Let us go to the next best:—there is nobody;—no man can be said to put you in mind of Johnson." It is a compliment indeed, but it cannot match in detail and sensitivity Boswell's own remarks toward the end of his own biography, as he pays tribute to ". . . . a man whose talents, acquirements, and virtues, were so extraordinary that the more his character is considered, the more he will be regarded by the present age, and by posterity, with admiration and reverence." Seldom has a biographer been more prophetic!

Suggestions for Further Reading

As already suggested in the introduction, Johnson has been splendidly treated by his biographers right from the start. Students will, of course, find selections from James Boswell's monumental work *The Life of Samuel Johnson, L.L.D.* in this anthology. Also especially recommended are Joseph Wood Krutch, *Samuel Johnson* (1944); James Clifford, *Young Sam Johnson* (1955), even though it covers only the years before the meeting with Boswell; John Wain, *Samuel Johnson* (1975); and, for this editor, the premier critical biography, W. J. Bate, *Samuel Johnson* (1977).

Jean Hagstrum, *Samuel Johnson's Literary Criticism* (1952); W. J. Bate, *The Achievement of Samuel Johnson* (1955), are especially helpful for students of Johnson's criticism, and Robert Voitle, *Samuel Johnson the Moralist* (1961); Maurice Quinlan, *Samuel Johnson's: A Layman's Religion* (1964); Donald J. Greene, *The Politics of Samuel Johnson* (1960); and William K. Wimsatt, *The Prose Style of Samuel Johnson* (1942) are superior studies of their respective areas of concern.

Two essays deal successfully with Johnson's major poetry: Frederick W. Hilles, "Johnson's Poetic Fire" in *From Sensibility to Romanticism,* eds. Frederick W. Hilles and Harold Bloom (1965); and Ian Jack, *Augustan Satire* (1952), pp. 135–145.

Donald J. Greene, ed., *Samuel Johnson: A Collection of Critical Essays* (1965), is a thoughtful and comprehensive compilation of some of the best critical writing on Johnson and should be immensely valuable for beginning students.

Students interested in further study of Boswell, the man and his art, will find the following works helpful: Chauncey B. Tinker, *Young Boswell* (1922); Frederick Pottle and Frank Brady, *James Boswell* (1966); Bertrand Bronson, "Boswell's Boswell" in his *Johnson Agonistes and Other Essays* (1946); Mary Lascelles, "Notions and Facts: Johnson and Boswell on Their Travels," and Ian Jack, "Two Biographers: Lockhart and Boswell" in *Johnson, Boswell and Their Circle: Essays Presented to Lawrence Fitzroy Powell* (1965). James Clifford, ed., *Twentieth-Century Interpretations of Boswell's Life of Johnson* (1970), is a fine collection of essays on Boswell, his life, and his work.

THE VANITY OF HUMAN WISHES

THE TENTH SATIRE OF JUVENAL IMITATED

Let observation with extensive view,
Survey mankind, from China to Peru;
Remark each anxious toil, each eager strife,
And watch the busy scenes of crouded life;
Then say how hope and fear, desire and hate,
O'erspread with snares the clouded maze of fate,
Where wav'ring man, betray'd by vent'rous pride,
To tread the dreary paths without a guide,
As treach'rous phantoms in the mist delude,
Shuns fancied ills, or chases airy good;
How rarely reason guides the stubborn choice,
Rules the bold hand, or prompts the suppliant voice;
How nations sink, by darling schemes oppress'd,
When vengeance listens to the fool's request.
Fate wings with ev'ry wish th' afflictive dart,
Each gift of nature, and each grace of art,
With fatal heat impetuous courage glows,
With fatal sweetness elocution flows,
Impeachment stops the speaker's pow'rful breath,
And restless fire precipitates on death.
  But scarce observ'd, the knowing and the bold
Fall in the gen'ral massacre of gold;
Wide-wasting pest! that rages unconfin'd,
And crouds with crimes the records of mankind;
For gold his sword the hireling ruffian draws,
For gold the hireling judge distorts the laws;
Wealth heap'd on wealth, nor truth nor safety buys,
The dangers gather as the treasures rise.
  Let hist'ry tell where rival kings command,
And dubious title shakes the madded land,
When statutes glean the refuse of the sword,
How much more safe the vassal than the lord;
Low skulks the hind beneath the rage of pow'r,
And leaves the wealthy traytor in the Tow'r,
Untouch'd his cottage, and his slumbers sound,
Tho' confiscation's vultures hover round.
  The needy traveller, serene and gay,
Walks the wild heath, and sings his toil away.
Does envy seize thee? crush th' upbraiding joy,
Increase his riches and his peace destroy;
Now fears in dire vicissitude invade,
The rustling brake alarms, and quiv'ring shade,
Nor light nor darkness bring his pain relief,
One shews the plunder, and one hides the thief.
  Yet still one gen'ral cry the skies assails,
And gain and grandeur load the tainted gales;
Few know the toiling statesman's fear or care,
Th' insidious rival and the gaping heir.
  Once more, Democritus, arise on earth,
With chearful wisdom and instructive mirth,
See motley life in modern trappings dress'd,
And feed with varied fools th' eternal jest:
Thou who couldst laugh where want enchain'd caprice,
Toil crush'd conceit, and man was of a piece;
Where wealth unlov'd without a mourner dy'd,
And scarce a sycophant was fed by pride;
Where ne'er was known the form of mock debate,
Or seen a new-made mayor's unwieldy state;
Where change of fav'rites made no change of laws,
And senates heard before they judg'd a cause;
How wouldst thou shake at Britain's modish tribe,
Dart the quick taunt, and edge the piercing gibe?
Attentive truth and nature to descry,
And pierce each scene with philosophic eye.
To thee were solemn toys or empty shew,
The robes of pleasure and the veils of woe:
All aid the farce, and all thy mirth maintain,
Whose joys are causeless, or whose griefs are vain.
  Such was the scorn that fill'd the sage's mind,
Renew'd at ev'ry glance on humankind;
How just that scorn ere yet thy voice declare,
Search every state, and canvass ev'ry pray'r.
  Unnumber'd suppliants croud Preferment's gate,
Athirst for wealth, and burning to be great;
Delusive Fortune hears th' incessant call,
They mount, they shine, evaporate, and fall.
On ev'ry stage the foes of peace attend,
Hate dogs their flight, and insult mocks their end.
Love ends with hope, the sinking statesman's door
Pours in the morning worshiper no more;
For growing names the weekly scribbler lies,
To growing wealth the dedicator flies,
From every room descends the painted face,
That hung the bright Palladium of the place,

THE VANITY OF HUMAN WISHES. **42. brake:** a thicket. **49. Democritus:** (460–357? B.C.), the celebrated "laughing" Greek philosopher, known for his cheerful, but pointed satire. **84. Palladium:** the great statue of Athena that supposedly protected Troy. It was stolen by Diomedes so that Troy might be captured.

And smok'd in kitchens, or in auctions sold,
To better features yields the frame of gold;
For now no more we trace in ev'ry line
Heroic worth, benevolence divine:
The form distorted justifies the fall.
And detestation rids th' indignant wall.
But will not Britain hear the last appeal,
Sign her foes doom, or guard her fav'rites zeal?
Through Freedom's sons no more remonstrance rings,
Degrading nobles and controuling kings;
Our supple tribes repress their patriot throats,
And ask no questions but the price of votes;
With weekly libels and septennial ale,
Their wish is full to riot and to rail.
In full-blown dignity, see Wolsey stand,
Law in his voice, and fortune in his hand:
To him the church, the realm, their pow'rs consign,
Thro' him the rays of regal bounty shine,
Turn'd by his nod the stream of honour flows,
His smile alone security bestows:
Still to new heights his restless wishes tow'r,
Claim leads to claim, and pow'r advances pow'r;
Till conquest unresisted ceas'd to please,
And rights submitted, left him none to seize.
At length his sov'reign frowns—the train of state
Mark the keen glance, and watch the sign to hate.
Where-e'er he turns he meets a stranger's eye,
His suppliants scorn him, and his followers fly;
At once is lost the pride of aweful state,
The golden canopy, the glitt'ring plate,
The regal palace, the luxurious board,
The liv'ried army, and the menial lord.
With age, with cares, with maladies oppress'd,
He seeks the refuge of monastic rest.
Grief aids disease, remember'd folly stings,
And his last sighs reproach the faith of kings.
Speak thou, whose thoughts at humble peace repine,
Shall Wolsey's wealth, with Wolsey's end be thine?
Or liv'st thou now, with safer pride content,
The wisest justice on the banks of Trent?
For why did Wolsey near the steeps of fate,
On weak foundations raise th' enormous weight?
Why but to sink beneath misfortune's blow,
With louder ruin to the gulphs below?
What gave great Villiers to th' assassin's knife,
And fixed disease on Harley's closing life?
What murder'd Wentworth, and what exil'd Hyde,
By kings protected, and to kings ally'd?
What but their wish indulg'd in courts to shine,
And pow'r too great to keep, or to resign?
When first the college rolls receive his name,
The young enthusiast quits his ease for fame;
Through all his veins the fever of renown
Burns from the strong contagion of the gown;
O'er Bodley's dome his future labours spread,
And Bacon's mansion trembles o'er his head.
Are these thy views? proceed, illustrious youth,
And virtue guard thee to the throne of Truth!
Yet should thy soul indulge the gen'rous heat,
Till captive Science yields her last retreat;
Should Reason guide thee with her brightest ray,
And pour on misty Doubt resistless day;
Should no false Kindness lure to loose delight,
Nor Praise relax, nor Difficulty fright;
Should tempting Novelty thy cell refrain,
And Sloth effuse her opiate fumes in vain;
Should Beauty blunt on fops her fatal dart,
Nor claim the triumph of a letter'd heart;
Should no Disease thy torpid veins invade,
Nor Melancholy's phantoms haunt thy shade;
Yet hope not life from grief or danger free,
Nor think the doom of man revers'd for thee:
Deign on the passing world to turn thine eyes,
And pause awhile from letters, to be wise;
There mark what ills the scholar's life assail,
Toil, envy, want, the patron, and the jail.

97. septennial: every seven years. Politicians provided bribes of various kinds at the time of Parliamentary elections, which were held at least every seven years. **99. Wolsey:** the famous Thomas Wolsey (1472–1530), Cardinal of the Church and Lord Chancellor under Henry VIII.

129. Villiers: George Villiers (1592–1628), first Duke of Buckingham and a court favorite of James I and George I. He was assassinated. **130. Harley:** Robert Harley (1661–1724), Earl of Oxford and member of the Tory Ministry of Queen Anne. He was imprisoned when George I and the Whigs came to power in 1714. **131. Wentworth . . . Hyde:** Thomas Wentworth (1593–1641), Earl of Strafford, advisor to Charles I, was executed under the Long Parliament in 1641. Edward Hyde (1609–1674), Earl of Clarendon, Chancellor to Charles II, was exiled in 1667. **139. Bodley's dome:** the great Bodleian Library at Oxford. **140. Bacon's mansion:** Johnson notes: "There is a tradition that the study of Friar Bacon, built on an arch over the bridge, will fall, when a man greater than Bacon shall pass under it." Roger Bacon was the famous medieval Oxford philosopher.

See nations slowly wise, and meanly just,
To buried merit raise the tardy bust.
If dreams yet flatter, once again attend,
Hear Lydiat's life, and Galileo's end.
Nor deem, when learning her last prize bestows,
The glitt'ring eminence exempt from foes;
See when the vulgar 'scape, despis'd or aw'd,
Rebellion's vengeful talons seize on Laud.
From meaner minds, tho' smaller fines content,
The plunder'd palace or sequester'd rent;
Mark'd out by dangerous parts he meets the shock,
And fatal Learning leads him to the block:
Around his tomb let Art and Genius weep,
But hear his death, ye blockheads, hear and sleep.
The festal blazes, the triumphal show,
The ravish'd standard, and the captive foe,
The senate's thanks, the gazette's pompous tale,
With force resistless o'er the brave prevail.
Such bribes the rapid Greek o'er Asia whirl'd,
For such the steady Romans shook the world;
For such in distant lands the Britons shine,
And stain with blood the Danube or the Rhine;
This pow'r has praise, that virtue scarce can warm,
Till fame supplies the universal charm.
Yet Reason frowns on War's unequal game,
Where wasted nations raise a single name,
And mortgag'd states their grandsires wreaths regret,
From age to age in everlasting debt;
Wreaths which at last the dear-bought right convey
To rust on medals, or on stones decay.
On what foundation stands the warrior's pride,
How just his hopes let Swedish Charles decide;
A frame of adamant, a soul of fire,
No dangers fright him, and no labours tire;
O'er love, o'er fear, extends his wide domain,
Unconquer'd lord of pleasure and of pain;
No joys to him pacific scepters yield,
War sounds the trump, he rushes to the field;
Behold surrounding kings their pow'r combine,
And one capitulate, and one resign;
Peace courts his hand, but spreads her charms in vain;
"Think nothing gain'd," he cries, 'till nought remain,
"On Moscow's walls till Gothic standards fly,
"And all be mine beneath the polar sky."
The march begins in military state,
And nations on his eye suspended wait;
Stern Famine guards the solitary coast,
And Winter barricades the realms of Frost;
He comes, not want and cold his course delay;—
Hide, blushing Glory, hide Pultowa's day:
The vanquish'd hero leaves his broken bands,
And shews his miseries in distant lands;
Condemn'd a needy supplicant to wait,
While ladies interpose, and slaves debate.
But did not Chance at length her error mend?
Did no subverted empire mark his end?
Did rival monarchs give the fatal wound?
Or hostile millions press him to the ground?
His fall was destin'd to a barren strand,
A petty fortress, and a dubious hand;
He left the name, at which the world grew pale,
To point a moral, or adorn a tale.
All times their scenes of pompous woes afford,
From Persia's tyrant to Bavaria's lord.
In gay hostility, and barb'rous pride,
With half mankind embattled at his side,
Great Xerxes comes to seize the certain prey,
And starves exhausted regions in his way;
Attendant Flatt'ry counts his myriads o'er,
Till counted myriads sooth his pride no more;
Fresh praise is try'd till madness fires his mind,
The waves he lashes, and enchains the wind;
New pow'rs are claim'd, new pow'rs are still bestow'd,
Till rude resistance lops the spreading god;
The daring Greeks deride the martial show,
And heap their vallies with the gaudy foe;
Th' insulted sea with humbler thoughts he gains,

164. Lydiat . . . Galileo: references to Thomas Lydiat (1572–1646), the celebrated Oxford professor who died poor and forgotten, and to the famed Galileo (1564–1642), astronomer and discoverer of the telescope, who was declared a heretic and imprisoned by the Inquisition. **168. Laud:** William Laud was Archbishop of Canterbury under Charles I. A moderate Anglican churchman, he was executed by the Puritans in 1645. **170. sequester'd rent:** appropriated income. **179. rapid Greek:** Alexander the Great. **192. Swedish Charles:** King Charles XII of Sweden (1682–1718).

210. Pultowa's day: Charles was defeated by Peter the Great at Pultowa in Russia in 1709. **224. Persia's tyrant . . . Bavaria's lord:** The famous Xerxes, who invaded Greece and was defeated at Salamis in 480 B.C. Charles Albert, Elector of Bavaria, laid claim to the Holy Roman Empire, and was crowned Charles VII in 1742. He was manipulated and exploited by his allies, however, and died in disgrace in 1745.

A single skiff to speed his flight remains;
Th' incumber'd oar scarce leaves the dreaded coast
Through purple billows and a floating host.
The bold Bavarian, in a luckless hour,
Tries the dread summits of Cesarean pow'r,
With unexpected legions bursts away,
And sees defenceless realms receive his sway;
Short sway! fair Austria spreads her mournful charms,
The queen, the beauty, sets the world in arms;
From hill to hill the beacons rousing blaze
Spreads wide the hope of plunder and of praise;
The fierce Croatian, and the wild Hussar,
And all the sons of ravage croud the war;
The baffled prince in honour's flatt'ring bloom
Of hasty greatness finds the fatal doom,
His foes derision, and his subjects blame,
And steals to death from anguish and from shame.
Enlarge my life with multitude of days,
In health, in sickness, thus the suppliant prays;
Hides from himself his state, and shuns to know,
That life protracted is protracted woe.
Time hovers o'er, impatient to destroy,
And shuts up all the passages of joy:
In vain their gifts the bounteous seasons pour,
The fruit autumnal, and the vernal flow'r,
With listless eyes the dotard views the store,
He views, and wonders that they please no more;
Now pall the tasteless meats, and joyless wines,
And Luxury with sighs her slave resigns.
Approach, ye minstrels, try the soothing strain,
Diffuse the tuneful lenitives of pain:
No sounds alas would touch th' impervious ear,
Though dancing mountains witness'd Orpheus near;
Nor lute nor lyre his feeble pow'rs attend,
Nor sweeter musick of a virtuous friend,
But everlasting dictates croud his tongue,
Perversely grave, or positively wrong.
The still returning tale, and ling'ring jest,
Perplex the fawning niece and pamper'd guest,
While growing hopes scarce awe the gath'ring sneer,
And scarce a legacy can bribe to hear;
The watchful guests still hint the last offence,
The daughter's petulance, the son's expence,
Improve his heady rage with treach'rous skill,
And mould his passions till they make his will.
Unnumber'd maladies his joints invade,
Lay siege to life and press the dire blockade;
But unextinguish'd Avarice still remains,
And dreaded losses aggravate his pains;
He turns, with anxious heart and cripled hands,
His bonds of debt, and mortgages of lands;
Or views his coffers with suspicious eyes,
Unlocks his gold, and counts it till he dies.
But grant, the virtues of a temp'rate prime
Bless with an age exempt from scorn or crime;
An age that melts with unperceiv'd decay,
And glides in modest Innocence away;
Whose peaceful day Benevolence endears,
Whose night congratulating Conscience cheers;
The gen'ral fav'rite as the gen'ral friend:
Such age there is, and who shall wish its end?
Yet ev'n on this her load Misfortune flings,
To press the weary minutes flagging wings:
New sorrow rises as the day returns,
A sister sickens, or a daughter mourns.
Now kindred Merit fills the sable bier,
Now lacerated Friendship claims a tear.
Year chases year, decay pursues decay,
Still drops some joy from with'ring life away;
New forms arise, and diff'rent views engage,
Superfluous lags the vet'ran on the stage,
Till pitying Nature signs the last release,
And bids afflicted worth retire to peace.
But few there are whom hours like these await,
Who set unclouded in the gulphs of fate.
From Lydia's monarch should the search descend,
By Solon caution'd to regard his end,
In life's last scene what prodigies surprise,
Fears of the brave, and follies of the wise?
From Marlb'rough's eyes the streams of dotage flow,
And Swift expires a driv'ler and a show.
The teeming mother, anxious for her race,
Begs for each birth the fortune of a face:
Yet Vane could tell what ills from beauty spring;

245. fair Austria: Maria Theresa. **268. lenitives:** soothers. **270. Orpheus:** the legendary Greek musician whose art had the power to enthrall the listener.

313. Lydia's monarch: Croesus. Solon, the famous Athenian lawgiver, advised him to regard no living man as completely happy. He was later deposed by Cyrus. **317. Marlb'rough:** John Churchill, Duke of Marlborough (1650–1722), military master and victor at the Battle of Blenheim. His physical and mental condition deteriorated in his last years. **321. Vane:** Anne Vane, mistress of Frederick, Prince of Wales. He later deserted her, and she died in 1736 at the age of thirty-one.

And Sedley curs'd the form that pleas'd a king.
Ye nymphs of rosy lips and radiant eyes,
Whom Pleasure keeps too busy to be wise,
Whom Joys with soft varieties invite,
By day the frolick, and the dance by night,
Who frown with vanity, who smile with art,
And ask the latest fashion of the heart,
What care, what rules your heedless charms shall save,
Each nymph your rival, and each youth your slave?
Against your fame with fondness hate combines,
The rival batters, and the lover mines.
With distant voice neglected Virtue calls,
Less heard and less, the faint remonstrance falls;
Tir'd with contempt, she quits the slipp'ry reign,
And Pride and Prudence take her seat in vain.
In croud at once, where none the pass defend,
The harmless Freedom, and the private Friend.
The guardians yield, by force superior ply'd;
By Int'rest, Prudence; and by Flatt'ry, Pride.
Now beauty falls betray'd, despis'd, distress'd,
And hissing Infamy proclaims the rest.

Where then shall Hope and Fear their objects find?
Must dull Suspence corrupt the stagnant mind?
Must helpless man, in ignorance sedate,
Roll darkling down the torrent of his fate?
Must no dislike alarm, no wishes rise,
No cries attempt the mercies of the skies?
Enquirer, cease, petitions yet remain,
Which heav'n may hear, nor deem religion vain.
Still raise for good the supplicating voice,
But leave to heav'n the measure and the choice,
Safe in his pow'r, whose eyes discern afar
The secret ambush of a specious pray'r.
Implore his aid, in his decisions rest,
Secure whate'er he gives, he gives the best.
Yet when the sense of sacred presence fires,
And strong devotion to the skies aspires,
Pour forth thy fervours for a healthful mind,
Obedient passions, and a will resign'd;
For love, which scarce collective man can fill;
For patience sov'reign o'er transmuted ill;
For faith, that panting for a happier seat,
Counts death kind Nature's signal of retreat:
These goods for man the laws of heav'n ordain,
These goods he grants, who grants the pow'r to gain;
With these celestial wisdom calms the mind,
And makes the happiness she does not find.

(1748)

322. Sedley: Catherine Sedley was the mistress of the Duke of York, but was deserted by him when he became James II.

ON THE DEATH OF DR. ROBERT LEVET*

Condemn'd to hope's delusive mine,
As on we toil from day to day,
By sudden blasts, or slow decline,
Our social comforts drop away.

Well tried through many a varying year,
See LEVET to the grave descend;
Officious, innocent, sincere,
Of ev'ry friendless name the friend.

Yet still he fills affection's eye,
Obscurely wise, and coarsely kind;
Nor, letter'd arrogance, deny
Thy praise to merit unrefin'd.

When fainting nature call'd for aid,
And hov'ring death prepar'd the blow,
His vig'rous remedy display'd
The power of art without the show.

In misery's darkest cavern known,
His useful care was ever nigh,
Where hopeless anguish pour'd his groan,
And lonely want retir'd to die.

No summons mock'd by chill delay,
No petty gain disdain'd by pride,
The modest wants of ev'ry day
The toil of ev'ry day supplied.

His virtues walk'd their narrow round,
Nor made a pause, nor left a void;
And sure th' Eternal Master found
The single talent well employ'd.

The busy day, the peaceful night,
Unfelt, uncounted, glided by;

---

* Robert Levet (1705–1782), a poor but generous practitioner, lived for many years in Johnson's household.

ON THE DEATH OF DR. ROBERT LEVET. **7. officious:** helpful.

His frame was firm, his powers were bright,
 Tho' now his eightieth year was nigh.

Then with no throbbing fiery pain,
 No cold gradations of decay,
Death broke at once the vital chain,
 And free'd his soul the nearest way.

(1782)

FROM

The Rambler

NO. 4. SATURDAY, MARCH 31, 1750

Simul et jucunda et idonea dicere Vitæ.

HOR. [*Ars. Poet.* 334.]

And join both profit and delight in one.

CREECH.

The works of fiction, with which the present generation seems more particularly delighted, are such as exhibit life in its true state, diversified only by accidents that daily happen in the world, and influenced by passions and qualities which are really to be found in conversing with mankind.

This kind of writing may be termed not improperly the comedy of romance, and is to be conducted nearly by the rules of comic poetry. Its province is to bring about natural events by easy means, and to keep up curiosity without the help of wonder: it is therefore precluded from the machines and expedients of the heroic romance, and can neither employ giants to snatch away a lady from the nuptial rites, nor knights to bring her back from captivity; it can neither bewilder its personages in desarts, nor lodge them in imaginary castles.

I remember a remark made by Scaliger upon Pontanus,[1] that all his writings are filled with the same images; and that if you take from him his lillies and his roses, his satyrs and his dryads, he will have nothing left that can be called poetry. In like manner, almost all the fictions of the last age will vanish, if you deprive them of a hermit and a wood, a battle and a shipwreck.

Why this wild strain of imagination found reception so long, in polite and learned ages, it is not easy to conceive; but we cannot wonder that, while readers could be procured, the authors were willing to continue it: for when a man had by practice gained some fluency of language, he had no further care than to retire to his closet, let loose his invention, and heat his mind with incredibilities; a book was thus produced without fear of criticism, without the toil of study, without knowledge of nature, or acquaintance with life.

The task of our present writers is very different; it requires, together with that learning which is to be gained from books, that experience which can never be attained by solitary diligence, but must arise from general converse, and accurate observation of the living world. Their performances have, as Horace expresses it, *plus oneris quantum veniæ minus*,[2] little indulgence, and therefore more difficulty. They are engaged in portraits of which every one knows the original, and can detect any deviation from exactness of resemblance. Other writings are safe, except from the malice of learning, but these are in danger from every common reader; as the slipper ill executed was censured by a shoemaker who happened to stop in his way at the Venus of Apelles.[3]

But the fear of not being approved as just copyers of human manners, is not the most important concern that an author of this sort ought to have before him. These books are written chiefly to the young, the ignorant, and the idle, to whom they serve as lectures of conduct, and introductions into life. They are the entertainment of minds unfurnished with ideas, and therefore easily susceptible of impressions; not fixed by principles, and therefore easily following the current of fancy; not informed by experience, and consequently open to every false suggestion and partial account.

That the highest degree of reverence should be paid to youth, and that nothing indecent should be

THE RAMBLER, NO. 4. **1. Pontanus:** See Julius Caesar Scaliger, *Poetics*, V, iv.

2. plus . . . minus: *Epistles*, II, i, 170. **3. Apelles:** Apelles was a fourth-century B.C. painter from Colophon and later Ephesus. He did a famous painting of Venus rising from the sea. See Pliny, *Natural History*, XXXV, 36, 85.

suffered to approach their eyes or ears; are precepts extorted by sense and virtue from an ancient writer,[4] by no means eminent for chastity of thought. The same kind, tho' not the same degree of caution, is required to every thing which is laid before them, to secure them from unjust prejudices, perverse opinions, and incongruous combinations of images.

In the romances formerly written, every transaction and sentiment was so remote from all that passes among men, that the reader was in very little danger of making any applications to himself; the virtues and crimes were equally beyond his sphere of activity; and he amused himself with heroes and with traitors, deliverers and persecutors, as with beings of another species, whose actions were regulated upon motives of their own, and who had neither faults nor excellencies in common with himself.

But when an adventurer is levelled with the rest of the world, and acts in such scenes of the universal drama, as may be the lot of any other man; young spectators fix their eyes upon him with closer attention, and hope by observing his behaviour and success to regulate their own practices, when they shall be engaged in the like part.

For this reason these familiar histories may perhaps be made of greater use than the solemnities of professed morality, and convey the knowledge of vice and virtue with more efficacy than axioms and definitions. But if the power of example is so great, as to take possession of the memory by a kind of violence, and produce effects almost without the intervention of the will, care ought to be taken that, when the choice is unrestrained, the best examples only should be exhibited; and that which is likely to operate so strongly, should not be mischievous or uncertain in its effects.

The chief advantage which these fictions have over real life is, that their authors are at liberty, tho' not to invent, yet to select objects, and to cull from the mass of mankind, those individuals upon which the attention ought most to be employ'd; as a diamond, though it cannot be made, may be polished by art, and placed in such a situation, as to display that lustre which before was buried among common stones.

It is justly considered as the greatest excellency of art, to imitate nature; but it is necessary to distinguish those parts of nature, which are most proper for imitation: greater care is still required in representing life, which is so often discoloured by passion, or deformed by wickedness. If the world be promiscuously described, I cannot see of what use it can be to read the account; or why it may not be as safe to turn the eye immediately upon mankind, as upon a mirror which shows all that presents itself without discrimination.

It is therefore not a sufficient vindication of a character, that it is drawn as it appears, for many characters ought never to be drawn; nor of a narrative, that the train of events is agreeable to observation and experience, for that observation which is called knowledge of the world, will be found much more frequently to make men cunning than good. The purpose of these writings is surely not only to show mankind, but to provide that they may be seen hereafter with less hazard; to teach the means of avoiding the snares which are laid by TREACHERY for INNOCENCE, without infusing any wish for that superiority with which the betrayer flatters his vanity; to give the power of counteracting fraud, without the temptation to practise it; to initiate youth by mock encounters in the art of necessary defence, and to increase prudence without impairing virtue.

Many writers, for the sake of following nature, so mingle good and bad qualities in their principal personages, that they are both equally conspicuous; and as we accompany them through their adventures with delight, and are led by degrees to interest ourselves in their favour, we lose the abhorrence of their faults, because they do not hinder our pleasure, or, perhaps, regard them with some kindness for being united with so much merit.

There have been men indeed splendidly wicked, whose endowments threw a brightness on their crimes, and whom scarce any villainy made perfectly detestable, because they never could be wholly divested of their excellencies; but such have been in all ages the great corrupters of the world, and their resemblance ought no more to be preserved, than the art of murdering without pain.

Some have advanced, without due attention to the consequences of this notion, that certain virtues have their correspondent faults, and therefore that to exhibit either apart is to deviate from probability. Thus men are observed by Swift to be "grate-

4. ancient writer: Juvenal, *Satires,* xiv.

ful in the same degree as they are resentful." This principle, with others of the same kind, supposes man to act from a brute impulse, and persue a certain degree of inclination, without any choice of the object; for, otherwise, though it should be allowed that gratitude and resentment arise from the same constitution of the passions, it follows not that they will be equally indulged when reason is consulted; yet unless that consequence be admitted, this sagacious maxim becomes an empty sound, without any relation to practice or to life.

Nor is it evident, that even the first motions to these effects are always in the same proportion. For pride, which produces quickness of resentment, will obstruct gratitude, by unwillingness to admit that inferiority which obligation implies; and it is very unlikely, that he who cannot think he receives a favour will acknowledge or repay it.

It is of the utmost importance to mankind, that positions of this tendency should be laid open and confuted; for while men consider good and evil as springing from the same root, they will spare the one for the sake of the other, and in judging, if not of others at least of themselves, will be apt to estimate their virtues by their vices. To this fatal error all those will contribute, who confound the colours of right and wrong, and instead of helping to settle their boundaries, mix them with so much art, that no common mind is able to disunite them.

In narratives, where historical veracity has no place, I cannot discover why there should not be exhibited the most perfect idea of virtue; of virtue not angelical, nor above probability, for what we cannot credit we shall never imitate, but the highest and purest that humanity can reach, which, exercised in such trials as the various revolutions of things shall bring upon it, may, by conquering some calamities, and enduring others, teach us what we may hope, and what we can perform. Vice, for vice is necessary to be shewn, should always disgust; nor should the graces of gaiety, or the dignity of courage, be so united with it, as to reconcile it to the mind. Wherever it appears, it should raise hatred by the malignity of its practices, and contempt by the meanness of its stratagems; for while it is supported by either parts or spirit, it will be seldom heartily abhorred. The Roman tyrant was content to be hated, if he was but feared; and there are thousands of the readers of romances willing to be thought wicked, if they may be allowed to be wits. It is therefore to be steadily inculcated, that virtue is the highest proof of understanding, and the only solid basis of greatness; and that vice is the natural consequence of narrow thoughts, that it begins in mistake, and ends in ignominy.

NO. 60. SATURDAY, OCTOBER 13, 1750

—Quid sit pulchrum, quid turpe, quid utile, quid non,
Plenius et melius Chrysippo et Crantore dicit.

HOR. [*Epist.* I. ii. 3.]

Whose works the beautiful and base contain;
Of vice and virtue more instructive rules,
Than all the sober sages of the schools.

FRANCIS.

All joy or sorrow for the happiness or calamities of others is produced by an act of the imagination, that realises the event however fictitious, or approximates it however remote, by placing us, for a time, in the condition of him whose fortune we contemplate; so that we feel, while the deception lasts, whatever motions would be excited by the same good or evil happening to ourselves.

Our passions are therefore more strongly moved, in proportion as we can more readily adopt the pains or pleasure proposed to our minds, by recognising them as once our own, or considering them as naturally incident to our state of life. It is not easy for the most artful writer to give us an interest in happiness or misery, which we think ourselves never likely to feel, and with which we have never yet been made acquainted. Histories of the downfall of kingdoms, and revolutions of empires, are read with great tranquillity; the imperial tragedy pleases common auditors only by its pomp of ornament, and grandeur of ideas; and the man whose faculties have been engrossed by business, and whose heart never fluttered but at the rise or fall of stocks, wonders how the attention can be seized, or the affection agitated by a tale of love.

Those parallel circumstances, and kindred images, to which we readily conform our minds, are, above all other writings, to be found in narratives of the lives of particular persons; and therefore no species of writing seems more worthy of cultivation than biography, since none can be more delightful or more useful, none can more certainly enchain the heart by irresistible interest, or more widely diffuse instruction to every diversity of condition.

The general and rapid narratives of history, which involve a thousand fortunes in the business of a day, and complicate innumerable incidents in one great transaction, afford few lessons applicable to private life, which derives its comforts and its wretchedness from the right or wrong management of things which nothing but their frequency makes considerable, *Parva, si non fiunt quotidie,* says Pliny,[1] and which can have no place in those relations which never descend below the consultation of senates, the motions of armies, and the schemes of conspirators.

I have often thought that there has rarely passed a life of which a judicious and faithful narrative would not be useful. For, not only every man has, in the mighty mass of the world, great numbers in the same condition with himself, to whom his mistakes and miscarriages, escapes and expedients, would be of immediate and apparent use; but there is such an uniformity in the state of man, considered apart from adventitious and separable decorations and disguises, that there is scarce any possibility of good or ill, but is common to human kind. A great part of the time of those who are placed at the greatest distance by fortune, or by temper, must unavoidably pass in the same manner; and though, when the claims of nature are satisfied, caprice, and vanity, and accident, begin to produce discriminations and peculiarities, yet the eye is not very heedful, or quick, which cannot discover the same causes still terminating their influence in the same effects, though sometimes accelerated, sometimes retarded, or perplexed by multiplied combinations. We are all prompted by the same motives, all deceived by the same fallacies, all animated by hope, obstructed by danger, entangled by desire, and seduced by pleasure.

It is frequently objected to relations of particular lives, that they are not distinguished by any striking or wonderful vicissitudes. The scholar who passed his life among his books, the merchant who conducted only his own affairs, the priest, whose sphere of action was not extended beyond that of his duty, are considered as no proper objects of publick regard, however they might have excelled in their several stations, whatever might have been their learning, integrity, and piety. But this notion arises from false measures of excellence and dignity, and must be eradicated by considering, that, in the esteem of uncorrupted reason, what is of most use is of most value.

It is, indeed, not improper to take honest advantages of prejudice, and to gain attention by a celebrated name; but the business of the biographer is often to pass slightly over those performances and incidents, which produce vulgar greatness, to lead the thoughts into domestick privacies, and display the minute details of daily life, where exterior appendages are cast aside, and men excel each other only by prudence and by virtue. The account of Thuanus is, with great propriety, said by its author[2] to have been written, that it might lay open to posterity the private and familiar character of that man, *cujus ingenium et candorem ex ipsius scriptis sunt olim semper miraturi,* whose candour and genius will to the end of time be by his writings preserved in admiration.

There are many invisible circumstances which, whether we read as inquirers after natural or moral knowledge, whether we intend to enlarge our science, or increase our virtue, are more important than publick occurrences. Thus Salust, the great master of nature, has not forgot, in his account of Catiline,[3] to remark that *his walk was now quick, and again slow,* as an indication of a mind revolving something with violent commotion. Thus the story of Melancthon affords a striking lecture on the value of time, by informing us, that when he made an appointment, he expected not only the hour, but the minute to be fixed, that the day might not run out in the idleness of suspense; and all the plans and enterprizes of De Wit are now of less importance to the world, than that part of his personal character which represents him as *careful of his health, and negligent of his life.*

But biography has often been allotted to writers who seem very little acquainted with the nature of their task, or very negligent about the performance. They rarely afford any other account than might be

NO. 60. **1. Pliny:** *Epistles,* III, i.

2. Thuanus was one of the noted Continental Renaissance humanists. See Note 2 in *Samuel Johnson: Essays from the Rambler, Adventurer, Idler,* ed. W. J. Bate (New Haven and London, 1968), p. 112. **3. Catiline:** *Conspiracy of Catiline,* xv, 5.

collected from publick papers, but imagine themselves writing a life when they exhibit a chronological series of actions or preferments; and so little regard the manners or behaviour of their heroes, that more knowledge may be gained of a man's real character, by a short conversation with one of his servants, than from a formal and studied narrative, begun with his pedigree, and ended with his funeral.

If now and then they condescend to inform the world of particular facts, they are not always so happy as to select the most important. I know not well what advantage posterity can receive from the only circumstance by which Tickell has distinguished Addison from the rest of mankind, *the irregularity of his pulse:* nor can I think myself overpaid for the time spent in reading the life of Malherb, by being enabled to relate, after the learned biographer, that Malherb had two predominant opinions; one, that the looseness of a single woman might destroy all her boast of ancient descent; the other, that the French beggars made use very improperly and barbarously of the phrase *noble Gentleman,* because either word included the sense of both.

There are, indeed, some natural reasons why these narratives are often written by such as were not likely to give much instruction or delight, and why most accounts of particular persons are barren and useless. If a life be delayed till interest and envy are at an end, we may hope for impartiality, but must expect little intelligence; for the incidents which give excellence to biography are of a volatile and evanescent kind, such as soon escape the memory, and are rarely transmitted by tradition. We know how few can portray a living acquaintance, except by his most prominent and observable particularities, and the grosser features of his mind; and it may be easily imagined how much of this little knowledge may be lost in imparting it, and how soon a succession of copies will lose all resemblance of the original.

If the biographer writes from personal knowledge, and makes haste to gratify the publick curiosity, there is danger lest his interest, his fear, his gratitude, or his tenderness, overpower his fidelity, and tempt him to conceal, if not to invent. There are many who think it an act of piety to hide the faults or failings of their friends, even when they can no longer suffer by their detection; we therefore see whole ranks of characters adorned with uniform panegyrick, and not to be known from one another, but by extrinsick and casual circumstances. "Let me remember, says Hale, when I find myself inclined to pity a criminal, that there is likewise a pity due to the country." If we owe regard to the memory of the dead, there is yet more respect to be paid to knowledge, to virtue, and to truth.

NO. 117. TUESDAY, APRIL 30, 1751

῎Οσσαν ἐπ' Οὐλύμπῳ μέμασαν θέμεν, αὐτὰρ ἐπ' ῎Οσσῃ
Πήλιον εἰνοσίφυλλον, ἵν' οὐρανὸς αμβατὸς εἴη. Λ.

[HOMER, *Od.* XI. 315.]

The gods they challenge, and affect the skies:
Heav'd on *Olympus* tott'ring *Ossa* stood;
On *Ossa, Pelion* nods with all his wood.

POPE.

To the RAMBLER

Sir,

Nothing has more retarded the advancement of learning than the disposition of vulgar minds to ridicule and vilify what they cannot comprehend. All industry must be excited by hope; and as the student often proposes no other reward to himself than praise, he is easily discouraged by contempt and insult. He who brings with him into a clamorous multitude the timidity of recluse speculation, and has never hardened his front in publick life, or accustomed his passions to the vicissitudes and accidents, the triumphs and defeats of mixed conversation, will blush at the stare of petulant incredulity, and suffer himself to be driven, by a burst of laughter, from the fortresses of demonstration. The mechanist will be afraid to assert before hardy contradiction, the possibility of tearing down bulwarks with a silk-worm's thread; and the astronomer of relating the rapidity of light, the distance of the fixed stars, and the height of the lunar mountains.

If I could by any efforts have shaken off this cowardice, I had not sheltered myself under a borrowed name, nor applied to you for the means of communicating to the public the theory of a garret; a subject which, except some slight and transient strictures, has been hitherto neglected by those who were best qualified to adorn it, either for want of leisure to prosecute the various researches in which a nice discussion must engage them, or because it requires such diversity of knowledge, and such extent of curiosity, as is scarcely to be found in any single intellect: Or perhaps others foresaw the tumults which would be raised against them, and confined their knowledge to their own breasts, and abandoned prejudice and folly to the direction of chance.

That the professors of literature generally reside in the highest stories, has been immemorially observed. The wisdom of the ancients was well acquainted with the intellectual advantages of an elevated situation: why else were the *Muses* stationed on *Olympus* or *Parnassus* by those who could with equal right have raised them bowers in the vale of *Tempe*, or erected their altars among the flexures of *Meander*? [1] Why was *Jove* himself nursed upon a mountain? or why did the goddesses, when the prize of beauty was contested, try the cause upon the top of *Ida*? [2] Such were the fictions by which the great masters of the earlier ages endeavoured to inculcate to posterity the importance of a garret, which, though they had been long obscured by the negligence and ignorance of succeeding times, were well enforced by the celebrated symbol of *Pythagoras*, ἀνεμῶν πνεόντων, τὴν ἠχὼ προσκύνει; "when the wind blows, worship its echo." This could not but be understood by his disciples as an inviolable injunction to live in a garret, which I have found frequently visited by the echo and the wind. Nor was the tradition wholly obliterated in the age of *Augustus*, for *Tibullus* evidently congratulates himself upon his garret, not without some allusion to the *Pythagorean* precept.

Quàm juvat immites ventos audire cubantem——
Aut, gelidas hybernus aquas cum fuderit auster,
Securum somnos, imbre juvante, sequi!

[*El.* I. i. 45.]

How sweet in sleep to pass the careless hours,
Lull'd by the beating winds and dashing show'rs!

And it is impossible not to discover the fondness of *Lucretius*, an earlier writer, for a garret, in his description of the lofty towers of serene learning, and of the pleasure with which a wise man looks down upon the confused and erratic state of the world moving below him

Sed nil dulcius est, bene quàm munita tenere
Editâ doctrinâ sapientum templa serena;
Despicere unde queas alios, passimque videre
Errare, atque viam palanteis quærere vitæ.

[Bk. II. 7.]

——'Tis sweet thy lab'ring steps to guide
To virtue's heights, with wisdom well supply'd,
And all the magazines of learning fortify'd:
From thence to look below on human kind,
Bewilder'd in the maze of life, and blind.

DRYDEN.

The institution has, indeed, continued to our own time; the garret is still the usual receptacle of the philosopher and poet; but this, like many ancient customs, is perpetuated only by an accidental imitation, without knowledge of the original reason for which it was established.

Causa latet; res est notissima.

[VIRG. *Æn.* V. 5.]

The cause is secret, but th' effect is known.

ADDISON.

Conjectures have, indeed, been advanced concerning these habitations of literature, but without much satisfaction to the judicious enquirer. Some have imagined, that the garret is generally chosen by the wits, as most easily rented; and concluded that no man rejoices in his aereal abode, but on the days of payment. Others suspect, that a garret is chiefly convenient, as it is remoter than any other part of the house from the outer door, which is often observed to be infested by visitants, who talk incessantly of beer, or linen, or a coat, and repeat the same sounds every morning, and sometimes again in the afternoon, without any variation, except that they grow daily more importunate and clamorous, and raise their voices in time from mournful murmurs to raging vociferations. This eternal monotony is always detestable to a man

NO. 117. **1. flexures . . . *Meander:*** "flexures" are bends. A famous winding river in ancient geography, the Meander flowed into the Aegean Sea. **2. *Ida:*** an ancient mountain in Crete associated with the worship of Zeus.

whose chief pleasure is to enlarge his knowledge, and vary his ideas. Others talk of freedom from noise, and abstraction from common business or amusements; and some, yet more visionary, tell us, that the faculties are inlarged by open prospects, and that the fancy is more at liberty, when the eye ranges without confinement.

These conveniencies may perhaps all be found in a well chosen garret; but surely they cannot be supposed sufficiently important to have operated unvariably upon different climates, distant ages, and separate nations. Of an universal practice, there must still be presumed an universal cause, which, however recondite and abstruse, may be perhaps reserved to make me illustrious by its discovery, and you by its promulgation.

It is universally known, that the faculties of the mind are invigorated or weakened by the state of the body, and that the body is in a great measure regulated by the various compressions of the ambient [3] element. The effects of the air in the production or cure of corporal maladies have been acknowledged from the time of *Hippocrates*; but no man has yet sufficiently considered how far it may influence the operations of the genius, though every day affords instances of local understanding, of wits and reasoners, whose faculties are adapted to some single spot, and who, when they are removed to any other place, sink at once into silence and stupidity. I have discovered, by a long series of observations, that invention and elocution suffer great impediments from dense and impure vapours, and that the tenuity of a defecated [4] air at a proper distance from the surface of the earth, accelerates the fancy, and sets at liberty those intellectual powers which were before shackled by too strong attraction, and unable to expand themselves under the pressure of a gross atmosphere. I have found dulness to quicken into sentiment in a thin ether, as water, though not very hot, boils in a receiver partly exhausted; and heads in appearance empty have teemed with notions upon rising ground, as the flaccid [5] sides of a football would have swelled out into stiffness and extension.

For this reason I never think myself qualified to judge decisively of any man's faculties, whom I have only known in one degree of elevation; but take some opportunity of attending him from the cellar to the garret, and try upon him all the various degrees of rarefaction and condensation, tension and laxity. If he is neither vivacious aloft, nor serious below, I then consider him as hopeless; but as it seldom happens, that I do not find the temper to which the texture of his brain is fitted, I accommodate him in time with a tube of mercury, first marking the point most favourable to his intellects, according to rules which I have long studied, and which I may, perhaps, reveal to mankind in a complete treatise of barometrical pneumatology.[6]

Another cause of the gaiety and sprightliness of the dwellers in garrets is probably the encrease of that vertiginous[7] motion, with which we are carried round by the diurnal [8] revolution of the earth. The power of agitation upon the spirits is well known; every man has felt his heart lightened in a rapid vehicle, or on a galloping horse; and nothing is plainer, than that he who towers to the fifth story, is whirled through more space by every circumrotation, than another that grovels upon the groundfloor. The nations between the tropicks are known to be fiery, inconstant, inventive and fanciful; because, living at the utmost length of the earth's diameter, they are carried about with more swiftness than those whom nature has placed nearer to the poles; and therefore, as it becomes a wise man to struggle with the inconveniencies of his country, whenever celerity and acuteness are requisite, we must actuate our languor by taking a few turns round the centre in a garret.

If you imagine that I ascribe to air and motion effects which they cannot produce, I desire you to consult your own memory, and consider whether you have never known a man acquire reputation in his garret, which, when fortune or a patron had placed him upon the first floor, he was unable to maintain; and who never recovered his former vigour of understanding till he was restored to his original situation. That a garret will make every man a wit, I am very far from supposing; I know there are some who would continue blockheads even on the summit of the *Andes*, or on the peak of *Teneriffe*.[9] But let not any man be considered

3. **ambient**: all-encompassing. 4. **defecated**: purified. 5. **flaccid**: soft, flabby.

6. **pneumatology**: the science of spiritual beings. 7. **vertiginous**: whirling. 8. **diurnal**: daily. 9. ***Teneriffe***: Teneriffe is the largest of the Canary Islands.

as unimproveable till this potent remedy has been tried; for perhaps he was formed to be great only in a garret, as the joiner[10] of *Aretæus*[11] was rational in no other place but his own shop.

I think a frequent removal to various distances from the center so necessary to a just estimate of intellectual abilities, and consequently of so great use in education, that if I hoped that the public could be persuaded to so expensive an experiment, I would propose, that there should be a cavern dug, and a tower erected, like those which *Bacon* describes in *Solomon's* house,[12] for the expansion and concentration of understanding, according to the exigence of different employments, or constitutions. Perhaps some that fume away in meditations upon time and space in the tower, might compose tables of interest at a certain depth; and he that upon level ground stagnates in silence, or creeps in narrative, might at the height of half a mile, ferment into merriment, sparkle with repartee, and froth with declamation.

Addison observes, that we may find the heat of *Virgil's* climate, in some lines of his *Georgic*: so, when I read a composition, I immediately determine the height of the author's habitation. As an elaborate performance is commonly said to smell of the lamp, my commendation of a noble thought, a sprightly sally, or a bold figure, is to pronounce it fresh from the garret; an expression which would break from me upon the perusal of most of your papers, did I not believe, that you sometimes quit the garret, and ascend into the cock-loft.

Hypertatus

NO. 134. SATURDAY, JUNE 29, 1751

Quis scit, an adjiciant hodiernæ crastina summæ
Tempora Dî superi!

HOR. [*Odes.* IV. vii. 17.]

Who knows if Heav'n, with ever-bounteous pow'r,
Shall add to-morrow to the present hour.

FRANCIS.

I sat yesterday morning employed in deliberating on which, among the various subjects that occurred to my imagination, I should bestow the paper of to-day. After a short effort of meditation by which nothing was determined, I grew every moment more irresolute, my ideas wandered from the first intention, and I rather wished to think, than thought, upon any settled subject; till at last I was awakened from this dream of study by a summons from the press: the time was come for which I had been thus negligently purposing to provide, and, however dubious or sluggish, I was now necessitated to write.

Though to a writer whose design is so comprehensive and miscellaneous, that he may accommodate himself with a topick from every scene of life, or view of nature, it is no great aggravation of his task to be obliged to a sudden composition, yet I could not forbear to reproach myself for having so long neglected what was unavoidably to be done, and of which every moment's idleness increased the difficulty. There was however some pleasure in reflecting that I, who had only trifled till diligence was necessary, might still congratulate myself upon my superiority to multitudes, who have trifled till diligence is vain; who can by no degree of activity or resolution recover the opportunities which have slipped away; and who are condemned by their own carelessness to hopeless calamity and barren sorrow.

The folly of allowing ourselves to delay what we know cannot be finally escaped, is one of the general weaknesses, which, in spite of the instruction of moralists, and the remonstrances of reason, prevail to a greater or less degree in every mind: even they who most steadily withstand it, find it, if not the most violent, the most pertinacious of their passions, always renewing its attacks, and though often vanquished, never destroyed.

It is indeed natural to have particular regard to the time present, and to be most solicitous for that which is by its nearness enabled to make the strongest impressions. When therefore any sharp pain is to be suffered, or any formidable danger to be incurred, we can scarcely exempt ourselves wholly from the seducements of imagination; we readily believe that another day will bring some support or advantage which we now want; and are easily persuaded, that the moment of necessity which we desire never to arrive, is at a great distance from us.

Thus life is languished away in the gloom of

10. joiner: carpenter. **11. *Aretæus:*** Aretæus was a Greek writer of the first and second century. **12.** The description is in Sir Francis Bacon's *The New Atlantis.*

anxiety, and consumed in collecting resolution which the next morning dissipates; in forming purposes which we scarcely hope to keep, and reconciling ourselves to our own cowardice by excuses, which, while we admit them, we know to be absurd. Our firmness is by the continual contemplation of misery hourly impaired; every submission to our fear enlarges its dominion; we not only waste that time in which the evil we dread might have been suffered and surmounted, but even where procrastination produces no absolute encrease of our difficulties, make them less superable to ourselves by habitual terrors. When evils cannot be avoided, it is wise to contract the interval of expectation; to meet the mischiefs which will overtake us if we fly; and suffer only their real malignity without the conflicts of doubt and anguish of anticipation.

To act is far easier than to suffer, yet we every day see the progress of life retarded by the *vis inertiæ,* the mere repugnance to motion, and find multitudes repining at the want of that which nothing but idleness hinders them from enjoying. The case of *Tantalus,* in the region of poetick punishment, was somewhat to be pitied, because the fruits that hung about him retired from his hand; but what tenderness can be claimed by those who though perhaps they suffer the pains of *Tantalus* will never lift their hands for their own relief?

There is nothing more common among this torpid generation than murmurs and complaints; murmurs at uneasiness which only vacancy and suspicion expose them to feel, and complaints of distresses which it is in their own power to remove. Laziness is commonly associated with timidity. Either fear originally prohibits endeavours by infusing despair of success; or the frequent failure of irresolute struggles, and the constant desire of avoiding labour, impress by degrees false terrors on the mind. But fear, whether natural or acquired, when once it has full possession of the fancy, never fails to employ it upon visions of calamity, such as if they are not dissipated by useful employment, will soon overcast it with horrors, and imbitter life not only with those miseries by which all earthly beings are really more or less tormented, but with those which do not yet exist, and which can only be discerned by the perspicacity of cowardice.

Among all who sacrifice future advantage to present inclination, scarcely any gain so little as those that suffer themselves to freeze in idleness. Others are corrupted by some enjoyment of more or less power to gratify the passions; but to neglect our duties, merely to avoid the labour of performing them, a labour which is always punctually rewarded, is surely to sink under weak temptations. Idleness never can secure tranquillity; the call of reason and of conscience will pierce the closest pavilion of the sluggard, and, though it may not have force to drive him from his down, will be loud enough to hinder him from sleep. Those moments which he cannot resolve to make useful by devoting them to the great business of his being, will still be usurped by powers that will not leave them to his disposal; remorse and vexation will seize upon them, and forbid him to enjoy what he is so desirous to appropriate.

There are other causes of inactivity incident to more active faculties and more acute discernment. He to whom many objects of persuit arise at the same time, will frequently hesitate between different desires, till a rival has precluded him, or change his course as new attractions prevail, and harrass himself without advancing. He who sees different ways to the same end, will, unless he watches carefully over his own conduct, lay out too much of his attention upon the comparison of probabilities, and the adjustment of expedients, and pause in the choice of his road, till some accident intercepts his journey. He whose penetration extends to remote consequences, and who, whenever he applies his attention to any design, discovers new prospects of advantage, and possibilities of improvement, will not easily be persuaded that his project is ripe for execution; but will superadd one contrivance to another, endeavour to unite various purposes in one operation, multiply complications, and refine niceties, till he is entangled in his own scheme, and bewildered in the perplexity of various intentions. He that resolves to unite all the beauties of situation in a new purchase, must waste his life in roving to no purpose from province to province. He that hopes in the same house to obtain every convenience, may draw plans and study *Palladio,*[1] but will never lay

NO. 134. 1. Palladio (1518–1580) was an Italian architect.

a stone. He will attempt a treatise on some important subject, and amass materials, consult authors, and study all the dependent and collateral parts of learning, but never conclude himself qualified to write. He that has abilities to conceive perfection, will not easily be content without it; and since perfection cannot be reached, will lose the opportunity of doing well in the vain hope of unattainable excellence.

The certainty that life cannot be long, and the probability that it will be much shorter than nature allows, ought to awaken every man to the active prosecution of whatever he is desirous to perform. It is true that no diligence can ascertain success; death may intercept the swiftest career; but he who is cut off in the execution of an honest undertaking, has at least the honour of falling in his rank, and has fought the battle, though he missed the victory.

NO. 148. SATURDAY, AUGUST 17, 1751

Me pater sævis oneret catenis
Quod viro clemens misero peperci,
Me vel extremis Numidarum in oris
Classe releget.

HOR. [*Odes.* III. xi. 45.]

Me let my father load with chains,
Or banish to *Numidia*'s farthest plains;
—My crime, that I a loyal wife,
In kind compassion sav'd my husband's life.

FRANCIS.

Politicians remark that no oppression is so heavy or lasting as that which is inflicted by the perversion and exorbitance of legal authority. The robber may be seized, and the invader repelled whenever they are found; they who pretend no right but that of force, may by force be punished or suppressed. But when plunder bears the name of impost, and murder is perpetrated by a judicial sentence, fortitude is intimidated and wisdom confounded; resistance shrinks from an alliance with rebellion, and the villain remains secure in the robes of the magistrate.

Equally dangerous and equally detestable are the cruelties often exercised in private families, under the venerable sanction of parental authority; the power which we are taught to honour from the first moments of reason; which is guarded from insult and violation by all that can impress awe upon the mind of man; and which therefore may wanton in cruelty without controul, and trample the bounds of right with innumerable transgressions, before duty and piety will dare to seek redress, or think themselves at liberty to recur to any other means of deliverance than supplications by which insolence is elated, and tears by which cruelty is gratified.

It was for a long time imagined by the *Romans*, that no son could be the murderer of his father, and they had therefore no punishment appropriated to parricide. They seem likewise to have believed with equal confidence that no father could be cruel to his child, and therefore they allowed every man the supreme judicature in his own house, and put the lives of his offspring into his hands. But experience informed them by degrees, that they had determined too hastily in favour of human nature; they found that instinct and habit were not able to contend with avarice or malice; that the nearest relation might be violated; and that power, to whomsoever entrusted, might be ill employed. They were therefore obliged to supply and to change their institutions; to deter the parricide by a new law, and to transfer capital punishments from the parent to the magistrate.

There are indeed many houses which it is impossible to enter familiarly, without discovering that parents are by no means exempt from the intoxications of dominion; and that he who is in no danger of hearing remonstrances but from his own conscience, will seldom be long without the art of controlling his convictions, and modifying justice by his own will.

If in any situation the heart were inaccessible to malignity, it might be supposed to be sufficiently secured by parental relation. To have voluntarily become to any being the occasion of its existence, produces an obligation to make that existence happy. To see helpless infancy stretching out her hands and pouring out her cries in testimony of dependance, without any powers to alarm jealousy, or any guilt to alienate affection, must surely awaken tenderness in every human mind; and tenderness once excited will be hourly encreased by the natural contagion of felicity, by the repercussion of communicated pleasure, and the consciousness of the dignity of benefaction. I believe no generous or benevolent man can see the vilest animal courting his regard, and shrinking at his anger, playing his gambols[1] of delight before him, calling on him in distress, and flying to him in danger, without more kindness than he can persuade himself to feel for the wild and unsocial inhabitants of the air and water. We naturally endear to ourselves those to whom we impart any kind of pleasure, because we imagine their affection and esteem secured to us by the benefits which they receive.

There is indeed another method by which the pride of superiority may be likewise gratified. He that has extinguished all the sensations of humanity, and has no longer any satisfaction in the reflection that he is loved as the distributor of happiness, may please himself with exciting terror as the inflicter of pain; he may delight his solitude with contemplating the extent of his power and the force of his commands, in imagining the desires that flutter on the tongue which is forbidden to utter them, or the discontent which preys on the heart in which fear confines it; he may amuse himself with new contrivances of detection, multiplications of prohibition, and varieties of punishment; and swell with exultation when he considers how little of the homage that he receives he owes to choice.

That princes of this character have been known, the history of all absolute kingdoms will inform us; and since, as *Aristotle* observes, *ἡ οἰκονομικὴ μοναρχία, the government of a family is naturally monarchical,*[2] it is like other monarchies too often arbitrarily administered. The regal and parental tyrant differ only in the extent of their dominions, and the number of their slaves. The same passions cause the same miseries; except that seldom any prince, however despotick, has so far shaken off all awe of the publick eye as to venture upon those freaks of injustice, which are sometimes indulged under the secrecy of a private dwelling. Capricious injunctions, partial decisions, unequal allotments, distributions of reward not by merit but by fancy, and punishments regulated not by the degree of the offence, but by the humour of the judge, are too frequent where no power is known but that of a father.

NO. 148. 1. **gambols:** games, frolics. 2. *Politics,* I, ii, 21.

That he delights in the misery of others no man will confess, and yet what other motive can make a father cruel? The king may be instigated by one man to the destruction of another; he may sometimes think himself endangered by the virtues of a subject; he may dread the successful general or the popular orator; his avarice may point out golden confiscations; and his guilt may whisper that he can only be secure, by cutting off all power of revenge.

But what can a parent hope from the oppression of those who were born to his protection, of those who can disturb him with no competition, who can enrich him with no spoils? Why cowards are cruel may be easily discovered; but for what reason not more infamous than cowardice can that man delight in oppression who has nothing to fear?

The unjustifiable severity of a parent is loaded with this aggravation, that those whom he injures are always in his sight. The injustice of a prince is often exercised upon those of whom he never had any personal or particular knowledge; and the sentence which he pronounces, whether of banishment, imprisonment, or death, removes from his view the man whom he condemns. But the domestick oppressor dooms himself to gaze upon those faces which he clouds with terror and with sorrow; and beholds every moment the effects of his own barbarities. He that can bear to give continual pain to those who surround him, and can walk with satisfaction in the gloom of his own presence; he that can see submissive misery without relenting, and meet without emotion the eye that implores mercy, or demands justice, will scarcely be amended by remonstrance or admonition; he has found means of stopping the avenues of tenderness, and arming his heart against the force of reason.

Even though no consideration should be paid to the great law of social beings, by which every individual is commanded to consult the happiness of others, yet the harsh parent is less to be vindicated than any other criminal, because he less provides for the happiness of himself. Every man, however little he loves others, would willingly be loved; every man hopes to live long, and therefore hopes for that time at which he shall sink back to imbecillity, and must depend for ease and chearfulness upon the officiousness of others. But how has he obviated the inconveniencies of old age, who alienates from him the assistance of his children, and whose bed must be surrounded in his last hours, in the hours of languor and dejection, of impatience and of pain, by strangers to whom his life is indifferent, or by enemies to whom his death is desirable?

Piety will indeed in good minds overcome provocation, and those who have been harrassed by brutality will forget the injuries which they have suffered so far as to perform the last duties with alacrity and zeal. But surely no resentment can be equally painful with kindness thus undeserved, nor can severer punishment be imprecated upon a man not wholly lost in meanness and stupidity, than through the tediousness of decrepitude, to be reproached by the kindness of his own children, to receive not the tribute but the alms of attendance, and to owe every relief of his miseries not to gratitude but to mercy.

NO. 154. SATURDAY, SEPTEMBER 7, 1751

—Tibi res antiquæ laudis & artis
Aggredior, sanctos ausus recludere fontes.

VIRG. [*Georg.* II. 174.]

For thee my tuneful accents will I raise,
And treat of arts disclos'd in ancient days;
Once more unlock for thee the sacred spring.

DRYDEN.

The direction of *Aristotle* to those that study politicks, is, first to examine and understand what has been written by the ancients upon government; then to cast their eyes round upon the world, and consider by what causes the prosperity of communities is visibly influenced, and why some are worse, and others better administered.

The same method must be pursued by him who hopes to become eminent in any other part of knowledge. The first task is to search books, the next to contemplate nature. He must first possess himself of the intellectual treasures which the diligence of former ages has accumulated, and then endeavour to encrease them by his own collections.

The mental disease of the present generation, is impatience of study, contempt of the great masters of ancient wisdom, and a disposition to rely wholly upon unassisted genius and natural sagacity. The wits of these happy days have discovered a way to fame, which the dull caution of our laborious ancestors durst never attempt; they cut the knots of sophistry which it was formerly the business of years to untie, solve difficulties by sudden irradiations of intelligence, and comprehend long processes of argument by immediate intuition.

Men who have flattered themselves into this opinion of their own abilities, look down on all who waste their lives over books, as a race of inferior beings condemned by nature to perpetual pupillage, and fruitlessly endeavouring to remedy their barrenness by incessant cultivation, or succour their feebleness by subsidiary strength. They presume that none would be more industrious than they, if they were not more sensible of deficiencies, and readily conclude, that he who places no confidence in his own powers, owes his modesty only to his weakness.

It is however certain that no estimate is more in danger of erroneous calculations than those by which a man computes the force of his own genius. It generally happens at our entrance into the world, that by the natural attraction of similitude, we associate with men like ourselves young, sprightly, and ignorant, and rate our accomplishments by comparison with theirs; when we have once obtained an acknowledged superiority over our acquaintances, imagination and desire easily extend it over the rest of mankind, and if no accident forces us into new emulations, we grow old, and die in admiration of ourselves.

Vanity, thus confirmed in her dominion, readily listens to the voice of idleness, and sooths the slumber of life with continual dreams of excellence and greatness. A man elated by confidence in his natural vigour of fancy and sagacity of conjecture, soon concludes that he already possesses whatever toil and enquiry can confer. He then listens with eagerness to the wild objections which folly has raised against the common means of improvement; talks of the dark chaos of indigested knowledge; describes the mischievous effects of heterogeneous sciences fermenting in the mind; relates the blunders of lettered ignorance; expatiates on the heroick merit of those who deviate from prescription, or shake off authority; and gives vent to the inflations of his heart by declaring that he owes nothing to pedants and universities.

All these pretensions, however confident, are very often vain. The laurels which superficial acuteness gains in triumphs over ignorance unsupported by vivacity, are observed by *Locke* to be lost whenever real learning and rational diligence appear against her; the sallies of gaiety are soon repressed by calm confidence, and the artifices of subtilty are readily detected by those who having carefully studied the question, are not easily confounded or surprised.

But though the contemner of books had neither been deceived by others nor himself, and was really born with a genius surpassing the ordinary abilities of mankind; yet surely such gifts of providence may be more properly urged as incitements to labour, than encouragements to negligence. He that neglects the culture of ground, naturally fertile, is more shamefully culpable than he whose field would scarcely recompence his husbandry.

Cicero remarks, that not to know what has been transacted in former times is to continue always a child. If no use is made of the labours of past ages, the world must remain always in the infancy of knowledge. The discoveries of every man must terminate in his own advantage, and the studies of every age be employed on questions which the past generation had discussed and determined. We may with as little reproach borrow science as manufactures from our ancestors; and it is as rational to live in caves till our own hands have erected a palace, as to reject all knowledge of architecture, which our understandings will not supply.

To the strongest and quickest mind it is far easier to learn than to invent. The principles of arithmetick and geometry may be comprehended by a close attention in a few days; yet who can flatter himself that the study of a long life would have enabled him to discover them, when he sees them yet unknown to so many nations, whom he cannot suppose less liberally endowed with natural reason, than the *Grecians* or *Egyptians*?

Every science was thus far advanced towards perfection, by the emulous diligence of contemporary students, and the gradual discoveries of one age improving on another. Sometimes unexpected flashes of instruction were struck out by the fortuitous collision of happy incidents, or an involuntary concurrence of ideas, in which the philosopher to whom they happened had no other merit than that of knowing their value, and transmitting unclouded to posterity that light which had been kindled by causes out of his power. The happiness of these casual illuminations no man can promise to himself, because no endeavours can procure them; and therefore, whatever be our abilities or application, we must submit to learn from others what perhaps would have lain hid for ever from human penetration, had not some remote enquiry brought it to view; as treasures are thrown up by the ploughman and the digger in the rude exercise of their common occupations.

The man whose genius qualifies him for great undertakings, must at least be content to learn from books the present state of human knowledge; that he may not ascribe to himself the invention of arts generally known; weary his attention with experiments of which the event has been long registered; and waste, in attempts which have already succeeded or miscarried, that time which might have been spent with usefulness and honour upon new undertakings.

But though the study of books is necessary, it is not sufficient to constitute literary eminence. He that wishes to be counted among the benefactors of posterity, must add by his own toil to the acquisitions of his ancestors, and secure his memory from neglect by some valuable improvement. This can only be effected by looking out upon the wastes of the intellectual world, and extending the power of learning over regions yet undisciplined and barbarous; or by surveying more exactly her antient dominions, and driving ignorance from the fortresses and retreats where she skulks undetected and undisturbed. Every science has its difficulties which yet call for solution before we attempt new systems of knowledge; as every country has its forests and marshes, which it would be wise to cultivate and drain, before distant colonies are projected as a necessary discharge of the exuberance of inhabitants.

No man ever yet became great by imitation. Whatever hopes for the veneration of mankind must have invention in the design or the execution; either the effect must itself be new, or the means by which it is produced. Either truths hitherto unknown must be discovered, or those which are already known enforced by stronger evidence, facilitated by clearer method, or ellucidated by brighter illustrations.

Fame cannot spread wide or endure long that is not rooted in nature, and manured by art. That which hopes to resist the blast of malignity, and stand firm against the attacks of time, must contain in itself some original principle of growth. The reputation which arises from the detail or transposition of borrowed sentiments, may spread for a while, like ivy on the rind of antiquity, but will be torn away by accident or contempt, and suffered to rot unheeded on the ground.

NO. 155. TUESDAY, SEPTEMBER 10, 1751

———*Steriles transmisimus annos,*
Hæc ævi mihi prima dies, hæc limina vitæ.

STAT. [I. 362.]

———Our barren years are past;
Be this of life the first, of sloth the last.

ELPHINSTON.

No weakness of the human mind has more frequently incurred animadversion,[1] than the negligence with which men overlook their own faults, however flagrant, and the easiness with which they pardon them, however frequently repeated.

It seems generally believed, that, as the eye cannot see itself, the mind has no faculties by which it can contemplate its own state, and that therefore we have not means of becoming acquainted with our real characters; an opinion which, like innumerable other postulates, an enquirer finds himself inclined to admit upon very little evidence, because it affords a ready solution of many difficulties. It will explain why the greatest abilities frequently fail to promote the happiness of those who possess them; why those who can distinguish with the utmost nicety the boundaries of vice and virtue, suffer them to be confounded in their own conduct; why the active and vigilant resign their affairs implicitly to the management of others; and why the cautious and fearful make hourly approaches towards ruin, without one sigh of solicitude or struggle for escape.

When a position teems thus with commodious consequences, who can without regret confess it to be false? Yet it is certain that declaimers have indulged a disposition to describe the dominion of the passions as extended beyond the limits that nature assigned. Self-love is often rather arrogant than blind; it does not hide our faults from ourselves, but persuades us that they escape the notice of others, and disposes us to resent censures lest we should confess them to be just. We are secretly conscious of defects and vices which we hope to conceal from the publick eye, and please ourselves with innumerable impostures, by which, in reality, no body is deceived.

In proof of the dimness of our internal sight, or the general inability of man to determine rightly concerning his own character, it is common to urge the success of the most absurd and incredible flattery, and the resentment always raised by advice, however soft, benevolent, and reasonable. But flattery, if its operation be nearly examined, will be found to owe its acceptance not to our ignorance but knowledge of our failures, and to delight us rather as it consoles our wants than displays our possessions. He that shall solicit the favour of his patron by praising him for qualities which he can find in himself, will be defeated by the more daring panegyrist who enriches him with adscititious[2] excellence. Just praise is only a debt, but flattery is a present. The acknowledgement of those virtues on which conscience congratulates us, is a tribute that we can at any time exact with confidence, but the celebration of those which we only feign, or desire without any vigorous endeavours to attain them, is received as a confession of sovereignty over regions never conquered, as a favourable decision of disputable claims, and is more welcome as it is more gratuitous.

Advice is offensive, not because it lays us open to unexpected regret, or convicts us of any fault which had escaped our notice, but because it shows us that we are known to others as well as to ourselves; and the officious monitor is persecuted with hatred, not because his accusation is false, but because he assumes that superiority which we are not willing to grant him, and has dared to detect what we desired to conceal.

For this reason advice is commonly ineffectual. If those who follow the call of their desires, without enquiry whither they are going, had deviated

NO. 155. **1. animadversion:** notice, attention.

2. adscititious: supplementary.

ignorantly from the paths of wisdom, and were rushing upon dangers unforeseen, they would readily listen to information that recalls them from their errors, and catch the first alarm by which destruction or infamy is denounced. Few that wander in the wrong way mistake it for the right; they only find it more smooth and flowery, and indulge their own choice rather than approve it: therefore few are persuaded to quit it by admonition or reproof, since it impresses no new conviction, nor confers any powers of action or resistance. He that is gravely informed how soon profusion will annihilate his fortune, hears with little advantage what he knew before, and catches at the next occasion of expence, because advice has no force to suppress his vanity. He that is told how certainly intemperance will hurry him to the grave, runs with his usual speed to a new course of luxury, because his reason is not invigorated, nor his appetite weakened.

The mischief of flattery is, not that it persuades any man that he is what he is not, but that it suppresses the influence of honest ambition, by raising an opinion that honour may be gained without the toil of merit; and the benefit of advice arises commonly, not from any new light imparted to the mind, but from the discovery which it affords of the publick suffrages. He that could withstand conscience, is frighted at infamy, and shame prevails when reason was defeated.

As we all know our own faults, and know them commonly with many aggravations which human perspicacity cannot discover, there is, perhaps, no man, however hardened by impudence or dissipated by levity, sheltered by hypocrisy, or blasted by disgrace, who does not intend some time to review his conduct, and to regulate the remainder of his life by the laws of virtue. New temptations indeed attack him, new invitations are offered by pleasure and interest, and the hour of reformation is always delayed; every delay gives vice another opportunity of fortifying itself by habit; and the change of manners, though sincerely intended and rationally planned, is referred to the time when some craving passion shall be fully gratified, or some powerful allurement cease its importunity.

Thus procrastination is accumulated on procrastination, and one impediment succeeds another, till age shatters our resolution, or death intercepts the project of amendment. Such is often the end of salutary purposes, after they have long delighted the imagination, and appeased that disquiet which every mind feels from known misconduct, when the attention is not diverted by business or by pleasure.

Nothing surely can be more unworthy of a reasonable nature, than to continue in a state so opposite to real happiness, as that all the peace of solitude and felicity of meditation, must arise from resolutions of forsaking it. Yet the world will often afford examples of men, who pass months and years in a continual war with their own convictions, and are daily dragged by habit or betrayed by passion into practices, which they closed and opened their eyes with purposes to avoid; purposes which, though settled on conviction, the first impulse of momentary desire totally overthrows.

The influence of custom is indeed such that to conquer it will require the utmost efforts of fortitude and virtue, nor can I think any man more worthy of veneration and renown, than those who have burst the shackles of habitual vice. This victory however has different degrees of glory as of difficulty; it is more heroic as the objects of guilty gratification are more familiar, and the recurrence of solicitation more frequent. He that from experience of the folly of ambition resigns his offices, may set himself free at once from temptation to squander his life in courts, because he cannot regain his former station. He who is inslaved by an amorous passion, may quit his tyrant in disgust, and absence will without the help of reason overcome by degrees the desire of returning. But those appetites to which every place affords their proper object, and which require no preparatory measures or gradual advances, are more tenaciously adhesive; the wish is so near the enjoyment, that compliance often precedes consideration, and before the powers of reason can be summoned, the time for employing them is past.

Indolence is therefore one of the vices from which those whom it once infects are seldom reformed. Every other species of luxury operates upon some appetite that is quickly satiated, and requires some concurrence of art or accident which every place will not supply; but the desire of ease acts equally at all hours, and the longer it is indulged is the more encreased. To do nothing is in every man's power; we can never want an opportunity of omitting duties. The lapse to indolence is soft and imperceptible, because it is only a mere cessation of activity; but the return to diligence is difficult, because it implies a change from rest to motion, from privation to reality.

————Facilis descensus Averni:
Noctes atque dies patet atri janua Ditis:
Sed revocare gradum, superasque evadere ad auras,
Hoc opus, hic labor est.————

[VIR. *Æn.* VI. 126.]

The gates of *Hell* are open night and day;
Smooth the descent, and easy is the way:
But, to return, and view the chearful skies;
In this, the task and mighty labour lies.

DRYDEN.

Of this vice, as of all others, every man who indulges it is conscious; we all know our own state, if we could be induced to consider it; and it might perhaps be useful to the conquest of all these ensnarers of the mind, if at certain stated days life was reviewed. Many things necessary are omitted, because we vainly imagine that they may be always performed, and what cannot be done without pain will for ever be delayed if the time of doing it be left unsettled. No corruption is great but by long negligence, which can scarcely prevail in a mind regularly and frequently awakened by periodical remorse. He that thus breaks his life into parts, will find in himself a desire to distinguish every stage of his existence by some improvement, and delight himself with the approach of the day of recollection, as of the time which is to begin a new series of virtue and felicity.

NO. 183. TUESDAY, DECEMBER 17, 1751

Nulla fides regni sociis, omnisque potestas
Impatiens consortis erit.

LUCAN [*Phar.* I. 92.]

No faith of partnership dominion owns;
Still discord hovers o'er divided thrones.

The hostility perpetually exercised between one man and another, is caused by the desire of many for that which only few can possess. Every man would be rich, powerful, and famous; yet fame, power, and riches, are only the names of relative conditions, which imply the obscurity, dependence, and poverty of greater numbers.

This universal and incessant competition, produces injury and malice by two motives, interest, and envy; the prospect of adding to our possessions what we can take from others, and the hope of alleviating the sense of our disparity by lessening others, though we gain nothing to ourselves.

Of these two malignant and destructive powers, it seems probable at the first view, that interest has the strongest and most extensive influence. It is easy to conceive that opportunities to seize what has been long wanted, may excite desires almost irresistible; but surely, the same eagerness cannot be kindled by an accidental power of destroying that which gives happiness to another. It must be more natural to rob for gain, than to ravage only for mischief.

Yet I am inclined to believe, that the great law of mutual benevolence is oftener violated by envy than by interest, and that most of the misery which the defamation of blameless actions, or the obstruction of honest endeavours brings upon the world, is inflicted by men that propose no advantage to themselves but the satisfaction of poisoning the banquet which they cannot taste, and blasting the harvest which they have no right to reap.

Interest can diffuse itself but to a narrow compass. The number is never large of those who can hope to fill the posts of degraded power, catch the fragments of shattered fortune, or succeed to the honours of depreciated beauty. But the empire of envy has no limits, as it requires to its influence very little help from external circumstances. Envy may always be produced by idleness and pride, and in what place will not they be found?

Interest requires some qualities not universally bestowed. The ruin of another will produce no profit to him, who has not discernment to mark his advantage, courage to seize, and activity to pursue it; but the cold malignity of envy may be exerted in a torpid and quiescent state, amidst the gloom of stupidity, in the coverts of cowardice. He that falls by the attacks of interest, is torn by hungry tigers; he may discover and resist his enemies. He that perishes in the ambushes of envy, is destroyed by unknown and invisible assailants, and dies like a man suffocated by a poisonous vapour, without knowledge of his danger, or possibility of contest.

Interest is seldom pursued but at some hazard. He that hopes to gain much, has commonly something to lose, and when he ventures to attack superiority, if he fails to conquer, is irrecoverably crushed. But envy may act without expence, or danger. To spread suspicion, to invent calumnies, to propagate scandal, requires neither labour nor courage. It is easy for the author of a lye, however malignant, to escape detection, and infamy needs very little industry to assist its circulation.

Envy is almost the only vice which is practicable at all times, and in every place; the only passion which can never lie quiet for want of irritation: its effects therefore are every where discoverable, and its attempts always to be dreaded.

It is impossible to mention a name which any advantageous distinction has made eminent, but some latent animosity will burst out. The wealthy trader, however he may abstract himself from publick affairs, will never want those who hint, with *Shylock,* that ships are but boards. The beauty, adorned only with the unambitious graces of innocence and modesty, provokes, whenever she appears, a thousand murmurs of detraction. The genius, even when he endeavours only to entertain or instruct, yet suffers persecution from innumerable criticks, whose acrimony is excited merely by the pain of seeing others pleased, and of hearing applauses which another enjoys.

The frequency of envy makes it so familiar, that it escapes our notice; nor do we often reflect upon its turpitude or malignity, till we happen to feel its influence. When he that has given no provocation to malice, but by attempting to excel, finds himself pursued by multitudes whom he never saw with all the implacability of personal resentment; when he perceives clamour and malice let loose upon him as a publick enemy, and incited by every stratagem of defamation; when he hears the misfortunes of his family, or the follies of his youth exposed to the world; and every failure of conduct, or defect of nature aggravated and ridiculed; he then learns to abhor those artifices at which he only laughed before, and discovers how much the happiness of life would be advanced by the eradiction of envy from the human heart.

Envy is, indeed, a stubborn weed of the mind, and seldom yields to the culture of philosophy. There are, however, considerations, which if carefully implanted and diligently propagated, might in time overpower and repress it, since no one can nurse it for the sake of pleasure, as its effects are only shame, anguish, and perturbation.

It is above all other vices inconsistent with the character of a social being, because it sacrifices truth and kindness to very weak temptations. He that plunders a wealthy neighbour, gains as much as he takes away, and may improve his own condition in the same proportion as he impairs another's; but he that blasts a flourishing reputation, must be content with a small dividend of additional fame, so small as can afford very little consolation to balance the guilt by which it is obtained.

I have hitherto avoided that dangerous and empirical morality, which cures one vice by means of another. But envy is so base and detestable, so vile in its original, and so pernicious in its effects, that the predominance of almost any other quality is to be preferred. It is one of those lawless enemies of society, against which poisoned arrows may honestly be used. Let it, therefore, be constantly remembered, that whoever envies another, confesses his superiority, and let those be reformed by their pride who have lost their virtue.

It is no slight aggravation of the injuries which envy incites, that they are committed against those who have given no intentional provocation; and that the sufferer is often marked out for ruin, not because he has failed in any duty, but because he has dared to do more than was required.

Almost every other crime is practised by the help of some quality which might have produced esteem or love, if it had been well employed; but envy is mere unmixed and genuine evil; it pursues a hateful end by despicable means, and desires not so much its own happiness as another's misery. To avoid depravity like this, it is not necessary that any one should aspire to heroism or sanctity, but only, that he should resolve not to quit the rank which nature assigns him, and wish to maintain the dignity of a human being.

NO. 184. SATURDAY, DECEMBER 21, 1751

Permittes ipsis expendere numinibus, quid
Conveniat nobis, rebusque sit utile nostris.

JUV. [*Sat.* X. 347.]

Intrust thy fortune to the pow'rs above:
Leave them to manage for thee, and to grant
What their unerring wisdom sees thee want.

DRYDEN.

As every scheme of life, so every form of writing has its advantages and inconveniencies, though not mingled in the same proportions. The writer of essays, escapes many embarrassments to which a large work would have exposed him; he seldom harrasses his reason with long trains of consequence, dims his eyes with the perusal of antiquated volumes, or burthens his memory with great accumulations of preparatory knowledge. A careless glance upon a favourite author, or transient survey of the varieties of life, is sufficient to supply the first hint or seminal idea, which enlarged by the gradual accretion of matter stored in the mind, is by the warmth of fancy easily expanded into flowers, and sometimes ripened into fruit.

The most frequent difficulty, by which the authors of these petty compositions are distressed, arises from the perpetual demand of novelty and change. The compiler of a system of science lays his invention at rest, and employs only his judgment, the faculty exerted with least fatigue. Even the relator of feigned adventures, when once the principal characters are established, and the great events regularly connected, finds incidents and episodes crouding upon his mind; every change opens new views, and the latter part of the story grows without labour out of the former. But he that attempts to entertain his reader with unconnected pieces, finds the irksomeness of his task rather encreased than lessened by every production. The day calls afresh upon him for a new topick, and he is again obliged to choose, without any principle to regulate his choice.

It is indeed true, that there is seldom any necessity of looking far, or enquiring long for a proper subject. Every diversity of art or nature, every public blessing or calamity, every domestick pain or gratification, every sally of caprice, blunder of absurdity, or stratagem of affectation may supply matter to him whose only rule is to avoid uniformity. But it often happens, that the judgment is distracted with boundless multiplicity, the imagination ranges from one design to another, and the hours pass imperceptibly away till the composition can be no longer delayed, and necessity enforces the use of those thoughts which then happen to be at hand. The mind rejoicing at deliverance on any terms from perplexity and suspense, applies herself vigorously to the work before her, collects embellishments and illustrations, and sometimes finishes with great elegance and happiness what in a state of ease and leisure she never had begun.

It is not commonly observed, how much, even of actions considered as particularly subject to choice, is to be attributed to accident, or some cause out of our own power, by whatever name it be distinguished. To close tedious deliberations with hasty resolves, and after long consultations with reason to refer the question to caprice, is by no means peculiar to the essayist. Let him that peruses this paper, review the series of his life, and enquire how he was placed in his present condition. He will find that of the good or ill which he has experienced, a great part came unexpected, without any visible gradations of approach; that every event has been influenced by causes acting without his intervention; and that whenever he pretended to the prerogative of foresight, he was mortified with new conviction of the shortness of his views.

The busy, the ambitious, the inconstant, and the adventurous, may be said to throw themselves by design into the arms of fortune, and voluntarily to quit the power of governing themselves; they engage in a course of life in which little can be ascertained by previous measures; nor is it any wonder that their time is past between elation and despondency, hope and disappointment.

Some there are who appear to walk the road of life with more circumspection, and make no step till they think themselves secure from the hazard of a precipice; when neither pleasure nor profit can tempt them from the beaten path; who refuse to climb lest they should fall, or to run lest they should stumble, and move slowly forward without any compliance with those passions by which the heady and vehement are seduced and betrayed.

Yet even the timorous prudence of this judicious class is far from exempting them from the dominion of chance, a subtle and insidious power, who will intrude upon privacy and embarrass caution. No course of life is so prescribed and limited, but that many actions must result from arbitrary election. Every one must form the general plan of his conduct by his own reflections; he must resolve whether he will endeavour at riches or at content;

whether he will exercise private or publick virtues; whether he will labour for the general benefit of mankind, or contract his beneficence to his family and dependants.

This question has long exercised the schools of philosophy, but remains yet undecided; and what hope is there that a young man, unacquainted with the arguments on either side, should determine his own destiny otherwise than by chance?

When chance has given him a partner of his bed, whom he prefers to all other women, without any proof of superior desert, chance must again direct him in the education of his children; for, who was ever able to convince himself by arguments, that he had chosen for his son that mode of instruction to which his understanding was best adapted, or by which he would most easily be made wise or virtuous?

Whoever shall enquire by what motives he was determined on these important occasions, will find them such, as his pride will scarcely suffer him to confess; some sudden ardour of desire, some uncertain glimpse of advantage, some petty competition, some inaccurate conclusion, or some example implicitly reverenced. Such are often the first causes of our resolves; for it is necessary to act, but impossible to know the consequences of action, or to discuss all the reasons which offer themselves on every part to inquisitiveness and solicitude.

Since life itself is uncertain, nothing which has life for its basis, can boast much stability. Yet this is but a small part of our perplexity. We set out on a tempestuous sea, in quest of some port, where we expect to find rest, but where we are not sure of admission; we are not only in danger of sinking in the way, but of being misled by meteors mistaken for stars, of being driven from our course by the changes of the wind, and of losing it by unskilful steerage; yet it sometimes happens, that cross winds blow us to a safer coast, that meteors draw us aside from whirlpools, and that negligence or error contributes to our escape from mischiefs to which a direct course would have exposed us. Of those that by precipitate conclusions, involve themselves in calamities without guilt, very few, however they may reproach themselves, can be certain that other measures would have been more successful.

In this state of universal uncertainty, where a thousand dangers hover about us, and none can tell whether the good that he persues is not evil in disguise, or whether the next step will lead him to safety or destruction, nothing can afford any rational tranquillity, but the conviction that, however we amuse ourselves with unideal sounds, nothing in reality is governed by chance, but that the universe is under the perpetual superintendence of him who created it; that our being is in the hands of omnipotent goodness, by whom what appears casual to us is directed for ends ultimately kind and merciful; and that nothing can finally hurt him who debars not himself from the divine favour.

NO. 208. SATURDAY, MARCH 14, 1752

Ἡράκλειτος ἐγώ· τί με ὦ κάτω ἕλκετ᾽ ἄμουσι;
Οὐχ᾽ ὑμῖν ἐπόνουν, τοῖς δὲ μ᾽ ἐπισταμένοις·
Εἷς ἐμοὶ ἄνθρωπος τρισμύριοι· οἱ δ᾽ ἀνάριθμοι
Οὐδείς· ταῦτ᾽ αὐδῶ καὶ παρὰ Περσεφόνῃ·

DIOG. LAERT.

Begone, ye blockheads, *Heraclitus* cries,
And leave my labours to the learn'd and wise,
By wit, by knowledge, studious to be read,
I scorn the multitude, alive and dead.

Time, which puts an end to all human pleasures and sorrows, has likewise concluded the labours of the RAMBLER. Having supported, for two years, the anxious employment of a periodical writer, and multiplied my essays to four volumes, I have now determined to desist.

The reasons of this resolution it is of little importance to declare, since justification is unnecessary when no objection is made. I am far from supposing, that the cessation of my performances will raise any inquiry, for I have never been much a favourite of the publick, nor can boast that, in the progress of my undertaking, I have been animated by the rewards of the liberal, the caresses of the great, or the praises of the eminent.

But I have no design to gratify pride by submission, or malice by lamentation; nor think it reasonable to complain of neglect from those whose regard I never solicited. If I have not been distinguished by the distributers of literary honours, I have seldom descended to the arts by which favour is obtained. I have seen the meteors of fashion rise and fall, without any attempt to add a moment to their duration. I have never complied with temporary curiosity, nor enabled my readers to discuss the topick of the day; I have rarely exempl[if]ied my assertions by living characters; in my papers, no man could look for censures of his enemies, or praises of himself; and they only were expected to peruse them, whose passions left them leisure for abstracted truth, and whom virtue could please by its naked dignity.

To some, however, I am indebted for encouragement, and to others for assistance. The number of my friends was never great, but they have been such as would not suffer me to think that I was writing in vain, and I did not feel much dejection from the want of popularity.

My obligations having not been frequent, my acknowledgements may be soon dispatched. I can restore to all my correspondents their productions, with little diminution of the bulk of my volumes, though not without the loss of some pieces to which particular honours have been paid.

The parts from which I claim no other praise than that of having given them an opportunity of appearing, are the four billets in the tenth paper, the second letter in the fifteenth, the thirtieth, the forty-fourth, the ninety-seventh, and the hundredth papers, and the second letter in the hundred and seventh.

Having thus deprived myself of many excuses which candor might have admitted for the inequality of my compositions, being no longer able to alledge the necessity of gratifying correspondents, the importunity with which publication was solicited, or obstinacy with which correction was rejected, I must remain accountable for all my faults, and submit, without subterfuge, to the censures of criticism, which, however, I shall not endeavour to soften by a formal deprecation, or to overbear by the influence of a patron. The supplications of an author never yet reprieved him a moment from oblivion; and, though greatness has sometimes sheltered guilt, it can afford no protection to ignorance or dulness. Having hitherto attempted only the propagation of truth, I will not at last violate it by the confession of terrors which I do not feel: Having laboured to maintain the dignity of virtue, I will not now degrade it by the meanness of dedication.

The seeming vanity with which I have sometimes spoken of myself, would perhaps require an apology, were it not extenuated by the example of those who have published essays before me, and by the privilege which every nameless writer has been hitherto allowed. "A mask," says *Castiglione*, "confers a right of acting and speaking with less restraint, even when the wearer happens to be known." [1] He that is discovered without his own consent, may claim some indulgence, and cannot be rigorously called to justify those sallies or frolicks which his disguise must prove him desirous to conceal.

But I have been cautious lest this offence should be frequently or grossly committed; for, as one of the philosophers directs us to live with a friend, as with one that is some time to become an enemy, I have always thought it the duty of an anonymous author to write, as if he expected to be hereafter known.

I am willing to flatter myself with hopes, that, by collecting these papers, I am not preparing for my future life, either shame or repentance. That all are happily imagined, or accurately polished, that the same sentiments have not sometimes recurred, or the same expressions been too frequently repeated, I have not confidence in my abilities sufficient to warrant. He that condemns himself to compose on a stated day, will often bring to his task an attention dissipated, a memory embarrassed, an imagination overwhelmed, a mind distracted with anxieties, a body languishing with disease: He will labour on a barren topick, till it is too late to change it; or in the ardour of invention, diffuse his thoughts into wild exuberance, which the pressing hour of publication cannot suffer judgment to examine or reduce.

Whatever shall be the final sentence of mankind, I have at least endeavoured to deserve their kindness. I have laboured to refine our language to grammatical purity, and to clear it from colloquial barbarisms, licentious idioms, and irregular combinations. Something, perhaps, I have added to the elegance of its construction, and something to the harmony of its cadence. When common words were less pleasing to the ear, or less distinct in their signification, I have familiarized the terms of philosophy by applying them to popular ideas, but have rarely admitted any word not authorized by former writers; for I believe that whoever knows the *En-*

NO. 208. 1. In *The Courtier*, II, ii.

glish tongue in its present extent, will be able to express his thoughts without further help from other nations.

As it has been my principal design to inculcate wisdom or piety, I have allotted few papers to the idle sports of imagination. Some, perhaps, may be found, of which the highest excellence is harmless merriment, but scarcely any man is so steadily serious, as not to complain, that the severity of dictatorial instruction has been too seldom relieved, and that he is driven by the sternness of the Rambler's philosophy to more chearful and airy companions.

Next to the excursions of fancy are the disquisitions of criticism, which, in my opinion, is only to be ranked among the subordinate and instrumental arts. Arbitrary decision and general exclamation I have carefully avoided, by asserting nothing without a reason, and establishing all my principles of judgment on unalterable and evident truth.

In the pictures of life I have never been so studious of novelty or surprize, as to depart wholly from all resemblance; a fault which writers deservedly celebrated frequently commit, that they may raise, as the occasion requires, either mirth or abhorrence. Some enlargement may be allowed to declamation, and some exaggeration to burlesque; but as they deviate farther from reality, they become less useful, because their lessons will fail of application. The mind of the reader is carried away from the contemplation of his own manners; he finds in himself no likeness to the phantom before him; and though he laughs or rages, is not reformed.

The essays professedly serious, if I have been able to execute my own intentions, will be found exactly conformable to the precepts of Christianity, without any accommodation to the licentiousness and levity of the present age. I therefore look back on this part of my work with pleasure, which no blame or praise of man shall diminish or augment. I shall never envy the honours which wit and learning obtain in any other cause, if I can be numbered among the writers who have given ardour to virtue, and confidence to truth.

Αὐτῶν ἐκ μακάρων ἀντάξιος εἴη ἀμοιβή.[2]

Celestial pow'rs! that piety regard,
From you my labours wait their last reward.

2. See Dionysius Periegetes, 1, 1186.

Preface to Shakespeare

That praises are without reason lavished on the dead, and that the honours due only to excellence are paid to antiquity, is a complaint likely to be always continued by those, who, being able to add nothing to truth, hope for eminence from the heresies of paradox; or those, who, being forced by disappointment upon consolatory expedients, are willing to hope from posterity what the present age refuses, and flatter themselves that the regard which is yet denied by envy, will be at last bestowed by time.

Antiquity, like every other quality that attracts the notice of mankind, has undoubtedly votaries that reverence it, not from reason, but from prejudice. Some seem to admire indiscriminately whatever has been long preserved, without considering that time has sometimes co-operated with chance; all perhaps are more willing to honour past than present excellence; and the mind contemplates genius through the shades of age, as the eye surveys the sun through artificial opacity. The great contention of criticism is to find the faults of the moderns, and the beauties of the ancients. While an authour is yet living we estimate his powers by his worst performance, and when he is dead we rate them by his best.

To works, however, of which the excellence is not absolute and definite, but gradual and comparative; to works not raised upon principles demonstrative and scientifick, but appealing wholly to observation and experience, no other test can be applied than length of duration and continuance of esteem. What mankind have long possessed they have often examined and compared, and if they persist to value the possession, it is because frequent comparisons have confirmed opinion in its favour. As among the works of nature no man can properly call a river deep or a mountain high, without the knowledge of many mountains and many rivers; so in the productions of genius, nothing can be stiled excellent till it has been compared with other works of the same kind. Demonstration immediately displays its power, and has nothing to hope or fear from the flux of years; but works tentative and experimental must be estimated by their proportion to the general and collective ability of man, as it is discovered in a long succession of endeavours. Of the first building that was raised, it might be with certainty determined that it was round or square, but whether it was spacious or lofty must have been referred to time. The Pythagorean scale of numbers was at once discovered to be perfect;[1] but the poems of *Homer* we yet know not to transcend the common limits of human intelligence, but by remarking, that nation after nation, and century after century, has been able to do little more than transpose his incidents, new name his characters, and paraphrase his sentiments.

The reverence due to writings that have long subsisted arises therefore not from any credulous confidence in the superior wisdom of past ages, or gloomy persuasion of the degeneracy of mankind, but is the consequence of acknowledged and indubitable positions, that what has been longest known has been most considered, and what is most considered is best understood.

The Poet, of whose works I have undertaken the revision, may now begin to assume the dignity of an ancient, and claim the privilege of established fame and prescriptive veneration. He has long outlived his century, the term commonly fixed as the test of literary merit. Whatever advantages he might once derive from personal allusions, local customs, or temporary opinions, have for many years been lost; and every topick of merriment or motive of sorrow, which the modes of artificial life afforded him, now only obscure the scenes which they once illuminated. The effects of favour and competition are at an end; the tradition of his friendships and his enmities has perished; his works support no opinion with arguments, nor supply any faction with invectives; they can neither indulge vanity nor gratify malignity, but are read without any other reason than the desire of pleasure, and are therefore praised only as pleasure is obtained; yet, thus unassisted by interest or passion, they have past through variations of taste and changes of manners, and, as they devolved from one generation to another, have received new honours at every transmission.

But because human judgment, though it be gradually gaining upon certainty, never becomes infallible; and approbation, though long continued, may yet be only the approbation of prejudice or fashion; it is proper to inquire, by what peculiarities of excellence *Shakespeare* has gained and kept the favour of his countrymen.

Nothing can please many, and please long, but just representations of general nature. Particular manners can be known to few, and therefore few only can judge how nearly they are copied. The irregular combinations of fanciful invention may delight a-while, by that novelty of which the common satiety of life sends us all in quest; but the pleasures of sudden wonder are soon exhausted, and the mind can only repose on the stability of truth.

Shakespeare is above all writers, at least above all modern writers, the poet of nature; the poet that holds up to his readers a faithful mirrour of manners and of life. His characters are not modified by the customs of particular places, unpractised by the rest of the world; by the peculiarities of studies or professions, which can operate but upon small numbers; or by the accidents of transient fashions or temporary opinions: they are the genuine progeny of common humanity, such as the world will always supply, and observation will always find. His persons act and speak by the influence of those general passions and principles by which all minds are agitated, and the whole system of life is continued in motion. In the writings of other poets a character is too often an individual; in those of *Shakespeare* it is commonly a species.

It is from this wide extension of design that so much instruction is derived. It is this which fills the plays of *Shakespeare* with practical axioms and domestick wisdom. It was said of *Euripides*, that every verse was a precept;[2] and it may be said of *Shakespeare*, that from his works may be collected a system of civil and economical prudence. Yet his real power is not shown in the splendour of particular passages, but by the progress of his fable, and the tenour of his dialogue; and he that tries to recommend him by select quotations, will succeed like the pedant in *Hierocles*,[3] who, when he offered his house to sale, carried a brick in his pocket as a specimen.

It will not easily be imagined how much *Shakespeare* excells in accommodating his sentiments to real life, but by comparing him with other authours. It was observed of the ancient schools of

PREFACE TO SHAKESPEARE. 1. Aristotle, *Metaphysics*, I, 5.

2. Cicero, *Familiar Letters*, xvi, 8. 3. ***Hierocles:*** see *Hieroclis Commentarius in Aurea Carmina*, ed. Needham (1709), p. 462.

declamation, that the more diligently they were frequented, the more was the student disqualified for the world, because he found nothing there which he should ever meet in any other place. The same remark may be applied to every stage but that of *Shakespeare*. The theatre, when it is under any other direction, is peopled by such characters as were never seen, conversing in a language which was never heard, upon topicks which will never arise in the commerce of mankind. But the dialogue of this authour is often so evidently determined by the incident which produces it, and is pursued with so much ease and simplicity, that it seems scarcely to claim the merit of fiction, but to have been gleaned by diligent selection out of common conversation, and common occurrences.

Upon every other stage the universal agent is love, by whose power all good and evil is distributed, and every action quickened or retarded. To bring a lover, a lady and a rival into the fable; to entangle them in contradictory obligations, perplex them with oppositions of interest, and harrass them with violence of desires inconsistent with each other; to make them meet in rapture and part in agony; to fill their mouths with hyperbolical joy and outrageous sorrow; to distress them as nothing human ever was distressed; to deliver them as nothing human ever was delivered, is the business of a modern dramatist. For this probability is violated, life is misrepresented, and language is depraved. But love is only one of many passions, and as it has no great influence upon the sum of life, it has little operation in the dramas of a poet, who caught his ideas from the living world, and exhibited only what he saw before him. He knew, that any other passion, as it was regular or exorbitant, was a cause of happiness or calamity.

Characters thus ample and general were not easily discriminated and preserved, yet perhaps no poet ever kept his personages more distinct from each other. I will not say with *Pope*, that every speech may be assigned to the proper speaker,[4] because many speeches there are which have nothing characteristical; but, perhaps, though some may be equally adapted to every person, it will be difficult to find any that can be properly transferred from the present possessor to another claimant. The choice is right, when there is reason for choice.

Other dramatists can only gain attention by hyperbolical or aggravated characters, by fabulous and unexampled excellence or depravity, as the writers of barbarous romances invigorated the reader by a giant and a dwarf; and he that should form his expectations of human affairs from the play, or from the tale, would be equally deceived. *Shakespeare* has no heroes; his scenes are occupied only by men, who act and speak as the reader thinks that he should himself have spoken or acted on the same occasion: Even where the agency is supernatural the dialogue is level with life. Other writers disguise the most natural passions and most frequent incidents; so that he who contemplates them in the book will not know them in the world: *Shakespeare* approximates the remote, and familiarizes the wonderful; the event which he represents will not happen, but if it were possible, its effects would be probably such as he has assigned; and it may be said, that he has not only shewn human nature as it acts in real exigences, but as it would be found in trials, to which it cannot be exposed.

This therefore is the praise of *Shakespeare*, that his drama is the mirrour of life; that he who has mazed his imagination, in following the phantoms which other writers raise up before him, may here be cured of his delirious extasies, by reading human sentiments in human language; by scenes from which a hermit may estimate the transactions of the world, and a confessor predict the progress of the passions.

His adherence to general nature has exposed him to the censure of criticks, who form their judgments upon narrower principles. *Dennis* and *Rhymer* think his *Romans* not sufficiently Roman;[5] and *Voltaire* censures his kings as not completely royal. *Dennis* is offended, that *Menenius*, a senator of *Rome*, should play the buffoon; and *Voltaire* perhaps thinks decency violated when the *Danish* Usurper is represented as a drunkard.[6] But *Shake-*

4. ***Pope* . . . speaker:** See Alexander Pope's *Preface to Shakespeare* (1725).

5. ***Dennis* . . . Roman:** See John Dennis (1657–1734) in his *Essay on the Genius and Writings of Shakespeare* (1712), ed. Hooker (1943), II, 5; and Thomas Rymer (1641–1713), *A Short View of Tragedy* (1692), ed. Zimansky (1956), pp. 164–169. Dennis and Rymer typified for Johnson the kind of narrow, rule-mongering criticism that he deplored. **6. drunkard:** Voltaire (François Marie Arouet) (1694–1778), the great French Enlightenment thinker and critic, consistently berated Shakespeare for violations of classical rules of art.

speare always makes nature predominate over accident; and if he preserves the essential character, is not very careful of distinctions superinduced and adventitious. His story requires Romans or kings, but he thinks only on men. He knew that *Rome,* like every other city, had men of all dispositions; and wanting a buffoon, he went into the senate-house for that which the senate-house would certainly have afforded him. He was inclined to shew an usurper and a murderer not only odious but despicable, he therefore added drunkenness to his other qualities, knowing that kings love wine like other men, and that wine exerts its natural power upon kings. These are the petty cavils of petty minds; a poet overlooks the casual distinction of country and condition, as a painter, satisfied with the figure, neglects the drapery.

The censure which he has incurred by mixing comick and tragick scenes, as it extends to all his works, deserves more consideration. Let the fact be first stated, and then examined.

Shakespeare's plays are not in the rigorous and critical sense either tragedies or comedies, but compositions of a distinct kind; exhibiting the real state of sublunary nature, which partakes of good and evil, joy and sorrow, mingled with endless variety of proportion and innumerable modes of combination; and expressing the course of the world, in which the loss of one is the gain of another; in which, at the same time, the reveller is hasting to his wine, and the mourner burying his friend; in which the malignity of one is sometimes defeated by the frolick of another; and many mischiefs and many benefits are done and hindered without design.

Out of this chaos of mingled purposes and casualties the ancient poets, according to the laws which custom had prescribed, selected some the crimes of men, and some their absurdities; some the momentous vicissitudes of life, and some the lighter occurrences; some the terrours of distress, and some the gayeties of prosperity. Thus rose the two modes of imitation, known by the names of *tragedy* and *comedy,* compositions intended to promote different ends by contrary means, and considered as so little allied, that I do not recollect among the *Greeks* or *Romans* a single writer who attempted both.

Shakespeare has united the powers of exciting laughter and sorrow not only in one mind, but in one composition. Almost all his plays are divided between serious and ludicrous characters, and, in the successive evolutions of the design, sometimes produce seriousness and sorrow, and sometimes levity and laughter.

That this is a practice contrary to the rules of criticism will be readily allowed; but there is always an appeal open from criticism to nature. The end of writing is to instruct; the end of poetry is to instruct by pleasing. That the mingled drama may convey all the instruction of tragedy or comedy cannot be denied, because it includes both in its alterations of exhibition, and approaches nearer than either to the appearance of life, by shewing how great machinations and slender designs may promote or obviate one another, and the high and the low co-operate in the general system by unavoidable concatenation.

It is objected, that by this change of scenes the passions are interrupted in their progression, and that the principal event, being not advanced by a due gradation of preparatory incidents, wants at last the power to move, which constitutes the perfection of dramatick poetry. This reasoning is so specious, that it is received as true even by those who in daily experience feel it to be false. The interchanges of mingled scenes seldom fail to produce the intended vicissitudes of passion. Fiction cannot move so much, but that the attention may be easily transferred; and though it must be allowed that pleasing melancholy be sometimes interrupted by unwelcome levity, yet let it be considered likewise, that melancholy is often not pleasing, and that the disturbance of one man may be the relief of another; that different auditors have different habitudes; and that, upon the whole, all pleasure consists in variety.

The players, who in their edition[7] divided our authour's works into comedies, histories, and tragedies, seem not to have distinguished the three kinds, by any very exact or definite ideas.

An action which ended happily to the principal persons, however serious or distressful through its intermediate incidents, in their opinion constituted a comedy. This idea of a comedy continued long amongst us, and plays were written, which, by

7. The reference here is to John Heming and Henry Condell, fellow-members of Shakespeare's acting company, who edited the first folio in 1623.

changing the catastrophe, were tragedies to-day and comedies to-morrow.

Tragedy was not in those times a poem of more general dignity or elevation than comedy; it required only a calamitous conclusion, with which the common criticism of that age was satisfied, whatever lighter pleasure it afforded in its progress.

History was a series of actions, with no other than chronological succession, independent of each other, and without any tendency to introduce or regulate the conclusion. It is not always very nicely distinguished from tragedy. There is not much nearer approach to unity of action in the tragedy of *Antony and Cleopatra,* than in the history of *Richard the Second.* But a history might be continued through many plays; as it had no plan, it had no limits.

Through all these denominations of the drama, *Shakespeare*'s mode of composition is the same; an interchange of seriousness and merriment, by which the mind is softened at one time, and exhilarated at another. But whatever be his purpose, whether to gladden or depress, or to conduct the story, without vehemence or emotion, through tracts of easy and familiar dialogue, he never fails to attain his purpose; as he commands us, we laugh or mourn, or sit silent with quiet expectation, in tranquillity without indifference.

When *Shakespeare*'s plan is understood, most of the criticisms of *Rhymer* and *Voltaire* vanish away. The play of *Hamlet* is opened, without impropriety, by two sentinels; *Iago* bellows at *Brabantio*'s window, without injury to the scheme of the play, though in terms which a modern audience would not easily endure; the character of *Polonius* is seasonable and useful; and the Grave-diggers themselves may be heard with applause.

Shakespeare engaged in dramatick poetry with the world open before him; the rules of the ancients were yet known to few; the publick judgment was unformed; he had no example of such fame as might force him upon imitation, nor criticks of such authority as might restrain his extravagance: He therefore indulged his natural disposition, and his disposition, as *Rhymer* has remarked, led him to comedy. In tragedy he often writes with great appearance of toil and study, what is written at last with little felicity; but in his comick scenes, he seems to produce without labour, what no labour can improve. In tragedy he is always struggling after some occasion to be comick, but in comedy he seems to repose, or to luxuriate, as in a mode of thinking congenial to his nature. In his tragick scenes there is always something wanting, but his comedy often surpasses expectation or desire. His comedy pleases by the thoughts and the language, and his tragedy for the greater part by incident and action. His tragedy seems to be skill, his comedy to be instinct.

The force of his comick scenes has suffered little diminution from the changes made by a century and a half, in manners or in words. As his personages act upon principles arising from genuine passion, very little modified by particular forms, their pleasures and vexations are communicable to all times and to all places; they are natural, and therefore durable; the adventitious peculiarities of personal habits, are only superficial dies, bright and pleasing for a little while, yet soon fading to a dim tinct, without any remains of former lustre; but the discriminations of true passion are the colours of nature; they pervade the whole mass, and can only perish with the body that exhibits them. The accidental compositions of heterogeneous modes are dissolved by the chance which combined them; but the uniform simplicity of primitive qualities neither admits increase, nor suffers decay. The sand heaped by one flood is scattered by another, but the rock always continues in its place. The stream of time, which is continually washing the dissoluble fabricks of other poets, passes without injury by the adamant[8] of *Shakespeare.*

If there be, what I believe there is, in every nation, a stile which never becomes obsolete, a certain mode of phraseology so consonant and congenial to the analogy and principles of its respective language as to remain settled and unaltered; this stile is probably to be sought in the common intercourse of life, among those who speak only to be understood, without ambition of elegance. The polite are always catching modish innovations, and the learned depart from established forms of speech, in hope of finding or making better; those who wish for distinction forsake the vulgar, when the vulgar is right; but there is a conversation above grossness and below refinement, where propriety resides, and where this poet seems to have gathered his comick dialogue. He is therefore more

8. **adamant:** stone believed to be impenetrable.

agreeable to the ears of the present age than any other authour equally remote, and among his other excellencies deserves to be studied as one of the original masters of our language.

These observations are to be considered not as unexceptionably constant, but as containing general and predominant truth. *Shakespeare*'s familiar dialogue is affirmed to be smooth and clear, yet not wholly without ruggedness or difficulty; as a country may be eminently fruitful, though it has spots unfit for cultivation: His characters are praised as natural, though their sentiments are sometimes forced, and their actions improbable; as the earth upon the whole is spherical, though its surface is varied with protuberances and cavities.

Shakespeare with his excellencies has likewise faults, and faults sufficient to obscure and overwhelm any other merit. I shall shew them in the proportion in which they appear to me, without envious malignity or superstitious veneration. No question can be more innocently discussed than a dead poet's pretensions to renown; and little regard is due to that bigotry which sets candour higher than truth.

His first defect is that to which may be imputed most of the evil in books or in men. He sacrifices virtue to convenience, and is so much more careful to please than to instruct, that he seems to write without any moral purpose. From his writings indeed a system of social duty may be selected, for he that thinks reasonably must think morally; but his precepts and axioms drop casually from him; he makes no just distribution of good or evil, nor is always careful to shew in the virtuous a disapprobation of the wicked; he carries his persons indifferently through right and wrong, and at the close dismisses them without further care, and leaves their examples to operate by chance. This fault the barbarity of his age cannot extenuate; for it is always a writer's duty to make the world better, and justice is a virtue independant on time or place.

The plots are often so loosely formed, that a very slight consideration may improve them, and so carelessly pursued, that he seems not always fully to comprehend his own design. He omits opportunities of instructing or delighting which the train of his story seems to force upon him, and apparently rejects those exhibitions which would be more affecting, for the sake of those which are more easy.

It may be observed, that in many of his plays the latter part is evidently neglected. When he found himself near the end of his work, and, in view of his reward, he shortened the labour, to snatch the profit. He therefore remits his efforts where he should most vigorously exert them, and his catastrophe is improbably produced or imperfectly represented.

He had no regard to distinction of time or place, but gives to one age or nation, without scruple, the customs, institutions, and opinions of another, at the expence not only of likelihood, but of possibility. These faults *Pope* has endeavoured, with more zeal than judgment, to transfer to his imagined interpolators. We need not wonder to find *Hector* quoting *Aristotle*, when we see the loves of *Theseus* and *Hippolyta* combined with the *Gothick* mythology of fairies. *Shakespeare*, indeed, was not the only violator of chronology, for in the same age *Sidney*, who wanted not the advantages of learning, has, in his *Arcadia*, confounded the pastoral with the feudal times, the days of innocence, quiet and security, with those of turbulence, violence and adventure.

In his comick scenes he is seldom very successful, when he engages his characters in reciprocations of smartness and contests of sarcasm; their jests are commonly gross, and their pleasantry licentious; neither his gentlemen nor his ladies have much delicacy, nor are sufficiently distinguished from his clowns by any appearance of refined manners. Whether he represented the real conversation of his time is not easy to determine; the reign of *Elizabeth* is commonly supposed to have been a time of stateliness, formality and reserve, yet perhaps the relaxations of that severity were not very elegant. There must, however, have been always some modes of gayety preferable to others, and a writer ought to chuse the best.

In tragedy his performance seems constantly to be worse, as his labour is more. The effusions of passion which exigence forces out are for the most part striking and energetick; but whenever he solicits his invention, or strains his faculties, the offspring of his throes is tumour, meanness, tediousness, and obscurity.

In narration he affects a disproportionate pomp of diction and a wearisome train of circumlocution, and tells the incident imperfectly in many words, which might have been more plainly delivered in few. Narration in dramatick poetry is naturally tedious, as it is unanimated and inactive, and obstructs the progress of the action; it should therefore always be rapid, and enlivened by frequent interruption. *Shakespeare* found it an encumbrance, and instead of lightening it by brevity, endeavoured to recommend it by dignity and splendour.

His declamations or set speeches are commonly cold and weak, for his power was the power of nature; when he endeavoured, like other tragick writers, to catch opportunities of amplification, and instead of inquiring what the occasion demanded, to show how much his stores of knowledge could supply, he seldom escapes without the pity or resentment of his reader.

It is incident to him to be now and then entangled with an unwieldy sentiment, which he cannot well express, and will not reject; he struggles with it a while, and if it continues stubborn, comprises it in words such as occur, and leaves it to be disentangled and evolved by those who have more leisure to bestow upon it.

Not that always where the language is intricate the thought is subtle, or the image always great where the line is bulky; the equality of words to things is very often neglected, and trivial sentiments and vulgar ideas disappoint the attention, to which they are recommended by sonorous epithets and swelling figures.

But the admirers of this great poet have most reason to complain when he approaches nearest to his highest excellence, and seems fully resolved to sink them in dejection, and mollify them with tender emotions by the fall of greatness, the danger of innocence, or the crosses of love. He is not long soft and pathetick without some idle conceit, or contemptible equivocation. He no sooner begins to move, than he counteracts himself; and terrour and pity, as they are rising in the mind, are checked and blasted by sudden frigidity.

A quibble is to *Shakespeare,* what luminous vapours are to the traveller; he follows it at all adventures, it is sure to lead him out of his way, and sure to engulf him in the mire. It has some malignant power over his mind, and its fascinations are irresistible. Whatever be the dignity or profundity of his disquisition, whether he be enlarging knowledge or exalting affection, whether he be amusing attention with incidents, or enchaining it in suspense, let but a quibble spring up before him, and he leaves his work unfinished. A quibble is the golden apple for which he will always turn aside from his career, or stoop from his elevation. A quibble poor and barren as it is, gave him such delight, that he was content to purchase it, by the sacrifice of reason, propriety and truth. A quibble was to him the fatal *Cleopatra* for which he lost the world, and was content to lose it.

It will be thought strange, that, in enumerating the defects of this writer, I have not yet mentioned his neglect of the unities; his violation of those laws which have been instituted and established by the joint authority of poets and of criticks.

For his other deviations from the art of writing, I resign him to critical justice, without making any other demand in his favour, than that which must be indulged to all human excellence; that his virtues be rated with his failings: But, from the censure which this irregularity may bring upon him, I shall, with due reverence to that learning which I must oppose, adventure to try how I can defend him.

His histories, being neither tragedies nor comedies, are not subject to any of their laws; nothing more is necessary to all the praise which they expect, than that the changes of action be so prepared as to be understood, that the incidents be various and affecting, and the characters consistent, natural and distinct. No other unity is intended, and therefore none is to be sought.

In his other works he has well enough preserved the unity of action. He has not, indeed, an intrigue regularly perplexed and regularly unravelled; he does not endeavour to hide his design only to discover it, for this is seldom the order of real events, and *Shakespeare* is the poet of nature: But his plan has commonly what *Aristotle* requires, a beginning, a middle, and an end; one event is concatenated[9] with another, and the conclusion follows by easy consequence. There are perhaps some incidents that might be spared, as in other poets there is much talk that only fills up time upon the stage; but the general system makes gradual advances, and the end of the play is the end of expectation.

To the unities of time and place he has shewn no regard, and perhaps a nearer view of the principles on which they stand will diminish their

9. concatenated: blended.

value, and withdraw from them the veneration which, from the time of *Corneille,*[10] they have very generally received by discovering that they have given more trouble to the poet, than pleasure to the auditor.

The necessity of observing the unities of time and place arises from the supposed necessity of making the drama credible. The criticks hold it impossible, that an action of months or years can be possibly believed to pass in three hours; or that the spectator can suppose himself to sit in the theatre, while ambassadors go and return between distant kings, while armies are levied and towns besieged, while an exile wanders and returns, or till he whom they saw courting his mistress, shall lament the untimely fall of his son. The mind revolts from evident falsehood, and fiction loses its force when it departs from the resemblance of reality.

From the narrow limitation of time necessarily arises the contraction of place. The spectator, who knows that he saw the first act at *Alexandria*, cannot suppose that he sees the next at *Rome*, at a distance to which not the dragons of *Medea* could, in so short a time, have transported him; he knows with certainty that he has not changed his place; and he knows that place cannot change itself; that what was a house cannot become a plain; that what was *Thebes* can never be *Persepolis*.

Such is the triumphant language with which a critick exults over the misery of an irregular poet, and exults commonly without resistance or reply. It is time therefore to tell him, by the authority of *Shakespeare*, that he assumes, as an unquestionable principle, a position, which, while his breath is forming it into words, his understanding pronounces to be false. It is false, that any representation is mistaken for reality; that any dramatick fable in its materiality was ever credible, or, for a single moment, was ever credited.

The objection arising from the impossibility of passing the first hour at *Alexandria*, and the next at *Rome*, supposes, that when the play opens the spectator really imagines himself at *Alexandria*, and believes that his walk to the theatre has been a voyage to *Egypt*, and that he lives in the days of *Antony* and *Cleopatra*. Surely he that imagines this, may imagine more. He that can take the stage at one time for the palace of the *Ptolemies*, may take it in half an hour for the promontory of *Actium*. Delusion, if delusion be admitted, has no certain limitation; if the spectator can be once persuaded, that his old acquaintance are *Alexander* and *Cæsar*, that a room illuminated with candles is the plain of *Pharsalia*, or the bank of *Granicus*, he is in a state of elevation above the reach of reason, or of truth, and from the heights of empyrean poetry, may despise the circumscriptions of terrestrial nature. There is no reason why a mind thus wandering in extasy should count the clock, or why an hour should not be a century in that calenture[11] of the brains that can make the stage a field.

The truth is, that the spectators are always in their senses, and know, from the first act to the last, that the stage is only a stage, and that the players are only players. They come to hear a certain number of lines recited with just gesture and elegant modulation. The lines relate to some action, and an action must be in some place; but the different actions that compleat a story may be in places very remote from each other; and where is the absurdity of allowing that space to represent first *Athens*, and then *Sicily*, which was always known to be neither *Sicily* nor *Athens*, but a modern theatre?

By supposition, as place is introduced, time may be extended; the time required by the fable elapses for the most part between the acts; for, of so much of the action as is represented, the real and poetical duration is the same. If, in the first act, preparations for war against *Mithridates* are represented to be made in *Rome*, the event of the war may, without absurdity, be represented, in the catastrophe, as happening in *Pontus*; we know that there is neither war, nor preparation for war; we know that we are neither in *Rome* nor *Pontus*; that neither *Mithridates* nor *Lucullus* are before us. The drama exhibits successive imitations of successive actions, and why may not the second imitation represent an action that happened years after the first; if it be so connected with it, that nothing but time can be supposed to intervene? Time is, of all modes of existence, most obsequious

10. *Corneille:* Pierre Corneille (1606–1684), celebrated French dramatist and critic, who urged strict following of the unities of time, place, and action.

11. calenture: fever, passion.

to the imagination; a lapse of years is as easily conceived as a passage of hours. In contemplation we easily contract the time of real actions, and therefore willingly permit it to be contracted when we only see their imitation.

It will be asked, how the drama moves, if it is not credited. It is credited with all the credit due to a drama. It is credited, whenever it moves, as a just picture of a real original; as representing to the auditor what he would himself feel, if he were to do or suffer what is there feigned to be suffered or to be done. The reflection that strikes the heart is not, that the evils before us are real evils, but that they are evils to which we ourselves may be exposed. If there be any fallacy, it is not that we fancy the players, but that we fancy ourselves unhappy for a moment; but we rather lament the possibility than suppose the presence of misery, as a mother weeps over her babe, when she remembers that death may take it from her. The delight of tragedy proceeds from our consciousness of fiction; if we thought murders and treasons real, they would please no more.

Imitations produce pain or pleasure, not because they are mistaken for realities, but because they bring realities to mind. When the imagination is recreated by a painted landscape, the trees are not supposed capable to give us shade, or the fountains coolness; but we consider, how we should be pleased with such fountains playing beside us, and such woods waving over us. We are agitated in reading the history of *Henry* the Fifth, yet no man takes his book for the field of *Agencourt*. A dramatick exhibition is a book recited with concomitants that encrease or diminish its effect. Familiar comedy is often more powerful in the theatre, than on the page; imperial tragedy is always less. The humour of *Petruchio* may be heightened by grimace; but what voice or what gesture can hope to add dignity or force to the soliloquy of *Cato*.[12]

A play read, affects the mind like a play acted. It is therefore evident, that the action is not supposed to be real, and it follows that between the acts a longer or shorter time may be allowed to pass, and that no more account of space or duration is to be taken by the auditor of a drama, than by the reader of a narrative, before whom may pass in an hour the life of a hero, or the revolutions of an empire.

Whether *Shakespeare* knew the unities, and rejected them by design, or deviated from them by happy ignorance, it is, I think, impossible to decide, and useless to inquire. We may reasonably suppose, that, when he rose to notice, he did not want the counsels and admonitions of scholars and criticks, and that he at last deliberately persisted in a practice, which he might have begun by chance. As nothing is essential to the fable, but unity of action, and as the unities of time and place arise evidently from false assumptions, and, by circumscribing the extent of the drama, lessen its variety, I cannot think it much to be lamented, that they were not known by him, or not observed: Nor, if such another poet could arise, should I very vehemently reproach him, that his first act passed at *Venice*, and his next in *Cyprus*. Such violations of rules merely positive, become the comprehensive genius of *Shakespeare*, and such censures are suitable to the minute and slender criticism of *Voltaire*:

Non usque adeo permiscuit imis
Longus summa dies, ut non, si voce Metelli
Serventur leges, malint a Cæsare tolli.[13]

Yet when I speak thus slightly of dramatick rules, I cannot but recollect how much wit and learning may be produced against me; before such authorities I am afraid to stand, not that I think the present question one of those that are to be decided by mere authority, but because it is to be suspected, that these precepts have not been so easily received but for better reasons than I have yet been able to find. The result of my enquiries, in which it would be ludicrous to boast of impartiality, is, that the unities of time and place are not essential to a just drama, that though they may sometimes conduce to pleasure, they are always to be sacrificed to the nobler beauties of variety and instruction; and that a play, written with nice observation of critical rules, is to be contemplated as an elaborate curiosity, as the product of super-

12. ***Cato:*** see Joseph Addison's drama *Cato,* V, i.

13. ***Non . . . tolli:*** from Lucan's *Pharsalia,* III, 138–140. J. D. Duff translates the lines as follows: "The course of time has not wrought such confusion that the laws would not rather be trampled on by Caesar than saved by Metellus."

fluous and ostentatious art, by which is shewn, rather what is possible, than what is necessary.

He that, without diminution of any other excellence, shall preserve all the unities unbroken, deserves the like applause with the architect, who shall display all the orders of architecture in a citadel, without any deduction from its strength; but the principal beauty of a citadel is to exclude the enemy; and the greatest graces of a play, are to copy nature and instruct life.

Perhaps, what I have here not dogmatically but deliberately written, may recal the principles of the drama to a new examination. I am almost frighted at my own temerity; and when I estimate the fame and the strength of those that maintain the contrary opinion, am ready to sink down in reverential silence; as *Æneas* withdrew from the defence of *Troy,* when he saw *Neptune* shaking the wall, and *Juno* heading the besiegers.[14]

Those whom my arguments cannot persuade to give their approbation to the judgment of *Shakespeare,* will easily, if they consider the condition of his life, make some allowance for his ignorance.

Every man's performances, to be rightly estimated, must be compared with the state of the age in which he lived, and with his own particular opportunities; and though to the reader a book be not worse or better for the circumstances of the authour, yet as there is always a silent reference of human works to human abilities, and as the enquiry, how far man may extend his designs, or how high he may rate his native force, is of far greater dignity than in what rank we shall place any particular performance, curiosity is always busy to discover the instruments, as well as to survey the workmanship, to know how much is to be ascribed to original powers, and how much to casual and adventitious help. The palaces of *Peru* or *Mexico* were certainly mean and incommodious habitations, if compared to the houses of *European* monarchs; yet who could forbear to view them with astonishment, who remembered that they were built without the use of iron?

The *English* nation, in the time of *Shakespeare,* was yet struggling to emerge from barbarity. The philology of *Italy* had been transplanted hither in the reign of *Henry* the Eighth; and the learned languages had been successfully cultivated by *Lilly,*[15] *Linacer,*[16] and *More;*[17] by *Pole,*[18] *Cheke,*[19] and *Gardiner;*[20] and afterwards by *Smith,*[21] *Clerk,*[22] *Haddon,*[23] and *Ascham.*[24] Greek was now taught to boys in the principal schools; and those who united elegance with learning, read, with great diligence, the *Italian* and *Spanish* poets. But literature was yet confined to professed scholars, or to men and women of high rank. The publick was gross and dark; and to be able to read and write, was an accomplishment still valued for its rarity.

Nations, like individuals, have their infancy. A people newly awakened to literary curiosity, being yet unacquainted with the true state of things, knows not how to judge of that which is proposed as its resemblance. Whatever is remote from common appearances is always welcome to vulgar, as to childish credulity; and of a country unenlightened by learning, the whole people is the vulgar. The study of those who then aspired to plebeian learning was laid out upon adventures, giants, dragons, and enchantments. *The Death of Arthur* was the favourite volume.

The mind, which has feasted on the luxurious wonders of fiction, has no taste of the insipidity of truth. A play which imitated only the common occurrences of the world, would, upon the admirers of *Palmerin* and *Guy* of *Warwick,* have made little impression; he that wrote for such an audience was under the necessity of looking round for strange events and fabulous transactions, and that incredibility, by which maturer knowledge is of-

14. *Aeneid,* II, 610–615.

15. ***Lilly:*** William Lily (1468?–1522), first master of St. Paul's School and author of a famous Latin grammar. **16. *Linacer:*** Thomas Linacre (1460?–1524), physician and classical scholar, teacher at Oxford, author of a Latin grammar. **17. *More:*** Sir Thomas More (1478–1535) succeeded Wolsey as Lord Chancellor in 1529, was later indicted for treason, convicted, and beheaded in 1535. More was a classical scholar, author and translator of Latin works. **18. *Pole:*** Reginald Pole (1500–1558), also a scholar-statesman who became Chancellor of Cambridge. **19. *Cheke:*** Sir John Cheke (1514–1557), classical scholar, Professor of Greek at Cambridge. **20. *Gardiner:*** Stephen Gardiner (1483?–1555), statesman and scholar, was a Chancellor of Cambridge University. **21. *Smith:*** Sir Thomas Smith (1513–1577), still another scholar-statesman, was Vice-Chancellor at Cambridge. **22. *Clerk:*** John Clerk (d. 1541) was chaplain to Cardinal Wolsey and Bishop of Bath and Wells. **23. *Haddon:*** Walter Haddon (1516–1572), Vice-Chancellor of Cambridge. **24. *Ascham:*** Roger Ascham (1515–1568), classical scholar, author of the famous *Scholemaster* on the education of boys.

fended, was the chief recommendation of writings, to unskilful curiosity.

Our authour's plots are generally borrowed from novels, and it is reasonable to suppose, that he chose the most popular, such as were read by many, and related by more; for his audience could not have followed him through the intricacies of the drama, had they not held the thread of the story in their hands.

The stories, which we now find only in remoter authours, were in his time accessible and familiar. The fable of *As you like it,* which is supposed to be copied from *Chaucer*'s Gamelyn, was a little pamphlet of those times,[25] and old Mr. *Cibber*[26] remembered the tale of *Hamlet* in plain *English* prose, which the criticks have now to seek in *Saxo Grammaticus*.[27]

His *English* histories he took from *English* chronicles and *English* ballads; and as the ancient writers were made known to his countrymen by versions, they supplied him with new subjects; he dilated some of *Plutarch*'s lives into plays, when they had been translated by *North*.[28]

His plots, whether historical or fabulous, are always crouded with incidents, by which the attention of a rude people was more easily caught than by sentiment or argumentation; and such is the power of the marvellous even over those who despise it, that every man finds his mind more strongly seized by the tragedies of *Shakespeare* than of any other writer; others please us by particular speeches, but he always makes us anxious for the event, and has perhaps excelled all but *Homer* in securing the first purpose of a writer, by exciting restless and unquenchable curiosity, and compelling him that reads his work to read it through.

The shows and bustle with which his plays abound have the same original. As knowledge advances, pleasure passes from the eye to the ear, but returns, as it declines, from the ear to the eye. Those to whom our authour's labours were exhibited had more skill in pomps or processions than in poetical language, and perhaps wanted some visible and discriminated events, as comments on the dialogue. He knew how he should most please; and whether his practice is more agreeable to nature, or whether his example has prejudiced the nation, we still find that on our stage something must be done as well as said, and inactive declamation is very coldly heard, however musical or elegant, passionate or sublime.

Voltaire expresses his wonder, that our authour's extravagancies are endured by a nation, which has seen the tragedy of *Cato*. Let him be answered, that *Addison* speaks the language of poets, and *Shakespeare,* of men. We find in *Cato* innumerable beauties which enamour us of its authour, but we see nothing that acquaints us with human sentiments or human actions; we place it with the fairest and the noblest progeny which judgment propagates by conjunction with learning, but *Othello* is the vigorous and vivacious offspring of observation impregnated by genius. *Cato* affords a splendid exhibition of artificial and fictitious manners, and delivers just and noble sentiments, in diction easy, elevated and harmonious, but its hopes and fears communicate no vibration to the heart; the composition refers us only to the writer; we pronounce the name of *Cato,* but we think on *Addison.*

The work of a correct and regular writer is a garden accurately formed and diligently planted, varied with shades, and scented with flowers; the composition of *Shakespeare* is a forest, in which oaks extend their branches, and pines tower in the air, interspersed sometimes with weeds and brambles, and sometimes giving shelter to myrtles and to roses; filling the eye with awful pomp, and gratifying the mind with endless diversity. Other poets display cabinets of precious rarities, minutely finished, wrought into shape, and polished unto brightness. *Shakespeare* opens a mine which contains gold and diamonds in unexhaustible plenty, though clouded by incrustations, debased by impurities, and mingled with a mass of meaner minerals.

It has been much disputed, whether *Shakespeare* owed his excellence to his own native force, or whether he had the common helps of scholastick education, the precepts of critical science, and the examples of ancient authours.

25. Chaucer was not the author of the famous tale of Gamelyn, which was the source of Thomas Lodge's *Rosalynde,* which in turn was the source of Shakespeare's *As You Like It.* **26.** ***Cibber:*** Colley Cibber. See earlier notes in the selections from Pope. **27.** The *Historia Danica* of Saxo Grammaticus was a major source of *Hamlet.* **28.** ***North:*** Sir Thomas North (1535?–1601?), translator of Plutarch's *Parallel Lives.*

There has always prevailed a tradition, that *Shakespeare* wanted learning, that he had no regular education, nor much skill in the dead languages. *Jonson,*[29] his friend, affirms, that *he had small Latin, and no Greek;* who, besides that he had no imaginable temptation to falsehood, wrote at a time when the character and acquisitions of *Shakespeare* were known to multitudes. His evidence ought therefore to decide the controversy, unless some testimony of equal force could be opposed.

Some have imagined, that they have discovered deep learning in many imitations of old writers; but the examples which I have known urged, were drawn from books translated in his time; or were such easy coincidencies of thought, as will happen to all who consider the same subjects; or such remarks on life or axioms of morality as float in conversation, and are transmitted through the world in proverbial sentences.

I have found it remarked, that, in this important sentence, *Go before, I'll follow,* we read a translation of, *I prae, sequar.* I have been told, that when *Caliban,* after a pleasing dream, says, *I cry'd to sleep again,* the authour imitates *Anacreon,*[30] who had, like every other man, the same wish on the same occasion.

There are a few passages which may pass for imitations, but so few, that the exception only confirms the rule; he obtained them from accidental quotations, or by oral communication, and as he used what he had, would have used more if he had obtained it.

The *Comedy of Errors* is confessedly taken from the *Menæchmi* of *Plautus*; from the only play of *Plautus* which was then in *English*. What can be more probable, than that he who copied that, would have copied more; but that those which were not translated were inaccessible?

Whether he knew the modern languages is uncertain. That his plays have some *French* scenes proves but little; he might easily procure them to be written, and probably, even though he had known the language in the common degree, he could not have written it without assistance. In the story of *Romeo* and *Juliet* he is observed to have followed the *English* translation, where it deviates from the *Italian;* but this on the other part proves nothing against his knowledge of the original. He was to copy, not what he knew himself, but what was known to his audience.

It is most likely that he had learned *Latin* sufficiently to make him acquainted with construction, but that he never advanced to an easy perusal of the *Roman* authours. Concerning his skill in modern languages, I can find no sufficient ground of determination; but as no imitations of *French* or *Italian* authours have been discovered, though the *Italian* poetry was then high in esteem, I am inclined to believe, that he read little more than *English,* and chose for his fables only such tales as he found translated.

That much knowledge is scattered over his works is very justly observed by *Pope,* but it is often such knowledge as books did not supply. He that will understand *Shakespeare,* must not be content to study him in the closet, he must look for his meaning sometimes among the sports of the field, and sometimes among the manufactures of the shop.

There is however proof enough that he was a very diligent reader, nor was our language then so indigent of books, but that he might very liberally indulge his curiosity without excursion into foreign literature. Many of the *Roman* authours were translated, and some of the *Greek;* the reformation had filled the kingdom with theological learning; most of the topicks of human disquisition had found *English* writers; and poetry had been cultivated, not only with diligence, but success. This was a stock of knowledge sufficient for a mind so capable of appropriating and improving it.

But the greater part of his excellence was the product of his own genius. He found the *English* stage in a state of the utmost rudeness; no essays either in tragedy or comedy had appeared, from which it could be discovered to what degree of delight either one or other might be carried. Neither character nor dialogue were yet understood. *Shakespeare* may be truly said to have introduced them both amongst us, and in some of his happier scenes to have carried them both to the utmost height.

By what gradations of improvement he proceeded, is not easily known; for the chronology of his works is yet unsettled. *Rowe* is of opinion, that

29. ***Jonson:*** Ben Jonson is responsible for this oft-quoted remark made in his verses on Shakespeare in the *First Folio.* 30. ***Anacreon:*** a famous lyric poet of the sixth century B.C.

perhaps we are not to look for his beginning, like those of other writers, in his least perfect works; art had so little, and nature so large a share in what he did, that for ought I know, says he, *the performances of his youth, as they were the most vigorous, were the best.*[31] But the power of nature is only the power of using to any certain purpose the materials which diligence procures, or opportunity supplies. Nature gives no man knowledge, and when images are collected by study and experience, can only assist in combining or applying them. *Shakespeare,* however favoured by nature, could impart only what he had learned; and as he must increase his ideas, like other mortals, by gradual acquisition, he, like them, grew wiser as he grew older, could display life better, as he knew it more, and instruct with more efficacy, as he was himself more amply instructed.

There is a vigilance of observation and accuracy of distinction which books and precepts cannot confer; from this almost all original and native excellence proceeds. *Shakespeare* must have looked upon mankind with perspicacity, in the highest degree curious and attentive. Other writers borrow their characters from preceding writers, and diversify them only by the accidental appendages of present manners; the dress is a little varied, but the body is the same. Our authour had both matter and form to provide; for except the characters of *Chaucer,* to whom I think he is not much indebted, there were no writers in *English,* and perhaps not many in other modern languages, which shewed life in its native colours.

The contest about the original benevolence or malignity of man had not yet commenced. Speculation had not yet attempted to analyse the mind, to trace the passions to their sources, to unfold the seminal principles of vice and virtue, or sound the depths of the heart for the motives of action. All those enquiries, which from that time that human nature became the fashionable study, have been made sometimes with nice discernment, but often with idle subtilty, were yet unattempted. The tales, with which the infancy of learning was satisfied, exhibited only the superficial appearances of action, related the events but omitted the causes, and were formed for such as delighted in wonders rather than in truth. Mankind was not then to be studied in the closet; he that would know the world, was under the necessity of gleaning his own remarks, by mingling as he could in its business and amusements.

Boyle[32] congratulated himself upon his high birth, because it favoured his curiosity, by facilitating his access. *Shakespeare* had no such advantage; he came to *London* a needy adventurer, and lived for a time by very mean employments. Many works of genius and learning have been performed in states of life, that appear very little favourable to thought or to enquiry; so many, that he who considers them is inclined to think that he sees enterprise and perseverance predominating over all external agency, and bidding help and hindrance vanish before them. The genius of *Shakespeare* was not to be depressed by the weight of poverty, nor limited by the narrow conversation to which men in want are inevitably condemned; the incumbrances of his fortune were shaken from his mind, *as dewdrops from a lion's mane.*[33]

Though he had so many difficulties to encounter, and so little assistance to surmount them, he has been able to obtain an exact knowledge of many modes of life, and many casts of native dispositions; to vary them with great multiplicity; to mark them by nice distinctions; and to shew them in full view by proper combinations. In this part of his performances he had none to imitate, but has himself been imitated by all succeeding writers; and it may be doubted, whether from all his successors more maxims of theoretical knowledge, or more rules of practical prudence, can be collected, than he alone has given to his country.

Nor was his attention confined to the actions of men; he was an exact surveyor of the inanimate world; his descriptions have always some peculiarities, gathered by contemplating things as they really exist. It may be observed, that the oldest poets of many nations preserve their reputation, and that the following generations of wit, after a short celebrity, sink into oblivion. The first, whoever they be, must take their sentiments and descriptions immediately from knowledge; the resemblance is therefore just, their descriptions are verified by every eye, and their sentiments ac-

31. Nicholas Rowe (1674–1718), Poet Laureate, dramatist, editor of Shakespeare's plays.

32. ***Boyle:*** Robert Boyle (1627–1691), English physicist and chemist. **33.** *Troilus and Cressida,* III, iii, 224.

knowledged by every breast. Those whom their fame invites to the same studies, copy partly them, and partly nature, till the books of one age gain such authority, as to stand in the place of nature to another, and imitation, always deviating a little, becomes at last capricious and casual. *Shakespeare*, whether life or nature be his subject, shews plainly, that he has seen with his own eyes; he gives the image which he receives, not weakened or distorted by the intervention of any other mind; the ignorant feel his representations to be just, and the learned see that they are compleat.

Perhaps it would not be easy to find any authour, except *Homer*, who invented so much as *Shakespeare*, who so much advanced the studies which he cultivated, or effused so much novelty upon his age or country. The form, the characters, the language, and the shows of the *English* drama are his. *He seems*, says *Dennis*, *to have been the very original of our* English *tragical harmony, that is, the harmony of blank verse, diversified often by dissyllable and trissyllable terminations. For the diversity distinguishes it from heroick harmony, and by bringing it nearer to common use makes it more proper to gain attention, and more fit for action and dialogue. Such verse we make when we are writing prose; we make such verse in common conversation.*[34]

I know not whether this praise is rigorously just. The dissyllable termination, which the critick rightly appropriates to the drama, is to be found, though, I think, not in *Gorboduc*[35] which is confessedly before our authour; yet in *Hieronnymo*,[36] of which the date is not certain, but which there is reason to believe at least as old as his earliest plays. This however is certain, that he is the first who taught either tragedy or comedy to please, there being no theatrical piece of any older writer, of which the name is known, except to antiquaries and collectors of books, which are sought because they are scarce, and would not have been scarce, had they been much esteemed.

To him we must ascribe the praise, unless *Spenser* may divide it with him, of having first discovered to how much smoothness and harmony the *English* language could be softened. He has speeches, perhaps sometimes scenes, which have all the delicacy of *Rowe*, without his effeminacy. He endeavours indeed commonly to strike by the force and vigour of his dialogue, but he never executes his purpose better, than when he tries to sooth by softness.

Yet it must be at last confessed, that as we owe every thing to him, he owes something to us; that, if much of his praise is paid by perception and judgement, much is likewise given by custom and veneration. We fix our eyes upon his graces, and turn them from his deformities, and endure in him what we should in another loath or despise. If we endured without praising, respect for the father of our drama might excuse us; but I have seen, in the book of some modern critick,[37] a collection of anomalies which shew that he has corrupted language by every mode of depravation, but which his admirer has accumulated as a monument of honour.

He has scenes of undoubted and perpetual excellence, but perhaps not one play, which, if it were now exhibited as the work of a contemporary writer, would be heard to the conclusion. I am indeed far from thinking, that his works were wrought to his own ideas of perfection; when they were such as would satisfy the audience, they satisfied the writer. It is seldom that authours, though more studious of fame than *Shakespeare*, rise much above the standard of their own age; to add a little of what is best will always be sufficient for present praise, and those who find themselves exalted into fame, are willing to credit their encomiasts, and to spare the labour of contending with themselves.

It does not appear, that *Shakespeare* thought his works worthy of posterity, that he levied any ideal tribute upon future times, or had any further prospect, than of present popularity and present profit. When his plays had been acted, his hope was at an end; he solicited no addition of honour from the reader. He therefore made no scruple to repeat the same jests in many dialogues, or to entangle different plots by the same knot of perplexity, which may be at least forgiven him, by

34. John Dennis (1657–1734), *An Essay on the Genius and Writings of Shakespeare* (1712). **35.** ***Gorboduc:*** the play by Norton and Sackville. **36.** ***Hieronnymo:*** a reference to Thomas Kyd's *The Spanish Tragedy* (1592). Hieronimo was the principal character.

37. A reference to John Upton, *Critical Observations on Shakespeare* (1746).

those who recollect, that of *Congreve*'s[38] four comedies, two are concluded by a marriage in a mask, by a deception, which perhaps never happened, and which, whether likely or not, he did not invent.

So careless was this great poet of future fame, that, though he retired to ease and plenty, while he was yet little *declined into the vale of years,*[39] before he could be disgusted with fatigue, or disabled by infirmity, he made no collection of his works, nor desired to rescue those that had been already published from the depravations that obscured them, or secure to the rest a better destiny, by giving them to the world in their genuine state.

Of the plays which bear the name of *Shakespeare* in the late editions, the greater part were not published till about seven years after his death, and the few which appeared in his life are apparently thrust into the world without the care of the authour, and therefore probably without his knowledge.

Of all the publishers, clandestine or professed, their negligence and unskilfulness has by the late revisers been sufficiently shown. The faults of all are indeed numerous and gross, and have not only corrupted many passages perhaps beyond recovery, but have brought others into suspicion, which are only obscured by obsolete phraseology, or by the writer's unskilfulness and affectation. To alter is more easy than to explain, and temerity is a more common quality than diligence. Those who saw that they must employ conjecture to a certain degree, were willing to indulge it a little further. Had the authour published his own works, we should have sat quietly down to disentangle his intricacies, and clear his obscurities; but now we tear what we cannot loose, and eject what we happen not to understand.

The faults are more than could have happened without the concurrence of many causes. The stile of *Shakespeare* was in itself ungrammatical, perplexed and obscure; his works were transcribed for the players by those who may be supposed to have seldom understood them; they were transmitted by copiers equally unskilful, who still multiplied errours; they were perhaps sometimes mutilated by the actors, for the sake of shortening the speeches; and were at last printed without correction of the press.

In this state they remained, not as Dr. *Warburton*[40] supposes, because they were unregarded, but because the editor's art was not yet applied to modern languages, and our ancestors were accustomed to so much negligence of *English* printers, that they could very patiently endure it. At last an edition was undertaken by *Rowe*; not because a poet was to be published by a poet, for *Rowe* seems to have thought very little on correction or explanation, but that our authour's works might appear like those of his fraternity, with the appendages of a life and recommendatory preface. *Rowe* has been clamorously blamed for not performing what he did not undertake, and it is time that justice be done him, by confessing, that though he seems to have had no thought of corruption beyond the printer's errours, yet he has made many emendations, if they were not made before, which his successors have received without acknowledgment, and which, if they had produced them, would have filled pages and pages with censures of the stupidity by which the faults were committed, with displays of the absurdities which they involved, with ostentatious expositions of the new reading, and self congratulations on the happiness of discovering it.

Of *Rowe*, as of all the editors, I have preserved the preface, and have likewise retained the authour's life, though not written with much elegance or spirit; it relates however what is now to be known, and therefore deserves to pass through all succeeding publications.

The nation had been for many years content enough with Mr. *Rowe*'s performance, when Mr. *Pope* made them acquainted with the true state of *Shakespear*[*e*]'s text, shewed that it was extremely corrupt, and gave reason to hope that there were means of reforming it. He collated the old copies, which none had thought to examine before, and restored many lines to their integrity; but, by a very compendious criticism, he rejected whatever he disliked, and thought more of amputation than of cure.

38. ***Congreve:*** William Congreve (1670–1729), famous Restoration dramatist. 39. *Othello,* III, iii, 264–265.

40. ***Warburton:*** William Warburton (1698–1779), editor of Shakespeare.

I know not why he is commended by Dr. *Warburton* for distinguishing the genuine from the spurious plays. In this choice he exerted no judgement of his own; the plays which he received, were given by *Hemings* and *Condel,* the first editors; and those which he rejected, though, according to the licentiousness of the press in those times, they were printed during *Shakespear*[*e*]'s life, with his name, had been omitted by his friends, and were never added to his works before the edition of 1664, from which they were copied by the later printers.

This was a work which *Pope* seems to have thought unworthy of his abilities, being not able to suppress his contempt of *the dull duty of an editor.* He understood but half his undertaking. The duty of a collator is indeed dull, yet, like other tedious tasks, is very necessary; but an emendatory critick would ill discharge his duty, without qualities very different from dulness. In perusing a corrupted piece, he must have before him all possibilities of meaning, with all possibilities of expression. Such must be his comprehension of thought, and such his copiousness of language. Out of many readings possible, he must be able to select that which best suits with the state, opinions, and modes of language prevailing in every age, and with his authour's particular cast of thought, and turn of expression. Such must be his knowledge, and such his taste. Conjectural criticism demands more than humanity possesses, and he that exercises it with most praise has very frequent need of indulgence. Let us now be told no more of the dull duty of an editor.

Confidence is the common consequence of success. They whose excellence of any kind has been loudly celebrated, are ready to conclude, that their powers are universal. *Pope*'s edition fell below his own expectations, and he was so much offended, when he was found to have left any thing for others to do, that he past the latter part of his life in a state of hostility with verbal criticism.

I have retained all his notes, that no fragment of so great a writer may be lost; his preface, valuable alike for elegance of composition and justness of remark, and containing a general criticism on his authour, so extensive that little can be added, and so exact, that little can be disputed, every editor has an interest to suppress, but that every reader would demand its insertion.

Pope was succeeded by *Theobald,*[41] a man of narrow comprehension and small acquisitions, with no native and intrinsick splendour of genius, with little of the artificial light of learning, but zealous for minute accuracy, and not negligent in pursuing it. He collated the ancient copies, and rectified many errors. A man so anxiously scrupulous might have been expected to do more, but what little he did was commonly right.

In his report of copies and editions he is not to be trusted, without examination. He speaks sometimes indefinitely of copies, when he has only one. In his enumeration of editions, he mentions the two first folios as of high, and the third folio as of middle authority; but the truth is, that the first is equivalent to all others, and that the rest only deviate from it by the printer's negligence. Whoever has any of the folios has all, excepting those diversities which mere reiteration of editions will produce. I collated them all at the beginning, but afterwards used only the first.

Of his notes I have generally retained those which he retained himself in his second edition, except when they were confuted by subsequent annotators, or were too minute to merit preservation. I have sometimes adopted his restoration of a comma, without inserting the panegyrick in which he celebrated himself for his achievement. The exuberant excrescence of [his] diction I have often lopped, his triumphant exultations over *Pope* and *Rowe* I have sometimes suppressed, and his contemptible ostentation I have frequently concealed; but I have in some places shewn him, as he would have shewn himself, for the reader's diversion, that the inflated emptiness of some notes may justify or excuse the contraction of the rest.

Theobald, thus weak and ignorant, thus mean and faithless, thus petulant and ostentatious, by the good luck of having *Pope* for his enemy, has escaped, and escaped alone, with reputation, from this undertaking. So willingly does the world support those who solicite favour, against those who command reverence; and so easily is he praised, whom no man can envy.

Our authour fell then into the hands of Sir *Thomas Hanmer,*[42] the *Oxford* editor, a man, in

41. ***Theobald:*** Lewis Theobald (1688–1744), editor of Shakespeare, who is generally regarded highly by scholars. 42. ***Hanmer:*** Sir Thomas Hammer.

my opinion, eminently qualified by nature for such studies. He had, what is the first requisite to emendatory criticism, that intuition by which the poet's intention is immediately discovered, and that dexterity of intellect which dispatches its work by the easiest means. He had undoubtedly read much; his acquaintance with customs, opinions, and traditions, seems to have been large; and he is often learned without shew. He seldom passes what he does not understand, without an attempt to find or to make a meaning, and sometimes hastily makes what a little more attention would have found. He is solicitous to reduce to grammar, what he could not be sure that his authour intended to be grammatical. *Shakespeare* regarded more the series of ideas, than of words; and his language, not being designed for the reader's desk, was all that he desired it to be, if it conveyed his meaning to the audience.

Hanmer's care of the metre has been too violently censured. He found the measures reformed in so many passages, by the silent labours of some editors, with the silent acquiescence of the rest, that he thought himself allowed to extend a little further the license, which had already been carried so far without reprehension; and of his corrections in general, it must be confessed, that they are often just, and made commonly with the least possible violation of the text.

But, by inserting his emendations, whether invented or borrowed, into the page, without any notice of varying copies, he has appropriated the labour of his predecessors, and made his own edition of little authority. His confidence indeed, both in himself and others, was too great; he supposes all to be right that was done by *Pope* and *Theobald*; he seems not to suspect a critick of fallibility, and it was but reasonable that he should claim what he so liberally granted.

As he never writes without careful enquiry and diligent consideration, I have received all his notes, and believe that every reader will wish for more.

Of the last editor[43] it is more difficult to speak. Respect is due to high place, tenderness to living reputation, and veneration to genius and learning; but he cannot be justly offended at that liberty of which he has himself so frequently given an example, nor very solicitous what is thought of notes, which he ought never to have considered as part of his serious employments, and which, I suppose, since the ardour of composition is remitted, he no longer numbers among his happy effusions.

The original and predominant errour of his commentary, is acquiescence in his first thoughts; that precipitation which is produced by consciousness of quick discernment; and that confidence which presumes to do, by surveying the surface, what labour only can perform, by penetrating the bottom. His notes exhibit sometimes perverse interpretations, and sometimes improbable conjectures; he at one time gives the authour more profundity of meaning than the sentence admits, and at another discovers absurdities, where the sense is plain to every other reader. But his emendations are likewise often happy and just; and his interpretation of obscure passages learned and sagacious.

Of his notes, I have commonly rejected those, against which the general voice of the publick has exclaimed, or which their own incongruity immediately condemns, and which, I suppose, the authour himself would desire to be forgotten. Of the rest, to part I have given the highest approbation, by inserting the offered reading in the text; part I have left to the judgment of the reader, as doubtful, though specious; and part I have censured without reserve, but I am sure without bitterness of malice, and, I hope, without wantonness of insult.

It is no pleasure to me, in revising my volumes, to observe how much paper is wasted in confutation. Whoever considers the revolutions of learning, and the various questions of greater or less importance, upon which wit and reason have exercised their powers, must lament the unsuccessfulness of enquiry, and the slow advances of truth, when he reflects, that great part of the labour of every writer is only the destruction of those that went before him. The first care of the builder of a new system, is to demolish the fabricks which are standing. The chief desire of him that comments an authour, is to shew how much other commentators have corrupted and obscured him. The opinions prevalent in one age, as truths above the reach of controversy, are confuted and rejected in another, and rise again to reception in remoter times. Thus the human mind is kept in motion without progress. Thus sometimes truth and errour, and sometimes contrarieties of errour, take each other's place by reciprocal invasion. The tide of seeming

43. Warburton.

knowledge which is poured over one generation, retires and leaves another naked and barren; the sudden meteors of intelligence which for a while appear to shoot their beams into the regions of obscurity, on a sudden withdraw their lustre, and leave mortals again to grope their way.

These elevations and depressions of renown, and the contradictions to which all improvers of knowledge must for ever be exposed, since they are not escaped by the highest and brightest of mankind, may surely be endured with patience by criticks and annotators, who can rank themselves but as the satellites of their authours. How canst thou beg for life, says *Achilles* to his captive, when thou knowest that thou art now to suffer only what must another day be suffered by *Achilles*?[44]

Dr. *Warburton* had a name sufficient to confer celebrity on those who could exalt themselves into antagonists, and his notes have raised a clamour too loud to be distinct. His chief assailants are the authours of *the Canons of criticism* and of the *Review* of Shakespeare*'s text*;[45] of whom one ridicules his errours with airy petulance, suitable enough to the levity of the controversy; the other attacks them with gloomy malignity, as if he were dragging to justice an assassin or incendiary. The one stings like a fly, sucks a little blood, takes a gay flutter, and returns for more; the other bites like a viper, and would be glad to leave inflammations and gangrene behind him. When I think on one, with his confederates, I remember the danger of *Coriolanus*, who was afraid that *girls with spits, and boys with stones, should slay him in puny battle*;[46] when the other crosses my imagination, I remember the prodigy in *Macbeth*,

An eagle tow'ring in his pride of place,
Was by a mousing owl hawk'd at and kill'd.[47]

Let me however do them justice. One is a wit, and one a scholar. They have both shewn acuteness sufficient in the discovery of faults, and have both advanced some probable interpretations of obscure passages; but when they aspire to conjecture and emendation, it appears how falsely we all estimate our own abilities, and the little which they have been able to perform might have taught them more candour to the endeavours of others.

Before Dr. *Warburton*'s edition, *Critical observations on Shakespeare* had been published by Mr. *Upton*, a man skilled in languages, and acquainted with books, but who seems to have had no great vigour of genius or nicety of taste. Many of his explanations are curious and useful, but he likewise, though he professed to oppose the licentious confidence of editors, and adhere to the old copies, is unable to restrain the rage of emendation, though his ardour is ill seconded by his skill. Every cold empirick, when his heart is expanded by a successful experiment, swells into a theorist, and the laborious collator at some unlucky moment frolicks in conjecture.

Critical, historical and explanatory notes have been likewise published upon *Shakespeare* by Dr. *Grey*,[48] whose diligent perusal of the old *English* writers has enabled him to make some useful observations. What he undertook he has well enough performed, but as he neither attempts judicial nor emendatory criticism, he employs rather his memory than his sagacity. It were to be wished that all would endeavour to imitate his modesty who have not been able to surpass his knowledge.

I can say with great sincerity of all my predecessors, what I hope will hereafter be said of me, that not one has left *Shakespeare* without improvement, nor is there one to whom I have not been indebted for assistance and information. Whatever I have taken from them it was my intention to refer to its original authour, and it is certain, that what I have not given to another, I believed when I wrote it to be my own. In some perhaps I have been anticipated; but if I am ever found to encroach upon the remarks of any other commentator, I am willing that the honour, be it more or less, should be transferred to the first claimant, for his right, and his alone, stands above dispute; the second can prove his pretensions only to himself, nor can himself always distinguish invention, with sufficient certainty, from recollection.

They have all been treated by me with candour, which they have not been careful of observing to one another. It is not easy to discover from what cause the acrimony of a scholiast can naturally proceed. The subjects to be discussed by him are of

44. *Iliad,* xxi, 106–114. **45.** Thomas Edwards and Benjamin Heath. **46.** *Coriolanus,* IV, iv, 5–6. Not an exact quotation. **47.** *Macbeth,* II, iv, 12–13.

48. Zachary Grey.

very small importance; they involve neither property nor liberty; nor favour the interest of sect or party. The various readings of copies, and different interpretations of a passage, seem to be questions that might exercise the wit, without engaging the passions. But, whether it be, that *small things make mean men proud*,[49] and vanity catches small occasions; or that all contrariety of opinion, even in those that can defend it no longer, makes proud men angry; there is often found in commentaries a spontaneous strain of invective and contempt, more eager and venomous than is vented by the most furious controvertist in politicks against those whom he is hired to defame.

Perhaps the lightness of the matter may conduce to the vehemence of the agency; when the truth to be investigated is so near to inexistence, as to escape attention, its bulk is to be enlarged by rage and exclamation: That to which all would be indifferent in its original state, may attract notice when the fate of a name is appended to it. A commentator has indeed great temptations to supply by turbulence what he wants of dignity, to beat his little gold to a spacious surface, to work that to foam which no art or diligence can exalt to spirit.

The notes which I have borrowed or written are either illustrative, by which difficulties are explained; or judicial, by which faults and beauties are remarked; or emendatory, by which depravations are corrected.

The explanations transcribed from others, if I do not subjoin any other interpretation, I suppose commonly to be right, at least I intend by acquiescence to confess, that I have nothing better to propose.

After the labours of all the editors, I found many passages which appeared to me likely to obstruct the greater number of readers, and thought it my duty to facilitate their passage. It is impossible for an expositor not to write too little for some, and too much for others. He can only judge what is necessary by his own experience; and how long soever he may deliberate, will at last explain many lines which the learned will think impossible to be mistaken, and omit many for which the ignorant will want his help. These are censures merely relative, and must be quietly endured. I have endeavoured to be neither superfluously copious, nor scrupulously reserved, and hope that I have made my authour's meaning accessible to many who before were frighted from perusing him, and contributed something to the publick, by diffusing innocent and rational pleasure.

The compleat explanation of an authour not systematick and consequential, but desultory and vagrant, abounding in casual allusions and light hints, is not to be expected from any single scholiast. All personal reflections, when names are suppressed, must be in a few years irrecoverably obliterated; and customs, too minute to attract the notice of law, such as modes of dress, formalities of conversation, rules of visits, disposition of furniture, and practices of ceremony, which naturally find places in familiar dialogue, are so fugitive and unsubstantial, that they are not easily retained or recovered. What can be known, will be collected by chance, from the recesses of obscure and obsolete papers, perused commonly with some other view. Of this knowledge every man has some, and none has much; but when an authour has engaged the publick attention, those who can add any thing to his illustration, communicate their discoveries, and time produces what had eluded diligence.

To time I have been obliged to resign many passages, which, though I did not understand them, will perhaps hereafter be explained, having, I hope, illustrated some, which others have neglected or mistaken, sometimes by short remarks, or marginal directions, such as every editor has added at his will, and often by comments more laborious than the matter will seem to deserve; but that which is most difficult is not always most important, and to an editor nothing is a trifle by which his authour is obscured.

The poetical beauties or defects I have not been very diligent to observe. Some plays have more, and some fewer judicial observations, not in proportion to their difference of merit, but because I gave this part of my design to chance and to caprice. The reader, I believe, is seldom pleased to find his opinion anticipated; it is natural to delight more in what we find or make, than in what we receive. Judgement, like other faculties, is improved by practice, and its advancement is hindered by submission to dictatorial decisions, as the memory grows torpid by the use of a table book. Some initiation is however necessary; of all skill,

49. *2 Henry VI*, IV, i, 106.

part is infused by precept, and part is obtained by habit; I have therefore shewn so much as may enable the candidate of criticism to discover the rest.

To the end of most plays, I have added short strictures, containing a general censure of faults, or praise of excellence; in which I know not how much I have concurred with the current opinion; but I have not, by any affectation of singularity, deviated from it. Nothing is minutely and particularly examined, and therefore it is to be supposed, that in the plays which are condemned there is much to be praised, and in these which are praised much to be condemned.

The part of criticism in which the whole succession of editors has laboured with the greatest diligence, which has occasioned the most arrogant ostentation, and excited the keenest acrimony, is the emendation of corrupted passages, to which the publick attention having been first drawn by the violence of contention between *Pope* and *Theobald,* has been continued by the persecution, which, with a kind of conspiracy, has been since raised against all the publishers of *Shakespeare*.

That many passages have passed in a state of depravation through all the editions is indubitably certain; of these the restoration is only to be attempted by collation of copies or sagacity of conjecture. The collator's province is safe and easy, the conjecturer's perilous and difficult. Yet as the greater part of the plays are extant only in one copy, the peril must not be avoided, nor the difficulty refused.

Of the readings which this emulation of amendment has hitherto produced, some from the labours of every publisher I have advanced into the text; those are to be considered as in my opinion sufficiently supported; some I have rejected without mention, as evidently erroneous; some I have left in the notes without censure or approbation, as resting in equipoise between objection and defence; and some, which seemed specious but not right, I have inserted with a subsequent animadversion.

Having classed the observations of others, I was at last to try what I could substitute for their mistakes, and how I could supply their omissions. I collated such copies as I could procure, and wished for more, but have not found the collectors of these rarities very communicative. Of the editions which chance or kindness put into my hands I have given an enumeration, that I may not be blamed for neglecting what I had not the power to do.

By examining the old copies, I soon found that the later publishers, with all their boasts of diligence, suffered many passages to stand unauthorised, and contented themselves with *Rowe*'s regulation of the text, even where they knew it to be arbitrary, and with a little consideration might have found it to be wrong. Some of these alterations are only the ejection of a word for one that appeared to him more elegant or more intelligible. These corruptions I have often silently rectified; for the history of our language, and the true force of our words, can only be preserved, by keeping the text of authours free from adulteration. Others, and those very frequent, smoothed the cadence, or regulated the measure; on these I have not exercised the same rigour; if only a word was transposed, or a particle inserted or omitted, I have sometimes suffered the line to stand; for the inconstancy of the copies is such, as that some liberties may be easily permitted. But this practice I have not suffered to proceed far, having restored the primitive diction wherever it could for any reason be preferred.

The emendations, which comparison of copies supplied, I have inserted in the text; sometimes where the improvement was slight, without notice, and sometimes with an account of the reasons of the change.

Conjecture, though it be sometimes unavoidable, I have not wantonly nor licentiously indulged. It has been my settled principle, that the reading of the ancient books is probably true, and therefore is not to be disturbed for the sake of elegance, perspicuity, or mere improvement of the sense. For though much credit is not due to the fidelity, nor any to the judgement of the first publishers, yet they who had the copy before their eyes were more likely to read it right, than we who only read it by imagination. But it is evident that they have often made strange mistakes by ignorance or negligence, and that therefore something may be properly attempted by criticism, keeping the middle way between presumption and timidity.

Such criticism I have attempted to practise, and where any passage appeared inextricably perplexed, have endeavoured to discover how it may be recalled to sense, with least violence. But my first labour is, always to turn the old text on every side, and try if there be any interstice, through which light can find its way; nor would *Huetius*[50] himself condemn me, as refusing the trouble of research, for the ambition of alteration. In this modest industry I have not been unsuccessful. I have rescued many lines from the violations of temerity, and secured many scenes from the inroads of correction. I have adopted the *Roman* sentiment, that it is more honourable to save a citizen, than to kill an enemy, and have been more careful to protect than to attack.

I have preserved the common distribution of the plays into acts, though I believe it to be in almost all the plays void of authority. Some of those which are divided in the later editions have no division in the first folio, and some that are divided in the folio have no division in the preceding copies. The settled mode of the theatre requires four intervals in the play, but few, if any, of our authour's compositions can be properly distributed in that manner. An act is so much of the drama as passes without intervention of time or change of place. A pause makes a new act. In every real, and therefore in every imitative action, the intervals may be more or fewer, the restriction of five acts being accidental and arbitrary. This *Shakespeare* knew, and this he practised; his plays were written, and at first printed in one unbroken continuity, and ought now to be exhibited with short pauses, interposed as often as the scene is changed, or any considerable time is required to pass. This method would at once quell a thousand absurdities.

In restoring the authour's works to their integrity, I have considered the punctuation as wholly in my power; for what could be their care of colons and commas, who corrupted words and sentences. Whatever could be done by adjusting points is therefore silently performed, in some plays with much diligence, in others with less; it is hard to keep a busy eye steadily fixed upon evanescent atoms, or a discursive mind upon evanescent truth.

The same liberty has been taken with a few particles, or other words of slight effect. I have sometimes inserted or omitted them without notice. I have done that sometimes, which the other editors have done always, and which indeed the state of the text may sufficiently justify.

The greater part of readers, instead of blaming us for passing trifles, will wonder that on mere trifles so much labour is expended, with such importance of debate, and such solemnity of diction. To these I answer with confidence, that they are judging of an art which they do not understand; yet cannot much reproach them with their ignorance, nor promise that they would become in general, by learning criticism, more useful, happier or wiser.

As I practised conjecture more, I learned to trust it less; and after I had printed a few plays, resolved to insert none of my own readings in the text. Upon this caution I now congratulate myself, for every day encreases my doubt of my emendations.

Since I have confined my imagination to the margin, it must not be considered as very reprehensible, if I have suffered it to play some freaks in its own dominion. There is no danger in conjecture, if it be proposed as conjecture; and while the text remains uninjured, those changes may be safely offered, which are not considered even by him that offers them as necessary or safe.

If my readings are of little value, they have not been ostentatiously displayed or importunately obtruded. I could have written longer notes, for the art of writing notes is not of difficult attainment. The work is performed, first by railing at the stupidity, negligence, ignorance, and asinine tastelessness of the former editors, and shewing, from all that goes before and all that follows, the inelegance and absurdity of the old reading; then by proposing something, which to superficial readers would seem specious, but which the editor rejects with indignation; then by producing the true reading, with a long paraphrase, and concluding with loud acclamations on the discovery, and a sober wish for the advancement and prosperity of genuine criticism.

All this may be done, and perhaps done sometimes without impropriety. But I have always suspected that the reading is right, which requires many words to prove it wrong; and the emendation wrong, that cannot without so much labour appear to be right. The justness of a happy restora-

50. ***Huetius:*** a reference to the distinguished French scholar Pierre Daniel Huet.

tion strikes at once, and the moral precept may be well applied to criticism, *quod dubitas ne feceris.*[51]

To dread the shore which he sees spread with wrecks, is natural to the sailor. I had before my eye, so many critical adventures ended in miscarriage, that caution was forced upon me. I encountered in every page Wit struggling with its own sophistry, and Learning confused by the multiplicity of its views. I was forced to censure those whom I admired, and could not but reflect, while I was dispossessing their emendations, how soon the same fate might happen to my own, and how many of the readings which I have corrected may be by some other editor defended and established.

Criticks, I saw, that other's names efface,
And fix their own, with labour, in the place;
Their own, like others, soon their place resign'd,
Or disappear'd, and left the first behind.[52]

POPE.

That a conjectural critick should often be mistaken, cannot be wonderful, either to others or himself, if it be considered, that in his art there is no system, no principal and axiomatical truth that regulates subordinate positions. His chance of errour is renewed at every attempt; an oblique view of the passage, a slight misapprehension of a phrase, a casual inattention to the parts connected, is sufficient to make him not only fail, but fail ridiculously; and when he succeeds best, he produces perhaps but one reading of many probable, and he that suggests another will always be able to dispute his claims.

It is an unhappy state, in which danger is hid under pleasure. The allurements of emendation are scarcely resistible. Conjecture has all the joy and all the pride of invention, and he that has once started a happy change, is too much delighted to consider what objections may rise against it.

Yet conjectural criticism has been of great use in the learned world; nor is it my intention to depreciate a study, that has exercised so many mighty minds, from the revival of learning to our own age, from the Bishop of *Aleria*[53] to English *Bentley*. The criticks on ancient authours have, in the exercise of their sagacity, many assistances, which the editor of *Shakespeare* is condemned to want. They are employed upon grammatical and settled languages, whose construction contributes so much to perspicuity, that *Homer* has fewer passages unintelligible than *Chaucer*. The words have not only a known regimen, but invariable quantities, which direct and confine the choice. There are commonly more manuscripts than one; and they do not often conspire in the same mistakes. Yet *Scaliger* could confess to *Salmasius* how little satisfaction his emendations gave him. *Illudunt nobis conjecturæ nostræ, quarum nos pudet, posteaquam in meliores codices incidimus.*[54] And *Lipsius* could complain, that criticks were making faults, by trying to remove them, *Ut olim vitiis, ita nunc remediis laboratur.*[55] And indeed, where mere conjecture is to be used, the emendations of *Scaliger* and *Lipsius,* notwithstanding their wonderful sagacity and erudition, are often vague and disputable, like mine or *Theobald's.*

Perhaps I may not be more censured for doing wrong, than for doing little; for raising in the publick expectations, which at last I have not answered. The expectation of ignorance is indefinite, and that of knowledge is often tyrannical. It is hard to satisfy those who know not what to demand, or those who demand by design what they think impossible to be done. I have indeed disappointed no opinion more than my own; yet I have endeavoured to perform my task with no slight solicitude. Not a single passage in the whole work has appeared to me corrupt, which I have not attempted to restore; or obscure, which I have not endeavoured to illustrate. In many I have failed like others; and from many, after all my efforts, I have retreated, and confessed the repulse. I have not passed over, with affected superiority, what is equally difficult to the reader and to myself, but where I could not instruct him, have owned my ignorance. I might easily have accumulated a mass

---

51. ***Quod . . . feceris:*** "When you are in doubt, don't do it." Pliny, *Epistles,* I, xviii. 52. *Temple of Fame,* ll. 37–40. Not an exact quotation. 53. The reference here is to Joannes Andreas (1417–c. 1480), who was librarian to Pope Sixtus IV, and a distinguished textual editor. 54. ***Illudunt . . . incidimus:*** "Our conjectures make fools of us, shaming us, when afterwards we come upon better manuscripts." 55. ***Ut . . . laboratur:*** "As formerly we labored with faults, so now we deal with corrections."

of seeming learning upon easy scenes; but it ought not to be imputed to negligence, that, where nothing was necessary, nothing has been done, or that, where others have said enough, I have said no more.

Notes are often necessary, but they are necessary evils. Let him, that is yet unacquainted with the powers of *Shakespeare,* and who desires to feel the highest pleasure that the drama can give, read every play from the first scene to the last, with utter negligence of all his commentators. When his fancy is once on the wing, let it not stoop at correction or explanation. When his attention is strongly engaged, let it disdain alike to turn aside to the name of *Theobald* and of *Pope*. Let him read on through brightness and obscurity, through integrity and corruption; let him preserve his comprehension of the dialogue and his interest in the fable. And when the pleasures of novelty have ceased, let him attempt exactness; and read the commentators.

Particular passages are cleared by notes, but the general effect of the work is weakened. The mind is refrigerated by interruption; the thoughts are diverted from the principal subject; the reader is weary, he suspects not why; and at last throws away the book, which he has too diligently studied.

Parts are not to be examined till the whole has been surveyed; there is a kind of intellectual remoteness necessary for the comprehension of any great work in its full design and its true proportions; a close approach shews the smaller niceties, but the beauty of the whole is discerned no longer.

It is not very grateful to consider how little the succession of editors has added to this authour's power of pleasing. He was read, admired, studied, and imitated, while he was yet deformed with all the improprieties which ignorance and neglect could accumulate upon him; while the reading was yet not rectified, nor his allusions understood; yet then did *Dryden* pronounce "that *Shakespeare* was the man, who, of all modern and perhaps ancient poets, had the largest and most comprehensive soul. All the images of nature were still present to him, and he drew them not laboriously, but luckily: When he describes any thing, you more than see it, you feel it too. Those who accuse him to have wanted learning, give him the greater commendation: he was naturally learned: he needed not the spectacles of books to read nature; he looked inwards, and found her there. I cannot say he is every where alike; were he so, I should do him injury to compare him with the greatest of mankind. He is many times flat and insipid; his comick wit degenerating into clenches, his serious swelling into bombast. But he is always great, when some great occasion is presented to him: No man can say, he ever had a fit subject for his wit, and did not then raise himself as high above the rest of poets,

> *Quantum lenta solent inter viburna*
> *cupressi.*"[56]

It is to be lamented, that such a writer should want a commentary; that his language should become obsolete, or his sentiments obscure. But it is vain to carry wishes beyond the condition of human things; that which must happen to all, has happened to *Shakespeare,* by accident and time; and more than has been suffered by any other writer since the use of types, has been suffered by him through his own negligence of fame, or perhaps by that superiority of mind, which despised its own performances, when it compared them with its powers, and judged those works unworthy to be preserved, which the criticks of following ages were to contend for the fame of restoring and explaining.

Among these candidates of inferiour fame, I am now to stand the judgment of the publick; and wish that I could confidently produce my commentary as equal to the encouragement which I have had the honour of receiving. Every work of this kind is by its nature deficient, and I should feel little solicitude about the sentence, were it to be pronounced only by the skilful and the learned.

FROM

The Lives of the Poets

From THE LIFE OF POPE

. . .

A man of such exalted superiority and so little moderation would naturally have all his delin-

56. ***Quantum . . . cupressi:*** End of the celebrated tribute to Shakespeare in John Dryden's *Essay of Dramatic Poesy.* The Latin is from Virgil, *Eclogues,* I, 25: "As do cypresses among pliant shrubs."

quences observed and aggravated: those who could not deny that he was excellent would rejoice to find that he was not perfect.

Perhaps it may be imputed to the unwillingness with which the same man is allowed to possess many advantages that his learning has been depreciated. He certainly was in his early life a man of great literary curiosity, and when he wrote his *Essay on Criticism* had for his age a very wide acquaintance with books. When he entered into the living world it seems to have happened to him as to many others that he was less attentive to dead masters: he studied in the academy of Paracelsus,[1] and made the universe his favourite volume. He gathered his notions fresh from reality, not from the copies of authors, but the originals of Nature. Yet there is no reason to believe that literature ever lost his esteem; he always professed to love reading, and Dobson, who spent some time at his house translating his *Essay on Man*, when I asked him what learning he found him to possess, answered, "More than I expected." His frequent references to history, his allusions to various kinds of knowledge, and his images selected from art and nature, with his observations on the operations of the mind and the modes of life, shew an intelligence perpetually on the wing, excursive, vigorous, and diligent, eager to pursue knowledge, and attentive to retain it.

From this curiosity arose the desire of travelling, to which he alludes in his verses to Jervas, and which, though he never found an opportunity to gratify it, did not leave him till his life declined.

Of his intellectual character the constituent and fundamental principle was Good Sense, a prompt and intuitive perception of consonance and propriety. He saw immediately, of his own conceptions, what was to be chosen, and what to be rejected; and, in the works of others, what was to be shunned, and what was to be copied.

But good sense alone is a sedate and quiescent quality, which manages its possessions well, but does not increase them; it collects few materials for its own operations, and preserves safety, but never gains supremacy. Pope had likewise genius; a mind active, ambitious, and adventurous, always investigating, always aspiring; in its widest searches still longing to go forward, in its highest flights still wishing to be higher; always imagining something greater than it knows, always endeavouring more than it can do.

To assist these powers he is said to have had great strength and exactness of memory. That which he had heard or read was not easily lost; and he had before him not only what his own meditation suggested, but what he had found in other writers that might be accommodated to his present purpose.

These benefits of nature he improved by incessant and unwearied diligence; he had recourse to every source of intelligence, and lost no opportunity of information; he consulted the living as well as the dead; he read his compositions to his friends, and was never content with mediocrity when excellence could be attained. He considered poetry as the business of his life, and, however he might seem to lament his occupation, he followed it with constancy: to make verses was his first labour, and to mend them was his last.

From his attention to poetry he was never diverted. If conversation offered anything that could be improved he committed it to paper; if a thought, or perhaps an expression more happy than was common, rose to his mind, he was careful to write it; an independent distich[2] was preserved for an opportunity of insertion, and some little fragments have been found containing lines, or parts of lines, to be wrought upon at some other time.

He was one of those few whose labour is their pleasure; he was never elevated to negligence, nor wearied to impatience; he never passed a fault unamended by indifference, nor quitted it by despair. He laboured his works first to gain reputation, and afterwards to keep it.

Of composition there are different methods. Some employ at once memory and invention, and, with little intermediate use of the pen, form and polish large masses by continued meditation, and write their productions only when, in their own opinion, they have completed them. It is related of Virgil that his custom was to pour out a great number of verses in the morning, and pass the day in retrenching exuberances and correcting inaccuracies. The method of Pope, as may be collected

LIVES OF THE POETS: LIFE OF POPE. **1. Paracelsus:** the noted Swiss scientist.

2. distich: a couple of lines of verse, usually making good sense.

from his translation, was to write his first thoughts in his first words, and gradually to amplify, decorate, rectify, and refine them.

With such faculties and such dispositions he excelled every other writer in *poetical prudence;* he wrote in such a manner as might expose him to few hazards. He used almost always the same fabrick of verse; and, indeed, by those few essays which he made of any other, he did not enlarge his reputation. Of this uniformity the certain consequence was readiness and dexterity. By perpetual practice language had in his mind a systematical arrangement; having always the same use for words, he had words so selected and combined as to be ready at his call. This increase of facility he confessed himself to have perceived in the progress of his translation.

But what was yet of more importance, his effusions were always voluntary, and his subjects chosen by himself. His independence secured him from drudging at a task, and labouring upon a barren topick: he never exchanged praise for money, nor opened a shop of condolence or congratulation. His poems, therefore, were scarce ever temporary. He suffered coronations and royal marriages to pass without a song, and derived no opportunities from recent events, nor any popularity from the accidental disposition of his readers. He was never reduced to the necessity of soliciting the sun to shine upon a birthday, of calling the Graces and Virtues to a wedding, or of saying what multitudes have said before him. When he could produce nothing new, he was at liberty to be silent.

His publications were for the same reason never hasty. He is said to have sent nothing to the press till it had lain two years under his inspection: it is at least certain that he ventured nothing without nice examination. He suffered the tumult of imagination to subside, and the novelties of invention to grow familiar. He knew that the mind is always enamoured of its own productions, and did not trust his first fondness. He consulted his friends, and listened with great willingness to criticism; and, what was of more importance, he consulted himself, and let nothing pass against his own judgement.

He professed to have learned his poetry from Dryden, whom, whenever an opportunity was presented, he praised through his whole life with unvaried liberality; and perhaps his character may receive some illustration if he be compared with his master.

Integrity of understanding and nicety of discernment were not allotted in a less proportion to Dryden than to Pope. The rectitude of Dryden's mind was sufficiently shewn by the dismission of his poetical prejudices, and the rejection of unnatural thoughts and rugged numbers. But Dryden never desired to apply all the judgement that he had. He wrote, and professed to write, merely for the people; and when he pleased others, he contented himself. He spent no time in struggles to rouse latent powers; he never attempted to make that better which was already good, nor often to mend what he must have known to be faulty. He wrote, as he tells us, with very little consideration; when occasion or necessity called upon him, he poured out what the present moment happened to supply, and, when once it had passed the press, ejected it from his mind; for when he had no pecuniary interest, he had no further solicitude.

Pope was not content to satisfy; he desired to excel, and therefore always endeavoured to do his best: he did not court the candour, but dared the judgement of his reader, and, expecting no indulgence from others, he shewed none to himself. He examined lines and words with minute and punctilious observation, and retouched every part with indefatigable diligence, till he had left nothing to be forgiven.

For this reason he kept his pieces very long in his hands, while he considered and reconsidered them. The only poems which can be supposed to have been written with such regard to the times as might hasten their publication, were the two satires of *Thirty-eight;* of which Dodsley told me that they were brought to him by the author, that they might be fairly copied. "Almost every line," he said, "was then written twice over; I gave him a clean transcript, which he sent some time afterwards to me for the press, with almost every line written twice over a second time."

His declaration that his care for his works ceased at their publication was not strictly true. His parental attention never abandoned them; what he found amiss in the first edition, he silently corrected in those that followed. He appears to have revised the *Iliad,* and freed it from some of its imperfections; and the *Essay on Criticism* received many improvements after its first appearance. It will seldom be found that he altered without adding clearness, elegance, or vigour. Pope had perhaps the judgement of Dryden; but Dryden certainly wanted the diligence of Pope.

In acquired knowledge the superiority must be allowed to Dryden, whose education was more scholastick, and who before he became an author had been allowed more time for study, with better means of information. His mind has a larger range, and he collects his images and illustrations from a more extensive circumference of science. Dryden knew more of man in his general nature, and Pope in his local manners. The notions of Dryden were formed by comprehensive speculation, and those of Pope by minute attention. There is more dignity in the knowledge of Dryden, and more certainty in that of Pope.

Poetry was not the sole praise of either, for both excelled likewise in prose; but Pope did not borrow his prose from his predecessor. The style of Dryden is capricious and varied, that of Pope is cautious and uniform; Dryden obeys the motions of his own mind, Pope constrains his mind to his own rules of composition. Dryden is sometimes vehement and rapid; Pope is always smooth, uniform, and gentle. Dryden's page is a natural field, rising into inequalities, and diversified by the varied exuberance of abundant vegetation; Pope's is a velvet lawn, shaven by the scythe, and levelled by the roller.

Of genius, that power which constitutes a poet; that quality without which judgement is cold and knowledge is inert; that energy which collects, combines, amplifies, and animates—the superiority must, with some hesitation, be allowed to Dryden. It is not to be inferred that of this poetical vigour Pope had only a little, because Dryden had more, for every other writer since Milton must give place to Pope; and even of Dryden it must be said that if he has brighter paragraphs, he has not better poems. Dryden's performances were always hasty, either excited by some external occasion, or extorted by domestick necessity; he composed without consideration, and published without correction. What his mind could supply at call, or gather in one excursion, was all that he sought, and all that he gave. The dilatory caution of Pope enabled him to condense his sentiments, to multiply his images, and to accumulate all that study might produce, or chance might supply. If the flights of Dryden therefore are higher, Pope continues longer on the wing. If of Dryden's fire the blaze is brighter, of Pope's the heat is more regular and constant. Dryden often surpasses expectation, and Pope never falls below it. Dryden is read with frequent astonishment, and Pope with perpetual delight.

This parallel will, I hope, when it is well considered, be found just; and if the reader should suspect me, as I suspect myself, of some partial fondness for the memory of Dryden, let him not too hastily condemn me; for meditation and enquiry may, perhaps, shew him the reasonableness of my determination.

The works of Pope are now to be distinctly examined, not so much with attention to slight faults or petty beauties, as to the general character and effect of each performance.

It seems natural for a young poet to initiate himself by Pastorals, which, not professing to imitate real life, require no experience, and, exhibiting only the simple operation of unmingled passions, admit no subtle reasoning or deep enquiry. Pope's *Pastorals* are not however composed but with close thought; they have reference to the times of the day, the seasons of the year, and the periods of human life. The last, that which turns the attention upon age and death, was the author's favourite. To tell of disappointment and misery, to thicken the darkness of futurity, and perplex the labyrinth of uncertainty, has been always a delicious employment of the poets. His preference was probably just. I wish, however, that his fondness had not overlooked a line in which the "Zephyrs" are made "to lament in silence." [3]

To charge these *Pastorals* with want of invention is to require what never was intended. The imitations are so ambitiously frequent that the writer evidently means rather to shew his literature than his wit. It is surely sufficient for an author of sixteen not only to be able to copy the poems of antiquity with judicious selection, but to have obtained sufficient power of language and skill in metre to exhibit a series of versification, which had in English poetry no precedent, nor has since had an imitation.

3. *Pastorals,* IV, 49.

The design of *Windsor Forest* is evidently derived from *Cooper's Hill*, with some attention to Waller's poem on *The Park*; but Pope cannot be denied to excel his masters in variety and elegance, and the art of interchanging description, narrative, and morality. The objection made by Dennis is the want of plan, of a regular subordination of parts terminating in the principal and original design.[4] There is this want in most descriptive poems, because as the scenes, which they must exhibit successively, are all subsisting at the same time, the order in which they are shewn must by necessity be arbitrary, and more is not to be expected from the last part than from the first. The attention, therefore, which cannot be detained by suspense, must be excited by diversity, such as his poem offers to its reader.

But the desire of diversity may be too much indulged: the parts of *Windsor Forest* which deserve least praise are those which were added to enliven the stillness of the scene, the appearance of Father Thames, and the transformation of Lodona. Addison had in his *Campaign* derided the "Rivers" that "rise from their oozy beds" to tell stories of heroes, and it is therefore strange that Pope should adopt a fiction not only unnatural but lately censured. The story of Lodona is told with sweetness; but a new metamorphosis is a ready and puerile expedient: nothing is easier than to tell how a flower was once a blooming virgin, or a rock an obdurate tyrant.

The Temple of Fame has, as Steele warmly declared, "a thousand beauties." Every part is splendid; there is great luxuriance of ornaments; the original vision of Chaucer was never denied to be much improved; the allegory is very skilfully continued, the imagery is properly selected and learnedly displayed: yet, with all this comprehension of excellence, as its scene is laid in remote ages, and its sentiments, if the concluding paragraph be excepted, have little relation to general manners or common life, it never obtained much notice, but is turned silently over, and seldom quoted or mentioned with either praise or blame.

That *The Messiah* excels the *Pollio*[5] is no great praise, if it be considered from what original[6] the improvements are derived.

The *Verses on the unfortunate Lady* have drawn much attention by the illaudable singularity of treating suicide with respect, and they must be allowed to be written in some parts with vigorous animation, and in others with gentle tenderness; nor has Pope produced any poem in which the sense predominates more over the diction. But the tale is not skilfully told: it is not easy to discover the character of either the lady or her guardian. History relates that she was about to disparage herself by a marriage with an inferior; Pope praises her for the dignity of ambition, and yet condemns the unkle to detestation for his pride: the ambitious love of a niece may be opposed by the interest, malice, or envy of an unkle, but never by his pride. On such an occasion a poet may be allowed to be obscure, but inconsistency never can be right.

The *Ode for St. Cecilia's Day* was undertaken at the desire of Steele: in this the author is generally confessed to have miscarried, yet he has miscarried only as compared with Dryden; for he has far outgone other competitors. Dryden's plan is better chosen; history will always take stronger hold of the attention than fable: the passions excited by Dryden are the pleasures and pains of real life, the scene of Pope is laid in imaginary existence. Pope is read with calm acquiescence, Dryden with turbulent delight; Pope hangs upon the ear, and Dryden finds the passes of the mind.

Both the odes want the essential constituent of metrical compositions, the stated recurrence of settled numbers. It may be alleged that Pindar is said by Horace to have written "numeris lege solutis,"[7] but as no such lax performances have been transmitted to us, the meaning of that expression cannot be fixed; and perhaps the like return might properly be made to a modern Pindarist, as Mr. Cobb[8] received from Bentley, who, when he found his criticisms upon a Greek exercise, which Cobb had presented, refuted one after another by Pindar's authority, cried out at last, "Pindar was a bold fellow, but thou art an impudent one."

If Pope's *Ode* be particularly inspected it will be found that the first stanza consists of sounds well chosen indeed, but only sounds.

The second consists of hyperbolical common-

4. *Pastorals,* II, 136. **5.** Virgil's *Eclogue IV.* **6.** Book of Isaiah.

7. "numeris . . . solutis": *Odes,* IV, ii, 11–12: "in free verse." **8. Mr. Cobb:** Samuel Cobb (1675–1713), poet and translator.

places, easily to be found, and perhaps without much difficulty to be as well expressed.

In the third, however, there are numbers, images, harmony, and vigour, not unworthy the antagonist of Dryden. Had all been like this—but every part cannot be the best.

The next stanzas place and detain us in the dark and dismal regions of mythology, where neither hope nor fear, neither joy nor sorrow can be found: the poet however faithfully attends us; we have all that can be performed by elegance of diction or sweetness of versification; but what can form avail without better matter?

The last stanza recurs again to common-places. The conclusion is too evidently modelled by that of Dryden; and it may be remarked that both end with the same fault, the comparison of each is literal on one side, and metaphorical on the other.

Poets do not always express their own thoughts; Pope, with all this labour in the praise of musick, was ignorant of its principles, and insensible of its effects.

One of his greatest though of his earliest works is the *Essay on Criticism,* which if he had written nothing else would have placed him among the first criticks and the first poets, as it exhibits every mode of excellence that can embellish or dignify didactick composition, selection of matter, novelty of arrangement, justness of precept, splendour of illustration, and propriety of digression. I know not whether it be pleasing to consider that he produced this piece at twenty, and never afterwards excelled it: he that delights himself with observing that such powers may be so soon attained, cannot but grieve to think that life was ever after at a stand.

To mention the particular beauties of the *Essay* would be unprofitably tedious; but I cannot forbear to observe that the comparison of a student's progress in the sciences with the journey of a traveller in the Alps is perhaps the best that English poetry can shew.[9] A simile, to be perfect, must both illustrate and ennoble the subject; must shew it to the understanding in a clearer view, and display it to the fancy with greater dignity: but either of these qualities may be sufficient to recommend it. In didactick poetry, of which the great purpose is instruction, a simile may be praised which illustrates, though it does not ennoble; in heroicks, that may be admitted which ennobles, though it does not illustrate. That it may be complete it is required to exhibit, independently of its references, a pleasing image; for a simile is said to be a short episode. To this antiquity was so attentive that circumstances were sometimes added, which, having no parallels, served only to fill the imagination, and produced what Perrault[10] ludicrously called "comparisons with a long tail." In their similes the greatest writers have sometimes failed: the ship-race,[11] compared with the chariot-race, is neither illustrated nor aggrandised; land and water make all the difference: when Apollo running after Daphne is likened to a greyhound chasing a hare,[12] there is nothing gained; the ideas of pursuit and flight are too plain to be made plainer, and a god and the daughter of a god are not represented much to their advantage by a hare and dog. The simile of the Alps has no useless parts, yet affords a striking picture by itself: it makes the foregoing position better understood, and enables it to take faster hold on the attention; it assists the apprehension, and elevates the fancy.

Let me likewise dwell a little on the celebrated paragraph,[13] in which it is directed that "the sound should seem an echo to the sense"; a precept which Pope is allowed to have observed beyond any other English poet.

This notion of representative metre, and the desire of discovering frequent adaptations of the sound to the sense, have produced, in my opinion, many wild conceits and imaginary beauties. All that can furnish this representation are the sounds of the words considered singly, and the time in which they are pronounced. Every language has some words framed to exhibit the noises which they express, as *thump, rattle, growl, hiss.* These, however, are but few, and the poet cannot make them more, nor can they be of any use but when sound is to be mentioned. The time of pronunciation was in the dactylick measures of the learned languages capable of considerable variety; but that variety could be accommodated only to motion or duration, and different degrees of motion were perhaps expressed by verses rapid or slow, without

9. The simile in *An Essay on Criticism,* ll. 219 ff.

10. Perrault: Charles Perrault (1628–1703), French writer of fairy tales. **11. ship-race:** in Book V of Virgil's *Aeneid.* **12.** Ovid, *Metamorphoses,* I, 533–538. **13. celebrated paragraph:** *Essay on Criticism,* II, 337–383.

much attention of the writer, when the image had full possession of his fancy: but our language having little flexibility our verses can differ very little in their cadence. The fancied resemblances, I fear, arise sometimes merely from the ambiguity of words; there is supposed to be some relation between a *soft* line and a *soft* couch, or between *hard* syllables and *hard* fortune.

Motion, however, may be in some sort exemplified; and yet it may be suspected that even in such resemblances the mind often governs the ear, and the sounds are estimated by their meaning. One of the most successful attempts has been to describe the labour of Sisyphus:[14]

> With many a weary step, and many a groan,
> Up a high hill he heaves a huge round stone;
> The huge round stone, resulting with a bound,
> Thunders impetuous down, and smoaks along the ground.[15]

Who does not perceive the stone to move slowly upward, and roll violently back? But set the same numbers to another sense;

> While many a merry tale, and many a song,
> Chear'd the rough road, we wish'd the rough road long.
> The rough road then, returning in a round,
> Mock'd our impatient steps, for all was fairy ground.

We have now surely lost much of the delay, and much of the rapidity.

But to shew how little the greatest master of numbers can fix the principles of representative harmony, it will be sufficient to remark that the poet, who tells us that

> When Ajax strives some rock's vast weight to throw,
> The line too labours and the words move slow:
> Not so when swift Camilla scours the plain,
> Flies o'er th' unbending corn, and skims along the main;[16]

when he had enjoyed for about thirty years the praise of Camilla's lightness of foot, tried another experiment upon *sound* and *time*, and produced this memorable triplet:

> Waller was smooth; but Dryden taught to join
> The varying verse, the full resounding line,
> The long majestick march, and energy divine.[17]

Here are the swiftness of the rapid race and the march of slow-paced majesty exhibited by the same poet in the same sequence of syllables, except that the exact prosodist will find the line of *swiftness* by one time longer than that of *tardiness*.

Beauties of this kind are commonly fancied; and when real are technical and nugatory, not to be rejected and not to be solicited.

To the praises which have been accumulated on *The Rape of the Lock* by readers of every class, from the critick to the waiting-maid, it is difficult to make any addition. Of that which is universally allowed to be the most attractive of all ludicrous compositions, let it rather be now enquired from what sources the power of pleasing is derived.

Dr. Warburton, who excelled in critical perspicacity, has remarked that the preternatural agents are very happily adapted to the purposes of the poem. The heathen deities can no longer gain attention: we should have turned away from a contest between Venus and Diana. The employment of allegorical persons always excites conviction of its own absurdity: they may produce effects, but cannot conduct actions; when the phantom is put in motion, it dissolves; thus Discord may raise a mutiny, but Discord cannot conduct a march, nor besiege a town. Pope brought into view a new race of Beings, with powers and passions proportionate to their operation. The sylphs and gnomes act at the toilet and the tea-table, what more terrifick and more powerful phantoms perform on the stormy ocean or the field of battle; they give their proper help, and do their proper mischief.

Pope is said by an objector not to have been the inventer of this petty nation; a charge which might with more justice have been brought against the author of the *Iliad*, who doubtless adopted the religious system of his country; for what is there but the names of his agents which Pope has not

14. Sisyphus: In the ancient story, Sisyphus, legendary King of Corinth, was condemned to an eternal punishment of pushing a huge stone up a hill only to have it roll back down when it reached the top. **15.** Pope's *Odyssey*, xi, 735–738. **16.** *Essay on Criticism*, ll. 370–373. Camilla was a Volscian princess, a devotee of Diana. She was so swift of foot that she could run over a field of corn without hurting the blades, and over the ocean without wetting her feet.

17. *Imitations of Horace, Epistles*, II, i, 267–269.

invented? Has he not assigned them characters and operations never heard of before? Has he not, at least, given them their first poetical existence? If this is not sufficient to denominate his work original, nothing original ever can be written.

In this work are exhibited in a very high degree the two most engaging powers of an author: new things are made familiar, and familiar things are made new. A race of aerial people never heard of before is presented to us in a manner so clear and easy, that the reader seeks for no further information, but immediately mingles with his new acquaintance, adopts their interests, and attends their pursuits, loves a sylph and detests a gnome.

That familiar things are made new every paragraph will prove. The subject of the poem is an event below the common incidents of common life; nothing real is introduced that is not seen so often as to be no longer regarded, yet the whole detail of a female-day is here brought before us invested with so much art of decoration that, though nothing is disguised, every thing is striking, and we feel all the appetite of curiosity for that from which we have a thousand times turned fastidiously away.

The purpose of the Poet is, as he tells us, to laugh at "the little unguarded follies of the female sex." It is therefore without justice that Dennis charges *The Rape of the Lock* with the want of a moral, and for that reason sets it below *The Lutrin*,[18] which exposes the pride and discord of the clergy. Perhaps neither Pope nor Boileau has made the world much better than he found it; but if they had both succeeded, it were easy to tell who would have deserved most from publick gratitude. The freaks, and humours, and spleen, and vanity of women, as they embroil families in discord and fill houses with disquiet, do more to obstruct the happiness of life in a year than the ambition of the clergy in many centuries. It has been well observed that the misery of man proceeds not from any single crush of overwhelming evil, but from small vexations continually repeated.

It is remarked by Dennis likewise that the machinery is superfluous; that by all the bustle of preternatural operation the main event is neither hastened nor retarded. To this charge an efficacious answer is not easily made. The sylphs cannot be said to help or to oppose, and it must be allowed to imply some want of art that their power has not been sufficiently intermingled with the action. Other parts may likewise be charged with want of connection; the game at *ombre* might be spared, but if the lady had lost her hair while she was intent upon her cards, it might have been inferred that those who are too fond of play will be in danger of neglecting more important interests. Those perhaps are faults; but what are such faults to so much excellence!

The *Epistle of Eloise to Abelard* is one of the most happy productions of human wit: the subject is so judiciously chosen, that it would be difficult, in turning over the annals of the world, to find another which so many circumstances concur to recommend. We regularly interest ourselves most in the fortune of those who most deserve our notice. Abelard and Eloise were conspicuous in their days for eminence of merit. The heart naturally loves truth. The adventures and misfortunes of this illustrious pair are known from undisputed history. Their fate does not leave the mind in hopeless dejection; for they both found quiet and consolation in retirement and piety. So new and so affecting is their story that it supersedes invention, and imagination ranges at full liberty without straggling into scenes of fable.

The story thus skilfully adopted has been diligently improved. Pope has left nothing behind him which seems more the effect of studious perseverance and laborious revisal. Here is particularly observable the "curiosa felicitas,"[19] a fruitful soil, and careful cultivation. Here is no crudeness of sense, nor asperity of language.

The sources from which sentiments which have so much vigour and efficacy have been drawn are shewn to be the mystick writers by the learned author of the *Essay on the Life and Writings of Pope*;[20] a book which teaches how the brow of criticism may be smoothed, and how she may be enabled, with all her severity, to attract and to delight.

The train of my disquisition has now conducted me to that poetical wonder, the translation of the *Iliad*; a performance which no age or nation can pretend to equal. To the Greeks translation was almost unknown; it was totally unknown to the

18. ***The Lutrin:*** a mock-heroic poem by Boileau.

19. **"curiosa felicitas":** "planned happy touch." **20.** Joseph Warton (1722–1800).

inhabitants of Greece. They had no recourse to the Barbarians for poetical beauties, but sought for every thing in Homer, where, indeed, there is but little which they might not find.

The Italians have been very diligent translators; but I can hear of no version, unless perhaps Anguillara's *Ovid* may be excepted, which is read with eagerness. The *Iliad* of Salvini every reader may discover to be punctiliously exact; but it seems to be the work of a linguist skilfully pedantick, and his countrymen, the proper judges of its power to please, reject it with disgust.

Their predecessors the Romans have left some specimens of translation behind them, and that employment must have had some credit in which Tully and Germanicus engaged; but unless we suppose, what is perhaps true, that the plays of Terence were versions of Menander,[21] nothing translated seems ever to have risen to high reputation. The French, in the meridian hour of their learning, were very laudably industrious to enrich their own language with the wisdom of the ancients; but found themselves reduced, by whatever necessity, to turn the Greek and Roman poetry into prose. Whoever could read an author could translate him. From such rivals little can be feared.

The chief help of Pope in this arduous undertaking was drawn from the versions of Dryden. Virgil had borrowed much of his imagery from Homer, and part of the debt was now paid by his translator. Pope searched the pages of Dryden for happy combinations of heroick diction, but it will not be denied that he added much to what he found. He cultivated our language with so much diligence and art that he has left in his *Homer* a treasure of poetical elegances to posterity. His version may be said to have tuned the English tongue, for since its appearance no writer, however deficient in other powers, has wanted melody. Such a series of lines so elaborately corrected and so sweetly modulated took possession of the publick ear; the vulgar was enamoured of the poem, and the learned wondered at the translation.

But in the most general applause discordant voices will always be heard. It has been objected by some, who wish to be numbered among the sons of learning, that Pope's version of Homer is not Homerical; that it exhibits no resemblance of the original and characteristick manner of the Father of Poetry, as it wants his awful simplicity, his artless grandeur, his unaffected majesty. This cannot be totally denied, but it must be remembered that "necessitas quod cogit defendit," that may be lawfully done which cannot be forborne. Time and place will always enforce regard. In estimating this translation consideration must be had of the nature of our language, the form of our metre, and, above all, of the change which two thousand years have made in the modes of life and the habits of thought. Virgil wrote in a language of the same general fabrick with that of Homer, in verses of the same measure, and in an age nearer to Homer's time by eighteen hundred years; yet he found even then the state of the world so much altered, and the demand for elegance so much increased, that mere nature would be endured no longer; and perhaps, in the multitude of borrowed passages, very few can be shewn which he has not embellished.

There is a time when nations emerging from barbarity, and falling into regular subordination, gain leisure to grow wise, and feel the shame of ignorance and the craving pain of unsatisfied curiosity. To this hunger of the mind plain sense is grateful; that which fills the void removes uneasiness, and to be free from pain for a while is pleasure; but repletion generates fastidiousness, a saturated intellect soon becomes luxurious, and knowledge finds no willing reception till it is recommended by artificial diction. Thus it will be found in the progress of learning that in all nations the first writers are simple, and that every age improves in elegance. One refinement always makes way for another, and what was expedient to Virgil was necessary to Pope.

I suppose many readers of the English *Iliad*, when they have been touched with some unexpected beauty of the lighter kind, have tried to enjoy it in the original, where, alas! it was not to be found. Homer doubtless owes to his translator many Ovidian graces not exactly suitable to his character; but to have added can be no great crime if nothing be taken away. Elegance is surely to be desired if it be not gained at the expence of dignity. A hero would wish to be loved as well as to be reverenced.

21. Terence . . . Menander: Terence (c. 190–159 B.C.) and Menander (c. 342–292 B.C.), the first, a great Roman, and the second, a great Greek comic dramatist.

To a thousand cavils one answer is sufficient; the purpose of a writer is to be read, and the criticism which would destroy the power of pleasing must be blown aside. Pope wrote for his own age and his own nation: he knew that it was necessary to colour the images and point the sentiments of his author; he therefore made him graceful, but lost him some of his sublimity.

The copious notes with which the version is accompanied and by which it is recommended to many readers, though they were undoubtedly written to swell the volumes, ought not to pass without praise: commentaries which attract the reader by the pleasure of perusal have not often appeared; the notes of others are read to clear difficulties, those of Pope to vary entertainment.

It has, however, been objected with sufficient reason that there is in the commentary too much of unseasonable levity and affected gaiety; that too many appeals are made to the ladies, and the ease which is so carefully preserved is sometimes the ease of a trifler. Every art has its terms and every kind of instruction its proper style; the gravity of common criticks may be tedious, but is less despicable than childish merriment.

Of the *Odyssey* nothing remains to be observed; the same general praise may be given to both translations, and a particular examination of either would require a large volume. The notes were written by Broome, who endeavoured not unsuccessfully to imitate his master.

Of *The Dunciad* the hint is confessedly taken from Dryden's *Mac Flecknoe,* but the plan is so enlarged and diversified as justly to claim the praise of an original, and affords perhaps the best specimen that has yet appeared of personal satire ludicrously pompous.

That the design was moral, whatever the author might tell either his readers or himself, I am not convinced. The first motive was the desire of revenging the contempt with which Theobald had treated his *Shakespeare,* and regaining the honour which he had lost, by crushing his opponent. Theobald was not of bulk enough to fill a poem, and therefore it was necessary to find other enemies with other names, at whose expence he might divert the publick.

In this design there was petulance and malignity enough; but I cannot think it very criminal. An author places himself uncalled before the tribunal of criticism, and solicits fame at the hazard of disgrace. Dulness or deformity are not culpable in themselves, but may be very justly reproached when they pretend to the honour of wit or the influence of beauty. If bad writers were to pass without reprehension what should restrain them? "impune diem consumpserit ingens Telephus";[22] and upon bad writers only will censure have much effect. The satire which brought Theobald and Moore into contempt, dropped impotent from Bentley, like the javelin of Priam.

All truth is valuable, and satirical criticism may be considered as useful when it rectifies error and improves judgement: he that refines the publick taste is a publick benefactor.

The beauties of this poem are well known; its chief fault is the grossness of its images. Pope and Swift had an unnatural delight in ideas physically impure, such as every other tongue utters with unwillingness, and of which every ear shrinks from the mention.

But even this fault, offensive as it is, may be forgiven for the excellence of other passages; such as the formation and dissolution of Moore, the account of the Traveller, the misfortune of the Florist, and the crowded thoughts and stately numbers which dignify the concluding paragraph.

The alterations which have been made in *The Dunciad,* not always for the better, require that it should be published, as in the last collection, with all its variations.

The *Essay on Man* was a work of great labour and long consideration, but certainly not the happiest of Pope's performances. The subject is perhaps not very proper for poetry, and the poet was not sufficiently master of his subject; metaphysical morality was to him a new study, he was proud of his acquisitions, and, supposing himself master of great secrets, was in haste to teach what he had not learned. Thus he tells us, in the first Epistle, that from the nature of the Supreme Being may be deduced an order of beings such as mankind, because Infinite Excellence can do only what is best. He finds out that these beings must be "somewhere," and that "all the question is whether man be in a wrong place." Surely if, according to the

22. "impune . . . Telephus": "Shall a huge Telephus use up a whole day with impunity?" Juvenal, *Satires,* I, 5.

poet's Leibnitian[23] reasoning, we may infer that man ought to be only because he is, we may allow that his place is the right place, because he has it. Supreme Wisdom is not less infallible in disposing than in creating. But what is meant by "somewhere" and "place" and "wrong place" it had been vain to ask Pope, who probably had never asked himself.

Having exalted himself into the chair of wisdom he tells us much that every man knows, and much that he does not know himself; that we see but little, and that the order of the universe is beyond our comprehension, an opinion not very uncommon; and that there is a chain of subordinate beings "from infinite to nothing," of which himself and his readers are equally ignorant. But he gives us one comfort which, without his help, he supposes unattainable, in the position "that though we are fools, yet God is wise."

This *Essay* affords an egregious instance of the predominance of genius, the dazzling splendour of imagery, and the seductive powers of eloquence. Never were penury of knowledge and vulgarity of sentiment so happily disguised. The reader feels his mind full, though he learns nothing; and when he meets it in its new array no longer knows the talk of his mother and his nurse. When these wonder-working sounds sink into sense and the doctrine of the *Essay*, disrobed of its ornaments, is left to the powers of its naked excellence, what shall we discover? That we are, in comparison with our Creator, very weak and ignorant; that we do not uphold the chain of existence; and that we could not make one another with more skill than we are made. We may learn yet more: that the arts of human life were copied from the instinctive operations of other animals; that if the world be made for man, it may be said that man was made for geese. To these profound principles of natural knowledge are added some moral instructions equally new: that self-interest well understood will produce social concord; that men are mutual gainers by mutual benefits; that evil is sometimes balanced by good; that human advantages are unstable and fallacious, of uncertain duration and doubtful effect; that our true honour is not to have a great part, but to act it well; that virtue only is our own; and that happiness is always in our power.

Surely a man of no very comprehensive search may venture to say that he has heard all this before, but it was never till now recommended by such a blaze of embellishment or such sweetness of melody. The vigorous contraction of some thoughts, the luxuriant amplification of others, the incidental illustrations, and sometimes the dignity, sometimes the softness of the verses, enchain philosophy, suspend criticism, and oppress judgement by overpowering pleasure.

This is true of many paragraphs; yet if I had undertaken to exemplify Pope's felicity of composition before a rigid critick I should not select the *Essay on Man*, for it contains more lines unsuccessfully laboured, more harshness of diction, more thoughts imperfectly expressed, more levity without elegance, and more heaviness without strength, than will easily be found in all his other works.

The *Characters of Men and Women* are the product of diligent speculation upon human life; much labour has been bestowed upon them, and Pope very seldom laboured in vain. That his excellence may be properly estimated I recommend a comparison of his *Characters of Women* with Boileau's *Satire*; it will then be seen with how much more perspicacity female nature is investigated and female excellence selected; and he surely is no mean writer to whom Boileau shall be found inferior. The *Characters of Men*, however, are written with more, if not with deeper, thought, and exhibit many passages exquisitely beautiful. "The Gem and the Flower" will not easily be equalled.[24] In the women's part are some defects: the character of Atossa is not so neatly finished as that of Clodio, and some of the female characters may be found perhaps more frequently among men; what is said of Philomede was true of Prior.

In the *Epistles to Lord Bathurst* and *Lord Burlington* Dr. Warburton has endeavoured to find a train of thought which was never in the writer's head, and, to support his hypothesis, has printed that first which was published last. In one the most valuable passage is perhaps the elogy on Good Sense, and the other the End of the Duke of Buckingham.

The *Epistle to Arbuthnot,* now arbitrarily called

23. Gottfried Leibnitz (1646–1716), the German philosopher who had a good deal of influence on Pope's thinking.

24. See *Moral Essays*, I, 141–148.

the *Prologue to the Satires*, is a performance consisting, as it seems, of many fragments wrought into one design, which by this union of scattered beauties contains more striking paragraphs than could probably have been brought together into an occasional work. As there is no stronger motive to exertion than self-defence, no part has more elegance, spirit, or dignity than the poet's vindication of his own character. The meanest passage is the satire upon Sporus.

Of the two poems which derived their names from the year, and which are called the *Epilogue to the Satires*, it was very justly remarked by Savage that the second was in the whole more strongly conceived and more equally supported, but that it had no single passages equal to the contention in the first for the dignity of Vice, and the celebration of the triumph of Corruption.

The *Imitations of Horace* seem to have been written as relaxations of his genius. This employment became his favourite by its facility; the plan was ready to his hand, and nothing was required but to accommodate as he could the sentiments of an old author to recent facts or familiar images; but what is easy is seldom excellent: such imitations cannot give pleasure to common readers. The man of learning may be sometimes surprised and delighted by an unexpected parallel; but the comparison requires knowledge of the original, which will likewise often detect strained applications. Between Roman images and English manners there will be an irreconcileable dissimilitude, and the work will be generally uncouth and party-coloured; neither original nor translated, neither ancient nor modern.

Pope had, in proportions very nicely adjusted to each other, all the qualities that constitute genius. He had Invention, by which new trains of events are formed and new scenes of imagery displayed, as in *The Rape of the Lock*, and by which extrinsick and adventitious embellishments and illustrations are connected with a known subject, as in the *Essay on Criticism*; he had Imagination, which strongly impresses on the writer's mind and enables him to convey to the reader the various forms of nature, incidents of life, and energies of passion, as in his *Eloisa, Windsor Forest*, and the *Ethick Epistles*; he had Judgement, which selects from life or nature what the present purpose requires, and, by separating the essence of things from its concomitants, often makes the representation more powerful than the reality; and he had colours of language always before him ready to decorate his matter with every grace of elegant expression, as when he accommodates his diction to the wonderful multiplicity of Homer's sentiments and descriptions.

Poetical expression includes sound as well as meaning. "Musick," says Dryden, "is inarticulate poetry"; among the excellences of Pope, therefore, must be mentioned the melody of his metre. By perusing the works of Dryden he discovered the most perfect fabrick of English verse, and habituated himself to that only which he found the best; in consequence of which restraint his poetry has been censured as too uniformly musical, and as glutting the ear with unvaried sweetness. I suspect this objection to be the cant of those who judge by principles rather than perception; and who would even themselves have less pleasure in his works if he had tried to relieve attention by studied discords, or affected to break his lines and vary his pauses.

But though he was thus careful of his versification he did not oppress his powers with superfluous rigour. He seems to have thought with Boileau that the practice of writing might be refined till the difficulty should overbalance the advantage. The construction of his language is not always strictly grammatical; with those rhymes which prescription had conjoined he contented himself, without regard to Swift's remonstrances,[25] though there was no striking consonance; nor was he very careful to vary his terminations or to refuse admission at a small distance to the same rhymes.

To Swift's edict for the exclusion of alexandrines and triplets he paid little regard; he admitted them, but, in the opinion of Fenton, too rarely: he uses them more liberally in his translation than his poems.

He has a few double rhymes, and always, I think, unsuccessfully, except once in *The Rape of the Lock*.

Expletives he very early ejected from his verses; but he now and then admits an epithet rather commodious than important. Each of the six first lines of the *Iliad* might lose two syllables with very little

25. Swift's remonstrances: see Swift's letter to Pope, June 28, 1715.

diminution of the meaning; and sometimes, after all his art and labour, one verse seems to be made for the sake of another. In his latter productions the diction is sometimes vitiated by French idioms, with which Bolingbroke had perhaps infected him.

I have been told that the couplet by which he declared his own ear to be most gratified was this:

Lo, where Mæotis sleeps, and hardly flows
The freezing Tanais thro' a waste of snows.[26]

But the reason of this preference I cannot discover.

It is remarked by Watts[27] that there is scarcely a happy combination of words or a phrase poetically elegant in the English language which Pope has not inserted into his version of Homer. How he obtained possession of so many beauties of speech it were desirable to know. That he gleaned from authors, obscure as well as eminent, what he thought brilliant or useful, and preserved it all in a regular collection, is not unlikely. When, in his last years, Hall's *Satires*[28] were shewn him he wished that he had seen them sooner.

New sentiments and new images others may produce, but to attempt any further improvement of versification will be dangerous. Art and diligence have now done their best, and what shall be added will be the effort of tedious toil and needless curiosity.

After all this it is surely superfluous to answer the question that has once been asked, Whether Pope was a poet? otherwise than by asking in return, If Pope be not a poet, where is poetry to be found? To circumscribe poetry by a definition will only shew the narrowness of the definer, though a definition which shall exclude Pope will not easily be made. Let us look round upon the present time, and back upon the past; let us enquire to whom the voice of mankind has decreed the wreath of poetry; let their productions be examined and their claims stated, and the pretensions of Pope will be no more disputed. Had he given the world only his version the name of poet must have been allowed him; if the writer of the *Iliad* were to class his successors he would assign a very high place to his translator, without requiring any other evidence of genius.

26. *Dunciad,* III, 87–88. **27. Watts:** Isaac Watts (1674–1748), poet and hymn writer. **28.** Joseph Hall (1574–1656), the bitter satirist, author of *Virgidemiarum Sex Libri.*

From THE LIFE OF GRAY

. . .

Gray's poetry is now to be considered, and I hope not to be looked on as an enemy to his name if I confess that I contemplate it with less pleasure than his life.

His *Ode on Spring* has something poetical, both in the language and the thought; but the language is too luxuriant, and the thoughts have nothing new. There has of late arisen a practice of giving to adjectives, derived from substantives, the termination of participles, such as the *cultured* plain, the *daisied* bank; but I was sorry to see, in the lines of a scholar like Gray, "the *honied* Spring." The morality is natural, but too stale; the conclusion is pretty.

The poem on the Cat was doubtless by its author considered as a trifle, but it is not a happy trifle. In the first stanza "the azure flowers that blow," shew resolutely a rhyme is sometimes made when it cannot easily be found. Selima, the Cat, is called a nymph, with some violence both to language and sense; but there is good use made of it when it is done; for of the two lines,

What female heart can gold despise?
What cat's averse to fish?

the first relates merely to the nymph, and the second only to the cat. The sixth stanza contains a melancholy truth, that "a favourite has no friend," but the last ends in a pointed sentence of no relation to the purpose; if what glistered had been "gold," the cat would not have gone into the water; and, if she had, would not less have been drowned.

The Prospect of Eton College suggests nothing to Gray which every beholder does not equally think and feel. His supplication to father Thames, to tell him who drives the hoop or tosses the ball, is useless and puerile. Father Thames has no better means of knowing than himself. His epithet "buxom health" is not elegant; he seems not to understand the word. Gray thought his language more poetical as it was more remote from common use: finding in Dryden "honey redolent of Spring," an expression that reaches the utmost limits of our language, Gray drove it a little more beyond common apprehension, by making "gales" to be "redolent of joy and youth."

Of the *Ode on Adversity* the hint was at first taken from "O Diva, gratum quæ regis Antium";[1] but Gray has excelled his original by the variety of his sentiments and by their moral application. Of this piece, at once poetical and rational, I will not by slight objections violate the dignity.

My process has now brought me to the "Wonderful Wonder of Wonders," the two Sister Odes; by which, though either vulgar ignorance or common sense at first universally rejected them, many have been since persuaded to think themselves delighted. I am one of those that are willing to be pleased, and therefore would gladly find the meaning of the first stanza of *The Progress of Poetry*.

Gray seems in his rapture to confound the images of "spreading sound" and "running water." A "stream of musick" may be allowed; but where does Musick, however "smooth and strong," after having visited the "verdant vales," "rowl down the steep amain," so as that "rocks and nodding groves rebellow to the roar"? If this be said of Musick, it is nonsense; if it be said of Water, it is nothing to the purpose.

The second stanza, exhibiting Mars's car and Jove's eagle, is unworthy of further notice. Criticism disdains to chase a school-boy to his commonplaces.

To the third it may likewise be objected that it is drawn from Mythology, though such as may be more easily assimilated to real life. "Idalia's velvet-green" has something of cant. An epithet or metaphor drawn from Nature ennobles Art; an epithet or metaphor drawn from Art degrades Nature. Gray is too fond of words arbitrarily compounded. "Many-twinkling" was formerly censured as not analogical; we may say *many spotted*, but scarcely *many-spotting*. The stanza, however, has something pleasing.

Of the second ternary[2] of stanzas the first endeavours to tell something, and would have told it had it not been crossed by Hyperion; the second describes well enough the universal prevalence of poetry, but I am afraid that the conclusion will not rise from the premises. The caverns of the North and the plains of Chili are not the residences of "Glory" and "generous Shame." But that Poetry and Virtue go always together is an opinion so pleasing that I can forgive him who resolves to think it true.

The third stanza sounds big with Delphi, and Egean, and Ilissus, and Meander, and "hallowed fountain" and "solemn sound"; but in all Gray's odes there is a kind of cumbrous splendour which we wish away. His position is at last false: in the time of Dante and Petrarch, from whom he derives our first school of poetry, Italy was overrun by "tyrant power" and "coward vice"; nor was our state much better when we first borrowed the Italian arts.

Of the third ternary the first gives a mythological birth of Shakespeare. What is said of that mighty genius is true; but it is not said happily: the real effects of this poetical power are put out of sight by the pomp of machinery. Where truth is sufficient to fill the mind, fiction is worse than useless; the counterfeit debases the genuine.

His account of Milton's blindness, if we suppose it caused by study in the formation of his poem, a supposition surely allowable, is poetically true, and happily imagined. But the "car" of Dryden, with his "two coursers," has nothing in it peculiar; it is a car in which any other rider may be placed.

The Bard appears at the first view to be, as Algarotti[3] and others have remarked, an imitation of the prophecy of Nereus.[4] Algarotti thinks it superior to its original, and, if preference depends only on the imagery and animation of the two poems, his judgement is right. There is in *The Bard* more force, more thought, and more variety. But to copy is less than to invent, and the copy has been unhappily produced at a wrong time. The fiction of Horace was to the Romans credible; but its revival disgusts us with apparent and unconquerable falsehood. "Incredulus odi." [5]

To select a singular event, and swell it to a giant's bulk by fabulous appendages of spectres and predictions, has little difficulty, for he that forsakes the probable may always find the marvellous. And it has little use: we are affected only as we believe; we are improved only as we find something

LIFE OF GRAY. 1. **"O Diva . . . Antium"**: "O goddess who rules over delightful Antium." Horace, *Odes,* I, 35. 2. **ternary:** set of three.

3. **Algarotti:** Francesco Algarotti (1712–1764), Italian scientist, essayist, critic. 4. **Nereus:** Nereus, an old sea god with the gift of prophecy. See Horace, *Odes,* I, 15. 5. **"Incredulus odi"**: "I hate it when I can't believe." Horace, *Ars Poetica,* 1. 188.

to be imitated or declined. I do not see that *The Bard* promotes any truth, moral or political.

His stanzas are too long, especially his epodes; the ode is finished before the ear has learned its measures, and consequently before it can receive pleasure from their consonance and recurrence.

Of the first stanza the abrupt beginning has been celebrated, but technical beauties can give praise only to the inventor. It is in the power of any man to rush abruptly upon his subject, that has read the ballad of *Johnny Armstrong*,

Is there ever a man in all Scotland—

The initial resemblances, or alliterations, "ruin," "ruthless," "helm or hauberk," are below the grandeur of a poem that endeavours at sublimity.

In the second stanza the Bard is well described; but in the third we have the puerilities of obsolete mythology. When we are told that Cadwallo "hush'd the stormy main," and that Modred "made huge Plinlimmon bow his cloud-top'd head," attention recoils from the repetition of a tale that, even when it was first heard, was heard with scorn.

The "weaving" of the "winding sheet" he borrowed, as he owns, from the northern Bards; but their texture, however, was very properly the work of female powers, as the art of spinning the thread of life in another mythology. Theft is always dangerous; Gray has made weavers of his slaughtered bards by a fiction outrageous and incongruous. They are then called upon to "Weave the warp, and weave the woof," perhaps with no great propriety; for it is by crossing the woof with the warp that men weave the web or piece; and the first line was dearly bought by the admission of its wretched correspondent, "Give ample room and verge enough." He has, however, no other line as bad.

The third stanza of the second ternary is commended, I think, beyond its merit. The personification is indistinct. Thirst and Hunger are not alike, and their features, to make the imagery perfect, should have been discriminated. We are told, in the same stanza, how "towers" are "fed." But I will no longer look for particular faults; yet let it be observed that the ode might have been concluded with an action of better example: but suicide is always to be had without expence of thought.

These odes are marked by glittering accumulations of ungraceful ornaments: they strike, rather than please; the images are magnified by affectation; the language is laboured into harshness. The mind of the writer seems to work with unnatural violence. "Double, double, toil and trouble." He has a kind of strutting dignity, and is tall by walking on tiptoe. His art and his struggle are too visible, and there is too little appearance of ease and nature.

To say that he has no beauties would be unjust: a man like him, of great learning and great industry, could not but produce something valuable. When he pleases least, it can only be said that a good design was ill directed.

His translations of Northern and Welsh poetry deserve praise: the imagery is preserved, perhaps often improved; but the language is unlike the language of other poets.

In the character of his *Elegy* I rejoice to concur with the common reader; for by the common sense of readers uncorrupted with literary prejudices, after all the refinements of subtilty and the dogmatism of learning, must be finally decided all claim to poetical honours. The *Church-yard* abounds with images which find a mirrour in every mind, and with sentiments to which every bosom returns an echo. The four stanzas beginning "Yet even these bones" are to me original: I have never seen the notions in any other place; yet he that reads them here persuades himself that he has always felt them. Had Gray written often thus it had been vain to blame, and useless to praise him.

From THE LIFE OF MILTON

. . .

His literature was unquestionably great. He read all the languages which are considered either as learned or polite: Hebrew, with its two dialects, Greek, Latin, Italian, French, and Spanish. In Latin his skill was such as places him in the first rank of writers and criticks; and he appears to have cultivated Italian with uncommon diligence. The books in which his daughter, who used to read to him, represented him as most delighting, after Homer, which he could almost repeat, were Ovid's *Metamorphoses* and Euripides. His Euripides is, by Mr. Cradock's kindness,[1] now in my hands: the

LIFE OF MILTON. 1. The writer Joseph Cradock (1742–1826).

margin is sometimes noted; but I have found nothing remarkable.

Of the English poets he set most value upon Spenser, Shakespeare, and Cowley. Spenser was apparently his favourite; Shakespeare he may easily be supposed to like, with every other skilful reader, but I should not have expected that Cowley, whose ideas of excellence were different from his own, would have had much of his approbation. His character of Dryden, who sometimes visited him, was that he was a good rhymist, but no poet.

His theological opinions are said to have been first Calvinistical, and afterwards, perhaps when he began to hate the Presbyterians, to have extended towards Arminianism.[2] In the mixed questions of theology and government he never thinks that he can recede far enough from popery or prelacy; but what Baudius says of Erasmus[3] seems applicable to him: "magis habuit quod fugeret, quam quod sequeretur." He had determined rather what to condemn than what to approve. He has not associated himself with any denomination of Protestants: we know rather what he was not, than what he was. He was not of the church of Rome; he was not of the church of England.

To be of no church is dangerous. Religion, of which the rewards are distant and which is animated only by Faith and Hope, will glide by degrees out of the mind unless it be invigorated and reimpressed by external ordinances, by stated calls to worship, and the salutary influence of example. Milton, who appears to have had full conviction of the truth of Christianity, and to have regarded the Holy Scriptures with the profoundest veneration, to have been untainted by any heretical peculiarity of opinion, and to have lived in a confirmed belief of the immediate and occasional agency of Providence, yet grew old without any visible worship. In the distribution of his hours, there was no hour of prayer, either solitary or with his household; omitting publick prayers, he omitted all.

Of this omission the reason has been sought, upon a supposition which ought never to be made, that men live with their own approbation, and justify their conduct to themselves. Prayer certainly was not thought superfluous by him, who represents our first parents as praying acceptably in the state of innocence, and efficaciously after their fall. That he lived without prayer can hardly be affirmed; his studies and meditations were an habitual prayer. The neglect of it in his family was probably a fault for which he condemned himself, and which he intended to correct, but that death, as too often happens, intercepted his reformation.

His political notions were those of an acrimonious and surly republican, for which it is not known that he gave any better reason than that "a popular government was the most frugal; for the trappings of a monarchy would set up an ordinary commonwealth." It is surely very shallow policy, that supposes money to be the chief good; and even this without considering that the support and expence of a Court is for the most part only a particular kind of traffick, by which money is circulated without any national impoverishment.

Milton's republicanism was, I am afraid, founded in an envious hatred of greatness, and a sullen desire of independence; in petulance impatient of controul, and pride disdainful of superiority. He hated monarchs in the state and prelates in the church; for he hated all whom he was required to obey. It is to be suspected that his predominant desire was to destroy rather than establish, and that he felt not so much the love of liberty as repugnance to authority.

It has been observed that they who most loudly clamour for liberty do not most liberally grant it. What we know of Milton's character in domestick relations is, that he was severe and arbitrary. His family consisted of women; and there appears in his books something like a Turkish contempt of females, as subordinate and inferior beings. That his own daughters might not break the ranks, he suffered them to be depressed by a mean and penurious education. He thought woman made only for obedience, and man only for rebellion. . . .

. . .

One of the poems on which much praise has been bestowed is *Lycidas*; of which the diction is harsh, the rhymes uncertain, and the numbers unpleasing. What beauty there is, we must therefore

2. **Arminianism:** the teachings of James Arminius (1560–1609), a Dutch Protestant theologian. Arminius opposed Calvin's doctrine of predestination. 3. **Baudius . . . Erasmus:** Dominic Baudius (1561–1613), poet and scholar; Desiderius Erasmus (1466–1536), the great Dutch Renaissance scholar and humanist.

seek in the sentiments and images. It is not to be considered as the effusion of real passion; for passion runs not after remote allusions and obscure opinions. Passion plucks no berries from the myrtle and ivy, nor calls upon Arethuse and Mincius, nor tells of "rough satyrs and fauns with cloven heel." Where there is leisure for fiction there is little grief.

In this poem there is no nature, for there is no truth; there is no art, for there is nothing new. Its form is that of a pastoral, easy, vulgar, and therefore disgusting: whatever images it can supply are long ago exhausted; and its inherent improbability always forces dissatisfaction on the mind. When Cowley tells of Hervey that they studied together, it is easy to suppose how much he must miss the companion of his labours and the partner of his discoveries; but what image of tenderness can be excited by these lines!

> We drove afield, and both together heard
> What time the grey fly winds her sultry horn,
> Battening our flocks with the fresh dews of night.

We know that they never drove afield, and that they had no flocks to batten; and though it be allowed that the representation may be allegorical, the true meaning is so uncertain and remote that it is never sought because it cannot be known when it is found.

Among the flocks and copses and flowers appear the heathen deities, Jove and Phœbus, Neptune and Æolus, with a long train of mythological imagery, such as a College easily supplies. Nothing can less display knowledge or less exercise invention than to tell how a shepherd has lost his companion and must now feed his flocks alone, without any judge of his skill in piping; and how one god asks another god what is become of Lycidas, and how neither god can tell. He who thus grieves will excite no sympathy; he who thus praises will confer no honour.

This poem has yet a grosser fault. With these trifling fictions are mingled the most awful and sacred truths, such as ought never to be polluted with such irreverent combinations. The shepherd likewise is now a feeder of sheep, and afterwards an ecclesiastical pastor, a superintendent of a Christian flock. Such equivocations are always unskilful; but here they are indecent, and at least approach to impiety, of which, however, I believe the writer not to have been conscious.

Such is the power of reputation justly acquired that its blaze drives away the eye from nice examination. Surely no man could have fancied that he read *Lycidas* with pleasure had he not known its author.

Of the two pieces, *L'Allegro* and *Il Penseroso*, I believe opinion is uniform; every man that reads them, reads them with pleasure. The author's design is not, what Theobald has remarked, merely to shew how objects derived their colours from the mind, by representing the operation of the same things upon the gay and the melancholy temper, or upon the same man as he is differently disposed; but rather how, among the successive variety of appearances, every disposition of mind takes hold on those by which it may be gratified.

The *chearful* man hears the lark in the morning; the *pensive* man hears the nightingale in the evening. The *chearful* man sees the cock strut, and hears the horn and hounds echo in the wood; then walks "not unseen" to observe the glory of the rising sun or listen to the singing milk-maid, and view the labours of the plowman and the mower; then casts his eyes about him over scenes of smiling plenty, and looks up to the distant tower, the residence of some fair inhabitant: thus he pursues rural gaiety through a day of labour or of play, and delights himself at night with the fanciful narratives of superstitious ignorance.

The *pensive* man at one time walks "unseen" to muse at midnight, and at another hears the sullen curfew. If the weather drives him home he sits in a room lighted only by "glowing embers"; or by a lonely lamp outwatches the North Star to discover the habitation of separate souls, and varies the shades of meditation by contemplating the magnificent or pathetick scenes of tragick and epick poetry. When the morning comes, a morning gloomy with rain and wind, he walks into the dark trackless woods, falls asleep by some murmuring water, and with melancholy enthusiasm expects some dream of prognostication or some musick played by aerial performers.

Both Mirth and Melancholy are solitary, silent inhabitants of the breast that neither receive nor transmit communication: no mention is therefore made of a philosophical friend or a pleasant companion. The seriousness does not arise from any participation of calamity, nor the gaiety from the pleasures of the bottle.

The man of *chearfulness* having exhausted the country tries what "towered cities" will afford, and mingles with scenes of splendor, gay assemblies, and nuptial festivities; but he mingles a mere spectator as, when the learned comedies of Jonson or the wild dramas of Shakespeare are exhibited, he attends the theatre.

The *pensive* man never loses himself in crowds, but walks the cloister or frequents the cathedral. Milton probably had not yet forsaken the Church.

Both his characters delight in musick; but he seems to think that chearful notes would have obtained from Pluto a compleat dismission of Eurydice,[4] of whom solemn sounds only procured a conditional release.

For the old age of Chearfulness he makes no provision; but Melancholy he conducts with great dignity to the close of life. His Chearfulness is without levity, and his Pensiveness without asperity.

Through these two poems the images are properly selected and nicely distinguished, but the colours of the diction seem not sufficiently discriminated. I know not whether the characters are kept sufficiently apart. No mirth can, indeed, be found in his melancholy; but I am afraid that I always meet some melancholy in his mirth. They are two noble efforts of imagination. . . .

Those little pieces may be dispatched without much anxiety; a greater work calls for greater care. I am now to examine *Paradise Lost,* a poem which, considered with respect to design, may claim the first place, and with respect to performance the second, among the productions of the human mind.

By the general consent of criticks the first praise of genius is due to the writer of an epick poem, as it requires an assemblage of all the powers which are singly sufficient for other compositions. Poetry is the art of uniting pleasure with truth, by calling imagination to the help of reason. Epick poetry undertakes to teach the most important truths by the most pleasing precepts, and therefore relates some great event in the most affecting manner. History must supply the writer with the rudiments of narration, which he must improve and exalt by a nobler art, must animate by dramatick energy, and diversify by retrospection and anticipation; morality must teach him the exact bounds and different shades of vice and virtue; from policy and the practice of life he has to learn the discriminations of character and the tendency of the passions, either single or combined; and physiology must supply him with illustrations and images. To put these materials to poetical use is required an imagination capable of painting nature and realizing fiction. Nor is he yet a poet till he has attained the whole extension of his language, distinguished all the delicacies of phrase, and all the colours of words, and learned to adjust their different sounds to all the varieties of metrical modulation.

Bossu[5] is of opinion that the poet's first work is to find a *moral,* which his fable is afterwards to illustrate and establish. This seems to have been the process only of Milton: the moral of other poems is incidental and consequent; in Milton's only it is essential and intrinsick. His purpose was the most useful and the most arduous: "to vindicate the ways of God to man"; to shew the reasonableness of religion, and the necessity of obedience to the Divine Law.

To convey this moral there must be a *fable,* a narration artfully constructed, so as to excite curiosity and surprise expectation. In this part of his work Milton must be confessed to have equalled every other poet. He has involved in his account of the Fall of Man the events which preceded, and those that were to follow it: he has interwoven the whole system of theology with such propriety that every part appears to be necessary, and scarcely any recital is wished shorter for the sake of quickening the progress of the main action.

The subject of an epick poem is naturally an event of great importance. That of Milton is not the destruction of a city, the conduct of a colony, or the foundation of an empire. His subject is the fate of worlds, the revolutions of heaven and of earth; rebellion against the Supreme King raised by the highest order of created beings; the overthrow of their host and the punishment of their

4. Eurydice: Eurydice, wife of Orpheus, whose power of music secured an agreement from Pluto, god of the underworld, to bring her back from the dead. There was one condition: that Orpheus not look back at her. Glancing back to see whether she was following, however, he lost her forever.

5. Bossu: René Le Bossu (1631–1680), French neoclassical critic and author of a *Treatise on the Epic Poem.*

crime; the creation of a new race of reasonable creatures; their original happiness and innocence, their forfeiture of immortality, and their restoration to hope and peace.

Great events can be hastened or retarded only by persons of elevated dignity. Before the greatness displayed in Milton's poem all other greatness shrinks away. The weakest of his agents are the highest and noblest of human beings, the original parents of mankind; with whose actions the elements consented; on whose rectitude or deviation of will depended the state of terrestrial nature and the condition of all the future inhabitants of the globe.

Of the other agents in the poem, the chief are such as it is irreverence to name on slight occasions. The rest were lower powers;

> of which the least could wield
> Those elements, and arm him with the force
> Of all their regions;

powers which only the controul of Omnipotence restrains from laying creation waste, and filling the vast expanse of space with ruin and confusion. To display the motives and actions of beings thus superiour, so far as human reason can examine them or human imagination represent them, is the task which this mighty poet has undertaken and performed.

In the examination of epick poems much speculation is commonly employed upon the *characters*. The characters in the *Paradise Lost* which admit of examination are those of angels and of man; of angels good and evil, of man in his innocent and sinful state.

Among the angels the virtue of Raphael is mild and placid, of easy condescension and free communication; that of Michael is regal and lofty, and, as may seem, attentive to the dignity of his own nature. Abdiel and Gabriel appear occasionally, and act as every incident requires; the solitary fidelity of Abdiel is very amiably painted.

Of the evil angels the characters are more diversified. To Satan, as Addison observes, such sentiments are given as suit "the most exalted and most depraved being." [6] Milton has been censured by Clarke for the impiety which sometimes breaks from Satan's mouth. For there are thoughts, as he justly remarks, which no observation of character can justify, because no good man would willingly permit them to pass, however transiently, through his own mind.[7] To make Satan speak as a rebel, without any such expressions as might taint the reader's imagination, was indeed one of the great difficulties in Milton's undertaking, and I cannot but think that he has extricated himself with great happiness. There is in Satan's speeches little that can give pain to a pious ear. The language of rebellion cannot be the same with that of obedience. The malignity of Satan foams in haughtiness and obstinacy; but his expressions are commonly general, and not otherwise offensive than as they are wicked.

The other chiefs of the celestial rebellion are very judiciously discriminated in the first and second books; and the ferocious character of Moloch appears, both in the battle and the council, with exact consistency.

To Adam and to Eve are given during their innocence such sentiments as innocence can generate and utter. Their love is pure benevolence and mutual veneration; their repasts are without luxury and their diligence without toil. Their addresses to their Maker have little more than the voice of admiration and gratitude. Fruition left them nothing to ask, and Innocence left them nothing to fear.

But with guilt enter distrust and discord, mutual accusation, and stubborn self-defence; they regard each other with alienated minds, and dread their Creator as the avenger of their transgression. At last they seek shelter in his mercy, soften to repentance, and melt in supplication. Both before and after the Fall the superiority of Adam is diligently sustained.

Of the *probable* and the *marvellous*, two parts of a vulgar epick poem which immerge the critick in deep consideration, the *Paradise Lost* requires little to be said. It contains the history of a miracle, of Creation and Redemption; it displays the power and the mercy of the Supreme Being; the probable therefore is marvellous, and the marvellous is probable. The substance of the narrative is truth; and as truth allows no choice, it is, like necessity, superior to rule. To the accidental or adventitious

6. See *Spectator*, No. 303.

7. John Clarke (1687–1734), classical scholar. Clarke's observation is made in his *Essay upon Study* (1731), pp. 204–207.

parts, as to every thing human, some slight exceptions may be made. But the main fabrick is immovably supported.

It is justly remarked by Addison[8] that this poem has, by the nature of its subject, the advantage above all others, that it is universally and perpetually interesting. All mankind will, through all ages, bear the same relation to Adam and to Eve, and must partake of that good and evil which extend to themselves.

Of the *machinery,* so called from θεὸς ἀπὸ μηχανῆς[9] by which is meant the occasional interposition of supernatural power, another fertile topic of critical remarks, here is no room to speak, because every thing is done under the immediate and visible direction of Heaven; but the rule is so far observed that no part of the action could have been accomplished by any other means.

Of *episodes* I think there are only two, contained in Raphael's relation of the war in heaven and Michael's prophetick account of the changes to happen in this world. Both are closely connected with the great action; one was necessary to Adam as a warning, the other as a consolation.

To the compleatness or *integrity* of the design nothing can be objected; it has distinctly and clearly what Aristotle requires, a beginning, a middle, and an end. There is perhaps no poem of the same length from which so little can be taken without apparent mutilation. Here are no funeral games, nor is there any long description of a shield. The short digressions at the beginning of the third, seventh, and ninth books might doubtless be spared; but superfluities so beautiful who would take away? or who does not wish that the author of the *Iliad* had gratified succeeding ages with a little knowledge of himself? Perhaps no passages are more frequently or more attentively read than those extrinsick paragraphs; and, since the end of poetry is pleasure, that cannot be unpoetical with which all are pleased.

The questions, whether the action of the poem be strictly *one,* whether the poem can be properly termed *heroick,* and who is the hero, are raised by such readers as draw their principles of judgement rather from books than from reason. Milton, though he intituled *Paradise Lost* only a "poem," yet calls it himself "heroick song." Dryden, petulantly and indecently, denies the heroism of Adam because he was overcome; but there is no reason why the hero should not be unfortunate except established practice, since success and virtue do not go necessarily together. Cato is the hero of Lucan, but Lucan's authority will not be suffered by Quintilian to decide. However, if success be necessary, Adam's deceiver was at last crushed; Adam was restored to his Maker's favour, and therefore may securely resume his human rank.

After the scheme and fabrick of the poem must be considered its component parts, the sentiments, and the diction.

The *sentiments,* as expressive of manners or appropriated to characters, are for the greater part unexceptionably just.

Splendid passages containing lessons of morality or precepts of prudence occur seldom. Such is the original formation of this poem that as it admits no human manners till the Fall, it can give little assistance to human conduct. Its end is to raise the thoughts above sublunary cares or pleasures. Yet the praise of that fortitude, with which Abdiel maintained his singularity of virtue against the scorn of multitudes, may be accommodated to all times; and Raphael's reproof of Adam's curiosity after the planetary motions, with the answer returned by Adam, may be confidently opposed to any rule of life which any poet has delivered.

The thoughts which are occasionally called forth in the progress are such as could only be produced by an imagination in the highest degree fervid and active, to which materials were supplied by incessant study and unlimited curiosity. The heat of Milton's mind might be said to sublimate his learning, to throw off into his work the spirit of science, unmingled with its grosser parts.

He had considered creation in its whole extent, and his descriptions are therefore learned. He had accustomed his imagination to unrestrained indulgence, and his conceptions therefore were extensive. The characteristick quality of his poem is sublimity. He sometimes descends to the elegant, but his element is the great. He can occasionally invest himself with grace; but his natural port is gigantick loftiness. He can please when pleasure is required; but it is his peculiar power to astonish.

He seems to have been well acquainted with his

8. *Spectator,* No. 273. 9. The familiar *deus ex machina* (god coming from a machine). See Aristotle, *Poetics,* xv, 10.

own genius, and to know what it was that Nature had bestowed upon him more bountifully than upon others; the power of displaying the vast, illuminating the splendid, enforcing the awful, darkening the gloomy, and aggravating the dreadful: he therefore chose a subject on which too much could not be said, on which he might tire his fancy without the censure of extravagance.

The appearances of nature, and the occurrences of life did not satiate his appetite of greatness. To paint things as they are requires a minute attention, and employs the memory rather than the fancy. Milton's delight was to sport in the wide regions of possibility; reality was a scene too narrow for his mind. He sent his faculties out upon discovery, into worlds where only imagination can travel, and delighted to form new modes of existence, and furnish sentiment and action to superior beings, to trace the counsels of hell, or accompany the choirs of heaven.

But he could not be always in other worlds: he must sometimes revisit earth, and tell of things visible and known. When he cannot raise wonder by the sublimity of his mind he gives delight by its fertility.

Whatever be his subject he never fails to fill the imagination. But his images and descriptions of the scenes or operations of Nature do not seem to be always copied from original form, nor to have the freshness, raciness, and energy of immediate observation. He saw Nature, as Dryden expresses it, "through the spectacles of books"; and on most occasions calls learning to his assistance. The garden of Eden brings to his mind the vale of Enna, where Proserpine was gathering flowers. Satan makes his way through fighting elements, like Argo between the Cyanean rocks or Ulysses between the two *Sicilian* whirlpools, when he shunned Charybdis "on the larboard." The mythological allusions have been justly censured, as not being always used with notice of their vanity; but they contribute variety to the narration, and produce an alternate exercise of the memory and the fancy.

His similes are less numerous and more various than those of his predecessors. But he does not confine himself within the limits of rigorous comparison: his great excellence is amplitude, and he expands the adventitious image beyond the dimensions which the occasion required. Thus, comparing the shield of Satan to the orb of the Moon, he crowds the imagination with the discovery of the telescope and all the wonders which the telescope discovers.

Of his moral sentiments it is hardly praise to affirm that they excel those of all other poets; for this superiority he was indebted to his acquaintance with the sacred writings. The ancient epick poets, wanting the light of Revelation, were very unskilful teachers of virtue: their principal characters may be great, but they are not amiable. The reader may rise from their works with a greater degree of active or passive fortitude, and sometimes of prudence; but he will be able to carry away few precepts of justice, and none of mercy.

From the Italian writers it appears that the advantages of even Christian knowledge may be possessed in vain. Ariosto's pravity[10] is generally known; and, though the *Deliverance of Jerusalem* may be considered as a sacred subject, the poet[11] has been very sparing of moral instruction.

In Milton every line breathes sanctity of thought and purity of manners, except when the train of the narration requires the introduction of the rebellious spirits; and even they are compelled to acknowledge their subjection to God in such a manner as excites reverence and confirms piety.

Of human beings there are but two; but those two are the parents of mankind, venerable before their fall for dignity and innocence, and amiable after it for repentance and submission. In their first state their affection is tender without weakness, and their piety sublime without presumption. When they have sinned they shew how discord begins in mutual frailty, and how it ought to cease in mutual forbearance; how confidence of the divine favour is forfeited by sin, and how hope of pardon may be obtained by penitence and prayer. A state of innocence we can only conceive, if indeed in our present misery it be possible to conceive it; but the sentiments and worship proper to a fallen and offending being we have all to learn, as we have all to practise.

The poet whatever be done is always great. Our progenitors in their first state conversed with angels; even when folly and sin had degraded them

10. pravity: depravity. Ludovico Ariosto (1474–1533), Italian poet, author of the epic *Orlando Furioso.* **11.** Torquato Tasso (1544–1595), Italian epic poet, author of *Jerusalem Delivered.*

they had not in their humiliation "the port of mean suitors"; and they rise again to reverential regard when we find that their prayers were heard.

As human passions did not enter the world before the Fall, there is in the *Paradise Lost* little opportunity for the pathetick; but what little there is has not been lost. That passion which is peculiar to rational nature, the anguish arising from the consciousness of transgression and the horrours attending the sense of the Divine Displeasure, are very justly described and forcibly impressed. But the passions are moved only on one occasion; sublimity is the general and prevailing quality in this poem—sublimity variously modified, sometimes descriptive, sometimes argumentative.

The defects and faults of *Paradise Lost,* for faults and defects every work of man must have, it is the business of impartial criticism to discover. As in displaying the excellence of Milton I have not made long quotations, because of selecting beauties there had been no end, I shall in the same general manner mention that which seems to deserve censure; for what Englishman can take delight in transcribing passages, which, if they lessen the reputation of Milton, diminish in some degree the honour of our country?

The generality of my scheme does not admit the frequent notice of verbal inaccuracies which Bentley, perhaps better skilled in grammar than in poetry, has often found, though he sometimes made them, and which he imputed to the obtrusions of a reviser whom the author's blindness obliged him to employ. A supposition rash and groundless, if he thought it true; and vile and pernicious if, as is said, he in private allowed it to be false.

The plan of *Paradise Lost* has this inconvenience, that it comprises neither human actions nor human manners. The man and woman who act and suffer are in a state which no other man or woman can ever know. The reader finds no transaction in which he can be engaged, beholds no condition in which he can by any effort of imagination place himself; he has, therefore, little natural curiosity or sympathy.

We all, indeed, feel the effects of Adam's disobedience; we all sin like Adam, and like him must all bewail our offences; we have restless and insidious enemies in the fallen angels, and in the blessed spirits we have guardians and friends; in the Redemption of mankind we hope to be included: in the description of heaven and hell we are surely interested, as we are all to reside hereafter either in the regions of horrour or of bliss.

But these truths are too important to be new: they have been taught to our infancy; they have mingled with our solitary thoughts and familiar conversation, and are habitually interwoven with the whole texture of life. Being therefore not new they raise no unaccustomed emotion in the mind: what we knew before we cannot learn; what is not unexpected, cannot surprise.

Of the ideas suggested by these awful scenes, from some we recede with reverence, except when stated hours require their association; and from others we shrink with horrour, or admit them only as salutary inflictions, as counterpoises to our interests and passions. Such images rather obstruct the career of fancy than incite it.

Pleasure and terrour are indeed the genuine sources of poetry; but poetical pleasure must be such as human imagination can at least conceive, and poetical terrour such as human strength and fortitude may combat. The good and evil of Eternity are too ponderous for the wings of wit; the mind sinks under them in passive helplessness, content with calm belief and humble adoration.

Known truths however may take a different appearance, and be conveyed to the mind by a new train of intermediate images. This Milton has undertaken, and performed with pregnancy and vigour of mind peculiar to himself. Whoever considers the few radical positions which the Scriptures afforded him will wonder by what energetick operation he expanded them to such extent and ramified them to so much variety, restrained as he was by religious reverence from licentiousness of fiction.

Here is a full display of the united force of study and genius; of a great accumulation of materials, with judgement to digest and fancy to combine them: Milton was able to select from nature or from story, from ancient fable or from modern science, whatever could illustrate or adorn his thoughts. An accumulation of knowledge impregnated his mind, fermented by study and exalted by imagination.

It has been therefore said without an indecent hyperbole by one of his encomiasts, that in reading *Paradise Lost* we read a book of universal knowledge.

But original deficience cannot be supplied. The want of human interest is always felt. *Paradise Lost* is one of the books which the reader admires and lays down, and forgets to take up again. None ever wished it longer than it is. Its perusal is a duty rather than a pleasure. We read Milton for instruction, retire harassed and overburdened, and look elsewhere for recreation; we desert our master, and seek for companions.

Another inconvenience of Milton's design is that it requires the description of what cannot be described, the agency of spirits. He saw that immateriality supplied no images, and that he could not show angels acting but by instruments of action; he therefore invested them with form and matter. This being necessary was therefore defensible; and he should have secured the consistency of his system by keeping immateriality out of sight, and enticing his reader to drop it from his thoughts. But he has unhappily perplexed his poetry with his philosophy. His infernal and celestial powers are sometimes pure spirit and sometimes animated body. When Satan walks with his lance upon the "burning marle" [12] he has a body; when in his passage between hell and the new world he is in danger of sinking in the vacuity and is supported by a gust of rising vapours he has a body; when he animates the toad he seems to be mere spirit that can penetrate matter at pleasure; when he "starts up in his own shape," he has at least a determined form; and when he is brought before Gabriel he has "a spear and a shield," which he had the power of hiding in the toad, though the arms of the contending angels are evidently material.

The vulgar inhabitants of Pandæmonium,[13] being "incorporeal spirits," are "at large though without number" in a limited space, yet in the battle when they were overwhelmed by mountains their armour hurt them, "crushed in upon their substance, now grown gross by sinning." This likewise happened to the uncorrupted angels, who were overthrown "the sooner for their arms, for unarmed they might easily as spirits have evaded by contraction or remove." Even as spirits they are hardly spiritual, for "contraction" and "remove" are images of matter; but if they could have escaped without their armour, they might have escaped from it and left only the empty cover to be battered. Uriel, when he rides on a sun-beam, is material; Satan is material when he is afraid of the prowess of Adam.

The confusion of spirit and matter which pervades the whole narration of the war of heaven fills it with incongruity; and the book in which it is related is, I believe, the favourite of children, and gradually neglected as knowledge is increased.

After the operation of immaterial agents which cannot be explained may be considered that of allegorical persons, which have no real existence. To exalt causes into agents, to invest abstract ideas with form, and animate them with activity has always been the right of poetry. But such airy beings are for the most part suffered only to do their natural office, and retire. Thus Fame tells a tale and Victory hovers over a general or perches on a standard; but Fame and Victory can do no more. To give them any real employment or ascribe to them any material agency is to make them allegorical no longer, but to shock the mind by ascribing effects to non-entity. In the *Prometheus* of Æschylus we see Violence and Strength, and in the *Alcestis* of Euripides we see Death, brought upon the stage, all as active persons of the drama; but no precedents can justify absurdity.

Milton's allegory of Sin and Death is undoubtedly faulty. Sin is indeed the mother of Death, and may be allowed to be the portress of hell; but when they stop the journey of Satan, a journey described as real, and when Death offers him battle, the allegory is broken. That Sin and Death should have shewn the way to hell might have been allowed; but they cannot facilitate the passage by building a bridge, because the difficulty of Satan's passage is described as real and sensible, and the bridge ought to be only figurative. The hell assigned to the rebellious spirits is described as not less local than the residence of man. It is placed in some distant part of space, separated from the regions of harmony and order by a chaotick waste and an unoccupied vacuity; but Sin and Death worked up a "mole of aggregated soil," cemented with asphaltus; a work too bulky for ideal architects.

This unskilful allegory appears to me one of the greatest faults of the poem; and to this there was no temptation, but the author's opinion of its beauty.

To the conduct of the narrative some objections may be made. Satan is with great expectation

12. "burning marle": "burning earth." **13. Pandæmonium:** Pandæmonium is the home of all demons, the capital of Hell. See *Paradise Lost,* I, 756.

brought before Gabriel in Paradise, and is suffered to go away unmolested. The creation of man is represented as the consequence of the vacuity left in heaven by the expulsion of the rebels; yet Satan mentions it as a report "rife in heaven" before his departure.

To find sentiments for the state of innocence was very difficult; and something of anticipation perhaps is now and then discovered. Adam's discourse of dreams seems not to be the speculation of a new-created being. I know not whether his answer to the angel's reproof for curiosity does not want something of propriety: it is the speech of a man acquainted with many other men. Some philosophical notions, especially when the philosophy is false, might have been better omitted. The angel in a comparison speaks of "timorous deer," before deer were yet timorous, and before Adam could understand the comparison.

Dryden remarks that Milton has some flats among his elevations. This is only to say that all the parts are not equal. In every work one part must be for the sake of others; a palace must have passages, a poem must have transitions. It is no more to be required that wit should always be blazing than that the sun should always stand at noon. In a great work there is a vicissitude of luminous and opaque parts, as there is in the world a succession of day and night. Milton, when he has expatiated in the sky, may be allowed sometimes to revisit earth; for what other author ever soared so high or sustained his flight so long?

Milton, being well versed in the Italian poets, appears to have borrowed often from them; and, as every man catches something from his companions, his desire of imitating Ariosto's levity has disgraced his work with the "Paradise of Fools"; a fiction not in itself ill-imagined, but too ludicrous for its place.

His play on words, in which he delights too often; his equivocations, which Bentley endeavours to defend by the example of the ancients; his unnecessary and ungraceful use of terms of art it is not necessary to mention, because they are easily remarked and generally censured, and at last bear so little proportion to the whole that they scarcely deserve the attention of a critick.

Such are the faults of that wonderful performance *Paradise Lost*; which he who can put in balance with its beauties must be considered not as nice but as dull, as less to be censured for want of candour than pitied for want of sensibility. . . .

. . .

The highest praise of genius is original invention. Milton cannot be said to have contrived the structure of an epick poem, and therefore owes reverence to that vigour and amplitude of mind to which all generations must be indebted for the art of poetical narration, for the texture of the fable, the variation of incidents, the interposition of dialogue, and all the stratagems that surprise and enchain attention. But of all the borrowers from Homer Milton is perhaps the least indebted. He was naturally a thinker for himself, confident of his own abilities and disdainful of help or hindrance; he did not refuse admission to the thoughts or images of his predecessors, but he did not seek them. From his contemporaries he neither courted nor received support; there is in his writings nothing by which the pride of other authors might be gratified or favour gained, no exchange of praise or solicitation of support. His great works were performed under discountenance and in blindness, but difficulties vanished at his touch; he was born for whatever is arduous; and his work is not the greatest of heroick poems, only because it is not the first.

From THE LIFE OF COWLEY

Cowley, like other poets who have written with narrow views, and instead of tracing intellectual pleasure to its natural sources in the mind of man, paid their court to temporary prejudices, has been at one time too much praised, and too much neglected at another.

Wit, like all other things subject by their nature to the choice of man, has its changes and fashions, and at different times takes different forms. About the beginning of the seventeenth century appeared a race of writers that may be termed the metaphysical poets, of whom in a criticism on the works of Cowley it is not improper to give some account.

The metaphysical poets were men of learning, and to shew their learning was their whole endeavor; but, unluckily resolving to shew it in rhyme, instead of writing poetry they only wrote verses, and very often such verses as stood the trial of the finger better than of the ear; for the modulation was so imperfect that they were only found to be verses by counting the syllables.

If the father of criticism has rightly denominated poetry τέχνη μιμητική, *an imitative art*, these writers will without great wrong lose their right to the name of poets, for they cannot be said to have imitated any thing: they neither copied nature nor life; neither painted the forms of matter nor represented the operations of intellect.

Those however who deny them to be poets allow them to be wits. Dryden confesses of himself and his contemporaries that they fall below Donne in wit, but maintains that they surpass him in poetry.[1]

If Wit be well described by Pope as being "that which has been often thought, but was never before so well expressed,"[2] they certainly never attained nor ever sought it, for they endeavoured to be singular in their thoughts, and were careless of their diction. But Pope's account of wit is undoubtedly erroneous; he depresses it below its natural dignity, and reduces it from strength of thought to happiness of language.

If by a more noble and more adequate conception that be considered as Wit which is at once natural and new, that which though not obvious is, upon its first production, acknowledged to be just; if it be that, which he that never found it, wonders how he missed; to wit of this kind the metaphysical poets have seldom risen. Their thoughts are often new, but seldom natural; they are not obvious, but neither are they just; and the reader, far from wondering that he missed them, wonders more frequently by what perverseness of industry they were ever found.

But Wit, abstracted from its effects upon the hearer, may be more rigorously and philosophically considered as a kind of *discordia concors;* a combination of dissimilar images, or discovery of occult resemblances in things apparently unlike. Of wit, thus defined, they have more than enough. The most heterogeneous ideas are yoked by violence together; nature and art are ransacked for illustrations, comparisons, and allusions; their learning instructs, and their subtilty surprises; but the reader commonly thinks his improvement dearly bought, and, though he sometimes admires, is seldom pleased.

From this account of their compositions it will be readily inferred that they were not successful in representing or moving the affections. As they were wholly employed on something unexpected and surprising they had no regard to that uniformity of sentiment, which enables us to conceive and to excite the pains and the pleasure of other minds: they never enquired what on any occasion they should have said or done, but wrote rather as beholders than partakers of human nature; as beings looking upon good and evil, impassive and at leisure; as Epicurean deities making remarks on the actions of men and the vicissitudes of life, without interest and without emotion. Their courtship was void of fondness and their lamentation of sorrow. Their wish was only to say what they hoped had been never said before.

Nor was the sublime more within their reach than the pathetick; for they never attempted that comprehension and expanse of thought which at once fills the whole mind, and of which the first effect is sudden astonishment, and the second rational admiration. Sublimity is produced by aggregation, and littleness by dispersion. Great thoughts are always general, and consist in positions not limited by exceptions, and in descriptions not descending to minuteness. It is with great propriety that subtlety, which in its original import means exility of particles, is taken in its metaphorical meaning for nicety of distinction. Those writers who lay on the watch for novelty could have little hope of greatness; for great things cannot have escaped former observation. Their attempts were always analytick: they broke every image into fragments, and could no more represent by their slender conceits and laboured particularities the prospects of nature or the scenes of life, than he who dissects a sun-beam with a prism can exhibit the wide effulgence of a summer noon.

What they wanted however of the sublime they endeavoured to supply by hyperbole; their amplification had no limits: they left not only reason but fancy behind them, and produced combinations of confused magnificence that not only could not be credited, but could not be imagined.

Yet great labour directed by great abilities is never wholly lost: if they frequently threw away their wit upon false conceits, they likewise sometimes struck out unexpected truth: if their conceits were far-fetched, they were often worth the car-

LIFE OF COWLEY. 1. *Essays*, ed. W. P. Ker (New York, 1961), II, 102. 2. *Essay on Criticism*, ll. 297–298.

riage. To write on their plan it was at least necessary to read and think. No man could be born a metaphysical poet, nor assume the dignity of a writer by descriptions copied from descriptions, by imitations borrowed from imitations, by traditional imagery and hereditary similes, by readiness of rhyme and volubility of syllables.

In perusing the works of this race of authors the mind is exercised either by recollection or inquiry; either something already learned is to be retrieved, or something new is to be examined. If their greatness seldom elevates their acuteness often surprises; if the imagination is not always gratified, at least the powers of reflection and comparison are employed; and in the mass of materials, which ingenious absurdity has thrown together, genuine wit and useful knowledge may be sometimes found, buried perhaps in grossness of expression, but useful to those who know their value, and such as, when they are expanded to perspicuity and polished to elegance, may give lustre to works which have more propriety though less copiousness of sentiment.

From THE LIFE OF SAVAGE

. . .

Such were the life and death of Richard Savage, a man equally distinguished by his virtues and vices; and at once remarkable for his weaknesses and abilities.

He was of a middle stature, of a thin habit of body, a long visage, coarse features, and melancholy aspect; of a grave and manly deportment, a solemn dignity of mien, but which, upon a nearer acquaintance, softened into an engaging easiness of manners. His walk was slow, and his voice tremulous and mournful. He was easily excited to smiles, but very seldom provoked to laughter.

His mind was in an uncommon degree vigorous and active. His judgement was accurate, his apprehension quick, and his memory so tenacious that he was frequently observed to know what he had learned from others in a short time, better than those by whom he was informed; and could frequently recollect incidents with all their combination of circumstances, which few would have regarded at the present time, but which the quickness of his apprehension impressed upon him. He had the peculiar felicity that his attention never deserted him: he was present to every object, and regardful of the most trifling occurrences. He had the art of escaping from his own reflections, and accommodating himself to every new scene.

To this quality is to be imputed the extent of his knowledge, compared with the small time which he spent in visible endeavours to acquire it. He mingled in cursory conversation with the same steadiness of attention as others apply to a lecture; and, amidst the appearance of thoughtless gaiety, lost no new idea that was started, nor any hint that could be improved. He had therefore made in coffee-houses the same proficiency as others in their closets; and it is remarkable that the writings of a man of little education and little reading have an air of learning scarcely to be found in any other performances, but which perhaps as often obscures as embellishes them.

His judgement was eminently exact both with regard to writings and to men. The knowledge of life was indeed his chief attainment; and it is not without some satisfaction that I can produce the suffrage of Savage in favour of human nature, of which he never appeared to entertain such odious ideas as some, who perhaps had neither his judgement nor experience, have published, either in ostentation of their sagacity, vindication of their crimes, or gratification of their malice.

His method of life particularly qualified him for conversation, of which he knew how to practise all the graces. He was never vehement or loud, but at once modest and easy, open and respectful; his language was vivacious and elegant, and equally happy upon grave or humorous subjects. He was generally censured for not knowing when to retire, but that was not the defect of his judgement, but of his fortune; when he left his company he was frequently to spend the remaining part of the night in the street, or at least was abandoned to gloomy reflections, which it is not strange that he delayed as long as he could; and sometimes forgot that he gave others pain to avoid it himself.

It cannot be said that he made use of his abilities for the direction of his own conduct: an irregular and dissipated manner of life had made him the slave of every passion that happened to be excited by the presence of its object, and that slavery to his passions reciprocally produced a life irregular and dissipated. He was not master of his own motions, nor could promise any thing for the next day.

With regard to his economy nothing can be added to the relation of his life. He appeared to think himself born to be supported by others, and dispensed from all necessity of providing for himself; he therefore never prosecuted any scheme of advantage, nor endeavoured even to secure the profits which his writings might have afforded him. His temper was, in consequence of the dominion of his passions, uncertain and capricious: he was easily engaged, and easily disgusted; but he is accused of retaining his hatred more tenaciously than his benevolence.

He was compassionate both by nature and principle, and always ready to perform offices of humanity; but when he was provoked (and very small offences were sufficient to provoke him), he would prosecute his revenge with the utmost acrimony till his passion had subsided.

His friendship was therefore of little value; for though he was zealous in the support or vindication of those whom he loved, yet it was always dangerous to trust him, because he considered himself as discharged by the first quarrel from all ties of honour or gratitude, and would betray those secrets which, in the warmth of confidence, had been imparted to him. This practice drew upon him an universal accusation of ingratitude: nor can it be denied that he was very ready to set himself free from the load of an obligation, for he could not bear to conceive himself in a state of dependence; his pride being equally powerful with his other passions, and appearing in the form of insolence at one time, and of vanity at another. Vanity, the most innocent species of pride, was most frequently predominant: he could not easily leave off when he had once begun to mention himself or his works; nor ever read his verses without stealing his eyes from the page, to discover, in the faces of his audience, how they were affected with any favourite passage.

A kinder name than that of vanity ought to be given to the delicacy with which he was always careful to separate his own merit from every other man's, and to reject that praise to which he had no claim. He did not forget, in mentioning his performances, to mark every line that had been suggested or amended; and was so accurate as to relate that he owed *three words* in THE WANDERER to the advice of his friends.

His veracity was questioned, but with little reason; his accounts, though not indeed always the same, were generally consistent. When he loved any man he suppressed all his faults; and, when he had been offended by him, concealed all his virtues: but his characters were generally true, so far as he proceeded; though it cannot be denied that his partiality might have sometimes the effect of falsehood.

In cases indifferent he was zealous for virtue, truth, and justice: he knew very well the necessity of goodness to the present and future happiness of mankind; nor is there perhaps any writer who has less endeavoured to please by flattering the appetites or perverting the judgement.

As an author therefore, and he now ceases to influence mankind in any other character, if one piece which he had resolved to suppress be excepted, he has very little to fear from the strictest moral or religious censure. And though he may not be altogether secure against the objections of the critick, it must, however, be acknowledged that his works are the productions of a genius truly poetical, and, what many writers who have been more lavishly applauded cannot boast, that they have an original air, which has no resemblance of any foregoing work; that the versification and sentiments have a cast peculiar to themselves, which no man can imitate with success, because what was nature in Savage would in another be affectation. It must be confessed that his descriptions are striking, his images animated, his fictions justly imagined, and his allegories artfully pursued; that his diction is elevated, though sometimes forced, and his numbers sonorous and majestick, though frequently sluggish and encumbered. Of his style, the general fault is harshness, and its general excellence is dignity; of his sentiments, the prevailing beauty is sublimity, and uniformity the prevailing defect.

For his life or for his writings none, who candidly consider his fortune, will think an apology either necessary or difficult. If he was not always sufficiently instructed in his subject, his knowledge was at least greater than could have been attained by others in the same state. If his works were sometimes unfinished, accuracy cannot reasonably be exacted from a man oppressed with want, which he has no hope of relieving but by a speedy publication. The insolence and resentment of which he is accused were not easily to be avoided by a great mind, irritated by perpetual hardships, and constrained hourly to return the spurns of contempt and repress the insolence of prosperity; and vanity may surely readily be pardoned in him, to whom life afforded no other comforts than barren praises, and the consciousness of deserving them.

Those are no proper judges of his conduct who have slumbered away their time on the down of plenty, nor will any wise man presume to say, "Had I been in Savage's condition, I should have lived or written better than Savage."

This relation will not be wholly without its use if those who languish under any part of his sufferings shall be enabled to fortify their patience by reflecting that they feel only those afflictions from which the abilities of Savage did not exempt him; or those who, in confidence of superior capacities or attainments, disregard the common maxims of life, shall be reminded that nothing will supply the want of prudence, and that negligence and irregularity long continued will make knowledge useless, wit ridiculous, and genius contemptible.

(1784)

The History of Rasselas,

PRINCE OF ABISSINIA

I

DESCRIPTION OF A PALACE IN A VALLEY

Ye who listen with credulity to the whispers of fancy, and persue with eagerness the phantoms of hope; who expect that age will perform the promises of youth, and that the deficiencies of the present day will be supplied by the morrow; attend to the history of Rasselas prince of Abissinia.

Rasselas was the fourth son of the mighty emperour, in whose dominions the Father of waters begins his course; whose bounty pours down the streams of plenty, and scatters over half the world the harvests of Egypt.

According to the custom which has descended from age to age among the monarchs of the torrid zone, Rasselas was confined in a private palace, with the other sons and daughters of Abissinian royalty, till the order of succession should call him to the throne.

The place, which the wisdom or policy of antiquity had destined for the residence of the Abissinian princes, was a spacious valley in the kingdom of Amhara, surrounded on every side by mountains, of which the summits overhang the middle part. The only passage, by which it could be entered, was a cavern that passed under a rock, of which it has long been disputed whether it was the work of nature or of human industry. The outlet of the cavern was concealed by a thick wood, and the mouth which opened into the valley was closed with gates of iron, forged by the artificers of ancient days, so massy that no man could, without the help of engines, open or shut them.

From the mountains on every side, rivulets descended that filled all the valley with verdure and fertility, and formed a lake in the middle inhabited by fish of every species, and frequented by every fowl whom nature has taught to dip the wing in water. This lake discharged its superfluities by a stream which entered a dark cleft of the mountain on the northern side, and fell with dreadful noise from precipice to precipice till it was heard no more.

The sides of the mountains were covered with trees, the banks of the brooks were diversified with flowers; every blast shook spices from the rocks, and every month dropped fruits upon the ground. All animals that bite the grass, or brouse the shrub, whether wild or tame, wandered in this extensive circuit, secured from beasts of prey by the mountains which confined them. On one part were flocks and herds feeding in the pastures, on another all the beasts of chase frisking in the lawns; the sprightly kid was bounding on the rocks, the subtle monkey frolicking in the trees, and the solemn elephant reposing in the shade. All the diversities of the world were brought together, the blessings of nature were collected, and its evils extracted and excluded.

The valley, wide and fruitful, supplied its inhabitants with the necessaries of life, and all delights and superfluities were added at the annual visit which the emperour paid his children, when the iron gate was opened to the sound of musick; and during eight days every one that resided in the valley was required to propose whatever might contribute to make seclusion pleasant, to fill up the vacancies of attention, and lessen the tediousness of time. Every desire was immediately granted. All the artificers of pleasure were called to gladden the festivity; the musicians exerted the power of harmony, and the dancers shewed their activity before the princes, in hope that they should pass their lives in this blissful captivity, to which th[o]se only were admitted whose performance was thought able to add novelty to luxury. Such was the appearance of security and delight which this retirement afforded, that they to whom it was new always desired that it might be perpetual; and as those, on whom the iron gate had once closed, were never suffered to return, the effect of longer experience could not be known. Thus every year produced new schemes of delight, and new competitors for imprisonment.

The palace stood on an eminence raised about thirty paces above the surface of the lake. It was divided into many squares or courts, built with greater or less magnificence according to the rank of those for whom they were designed. The roofs were turned into arches of massy stone joined with a cement that grew harder by time, and the building stood from century to century, deriding the solstitial rains and equinoctial hurricanes, without need of reparation.

This house, which was so large as to be fully known to none but some ancient officers who successively inherited the secrets of the place, was built as if suspicion herself had dictated the plan. To every room there was an open and secret passage, every square had a communication with the rest, either from the upper stories by private galleries, or by subterranean passages from the lower apartments. Many of the columns had unsuspected cavities, in which a long race of monarchs had reposited their treasures. They then closed up the opening with marble, which was never to be removed but in the utmost exigencies of the kingdom; and recorded their accumulations in a book which was itself concealed in a tower not entered but by the emperour, attended by the prince who stood next in succession.

II

THE DISCONTENT OF RASSELAS IN THE HAPPY VALLEY

Here the sons and daughters of Abissinia lived only to know the soft vicissitudes of pleasure and repose, attended by all that were skilful to delight, and gratified with whatever the senses can enjoy. They wandered in gardens of fragrance, and slept in the fortresses of security. Every art was practised to make them pleased with their own condition. The sages who instructed them, told them of nothing but the miseries of publick life, and described all beyond the mountains as regions of calamity, where discord was always raging, and where man preyed upon man.

To heighten their opinion of their own felicity, they were daily entertained with songs, the subject of which was the *happy valley*. Their appetites were excited by frequent enumerations of different enjoyments, and revelry and merriment was the business of every hour from the dawn of morning to the close of even.

These methods were generally successful; few of the Princes had ever wished to enlarge their bounds, but passed their lives in full conviction that they had all within their reach that art or nature could bestow, and pitied those whom fate had excluded from this seat of tranquility, as the sport of chance, and the slaves of misery.

Thus they rose in the morning, and lay down at night, pleased with each other and with themselves, all but Rasselas, who, in the twenty-sixth year of his age, began to withdraw himself from their pastimes and assemblies, and to delight in solitary walks and silent meditation. He often sat before tables covered with luxury, and forgot to taste the dainties that were placed before him: he rose abruptly in the midst of the song, and hastily retired beyond the sound of musick. His attendants observed the change and endeavoured to renew his love of pleasure: he neglected their officiousness, repulsed their invitations, and spent day after day on the banks of rivulets sheltered with trees, where he sometimes listened to the birds in the branches, sometimes observed the fish playing in the stream, and anon cast his eyes upon the pastures and mountains filled with animals, of which some were biting the herbage, and some sleeping among the bushes.

This singularity of his humour made him much observed. One of the Sages, in whose conversation he had formerly delighted, followed him secretly, in hope of discovering the cause of his disquiet. Rasselas, who knew not that any one was near him, having for some time fixed his eyes upon the goats that were brousing among the rocks, began to compare their condition with his own.

"What," said he, "makes the difference between man and all the rest of the animal creation? Every beast that strays beside me has the same corporal necessities with myself; he is hungry and crops the grass, he is thirsty and drinks the stream, his thirst and hunger are appeased, he is satisfied and sleeps; he rises again and is hungry, he is again fed and is at rest. I am hungry and thirsty like him, but when thirst and hunger cease I am not at rest; I am, like him, pained with want, but am not, like him, satisfied with fulness. The intermediate hours are tedious and gloomy; I long again to be hungry that I may again quicken my attention. The birds peck the berries or the corn, and fly away to the groves where they sit in seeming happiness on the branches, and waste their lives in tuning one unvaried series of sounds. I likewise can call the lutanist and the singer, but the sounds that pleased me yesterday weary me to day, and will grow yet more wearisome to morrow. I can discover within me no power of perception which is not glutted with its proper pleasure, yet I do not feel myself delighted. Man has surely some latent sense for which this place affords no gratification, or he has some desires distinct from sense which must be satisfied before he can be happy."

After this he lifted up his head, and seeing the moon rising, walked towards the palace. As he passed through the fields, and saw the animals around him, "Ye, said he, are happy, and need not envy me that walk thus among you, burthened with myself; nor do I, ye gentle beings, envy your felicity; for it is not the felicity of man. I have many distresses from which ye are free; I fear pain when I do not feel it; I sometimes shrink at evils recollected, and sometimes start at evils anticipated: surely the equity of providence has ballanced peculiar sufferings with peculiar enjoyments."

With observations like these the prince amused himself as he returned, uttering them with a plaintive voice, yet with a look that discovered him to feel some complacence in his own perspicacity, and to receive some solace of the miseries of life, from consciousness of the delicacy with which he felt, and the eloquence with which he bewailed them. He mingled cheerfully in the diversions of the evening, and all rejoiced to find that his heart was lightened.

III

THE WANTS OF HIM THAT WANTS NOTHING

On the next day his old instructor, imagining that he had now made himself acquainted with his disease of mind, was in hope of curing it by counsel, and officiously sought an opportunity of conference, which the prince, having long considered him as one whose intellects were exhausted, was not very willing to afford: "Why, said he, does this man thus intrude upon me; shall I be never suffered to forget those lectures which pleased only while they were new, and to become new again must be forgotten?" He then walked into the wood, and composed himself to his usual meditations; when, before his thoughts had taken any settled form, he perceived his persuer at his side, and was at first prompted by his impatience to go hastily away; but, being unwilling to offend a man whom he had once reverenced and still loved, he invited him to sit down with him on the bank.

The old man, thus encouraged, began to lament the change which had been lately observed in the prince, and to enquire why he so often retired from the pleasures of the palace, to loneliness and silence. "I fly from pleasure, said the prince, because pleasure has ceased to please; I am lonely because I am miserable, and am unwilling to cloud with my presence the happiness of others." "You, Sir, said the sage, are the first who has complained of misery in the *happy valley*. I hope to convince you that your complaints have no real cause. You are here in full possession of all that the emperour of Abissinia can bestow; here is neither labour to be endured nor danger to be dreaded, yet here is all that labour or danger can procure or purchase. Look round and tell me which of your wants is without supply: if you want nothing, how are you unhappy?"

"That I want nothing, said the prince, or that I

know not what I want, is the cause of my complaint; if I had any known want, I should have a certain wish; that wish would excite endeavour, and I should not then repine to see the sun move so slowly towards the western mountain, or lament when the day breaks and sleep will no longer hide me from myself. When I see the kids and the lambs chasing one another, I fancy that I should be happy if I had something to persue. But, possessing all that I can want, I find one day and one hour exactly like another, except that the latter is still more tedious than the former. Let your experience inform me how the day may now seem as short as in my childhood, while nature was yet fresh, and every moment shewed me what I never had observed before. I have already enjoyed too much; give me something to desire."

The old man was surprized at this new species of affliction, and knew not what to reply, yet was unwilling to be silent. "Sir, said he, if you had seen the miseries of the world, you would know how to value your present state." "Now, said the prince, you have given me something to desire; I shall long to see the miseries of the world, since the sight of them is necessary to happiness."

IV

THE PRINCE CONTINUES TO GRIEVE AND MUSE

At this time the sound of musick proclaimed the hour of repast, and the conversation was concluded. The old man went away sufficiently discontented to find that his reasonings had produced the only conclusion which they were intended to prevent. But in the decline of life shame and grief are of short duration; whether it be that we bear easily what we have born long, or that, finding ourselves in age less regarded, we less regard others; or, that we look with slight regard upon afflictions, to which we know that the hand of death is about to put an end.

The prince, whose views were extended to a wider space could not speedily quiet his emotions. He had been before terrified at the length of life which nature promised him, because he considered that in a long time much must be endured; he now rejoiced in his youth, because in many years much might be done.

This first beam of hope, that had been ever darted into his mind, rekindled youth in his cheeks, and doubled the lustre of his eyes. He was fired with the desire of doing something, though he knew not yet with distinctness, either end or means.

He was now no longer gloomy and unsocial; but, considering himself as master of a secret stock of happiness, which he could enjoy only by concealing it, he affected to be busy in all schemes of diversion, and endeavoured to make others pleased with the state of which he himself was weary. But pleasures never can be so multiplied or continued, as not to leave much of life unemployed; there were many hours, both of the night and day, which he could spend without suspicion in solitary thought. The load of life was much lightened: he went eagerly into the assemblies, because he supposed the frequency of his presence necessary to the success of his purposes; he retired gladly to privacy, because he had now a subject of thought.

His chief amusement was to picture to himself that world which he had never seen; to place himself in various conditions; to be entangled in imaginary difficulties, and to be engaged in wild adventures: but his benevolence always terminated his projects in the relief of distress, the detection of fraud, the defeat of oppression, and the diffusion of happiness.

Thus passed twenty months of the life of Rasselas. He busied himself so intensely in visionary bustle, that he forgot his real solitude; and, amidst hourly preparations for the various incidents of human affairs, neglected to consider by what means he should mingle with mankind.

One day, as he was sitting on a bank, he feigned to himself an orphan virgin robbed of her little portion by a treacherous lover, and crying after him for restitution and redress. So strongly was the image impressed upon his mind, that he started up in the maid's defence, and run forward to seize the plunderer with all the eagerness of real pursuit. Fear naturally quickens the flight of guilt. Rasselas could not catch the fugitive with his utmost efforts; but, resolving to weary, by perseverance, him whom he could not surpass in speed, he pressed on till the foot of the mountain stopped his course.

Here he recollected himself, and smiled at his own useless impetuosity. Then raising his eyes to the mountain, "This, said he, is the fatal obstacle that hinders at once the enjoyment of pleasure, and the exercise of virtue. How long is it that my hopes and wishes have flown beyond this boundary of my life, which yet I never have attempted to surmount!"

Struck with this reflection, he sat down to muse, and remembered, that since he first resolved to escape from his confinement, the sun had passed twice over him in his annual course. He now felt a degree of regret with which he had never been before acquainted. He considered how much might have been done in the time which had passed, and left nothing real behind it. He compared twenty months with the life of man. "In life, said he, is not to be counted the ignorance of infancy, or imbecility of age. We are long before we are able to think, and we soon cease from the power of acting. The true period of human existence may be reasonably estimated as forty years, of which I have mused away the four and twentieth part. What I have lost was certain, for I have certainly possessed it; but of twenty months to come who can assure me?"

The consciousness of his own folly pierced him deeply, and he was long before he could be reconciled to himself. "The rest of my time, said he, has been lost by the crime or folly of my ancestors, and the absurd institutions of my country; I remember it with disgust, yet without remorse: but the months that have passed since new light darted into my soul, since I formed a scheme of reasonable felicity, have been squandered by my own fault. I have lost that which can never be restored: I have seen the sun rise and set for twenty months, an idle gazer on the light of heaven: In this time the birds have left the nest of their mother, and committed themselves to the woods and to the skies: the kid has forsaken the teat, and learned by degrees to climb the rocks in quest of independant sustenance. I only have made no advances, but am still helpless and ignorant. The moon by more than twenty changes, admonished me of the flux of life; the stream that rolled before my feet upbraided my inactivity. I sat feasting on intellectual luxury, regardless alike of the examples of the earth, and the instructions of the planets. Twenty months are passed, who shall restore them!"

These sorrowful meditations fastened upon his mind; he past four months in resolving to lose no more time in idle resolves, and was awakened to more vigorous exertion by hearing a maid, who had broken a porcelain cup, remark, that what cannot be repaired is not to be regretted.

This was obvious; and Rasselas reproached himself that he had not discovered it, having not known, or not considered, how many useful hints are obtained by chance, and how often the mind, hurried by her own ardour to distant views, neglects the truths that lie open before her. He, for a few hours, regretted his regret, and from that time bent his whole mind upon the means of escaping the valley of happiness.

V

THE PRINCE MEDITATES HIS ESCAPE

He now found that it would be very difficult to effect that which it was very easy to suppose effected. When he looked round about him, he saw himself confined by the bars of nature which had never yet been broken, and by the gate, through which none that once had passed it were ever able to return. He was now impatient as an eagle in a grate. He passed week after week in clambering the mountains, to see if there was any aperture which the bushes might conceal, but found all the summits inaccessible by their prominence. The iron gate he despaired to open; for it was not only secured with all the power of art, but was always watched by successive sentinels, and was by its position exposed to the perpetual observation of all the inhabitants.

He then examined the cavern through which the waters of the lake were discharged; and, looking down at a time when the sun shone strongly upon its mouth, he discovered it to be full of broken rocks, which, though they permitted the stream to flow through many narrow passages, would stop any body of solid bulk. He returned discouraged and dejected; but, having now known the blessing of hope, resolved never to despair.

In these fruitless searches he spent ten months. The time, however, passed chearfully away: in the morning he rose with new hope, in the evening applauded his own diligence, and in the night slept sound after his fatigue. He met a thousand amusements which beguiled his labour, and diversified his thoughts. He discerned the various instincts of animals, and properties of plants, and found the place replete with wonders, of which he purposed to solace himself with the contemplation, if he should never be able to accomplish his flight; rejoicing that his endeavours, though yet unsuccessful, had supplied him with a source of inexhaustible enquiry.

But his original curiosity was not yet abated; he resolved to obtain some knowledge of the ways of men. His wish still continued, but his hope grew less. He ceased to survey any longer the walls of his prison, and spared to search by new toils for interstices which he knew could not be found, yet determined to keep his design always in view, and lay hold on any expedient that time should offer.

VI

A DISSERTATION ON THE ART OF FLYING

Among the artists that had been allured into the happy valley, to labour for the accommodation and pleasure of its inhabitants, was a man eminent for his knowledge of the mechanick powers, who had contrived many engines both of use and recreation. By a wheel, which the stream turned, he forced the water into a tower, whence it was distributed to all the apartments of the palace. He erected a pavillion in the garden, around which he kept the air always cool by artificial showers. One of the groves, appropriated to the ladies, was ventilated by fans, to which the rivulet that ran through it gave a constant motion; and instruments of soft musick were placed at proper distances, of which some played by the impulse of the wind, and some by the power of the stream.

This artist was sometimes visited by Rasselas, who was pleased with every kind of knowledge, imagining that the time would come when all his acquisitions should be of use to him in the open world. He came one day to amuse himself in his usual manner, and found the master busy in building a sailing chariot: he saw that the design was practicable upon a level surface, and with expressions of great esteem solicited its completion. The workman was pleased to find himself so much regarded by the prince, and resolved to gain yet higher honours. "Sir, said he, you have seen but a small part of what the mechanick sciences can perform. I have been long of opinion, that, instead of the tardy conveyance of ships and chariots, man might use the swifter migration of wings; that the fields of air are open to knowledge, and that only ignorance and idleness need crawl upon the ground."

This hint rekindled the prince's desire of passing the mountains; having seen what the mechanist had already performed, he was willing to fancy that he could do more; yet resolved to enquire further before he suffered hope to afflict him by disappointment. "I am afraid, said he to the artist, that your imagination prevails over your skill, and that you now tell me rather what you wish than what you know. Every animal has his element assigned him; the birds have the air, and man and beasts the earth." "So, replied the mechanist, fishes have the water, in which yet beasts can swim by nature, and men by art. He that can swim needs not despair to fly: to swim is to fly in a grosser fluid, and to fly is to swim in a subtler. We are only to proportion our power to resistance to the different density of the matter through which we are to pass. You will be necessarily upborn by the air, if you can renew any impulse upon it, faster than the air can recede from the pressure."

"But the exercise of swimming, said the prince, is very laborious; the strongest limbs are soon wearied; I am afraid the act of flying will be yet more violent, and wings will be of no great use, unless we can fly further than we can swim."

"The labour of rising from the ground, said the artist, will be great, as we see it in the heavier domestick fowls; but, as we mount higher, the earth's attraction, and the body's gravity, will be gradually diminished, till we shall arrive at a region where the man will float in the air without any tendency to fall: no care will then be necessary, but to move forwards, which the gentlest impulse will effect. You, Sir, whose curiosity is so extensive, will easily conceive with what pleasure a philosopher, furnished with wings, and hovering in the sky, would see the earth, and all its inhabitants, rolling beneath him, and presenting to him successively, by its diurnal motion, all the countries within the same parallel. How must it amuse the pendent spectator to see the moving scene of land and ocean, cities and desarts! To survey with equal security the marts of trade, and the fields of battle; mountains infested by barbarians, and fruitful regions gladdened by plenty, and lulled by peace! How easily shall we then trace the Nile through all his passage; pass over to distant regions, and examine the face of nature from one extremity of the earth to the other!"

"All this, said the prince, is much to be desired, but I am afraid that no man will be able to breathe in these regions of speculation and tranquility. I have been told, that respiration is difficult upon lofty mountains, yet from these precipices, though so high as to produce great tenuity of the air, it is very easy to fall: therefore I suspect, that from any height, where life can be supported, there may be danger of too quick descent."

"Nothing, replied the artist, will ever be attempted, if all possible objections must be first overcome. If you will favour my project I will try the first flight at my own hazard. I have considered the structure of all volant animals, and find the folding continuity of the bat's wings most easily accommodated to the human form. Upon this model I shall begin my task to morrow, and in a year expect to tower into the air beyond the malice or persuit of man. But I will work only on this condition, that the art shall not be divulged, and that you shall not require me to make wings for any but ourselves."

"Why, said Rasselas, should you envy others so great an advantage? All skill ought to be exerted for universal good; every man has owed much to others, and ought to repay the kindness that he has received."

"If men were all virtuous, returned the artist, I should with great alacrity teach them all to fly. But what would be the security of the good, if the bad could at pleasure invade them from the sky? Against an army sailing through the clouds neither walls, nor mountains, nor seas, could afford any security. A flight of northern savages might hover in the wind, and light at once with irresistible violence upon the capital of a fruitful region that was rolling under them. Even this valley, the retreat of princes, the abode of happiness, might be violated by the sudden descent of some of the naked nations that swarm on the coast of the southern sea."

The prince promised secrecy, and waited for the performance, not wholly hopeless of success. He visited the work from time to time, observed its progress, and remarked many ingenious contrivances to facilitate motion, and unite levity with strength. The artist was every day more certain that he should leave vultures and eagles behind him, and the contagion of his confidence seized upon the prince.

In a year the wings were finished, and, on a morning appointed, the maker appeared furnished for flight on a little promontory: he waved his pinions a while to gather air, then leaped from his stand, and in an instant dropped into the lake. His wings, which were of no use in the air, sustained him in the water, and the prince drew him to land, half dead with terrour and vexation.

VII

THE PRINCE FINDS A MAN OF LEARNING

The prince was not much afflicted by this disaster, having suffered himself to hope for a happier event, only because he had no other means of escape in view. He still persisted in his design to leave the happy valley by the first opportunity.

His imagination was now at a stand; he had no prospect of entering into the world; and, notwithstanding all his endeavours to support himself, discontent by degrees preyed upon him, and he began again to lose his thoughts in sadness, when the rainy season, which in these countries is periodical, made it inconvenient to wander in the woods.

The rain continued longer and with more violence than had been ever known: the clouds broke on the surrounding mountains, and the torrents streamed into the plain on every side, till the cavern was too narrow to discharge the water. The lake overflowed its banks, and all the level of the valley was covered with the inundation. The eminence, on which the palace was built, and some other spots of rising ground, were all that the eye could now discover. The herds and flocks left the pastures, and both the wild beasts and the tame retreated to the mountains.

This inundation confined all the princes to domestick amusements, and the attention of Rasselas was particularly seized by a poem, which Imlac rehearsed upon the various conditions of humanity. He commanded the poet to attend him in his apartment, and recite his verses a second time; then entering into familiar talk, he thought himself happy in having found a man who knew the world so well, and could so skilfully paint the scenes of life. He asked a thousand questions about things, to which, though common to all other mortals, his confinement from childhood had kept him a stranger. The poet pitied his ignorance, and loved his curiosity, and entertained him from day to day with novelty and instruction, so that the prince regretted the necessity of sleep, and longed till the morning should renew his pleasure.

As they were sitting together, the prince commanded Imlac to relate his history, and to tell by what accident he was forced, or by what motive induced, to close his life in the happy valley. As he was going to begin his narrative, Rasselas was called to a concert, and obliged to restrain his curiosity till the evening.

VIII

THE HISTORY OF IMLAC

The close of the day is, in the regions of the torrid zone, the only season of diversion and entertainment, and it was therefore mid-night before the musick ceased, and the princesses retired. Rasselas then called for his companion and required him to begin the story of his life.

"Sir, said Imlac, my history will not be long: the life that is devoted to knowledge passes silently away, and is very little diversified by events. To talk in publick, to think in solitude, to read and to hear, to inquire, and answer inquiries, is the business of a scholar. He wanders about the world without pomp or terrour, and is neither known nor valued but by men like himself.

"I was born in the kingdom of Goiama, at no great distance from the fountain of the Nile. My father was a wealthy merchant, who traded between the inland countries of Africk and the ports of the red sea. He was honest, frugal and diligent, but of mean sentiments, and narrow comprehension: he desired only to be rich, and to conceal his riches, lest he should be spoiled by the governours of the province."

"Surely, said the prince, my father must be negligent of his charge, if any man in his dominions dares take that which belongs to another. Does he not know that kings are accountable for injustice permitted as well as done? If I were emperour, not the meanest of my subjects should be oppressed with impunity. My blood boils when I am told that a merchant durst not enjoy his honest gains for fear of losing them by the rapacity of power. Name the governour who robbed the people, that I may declare his crimes to the emperour."

"Sir, said Imlac, your ardour is the natural effect of virtue animated by youth: the time will come when you will acquit your father, and perhaps hear with less impatience of the governour. Oppression is, in the Abissinian dominions, neither frequent nor tolerated; but no form of government has been yet discovered, by which cruelty can be wholly prevented. Subordination supposes power on one part and subjection on the other; and if power be in the hands of men, it will sometimes be abused. The vigilance of the supreme magistrate may do much, but much will still remain undone. He can never know all the crimes that are committed, and can seldom punish all that he knows."

"This, said the prince, I do not understand, but I had rather hear thee than dispute. Continue thy narration."

"My father, proceeded Imlac, originally intended that I should have no other education, than such as might qualify me for commerce; and discovering in me great strength of memory, and quickness of apprehension, often declared his hope that I should be some time the richest man is Abissinia."

"Why, said the prince, did thy father desire the increase of his wealth, when it was already greater than he durst discover or enjoy? I am unwilling to doubt thy veracity, yet inconsistencies cannot both be true."

"Inconsistencies, answered Imlac, cannot be right, but, imputed to man, they may both be true. Yet diversity is not inconsistency. My father might expect a time of greater security. However, some desire is necessary to keep life in motion, and he, whose real wants are supplied, must admit those of fancy."

"This, said the prince, I can in some measure conceive. I repent that I interrupted thee."

"With this hope, proceeded Imlac, he sent me to school; but when I had once found the delight of knowledge, and felt the pleasure of intelligence and the pride of invention, I began silently to despise riches, and determined to disappoint the purpose of my father, whose grossness of conception raised my pity. I was twenty years old before his tenderness would expose me to the fatigue of travel, in which time I had been instructed, by successive masters, in all the literature of my native country. As every hour taught me something new, I lived in a continual course of gratifications; but, as I advanced towards manhood, I lost much of the reverence with which I had been used to look on my instructors; because, when the lesson was ended, I did not find them wiser or better than common men.

"At length my father resolved to initiate me in commerce, and, opening one of his subterranean treasuries, counted out ten thousand pieces of gold. This, young man, said he, is the stock with which you must negotiate. I began with less than the fifth part, and you see how diligence and parsimony have increased it. This is your own to waste or to improve. If you squander it by negligence or caprice, you must wait for my death before you will be rich: if, in four years, you double your stock, we will thenceforward let subordination cease, and live together as friends and partners; for he shall always be equal with me, who is equally skilled in the art of growing rich.

"We laid our money upon camels, concealed in bales of cheap goods, and travelled to the shore of the red sea. When I cast my eye on the expanse of waters my heart bounded like that of a prisoner escaped. I felt an unextinguishable curiosity kindle in my mind, and resolved to snatch this opportunity of seeing the manners of other nations, and of learning sciences unknown in Abissinia.

"I remembered that my father had obliged me to the improvement of my stock, not by a promise which I ought not to violate, but by a penalty which I was at liberty to incur; and therefore determined to gratify my predominant desire, and by drinking at the fountains of knowledge, to quench the thirst of curiosity.

"As I was supposed to trade without connexion with my father, it was easy for me to become acquainted with the master of a ship, and procure a passage to some other country. I had no motives of choice to regulate my voyage; it was sufficient for me that, wherever I wandered, I should see a country which I had not seen before. I therefore entered a ship bound for Surat, having left a letter for my father declaring my intention.

IX

THE HISTORY OF IMLAC CONTINUED

"When I first entered upon the world of waters, and lost sight of land, I looked round about me with pleasing terrour, and thinking my soul enlarged by the boundless prospect, imagined that I could gaze round for ever without satiety; but, in a short time, I grew weary of looking on barren uniformity, where I could only see again what I had already seen. I then descended into the ship, and doubted for a while whether all my future pleasures would not end like this in disgust and disappointment. Yet, surely, said I, the ocean and the land are very different; the only variety of water is rest and motion, but the earth has mountains and vallies, desarts and cities: it is inhabited by men of different customs and contrary opinions; and I may hope to find variety in life, though I should miss it in nature.

"With this thought I quieted my mind; and amused myself during the voyage, sometimes by learning from the sailors the art of navigation, which I have never practised, and sometimes by forming schemes for my conduct in different situations, in not one of which I have been ever placed.

"I was almost weary of my naval amusements when we landed safely at Surat. I secured my money, and purchasing some commodities for show, joined myself to a caravan that was passing into the inland country. My companions, for some reason or other, conjecturing that I was rich, and, by my inquiries and admiration, finding that I was ignorant, considered me as a novice whom they had a right to cheat, and who was to learn at the usual expence the art of fraud. They exposed me to the theft of servants, and the exaction of officers, and saw me plundered upon false pretences, without any advantage to themselves, but that of rejoicing in the superiority of their own knowledge."

"Stop a moment, said the prince. Is there such depravity in man, as that he should injure another without benefit to himself? I can easily conceive that all are pleased with superiority; but your ignorance was merely accidental, which, being neither your crime nor your folly, could afford them no reason to applaud themselves; and the knowledge which they had, and which you wanted, they might as effectually have shewn by warning, as betraying you."

"Pride, said Imlac, is seldom delicate, it will please itself with very mean advantages; and envy feels not its own happiness, but when it may be compared with the misery of others. They were my enemies because they grieved to think me rich, and my oppressors because they delighted to find me weak."

"Proceed, said the prince: I doubt not of the facts which you relate, but imagine that you impute them to mistaken motives."

"In this company, said Imlac, I arrived at Agra, the capital of Indostan, the city in which the great Mogul commonly resides. I applied myself to the language of the country, and in a few months was able to converse with the learned men; some of whom I found morose and reserved, and others easy and communicative; some were unwilling to teach another what they had with difficulty learned themselves; and some shewed that the end of their studies was to gain the dignity of instructing.

"To the tutor of the young princes I recommended myself so much, that I was presented to the emperour as a man of uncommon knowledge. The emperour asked me many questions concerning my country and my travels; and though I cannot now recollect any thing that he uttered above the power of a common man, he dismissed me astonished at his wisdom, and enamoured of his goodness.

"My credit was now so high, that the merchants, with whom I had travelled, applied to me for recommendations to the ladies of the court. I was surprised at their confidence of solicitation, and gently reproached them with their practices on the road. They heard me with cold indifference, and shewed no tokens of shame or sorrow.

"They then urged their request with the offer of a bribe; but what I would not do for kindness I would not do for money; and refused them, not because they had injured me, but because I would not enable them to injure others; for I knew they would have made use of my credit to cheat those who should buy their wares.

"Having resided at Agra till there was no more to be learned, I travelled into Persia, where I saw many remains of ancient magnificence, and observed many new accommodations of life. The Persians are a nation eminently social, and their assemblies afforded me daily opportunities of remarking characters and manners, and of tracing human nature through all its variations.

"From Persia I passed into Arabia, where I saw a nation at once pastoral and warlike; who live without any settled habitation; whose only wealth is their flocks and herds; and who have yet carried on, through all ages, an hereditary war with all mankind, though they neither covet nor envy their possessions.

X

IMLAC'S HISTORY CONTINUED. A DISSERTATION UPON POETRY

"Wherever I went, I found that Poetry was considered as the highest learning, and regarded with a veneration somewhat approaching to that which man would pay to the Angelick Nature. And it yet fills me with wonder, that, in almost all countries, the most ancient poets are considered as the best: whether it be that every other kind of knowledge is an acquisition gradually attained, and poetry is a gift conferred at once; or that the first poetry of every nation surprised them as a novelty, and retained the credit by consent which it received by accident at first: or whether, as the province of poetry is to describe Nature and Passion, which are always the same, the first writers took possession of the most striking objects for description, and the most probable occurrences for fiction, and left nothing to those that followed them, but transcription of the same events, and new combinations of the same images. Whatever be the reason, it is commonly observed that the early writers are in possession of nature, and their followers of art: that the first excel in strength and invention, and the latter in elegance and refinement.

"I was desirous to add my name to this illustrious fraternity. I read all the poets of Persia and Arabia, and was able to repeat by memory the volumes that are suspended in the mosque of Mecca. But I soon found that no man was ever great by imitation. My desire of excellence impelled me to transfer my attention to nature and to life. Nature was to be my subject, and men to be my auditors: I could never describe what I had not seen: I could not hope to move those with delight or terrour, whose interests and opinions I did not understand.

"Being now resolved to be a poet, I saw every thing with a new purpose; my sphere of attention was suddenly magnified: no kind of knowledge was to be overlooked. I ranged mountains and deserts for images and resemblances, and pictured upon my mind every tree of the forest and flower of the valley. I observed with equal care the crags of the rock and the pinnacles of the palace. Sometimes I wandered along the mazes of the rivulet, and sometimes watched the changes of the summer clouds. To a poet nothing can be useless. Whatever is beautiful, and whatever is dreadful, must be familiar to his imagination: he must be conversant with all that is awfully vast or elegantly little. The plants of the garden, the animals of the wood, the minerals of the earth, and meteors of the sky, must all concur to store his mind with inexhaustible variety: for every idea is useful for the inforcement or decoration of moral or religious truth; and he, who knows most, will have most power of diversifying his scenes, and of gratifying his reader with remote allusions and unexpected instruction.

"All the appearances of nature I was therefore careful to study, and every country which I have surveyed has contributed something to my poetical powers."

"In so wide a survey, said the prince, you must surely have left much unobserved. I have lived, till now, within the circuit of these mountains, and yet cannot walk abroad without the sight of something which I had never beheld before, or never heeded."

"The business of a poet, said Imlac, is to examine, not the individual, but the species; to remark general properties and large appearances: he does not number the streaks of the tulip, or describe the different shades in the verdure of the forest. He is to exhibit in his portraits of nature such prominent and striking features, as recal the original to every mind; and must neglect the minuter discriminations, which one may have remarked, and another have neglected, for those characteristicks which are alike obvious to vigilance and carelessness.

"But the knowledge of nature is only half the task of a poet; he must be acquainted likewise with all the modes of life. His character requires that he estimate the happiness and misery of every condition; observe the power of all the passions in all their combinations, and trace the changes of the human mind as they are modified by various institutions and accidental influences of climate or custom, from the spriteliness of infancy to the despondence of decrepitude. He must divest himself of the prejudices of his age or country; he must consider right and wrong in their abstracted and invariable state; he must disregard present laws and opinions, and rise to general and transcendental truths, which will always be the same: he must therefore content himself with the slow progress of his name; contemn the applause of his own time, and commit his claims to the justice of posterity. He must write as the interpreter of nature, and the legislator of mankind, and consider himself as presiding over the thoughts and manners of future generations; as a being superiour to time and place.

"His labour is not yet at an end: he must know many languages and many sciences; and, that his stile may be worthy of his thoughts, must, by incessant practice, familiarize to himself every delicacy of speech and grace of harmony."

XI

IMLAC'S NARRATIVE CONTINUED. A HINT ON PILGRIMAGE

Imlac now felt the enthusiastic fit, and was proceeding to aggrandize his own profession, when the prince cried out, "Enough! Thou hast convinced me, that no human being can ever be a poet. Proceed with thy narration."

"To be a poet, said Imlac, is indeed very difficult." "So difficult, returned the prince, that I will at present hear no more of his labours. Tell me whither you went when you had seen Persia."

"From Persia, said the poet, I travelled through Syria, and for three years resided in Palestine, where I conversed with great numbers of the northern and western nations of Europe; the nations which are now in possession of all power and all knowledge; whose armies are irresistible, and whose fleets command the remotest parts of the globe. When I compared these men with the natives of our own kingdom, and those that surround us, they appeared almost another order of beings. In their countries it is difficult to wish for any thing that may not be obtained: a thousand arts, of which we never heard, are continually labouring for their convenience and pleasure; and whatever their own climate has denied them is supplied by their commerce."

"By what means, said the prince, are the Europeans thus powerful? or why, since they can so easily visit Asia and Africa for trade or conquest, cannot the Asiaticks and Africans invade their coasts, plant colonies in their ports, and give laws to their natural princes? The same wind that carries them back would bring us thither."

"They are more powerful, Sir, than we, answered Imlac, because they are wiser; knowledge will always predominate over ignorance, as man governs the other animals. But why their knowledge is more than ours, I know not what reason can be given, but the unsearchable will of the Supreme Being."

"When, said the prince with a sigh, shall I be able to visit Palestine, and mingle with this mighty confluence of nations? Till that happy moment shall arrive, let me fill up the time with such representations as thou canst give me. I am not ignorant of the motive that assembles such numbers in that place, and cannot but consider it as the center of wisdom and piety, to which the best and wisest men of every land must be continually resorting."

"There are some nations, said Imlac, that send few visitants to Palestine; for many numerous and learned sects in Europe, concur to censure pilgrimage as superstitious, or deride it as ridiculous."

"You know, said the prince, how little my life has made me acquainted with diversity of opinions: it will be too long to hear the arguments on both sides; you, that have considered them, tell me the result."

"Pilgrimage, said Imlac, like many other acts of piety, may be reasonable or superstitious, according to the principles upon which it is performed. Long journies in search of truth are not commanded. Truth, such as is necessary to the regulation of life, is always found where it is honestly sought. Change of place is no natural cause of the increase of piety, for it inevitably produces dissipation of mind. Yet, since men go every day to view the fields where great actions have been performed, and return with stronger impressions of the event, curiosity of the same kind may naturally dispose us to view that country whence our religion had its beginning; and I believe no man surveys those awful scenes without some confirmation of holy resolutions. That the Supreme Being may be more easily propitiated in one place than in another, is the dream of idle superstition; but that some places may operate upon our own minds in an uncommon manner, is an opinion which hourly experience will justify. He who supposes that his vices may be more successfully combated in Palestine, will, perhaps, find himself mistaken, yet he may go thither without folly: he who thinks they will be more freely pardoned, dishonours at once his reason and religion."

"These, said the prince, are European distinctions. I will consider them another time. What have you found to be the effect of knowledge? Are those nations happier than we?"

"There is so much infelicity, said the poet, in the world, that scarce any man has leisure from his own distresses to estimate the comparative happiness of others. Knowledge is certainly one of the means of pleasure, as is confessed by the natural desire which every mind feels of increasing its ideas. Ignorance is mere privation, by which nothing can be produced: it is a vacuity in which the soul sits motionless and torpid for want of attraction; and, without knowing why, we always rejoice when we learn, and grieve when we forget. I am therefore inclined to conclude, that, if nothing counteracts the natural consequence of learning, we grow more happy as our minds take a wider range.

"In enumerating the particular comforts of life we shall find many advantages on the side of the Europeans. They cure wounds and diseases with which we languish and perish. We suffer inclemencies of weather which they can obviate. They have engines for the despatch of many laborious works, which we must perform by manual industry. There is such communication between distant places, that one friend can hardly be said to be absent from another. Their policy removes all publick inconveniencies: they have roads cut through their mountains, and bridges laid upon their rivers. And, if we descend to the privacies of life, their habitations are more commodious, and their possessions are more secure."

"They are surely happy, said the prince, who have all these conveniencies, of which I envy none so much as the facility with which separated friends interchange their thoughts."

"The Europeans, answered Imlac, are less unhappy than we, but they are not happy. Human life is every where a state in which much is to be endured, and little to be enjoyed."

XII

THE STORY OF IMLAC CONTINUED

"I am not yet willing, said the prince, to suppose that happiness is so parsimoniously distributed to mortals; nor can believe but that, if I had the choice of life, I should be able to fill every day with pleasure. I would injure no man, and should provoke no resentment: I would relieve every distress, and should enjoy the benedictions of gratitude. I would choose my friends among the wise, and my wife among the virtuous; and therefore should be in no danger from treachery, or unkindness. My children should, by my care, be learned and pious, and would repay to my age what their childhood had received. What would dare to molest him who might call on every side to thousands enriched by his bounty, or assisted by his power? And why should not life glide quietly away in the soft reciprocation of protection and reverence? All this may be done without the help of European refinements, which appear by their effects to be rather specious than useful. Let us leave them and persue our journey."

"From Palestine, said Imlac, I passed through many regions of Asia; in the more civilized kingdoms as a trader, and among the Barbarians of the mountains as a pilgrim. At last I began to long for my native country, that I might repose after my travels, and fatigues, in the places where I had spent my earliest years, and gladden my old companions with the recital of my adventures. Often did I figure to myself those, with whom I had sported away the gay hours of dawning life, sitting round me in its evening, wondering at my tales, and listening to my counsels.

"When this thought had taken possession of my mind, I considered every moment as wasted which did not bring me nearer to Abissinia. I hastened into Egypt, and, notwithstanding my impatience, was detained ten months in the contemplation of its ancient magnificence, and in enquiries after the remains of its ancient learning. I found in Cairo a mixture of all nations; some brought thither by the love of knowledge, some by the hope of gain, and many by the desire of living after their own manner without observation, and of lying hid in the obscurity of multitudes: for, in a city, populous as Cairo, it is possible to obtain at the same time the gratifications of society, and the secrecy of solitude.

"From Cairo I travelled to Suez, and embarked on the Red sea, passing along the coast till I arrived at the port from which I had departed twenty years before. Here I joined myself to a caravan and re-entered my native country.

"I now expected the caresses of my kinsmen, and the congratulations of my friends, and was not without hope that my father, whatever value he had set upon riches, would own with gladness and pride a son who was able to add to the felicity and honour of the nation. But I was soon convinced that my thoughts were vain. My father had been dead fourteen years, having divided his wealth among my brothers, who were removed to some other provinces. Of my companions the greater part was in the grave, of the rest some could with difficulty remember me, and some considered me as one corrupted by foreign manners.

"A man used to vicissitudes is not easily dejected. I forgot, after a time, my disappointment, and endeavoured to recommend myself to the nobles of the kingdom: they admitted me to their tables, heard my story, and dismissed me. I opened a school, and was prohibited to teach. I then resolved to sit down in the quiet of domestick life, and addressed a lady that was fond of my conversation, but rejected my suit, because my father was a merchant.

"Wearied at last with solicitation and repulses, I resolved to hide myself for ever from the world, and depend no longer on the opinion or caprice of others. I waited for the time when the gate of the *happy valley* should open, that I might bid farewell to hope and fear: the day came; my performance was distinguished with favour, and I resigned myself with joy to perpetual confinement."

"Hast thou here found happiness at last? said Rasselas. Tell me without reserve; art thou content with thy condition? or, dost thou wish to be again wandering and inquiring? All the inhabitants of this valley celebrate their lot, and, at the annual visit of the emperour, invite others to partake of their felicity."

"Great prince, said Imlac, I shall speak the truth. I know not one of all your attendants who does not lament the hour when he entered this retreat. I am less unhappy than the rest, because I have a mind replete with images, which I can vary and combine at pleasure. I can amuse my solitude by the renovation of the knowledge which begins to fade from my memory, and by recollection of the accidents of my past life. Yet all this ends in the sorrowful consideration, that my acquirements are now useless, and that none of my pleasures can be again enjoyed. The rest, whose minds have no impression but of the present moment, are either corroded by malignant passions, or sit stupid in the gloom of perpetual vacancy."

"What passions can infest those, said the prince, who have no rivals? We are in a place where impotence precludes malice, and where all envy is repressed by community of enjoyments."

"There may be community, said Imlac, of material possessions, but there can never be community of love or of esteem. It must happen that one will please more than another; he that knows himself despised will always be envious; and still more envious and malevolent, if he is condemned to live in the presence of those who despise him. The invitations, by which they allure others to a state which they feel to be wretched, proceed from the natural malignity of hopeless misery. They are weary of themselves, and of each other, and expect to find relief in new companions. They envy the liberty which their folly has forfeited, and would gladly see all mankind imprisoned like themselves.

"From this crime, however, I am wholly free. No man can say that he is wretched by my persuasion. I look with pity on the crowds who are annually soliciting admission to captivity, and wish that it were lawful for me to warn them of their danger."

"My dear Imlac, said the prince, I will open to thee my whole heart. I have long meditated an escape from the happy valley. I have examined the mountains on every side, but find myself insuperably barred: teach me the way to break my prison; thou shalt be the companion of my flight, the guide of my rambles, the partner of my fortune, and my sole director in the *choice of life*."

"Sir, answered the poet, your escape will be difficult, and, perhaps, you may soon repent your curiosity. The world, which you figure to yourself smooth and quiet as the lake in the valley, you will find a sea foaming with tempests, and boiling with whirlpools: you will be sometimes overwhelmed by the waves of violence, and sometimes dashed against the rocks of treachery. Amidst wrongs and frauds, competitions and anxieties, you will wish a thousand times for these seats of quiet, and willingly quit hope to be free from fear."

"Do not seek to deter me from my purpose, said the prince: I am impatient to see what thou hast seen; and, since thou art thyself weary of the valley, it is evident, that thy former state was better than this. Whatever be the consequence of my experiment, I am resolved to judge with my own eyes of the various conditions of men, and then to make deliberately my *choice of life*."

"I am afraid, said Imlac, you are hindered by stronger restraints than my persuasions; yet, if your determination is fixed, I do not counsel you to despair. Few things are impossible to diligence and skill."

XIII

RASSELAS DISCOVERS THE MEANS OF ESCAPE

The prince now dismissed his favourite to rest, but the narrative of wonders and novelties filled his mind with perturbation. He revolved all that he had heard, and prepared innumerable questions for the morning.

Much of his uneasiness was now removed. He had a friend to whom he could impart his thoughts, and whose experience could assist him in his designs. His heart was no longer condemned to swell with silent vexation. He thought that even the *happy valley* might be endured with such a companion, and that, if they could range the world together, he should have nothing further to desire.

In a few days the water was discharged, and the ground dried. The prince and Imlac then walked out together to converse without the notice of the rest. The prince, whose thoughts were always on the wing, as he passed by the gate, said, with a countenance of sorrow, "Why art thou so strong, and why is man so weak?"

"Man is not weak, answered his companion; knowledge is more than equivalent to force. The master of mechanicks laughs at strength. I can burst the gate, but cannot do it secretly. Some other expedient must be tried."

As they were walking on the side of the mountain, they observed that the conies,[1] which the rain had driven from their burrows, had taken shelter among the bushes, and formed holes behind them,

RASSELAS. **1. conies:** rabbits.

tending upwards in an oblique line. "It has been the opinion of antiquity, said Imlac, that human reason borrowed many arts from the instinct of animals; let us, therefore, not think ourselves degraded by learning from the coney. We may escape by piercing the mountain in the same direction. We will begin where the summit hangs over the middle part, and labour upward till we shall issue out beyond the prominence."

The eyes of the prince, when he heard this proposal, sparkled with joy. The execution was easy, and the success certain.

No time was now lost. They hastened early in the morning to chuse a place proper for their mine. They clambered with great fatigue among crags and brambles, and returned without having discovered any part that favoured their design. The second and the third day were spent in the same manner, and with the same frustration. But, on the fourth, they found a small cavern, concealed by a thicket, where they resolved to make their experiment.

Imlac procured instruments proper to hew stone and remove earth, and they fell to their work on the next day with more eagerness than vigour. They were presently exhausted by their efforts, and sat down to pant upon the grass. The prince, for a moment, appeared to be discouraged. "Sir, said his companion, practice will enable us to continue our labour for a longer time; mark, however, how far we have advanced, and you will find that our toil will some time have an end. Great works are performed, not by strength, but perseverance: yonder palace was raised by single stones, yet you see its height and spaciousness. He that shall walk with vigour three hours a day will pass in seven years a space equal to the circumference of the globe."

They returned to their work day after day, and, in a short time, found a fissure in the rock, which enabled them to pass far with very little obstruction. This Rasselas considered as a good omen. "Do not disturb your mind, said Imlac, with other hopes or fears than reason may suggest: if you are pleased with prognosticks of good, you will be terrified likewise with tokens of evil, and your whole life will be a prey to superstition. Whatever facilitates our work is more than an omen, it is a cause of success. This is one of those pleasing surprises which often happen to active resolution. Many things difficult to design prove easy to performance."

XIV

RASSELAS AND IMLAC RECEIVE AN UNEXPECTED VISIT

They had now wrought their way to the middle, and solaced their toil with the approach of liberty, when the prince, coming down to refresh himself with air, found his sister Nekayah standing before the mouth of the cavity. He started and stood confused, afraid to tell his design, and yet hopeless to conceal it. A few moments determined him to repose on her fidelity, and secure her secrecy by a declaration without reserve.

"Do not imagine, said the princess, that I came hither as a spy. I had long observed from my window, that you and Imlac directed your walk every day towards the same point, but I did not suppose you had any better reason for the preference than a cooler shade, or more fragrant bank; nor followed you with any other design than to partake of your conversation. Since then not suspicion but fondness has detected you, let me not lose the advantage of my discovery. I am equally weary of confinement with yourself, and not less desirous of knowing what is done or suffered in the world. Permit me to fly with you from this tasteless tranquility, which will yet grow more loathsome when you have left me. You may deny me to accompany you, but cannot hinder me from following."

The prince, who loved Nekayah above his other sisters, had no inclination to refuse her request, and grieved that he had lost an opportunity of shewing his confidence by a voluntary communication. It was therefore agreed that she should leave the valley with them; and that, in the mean time, she should watch, lest any other straggler should, by chance or curiosity, follow them to the mountain.

At length their labour was at an end; they saw light beyond the prominence, and, issuing to the top of the mountain, beheld the Nile, yet a narrow current, wandering beneath them.

The prince looked round with rapture, anticipated all the pleasures of travel, and in thought was already transported beyond his father's dominions. Imlac, though very joyful at his escape, had less expectation of pleasure in the world, which he had before tried, and of which he had been weary.

Rasselas was so much delighted with a wider horizon, that he could not soon be persuaded to return into the valley. He informed his sister that the way was open, and that nothing now remained but to prepare for their departure.

XV

THE PRINCE AND PRINCESS LEAVE THE VALLEY, AND SEE MANY WONDERS

The prince and princess had jewels sufficient to make them rich whenever they came into a place of commerce, which, by Imlac's direction, they hid in their cloaths, and, on the night of the next full moon, all left the valley. The princess was followed only by a single favourite, who did not know whither she was going.

They clambered through the cavity, and began to go down on the other side. The princess and her maid turned their eyes towards every part, and, seeing nothing to bound their prospect, considered themselves as in danger of being lost in a dreary vacuity. They stopped and trembled. "I am almost afraid, said the princess, to begin a journey of which I cannot perceive an end, and to venture into this immense plain where I may be approached on every side by men whom I never saw." The prince felt nearly the same emotions, though he thought it more manly to conceal them.

Imlac smiled at their terrours, and encouraged them to proceed; but the princess continued irresolute till she had been imperceptibly drawn forward too far to return.

In the morning they found some shepherds in the field, who set milk and fruits before them. The princess wondered that she did not see a palace ready for her reception, and a table spread with delicacies; but, being faint and hungry, she drank the milk and ate the fruits, and thought them of a higher flavour than the products of the valley.

They travelled forward by easy journeys, being all unaccustomed to toil or difficulty, and knowing, that though they might be missed, they could not be persued. In a few days they came into a more populous region, where Imlac was diverted with the admiration which his companions expressed at the diversity of manners, stations and employments.

Their dress was such as might not bring upon them the suspicion of having any thing to conceal, yet the prince, wherever he came, expected to be obeyed, and the princess was frighted, because those that came into her presence did not prostrate themselves before her. Imlac was forced to observe them with great vigilance, lest they should betray their rank by their unusual behaviour, and detained them several weeks in the first village to accustom them to the sight of common mortals.

By degrees the royal wanderers were taught to understand that they had for a time laid aside their dignity, and were to expect only such regard as liberality and courtesy could procure. And Imlac, having, by many admonitions, prepared them to endure the tumults of a port, and the ruggedness of the commercial race, brought them down to the sea-coast.

The prince and his sister, to whom every thing was new, were gratified equally at all places, and therefore remained for some months at the port without any inclination to pass further. Imlac was content with their stay, because he did not think it safe to expose them, unpractised in the world, to the hazards of a foreign country.

At last he began to fear lest they should be discovered, and proposed to fix a day for their departure. They had no pretensions to judge for themselves, and referred the whole scheme to his direction. He therefore took passage in a ship to Suez; and, when the time came, with great difficulty prevailed on the princess to enter the vessel. They had a quick and prosperous voyage, and from Suez travelled by land to Cairo.

XVI

THEY ENTER CAIRO, AND FIND EVERY MAN HAPPY

As they approached the city, which filled the strangers with astonishment, "This, said Imlac to the prince, is the place where travellers and merchants assemble from all the corners of the earth. You will here find men of every character, and every occupation. Commerce is here honourable: I will act as a merchant, and you shall live as strangers, who have no other end of travel than curiosity; it will soon be observed that we are rich; our reputation will procure us access to all whom we shall desire to know; you will see all the conditions of humanity, and enable yourself at leisure to make your *choice of life*."

They now entered the town, stunned by the noise, and offended by the crowds. Instruction had not yet so prevailed over habit, but that they wondered to see themselves pass undistinguished along the street, and met by the lowest of the people without reverence or notice. The princess could not at first bear the thought of being levelled with the vulgar, and, for some days, continued in her chamber, where she was served by her favourite Pekuah as in the palace of the valley.

Imlac, who understood traffick, sold part of the jewels the next day, and hired a house, which he adorned with such magnificence, that he was immediately considered as a merchant of great wealth. His politeness attracted many acquaintance, and his generosity made him courted by many dependants. His table was crowded by men of every nation, who all admired his knowledge, and solicited his favour. His companions, not being able to mix in the conversation, could make no discovery of their ignorance or surprise, and were gradually initiated in the world as they gained knowledge of the language.

The prince had, by frequent lectures, been taught the use and nature of money; but the ladies could not, for a long time, comprehend what the merchants did with small pieces of gold and silver, or why things of so little use should be received as equivalent to the necessaries of life.

They studied the language two years, while Imlac was preparing to set before them the various ranks and conditions of mankind. He grew acquainted with all who had any thing uncommon in their fortune or conduct. He frequented the voluptuous and the frugal, the idle and the busy, the merchants and the men of learning.

The prince, being now able to converse with fluency, and having learned the caution necessary to be observed in his intercourse with strangers, began to accompany Imlac to places of resort, and to enter into all assemblies, that he might make his *choice of life*.

For some time he thought choice needless, because all appeared to him equally happy. Wherever he went he met gayety and kindness, and heard the song of joy, or the laugh of carelessness. He began to believe that the world overflowed with universal plenty, and that nothing was withheld either from want or merit; that every hand showered liberality, and every heart melted with benevolence: "and who then, says he, will be suffered to be wretched?"

Imlac permitted the pleasing delusion, and was unwilling to crush the hope of inexperience; till one day, having sat a while silent, "I know not, said the prince, what can be the reason that I am more unhappy than any of our friends. I see them perpetually and unalterably chearful, but feel my own mind restless and uneasy. I am unsatisfied with those pleasures which I seem most to court; I live in the crowds of jollity, not so much to enjoy company as to shun myself, and am only loud and merry to conceal my sadness."

"Every man, said Imlac, may, by examining his own mind, guess what passes in the minds of others: when you feel that your own gaiety is counterfeit, it may justly lead you to suspect that of your companions not to be sincere. Envy is commonly reciprocal. We are long before we are convinced that happiness is never to be found, and each believes it possessed by others, to keep alive the hope of obtaining it for himself. In the assembly, where you passed the last night, there appeared such spriteliness of air, and volatility of fancy, as might have suited beings of an higher order, formed to inhabit serener regions inaccessible to care or sorrow: yet, believe me, prince, there was not one who did not dread the moment when solitude should deliver him to the tyranny of reflection."

"This, said the prince, may be true of others, since it is true of me; yet, whatever be the general infelicity of man, one condition is more happy than another, and wisdom surely directs us to take the least evil in the *choice of life*."

"The causes of good and evil, answered Imlac, are so various and uncertain, so often entangled with each other, so diversified by various relations, and so much subject to accidents which cannot be foreseen, that he who would fix his condition upon incontestable reasons of preference, must live and die inquiring and deliberating."

"But surely, said Rasselas, the wise men, to whom we listen with reverence and wonder, chose that mode of life for themselves which they thought most likely to make them happy."

"Very few, said the poet, live by choice. Every man is placed in his present condition by causes which acted without his foresight, and with which he did not always willingly cooperate; and therefore you will rarely meet one who does not think the lot of his neighbour better than his own."

"I am pleased to think, said the prince, that my birth has given me at least one advantage over others, by enabling me to determine for myself. I have here the world before me; I will review it at leisure: surely happiness is somewhere to be found."

XVII

THE PRINCE ASSOCIATES WITH YOUNG MEN OF SPIRIT AND GAIETY

Rasselas rose next day, and resolved to begin his experiments upon life. "Youth, cried he, is the time of gladness: I will join myself to the young men, whose only business is to gratify their desires, and whose time is all spent in a succession of enjoyments."

To such societies he was readily admitted, but a few days brought him back weary and disgusted. Their mirth was without images, their laughter without motive; their pleasures were gross and sensual, in which the mind had no part; their conduct was at once wild and mean; they laughed at order and at law, but the frown of power rejected, and the eye of wisdom abashed them.

The prince soon concluded, that he should never be happy in a course of life of which he was ashamed. He thought it unsuitable to a reasonable being to act without a plan, and to be sad or chearful only by chance. "Happiness, said he, must be something solid and permanent, without fear and without uncertainty."

But his young companions had gained so much of his regard by their frankness and courtesy, that he could not leave them without warning and remonstrance. "My friends, said he, I have seriously considered our manners and our prospects, and find that we have mistaken our own interest. The first years of man must make provision for the last. He that never thinks never can be wise. Perpetual levity must end in ignorance; and intemperance, though it may fire the spirits for an hour, will make life short or miserable. Let us consider that youth is of no long duration, and that in maturer age, when the enchantments of fancy shall cease, and phantoms of delight dance no more about us, we shall have no comforts but the esteem of wise men, and the means of doing good. Let us, therefore, stop, while to stop is in our power: let us live as men who are sometime to grow old, and to whom it will be the most dreadful of all evils not to count their past years but by follies, and to be reminded of their former luxuriance of health only by the maladies which riot has produced."

They stared a while in silence one upon another, and, at last, drove him away by a general chorus of continued laughter.

The consciousness that his sentiments were just, and his intentions kind, was scarcely sufficient to support him against the horrour of derision. But he recovered his tranquility, and persued his search.

XVIII

THE PRINCE FINDS A WISE AND HAPPY MAN

As he was one day walking in the street, he saw a spacious building which all were, by the open doors, invited to enter: he followed the stream of people, and found it a hall or school of declamation, in which professors read lectures to their auditory. He fixed his eye upon a sage raised above the rest, who discoursed with great energy on the government of the passions. His look was venerable, his action graceful, his pronunciation clear, and his diction elegant. He shewed, with great strength of sentiment, and variety of illustration, that human nature is degraded and debased, when the lower faculties predominate over the higher; that when fancy, the parent of passion, usurps the dominion of the mind, nothing ensues but the natural effect of unlawful government, perturbation and confusion; that she betrays the fortresses of the intellect to rebels, and excites her children to sedition against reason their lawful sovereign. He compared reason to the sun, of which the light is constant, uniform, and lasting; and fancy to a meteor, of bright but transitory lustre, irregular in its motion, and delusive in its direction.

He then communicated the various precepts given from time to time for the conquest of passion, and displayed the happiness of those who had obtained the important victory, after which man is no longer the slave of fear, nor the fool of hope; is no more emaciated by envy, inflamed by anger, emasculated by tenderness, or depressed by grief; but walks on calmly through the tumults or the privacies of life, as the sun persues alike his course through the calm or the stormy sky.

He enumerated many examples of heroes immovable by pain or pleasure, who looked with indifference on those modes or accidents to which the vulgar give the names of good and evil. He exhorted his hearers to lay aside their prejudices, and arm themselves against the shafts of malice or misfortune, by invulnerable patience, concluding, that this state only was happiness, and that this happiness was in every one's power.

Rasselas listened to him with the veneration due to the instructions of a superiour being, and, waiting for him at the door, humbly implored the liberty of visiting so great a master of true wisdom. The lecturer hesitated a moment, when Rasselas put a purse of gold into his hand, which he received with a mixture of joy and wonder.

"I have found, said the prince at his return to Imlac, a man who can teach all that is necessary to be known, who, from the unshaken throne of rational fortitude, looks down on the scenes of life changing beneath him. He speaks, and attention watches his lips. He reasons, and conviction closes his periods. This man shall be my future guide: I will learn his doctrines, and imitate his life."

"Be not too hasty, said Imlac, to trust, or to admire, the teachers of morality: they discourse like angels, but they live like men."

Rasselas, who could not conceive how any man could reason so forcibly without feeling the cogency of his own arguments, paid his visit in a few days, and was denied admission. He had now learned the power of money, and made his way by a piece of gold to the inner apartment, where he found the philosopher in a room half darkened, with his eyes misty, and his face pale. "Sir, said he, you are come at a time when all human friendship is useless; what I suffer cannot be remedied, what I have lost cannot be supplied. My daughter, my only daughter, from whose tenderness I expected all the comforts of my age, died last night of a fever. My views, my purposes, my hopes are at an end: I am now a lonely being disunited from society."

"Sir, said the prince, mortality is an event by which a wise man can never be surprised: we know that death is always near, and it should therefore always be expected." "Young man, answered the philosopher, you speak like one that has never felt the pangs of separation." "Have you then forgot the precepts, said Rasselas, which you so powerfully enforced? Has wisdom no strength to arm the heart against calamity? Consider, that external things are naturally variable, but truth and reason are always the same." "What comfort, said the mourner, can truth and reason afford me? of what effect are they now, but to tell me, that my daughter will not be restored?"

The prince, whose humanity would not suffer him to insult misery with reproof, went away convinced of the emptiness of rhetorical sound, and the inefficacy of polished periods and studied sentences.

XIX

A GLIMPSE OF PASTORAL LIFE

He was still eager upon the same enquiry; and, having heard of a hermit, that lived near the lowest cataract of the Nile, and filled the whole country with the fame of his sanctity, resolved to visit his retreat, and enquire whether that felicity, which publick life could not afford, was to be found in solitude; and whether a man, whose age and virtue made him venerable, could teach any peculiar art of shunning evils, or enduring them.

Imlac and the princess agreed to accompany him, and, after the necessary preparations, they began their journey. Their way lay through fields, where shepherds tended their flocks, and the lambs were playing upon the pasture. "This, said the poet, is the life which has been often celebrated for its innocence and quiet: let us pass the heat of the day among the shepherds tents, and know whether all our searches are not to terminate in pastoral simplicity."

The proposal pleased them, and they induced the shepherds, by small presents and familiar questions, to tell their opinion of their own state: they were so rude and ignorant, so little able to compare the good with the evil of the occupation, and so indistinct in their narratives and descriptions, that very little could be learned from them. But it was evident that their hearts were cankered with discontent; that they considered themselves as condemned to labour for the luxury of the rich, and looked up with stupid malevolence toward those that were placed above them.

The princess pronounced with vehemence, that she would never suffer these envious savages to be her companions, and that she should not soon be desirous of seeing any more specimens of rustick happiness; but could not believe that all the accounts of primeval pleasures were fabulous, and was yet in doubt whether life had any thing that could be justly preferred to the placid gratifications of fields and woods. She hoped that the time would come, when with a few virtuous and elegant companions, she should gather flowers planted by her own hand, fondle the lambs of her own ewe, and listen, without care, among brooks and breezes, to one of her maidens reading in the shade.

XX

THE DANGER OF PROSPERITY

On the next day they continued their journey, till the heat compelled them to look round for shelter. At a small distance they saw a thick wood, which they no sooner entered than they perceived that they were approaching the habitations of men. The shrubs were diligently cut away to open walks where the shades were darkest; the boughs of opposite trees were artificially interwoven; seats of flowery turf were raised in vacant spaces, and a rivulet, that wantoned along the side of a winding path, had its banks sometimes opened into small basons and its stream sometimes obstructed by little mounds of stone heaped together to increase its murmurs.

They passed slowly through the wood, delighted with such unexpected accommodations, and entertained each other with conjecturing what, or who, he could be, that, in those rude and unfrequented regions, had leisure and art for such harmless luxury.

As they advanced, they heard the sound of musick, and saw youths and virgins dancing in the grove; and, going still further, beheld a stately palace built upon a hill surrounded with woods. The laws of eastern hospitality allowed them to enter, and the master welcomed them like a man liberal and wealthy.

He was skilful enough in appearances soon to discern that they were no common guests, and spread his table with magnificence. The eloquence of Imlac caught his attention, and the lofty courtesy of the princess excited his respect. When they offered to depart he entreated their stay, and was the next day still more unwilling to dismiss them than before. They were easily persuaded to stop, and civility grew up in time to freedom and confidence.

The prince now saw all the domesticks chearful, and all the face of nature smiling round the place, and could not forbear to hope that he should find here what he was seeking; but when he was congratulating the master upon his possessions, he answered with a sigh, "My condition has indeed the appearance of happiness, but appearances are delusive. My prosperity puts my life in danger; the Bassa of Egypt is my enemy, incensed only by my wealth and popularity. I have been hitherto protected against him by the princes of the country; but, as the favour of the great is uncertain, I know not how soon my defenders may be persuaded to share the plunder with the Bassa. I have sent my treasures into a distant country, and, upon the first alarm, am prepared to follow them. Then will my enemies riot in my mansion, and enjoy the gardens which I have planted."

They all joined in lamenting his danger, and deprecating his exile; and the princess was so much disturbed with the tumult of grief and indignation, that she retired to her apartment. They continued with their kind inviter a few days longer, and then went forward to find the hermit.

XXI

THE HAPPINESS OF SOLITUDE. THE HERMIT'S HISTORY

They came on the third day, by the direction of the peasants, to the hermit's cell: it was a cavern in the side of a mountain, over-shadowed with palm-trees; at such a distance from the cataract, that nothing more was heard than a gentle uniform murmur, such as composed the mind to pensive meditation, especially when it was assisted by the wind whistling among the branches. The first rude essay of nature had been so much improved by human labour, that the cave contained several apartments, appropriated to different uses, and often afforded lodging to travellers, whom darkness or tempests happened to overtake.

The hermit sat on a bench at the door, to enjoy

the coolness of the evening. On one side lay a book with pens and papers, on the other mechanical instruments of various kinds. As they approached him unregarded, the princess observed that he had not the countenance of a man that had found, or could teach, the way to happiness.

They saluted him with great respect, which he repaid like a man not unaccustomed to the forms of courts. "My children, said he, if you have lost your way, you shall be willingly supplied with such conveniencies for the night as this cavern will afford. I have all that nature requires, and you will not expect delicacies in a hermit's cell."

They thanked him, and entering, were pleased with the neatness and regularity of the place. The hermit set flesh and wine before them, though he fed only upon fruits and water. His discourse was chearful without levity, and pious without enthusiasm. He soon gained the esteem of his guests, and the princess repented of her hasty censure.

At last Imlac began thus: "I do not now wonder that your reputation is so far extended; we have heard at Cairo of your wisdom, and came hither to implore your direction for this young man and maiden in the *choice of life*."

"To him that lives well, answered the hermit, every form of life is good; nor can I give any other rule for choice, than to remove from all apparent evil."

"He will remove most certainly from evil, said the prince, who shall devote himself to that solitude which you have recommended by your example."

"I have indeed lived fifteen years in solitude, said the hermit, but have no desire that my example should gain any imitators. In my youth I professed arms, and was raised by degrees to the highest military rank. I have traversed wide countries at the head of my troops, and seen many battles and sieges. At last, being disgusted by the preferment of a younger officer, and feeling that my vigour was beginning to decay, I resolved to close my life in peace, having found the world full of snares, discord, and misery. I had once escaped from the persuit of the enemy by the shelter of this cavern, and therefore chose it for my final residence. I employed artificers to form it into chambers, and stored it with all that I was likely to want.

"For some time after my retreat, I rejoiced like a tempest-beaten sailor at his entrance into the harbour, being delighted with the sudden change of the noise and hurry of war, to stillness and repose. When the pleasure of novelty went away, I employed my hours in examining the plants which grow in the valley, and the minerals which I collected from the rocks. But that enquiry is now grown tasteless and irksome. I have been for some time unsettled and distracted: my mind is disturbed with a thousand perplexities of doubt, and vanities of imagination, which hourly prevail upon me, because I have no opportunities of relaxation or diversion. I am sometimes ashamed to think that I could not secure myself from vice, but by retiring from the exercise of virtue, and began to suspect that I was rather impelled by resentment, than led by devotion, into solitude. My fancy riots in scenes of folly, and I lament that I have lost so much, and have gained so little. In solitude, if I escape the example of bad men, I want likewise the counsel and conversation of the good. I have been long comparing the evils with the advantages of society, and resolve to return into the world to morrow. The life of a solitary man will be certainly miserable, but not certainly devout."

They heard his resolution with surprise, but, after a short pause, offered to conduct him to Cairo. He dug up a considerable treasure which he had hid among the rocks, and accompanied them to the city, on which, as he approached it, he gazed with rapture.

XXII

THE HAPPINESS OF A LIFE LED ACCORDING TO NATURE

Rasselas went often to an assembly of learned men, who met at stated times to unbend their minds, and compare their opinions. Their manners were somewhat coarse, but their conversation was instructive, and their disputations acute, though sometimes too violent, and often continued till neither controvertist remembered upon what question they began. Some faults were almost general among them: every one was desirous to dictate to the rest, and every one was pleased to hear the genius or knowledge of another depreciated.

In this assembly Rasselas was relating his interview with the hermit, and the wonder with which he heard him censure a course of life which he had so deliberately chosen, and so laudably followed. The sentiments of the hearers were various. Some were of opinion, that the folly of his choice had been justly punished by condemnation to perpetual perseverance. One of the youngest among them, with great vehemence, pronounced him an hypocrite. Some talked of the right of society to the labour of individuals, and considered retirement as a desertion of duty. Others readily allowed, that there was a time when the claims of the publick were satisfied, and when a man might properly sequester himself, to review his life, and purify his heart.

One, who appeared more affected with the narrative than the rest, thought it likely, that the hermit would, in a few years, go back to his retreat, and, perhaps, if shame did not restrain, or death intercept him, return once more from his retreat into the world: "For the hope of happiness, said he, is so strongly impressed, that the longest experience is not able to efface it. Of the present state, whatever it be, we feel, and are forced to confess, the misery, yet, when the same state is again at a distance, imagination paints it as desirable. But the time will surely come, when desire will be no longer our torment, and no man shall be wretched but by his own fault."

"This, said a philosopher, who had heard him with tokens of great impatience, is the present condition of a wise man. The time is already come, when none are wretched but by their own fault. Nothing is more idle, than to inquire after happiness, which nature has kindly placed within our reach. The way to be happy is to live according to nature, in obedience to that universal and unalterable law with which every heart is originally impressed; which is not written on it by precept, but engraven by destiny, not instilled by education, but infused at our nativity. He that lives according to nature will suffer nothing from the delusions of hope, or importunities of desire: he will receive and reject with equability of temper; and act or suffer as the reason of things shall alternately prescribe. Other men may amuse themselves with subtle definitions, or intricate raciocination. Let them learn to be wise by easier means: let them observe the hind of the forest, and the linnet of the grove: let them consider the life of animals, whose motions are regulated by instinct; they obey their guide and are happy. Let us therefore, at length, cease to dispute, and learn to live; throw away the incumbrance of precepts, which they who utter them with so much pride and pomp do not understand, and carry with us this simple and intelligible maxim, That deviation from nature is deviation from happiness."

When he had spoken, he looked round him with a placid air, and enjoyed the consciousness of his own beneficence. "Sir, said the prince, with great modesty, as I, like all the rest of mankind, am desirous of felicity, my closest attention has been fixed upon your discourse: I doubt not the truth of a position which a man so learned has so confidently advanced. Let me only know what it is to live according to nature."

"When I find young men so humble and so docile, said the philosopher, I can deny them no information which my studies have enabled me to afford. To live according to nature, is to act always with due regard to the fitness arising from the relations and qualities of causes and effects; to concur with the great and unchangeable scheme of universal felicity; to co-operate with the general disposition and tendency of the present system of things."

The prince soon found that this was one of the sages whom he should understand less as he heard him longer. He therefore bowed and was silent, and the philosopher, supposing him satisfied, and the rest vanquished, rose up and departed with the air of a man that had co-operated with the present system.

XXIII

THE PRINCE AND HIS SISTER DIVIDE BETWEEN THEM THE WORK OF OBSERVATION

Rasselas returned home full of reflexions, doubtful how to direct his future steps. Of the way to happiness he found the learned and simple equally ignorant; but, as he was yet young, he flattered himself that he had time remaining for more experiments, and further enquiries. He communicated to Imlac his observations and his doubts, but was answered by him with new doubts, and remarks that gave him no comfort. He therefore discoursed more frequently and freely with his sister, who had yet the same hope with himself, and always assisted him to give some reason why, though he had been hitherto frustrated, he might succeed at last.

"We have hitherto, said she, known but little of the world: we have never yet been either great or mean. In our own country, though we had royalty, we had no power, and in this we have not yet seen the private recesses of domestick peace. Imlac favours not our search, lest we should in time find him mistaken. We will divide the task between us: you shall try what is to be found in the splendour of courts, and I will range the shades of humbler life. Perhaps command and authority may be the supreme blessings, as they afford most opportunities of doing good: or, perhaps, what this world can give may be found in the modest habitations of middle fortune; too low for great designs, and too high for penury and distress."

XXIV

THE PRINCE EXAMINES THE HAPPINESS OF HIGH STATIONS

Rasselas applauded the design, and appeared next day with a splendid retinue at the court of the Bassa. He was soon distinguished for his magnificence, and admitted, as a prince whose curiosity had brought him from distant countries, to an intimacy with the great officers, and frequent conversation with the Bassa himself.

He was at first inclined to believe, that the man must be pleased with his own condition, whom all approached with reverence, and heard with obedience, and who had the power to extend his edicts to a whole kingdom. "There can be no pleasure, said he, equal to that of feeling at once the joy of thousands all made happy by wise administration. Yet, since, by the law of subordination, this sublime delight can be in one nation but the lot of one, it is surely reasonable to think that there is some satisfaction more popular and accessible, and that millions can hardly be subjected to the will of a single man, only to fill his particular breast with incommunicable content."

These thoughts were often in his mind, and he found no solution of the difficulty. But as presents and civilities gained him more familiarity, he found that almost every man who stood high in employment hated all the rest, and was hated by them, and that their lives were a continual succession of plots and detections, stratagems and escapes, faction and treachery. Many of those, who surrounded the Bassa, were sent only to watch and report his conduct; every tongue was muttering censure and every eye was searching for a fault.

At last the letters of revocation arrived, the Bassa was carried in chains to Constantinople, and his name was mentioned no more.

"What are we now to think of the prerogatives of power, said Rasselas to his sister; is it without any efficacy to good? or, is the subordinate degree only dangerous, and the supreme safe and glorious? Is the Sultan the only happy man in his dominions? or, is the Sultan himself subject to the torments of suspicion, and the dread of enemies?"

In a short time the second Bassa was deposed. The Sultan, that had advanced him, was murdered by the Janisaries,[2] and his successor had other views and different favourites.

XXV

THE PRINCESS PERSUES HER ENQUIRY WITH MORE DILIGENCE THAN SUCCESS

The princess, in the mean time, insinuated herself into many families; for there are few doors, through which liberality, joined with good humour, cannot find its way. The daughters of many houses were airy and chearful, but Nekayah had been too long accustomed to the conversation of Imlac and her brother to be much pleased with childish levity and prattle which had no meaning. She found their thoughts narrow, their wishes low, and their merriment often artificial. Their pleasures, poor as they were, could not be preserved pure, but were embittered by petty competitions and worthless emulation. They were always jealous of the beauty of each other: of a quality to which solicitude can add nothing, and from which detraction can take nothing away. Many were in love with triflers like themselves, and many fancied that they were in love when in truth they were only idle. Their affection was seldom fixed on sense or virtue, and therefore seldom ended but in vexation. Their

2. **Janisaries:** Turkish soldiers.

grief, however, like their joy, was transient; every thing floated in their mind unconnected with the past or future, so that one desire easily gave way to another, as a second stone cast into the water effaces and confounds the circles of the first.

With these girls she played as with inoffensive animals, and found them proud of her countenance, and weary of her company.

But her purpose was to examine more deeply, and her affability easily persuaded the hearts that were swelling with sorrow to discharge their secrets in her ear: and those whom hope flattered, or prosperity delighted, often courted her to partake their pleasures.

The princess and her brother commonly met in the evening in a private summer-house on the bank of the Nile, and related to each other the occurrences of the day. As they were sitting together, the princess cast her eyes upon the river that flowed before her. "Answer, said she, great father of waters, thou that rollest thy floods through eighty nations, to the invocations of the daughter of thy native king. Tell me if thou waterest, through all thy course, a single habitation from which thou dost not hear the murmurs of complaint?"

"You are then, said Rasselas, not more successful in private houses than I have been in courts." "I have, since the last partition of our provinces, said the princess, enabled myself to enter familiarly into many families, where there was the fairest show of prosperity and peace, and know not one house that is not haunted by some fury that destroys its quiet.

"I did not seek ease among the poor, because I concluded that there it could not be found. But I saw many poor whom I had supposed to live in affluence. Poverty has, in large cities, very different appearances: it is often concealed in splendour, and often in extravagance. It is the care of a very great part of mankind to conceal their indigence from the rest: they support themselves by temporary expedients, and every day is lost in contriving for the morrow.

"This, however, was an evil, which, though frequent, I saw with less pain, because I could relieve it. Yet some have refused my bounties; more offended with my quickness to detect their wants, than pleased with my readiness to succour them: and others, whose exigencies compelled them to admit my kindness, have never been able to forgive their benefactress. Many, however, have been sincerely grateful without the ostentation of gratitude, or the hope of other favours."

XXVI

THE PRINCESS CONTINUES HER REMARKS UPON PRIVATE LIFE

Nekayah perceiving her brother's attention fixed, proceeded in her narrative.

"In families, where there is or is not poverty, there is commonly discord: if a kingdom be, as Imlac tells us, a great family, a family likewise is a little kingdom, torn with factions and exposed to revolutions. An unpractised observer expects the love of parents and children to be constant and equal; but this kindness seldom continues beyond the years of infancy: in a short time the children become rivals to their parents. Benefits are allayed by reproaches, and gratitude debased by envy.

"Parents and children seldom act in concert: each child endeavours to appropriate the esteem or fondness of the parents, and the parents, with yet less temptation, betray each other to their children; thus some place their confidence in the father, and some in the mother, and, by degrees, the house is filled with artifices and feuds.

"The opinions of children and parents, of the young and the old, are naturally opposite, by the contrary effects of hope and despondence, of expectation and experience, without crime or folly on either side. The colours of life in youth and age appear different, as the face of nature in spring and winter. And how can children credit the assertions of parents, which their own eyes show them to be false?

"Few parents act in such a manner as much to enforce their maxims by the credit of their lives. The old man trusts wholly to slow contrivance and gradual progression: the youth expects to force his way by genius, vigour, and precipitance. The old man pays regard to riches, and the youth reverences virtue. The old man deifies prudence: the youth commits himself to magnanimity and chance. The young man, who intends no ill, believes that none is intended, and therefore acts with openness and candour: but his father, having suffered the injuries of fraud, is impelled to suspect, and too often allured to practice it. Age looks with anger on the temerity of youth, and youth with contempt on the scrupulosity of age. Thus parents and children, for the greatest part, live on to love less and less: and, if those whom nature has thus closely united are the torments of each other, where shall we look for tenderness and consolation?"

"Surely, said the prince, you must have been unfortunate in your choice of acquaintance: I am unwilling to believe, that the most tender of all relations is thus impeded in its effects by natural necessity."

"Domestick discord, answered she, is not inevitably and fatally necessary; but yet is not easily avoided. We seldom see that a whole family is virtuous: the good and evil cannot well agree; and the evil can yet less agree with one another: even the virtuous fall sometimes to variance, when their virtues are of different kinds, and tending to extremes. In general, those parents have most reverence who most deserve it: for he that lives well cannot be despised.

"Many other evils infest private life. Some are the slaves of servants whom they have trusted with their affairs. Some are kept in continual anxiety to the caprice of rich relations, whom they cannot please, and dare not offend. Some husbands are imperious, and some wives perverse: and, as it is always more easy to do evil than good, though the wisdom or virtue of one can very rarely make many happy, the folly or vice of one may often make many miserable."

"If such be the general effect of marriage, said the prince, I shall, for the future, think it dangerous to connect my interest with that of another, lest I should be unhappy by my partner's fault."

"I have met, said the princess, with many who live single for that reason; but I never found that their prudence ought to raise envy. They dream away their time without friendship, without fondness, and are driven to rid themselves of the day, for which they have no use, by childish amusements, or vicious delights. They act as beings under the constant sense of some known inferiority, that fills their minds with rancour, and their tongues with censure. They are peevish at home, and malevolent abroad; and, as the out-laws of human nature, make it their business and their pleasure to disturb that society which debars them from its privileges. To live without feeling or exciting sympathy, to be fortunate without adding to the felicity of others, or afflicted without tasting the balm of pity, is a state more gloomy than solitude: it is not retreat but exclusion from mankind. Marriage has many pains, but celibacy has no pleasures."

"What then is to be done? said Rasselas; the more we enquire, the less we can resolve. Surely he is most likely to please himself that has no other inclination to regard."

XXVII

DISQUISITION UPON GREATNESS

The conversation had a short pause. The prince, having considered his sister's observations, told her, that she had surveyed life with prejudice, and supposed misery where she did not find it. "Your narrative, says he, throws yet a darker gloom upon the prospects of futurity: the predictions of Imlac were but faint sketches of the evils painted by Nekayah. I have been lately convinced that quiet is not the daughter of grandeur, or of power: that her presence is not to be bought by wealth, nor enforced by conquest. It is evident, that as any man acts in a wider compass, he must be more exposed to opposition from enmity or miscarriage from chance; whoever has many to please or to govern, must use the ministry of many agents, some of whom will be wicked, and some ignorant; by some he will be misled, and by others betrayed. If he gratifies one he will offend another: those that are not favoured will think themselves injured; and, since favours can be conferred but upon few, the greater number will be always discontented."

"The discontent, said the princess, which is thus unreasonable, I hope that I shall always have spirit to despise, and you, power to repress."

"Discontent, answered Rasselas, will not always be without reason under the most just or vigilant administration of publick affairs. None, however attentive, can always discover that merit which indigence or faction may happen to obscure; and none, however powerful, can always reward it. Yet, he that sees inferiour desert advanced above him, will naturally impute that preference to partiality or caprice; and, indeed, it can scarcely be hoped that any man, however magnanimous by nature, or exalted by condition, will be able to persist for ever in fixed and inexorable justice of distribution: he will sometimes indulge his own affections, and sometimes those of his favourites; he will permit some to please him who can never serve him; he will discover in those whom he loves qualities which in reality they do not possess; and to those, from whom he receives pleasure, he will in turn endeavour to give it. Thus will recommendations sometimes prevail which were purchased by money, or by the more destructive bribery of flattery and servility.

"He that has much to do will do something wrong, and of that wrong must suffer the consequences; and, if it were possible that he should always act rightly, yet when such numbers are to judge of his conduct, the bad will censure and obstruct him by malevolence, and the good sometimes by mistake.

"The highest stations cannot therefore hope to be the abodes of happiness, which I would willingly believe to have fled from thrones and palaces to seats of humble privacy and placid obscurity. For what can hinder the satisfaction, or intercept the expectations, of him whose abilities are adequate to his employments, who sees with his own eyes the whole circuit of his influence, who chooses by his own knowledge all whom he trusts, and whom none are tempted to deceive by hope or fear? Surely he has nothing to do but to love and to be loved, to be virtuous and to be happy."

"Whether perfect happiness would be procured by perfect goodness, said Nekayah, this world will never afford an opportunity of deciding. But this, at least, may be maintained, that we do not always find visible happiness in proportion to visible virtue. All natural and almost all political evils, are incident alike to the bad and good: they are confounded in the misery of a famine, and not much distinguished in the fury of a faction; they sink together in a tempest, and are driven together from their country by invaders. All that virtue can afford is quietness of conscience, a steady prospect of a happier state; this may enable us to endure calamity with patience; but remember that patience must suppose pain."

XXVIII

RASSELAS AND NEKAYAH CONTINUE THEIR CONVERSATION

"Dear princess, said Rasselas, you fall into the common errours of exaggeratory declamation, by producing, in a familiar disquisition, examples of national calamities, and scenes of extensive misery, which are found in books rather than in the world, and which, as they are horrid, are ordained to be rare. Let us not imagine evils which we do not feel, nor injure life by misrepresentations. I cannot bear that querelous eloquence which threatens every city with a siege like that of Jerusalem, that makes famine attend on every flight of locusts, and suspends pestilence on the wing of every blast that issues from the south.

"On necessary and inevitable evils, which overwhelm kingdoms at once, all disputation is vain: when they happen they must be endured. But it is evident, that these bursts of universal distress are more dreaded than felt: thousands and ten thousands flourish in youth, and wither in age, without the knowledge of any other than domestick evils, and share the same pleasures and vexations whether their kings are mild or cruel, whether the armies of their country persue their enemies, or retreat before them. While courts are disturbed with intestine[3] competitions, and ambassadours are negotiating in foreign countries, the smith still plies his anvil, and the husbandman drives his plow forward; the necessaries of life are required and obtained, and the successive business of the seasons continues to make its wonted revolutions.

"Let us cease to consider what, perhaps, may never happen, and what, when it shall happen, will laugh at human speculation. We will not endeavour to modify the motions of the elements, or to fix the destiny of kingdoms. It is our business to consider what beings like us may perform; each labouring for his own happiness, by promoting within his circle, however narrow, the happiness of others.

"Marriage is evidently the dictate of nature; men and women were made to be companions of each other, and therefore I cannot be persuaded but that marriage is one of the means of happiness."

3. intestine: internal.

"I know not, said the princess, whether marriage be more than one of the innumerable modes of human misery. When I see and reckon the various forms of connubial infelicity, the unexpected causes of lasting discord, the diversities of temper, the oppositions of opinion, the rude collisions of contrary desire where both are urged by violent impulses, the obstinate contests of disagreeing virtues, where both are supported by consciousness of good intention, I am sometimes disposed to think with the severer casuists[4] of most nations, that marriage is rather permitted than approved, and that none, but by the instigation of a passion too much indulged, entangle themselves with indissoluble compacts."

"You seem to forget, replied Rasselas, that you have, even now, represented celibacy as less happy than marriage. Both conditions may be bad, but they cannot both be worst. Thus it happens when wrong opinions are entertained, that they mutually destroy each other, and leave the mind open to truth."

"I did not expect, answered the princess, to hear that imputed to falshood which is the consequence only of frailty. To the mind, as to the eye, it is difficult to compare with exactness objects vast in their extent, and various in their parts. Where we see or conceive the whole at once we readily note the discriminations and decide the preference: but of two systems, of which neither can be surveyed by any human being in its full compass of magnitude and multiplicity of complication, where is the wonder, that judging of the whole by parts, I am alternately affected by one and the other as either presses on my memory or fancy? We differ from ourselves just as we differ from each other, when we see only part of the question, as in the multifarious relations of politicks and morality: but when we perceive the whole at once, as in numerical computations, all agree in one judgment, and none ever varies his opinion."

"Let us not add, said the prince, to the other evils of life, the bitterness of controversy, nor endeavour to vie with each other in subtilties of argument. We are employed in a search, of which both are equally to enjoy the success, or suffer by the miscarriage. It is therefore fit that we assist each other. You surely conclude too hastily from the infelicity of marriage against its institution; will not the misery of life prove equally that life cannot be the gift of heaven? The world must be peopled by marriage, or peopled without it."

"How the world is to be peopled, returned Nekayah, is not my care, and needs not be yours. I see no danger that the present generation should omit to leave successors behind them: we are not now enquiring for the world, but for ourselves."

XXIX

THE DEBATE ON MARRIAGE CONTINUED

'The good of the whole says Rasselas, is the same with the good of all its parts. If marriage be best for mankind it must be evidently best for individuals, or a permanent and a necessary duty must be the cause of evil, and some must be inevitably sacrificed to the convenience of others. In the estimate which you have made of the two states, it appears that the incommodities of a single life are, in a great measure, necessary and certain, but those of the conjugal state accidental and avoidable.

"I cannot forbear to flatter myself that prudence and benevolence will make marriage happy. The general folly of mankind is the cause of general complaint. What can be expected but disappointment and repentance from a choice made in the immaturity of youth, in the ardour of desire, without judgment, without foresight, without enquiry after conformity of opinions, similarity of manners, rectitude of judgment, or purity of sentiment.

"Such is the common process of marriage. A youth and maiden meeting by chance, or brought together by artifice, exchange glances, reciprocate civilities, go home, and dream of one another. Having little to divert attention, or diversify thought, they find themselves uneasy when they are apart, and therefore conclude that they shall be happy together. They marry, and discover what nothing but voluntary blindness had before concealed; they wear out life in altercations, and charge nature with cruelty.

"From those early marriages proceeds likewise the rivalry of parents and children: the son is

4. **casuists:** students of ethical questions.

eager to enjoy the world before the father is willing to forsake it, and there is hardly room at once for two generations. The daughter begins to bloom before the mother can be content to fade, and neither can forbear to wish for the absence of the other.

"Surely all these evils may be avoided by that deliberation and delay which prudence prescribes to irrevocable choice. In the variety and jollity of youthful pleasures life may be well enough supported without the help of a partner. Longer time will increase experience, and wider views will allow better opportunities of enquiry and selection: one advantage, at least, will be certain; the parents will be visibly older than their children."

"What reason cannot collect, said Nekayah, and what experiment has not yet taught, can be known only from the report of others. I have been told that late marriages are not eminently happy. This is a question too important to be neglected, and I have often proposed it to those, whose accuracy of remark, and comprehensiveness of knowledge, made their suffrages worthy of regard. They have generally determined, that it is dangerous for a man and woman to suspend their fate upon each other, at a time when opinions are fixed, and habits are established; when friendships have been contracted on both sides, when life has been planned into method, and the mind has long enjoyed the contemplation of its own prospects.

"It is scarcely possible that two travelling through the world under the conduct of chance, should have been both directed to the same path, and it will not often happen that either will quit the track which custom has made pleasing. When the desultory levity of youth has settled into regularity, it is soon succeeded by pride ashamed to yield, or obstinacy delighting to contend. And even though mutual esteem produces mutual desire to please, time itself, as it modifies unchangeably the external mien, determines likewise the direction of the passions, and gives an inflexible rigidity to the manners. Long customs are not easily broken: he that attempts to change the course of his own life, very often labours in vain; and how shall we do that for others which we are seldom able to do for ourselves?"

"But surely, interposed the prince, you suppose the chief motive of choice forgotten or neglected. Whenever I shall seek a wife, it shall be my first question, whether she be willing to be led by reason?"

"Thus it is, said Nekayah, that philosophers are deceived. There are a thousand familiar disputes which reason never can decide; questions that elude investigation, and make logick ridiculous; cases where something must be done, and where little can be said. Consider the state of mankind, and enquire how few can be supposed to act upon any occasions, whether small or great, with all the reasons of action present to their minds. Wretched would be the pair above all names of wretchedness, who should be doomed to adjust by reason every morning all the minute detail of a domestick day.

"Those who marry at an advanced age, will probably escape the encroachments of their children; but, in diminution of this advantage, they will be likely to leave them, ignorant and helpless, to a guardian's mercy: or, if that should not happen, they must at least go out of the world before they see those whom they love best either wise or great.

"From their children, if they have less to fear, they have less also to hope, and they lose, without equivalent, the joys of early love, and the convenience of uniting with manners pliant, and minds susceptible of new impressions, which might wear away their dissimilitudes by long cohabitation, as soft bodies, by continual attrition, conform their surfaces to each other.

"I believe it will be found that those who marry late are best pleased with their children, and those who marry early with their partners."

"The union of these two affections, said Rasselas, would produce all that could be wished. Perhaps there is a time when marriage might unite them, a time neither too early for the father, nor too late for the husband."

"Every hour, answered the princess, confirms my prejudice in favour of the position so often uttered by the mouth of Imlac, 'That nature sets her gifts on the right hand and on the left.' Those conditions, which flatter hope and attract desire, are so constituted, that, as we approach one, we recede from another. There are goods so opposed that we cannot seize both, but, by too much prudence, may pass between them at too great a distance to reach either. This is often the fate of long consideration; he does nothing who endeavours to do more than is allowed to humanity. Flatter not yourself with contrarieties of pleasure. Of the blessings set before you make your choice, and be content. No man can taste the fruits of autumn while he is delighting his scent with the flowers of the spring: no man can, at the same time, fill his cup from the source and from the mouth of the Nile."

XXX

IMLAC ENTERS, AND CHANGES THE CONVERSATION

Here Imlac entered, and interrupted them. "Imlac, said Rasselas, I have been taking from the princess the dismal history of private life, and am almost discouraged from further search."

"It seems to me, said Imlac, that while you are making the choice of life, you neglect to live. You wander about a single city, which, however large and diversified, can now afford few novelties, and forget that you are in a country, famous among the earliest monarchies for the power and wisdom of its inhabitants; a country where the sciences first dawned that illuminate the world, and beyond which the arts cannot be traced of civil society or domestick life.

"The old Egyptians have left behind them monuments of industry and power before which all European magnificence is confessed to fade away. The ruins of their architecture are the schools of modern builders, and from the wonders, which time has spared we may conjecture, though uncertainly, what it has destroyed."

"My curiosity, said Rasselas, does not very strongly lead me to survey piles of stone, or mounds of earth; my business is with man. I came hither not to measure fragments of temples, or trace choaked aqueducts, but to look upon the various scenes of the present world."

"The things that are now before us, said the princess, require attention, and deserve it. What have I to do with the heroes or the monuments of ancient times? with times which never can return, and heroes, whose form of life was different from all that the present condition of mankind requires or allows."

"To know any thing, returned the poet, we must know its effects; to see men we must see their works, that we may learn what reason has dictated, or passion has incited, and find what are the most powerful motives of action. To judge rightly of the present we must oppose it to the past; for all judgment is comparative, and of the future nothing can be known. The truth is, that no mind is much employed upon the present: recollection and anticipation fill up almost all our moments. Our passions are joy and grief, love and hatred, hope and fear. Of joy and grief the past is the object, and the future of hope and fear; even love and hatred respect the past, for the cause must have been before the effect.

"The present state of things is the consequence of the former, and it is natural to inquire what were the sources of the good that we enjoy, or of the evil that we suffer. If we act only for ourselves, to neglect the study of history is not prudent: if we are entrusted with the care of others, it is not just. Ignorance, when it is voluntary, is criminal; and he may properly be charged with evil who refused to learn how he might prevent it.

"There is no part of history so generally useful as that which relates the progress of the human mind, the gradual improvement of reason, the successive advances of science, the vicissitudes of learning and ignorance, which are the light and darkness of thinking beings, the extinction and resuscitation of arts, and all the revolutions of the intellectual world. If accounts of battles and invasions are peculiarly the business of princes, the useful or elegant arts are not to be neglected; those who have kingdoms to govern, have understandings to cultivate.

"Example is always more efficacious than precept. A soldier is formed in war, and a painter must copy pictures. In this, contemplative life has the advantage: great actions are seldom seen, but the labours of art are always at hand for those who desire to know what art has been able to perform.

"When the eye or the imagination is struck with any uncommon work the next transition of an active mind is to the means by which it was performed. Here begins the true use of such contemplation; we enlarge our comprehension by new ideas, and perhaps recover some art lost to mankind, or learn what is less perfectly known in our own country. At least we compare our own with former times, and either rejoice at our improvements, or, what is the first motion towards good discover our defects."

"I am willing, said the prince, to see all that can deserve my search." "And I, said the princess, shall rejoice to learn something of the manners of antiquity."

"The most pompous monument of Egyptian greatness, and one of the most bulky works of manual industry, said Imlac, are the pyramids; fabricks raised before the time of history, and of which the earliest narratives afford us only uncertain traditions. Of these the greatest is still standing, very little injured by time."

"Let us visit them to morrow, said Nekayah. I have often heard of the Pyramids, and shall not rest, till I have seen them within and without with my own eyes."

XXXI

THEY VISIT THE PYRAMIDS

The resolution being thus taken, they set out the next day. They laid tents upon their camels, being resolved to stay among the pyramids till their curiosity was fully satisfied. They travelled gently, turned aside to every thing remarkable, stopped from time to time and conversed with the inhabitants, and observed the various appearances of towns, ruined and inhabited, of wild and cultivated nature.

When they came to the great pyramid they were astonished at the extent of the base, and the height of the top. Imlac explained to them the principles upon which the pyramidal form was chosen for a fabrick intended to co-extend its duration with that of the world: he showed that its gradual diminution gave it such stability, as defeated all the common attacks of the elements, and could scarcely be overthrown by earthquakes themselves, the least resistible of natural violence. A concussion that should shatter the pyramid would threaten the dissolution of the continent.

They measured all its dimensions, and pitched their tents at its foot. Next day they prepared to enter its interiour apartments, and having hired the common guides climbed up to the first passage, when the favourite of the princess, looking into the cavity, stepped back and trembled. "Pekuah, said the princess, of what art thou afraid?" "Of the narrow entrance, answered the lady, and of the dreadful gloom. I dare not enter a place which must surely be inhabited by unquiet souls. The original possessors of these dreadful vaults will start up before us, and, perhaps, shut us in for ever." She spoke, and threw her arms round the neck of her mistress.

"If all your fear be of apparitions, said the prince, I will promise you safety: there is no danger from the dead; he that is once buried will be seen no more."

"That the dead are seen no more, said Imlac, I will not undertake to maintain against the concurrent and unvaried testimony of all ages, and of all nations. There is no people, rude or learned, among whom apparitions of the dead are not related and believed. This opinion, which, perhaps, prevails as far as human nature is diffused, could become universal only by its truth: those, that never heard of one another, would not have agreed in a tale which nothing but experience can make credible. That it is doubted by single cavillers can very little weaken the general evidence, and some who deny it with their tongues confess it by their fears.

"Yet I do not mean to add new terrours to those which have already seized upon Pekuah. There can be no reason why spectres should haunt the pyramid more than other places, or why they should have power or will to hurt innocence and purity. Our entrance is no violation of their priviledges; we can take nothing from them, how then can we offend them?"

"My dear Pekuah, said the princess, I will always go before you, and Imlac shall follow you. Remember that you are the companion of the princess of Abissinia."

"If the princess is pleased that her servant should die, returned the lady, let her command some death less dreadful than enclosure in this horrid cavern. You know I dare not disobey you: I must go if you command me; but, if I once enter, I never shall come back."

The princess saw that her fear was too strong for expostulation or reproof, and embracing her, told her that she should stay in the tent till their return. Pekuah was yet not satisfied, but entreated the princess not to persue so dreadful a purpose as that of entering the recesses of the pyramid. "Though I cannot teach courage, said Nekayah, I must not learn cowardise; nor leave at last undone what I came hither only to do."

XXXII

THEY ENTER THE PYRAMID

Pekuah descended to the tents, and the rest entered the pyramid: they passed through the galleries, surveyed the vaults of marble, and examined the chest in which the body of the founder is supposed to have been reposited. They then sat down in one of the most spacious chambers to rest a while before they attempted to return.

"We have now, said Imlac, gratified our minds with an exact view of the greatest work of man, except the wall of China.

"Of the wall it is very easy to assign the motives. It secured a wealthy and timorous nation from the incursions of Barbarians, whose unskilfulness in arts made it easier for them to supply their wants by rapine than by industry, and who from time to time poured in upon the habitations of peaceful commerce, as vultures descend upon domestick fowl. Their celerity and fierceness made the wall necessary, and their ignorance made it efficacious.

"But for the pyramids no reason has ever been given adequate to the cost and labour of the work. The narrowness of the chambers proves that it could afford no retreat from enemies, and treasures might have been reposited at far less expence with equal security. It seems to have been erected only in compliance with that hunger of imagination which preys incessantly upon life, and must be always appeased by some employment. Those who have already all that they can enjoy, must enlarge their desires. He that has built for use, till use is supplied, must begin to build for vanity, and extend his plan to the utmost power of human performance, that he may not be soon reduced to form another wish.

"I consider this mighty structure as a monument of the insufficiency of human enjoyments. A king, whose power is unlimited, and whose treasures surmount all real and imaginary wants, is compelled to solace, by the erection of a pyramid, the satiety of dominion and tastelesness of pleasures, and to amuse the tediousness of declining life, by seeing thousands labouring without end, and one stone, for no purpose, laid upon another. Whoever thou art, that, not content with a moderate condition, imaginest happiness in royal magnificence, and dreamest that command or riches can feed the appetite of novelty with perpetual gratifications, survey the pyramids, and confess thy folly!"

XXXIII

THE PRINCESS MEETS WITH AN UNEXPECTED MISFORTUNE

They rose up, and returned through the cavity at which they had entered, and the princess prepared for her favourite a long narrative of dark labyrinths, and costly rooms, and of the different impressions which the varieties of the way had made upon her. But, when they came to their train, they found every one silent and dejected: the men discovered shame and fear in their countenances, and the women were weeping in the tents.

What had happened they did not try to conjecture, but immediately enquired. "You had scarcely entered into the pyramid, said one of the attendants, when a troop of Arabs rushed upon us: we were too few to resist them, and too slow to escape. They were about to search the tents, set us on our camels, and drive us along before them, when the approach of some Turkish horsemen put them to flight; but they seized the lady Pekuah with her two maids, and carried them away; the Turks are now persuing them by our instigation, but I fear they will not be able to overtake them."

The princess was overpowered with surprise and grief. Rasselas, in the first heat of his resentment, ordered his servants to follow him, and prepared to persue the robbers with his sabre in his hand. "Sir, said Imlac, what can you hope from violence or valour? the Arabs are mounted on horses trained to battle and retreat; we have only beasts of burden. By leaving our present station we may lose the princess, but cannot hope to regain Pekuah."

In a short time the Turks returned, having not been able to reach the enemy. The princess burst out into new lamentations, and Rasselas could scarcely forbear to reproach them with cowardice; but Imlac was of opinion, that the escape of the Arabs was no addition to their misfortune, for, perhaps, they would have killed their captives rather than have resigned them.

XXXIV

THEY RETURN TO CAIRO WITHOUT PEKUAH

There was nothing to be hoped from longer stay. They returned to Cairo repenting of their curiosity, censuring the negligence of the government, lamenting their own rashness which had neglected to procure a guard, imagining many expedients by which the loss of Pekuah might have been prevented, and resolving to do something for her recovery, though none could find any thing proper to be done.

Nekayah retired to her chamber, where her women attempted to comfort her, by telling her that all had their troubles, and that lady Pekuah had enjoyed much happiness in the world for a long time, and might reasonably expect a change of fortune. They hoped that some good would befal her wheresoever she was, and that their mistress would find another friend who might supply her place.

The princess made them no answer, and they continued the form of condolence, not much grieved in their hearts that the favourite was lost.

Next day the prince presented to the Bassa a memorial of the wrong which he had suffered, and a petition for redress. The Bassa threatened to punish the robbers, but did not attempt to catch them, nor, indeed, could any account or description be given by which he might direct the persuit.

It soon appeared that nothing would be done by authority. Governors, being accustomed to hear of more crimes than they can punish, and more wrongs than they can redress, set themselves at ease by indiscriminate negligence, and presently forget the request when they lose sight of the petitioner.

Imlac then endeavoured to gain some intelligence by private agents. He found many who pretended to an exact knowledge of all the haunts of the Arabs, and to regular correspondence with their chiefs, and who readily undertook the recovery of Pekuah. Of these, some were furnished with money for their journey, and came back no more; some were liberally paid for accounts which a few days discovered to be false. But the princess would not suffer any means, however improbable, to be left untried. While she was doing something she kept her hope alive. As one expedient failed, another was suggested; when one messenger returned unsuccessful, another was despatched to a different quarter.

Two months had now passed, and of Pekuah nothing had been heard; the hopes which they had endeavoured to raise in each other grew more languid, and the princess, when she saw nothing more to be tried, sunk down inconsolable in hopeless dejection. A thousand times she reproached herself with the easy compliance by which she permitted her favourite to stay behind her. "Had not my fondness, said she, lessened my authority, Pekuah had not dared to talk of her terrours. She ought to have feared me more than spectres. A severe look would have overpowered her; a peremptory command would have compelled obedience. Why did foolish indulgence prevail upon me? Why did I not speak and refuse to hear?"

"Great princess, said Imlac, do not reproach yourself for your virtue, or consider that as blameable by which evil has accidentally been caused. Your tenderness for the timidity of Pekuah was generous and kind. When we act according to our duty, we commit the event to him by whose laws our actions are governed, and who will suffer none to be finally punished for obedience. When, in prospect of some good, whether natural or moral, we break the rules prescribed us, we withdraw from the direction of superiour wisdom, and take all consequences upon ourselves. Man cannot so far know the connexion of causes and events, as that he may venture to do wrong in order to do right. When we persue our end by lawful means, we may always console our miscarriage by the hope of future recompense. When we consult only our own policy, and attempt to find a nearer way to good, by overleaping the settled boundaries of right and wrong, we cannot be happy even by success, because we cannot escape the consciousness of our fault; but, if we miscarry, the disappointment is irremediably embittered. How comfortless is the sorrow of him, who feels at once the pangs of guilt, and the vexation of calamity which guilt has brought upon him?

"Consider, princess, what would have been your condition, if the lady Pekuah had entreated to accompany you, and, being compelled to stay in the tents, had been carried away; or how would you have born the thought, if you had forced her into the pyramid, and she had died before you in agonies of terrour."

"Had either happened, said Nekayah, I could not have endured life till now: I should have been tortured to madness by the remembrance of such cruelty, or must have pined away in abhorrence of myself."

"This at least, said Imlac, is the present reward of virtuous conduct, that no unlucky consequence can oblige us to repent it."

XXV

THE PRINCESS LANGUISHES FOR WANT OF PEKUAH

Nekayah, being thus reconciled to herself, found that no evil is insupportable but that which is accompanied with consciousness of wrong. She was, from that time, delivered from the violence of tempestuous sorrow, and sunk into silent pensiveness and gloomy tranquillity. She sat from morning to evening recollecting all that had been done or said by her Pekuah, treasured up with care every trifle on which Pekuah had set an accidental value, and which might recal to mind any little incident or careless conversation. The sentiments of her, whom she now expected to see no more, were treasured in her memory as rules of life, and she deliberated to no other end than to conjecture on any occasion what would have been the opinion and counsel of Pekuah.

The women, by whom she was attended, knew nothing of her real condition, and therefore she could not talk to them but with caution and reserve. She began to remit her curiosity, having no great care to collect notions which she had no convenience of uttering. Rasselas endeavoured first to comfort and afterwards to divert her; he hired musicians, to whom she seemed to listen, but did not hear them, and procured masters to instruct her in various arts, whose lectures, when they visited her again, were again to be repeated. She had lost her taste of pleasure and her ambition of excellence. And her mind, though forced into short excursions, always recurred to the image of her friend.

Imlac was every morning earnestly enjoined to renew his enquiries, and was asked every night whether he had yet heard of Pekuah, till not being able to return the princess the answer that she desired, he was less and less willing to come into her presence. She observed his backwardness, and commanded him to attend her. "You are not, said she, to confound impatience with resentment, or to suppose that I charge you with negligence, because I repine at your unsuccessfulness. I do not much wonder at your absence; I know that the unhappy are never pleasing, and that all naturally avoid the contagion of misery. To hear complaints is wearisome alike to the wretched and the happy; for who would cloud by adventitious grief the short gleams of gaiety which life allows us? or who, that is struggling under his own evils, will add to them the miseries of another?

"The time is at hand, when none shall be disturbed any longer by the sighs of Nekayah: my search after happiness is now at an end. I am resolved to retire from the world with all its flatteries and deceits, and will hide myself in solitude, without any other care than to compose my thoughts, and regulate my hours by a constant succession of innocent occupations, till, with a mind purified from all earthly desires, I shall enter into that state, to which all are hastening, and in which I hope again to enjoy the friendship of Pekuah."

"Do not entangle your mind, said Imlac, by irrevocable determinations, nor increase the burthen of life by a voluntary accumulation of misery: the weariness of retirement will continue or increase when the loss of Pekuah is forgotten. That you have been deprived of one pleasure is no very good reason for rejection of the rest."

"Since Pekuah was taken from me, said the princess, I have no pleasure to reject or to retain. She that has no one to love or trust has little to hope. She wants the radical principle of happiness. We may, perhaps, allow that what satisfaction this world can afford, must arise from the conjunction of wealth, knowledge and goodness: wealth is nothing but as it is bestowed, and knowledge nothing but as it is communicated: they must therefore be imparted to others, and to whom could I now delight to impart them? Goodness affords the only comfort which can be enjoyed without a partner, and goodness may be practised in retirement."

"How far solitude may admit goodness, or advance it, I shall not, replied Imlac, dispute at present. Remember the confession of the pious hermit. You will wish to return into the world, when the image of your companion has left your thoughts." "That time, said Nekayah, will never come. The generous frankness, the modest obsequiousness, and the faithful secrecy of my dear Pekuah, will always be more missed, as I shall live longer to see vice and folly."

"The state of a mind oppressed with a sudden calamity, said Imlac, is like that of the fabulous inhabitants of the new created earth, who, when the first night came upon them, supposed that day never would return. When the clouds of sorrow gather over us, we see nothing beyond them, nor can imagine how they will be dispelled: yet a new day succeeded to the night, and sorrow is never long without a dawn of ease. But they who restrain themselves from receiving comfort, do as the savages would have done, had they put out their eyes when it was dark. Our minds, like our bodies, are in continual flux; something is hourly lost, and something acquired. To lose much at once is inconvenient to either, but while the vital powers remain uninjured, nature will find the means of reparation. Distance has the same effect on the mind as on the eye, and while we glide along the stream of time, whatever we leave behind us is always lessening, and that which we approach increasing in magnitude. Do not suffer life to stagnate; it will grow muddy for want of motion: commit yourself again to the current of the world; Pekuah will vanish by degrees; you will meet in your way some other favourite, or learn to diffuse yourself in general conversation."

"At least, said the prince, do not despair before all remedies have been tried: the enquiry after the unfortunate lady is still continued, and shall be carried on with yet greater diligence, on condition that you will promise to wait a year for the event, without any unalterable resolution."

Nekayah thought this a reasonable demand, and made the promise to her brother, who had been advised by Imlac to require it. Imlac had, indeed, no great hope of regaining Pekuah, but he supposed, that if he could secure the interval of a year, the princess would be then in no danger of a cloister.

XXXVI

PEKUAH IS STILL REMEMBERED. THE PROGRESS OF SORROW

Nekayah, seeing that nothing was omitted for the recovery of her favourite, and having, by her promise, set her intention of retirement at a distance, began imperceptibly to return to common cares and common pleasures. She rejoiced without her own consent at the suspension of her sorrows, and sometimes caught herself with indignation in the act of turning away her mind from the remembrance of her, whom yet she resolved never to forget.

She then appointed a certain hour of the day for meditation on the merits and fondness of Pekuah, and for some weeks retired constantly at the time fixed, and returned with her eyes swollen and her countenance clouded. By degrees she grew less scrupulous, and suffered any important and pressing avocation to delay the tribute of daily tears. She then yielded to less occasions; sometimes forgot what she was indeed afraid to remember, and, at last, wholly released herself from the duty of periodical affliction.

Her real love of Pekuah was yet not diminished. A thousand occurrences brought her back to memory, and a thousand wants, which nothing but the confidence of friendship can supply, made her frequently regretted. She, therefore, solicited Imlac never to desist from enquiry, and to leave no art of intelligence untried, that, at least, she might have the comfort of knowing that she did not suffer by negligence or sluggishness. "Yet what, said she, is to be expected from our persuit of happiness, when we find the state of life to be such, that happiness itself is the cause of misery? Why should we endeavour to attain that, of which the possession cannot be secured? I shall henceforward fear to yield my heart to excellence, however bright, or to fondness, however tender, lest I should lose again what I have lost in Pekuah."

XXXVII

THE PRINCESS HEARS NEWS OF PEKUAH

In seven months, one of the messengers, who had been sent away upon the day when the promise was drawn from the princess, returned, after many unsuccessful rambles, from the borders of Nubia, with an account that Pekuah was in the hands of an Arab chief, who possessed a castle or fortress on the extremity of Egypt. The Arab, whose revenue was plunder, was willing to restore her, with her two attendants, for two hundred ounces of gold.

The price was no subject of debate. The princess was in extasies when she heard that her favourite was alive, and might so cheaply be ransomed. She could not think of delaying for a moment Pekuah's happiness or her own, but entreated her brother to send back the messenger with the sum required. Imlac, being consulted, was not very confident of the veracity of the relator, and was still more doubtful of the Arab's faith, who might, if he were too liberally trusted, detain at once the money and the captives. He thought it dangerous to put themselves in the power of the Arab, by going into his district, and could not expect that the Rover would so much expose himself as to come into the lower country, where he might be seized by the forces of the Bassa.

It is difficult to negotiate where neither will trust. But Imlac, after some deliberation, directed the messenger to propose that Pekuah should be conducted by ten horsemen to the monastry of St. Anthony, which is situated in the deserts of Upper-Egypt, where she should be met by the same number, and her ransome should be paid.

That no time might be lost, as they expected that the proposal would not be refused, they immediately began their journey to the monastry; and, when they arrived, Imlac went forward with the former messenger to the Arab's fortress. Rasselas was desirous to go with them, but neither his sister nor Imlac would consent. The Arab, according to the custom of his nation, observed the laws of hospitality with great exactness to those who put themselves into his power, and, in a few days, brought Pekuah with her maids, by easy journeys, to their place appointed, where receiving the stipulated price, he restored her with great respect to liberty and her friends, and undertook to conduct them back towards Cairo beyond all danger of robbery or violence.

The princess and her favourite embraced each other with transport too violent to be expressed, and went out together to pour the tears of tenderness in secret, and exchange professions of kindness and gratitude. After a few hours they returned into the refectory of the convent, where, in the presence of the prior and his brethren, the prince required of Pekuah the history of her adventures.

XXXVIII

THE ADVENTURES OF THE LADY PEKUAH

"At what time, and in what manner, I was forced away, said Pekuah, your servants have told you. The suddenness of the event struck me with surprise, and I was at first rather stupified than agitated with any passion of either fear or sorrow. My confusion was encreased by the speed and tumult of our flight while we were followed by the Turks, who, as it seemed, soon despaired to overtake us, or were afraid of those whom they made a shew of menacing.

"When the Arabs saw themselves out of danger they slackened their course, and, as I was less harassed by external violence, I began to feel more uneasiness in my mind. After some time we stopped near a spring shaded with trees in a pleasant meadow, where we were set upon the ground, and offered such refreshments as our masters were partaking. I was suffered to sit with my maids apart from the rest, and none attempted to comfort or insult us. Here I first began to feel the full weight of my misery. The girls sat weeping in silence, and from time to time looked on me for succour. I knew not to what condition we were doomed, nor could conjecture where would be the place of our captivity, or whence to draw any hope of deliverance. I was in the hands of robbers and savages, and had no reason to suppose that their pity was more than their justice, or that they would forbear the gratification of any ardour of desire, or caprice of cruelty. I, however, kissed my maids, and endeavoured to pacify them by remarking, that we were yet treated with decency, and that, since we were now carried beyond persuit, there was no danger of violence to our lives.

"When we were to be set again on horseback, my maids clung round me, and refused to be parted, but I commanded them not to irritate those who had us in their power. We travelled the remaining part of the day through an unfrequented and pathless country, and came by moonlight to the side of a hill, where the rest of the troop was stationed. Their tents were pitched, and their fires kindled, and our chief was welcomed as a man much beloved by his dependants.

"We were received into a large tent, where we found women who had attended their husbands in the expedition. They set before us the supper which they had provided, and I eat it rather to encourage my maids than to comply with any appetite of my own. When the meat was taken away they spread the carpets for repose. I was weary, and hoped to find in sleep that remission of distress which nature seldom denies. Ordering myself therefore to be undrest, I observed that the women looked very earnestly upon me, not expecting, I suppose, to see me so submissively attended. When my upper vest was taken off, they were apparently struck with the splendour of my cloaths, and one of them timorously laid her hand upon the embroidery. She then went out, and, in a short time, came back with another woman, who seemed to be of higher rank, and greater authority. She did, at her entrance, the usual act of reverence, and, taking me by the hand, placed me in a smaller tent, spread with finer carpets, where I spent the night quietly with my maids.

"In the morning, as I was sitting on the grass, the chief of the troop came towards me. I rose up to receive him, and he bowed with great respect. "Illustrious lady, said he, my fortune is better than I had presumed to hope; I am told by my women, that I have a princess in my camp." Sir, answered I, your women have deceived themselves and you; I am not a princess, but an unhappy stranger who intended soon to have left this country, in which I am now to be imprisoned for ever. "Whoever, or whencesoever, you are, returned the Arab, your dress, and that of your servants, show your rank to be high, and your wealth to be great. Why should you, who can so easily procure your ransome, think yourself in danger of perpetual captivity? The purpose of my incursions is to encrease my riches, or more properly to gather tribute. The sons of Ishmael are the natural and hereditary lords of this part of the continent, which is usurped by late invaders, and low-born tyrants, from whom we are compelled to take by the sword what is denied to justice. The violence of war admits no distinction; the lance that is lifted at guilt and power will sometimes fall on innocence and gentleness."

"How little, said I, did I expect that yesterday it should have fallen upon me."

"Misfortunes, answered the Arab, should always be expected. If the eye of hostility could learn reverence or pity, excellence like yours had been exempt from injury. But the angels of affliction spread their toils alike for the virtuous and the wicked, for the mighty and the mean. Do not be disconsolate; I am not one of the lawless and cruel rovers of the desart; I know the rules of civil life: I will fix your ransome, give a pasport to your messenger, and perform my stipulation with nice punctuality."

"You will easily believe that I was pleased with this courtesy; and finding that his predominant passion was desire of money, I began now to think my danger less, for I knew that no sum would be thought too great for the release of Pekuah. I told him that he should have no reason to charge me with ingratitude, if I was used with kindness, and that any ransome, which could be expected for a maid of common rank, would be paid, but that he must not persist to rate me as a princess. He said, he would consider what he should demand, and then, smiling, bowed and retired.

"Soon after the women came about me, each contending to be more officious than the other, and my maids themselves were served with reverence. We travelled onward by short journeys. On the fourth day the chief told me, that my ransome must be two hundred ounces of gold, which I not only promised him, but told him, that I would add fifty more, if I and my maids were honourably treated.

"I never knew the power of gold before. From that time I was the leader of the troop. The march of every day was longer or shorter as I commanded, and the tents were pitched where I chose to rest. We now had camels and other conveniencies for travel, my own women were always at my side, and I amused myself with observing the manners of the vagrant nations, and with viewing remains of ancient edifices with which these deserted countries appear to have been, in some distant age, lavishly embellished.

"The chief of the band was a man far from illiterate: he was able to travel by the stars or the compass, and had marked in his erratick expeditions such places as are most worthy the notice of a passenger. He observed to me, that buildings are always best preserved in places little frequented, and difficult of access: for, when once a country declines from its primitive splendour, the more inhabitants are left, the quicker ruin will be made. Walls supply stones more easily than quarries, and palaces and temples will be demolished to make stables of granate, and cottages of porphyry.[5]

XXXIX

THE ADVENTURES OF PEKUAH CONTINUED

"We wandered about in this manner for some weeks, whether, as our chief pretended, for my gratification, or, as I rather suspected, for some convenience of his own. I endeavoured to appear contented where sullenness and resentment would have been of no use, and that endeavour conduced much to the calmness of my mind; but my heart was always with Nekayah, and the troubles of the night much overbalanced the amusements of the day. My women, who threw all their cares upon their mistress, set their minds at ease from the time when they saw me treated with respect, and gave themselves up to the incidental alleviations of our fatigue without solicitude or sorrow. I was pleased with their pleasure, and animated with their confidence. My condition had lost much of its terrour, since I found that the Arab ranged the country merely to get riches. Avarice is an uniform and tractable vice: other intellectual distempers are different in different constitutions of mind; that which sooths the pride of one will offend the pride of another; but to the favour of the covetous there is a ready way, bring money and nothing is denied.

"At last we came to the dwelling of our chief, a strong and spacious house built with stone in an island of the Nile, which lies, as I was told, under the tropick. "Lady, said the Arab, you shall rest after your journey a few weeks in this place, where you are to consider yourself as sovereign. My occupation is war: I have therefore chosen this obscure residence, from which I can issue unexpected, and to which I can retire unpersued. You may now repose in security: here are few pleasures, but here is no danger." He then led me into the inner apartments, and seating me on the richest couch, bowed to the ground. His women, who considered me as a rival, looked on me with malignity; but being soon informed that I was a great lady detained only for my ransome, they began to vie with each other in obsequiousness and reverence.

"Being again comforted with new assurances of speedy liberty, I was for some days diverted from impatience by the novelty of the place. The turrets overlooked the country to a great distance, and afforded a view of many windings of the stream. In the day I wandered from one place to another as the course of the sun varied the splendour of the prospect, and saw many things which I had never seen before. The crocodiles and river-horses are common in this unpeopled region, and I often looked upon them with terrour, though I knew that they could not hurt me. For some time I expected to see mermaids and tritons, which, as Imlac has told me, the European travellers have stationed in the Nile, but no such beings ever appeared, and the Arab, when I enquired after them, laughed at my credulity.

"At night the Arab always attended me to a tower set apart for celestial observations, where he endeavoured to teach me the names and courses of the stars. I had no great inclination to this study, but an appearance of attention was necessary to please my instructor, who valued himself for his skill, and, in a little while, I found some employment requisite to beguile the tediousness of time, which was to be passed always amidst the same objects. I was weary of looking in the morning on things from which I had turned away weary in the evening: I therefore was at last willing to observe the stars rather than do nothing, but could not always compose my thoughts, and was very often thinking on Nekayah when others imagined me contemplating the sky. Soon after the Arab went upon another expedition, and then my only pleasure was to talk with my maids about the accident by which we were carried away, and the happiness that we should all enjoy at the end of our captivity."

"There were women in your Arab's fortress, said the princess, why did you not make them your companions, enjoy their conversation, and partake their diversions? In a place where they found business or amusement, why should you alone sit corroded with idle melancholy? or why could not you

5. **porphyry**: a beautiful and hard rock.

bear for a few months that condition to which they were condemned for life?"

"The diversions of the women, answered Pekuah, were only childish play, by which the mind accustomed to stronger operations could not be kept busy. I could do all which they delighted in doing by powers merely sensitive, while my intellectual faculties were flown to Cairo. They ran from room to room as a bird hops from wire to wire in his cage. They danced for the sake of motion, as lambs frisk in a meadow. One sometimes pretended to be hurt that the rest might be alarmed, or hid herself that another might seek her. Part of their time passed in watching the progress of light bodies that floated on the river, and part in marking the various forms into which clouds broke in the sky.

"Their business was only needlework, in which I and my maids sometimes helped them; but you know that the mind will easily straggle from the fingers, nor will you suspect that captivity and absence from Nekayah could receive solace from silken flowers.

"Nor was much satisfaction to be hoped from their conversation: for of what could they be expected to talk? They had seen nothing; for they had lived from early youth in that narrow spot: of what they had not seen they could have no knowledge, for they could not read. They had no ideas but of the few things that were within their view, and had hardly names for any thing but their cloaths and their food. As I bore a superiour character, I was often called to terminate their quarrels, which I decided as equitably as I could. If it could have amused me to hear the complaints of each against the rest, I might have been often detained by long stories, but the motives of their animosity were so small that I could not listen without intercepting the tale."

"How, said Rasselas, can the Arab, whom you represented as a man of more than common accomplishments, take any pleasure in his seraglio, when it is filled only with women like these? Are they exquisitely beautiful?"

"They do not, said Pekuah, want that unaffecting and ignoble beauty which may subsist without spriteliness or sublimity, without energy of thought or dignity of virtue. But to a man like the Arab such beauty was only a flower casually plucked and carelessly thrown away. Whatever pleasures he might find among them, they were not those of friendship or society. When they were playing about him he looked on them with inattentive superiority: when they vied for his regard he sometimes turned away disgusted. As they had no knowledge, their talk could take nothing from the tediousness of life: as they had no choice, their fondness, or appearance of fondness, excited in him neither pride nor gratitude; he was not exalted in his own esteem by the smiles of a woman who saw no other man, nor was much obliged by that regard, of which he could never know the sincerity, and which he might often perceive to be exerted not so much to delight him as to pain a rival. That which he gave, and they received, as love, was only a careless distribution of superfluous time, such love as man can bestow upon that which he despises, such as has neither hope nor fear, neither joy nor sorrow."

"You have reason, lady, to think yourself happy, said Imlac, that you have been thus easily dismissed. How could a mind, hungry for knowledge, be willing, in an intellectual famine, to lose such a banquet as Pekuah's conversation?"

"I am inclined to believe, answered Pekuah, that he was for some time in suspense; for, notwithstanding his promise, whenever I proposed to dispatch a messenger to Cairo, he found some excuse for delay. While I was detained in his house he made many incursions into the neighbouring countries, and, perhaps, he would have refused to discharge me, had his plunder been equal to his wishes. He returned always courteous, related his adventures, delighted to hear my observations, and endeavoured to advance my acquaintance with the stars. When I importuned him to send away my letters, he soothed me with professions of honour and sincerity; and, when I could be no longer decently denied, put his troop again in motion, and left me to govern in his absence. I was much afflicted by this studied procrastination, and was sometimes afraid that I should be forgotten; that you would leave Cairo, and I must end my days in an island of the Nile.

"I grew at last hopeless and dejected, and cared so little to entertain him, that he for a while more frequently talked with my maids. That he should fall in love with them, or with me, might have been equally fatal, and I was not much pleased with the growing friendship. My anxiety was not long; for, as I recovered some degree of chearfulness, he returned to me, and I could not forbear to despise my former uneasiness.

"He still delayed to send for my ransome, and would, perhaps, never have determined, had not your agent found his way to him. The gold, which he would not fetch, he could not reject when it was offered. He hastened to prepare for our journey hither, like a man delivered from the pain of an intestine conflict. I took leave of my companions in the house, who dismissed me with cold indifference."

Nekayah, having heard her favourite's relation, rose and embraced her, and Rasselas gave her an hundred ounces of gold, which she presented to the Arab for the fifty that were promised.

XL

THE HISTORY OF A MAN OF LEARNING

They returned to Cairo, and were so well pleased at finding themselves together, that none of them went much abroad. The prince began to love learning, and one day declared to Imlac, that he intended to devote himself to science, and pass the rest of his days in literary solitude.

"Before you make your final choice, answered Imlac, you ought to examine its hazards, and converse with some of those who are grown old in the company of themselves. I have just left the observatory of one of the most learned astronomers in the world, who has spent forty years in unwearied attention to the motions and appearances of the celestial bodies, and has drawn out his soul in endless calculations. He admits a few friends once a month to hear his deductions and enjoy his discoveries. I was introduced as a man of knowledge worthy of his notice. Men of various ideas and fluent conversation are commonly welcome to those whose thoughts have been long fixed upon a single point, and who find the images of other things stealing away. I delighted him with my remarks, he smiled at the narrative of my travels, and was glad to forget the constellations, and descend for a moment into the lower world.

"On the next day of vacation I renewed my visit, and was so fortunate as to please him again. He relaxed from that time the severity of his rule, and permitted me to enter at my own choice. I found him always busy, and always glad to be relieved. As each knew much which the other was desirous of learning, we exchanged our notions with great delight. I perceived that I had every day more of his confidence, and always found new cause of admiration in the profundity of his mind. His comprehension is vast, his memory capacious and retentive, his discourse is methodical, and his expression clear.

"His integrity and benevolence are equal to his learning. His deepest researches and most favourite studies are willingly interrupted for any opportunity of doing good by his counsel or his riches. To his closest retreat, at his most busy moments, all are admitted that want his assistance: "For though I exclude idleness and pleasure, I will never, says he, bar my doors against charity. To man is permitted the contemplation of the skies, but the practice of virtue is commanded."

"Surely, said the princess, this man is happy."

"I visited him, said Imlac, with more and more frequency, and was every time more enamoured of his conversation: he was sublime without haughtiness, courteous without formality, and communicative without ostentation. I was at first, great princess, of your opinion, thought him the happiest of mankind, and often congratulated him on the blessing that he enjoyed. He seemed to hear nothing with indifference but the praises of his condition, to which he always returned a general answer, and diverted the conversation to some other topick.

"Amidst this willingness to be pleased, and labour to please, I had quickly reason to imagine that some painful sentiment pressed upon his mind. He often looked up earnestly towards the sun, and let his voice fall in the midst of his discourse. He would sometimes, when we were alone, gaze upon me in silence with the air of a man who longed to speak what he was yet resolved to suppress. He would often send for me with vehement injunctions of haste, though, when I came to him, he had nothing extraordinary to say. And sometimes, when I was leaving him, would call me back, pause a few moments and then dismiss me.

XLI

THE ASTRONOMER DISCOVERS THE CAUSE OF HIS UNEASINESS

"At last the time came when the secret burst his reserve. We were sitting together last night in the turret of his house, watching the emersion[6] of a satellite of Jupiter. A sudden tempest clouded the sky, and disappointed our observation. We sat a while silent in the dark, and then he addressed himself to me in these words: "Imlac, I have long considered thy friendship as the greatest blessing of my life. Integrity without knowledge is weak and useless, and knowledge without integrity is dangerous and dreadful. I have found in thee all the qualities requisite for trust, benevolence, experience, and fortitude. I have long discharged an office which I must soon quit at the call of nature, and shall rejoice in the hour of imbecility and pain to devolve it upon thee."

"I thought myself honoured by this testimony, and protested that whatever could conduce to his happiness would add likewise to mine."

"Hear, Imlac, what thou wilt not without difficulty credit. I have possessed for five years the regulation of weather, and the distribution of the seasons: the sun has listened to my dictates, and passed from tropick to tropick by my direction; the clouds, at my call, have poured their waters, and the Nile has overflowed at my command; I have restrained the rage of the dog-star, and mitigated the fervours of the crab. The winds alone, of all the elemental powers, have hitherto refused my authority, and multitudes have perished by equinoctial tempests which I found myself unable to prohibit or restrain. I have administered this great office with exact justice, and made to the different nations of the earth an impartial dividend of rain and sunshine. What must have been the misery of half the globe, if I had limited the clouds to particular regions, or confined the sun to either side of the equator?"

XLII

THE OPINION OF THE ASTRONOMER IS EXPLAINED AND JUSTIFIED

"I suppose he discovered in me, through the obscurity of the room, some tokens of amazement and doubt, for, after a short pause, he proceeded thus:"

"Not to be easily credited will neither surprise nor offend me; for I am, probably, the first of human beings to whom this trust has been imparted. Nor do I know whether to deem this distinction a reward or punishment; since I have possessed it I have been far less happy than before, and nothing but the consciousness of good intention could have enabled me to support the weariness of unremitted vigilance."

"How long, Sir, said I, has this great office been in your hands?"

"About ten years ago, said he, my daily observations of the changes of the sky led me to consider, whether, if I had the power of the seasons, I could confer greater plenty upon the inhabitants of the earth. This contemplation fastened on my mind, and I sat days and nights in imaginary dominion, pouring upon this country and that the showers of fertility, and seconding every fall of rain with a due proportion of sunshine. I had yet only the will to do good, and did not imagine that I should ever have the power.

"One day as I was looking on the fields withering with heat, I felt in my mind a sudden wish that I could send rain on the southern mountains, and raise the Nile to an inundation. In the hurry of my imagination I commanded rain to fall, and, by comparing the time of my command, with that of the inundation, I found that the clouds had listned to my lips."

"Might not some other cause, said I, produce this concurrence? the Nile does not always rise on the same day."

"Do not believe, said he with impatience, that such objections could escape me: I reasoned long against my own conviction, and laboured against truth with the utmost obstinacy. I sometimes suspected myself of madness, and should not have dared to impart this secret but to a man like you, capable of distinguishing the wonderful from the impossible, and the incredible from the false."

"Why, Sir, said I, do you call that incredible, which you know, or think you know, to be true?"

"Because, said he, I cannot prove it by any external evidence; and I know too well the laws of demonstration to think that my conviction ought to influence another, who cannot, like me, be conscious of its force. I, therefore, shall not attempt to

6. **emersion:** coming into view.

gain credit by disputation. It is sufficient that I feel this power, that I have long possessed, and every day exerted it. But the life of man is short, the infirmities of age increase upon me, and the time will soon come when the regulator of the year must mingle with the dust. The care of appointing a successor has long disturbed me; the night and the day have been spent in comparisons of all the characters which have come to my knowledge, and I have yet found none so worthy as thyself.

XLIII

THE ASTRONOMER LEAVES IMLAC HIS DIRECTIONS

"Hear therefore, what I shall impart, with attention, such as the welfare of a world requires. If the task of a king be considered as difficult, who has the care only of a few millions, to whom he cannot do much good or harm, what must be the anxiety of him, on whom depend the action of the elements, and the great gifts of light and heat!——Hear me therefore with attention.

"I have diligently considered the position of the earth and sun, and formed innumerable schemes in which I changed their situation. I have sometimes turned aside the axis of the earth, and sometimes varied the ecliptick of the sun: but I have found it impossible to make a disposition by which the world may be advantaged; what one region gains, another loses by any imaginable alteration, even without considering the distant parts of the solar system with which we are unacquainted. Do not, therefore, in thy administration of the year, indulge thy pride by innovation; do not please thyself with thinking that thou canst make thyself renowned to all future ages, by disordering the seasons. The memory of mischief is no desirable fame. Much less will it become thee to let kindness or interest prevail. Never rob other countries of rain to pour it on thine own. For us the Nile is sufficient."

"I promised that when I possessed the power, I would use it with inflexible integrity, and he dismissed me, pressing my hand." "My heart, said he, will be now at rest, and my benevolence will no more destroy my quiet: I have found a man of wisdom and virtue, to whom I can chearfully bequeath the inheritance of the sun."

The prince heard this narration with very serious regard, but the princess smiled, and Pekuah convulsed herself with laughter. "Ladies, said Imlac, to mock the heaviest of human afflictions is neither charitable nor wise. Few can attain this man's knowledge, and few practise his virtues; but all may suffer his calamity. Of the uncertainties of our present state, the most dreadful and alarming is the uncertain continuance of reason."

The princess was recollected, and the favourite was abashed. Rasselas, more deeply affected, enquired of Imlac, whether he thought such maladies of the mind frequent, and how they were contracted.

XLIV

THE DANGEROUS PREVALENCE OF IMAGINATION

"Disorders of intellect, answered Imlac, happen much more often than superficial observers will easily believe. Perhaps, if we speak with rigorous exactness, no human mind is in its right state. There is no man whose imagination does not sometimes predominate over his reason, who can regulate his attention wholly by his will, and whose ideas will come and go at his command. No man will be found in whose mind airy notions do not sometimes tyrannise, and force him to hope or fear beyond the limits of sober probability. All power of fancy over reason is a degree of insanity; but while this power is such as we can controul and repress, it is not visible to others, nor considered as any depravation of the mental faculties: it is not pronounced madness but when it comes ungovernable, and apparently influences speech or action.

"To indulge the power of fiction, and send imagination out upon the wing, is often the sport of those who delight too much in silent speculation. When we are alone we are not always busy; the labour of excogitation is too violent to last long; the ardour of enquiry will sometimes give way to idleness or satiety. He who has nothing external that can divert him, must find pleasure in his own thoughts, and must conceive himself what he is not; for who is pleased with what he is? He then expatiates in boundless futurity, and culls from all imaginable conditions that which for the present moment he should most desire, amuses his desires with impossible enjoyments, and confers upon his pride unattainable dominion. The mind dances from scene to scene, unites all pleasures in all combinations, and riots in delights which nature and fortune, with all their bounty, cannot bestow.

"In time some particular train of ideas fixes the attention, all other intellectual gratifications are rejected, the mind, in weariness or leisure, recurs constantly to the favourite conception, and feasts on the luscious falsehood whenever she is offended with the bitterness of truth. By degrees the reign of fancy is confirmed; she grows first imperious, and in time despotick. Then fictions begin to operate as realities, false opinions fasten upon the mind, and life passes in dreams of rapture or of anguish.

"This, Sir, is one of the dangers of solitude, which the hermit has confessed not always to promote goodness, and the astronomer's misery has proved to be not always propitious to wisdom."

"I will no more, said the favourite, imagine myself the queen of Abissinia. I have often spent the hours, which the princess gave to my own disposal, in adjusting ceremonies and regulating the court; I have repressed the pride of the powerful, and granted the petitions of the poor; I have built new palaces in more happy situations, planted groves upon the tops of mountains, and have exulted in the beneficence of royalty, till, when the princess entered, I had almost forgotten to bow down before her."

"And I, said the princess, will not allow myself any more to play the shepherdess in my waking dreams. I have often soothed my thoughts with the quiet and innocence of pastoral employments, till I have in my chamber heard the winds whistle, and the sheep bleat; sometimes freed the lamb entangled in the thicket, and sometimes with my crook encountered the wolf. I have a dress like that of the village maids, which I put on to help my imagination, and a pipe on which I play softly, and suppose myself followed by my flocks."

"I will confess, said the prince, an indulgence of fantastick delight more dangerous than yours. I have frequently endeavoured to image the possibility of a perfect government, by which all wrong should be restrained, all vice reformed, and all the subjects preserved in tranquility and innocence. This thought produced innumerable schemes of reformation, and dictated many useful regulations and salutary edicts. This has been the sport and sometimes the labour of my solitude; and I start, when I think with how little anguish I once supposed the death of my father and my brothers."

"Such, says Imlac, are the effects of visionary schemes: when we first form them we know them to be absurd, but familiarise them by degrees, and in time lose sight of their folly."

XLV

THEY DISCOURSE WITH AN OLD MAN

The evening was now far past, and they rose to return home. As they walked along the bank of the Nile, delighted with the beams of the moon quivering on the water, they saw at a small distance an old man, whom the prince had often heard in the assembly of the sages. "Yonder, said he, is one whose years have calmed his passions, but not clouded his reason: let us close the disquisitions of the night, by enquiring what are his sentiments of his own state, that we may know whether youth alone is to struggle with vexation, and whether any better hope remains for the latter part of life."

Here the sage approached and saluted them. They invited him to join their walk, and prattled a while as acquaintance that had unexpectedly met one another. The old man was chearful and talkative, and the way seemed short in his company. He was pleased to find himself not disregarded, accompanied them to their house, and, at the prince's request, entered with them. They placed him in the seat of honour, and set wine and conserves before him.

"Sir, said the princess, an evening walk must give to a man of learning, like you, pleasures which ignorance and youth can hardly conceive. You know the qualities and the causes of all that you behold, the laws by which the river flows, the periods in which the planets perform their revolutions. Every thing must supply you with contemplation, and renew the consciousness of your own dignity."

"Lady, answered he, let the gay and the vigorous expect pleasure in their excursions, it is enough that age can obtain ease. To me the world has lost its novelty: I look round, and see what I remember to have seen in happier days. I rest against a tree, and consider, that in the same shade I once disputed upon the annual overflow of the Nile with a friend who is now silent in the grave. I cast my eyes upwards, fix them on the changing moon, and think with pain on the vicissitudes of life. I have ceased to take much delight in physical truth; for what have I to do with those things which I am soon to leave?"

"You may at least recreate yourself, said Imlac, with the recollection of an honourable and useful life, and enjoy the praise which all agree to give you."

"Praise, said the sage, with a sigh, is to an old man an empty sound. I have neither mother to be delighted with the reputation of her son, nor wife to partake the honours of her husband. I have outlived my friends and my rivals. Nothing is now of much importance; for I cannot extend my interest beyond myself. Youth is delighted with applause, because it is considered as the earnest of some future good, and because the prospect of life is far extended: but to me, who am now declining to decrepitude, there is little to be feared from the malevolence of men, and yet less to be hoped from their affection or esteem. Something they may yet take away, but they can give me nothing. Riches would now be useless, and high employment would be pain. My retrospect of life recalls to my view many opportunities of good neglected, much time squandered upon trifles, and more lost in idleness and vacancy. I leave many great designs unattempted, and many great attempts unfinished. My mind is burthened with no heavy crime, and therefore I compose myself to tranquility; endeavour to abstract my thoughts from hopes and cares, which, though reason knows them to be vain, still try to keep their old possession of the heart; expect, with serene humility, that hour which nature cannot long delay; and hope to possess in a better state that happiness which here I could not find, and that virtue which here I have not attained."

He rose and went away, leaving his audience not much elated with the hope of long life. The prince consoled himself with remarking, that it was not reasonable to be disappointed by this account; for age had never been considered as the season of felicity, and, if it was possible to be easy in decline and weakness, it was likely that the days of vigour and alacrity might be happy: that the noon of life might be bright, if the evening could be calm.

The princess suspected that age was querulous and malignant, and delighted to repress the expectations of those who had newly entered the world. She had seen the possessors of estates look with envy on their heirs, and known many who enjoy pleasure no longer than they can confine it to themselves.

Pekuah conjectured, that the man was older than he appeared, and was willing to impute his complaints to delirious dejection; or else supposed that he had been unfortunate, and was therefore discontented: "For nothing, said she, is more common than to call our own condition, the condition of life."

Imlac, who had no desire to see them depressed, smiled at the comforts which they could so readily procure to themselves, and remembered, that at the same age, he was equally confident of unmingled prosperity, and equally fertile of consolatory expedients. He forbore to force upon them unwelcome knowledge, which time itself would too soon impress. The princess and her lady retired; the madness of the astronomer hung upon their minds, and they desired Imlac to enter upon his office, and delay next morning the rising of the sun.

XLVI

THE PRINCESS AND PEKUAH VISIT THE ASTRONOMER

The princess and Pekuah having talked in private of Imlac's astronomer, thought his character at once so amiable and so strange, that they could not be satisfied without a nearer knowledge, and Imlac was requested to find the means of bringing them together.

This was somewhat difficult; the philosopher had never received any visits from women, though he lived in a city that had in it many Europeans who followed the manners of their own countries, and many from other parts of the world that lived there with European liberty. The ladies would not be refused, and several schemes were proposed for the accomplishment of their design. It was proposed to introduce them as strangers in distress, to whom the sage was always accessible; but, after some deliberation, it appeared, that by this artifice, no acquaintance could be formed, for their conversation would be short, and they could not decently importune him often. "This, said Rasselas, is true; but I have yet a stronger objection against the misrepresentation of your state. I have always considered it as treason against the great republick of human nature, to make any man's virtues the means of deceiving him, whether on great or little occasions. All imposture weakens confidence and chills benevolence. When the sage finds that you are not what you seemed, he will feel the resentment natural to a man who, conscious of great abilities, discovers that he has been tricked by understandings meaner than his own, and, perhaps, the distrust, which he can never afterwards wholly lay aside, may stop the voice of counsel, and close the hand of charity; and where will you find the power of restoring his benefactions to mankind, or his peace to himself?"

To this no reply was attempted, and Imlac began to hope that their curiosity would subside; but, next day, Pekuah told him, she had now found an honest pretence for a visit to the astronomer, for she would solicite permission to continue under him the studies in which she had been initiated by the Arab, and the princess might go with her either as a fellow-student, or because a woman could not decently come alone. "I am afraid, said Imlac, that he will be soon weary of your company: men advanced far in knowledge do not love to repeat the elements of their art, and I am not certain that even of the elements, as he will deliver them connected with inferences, and mingled with reflections, you are a very capable auditress." "That, said Pekuah, must be my care: I ask of you only to take me thither. My knowledge is, perhaps, more than you imagine it, and by concurring always with his opinions I shall make him think it greater than it is."

The astronomer, in pursuance of this resolution, was told, that a foreign lady, travelling in search of knowledge, had heard of his reputation, and was desirous to become his scholar. The uncommonness of the proposal raised at once his surprize and curiosity, and when, after a short deliberation, he consented to admit her, he could not stay without impatience till the next day.

The ladies dressed themselves magnificently, and were attended by Imlac to the astronomer, who was pleased to see himself approached with respect by persons of so splendid an appearance. In the exchange of the first civilities he was timorous and bashful; but when the talk became regular, he recollected his powers, and justified the character which Imlac had given. Enquiring of Pekuah what could have turned her inclination towards astronomy, he received from her a history of her adventure at the pyramid, and of the time passed in the Arab's island. She told her tale with ease and elegance, and her conversation took possession of his heart. The discourse was then turned to astronomy: Pekuah displayed what she knew: he looked upon her as a prodigy of genius, and intreated her not to desist from a study which she had so happily begun.

They came again and again, and were every time more welcome than before. The sage endeavoured to amuse them, that they might prolong their visits, for he found his thoughts grow brighter in their company; the clouds of solicitude vanished by degrees, as he forced himself to entertain them, and he grieved when he was left at their departure to his old employment of regulating the seasons.

The princess and her favourite had now watched his lips for several months, and could not catch a single word from which they could judge whether he continued, or not, in the opinion of his preternatural commission. They often contrived to bring him to an open declaration, but he easily eluded all their attacks, and on which side soever they pressed him escaped from them to some other topick.

As their familiarity increased they invited him often to the house of Imlac, where they distinguished him by extraordinary respect. He began gradually to delight in sublunary pleasures. He came early and departed late; laboured to recommend himself by assiduity and compliance; excited their curiosity after new arts, that they might still want his assistance; and when they made any excursion of pleasure or enquiry, entreated to attend them.

By long experience of his integrity and wisdom, the prince and his sister were convinced that he might be trusted without danger; and lest he should draw any false hopes from the civilities which he received, discovered to him their condition, with the motives of their journey, and required his opinion on the choice of life.

"Of the various conditions which the world spreads before you, which you shall prefer, said the sage, I am not able to instruct you. I can only tell that I have chosen wrong. I have passed my time in study without experience; in the attainment of sciences which can, for the most part, be but remotely useful to mankind. I have purchased knowledge at the expence of all the common comforts of life: I have missed the endearing elegance of female friendship, and the happy commerce of domestick tenderness. If I have obtained any prerogatives above other students, they have been accompanied with fear, disquiet, and scrupulosity; but even of these prerogatives, whatever they were, I have, since my thoughts have been diversified by more intercourse with the world, begun to question the reality. When I have been for a few days lost in pleasing dissipation, I am always tempted to think that my enquiries have ended in errour, and that I have suffered much, and suffered it in vain."

Imlac was delighted to find that the sage's understanding was breaking through its mists, and resolved to detain him from the planets till he should forget his task of ruling them, and reason should recover its original influence.

From this time the astronomer was received into familiar friendship, and partook of all their projects and pleasures: his respect kept him attentive, and the activity of Rasselas did not leave much time unengaged. Something was always to be done; the day was spent in making observations which furnished talk for the evening, and the evening was closed with a scheme for the morrow.

The sage confessed to Imlac, that since he had mingled in the gay tumults of life, and divided his hours by a succession of amusements, he found the conviction of his authority over the skies fade gradually from his mind, and began to trust less to an opinion which he never could prove to others, and which he now found subject to variation from causes in which reason had no part. "If I am accidentally left alone for a few hours, said he, my inveterate persuasion rushes upon my soul, and my thoughts are chained down by some irresistible violence, but they are soon disentangled by the prince's conversation, and instantaneously released at the entrance of Pekuah. I am like a man habitually afraid of spectres, who is set at ease by a lamp, and wonders at the dread which harrassed him in the dark, yet, if his lamp be extinguished, feels again the terrours which he knows that when it is light he shall feel no more. But I am sometimes afraid lest I indulge my quiet by criminal negligence, and voluntarily forget the great charge with which I am intrusted. If I favour myself in a known errour, or am determined by my own ease in a doubtful question of this importance, how dreadful is my crime!"

"No disease of the imagination, answered Imlac, is so difficult of cure, as that which is complicated with the dread of guilt: fancy and conscience then act interchangeably upon us, and so often shift their places, that the illusions of one are not distinguished from the dictates of the other. If fancy presents images not moral or religious, the mind drives them away when they give it pain, but when melancholick notions take the form of duty, they lay hold on the faculties without opposition, because we are afraid to exclude or banish them. For this reason the superstitious are often melancholy, and the melancholy almost always superstitious.

"But do not let the suggestions of timidity overpower your better reason: the danger of neglect can be but as the probability of the obligation, which when you consider it with freedom, you find very little, and that little growing every day less. Open your heart to the influence of the light, which, from time to time, breaks in upon you: when scruples importune you, which you in your lucid moments know to be vain, do not stand to parley, but fly to business or to Pekuah, and keep this thought always prevalent, that you are only one atom of the mass of humanity, and have neither such virtue nor vice, as that you should be singled out for supernatural favours or afflictions."

XLVII

THE PRINCE ENTERS AND BRINGS A NEW TOPICK

"All this, said the astronomer, I have often thought, but my reason has been so long subjugated by an uncontrolable and overwhelming idea, that it durst not confide in its own decisions. I now see how fatally I betrayed my quiet, by suffering chimeras to prey upon me in secret; but melancholy shrinks from communication, and I never found a man before, to whom I could impart my troubles, though I had been certain of relief. I rejoice to find my own sentiments confirmed by yours, who are not easily deceived, and can have no motive or purpose to deceive. I hope that time and variety will dissipate the gloom that has so long surrounded me, and the latter part of my days will be spent in peace."

"Your learning and virtue, said Imlac, may justly give you hopes."

Rasselas then entered with the princess and Pekuah, and enquired whether they had contrived any new diversion for the next day. "Such, said Nekayah, is the state of life, that none are happy but by the anticipation of change: the change itself is nothing; when we have made it, the next wish is to change again. The world is not yet exhausted; let me see something tomorrow which I never saw before."

"Variety, said Rasselas, is so necessary to content, that even the happy valley disgusted me by the recurrence of its luxuries; yet I could not forbear to reproach myself with impatience, when I saw the monks of St. Anthony support without complaint, a life, not of uniform delight, but uniform hardship."

"Those men, answered Imlac, are less wretched in their silent convent than the Abissinian princes in their prison of pleasure. Whatever is done by the monks is incited by an adequate and reasonable motive. Their labour supplies them with necessaries; it therefore cannot be omitted, and is certainly rewarded. Their devotion prepares them for another state, and reminds them of its approach, while it fits them for it. Their time is regularly distributed; one duty succeeds another, so that they are not left open to the distraction of unguided choice, nor lost in the shades of listless inactivity. There is a certain task to be performed at an appropriated hour; and their toils are cheerful, because they consider them as acts of piety, by which they are always advancing towards endless felicity."

"Do you think, said Nekayah, that the monastick rule is a more holy and less imperfect state than any other? May not he equally hope for future happiness who converses openly with mankind, who succours the distressed by his charity, instructs the ignorant by his learning, and contributes by his industry to the general system of life; even though he should omit some of the mortifications which are practised in the cloister, and allow himself such harmless delights as his condition may place within his reach?"

"This, said Imlac, is a question which has long divided the wise, and perplexed the good. I am afraid to decide on either part. He that lives well in the world is better than he that lives well in a monastery. But, perhaps, every one is not able to stem the temptations of publick life; and, if he cannot conquer, he may properly retreat. Some have little power to do good, and have likewise little strength to resist evil. Many are weary of their conflicts with adversity, and are willing to eject those passions which have long busied them in vain. And many are dismissed by age and diseases from the more laborious duties of society. In monasteries the weak and timorous may be happily sheltered, the weary may repose, and the penitent may meditate. Those retreats of prayer and contemplation have something so congenial to the mind of man, that, perhaps, there is scarcely one that does not purpose to close his life in pious abstraction with a few associates serious as himself."

"Such, said Pekuah, has often been my wish, and I have heard the princess declare, that she should not willingly die in a croud."

"The liberty of using harmless pleasures, proceeded Imlac, will not be disputed; but it is still to be examined what pleasures are harmless. The evil of any pleasure that Nekayah can image is not in the act itself, but in its consequences. Pleasure, in itself harmless, may become mischievous, by endearing to us a state which we know to be transient and probatory, and withdrawing our thoughts from that, of which every hour brings us nearer to the beginning, and of which no length of time will bring us to the end. Mortification is not virtuous in itself, nor has any other use, but that it disengages us from the allurements of sense. In the state of future perfection, to which we all aspire, there will be pleasure without danger, and security without restraint."

The princess was silent, and Rasselas, turning to the astronomer, asked him, whether he could not delay her retreat, by shewing her something which she had not seen before.

"Your curiosity, said the sage, has been so general, and your pursuit of knowledge so vigorous, that novelties are not now very easily to be found: but what you can no longer procure from the living may be given by the dead. Among the wonders of this country are the catacombs, or the ancient repositories, in which the bodies of the earliest generations were lodged, and where, by the virtue of the gums which embalmed them, they yet remain without corruption."

"I know not, said Rasselas, what pleasure the sight of the catacombs can afford; but, since nothing else is offered, I am resolved to view them, and shall place this with many other things which I have done, because I would do something."

They hired a guard of horsemen, and the next day visited the catacombs. When they were about to descend into the sepulchral caves, "Pekuah, said the princess, we are now again invading the habitations of the dead; I know that you will stay behind; let me find you safe when I return." "No, I will not be left, answered Pekuah; I will go down between you and the prince."

They then all descended, and roved with wonder through the labyrinth of subterraneous passages, where the bodies were laid in rows on either side.

XLVIII

IMLAC DISCOURSES ON THE NATURE OF THE SOUL

"What reason, said the prince, can be given, why the Egyptians should thus expensively preserve those carcasses which some nations consume with fire, others lay to mingle with the earth, and all agree to remove from their sight, as soon as decent rites can be performed?"

"The original of ancient customs, said Imlac, is commonly unknown; for the practice often continues when the cause has ceased; and concerning superstitious ceremonies it is vain to conjecture; for what reason did not dictate reason cannot explain. I have long believed that the practice of embalming arose only from tenderness to the remains of relations or friends, and to this opinion I am more inclined, because it seems impossible that this care should have been general: had all the dead been embalmed, their repositories must in time have been more spacious than the dwellings of the living. I suppose only the rich or honourable were secured from corruption, and the rest left to the course of nature.

"But it is commonly supposed that the Egyptians believed the soul to live as long as the body continued undissolved, and therefore tried this method of eluding death."

"Could the wise Egyptians, said Nekayah, think so grosly of the soul? If the soul could once survive its separation, what could it afterwards receive or suffer from the body?"

"The Egyptians would doubtless think erroneously, said the astronomer, in the darkness of heathenism, and the first dawn of philosophy. The nature of the soul is still disputed amidst all our opportunities of clearer knowledge: some yet say, that it may be material, who, nevertheless, believe it to be immortal."

"Some, answered Imlac, have indeed said that the soul is material, but I can scarcely believe that any man has thought it, who knew how to think; for all the conclusions of reason enforce the immateriality of mind, and all the notices of sense and investigations of science concur to prove the unconsciousness of matter.

"It was never supposed that cogitation is inherent in matter, or that every particle is a thinking being. Yet, if any part of matter be devoid of thought, what part can we suppose to think? Matter can differ from matter only in form, density, bulk, motion, and direction of motion: to which of these, however varied or combined, can consciousness be annexed? To be round or square, to be solid or fluid, to be great or little, to be moved slowly or swiftly one way or another, are modes of material existence, all equally alien from the nature of cogitation. If matter be once without thought, it can only be made to think by some new modification, but all the modifications which it can admit are equally unconnected with cogitative powers."

"But the materialists, said the astronomer, urge that matter may have qualities with which we are unacquainted."

"He who will determine, returned Imlac, against that which he knows, because there may be something which he knows not; he that can set hypothetical possibility against acknowledged certainty, is not to be admitted among reasonable beings. All that we know of matter is, that matter is inert, senseless and lifeless; and if this conviction cannot be opposed but by referring us to something that we know not, we have all the evidence that human intellect can admit. If that which is known may be over-ruled by that which is unknown, no being, not omniscient, can arrive at certainty."

"Yet let us not, said the astronomer, too arrogantly limit the Creator's power."

"It is no limitation of omnipotence, replied the poet, to suppose that one thing is not consistent with another, that the same proposition cannot be at once true and false, that the same number cannot be even and odd, that cogitation cannot be conferred on that which is created incapable of cogitation."

"I know not, said Nekayah, any great use of this question. Does that immateriality, which, in my opinion, you have sufficiently proved, necessarily include eternal duration?"

"Of immateriality, said Imlac, our ideas are negative, and therefore obscure. Immateriality seems to imply a natural power of perpetual duration as a consequence of exemption from all causes of decay: whatever perishes, is destroyed by the solution of its contexture, and separation of its parts; nor can we conceive how that which has no parts, and therefore admits no solution, can be naturally corrupted or impaired."

"I know not, said Rasselas, how to conceive any thing without extension: what is extended must have parts, and you allow, that whatever has parts may be destroyed."

"Consider your own conceptions, replied Imlac, and the difficulty will be less. You will find substance without extension. An ideal form is no less real than material bulk: yet an ideal form has no extension. It is no less certain, when you think on a pyramid, that your mind possesses the idea of a pyramid, than that the pyramid itself is standing. What space does the idea of a pyramid occupy more than the idea of a grain of corn? or how can either idea suffer laceration? As is the effect such is the cause; as thought is, such is the power that thinks; a power impassive and indiscerptible." [7]

"But the Being, said Nekayah, whom I fear to name, the Being which made the soul, can destroy it."

"He, surely, can destroy it, answered Imlac, since, however unperishable, it receives from a superiour nature its power of duration. That it will not perish by any inherent cause of decay, or principle of corruption, may be shown by philosophy; but philosophy can tell no more. That it will not be annihilated by him that made it, we must humbly learn from higher authority."

The whole assembly stood a while silent and collected. "Let us return, said Rasselas, from this scene of mortality. How gloomy would be these mansions of the dead to him who did not know that he shall never die; that what now acts shall continue its agency, and what now thinks shall think on forever. Those that lie here stretched before us, the wise and the powerful of antient times, warn us to remember the shortness of our present state: they were, perhaps, snatched away while they were busy, like us, in the choice of life."

"To me, said the princess, the choice of life is become less important; I hope hereafter to think only on the choice of eternity."

They then hastened out of the caverns, and, under the protection of their guard, returned to Cairo.

XLIX

THE CONCLUSION, IN WHICH NOTHING IS CONCLUDED

It was now the time of the inundation of the Nile: a few days after their visit to the catacombs, the river began to rise.

They were confined to their house. The whole region being under water gave them no invitation to any excursions, and, being well supplied with materials for talk, they diverted themselves with comparisons of the different forms of life which they had observed, and with various schemes of happiness which each of them had formed.

Pekuah was never so much charmed with any place as the convent of St. Anthony, where the Arab restored her to the princess, and wished only to fill it with pious maidens, and to be made prioress of the order: she was weary of expectation and disgust, and would gladly be fixed in some unvariable state.

The princess thought, that of all sublunary things, knowledge was the best: She desired first to learn all sciences, and then purposed to found a college of learned women, in which she would pre-

7. **indiscerptible**: incapable of being divided into parts.

side, that, by conversing with the old, and educating the young, she might divide her time between the acquisition and communication of wisdom, and raise up for the next age models of prudence, and patterns of piety.

The prince desired a little kingdom, in which he might administer justice in his own person, and see all the parts of government with his own eyes; but he could never fix the limits of his dominion, and was always adding to the number of his subjects.

Imlac and the astronomer were contented to be driven along the stream of life without directing their course to any particular port.

Of these wishes that they had formed they well knew that none could be obtained. They deliberated a while what was to be done, and resolved, when the inundation should cease, to return to Abissinia.

FINIS

James Boswell
1740–1795

FROM

The Life of Samuel Johnson, LL.D.

To write the Life of him who excelled all mankind in writing the lives of others, and who, whether we consider his extraordinary endowments, or his various works, has been equalled by few in any age, is an arduous, and may be reckoned in me a presumptuous task.

Had Dr. Johnson written his own Life, in conformity with the opinion which he has given,[1] that every man's life may be best written by himself; had he employed in the preservation of his own history, that clearness of narration and elegance of language in which he has embalmed so many eminent persons, the world would probably have had the most perfect example of biography that was ever exhibited. But although he at different times, in a desultory manner, committed to writing many particulars of the progress of his mind and fortunes, he never had persevering diligence enough to form them into a regular composition. Of these memorials a few have been preserved; but the greater part was consigned by him to the flames, a few days before his death.

As I had the honour and happiness of enjoying his friendship for upwards of twenty years; as I had the scheme of writing his life constantly in view; as he was well apprised of this circumstance, and from time to time obligingly satisfied my enquiries, by communicating to me the incidents of his early years; as I acquired a facility in recollecting, and was very assiduous in recording, his conversation, of which the extraordinary vigour and vivacity constituted one of the first features of his character; and as I have spared no pains in obtaining materials concerning him, from every quarter where I could discover that they were to be found, and have been favoured with the most liberal communications by his friends; I flatter myself that few biographers have entered upon such a work as this, with more advantages; independent of literary abilities, in which I am not vain enough to compare myself with some great names who have gone before me in this kind of writing.

Since my work was announced, several Lives and Memoirs of Dr. Johnson have been published, the most voluminous of which is one compiled for the booksellers of London, by Sir John Hawkins,

[Throughout the selections from *The Life of Samuel Johnson, LL.D.*, Boswell's footnotes are indicated by asterisks, the editor's by Arabic numerals.]

LIFE OF JOHNSON. 1. See Johnson's *Idler*, No. 84.

Knight,* a man, whom, during my long intimacy with Dr. Johnson, I never saw in his company, I think, but once, and I am sure not above twice. Johnson might have esteemed him for his decent, religious demeanour, and his knowledge of books and literary history; but from the rigid formality of his manners, it is evident that they never could have lived together with companionable ease and familiarity; nor had Sir John Hawkins that nice perception which was necessary to mark the finer and less obvious parts of Johnson's character. His being appointed one of his executors, gave him an opportunity of taking possession of such fragments of a diary and other papers as were left; of which, before delivering them up to the residuary legatee, whose property they were, he endeavoured to extract the substance. In this he has not been very successful, as I have found upon a perusal of those papers, which have been since transferred to me. Sir John Hawkins's ponderous labours, I must acknowledge, exhibit a *farrago,* of which a considerable portion is not devoid of entertainment to the lovers of literary gossiping; but besides its being swelled out with long unnecessary extracts from various works, (even one of several leaves from Osborne's Harleian Catalogue, and those not compiled by Johnson, but by Oldys,) a very small part of it relates to the person who is the subject of the book; and, in that, there is such an inaccuracy in the statement of facts, as in so solemn an authour is hardly excusable, and certainly makes his narrative very unsatisfactory. But what is still worse, there is throughout the whole of it a dark uncharitable cast, by which the most unfavourable construction is put upon almost every circumstance in the character and conduct of my illustrious friend; who, I trust, will, by a true and fair delineation, be vindicated both from the injurious misrepresentations of this authour, and from the slighter aspersions of a lady who once lived in great intimacy with him.

There is, in the British Museum, a letter from Bishop Warburton to Dr. Birch, on the subject of biography; which, though I am aware it may expose me to a charge of artfully raising the value of my own work, by contrasting it with that of which I have spoken, is so well conceived and expressed, that I cannot refrain from here inserting it:

> I shall endeavour, (says Dr. Warburton,) to give you what satisfaction I can in any thing you want to be satisfied in any subject of Milton, and am extremely glad you intend to write his life. Almost all the life-writers we have had before Toland and Desmaiseaux, are indeed strange insipid creatures; and yet I had rather read the worst of them, than be obliged to go through with this of Milton's, or the other's life of Boileau, where there is such a dull, heavy succession of long quotations of disinteresting passages, that it makes their method quite nauseous. But the verbose, tasteless Frenchman seems to lay it down as a principle, that every life must be a book, and what's worse, it proves a book without a life; for what do we know of Boileau, after all his tedious stuff? You are the only one, (and I speak it without a compliment,) that by the vigour of your stile and sentiments, and the real importance of your materials, have the art, (which one would imagine no one could have missed,) of adding agreements to the most agreeable subject in the world, which is literary history.
>
> *Nov. 24, 1737.*

Instead of melting down my materials into one mass, and constantly speaking in my own person, by which I might have appeared to have more merit in the execution of the work, I have resolved to adopt and enlarge upon the excellent plan of Mr. Mason, in his Memoirs of Gray. Wherever narrative is necessary to explain, connect, and supply, I furnish it to the best of my abilities; but in the chronological series of Johnson's life, which I trace as distinctly as I can, year by year, I produce, wherever it is in my power, his own minutes, letters, or conversation, being convinced that this mode is more lively, and will make my readers better acquainted with him, than even most of those

---

* The greatest part of this book was written while Sir John Hawkins was alive: and I vow, that one object of my strictures was to make him feel some compunction for his illiberal treatment of Dr. Johnson. Since his decease, I have suppressed several of my remarks upon his work. But though I would not "war with the dead" *offensively,* I think it necessary to be strenuous in *defence* of my illustrious friend, which I cannot be, without strong animadversions upon a writer who has greatly injured him. Let me add, that though I doubt I should not have been very prompt to gratify Sir John Hawkins with any compliment in his life-time, I do now frankly acknowledge, that, in my opinion, his volume, however inadequate and improper as a life of Dr. Johnson, and however discredited by unpardonable inaccuracies in other respects, contains a collection of curious anecdotes and observations, which few men but its authour could have brought together.

were who actually knew him, but could know him only partially; whereas there is here an accumulation of intelligence from various points, by which his character is more fully understood and illustrated.

Indeed I cannot conceive a more perfect mode of writing any man's life, than not only relating all the most important events of it in their order, but interweaving what he privately wrote, and said, and thought; by which mankind are enabled as it were to see him live, and to "live o'er each scene" with him, as he actually advanced through the several stages of his life. Had his other friends been as diligent and ardent as I was, he might have been almost entirely preserved. As it is, I will venture to say that he will be seen in this work more completely than any man who has ever yet lived.

And he will be seen as he really was; for I profess to write, not his panegyrick, which must be all praise, but his Life; which, great and good as he was, must not be supposed to be entirely perfect. To be as he was, is indeed subject of panegyrick enough to any man in this state of being; but in every picture there should be shade as well as light, and when I delineate him without reserve, I do what he himself recommended, both by his precept and his example.

"If the biographer writes from personal knowledge, and makes haste to gratify the publick curiosity, there is danger lest his interest, his fear, his gratitude, or his tenderness, overpower his fidelity, and tempt him to conceal, if not to invent. There are many who think it an act of piety to hide the faults or failings of their friends, even when they can no longer suffer by their detection; we therefore see whole ranks of characters adorned with uniform panegyrick, and not to be known from one another but by extrinsick and casual circumstances. 'Let me remember, (says Hale,) when I find myself inclined to pity a criminal, that there is likewise a pity due to the country.' If we owe regard to the memory of the dead, there is yet more respect to be paid to knowledge, to virtue, and to truth." [2]

What I consider as the peculiar value of the following work, is, the quantity it contains of Johnson's conversation; which is universally acknowledged to have been eminently instructive and entertaining; and of which the specimens that I have given upon a former occasion, have been received with so much approbation, that I have good grounds for supposing that the world will not be indifferent to more ample communications of a similar nature.

2. See Johnson's *Rambler*, No. 60.

A.D. 1709–1727

EARLY YEARS

Samuel Johnson was born in Lichfield, in Staffordshire, on the 18th of September, N.S. 1709; and his initiation into the Christian church was not delayed; for his baptism is recorded in the register of St. Mary's parish in that city, to have been performed on the day of his birth: His father is there stiled *Gentleman*, a circumstance of which an ignorant panegyrist has praised him for not being proud; when the truth is, that the appellation of Gentleman, though now lost in the indiscriminate assumption of *Esquire*, was commonly taken by those who could not boast of gentility. His father was Michael Johnson, a native of Derbyshire, of obscure extraction, who settled in Lichfield as a bookseller and stationer. His mother was Sarah Ford, descended of an ancient race of substantial yeomanry in Warwickshire. They were well advanced in years when they married, and never had more than two children, both sons, Samuel, their first-born, who lived to be the illustrious character whose various excellence I am to endeavour to record, and Nathanael, who died in his twenty-fifth year.

Mr. Michael Johnson was a man of a large and robust body, and of a strong and active mind; yet, as in the most solid rocks, veins of unsound substance are often discovered, there was in him a mixture of that disease, the nature of which eludes the most minute enquiry, though the effects are well known to be a weariness of life, an unconcern about those things which agitate the greater part of mankind, and a general sensation of gloomy wretchedness. From him then his son inherited, with some other qualities, "a vile melancholy," which in his too strong expression of any disturbance of mind, "made him mad all his life, at least not sober." Michael was, however, forced by the narrowness of his circumstances to be very diligent in business, not only in his shop, but by occasionally resorting to several towns in the neighbourhood, some of which were at a considerable distance from Lichfield. At that time booksellers' shops in the provincial towns of England were very rare, so that there was not one even in Birmingham, in which town old Mr. Johnson used to open a shop every market-day. He was a pretty good Latin scholar, and a citizen so creditable as to be made one of the magistrates of Lichfield; and, being a man of good sense, and skill in his trade, he acquired a reasonable share of wealth, of which however he afterwards lost the greatest part, by engaging unsuccessfully in a manufacture of parchment. He was a zealous high-church man and royalist, and retained his attachment to the unfortunate house of Stuart, though he reconciled himself, by casuistical arguments of expediency and necessity, to take the oaths imposed by the prevailing power.

There is a circumstance in his life somewhat romantick, but so well authenticated, that I shall not omit it. A young woman of Leek, in Staffordshire, while he served his apprenticeship there, conceived a violent passion for him; and though it met with no favourable return, followed him to Lichfield, where she took lodgings opposite to the house in which he lived, and indulged her hopeless flame. When he was informed that it so preyed upon her mind that her life was in danger, he with a generous humanity went to her and offered to marry her, but it was then too late: Her vital power was exhausted; and she actually exhibited one of the very rare instances of dying for love. She was buried in the cathedral of Lichfield; and he, with a tender regard, placed a stone over her grave with this inscription:

Here lies the body of
Mrs. ELIZABETH BLANEY, a stranger:
She departed this life
20 of September, 1694.

Johnson's mother was a woman of distinguished understanding. I asked his old school-fellow, Mr. Hector, surgeon, of Birmingham, if she was not vain of her son. He said, "she had too much good sense to be vain, but she knew her son's value." Her piety was not inferiour to her understanding; and to her must be ascribed those early impressions of religion upon the mind of her son, from which the world afterwards derived so much benefit. He told me, that he remembered distinctly having had the first notice of Heaven, "a place to which good people went," and hell, "a place to which bad people went," communicated to him by her, when a little child in bed with her, and that it might be the better fixed in his memory, she sent him to repeat it to Thomas Jackson, their man-servant; he not being in the way, this was not done; but there was no occasion for any artificial aid for its preservation.

. . .

Young Johnson had the misfortune to be much afflicted with the scrophula, or king's-evil, which disfigured a countenance naturally well formed, and hurt his visual nerves so much, that he did not see at all with one of his eyes, though its appearance was little different from that of the other. There is amongst his prayers, one inscribed "*When my* EYE *was restored to its use*," which ascertains a defect that many of his friends knew he had, though I never perceived it. I supposed him to be only near-sighted; and indeed I must observe, that in no other respect could I discern any defect in his vision; on the contrary, the force of his attention and perceptive quickness made him see and distinguish all manner of objects, whether of nature or of art, with a nicety that is rarely to be found. When he and I were travelling in the Highlands of Scotland, and I pointed out to him a mountain which I observed resembled a cone, he corrected my inaccuracy, by shewing me, that it was indeed pointed at the top, but that one side of it was larger than the other. And the ladies with whom he was acquainted agree, that no man was more nicely and minutely critical in the elegance of female dress. When I found that he saw the romantick beauties of Islam, in Derbyshire, much better than I did, I told him that he resembled an able performer upon a bad instrument. How false and contemptible then are all the remarks which have been made to the prejudice either of his candour or of his philosophy, founded upon a supposition that he was almost blind. It has been said, that he contracted this grievous malady from his nurse. His mother, yielding to the superstitious notion, which, it is wonderful to think, prevailed so long in this country, as to the virtue of the regal touch; a notion, which our kings encouraged, and to which a man of such enquiry and such judgement as Carte could give credit; carried him to London, where he was actually touched by Queen Anne.

. . .

That superiority over his fellows, which he maintained with so much dignity in his march through life, was not assumed from vanity and ostentation, but was the natural and constant effect of those extraordinary powers of mind, of which he could not but be conscious by comparison; the intellectual difference, which in other cases of comparison of characters, is often a matter of undecided contest, being as clear in his case as the superiority of stature in some men above others. Johnson did not strut or stand on tip-toe; he only did not stoop. From his earliest years, his superiority was perceived and acknowledged. He was from the beginning, *Ἄναξ ανδρῶν*, a king of men. His schoolfellow, Mr. Hector, has obligingly furnished me with many particulars of his boyish days; and assured me that he never knew him corrected at school, but for talking and diverting other boys from their business. He seemed to learn by intuition; for though indolence and procrastination were inherent in his constitution, whenever he made an exertion he did more than any one else. In short, he is a memorable instance of what has been often observed, that the boy is the man in miniature: and that the distinguishing characteristicks of each individual are the same, through the whole course of life. His favourites used to receive very liberal assistance from him; and such was the submission and deference with which he was treated, such the desire to obtain his regard, that three of the boys, of whom Mr. Hector was sometimes one, used to come in the morning as his humble attendants, and carry him to school. One in the middle stooped, while he sat upon his back, and one on each side supported him; and thus he was borne triumphant. Such a proof of the early predominance of intellectual vigour is very remarkable, and does honour to human nature.—Talking to me once himself of his being much distinguished at school, he told me, "they never thought to raise me by comparing me to any one; they never said, Johnson is as good a scholar as such a one; but such a one is as good a scholar as Johnson; and this was said but of one, but of Lowe; and I do not think he was as good a scholar."

He discovered a great ambition to excel, which roused him to counteract his indolence. He was uncommonly inquisitive; and his memory was so tenacious, that he never forgot anything that he either heard or read. Mr. Hector remembers having recited to him eighteen verses, which, after a little pause, he repeated *verbatim*, varying only one epithet, by which he improved the line.

He never joined with the other boys in their ordinary diversions: his only amusement was in winter, when he took a pleasure in being drawn upon the ice by a boy barefooted, who pulled him along by a garter fixed around him; no very easy operation, as his size was remarkably large. His defective sight, indeed, prevented him from enjoying the common sports; and he once pleasantly remarked to me, "how wonderfully well he had contrived to be idle without them." Lord Chesterfield, however, has justly observed in one of his letters, when earnestly cautioning a friend against the pernicious effects of idleness, that active sports are not to be reckoned idleness in young people; and that the listless torpor of doing nothing alone deserves that name. Of this dismal inertness of disposition, Johnson had all his life too great a share. Mr. Hector relates, that "he could not oblige him more than by sauntering away the hours of vacation in the fields, during which he was more engaged in talking to himself than to his companion."

. . .

A.D. 1729

AGE 20

The "morbid melancholy," which was lurking in his constitution, and to which we may ascribe those particularities, and that aversion to regular life, which, at a very early period, marked his character, gathered such strength in his twentieth year, as to afflict him in a dreadful manner. While he was at Lichfield, in the college vacation of the year 1729, he felt himself overwhelmed with an horrible hypochondria, with perpetual irritation, fretfulness, and impatience; and with a dejection, gloom, and despair, which made existence misery. From this dismal malady he never afterwards was perfectly relieved; and all his labours, and all his enjoyments, were but temporary interruptions of its baleful influence. How wonderful, how unsearchable are the ways of God! Johnson, who was blest with all the powers of genius and understanding in a degree far above the ordinary state of human nature, was at the same time visited with a disorder so afflictive, that they who know it by dire experience, will not envy his exalted endowments. That it was, in some degree, occasioned by a defect in his nervous system, that inexplicable part of our frame, appears highly probable. He told Mr. Paradise that he was sometimes so languid and inefficient, that he could not distinguish the hour upon the town-clock.

Johnson, upon the first violent attack of this disorder, strove to overcome it by forcible exertions. He frequently walked to Birmingham and back again, and tried many other expedients, but all in vain. His expression concerning it to me was "I did not then know how to manage it." His distress became so intolerable, that he applied to Dr. Swinfen, physician in Lichfield, his godfather, and put into his hands a state of his case, written in Latin. Dr. Swinfen was so much struck with the extraordinary acuteness, research, and eloquence of this paper, that in his zeal for his godson he shewed it to several people. His daughter, Mrs. Desmoulins, who was many years humanely supported in Dr. Johnson's house in London, told me, that upon his discovering that Dr. Swinfen had communicated his case, he was so much offended, that he was never afterwards fully reconciled to him. He indeed had good reason to be offended; for though Dr. Swinfen's motive was good, he inconsiderately betrayed a matter deeply interesting and of great delicacy, which had been entrusted to him in confidence: and exposed a complaint of his young friend and patient, which, in the superficial opinion of the generality of mankind, is attended with contempt and disgrace.

But let not little men triumph upon knowing that Johnson was an HYPOCHONDRIACK, was subject to what the learned, philosophical, and pious Dr. Cheyne has so well treated under the title of "The English Malady." Though he suffered severely from it, he was not therefore degraded. The powers of his great mind might be troubled, and their full exercise suspended at times; but the mind itself was ever entire. As a proof of this, it is only necessary to consider, that, when he was at the very worst, he composed that state of his own case, which shewed an uncommon vigour, not only of fancy and taste, but of judgement. I am aware that he himself was too ready to call such a complaint by the name of *madness;* in conformity with which notion, he has traced its gradations, with exquisite nicety, in one of the chapters of his RASSELAS. But there is surely a clear distinction between a disorder which affects only the imagination and spirits, while the judgement is sound, and a disorder by which the judgement itself is impaired. The distinction was made to me by the late Professor Gaubius of Leyden, physician to the Prince of Orange, in a conversation which I had with him several years ago, and he explained it thus: "If (said he) a man tells me that he is grievously disturbed, for that he *imagines* he sees a ruffian coming against him with a drawn sword, though at the same time he is *conscious* it is a delusion, I pronounce him to have a disordered imagination; but if a man tells me that he *sees* this, and in consternation calls to me to look at it, I pronounce him to be *mad.*"

It is a common effect of low spirits or melancholy, to make those who are afflicted with it imagine that they are actually suffering those evils which happen to be most strongly presented to their minds. Some have fancied themselves to be deprived of the use of their limbs, some to labour under acute diseases, others to be in extreme poverty; when, in truth, there was not the least reality in any of the suppositions; so that when the vapours were dispelled, they were convinced of the delusion. To Johnson, whose supreme enjoyment was the exercise of his reason, the disturbance or obscuration of that faculty was the evil most to be dreaded. Insanity, therefore, was the object of his most dismal apprehension; and he fancied himself seized by it, or approaching to it, at the very time when he was giving proofs of a more than ordinary soundness and vigour of judgement. That his own diseased imagination should have so far deceived him, is strange; but it is stranger still that some of his friends should have given credit to his groundless opinion, when they had such undoubted proofs that it was totally fallacious; though it is by no means surprising that those who wish to depreciate him, should, since his death, have laid hold of this circumstance, and insisted upon it with very unfair aggravation.

Amidst the oppression and distraction of a disease which very few have felt in its full extent, but many have experienced in a slighter degree, Johnson, in his writings, and in his conversation, never failed to display all the varieties of intellectual excellence. In his march through this world to a better, his mind still appeared grand and brilliant, and impressed all around him with the truth of Virgil's noble sentiment—

Igneus est ollis vigor et cælestis origo.[3]

The history of his mind as to religion is an important article. I have mentioned the early impressions made upon his tender imagination by his mother, who continued her pious cares with assiduity, but, in his opinion, not with judgement. "Sunday (said he) was a heavy day to me when I was a boy. My mother confined me on that day, and made me read 'The Whole Duty of Man,' from a great part of which I could derive no instruction. When, for instance, I had read the chapter on theft, which from my infancy I had been taught was wrong, I was no more convinced that theft was wrong than before; so there was no accession of knowledge. A boy should be introduced to such books by having his attention directed to the arrangement, to the style, and other excellencies of composition; that the mind being thus engaged by an amusing variety of objects may not grow weary."

He communicated to me the following particulars upon the subject of his religious progress. "I fell into an inattention to religion, or an indifference about it, in my ninth year. The church at Lichfield, in which we had a seat, wanted reparation, so I was to go and find a seat in other churches; and having bad eyes, and being awkward about this, I used to go and read in the fields on Sunday. This habit continued till my fourteenth year; and still I find a great reluctance to go to church. I then became a sort of lax *talker* against religion, for I did not much *think* against it; and this lasted till I went to Oxford, where it would not be *suffered.* When at Oxford, I took up Law's 'Serious Call to a Holy Life,' expecting to find it a dull book, (as such books generally are,) and perhaps to laugh at it. But I found Law quite an overmatch for me; and this was the first occasion of my thinking in earnest of religion, after I became capable of rational enquiry." From this time forward religion was the predominant object of his thoughts; though, with the just sentiments of a conscientious christian, he lamented that his practice of its duties fell far short of what it ought to be.

. . .

A.D. 1736

AGE 27

In a man whom religious education has secured from licentious indulgences, the passion of love, when once it has seized him, is exceedingly strong; being unimpaired by dissipation, and totally concentrated in one object. This was experienced by Johnson, when he became the fervent admirer of Mrs. Porter, after her first husband's death. Miss Porter told me, that when he was first introduced to her mother, his appearance was very forbidding: he was then lean and lank, so that his immense structure of bones was hideously striking to the eye, and the scars of the scrophula were deeply visible. He also wore his hair, which was straight and stiff, and separated behind: and he often had, seemingly, convulsive starts and odd gesticulations, which tended to excite at once surprise and ridicule. Mrs. Porter was so much engaged by his conversation that she overlooked all these external disadvantages, and said to her daughter, "this is the most sensible man that I ever saw in my life."

Though Mrs. Porter was double the age of Johnson, and her person and manner, as described to me by the late Mr. Garrick, were by no means pleasing to others, she must have had a superiority of understanding and talents as she certainly inspired him with a more than ordinary passion; and she having signified her willingness to accept of his hand, he went to Lichfield to ask his mother's consent to the marriage; which he could not but be conscious was a very imprudent scheme, both on account of their disparity of years, and her want of fortune. But Mrs. Johnson knew too well the ardour of her son's temper, and was too tender a parent to oppose his inclinations.

I know not for what reason the marriage ceremony was not performed at Birmingham; but a resolution was taken that it should be at Derby, for which place the bride and bridegroom set out on horseback, I suppose in very good humour. But

3. ***Igneus . . . origo:*** "With these seeds a flaming vigor and heavenly source is associated." See *Aeneid,* vi, 730.

though Mr. Topham Beauclerk used archly to mention Johnson's having told him with much gravity, "Sir, it was a love marriage on both sides," I have had from my illustrious friend the following curious account of their journey to church upon the nuptial morn:—"Sir, she had read the old romances, and had got into her head the fantastical notion that a woman of spirit should use her lover like a dog. So, Sir, at first she told me that I rode too fast, and she could not keep up with me: and, when I rode a little slower, she passed me, and complained that I lagged behind. I was not to be made the slave of caprice; and I resolved to begin as I meant to end. I therefore pushed on briskly, till I was fairly out of her sight. The road lay between two hedges, so I was sure she could not miss it; and I contrived that she should soon come up with me. When she did, I observed her to be in tears."

This, it must be allowed, was a singular beginning of connubial felicity; but there is no doubt that Johnson, though he thus shewed a manly firmness, proved a most affectionate and indulgent husband to the last moment of Mrs. Johnson's life: and in his "Prayers and Meditations," we find very remarkable evidence that his regard and fondness for her never ceased, even after her death.

He now set up a private academy, for which purpose he hired a large house, well situated near his native city. In the Gentleman's Magazine for 1736, there is the following advertisement: "At Edial, near Lichfield, in Staffordshire, young gentlemen are boarded and taught the Latin and Greek Languages, by SAMUEL JOHNSON." But the only pupils that were put under his care were the celebrated David Garrick and his brother George, and a Mr. Offely, a young gentleman of good fortune who died early. As yet, his name had nothing of that celebrity which afterwards commanded the highest attention and respect of mankind. Had such an advertisement appeared after the publication of his LONDON, or his RAMBLER, or his DICTIONARY, how would it have burst upon the world! with what eagerness would the great and the wealthy have embraced an opportunity of putting their sons under the learned tuition of SAMUEL JOHNSON. The truth, however, is, that he was not so well qualified for being a teacher of elements, and a conductor in learning by regular gradations, as men of inferiour powers of mind. His own acquisitions had been made by fits and starts, by violent irruptions into the regions of knowledge; and it could not be expected that his impatience would be subdued, and his impetuosity restrained, so as to fit him for a quiet guide to novices. The art of communicating instruction, of whatever kind, is much to be valued; and I have ever thought that those who devote themselves to this employment, and do their duty with diligence and success, are entitled to very high respect from the community, as Johnson himself often maintained. Yet I am of opinion, that the greatest abilities are not only not required for this office, but render a man less fit for it.

. . .

A.D. 1737–1738

AGE 28–29

How he employed himself upon his first coming to London is not particularly known. I never heard that he found any protection or encouragement by the means of Mr. Colson, to whose academy David Garrick went. Mrs. Lucy Porter told me, that Mr. Walmsley gave him a letter of introduction to Lintot his bookseller, and that Johnson wrote some things for him; but I imagine this to be a mistake, for I have discovered no trace of it, and I am pretty sure he told me, that Mr. Cave was the first publisher by whom his pen was engaged in London.

He had a little money when he came to town, and he knew how he could live in the cheapest manner. His first lodgings were at the house of Mr. Norris, a staymaker, in Exeter-street, adjoining Catharine-street, in the Strand. "I dined (said he) very well for eight-pence, with very good company, at the Pine-Apple in New-street, just by. Several of them had travelled. They expected to meet every day; but did not know one another's names. It used to cost the rest a shilling, for they drank wine; but I had a cut of meat for six-pence, and bread for a penny, and gave the waiter a penny; so that I was quite well served, nay, better than the rest, for they gave the waiter nothing."

He at this time, I believe, abstained entirely from fermented liquors: a practice to which he rigidly conformed for many years together, at different periods of his life.

. . .

It appears that he was now enlisted by Mr. Cave as a regular coadjutor in his magazine, by which he probably obtained a tolerable livelihood. At what time, or by what means, he had acquired a competent knowledge both of French and Italian, I do not know; but he was so well skilled in them, as to be sufficiently qualified for a translator. That part of his labour which consisted in emendation and improvement of the productions of other contributors, like that employed in levelling ground, can be perceived only by those who had an opportunity of comparing the original with the altered copy. What we certainly know to have been done by him in this way, was the Debates in both houses of Parliament, under the name of "The Senate of Lilliput," sometimes with feigned denominations of the several speakers, sometimes with denominations formed of the letters of their real names, in the manner of what is called anagram, so that they might easily be decyphered. Parliament then kept the press in a kind of mysterious awe, which made it necessary to have recourse to such devices. In our time it has acquired an unrestrained freedom, so that the people in all parts of the kingdom have a fair, open, and exact report of the actual proceedings of their representatives and legislators, which in our constitution is highly to be valued; though, unquestionably, there has of late been too much reason to complain of the petulance with which obscure scribblers have presumed to treat men of the most respectable character and situation.

This important article of the Gentleman's Magazine was, for several years, executed by Mr. William Guthrie, a man who deserves to be respectably recorded in the literary annals of this country. He was descended of an ancient family in Scotland; but having a small patrimony, and being an adherent of the unfortunate house of Stuart, he could not accept of any office in the state; he therefore came to London, and employed his talents and learning as an "Authour by profession." His writings in history, criticism, and politicks, had considerable merit. He was the first English historian who had recourse to that authentick source of information, the Parliamentary Journals; and such was the power of his political pen, that, at an early period, Government thought it worth their while to keep it quiet by a pension, which he enjoyed till his death. Johnson esteemed him enough to wish that his life should be written. The debates in Parliament, which were brought home and digested by Guthrie, whose memory, though surpassed by others who have since followed him in the same department, was yet very quick and tenacious, were sent by Cave to Johnson for his revision; and, after some time, when Guthrie had attained to greater variety of employment, and the speeches were more and more enriched by the accession of Johnson's genius, it was resolved that he should do the whole himself, from the scanty notes furnished by persons employed to attend in both houses of Parliament. Sometimes, however, as he himself told me, he had nothing more communicated to him than the names of the several speakers, and the part which they had taken in the debate.

Thus was Johnson employed during some of the best years of his life, as a mere literary labourer "for gain, not glory," solely to obtain an honest support. He however indulged himself in occasional little sallies, which the French so happily express by the term *jeux d'esprit*, and which will be noticed in their order, in the progress of this work.

. . .

A.D. 1744

AGE 35

It does not appear that he wrote anything in 1744 for the Gentleman's Magazine, but the Preface. His life of Barretier was now re-published in a pamphlet by itself. But he produced one work this year, fully sufficient to maintain the high reputation which he had acquired. This was "THE LIFE OF RICHARD SAVAGE," a man, of whom it is difficult to speak impartially, without wondering that he was for some time the intimate companion of Johnson; for his character was marked by profligacy, insolence, and ingratitude: yet, as he undoubtedly had a warm and vigorous, though unregulated mind, had seen life in all its varieties, and been much in the company of the statesmen and wits of his time, he could communicate to Johnson an abundant supply of such materials as his philosophical curiosity most eagerly desired; and as Savage's misfortunes and misconduct had reduced him to the lowest state of wretchedness as a writer for bread, his visits to St. John's Gate naturally brought Johnson and him together.

It is melancholy to reflect, that Johnson and Savage were sometimes in such extreme indigence, that they could not pay for a lodging; so that they have wandered together whole nights in the streets. Yet in these almost incredible scenes of distress, we may suppose that Savage mentioned many of the anecdotes with which Johnson afterwards enriched the life of his unhappy companion, and those of other Poets.

He told Sir Joshua Reynolds, that one night in particular, when Savage and he walked round St. James's-square for want of a lodging, they were not at all depressed by their situation; but in high spirits and brimful of patriotism, traversed the square for several hours, inveighed against the minister, and "resolved they would *stand by their country*."

I am afraid, however, that by associating with Savage, who was habituated to the dissipation and licentiousness of the town, Johnson, though his good principles remained steady, did not entirely preserve that conduct, for which, in days of greater simplicity, he was remarked by his friend Mr. Hector; but was imperceptibly led into some indulgences which occasioned much distress to his virtuous mind.

That Johnson was anxious that an authentick and favourable account of his extraordinary friend should first get possession of the publick attention, is evident from a letter which he wrote in the Gentleman's Magazine for August of the year preceding its publication.

Mr. Urban,

As your collections show how often you have owed the ornaments of your poetical pages to the correspondence of the unfortunate and ingenious Mr. Savage, I doubt not but you have so much regard to his memory as to encourage any design that may have a tendency to the preservation of it from insults or calumnies; and therefore, with some degree of assurance, intreat you to inform the publick, that his life will speedily be published by a person who was favoured with his confidence, and received from himself an account of most of the transactions which he proposes to mention, to the time of his retirement to Swansea in Wales.

"From that period, to his death in the prison of Bristol, the account will be continued from materials still less liable to objection; his own letters, and those of his friends, some of which will be inserted in the work, and abstracts of others subjoined in the margin.

"It may be reasonably imagined, that others may have the same design; but as it is not credible that they can obtain the same materials, it must be expected they will supply from invention the want of intelligence; and that under the title of 'The Life of Savage,' they will publish only a novel, filled with romantick adventures, and imaginary amours. You may therefore, perhaps gratify the lovers of truth and wit, by giving me leave to inform them in your Magazine, that my account will be published in 8vo. by Mr. Roberts, in Warwick-lane.

[*No signature.*]

In February, 1744, it accordingly came forth from the shop of Roberts, between whom and Johnson I have not traced any connection, except the casual one of this publication. In Johnson's "Life of Savage," although it must be allowed that its moral is the reverse of—"*Respicere exemplar vitæ morumque jubebo,*"[4] a very useful lesson is inculcated, to guard men of warm passions from a too free indulgence of them; and the various incidents are related in so clear and animated a manner, and illuminated throughout with so much philosophy, that it is one of the most interesting narratives in the English language. Sir Joshua Reynolds told me, that upon his return from Italy he met with it in Devonshire, knowing nothing of its authour, and began to read it while he was standing with his arm leaning against a chimney-piece. It seized his attention so strongly, that, not being able to lay down the book till he had finished it, when he attempted to move, he found his arm totally benumbed. The rapidity with which this work was composed, is a wonderful circumstance. Johnson has been heard to say, "I wrote forty-eight of the

4. ***"Respicere . . . jubebo":*** "I shall command you to behold a model of life and morality." See Horace, *Ars Poetica,* l. 317.

printed octavo pages of the Life of Savage at a sitting; but then I sat up all night."

. . .

A.D. 1749

AGE 40

. . .

In January, 1749, he published "THE VANITY OF HUMAN WISHES, being the Tenth Satire of Juvenal imitated." He, I believe, composed it the preceding year. Mrs. Johnson, for the sake of country air, had lodgings at Hampstead, to which he resorted occasionally, and there the greatest part, if not the whole, of this Imitation was written. The fervid rapidity with which it was produced, is scarcely credible. I have heard him say, that he composed seventy lines of it in one day, without putting one of them upon paper till they were finished. I remember when I once regretted to him that he had not given us more of Juvenal's Satires, he said, he probably should give more, for he had them all in his head; by which I understood, that he had the originals and correspondent allusions floating in his mind, which he could, when he pleased, embody and render permanent without much labour. Some of them, however, he observed were too gross for imitation.

The profits of a single poem, however excellent, appear to have been very small in the last reign, compared with what a publication of the same size has since been known to yield. I have mentioned upon Johnson's own authority, that for his LONDON he had only ten guineas; and now, after his fame was established, he got for his "Vanity of Human Wishes" but five guineas more, as is proved by an authentick document in my possession.

It will be observed, that he reserves to himself the right of printing one edition of this satire, which was his practice upon occasion of the sale of all his writings; it being his fixed intention to publish at some period, for his own profit, a complete collection of his works.

His "Vanity of Human Wishes" has less of common life, but more of a philosophick dignity than his "London." More readers, therefore, will be delighted with the pointed spirit of "London," than with the profound reflection of "The Vanity of Human Wishes." Garrick, for instance, observed in his sprightly manner, with more vivacity than regard to just discrimination, as is usual with wits, "When Johnson lived much with the Herveys, and saw a good deal of what was passing in life, he wrote his 'London,' which is lively and easy: when he became more retired, he gave us his 'Vanity of Human Wishes,' which is as hard as Greek. Had he gone on to imitate another satire, it would have been as hard as Hebrew."

But "The Vanity of Human Wishes" is, in the opinion of the best judges, as high an effort of ethick poetry as any language can shew. The instances of variety of disappointment are chosen so judiciously, and painted so strongly, that, the moment they are read, they bring conviction to every thinking mind. That of the scholar must have depressed the too sanguine expectations of many an ambitious student. That of the warrior, Charles of Sweden, is, I think, as highly finished a picture as can possibly be conceived.

. . .

A.D. 1750

AGE 41

. . .

In 1750 he came forth in the character for which he was eminently qualified, a majestick teacher of moral and religious wisdom. The vehicle which he chose was that of a periodical paper, which he knew had been, upon former occasions, employed with great success. The Tatler, Spectator, and Guardian, were the last of the kind published in England, which had stood the test of a long trial; and such an interval had now elapsed since their publication, as made him justly think that, to many of his readers, this form of instruction would, in some degree, have the advantage of novelty. A few days before the first of his Essays came out, there started another competitor for fame in the same form, under the title of "The Tatler Revived," which I believe was "born but to die." Johnson was, I think, not very happy in the choice of his title,—"The Rambler;" which certainly is not suited to a series of grave and moral discourses; which the Italians have literally, but ludicrously, translated by *Il Vagabondo;* and which has been lately assumed as the denomination of a vehicle of licentious tales, "The Rambler's Magazine." He gave Sir Joshua Reynolds the following account of its getting this name: "What *must* be done, Sir, *will* be done. When I was to begin publishing that paper, I was at a loss how to name it. I sat down at night upon my bedside, and resolved that I would not go to sleep till I had fixed its title. The Rambler seemed the best that occurred, and I took it."

With what devout and conscientious sentiments this paper was undertaken, is evidenced by the following prayer, which he composed and offered up on the occasion: "Almighty God, the giver of all good things, without whose help all labour is ineffectual, and without whose grace all wisdom is folly: grant, I beseech Thee, that in this undertaking thy Holy Spirit may not be with-held from me, but that I may promote thy glory, and the salvation of myself and others: grant this, O Lord, for the sake of thy son, JESUS CHRIST. Amen."

. . .

Posterity will be astonished when they are told, upon the authority of Johnson himself, that many of these discourses, which we should suppose had been laboured with all the slow attention of literary leisure, were written in haste as the moment pressed, without even being read over by him before they were printed. It can be accounted for only in this way; that by reading and meditation, and a very close inspection of life, he had accumulated a great fund of miscellaneous knowledge, which, by a peculiar promptitude of mind, was ever ready at his call, and which he had constantly accustomed himself to clothe in the most apt and energetick expression. Sir Joshua Reynolds once asked him by what means he had attained his extraordinary accuracy and flow of language. He told him, that he had early laid it down as a fixed rule to do his best on every occasion, and in every company: to impart whatever he knew in the most forcible language he could put it in; and that by constant practice, and never suffering any careless expressions to escape him, or attempting to deliver his thoughts without arranging them in the clearest manner, it became habitual to him.

. . .

A.D. 1754, 1755

AGE 45–46

. . .

The Dictionary, we may believe, afforded Johnson full occupation this year. As it approached to its conclusion, he probably worked with redoubled vigour, as seamen increase their exertion and alacrity when they have a near prospect of their haven.

Lord Chesterfield,[5] to whom Johnson had paid the high compliment of addressing to his Lordship the Plan of his Dictionary, had behaved to him in such a manner as to excite his contempt and indignation. The world has been for many years amused with a story confidently told, and as confidently repeated with additional circumstances, that a sudden disgust was taken by Johnson upon occasion of his having been one day kept long in waiting in his Lordship's antechamber, for which the reason assigned was, that he had company with him; and that at last, when the door opened, out walked Colley Cibber; and that Johnson was so violently provoked when he found for whom he had been so long excluded, that he went away in a passion, and never would return. I remember having mentioned this story to George Lord Lyttelton, who told me, he was very intimate with Lord Chesterfield; and holding it as a well-known truth, defended Lord Chesterfield by saying, that "Cibber, who had been introduced familiarly by the backstairs, had probably not been there above ten minutes." It may seem strange even to entertain a doubt concerning a story so long and so wildly current, and thus implicitly adopted, if not sanctioned, by the authority which I have mentioned; but Johnson himself assured me, that there was not the least foundation for it. He told me, that there never was any particular incident which produced a quarrel between Lord Chesterfield and him; but that his Lordship's continued neglect was the reason why he resolved to have no connexion with him. When the Dictionary was upon the eve of publication, Lord Chesterfield, who, it is said, had flattered himself with expectations that Johnson would dedicate the work to him, attempted, in

5. **Chesterfield:** Philip Dormer Stanhope, Lord Chesterfield (1694–1773), statesman and famous wit and man-of-letters.

a courtly manner, to soothe and insinuate himself with the Sage, conscious, as it should seem, of the old indifference with which he had treated its learned authour; and further attempted to conciliate him, by writing two papers in "The World," in recommendation of the work; and it must be confessed, that they contain some studied compliments, so finely turned, that if there had been no previous offence, it is probable that Johnson would have been highly delighted. Praise, in general, was pleasing to him; but by praise from a man of rank and elegant accomplishments, he was peculiarly gratified.

His Lordship says, "I think the publick in general, and the republick of letters in particular, are greatly obliged to Mr. Johnson, for having undertaken, and executed so great and desirable a work. Perfection is not to be expected from man: but if we are to judge by the various works of Johnson already published, we have good reason to believe, that he will bring this as near to perfection as any man could do. The plan of it, which he published some years ago, seems to me to be a proof of it. Nothing can be more rationally imagined, or more accurately and elegantly expressed. I therefore recommend the previous perusal of it to all those who intend to buy the Dictionary, and who, I suppose, are all those who can afford it."

. . .

"It must be owned, that our language is, at present, in a state of anarchy, and hitherto, perhaps, it may not have been the worse for it. During our free and open trade, many words and expressions have been imported, adopted, and naturalized from other languages, which have greatly enriched our own. Let it still preserve what real strength and beauty it may have borrowed from others; but let it not, like the Tarpeian maid, be overwhelmed and crushed by unnecessary ornaments. The time for discrimination seems to be now come. Toleration, adoption, and naturalization have run their lengths. Good order and authority are now necessary. But where shall we find them, and at the same time, the obedience due to them? We must have recourse to the old Roman expedient in times of confusion, and chuse a dictator. Upon this principle, I give my vote for Mr. Johnson, to fill that great and arduous post, and I hereby declare, that I make a total surrender of all my rights and privileges in the English language, as a free-born British subject, to the said Mr. Johnson, during the term of his dictatorship. Nay more, I will not only obey him like an old Roman, as my dictator, but, like a modern Roman, I will implicitly believe in him as my Pope, and hold him to be infallible while in the chair, but no longer. More than this he cannot well require; for, I presume, that obedience can never be expected, where there is neither terrour to enforce, nor interest to invite it."

. . .

"But a Grammar, a Dictionary, and a History of our Language, through its several stages, were still wanting at home, and importunately called for from abroad. Mr. Johnson's labours will now, I dare say, very fully supply that want, and greatly contribute to the farther spreading of our language in other countries. Learners were discouraged, by finding no standard to resort to; and, consequently, thought it incapable of any. They will now be undeceived and encouraged."

This courtly device failed of its effect. Johnson, who thought that "all was false and hollow," despised the honeyed words, and was even indignant that Lord Chesterfield should, for a moment, imagine, that he could be the dupe of such an artifice. His expression to me concerning Lord Chesterfield, upon this occasion, was, "Sir, after making great professions, he had, for many years, taken no notice of me; but when my Dictionary was coming out, he fell a scribbling in 'The World' about it. Upon which, I wrote him a letter expressed in civil terms, but such as might shew him that I did not mind what he said or wrote, and that I had done with him."

This is that celebrated letter of which so much has been said, and about which curiosity has been so long excited, without being gratified. I for many years solicited Johnson to favour me with a copy of it, that so excellent a composition might not be lost to posterity. He delayed from time to time to give it me;* till at last in 1781, when we were on

* Dr. Johnson appeared to have had a remarkable delicacy with respect to the circulation of this letter; for Dr. Douglas, Bishop of Salisbury, informs me, that having many years ago pressed him to be allowed to read

a visit at Mr. Dilly's, at Southill in Bedfordshire, he was pleased to dictate it to me from memory. He afterwards found among his papers a copy of it, which he had dictated to Mr. Baretti, with its title and corrections, in his own hand-writing. This he gave to Mr. Langton; adding that if it were to come into print, he wished it to be from that copy. By Mr. Langton's kindness, I am enabled to enrich my work with a perfect transcript of what the world has so eagerly desired to see.

TO THE RIGHT HONOURABLE
THE EARL OF CHESTERFIELD.

My Lord, *February 7, 1755.*

I HAVE been lately informed, by the proprietor of the World, that two papers, in which my Dictionary is recommended to the publick, were written by your Lordship. To be so distinguished, is an honour, which, being very little accustomed to favours from the great, I know not well how to receive, or in what terms to acknowledge.

When, upon some slight encouragement, I first visited your Lordship, I was overpowered, like the rest of mankind, by the enchantment of your address, and could not forbear to wish that I might boast myself *Le vainqueur du vainqueur de la terre;*[6]—that I might obtain that regard for which I saw the world contending; but I found my attendance so little encouraged, that neither pride nor modesty would suffer me to continue it. When I had once addressed your Lordship in publick, I had exhausted all the art of pleasing which a retired and uncourtly scholar can possess. I had done all that I could; and no man is well pleased to have his all neglected, be it ever so little.

Seven years, my Lord, have now past, since I waited in your outward rooms, or was repulsed from your door; during which time I have been pushing on my work through difficulties, of which it is useless to complain, and have brought it, at last, to the verge of publication, without one act of assistance, one word of encouragement, or one smile of favour. Such treatment I did not expect, for I never had a Patron before.

The shepherd in Virgil grew at last acquainted with Love, and found him a native of the rocks.

Is not a Patron, my Lord, one who looks with unconcern on a man struggling for life in the water, and, when he has reached ground, encumbers him with help? The notice which you have been pleased to take of my labours, had it been early, had been kind; but it has been delayed till I am indifferent, and cannot enjoy it; till I am solitary, and cannot impart it; till I am known, and do not want it. I hope it is no very cynical asperity, not to confess obligations where no benefit has been received, or to be unwilling that the Publick should consider me as owing that to a Patron, which Providence has enabled me to do for myself.

Having carried on my work thus far with so little obligation to any favourer of learning, I shall not be disappointed though I should conclude it, if less be possible, with less; for I have been long wakened from that dream of hope, in which I once boasted myself with so much exultation,

My Lord,
Your Lordship's most humble
Most obedient servant,
Sam Johnson.

While this was the talk of the town, (says Dr. Adams, in a letter to me) I happened to visit Dr. Warburton, who finding that I was acquainted with Johnson, desired me earnestly to carry his compliments to him, and to tell him, that he honoured him for his manly behaviour in rejecting these condescensions of Lord Chesterfield, and for resenting the treatment he had received from him with a proper spirit. Johnson was visibly pleased with this compliment, for he had always a high opinion of Warburton.

. . .

The Dictionary, with a Grammar and History of the English Language, being now at length published, in two volumes folio, the world contemplated with wonder so stupendous a work atchieved by one man, while other countries had thought such undertakings fit only for whole academies.

---

it to the second Lord Hardwicke, who was very desirous to hear it, (promising at the same time, that no copy of it should be taken,) Johnson seemed much pleased that it had attracted the attention of a nobleman of such a respectable character; but after pausing some time, declined to comply with the request, saying, with a smile, "No, Sir; I have hurt the dog too much already;" or words to that purpose.

6. ***Le vainqueur . . . terre:*** "The conqueror of the conqueror of the earth."

Vast as his powers were, I cannot but think that his imagination deceived him, when he supposed that by constant application he might have performed the task in three years. Let the Preface be attentively perused, in which is given, in a clear, strong, and glowing style, a comprehensive, yet particular view of what he had done; and it will be evident, that the time he employed upon it was comparatively short. I am unwilling to swell my book with long quotations from what is in every body's hands, and I believe there are few prose compositions in the English language that are read with more delight, or are more impressed upon the memory, than that preliminary discourse. One of its excellencies has always struck me with peculiar admiration; I mean the perspicuity with which he has expressed abstract scientifick notions. As an instance of this, I shall quote the following sentence: "When the radical idea branches out into parallel ramifications, how can a consecutive series be formed of senses in their own nature collateral?" We have here an example of what has been often said, and I believe with justice, that there is for every thought a certain nice adaptation of words which none other could equal, and which, when a man has been so fortunate as to hit, he has attained, in that particular case, the perfection of language.

. . .

A.D. 1759

AGE 50

. . .

Soon after this event, he wrote his "RASSELAS, PRINCE OF ABYSSINIA:" concerning the publication of which Sir John Hawkins guesses vaguely and idly, instead of having taken the trouble to inform himself with authentick precision. Not to trouble my readers with a repetition of the Knight's reveries, I have to mention, that the late Mr. Strahan the printer told me, that Johnson wrote it, that with the profits he might defray the expence of his mother's funeral, and pay some little debts which she had left. He told Sir Joshua Reynolds, that he composed it in the evenings of one week, sent it to the press in portions as it was written, and had never since read it over. Mr. Strahan, Mr. Johnson, and Mr. Dodsley, purchased it for a hundred pounds, but afterwards paid him twenty-five pounds more, when it came to a second edition.

Considering the large sums which have been received for compilations, and works requiring not much more genius than compilations, we cannot but wonder at the very low price which he was content to receive for this admirable performance; which, though he had written nothing else, would have rendered his name immortal in the world of literature. None of his writings has been so extensively diffused over Europe; for it has been translated into most, if not all, of the modern languages. This Tale, with all the charms of oriental imagery, and all the force and beauty of which the English language is capable, leads us through the most important scenes of human life, and shews us that this stage of our being is full of "vanity and vexation of spirit." To those who look no further than the present life, or who maintain that human nature has not fallen from the state in which it was created, the instruction of this sublime story will be of no avail. But they who think justly, and feel with strong sensibility, will listen with eagerness and admiration to its truth and wisdom. Voltaire's CANDIDE, written to refute the system of Optimism, which it has accomplished with brilliant success, is wonderfully similar in its plan and conduct to Johnson's RASSELAS; insomuch, that I have heard Johnson say, that if they had not been published so closely one after the other that there was not time for imitation, it would have been in vain to deny that the scheme of that which came latest was taken from the other. Though the proposition illustrated by both these works was the same, namely, that in our present state there is more evil than good, the intention of the writers was very different. Voltaire, I am afraid, meant only by wanton profaneness to obtain a sportive victory over religion, and to discredit the belief of a superintending Providence: Johnson meant, by shewing the unsatisfactory nature of things temporal, to direct the hopes of man to things eternal. Rasselas, as was observed to me by a very accomplished lady, may be considered as a more enlarged and more deeply philosophical discourse in prose, upon the interesting truth, which in his "Vanity of Human Wishes" he had so successfully enforced in verse.

The fund of thinking which this work contains

is such, that almost every sentence of it may furnish a subject of long meditation. I am not satisfied if a year passes without my having read it through; and at every perusal, my admiration of the mind which produced it is so highly raised, that I can scarcely believe that I had the honour of enjoying the intimacy of such a man.

. . .

This is to me a memorable year [1763]; for in it I had the happiness to obtain the acquaintance of that extraordinary man whose memoirs I am now writing; an acquaintance which I shall ever esteem as one of the most fortunate circumstances in my life. Though then but two-and-twenty, I had for several years read his works with delight and instruction, and had the highest reverence for their authour, which had grown up in my fancy into a kind of mysterious veneration, by figuring to myself a state of solemn elevated abstraction, in which I supposed him to live in the immense metropolis of London. Mr. Gentleman, a native of Ireland, who passed some years in Scotland as a player, and as an instructor in the English language, a man whose talents and worth were depressed by misfortunes, had given me a representation of the figure and manner of DICTIONARY JOHNSON! as he was then generally called;* and during my first visit to London, which was for three months in 1760, Mr. Derrick the poet, who was Gentleman's friend and countryman, flattered me with hopes that he would introduce me to Johnson, an honour of which I was very ambitious. But he never found an opportunity; which made me doubt that he had promised to do what was not in his power; till Johnson some years afterwards told me, "Derrick, Sir, might very well have introduced you. I had a kindness for Derrick, and am sorry he is dead."

. . .

Mr. Thomas Davies the actor, who then kept a bookseller's shop in Russel-street, Covent-garden, told me that Johnson was very much his friend, and came frequently to his house, where he more than once invited me to meet him: but by some unlucky accident or other he was prevented from coming to us.

Mr. Thomas Davies was a man of good understanding and talents, with the advantage of a liberal education. Though somewhat pompous, he was an entertaining companion; and his literary performances have no inconsiderable share of merit. He was a friendly and very hospitable man. Both he and his wife, (who has been celebrated for her beauty,) though upon the stage for many years, maintained an uniform decency of character; and Johnson esteemed them, and lived in as easy an intimacy with them as with any family which he used to visit. Mr. Davies recollected several of Johnson's remarkable sayings, and was one of the best of the many imitators of his voice and manner, while relating them. He increased my impatience more and more to see the extraordinary man whose works I highly valued, and whose conversation was reported to be so peculiarly excellent.

At last, on Monday the 16th of May, when I was sitting in Mr. Davies's back-parlour, after having drunk tea with him and Mrs. Davies, Johnson unexpectedly came into the shop; and Mr. Davies having perceived him through the glass-door in the room in which we were sitting, advancing towards us,—he announced his awful approach to me, somewhat in the manner of an actor in the part of Horatio, when he addresses Hamlet on the appearance of his father's ghost, "Look, my Lord, it comes." I found that I had a very perfect idea of Johnson's figure, from the portrait of him painted by Sir Joshua Reynolds soon after he had published his Dictionary, in the attitude of sitting in his easy chair in deep meditation; which was the first picture his friend did for him, which Sir Joshua very kindly presented to me, and from which an engraving has been made for this work. Mr. Davies mentioned my name, and respectfully introduced me to him. I was much agitated; and recollecting his prejudice against the Scotch, of which I had heard much, I said to Davies, "Don't tell where I come from."—"From Scotland," cried Davies, roguishly. "Mr. Johnson, (said I) I do indeed come from Scotland, but I cannot help it." I am willing to flatter myself that I meant this as light pleasantry to soothe and conciliate him, and

* As great men of antiquity such as Scipio *Africanus* had an epithet added to their names, in consequence of some celebrated action, so my illustrious friend was often called DICTIONARY JOHNSON, from that wonderful achievement of genius and labour, his "Dictionary of the English Language;" the merit of which I contemplate with more and more admiration.

not as an humiliating abasement at the expence of my country. But however that might be, this speech was somewhat unlucky; for with that quickness of wit for which he was so remarkable, he seized the expression "come from Scotland," which I used in the sense of being of that country; and, as if I had said that I had come away from it, or left it, retorted, "That, Sir, I find, is what a very great many of your countrymen cannot help." This stroke stunned me a good deal; and when we had sat down, I felt myself not a little embarrassed, and apprehensive of what might come next. He then addressed himself to Davies: "What do you think of Garrick? He has refused me an order for the play for Miss Williams, because he knows the house will be full, and that an order would be worth three shillings." Eager to take any opening to get into conversation with him, I ventured to say, "O, Sir, I cannot think Mr. Garrick would grudge such a trifle to you." "Sir, (said he, with a stern look,) I have known David Garrick longer than you have done: and I know no right you have to talk to me on the subject." Perhaps I deserved this check; for it was rather presumptuous in me, an entire stranger, to express any doubt of the justice of his animadversion upon his old acquaintance and pupil. I now felt myself much mortified, and began to think, that the hope which I had long indulged of obtaining his acquaintance was blasted. And, in truth, had not my ardour been uncommonly strong, and my resolution uncommonly persevering, so rough a reception might have deterred me for ever from making any further attempts. Fortunately, however, I remained upon the field not wholly discomfited; and was soon rewarded by hearing some of his conversation, of which I preserved the following short minute, without marking the questions and observations by which it was produced.

"People (he remarked) may be taken in once, who imagine that an authour is greater in private life than other men. Uncommon parts require uncommon opportunities for their exertion.

"In barbarous society, superiority of parts is of real consequence. Great strength or great wisdom is of much value to an individual. But in more polished times there are people to do every thing for money; and then there are a number of other superiorities, such as those of birth and fortune, and rank; that dissipate men's attention, and leave no extraordinary share of respect for personal and intellectual superiority. This is wisely ordered by Providence, to preserve some equality among mankind."

"Sir, this book ('The Elements of Criticism,' which he had taken up,) is a pretty essay, and deserves to be held in some estimation, though much of it is chimerical."

Speaking of one who with more than ordinary boldness attacked publick measures and the royal family, he said, "I think he is safe from the law, but he is an abusive scoundrel; and instead of applying to my Lord Chief Justice to punish him, I would send half a dozen footmen and have him well ducked."

"The notion of liberty amuses the people of England, and helps to keep off the *tedium vitæ*. When a butcher tells you that *his heart bleeds for his country*, he has, in fact, no uneasy feeling."

"Sheridan will not succeed at Bath with his oratory. Ridicule has gone down before him, and I doubt, Derrick is his enemy."

"Derrick may do very well, as long as he can outrun his character; but the moment his character gets up with him, it is all over."

It is, however, but just to record, that some years afterwards, when I reminded him of this sarcasm, he said, "Well, but Derrick has now got a character that he need not run away from."

I was highly pleased with the extraordinary vigour of his conversation, and regretted that I was drawn away from it by an engagement at another place. I had, for a part of the evening, been left alone with him, and had ventured to make an observation now and then, which he received very civilly; so that I was satisfied that though there was a roughness in his manner, there was no ill-nature in his disposition. Davies followed me to the door, and when I complained to him a little of the hard blows which the great man had given me, he kindly took upon him to console me by saying, "Don't be uneasy. I can see he likes you very well."

A few days afterwards I called on Davies, and asked him if he thought I might take the liberty of waiting on Mr. Johnson at his chambers in the Temple. He said I certainly might, and that Mr. Johnson would take it as a compliment. So on Tuesday the 24th of May, after having been enlivened by the witty sallies of Messieurs Thornton,

Wilkes, Churchill, and Lloyd, with whom I had passed the morning, I boldly repaired to Johnson. His chambers were on the first floor of No. 1, Inner-Temple-lane, and I entered them with an impression given me by the Reverend Dr. Blair, of Edinburgh, who had been introduced to him not long before, and described his having "found the Giant in his den"; an expression which, when I came to be pretty well acquainted with Johnson, I repeated to him, and he was diverted at this picturesque account of himself. Dr. Blair had been presented to him by Dr. James Fordyce. At this time the controversy concerning the pieces published by Mr. James Macpherson, as translations of Ossian, was at its height. Johnson had all along denied their authenticity; and, what was still more provoking to their admirers, maintained that they had no merit. The subject having been introduced by Dr. Fordyce, Dr. Blair, relying on the internal evidence of their antiquity, asked Dr. Johnson whether he thought any man of a modern age could have written such poems? Johnson replied, "Yes, Sir, many men, many women, and many children." Johnson at this time, did not know that Dr. Blair had just published a Dissertation, not only defending their authenticity, but seriously ranking them with the poems of Homer and Virgil; and when he was afterwards informed of this circumstance, he expressed some displeasure at Dr. Fordyce's having suggested the topick, and said, "I am not sorry that they got thus much for their pains. Sir, it was like leading one to talk of a book, when the authour is concealed behind the door."

He received me very courteously: but, it must be confessed, that his apartment, and furniture, and morning dress, were sufficiently uncouth. His brown suit of cloaths looked very rusty: he had on a little old shrivelled unpowdered wig, which was too small for his head; his shirt-neck and knees of his breeches were loose; his black worsted stockings ill drawn up; and he had a pair of unbuckled shoes by way of slippers. But all these slovenly particularities were forgotten the moment that he began to talk. Some gentlemen, whom I do not recollect, were sitting with him; and when they went away, I also rose; but he said to me, "Nay, don't go."—"Sir, (said I), I am afraid that I intrude upon you. It is benevolent to allow me to sit and hear you." He seemed pleased with this compliment, which I sincerely paid him, and answered, "Sir, I am obliged to any man who visits me."—I have preserved the following short minute of what passed this day.

"Madness frequently discovers itself merely by unnecessary deviation from the usual modes of the world. My poor friend Smart showed the disturbance of his mind, by falling upon his knees, and saying his prayers in the street, or in any other unusual place. Now although, rationally speaking, it is greater madness not to pray at all, than to pray as Smart did, I am afraid there are so many who do not pray, that their understanding is not called in question."

Concerning this unfortunate poet, Christopher Smart, who was confined in a mad-house, he had, at another time, the following conversation with Dr. Burney.—BURNEY. "How does poor Smart do, Sir; is he likely to recover?" JOHNSON. "It seems as if his mind had ceased to struggle with the disease; for he grows fat upon it." BURNEY. "Perhaps, Sir, that may be from want of exercise." JOHNSON. "No, Sir; he has partly as much exercise as he used to have, for he digs in the garden. Indeed, before his confinement, he used for exercise to walk to the alehouse; but he was *carried* back again. I did not think he ought to be shut up. His infirmities were not noxious to society. He insisted on people praying with him; and I'd as lief pray with Kit Smart as any one else. Another charge was, that he did not love clean linen; and I have no passion for it."

. . .

Finding him in a placid humour, and wishing to avail myself of the opportunity which I fortunately had of consulting a sage, to hear whose wisdom, I conceived, in the ardour of youthful imagination, that men filled with a noble enthusiasm for intellectual improvement would gladly have resorted from distant lands;—I opened my mind to him ingenuously, and gave him a little sketch of my life, to which he was pleased to listen with great attention.

I acknowledged, that though educated very strictly in the principles of religion, I had for some time been misled into a certain degree of infidelity; but that I was come now to a better way of thinking, and was fully satisfied of the truth of the Christian revelation, though I was not clear as to every point considered to be orthodox. Being at all times a curious examiner of the human mind, and pleased with an undisguised display of what had passed in it, he called to me with warmth, "Give me your hand; I have taken a liking to you." He then began to descant upon the force of testimony, and the little we could know of final causes; so that the objections of, why was it so? or why was it not so? ought not to disturb us; adding, that he himself had at one period been guilty of a temporary neglect of religion, but that it was not the result of argument, but mere absence of thought.

After having given credit to reports of his bigotry, I was agreeably surprised when he expressed the following very liberal sentiment, which has the additional value of obviating an objection to our holy religion, founded upon the discordant tenets of Christians themselves: "For my part, Sir, I think all Christians, whether Papists or Protestants, agree in the essential articles, and that their differences are trivial, and rather political than religious."

We talked of belief in ghosts. He said, "Sir, I make a distinction between what a man may experience by the mere strength of his imagination, and what imagination cannot possibly produce. Thus, suppose I should think that I saw a form, and heard a voice cry, 'Johnson, you are a very wicked fellow, and unless you repent you will certainly be punished;' my own unworthiness is so deeply impressed upon my mind, that I might *imagine* I thus saw and heard, and therefore I should not believe that an external communication had been made to me. But if a form should appear, and a voice should tell me that a particular man had died at a particular place, and a particular hour, a fact which I had no apprehension of, nor any means of knowing, and this fact, with all its circumstances, should afterwards be unquestionably proved, I should, in that case, be persuaded that I had supernatural intelligence imparted to me."

Here is it proper, once for all, to give a true and fair statement of Johnson's way of thinking upon the question, whether departed spirits are ever permitted to appear in this world, or in any way to operate upon human life. He has been ignorantly misrepresented as weakly credulous upon that subject; and, therefore, though I feel an inclination to disdain and treat with silent contempt so foolish a notion concerning my illustrious friend, yet as I find it has gained ground, it is necessary to refute it. The real fact then is, that Johnson had a very philosophical mind, and such a rational respect for testimony, as to make him submit his understanding to what was authentically proved, though he could not comprehend why it was so. Being thus disposed, he was willing to inquire into the truth of any relation of supernatural agency, a general belief of which has prevailed in all nations and ages. But so far was he from being the dupe of implicit faith, that he examined the matter with a jealous attention, and no man was more ready to refute its falsehood when he had discovered it.

. . .

A.D. 1764

AGE 55

In this year, except what he may have done in revising Shakspeare, we do not find that he laboured much in literature. He wrote a review of Grainger's "Sugar Cane, a Poem," in the London Chronicle. He told me, that Dr. Percy wrote the greatest part of this review; but, I imagine, he did not recollect it distinctly, for it appears to be mostly, if not altogether, his own. He also wrote in the Critical Review, an account of Goldsmith's excellent poem, "The Traveller."

The ease and the independence to which he had at last attained by royal munificence, increased his natural indolence. In his "Meditations," he thus accuses himself: "GOOD FRIDAY, April 20, 1764. I have made no reformation; I have lived totally useless, more sensual in thought, and more addicted to wine and meat." And next morning he thus feelingly complains: "My indolence, since my last reception of the sacrament, has sunk into grosser sluggishness, and my dissipation spread into wilder negligence. My thoughts have been clouded with sensuality; and, except that from the beginning of this year I have, in some measure, forborne excess of strong drink, my appetites have predominated over my reason. A kind of strange oblivion has overspread me, so that I know not what has become of the last year; and perceive that incidents and intelligence pass over me without leaving any impression." He then solemnly says, "This is not the life to which heaven is promised;" and he earnestly resolves an amendment.

It was his custom to observe certain days with

a pious abstraction: viz, New-year's day, the day of his wife's death, Good Friday, Easter-day, and his own birth-day. He this year says, "I have now spent fifty-five years in resolving: having, from the earliest time almost that I can remember, been forming schemes of a better life. I have done nothing. The need of doing, therefore, is pressing, since the time of doing is short. O GOD, grant me to resolve aright, and to keep my resolutions, for JESUS CHRIST's sake. Amen." Such a tenderness of conscience, such a fervent desire of improvement, will rarely be found. It is, surely, not decent in those who are hardened in indifference to spiritual improvement, to treat this pious anxiety of Johnson with contempt.

About this time he was afflicted with a very severe return of the hypochondriack disorder, which was ever lurking about him. He was so ill, as, notwithstanding his remarkable love of company, to be entirely averse to society, the most fatal symptom of that malady. Dr. Adams told me, that, as an old friend he was admitted to visit him, and that he found him in a deplorable state, sighing, groaning, talking to himself, and restlessly walking from room to room. He then used this emphatical expression of the misery which he felt: "I would consent to have a limb amputated to recover my spirits."

Talking to himself was, indeed, one of his singularities ever since I knew him. I was certain that he was frequently uttering pious ejaculations; for fragments of the Lord's Prayer have been distinctly overheard. His friend Mr. Thomas Davies, of whom Churchill says,

> That Davies hath a very pretty wife,——

when Dr. Johnson muttered—"lead us not into temptation," used with waggish and gallant humour to whisper [to] Mrs. Davies, "You, my dear, are the cause of this."

He had another particularity, of which none of his friends even ventured to ask an explanation. It appeared to me some superstitious habit, which he had contracted early, and from which he had never called upon his reason to disentangle him. This was his anxious care to go out or in at a door or passage, by a certain number of steps from a certain point, or at least so as that either his right or his left foot, (I am not certain which,) should constantly make the first actual movement when he came close to the door or passage. Thus I conjecture: for I have, upon innumerable occasions, observed him suddenly stop, and then seem to count his steps with a deep earnestness; and when he had neglected or gone wrong in this sort of magical movement, I have seen him go back again, put himself in a proper posture to begin the ceremony, and, having gone through it, break from his abstraction, walk briskly on, and join his companion. A strange instance of something of this nature, even when on horseback, happened when he was in the Isle of Sky. Sir Joshua Reynolds has observed him to go a good way about, rather than cross a particular alley in Leicesterfields; but this Sir Joshua imputed to his having had some disagreeable recollection associated with it.

That the most minute singularities which belonged to him, and made very observable parts of his appearance and manner, may not be omitted, it is requisite to mention, that while talking or even musing as he sat in his chair, he commonly held his head to one side towards his right shoulder, and shook it in a tremulous manner, moving his body backwards and forwards, and rubbing his left knee in the same direction, with the palm of his hand. In the intervals of articulating he made various sounds with his mouth; sometimes as if ruminating, or what is called chewing the cud, sometimes giving a half whistle, sometimes making his tongue play backwards from the roof of his mouth, as if clucking like a hen, and sometimes protruding it against his upper gums in front, as if pronouncing quickly under his breath, *too, too, too:* all this accompanied sometimes with a thoughtful look, but more frequently with a smile. Generally when he had concluded a period, in the course of a dispute, by which time he was a good deal exhausted by violence and vociferation, he used to blow out his breath like a whale. This I suppose was a relief to his lungs; and seemed in him to be a contemptuous mode of expression, as if he had made the arguments of his opponent fly like chaff before the wind.

I am fully aware how very obvious an occasion I here give for the sneering jocularity of such as have no relish of an exact likeness; which to render complete, he who draws it must not disdain the slightest strokes. But if witlings should be inclined to attack this account, let them have the candour to quote what I have offered in my defence.

. . .

A.D. 1765

AGE 56

. . .

This year was distinguished by his being introduced into the family of Mr. Thrale, one of the most eminent brewers in England, and member of Parliament for the borough of Southwark. Foreigners are not a little amazed, when they hear of brewers, distillers, and men in similar departments of trade, held forth as persons of considerable consequence. In this great commercial country it is natural that a situation which produces much wealth should be considered as very respectable; and, no doubt, honest industry is entitled to esteem. But, perhaps, the too rapid advances of men of low extraction tends to lessen the value of that distinction by birth and gentility, which has ever been found beneficial to the grand scheme of subordination. Johnson used to give this account of the rise of Mr. Thrale's father: "He worked at six shillings a week for twenty years in the great brewery, which afterwards was his own. The proprietor of it had an only daughter, who was married to a nobleman. It was not fit that a peer should continue the business. On the old man's death, therefore, the brewery was to be sold. To find a purchaser for so large a property was a difficult matter; and, after some time, it was suggested, that it would be adviseable to treat with Thrale, a sensible, active, honest man, who had been employed in the house, and to transfer the whole to him for thirty thousand pounds, security being taken upon the property. This was accordingly settled. In eleven years Thrale paid the purchase-money. He acquired a large fortune, and lived to be a member of Parliament for Southwark. But what was most remarkable was the liberality with which he used his riches. He gave his son and daughters the best education. The esteem which his good conduct procured him from the nobleman who had married his master's daughter, made him to be treated with much attention; and his son, both at school and at the University of Oxford, associated with young men of the first rank. His allowance from his father, after he left college, was splendid; not less than a thousand a year. This, in a man who had risen as old Thrale did, was a very extraordinary instance of generosity. He used to say, 'If this young dog does not find so much after I am gone as he expects, let him remember that he has had a great deal in my own time.' "

The son, though in affluent circumstances, had good sense enough to carry on his father's trade, which was of such extent, that I remember he once told me, he would not quit it for an annuity of ten thousand a year; "Not (said he,) that I get ten thousand a year by it, but it is an estate to a family." Having left daughters only, the property was sold for the immense sum of one hundred and thirty-five thousand pounds; a magnificent proof of what may be done by fair trade in a long period of time.

There may be some who think that a new system of gentility might be established, upon principles totally different from what have hitherto prevailed. Our present heraldry, it may be said, is suited to the barbarous times in which it had its origin. It is chiefly founded upon ferocious merit, upon military excellence. Why, in civilised times, we may be asked, should there not be rank and honours, upon principles, which, independent of long custom, are certainly not less worthy, and which, when once allowed to be connected with elevation and precedency, would obtain the same dignity in our imagination? Why should not the knowledge, the skill, the expertness, the assiduity, and the spirited hazards of trade and commerce, when crowned with success, be entitled to give those flattering distinctions by which mankind are so universally captivated?

Such are the specious, but false, arguments for a proposition which always will find numerous advocates, in a nation where men are every day starting up from obscurity to wealth. To refute them is needless. The general sense of mankind cries out, with irresistible force, "*Un gentilhomme est toujours gentilhomme.*"

Mr. Thrale had married Miss Hester Lynch Salusbury, of good Welch extraction, a lady of lively talents, improved by education. That Johnson's introduction into Mr. Thrale's family, which contributed so much to the happiness of his life, was owing to her desire for his conversation, is a very probable and the general supposition: but it is not the truth. Mr. Murphy, who was intimate with Mr. Thrale, having spoken very highly of Dr. Johnson, he was requested to make them acquainted. This being mentioned to Johnson, he accepted of an invitation to dinner at Thrale's, and was so much pleased with his reception, both by Mr. and Mrs. Thrale, and they so much pleased with him, that his invitations to their house were more and more frequent, till at last he became one of the family, and an apartment was appropriated to him, both in their house at Southwark and in their villa at Streatham.

Johnson had a very sincere esteem for Mr. Thrale, as a man of excellent principles, a good scholar, well skilled in trade, of a sound understanding, and of manners such as presented the character of a plain independent English 'Squire. As this family will frequently be mentioned in the course of the following pages, and as a false notion has prevailed that Mr. Thrale was inferiour, and in some degree insignificant, compared with Mrs. Thrale, it may be proper to give a true state of the case from the authority of Johnson himself in his own words.

"I know no man, (said he,) who is more master of his wife and family than Thrale. If he but holds up a finger, he is obeyed. It is a great mistake to suppose that she is above him in literary attainments. She is more flippant; but he has ten times her learning: he is a regular scholar; but her learning is that of a school-boy in one of the lower forms." My readers may naturally wish for some representation of the figures of this couple. Mr. Thrale was tall, well proportioned, and stately. As for *Madam,* or *my Mistress,* by which epithets Johnson used to mention Mrs. Thrale, she was short, plump, and brisk. She has herself given us a lively view of the idea which Johnson had of her person, on her appearing before him in a dark-coloured gown: "You little creatures should never wear those sort of clothes, however; they are unsuitable in every way. What! have not all insects gay colours!" Mr. Thrale gave his wife a liberal indulgence, both in the choice of their company, and in the mode of entertaining them. He understood and valued Johnson, without remission, from their first acquaintance to the day of his death. Mrs. Thrale was enchanted with Johnson's conversation for its own sake, and had also a very allowable vanity in appearing to be honoured with the attention of so celebrated a man.

Nothing could be more fortunate for Johnson than this connection. He had at Mr. Thrale's all the comforts and even luxuries of life: his melancholy was diverted, and his irregular habits lessened by association with an agreeable and well ordered family. He was treated with the utmost respect, and even affection. The vivacity of Mrs. Thrale's literary talk roused him to cheerfulness and exertion, even when they were alone. But this was not often the case; for he found here a constant succession of what gave him the highest enjoyment, the society of the learned, the witty, and the eminent in every way; who were assembled in numerous companies; called forth his wonderful powers, and gratified him with admiration, to which no man could be insensible.

In the October of this year he at length gave to the world his edition of Shakspeare, which, if it had no other merit but that of producing his Preface, in which the excellencies and defects of that immortal bard are displayed with a masterly hand, the nation would have had no reason to complain. A blind indiscriminate admiration of Shakspeare had exposed the British nation to the ridicule of foreigners. Johnson, by candidly admitting the faults of his poet, had the more credit in bestowing on him deserved and indisputable praise; and doubtless none of all his panegyrists have done him half so much honour. Their praise was like that of a counsel, upon his own side of the cause; Johnson's was like the grave, well considered, and impartial opinion of the judge, which falls from his lips with weight, and is received with reverence. What he did as a commentator has no small share of merit, though his researches were not so ample, and his investigations so acute as they might have been; which we now certainly know from the labours of other able and ingenious criticks who have followed him. He has enriched his edition with a concise account of each play, and of his characteristick excellence. Many of his notes have illustrated obscurities in the text, and placed passages eminent for beauty in a more conspicuous light; and he has, in general, exhibited such a mode of annotation, as may be beneficial to all subsequent editors.

. . .

A.D. 1767

AGE 58

. . .

In February, 1767, there happened one of the most remarkable incidents of Johnson's life, which gratified his monarchical enthusiasm, and which he loved to relate with all its circumstances, when requested by his friends. This was his being honoured by a private conversation with his Majesty, in the library at the Queen's house. He had frequently visited those splendid rooms, and noble collection of books,* which he used to say was more numerous and curious than he supposed any person could have made in the time which the King had employed. Mr. Barnard, the librarian, took care that he should have every accommodation that should contribute to his ease and convenience, while indulging his literary taste in that place: so that he had here a very agreeable resource at leisure hours.

His Majesty having been informed of his occasional visits, was pleased to signify a desire that he should be told when Dr. Johnson came next to the library. Accordingly, the next time that Johnson did come, as soon as he was fairly engaged with a book, on which, while he sat by the fire, he seemed quite intent, Mr. Barnard stole round to the apartment where the King was, and, in obedience to his Majesty's commands, mentioned that Dr. Johnson was then in the library. His Majesty said he was at leisure, and would go to him: upon which Mr. Barnard took one of the candles that stood on the King's table, and lighted his Majesty through a suite of rooms, till they came to a private door into the library, of which his Majesty had the key. Being entered, Mr. Barnard stepped forward hastily to Dr. Johnson, who was still in a profound study, and whispered to him, "Sir, here is the King." Johnson started up, and stood still. His Majesty approached him, and at once was courteously easy.*

His Majesty began by observing, that he understood he came sometimes to the library; and then mentioned his having heard that the Doctor had been lately at Oxford, asked him if he was not fond of going thither. To which Johnson answered, that he was indeed fond of going to Oxford sometimes, but was likewise glad to come back again. The King then asked him what they were doing at Oxford. Johnson answered, he could not much commend their diligence, but that in some respects they were mended, for they had put their press under better regulations, and were at that time printing Polybius. He was then asked whether there were better libraries at Oxford or Cambridge. He answered, he believed the Bodleian was larger than any they had at Cambridge; at the same time adding, "I hope, whether we have more books or not than they have at Cambridge, we shall make

* Dr. Johnson had the honour of contributing his assistance towards the formation of this library; for I have read a long letter from him to Mr. Barnard, giving the most masterly instructions on the subject. I wished much to have gratified my readers with the perusal of his letter, and have reason to think that his Majesty would have been graciously pleased to permit its publication; but Mr. Barnard, to whom I applied, declined it "on his own account."

* The particulars of this conversation I have been at great pains to collect with the utmost authenticity, from Dr. Johnson's own detail to myself; from Mr. Langton who was present when he gave an account of it to Dr. Joseph Warton, and several other friends at Sir Joshua Reynolds's; from Mr. Barnard; from the copy of a letter written by the late Mr. Strahan the printer, to Bishop Warburton; and from a minute, the original of which is among the papers of the late Sir James Caldwell, and a copy of which was most obligingly obtained for me from his son Sir John Caldwell, by Sir Francis Lumm. To all these gentlemen I beg leave to make my grateful acknowledgements, and particularly to Sir Francis Lumm, who was pleased to take a great deal of trouble, and even had the minute laid before the King by Lord Caermarthen, now Duke of Leeds, then one of his Majesty's Principal Secretaries of State, who announced to Sir Francis the Royal pleasure concerning it by a letter, in these words: "I have the King's commands to assure you, Sir, how sensible his Majesty is of your attention in communicating the minute of the conversation previous to its publication. As there appears no objection to your complying with Mr. Boswell's wishes on the subject, you are at full liberty to deliver it to that gentleman, to make such use of in his Life of Dr. Johnson, as he may think proper."

as good use of them as they do." Being asked whether All-Souls or Christ-Church library was the largest, he answered, "All-Souls library is the largest we have, except the Bodleian." "Ay, (said the King,) that is the publick library."

His Majesty enquired if he was then writing any thing. He answered, he was not, for he had pretty well told the world what he knew, and must now read to acquire more knowledge. The King, as it should seem with a view to urge him to rely on his own stores as an original writer, and to continue his labours, then said, "I do not think you borrow much from any body." Johnson said, he thought he had already done his part as a writer. "I should have thought so too, (said the King,) if you had not written so well."—Johnson observed to me, upon this, that "No man could have paid a handsomer compliment; and it was fit for a King to pay. It was decisive." When asked by another friend, at Sir Joshua Reynolds's, whether he made any reply to this high compliment, he answered, "No, Sir. When the King had said it, it was to be so. It was not for me to bandy civilities with my Sovereign." Perhaps no man who had spent his whole life in courts could have shewn a more nice and dignified sense of true politeness than Johnson did in this instance.

His Majesty having observed to him that he supposed he must have read a great deal; Johnson answered, that he thought more than he read; that he had read a great deal in the early part of his life, but having fallen into ill health, he had not been able to read much, compared with others: for instance, he said he had not read much, compared with Dr. Warburton. Upon which the King said, that he heard Dr. Warburton was a man of such general knowledge, that you could scarce talk with him on any subject on which he was not qualified to speak; and that his learning resembled Garrick's acting, in its universality. His Majesty then talked of the controversy between Warburton and Lowth, which he seemed to have read, and asked Johnson what he thought of it. Johnson answered, "Warburton has most general, most scholastic learning; Lowth is the more correct scholar. I do not know which of them calls names best." The King was pleased to say he was of the same opinion; adding, "You do not think, then, Dr. Johnson, that there was much argument in the case." Johnson said, he did not think there was. "Why truly, (said the King,) when once it comes to calling names, argument is pretty well at an end."

His Majesty then asked him what he thought of Lord Lyttelton's history, which was then just published. Johnson said, he thought his style pretty good, but that he had blamed Henry the Second rather too much. "Why, (said the King), they seldom do these things by halves." "No, Sir, (answered Johnson), not to Kings." But fearing to be misunderstood, he proceeded to explain himself; and immediately subjoined, "That for those who spoke worse of Kings than they deserved, he could find no excuse; but that he could more easily conceive how some might speak better of them than they deserved, without any ill intention; for, as Kings had much in their power to give, those who were favoured by them would frequently, from gratitude, exaggerate their praises: and as this proceeded from a good motive, it was certainly excusable, as far as errour could be excusable."

The King then asked him what he thought of Dr. Hill. Johnson answered, that he was an ingenious man, but had no veracity; and immediately mentioned, as an instance of it, an assertion of that writer, that he had seen objects magnified to a much greater degree by using three or four microscopes at a time than by using one. "Now, (added Johnson,) every one acquainted with microscopes knows, that the more of them he looks through, the less the object will appear." "Why, (replied the King,) this is not only telling an untruth, but telling it clumsily; for, if that be the case, every one who can look through a microscope will be able to detect him."

"I now, (said Johnson to his friends, when relating what had passed,) began to consider that I was deprecating this man in the estimation of his Sovereign, and thought it was time for me to say something that might be more favourable." He added, therefore, that Dr. Hill was, notwithstanding, a very curious observer; and if he would have been contented to tell the world no more than he knew, he might have been a very considerable man, and needed not to have recourse to such mean expedients to raise his reputation.

The King then talked of literary journals, mentioned particularly the *Journal des Savans,* and asked Johnson if it was well done. Johnson said, it was formerly very well done, and gave some account of the persons who began it, and carried it on for some years: enlarging at the same time, on the nature and use of such works. The King asked him if it was well done now. Johnson answered, he had no reason to think that it was. The King then asked him if there were any other literary journals published in this kingdom, except the Monthly and Critical Reviews; and on being answered there was no other, his Majesty asked which of them was the best: Johnson answered, that the Monthly Review was done with most care, the Critical upon the best principles; adding that the authours of the Monthly Review were enemies to the Church. This the King said he was sorry to hear.

The conversation next turned on the Philosophical Transactions, when Johnson observed that they had now a better method of arranging their materials than formerly. "Ay, (said the King), they are obliged to Dr. Johnson for that;" for his Majesty had heard and remembered the circumstance, which Johnson himself had forgot.

His Majesty expressed a desire to have the literary biography of this country ably executed, and proposed to Dr. Johnson to undertake it. Johnson signified his readiness to comply with his Majesty's wishes.

During the whole of this interview, Johnson talked to his Majesty with profound respect, but still in his firm manly manner, with a sonorous voice, and never in that subdued tone which is commonly used at the levee and in the drawing room. After the King withdrew, Johnson shewed himself highly pleased with his Majesty's conversation, and gracious behaviour. He said to Mr. Barnard, "Sir, they may talk of the King as they will; but he is the finest gentleman I have ever seen." And he afterwards observed to Mr. Langton, "Sir, his manners are those of as fine a gentleman as we may suppose Lewis the Fourteenth or Charles the Second."

At Sir Joshua Reynolds's, where a circle of Johnson's friends was collected round him to hear his account of this memorable conversation, Dr. Joseph Warton, in his frank and lively manner, was very active in pressing him to mention the particulars. "Come now, Sir, this is an interesting matter; do favour us with it." Johnson with great good humour, complied.

He told them, "I found his Majesty wished I should talk and I made it my business to talk. I find it does a man good to be talked to by his sovereign. In the first place, a man cannot be in a passion—." Here some question interrupted him, which is to be regretted, as he certainly would have pointed out and illustrated many circumstances of advantage, from being in a situation, where the powers of the mind are at once excited to vigorous exertion, and tempered by reverential awe.

. . .

A.D. 1769

AGE 60

. . .

Talking of a London life, he said, "The happiness of London is not to be conceived but by those who have been in it. I will venture to say, there is more learning and science within the circumference of ten miles from where we now sit, than in all the rest of the kingdom." Boswell. "The only disadvantage is the great distance at which people live from one another." Johnson. "Yes, Sir; but that is occasioned by the largeness of it, which is the cause of all the other advantages." Boswell. "Sometimes I have been in the humour of wishing to retire to a desart." Johnson. "Sir, you have desart enough in Scotland."

Although I had promised myself a great deal of instructive conversation with him on the conduct of the married state, of which I had then a near prospect, he did not say much upon that topick. Mr. Seward heard him once say, that "a man has a very bad chance for happiness in that state, unless he marries a woman of very strong and fixed principles of religion." He maintained to me contrary to the common notion, that a woman would not be the worse wife for being learned; in which, from all that I have observed of *Artemisias,* I humbly differed from him. That a woman should be sensible and well informed, I allow to be a great advantage; and think that Sir Thomas Overbury,[7] in his rude versification, has very judiciously

7. Sir Thomas Overbury: poet (1581–1613), chiefly famous for his prose sketches of types of character.

pointed out that degree of intelligence which is to be desired in a female companion:

Give me, next *good*, an *understanding wife*,
By Nature *wise*, not *learned* by much art;
Some *knowledge* on her side will all my life
More scope of conversation impart;
Besides, her inborne virtue fortifie;
They are most firmly good, who best know
why.[8]

When I censured a gentleman of my acquaintance for marrying a second time, as it shewed a disregard of his first wife, he said "Not at all, Sir. On the contrary, were he not to marry again, it might be concluded that his first wife had given him a disgust to marriage; but by taking a second wife he pays the highest compliment to the first, by shewing that she made him so happy as a married man, that he wishes to be so a second time." So ingenious a turn did he give to this delicate question. And yet, on another occasion, he owned that he once had almost asked a promise of Mrs. Johnson that she would not marry again, but had checked himself. Indeed I cannot help thinking, that in his case the request would have been unreasonable; for if Mrs. Johnson forgot, or thought it no injury to the memory of her first love,—the husband of her youth and the father of her children,—to make a second marriage, why should she be precluded from a third, should she be so inclined? In Johnson's persevering fond appropriation of his *Tetty*, even after her decease, he seems totally to have overlooked the prior claim of the honest Birmingham trader. I presume that her having been married before had, at times, given him some uneasiness; for I remember his observing upon the marriage of one of our common friends, "He has done a very foolish thing, Sir; he has married a widow, when he might have had a maid."

. . .

I had hired a Bohemian as my servant while I remained in London, and being much pleased with him, I asked Dr. Johnson whether his being a Roman Catholick should prevent my taking him with me to Scotland. JOHNSON. "Why no, Sir. If *he* has no objections, you can have none." BOSWELL. "So, Sir, you are no great enemy to the Roman Catholick Religion." JOHNSON. "No more, Sir, than to the Presbyterian religion." BOSWELL. "You are joking." JOHNSON. "No, Sir, I really think so. Nay, Sir, of the two, I prefer the Popish." BOSWELL. "How so, Sir?" JOHNSON. "Why, Sir, the Presbyterians have no church, no apostolical ordination." BOSWELL. "And do you think that absolutely essential, Sir?" JOHNSON. "Why, Sir, as it was an apostolical institution, I think it is dangerous to be without it. And, Sir, the Presbyterians have no publick worship: they have no form of prayer in which they know they are to join. They go to hear a man pray, and are to judge whether they will join with him." BOSWELL. "But, Sir, their doctrine is the same with that of the Church of England. Their confession of faith, and the thirty-nine articles contain the same points, even the doctrine of predestination." JOHNSON. "Why, yes, Sir; predestination was a part of the clamour of the times, so it is mentioned in our articles, but with as little positiveness as could be." BOSWELL. "Is it necessary, Sir, to believe all the thirty-nine articles?" JOHNSON. "Why, Sir, that is a question which has been much agitated. Some have thought it necessary that they should all be believed; others have considered them to be only articles of peace, that is to say, you are not to preach against them." BOSWELL. "It appears to me, Sir, that predestination, or what is equivalent to it, cannot be avoided, if we hold an universal prescience in the Deity." JOHNSON. "Why, Sir, does not GOD every day see things going on without preventing them?" BOSWELL. "True, Sir, but if a thing be *certainly* foreseen, it must be fixed, and cannot happen otherwise; and if we apply this consideration to the human mind, there is no free will, nor do I see how prayer can be of any avail." He mentioned Dr. Clarke, and Bishop Bramhall on Liberty and Necessity, and bid me read South's Sermons on Prayer; but avoided the question which has excruciated philosophers and divines, beyond any other. I did not press it further, when I perceived that he was displeased, and shrunk from any abridgement of an attribute usually ascribed to the Divinity, however irreconcileable in its full extent with the grand system of moral government. His supposed orthodoxy here cramped the vigourous powers of his understanding. He was confined by a chain which early imagination and long habit made him think massy and strong, but which, had he ventured to try, he could at once have snapt asunder.

8. Sir Thomas Overbury's poem "A Wife" (1614).

I proceeded: "What do you think, Sir, of Purgatory, as believed by the Roman Catholicks?" JOHNSON. "Why, Sir, it is a very harmless doctrine. They are of opinion that the generality of mankind are neither so obstinately wicked as to deserve everlasting punishment, nor so good as to merit being admitted into the society of blessed spirits; and therefore that GOD is graciously pleased to allow of a middle state, where they may be purified by certain degrees of suffering. You see, Sir, there is nothing unreasonable in this." BOSWELL. "But then, Sir, their masses for the dead?" JOHNSON. "Why, Sir, if it be once establishd that there are souls in purgatory, it is as proper to pray for *them,* as for our brethren of mankind who are yet in this life." BOSWELL. "The idolatry of the Mass?" JOHNSON. "Sir, there is no idolatry in the Mass. They believe GOD to be there, and they adore him." BOSWELL. "The worship of Saints?" JOHNSON. "Sir, they do not worship saints; they invoke them; they only ask their prayers. I am talking all this time of the *doctrines* of the Church of Rome. I grant you that in *practice,* Purgatory is made a lucrative imposition, and that the people do become idolatrous as they recommend themselves to the tutelary protection of particular saints. I think their giving the sacrament only in one kind is criminal, because it is contrary to the express institution of CHRIST, and I wonder how the Council of Trent admitted it." BOSWELL. "Confession?" JOHNSON. "Why, I don't know but that is a good thing. The scripture says, 'Confess your faults one to another,' and the priests confess as well as the laity. Then it must be considered that their absolution is only upon repentance, and often upon penance also. You think your sins may be forgiven without penance, upon repentance alone."

I thus ventured to mention all the common objections against the Roman Catholic Church, that I might hear so great a man upon them. What he said is here accurately recorded. But it is not improbable that if one had taken the other side, he might have reasoned differently.

. . .

A.D. 1776

AGE 67

I am now to record a very curious incident in Dr. Johnson's life, which fell under my own observation; of which *pars magna fui,*[9] and which I am persuaded will, with the liberal-minded, be much to his credit.

My desire of being acquainted with celebrated men of every description, had made me, much about the same time, obtain an introduction to Dr. Samuel Johnson and to John Wilkes, Esq.[10] Two men more different could perhaps not be selected out of all mankind. They had even attacked one another with some asperity in their writings; yet I lived in habits of friendship with both. I could fully relish the excellence of each; for I have ever delighted in that intellectual chymistry, which can separate good qualities from evil in the same person.

Sir John Pringle, "mine own friend and my Father's friend," between whom and Dr. Johnson I in vain wished to establish an acquaintance, as I respected and lived in intimacy with both of them, observed to me once, very ingeniously, "It is not in friendship as in mathematicks, where two things, each equal to a third, are equal between themselves. You agree with Johnson as a middle quality, and you agree with me as a middle quality; but Johnson and I should not agree." Sir John was not sufficiently flexible; so I desisted; knowing, indeed, that the repulsion was equally strong on the part of Johnson; who, I know not from what cause, unless his being a Scotchman, had formed a very erroneous opinion of Sir John. But I conceived an irresistible wish, if possible, to bring Dr. Johnson and Mr. Wilkes together. How to manage it, was a nice and difficult matter.

My worthy booksellers and friends, Messieurs Dilly in the Poultry, at whose hospitable and well-covered table I have seen a greater number of lit-

9. ***pars . . . fui:*** "I was a great part." See Virgil, *Aeneid,* ii, 5. **10.** John Wilkes (1727–1797), rabble-rousing member of the House of Commons, twice expelled for libelous publications. He became Sheriff of London and Middlesex, finally took his seat in 1774, in which year he was Lord Mayor of London. Wilkes, always the flamboyant politician, was nevertheless a champion of political rights.

erary men, than at any other, except that of Sir Joshua Reynolds, had invited me to meet Mr. Wilkes and some more gentlemen, on Wednesday, May 15. "Pray (said I,) let us have Dr. Johnson." —"What with Mr. Wilkes? not for the world, (said Mr. Edward Dilly;) Dr. Johnson would never forgive me."—"Come, (said I,) if you'll let me negociate for you, I will be answerable that all shall go well." Dilly. "Nay, if you will take it upon you, I am sure I shall be very happy to see them both here."

Notwithstanding the high veneration which I entertained for Dr. Johnson, I was sensible that he was sometimes a little actuated by the spirit of contradiction, and by means of that I hoped I should gain my point. I was persuaded that if I had come upon him with a direct proposal, "Sir, will you dine in company with Jack Wilkes?" he would have flown into a passion, and would probably have answered, "Dine with Jack Wilkes, Sir! I'd as soon dine with Jack Ketch."[11] I therefore, while we were sitting quietly by ourselves at his house in an evening, took occasion to open my plan thus:— "Mr. Dilly, Sir, sends his respectful compliments to you, and would be happy if you would do him the honour to dine with him on Wednesday next along with me, as I must soon go to Scotland." Johnson. "Sir, I am obliged to Mr. Dilly. I will wait upon him—" Boswell. "Provided, Sir, I suppose, that the company which he is to have, is agreeable to you." Johnson. "What do you mean, Sir? What do you take me for? Do you think I am so ignorant of the world, as to imagine that I am to prescribe to a gentleman what company he is to have at his table?" Boswell. "I beg your pardon, Sir, for wishing to prevent you from meeting people whom you might not like. Perhaps he may have some of what he calls his patriotick friends with him." Johnson. "Well, Sir, and what then? What care *I* for his *patriotick friends*? Poh!" Boswell. "I should not be surprized to find Jack Wilkes there." Johnson. "And if Jack Wilkes *should* be there, what is that to *me*, Sir? My dear friend, let us have no more of this. I am sorry to be angry with you; but really it is treating me strangely to talk to me as if I could not meet any company whatever, occasionally." Boswell. "Pray, forgive me, Sir: I meant well. But you shall meet whoever comes, for me." Thus I secured him, and told Dilly that he would find him very well pleased to be one of his guests on the day appointed.

Upon the much expected Wednesday, I called on him about half an hour before dinner, as I often did when we were to dine out together, to see that he was ready in time, and to accompany him. I found him buffeting his books, as upon a former occasion, covered with dust, and making no preparation for going abroad. "How is this, Sir? (said I). Don't you recollect that you are to dine at Mr. Dilly's?" Johnson. "Sir, I did not think of going to Dilly's: it went out of my head. I have ordered dinner at home with Mrs. Williams." Boswell. "But, my dear Sir, you know you were engaged to Mr. Dilly, and I told him so. He will expect you, and will be much disappointed if you don't come." Johnson. "You must talk to Mrs. Williams about this."

Here was a sad dilemma. I feared that what I was so confident I had secured, would yet be frustrated. He had accustomed himself to shew Mrs. Williams such a degree of humane attention, as frequently imposed some restraint upon him; and I knew that if she should be obstinate, he would not stir. I hastened down stairs to the blind lady's room, and told her I was in great uneasiness, for Dr. Johnson had engaged to me to dine this day at Mr. Dilly's, but that he had told me he had forgotten his engagement, and had ordered dinner at home. "Yes, Sir, (said she, pretty peevishly,) Dr. Johnson is to dine at home."—"Madam, (said I,) his respect for you is such, that I know he will not leave you, unless you absolutely desire it. But as you have so much of his company, I hope you will be good enough to forego it for a day: as Mr. Dilly is a very worthy man, has frequently had agreeable parties at his house for Dr. Johnson, and will be vexed if the Doctor neglects him to-day. And then, Madam, be pleased to consider my situation; I carried the message, and I assured Mr. Dilly that Dr. Johnson was to come; and no doubt he has made a dinner, and invited a company, and boasted of the honour he expected to have. I shall be quite disgraced if the Doctor is not there." She gradually softened to my solicitations, which were certainly as earnest as most entreaties to ladies upon any occasion, and was graciously pleased to empower me to tell Dr. Johnson, "That all things considered, she thought he should certainly go."

11. Jack Ketch was the executioner at Tyburn.

I flew back to him, still in dust, and careless of what should be the event, "indifferent in his choice to go or stay;" but as soon as I had announced to him Mrs. Williams's consent, he roared, "Frank, a clean shirt," and was very soon drest. When I had him fairly seated in a hackney-coach with me, I exulted as much as a fortune-hunter who has got an heiress into a post-chaise with him to set out for Gretna-Green.

When we entered Mr. Dilly's drawing-room, he found himself in the midst of a company he did not know. I kept myself snug and silent, watching how he would conduct himself. I observed him whispering to Mr. Dilly, "Who is that gentleman, sir?"—"Mr. Arthur Lee."—JOHNSON. "Too, too, too," (under his breath,) which was one of his habitual mutterings. Mr. Arthur Lee could not but be very obnoxious to Johnson, for he was not only a *patriot*, but an *American*. He was afterwards minister from the United States at the court of Madrid. "And who is the gentleman in lace?"—"Mr. Wilkes, Sir." This information confounded him still more; he had some difficulty to restrain himself, and taking up a book, sat down upon a window-seat and read, or at least kept his eye upon it intently for some time, till he composed himself. His feelings, I dare say, were awkward enough. But he no doubt recollected his having rated me for supposing that he could be at all disconcerted by any company, and he, therefore, resolutely set himself to behave quite as an easy man of the world, who could adapt himself at once to the disposition and manners of those whom he might chance to meet.

The cheering sound of "Dinner is upon the table," dissolved his reverie, and we *all* sat down without any symptom of ill humour. There were present, beside Mr. Wilkes, and Mr. Arthur Lee, who was an old companion of mine when he studied physick at Edinburgh, Mr. (now Sir John) Miller, Dr. Lettsom, and Mr. Slater, the druggist. Mr. Wilkes placed himself next to Dr. Johnson, and behaved to him with so much attention and politeness, that he gained upon him insensibly. No man eat more heartily than Johnson, or loved better what was nice and delicate. Mr. Wilkes was very assiduous in helping him to some fine veal. "Pray give me leave, Sir;—It is better here—A little of the brown—Some fat, Sir—A little of the stuffing—Some gravy—Let me have the pleasure of giving you some butter—Allow me to recommend a squeeze of this orange;—or the lemon, perhaps, may have more zest."—"Sir, Sir, I am obliged to you, Sir," cried Johnson, bowing, and turning his head to him with a look for some time of "surly virtue," [12] but, in a short while, of complacency.

Foote being mentioned, Johnson said, "He is not a good mimick." One of the company added, "A merry Andrew, a buffoon." JOHNSON. "But he has wit too, and is not deficient in ideas, or in fertility and variety of imagery, and not empty of reading; he has knowledge enough to fill up his part. One species of wit he has in an eminent degree, that of escape. You drive him into a corner with both hands; but he's gone, Sir, when you think you have got him—like an animal that jumps over your head. Then he has a great range for wit; he never lets truth stand between him and a jest, and he is sometimes mighty coarse. Garrick is under many restraints from which Foote is free." WILKES. "Garrick's wit is more like Lord Chesterfield's." JOHNSON. "The first time I was in company with Foote was at Fitzherbert's. Having no good opinion of the fellow, I was resolved not to be pleased; and it is very difficult to please a man against his will. I went on eating my dinner pretty sullenly, affecting not to mind him. But the dog was so very comical, that I was obliged to lay down my knife and fork, throw myself back upon my chair, and fairly laugh it out. No, Sir, he was irresistible. He upon one occasion experienced, in an extraordinary degree, the efficacy of his powers of entertaining. Amongst the many and various modes which he tried of getting money, he became a partner with a small-beer brewer, and he was to have a share of the profits for procuring customers amongst his numerous acquaintance. Fitzherbert was one who took his small-beer; but it was so bad that the servants resolved not to drink it. They were at some loss how to notify their resolution, being afraid of offending their master, who they knew liked Foote much as a companion. At last they fixed upon a little black boy, who was rather a favourite, to be their deputy, and deliver their remonstrance; and having invested him with the whole authority of the kitchen, he was to inform Mr. Fitzherbert, in all their names, upon a certain day, that they would drink Foote's small-beer no longer. On that day Foote

12. **"surly virtue"**: see Johnson's "London, a Poem."

happened to dine at Fitzherbert's, and this boy served at table; he was so delighted with Foote's stories, and merriment, and grimace, that when he went down stairs, he told them, "This is the finest man I have ever seen. I will not deliver your message. I will drink his small-beer."

Somebody observed that Garrick could not have done this. WILKES. "Garrick would have made the small-beer still smaller. He is now leaving the stage; but he will play *Scrub* all his life." I knew that Johnson would let nobody attack Garrick but himself, as Garrick said to me, and I had heard him praise his liberality; so to bring out his commendation of his celebrated pupil, I said, loudly, "I have heard Garrick is liberal." JOHNSON. "Yes, Sir, I know that Garrick has given away more money than any man in England that I am acquainted with, and that not from ostentatious views. Garrick was very poor when he began life; so when he came to have money, he probably was very unskilful in giving away, and saved when he should not. But Garrick began to be liberal as soon as he could; and I am of opinion, the reputation of avarice which he has had, has been very lucky for him, and prevented his having many enemies. You despise a man for avarice, but do not hate him. Garrick might have been much better attacked for living with more splendour than is suitable to a player: if they had had the wit to have assaulted him in that quarter, they might have galled him more. But they have kept clamouring about his avarice, which has rescued him from much obloquy and envy."

Talking of the great difficulty of obtaining authentick information for biography, Johnson told us, "When I was a young fellow I wanted to write the 'Life of Dryden,' and in order to get materials, I applied to the only two persons then alive who had seen him; these were old Swinney,[13] and old Cibber. Swinney's information was no more than this, 'That at Will's coffee-house Dryden had a particular chair for himself, which was set by the fire in winter, and was then called his winter-chair; and that it was carried out for him to the balcony in summer, and was then called his summer-chair.' Cibber could tell no more but 'That he remembered him a decent old man, arbiter of critical disputes at Will's.' You are to consider that Cibber was then at a great distance from Dryden, had perhaps one leg only in the room, and durst not draw in the other." BOSWELL. "Yet Cibber was a man of observation?" JOHNSON. "I think not." BOSWELL. "You will allow his 'Apology' to be well done." JOHNSON. "Very well done, to be sure, Sir. That book is a striking proof of the justice of Pope's remark:

> Each might his several province well
> command,
> Would all but stoop to what they understand.[14]

BOSWELL. "And his plays are good." JOHNSON. "Yes; but that was his trade; *l'esprit du corps;* he had been all his life among players and play-writers. I wondered that he had so little to say in conversation, for he had kept the best company, and learnt all that can be got by the ear. He abused Pindar to me, and then shewed me an ode of his own, with an absurd couplet, making a linnet soar on an eagle's wing. I told him that when the ancients made a simile, they always made it like something real."

Mr. Wilkes remarked, that "among all the bold flights of Shakspeare's imagination, the boldest was making Birnamwood march to Dunsinane; creating a wood where there never was a shrub; a wood in Scotland! ha! ha! ha!" And he also observed, that "the clannish slavery of the Highlands of Scotland was the single exception to Milton's remark of 'The Mountain Nymph sweet Liberty,' being worshipped in all hilly countries."—"When I was at Inverary (said he,) on a visit to my old friend Archibald, Duke of Argyle, his dependents congratulated me on being such a favourite of his Grace. I said, 'It is then, gentlemen, truly lucky for me; for if I had displeased the Duke, and he had wished it, there is not a Campbell among you but would have been ready to bring John Wilkes's head to him in a charger. It would have been only

> Off with his head! so much for *Aylesbury.*

I was then member for Aylesbury."

Dr. Johnson and Mr. Wilkes talked of the contested passage in Horace's Art of Poetry, "*Difficile est propriè communia dicere.*" Mr. Wilkes, according to my note, gave the interpretation thus: "It is

13. Swinney: the reference is to Owen Mac Swinney who managed the Haymarket and Drury Lane Theaters.

14. See Pope's *Essay on Criticism,* ll. 66–67.

difficult to speak with propriety of common things; as, if a poet had to speak of Queen Caroline drinking tea, he must endeavour to avoid the vulgarity of cups and saucers." But upon reading my note, he tells me that he meant to say, that "the word *communia,* being a Roman law-term, signifies here things *communis juris,* that is to say, what have never yet been treated by any body; and this appears clearly from what followed,

———Tuque
Rectiùs Iliacum carmen deducis in actus
Quàm si proferres ignota indictaque primus.[15]

You will easier make a tragedy out of the Iliad than on any subject not handled before." JOHNSON. "He means that it is difficult to appropriate to particular persons qualities which are common to all mankind, as Homer has done."

WILKES. "We have no City-Poet now: that is an office which has gone into disuse. The last was Elkanah Settle. There is something in *names* which one cannot help feeling. Now *Elkanah Settle* sounds so *queer,* who can expect much from that name? We should have no hesitation to give it for John Dryden, in preference to Elkanah Settle, from the names only, without knowing their different merits." JOHNSON. "I suppose Sir, Settle did as well for Aldermen in his time, as John Home could do now. Where did Beckford, and Trecothick learn English?"

Mr. Arthur Lee mentioned some Scotch who had taken possession of a barren part of America, and wondered why they should choose it. JOHNSON. "Why, Sir, all barrenness is comparative. The *Scotch* would not know it to be barren." BOSWELL. "Come, come, he is flattering the English. You have now been in Scotland, Sir, and say if you did not see meat and drink enough there." JOHNSON. "Why yes, Sir; meat and drink enough to give the inhabitants sufficient strength to run away from home." All these quick and lively sallies were said sportively, quite in jest, and with a smile, which showed that he meant only wit. Upon this topick he and Mr. Wilkes could perfectly assimilate; here was a bond of union between them, and I was conscious that as both of them had visited Caledonia, both were fully satisfied of the strange narrow ignorance of those who imagine that it is a land of famine. But they amused themselves with persevering in the old jokes. When I claimed a superiority for Scotland over England in one respect, that no man can be arrested there for a debt merely because another swears it against him; but there must first be the judgement of a court of law ascertaining its justice; and that a seizure of the person, before judgement is obtained, can take place only, if his creditor should swear that he is about to fly from the country, or, as it is technically expressed, is *in meditatione fugæ:* WILKES. "That, I should think, may be safely sworn of all the Scotch nation." JOHNSON. (To Mr. Wilkes) "You must know, Sir, I lately took my friend Boswell, and shewed him genuine civilised life in an English provincial town. I turned him loose at Lichfield, my native city, that he might see for once real civility: for you know he lives among savages in Scotland, and among rakes in London." WILKES. "Except when he is with grave, sober, decent people, like you and me." JOHNSON. (smiling) "And we ashamed of him."

They were quite frank and easy. Johnson told the story of his asking Mrs. Macaulay to allow her footman to sit down with them, to prove the ridiculousness of the arguments for the equality of mankind; and he said to me afterwards, with a nod of satisfaction, "You saw Mr. Wilkes acquiesced." Wilkes talked with all imaginable freedom of the ludicrous title given to the Attorney-General, *Diabolus Regis*; adding, "I have reason to know something about that officer; for I was prosecuted for a libel." Johnson, who many people would have supposed must have been furiously angry at hearing this talked of so lightly, said not a word. He was now, *indeed,* "a good-humoured fellow."

After dinner we had an accession of Mrs. Knowles, the Quaker lady, well known for her various talents, and of Mr. Alderman Lee. Amidst some patriotick groans, somebody (I think the Alderman) said, "Poor old England is lost." JOHNSON. "Sir, it is not so much to be lamented that old England is lost, as that the Scotch have found it." WILKES. "Had Lord Bute governed Scotland only, I should not have taken the trouble to write his eulogy, and dedicate 'MORTIMER' to him."

Mr. Wilkes held a candle to shew a fine print of a beautiful female figure which hung in the

15. Tuque . . . primus: "And you proceed more correctly in dividing the tale of Troy into acts than in offering a new story of your own making." See *Ars Poetica,* ll. 128–130.

room, and pointed out the elegant contour of the bosom with the finger of an arch connoisseur. He afterwards in a conversation with me waggishly insisted, that all the time Johnson shewed visible signs of a fervent admiration of the corresponding charms of the fair Quaker.

This record, though by no means so perfect as I could wish, will serve to give a notion of a very curious interview, which was not only pleasing at the time, but had the agreeable and benignant effect of reconciling any animosity, and sweetening any acidity, which, in the various bustle of political contest, had been produced in the minds of two men, who though widely different, had so many things in common—classical learning, modern literature, wit and humour, and ready repartee—that it would have been much to be regretted if they had been for ever at a distance from each other.

Mr. Burke gave me much credit for this successful *negotiation;* and pleasantly said, "that there was nothing equal to it in the whole history of the *Corps Diplomatique.*"

I attended Dr. Johnson home, and had the satisfaction to hear him tell Mrs. Williams how much he had been pleased with Mr. Wilkes's company, and what an agreeable day he had passed.

. . .

A.D. 1784

AGE 75

. . .

My readers are now, at last, to behold SAMUEL JOHNSON preparing himself for that doom, from which the most exalted powers afford no exemption to man. Death had always been to him an object of terrour; so that though by no means happy, he still clung to life with an eagerness at which many have wondered. At any time when he was ill, he was very pleased to be told that he looked better. An ingenious member of the *Eumelian Club* [16] informs me, that upon one occasion, when he said to him that he saw health returning to his cheek, Johnson seized him by the hand and exclaimed, "Sir, you are one of the kindest friends I ever had."

His own state of his views of futurity will appear truly rational; and may, perhaps, impress the unthinking with seriousness.

"You know, (says he,) I never thought confidence with respect to futurity, any part of the character of a brave, a wise, or a good man. Bravery has no place where it can avail nothing; wisdom impresses strongly the consciousness of those faults, of which it is, perhaps, itself an aggravation; and goodness, always wishing to be better, and imputing every deficience to criminal negligence, and every fault to voluntary corruption, never dares to suppose the condition of forgiveness fulfilled, nor what is wanting in the crime supplied by penitence.

"This is the state of the best; but what must be the condition of him whose heart will not suffer him to rank himself among the best, or among the good? Such must be his dread of the approaching trial as will leave him little attention to the opinion of those whom he is leaving for ever; and the serenity that is not felt, it can be no virtue to feign."

His great fear of death, and the strange dark manner in which Sir John Hawkins imparts the uneasiness which he expressed on account of offences with which he charged himself, may give occasion to injurious suspicions, as if there had been something of more than ordinary criminality weighing upon his conscience. On that account, therefore, as well as from the regard to truth which he inculcated, I am to mention, (with all possible respect and delicacy, however,) that his conduct after he came to London, and had associated with Savage and others, was not so strictly virtuous, in one respect, as when he was a younger man. It was well known, that his amorous inclinations were uncommonly strong and impetuous. He owned to many of his friends, that he used to take women of the town to taverns, and hear them relate their history. —In short, it must not be concealed, that like many other good and pious men, among whom we may place the apostle Paul upon his own authority, Johnson was not free from propensities which were ever "warring against the law of his mind."—and that in his combats with them, he was sometimes overcome.

Here let the profane and licentious pause; let them not thoughtlessly say that Johnson was an

16. ***Eumelian Club:*** a club in London founded by a Dr. Ash, a learned and talented physician.

hypocrite, or that his *principles* were not firm, because his *practice* was not uniformly conformable to what he professed.

. . .

Dr. Brocklesby, who will not be suspected of fanaticism, obliged me with the following accounts:

"For some time before his death, all his fears were calmed and absorbed by the prevalence of his faith, and his trust in the merits and *propitiation* of JESUS CHRIST.

"He talked often to me about the necessity of faith in the *sacrifice* of Jesus, as necessary beyond all good works whatever, for the salvation of mankind.

"He pressed me to study Dr. Clarke and to read his sermons. I asked him why he pressed Dr. Clarke, an Arian.* Because, (said he,) he is fullest on the *propitiatory sacrifice.*'"

Johnson having thus in his mind the true Christian scheme, at once rational and consolatory, uniting justice and mercy in the DIVINITY, with the improvement of human nature, previous to his receiving the Holy Sacrament, in his apartment, composed and fervently uttered his prayer:

"Almighty and most merciful Father, I am now as to human eyes it seems, about to commemorate, for the last time, the death of thy Son JESUS CHRIST, our Saviour and Redeemer. Grant, O LORD, that my whole hope and confidence may be in his merits, and thy mercy; enforce and accept my imperfect repentance; make this commemoration available to the confirmation of my faith, the establishment of my hope, and the enlargement of my charity; and make the death of thy Son JESUS CHRIST effectual to my redemption. Have mercy upon me, and pardon the multitude of my offences. Bless my friends; have mercy upon all men. Support me, by thy Holy Spirit, in the days of weakness, and at the hour of death; and receive me, at my death, to everlasting happiness, for the sake of JESUS CHRIST. Amen."

Having, as has been already mentioned, made his will on the 8th and 9th of December, and settled all his worldly affairs, he languished till Monday, the 13th of that month, when he expired, about seven o'clock in the evening, with so little apparent pain that his attendants hardly perceived when his dissolution took place.

Of his last moments, my brother, Thomas David, has furnished me with the following particulars:

"The Doctor, from the time that he was certain his death was near, appeared to be perfectly resigned, was seldom or never fretful or out of temper, and often said to his faithful servant, who gave me this account, 'Attend, Francis, to the salvation of your soul, which is the object of greatest importance:' he also explained to him passages in the scripture, and seemed to have pleasure in talking upon religious subjects.

"On Monday, the 13th of December, the day on which he died, a Miss Morris, daughter to a particular friend of his, called, and said to Francis, that she begged to be permitted to see the Doctor, that she might earnestly request him to give her his blessing. Francis went into his room, followed by the young lady, and delivered the message. The Doctor turned himself in the bed, and said, 'GOD bless you, my dear!' These were the last words he spoke.—His difficulty of breathing increased till about seven o'clock in the evening, when Mr. Barber and Mrs. Desmoulins, who were sitting in the room, observing that the noise he made in breathing had ceased, went to the bed, and found he was dead."

. . .

I trust, I shall not be accused of affectation, when I declare, that I find myself unable to express all that I felt upon the loss of such a "Guide, Philosopher, and Friend." I shall, therefore, not say one word of my own, but adopt those of an eminent

* The change of his sentiments with regard to Dr. Clarke, is thus mentioned to me in a letter from the late Dr. Adams, Master of Pembroke College, Oxford.—"The Doctor's prejudices were the strongest, and certainly in another sense the weakest, that ever possessed a sensible man. You know his extreme zeal for orthodoxy. But did you ever hear what he told me himself? That he had made it a rule not to admit Dr. Clarke's name in his Dictionary. This, however, wore off. At some distance of time he advised with me what books he should read in defence of the Christian Religion. I recommended 'Clarke's Evidences of Natural and Revealed Religion,' as the best of the kind; and I find in what is called his 'Prayers and Meditations,' that he was frequently employed in the latter part of his time in reading Clarke's Sermons."

friend,[17] which he uttered with an abrupt felicity, superiour to all studied compositions:—"He has made a chasm, which not only nothing can fill up, but which nothing has a tendency to fill up.—Johnson is dead.—Let us go to the next best:—there is nobody; no man can be said to put you in mind of Johnson."

As Johnson had abundant homage paid to him during his life, so no writer in this nation ever had such an accumulation of literary honours after his death. A sermon upon that event was preached in St. Mary's church, Oxford, before the University, by the Reverend Mr. Agutter, of Magdalen College. The Lives, the Memoirs, the Essays, both in prose and verse, which have been published concerning him, would make many volumes. The numerous attacks too upon him, I consider as part of his consequence, upon the principle which he himself so well knew and asserted. Many who trembled at his presence, were forward in assault, when they no longer apprehended danger. When one of his little pragmatical foes was invidiously snarling at his fame, at Sir Joshua Reynolds's table, the Reverend Dr. Parr exclaimed, with his usual bold animation, "Ay, now that the old lion is dead, every ass thinks he may kick at him."

A monument for him, in Westminster-Abbey, was resolved upon soon after his death, and was supported by a most respectable contribution; but the Dean and Chapter of St. Paul's, having come to a resolution of admitting monuments there, upon a liberal and magnificent plan, that Cathedral was afterwards fixed on, as the place in which a cenotaph should be erected to his memory: and in the cathedral of his native city of Lichfield, a smaller one is to be erected. To compose his epitaph, could not but excite the warmest competition of genius. If *laudari à laudato viro* be praise which is highly estimable, I should not forgive myself were I to omit the following sepulchral verses on the authour of THE ENGLISH DICTIONARY, written by the Right Honourable Henry Flood:

> No need of Latin or of Greek to grace
> Our JOHNSON's memory, or inscribe his grave;
> His native language claims this mournful space,
> To pay the immortality he gave.

The character of SAMUEL JOHNSON has, I trust, been so developed in the course of this work, that they, who have honoured it with a perusal, may be considered as well acquainted with him. As, however, it may be expected that I should collect into one view the capital and distinguishing features of this extraordinary man, I shall endeavour to acquit myself of that part of my biographical undertaking, however difficult it may be to do that which many of my readers will do better for themselves.

His figure was large and well formed, and his countenance of the cast of an ancient statue; yet his appearance was rendered strange and somewhat uncouth, by convulsive cramps, by the scars of that distemper which it was once imagined the royal touch could cure, and by a slovenly mode of dress. He had the use only of one eye; yet so much does mind govern, and even supply the deficiency of organs, that his visual perceptions, as far as they extended, were uncommonly quick and accurate. So morbid was his temperament, that he never knew the natural joy of a free and vigourous use of his limbs; when he walked, it was like the struggling gait of one in fetters; when he rode, he had no command or direction of his horse, but was carried as if in a balloon. That with his constitution and habits of life he should have lived seventy-five years, is a proof that an inherent *vivida vis*[18] is a powerful preservative of the human frame.

Man is, in general, made up of contradictory qualities; and these will ever shew themselves in strange succession, where a consistency in appearance at least, if not reality, has not been attained by long habits of philosophical discipline. In proportion to the native vigour of the mind, the contradictory qualities will be the more prominent, and more difficult to be adjusted: and, therefore, we are not to wonder, that Johnson exhibited an eminent example of this remark which I have made upon human nature. At different times, he seemed a different man, in some respects; not, however, in any great or essential article, upon which he had fully employed his mind, and settled certain principles of duty, but only in his manners, and in the display of argument and fancy in his talk. He was

17. eminent friend: William Gerard Hamilton (1729–1796), the famous "Single Speech Hamilton," who, as a Member of Parliament for Petersfield, made a notable maiden speech. Johnson had high praise for his power as a conversationalist.

18. *vivida vis:* strong force.

prone to superstition, but not to credulity. Though his imagination might incline him to a belief of the marvellous and the mysterious, his vigorous reason examined the evidence with jealousy. He was a sincere and zealous Christian, of high Church-of-England and monarchical principles, which he would not tamely suffer to be questioned; and had, perhaps, at an early period, narrowed his mind somewhat too much, both as to religion and politicks. His being impressed with the danger of extreme latitude in either, though he was of a very independent spirit, occasioned his appearing somewhat unfavourable to the prevalence of that noble freedom of sentiment which is the best possession of man. Nor can it be denied, that he had many prejudices; which, however, frequently suggested many of his pointed sayings, that rather shew a playfulness of fancy than any settled malignity. He was steady and inflexible in maintaining the obligations of religion and morality; both from a regard for the order of society, and from a veneration for the GREAT SOURCE of all order; correct, nay stern in his taste; hard to please, and easily offended; impetuous and irritable in his temper, but of a most humane and benevolent heart, which shewed itself not only in a most liberal charity, as far as his circumstances would allow, but in a thousand instances of active benevolence. He was afflicted with a bodily disease, which made him often restless and fretful; and with a constitutional melancholy, the clouds of which darkened the brightness of his fancy, and gave a gloomy cast to his whole course of thinking: we, therefore, ought not to wonder at his sallies of impatience and passion at any time; especially when provoked by obtrusive ignorance, or presuming petulance; and allowance must be made for his uttering hasty and satirical sallies even against his best friends. And, surely, when it is considered, that, "amidst sickness and sorrow," he exerted his faculties in so many works for the benefit of mankind, and particularly that he achieved the great and admirable DICTIONARY of our language, we must be astonished at his resolution. The solemn text, "of him to whom much is given, much will be required," seems to have been ever present to his mind, in a rigourous sense, and to have made him dissatisfied with his labours and acts of goodness, however comparatively great; so that the unavoidable consciousness of his superiority was, in that respect, a cause of disquiet. He suffered so much from this, and from the gloom which perpetually haunted him, and made solitude frightful, that it may be said of him, "If in this life only he had hope, he was of all men most miserable." He loved praise, when it was brought to him; but was too proud to seek for it. He was somewhat susceptible of flattery. As he was general and unconfined in his studies, he cannot be considered as master of any one particular science; but he had accumulated a vast and various collection of learning and knowledge, which was so arranged in his mind, as to be ever in readiness to be brought forth. But his superiority over other learned men consisted chiefly in what may be called the art of thinking, the art of using his mind; a certain continual power of seizing the useful substance of all that he knew, and exhibiting it in a clear and forcible manner; so that knowledge, which we often see to be no better than lumber in men of dull understanding, was, in him, true, evident, and actual wisdom. His moral precepts are practical; for they are drawn from an intimate acquaintance with human nature. His maxims carry conviction; for they are founded on the basis of common sense, and a very attentive and minute survey of real life. His mind was so full of imagery, that he might have been perpetually a poet; yet it is remarkable, that, however rich his prose is in this respect, his poetical pieces, in general, have not much of that splendour, but are rather distinguished by strong sentiment, and acute observation, conveyed in harmonious and energetick verse, particularly in heroick couplets. Though usually grave, and even awful in his deportment, he possessed uncommon and peculiar powers of wit and humour; he frequently indulged himself in colloquial pleasantry; and the heartiest merriment was often enjoyed in his company; with this great advantage, that, as it was entirely free from any poisonous tincture of vice or impiety, it was salutary to those who shared in it. He had accustomed himself to such accuracy in his common conversation, that he at all times expressed his thoughts with great force, and an elegant choice of language, the effect of which was aided by his having a loud voice, and a slow deliberate utterance. In him were united a most logical head with a most fertile imagination, which gave him an extraordinary advantage in arguing: for he could reason close or wide, as he saw best for the moment. Exulting in his intellectual strength and dexterity, he could, when he pleased, be the greatest sophist that ever contended in the lists of declamation; and, from a spirit of contradiction, and a delight in shewing his powers, he would often maintain the wrong side with equal warmth and ingenuity; so that, when there was an audience, his real opinions could seldom be gathered from his talk; though when he was in company with a single friend, he would discuss a subject with genuine fairness; but he was too conscientious to make errour permanent and pernicious, by deliberately writing it; and, in all his numerous works, he earnestly inculcated what appeared to him to be the truth; his piety being constant, and the ruling principle of all his conduct.

Such was SAMUEL JOHNSON, a man whose talents, acquirements, and virtues were so extraordinary, that the more his character is considered the more he will be regarded by the present age, and by posterity, with admiration and reverence.

Edmund Burke

1729–1797

It is difficult to restrict Edmund Burke to any one field of endeavor. In a long and extremely active career he was a statesman, an orator, a political philosopher, and a literary theorist. To neglect any one of these fields in a study of his work is to miss the wide-ranging genius of the man, his special role in eighteenth-century affairs in particular, and the Enlightenment in general. Samuel Johnson's tributes to Burke—"Take up whatever topic you please, he is ready to meet you" or "Burke is an extraordinary man. His stream of mind is perpetual."—are vivid reminders to all who read this remarkable writer.

Burke was born in Dublin, Ireland, on January 12, 1729, the son of a Protestant lawyer father and a Roman Catholic mother. He was raised in the Church of England, but was keenly aware of the strongly discriminatory laws under which Catholics lived. Indeed, from his earliest days one can observe in his many activities a keen sensitivity to prejudice and injustice and a vehement hatred of tyranny. No simplistic portrait will do. Burke, as Isaac Krammick has recently argued in his book *The Rage of Edmund Burke,* is an ambivalent man; on the one hand, a vigorous defender of tradition, and on the other, an outspoken pleader for Irish Catholics, American colonists, exploited Bengalese, French aristocrats, and others victimized by the selfishness of entrenched interests. There is also, in his writing and political activities, a spirit that links him, in spite of obvious differences, with Pope, Swift, and Johnson. A figure of the Enlightenment, he nevertheless shares their amusement and scorn at those vain dreams and abstract theories so contrary to a truly enlightened outlook and sets his trust in those fundamental truths of human nature as they have persisted through human history. In W. J. Bate's words, "The extraordinary appeal of his example, continuing throughout the changes of almost two centuries, lies in what can only be called a generous capaciousness of mind, and secondly, in his unrivalled power to distill creative principles of thought and action from the concrete, practical facts of a situation."

Burke's first schooling was at Ballitore, County Kildare, under the direction of the Quaker educator Abraham Shackleton. Shackleton, both as teacher and human being, was a model of tolerance; Burke developed a strong and lasting friendship with his son, Richard. Entering Trinity College in 1744, Burke pursued literary and philosophical studies; his father's great dream was to have his son follow his own profession of law. In spite of the disarray and decadence of much university education at the time, classical studies were still very much the heart of the curriculum, and he read widely in Aristotle, Demosthenes, Cicero, and Quintilian, rhetorical theorists and master orators who influenced him greatly. It was also at Trinity that Burke, strongly interested in human motivation, imaginative and emotional response, and other psychological issues, began to explore in some depth the questions raised in Longinus' ancient treatise *On the Sublime* and to formulate new ways of thinking about the subject that were to become central in his own document, *A Philosophical Inquiry into the Origin of Our Ideas of the Sublime and Beautiful,* published in 1757.

Burke completed his A.B. in February, 1748, and two years later, still strongly influenced by his father, he began the study of law at the Middle Temple. By this time the breadth of his reading background, from the classical to the contemporary, was so remarkable that he found the legal curriculum and the teaching techniques unimaginative and restrictive. Eventually he abandoned any ideas about a legal career and focused more sharply on the literary life. He had demonstrated a great satiric talent in his *A Vindication of Natural Society* (1756), a delightful and shattering parody of Lord Bolingbroke's rigidly theoretical scheme for the description of nature and the organization of government. On March 12, 1757, he married Jane Nugent; a son Richard was born to them on February 8, 1758. It was about this time that further impetus was given to his literary leanings as he became acquainted with Samuel Johnson and became part of that legendary Literary Club of which we have already spoken.

Burke's political career began in 1765, when the Marquis of Rockingham, on becoming First Lord of the Treasury, made him his private secretary. Rockingham was the leader of that faction of moderate Whigs, called by many students of the period liberal conservatives, who looked to the Glorious Revolution of 1688 as their model for reform and change, and Burke became a leading light and intellectual spokesman for the group. He had in 1765 been elected to Parliament from Wendover, and in 1774 he was elected from Bristol. Finally, when his independent political views and his record of voting against the wishes of his constituents made reelection from Bristol impossible, Rockingham nominated him for membership from the borough of Malton. All told, he sat in Parliament for nearly thirty years, almost always among the loyal opposition, since the Rockingham group was out of favor during the administration of George III. While his party was briefly in power in 1782 and he was Paymaster General, he turned his attention to India and to the scandalous corruption of the East India Company and the outrageous conduct of Warren Hastings, the Governor-General. He moved the impeachment of Hastings and delivered some of his most stirring speeches during the trial. After seven years of maneuvering and the new distraction of the French Revolution, however, he lost the case, and Hastings went free.

His great eloquence, his brilliant prose style, his ability to marshal arguments in the fashion of the classical rhetoricians did not always guarantee the success of his positions and causes. He was all too often on the losing side, as political dealing won the battle with philosophy. Yet Burke consistently took the high ground, arguing for the values of justice, tolerance, conciliation, the rule of law, the importance of sound reform with a view to strengthening institutions that have survived the test of the ages. As he grew older, he was often savagely criticized and cruelly caricatured. He even incurred the wrath of his own party when he sharply attacked Charles James Fox's praise of the French Constitution during a Parliamentary discussion of the Quebec Bill in 1791. In April of 1794 he lost his son Richard and now seemed a truly broken man. Physically weak and deeply disillusioned, he retired from Parliament and returned to his home in Beaconsfield, receiving a pension from the Prime Minister, William Pitt the Younger. Still a final blow was delivered as the proud Burke, now mocked and reduced almost to a figure of fun, was scathingly attacked by the Duke of Bedford for his acceptance of the pension. Rousing himself for one final burst of artistry, he answered Bedford in his classic *Letter to a Noble Lord* in 1796. Burke died in Beaconsfield on July 9, 1797.

Burke's long career was characterized, as many commentators have argued, by a flexible conservatism rooted in principle, in a deep respect for established traditions and institutions, and yet also, as already suggested, by a deep suspicion of that abstract theorizing that ignores the overriding importance of human psychology, of concrete circumstances, and of the evolving process of life. Gerald Chapman speaks of Burke's practical imagination. Bate consistently reminds us of the modernity of the man, of his strong sense of change in the nature of things, ". . . the fact that there is always the sense of a large finished past which can be rescued only by the interpretative imagination that meditates on it, as music can come alive only when the printed pattern of notes is scanned and repeated, for a little time, by some later intelligence." As early as 1757, in his famous treatise *On the Sublime,* he sharply distinguishes the beautiful from the sublime and confronts human response directly in his analysis. For him, the sublime is radically different from the beautiful; it is not dependent on objective formulae, but is essentially a state of mind stirred by vastness, power, infinity, obscurity, and similar forces. It does not bring to the spirit the calm associated with the beautiful, but rather provokes and stirs the imagination to effort and struggle. "The passion," he writes, "caused by the great and sublime in *nature,* when those causes operate most powerfully, is astonishment; and astonishment is that state of the soul, in which all its motions are suspended, with some degree of horror."

Burke's concerns were extremely varied, moving from domestic politics to the great issues of his age involving America, France, and India. Reform was his consistent theme, although reform was always seen as a positive, constructive force.

While supporting economic reform in England, he opposed policies for Parliamentary change that would allow for unjustified royal influence in the workings of Parliament and would seriously weaken political parties. In words that staunchly defend the ancient and sacred prerogatives of Parliament and just as vigorously oppose the idea of royal appointees, a very modern-sounding Burke cries out against "... a cabal of the closet and the back-stairs" and reminds his fellow Englishmen that "... although government certainly is an institution of divine authority, yet its forms, and the persons who administer it, all originate from the people."

His great speeches on *American Taxation* of 1774 and on *Conciliation with the Colonies* of 1775, especially the latter, show him arguing for a generous-spirited Great Britain to recognize the reality of the colonies and to abolish all petty and vindictive schemes of taxation. The *Conciliation* speech is quite simply a masterpiece of classical rhetorical construction that represents the high point of Burke's vision of the American colonies as an organic part of a healthy and vigorous British empire. Occasioned by still another "Modest Proposal" for conciliating the colonies, this time from First Lord of the Treasury North, Burke's speech cleverly turns North's arguments around. His scheme would allow any colony that provided for its own government, raised a fair proportion for the common defense and put it at the disposal of Parliament to be free from all taxes except those required for the proper regulation of commerce.

Burke argued that North's plan would divide rather than unite the colonies and ultimately render them hopelessly subservient. He skillfully uses the idea of conciliation as a point of departure, but argues for a true conciliation based on a recognition of the background, development, and spirit of America. How striking and poignant is Burke's question to his colleagues, a question grounded as always in a recognition of the realities of a human situation: "But the question is not, whether their spirit deserves praise or blame,—what, in the name of God, shall we do with it?" And how humane and reasonable his answer. Let our conciliation be magnanimous, says Burke, not mean and exploitative. "Let the colonies always keep the idea of their civil rights associated with your government,—they will cling and grapple to you and no force under heaven will be of power to tear them from their allegiance."

Burke's opposition to unjust restrictions on Irish trade and to the various discriminatory penal laws against Roman Catholics as well as his strong support of the Catholic Relief Acts of 1778 and 1782 are further evidence of his concern. He also fought for Charles James Fox's East India Bill, which was calculated to curb the unconscionable abuses of that company and to restore proper governmental control. He was, as suggested above, just as active and forceful in the move to impeach Warren Hastings, the Governor-General.

At the same time Burke rarely confused change with upheaval, reform with the undermining of established institutions. While supporting the cause of freedom in America, he nevertheless saw in the French Revolution the kind of violent change that threatened not only France, but the entire civilized world. This Revolution was unquestionably the major political event of his lifetime, and he addressed himself to it with intense concern in several documents, most notably the *Reflections on the Revolution in France* in 1790. While he could see the revolt of the American colonies as justified in terms of his "reform in order to preserve" principle, he attacked the French Revolution as a radical, ideological, and ultimately destructive action. Still clinging to his hatred of theory for the sake of theory, still, like Swift, horrified by those politicians more interested in efficiency than in human beings, still the defender of the true ideal of Enlightenment, he viewed the events in France as leading not to freedom, but to a new kind of tyranny that never really concerned itself with the reasoned, constructive reform of institutions so central to his philosophy. At times in the *Reflections*, the vividness of his prose startles; at times, and W. J. Bate makes this argument most convincingly, his prophetic vision of the Revolution as precursor to modern totalitarianism astounds. The Revolutionaries, he concludes, "... have found their punishment in their success. Laws overturned; tribunals subverted; industry without vigour; commerce expiring; the revenue unpaid, yet the people impoverished; a church pillaged, and a state not relieved; civil and military anarchy made the constitution of the kingdom." He exhorted the English, observant and enlightened, to take note; to keep in mind the example of their own Constitution and to be wary of new models.

> Our people will find employment enough for a truly patriotic, free, and independent spirit, in guarding what they possess from violation. I would not exclude alteration neither; but even when I changed, it should be to preserve. I should be led to my remedy by a great grievance. In what I did, I should follow the example of our ancestors.... Not being illuminated with the light of which the gentlemen of France tell us they have got so abundant a share, they acted under a strong impression of the ignorance and fallibility of mankind. He that had made them thus fallible, rewarded them for having in their conduct attended to their nature. Let us imitate their caution, if we wish to deserve their fortune, or to retain their bequests. Let us add, if we please, but let us preserve what they have left; and standing on the firm ground of the British Constitution, let us be satisfied to admire, rather than attempt to follow in their desperate flights, the aeronauts of France.

Edmund Burke stands as the statesman/man-of-letters *par excellence*, a man whose astute political sense and varied artistic gifts were committed, if not always successfully, certainly unrelentingly to the vision of a good society that is tolerant, generous, and responsive to the basic needs of human beings. "The situation of man is the preceptor of his duty" is very close to his guiding principle. His own words come very close to describing his ideal of Enlightenment as well as the progress of his career: "When I see in any of these detached gentlemen of our times the angelic purity, power, and beneficence, I shall admit them to be angels. In the meantime we are born only to be men. We shall do enough if we form ourselves to be good ones. It is therefore our business carefully to cultivate in our minds, to rear to the most perfect vigor and maturity, every sort of generous and honest feeling, that belongs to our nature."

Suggestions for Further Reading

While there is still no truly great biography of Burke, John Morley, *Burke* (1879), Philip Magnus, *Edmund Burke* (1939), and especially Thomas Copeland, *Our Eminent Friend Edmund Burke* (1949), are helpful. W. J. Bate's introduction to *Edmund Burke: Selected Works* (1960) is still the best interpretation of Burke's overall philosophy, a penetrating and superbly written analysis.

Also recommended for further study are Thomas H. D. Mahoney, *Edmund Burke and Ireland* (1960); Russell Kirk, *Edmund Burke: A Genius Reconsidered* (1967); Gerald Chapman, *Edmund Burke: The Practical Imagination* (1967); and Isaac Kramnick, *The Rage of Edmund Burke: Portrait of an Ambivalent Conservative* (1977).

FROM

A Philosophical Enquiry Into the Origin of Our Ideas of the Sublime and the Beautiful

PART I

SECTION VII

OF THE SUBLIME

Whatever is fitted in any sort to excite the ideas of pain and danger, that is to say, whatever is in any sort terrible, or is conversant about terrible objects, or operates in a manner analogous to terror, is a source of the *sublime;* that is, it is productive of the strongest emotion which the mind is capable of feeling. I say the strongest emotion, because I am satisfied the ideas of pain are much more powerful than those which enter on the part of pleasure. Without all doubt, the torments which we may be made to suffer are much greater in their effect on the body and mind, than any pleasures which the most learned voluptuary could suggest, or than the liveliest imagination, and the most sound and exquisitely sensible body, could enjoy. Nay, I am in great doubt whether any man could be found, who would earn a life of the most perfect satisfaction at the price of ending it in the torments, which justice inflicted in a few hours on the late unfortunate regicide in France.[1] But as pain is stronger in its operation than pleasure, so death is in general a much more affecting idea than pain; because there are very few pains, however exquisite, which are not preferred to death: nay, what generally makes pain itself, if I may say so, more painful, is, that it is considered as an emissary of this king of terrors. When danger or pain press too nearly, they are incapable of giving any delight, and are simply terrible; but at certain distances, and with certain modifications, they may be, and they are, delightful, as we every day experience. The cause of this I shall endeavor to investigate hereafter.

THE SUBLIME. 1. A reference to Robert Francis Damiess, who failed in an assassination attempt on Louis XV and was executed in 1757 after excruciating torture.

SECTION X

OF BEAUTY

The passion which belongs to generation, merely as such, is lust only. This is evident in brutes, whose passions are more unmixed, and which pursue their purposes more directly than ours. The only distinction they observe with regard to their mates, is that of sex. It is true, that they stick severally to their own species in preferences to all others. But this preference, I imagine, does not arise from any sense of beauty which they find in their species, as Mr. Addison supposes,[2] but from a law of some other kind, to which they are subject; and this we may fairly conclude, from their apparent want of choice amongst those objects to which the barriers of their species have confined them. But man, who is a creature adapted to a greater variety and intricacy of relation, connects with the general passion the idea of some *social* qualities, which direct

2. See *Spectator* No. 413.

and heighten the appetite which he has in common with all other animals; and as he is not designed like them to live at large, it is fit that he should have some thing to create a preference, and fix his choice; and this in general should be some sensible quality; as no other can so quickly, so powerfully, or so surely produce its effect. The object therefore of this mixed passion, which we call love, is the *beauty* of the *sex*. Men are carried to the sex in general, as it is the sex, and by the common law of nature; but they are attached to particulars by personal *beauty*. I call beauty a social quality; for where women and men, and not only they, but when other animals give us a sense of joy and pleasure in beholding them (and there are many that do so), they inspire us with sentiments of tenderness and affection towards their persons; we like to have them near us, and we enter willingly into a kind of relation with them, unless we should have strong reasons to the contrary. But to what end, in many cases, this was designed, I am unable to discover; for I see no greater reason for a connection between man and several animals who are attired in so engaging a manner, than between him and some others who entirely want this attraction, or possess it in a far weaker degree. But it is probable that Providence did not make even this distinction, but with a view to some great end; though we cannot perceive distinctly what it is, as his wisdom is not our wisdom, nor our way his ways.

PART II

SECTION I

OF THE PASSION CAUSED BY THE SUBLIME

The passion caused by the great and sublime in *nature*, when those causes operate most powerfully, is astonishment: and astonishment is that state of the soul in which all its motions are suspended, with some degree of horror. In this case the mind is so entirely filled with its object, that it cannot entertain any other, nor by consequence reason on that object which employs it. Hence arises the great power of the sublime, that, far from being produced by them, it anticipates our reasonings, and hurries us on by an irresistible force. Astonishment, as I have said, is the effect of the sublime in its highest degree; the inferior effects are admiration, reverence, and respect.

SECTION II

TERROR

No passion so effectually robs the mind of all its powers of acting and reasoning as *fear*. For fear being an apprehension of pain or death, it operates in a manner that resembles actual pain. Whatever therefore is terrible, with regard to sight, is sublime too, whether this cause of terror be endued with greatness of dimensions or not; for it is impossible to look on anything as trifling, or contemptible, that may be dangerous. There are many animals, who, though far from being large, are yet capable of raising ideas of the sublime, because they are considered as objects of terror. As serpents and poisonous animals of almost all kinds. And to things of great dimensions, if we annex an adventitious idea of terror, they become without comparison greater. A level plain of a vast extent on land, is certainly no mean idea; the prospect of such a plain may be as extensive as a prospect of the ocean; but can it ever fill the mind with anything so great as the ocean itself? This is owing to several causes; but it is owing to none more than this, that the ocean is an object of no small terror. Indeed terror is in all cases whatsoever, either more openly or latently, the ruling principle of the sublime. Several languages bear a strong testimony to the affinity of these ideas. They frequently use the same word to signify indifferently the modes of astonishment or admiration and those of terror. Θάμβος is in Greek either fear or wonder; δεινός is terrible or respectable; αἰδέω, to reverence or to fear. *Vereor* in Latin is what αἰδέω is in Greek. The Romans used the verb *stupeo*, a term which strongly marks the state of an astonished mind, to express the effect either of simple fear, or of astonishment; the word *attonitus* (thunderstruck) is equally expressive of the alliance of these ideas; and do not the French *étonnement*, and the English *astonishment* and *amazement*, point out as clearly the kindred emotions which attend fear and wonder? They who have a more general knowledge of languages, could produce, I make no doubt, many other and equally striking examples.

SECTION III

OBSCURITY

To make anything very terrible, obscurity seems in general to be necessary. When we know the full extent of any danger, when we can accustom our eyes to it, a great deal of the apprehension vanishes. Every one will be sensible of this, who considers how greatly night adds to our dread, in all cases of danger, and how much the notions of ghosts and goblins, of which none can form clear ideas, affect minds which give credit to the popular tales concerning such sorts of beings. Those despotic governments which are founded on the passions of men, and principally upon the passion of fear, keep their chief as much as may be from the public eye. The policy has been the same in many cases of religion. Almost all the heathen temples were dark. Even in the barbarous temples of the Americans at this day, they keep their idol in a dark part of the hut, which is consecrated to his worship. For this purpose too the Druids performed all their ceremonies in the bosom of the darkest woods, and in the shade of the oldest and most spreading oaks. No person seems better to have understood the secret of heightening, or of setting terrible things, if I may use the expression, in their strongest light, by the force of a judicious obscurity than Milton. His description of death in the second book is admirably studied; it is astonishing with what a gloomy pomp, with what a significant and expressive uncertainty of strokes and coloring, he has finished the portrait of the king of terrors:

The other shape,
If shape it might be called that shape had none
Distinguishable, in member, joint, or limb;
Or substance might be called that shadow
seemed;
For each seemed either; black he stood as
night;
Fierce as ten furies; terrible as hell;
And shook a deadly dart. What seemed his
head
The likeness of a kingly crown had on.[3]

In this description all is dark, uncertain, confused, terrible, and sublime to the last degree.

3. See *Paradise Lost,* II, 666–673.

SECTION IV

OF THE DIFFERENCE BETWEEN CLEARNESS AND OBSCURITY WITH REGARD TO THE PASSIONS

It is one thing to make a idea clear, and another to make it *affecting* to the imagination. If I make a drawing of a palace, or a temple, or a landscape, I present a very clear idea of those objects; but then (allowing for the effect of imitation which is something) my picture can at most affect only as the palace, temple, or landscape, would have affected in the reality. On the other hand, the most lively and spirited verbal description I can give raises a very obscure and imperfect *idea* of such objects; but then it is in my power to raise a stronger *emotion* by the description than I could do by the best painting. This experience constantly evinces. The proper manner of conveying the *affections* of the mind from one to another is by words; there is a great insufficiency in all other methods of communication; and so far is a clearness of imagery from being absolutely necessary to an influence upon the passions, that they may be considerably operated upon, without presenting any image at all, by certain sounds adapted to that purpose; of which we have a sufficient proof in the acknowledged and powerful effects of instrumental music. In reality, a great clearness helps but little towards affecting the passions, as it is in some sort an enemy to all enthusiasms whatsoever.

SECTION [IV]

THE SAME SUBJECT CONTINUED

There are two verses in Horace's Art of Poetry that seem to contradict this opinion; for which reason I shall take a little more pains in clearing it up. The verses are,

Segnius irritant animos demissa per aures,
Quam quæ sunt oculis subjecta fidelibus.[4]

On this the Abbé du Bos founds a criticism, wherein he gives painting the preference to poetry in the article of moving the passions; principally on account of the greater *clearness* of the ideas it rep-

4. **Segnius . . . fidelibus:** "The spirit is moved less strongly by what strikes the ears rather than the trusty eyes." See *Ars Poetica,* ll. 180–181.

resents. I believe this excellent judge was led into this mistake (if it be a mistake) by his system; to which he found it more comformable than I imagine it will be found to experience. I know several who admire and love painting, and yet who regard the objects of their admiration in that art with coolness enough in comparison of that warmth with which they are animated by affecting pieces of poetry or rhetoric. Among the common sort of people, I never could perceive that painting had much influence on their passions. It is true that the best sorts of painting, as well as the best sorts of poetry, are not much understood in that sphere. But it is most certain that their passions are very strongly roused by a fanatic preacher, or by the ballads of Chevy Chase, or the Children in the Wood, and by other little popular poems and tales that are current in that rank of life. I do not know of any paintings, bad or good, that produce the same effect. So that poetry, with all its obscurity, has a more general, as well as a more powerful dominion over the passions, than the other art. And I think there are reasons in nature, why the obscure idea, when properly conveyed, should be more affecting than the clear. It is our ignorance of things that causes all our admiration, and chiefly excites our passions. Knowledge and acquaintance make the most striking causes affect but little. It is thus with the vulgar; and all men are as the vulgar in what they do not understand. The ideas of eternity, and infinity, are among the most affecting we have: and yet perhaps there is nothing of which we really understand so little, as of infinity and eternity. We do not anywhere meet a more sublime description than this justly-celebrated one of Milton, wherein he gives the portrait of Satan with a dignity so suitable to the subject:

He above the rest
In shape and gesture proudly eminent
Stood like a tower; his form had yet not lost
All her original brightness, nor appeared
Less than archangel ruined, and th' excess
Of glory obscured: as when the sun new risen
Looks through the horizontal misty air
Shorn of his beams; or from behind the moon
In dim eclipse disastrous twilight sheds
On half the nations; and with fear of change
Perplexes monarchs.[5]

Here is a very noble picture; and in what does this poetical picture consist? In images of a tower, an archangel, the sun rising through mists, or in an eclipse, the ruin of monarchs and the revolutions of kingdoms. The mind is hurried out of itself, by a crowd of great and confused images; which affect because they are crowded and confused. For separate them, and you lose much of the greatness; and join them, and you infallibly lose the clearness. The images raised by poetry are always of this obscure kind; though in general the effects of poetry are by no means to be attributed to the images it raises; which point we shall examine more at large hereafter. But painting, when we have allowed for the pleasure of imitation, can only affect simply by the images it presents; and even in painting, a judicious obscurity in some things contributes to the effect of the picture; because the images of painting are exactly similar to those in nature; and in nature, dark, confused, uncertain images have a greater power on the fancy to form the grander passions, than those have which are more clear and determinate. But where and when this observation may be applied to practice, and how far it shall be extended, will be better deduced from the nature of the subject, and from the occasion, than from any rules that can be given.

I am sensible that this idea has met with opposition, and is likely still to be rejected by several. But let it be considered that hardly anything can strike the mind with its greatness, which does not make some sort of approach towards infinity; which nothing can do whilst we are able to perceive its bounds; but to see an object distinctly, and to perceive its bounds, is one and the same thing. A clear idea is therefore another name for a little idea. There is a passage in the book of Job amazingly sublime, and this sublimity is principally due to the terrible uncertainty of the thing described: *In thoughts from the visions of the night, when deep sleep falleth upon men, fear came upon me and trembling, which made all my bones to shake. Then a spirit passed before my face. The hair of my flesh stood up. It stood still, but I could not discern the form thereof; an image was before mine eyes; there was silence; and I heard a voice,—Shall mortal man be more just than God?*[6] We are first prepared with

5. See *Paradise Lost,* I, 589–599.

6. See Job 4:13–17.

the utmost solemnity for the vision; we are first terrified, before we are let even into the obscure cause of our emotion; but when this grand cause of terror makes its appearance, what is it? Is it not wrapt up in the shades of its own incomprehensible darkness, more awful, more striking, more terrible, than the liveliest description, than the clearest painting, could possible represent it? When painters have attempted to give us clear representations of these very fanciful and terrible ideas, they have, I think, almost always failed; insomuch that I have been at a loss, in all the pictures I have seen of hell, to determine whether the painter did not intend something ludicrous. Several painters have handled a subject of this kind, with a view of assembling as many horrid phantoms as their imagination could suggest; but all the designs I have chanced to meet of the temptations of St. Anthony were rather a sort of odd, wild grotesques, than any thing capable of producing a serious passion. In all these subjects poetry is very happy. Its apparitions, its chimeras, its harpies, its allegorical figures, are grand and affecting; and though Virgil's Fame and Homer's Discord are obscure, they are magnificent figures. These figures in painting would be clear enough, but I fear they might become ridiculous.

SECTION V

POWER

Besides those things which *directly* suggest the idea of danger, and those which produce a similar effect from a mechanical cause, I know of nothing sublime, which is not some modification of power. And this branch rises, as naturally as the other two branches, from terror, the common stock of everything that is sublime. The idea of power, at first view, seems of the class of those indifferent ones, which may equally belong to pain or to pleasure. But in reality, the affection arising from the idea of vast power is extremely remote from that neutral character. For first, we must remember that the idea of pain, in its highest degree, is much stronger than the highest degree of pleasure; and that it preserves the same superiority through all the subordinate gradations. From hence it is, that where the chances for equal degrees of suffering or enjoyment are in any sort equal, the idea of the suffering must always be prevalent. And indeed the ideas of pain, and, above all, of death, are so very affecting, that whilst we remain in the presence of whatever is supposed to have the power of inflicting either, it is impossible to be perfectly free from terror. Again, we know by experience, that, for the enjoyment of pleasure, no great efforts of power are at all necessary; nay, we know that such efforts would go a great way towards destroying our satisfaction: for pleasure must be stolen, and not forced upon us; pleasure follows the will; and therefore we are generally affected with it by many things of a force greatly inferior to our own. But pain is always inflicted by a power in some way superior, because we never submit to pain willingly. So that strength, violence, pain, and terror, are ideas that rush in upon the mind together. Look at a man, or any other animal of prodigious strength, and what is your idea before reflection? Is it that this strength will be subservient to you, to your ease, to your pleasure, to your interest in any sense? No; the emotion you feel is, lest this enormous strength should be employed to the purposes of rapine and destruction. That power derives all its sublimity from the terror with which it is generally accompanied, will appear evidently from its effect in the very few cases, in which it may be possible to strip a considerable degree of strength of its ability to hurt. When you do this, you spoil it of everything sublime, and it immediately becomes contemptible. An ox is a creature of vast strength; but he is an innocent creature, extremely serviceable, and not at all dangerous; for which reason the idea of an ox is by no means grand. A bull is strong too; but his strength is of another kind; often very destructive, seldom (at least amongst us) of any use in our business; the idea of a bull is therefore great, and it has frequently a place in sublime descriptions, and elevating comparisons. Let us look at another strong animal, in the two distinct lights in which we may consider him. The horse in the light of an useful beast, fit for the plough, the road, the draft; in every social useful light, the horse has nothing sublime; but is it thus that we are affected with him, *whose neck is clothed with thunder, the glory of whose nostrils is terrible, who swalloweth the ground with fierceness and rage, neither believeth that it is the sound of the trumpet?*[7] In this description, the useful character of the horse entirely

7. See Job 39:19, 20, 24.

disappears, and the terrible and sublime blaze out together. We have continually about us animals of a strength that is considerable, but not pernicious. Amongst these we never look for the sublime; it comes upon us in the gloomy forest, and in the howling wilderness, in the form of the lion, the tiger, the panther, or rhinoceros. Whenever strength is only useful, and employed for our benefit or our pleasure, then it is never sublime; for nothing can act agreeably to us, that does not act in conformity to our will; but to act agreeably to our will, it must be subject to us, and therefore can never be the cause of a grand and commanding conception. The description of the wild ass, in Job, is worked up into no small sublimity, merely by insisting on his freedom, and his setting mankind at defiance; otherwise the description of such an animal could have had nothing noble in it. *Who hath loosed* (says he) *the bands of the wild ass? whose house I have made the wilderness and the barren land his dwellings. He scorneth the multitude of the city, neither regardeth he the voice of the driver. The range of the mountains is his pasture.*[8] The magnificent description of the unicorn and of leviathan, in the same book, is full of the same heightening circumstances: *Will the unicorn be willing to serve thee? canst thou bind the unicorn with his band in the furrow? wilt thou trust him because his strength is great?—Canst thou draw out leviathan with an hook? will he make a covenant with thee? wilt thou take him for a servant forever? shall not one be cast down even at the sight of him?*[9] In short, wherever we find strength, and in what light soever we look upon power, we shall all along observe the sublime the concomitant of terror, and contempt the attendant on a strength that is subservient and innoxious. The race of dogs, in many of their kinds, have generally a competent degree of strength and swiftness; and they exert these and other valuable qualities which they possess, greatly to our convenience and pleasure. Dogs are indeed the most social, affectionate, and amiable animals of the whole brute creation; but love approaches much nearer to contempt than is commonly imagined; and accordingly, though we caress dogs, we borrow from them an appellation of the most despicable kind, when we employ terms of reproach; and this appellation is the common mark of the last vileness and contempt in every language. Wolves have not more strength than several species of dogs; but, on account of their unmanageable fierceness, the idea of a wolf is not despicable; it is not excluded from grand descriptions and similitudes. Thus we are affected by strength, which is *natural* power. The power which arises from institution in kings and commanders, has the same connection with terror. Sovereigns are frequently addressed with the title of *dread majesty*. And it may be observed, that young persons, little acquainted with the world, and who have not been used to approach men in power, are commonly struck with an awe which takes away the free use of their faculties. *When I prepared my seat in the street,* (says Job,) *the young men saw me, and hid themselves.*[10] Indeed so natural is this timidity with regard to power, and so strongly does it inhere in our constitution, that very few are able to conquer it, but by mixing much in the business of the great world, or by using no small violence to their natural dispositions. I know some people are of opinion, that no awe, no degree of terror, accompanies the idea of power; and have hazarded to affirm, that we can contemplate the idea of God himself without any such emotion. I purposely avoided, when I first considered this subject, to introduce the idea of that great and tremendous Being, as an example in an argument so light as this; though it frequently occurred to me, not as an objection to, but as a strong confirmation of, my notions in this matter. I hope, in what I am going to say, I shall avoid presumption, where it is almost impossible for any mortal to speak with strict propriety. I say then, that whilst we consider the Godhead merely as he is an object of the understanding, which forms a complex idea of power, wisdom, justice, goodness, all stretched to a degree far exceeding the bounds of our comprehension, whilst we consider the divinity in this refined and abstracted light, the imagination and passions are little or nothing affected. But because we are bound, by the condition of our nature, to ascend to these pure and intellectual ideas, through the medium of sensible images, and to judge of these divine qualities by their evident acts and exertions, it becomes extremely hard to disentangle our idea of the cause from the effect by which we are led to know it. Thus, when we contemplate the Deity, his at-

8. See Job 39:5–8. **9.** See Job 39:9–11; 41:1, 4, 9.

10. See Job 29:7–8.

tributes and their operation, coming united on the mind, form a sort of sensible image, and as such are capable of affecting the imagination. Now, though in a just idea of the Deity, perhaps none of his attributes are predominant, yet, to our imagination, his power is by far the most striking. Some reflection, some comparing, is necessary to satisfy us of his wisdom, his justice, and his goodness. To be struck with his power, it is only necessary that we should open our eyes. But whilst we contemplate so vast an object, under the arm, as it were, of almighty power, and invested upon every side with omnipresence, we shrink into the minuteness of our own nature, and are, in a manner, annihilated before him. And though a consideration of his other attributes may relieve, in some measure, our apprehensions; yet no conviction of the justice with which it is exercised, nor the mercy with which it is tempered, can wholly remove the terror that naturally arises from a force which nothing can withstand. If we rejoice, we rejoice with trembling; and even whilst we are receiving benefits, we cannot but shudder at a power which can confer benefits of such mighty importance. When the prophet David contemplated the wonders of wisdom and power which are displayed in the economy of man, he seems to be struck with a sort of divine horror, and cries out, *fearfully and wonderfully am I made.*[11] An heathen poet has a sentiment of a similar nature; Horace looks upon it as the last effort of philosophical fortitude, to behold without terror and amazement, this immense and glorious fabric of the universe:

> Hunc solem, et stellas, et decedentia certis
> Tempora momentis suni qui formidine nulla
> Imbuti spectent.[12]

Lucretius is a poet not to be suspected of giving way to superstitious terrors; yet, when he supposes the whole mechanism of nature laid open by the master of his philosophy, his transport on this magnificent view, which he has represented in the colors of such bold and lively poetry, is overcast with a shade of secret dread and horror:

> His ibi me rebus quædum divina voluptas
> Percipit, atque horror; quod sic natura, tua vi
> Tam manifesta patens, ex omni parte retecta
> est.[13]

But the Scripture alone can supply ideas answerable to the majesty of this subject. In the Scripture, wherever God is represented as appearing or speaking, everything terrible in nature is called up to heighten the awe and solemnity of the Divine presence. The Psalms, and the prophetical books, are crowded with instances of this kind. *The earth shook,* (says the Psalmist,) *the heavens also dropped at the presence of the Lord.*[14] And what is remarkable, the painting preserves the same character, not only when he is supposed descending to take vengeance upon the wicked, but even when he exerts the like plenitude of power in acts of beneficence to mankind. *Tremble, thou earth! at the presence of the Lord; at the presence of the God of Jacob; which turned the rock into standing water, the flint into a fountain of waters!* [15] It were endless to enumerate all the passages, both in the sacred and profane writers, which establish the general sentiment of mankind, concerning the inseparable union of a sacred and reverential awe, with our ideas of the divinity. Hence the common maxim, *Primus in orbe deos fecit timor.*[16] This maxim may be, as I believe it is, false with regard to the origin of religion. The maker of the maxim saw how inseparable these ideas were, without considering that the notion of some great power must be always precedent to our dread of it. But this dread must necessarily follow the idea of such a power, when it is once excited in the mind. It is on this principle that true religion has, and must have, so large a mixture of salutary fear; and that false religions have generally nothing else but fear to support them. Before the Christian religion had, as it were, humanized the idea of the Divinity, and brought it somewhat nearer to us, there was very little said of the love of God. The followers of Plato have something of it, and only something; the other writers of pagan antiquity, whether poets or philosophers, nothing at all. And they who consider with what infinite attention, by what a disregard of every

11. See Psalms 139:14. **12. Hunc . . . spectent:** "Some can behold yon sun, and stars and seasons that pass at given moments with no sense of fear." See Epistles, I, vi, 3–5.

13. His . . . est: "Here in these events some divine pleasure and awe touches me, and so Nature, by your power now so clear, has been revealed on every side." See Lucretius, *De Rerum Natura,* III, 38–40. **14.** Psalms 68:8. **15.** Psalms 114:7–8. **16. *Primus . . . timor:*** "Fear first created gods in the world." See Statius, *Thebaid,* III, 661.

perishable object, through what long habits of piety and contemplation it is that any man is able to attain an entire love and devotion to the Deity, will easily perceive that it is not the first, the most natural, and the most striking effect which proceeds from that idea. Thus we have traced power through its several gradations unto the highest of all, where our imagination is finally lost; and we find terror, quite throughout the progress, its inseparable companion, and growing along with it, as far as we can possibly trace them. Now, as power is undoubtedly a capital source of the sublime, this will point out evidently from whence its energy is derived, and to what class of ideas we ought to unite it.

SECTION VII

VASTNESS

Greatness of dimension is a powerful cause of the sublime. This is too evident, and the observation too common, to need any illustration; it is not so common to consider in what ways greatness of dimension, vastness of extent or quantity, has the most striking effect. For, certainly, there are ways and modes wherein the same quantity of extension shall produce greater effects than it is found to do in others. Extension is either in length, height, or depth. Of these the length strikes least; a hundred yards of even ground will never work such an effect as a tower a hundred yards high, or a rock or mountain of that altitude. I am apt to imagine, likewise, that height is less grand than depth; and that we are more struck at looking down from a precipice, than looking up at an object of equal height; but of that I am not very positive. A perpendicular has more force in forming the sublime, than an inclined plane, and the effects of a rugged and broken surface seem stronger than where it is smooth and polished. It would carry us out of our way to enter in this place into the cause of these appearances, but certain it is they afford a large and fruitful field of speculation. However, it may not be amiss to add to these remarks upon magnitude, that as the great extreme of dimension is sublime, so the last extreme of littleness is in some measure sublime likewise; when we attend to the infinite divisibility of matter, when we pursue animal life into these excessively small, and yet organized beings, that escape the nicest inquisition of the sense; when we push our discoveries yet downward, and consider those creatures so many degrees yet smaller, and the still diminishing scale of existence, in tracing which the imagination is lost as well as the sense; we become amazed and confounded at the wonders of minuteness; nor can we distinguish in its effect this extreme of littleness from the vast itself. For division must be infinite as well as addition; because the idea of a perfect unity can no more be arrived at, than that of a complete whole, to which nothing may be added.

SECTION VIII

INFINITY

Another source of the sublime is *infinity,* if it does not rather belong to the last. Infinity has a tendency to fill the mind with that sort of delightful horror, which is the most genuine effect, and truest test of the sublime. There are scarce any things which can become the objects of our senses, that are really and in their own nature infinite. But the eye not being able to perceive the bounds of many things, they seem to be infinite, and they produce the same effects as if they were really so. We are deceived in the like manner, if the parts of some large object are so continued to any indefinite number, that the imagination meets no check which may hinder its extending them at pleasure.

Whenever we repeat any idea frequently, the mind, by a sort of mechanism, repeats it long after the first cause has ceased to operate. After whirling about when we sit down, the objects about us still seem to whirl. After a long succession of noises, as the fall of waters, or the beating of forge-hammers, the hammers beat and the waters roar in the imagination long after the first sounds have ceased to affect it; and they die away at last by gradations which are scarcely perceptible. If you hold up a straight pole, with your eye to one end, it will seem extended to a length almost incredible. Place a number of uniform and equi-distant marks on this pole, they will cause the same deception, and seem multiplied without end. The senses, strongly affected in some one manner, cannot quickly change their tenor, or adapt themselves to other things; but they continue in their old channel until the strength of the first mover decays. This is the reason of an appearance very frequent in madmen; that they remain whole days and nights, sometimes whole years, in the constant repetition of some remark, some complaint, or song; which having struck powerfully on their disordered imagination in the beginning of their frenzy, every repetition reinforces it with new strength, and the hurry of their spirits, unrestrained by the curb of reason, continues it to the end of their lives.

SECTION XIV

LIGHT

Having considered extension, so far as it is capable of raising ideas of greatness; *color* comes next under consideration. All colors depend on *light.* Light therefore ought previously to be examined; and with it its opposite, darkness. With regard to light, to make it a cause capable of producing the sublime, it must be attended with some circumstances, besides its bare faculty of showing other objects. Mere light is too common a thing to make a strong impression on the mind, and without a strong impression nothing can be sublime. But such a light as that of the sun, immediately exerted on the eye, as it overpowers the sense, is a very great idea. Light of an inferior strength to this, if it moves with great celerity, has the same power; for lightning is certainly productive of grandeur, which it owes chiefly to the extreme velocity of its motion. A quick transition from light to darkness, or from darkness to light, has yet a greater effect. But darkness is more productive of sublime ideas than light. Our great poet was convinced of this; and indeed so full was he of this idea, so entirely possessed with the power of a well-managed darkness, that in describing the appearance of the Deity, amidst that profusion of magnificent images, which the grandeur of his subject provokes him to pour out upon every side, he is far from forgetting the obscurity which surrounds the most incomprehensible of all beings, but

With majesty of *darkness* round
Circles his throne.[17]

And what is no less remarkable, our author had the secret of preserving this idea, even when he seemed to depart the farthest from it, when he describes the light and glory which flows from the Divine presence; a light which by its very excess is converted into a species of darkness:—

Dark with excessive *light* thy skirts appear.[18]

Here is an idea not only poetical in a high degree, but strictly and philosophically just. Extreme light, by overcoming the organs of sight, obliterates all objects, so as in its effect exactly to resemble darkness. After looking for some time at the sun, two black spots, the impression which it leaves, seem to dance before our eyes. Thus are two ideas as opposite as can be imagined reconciled in the extremes of both; and both, in spite of their opposite nature, brought to concur in producing the sublime. And this is not the only instance wherein the opposite extremes operate equally in favor of the sublime, which in all things abhors mediocrity.

PART III

SECTION I

OF BEAUTY

It is my design to consider beauty as distinguished from the sublime; and, in the course of the inquiry, to examine how far it is consistent with it. But previous to this, we must take a short review of the opinions already entertained of this quality; which I think are hardly to be reduced to any fixed principles; because men are used to talk of beauty in a figurative manner, that is to say, in a manner extremely uncertain, and indeterminate. By beauty, I mean that quality, or those qualities in bodies, by which they cause love, or some passion similar to it. I confine this definition to the merely sensible qualities of things, for the sake of preserving the utmost simplicity in a subject, which must always distract us whenever we take in those various causes of sympathy which attach us to any persons or things from secondary considerations, and not from the direct force which they have merely on being viewed. I likewise distinguish love, (by which I mean that satisfaction which arises to the mind upon contemplating anything beautiful, of whatsoever nature it may be,) from desire or lust, which is an energy of the mind, that hurries us on to the

17. See *Paradise Lost,* II, 266–267.

18. See *Paradise Lost,* III, 380.

possession of certain objects, that do not affect us as they are beautiful, but by means altogether different. We shall have a strong desire for a woman of no remarkable beauty; whilst the greatest beauty in men, or in other animals, though it causes love, yet excites nothing at all of desire. Which shows that beauty, and the passion caused by beauty, which I call love, is different from desire, though desire may sometimes operate along with it; but it is to this latter that we must attribute those violent and tempestuous passions, and the consequent emotions of the body which attend what is called love in some of its ordinary acceptations, and not to the effects of beauty merely as it is such.

SECTION XII

THE REAL CAUSE OF BEAUTY

Having endeavored to show what beauty is not, it remains that we should examine, at least with equal attention, in what it really consists. Beauty is a thing much too affecting not to depend upon some positive qualities. And since it is no creature of our reason, since it strikes us without any reference to use, and even where no use at all can be discerned, since the order and method of nature is generally very different from our measures and proportions, we must conclude that beauty is, for the greater part, some quality in bodies acting mechanically upon the human mind by the intervention of the senses. We ought, therefore, to consider attentively in what manner those sensible qualities are disposed, in such things as by experience we find beautiful, or which excite in us the passion of love, or some correspondent affection.

SECTION XVIII

RECAPITULATION

On the whole, the qualities of beauty, as they are merely sensible qualities, are the following: First, to be comparatively small. Secondly, to be smooth. Thirdly, to have a variety in the direction of the parts; but, fourthly, to have those parts not angular, but melted, as it were, into each other. Fifthly, to be of a delicate frame, without any remarkable appearance of strength. Sixthly, to have its colors clear and bright, but not very strong and glaring. Seventhly, or if it should have any glaring color, to have it diversified with others. These are, I believe, the properties on which beauty depends; properties that operate by nature, and are less liable to be altered by caprice, or confounded by a diversity of tastes, than any other.

SECTION XXVII

THE SUBLIME AND BEAUTIFUL COMPARED

On closing this general view of beauty, it naturally occurs that we should compare it with the sublime; and in this comparison there appears a remarkable contrast. For sublime objects are vast in their dimensions, beautiful ones comparatively small; beauty should be smooth and polished; the great, rugged and negligent: beauty should shun the right line, yet deviate from it insensibly; the great in many cases loves the right line; and when it deviates, it often makes a strong deviation: beauty should not be obscure; the great ought to be dark and gloomy: beauty should be light and delicate; the great ought to be solid, and even massive. They are indeed ideas of a very different nature, one being founded on pain, the other on pleasure; and, however they may vary afterwards from the direct nature of their causes, yet these causes keep up an eternal distinction between them, a distinction never to be forgotten by any whose business it is to affect the passions. In the infinite variety of natural combinations, we must expect to find the qualities of things the most remote imaginable from each other united in the same object. We must expect also to find combinations of the same kind in the works of art. But when we consider the power of an object upon our passions, we must know that when anything is intended to affect the mind by the force of some predominant property, the affection produced is like to be the more uniform and perfect, if all the other properties or qualities of the object be of the same nature, and tending to the same design as the principal.

> If black and white blend, soften, and unite
> A thousand ways, are there no black and
> white?[19]

If the qualities of the sublime and beautiful are sometimes found united, does this prove that they are the same; does it prove that they are any way

19. See Pope, *Essay on Man*, II, 213–214.

allied; does it prove even that they are not opposite and contradictory? Black and white may soften, may blend; but they are not therefore the same. Nor, when they are so softened and blended with each other, or with different colors, is the power of black as black, or of white as white, so strong as when each stands uniform and distinguished.

PART IV

SECTION I

OF THE EFFICIENT CAUSE OF THE SUBLIME AND BEAUTIFUL

When I say, I intend to inquire into the efficient cause of sublimity and beauty, I would not be understood to say, that I can come to the ultimate cause. I do not pretend that I shall ever be able to explain why certain affections of the body produce such a distinct emotion of mind, and no other; or why the body is at all affected by the mind, or the mind by the body. A little thought will show this to be impossible. But I conceive, if we can discover what affections of the mind produce certain emotions of the body; and what distinct feelings and qualities of body shall produce certain determinate passions in the mind, and no others, I fancy a great deal will be done; something not unuseful towards a distinct knowledge of our passions, so far at least as we have them at present under our consideration. This is all, I believe, we can do. If we could advance a step farther, difficulties would still remain, as we should be still equally distant from the first cause. When Newton first discovered the property of attraction, and settled its laws, he found it served very well to explain several of the most remarkable phenomena in nature; but yet, with reference to the general system of things, he could consider attraction but as an effect, whose cause at that time he did not attempt to trace. But when he afterwards began to account for it by a subtle elastic ether, this great man (if in so great a man it be not impious to discover anything like a blemish) seemed to have quitted his usual cautious manner of philosophizing; since, perhaps, allowing all that has been advanced on this subject to be sufficiently proved, I think it leaves us with as many difficulties as it found us. That great chain of causes, which, linking one to another, even to the throne of God himself, can never be unravelled by any industry of ours. When we go but one step beyond the immediate sensible qualities of things, we go out of our depth. All we do after is but a faint struggle, that shows we are in an element which does not belong to us. So that when I speak of cause, and efficient cause, I only mean certain affections of the mind, that cause certain changes in the body; or certain powers and properties in bodies, that work a change in the mind. As, if I were to explain the motion of a body falling to the ground, I would say it was caused by gravity; and I would endeavor to show after what manner this power operated, without attempting to show why it operated in this manner: or, if I were to explain the effects of bodies striking one another by the common laws of percussion, I should not endeavor to explain how motion itself is communicated.

PART V

SECTION V

EXAMPLES THAT WORDS MAY AFFECT WITHOUT RAISING IMAGES

I find it very hard to persuade several that their passions are affected by words from whence they have no ideas; and yet harder to convince them that in the ordinary course of conversation we are sufficiently understood without raising any images of the things concerning which we speak. It seems to be an odd subject of dispute with any man, whether he has ideas in his mind or not. Of this, at first view, every man, in his own forum, ought to judge without appeal. But, strange as it may appear, we are often at a loss to know what ideas we have of things, or whether we have any ideas at all upon some subjects. It even requires a good deal of attention to be thoroughly satisfied on this head. Since I wrote these papers, I found two very striking instances of the possibility there is, that a man may hear words without having any idea of the things which they represent, and yet afterwards be capable of returning them to others, combined in a new way, and with great propriety, energy, and instruction. The first instance is that of Mr.

Blacklock, a poet blind from his birth.[20] Few men blessed with the most perfect sight can describe visual objects with more spirit and justness than this blind man; which cannot possibly be attributed to his having a clearer conception of the things he describes than is common to other persons. Mr. Spence, in an elegant preface which he has written to the works of this poet, reasons very ingeniously, and, I imagine, for the most part, very rightly upon the cause of this extraordinary phenomenon; but I cannot altogether agree with him, that some improprieties in language and thought, which occur in these poems, have arisen from the blind poet's imperfect conception of visual objects, since such improprieties, and much greater, may be found in writers even of a higher class than Mr. Blacklock, and who, notwithstanding, possessed the faculty of seeing in its full perfection. Here is a poet doubtless as much affected by his own descriptions as any that reads them can be; and yet he is affected with this strong enthusiasm by things of which he neither has, nor can possibly have, any idea further than that of a bare sound: and why may not those who read his works be affected in the same manner that he was; with as little of any real ideas of the things described? The second instance is of Mr. Saunderson, professor of mathematics in the University of Cambridge.[21] This learned man had acquired great knowledge in natural philosophy, in astronomy, and whatever sciences depend upon mathematical skill. What was the most extraordinary and the most to my purpose, he gave excellent lectures upon light and colors; and this man taught others the theory of those ideas which they had, and which he himself undoubtedly had not. But it is probable that the words red, blue, green, answered to him as well as the ideas of the colors themselves; for the ideas of greater or lesser degrees of refrangibility being applied to these words, and the blind man being instructed in what other respects they were found to agree or to disagree, it was as easy for him to reason upon the words as if he had been fully master of the ideas. Indeed it must be owned he could make no new discoveries in the way of experiment. He did nothing but what we do every day in common discourse. When I wrote this last sentence, and used the words *every day* and *common discourse,* I had no images in my mind of any succession of time; nor of men in conference with each other; nor do I imagine that the reader will have any such ideas on reading it. Neither when I spoke of red, or blue, and green, as well as refrangibility, had I these several colors, or the rays of light passing into a different medium, and there diverted from their course, painted before me in the way of images. I know very well that the mind possesses a faculty of raising such images at pleasure; but then an act of the will is necessary to this; and in ordinary conversation or reading it is very rarely that any image at all is excited in the mind. If I say, "I shall go to Italy next summer," I am well understood. Yet I believe nobody has by this painted in his imagination the exact figure of the speaker passing by land or by water, or both; sometimes on horseback, sometimes in a carriage: with all the particulars of the journey. Still less has he any idea of Italy, the country to which I proposed to go; or of the greenness of the fields, the ripening of the fruits, and the warmth of the air, with the change to this from a different season, which are the ideas for which the word *summer* is substituted; but least of all has he any image from the word *next;* for this word stands for the idea of many summers, with the exclusion of all but one: and surely the man who says *next summer* has no images of such a succession, and such an exclusion. In short, it is not only of those ideas which are commonly called abstract, and of which no image at all can be formed, but even of particular, real beings, that we converse without having any idea of them excited in the imagination; as will certainly appear on a diligent examination of our own minds. Indeed, so little does poetry depend for its effect on the power of raising sensible images, that I am convinced it would lose a very considerable part of its energy, if this were the necessary result of all description. Because that union of affecting words, which is the most powerful of all poetical instruments, would frequently

20. Mr. Blacklock . . . birth: a reference to Thomas Blacklock (1721–1791), a Scottish poet who was blind from the age of six months and who published his *Poems* in 1746. Joseph Spence, the celebrated eighteenth-century man of letters, published a critical preface to the second edition of Blacklock's *Poems* in 1756. **21. Mr. Saunderson . . . Cambridge:** Nicolas Saunderson (1682–1739), a Professor of Mathematics at Cambridge University.

lose its force along with its propriety and consistency, if the sensible images were always excited. There is not, perhaps, in the whole *Æneid* a more grand and labored passage than the description of Vulcan's cavern in Etna, and the works that are there carried on. Virgil dwells particularly on the formation of the thunder which he describes unfinished under the hammers of the Cyclops. But what are the principles of this extraordinary composition?

> Tres imbris torti radios, tres nubis aquosæ
> Addiderant; rutili tres ignis, et alitis austri:
> Fulgores nunc terrificos, sonitumque,
> metumque
> Miscebant operi, flammisque sequacibus iras.[22]

This seems to me admirably sublime: yet if we attend coolly to the kind of sensible images which a combination of ideas of this sort must form, the chimeras of madmen cannot appear more wild and absurd than such a picture. *"Three rays of twisted showers, three of watery clouds, three of fire, and three of the winged south wind; then mixed they in the work terrific lightnings, and sound, and fear, and anger, with pursuing flames."* This strange composition is formed into a gross body; it is hammered by the Cyclops, it is in part polished, and partly continues rough. The truth is, if poetry gives us a noble assemblage of words corresponding to many noble ideas, which are connected by circumstances of time or place, or related to each other as cause and effect, or associated in any natural way, they may be moulded together in any form, and perfectly answer their end. The picturesque connection is not demanded; because no real picture is formed; nor is the effect of the description at all the less upon this account. What is said of Helen by Priam and the old men of his council, is generally thought to give us the highest possible idea of that fatal beauty.

> Οὐ νέμεσις, Τρῶας καὶ ἐϋκνήμιδας Ἀχαιοὺς
> Τοιῇδ' ἀμφὶ γυναικὶ πολὺν χρόνον ἄλγεα πάσχειν·
> Αἰνῶς ἀθανάτῃσι θεῇς εἰς ὦπα ἔοικεν·

> They cried, No wonder such celestial charms
> For nine long years have set the world in arms;
> What winning graces! what majestic mien!
> She moves a goddess, and she looks a queen.
>
> POPE.[23]

Here is not one word said of the particulars of her beauty; nothing which can in the least help us to any precise idea of her person; but yet we are much more touched by this manner of mentioning her, than by those long and labored descriptions of Helen, whether handed down by tradition, or formed by fancy, which are to be met with in some authors. I am sure it affects me much more than the minute description which Spenser has given of Belphebe;[24] though I own that there are parts, in that description, as there are in all the descriptions of that excellent writer, extremely fine and poetical. The terrible picture which Lucretius has drawn of religion in order to display the magnanimity of his philosophical hero in opposing her, is thought to be designed with great boldness and spirit:—

> Humana ante oculos fœdè cum vita jaceret,
> In terris, oppressa gravi sub religione,
> Quæ caput e cœli regionibus ostendebat
> Horribili super aspectu mortalibus instans;
> Primus Graius homo mortales tollere contra
> Est oculos ausus.[25]

What idea do you derive from so excellent a picture? none at all, most certainly: neither has the poet said a single word which might in the least serve to mark a single limb or feature of the phantom, which he intended to represent in all the horrors imagination can conceive. In reality, poetry and rhetoric do not succeed in exact description so well as painting does; their business is, to affect rather by sympathy than imitation; to display rather the effect of things on the mind of the speaker, or of others, than to present a clear idea of the things themselves. This is their most extensive province, and that in which they succeed the best.

SECTION VI

POETRY NOT STRICTLY AN IMITATIVE ART

Hence we may observe that poetry, taken in its most general sense, cannot with strict propriety be called an art of imitation. It is indeed an imitation

22. See *Aeneid,* VIII, 429–432. **23.** Pope's translation (ll. 205–208) of the *Iliad,* III (ll. 156–158).

24. See *Faerie Queene,* II, iii, 21–31. **25. Humana . . . ausus:** "When human life lay across the earth crushed by grave religion before all eyes, who would show her head from heaven scowling at mortals with horrible aspect, a Greek it was who first dared to lift his eyes in opposition." See *De Rerum Natura,* I, 62–67.

so far as it describes the manners and passions of men which their words can express; where *animi motus effert interprete lingua.*[26] There it is strictly imitation; and all merely *dramatic* poetry is of this sort. But *descriptive* poetry operates chiefly by *substitution;* by the means of sounds, which by custom have the effect of realities. Nothing is an imitation further than as it resembles some other thing; and words undoubtedly have no sort of resemblance to the ideas for which they stand.

SECTION VII

HOW WORDS INFLUENCE THE PASSIONS

Now, as words affect, not by any original power, but by representation, it might be supposed, that their influence over the passions should be but light; yet it is quite otherwise; for we find by experience, that eloquence and poetry are as capable, nay indeed much more capable, of making deep and lively impressions than any other arts, and even than nature itself in very many cases. And this arises chiefly from these three causes. First, that we take an extraordinary part in the passions of others, and that we are easily affected and brought into sympathy by any tokens which are shown of them; and there are no tokens which can express all the circumstances of most passions so fully as words; so that if a person speaks upon any subject, he can not only convey the subject to you, but likewise the manner in which he is himself affected by it. Certain it is, that the influence of most things on our passions is not so much from the things themselves, as from our opinions concerning them; and these again depend very much on the opinions of other men, conveyable for the most part by words only. Secondly, there are many things of a very affecting nature, which can seldom occur in the reality, but the words that represent them often do; and thus they have an opportunity of making a deep impression and taking root in the mind, whilst the idea of the reality was transient; and to some perhaps never really occurred in any shape, to whom it is notwithstanding very affecting, as war, death, famine, &c. Besides many ideas have never been at all presented to the senses of any men but by words, as God, angels, devils, heaven, and hell, all of which have however a great influence over the passions. Thirdly, by words we have it in our power to make such *combinations* as we cannot possibly do otherwise. By this power of combining we are able, by the addition of well-chosen circumstances, to give a new life and force to the simple object. In painting we may represent any fine figure we please; but we never can give it those enlivening touches which it may receive from words. To represent an angel in a picture, you can only draw a beautiful young man winged: but what painting can furnish out anything so grand as the addition of one word, "the angel of the *Lord*"? It is true, I have here no clear idea; but these words affect the mind more than the sensible image did; which is all I contend for. A picture of Priam dragged to the altar's foot, and there murdered, if it were well executed, would undoubtedly be very moving; but there are very aggravating circumstances, which it could never represent:

> Sanguine fœdantem *quos ipse sacraverat* ignes.[27]

As a further instance, let us consider those lines of Milton, where he describes the travels of the fallen angels through their dismal habitation:

> O'er many a dark and dreary vale
> They passed, and many a region dolorous;
> O'er many a frozen, many a fiery Alp;
> Rocks, caves, lakes, fens, bogs, dens, and shades of death,
> A universe of death.[28]

Here is displayed the force of union in

> Rocks, caves, lakes, dens, bogs, fens, and shades

which yet would lose the greatest part of their effect, if they were not the

> Rocks, caves, lakes, dens, bogs, fens, and shades—of *Death.*

This idea or this affection caused by a word, which nothing but a word could annex to the others, raises a very great degree of the sublime,

26. ***animi . . . lingua:*** "With the tongue as interpreter she conveys the movement of the spirit." See Horace, *Ars Poetica,* l. 111.

27. **Sanguine . . . ignes:** "Corrupting with his blood the fires he himself had made sacred." See *Aeneid,* II, 502.

28. See *Paradise Lost,* II, 618–622.

and this sublime is raised yet higher by what follows, a "*universe of death.*" Here are again two ideas not presentable but by language, and an union of them great and amazing beyond conception; if they may properly be called ideas which present no distinct image to the mind; but still it will be difficult to conceive how words can move the passions which belong to real objects, without representing these objects clearly. This is difficult to us, because we do not sufficiently distinguish, in our observations upon language, between a clear expression and a strong expression. These are frequently confounded with each other, though they are in reality extremely different. The former regards the understanding, the latter belongs to the passions. The one describes a thing as it is, the latter describes it as it is felt. Now, as there is a moving tone of voice, an impassioned countenance, an agitated gesture, which affect independently of the things about which they are exerted, so there are words, and certain dispositions of words, which being peculiarly devoted to passionate subjects, and always used by those who are under the influence of any passion, touch and move us more than those which far more clearly and distinctly express the subject-matter. We yield to sympathy what we refuse to description. The truth is, all verbal description, merely as naked description, though never so exact, conveys so poor and insufficient an idea of the thing described, that it could scarcely have the smallest effect, if the speaker did not call in to his aid those modes of speech that mark a strong and lively feeling in himself. Then, by the contagion of our passions, we catch a fire already kindled in another, which probably might never have been struck out by the object described. Words, by strongly conveying the passions by those means which we have already mentioned, fully compensate for their weakness in other respects. It may be observed, that very polished languages, and such as are praised for their superior clearness and perspicuity, are generally deficient in strength. The French language has that perfection and that defect. Whereas the Oriental tongues, and in general the languages of most unpolished people, have a great force and energy of expression, and this is but natural. Uncultivated people are but ordinary observers of things, and not critical in distinguishing them; but, for that reason they admire more, and are more affected with what they see, and therefore express themselves in a warmer and more passionate manner. If the affection be well conveyed, it will work its effect without any clear idea, often without any idea at all of the thing which has originally given rise to it.

It might be expected, from the fertility of the subject, that I should consider poetry, as it regards the sublime and beautiful, more at large; but it must be observed, that in this light it has been often and well handled already. It was not my design to enter into the criticism of the sublime and beautiful in any art, but to attempt to lay down such principles as may tend to ascertain, to distinguish, and to form a sort of standard for them; which purposes I thought might be best effected by an inquiry into the properties of such things in nature, as raise love and astonishment in us; and by showing in what manner they operated to produce these passions. Words were only so far to be considered as to show upon what principle they were capable of being the representatives of these natural things, and by what powers they were able to affect us often as strongly as the things they represent, and sometimes much more strongly.

FROM

Speech on Moving His Resolutions for Conciliation with the Colonies

MARCH 22, 1775

I hope, Sir, that, notwithstanding the austerity of the Chair, your good-nature will incline you to some degree of indulgence towards human frailty. You will not think it unnatural, that those who have an object depending,[1] which strongly engages their hopes and fears, should be somewhat inclined to superstition. As I came into the House, full of anxiety about the event of my motion, I found, to my infinite surprise, that the grand penal bill by which we had passed sentence on the trade and sustenance of America is to be returned to us from

SPEECH ON CONCILIATION. **1. depending:** pending, unsettled.

the other House.* I do confess, I could not help looking on this event as a fortunate omen. I look upon it as a sort of Providential favor by which we are put once more in possession of our deliberative capacity, upon a business so very questionable in its nature, so very uncertain in its issue. By the return of this bill, which seemed to have taken its flight forever, we are at this very instant nearly as free to choose a plan for our American government as we were on the first day of the session. If, Sir, we incline to the side of conciliation, we are not at all embarrassed (unless we please to make ourselves so) by any incongruous mixture of coercion and restraint. We are therefore called upon, as it were by a superior warning voice, again to attend to America,—to attend to the whole of it together,—and to review the subject with an unusual degree of care and calmness.

Surely it is an awful subject,—or there is none so on this side of the grave. When I first had the honor of a seat in this House, the affairs of that continent pressed themselves upon us as the most important and most delicate object of Parliamentary attention. My little share in this great deliberation oppressed me. I found myself a partaker in a very high trust; and having no sort of reason to rely on the strength of my natural abilities for the proper execution of that trust, I was obliged to take more than common pains to instruct myself in everything which relates to our colonies. I was not less under the necessity of forming some fixed ideas concerning the general policy of the British empire. Something of this sort seemed to be indispensable, in order, amidst so vast a fluctuation of passions and opinions, to concentre my thoughts, to ballast my conduct, to preserve me from being blown about by every wind of fashionable doctrine. I really did not think it safe or manly to have fresh principles to seek upon every fresh mail which should arrive from America.

At that period I had the fortune to find myself in perfect concurrence with a large majority in this House. Bowing under that high authority, and penetrated with the sharpness and strength of that early impression, I have continued ever since, without the least deviation, in my original sentiments. Whether this be owing to an obstinate perseverance in error, or to a religious adherence to what appears to me truth and reason, it is in your equity to judge.

Sir, Parliament, having an enlarged view of objects, made, during this interval, more frequent changes in their sentiments and their conduct than could be justified in a particular person upon the contracted scale of private information. But though I do not hazard anything approaching to a censure on the motives of former Parliaments to all those alterations, one fact is undoubted,—that under them the state of America has been kept in continual agitation. Everything administered as remedy to the public complaint, if it did not produce, was at least followed by, an heightening of the distemper, until, by a variety of experiments, that important country has been brought into her present situation,—a situation which I will not miscall, which I dare not name, which I scarcely know how to comprehend in the terms of any description.

In this posture, Sir, things stood at the beginning of the session. About that time, a worthy member,[2] of great Parliamentary experience, who in the year 1766 filled the chair of the American Committee with much ability, took me aside, and, lamenting the present aspect of our politics, told me, things were come to such a pass that our former methods of proceeding in the House would be no longer tolerated,—that the public tribunal (never too indulgent to a long and unsuccessful opposition) would now scrutinize our conduct with unusual severity,—that the very vicissitudes and shiftings of ministerial measures, instead of convicting their authors of inconstancy and want of system, would be taken as an occasion of charging us with a predetermined discontent which nothing could satisfy, whilst we accused every measure of vigor as cruel and every proposal of lenity as weak and irresolute. The public, he said, would not have patience to see us play the game out with our adversaries; we must

* The act to restrain the trade and commerce of the provinces of Massachusetts Bay and New Hampshire, and colonies of Connecticut and Rhode Island and Providence Plantation, in North America, to Great Britain, Ireland, and the British Islands in the West Indies; and to prohibit such provinces and colonies from carrying on any fishery on the banks of Newfoundland, and other places therein mentioned, under certain conditions and limitations.

2. **worthy member:** Rose Fuller.

produce our hand. It would be expected that those who for many years had been active in such affairs should show that they had formed some clear and decided idea of the principles of colony government, and were capable of drawing out something like a platform of the ground which might be laid for future and permanent tranquillity.

I felt the truth of what my honorable friend represented; but I felt my situation, too. His application might have been made with far greater propriety to many other gentlemen. No man was, indeed, ever better disposed, or worse qualified, for such an undertaking, than myself. Though I gave so far into his opinion, that I immediately threw my thoughts into a sort of Parliamentary form, I was by no means equally ready to produce them. It generally argues some degree of natural impotence of mind, or some want of knowledge of the world, to hazard plans of government, except from a seat of authority. Propositions are made, not only ineffectually, but somewhat disreputably, when the minds of men are not properly disposed for their reception; and for my part, I am not ambitious of ridicule, not absolutely a candidate for disgrace.

Besides, Sir, to speak the plain truth, I have in general no very exalted opinion of the virtue of paper government, nor of any politics in which the plan is to be wholly separated from the execution. But when I saw that anger and violence prevailed every day more and more, and that things were hastening towards an incurable alienation of our colonies, I confess my caution gave way. I felt this as one of those few moments in which decorum yields to an higher duty. Public calamity is a mighty leveller; and there are occasions when any, even the slightest, chance of doing good must be laid hold on, even by the most inconsiderable person.

To restore order and repose to an empire so great and so distracted as ours is, merely an attempt, an undertaking that would ennoble the flights of the highest genius, and obtain pardon for the efforts of the meanest understanding. Struggling a good while with these thoughts, by degrees I felt myself more firm. I derived, at length, some confidence from what in other circumstances usually produces timidity. I grew less anxious, even from the idea of my own insignificance. For, judging of what you are by what you ought to be, I persuaded myself that you would not reject a reasonable proposition because it had nothing but its reason to recommend it. On the other hand, being totally destitute of all shadow of influence, natural or adventitious, I was very sure, that, if my proposition were futile or dangerous, if it were weakly conceived or improperly timed, there was nothing exterior to it of power to awe, dazzle, or delude you. You will see it just as it is, and you will treat it just as it deserves.

The proposition is peace. Not peace through the medium of war; not peace to be hunted through the labyrinth of intricate and endless negotiations; not peace to arise out of universal discord, fomented from principle, in all parts of the empire; not peace to depend on the juridical determination of perplexing questions, or the precise marking the shadowy boundaries of a complex government. It is simple peace, sought in its natural course and in its ordinary haunts. It is peace sought in the spirit of peace, and laid in principles purely pacific. I propose, by removing the ground of the difference, and by restoring the *former unsuspecting confidence of the colonies in the mother country,* to give permanent satisfaction to your people,—and (far from a scheme of ruling by discord) to reconcile them to each other in the same act and by the bond of the very same interest which reconciles them to British government.

My idea is nothing more. Refined policy ever has been the parent of confusion,—and ever will be so, as long as the world endures. Plain good intention, which is as easily discovered at the first view as fraud is surely detected at last, is, let me say, of no mean force in the government of mankind. Genuine simplicity of heart is an healing and cementing principle. My plan, therefore, being formed upon the most simple grounds imaginable, may disappoint some people, when they hear it. It has nothing to recommend it to the pruriency of curious ears. There is nothing at all new and captivating in it. It has nothing of the splendor of the project which has been lately laid upon your table by the noble lord in the blue riband.[3] It does not propose to fill your lobby with squabbling colony

3. lord . . . riband: a reference to Lord North, who had moved the resolution, passed by the House, not to impose taxes on any colony that contributed voluntarily to the common defense and well-being. The blue riband refers to North's membership in the Knights of the Garter.

agents, who will require the interposition of your mace at every instant to keep the peace amongst them. It does not institute a magnificent auction of finance, where captivated provinces come to general ransom by bidding against each other, until you knock down the hammer, and determine a proportion of payments beyond all the powers of algebra to equalize and settle.

The plan which I shall presume to suggest derives, however, one great advantage from the proposition and registry of that noble lord's project. The idea of conciliation is admissible. First, the House, in accepting the resolution moved by the noble lord, has admitted, notwithstanding the menacing front of our address, notwithstanding our heavy bill of pains and penalties, that we do not think ourselves precluded from all ideas of free grace and bounty.

The House has gone farther: it has declared conciliation admissible *previous* to any submission on the part of America. It has even shot a good deal beyond that mark, and has admitted that the complaints of our former mode of exerting the right of taxation were not wholly unfounded. That right thus exerted is allowed to have had something reprehensible in it,—something unwise, or something grievous; since, in the midst of our heat and resentment, we, of ourselves, have proposed a capital alteration, and, in order to get rid of what seemed so very exceptionable, have instituted a mode that is altogether new,—one that is, indeed, wholly alien from all the ancient methods and forms of Parliament.

The *principle* of this proceeding is large enough for my purpose. The means proposed by the noble lord for carrying his ideas into execution, I think, indeed, are very indifferently suited to the end; and this I shall endeavor to show you before I sit down. But, for the present, I take my ground on the admitted principle. I mean to give peace. Peace implies reconciliation; and where there has been a material dispute, reconciliation does in a manner always imply concession on the one part or on the other. In this state of things I make no difficulty in affirming that the proposal ought to originate from us. Great and acknowledged force is not impaired, either in effect or in opinion, by an unwillingness to exert itself. The superior power may offer peace with honor and with safety. Such an offer from such a power will be attributed to magnanimity. But the concessions of the weak are the concessions of fear. When such a one is disarmed, he is wholly at the mercy of his superior; and he loses forever that time and those chances which, as they happen to all men, are the strength and resources of all inferior power.

The capital leading questions on which you must this day decide are these two: First, whether you ought to concede: and secondly, what your concession ought to be. On the first of these questions we have gained (as I have just taken the liberty of observing to you) some ground. But I am sensible that a good deal more is still to be done. Indeed, Sir, to enable us to determine both on the one and the other of these great questions with a firm and precise judgment, I think it may be necessary to consider distinctly the true nature and the peculiar circumstances of the object which we have before us: because, after all our struggle, whether we will or not, we must govern America according to that nature and to those circumstances, and not according to our own imaginations, not according to abstract ideas of right, by no means according to mere general theories of government, the resort to which appears to me, in our present situation, no better than arrant trifling. I shall therefore endeavor, with your leave, to lay before you some of the most material of these circumstances in as full and as clear a manner as I am able to state them.

The first thing that we have to consider with regard to the nature of the object is the number of people in the colonies. I have taken for some years a good deal of pains on that point. I can by no calculation justify myself in placing the number below two millions of inhabitants of our own European blood and color,—besides at least 500,000 others, who form no inconsiderable part of the strength and opulence of the whole. This, Sir, is, I believe, about the true number. There is no occasion to exaggerate, where plain truth is of so much weight and importance. But whether I put the present numbers too high or too low is a matter of little moment. Such is the strength with which population shoots in that part of the world, that, state the numbers as high as we will, whilst the dispute continues, the exaggeration ends. Whilst we are discussing any given magnitude, they are grown to it. Whilst we spend our time in deliberating on the mode of governing two millions, we shall find we have millions more to manage. Your children do not grow faster from infancy to manhood than they spread from families to communities, and from villages to nations.

I put this consideration of the present and the growing numbers in the front of our deliberation, because, Sir, this consideration will make it evident to a blunter discernment than yours, that no partial, narrow, contracted, pinched, occasional system will be at all suitable to such an object. It will show you that it is not to be considered as one of those *minima*[4] which are out of the eye and consideration of the law,—not a paltry excrescence of the state,—not a mean dependant, who may be neglected with little damage and provoked with little danger. It will prove that some degree of care and caution is required in the handling such an object; it will show that you ought not, in reason, to trifle with so large a mass of the interests and feelings of the human race. You could at no time do so without guilt; and be assured you will not be able to do it long with impunity.

But the population of this country, the great and growing population, though a very important consideration, will lose much of its weight, if not combined with other circumstances. The commerce of your colonies is out of all proportion beyond the numbers of the people. This ground of their commerce, indeed, has been trod some days ago, and with great ability, by a distinguished person,[5] at your bar. This gentleman, after thirty-five years,—it is so long since he first appeared at the same place to plead for the commerce of Great Britain,—has come again before you to plead the same cause, without any other effect of time than that to the fire of imagination and extent of erudition, which even then marked him as one of the first literary characters of his age, he has added a consummate knowledge in the commercial interest of his country, formed by a long course of enlightened and discriminating experience.

Sir, I should be inexcusable in coming after such a person with any detail, if a great part of the members who now fill the House had not the misfortune to be absent when he appeared at your bar. Besides, Sir, I propose to take the matter at periods of time somewhat different from his. There is, if I mistake not, a point of view from whence, if you will look at this subject, it is impossible that it should not make an impression upon you.

I have in my hand two accounts: one a comparative state of the export trade of England to its colonies as it stood in the year 1704, and as it stood in the year 1772; the other a state of the export trade of this country to its colonies alone, as it stood in 1772, compared with the whole trade of England to all parts of the world (the colonies included) in the year 1704. They are from good vouchers: the latter period from the accounts on your table; the earlier from an original manuscript of Davenant, who first established the Inspector-General's office, which has been ever since his time so abundant a source of Parliamentary information.

The export trade to the colonies consists of three great branches: the African, which, terminating almost wholly in the colonies, must be put to the account of their commerce; the West Indian; and the North American. All these are so interwoven, that the attempt to separate them would tear to pieces the contexture of the whole, and, if not entirely destroy, would very much depreciate, the value of all the parts. I therefore consider these three denominations to be, what in effect they are, one trade.

The trade to the colonies, taken on the export side, at the beginning of this century, that is, in the year 1704, stood thus:—

Exports to North America and the West Indies	£483,265
To Africa	86,665
	£569,930

In the year 1772, which I take as a middle year between the highest and lowest of those lately laid on your table, the account was as follows:—

To North America and the West Indies	£4,791,734
To Africa	866,398
To which if you add the export trade from Scotland, which had in 1704 no existence	364,000
	£6,022,132

From five hundred and odd thousand, it has grown to six millions. It has increased no less than twelvefold. This is the state of the colony trade,

4. ***minima:*** small matters. 5. **distinguished person:** Richard Glover (1712–1785), Member of Parliament for Weymouth and Melcombe Regis.

as compared with itself at these two periods, within this century;—and this is matter for meditation. But this is not all. Examine my second account. See how the export trade to the colonies alone in 1772 stood in the other point of view, that is, as compared to the whole trade of England in 1704.

The whole export trade of England, including that to the colonies, in 1704	£6,509,000
Export to the colonies alone, in 1772	6,024,000
Difference	£ 485,000

The trade with America alone is now within less than £500,000 of being equal to what this great commercial nation, England, carried on at the beginning of this century with the whole world! If I had taken the largest year of those on your table, it would rather have exceeded. But, it will be said, is not this American trade an unnatural protuberance, that has drawn the juices from the rest of the body? The reverse. It is the very food that has nourished every other part into its present magnitude. Our general trade has been greatly augmented, and augmented more or less in almost every part to which it ever extended, but with this material difference: that of the six millions which in the beginning of the century constituted the whole mass of our export commerce the colony trade was but one twelfth part; it is now (as a part of sixteen millions) considerably more than a third of the whole. This is the relative proportion of the importance of the colonies at these two periods: and all reasoning concerning our mode of treating them must have this proportion as its basis, or it is a reasoning weak, rotten, and sophistical.

Mr. Speaker, I cannot prevail on myself to hurry over this great consideration. It is good for us to be here. We stand where we have an immense view of what is, and what is past. Clouds indeed, and darkness, rest upon the future. Let us, however, before we descend from this noble eminence, reflect that this growth of our national prosperity has happened within the short period of the life of man. It has happened within sixty-eight years. There are those alive whose memory might touch the two extremities. For instance, my Lord Bathurst might remember all the stages of the progress. He was in 1704 of an age at least to be made to comprehend such things. He was then old enough *acta parentum jam legere, et quæ sit poterit cognoscere virtus*.[6] Suppose, Sir, that the angel of this auspicious youth, foreseeing the many virtues which made him one of the most amiable, as he is one of the most fortunate men of his age, had opened to him in vision, that, when, in the fourth generation, the third prince of the House of Brunswick had sat twelve years on the throne of the nation which (by the happy issue of moderate and healing councils) was to be made Great Britain,[7] he should see his son, Lord Chancellor of England,[8] turn back the current of hereditary dignity to its fountain, and raise him to an higher rank of peerage, whilst he enriched the family with a new one,—if, amidst these bright and happy scenes of domestic honor and prosperity, that angel should have drawn up the curtain, and unfolded the rising glories of his country, and whilst he was gazing with admiration on the then commercial grandeur of England, the genius should point out to him a little speck, scarce visible in the mass of the national interest, a small seminal principle rather than a formed body, and should tell him,—"Young man, there is America,—which at this day serves for little more than to amuse you with stories of savage men and uncouth manners, yet shall, before you taste of death, show itself equal to the whole of that commerce which now attracts the envy of the world. Whatever England has been growing to by a progressive increase of improvement, brought in by varieties of people, by succession of civilizing conquests and civilizing settlements in a series of seventeen hundred years, you shall see as much added to her by America in the course of a single life!" If this state of his country had been foretold to him, would it not require all the sanguine credulity of youth, and all the fervid glow of enthusiasm, to make him believe it? Fortunate man, he has lived to see it! Fortunate indeed, if he lives to see nothing that shall vary the prospect, and cloud the setting of his day!

6. ***acta . . . virtus:*** "To read of the deeds of his ancestors, and to know what virtue is." See Virgil, *Eclogues*, IV, 26. **7.** King George I (1660–1727), the first of the House of Brunswick to assume the throne of Great Britain. The union referred to is that of England and Scotland. **8.** Henry, the eldest surviving son of Lord Bathurst, became Lord Chancellor in 1771. He was elevated to the peerage as Baron Apsley.

Excuse me, Sir, if, turning from such thoughts, I resume this comparative view once more. You have seen it on a large scale; look at it on a small one. I will point out to your attention a particular instance of it in the single province of Pennsylvania. In the year 1704, that province called for £11,459 in value of your commodities, native and foreign. This was the whole. What did it demand in 1772? Why, nearly fifty times as much; for in that year the export to Pennsylvania was £507,909, nearly equal to the export to all the colonies together in the first period.

I choose, Sir, to enter into these minute and particular details; because generalities, which in all other cases are apt to heighten and raise the subject, have here a tendency to sink it. When we speak of the commerce with our colonies, fiction lags after truth, invention is unfruitful, and imagination cold and barren.

So far, Sir, as to the importance of the object in the view of its commerce, as concerned in the exports from England. If I were to detail the imports, I could show how many enjoyments they procure which deceive the burden of life, how many materials which invigorate the springs of national industry and extend and animate every part of our foreign and domestic commerce. This would be a curious subject indeed,—but I must prescribe bounds to myself in a matter so vast and various.

I pass, therefore, to the colonies in another point of view,—their agriculture. This they have prosecuted with such a spirit, that, besides feeding plentifully their own growing multitude, their annual export of grain, comprehending rice, has some years ago exceeded a million value. Of their last harvest, I am persuaded, they will export much more. At the beginning of the century some of these colonies imported corn from the mother country. For some time past the Old World has been fed from the New. The scarcity which you have felt would have been a desolating famine, if this child of your old age, with a true filial piety, with a Roman charity, had not put the full breast of its youthful exuberance to the mouth of its exhausted parent.

As to the wealth, which the colonies have drawn from the sea by their fisheries, you had all that matter fully opened at your bar. You surely thought those acquisitions of value, for they seemed even to excite your envy; and yet the spirit by which that enterprising employment has been exercised ought rather, in my opinion, to have raised your esteem and admiration. And pray, Sir, what in the world is equal to it? Pass by the other parts, and look at the manner in which the people of New England have of late carried on the whale-fishery. Whilst we follow them among the tumbling mountains of ice, and behold them penetrating into the deepest frozen recesses of Hudson's Bay and Davis's Straits, whilst we are looking for them beneath the arctic circle, we hear that they have pierced into the opposite region of polar cold, that they are at the antipodes, and engaged under the frozen serpent of the South. Falkland Island, which seemed too remote and romantic an object for the grasp of national ambition, is but a stage and resting-place in the progress of their victorious industry. Nor is the equinoctial heat more discouraging to them than the accumulated winter of both the poles. We know, that, whilst some of them draw the line and strike the harpoon on the coast of Africa, others run the longitude, and pursue their gigantic game along the coast of Brazil. No sea but what is vexed by their fisheries. No climate that is not witness to their toils. Neither the perseverance of Holland, nor the activity of France, nor the dexterous and firm sagacity of English enterprise, ever carried this most perilous mode of hardy industry to the extent to which it has been pushed by this recent people,—a people who are still, as it were, but in the gristle, and not yet hardened into the bone of manhood. When I contemplate these things,—when I know that the colonies in general owe little or nothing to any care of ours, and that they are not squeezed into this happy form by the constraint of watchful and suspicious government, but that, through a wise and salutary neglect, a generous nature has been suffered to take her own way to perfection,—when I reflect upon these effects, when I see how profitable they have been to us, I feel all the pride of power sink, and all presumption in the wisdom of human contrivances melt and die away within me,—my rigor relents,—I pardon something to spirit of liberty.

I am sensible, Sir, that all which I have asserted in my detail is admitted in the gross, but that quite a different conclusion is drawn from it. America, gentlemen say, is a noble object,—it is an object well worth fighting for. Certainly it is, if fighting a people be the best way of gaining them. Gentlemen in this respect will be led to their choice of means by their complexions and their habits. Those who understand the military art will of course have some predilection for it. Those who wield the thunder of the state may have more confidence in the efficacy of arms. But I confess, possibly for want of this knowledge, my opinion is much more in favor of prudent management than of force,—considering force not as an odious, but a feeble instrument, for preserving a people so numerous, so active, so growing, so spirited as this, in a profitable and subordinate connection with us.

First, Sir, permit me to observe, that the use of force alone is but temporary. It may subdue for a moment; but it does not remove the necessity of subduing again: and a nation is not governed which is perpetually to be conquered.

My next objection is its uncertainty. Terror is not always the effect of force, and an armament is not a victory. If you do not succeed, you are without resource: for, conciliation failing, force remains; but, force failing, no further hope of reconciliation is left. Power and authority are sometimes bought by kindness; but they can never be begged as alms by an impoverished and defeated violence.

A further objection to force is, that you impair the object by your very endeavors to preserve it. The thing you fought for is not the thing which you recover, but depreciated, sunk, wasted, and consumed in the contest. Nothing less will content me than *whole America*. I do not choose to consume its strength along with our own; because in all parts it is the British strength that I consume. I do not choose to be caught by a foreign enemy at the end of this exhausting conflict, and still less in the midst of it. I may escape, but I can make no insurance against such an event. Let me add, that I do not choose wholly to break the American spirit; because it is the spirit that has made the country.

Lastly, we have no sort of *experience* in favor of force as an instrument in the rule of our colonies. Their growth and their utility has been owing to methods altogether different. Our ancient indulgence has been said to be pursued to a fault. It may be so; but we know, if feeling is evidence, that our fault was more tolerable than our attempt to mend it, and our sin far more salutary than our penitence.

These, Sir, are my reasons for not entertaining that high opinion of untried force by which many gentlemen, for whose sentiments in other particulars I have great respect, seem to be so greatly captivated. But there is still behind a third consideration concerning this object, which serves to determine my opinion on the sort of policy which ought to be pursued in the management of America, even more than its population and its commerce: I mean its *temper and character*.

In this character of the Americans a love of freedom is the predominating feature which marks and distinguishes the whole: and as an ardent is always a jealous affection, your colonies become suspicious, restive, and untractable, whenever they see the least attempt to wrest from them by force, or shuffle from them by chance, what they think the only advantage worth living for. This fierce spirit of liberty is stronger in the English colonies, probably, than in any other people of the earth, and this from a great variety of powerful causes; which, to understand the true temper of their minds, and the direction which this spirit takes, it will not be amiss to lay open somewhat more largely.

First, the people of the colonies are descendants of Englishmen. England, Sir, is a nation which still, I hope, respects, and formerly adored, her freedom. The colonists emigrated from you when this part of your character was most predominant; and they took this bias and direction the moment they parted from your hands. They are therefore not only devoted to liberty, but to liberty according to English ideas and on English principles. Abstract liberty, like other mere abstractions, is not to be found. Liberty inheres in some sensible object; and every nation has formed to itself some favorite point, which by way of eminence becomes the criterion of their happiness. It happened, you know, Sir, that the great contests for freedom in this country were from the earliest times chiefly upon the question of taxing. Most of the contests in the ancient commonwealths turned primarily on the right of election of magistrates, or on the balance among the several orders of the state. The question of money was not with them so immediate. But in England it was otherwise. On this point of taxes the ablest pens and most eloquent tongues have been exercised, the greatest spirits have acted and suffered. In order to give the fullest satisfaction concerning the importance of this point, it was not only necessary for those who in argument defended the excellence of the English Constitution to insist on this privilege of granting money as a dry point of fact, and to prove that the right had been acknowledged in ancient parchments and blind usages to reside in a certain body called an House of Commons: they went much further: they attempted to prove, and they succeeded, that in theory it ought to be so, from the particular nature of a House of Commons, as an immediate representative of the people, whether the old records had delivered this oracle or not. They took infinite pains to inculcate, as a fundamental principle, that in all monarchies the people must in effect themselves, mediately or immediately, possess the power of granting their own money, or no shadow of liberty could subsist. The colonies draw from you, as with their life-blood, these ideas and principles. Their love of liberty, as with you, fixed and attached on this specific point of taxing. Liberty might be safe or might be endangered in twenty other particulars without their being much pleased or alarmed. Here they felt its pulse; and as they found that beat, they thought themselves sick or sound. I do not say whether they were right or wrong in applying your general arguments to their own case. It is not easy, indeed, to make a monopoly of theorems and corollaries. The fact is, that they did thus apply those general arguments; and your mode of governing them, whether through lenity or indolence, through wisdom or mistake, confirmed them in the imagination, that they, as well as you, had an interest in these common principles.

They were further confirmed in this pleasing error by the form of their provincial legislative assemblies. Their governments are popular in an high degree: some are merely popular; in all, the popular representative is the most weighty; and this share of the people in their ordinary government never fails to inspire them with lofty sentiments, and with a strong aversion from whatever tends to deprive them of their chief importance.

If anything were wanting to this necessary operation of the form of government, religion would have given it a complete effect. Religion, always a principle of energy, in this new people is no way worn out or impaired; and their mode of professing it is also one main cause of this free spirit. The people are Protestants, and of that kind which is the most adverse to all implicit submission of mind and opinion. This is a persuasion not only favorable to liberty, but built upon it. I do not think, Sir, that the reason of this averseness in the dissenting churches from all that looks like absolute government is so much to be sought in their religious tenets as in their history. Every one knows that the Roman Catholic religion is at least coeval with most of the governments where it prevails, that it has generally gone hand in hand with them, and received great favor and every kind of support from authority. The Church of England, too, was formed from her cradle under the nursing care of regular government. But the dissenting interests have sprung up in direct opposition to all the ordinary powers of the world, and could justify that opposition only on a strong claim to natural liberty. Their very existence depended on the powerful and unremitted assertion of that claim. All Protestantism, even the most cold and passive, is a sort of dissent. But the religion most prevalent in our northern colonies is a refinement on the principle of resistance: it is the dissidence of dissent, and the protestantism of the Protestant religion. This religion, under a variety of denominations agreeing in nothing but in the communion of the spirit of liberty, is predominant in most of the northern provinces, where the Church of England, notwithstanding its legal rights, is in reality no more than a sort of private sect, not composing, most probably, the tenth of the people. The colonists left England when this spirit was high, and in the emigrants was the highest of all; and even that stream of foreigners which has been constantly flowing into these colonies has, for the greatest part, been composed of dissenters from the establishments of their several countries, and have brought with them a temper and character far from alien to that of the people with whom they mixed.

Sir, I can perceive, by their manner, that some gentlemen object to the latitude of this description, because in the southern colonies the Church of England forms a large body, and has a regular establishment. It is certainly true. There is, however, a circumstance attending these colonies, which, in my opinion, fully counterbalances this difference, and makes the spirit of liberty still more high and haughty than in those to the northward. It is, that in Virginia and the Carolinas they have a vast multitude of slaves. Where this is the case in any part of the world, those who are free are by far the most proud and jealous of their freedom. Freedom is to them not only an enjoyment, but a kind of rank and privilege. Not seeing there, that freedom, as in countries where it is a common blessing, and as broad and general as the air, may be united with much abject toil, with great misery, with all the exterior of servitude, liberty looks, amongst them, like something that is more noble and liberal. I do not mean, Sir, to commend the superior morality of this sentiment, which has at least as much pride as virtue in it; but I cannot alter the nature of man. The fact is so; and these people of the southern colonies are much more strongly, and with an higher and more stubborn spirit, attached to liberty, than those to the northward. Such were all the ancient commonwealths; such were our Gothic ancestors; such in our days were the Poles; and such will be all masters of slaves, who are not slaves themselves. In such a people, the haughtiness of domination combines with the spirit of freedom, fortifies it, and renders it invincible.

Permit me, Sir, to add another circumstance in our colonies, which contributes no mean part towards the growth and effect of this untractable spirit: I mean their education. In no country, perhaps, in the world is the law so general a study. The profession itself is numerous and powerful, and in most provinces it takes the lead. The greater number of the deputies sent to the Congress were lawyers. But all who read, and most do read, endeavor to obtain some smattering in that science. I have been told by an eminent bookseller, that in no branch of his business, after tracts of popular devotion, were so many books as those on the law exported to the plantations. The colonists have now fallen into the way of printing them for their own use. I hear that they have sold nearly as many of Blackstone's "Commentaries" [9] in America as in England. General Gage marks out this disposition very particularly in a letter on your table. He states, that all the people in his government are lawyers, or smatterers in law,—and that in Boston they have been enabled, by successful chicane, wholly to evade many parts of one of your capital penal constitutions. The smartness of debate will say, that this knowledge ought to teach them more clearly the rights of legislature, their obligations to obedience, and the penalties of rebellion. All this is mighty well. But my honorable and learned friend [10] on the floor, who condescends to mark what I say for animadversion, will disdain that ground. He has heard, as well as I, that, when great honors and great emoluments do not win over this knowledge to the service of the state, it is a formidable adversary to government. If the spirit be not tamed and broken by these happy methods, it is stubborn and litigious. *Abeunt studia in mores.*[11] This study renders men acute, inquisitive, dexterous, prompt in attack, ready in defence, full of resources. In other countries, the people, more simple, and of a less mercurial cast, judge of an ill principle in government only by an actual grievance; here they anticipate the evil, and judge of the pressure of the grievance by the badness of the principle. They augur misgovernment at a distance, and snuff the approach of tyranny in every tainted breeze.

The last cause of this disobedient spirit in the colonies is hardly less powerful than the rest, as it is not merely moral, but laid deep in the natural constitution of things. Three thousand miles of ocean lie between you and them. No contrivance can prevent the effect of this distance in weakening government. Seas roll, and months pass, between the order and the execution; and the want of a speedy explanation of a single point is enough to defeat an whole system. You have, indeed, winged ministers of vengeance, who carry your bolts in their pounces to the remotest verge of the sea: but there a power steps in, that limits the arrogance of raging passions and furious elements, and says, "So far shalt thou go, and no farther." Who are you, that should fret and rage, and bite the chains of Nature? Nothing worse happens to you than does to all nations who have extensive empire; and it happens in all the forms into which empire can be thrown. In large bodies, the circulation of power must be less vigorous at the extremities. Nature has said it. The Turk cannot govern

9. Blackstone's "Commentaries": a reference to Sir William Blackstone (1723–1780) and his famous *Commentaries on the Laws of England* (1765–1769), a comprehensive study of the English law and constitution.

10. the Attorney-General. **11.** ***Abeunt . . . mores:*** "Studies become a part of one's spirit." See Ovid, *Heroides, Ep.* XV, 83.

Egypt, and Arabia, and Kurdistan, as he governs Thrace; nor has he the same dominion in Crimea and Algiers which he has at Brusa and Smyrna. Despotism itself is obliged to truck and huckster. The Sultan gets such obedience as he can. He governs with a loose rein, that he may govern at all; and the whole of the force and vigor of his authority in his centre is derived from a prudent relaxation in all his borders. Spain, in her provinces, is perhaps not so well obeyed as you are in yours. She complies, too; she submits; she watches times. This is the immutable condition, the eternal law, of extensive and detached empire.

Then, Sir, from these six capital sources, of descent, of form of government, of religion in the northern provinces, of manners in the southern, of education, of the remoteness of situation from the first mover of government,—from all these causes a fierce spirit of liberty has grown up. It has grown with the growth of the people in your colonies, and increased with the increase of their wealth: a spirit, that, unhappily meeting with an exercise of power in England, which, however lawful, is not reconcilable to any ideas of liberty, much less with theirs, has kindled this flame that is ready to consume us.

I do not mean to commend either the spirit in this excess, or the moral causes which produce it. Perhaps a more smooth and accommodating spirit of freedom in them would be more acceptable to us. Perhaps ideas of liberty might be desired more reconcilable with an arbitrary and boundless authority. Perhaps we might wish the colonists to be persuaded that their liberty is more secure when held in trust for them by us (as their guardians during a perpetual minority) than with any part of it in their own hands. But the question is not, whether their spirit deserves praise or blame,—what, in the name of God, shall we do with it? You have before you the object, such as it is,—with all its glories, with all its imperfections on its head. You see the magnitude, the importance, the temper, the habits, the disorders. By all these considerations we are strongly urged to determine something concerning it. We are called upon to fix some rule and line for our future conduct, which may give a little stability to our politics, and prevent the return of such unhappy deliberations as the present. Every such return will bring the matter before us in a still more untractable form. For what astonishing and incredible things have we not seen already! What monsters have not been generated from this unnatural contention! Whilst every principle of authority and resistance has been pushed, upon both sides, as far as it would go, there is nothing so solid and certain, either in reasoning or in practice, that has not been shaken. Until very lately, all authority in America seemed to be nothing but an emanation from yours. Even the popular part of the colony constitution derived all its activity, and its first vital movement, from the pleasure of the crown. We thought, Sir, that the utmost which the discontented colonists could do was to disturb authority; we never dreamt they could of themselves supply it, knowing in general what an operose[12] business it is to establish a government absolutely new. But having, for our purposes in this contention, resolved that none but an obedient assembly should sit, the humors of the people there, finding all passage through the legal channel stopped, with great violence broke out another way. Some provinces have tried their experiment, as we have tried ours; and theirs has succeeded. They have formed a government sufficient for its purposes, without the bustle of a revolution, or the troublesome formality of an election. Evident necessity and tacit consent have done the business in an instant. So well they have done it, that Lord Dunmore (the account is among the fragments on your table) tells you that the new institution is infinitely better obeyed than the ancient government ever was in its most fortunate periods. Obedience is what makes government, and not the names by which it is called: not the name of the Governor, as formerly, or Committee, as at present. This new government has originated directly from the people, and was not transmitted through any of the ordinary artificial media of a positive constitution. It was not a manufacture ready formed, and transmitted to them in that condition from England. The evil arising from hence is this: that the colonists having once found the possibility of enjoying the advantages of order in the midst of a struggle for liberty, such struggles will not henceforward seem so terrible to the settled and sober part of mankind as they had appeared before the trial.

Pursuing the same plan of punishing by the denial of the exercise of government to still greater

12. operose: laborious.

lengths, we wholly abrogated the ancient government of Massachusetts. We were confident that the first feeling, if not the very prospect of anarchy, would instantly enforce a complete submission. The experiment was tried. A new, strange, unexpected face of things appeared. Anarchy is found tolerable. A vast province has now subsisted, and subsisted in a considerable degree of health and vigor, for near a twelvemonth, without governor, without public council, without judges, without executive magistrates. How long it will continue in this state, or what may arise out of this unheard-of situation, how can the wisest of us conjecture? Our late experience has taught us that many of those fundamental principles formerly believed infallible are either not of the importance they were imagined to be, or that we have not at all adverted to some other far more important and far more powerful principles which entirely overrule those we had considered as omnipotent. I am much against any further experiments which tend to put to the proof any more of these allowed opinions which contribute so much to the public tranquillity. In effect, we suffer as much at home by this loosening of all ties, and this concussion of all established opinions, as we do abroad. For, in order to prove that the Americans have no right to their liberties, we are every day endeavoring to subvert the maxims which preserve the whole spirit of our own. To prove that the Americans ought not to be free, we are obliged to depreciate the value of freedom itself; and we never seem to gain a paltry advantage over them in debate, without attacking some of those principles, or deriding some of those feelings, for which our ancestors have shed their blood.

But, Sir, in wishing to put an end to pernicious experiments, I do not mean to preclude the fullest inquiry. Far from it. Far from deciding on a sudden or partial view, I would patiently go round and round the subject, and survey it minutely in every possible aspect. Sir, if I were capable of engaging you to an equal attention, I would state, that, as far as I am capable of discerning, there are but three ways of proceeding relative to this stubborn spirit which prevails in your colonies and disturbs your government. These are,—to change that spirit, as inconvenient, by removing the causes,—to prosecute it, as criminal,—or to comply with it, as necessary. I would not be guilty of an imperfect enumeration; I can think of but these three. Another has, indeed been started,—that of giving up the colonies; but it met so slight a reception that I do not think myself obliged to dwell a great while upon it. It is nothing but a little sally of anger, like the frowardness of peevish children, who, when they cannot get all they would have, are resolved to take nothing.

The first of these plans—to change the spirit, as inconvenient, by removing the causes—I think is the most like a systematic proceeding. It is radical in its principle; but it is attended with great difficulties: some of them little short, as I conceive, of impossibilities. This will appear by examining into the plans which have been proposed.

As the growing population of the colonies is evidently one cause of their resistance, it was last session mentioned in both Houses, by men of weight, and received not without applause, that, in order to check this evil, it would be proper for the crown to make no further grants of land. But to this scheme there are two objections. The first, that there is already so much unsettled land in private hands as to afford room for an immense future population, although the crown not only withheld its grants, but annihilated its soil. If this be the case, then the only effect of this avarice of desolation, this hoarding of a royal wilderness, would be to raise the value of the possessions in the hands of the great private monopolists, without any adequate check to the growing and alarming mischief of population.

But if you stopped your grants, what would be the consequence? The people would occupy without grants. They have already so occupied in many places. You cannot station garrisons in every part of these deserts. If you drive the people from one place, they will carry on their annual tillage, and remove with their flocks and herds to another. Many of the people in the back settlements are already little attached to particular situations. Already they have topped the Appalachian mountains. From thence they behold before them an immense plain, one vast, rich, level meadow: a square of five hundred miles. Over this they would wander without a possibility of restraint; they would change their manners with the habits of their life; would soon forget a government by which they were disowned; would become hordes of English Tartars, and, pouring down upon your unfortified frontiers a fierce and irresistible cavalry, become masters of your governors and your counsellors, your collectors and comptrollers, and of all the slaves that adhered to them. Such would, and, in no long time, must be, the effect of attempting to forbid as a crime, and to suppress as an evil, the command and blessing of Providence, "Increase and multiply." Such would be the happy result of an endeavor to keep as a lair of wild beasts that earth which God by an express charter has given to the children of men. Far different, and surely much wiser, has been our policy hitherto. Hitherto we have invited our people, by every kind of bounty, to fixed establishments. We have invited the husbandman to look to authority for his title. We have taught him piously to believe in the mysterious virtue of wax and parchment. We have thrown each tract of land, as it was peopled, into districts, that the ruling power should never be wholly out of sight. We have settled all we could; and we have carefully attended every settlement with government.

Adhering, Sir, as I do, to this policy, as well as for the reasons I have just given, I think this new project of hedging in population to be neither prudent nor practicable.

To impoverish the colonies in general, and in particular to arrest the noble course of their marine enterprises, would be a more easy task. I freely confess it. We have shown a disposition to a system of this kind,—a disposition even to continue the restraint after the offence,—looking on ourselves as rivals to our colonies, and persuaded that of course we must gain all that they shall lose. Much mischief we may certainly do. The power inadequate to all other things is often more than sufficient for this. I do not look on the direct and immediate power of the colonies to resist our violence as very formidable. In this, however, I may be mistaken. But when I consider that we have colonies for no purpose but to be serviceable to us, it seems to my poor understanding a little preposterous to make them unserviceable, in order to keep them obedient. It is, in truth, nothing more than the old, and, as I thought, exploded problem of tyranny, which proposes to beggar its subjects into submission. But remember, when you have completed your system of impoverishment, that Nature still proceeds in her ordinary course; that discontent will increase with misery; and that there are critical moments in the fortune of all states, when they who are too weak to contribute to your prosperity may be strong enough to complete your ruin. *Spoliatis arma supersunt.*[13]

The temper and character which prevail in our colonies are, I am afraid, unalterable by any human art. We cannot, I fear, falsify the pedigree of this fierce people, and persuade them that they are not sprung from a nation in whose veins the blood of freedom circulates. The language in which they would hear you tell them this tale would detect the imposition; your speech would betray you. An Englishman is the unfittest person on earth to argue another Englishman into slavery.

I think it is nearly as little in our power to change their republican religion as their free descent, or to substitute the Roman Catholic as a penalty, or the Church of England as an improvement. The mode of inquisition and dragooning is going out of fashion in the Old World, and I should not confide much to their efficacy in the New. The education of the Americans is also on the same unalterable bottom with their religion. You cannot persuade them to burn their books of curious science, to banish their lawyers from their courts of law, or to quench the lights of their assemblies by refusing to choose those persons who are best read in their privileges. It would be no less impracticable to think of wholly annihilating the popular assemblies in which these lawyers sit. The army, by which we must govern in their place, would be far more chargeable to us, not quite so effectual, and perhaps, in the end, full as difficult to be kept in obedience.

With regard to the high aristocratic spirit of Virginia and the southern colonies, it has been proposed, I know, to reduce it by declaring a general enfranchisement of their slaves. This project has had its advocates and panegyrists; yet I never could argue myself into any opinion of it. Slaves are often much attached to their masters. A general wild offer of liberty would not always be accepted. History furnishes few instances of it. It is sometimes as hard to persuade slaves to be free as it is to compel freemen to be slaves; and in this auspicious scheme we should have both these pleasing tasks on our hands at once. But when we talk of en-

13. ***Spoliatis . . . supersunt:*** "Arms still remain to those who have been plundered." See Juvenal, *Satires*, VIII, 124.

franchisement, do we not perceive that the American master may enfranchise, too, and arm servile hands in defence of freedom?—a measure to which other people have had recourse more than once, and not without success, in a desperate situation of their affairs.

Slaves as these unfortunate black people are, and dull as all men are from slavery, must they not a little suspect the offer of freedom from that very nation which has sold them to their present masters,—from that nation, one of whose causes of quarrel with those masters is their refusal to deal any more in that inhuman traffic? An offer of freedom from England would come rather oddly, shipped to them in an African vessel, which is refused an entry into the ports of Virginia or Carolina, with a cargo of three hundred Angola negroes. It would be curious to see the Guinea captain attempting at the same instant to publish his proclamation of liberty and to advertise his sale of slaves.

But let us suppose all these moral difficulties got over. The ocean remains. You cannot pump this dry; and as long as it continues in its present bed, so long all the causes which weaken authority by distance will continue.

> Ye Gods! annihilate but space and time,
> And make two lovers happy,[14]

was a pious and passionate prayer,—but just as reasonable as many of the serious wishes of very grave and solemn politicians.

If, then, Sir, it seems almost desperate to think of any alternative course for changing the moral causes (and not quite easy to remove the natural) which produce prejudices irreconcilable to the late exercise of our authority, but that the spirit infallibly will continue, and, continuing, will produce such effects as now embarrass us,—the second mode under consideration is, to prosecute that spirit in its overt acts, as *criminal*.

At this proposition I must pause a moment. The thing seems a great deal too big for my ideas of jurisprudence. It should seem, to my way of conceiving such matters, that there is a very wide difference, in reason and policy, between the mode of proceeding on the irregular conduct of scattered individuals, or even of bands of men, who disturb order within the state, and the civil dissensions which may, from time to time, on great questions, agitate the several communities which compose a great empire. It looks to me to be narrow and pedantic to apply the ordinary ideas of criminal justice to this great public contest. I do not know the method of drawing up an indictment against an whole people. I cannot insult and ridicule the feelings of millions of my fellow-creatures as Sir Edward Coke insulted one excellent individual (Sir Walter Raleigh) at the bar.[15] I am not ripe to pass sentence on the gravest public bodies, intrusted with magistracies of great authority and dignity, and charged with the safety of their fellow-citizens, upon the very same title that I am. I really think that for wise men this is not judicious, for sober men not decent, for minds tinctured with humanity not mild and merciful.

Perhaps, Sir, I am mistaken in my idea of an empire, as distinguished from a single state or kingdom. But my idea of it is this: that an empire is the aggregate of many states under one common head, whether this head be a monarch or a presiding republic. It does, in such constitutions, frequently happen (and nothing but the dismal, cold, dead uniformity of servitude can prevent its happening) that the subordinate parts have many local privileges and immunities. Between these privileges and the supreme common authority the line may be extremely nice. Of course disputes, often, too, very bitter disputes, and much ill blood, will arise. But though every privilege is an exemption (in the case) from the ordinary exercise of the supreme authority, it is no denial of it. The claim of a privilege seems rather, *ex vi termini*,[16] to imply a superior power: for to talk of the privileges of a state or of a person who has no superior is hardly any better than speaking nonsense. Now in such unfortunate quarrels among the component parts of a great political union of communities, I can scarcely conceive anything more completely imprudent than for the head of the empire to insist, that if any privilege is pleaded against his will or his acts, that his whole authority is denied,—instantly to proclaim rebellion, to beat to arms, and to put the offending

14. See Alexander Pope, *On the Art of Sinking in Poetry.*

15. Sir Edward Coke (1552–1634) was Attorney-General, and later Chief Justice of the Common Pleas (1606) and of the King's Bench (1613). **16.** ***ex . . . termini:*** "From the power of the term."

provinces under the ban. Will not this, Sir, very soon teach the provinces to make no distinctions on their part? Will it not teach them that the government against which a claim of liberty is tantamount to high treason is a government to which submission is equivalent to slavery? It may not always be quite convenient to impress dependent communities with such an idea.

We are, indeed, in all disputes with the colonies, by the necessity of things, the judge. It is true, Sir. But I confess that the character of judge in my own cause is a thing that frightens me. Instead of filling me with pride, I am exceedingly humbled by it. I cannot proceed with a stern, assured judicial confidence, until I find myself in something more like a judicial character. I must have these hesitations as long as I am compelled to recollect, that, in my little reading upon such contests as these, the sense of mankind has at least as often decided against the superior as the subordinate power. Sir, let me add, too, that the opinion of my having some abstract right in my favor would not put me much at my ease in passing sentence, unless I could be sure that there were no rights which, in their exercise under certain circumstances, were not the most odious of all wrongs and the most vexatious of all injustice. Sir, these considerations have great weight with me, when I find things so circumstanced that I see the same party at once a civil litigant against me in a point of right and a culprit before me, while I sit as criminal judge on acts of his whose moral quality is to be decided upon the merits of that very litigation. Men are every now and then put, by the complexity of human affairs, into strange situations; but justice is the same, let the judge be in what situation he will.

There is, Sir, also a circumstance which convinces me that this mode of criminal proceeding is not (at least in the present stage of our contest) altogether expedient,—which is nothing less than the conduct of those very persons who have seemed to adopt that mode, by lately declaring a rebellion in Massachusetts Bay, as they had formerly addressed to have traitors brought hither, under an act of Henry the Eighth, for trial. For, though rebellion is declared, it is not proceeded against as such; nor have any steps been taken towards the apprehension or conviction of any individual offender, either on our late or our former address; but modes of public coercion have been adopted, and such as have much more resemblance to a sort of qualified hostility towards an independent power than the punishment of rebellious subjects. All this seems rather inconsistent; but it shows how difficult it is to apply these juridical ideas to our present case.[17]

In this situation, let us seriously and coolly ponder. What is it we have got by all our menaces, which have been many and ferocious? What advantage have we derived from the penal laws we have passed, and which, for the time, have been severe and numerous? What advances have we made towards our object, by the sending of a force, which, by land and sea, is no contemptible strength? Has the disorder abated? Nothing less.—When I see things in this situation, after such confident hopes, bold promises, and active exertions, I cannot, for my life, avoid a suspicion that the plan itself is not correctly right.

If, then, the removal of the causes of this spirit of American liberty be, for the greater part, or rather entirely, impracticable,—if the ideas of criminal process be inapplicable, or, if applicable, are in the highest degree inexpedient, what way yet remains? No way is open, but the third and last,—to comply with the American spirit as necessary, or, if you please, to submit to it as a necessary evil.

If we adopt this mode, if we mean to conciliate and concede, let us see of what nature the concession ought to be. To ascertain the nature of our concession, we must look at their complaint. The colonies complain that they have not the characteristic mark and seal of British freedom. They complain that they are taxed in a Parliament in which they are not represented. If you mean to satisfy them at all, you must satisfy them with regard to this complaint. If you mean to please any people, you must give them the boon which they ask,—not what you may think better for them, but of a kind totally different. Such an act may be a wise regulation, but it is no concession; whereas our present theme is the mode of giving satisfaction.

Sir, I think you must perceive that I am resolved this day to have nothing at all to do with the question of the right of taxation. Some gentlemen

17. A reference to a request by the House of Commons to the King on February 8, 1769. The House wanted to revive the power provided in an act of 1544 to bring disruptive persons back to England for trial.

startle,—but it is true: I put it totally out of the question. It is less than nothing in my consideration. I do not indeed wonder, nor will you, Sir, that gentlemen of profound learning are fond of displaying it on this profound subject. But my consideration is narrow, confined, and wholly limited to the policy of the question. I do not examine whether the giving away a man's money be a power excepted and reserved out of the general trust of government, and how far all mankind, in all forms of polity, are entitled to an exercise of that right by the charter of Nature,—or whether, on the contrary, a right of taxation is necessarily involved in the general principle of legislation, and inseparable from the ordinary supreme power. These are deep questions, where great names militate against each other, where reason is perplexed, and an appeal to authorities only thickens the confusion: for high and reverend authorities lift up their heads on both sides, and there is no sure footing in the middle. This point is the *great Serbonian bog, betwixt Damiata and Mount Casius old, where armies whole have sunk.*[18] I do not intend to be overwhelmed in that bog, though in such respectable company. The question with me is not whether you have a right to render your people miserable, but whether it is not your interest to make them happy. It is not what a lawyer tells me I *may* do, but what humanity, reason, and justice tell me I ought to do. Is a politic act the worse for being a generous one? Is no concession proper, but that which is made from your want of right to keep what you grant? Or does it lessen the grace or dignity of relaxing in the exercise of an odious claim, because you have your evidence-room full of titles, and your magazines stuffed with arms to enforce them? What signify all those titles and all those arms? Of what avail are they, when the reason of the thing tells me that the assertion of my title is the loss of my suit, and that I could do nothing but wound myself by the use of my own weapons?

Such is steadfastly my opinion of the absolute necessity of keeping up the concord of this empire by a unity of spirit, though in a diversity of operations, that, if I were sure the colonists had, at their leaving this country, sealed a regular compact of servitude, that they had solemnly abjured all the rights of citizens, that they had made a vow to renounce all ideas of liberty for them and their posterity to all generations, yet I should hold myself obliged to conform to the temper I found universally prevalent in my own day, and to govern two million of men, impatient of servitude, on the principles of freedom. I am not determining a point of law; I am restoring tranquillity: and the general character and situation of a people must determine what sort of government is fitted for them. That point nothing else can or ought to determine.

My idea, therefore, without considering whether we yield as matter of right or grant as matter of favor, is, *to admit the people of our colonies into an interest in the Constitution,* and, by recording that admission in the journals of Parliament, to give them as strong an assurance as the nature of the thing will admit that we mean forever to adhere to that solemn declaration of systematic indulgence.

Some years ago, the repeal of a revenue act, upon its understood principle, might have served to show that we intended an unconditional abatement of the exercise of a taxing power. Such a measure was then sufficient to remove all suspicion and to give perfect content. But unfortunate events since that time may make something further necessary,—and not more necessary for the satisfaction of the colonies than for the dignity and consistency of our own future proceedings.

I have taken a very incorrect measure of the disposition of the House, if this proposal in itself would be received with dislike. I think, Sir, we have few American financiers. But our misfortune is, we are too acute, we are too exquisite in our conjectures of the future, for men oppressed with such great and present evils. The more moderate among the opposers of Parliamentary concession freely confess that they hope no good from taxation; but they apprehend the colonists have further views, and if this point were conceded, they would instantly attack the trade laws. These gentlemen are convinced that this was the intention from the beginning, and the quarrel of the Americans with taxation was no more than a cloak and cover to this design. Such has been the language even of a gentleman of real moderation, and of a natural temper well adjusted to fair and equal government. I am, however, Sir, not a little surprised at this kind of discourse, whenever I hear it; and I am the more surprised on account of the arguments

18. See *Paradise Lost,* II, 592.

which I constantly find in company with it, and which are often urged from the same mouths and on the same day.

For instance, when we allege that it is against reason to tax a people under so many restraints in trade as the Americans, the noble lord [19] in the blue riband shall tell you that the restraints on trade are futile and useless, of no advantage to us, and of no burden to those on whom they are imposed,—that the trade to America is not secured by the Acts of Navigation, but by the natural and irresistible advantage of a commercial preference.

Such is the merit of the trade laws in this posture of the debate. But when strong internal circumstances are urged against the taxes,—when the scheme is dissected,—when experience and the nature of things are brought to prove, and do prove, the utter impossibility of obtaining an effective revenue from the colonies,—when these things are pressed, or rather press themselves, so as to drive the advocates of colony taxes to a clear admission of the futility of the scheme,—then, Sir, the sleeping trade laws revive from their trance, and this useless taxation is to be kept sacred, not for its own sake, but as a counter-guard and security of the laws of trade.

Then, Sir, you keep up revenue laws which are mischievous in order to preserve trade laws that are useless. Such is the wisdom of our plan in both its members. They are separately given up as of no value; and yet one is always to be defended for the sake of the other. But I cannot agree with the noble lord, nor with the pamphlet from whence he seems to have borrowed these ideas concerning the inutility of the trade laws. For, without idolizing them, I am sure they are still, in many ways, of great use to us; and in former times they have been of the greatest. They do confine, and they do greatly narrow, the market for the Americans. But my perfect conviction of this does not help me in the least to discern how the revenue laws form any security whatsoever to the commercial regulations,—or that these commercial regulations are the true ground of the quarrel,—or that the giving way, in any one instance, of authority is to lose all that may remain unconceded.

One fact is clear and indisputable: the public and avowed origin of this quarrel was on taxation. This quarrel has, indeed, brought on new disputes on new questions, but certainly the least bitter, and the fewest of all, on the trade laws. To judge which of the two be the real, radical cause of quarrel, we have to see whether the commercial dispute did, in order of time, precede the dispute on taxation. There is not a shadow of evidence for it. Next, to enable us to judge whether at this moment a dislike to the trade laws be the real cause of quarrel, it is absolutely necessary to put the taxes out of the question by a repeal. See how the Americans act in this position, and then you will be able to discern correctly what is the true object of the controversy, or whether any controversy at all will remain. Unless you consent to remove this cause of difference, it is impossible, with decency, to assert that the dispute is not upon what it is avowed to be. And I would, Sir, recommend to your serious consideration, whether it be prudent to form a rule for punishing people, not on their own acts, but on your conjectures. Surely it is preposterous, at the very best. It is not justifying your anger by their misconduct, but it is converting your ill-will into their delinquency.

But the colonies will go further.—Alas! alas! when will this speculating against fact and reason end? What will quiet these panic fears which we entertain of the hostile effect of a conciliatory conduct? Is it true that no case can exist in which it is proper for the sovereign to accede to the desires of his discontented subjects? Is there anything peculiar in this case, to make a rule for itself? Is all authority of course lost, when it is not pushed to the extreme? Is it a certain maxim, that, the fewer causes of dissatisfaction are left by government, the more the subject will be inclined to resist and rebel?

All these objections being in fact no more than suspicions, conjectures, divinations, formed in defiance of fact and experience, they did not, Sir, discourage me from entertaining the idea of a conciliatory concession, founded on the principles which I have just stated.

In forming a plan for this purpose, I endeavored to put myself in that frame of mind which was the most natural and the most reasonable, and which was certainly the most probable means of securing me from all error. I set out with a perfect distrust of my own abilities, a total renunciation of every speculation of my own, and with a pro-

19. noble lord: Lord North.

found reverence for the wisdom of our ancestors, who have left us the inheritance of so happy a Constitution and so flourishing an empire, and, what is a thousand times more valuable, the treasury of the maxims and principles which formed the one and obtained the other.

During the reigns of the kings of Spain of the Austrian family, whenever they were at a loss in the Spanish councils, it was common for their statesmen to say that they ought to consult the genius of Philip the Second. The genius of Philip the Second might mislead them; and the issue of their affairs showed that they had not chosen the most perfect standard. But, Sir, I am sure that I shall not be misled, when, in a case of constitutional difficulty, I consult the genius of the English Constitution. Consulting at that oracle, (it was with all due humility and piety,) I found four capital examples in a similar case before me: those of Ireland, Wales, Chester, and Durham.

Ireland, before the English conquest, though never governed by a despotic power, had no Parliament. How far the English Parliament itself was at that time modelled according to the present form is disputed among antiquarians. But we have all the reason in the world to be assured, that a form of Parliament, such as England then enjoyed, she instantly communicated to Ireland; and we are equally sure that almost every successive improvement in constitutional liberty, as fast as it was made here, was transmitted thither. The feudal baronage, and the feudal knighthood, the roots of our primitive Constitution, were early transplanted into that soil, and grew and flourished there. Magna Charta, if it did not give us originally the House of Commons, gave us at least an House of Commons of weight and consequence. But your ancestors did not churlishly sit down alone to the feast of Magna Charta. Ireland was made immediately a partaker. This benefit of English laws and liberties, I confess, was not at first extended to *all* Ireland. Mark the consequence. English authority and English liberty had exactly the same boundaries. Your standard could never be advanced an inch before your privileges. Sir John Davies[20] shows beyond a doubt, that the refusal of a general communication of these rights was the true cause why Ireland was five hundred years in subduing; and after the vain projects of a military government, attempted in the reign of Queen Elizabeth, it was soon discovered that nothing could make that country English, in civility and allegiance, but your laws and your forms of legislature. It was not English arms, but the English Constitution, that conquered Ireland. From that time, Ireland has ever had a general Parliament, as she had before a partial Parliament. You changed the people, you altered the religion, but you never touched the form or the vital substance of free government in that kingdom. You deposed kings; you restored them; you altered the succession to theirs, as well as to your own crown; but you never altered their Constitution, the principle of which was respected by usurpation, restored with the restoration of monarchy, and established, I trust, forever by the glorious Revolution.[21] This has made Ireland the great and flourishing kingdom that it is, and, from a disgrace and a burden intolerable to this nation, has rendered her a principal part of our strength and ornament. This country cannot be said to have ever formally taxed her. The irregular things done in the confusion of mighty troubles, and on the hinge of great revolutions, even if all were done that is said to have been done, form no example. If they have any effect in argument, they make an exception to prove the rule. None of your own liberties could stand a moment, if the casual deviations from them, at such times, were suffered to be used as proofs of their nullity. By the lucrative amount of such casual breaches in the Constitution, judge what the stated and fixed rule of supply has been in that kingdom. Your Irish pensioners would starve, if they had no other fund to live on than taxes granted by English authority. Turn your eyes to those popular grants from whence all your great supplies are come, and learn to respect that only source of public wealth in the British empire.

My next example is Wales. This country was said to be reduced by Henry the Third. It was said more truly to be so by Edward the First. But

20. Sir John Davies (1569–1626), poet, Solicitor- and Attorney-General for Ireland, author of *Discoverie of the true causes why Ireland was never entirely subdued until the beginning of his Majestie's happy reign* in 1604.

21. glorious Revolution: the famous Glorious Revolution of 1688 in which James II was deposed and replaced by William and Mary. Burke uses this bloodless revolution as a standard against which to measure the violence and bloodshed of the French Revolution.

though then conquered, it was not looked upon as any part of the realm of England. Its old Constitution, whatever that might have been, was destroyed; and no good one was substituted in its place. The care of that tract was put into the hands of Lords Marchers: a form of government of a very singular kind; a strange, heterogeneous monster, something between hostility and government: perhaps it has a sort of resemblance, according to the modes of those times, to that of commander-in-chief at present, to whom all civil power is granted as secondary. The manners of the Welsh nation followed the genius of the government: the people were ferocious, restive, savage, and uncultivated; sometimes composed, never pacified. Wales, within itself, was in perpetual disorder; and it kept the frontier of England in perpetual alarm. Benefits from it to the state there were none. Wales was only known to England by incursion and invasion.

Sir, during that state of things, Parliament was not idle. They attempted to subdue the fierce spirit of the Welsh by all sorts of rigorous laws. They prohibited by statute the sending all sorts of arms into Wales, as you prohibit by proclamation (with something more of doubt on the legality) the sending arms to America. They disarmed the Welsh by statute, as you attempted (but still with more question on the legality) to disarm New England by an instruction. They made an act to drag offenders from Wales into England for trial, as you have done (but with more hardship) with regard to America. By another act, where one of the parties was an Englishman, they ordained that his trial should be always by English. They made acts to restrain trade, as you do; and they prevented the Welsh from the use of fairs and markets, as you do the Americans from fisheries and foreign ports. In short, when the statute-book was not quite so much swelled as it is now, you find no less than fifteen acts of penal regulation on the subject of Wales.

Here we rub our hands,—A fine body of precedents for the authority of Parliament and the use of it!—I admit it fully; and pray add likewise to these precedents, that all the while Wales rid this kingdom like an *incubus;*[22] that it was an unprofitable and oppressive burden; and that an Englishman travelling in that country could not go six yards from the highroad without being murdered.

The march of the human mind is slow. Sir, it was not until after two hundred years discovered, that, by an eternal law, Providence had decreed vexation to violence, and poverty to rapine. Your ancestors did, however, at length open their eyes to the ill husbandry of injustice. They found that the tyranny of a free people could of all tyrannies the least be endured, and that laws made against an whole nation were not the most effectual methods for securing its obedience. Accordingly, in the twenty-seventh year of Henry the Eighth the course was entirely altered. With a preamble stating the entire and perfect rights of the crown of England, it gave to the Welsh all the rights and privileges of English subjects. A political order was established; the military power gave way to the civil; the marches were turned into counties. But that a nation should have a right to English liberties, and yet no share at all in the fundamental security of these liberties,—the grant of their own property, —seemed a thing so incongruous, that eight years after, that is, in the thirty-fifth of that reign, a complete and not ill-proportioned representation by counties and boroughs was bestowed upon Wales by act of Parliament. From that moment, as by a charm, the tumults subsided; obedience was restored; peace, order, and civilization followed in the train of liberty. When the day-star of the English Constitution had arisen in their hearts, all was harmony within and without;—

> Simul alba nautis
> Stella refulsit,
> Defluit saxis agitatus humor,
> Concidunt venti, fugiuntque nubes,
> Et minax (quod sic voluere) ponto
> Unda recumbit.[23]

The very same year the County Palatine of Chester received the same relief from its oppressions, and the same remedy to its disorders. Before this time Chester was little less distempered than Wales. The inhabitants, without rights themselves, were the fittest to destroy the rights of others; and from thence Richard the Second drew the standing army

22. ***incubus:*** an evil spirit.

23. **Simul . . . recumbit:** "As soon as the white star beamed on the sailors, the raging waters flow down from the rocks, the winds die down, the clouds disappear, and (since so they desire) the ominous waves grow peaceful on the sea." See Horace, *Odes,* I, 12, 27.

of archers with which for a time he oppressed England. The people of Chester applied to Parliament in a petition penned as I shall read to you.

> To the king our sovereign lord, in most humble wise shown unto your most excellent Majesty, the inhabitants of your Grace's County Palatine of Chester: That where the said County Palatine of Chester is and hath been alway hitherto exempt, excluded, and separated out and from your high court of Parliament, to have any knights and burgesses within the said court; by reason whereof the said inhabitants have hitherto sustained manifold disherisons, losses, and damages, as well in their lands, goods, and bodies, as in the good, civil, and politic governance and maintenance of the common wealth of their said country: And forasmuch as the said inhabitants have always hitherto been bound by the acts and statutes made and ordained by your said Highness, and your most noble progenitors, by authority of the said court, as far forth as other counties, cities, and boroughs have been, that have had their knights and burgesses within your said court of Parliament, and yet have had neither knight nor burgess there for the said County Palatine; the said inhabitants, for lack thereof, have been oftentimes touched and grieved with acts and statutes made within the said court, as well derogatory unto the most ancient jurisdictions, liberties, and privileges of your said County Palatine, as prejudicial unto the common wealth, quietness, rest, and peace of your Grace's most bounden subjects inhabiting within the same.

What did Parliament with this audacious address?—Reject it as a libel? Treat it as an affront to government? Spurn it as a derogation from the rights of legislature? Did they toss it over the table? Did they burn it by the hands of the common hangman?—They took the petition of grievance, all rugged as it was, without softening or temperament, unpurged of the original bitterness and indignation of complaint; they made it the very preamble to their act of redress, and consecrated its principle to all ages in the sanctuary of legislation.

Here is my third example. It was attended with the success of the two former. Chester, civilized as well as Wales, has demonstrated that freedom, and not servitude, is the cure of anarchy; as religion, and not atheism, is the true remedy for superstition. Sir, this pattern of Chester was followed in the reign of Charles the Second with regard to the County Palatine of Durham, which is my fourth example. This county had long lain out of the pale of free legislation. So scrupulously was the example of Chester followed, that the style of the preamble is nearly the same with that of the Chester act; and, without affecting the abstract extent of the authority of Parliament, it recognizes the equity of not suffering any considerable district, in which the British subjects may act as a body, to be taxed without their own voice in the grant.

Now if the doctrines of policy contained in these preambles, and the force of these examples in the acts of Parliament, avail anything, what can be said against applying them with regard to America? Are not the people of America as much Englishmen as the Welsh? The preamble of the act of Henry the Eighth says, the Welsh speak a language no way resembling that of his Majesty's English subjects. Are the Americans not as numerous? If we may trust the learned and accurate Judge Barrington's account of North Wales, and take that as a standard to measure the rest, there is no comparison. The people cannot amount to above 200,000: not a tenth part of the number in the colonies. Is America in rebellion? Wales was hardly ever free from it. Have you attempted to govern America by penal statutes? You made fifteen for Wales. But your legislative authority is perfect with regard to America: was it less perfect in Wales, Chester, and Durham? But America is virtually represented. What! does the electric force of virtual representation[24] more easily pass over the Atlantic than pervade Wales, which lies in your neighborhood? or than Chester and Durham, surrounded by abundance of representation that is actual and palpable? But, Sir, your ancestors thought this sort of virtual representation, however ample, to be totally insufficient for the freedom of the inhabitants of territories that are so near, and comparatively so inconsiderable. How, then, can I think it sufficient for those which are infinitely greater, and infinitely more remote?

You will now, Sir, perhaps imagine that I am on the point of proposing to you a scheme for a representation of the colonies in Parliament. Perhaps I

24. **virtual representation:** According to the theory of "virtual representation," members of Parliament supposedly represented the whole country, not just their own enfranchised constituents. The fact of the matter was, of course, that relatively few men had the vote at this time.

might be inclined to entertain some such thought; but a great flood stops me in my course. *Opposuit Natura.*[25] I cannot remove the eternal barriers of the creation. The thing, in that mode, I do not know to be possible. As I meddle with no theory, I do not absolutely assert the impracticability of such a representation; but I do not see my way to it; and those who have been more confident have not been more successful. However, the arm of public benevolence is not shortened; and there are often several means to the same end. What Nature has disjoined in one way wisdom may unite in another. When we cannot give the benefit as we would wish, let us not refuse it altogether. If we cannot give the principal, let us find a substitute. But how? where? what substitute?

Fortunately, I am not obliged, for the ways and means of this substitute, to tax my own unproductive invention. I am not even obliged to go to the rich treasury of the fertile framers of imaginary commonwealths: not to the Republic of Plato, not to the Utopia of More, not to the Oceana of Harrington.[26] It is before me,—it is at my feet,—

And the rude swain
Treads daily on it with his clouted shoon.[27]

I only wish you to recognize, for the theory, the ancient constitutional policy of this kingdom with regard to representation, as that policy has been declared in acts of Parliament,—and as to the practice, to return to that mode which an uniform experience has marked out to you as best, and in which you walked with security, advantage, and honor, until the year 1763.

My resolutions, therefore, mean to establish the equity and justice of a taxation of America by *grant,* and not by *imposition;* to mark the *legal competency* of the colony assemblies for the support of their government in peace, and for public aids in time of war; to acknowledge that this legal competency has had *a dutiful and beneficial exercise,* and that experience has shown *the benefit of their grants,* and *the futility of Parliamentary taxation, as a method of supply.*

These solid truths compose six fundamental propositions. There are three more resolutions corollary to these. If you admit the first set, you can hardly reject the others. But if you admit the first, I shall be far from solicitous whether you accept or refuse the last. I think these six massive pillars will be of strength sufficient to support the temple of British concord. I have no more doubt than I entertain of my existence, that, if you admitted these, you would command an immediate peace, and, with but tolerable future management, a lasting obedience in America. I am not arrogant in this confident assurance. The propositions are all mere matters of fact; and if they are such facts as draw irresistible conclusions even in the stating, this is the power of truth, and not any management of mine.

Sir, I shall open the whole plan to you together, with such observations on the motions as may tend to illustrate them, where they may want explanation.

The first is a resolution,—"That the colonies and plantations of Great Britain in North America, consisting of fourteen separate governments, and containing two millions and upwards of free inhabitants, have not had the liberty and privilege of electing and sending any knights and burgesses, or others, to represent them in the high court of Parliament."

This is a plain matter of fact, necessary to be laid down, and (excepting the description) it is laid down in the language of the Constitution; it is taken nearly *verbatim* from acts of Parliament.

The second is like unto the first,—"That the said colonies and plantations have been made liable to, and bounden by, several subsidies, payments, rates, and taxes, given and granted by Parliament, though the said colonies and plantations have not their knights and burgesses in the said high court of Parliament, of their own election, to represent the condition of their country; by lack whereof they have been oftentimes touched and grieved by subsidies, given, granted, and assented to, in the said court, in a manner prejudicial to the common wealth, quietness, rest, and peace of the subjects inhabiting within the same."

Is this description too hot or too cold, too strong or too weak? Does it arrogate too much to the supreme legislature? Does it lean too much to the

25. *Opposuit Natura:* "Nature opposed it." See Juvenal, *Satires,* X, 152. **26. Republic . . . Harrington:** famous treatises on ideal systems of government. **27.** Milton, *Comus,* ll. 633–634. Not an exact quotation.

claims of the people? If it runs into any of these errors, the fault is not mine. It is the language of your own ancient acts of Parliament.

Non meus hic sermo, sed quæ præcepit Ofellus
Rusticus, abnormis sapiens.[28]

It is the genuine produce of the ancient, rustic, manly, home-bred sense of this country. I did not dare to rub off a particle of the venerable rust that rather adorns and preserves than destroys the metal. It would be a profanation to touch with a tool the stones which construct the sacred altar of peace. I would not violate with modern polish the ingenuous and noble roughness of these truly constitutional materials. Above all things, I was resolved not to be guilty of tampering,—the odious vice of restless and unstable minds. I put my foot in the tracks of our forefathers, where I can neither wander nor stumble. Determining to fix articles of peace, I was resolved not to be wise beyond what was written; I was resolved to use nothing else than the form of sound words, to let others abound in their own sense, and carefully to abstain from all expressions of my own. What the law has said, I say. In all things else I am silent. I have no organ but for her words. This, if it be not ingenious, I am sure is safe.

There are, indeed, words expressive of grievance in this second resolution, which those who are resolved always to be in the right will deny to contain matter of fact, as applied to the present case; although Parliament thought them true with regard to the Counties of Chester and Durham. They will deny that the Americans were ever "touched and grieved" with the taxes. If they consider nothing in taxes but their weight as pecuniary impositions, there might be some pretence for this denial. But men may be sorely touched and deeply grieved in their privileges, as well as in their purses. Men may lose little in property by the act which takes away all their freedom. When a man is robbed of a trifle on the highway, it is not the twopence lost that constitutes the capital outrage. This is not confined to privileges. Even ancient indulgences withdrawn, without offence on the part of those who enjoyed such favors, operate as grievances. But were the Americans, then, not touched and grieved by the taxes, in some measure, merely as taxes? If so, why were they almost all either wholly repealed or exceedingly reduced? Were they not touched and grieved even by the regulating duties of the sixth of George the Second? Else why were the duties first reduced to one third in 1764, and afterwards to a third of that third in the year 1766? Were they not touched and grieved by the Stamp Act? I shall say they were, until that tax is revived. Were they not touched and grieved by the duties of 1767, which were likewise repealed, and which Lord Hillsborough tells you (for the ministry) were laid contrary to the true principle of commerce? Is not the assurance given by that noble person to the colonies of a resolution to lay no more taxes on them an admission that taxes would touch and grieve them? Is not the resolution of the noble lord in the blue riband, now standing on your journals, the strongest of all proofs that Parliamentary subsidies really touched and grieved them? Else why all these changes, modifications, repeals, assurances, and resolutions?

The next proposition is,—"That, from the distance of the said colonies, and from other circumstances, no method hath hitherto been devised for procuring a representation in Parliament for the said colonies."

This is an assertion of a fact. I go no further on the paper; though, in my private judgment, an useful representation is impossible; I am sure it is not desired by them, nor ought it, perhaps, by us: but I abstain from opinions.

The fourth resolution is,—"That each of the said colonies hath within itself a body, chosen, in part or in the whole, by the freemen, freeholders, or other free inhabitants thereof, commonly called the General Assembly, or General Court, with powers legally to raise, levy, and assess, according to the several usages of such colonies, duties and taxes towards defraying all sorts of public services."

This competence in the colony assemblies is certain. It is proved by the whole tenor of their acts of supply in all the assemblies, in which the constant style of granting is, "An aid to his Majesty"; and acts granting to the crown have regularly, for near a century, passed the public offices without dispute. Those who have been pleased paradoxically to deny this right, holding that none but

28. **Non . . . sapiens:** "This proposal is not mine, but Ofellus, a rustic man of extraordinary wisdom, advances it." See Horace, *Satires,* II, 2, 3.

the British Parliament can grant to the crown, are wished to look to what is done, not only in the colonies, but in Ireland, in one uniform, unbroken tenor, every session. Sir, I am surprised that this doctrine should come from some of the law servants of the crown. I say, that if the crown could be responsible, his Majesty,—but certainly the ministers, and even these law officers themselves, through whose hands the acts pass biennially in Ireland, or annually in the colonies, are in an habitual course of committing impeachable offences. What habitual offenders have been all Presidents of the Council, all Secretaries of State, all First Lords of Trade, all Attorneys and all Solicitors General! However, they are safe, as no one impeaches them; and there is no ground of charge against them, except in their own unfounded theories.

The fifth resolution is also a resolution of fact,—"That the said general assemblies, general courts, or other bodies legally qualified as aforesaid, have at sundry times freely granted several large subsidies and public aids for his Majesty's service, according to their abilities, when required thereto by letter from one of his Majesty's principal Secretaries of State; and that their right to grant the same, and their cheerfulness and sufficiency in the said grants, have been at sundry times acknowledged by Parliament."

To say nothing of their great expenses in the Indian wars, and not to take their exertion in foreign ones, so high as the supplies in the year 1695, not to go back to their public contributions in the year 1710, I shall begin to travel only where the journals give me light,—resolving to deal in nothing but fact authenticated by Parliamentary record, and to build myself wholly on that solid basis.

On the 4th of April, 1748, a committee of this House came to the following resolution:—

> *Resolved*, That it is the opinion of this committee, *that it is just and reasonable*, that the several provinces and colonies of Massachusetts Bay, New Hampshire, Connecticut, and Rhode Island be reimbursed the expenses they have been at in taking and securing to the crown of Great Britain the island of Cape Breton and its dependencies.

These expenses were immense for such colonies. They were above £200,000 sterling: money first raised and advanced on their public credit.

On the 28th of January, 1756, a message from the king came to us, to this effect:—"His Majesty, being sensible of the zeal and vigor with which his faithful subjects of certain colonies in North America have exerted themselves in defence of his Majesty's just rights and possessions, recommends it to this House to take the same into their consideration, and to enable his Majesty to give them such assistance as may be a *proper reward and encouragement*."

On the 3d of February, 1756, the House came to a suitable resolution, expressed in words nearly the same as those of the message; but with the further addition, that the money then voted was as an *encouragement* to the colonies to exert themselves with vigor. It will not be necessary to go through all the testimonies which your own records have given to the truth of my resolutions. I will only refer you to the places in the journals:—

Vol. XXVII.—16th and 19th May, 1757.
Vol. XXVIII.—June 1st, 1758,—April 26th and 30th, 1759,—March 26th and 31st, and April 28th, 1760,—Jan. 9th and 20th, 1761.
Vol. XXIX.—Jan. 22d and 26th, 1762,—March 14th and 17th, 1763.

Sir, here is the repeated acknowledgment of Parliament, that the colonies not only gave, but gave to satiety. This nation has formally acknowledged two things: first, that the colonies had gone beyond their abilities, Parliament having thought it necessary to reimburse them; secondly, that they had acted legally and laudably in their grants of money, and their maintenance of troops, since the compensation is expressly given as reward and encouragement. Reward is not bestowed for acts that are unlawful; and encouragement is not held out to things that deserve reprehension. My resolution, therefore, does nothing more than collect into one proposition what is scattered through your journals. I give you nothing but your own; and you cannot refuse in the gross what you have so often acknowledged in detail. The admission of this, which will be so honorable to them and to you, will, indeed, be mortal to all the miserable stories by which the passions of the misguided people have been engaged in an unhappy system. The people heard, indeed, from the beginning of these disputes, one thing continually dinned in their ears: that reason and justice demanded, that the Americans, who paid no taxes, should be compelled to contribute. How did that fact, of their paying nothing, stand, when the taxing system began? When Mr. Grenville began to form his system of American revenue, he stated in this House that the colonies were then in debt two million six hundred thousand pounds sterling money, and was of opinion they would discharge that debt in four years. On this state, those untaxed people were actually subject to the payment of taxes to the amount of six hundred and fifty thousand a year. In fact, however, Mr. Grenville was mistaken. The funds given for sinking the debt did not prove quite so ample as both the colonies and he expected. The calculation was too sanguine: the reduction was not completed till some years after, and at different times in different colonies. However, the taxes after the war continued too great to bear any addition, with prudence or propriety; and when the burdens imposed in consequence of former requisitions were discharged, our tone became too high to resort again to requisition. No colony, since that time, ever has had any requisition whatsoever made to it.

We see the sense of the crown, and the sense of Parliament, on the productive nature of a *revenue by grant.* Now search the same journals for the produce of the *revenue by imposition.* Where is it?—let us know the volume and the page. What is the gross, what is the net produce? To what service is it applied? How have you appropriated its surplus?—What! can none of the many skilful index-makers that we are now employing find any trace of it?—Well, let them and that rest together. —But are the journals, which say nothing of the revenue, as silent on the discontent?—Oh, no! a child may find it. It is the melancholy burden and blot of every page.

I think, then, I am, from those journals, justified in the sixth and last resolution, which is,—"That it hath been found by experience, that the manner of granting the said supplies and aids by the said general assemblies hath been more agreeable to the inhabitants of the said colonies, and more beneficial and conducive to the public service, than the mode of giving and granting aids and subsidies in Parliament, to be raised and paid in the said colonies."

This makes the whole of the fundamental part of the plan. The conclusion is irresistible. You cannot say that you were driven by any necessity to an exercise of the utmost rights of legislature. You cannot assert that you took on yourselves the task of imposing colony taxes, from the want of another legal body that is competent to the purpose of supplying the exigencies of the state without wounding the prejudices of the people. Neither is it true that the body so qualified, and having that competence, had neglected the duty.

The question now, on all this accumulated matter, is,—Whether you will choose to abide by a profitable experience or a mischievous theory? whether you choose to build on imagination or fact? whether you prefer enjoyment or hope? satisfaction in your subjects, or discontent?

If these propositions are accepted, everything which has been made to enforce a contrary system must, I take it for granted, fall along with it. On that ground, I have drawn the following resolution, which, when it comes to be moved, will naturally be divided in a proper manner:—"That it may be proper to repeal an act, made in the seventh year of the reign of his present Majesty, intituled, 'An act for granting certain duties in the British colonies and plantations in America; for allowing a drawback of the duties of customs, upon the exportation from this kingdom, of coffee and cocoa-nuts, of the produce of the said colonies or plantations; for discontinuing the drawbacks payable on China earthen ware exported to America; and for more effectually preventing the clandestine running of goods in the said colonies and plantations.'—And also, that it may be proper to repeal an act, made in the fourteenth year of the reign of his present Majesty, intituled, 'An act to discontinue, in such manner and for such time as are therein mentioned, the landing and discharging, lading or shipping, of goods, wares, and merchandise, at the town and within the harbor of Boston, in the province of Massachusetts Bay, in North America.'—And also, that it may be proper to repeal an act, made in the fourteenth year of the reign of his present Majesty, intituled, 'An act for the impartial administration of justice, in the cases of persons questioned for any acts done by them, in the execution of the law, or for the suppression of riots and tumults, in the province of the Massachusetts Bay, in New England.'—And also, that it may be proper to repeal an act, made in the fourteenth year of the reign of his present Majesty, intituled, 'An act for the better regulating the government of the province of the Massachusetts Bay, in New England.'—And also, that it may be proper to explain and amend an act, made in the thirty-fifth year of the reign of King Henry the Eighth, intituled, 'An Act for the trial of treasons committed out of the king's dominions.' "

I wish, Sir, to repeal the Boston Port Bill, because (independently of the dangerous precedent of suspending the rights of the subject during the king's pleasure) it was passed, as I apprehend, with less regularity, and on more partial principles, than it ought. The corporation of Boston was not heard before it was condemned. Other towns, full as guilty as she was, have not had their ports blocked up. Even the Restraining Bill of the present session does not go to the length of the Boston Port Act. The same ideas of prudence, which induced you not to extend equal punishment to equal guilt, even when you were punishing, induce me, who mean not to chastise, but to reconcile, to be satisfied with the punishment already partially inflicted.

Ideas of prudence and accomodation to circumstances prevent you from taking away the charters of Connecticut and Rhode Island, as you have taken away that of Massachusetts Colony, though the crown has far less power in the two former provinces than it enjoyed in the latter, and though the abuses have been full as great and as flagrant in the exempted as in the punished. The same reasons of prudence and accommodation have weight with me in restoring the charter of Massachusetts Bay. Besides, Sir, the act which changes the charter of Massachusetts is in many particulars so exceptionable, that, if I did not wish absolutely to repeal, I would by all means desire to alter it; as several of its provisions tend to the subversion of all public and private justice. Such, among others, is the power in the governor to change the sheriff at his pleasure, and to make a new returning officer for every special cause. It is shameful to behold such a regulation standing among English laws.

The act for bringing persons accused of committing murder under the orders of government to England for trial is but temporary. That act has calculated the probable duration of our quarrel with the colonies, and is accommodated to that supposed duration. I would hasten the happy moment of reconciliation, and therefore must, on my principle, get rid of that most justly obnoxious act.

The act of Henry the Eighth for the trial of treasons I do not mean to take away, but to confine it to its proper bounds and original intention: to make it expressly for trial of treasons (and the greatest treasons may be committed) in places where the jurisdiction of the crown does not extend.

Having guarded the privileges of local legislature, I would next secure to the colonies a fair and unbiased judicature; for which purpose, Sir, I propose the following resolution:—"That, from the time when the general assembly, or general court, of any colony or plantation in North America shall have appointed, by act of assembly duly confirmed, a settled salary to the offices of the chief justice and other judges of the superior courts, it may be proper that the said chief justice and other judges of the superior courts of such colony shall hold his and their office and offices during their good behavior, and shall not be removed therefrom, but when the said removal shall be adjudged by his Majesty in council, upon a hearing on complaint from the general assembly, or on a complaint from the governor, or the council, or the house of representatives, severally, of the colony in which the said chief justice and other judges have exercised the said offices."

The next resolution relates to the courts of admiralty. It is this:—"That it may be proper to regulate the courts of admiralty or vice-admiralty, authorized by the 15th chapter of the 4th George the Third, in such a manner as to make the same more commodious to those who sue or are sued in the said courts, and to provide for the more decent maintenance of the judges of the same."

These courts I do not wish to take away: they are in themselves proper establishments. This court is one of the capital securities of the Act of Navigation. The extent of its jurisdiction, indeed, has been increased; but this is altogether as proper, and is, indeed, on many accounts, more eligible, where new powers were wanted, than a court absolutely new. But courts incommodiously situated, in effect, deny justice; and a court partaking in the fruits of its own condemnation is a robber. The Congress complain, and complain justly, of this grievance.

These are the three consequential propositions. I have thought of two or three more; but they come rather too near detail, and to the province of executive government, which I wish Parliament always to superintend, never to assume. If the first six are granted, congruity will carry the latter three. If not, the things that remain unrepealed will be, I hope, rather unseemly incumbrances on the building than very materially detrimental to its strength and stability.

Here, Sir, I should close, but that I plainly perceive some objections remain, which I ought, if possible, to remove. The first will be, that, in resorting to the doctrine of our ancestors, as contained in the preamble to the Chester act, I prove too much: that the grievance from a want of representation, stated in that preamble, goes to the whole of legislation as well as to taxation; and that the colonies, grounding themselves upon that doctrine, will apply it to all parts of legislative authority.

To this objection, with all possible deference and humility, and wishing as little as any man living to impair the smallest particle of our supreme authority, I answer, that *the words are the words of Parliament, and not mine;* and that all false and inconclusive inferences drawn from them are not mine; for I heartily disclaim any such inference. I have chosen the words of an act of Parliament, which Mr. Grenville, surely a tolerably zealous and very judicious advocate for the sovereignty of Parliament, formerly moved to have read at your table in confirmation of his tenets. It is true that Lord Chatham[29] considered these preambles as declaring strongly in favor of his opinions. He was a no less powerful advocate for the privileges of the Americans. Ought I not from hence to presume that these preambles are as favorable as possible to both, when properly understood: favorable both to the rights of Parliament, and to the privilege of the dependencies of this crown? But, Sir, the object of grievance in my resolution I have not taken from the Chester, but from the Durham act, which confines the hardship of want of representation to the case of subsidies, and which therefore falls in exactly with the case of the colonies. But whether the unrepresented counties were *de jure* or *de facto*[30] bound the preambles do not accurately distinguish; nor, indeed, was it necessary: for, whether *de jure* or *de facto,* the legislature thought the exercise of the power of taxing, as of right, or as of fact without right, equally a grievance, and equally oppressive.

I do not know that the colonies have, in any general way, or in any cool hour, gone much beyond the demand of immunity in relation to taxes. It is not fair to judge of the temper or dispositions of any man or any set of men, when they are composed and at rest, from their conduct or their expressions in a state of disturbance and irritation. It is, besides, a very great mistake to imagine that mankind follow up practically any speculative principle, either of government or of freedom, as far as it will go in argument and logical illation.[31] We Englishmen stop very short of the principles upon which we support any given part of our Constitution, or even the whole of it together. I could easily, if I had not already tired you, give you very striking and convincing instances of it. This is nothing but what is natural and proper. All government, indeed every human benefit and enjoyment, every virtue and every prudent act, is founded on compromise and barter. We balance inconveniences; we give and take; we remit some rights, that we may enjoy others; and we choose rather to be happy citizens than subtle disputants. As we must give away some natural liberty, to enjoy civil advantages, so we must sacrifice some civil liberties, for the advantages to be derived from the communion and fellowship of a great empire. But, in all fair dealings, the thing bought must bear some proportion to the purchase paid. None will barter away the immediate jewel of his soul. Though a great house is apt to make slaves haughty, yet it is purchasing a part of the artificial importance of a great empire too dear, to pay for it all essential rights, and all the intrinsic dignity of human nature. None of us who would not risk his life rather than fall under a government purely arbitrary. But although there are some amongst us who think our Constitution wants many improvements to make it a complete system of liberty, perhaps none who are of that opinion would think it right to aim at such improvement by disturbing his country and risking everything that is dear to him. In every arduous enterprise, we con-

29. Lord Chatham: William Pitt, First Earl of Chatham (1708–1778). **30.** ***de jure . . . de facto:*** "by law or by the fact of the matter."

31. illation: inference, deduction.

sider what we are to lose, as well as what we are to gain; and the more and better stake of liberty every people possess, the less they will hazard in a vain attempt to make it more. These are *the cords of man.* Man acts from adequate motives relative to his interest, and not on metaphysical speculations. Aristotle, the great master of reasoning, cautions us, and with great weight and propriety, against this species of delusive geometrical accuracy in moral arguments, as the most fallacious of all sophistry.

The Americans will have no interest contrary to the grandeur and glory of England, when they are not oppressed by the weight of it; and they will rather be inclined to respect the acts of a superintending legislature, when they see them the acts of that power which is itself the security, not the rival, of their secondary importance. In this assurance my mind most perfectly acquiesces, and I confess I feel not the least alarm from the discontents which are to arise from putting people at their ease; nor do I apprehend the destruction of this empire from giving, by an act of free grace and indulgence, to two millions of my fellow-citizens some share of those rights upon which I have always been taught to value myself.

It is said, indeed, that this power of granting, vested in American assemblies, would dissolve the unity of the empire,—which was preserved entire, although Wales, and Chester, and Durham were added to it. Truly, Mr. Speaker, I do not know what this unity means; nor has it ever been heard of, that I know, in the constitutional policy of this country. The very idea of subordination of parts excludes this notion of simple and undivided unity. England is the head; but she is not the head and the members too. Ireland has ever had from the beginning a separate, but not an independent legislature, which, far from distracting, promoted the union of the whole. Everything was sweetly and harmoniously disposed through both islands for the conservation of English dominion and the communication of English liberties. I do not see that the same principles might not be carried into twenty islands, and with the same good effect. This is my model with regard to America, as far as the internal circumstances of the two countries are the same. I know no other unity of this empire than I can draw from its example during these periods, when it seemed to my poor understanding more united than it is now, or than it is likely to be by the present methods.

But since I speak of these methods, I recollect, Mr. Speaker, almost too late, that I promised, before I finished, to say something of the proposition of the noble lord on the floor, which has been so lately received, and stands on your journals. I must be deeply concerned, whenever it is my misfortune to continue a difference with the majority of this House. But as the reasons for that difference are my apology for thus troubling you, suffer me to state them in a very few words. I shall compress them into as small a body as I possibly can, having already debated that matter at large, when the question was before the committee.

First, then, I cannot admit that proposition of a ransom by auction,—because it is a mere project. It is a thing new, unheard of, supported by no experience, justified by no analogy, without example of our ancestors, or root in the Constitution. It is neither regular Parliamentary taxation nor colony grant. *Experimentum in corpore vili*[32] is a good rule, which will ever make me adverse to any trial of experiments on what is certainly the most valuable of all subjects, the peace of this empire.

Secondly, it is an experiment which must be fatal in the end to our Constitution. For what is it but a scheme for taxing the colonies in the antechamber of the noble lord and his successors? To settle the quotas and proportions in this House is clearly impossible. You, Sir, may flatter yourself you shall sit a state auctioneer, with your hammer in your hand, and knock down to each colony as it bids. But to settle (on the plan laid down by the noble lord) the true proportional payment for four or five and twenty governments, according to the absolute and the relative wealth of each, and according to the British proportion of wealth and burden, is a wild and chimerical notion. This new taxation must therefore come in by the back-door of the Constitution. Each quota must be brought to this House ready formed. You can neither add nor alter. You must register it. You can do nothing further. For on what grounds can you deliberate either before or after the proposition? You cannot hear the counsel for all these provinces, quarrelling each on its own quantity of payment, and its pro-

32. ***Experimentum . . . vili:*** "Experiment on an inferior body."

portion to others. If you should attempt it, the Committee of Provincial Ways and Means, or by whatever other name it will delight to be called, must swallow up all the time of Parliament.

Thirdly, it does not give satisfaction to the complaint of the colonies. They complain that they are taxed without their consent. You answer, that you will fix the sum at which they shall be taxed. That is, you give them the very grievance for the remedy. You tell them, indeed, that you will leave the mode to themselves. I really beg pardon; it gives me pain to mention it; but you must be sensible that you will not perform this part of the compact. For suppose the colonies were to lay the duties which furnished their contingent upon the importation of your manufactures; you know you would never suffer such a tax to be laid. You know, too, that you would not suffer many other modes of taxation. So that, when you come to explain yourself, it will be found that you will neither leave to themselves the quantum nor the mode, nor indeed anything. The whole is delusion, from one end to the other.

Fourthly, this method of ransom by auction, unless it be *universally* accepted, will plunge you into great and inextricable difficulties. In what year of our Lord are the proportions of payments to be settled? To say nothing of the impossibility that colony agents should have general powers of taxing the colonies at their discretion, consider, I implore you, that the communication by special messages and orders between these agents and their constituents on each variation of the case, when the parties come to contend together, and to dispute on their relative proportions, will be a matter of delay, perplexity, and confusion, that never can have an end.

If all the colonies do not appear at the outcry, what is the condition of those assemblies who offer, by themselves or their agents, to tax themselves up to your ideas of their proportion? The refractory colonies, who refuse all composition, will remain taxed only to your old impositions, which, however grievous in principle, are trifling as to production. The obedient colonies in this scheme are heavily taxed; the refractory remain unburdened. What will you do? Will you lay new and heavier taxes by Parliament on the disobedient? Pray consider in what way you can do it. You are perfectly convinced, that, in the way of taxing, you can do nothing but at the ports. Now suppose it is Virginia that refuses to appear at your auction, while Maryland and North Carolina bid handsomely for their ransom, and are taxed to your quota, how will you put these colonies on a par? Will you tax the tobacco of Virginia? If you do, you give its death-wound to your English revenue at home, and to one of the very greatest articles of your own foreign trade. If you tax the import of that rebellious colony, what do you tax but your own manufactures, or the goods of some other obedient and already well-taxed colony? Who has said one word on this labyrinth of detail, which bewilders you more and more as you enter into it? Who has presented, who can present, you with a clew to lead you out of it? I think, Sir, it is impossible that you should not recollect that the colony bounds are so implicated in one another (you know it by your other experiments in the bill for prohibiting the New England fishery) that you can lay no possible restraints on almost any of them which may not be presently eluded, if you do not confound the innocent with the guilty, and burden those whom upon every principle you ought to exonerate. He must be grossly ignorant of America, who thinks, that, without falling into this confusion of all rules of equity and policy, you can restrain any single colony, especially Virginia and Maryland, the central, and most important of them all.

Let it also be considered, that either in the present confusion you settle a permanent contingent, which will and must be trifling, and then you have no effectual revenue,—or you change the quota at every exigency, and then on every new repartition you will have a new quarrel.

Reflect besides, that, when you have fixed a quota for every colony, you have not provided for prompt and punctual payment. Suppose one, two, five, ten years' arrears. You cannot issue a Treasury extent against the failing colony. You must make new Boston port bills, new restraining laws, new acts for dragging men to England for trial. You must send out new fleets, new armies. All is to begin again. From this day forward the empire is never to know an hour's tranquillity. An intestine fire will be kept alive in the bowels of the colonies, which one time or other must consume this whole empire. I allow, indeed, that the Empire of Germany raises her revenue and her troops by quotas and contingents; but the revenue of the Empire and the army of the Empire is the worst revenue and the worst army in the world.

Instead of a standing revenue, you will therefore have a perpetual quarrel. Indeed, the noble lord who proposed this project of a ransom by auction seemed himself to be of that opinion. His project was rather designed for breaking the union of the colonies than for establishing a revenue. He confessed he apprehended that his proposal would not be to *their taste*. I say, this scheme of disunion seems to be at the bottom of the project; for I will not suspect that the noble lord meant nothing but merely to delude the nation by an airy phantom which he never intended to realize. But whatever his views may be, as I propose the peace and union of the colonies as the very foundation of my plan, it cannot accord with one whose foundation is perpetual discord.

Compare the two. This I offer to give you is plain and simple: the other full of perplexed and intricate mazes. This is mild: that harsh. This is found by experience effectual for its purposes: the other is a new project. This is universal: the other calculated for certain colonies only. This is immediate in its conciliatory operation: the other remote, contingent, full of hazard. Mine is what becomes the dignity of a ruling people: gratuitous, unconditional, and not held out as matter of bargain and sale. I have done my duty in proposing it to you. I have, indeed, tired you by a long discourse; but this is the misfortune of those to whose influence nothing will be conceded, and who must win every inch of their ground by argument. You have heard me with goodness. May you decide with wisdom! For my part, I feel my mind greatly disburdened by what I have done to-day. I have been the less fearful of trying your patience, because on this subject I mean to spare it altogether in future. I have this comfort,—that, in every stage of the American affairs, I have steadily opposed the measures that have produced the confusion, and may bring on the destruction, of this empire. I now go so far as to risk a proposal of my own. If I cannot give peace to my country, I give it to my conscience.

But what (says the financier) is peace to us without money? Your plan gives us no revenue.— No! But it does: for it secures to the subject the power of REFUSAL,—the first of all revenues. Experience is a cheat, and fact a liar, if this power in the subject, of proportioning his grant, or of not granting at all, has not been found the richest mine of revenue ever discovered by the skill or by the fortune of man. It does not, indeed, vote you £152,750: 11: 2¾ths, nor any other paltry limited sum; but it gives the strongbox itself, the fund, the bank, from whence only revenues can arise amongst a people sensible of freedom: *Posita luditur arca.*[33] Cannot you in England, cannot you at this time of day, cannot you, an House of Commons, trust to the principle which has raised so mighty a revenue, and accumulated a debt of near 140 millions in this country? Is this principle to be true in England and false everywhere else? Is it not true in Ireland? Has it not hitherto been true in the colonies? Why should you presume, that, in any country, a body duly constituted for any function will neglect to perform its duty, and abdicate its trust? Such a presumption would go against all government in all modes. But, in truth, this dread of penury of supply from a free assembly has no foundation in Nature. For first observe, that, besides the desire which all men have naturally of supporting the honor of their own government, that sense of dignity, and that security to property, which ever attends freedom, has a tendency to increase the stock of the free community. Most may be taken where most is accumulated. And what is the soil or climate where experience has not uniformly proved that the voluntary flow of heaped-up plenty, bursting from the weight of its own rich luxuriance, has ever run with a more copious stream of revenue than could be squeezed from the dry husks of oppressed indigence by the straining of all the politic machinery in the world?

Next, we know that parties must ever exist in a free country. We know, too, that the emulations of such parties, their contradictions, their reciprocal necessities, their hopes, and their fears, must send them all in their turns to him that holds the balance of the state. The parties are the gamesters; but government keeps the table, and is sure to be the winner in the end. When this game is played, I really think it is more to be feared that the people will be exhausted than that government will not be supplied. Whereas whatever is got by acts of absolute power ill obeyed because odious, or by

33. ***Posita . . . arca:*** "The treasure chest is the prize in the game." See Juvenal, *Satires,* I, 90.

contracts ill kept because constrained, will be narrow, feeble, uncertain, and precarious.

> East would retract
> Vows made in pain, as violent and void.[34]

I, for one, protest against compounding our demands: I declare against compounding, for a poor limited sum, the immense, ever-growing, eternal debt which is due to generous government from protected freedom. And so may I speed in the great object I propose to you, as I think it would not only be an act of injustice, but would be the worst economy in the world, to compel the colonies to a sum certain, either in the way of ransom, or in the way of compulsory compact.

But to clear up my ideas on this subject,—a revenue from America transmitted hither. Do not delude yourselves: you can never receive it,—no, not a shilling. We have experience that from remote countries it is not to be expected. If, when you attempted to extract revenue from Bengal, you were obliged to return in loan what you had taken in imposition, what can you expect from North America? For, certainly, if ever there was a country qualified to produce wealth, it is India; or an institution fit for the transmission, it is the East India Company. America has none of these aptitudes. If America gives you taxable objects on which you lay your duties here, and gives you at the same time a surplus by a foreign sale of her commodities to pay the duties on these objects which you tax at home, she has performed her part to the British revenue. But with regard to her own internal establishments, she may, I doubt not she will, contribute in moderation. I say in moderation; for she ought not to be permitted to exhaust herself. She ought to be reserved to a war; the weight of which, with the enemies that we are most likely to have, must be considerable in her quarter of the globe. There she may serve you, and serve you essentially.

For that service, for all service, whether of revenue, trade, or empire, my trust is in her interest in the British Constitution. My hold of the colonies is in the close affection which grows from common names, from kindred blood, from similar privileges, and equal protection. These are ties which, though light as air, are as strong as links of iron. Let the colonies always keep the idea of their civil rights associated with your government,—they will cling and grapple to you, and no force under heaven will be of power to tear them from their allegiance. But let it be once understood that your government may be one thing and their privileges another, that these two things may exist without any mutual relation,—the cement is gone, the cohesion is loosened, and everything hastens to decay and dissolution. As long as you have the wisdom to keep the sovereign authority of this country as the sanctuary of liberty, the sacred temple consecrated to our common faith, wherever the chosen race and sons of England worship freedom, they will turn their faces towards you. The more they multiply, the more friends you will have; the more ardently they love liberty, the more perfect will be their obedience. Slavery they can have anywhere. It is a weed that grows in every soil. They may have it from Spain, they may have it from Prussia. But, until you become lost to all feeling of your true interest and your natural dignity, freedom they can have from none but you. This is the commodity of price, of which you have the monopoly. This is the true Act of Navigation, which binds to you the commerce of the colonies, and through them secures to you the wealth of the world. Deny them this participation of freedom, and you break that sole bond which originally made, and must still preserve, the unity of the empire. Do not entertain so weak an imagination as that your registers and your bonds, your affidavits and your sufferances, your cockets[35] and your clearances, are what form the great securities of your commerce. Do not dream that your letters of office, and your instructions, and your suspending clauses are the things that hold together the great contexture of this mysterious whole. These things do not make your government. Dead instruments, passive tools as they are, it is the spirit of the English communion that gives all their life and efficacy to them. It is the spirit of the English Constitution, which, infused through the mighty mass, pervades, feeds, unites, invigorates, vivifies every part of the empire, even down to the minutest member.

Is it not the same virtue which does everything

34. Milton, *Paradise Lost,* IV, 96–97. Not an exact quotation.

35. cockets: sealed documents delivered to merchants to certify that their merchandise has been entered properly and that duty has been paid.

for us here in England? Do you imagine, then, that it is the Land-Tax Act which raises your revenue? that it is the annual vote in the Committee of Supply which gives you your army? or that it is the Mutiny Bill which inspires it with bravery and discipline? No! surely, no! It is the love of the people; it is their attachment to their government, from the sense of the deep stake they have in such a glorious institution, which gives you your army and your navy, and infuses into both that liberal obedience without which your army would be a base rabble and your navy nothing but rotten timber.

All this, I know well enough, will sound wild and chimerical to the profane herd of those vulgar and mechanical politicians who have no place among us: a sort of people who think that nothing exists but what is gross and material,—and who, therefore, far from being qualified to be directors of the great movement of empire, are not fit to turn a wheel in the machine. But to men truly initiated and rightly taught, these ruling and master principles, which in the opinion of such men as I have mentioned have no substantial existence, are in truth everything, and all in all. Magnanimity in politics is not seldom the truest wisdom; and a great empire and little minds go ill together. If we are conscious of our situation, and glow with zeal to fill our place as becomes our station and ourselves, we ought to auspicate[36] all our public proceedings on America with the old warning of the Church, *Sursum corda!* [37] We ought to elevate our minds to the greatness of that trust to which the order of Providence has called us. By adverting to the dignity of this high calling our ancestors have turned a savage wilderness into a glorious empire, and have made the most extensive and the only honorable conquests, not by destroying, but by promoting the wealth, the number, the happiness of the human race. Let us get an American revenue as we have got an American empire. English privileges have made it all that it is; English privileges alone will make it all it can be.

In full confidence of this unalterable truth, I now (*quod felix faustumque sit!*)[38] lay the first stone of the Temple of Peace; and I move you,—

36. auspicate: inaugurate. **37. *Sursum corda:*** "Lift up your hearts." **38. *quod . . . sit:*** "Let it be a happy and favorable sign." A familiar expression in Roman legal documents.

That the colonies and plantations of Great Britain in North America, consisting of fourteen separate governments, and containing two millions and upwards of free inhabitants, have not had the liberty and privilege of electing and sending any knights and burgesses, or others, to represent them in the high court of Parliament.

[Upon this Resolution, the previous question was put, and carried;— for the previous question 270, against it, 78.

The first four motions and the last had the previous question put on them. The others were negatived.]

FROM

Reflections on the Revolution in France *

. . .

I flatter myself that I love a manly, moral, regulated liberty as well as any gentleman of that society, be he who he will; and perhaps I have given as good proofs of my attachment to that cause, in the whole course of my public conduct. I think I envy liberty as little as they do, to any other nation. But I cannot stand forward, and give praise or blame to anything which relates to human actions, and human concerns, on a simple view of the object, as it stands stripped of every relation, in all the nakedness and solitude of metaphysical abstraction. Circumstances (which with some gentlemen pass for nothing) give in reality to every political principle its distinguishing colour and discriminating effect. The circumstances are what render every civil and political scheme beneficial or noxious to mankind. Abstractedly speaking, government, as well as liberty, is good; yet could I, in common sense, ten years ago, have felicitated France on her enjoyment of a government (for she then had a government) without inquiry what the nature of that government was, or how it was administered?

* The *Reflections* was in large part stirred by Richard Price (1723–1791), a nonconformist minister and liberal writer on politics, economics, and morals. His famous sermon, "On the Love of Our Country," offered a strong defense of the French Revolution.

Can I now congratulate the same nation upon its freedom? Is it because liberty in the abstract may be classed amongst the blessings of mankind, that I am seriously to felicitate a mad-man, who has escaped from the protecting restraint and wholesome darkness of his cell, on his restoration to the enjoyment of light and liberty? Am I to congratulate a highwayman and murderer, who has broke prison, upon the recovery of his natural rights? This would be to act over again the scene of the criminals condemned to the galleys, and their heroic deliverer, the metaphysic knight of the sorrowful countenance.

When I see the spirit of liberty in action, I see a strong principle at work; and this, for a while, is all I can possibly know of it. The wild *gas*, the fixed air, is plainly broke loose: but we ought to suspend our judgment until the first effervescence is a little subsided, till the liquor is cleared, and until we see something deeper than the agitation of a troubled and frothy surface. I must be tolerably sure, before I venture publicly to congratulate men upon a blessing, that they have really received one. Flattery corrupts both the receiver and the giver; and adulation is not of more service to the people than to kings. I should therefore suspend my congratulations on the new liberty of France, until I was informed how it had been combined with government; with public force; with the discipline and obedience of armies; with the collection of an effective and well-distributed revenue; with morality and religion; with the solidity of property; with peace and order; with civil and social manners. All these (in their way) are good things too; and, without them, liberty is not a benefit whilst it lasts, and is not likely to continue long. The effect of liberty to individuals is, that they may do what they please: we ought to see what it will please them to do, before we risk congratulations, which may be soon turned into complaints. Prudence would dictate this in the case of separate, insulated, private men; but liberty, when men act in bodies, is *power*. Considerate people, before they declare themselves, will observe the use which is made of *power;* and particularly of so trying a thing as *new* power in *new* persons, of whose principles, tempers, and dispositions they have little or no experience, and in situations, where those who appear the most stirring in the scene may possibly not be the real movers. . . .

On the forenoon of the 4th of November last, Doctor Richard Price, a non-conforming minister of eminence, preached at the dissenting meeting-house of the Old Jewry, to his club or society, a very extraordinary miscellaneous sermon, in which there are some good moral and religious sentiments, and not ill expressed, mixed up in a sort of porridge of various political opinions and reflections; but the Revolution in France is the grand ingredient in the cauldron. I consider the address transmitted by the Revolution Society to the National Assembly, through Earl Stanhope, as originating in the principles of the sermon, and as a corollary from them. It was moved by the preacher of that discourse. It was passed by those who came reeking from the effect of the sermon, without any censure or qualification, expressed or implied. If, however, any of the gentlemen concerned shall wish to separate the sermon from the resolution, they know how to acknowledge the one, and to disavow the other. They may do it: I cannot.

For my part, I looked on that sermon as the public declaration of a man much connected with literary caballers, and intriguing philosophers; with political theologians, and theological politicians, both at home and abroad. I know they set him up as a sort of oracle; because, with the best intentions in the world, he naturally *philippizes,*[1] and chants his prophetic songs in exact unison with their designs.

That sermon is in a strain which I believe has not been heard in this kingdom, in any of the pulpits which are tolerated or encouraged in it, since the year 1648; when a predecessor of Dr. Price, the Rev. Hugh Peters, made the vault of the king's own chapel at St. James's ring with the honour and privilege of the saints, who, with the "high praises of God in their mouths, and a *two*-edged sword in their hands, were to execute judgment on the heathen, and punishments upon the *people;* to bind their *kings* with chains, and their *nobles* with fetters of iron." [2] Few harangues from the pulpit, except in the days of your league in France, or in the days of our solemn league and covenant in England, have ever breathed less of the spirit of moderation than

REFLECTIONS. **1.** ***philippizes:*** delivers angry and insulting speeches. A word rooted in the famous speeches of the great Greek orator Demosthenes against Philip II of Macedonia. **2.** Psalm 149.

this lecture in the Old Jewry. Supposing, however, that something like moderation were visible in this political sermon; yet politics and the pulpit are terms that have little agreement. No sound ought to be heard in the church but the healing voice of Christian charity. The cause of civil liberty and civil government gains as little as that of religion by this confusion of duties. Those who quit their proper character, to assume what does not belong to them, are, for the greater part, ignorant both of the character they leave, and of the character they assume. Wholly unacquainted with the world in which they are so fond of meddling and inexperience in all its affairs, on which they pronounce with so much confidence, they have nothing of politics but the passions they excite. Surely the church is a place where one day's truce ought to be allowed to the dissensions and animosities of mankind.

This pulpit style, revived after so long a discontinuance, had to me the air of novelty, and of a novelty not wholly without danger. I do not charge this danger equally to every part of the discourse. The hint given to a noble and reverend lay-divine, who is supposed high in office in one of our universities,[3] and other lay-divines "of *rank* and literature," may be proper and seasonable, though somewhat new. If the noble *Seekers* should find nothing to satisfy their pious fancies in the old staple of the national church, or in all the rich variety to be found in the well-assorted warehouses of the dissenting congregations, Dr. Price advises them to improve upon non-conformity; and to set up, each of them, a separate meeting-house upon his own particular principles. It is somewhat remarkable that this reverend divine should be so earnest for setting up new churches, and so perfectly indifferent concerning the doctrine which may be taught in them. His zeal is of a curious character. It is not for the propagation of his own opinions, but of any opinions. It is not for the diffusion of truth, but for the spreading of contradiction. Let the noble teachers but dissent, it is no matter from whom or from what. This great point once secured, it is taken for granted their religion will be rational and manly. I doubt whether religion would reap all the benefits which the calculating divine computes from this "great company of great preachers." It would certainly be a valuable addition of non-descripts to the ample collection of known classes, genera and species, which at present beautify the *hortus siccus*[4] of dissent. A sermon from a noble duke, or a noble marquis, or a noble earl, or baron bold, would certainly increase and diversify the amusements of this town, which begins to grow satiated with the uniform round of its vapid dissipations. I should only stipulate that these new *Mess-Johns* in robes and coronets should keep some sort of bounds in the democratic and levelling principles which are expected from their titled pulpits. The new evangelists will, I dare say, disappoint the hopes that are conceived of them. They will not become, literally as well as figuratively, polemic divines, nor be disposed so to drill their congregations, that they may, as in former blessed times, preach their doctrines to regiments of dragoons and corps of infantry and artillery. Such arrangements, however favourable to the cause of compulsory freedom, civil and religious, may not be equally conducive to the national tranquillity. These few restrictions I hope are no great stretches of intolerance, no very violent exertions of despotism.

But I may say of our preacher, "*utinam nugis tota illa dedisset tempora sævitiæ.*"[5]—All things in this his fulminating bull are not of so innoxious a tendency. His doctrines affect our constitution in its vital parts. He tells the Revolution Society in this political sermon, that his Majesty "is almost the *only* lawful king in the world, because the *only* one who owes his crown to the *choice of his people.*" As to the kings of *the world,* all of whom (except one) this archpontiff of the *rights of men,* with all the plenitude, and with more than the boldness, of the papal deposing power in its meridian fervour of the twelfth century, puts into one sweeping clause of ban and anathema, and proclaims usurpers by circles of longitude and latitude, over the whole globe, it behoves them to consider how they admit into their territories these apostolic missionaries, who are to tell their subjects they are not lawful kings. That is their concern. It is ours, as a

3. Burke refers the reader to Dr. Richard Price's "Discourse on the Love of our Country," 3rd ed., November 4, 1789, pp. 17–18.

4. ***hortus siccus:*** dry garden. 5. ***utinam . . . sævitiæ:*** "Would that he had given all these times of bitterness to levity." See Juvenal, IV, 150.

domestic interest of some moment, seriously to consider the solidity of the *only* principle upon which these gentlemen acknowledge a king of Great Britain to be entitled to their allegiance.

This doctrine, as applied to the prince now on the British throne, either is nonsense, and therefore neither true nor false, or it affirms a most unfounded, dangerous, illegal, and unconstitutional position. According to this spiritual doctor of politics, if his Majesty does not owe his crown to the choice of his people, he is no *lawful king*. Now nothing can be more untrue than that the crown of this kingdom is so held by his Majesty. Therefore if you follow their rule, the king of Great Britain, who most certainly does not owe his high office to any form of popular election, is in no respect better than the rest of the gang of usurpers, who reign, or rather rob, all over the face of this our miserable world, without any sort of right or title to the allegiance of their people. The policy of this general doctrine, so qualified, is evident enough. The propagators of this political gospel are in hopes that their abstract principle (their principle that a popular choice is necessary to the legal existence of the sovereign magistracy) would be overlooked, whilst the king of Great Britain was not affected by it. In the meantime the ears of their congregations would be gradually habituated to it, as if it were a first principle admitted without dispute. For the present it would only operate as a theory, pickled in the preserving juices of pulpit eloquence, and laid by for future use. *Condo et compono quæ mox depromere possim.*[6] By this policy, whilst our government is soothed with a reservation in its favour, to which it has no claim, the security, which it has in common with all governments, so far as opinion is security, is taken away.

Thus these politicians proceed, whilst little notice is taken of their doctrines; but when they come to be examined upon the plain meaning of their words, and the direct tendency of their doctrines, then equivocations and slippery constructions come into play. When they say the king owes his crown to the choice of his people, and is therefore the only lawful sovereign in the world, they will perhaps tell us they mean to say no more than that some of the king's predecessors have been called to the throne by some sort of choice; and therefore he owes his crown to the choice of his people. Thus, by a miserable subterfuge, they hope to render their proposition safe, by rendering it nugatory. They are welcome to the asylum they seek for their offence, since they take refuge in their folly. For, if you admit this interpretation, how does their idea of election differ from our idea of inheritance? And how does the settlement of the crown in the Brunswick line derived from James the First come to legalize our monarchy, rather than that of any of the neighbouring countries? At some time or other, to be sure, all the beginners of dynasties were chosen by those who called them to govern. There is ground enough for the opinion that all the kingdoms of Europe were, at a remote period, elective, with more or fewer limitations in the objects of choice. But whatever kings might have been here, or elsewhere, a thousand years ago, or in whatever manner the ruling dynasties of England or France may have begun, the king of Great Britain is, at this day, king by a fixed rule of succession, according to the laws of his country; and whilst the legal conditions of the compact of sovereignty are performed by him, (as they are performed,) he holds his crown in contempt of the choice of the Revolution Society, who have not a single vote for a king amongst them, either individually or collectively; though I make no doubt they would soon erect themselves into an electoral college, if things were ripe to give effect to their claim. His Majesty's heirs and successors, each in his time and order, will come to the crown with the same contempt of their choice with which his Majesty has succeeded to that he wears.

Whatever may be the success of evasion in explaining away the gross error of *fact*, which supposes that his Majesty (though he holds it in concurrence with the wishes) owes his crown to the choice of his people, yet nothing can evade their full explicit declaration, concerning the principle of a right in the people to choose; which right is directly maintained, and tenaciously adhered to. All the oblique insinuations concerning election bottom in this proposition, and are referable to it. Lest the foundation of the king's exclusive legal title should pass for a mere rant of adulatory freedom, the political divine proceeds

6. ***Condo . . . possim:*** "I build and put together those things that I might soon draw from." See Horace, *Epistles,* I, 1.12.

dogmatically to assert, that, by the principles of the Revolution,[7] the people of England have acquired three fundamental rights, all which, with him, compose one system, and lie together in one short sentence; namely, that we have acquired a right,

1. "To choose our own governors."
2. "To cashier them for misconduct."
3. "To frame a government for ourselves."

This new, and hitherto unheard-of, bill of rights, though made in the name of the whole people, belongs to those gentlemen and their faction only. The body of the people of England have no share in it. They utterly disclaim it. They will resist the practical assertion of it with their lives and fortunes. They are bound to do so by the laws of their country, made at the time of that very Revolution which is appealed to in favour of the fictitious rights claimed by the Society which abuses its name.

These gentlemen of the Old Jewry, in all their reasonings on the Revolution of 1688, have a Revolution which happened in England about forty years before,[8] and the late French Revolution, so much before their eyes, and in their hearts, that they are constantly confounding all the three together. It is necessary that we should separate what they confound. We must recall their erring fancies to the *acts* of the Revolution which we revere, for the discovery of its true *principles.* If the *principles* of the Revolution of 1688 are anywhere to be found, it is in the statute called the *Declaration of Right.* In that most wise, sober, and considerate declaration, drawn up by great lawyers and great statesmen, and not by warm and inexperienced enthusiasts, not one word is said, nor one suggestion made, of a general right "to choose our own *governors;* to cashier them for misconduct; and to *form* a government for *ourselves.*"

This Declaration of Right (the act of the 1st of William and Mary, sess. 2, ch. 2) is the cornerstone of our constitution, as reinforced, explained, improved, and in its fundamental principles for ever settled. It is called "An Act for declaring the rights and liberties of the subject, and for *settling* the *succession* of the crown." You will observe, that these rights and this succession are declared in one body, and bound indissolubly together.

A few years after this period, a second opportunity offered for asserting a right of election to the crown. On the prospect of a total failure of issue from King William, and from the Princess, afterwards Queen Anne, the consideration of the settlement of the crown, and of a further security for the liberties of the people, again came before the legislature. Did they this second time make any provision for legalizing the crown on the spurious revolution principles of the Old Jewry? No. They followed the principles which prevailed in the Declaration of Right; indicating with more precision the persons who were to inherit in the Protestant line. This act also incorporated, by the same policy, our liberties, and an hereditary succession in the same act. Instead of a right to choose our own governors, they declared that the *succession* in that line (the Protestant line drawn from James the First) was absolutely necessary "for the peace, quiet, and security of the realm," and that it was equally urgent on them "to maintain a *certainty in the succession* thereof, to which the subjects may safely have recourse for their protection." Both these acts, in which are heard the unerring, unambiguous oracles of revolution policy, instead of countenancing the delusive, gipsy predictions of a "right to choose our governors," prove to a demonstration how totally adverse the wisdom of the nation was from turning a case of necessity into a rule of law.

Unquestionably there was at the Revolution, in the person of King William, a small and a temporary deviation from the strict order of a regular hereditary succession; but it is against all genuine principles of jurisprudence to draw a principle from a law made in a special case, and regarding an individual person. *Privilegium non transit in exemplum.*[9] If ever there was a time favourable for establishing the principle, that a king of popular choice was the only legal king, without all doubt it was at the Revolution. Its not being done at that time is a proof that the nation was of opinion it ought not to be done at any time. There is no person so completely ignorant of our history as not to know, that the majority in parliament of

7. **Revolution:** the Glorious Revolution of 1688. 8. The Puritan Revolution and Civil War of 1642–1649.

9. ***Privilegium . . . exemplum:*** "A privilege does not become a tradition."

both parties were so little disposed to anything resembling that principle, that at first they were determined to place the vacant crown, not on the head of the Prince of Orange, but on that of his wife Mary, daughter of King James, the eldest born of the issue of that king, which they acknowledged as undoubtedly his. It would be to repeat a very trite story, to recall to your memory all those circumstances which demonstrated that their accepting King William was not properly a *choice;* but to all those who did not wish, in effect, to recall King James, or to deluge their country in blood, and again to bring their religion, laws, and liberties into the peril they had just escaped, it was an act of *necessity,* in the strictest moral sense in which necessity can be taken. . . .

It is far from impossible to reconcile, if we do not suffer ourselves to be entangled in the mazes of metaphysic sophistry, the use both of a fixed rule and an occasional deviation; the sacredness of an hereditary principle of succession in our government, with a power of change in its application in cases of extreme emergency. Even in that extremity, (if we take the measure of our rights by our exercise of them at the Revolution,) the change is to be confined to the peccant [10] part only; to the part which produced the necessary deviation; and even then it is to be effected without a decomposition of the whole civil and political mass, for the purpose of originating a new civil order out of the first elements of society.

A state without the means of some change is without the means of its conservation. Without such means it might even risk the loss of that part of the constitution which it wished the most religiously to preserve. The two principles of conservation and correction operated strongly at the two critical periods of the Restoration and Revolution, when England found itself without a king. At both those periods the nation had lost the bond of union in their ancient edifice; they did not, however, dissolve the whole fabric. On the contrary, in both cases they regenerated the deficient part of the old constitution through the parts which were not impaired. They kept these old parts exactly as they were, that the part recovered might be suited to them. . . .

The second claim of the Revolution Society is "a right of cashiering their governors for *misconduct.*" Perhaps the apprehensions our ancestors entertained of forming such a precedent as that "of cashiering for misconduct," was the cause that the declaration of the act, which implied the abdication of King James, was, if it had any fault, rather too guarded, and too circumstantial. But all this guard, and all this accumulation of circumstances, serves to show the spirit of caution which predominated in the national councils in a situation in which men, irritated by oppression, and elevated by a triumph over it, are apt to abandon themselves to violent and extreme courses: it shows the anxiety of the great men who influenced the conduct of affairs at that great event to make the Revolution a parent of settlement, and not a nursery of future revolutions.

No government could stand a moment, if it could be blown down with anything so loose and indefinite as an opinion of *"misconduct."* They who led at the Revolution grounded the virtual abdication of King James upon no such light and uncertain principle. They charged him with nothing less than a design, confirmed by a multitude of illegal overt acts, to *subvert the Protestant church and state,* and their *fundamental,* unquestionable laws and liberties: they charged him with having broken the *original contract* between king and people. This was more than *misconduct.* A grave and overruling necessity obliged them to take the step they took, and took with infinite reluctance, as under the most rigorous of all laws. Their trust for the future preservation of the constitution was not in future revolutions. The grand policy of all their regulations was to render it almost impracticable for any future sovereign to compel the states of the kingdom to have again recourse to those violent remedies. They left the crown what, in the eye and estimation of law, it had ever been, perfectly irresponsible. In order to lighten the crown still further, they aggravated responsibility on ministers of state. By the statute of the 1st of King William, sess. 2nd, called *"the act for declaring the rights and liberties of the subject, and for settling the succession to the crown,"* they enacted, that the ministers should serve the crown on the terms of that declaration. They secured soon after the *frequent meetings of parliament,* by which the whole government would be under the constant inspection and active control of the popular representative and of the mag-

10. peccant: erring, sinning.

nates of the kingdom. In the next great constitutional act, that of the 12th and 13th of King William, for the further limitation of the crown, and *better* securing the rights and liberties of the subject, they provided, "that no pardon under the great seal of England should be pleadable to an impeachment by the Commons in parliament." The rule laid down for government in the Declaration of Right, the constant inspection of parliament, the practical claim of impeachment, they thought infinitely a better security not only for their constitutional liberty, but against the vices of administration, than the reservation of a right so difficult in the practice, so uncertain in the issue, and often so mischievous in the consequences, as that of "cashiering their governors." . . .

You will observe, that from Magna Charta to the Declaration of Right, it has been the uniform policy of our constitution to claim and assert our liberties, as an *entailed inheritance* derived to us from our forefathers, and to be transmitted to our posterity; as an estate specially belonging to the people of this kingdom, without any reference whatever to any other more general or prior right. By this means our constitution preserves a unity in so great a diversity of its parts. We have an inheritable crown; an inheritable peerage; and a House of Commons and a people inheriting privileges, franchises, and liberties, from a long line of ancestors.

This policy appears to me to be the result of profound reflection; or rather the happy effect of following nature, which is wisdom without reflection, and above it. A spirit of innovation is generally the result of a selfish temper, and confined views. People will not look forward to posterity, who never look backward to their ancestors. Besides, the people of England well know, that the idea of inheritance furnishes a sure principle of conservation, and a sure principle of transmission; without at all excluding a principle of improvement. It leaves acquisition free; but it secures what it acquires. Whatever advantages are obtained by a state proceeding on these maxims, are locked fast as in a sort of family settlement; grasped as in a kind of mortmain[11] for ever. By a constitutional policy, working after the pattern of nature, we receive, we hold, we transmit our government and our privileges, in the same manner in which we enjoy and transmit our property and our lives. The institutions of policy, the goods of fortune, the gifts of providence, are handed down to us, and from us, in the same course and order. Our political system is placed in a just correspondence and symmetry with the order of the world, and with the mode of existence decreed to a permanent body composed of transitory parts; wherein, by the disposition of a stupendous wisdom, moulding together the great mysterious incorporation of the human race, the whole, at one time, is never old, or middle-aged, or young, but, in a condition of unchangeable constancy, moves on through the varied tenor of perpetual decay, fall, renovation, and progression. Thus, by preserving the method of nature in the conduct of the state, in what we improve, we are never wholly new; in what we retain, we are never wholly obsolete. By adhering in this manner and on those principles to our forefathers, we are guided not by the superstition of antiquarians, but by the spirit of philosophic analogy. In this choice of inheritance we have given to our frame of polity the image of a relation in blood; binding up the constitution of our country with our dearest domestic ties; adopting our fundamental laws into the bosom of our family affections; keeping inseparable, and cherishing with the warmth of all their combined and mutually reflected charities, our state, our hearths, our sepulchres, and our altars.

Through the same plan of a conformity to nature in our artificial institutions, and by calling in the aid of her unerring and powerful instincts, to fortify the fallible and feeble contrivances of our reason, we have derived several other, and those no small benefits, from considering our liberties in the light of an inheritance. Always acting as if in the presence of cannonized forefathers, the spirit of freedom, leading in itself to misrule and excess, is tempered with an awful gravity. This idea of a liberal descent inspires us with a sense of habitual native dignity, which prevents that upstart insolence almost inevitably adhering to and disgracing those who are the first acquirers of any distinction. By this means our liberty becomes a noble freedom. It carries an imposing and majestic aspect. It has a pedigree and illustrating ancestors. It has its bearings and its ensigns armorial. It has its gallery of portraits; its monumental inscriptions; its records,

11. mortmain: an inalienable possession of lands or buildings by an ecclesiastical or other corporation.

evidences, and titles. We procure reverence to our civil institutions on the principle upon which nature teaches us to revere individual men; on account of their age, and on account of those from whom they are descended. All your sophisters cannot produce anything better adapted to preserve a rational and manly freedom than the course that we have pursued, who have chosen our nature rather than our speculations, our breasts rather than our inventions, for the great conservatories and magazines of our rights and privileges.

You might, if you pleased, have profited of our example, and have given to your recovered freedom a correspondent dignity. Your privileges, though discontinued, were not lost to memory. Your constitution, it is true, whilst you were out of possession, suffered waste and dilapidation; but you possessed in some parts the walls, and, in all, the foundations, of a noble and venerable castle. You might have repaired those walls; you might have built on those old foundations. Your constitution was suspended before it was perfected; but you had the elements of a constitution very nearly as good as could be wished. In your old states you possessed that variety of parts corresponding with the various descriptions of which your community was happily composed; you had all that combination, and all that opposition of interests, you had that action and counteraction, which, in the natural and in the political world, from the reciprocal struggle of discordant powers, draws out the harmony of the universe. These opposed and conflicting interests, which you considered as so great a blemish in your old and in our present constitution, interpose a salutary check to all precipitate resolutions. They render deliberation a matter not of choice, but of necessity; they make all change a subject of *compromise*, which naturally begets moderation; they produce *temperaments* preventing the sore evil of harsh, crude, unqualified reformations; and rendering all the headlong exertions of arbitrary power, in the few or in the many, for ever impracticable. Through that diversity of members and interests, general liberty had as many securities as there were separate views in the several orders; whilst by pressing down the whole by the weight of a real monarchy, the separate parts would have been prevented from warping, and starting from their allotted places.

You had all these advantages in your ancient states; but you chose to act as if you had never been moulded into civil society, and had everything to begin anew. You began ill, because you began by despising everything that belonged to you. You set up your trade without a capital. If the last generations of your country appeared without much lustre in your eyes, you might have passed them by, and derived your claims from a more early race of ancestors. Under a pious predilection for those ancestors, your imaginations would have realized in them a standard of virtue and wisdom, beyond the vulgar practice of the hour: and you would have risen with the example to whose imitation you aspired. Respecting your forefathers, you would have been taught to respect yourselves. You would not have chosen to consider the French as a people of yesterday, as a nation of low-born servile wretches until the emancipating year of 1789. In order to furnish, at the expense of your honour, an excuse to your apologists here for several enormities of yours, you would not have been content to be represented as a gang of Maroon slaves, suddenly broke loose from the house of bondage, and therefore to be pardoned for your abuse of the liberty to which you were not accustomed, and ill fitted. Would it not, my worthy friend, have been wiser to have you thought, what I, for one, always thought you, a generous and gallant nation, long misled to your disadvantage by your high and romantic sentiments of fidelity, honour, and loyalty; that events had been unfavourable to you, but that you were not enslaved through any illiberal or servile disposition; that in your most devoted submission, you were actuated by a principle of public spirit, and that it was your country you worshipped, in the person of your king? Had you made it to be understood, that in the delusion of this amiable error you had gone further than your wise ancestors; that you were resolved to resume your ancient privileges, whilst you preserved the spirit of your ancient and your recent loyalty and honour; or if, diffident of yourselves, and not clearly discerning the almost obliterated constitution of your ancestors, you had looked to your neighbours in this land, who had kept alive the ancient principles and models of the old common law of Europe meliorated and adapted to its present state—by following wise examples you would have given new examples of wisdom to the world. You would have rendered the cause of liberty venerable in the eyes of every worthy mind in every nation. You would have shamed despotism from the earth, by showing that freedom was not only reconcilable, but, as when well disciplined it is, auxiliary to law. You would have had an unoppressive but a productive revenue. You would have had a flourishing commerce to feed it. You would have had a free constitution; a potent monarchy; a disciplined army; a reformed and venerated clergy; a mitigated but spirited nobility, to lead your virtue, not to overlay it; you would have had a liberal order of commons, to emulate and to recruit that nobility; you would have had a protected, satisfied, laborious, and obedient people, taught to seek and to recognise the happiness that is to be found by virtue in all conditions; in which consists the true moral equality of mankind, and not in that monstrous fiction, which, by inspiring false ideas and vain expectations into men destined to travel in the obscure walk of laborious life, serves only to aggravate and embitter that real inequality, which it never can remove; and which the order of civil life establishes as much for the benefit of those whom it must leave in an humble state, as those whom it is able to exalt to a condition more splendid, but not more happy. You had a smooth and easy career of felicity and glory laid open to you, beyond anything recorded in the history of the world; but you have shown that difficulty is good for man.

Compute your gains: see what is got by those extravagant and presumptuous speculations which have taught your leaders to despise all their predecessors, and all their contemporaries, and even to despise themselves, until the moment in which they became truly despicable. By following those false lights, France has bought undisguised calamities at a higher price than any nation has purchased the most unequivocal blessings! France has bought poverty by crime! France has not sacrificed her virtue to her interest, but she has abandoned her interest, that she might prostitute her virtue. All other nations have begun the fabric of a new government, or the reformation of an old, by establishing originally, or by enforcing with greater exactness, some rites or other of religion. All other people have laid the foundations of civil freedom in severer manners, and a system of a more austere and masculine morality. France, when she let loose the reins of regal authority, doubled the licence of a ferocious dissoluteness in manners, and of an insolent irreligion in opinions and practices; and has extended through all ranks of life, as if she were communicating some privilege, or laying open some secluded benefit, all the unhappy corruptions that usually were the disease of wealth and power. This is one of the new principles of equality in France.

France, by the perfidy of her leaders, has utterly disgraced the tone of lenient council in the cabinets of princes, and disarmed it of its most potent topics. She has sanctified the dark, suspicious maxims of tyrannous distrust; and taught kings to tremble at (what will hereafter be called) the delusive plausibilities of moral politicians. Sovereigns will consider those, who advise them to place an unlimited confidence in their people, as subverters of their thrones; as traitors who aim at their destruction, by leading their easy good-nature, under specious pretences, to admit combinations of bold and faithless men into a participation of their power. This alone (if there were nothing else) is an irreparable calamity to you and to mankind. Remember that your parliament of Paris told your king, that, in calling the states together, he had nothing to fear but the prodigal excess of their zeal in providing for the support of the throne. It is right that these men should hide their heads. It is right that they should bear their part in the ruin which their counsel has brought on their sovereign and their country. Such sanguine declarations tend to lull authority asleep; to encourage it rashly to engage in perilous adventures of untried policy; to neglect those provisions, preparations, and precautions, which distinguished benevolence from imbecility; and without which no man can answer for the salutary effect of any abstract plan of government or of freedom. For want of these, they have seen the medicine of the state corrupted into its poison. They have seen the French rebel against a mild and unlawful monarch, with more fury, outrage, and insult, than ever any people has been known to rise against the most illegal usurper, or the most sanguinary tyrant. Their resistance was made to concession; their revolt was from protection; their blow was aimed at a hand holding out graces, favours, and immunities.

This was unnatural. The rest is in order. They have found their punishment in their success. Laws overturned; tribunals subverted; industry without vigour; commerce expiring; the revenue unpaid, yet the people impoverished; a church pillaged, and a state not relieved; civil and military anarchy made the constitution of the kingdom; everything human and divine sacrificed to the idol of public credit, and national bankruptcy the consequence; and, to crown all, the paper securities of new, precarious, tottering power, the discredited paper securities of impoverished fraud and beggared rapine, held out as a currency for the support of an empire, in lieu of the two great recognised species that represent the lasting, conventional credit of mankind, which disappeared and hid themselves in the earth from whence they came, when the principle of property, whose creatures and representatives they are, was systematically subverted.

Were all these dreadful things necessary? Were they the inevitable results of the desperate struggle of determined patriots, compelled to wade through blood and tumult, to the quiet shore of a tranquil and prosperous liberty? No! nothing like it. The fresh ruins of France, which shock our feelings wherever we can turn our eyes, are not the devastation of civil war; they are the sad but instructive monuments of rash and ignorant counsel in time of profound peace. They are the display of inconsiderate and presumptuous, because unresisted and irresistible, authority. The persons who have thus squandered away the precious treasure of their crimes, the persons who have made this prodigal and wild waste of public evils, (the last stake reserved for the ultimate ransom of the state,) have met in their progress with little, or rather with no opposition at all. Their whole march was more like a triumphal procession, than the progress of a war. Their pioneers have gone before them, and demolished and laid everything level at their feet. Not one drop of *their* blood have they shed in the cause of the country they have ruined. They have made no sacrifices to their projects of greater consequence than their shoebuckles, whilst they were imprisoning their king, murdering their fellow-citizens, and bathing in tears, and plunging in poverty and distress, thousands of worthy men and worthy families. Their cruelty has not ever been the base result of fear. It has been the effect of their sense of perfect safety, in authorizing treasons, robberies, rapes, assassinations, slaughters, and burnings, throughout their harassed land. But the cause of all was plain from the beginning.

This unforced choice, this fond election of evil, would appear perfectly unaccountable, if we did not consider the composition of the National Assembly: I do not mean its formal constitution, which, as it now stands, is exceptionable enough, but the materials of which, in a great measure, it is composed, which is of ten thousand times greater consequence than all the formalities in the world. If we were to know nothing of this assembly but by its title and function, no colours could paint to the imagination anything more venerable. In that light the mind of an inquirer, subdued by such an awful image as that of the virtue and wisdom of a whole people collected into a focus, would pause and hesitate in condemning things even of the very worst aspect. Instead of blameable, they would appear only mysterious. But no name, no power, no function, no artificial institution whatsoever, can make the men of whom any system of authority is composed, any other than God, and nature, and education, and their habits of life have made them. Capacities beyond these the people have not to give. Virtue and wisdom may be the objects of their choice; but their choice confers neither the one nor the other on those upon whom they lay their ordaining hands. They have not the engagement of nature, they have not the promise of revelation, for any such powers. . . .

. . .

You will smile here at the consistency of those democratists, who, when they are not on their guard, treat the humbler part of the community with the greatest contempt, whilst, at the same time, they pretend to make them the depositories of all power. It would require a long discourse to point out to you the many fallacies that lurk in the generality and equivocal nature of the terms "inadequate representation." I shall only say here, in justice to that old-fashioned constitution, under which we have long prospered, that our representation has been found perfectly adequate to all the purposes for which a representation of the people can be desired or devised. I defy the enemies of our constitution to show the contrary. To detail the particulars in which it is found so well to promote its ends, would demand a treatise on our practical constitution. I state here the doctrine of the Revolutionists, only that you and others may see what an opinion these gentlemen entertain of the constitution of their country, and why they seem to think that some great abuse of power, or some great calamity, as giving a chance for the blessing of a constitution according to their ideas, would be much palliated to their feelings; you see *why they* are so much enamoured of your fair and equal representation, which being once obtained, the same effects might follow. You see they consider our House of Commons as only "a semblance," "a form," "a theory," "a shadow," "a mockery," perhaps "a nuisance."

These gentlemen value themselves on being systematic; and not without reason. They must therefore look on this gross and palpable defect of representation, this fundamental grievance, (so they call it,) as a thing not only vicious in itself, but as rendering our whole government absolutely *illegitimate,* and not at all better than a downright *usurpation.* Another revolution, to get rid of this illegitimate and usurped government, would of course be perfectly justifiable, if not absolutely necessary. Indeed their principle, if you observe it with any attention, goes much further than to an alteration in the election of the House of Commons; for, if popular representation, or choice, is necessary to the *legitimacy* of all government, the House of Lords is, at one stroke, bastardized and corrupted in blood. That House is no representative of the people at all, even in "semblance or in form." The case of the crown is altogether as bad. In vain the crown may endeavour to screen itself against these gentlemen by the authority of the establishment made on the Revolution. The Revolution which is resorted to for a title, on their system, wants a title itself. The Revolution is built, according to their theory, upon a basis not more solid than our present formalities, as it was made by a House of Lords, not representing any one but themselves; and by a House of Commons exactly such as the present, that is, as they term it, by a mere "shadow and mockery" of representation.

Something they must destroy, or they seem to themselves to exist for no purpose. One set is for destroying the civil power through the ecclesiastical; another, for demolishing the ecclesiastic through the civil. They are aware that the worst consequences might happen to the public in accomplishing this double ruin of church and state; but they are so heated with their theories, that they give more than hints, that this ruin, with all the mischiefs that must lead to it and attend it, and which to themselves appear quite certain, would not be unacceptable to them, or very remote from their wishes. A man amongst them of great authority, and certainly of great talents, speaking of a supposed alliance between church and state, says, "perhaps *we must wait for the fall of the civil powers* before this most unnatural alliance be broken. Calamitous no doubt will that time be. But what convulsion in the political world ought to be a subject of lamentation, if it be attended with so desirable an effect?" You see with what a steady eye these gentlemen are prepared to view the greatest calamities which can befall their country. . . .

. . .

Far am I from denying in theory, full as far is my heart from withholding in practice, (if I were of power to give or to withhold,) the *real* rights of men. In denying their false claims of right, I do not mean to injure those which are real, and are such as their pretended rights would totally destroy. If civil society be made for the advantage of man, all the advantages for which it is made become his right. It is an institution of beneficence; and law itself is only beneficence acting by a rule. Men have a right to live by that rule; they have a right to do justice, as between their fellows, whether their fellows are in public function or in ordinary occupation. They have a right to the fruits of their industry; and to the means of making their industry fruitful. They have a right to the acquisitions of their parents; to the nourishment and improvement of their offspring; to instruction in life, and to consolation in death. Whatever each man can separately do, without trespassing upon others, he has a right to do for himself; and he has a right to a fair portion of all which society, with all its combinations of skill and force, can do in his favour. In this partnership all men have equal rights; but not to equal things. He that has but five shillings in the partnership, has as good a right to it, as he that has five hundred pounds has to his larger proportion. But he has not a right to an equal dividend in the product of the joint stock; and as to the share of power, authority, and direction which each individual ought to have in the management of the state, that I must deny to be amongst the direct original rights of man in civil society; for I have in my contemplation the civil social man, and no other. It is a thing to be settled by convention.

If civil society be the offspring of convention, that convention must be its law. That convention must limit and modify all the descriptions of constitution which are formed under it. Every sort of legislative, judicial, or executory power are its creatures. They can have no being in any other state of things; and how can any man claim under the conventions of civil society, rights which do not so much as suppose its existence? rights which are absolutely repugnant to it? One of the first motives to civil society, and which becomes one of its fundamental rules, is, *that no man should be judge in his own cause*. By this each person has at once divested himself of the first fundamental right of uncovenanted man, that is, to judge for himself, and to assert his own cause. He abdicates all rights to be his own governor. He inclusively, in a great measure, abandons the right of self-defence, the first law of nature. Men cannot enjoy the rights of an uncivil and of a civil state together. That he may obtain justice, he gives up his right of determining what it is in points the most essential to him. That he may secure some liberty, he makes a surrender in trust of the whole of it.

Government is not made in virtue of natural rights, which may and do exist in total independence of it; and exist in much greater clearness, and in a much greater degree of abstract perfection: but their abstract perfection is their practical defect. By having a right to everything they want everything. Government is a contrivance of human wisdom to provide for human *wants*. Men have a right that these wants should be provided for by this wisdom. Among these wants is to be reckoned the want, out of civil society, of a sufficient restraint upon their passions. Society requires not only that the passions of individuals should be subjected, but that even in the mass and body, as well as in the individuals, the inclinations of men should frequently be thwarted, their will controlled, and their passions brought into subjection. This can only be done *by a power out of themselves;* and not, in the exercise of its function, subject to that will and to those passions which it is its office to bridle and subdue. In this sense the restraints on men, as well as their liberties, are to be reckoned among their rights. But as the liberties and the restrictions vary with times and circumstances, and admit of infinite modifications, they cannot be settled upon any abstract rule; and nothing is so foolish as to discuss them upon that principle.

The moment you abate anything from the full rights of men, each to govern himself, and suffer any artificial, positive limitation upon those rights, from that moment the whole organization of government becomes a consideration of convenience. This it is which makes the constitution of a state, and the due distribution of its powers, a matter of the most delicate and complicated skill. It requires a deep knowledge of human nature and human necessities, and of the things which facilitate or obstruct the various ends, which are to be pursued by the mechanism of civil institutions. The state is to have recruits to its strength, and remedies to its distempers. What is the use of discussing a man's abstract right to food or medicine? The question is upon the method of procuring and administering them. In that deliberation I shall always advise to call in the aid of the farmer and the physician, rather than the professor of metaphysics.

The science of constructing a commonwealth, or renovating it, or reforming it, is, like every other experimental science, not to be taught *à priori*. Nor is it a short experience that can instruct us in that practical science; because the real effects of moral causes are not always immediate; but that which in the first instance is prejudicial may be excellent in its remoter operation; and its excellence may arise even from the ill effects it produces in the beginning. The reverse also happens: and very plausible schemes, with very pleasing commencements, have often shameful and lamentable conclusions. In states there are often some obscure and almost latent causes, things which appear at first view of little moment, on which a very great part of its prosperity or adversity may most essentially depend. The science of government being therefore so practical in itself, and intended for such practical purposes, a matter which requires experience, and even more experience than any person can gain in his whole life, however sagacious and observing he may be, it is with infinite caution that any man ought to venture upon pulling down an edifice, which has answered in any tolerable degree for ages the common purposes of society, or on building it up again, without having models and patterns of approved utility before his eyes.

These metaphysic rights entering into common life, like rays of light which pierce into a dense medium, are, by the laws of nature, refracted from their straight line. Indeed in the gross and complicated mass of human passions and concerns, the primitive rights of men undergo such a variety of refractions and reflections, that it becomes absurd to talk of them as if they continued in the simplicity of their original direction. The nature of man is intricate; the objects of society are of the greatest possible complexity: and therefore no simple disposition or direction of power can be suitable either to man's nature, or to the quality of his affairs. When I hear the simplicity of contrivance aimed at and boasted of in any new political constitutions, I am at no loss to decide that the artificers are grossly ignorant of their trade, or totally negligent of their duty. The simple governments are fundamentally defective, to say no worse of them. If you were to contemplate society in but one point of view, all these simple modes of polity are infinitely captivating. In effect each would answer its single end much more perfectly than the more complex is able to attain all its complex purposes. But it is better that the whole should be imperfectly and anomalously answered, than that, while some parts are provided for with great exactness, others might be totally neglected, or perhaps materially injured, by the over-care of a favourite member.

The pretended rights of these theorists are all extremes: and in proportion as they are metaphysically true, they are morally and politically false. The rights of men are in a sort of *middle,* incapable of definition, but not impossible to be discerned. The rights of men in governments are their advantages; and these are often in balances between differences of good; in compromises sometimes between good and evil, and sometimes between evil and evil. Political reason is a computing principle; adding, subtracting, multiplying, and dividing, morally and not metaphysically, or mathematically, true moral denominations.

By these theorists the right of the people is almost always sophistically confounded with their power. The body of the community, whenever it can come to act, can meet with no effectual resistance; but till power and right are the same, the whole body of them has no right inconsistent with virtue, and the first of all virtues, prudence. Men have no right to what is not reasonable, and to what is not for their benefit; for though a pleasant writer said, *Liceat perire poetis,*[12] when one of them, in cold blood, is said to have leaped into the flames of a volcanic revolution, *Ardentem frigidus Ætnam insiluit,*[13] I consider such a frolic rather as an unjustifiable poetic license, than as one of the franchises of Parnassus; and whether he were poet, or divine, or politician, that chose to exercise this kind of right, I think that more wise, because more charitable, thoughts would urge me rather to save the man, than to preserve his brazen slippers as the monuments of his folly.

The kind of anniversary sermons to which a great part of what I write refers, if men are not shamed out of their present course, in commemorating the fact, will cheat many out of the principles, and deprive them of the benefits, of the revolution they commemorate. I confess to you, Sir, I never liked this continual talk of resistance, and revolution, or the practice of making the extreme medicine of the constitution its daily bread. It renders the habit of society dangerously valetudinary: it is taking periodical doses of mercury sublimate, and swallowing down repeated provocatives of cantharides[14] to our love of liberty.

This distemper of remedy, grown habitual, relaxes and wears out, by a vulgar and prostituted use, the spring of that spirit which is to be exerted on great occasions. It was in the most patient period of Roman servitude that themes of tyrannicide made the ordinary exercise of boys at school—*cum perimit sævos classis numerosa tyrannos.*[15] In the ordinary state of things, it produces in a country like ours the worst effects, even on the cause of that liberty which it abuses with the dissoluteness of an extravagant speculation. Almost all the high-bred republicans of my time have, after a short space, become the most decided, thorough-paced courtiers; they soon left the business of a tedious, moderate, but practical resistance, to those of us whom, in the pride and intoxication of their theories, they

12. ***Liceat . . . poetis:*** "Poets have the right to destroy themselves." 13. ***Ardentem . . . insiluit:*** "Cold, he jumped into the burning Aetna." See Horace, *Art of Poetry,* ll. 465–466. 14. **cantharides:** the Spanish fly dried in quantity and employed externally as a blister and internally as an irritant, diuretic, and aphrodisiac. 15. See Juvenal, VII, 151.

have slighted as not much better than Tories. Hypocrisy, of course, delights in the most sublime speculations; for, never intending to go beyond speculation, it costs nothing to have it magnificent. But even in cases where rather levity than fraud was to be suspected in these ranting speculations, the issue has been much the same. These professors, finding their extreme principles not applicable to cases which call only for a qualified, or, as I may say, civil and legal resistance, in such cases employ no resistance at all. It is with them a war or a revolution, or it is nothing. Finding their schemes of politics not adapted to the state of the world in which they live, they often come to think lightly of all public principle; and are ready, on their part, to abandon for a very trivial interest what they find of very trivial value. Some indeed are of more steady and persevering natures; but these are eager politicians out of parliament, who have little to tempt them to abandon their favourite projects. They have some change in the church or state, or both, constantly in their view. When that is the case, they are always bad citizens, and perfectly unsure connexions. For, considering their speculative designs as of infinite value, and the actual arrangement of the state as of no estimation, they are at best indifferent about it. They see no merit in the good, and no fault in the vicious, management of public affairs; they rather rejoice in the latter, as more propitious to revolution. They see no merit or demerit in any man, or any action, or any political principle, any further than as they may forward or retard their design of change: they therefore take up, one day, the most violent and stretched prerogative, and another time the wildest democratic ideas of freedom, and pass from the one to the other without any sort of regard to cause, to person, or to party.

In France you are now in the crisis of a revolution, and in the transit from one form of government to another—you cannot see that character of men exactly in the same situation in which we see it in this country. With us it is militant; with you it is triumphant; and you know how it can act when its power is commensurate to its will. I would not be supposed to confine those observations to any description of men, or to comprehend all men of any description within them—No! far from it. I am as incapable of that injustice, as I am of keeping terms with those who profess principles of extremities; and who, under the name of religion, teach little else than wild and dangerous politics. The worst of these politics of revolution is this: they temper and harden the breast, in order to prepare it for the desperate strokes which are sometimes used in extreme occasions. But as these occasions may never arrive, the mind receives a gratuitous taint; and the moral sentiments suffer not a little, when no political purpose is served by the depravation. This sort of people are so taken up with their theories about the rights of man, that they have totally forgotten his nature. Without opening one new avenue to the understanding, they have succeeded in stopping up those that lead to the heart. They have perverted in themselves, and in those that attend to them, all the well-placed sympathies of the human breast.

This famous sermon of the Old Jewry breathes nothing but this spirit through all the political part. Plots, massacres, assassinations, seem to some people a trivial price for obtaining a revolution. A cheap, bloodless reformation, a guiltless liberty, appear flat and vapid to their taste. There must be a great change of scene; there must be a magnificent stage effect; there must be a grand spectacle to rouse the imagination, grown torpid with the lazy enjoyment of sixty years' security, and the still unanimating repose of public prosperity. The preacher found them all in the French Revolution. This inspires a juvenile warmth through his whole frame. His enthusiasm kindles as he advances; and when he arrives at his peroration it is in a full blaze. Then viewing, from the Pisgah[16] of his pulpit, the free, moral, happy, flourishing, and glorious state of France, as in a bird's-eye landscape of a promised land, he breaks out into the following rapture:

> What an eventful period is this! I am *thankful* that I have lived to it; I could almost say, *Lord, now lettest thou thy servant depart in peace, for mine eyes have seen thy salvation.*—I have lived to see a *diffusion* of knowledge, which has undermined superstition and error. —I have lived to see *the rights of men* better understood than ever; and nations panting for liberty which seemed to have lost the idea of it.—I have lived to see *thirty millions of people*, indignant and resolute, spurning at slavery, and demanding liberty with an irresistible

16. Pisgah: the point from which Moses viewed the Promised Land.

> voice. *Their king led in triumph, and an arbitrary monarch surrendering himself to his subjects.*

Before I proceed further, I have to remark, that Dr. Price seems rather to overvalue the great acquisitions of light which he has obtained and diffused in this age. The last century appears to me to have been quite as much enlightened. It had, though in a different place, a triumph as memorable as that of Dr. Price; and some of the great preachers of that period partook of it as eagerly as he has done in the triumph of France. On the trial of the Rev. Hugh Peters for high treason, it was deposed, that when King Charles was brought to London for his trial, the Apostle of Liberty in that day conducted the *triumph.* "I saw," says the witness, "his Majesty in the coach with six horses, and Peters riding before the king, *triumphing.*" Dr. Price, when he talks as if he had made a discovery, only follows a precedent; for, after the commencement of the king's trial, this precursor, the same Dr. Peters, concluding a long prayer at the Royal Chapel at Whitehall, (he had very triumphantly chosen his place,) said, "I have prayed and preached these twenty years; and now I may say with old Simeon, *Lord, now lettest thou thy servant depart in peace, for mine eyes have seen thy salvation.*" Peters had not the fruits of his prayer; for he neither departed so soon as he wished, nor in peace. He became (what I heartily hope none of his followers may be in this country) himself a sacrifice to the triumph which he led as pontiff. They dealt at the Restoration, perhaps, too hardly with this poor good man. But we owe it to his memory and his sufferings that he had as much illumination, and as much zeal, and had as effectually undermined all *the superstition and error* which might impede the great business he was engaged in, as any who follow and repeat after him, in this age, which would assume to itself an exclusive title to the knowledge of the rights of men, and all the glorious consequences of that knowledge.

After this sally of the preacher of the Old Jewry, which differs only in place and time, but agrees perfectly with the spirit and letter of the rapture of 1648, the Revolution Society, the fabricators of governments, the heroic band of *cashierers* of *monarchs,* electors of sovereigns, and leaders of kings in triumph, strutting with a proud consciousness of the diffusion of the knowledge of which every member had obtained so large a share in the donative, were in haste to make a generous diffusion of the knowledge they had thus gratuitously received. To make this bountiful communication, they adjourned from the church in the Old Jewry to the London Tavern; where the same Dr. Price, in whom the fumes of his oracular tripod were not entirely evaporated, moved and carried the resolution, or address of congratulation, transmitted by Lord Stanhope to the National Assembly of France.

I find a preacher of the gospel profaning the beautiful and prophetic ejaculation, commonly called *"nunc dimittis,"*[17] made on the first presentation of our Saviour in the temple, and applying it, with an inhuman and unnatural rapture, to the most horrid, atrocious, and afflicting spectacle that perhaps ever was exhibited to the pity and indignation of mankind. This *"leading in triumph,"* a thing in its best form unmanly and irreligious, which fills our preacher with such unhallowed transports, must shock, I believe, the moral taste of every well-born mind. Several English were the stupefied and indignant spectators of that triumph. It was (unless we have been strangely deceived) a spectacle more resembling a procession of American savages, entering into Onondaga,[18] after some of their murders called victories, and leading into hovels hung round with scalps, their captives, overpowered with the scoffs and buffets of women as ferocious as themselves, much more than it resembled the triumphal pomp of a civilized, martial nation;—if a civilized nation, or any men who had a sense of generosity, were capable of a personal triumph over the fallen and afflicted.

This, my dear Sir, was not the triumph of France. I must believe that, as a nation, it overwhelmed you with shame and horror. I must believe that the National Assembly find themselves in a state of the greatest humiliation in not being able to punish the authors of this triumph, or the actors in it; and that they are in a situation in which any inquiry

17. *nunc . . . dimittis:* the canticle of Simeon, beginning, "Lord, now lettest thou thy servant depart in peace" (Luke, ii, 29–32). **18. Onondaga:** territory of North American Indians of Iroquoian speech in New York State. British colonial representatives attended Onondaga congresses in the eighteenth century when a considerable group favoring the French had migrated to Catholic mission settlements on the St. Lawrence River. The conservative group remained loyal to the British.

they may make upon the subject must be destitute even of the appearance of liberty or impartiality. The apology of that assembly is found in their situation; but when we approve what they *must* bear, it is in us the degenerate choice of a vitiated mind.

With a compelled appearance of deliberation, they vote under the dominion of a stern necessity. They sit in the heart, as it were, of a foreign republic: they have their residence in a city whose constitution has emanated neither from the charter of their king, nor from their legislative power. There they are surrounded by an army not raised either by the authority of their crown, or by their command; and which, if they should order to dissolve itself, would instantly dissolve them. There they sit, after a gang of assassins had driven away some hundreds of the members; whilst those who held the same moderate principles, with more patience or better hope, continued every day exposed to outrageous insults and murderous threats. There a majority, sometimes real, sometimes pretended, captive itself, compels a captive king to issue as royal edicts, at third hand, the polluted nonsense of their most licentious and giddy coffeehouses. It is notorious, that all their measures are decided before they are debated. It is beyond doubt, that under the terror of the bayonet, and the lamp-post, and the torch to their houses, they are obliged to adopt all the crude and desperate measures suggested by clubs composed of a monstrous medley of all conditions, tongues, and nations. Among these are found persons, in comparison of whom Catiline[19] would be thought scrupulous, and Cethegus[20] a man of sobriety and moderation. Nor is it in these clubs alone that the public measures are deformed into monsters. They undergo a previous distortion in academies, intended as so many seminaries for these clubs, which are set up in all the places of public resort. In these meetings of all sorts, every counsel, in proportion as it is daring, and violent, and perfidious, is taken for the mark of superior genius. Humanity and compassion are ridiculed as the fruits of superstition and ignorance. Tenderness to individuals is considered as treason to the public. Liberty is always to be estimated perfect as property is rendered insecure. Amidst assassination, massacre, and confiscation, perpetrated or meditated, they are forming plans for the good order of future society. Embracing in their arms the carcases of base criminals, and promoting their relations on the title of their offences, they drive hundreds of virtuous persons to the same end, by forcing them to subsist by beggary or by crime.

The assembly, their organ, acts before them the farce of deliberation with as little decency as liberty. They act like the comedians of a fair before a riotous audience; they act amidst the tumultuous cries of a mixed mob of ferocious men, and of women lost to shame, who, according to their insolent fancies, direct, control, applaud, explode them; and sometimes mix and take their seats amongst them; domineering over them with a strange mixture of servile petulance and proud, presumptuous authority. As they have inverted order in all things, the gallery is in the place of the house. This assembly, which overthrows kings and kingdoms, has not even the physiognomy and aspect of a grave legislative body—*nec color imperii, nec frons ulla senatûs.*[21] They have a power given to them, like that of the evil principle, to subvert and destroy; but none to construct, except such machines as may be fitted for further subversion and further destruction.

Who is it that admires, and from the heart is attached to, national representative assemblies, but must turn with horror and disgust from such a profane burlesque, and abominable perversion of that sacred institute? Lovers of monarchy, lovers of republics, must alike abhor it. The members of your assembly must themselves groan under the tyranny of which they have all the shame, none of the direction, and little of the profit. I am sure many of the members who compose even the majority of that body must feel as I do, notwithstanding the applauses of the Revolution Society. Miserable king! miserable assembly! How must that assembly be silently scandalized with those of their members, who could call a day which seemed to blot the sun out of heaven, *"un beau jour!"*[22] How must they be inwardly indignant at hearing others, who

19. Catiline: Catiline was the notorious conspirator of the late Roman Republic. **20. Cethegus:** Marcus Cornelius Cethegus, Roman orator and general, who defeated the invading Carthaginian General Mago during the Second Punic War.

21. See Lucan, IX, 207. **22.** October 6, 1789.

thought fit to declare to them, "that the vessel of the state would fly forward in her course towards regeneration with more speed than ever," from the stiff gale of treason and murder, which preceded our preacher's triumph! What must they have felt, whilst, with outward patience, in inward indignation, they heard of the slaughter of innocent gentlemen in their houses, that "the blood spilled was not the most pure!" What must they have felt, when they were besieged by complaints of disorders which shook their country to its foundations, at being compelled coolly to tell the complainants, that they were under the protection of the law, and that they would address the king (the captive king) to cause the laws to be enforced for their protection; when the enslaved ministers of that captive king had formally notified to them, that there were neither law, nor authority, nor power left to protect! What must they have felt at being obliged, as a felicitation on the present new year, to request their captive king to forget the stormy period of the last, on account of the great good which *he* was likely to produce to his people; to the complete attainment of which good they adjourned the practical demonstrations of their loyalty, assuring him of their obedience, when he should no longer possess any authority to command!

This address was made with much good nature and affection, to be sure. But among the revolutions in France must be reckoned a considerable revolution in their ideas of politeness. In England we are said to learn manners at second-hand from your side of the water, and that we dress our behaviour in the frippery of France. If so, we are still in the old cut; and have not so far conformed to the new Parisian mode of good breeding, as to think it quite in the most refined strain of delicate compliment (whether in condolence or congratulation) to say, to the most humiliated creature that crawls upon the earth, that great public benefits are derived from the murder of his servants, the attempted assassination of himself and of his wife, and the mortification, disgrace, and degradation, that he has personally suffered. It is a topic of consolation which our ordinary of Newgate would be too humane to use to a criminal at the foot of the gallows. I should have thought that the hangman of Paris, now that he is liberalized by the vote of the National Assembly, and is allowed his rank and arms in the herald's college of the rights of men, would be too generous, too gallant a man, too full of the sense of his new dignity, to employ that cutting consolation to any of the persons whom the *lèze nation*[23] might bring under the administration of his *executive power*.

A man is fallen indeed, when he is thus flattered. The anodyne draught of oblivion, thus drugged, is well calculated to preserve a galling wakefulness, and to feel the living ulcer of a corroding memory. Thus to administer the opiate portion of amnesty, powdered with all the ingredients of scorn and contempt, is to hold to his lips, instead of "the balm of hurt minds," the cup of human misery full to the brim, and to force him to drink it to the dregs.

Yielding to reasons, at least as forcible as those which were so delicately urged in the compliment on the new year, the king of France will probably endeavour to forget these events and that compliment. But history, who keeps a durable record of all our acts, and exercises her awful censure over the proceedings of all sorts of sovereigns, will not forget either those events, or the era of this liberal refinement in the intercourse of mankind. History will record, that on the morning of the 6th of October, 1789, the king and queen of France, after a day of confusion, alarm, dismay, and slaughter, lay down, under the pledged security of public faith, to indulge nature in a few hours of respite, and troubled, melancholy repose. From this sleep the queen was first startled by the voice of the sentinel at her door, who cried out to her to save herself by flight—that this was the last proof of fidelity he could give—that they were upon him, and he was dead. Instantly he was cut down. A band of cruel ruffians and assassins, reeking with his blood, rushed into the chamber of the queen, and pierced with a hundred strokes of bayonets and poniards the bed, from thence this persecuted woman had but just time to fly almost naked, and, through ways unknown to the murderers, had escaped to seek refuge at the feet of a king and husband, not secure of his own life for a moment.

This king, to say no more of him, and this queen, and their infant children, (who once would have been the pride and hope of a great and generous people,) were then forced to abandon the sanctuary of the most splendid palace in the world,

23. ***lèze nation:*** treason.

which they left swimming in blood, polluted by massacre, and strewed with scattered limbs and mutilated carcases. Thence they were conducted into the capital of their kingdom. Two had been selected from the unprovoked, unresisted, promiscuous slaughter, which was made of the gentlemen of birth and family who composed the king's body guard. These two gentlemen, with all the parade of an execution of justice, were cruelly and publicly dragged to the block, and beheaded in the great court of the palace. Their heads were stuck upon spears, and led the procession; whilst the royal captives who followed in the train were slowly moved along, amidst the horrid yells, and shrilling screams, and frantic dances, and infamous contumelies, and all the unutterable abominations of the furies of hell, in the abused shape of the vilest of women. After they had been made to taste, drop by drop, more than the bitterness of death, in the slow torture of a journey of twelve miles, protracted to six hours, they were, under a guard, composed of those very soldiers who had thus conducted them through this famous triumph, lodged in one of the old palaces of Paris, now converted into a bastile for kings.

In this a triumph to be consecrated at altars? to be commemorated with grateful thanksgiving? to be offered to the divine humanity with fervent prayer and enthusiastic ejaculation?—These Theban and Thracian orgies, acted in France, and applauded only in the Old Jewry, I assure you, kindle prophetic enthusiasm in the minds but of very few people in this kingdom: although a saint and apostle, who may have revelations of his own, and who has so completely vanquished all the mean superstitions of the heart, may incline to think it pious and decorous to compare it with the entrance into the world of the Prince of Peace, proclaimed in a holy temple by a venerable sage, and not long before not worse announced by the voice of angels to the quiet innocence of shepherds.

At first I was at a loss to account for this fit of unguarded transport. I knew, indeed, that the sufferings of monarchs make a delicious repast to some sort of palates. There were reflections which might serve to keep this appetite within some bounds of temperance. But when I took one circumstance into my consideration, I was obliged to confess, that much allowance ought to be made for the society, and that the temptation was too strong for common discretion; I mean, the circumstance of the Io Pæan of the triumph, the animating cry which called "for *all* the BISHOPS to be hanged on the lamp-posts," might well have brought forth a burst of enthusiasm on the foreseen consequences of this happy day. I allow to so much enthusiasm some little deviation from prudence. I allow this prophet to break forth into hymns of joy and thanksgiving on an event which appears like the precursor of the Millennium, and the projected fifth monarchy, in the destruction of all church establishments. There was, however, (as in all human affairs there is,) in the midst of this joy, something to exercise the patience of these worthy gentlemen, and to try the long-suffering of their faith. The actual murder of the king and queen, and their child, was wanting to the other auspicious circumstances of this *"beautiful day."* The actual murder of the bishops, though called for by so many holy ejaculations, was also wanting. A group of regicide and sacrilegious slaughter, was indeed boldly sketched. It unhappily was left unfinished, in this great history-piece of the massacre of innocents. What hardy pencil of a great master, from the school of rights of men, will finish it, is to be seen hereafter. The age has not yet the complete benefit of that diffusion of knowledge that has undermined superstition and error; and the king of France wants another object or two to consign to oblivion, in consideration of all the good which is to arise from his own sufferings, and the patriotic crimes of an enlightened age.

Although this work of our new light and knowledge did not go to the length that in all probability it was intended it should be carried, yet I must think that such treatment of any human creatures must be shocking to any but those who are made for accomplishing revolutions. But I cannot stop here. Influenced by the inborn feelings of my nature, and not being illuminated by a single ray of this new-sprung modern light, I confess to you, Sir, that the exalted rank of the persons suffering, and particularly the sex, the beauty, and the amiable qualities of the descendant of so many kings and emperors, with the tender age of royal infants, insensible only through infancy and innocence of the cruel outrages to which their parents were exposed, instead of being a subject of exultation, adds not a little to my sensibility on that most melancholy occasion.

I hear that the august person, who was the principal object of our preacher's triumph, though he supported himself, felt much on that shameful occasion. As a man, it became him to feel for his wife and his children, and the faithful guards of his person, that were massacred in cold blood about him; as a prince, it became him to feel for the strange and frightful transformation of his civilized subjects, and to be more grieved for them than solicitous for himself. It derogates little from his fortitude, while it adds infinitely to the honour of his humanity. I am very sorry to say it, very sorry indeed, that such personages are in a situation in which it is not becoming in us to praise the virtues of the great.

I hear, and I rejoice to hear, that the great lady, the other object of the triumph, has borne that day, (one is interested that beings made for suffering should suffer well,) and that she bears all the succeeding days, that she bears the imprisonment of her husband, and her own captivity, and the exile of her friends, and the insulting adulation of addresses, and the whole weight of her accumulated wrongs, with a serene patience, in a manner suited to her rank and race, and becoming the offspring of a sovereign distinguished for her piety and her courage: that, like her, she has lofty sentiments; that she feels with the dignity of a Roman matron; that in the last extremity she will save herself from the last disgrace; and that, if she must fall, she will fall by no ignoble hand.

It is now sixteen or seventeen years since I saw the queen of France, then the dauphiness, at Versailles; and surely never lighted on this orb, which she hardly seemed to touch, a more delightful vision. I saw her just above the horizon, decorating and cheering the elevated sphere she just began to move in,—glittering like the morning-star, full of life, and splendour, and joy. Oh! what a revolution! and what a heart must I have to contemplate without emotion that elevation and that fall! Little did I dream when she added titles of veneration to those of enthusiastic, distant, respectful love, that she should ever be obliged to carry the sharp antidote against disgrace concealed in that bosom; little did I dream that I should have lived to see such disasters fallen upon her in a nation of gallant men, in a nation of men of honour, and of cavaliers. I thought ten thousand swords must have leaped from their scabbards to avenge even a look that threatened her with insult. But the age of chivalry is gone. That of sophisters, economists, and calculators, has succeeded; and the glory of Europe is extinguished for ever. Never, never more shall we behold that generous loyalty to rank and sex, that proud submission, that dignified obedience, that subordination of the heart, which kept alive, even in servitude itself, the spirit of an exalted freedom. The unbought grace of life, the cheap defence of nations, the nurse of manly sentiment and heroic enterprise, is gone! It is gone, that sensibility of principle, that chastity of honour, which felt a stain like a wound, which inspired courage whilst it mitigated ferocity, which ennobled whatever it touched, and under which vice itself lost half its evil, by losing all its grossness.

This mixed system of opinion and sentiment had its origin in the ancient chivalry; and the principle, though varied in its appearance by the varying state of human affairs, subsisted and influenced through a long succession of generations, even to the time we live in. If it should ever be totally extinguished, the loss I fear will be great. It is this which has given its character to modern Europe. It is this which has distinguished it under all its forms of government, and distinguished it to its advantage, from the states of Asia, and possibly from those states which flourished in the most brilliant periods of the antique world. It was this, which, without confounding ranks, had produced a noble equality, and handed it down through all the gradations of social life. It was this opinion which mitigated kings into companions, and raised private men to be fellows with kings. Without force or opposition, it subdued the fierceness of pride and power; it obliged sovereigns to submit to the soft collar of social esteem, compelled stern authority to submit to elegance, and gave a dominating vanquisher of laws to be subdued by manners.

But now all is to be changed. All the pleasing illusions, which made power gentle and obedience liberal, which harmonized the different shades of life, and which, by a bland assimilation, incorporated into politics the sentiments which beautify and soften private society, are to be dissolved by this new conquering empire of light and reason. All the decent drapery of life is to be rudely torn off. All the super-added ideas, furnished from the wardrobe of a moral imagination, which the heart owns, and the understanding ratifies, as necessary to cover the defects of our naked, shivering nature, and to raise it to dignity in our own estimation, are to be exploded as a ridiculous, absurd, and antiquated fashion.

On this scheme of things, a king is but a man, a queen is but a woman; a woman is but an animal, and an animal not of the highest order. All homage paid to the sex in general as such, and without distinct views, is to be regarded as romance and folly. Regicide, and parricide, and sacrilege, are but fictions of superstition, corrupting jurisprudence by destroying its simplicity. The murder of a king, or a queen, or a bishop, or a father, are only common homicide; and if the people are by any chance, or in any way, gainers by it, a sort of homicide much the most pardonable, and into which we ought not to make too severe a scrutiny.

On the scheme of this barbarous philosophy, which is the offspring of cold hearts and muddy understandings, and which is as void of solid wisdom as it is destitute of all taste and elegance, laws are to be supported only by their own terrors, and by the concern which each individual may find in them from his own private speculations, or can spare to them from his own private interests. In the groves of *their* academy, at the end of every vista, you see nothing but the gallows. Nothing is left which engages the affections on the part of the commonwealth. On the principles of this mechanic philosophy, our institutions can never be embodied, if I may use the expression, in persons; so as to create in us love, veneration, admiration, or attachment. But that sort of reason which banishes the affections is incapable of filling their place. These public affections, combined with manners, are required sometimes as supplements, sometimes as correctives, always as aids to law. The precept given by a wise man, as well as a great critic, for the construction of poems, is equally true as to states:—*Non satis est pulchra esse poemata, dulcia sunto.*[24] There ought to be a system of manners in every nation, which a well-formed mind would be disposed to relish. To make us love our country, our country ought to be lovely.

But power, of some kind or other, will survive the shock in which manners and opinions perish; and it will find other and worse means for its support. The usurpation which, in order to subvert ancient institutions, has destroyed ancient principles, will hold power by arts similar to those by which it has acquired it. When the old feudal and chivalrous spirit of *fealty,* which, by freeing kings from fear, freed both kings and subjects from the precautions of tyranny, shall be extinct in the minds of men, plots and assassinations will be anticipated by preventive murder and preventive confiscation, and that long roll of grim and bloody maxims, which form the political code of all power, not standing on its own honour, and the honour of those who are to obey it. Kings will be tyrants from policy, when subjects are rebels from principle.

When ancient opinions and rules of life are taken away, the loss cannot possibly be estimated. From that moment we have no compass to govern us; nor can we know distinctly to what port we steer. Europe, undoubtedly, taken in a mass, was in a flourishing condition the day on which your revolution was completed. How much of that prosperous state was owing to the spirit of our old manners and opinions is not easy to say; but as such causes cannot be indifferent in their operation, we must presume, that, on the whole, their operation was beneficial.

We are but too apt to consider things in the state in which we find them, without sufficiently adverting to the causes by which they have been produced, and possibly may be upheld. Nothing is more certain, than that our manners, our civilization, and all the good things which are connected with manners and with civilization, have, in this European world of ours, depended for ages upon two principles; and were indeed the result of both combined; I mean the spirit of a gentleman, and the spirit of religion. The nobility and the clergy, the one by profession, the other by patronage, kept learning in existence, even in the midst of arms and confusions, and whilst governments were rather in their causes, than formed. Learning paid back what it received to nobility and to priesthood; and paid it with usury, by enlarging their ideas, and by furnishing their minds. Happy if they had all continued to know their indissoluble union, and their proper place! Happy if learning, not debauched by ambition, had been satisfied to continue the instructor, and not aspired to be the

24. ***Non . . . sunto:*** "It is not enough that poems be beautiful, let them also be moving." See Horace, *Art of Poetry,* l. 99.

master! Along with its natural protectors and guardians, learning will be cast into the mire, and trodden down under the hoofs of a swinish multitude.

If, as I suspect, modern letters owe more than they are always willing to own to ancient manners, so do other interests which we value full as much as they are worth. Even commerce, and trade, and manufacture, the gods of our economical politicians, are themselves perhaps but creatures; are themselves but effects, which, as first causes, we choose to worship. They certainly grew under the same shade in which learning flourished. They too may decay with their natural protecting principles. With you, for the present at least, they all threaten to disappear together. Where trade and manufactures are wanting to a people, and the spirit of nobility and religion remains, sentiment supplies, and not always ill supplies, their place; but if commerce and the arts should be lost in an experiment to try how well a state may stand without these old fundamental principles, what sort of a thing must be a nation of gross, stupid, ferocious, and, at the same time, poor and sordid, barbarians, destitute of religion, honour, or manly pride, possessing nothing at present, and hoping for nothing hereafter?

I wish you may not be going fast, and by the shortest cut, to that horrible and disgustful situation. Already there appears a poverty of conception, a coarseness and vulgarity, in all the proceedings of the Assembly and of all their instructors. Their liberty is not liberal. Their science is presumptuous ignorance. Their humanity is savage and brutal.

It is not clear, whether in England we learned those grand and decorous principles and manners, of which considerable traces yet remain, from you, or whether you took them from us. But to you, I think, we trace them best. You seem to me to be—*gentis incunabula nostræ.*[25] France has always more or less influenced manners in England; and when your fountain is choked up and polluted, the stream will not run long, or not run clear, with us, or perhaps with any nation. This gives all Europe, in my opinion, but too close and connected a concern in what is done in France. Excuse me, therefore, if I have dwelt too long on the atrocious spectacle of the 6th of October, 1789, or have given too much scope to the reflections which have arisen in my mind on occasion of the most important of all revolutions, which may be dated from that day, I mean a revolution in sentiments, manners, and moral opinions. As things now stand, with everything respectable destroyed without us, and an attempt to destroy within us every principle of respect, one is almost forced to apologize for harbouring the common feelings of men.

Why do I feel so differently from the Reverend Dr. Price, and those of his lay flock who will choose to adopt the sentiments of his discourse?—For this plain reason—because it is *natural* I should; because we are so made, as to be affected at such spectacles with melancholy sentiments upon the unstable condition of mortal prosperity, and the tremendous uncertainty of human greatness; because in those natural feelings we learn great lessons; because in events like these our passions instruct our reason; because when kings are hurled from their thrones by the Supreme Director of this great drama, and become the objects of insult to the base, and of pity to the good, we behold such disasters in the moral, as we should behold a miracle in the physical, order of things. We are alarmed into reflection; our minds (as it has long since been observed) are purified by terror and pity; our weak, unthinking pride is humbled under the dispensations of a mysterious wisdom. Some tears might be drawn from me, if such a spectacle were exhibited on the stage. I should be truly ashamed of finding in myself that superficial, theatric sense of painted distress, whilst I could exult over it in real life. With such a perverted mind, I could never venture to show my face at a tragedy. People would think the tears that Garrick formerly, or that Siddons[26] not long since, have extorted from me, were the tears of hypocrisy; I should know them to be the tears of folly.

Indeed the theatre is a better school of moral sentiments than churches, where the feelings of humanity are thus outraged. Poets who have to deal with an audience not yet graduated in the school of the rights of men, and who must apply

25. *gentis . . . nostræ:* "the birthplace of our race." See Virgil, *Aeneid,* III, 105.

26. Garrick . . . Siddons: David Garrick (1717–1779) and Sarah Siddons (1755–1831), outstanding among actors and actresses of their age.

themselves to the moral constitution of the heart, would not dare to produce such a triumph as a matter of exultation. There, where men follow their natural impulses, they would not bear the odious maxims of a Machiavelian policy, whether applied to the attainment of monarchial or democratic tyranny. They would reject them on the modern, as they once did on the ancient stage, where they could not bear even the hypothetical proposition of such wickedness in the mouth of a personated tyrant, though suitable to the character he sustained. No theatric audience in Athens would bear what has been borne, in the midst of the real tragedy of this triumphal day; a principal actor weighing, as it were in scales hung in a shop of horrors,—so much actual crime against so much contingent advantage,—and after putting in and out weights, declaring that the balance was on the side of the advantages. They would not bear to see the crimes of new democracy posted as in a ledger against the crimes of old despotism, and the bookkeepers of politics finding democracy still in debt, but by no means unable or unwilling to pay the balance. In the theatre, the first intuitive glance, without any elaborate process of reasoning, will show, that this method of political computation would justify every extent of crime. They would see, that on these principles, even where the very worst were not perpetrated, it was owing rather to the fortune of the conspirators, than to their parsimony in the expenditure of treachery and blood. They would soon see, that criminal means once tolerated are soon preferred. They present a shorter cut to the object than through the highway of the moral virtues. Justifying perfidy and murder for public benefit, public benefit would soon become the pretext, and perfidy and murder the end; until rapacity, malice, revenge, and fear more dreadful than revenge, could satiate their insatiable appetites. Such must be the consequences of losing, in the splendour of these triumphs of the rights of men, all natural sense of wrong and right.

. . .

I almost venture to affirm, that not one in a hundred amongst us participates in the "triumph" of the Revolution Society. If the king and queen of France, and their children, were to fall into our hands by the chance of war, in the most acrimonious of all hostilities, (I deprecate such an event, I deprecate such hostility,) they would be treated with another sort of triumphal entry into London. We formerly have had a king of France in that situation; you have read how he was treated by the victor in the field; and in what manner he was afterwards received in England. Four hundred years have gone over us; but I believe we are not materially changed since that period. Thanks to our sullen resistance to innovation, thanks to the cold sluggishness of our national character, we still bear the stamp of our forefathers. We have not (as I conceive) lost the generosity and dignity of thinking of the fourteenth century; nor as yet have we subtilized ourselves into savages. We are not the converts of Rousseau; we are not the disciples of Voltaire; Helvetius[27] has made no progress amongst us. Atheists are not our preachers; madmen are not our lawgivers. We know that *we* have made no discoveries, and we think that no discoveries are to be made, in morality; nor many in the great principles of government, nor in the ideas of liberty, which were understood long before we were born, altogether as well as they will be after the grave has heaped its mould upon our presumption, and the silent tomb shall have imposed its law on our pert loquacity. In England we have not yet been completely embowelled of our natural entrails; we still feel within us, and we cherish and cultivate, those inbred sentiments which are the faithful guardians, the active monitors of our duty, the true supporters of all liberal and manly morals. We have not been drawn and trussed, in order that we may be filled, like stuffed birds in a museum, with chaff and rags and paltry blurred shreds of paper about the rights of man. We preserve the whole of our feelings still native and entire, unsophisticated by pedantry and infidelity. We have real hearts of flesh and blood beating in our bosoms. We fear God; we look up with awe to kings; with affection to parliaments; with duty to magistrates; with reverence to priests; and with respect to nobility. Why? Because such ideas are brought before our minds, it is *natural* to be so affected; because all other feelings are false and spurious, and tend to corrupt our minds, to vitiate our primary morals, to render us unfit for rational liberty; and by teaching us a servile, licen-

27. **Rousseau . . . Helvetius:** Rousseau, Voltaire, and Helvetius were among the philosophical architects of the French Revolution.

tious, and abandoned insolence, to be our low sport for a few holidays, to make us perfectly fit for, and justly deserving of, slavery, through the whole course of our lives.

You see, Sir, that in this enlightened age I am bold enough to confess, that we are generally men of untaught feeling; that instead of casting away all our old prejudices, we cherish them to a very considerable degree, and, to take more shame to ourselves, we cherish them because they are prejudices; and the longer they have lasted, and the more generally they have prevailed, the more we cherish them. We are afraid to put men to live and trade each on his own private stock of reason; because we suspect that this stock in each man is small, and that the individuals would do better to avail themselves of the general bank and capital of nations and of ages. Many of our men of speculation, instead of exploding general prejudices, employ their sagacity to discover the latent wisdom which prevails in them. If they find what they seek, and they seldom fail, they think it more wise to continue the prejudice, with the reason involved, than to cast away the coat of prejudice, and to leave nothing but the naked reason; because prejudice, with its reason, has a motive to give action to that reason, and an affection which will give it permanence. Prejudice is of ready application in the emergency; it previously engages the mind in a steady course of wisdom and virtue, and does not leave the man hesitating in the moment of decision, sceptical, puzzled, and unresolved. Prejudice renders a man's virtue his habit; and not a series of unconnected acts. Through just prejudice, his duty becomes a part of his nature.

Your literary men, and your politicians, and so do the whole clan of the enlightened among us, essentially differ in these points. They have no respect for the wisdom of others; but they pay it off by a very full measure of confidence in their own. With them it is a sufficient motive to destroy an old scheme of things, because it is an old one. As to the new, they are in no sort of fear with regard to the duration of a building run up in haste; because duration is no object to those who think little or nothing has been done before their time, and who place all their hopes in discovery. They conceive, very systematically, that all things which give perpetuity are mischievous, and therefore they are at inexpiable war with all establishments. They think that government may vary like modes of dress, and with as little ill effect: that there needs no principle of attachment, except a sense of present conveniency, to any constitution of the state. They always speak as if they were of opinion that there is a singular species of compact between them and their magistrates, which binds the magistrate, but which has nothing reciprocal in it, but that the majesty of the people has a right to dissolve it without any reason, but its will. Their attachment to their country itself is only so far as it agrees with some of their fleeting projects; it begins and ends with that scheme of polity which falls in with their momentary opinion.

These doctrines, or rather sentiments, seem prevalent with your new statesmen. But they are wholly different from those on which we have always acted in this country.

I hear it is sometimes given out in France, that what is doing among you is after the example of England. I beg leave to affirm, that scarcely anything done with you has originated from the practice or the prevalent opinions of this people, either in the act or in the spirit of the proceeding. Let me add, that we are as unwilling to learn these lessons from France, as we are sure that we never taught them to that nation. The cabals here, who take a sort of share in your transactions, as yet consist of but a handful of people. If unfortunately by their intrigues, their sermons, their publications, and by a confidence derived from an expected union with the counsels and forces of the French nation, they should draw considerable numbers into their faction, and in consequence should seriously attempt anything here in imitation of what has been done with you, the event, I dare venture to prophesy, will be, that, with some trouble to their country, they will soon accomplish their own destruction. This people refused to change their law in remote ages from respect to the infallibility of popes; and they will not now alter it from a pious implicit faith in the dogmatism of philosophers; though the former was armed with the anathema and crusade, and though the latter should act with the libel and the lamp-iron.

Formerly your affairs were your own concern only. We felt for them as men; but we kept aloof from them, because we were not citizens of France. But when we see the model held up to ourselves, we must feel as Englishmen, and feeling, we must provide as Englishmen. Your affairs, in spite of us, are made a part of our interest; so far at least as to keep at a distance your panacea, or your plague. If it be a panacea, we do not want it. We know the consequences of unnecessary physic. If it be a plague, it is such a plague that the precautions of the most severe quarantine ought to be established against it.

I hear on all hands that a cabal, calling itself philosophic, receives the glory of many of the late proceedings; and that their opinions and systems are the true actuating spirit of the whole of them. I have heard of no party in England, literary or political, at any time, known by such a description. It is not with you composed of those men, is it? whom the vulgar, in their blunt, homely style, commonly call atheists and infidels? If it be, I admit that we too have had writers of that description, who made some noise in their day. At present they repose in lasting oblivion. Who, born within the last forty years, has read one word of Collins, and Toland, and Tindal, and Chubb, and Morgan, and that whole race who called themselves Freethinkers? Who now reads Bolingbroke? Who ever read him through? Ask the booksellers of London what is become of all these lights of the world. In a few years their few successors will go to the family vault of "all the Capulets." But whatever they were, or are, with us, they were and are wholly unconnected individuals. With us they kept the common nature of their kind, and were not gregarious. They never acted in corps, or were known as a faction in the state, nor presumed to influence in that name or character, or for the purposes of such a faction, on any of our public concerns. Whether they ought so to exist, and so be permitted to act, is another question. As such cabals have not existed in England, so neither has the spirit of them had any influence in establishing the original frame of our constitution, or in any one of the several reparations and improvements it has undergone. The whole has been done under the auspices, and is confirmed by the sanctions, of religion and piety. The whole has emanated from the simplicity of our national character, and from a sort of native plainness and directness of understanding, which for a long time characterized those men who have successively obtained authority amongst us. This disposition still remains; at least in the great body of the people.

We know, and what is better, we feel inwardly, that religion is the basis of civil society, and the source of all good and of all comfort. In England we are so convinced of this, that there is no rust of superstition, with which the accumulated absurdity of the human mind might have crusted it over in the course of ages, that ninety-nine in a hundred of the people of England would not prefer to impiety. We shall never be such fools as to call in an enemy to the substance of any system to remove its corruptions, to supply its defects, or to perfect its construction. If our religious tenets should ever want a further elucidation, we shall not call on atheism to explain them. We shall not light up our temple from that unhallowed fire. It will be illuminated with other lights. It will be perfumed with other incense, than the infectious stuff which is imported by the smugglers of adulterated metaphysics. If our ecclesiastical establishment should want a revision, it is not avarice or rapacity, public or private, that we shall employ for the audit, or receipt, or application of its consecrated revenue. Violently condemning neither the Greek nor the Armenian, nor, since heats are subsided, the Roman system of religion, we prefer the Protestant; not because we think it has less of the Christian religion in it, but because, in our judgment, it has more. We are Protestants, not from indifference, but from zeal.

We know, and it is our pride to know, that man is by his constitution a religious animal; that atheism is against, not only our reason, but our instincts; and that it cannot prevail long. But if, in the moment of riot, and in a drunken delirium from the hot spirit drawn out of the alembic[28] of hell, which in France is now so furiously boiling, we should uncover our nakedness, by throwing off that Christian religion which has hitherto been our boast and comfort, and one great source of civilization amongst us, and amongst many other nations, we are apprehensive (being well aware that the mind will not endure a void) that some uncouth, pernicious, and degrading superstition might take place of it.

For that reason, before we take from our establishment the natural, human means of estimation, and give it up to contempt, as you have done, and

28. alembic: an apparatus for distilling.

in doing it have incurred the penalties you well deserve to suffer, we desire that some other may be presented to us in the place of it. We shall then form our judgment.

On these ideas, instead of quarreling with establishments, as some do, who have made a philosophy and a religion of their hostility to such institutions, we cleave closely to them. We are resolved to keep an established church, an established monarchy, an established aristocracy, and an established democracy, each in the degree it exists, and in no greater. I shall show you presently how much of each of these we possess.

It has been the misfortune (not, as these gentlemen think it, the glory) of this age, that everything is to be discussed, as if the constitution of our country were to be always a subject rather of altercation, than enjoyment. For this reason, as well as for the satisfaction of those among you (if any such you have among you) who may wish to profit of examples, I venture to trouble you with a few thoughts upon each of these establishments. I do not think they were unwise in ancient Rome, who, when they wished to new-model their laws, set commissioners to examine the best constituted republics within their reach.

First, I beg leave to speak of our church establishment, which is the first of our prejudices, not a prejudice destitute of reason, but involving in it profound and extensive wisdom. I speak of it first. It is first, and last, and midst in our minds. For, taking ground on that religious system, of which we are now in possession, we continue to act on the early received and uniformly continued sense of mankind. That sense not only, like a wise architect, hath built up the august fabric of states, but like a provident proprietor, to preserve the structure from profanation and ruin, as a sacred temple purged from all the impurities of fraud, and violence, and injustice, and tyranny, hath solemnly and for ever consecrated the commonwealth, and all that officiate in it. This consecration is made, that all who administer in the government of men, in which they stand in the person of God himself, should have high and worthy notions of their function and destination; that their hope should be full of immortality; that they should not look to the paltry pelf of the moment, nor to the temporary and transient praise of the vulgar, but to a solid, permanent existence, in the permanent part of their nature, and to a permanent fame and glory, in the example they leave as a rich inheritance to the world.

Such sublime principles ought to be infused into persons of exalted situations; and religious establishments provided, that may continually revive and enforce them. Every sort of moral, every sort of civil, every sort of politic institution, aiding the rational and natural ties that connect the human understanding and affections to the divine, are not more than necessary, in order to build up that wonderful structure, Man; whose prerogative it is, to be in a great degree a creature of his own making; and who, when made as he ought to be made, is destined to hold no trivial place in the creation. But whenever man is put over men, as the better nature ought ever to preside, in that case more particularly, he should as nearly as possible be approximated to his perfection.

The consecration of the state, by a state religious establishment, is necessary also to operate with a wholesome awe upon free citizens; because, in order to secure their freedom, they must enjoy some determinate portion of power. To them therefore a religion connected with the state, and with their duty towards it, becomes even more necessary than in such societies, where the people, by the terms of their subjection, are confined to private sentiments, and the management of their own family concerns. All persons possessing any portion of power ought to be strongly and awfully impressed with an idea that they act in trust: and that they are to account for their conduct in that trust to the one great Master, Author, and Founder of society.

This principle ought even to be more strongly impressed upon the minds of those who compose the collective sovereignty, than upon those of single princes. Without instruments, these princes can do nothing. Whoever uses instruments, in finding helps, finds also impediments. Their power is therefore by no means complete; nor are they safe in extreme abuse. Such persons, however elevated by flattery, arrogance, and self-opinion, must be sensible, that, whether covered or not by positive law, in some way or other they are accountable even here for the abuse of their trust. If they are not cut off by a rebellion of their people, they may be strangled by the very janissaries[29] kept for their security against all other rebellion. Thus we have seen the king of France sold by his soldiers for an increase of pay. But where popular authority is absolute and unrestrained, the people have an infinitely greater, because a far better founded, confidence in their own power. They are themselves, in a great measure, their own instruments. They are nearer to their objects. Besides, they are less under responsibility to one of the greatest controlling powers on earth, the sense of fame and estimation. The share of infamy, that is likely to fall to the lot of each individual in public acts, is small indeed; the operation of opinion being in the inverse ratio to the number of those who abuse power. Their own approbation of their own acts has to them the appearance of a public judgment in their favour. A perfect democracy is therefore the most shameless thing in the world. As it is the most shameless, it is also the most fearless. No man apprehends in his person that he can be made subject to punishment. Certainly the people at large never ought: for as all punishments are for example towards the conservation of the people at large, the people at large can never become the subject of punishment by human hand. It is therefore of infinite importance that they should not be suffered to imagine that their will, any more than that of kings, is the standard of right and wrong. They ought to be persuaded that they are full as little entitled, and far less qualified, with safety to themselves, to use any arbitrary power whatsoever; that therefore they are not under a false show of liberty, but in truth, to exercise an unnatural, inverted domination, tyrannically to exact, from those who officiate in the state, not an entire devotion to their interest, which is their right, but an abject submission to their occasional will; extinguishing thereby, in all those who serve them, all moral principle, all sense of dignity, all use of judgment, and all consistency of character; whilst by the very same process they give themselves up a proper, a suitable, but a most contemptible prey to the servile ambition of popular sycophants, or courtly flatterers.

When the people have emptied themselves of all the lust of selfish will, which without religion it is utterly impossible they ever should, when they are conscious that they exercise, and exercise perhaps in a higher link of the order of delegation, the power, which to be legitimate must be according to that eternal, immutable law, in which will and reason are the same, they will be more careful how they place power in base and incapable hands. In their nomination to office, they will not appoint to the exercise of authority, as to a pitiful job, but as to a holy function; not according to their sordid, selfish interest, nor to their wanton caprice, nor to their arbitrary will; but they will confer that power (which any man may well tremble to give or to receive) on those only, in whom they may discern that predominant proportion of active virtue and wisdom, taken together and fitted to the charge, such, as in the great and inevitable mixed mass of human imperfections and infirmities, is to be found.

When they are habitually convinced that no evil can be acceptable, either in the act or the permission, to him whose essence is good, they will be better able to extirpate out of the minds of all magistrates, civil, ecclesiastical, or military, anything that bears the least resemblance to a proud and lawless domination.

But one of the first and most leading principles on which the commonwealth and the laws are consecrated, is lest the temporary possessors and liferenters in it, unmindful of what they have received from their ancestors, or of what is due to their posterity, should act as if they were the entire masters; that they should not think it among their rights to cut off the entail, or commit waste on the inheritance, by destroying at their pleasure the whole original fabric of their society; hazarding to leave to those who come after them a ruin instead of an habitation—and teaching these successors as little to respect their contrivances, as they had themselves respected the institutions of their forefathers. By this unprincipled facility of changing the state as often, and as much, and in as many ways, as there are floating fancies or fashions, the whole chain and continuity of the commonwealth would be broken. No one generation could link with the other. Men would become little better than the flies of a summer.

And first of all, the science of jurisprudence, the pride of the human intellect, which, with all its

29. janissaries: soldiers in the Turkish sultan's guard established in the fourteenth century.

defects, redundancies, and errors, is the collected reason of ages, combining the principles of original justice with the infinite variety of human concerns, as a heap of old exploded errors, would be no longer studied. Personal self-sufficiency and arrogance (the certain attendants upon all those who have never experienced a wisdom greater than their own) would usurp the tribunal. Of course no certain laws, establishing invariable grounds of hope and fear, would keep the actions of men in a certain course, or direct them to a certain end. Nothing stable in the modes of holding property, or exercising function, could form a solid ground on which any parent could speculate in the education of his offspring, or in a choice for their future establishment in the world. No principles would be early worked into the habits. As soon as the most able instructor had completed his laborious course of instruction, instead of sending forth his pupil, accomplished in a virtuous discipline, fitted to procure him attention and respect, in his place in society, he would find everything altered; and that he had turned out a poor creature to the contempt and derision of the world, ignorant of the true grounds of estimation. Who would insure a tender and delicate sense of honour to beat almost with the first pulses of the heart, when no man could know what would be the test of honour in a nation, continually varying the standard of its coin? No part of life would retain its acquisitions. Barbarism with regard to science and literature, unskilfulness with regard to arts and manufactures, would infallibly succeed to the want of a steady education and settled principle; and thus the commonwealth itself would, in a few generations, crumble away, be disconnected into the dust and powder of individuality, and at length dispersed to all the winds of heaven.

To avoid therefore the evils of inconstancy and versatility, ten thousand times worse than those of obstinacy and the blindest prejudice, we have consecrated the state, that no man should approach to look into its defects or corruptions but with due caution; that he should never dream of beginning its reformation by its subversion; that he should approach to the faults of the state as to the wounds of a father, with pious awe and trembling solicitude. By this wise prejudice we are taught to look with horror on those children of their country, who are prompt rashly to hack that aged parent in pieces, and put him into the kettle of magicians, in hopes that by their poisonous weeds, and wild incantations, they may regenerate the paternal constitution, and renovate their father's life.

Society is indeed a contract. Subordinate contracts for objects of mere occasional interest may be dissolved at pleasure—but the state ought not to be considered as nothing better than a partnership agreement in a trade of pepper and coffee, calico or tobacco, or some other such low concern, to be taken up for a little temporary interest, and to be dissolved by the fancy of the parties. It is to be looked on with other reverence; because it is not a partnership in things subservient only to the gross animal existence of a temporary and perishable nature. It is a partnership in all science; a partnership in all art; a partnership in every virtue, and in all perfection. As the ends of such a partnership cannot be obtained in many generations, it becomes a partnership not only between those who are living, but between those who are living, those who are dead, and those who are to be born. Each contract of each particular state is but a clause in the great primæval contract of eternal society, linking the lower with the higher natures, connecting the visible and invisible world, according to a fixed compact sanctioned by the inviolable oath which holds all physical and all moral natures, each in their appointed place. This law is not subject to the will of those, who by an obligation above them, and infinitely superior, are bound to submit their will to that law. The municipal corporations of that universal kingdom are not morally at liberty at their pleasure, and on their speculations of a contingent improvement, wholly to separate and tear asunder the bands of their subordinate community, and to dissolve it into an unsocial, uncivil, unconnected chaos of elementary principles. It is the first and supreme necessity only, a necessity that is not chosen, but chooses, a necessity paramount to deliberation, that admits no discussion, and demands no evidence, which alone can justify a resort to anarchy. This necessity is no exception to the rule; because this necessity itself is a part too of that moral and physical disposition of things, to which man must be obedient by consent or force: but if that which is only submission to necessity should be made the object of choice, the law is broken, nature is disobeyed, and the rebellious are outlawed, cast forth, and exiled, from this world of reason, and order, and peace, and virtue, and fruitful penitence, into the antagonist world of madness, discord, vice, confusion, and unavailing sorrow. . . .

You may suppose that we do not approve your confiscation of the revenues of bishops, and deans, and chapters, and parochial clergy possessing independent estates arising from land, because we have the same sort of establishment in England. That objection, you will say, cannot hold as to the confiscation of the goods of monks and nuns, and the abolition of their order. It is true that this particular part of your general confiscation does not affect England, as a precedent in point: but the reason implies, and it goes a great way. The long parliament confiscated the lands of deans and chapters in England on the same ideas upon which your assembly set to sale the lands of the monastic orders. But it is in the principle of injustice that the danger lies, and not in the description of persons on whom it is first exercised. I see, in a country very near us, a course of policy pursued, which sets justice, the common concern of mankind, at defiance. With the National Assembly of France, possession is nothing, law and usage are nothing. I see the National Assembly openly reprobate the doctrine of prescription, which one of the greatest of their own lawyers tells us, with great truth, is a part of the law of nature. He tells us, that the positive ascertainment of its limits, and its security from invasion, were among the causes for which civil society itself has been instituted. If prescription be once shaken, no species of property is secure, when it once becomes an object large enough to tempt the cupidity of indigent power. I see a practice perfectly correspondent to their contempt of this great fundamental part of natural law. I see the confiscators begin with bishops, and chapters, and monasteries; but I do not see them end there. I see the princes of the blood, who, by the oldest usages of that kingdom, held large landed estates, (hardly with the compliment of a debate,) deprived of their possessions, and, in lieu of their stable, independent property, reduced to the hope of some precarious, charitable pension, at the pleasure of an assembly, which of course will pay little regard to the rights of pensioners at pleasure, when it despises those of legal proprietors. Flushed with the insolence of their first inglorious victories, and pressed by the distresses caused by their lust of unhallowed lucre, disappointed but not discouraged, they have at length ventured completely to subvert all property of all descriptions throughout the extent of a great kingdom. They have compelled all men, in all transactions of commerce, in the disposal of lands, in civil dealing, and through the whole communion of life, to accept as perfect payment and good and lawful tender, the symbols of their speculations on a projected sale of their plunder. What vestiges of liberty or property have they left? The tenant-right of a cabbage-garden, a year's interest in a hovel, the good-will of an ale-house or a baker's shop, the very shadow of a constructive property, are more ceremoniously treated in our parliament, than with you the oldest and most valuable landed possessions, in the hands of the most respectable personages, or than the whole body of the monied and commercial interest of your country. We entertain a high opinion of the legislative authority; but we have never dreamt that parliaments had any right whatever to violate property, to overrule prescription, or to force a currency of their own fiction in the place of that which is real, and recognised by the law of nations. But you, who began with refusing to submit to the most moderate restraints, have ended by establishing an unheard-of despotism. I find the ground upon which your confiscators go is this; that indeed their proceedings could not be supported in a court of justice; but that the rules of prescription cannot bind a legislative assembly. So that this legislative assembly of a free nation sits, not for the security, but for the destruction, of property, and not of property only, but of every rule and maxim which can give it stability, and of those instruments which can alone give it circulation.

When the Anabaptists of Munster, in the sixteenth century, had filled Germany with confusion, by their system of levelling, and their wild opinions concerning property, to what country in Europe did not the progress of their fury furnish just cause of alarm? Of all things, wisdom is the most terrified with epidemical fanaticism, because of all enemies it is that against which she is the least able to furnish any kind of resource. We cannot be ignorant of the spirit of atheistical fanaticism, that is inspired by a multitude of writings, dispersed with incredible assiduity and expense, and by sermons delivered in all the streets and places of public resort in Paris. These writings and sermons have filled the populace with a black and savage atrocity of mind, which supersedes in them the common feelings of nature, as well as all sentiments of morality and religion; insomuch that these wretches are induced to bear with a sullen patience the intolerable distresses brought upon them by the violent convulsions and permutations that have been made in property. The spirit of proselytism attends this spirit of fanaticism. They have societies to cabal and correspond at home and abroad for the propagation of their tenets. The republic of Berne, one of the happiest, the most prosperous, and the best governed countries upon earth, is one of the great objects, at the destruction of which they aim. I am told they have in some measure succeeded in sowing there the seeds of discontent. They are busy throughout Germany. Spain and Italy have not been untried. England is not left out of the comprehensive scheme of their malignant charity: and in England we find those who stretch out their arms to them, who recommend their example from more than one pulpit, and who choose in more than one periodical meeting, publicly to correspond with them, to applaud them, and to hold them up as objects for imitation; who receive from them tokens of confraternity, and standards consecrated amidst their rights and mysteries, who suggest to them leagues of perpetual amity, at the very time when the power, to which our constitution has exclusively delegated the federative capacity of this kingdom, may find it expedient to make war upon them.

It is not the confiscation of our church property from this example in France that I dread, though I think this would be no trifling evil. The great source of my solicitude is, lest it should ever be considered in England as the policy of a state to seek a resource in confiscations of any kind; or that any one description of citizens should be brought to regard any of the others as their proper prey. Nations are wading deeper and deeper into an ocean of boundless debt. Public debts, which at first were a security to governments, by interesting many in the public tranquillity, are likely in their excess to become the means of their subversion. If governments provide for these debts by heavy impositions, they perish by becoming odious to the people. If they do not provide for them they will be undone by the efforts of the most dangerous of all parties; I mean an extensive, discontented monied interest, injured and not destroyed. The men who compose this interest look for their security, in the first instance, to the fidelity of government; in the second, to its power. If they find the old governments effete, worn out, and with their springs relaxed, so as not to be of sufficient vigour for their purposes, they may seek new ones that shall be possessed of more energy; and this energy will be derived, not from an acquisition of resources, but from a contempt of justice. . . .

Rage and phrensy will pull down more in half an hour, than prudence, deliberation, and foresight can build up in a hundred years. The errors and defects of old establishments are visible and palpable. It calls for little ability to point them out; and where absolute power is given, it requires but a word wholly to abolish the vice and the establishment together. The same lazy but restless disposition, which loves sloth and hates quiet, directs the politicians, when they come to work for supplying the place of what they have destroyed. To make everything the reverse of what they have seen is quite as easy as to destroy. No difficulties occur in what has never been tried. Criticism is almost baffled in discovering the defects of what has not existed; and eager enthusiasm and cheating hope have all the wide field of imagination, in which they may expatiate with little or no opposition.

At once to preserve and to reform is quite another thing. When the useful parts of an old establishment are kept, and what is superadded is to be fitted to what is retained, a vigorous mind, steady, persevering attention, various powers of comparison and combination, and the resources of an understanding fruitful in expedients, are to be exercised; they are to be exercised in a continued conflict with the combined force of opposite vices, with the obstinacy that rejects all improvement, and the levity that is fatigued and disgusted with everything of which it is in possession. But you may object—"A process of this kind is slow. It is not fit for an assembly, which glories in performing in a few months the work of ages. Such a mode of reforming, possibly, might take up many years." Without question it might; and it ought. It is one of the excellencies of a method in which time is amongst the assistants, that its operation is slow, and in some cases almost imperceptible. If circumspection and caution are a part of wisdom, when we work only upon inanimate matter, surely they become a part of duty too, when the subject of our demolition and construction is not brick and timber, but sentient beings, by the sudden alteration of whose state, condition, and habits, multitudes may be rendered miserable. But it seems as if it were the prevalent opinion in Paris, that an unfeeling heart, and an undoubting confidence, are the sole qualifications for a perfect legislator. Far different are my ideas of that high office. The true lawgiver ought to have a heart full of sensibility. He ought to love and respect his kind, and to fear himself. It may be allowed to his temperament to catch his ultimate object with an intuitive glance; but his movements towards it ought to be deliberate. Political arrangement, as it is a work for social ends, is to be only wrought by social means. There mind must conspire with mind. Time is required to produce that union of minds which alone can produce all the good we aim at. Our patience will achieve more than our force. If I might venture to appeal to what is so much out of fashion in Paris, I mean to experience, I should tell you, that in my course I have known, and, according to my measure, have co-operated with great men; and I have never yet seen any plan which has not been mended by the observations of those who were inferior in understanding to the person who took the lead in the business. By a slow but well-sustained progress, the effect of each step is watched; the good or ill success of the first gives light to us in the second; and so, from light to light, we are conducted with safety through the whole series. We see that the parts of the system do not clash. The evils latent in the most promising contrivances are provided for as they arise. One advantage is as little as possible sacrificed to another. We compensate, we reconcile, we balance. We are enabled to unite into a consistent whole the various anomalies and contending principles that are found in the minds and affairs of men. From hence arises, not an excellence in simplicity, but one far superior, an excellence in composition. Where the great interests of mankind are concerned through a long succession of generations, that succession ought to be admitted into some share in the councils which are so deeply to affect them. If justice requires this, the work itself requires the aid of more minds than one age can furnish. It is from this view of things that the best legislators have been often satisfied with the establishment of some sure, solid, and ruling principle in government; a power like that which some of the philosophers have called a plastic nature; and having fixed the principle, they have left it afterwards to its own operation.

To proceed in this manner, that is, to proceed with a presiding principle, and a prolific energy, is with me the criterion of profound wisdom. What your politicians think the marks of a bold, hardy genius, are only proofs of a deplorable want of ability. By their violent haste and their defiance of the process of nature, they are delivered over blindly to every projector and adventurer, to every alchymist and empiric.[30] They despair of turning to account anything that is common. Diet is nothing in their system of remedy. The worst of it is, that this their despair of curing common distempers by regular methods, arises not only from defect of comprehension, but, I fear, from some malignity of disposition. Your legislators seem to have taken their opinions of all professions, ranks, and offices, from the declamations and buffooneries of satirists; who would themselves be astonished if they were held to the letter of their own descriptions. By listening only to these, your leaders regard all things only on the side of their vices and faults, and view those vices and faults under every colour of exaggeration. It is undoubtedly true, though it may seem paradoxical; but in general, those who are habitually employed in finding and displaying faults, are unqualified for the work of reformation: because their minds are not only unfurnished with patterns of the fair and good, but by habit they come to take no delight in the contemplation of those things. By hating vices too much, they come to love men too little. It is therefore not wonderful, that they should be indisposed and unable to serve them. From hence arises the complexional disposition of some of your guides to pull everything in pieces. At this malicious game they display the whole of their *quadrimanous*[31] activity. As to the rest, the paradoxes of eloquent writers, brought forth purely as a sport of fancy, to try their talents, to rouse attention and excite surprise, are taken up by these gentlemen, not in the spirit of the original authors, as means of cultivating their taste and improving their style. These paradoxes become with

30. empiric: a person, untrained in scientific procedure, who relies solely on practical experience. **31. *quadrimanous:*** having all four feet hand-like.

them serious grounds of action, upon which they proceed in regulating the most important concerns of the state. Cicero ludicrously describes Cato as endeavouring to act, in the commonwealth, upon the school paradoxes, which exercised the wits of the junior students in the Stoic philosophy. If this was true of Cato, these gentlemen copy after him in the manner of some persons who lived about his time—*pede nudo Catonem.*[32] Mr. Hume told me that he had from Rousseau himself the secret of his principles of composition. That acute though eccentric observer had perceived, that to strike and interest the public, the marvellous must be produced; that the marvellous of the heathen mythology had long since lost its effects; that giants, magicians, fairies, and heroes of romance which succeeded, had exhausted the portion of credulity which belonged to their age; that now nothing was left to the writer but that species of the marvellous which might still be produced, and with as great an effect as ever, though in another way; that is, the marvellous in life, in manners, in characters, and in extraordinary situations, giving rise to new and unlooked-for strokes in politics and morals. I believe, that were Rousseau alive, and in one of his lucid intervals, he would be shocked at the practical phrensy of his scholars, who in their paradoxes are servile imitators, and even in their incredulity discover an implicit faith. . . .

. . .

What you may do finally does not appear; nor is it of much moment, whilst the strange and contradictory relation between your army and all the parts of your republic, as well as the puzzled relation of those parts to each other and to the whole, remain as they are. You seem to have given the provisional nomination of the officers, in the first instance, to the king, with a reserve of approbation by the National Assembly. Men who have an interest to pursue are extremely sagacious in discovering the true seat of power. They must soon perceive that those, who can negative indefinitely, in reality appoint. The officers must therefore look to their intrigues in that Assembly, as the sole, certain road to promotion. Still, however, by your new constitution they must begin their solicitation at court. This double negotiation for military rank seems to me a contrivance as well adapted, as if it were studied for no other end, to promote faction in the Assembly itself, relative to this vast military patronage; and then to poison the corps of officers with factions of a nature still more dangerous to the safety of government, upon any bottom on which it can be placed, and destructive in the end to the efficiency of the army itself. Those officers, who lose the promotions intended for them by the crown, must become of a faction opposite to that of the Assembly which has rejected their claims, and must nourish discontents in the heart of the army against the ruling powers. Those officers, on the other hand, who, by carrying their point through an interest in the Assembly, feel themselves to be at best only second in the goodwill of the crown, though first in that of the Assembly, must slight an authority which would not advance and could not retard their promotion. If to avoid these evils you will have no other rule for command or promotion than seniority, you will have an army of formality; at the same time it will become more independent, and more of a military republic. Not they, but the king is the machine. A king is not to be deposed by halves. If he is not everything in the command of an army, he is nothing. What is the effect of a power placed nominally at the head of the army, who to that army is no object of gratitude, or of fear? Such a cipher is not fit for the administration of an object, of all things the most delicate, the supreme command of military men. They must be constrained (and their inclinations lead them to what their necessities require) by a real, vigorous, effective, decided, personal authority. The authority of the Assembly itself suffers by passing through such a debilitating channel as they have chosen. The army will not long look to an assembly acting through the organ of false show, and palpable imposition. They will not seriously yield obedience to a prisoner. They will either despise a pageant, or they will pity a captive king. This relation of your army to the crown will, if I am not greatly mistaken, become a serious dilemma in your politics.

It is besides to be considered, whether an assembly like yours, even supposing that it was in possession of another sort of organ through which its

32. ***pede . . . Catonem:*** see Horace, *Epistles,* I, 19, 12–14. The words are from a passage in which Horace is satirizing those who, by going about in "bare feet" (*pede nudo*) and with ascetic faces, claim to be capturing the virtue of Cato.

orders were to pass, is fit for promoting the obedience and discipline of an army. It is known, that armies have hitherto yielded a very precarious and uncertain obedience to any senate, or popular authority; and they will least of all yield it to an assembly which is only to have a continuance of two years. The officers must totally lose the characteristic disposition of military men, if they see with perfect submission and due admiration, the dominion of pleaders; especially when they find that they have a new court to pay to an endless succession of those pleaders; whose military policy, and the genius of whose command, (if they should have any,) must be as uncertain as their duration is transient. In the weakness of one kind of authority, and in the fluctuation of all, the officers of an army will remain for some time mutinous and full of faction, until some popular general, who understands the art of conciliating the soldiery, and who possesses the true spirit of command, shall draw the eyes of all men upon himself. Armies will obey him on his personal account. There is no other way of securing military obedience in this state of things. But the moment in which that event shall happen, the person who really commands the army is your master; the master (that is little) of your king, the master of your Assembly, the master of your whole republic. . . .

To make a government requires no great prudence. Settle the seat of power; teach obedience: and the work is done. To give freedom is still more easy. It is not necessary to guide; it only requires to let go the rein. But to form a *free government;* that is, to temper together these opposite elements of liberty and restraint in one consistent work, requires much thought, deep reflection, a sagacious, powerful, and combining mind. This I do not find in those who take the lead in the National Assembly. Perhaps they are not so miserably deficient as they appear. I rather believe it. It would put them below the common level of human understanding. But when the leaders choose to make themselves bidders at an auction of popularity, their talents, in the construction of the state, will be of no service. They will become flatterers instead of legislators; the instruments, not the guides, of the people. If any of them should happen to propose a scheme of liberty, soberly limited, and defined with proper qualifications, he will be immediately outbid by his competitors, who will produce something more splendidly popular. Suspicions will be raised of his fidelity to his cause. Moderation will be stigmatized as the virtue of cowards; and compromise as the prudence of traitors: until, in hopes of preserving the credit which may enable him to temper, and moderate, on some occasions, the popular leader is obliged to become active in propagating doctrines, and establishing powers, that will afterwards defeat any sober purpose at which he ultimately might have aimed.

But am I so unreasonable as to see nothing at all that deserves commendation in the indefatigable labours of this Assembly? I do not deny that, among an infinite number of acts of violence and folly, some good may have been done. They who destroy everything certainly will remove some grievance. They who make everything new, have a chance that they may establish something beneficial. To give them credit for what they have done in virtue of the authority they have usurped, or which can excuse them in the crimes by which that authority has been acquired, it must appear, that the same things could not have been accomplished without producing such a revolution. Most assuredly they might; because almost every one of the regulations made by them, which is not very equivocal, was either in the cession of the king, voluntarily made at the meeting of the states, or in the concurrent instructions to the orders. Some usages have been abolished on just grounds; but they were such, that if they had stood as they were to all eternity, they would little detract from the happiness and prosperity of any state. The improvements of the National Assembly are superficial, their errors fundamental.

Whatever they are, I wish my countrymen rather to recommend to our neighbours the example of the British constitution, than to take models from them for the improvement of our own. In the former they have got an invaluable treasure. They are not, I think, without some causes of apprehension and complaint; but these they do not owe to their constitution, but to their own conduct. I think our happy situation owing to our constitution; but owing to the whole of it, and not any part singly; owing in a great measure to what we have left standing in our several reviews and reformations, as well as to what we have altered or superadded. Our people will find employment enough for a truly patriotic, free, and independent spirit, in guarding what they possess from violation. I would not exclude alteration neither; but even when I changed, it should be to preserve. I should be led to my remedy by a great grievance. In what I did, I should follow the example of our ancestors. I would make the reparation as nearly as possible in the style of the building. A politic caution, a guarded circumspection, a moral rather than a complexional timidity, were among the ruling principles of our forefathers in their most decided conduct. Not being illuminated with the light of which the gentlemen of France tell us they have got so abundant a share, they acted under a strong impression of the ignorance and fallibility of mankind. He that had made them thus fallible, rewarded them for having in their conduct attended to their nature. Let us imitate their caution, if we wish to deserve their fortune, or to retain their bequests. Let us add, if we please, but let us preserve what they have left; and standing on the firm ground of the British constitution, let us be satisfied to admire, rather than attempt to follow in their desperate flights, the aëronauts of France.

I have told you candidly my sentiments. I think they are not likely to alter yours. I do not know that they ought. You are young; you cannot guide, but must follow the fortune of your country. But hereafter they may be of some use to you, in some future form which your commonwealth may take. In the present it can hardly remain; but before its final settlement it may be obliged to pass, as one of our poets says, "through great varieties of untried beings," and in all its transmigrations to be purified by fire and blood.

I have little to recommend my opinions but long observation and much impartiality. They come from one who has been no tool of power, no flatterer of greatness; and who in his last acts does not wish to belie the tenour of his life. They come from one, almost the whole of whose public exertion has been a struggle for the liberty of others; from one in whose breast no anger durable or vehement has ever been kindled, but by what he considered as tyranny; and who snatches from his share in the endeavours which are used by good men to discredit opulent oppression, the hours he has employed on your affairs; and who in so doing persuades himself he has not departed from his usual office: they come from one who desires honours, distinctions, and emoluments, but little; and who expects them not at all; who has no contempt for fame, and no fear of obloquy; who shuns contention, though he will hazard an opinion: from one who wishes to preserve consistency, but who would preserve consistency by varying his means to secure the unity of his end; and, when the equipoise of the vessel in which he sails may be endangered by overloading it upon one side, is desirous of carrying the small weight of his reasons to that which may preserve its equipoise.

(1790)

A Selection of Key Eighteenth-Century Minor Poetry

As already suggested in our General Introduction, simplistic approaches to the Enlightenment in England are readily available and can, unless carefully scrutinized, do a serious disservice to the richness and variety of the literature of the age. Nowhere is this more apparent than in the area of poetry. As we have noted, even the poetry of Alexander Pope, in so many ways the Neoclassic poet *par excellence,* encompasses a range of subject matter, a variety of genre, and a vitality of expression that belie any image of the coldly classical artist. He is, to be sure, the articulator of certain key ideas and values of his era, and he did set a dominant style that persisted for the better part of a century; his genius, however, could not be contained in any artificial mold, and it sought fresh ways of expressing his constantly developing vision of reality. Clearly the selections from Pope in this anthology reveal such a poet.

There is even greater variety of theme and technique in the minor poetry. On the one hand, the reader will find in great poems like Thomas Gray's *Elegy Written in a Country Churchyard* or in Oliver Goldsmith's *The Deserted Village* a fidelity to the rhythm of the iambic pentameter couplet and to the clear, denotative diction prized by writers of the age, as well as a strong sense of the poet's function as philosopher, teacher, and social critic. On the other hand, even in these poems one notices the touch of sentiment, the love of the simple and primitive, the sense of a closeness to nature, the slightly more private voice of the poet —all of which defy stereotyping.

Individuality and the spirit of innovation become the order of the day. Clearly there is an increasing interest in nature in its wilder and purer aspects, in nature untouched by human hands. The spectacular landscape, the rugged mountain, the primitive society—these and a number of other motifs become increasingly the object of the poet's attention in works like John Dyer's *Grongar Hill,* Joseph Warton's *The Enthusiast; or, The Lover of Nature,* or James Thomson's *The Seasons.* Witness Warton's great contrast between two views of nature in his poem:

> Rich in her weeping country's spoils, Versailles
> May boast a thousand fountains, that can cast
> The tortured waters to the distant heavens;
> Yet let me choose some pine-topped precipice
> Abrupt and shaggy, whence a foamy stream,
> Like Anio, tumbling roars; or some bleak heath,
> Where straggling stand the mournful juniper,
> Or yew-tree scathed; while in clear prospect round,
> From the grove's bosom spires emerge, and smoke
> In bluish wreaths ascends, ripe harvests wave,
> Herds low, and straw-roofed cots appear, and streams
> Beneath the sunbeams twinkle.

Listen to Dyer's philosophical ruminations on the delights of climbing Grongar Hill, his exclamation on reaching the height and looking down,

> Now I gain the mountain's brow,
> What a landscape lies below!
> No clouds, no vapours intervene,
> But the gay, the open scene
> Does the face of Nature show
> In all the hues of heaven's bow,
> And, swelling to embrace the light,
> Spreads around beneath the sight,

and his concluding lines on the wisdom to be gained from a moment close to nature.

A growing freedom of the imagination and the emotions from the restraining influence of judgment and a delight in the various powers and pleasures of the creative mind are apparent in a variety of poems. Mark Akenside's *The Pleasures of Imagination* is one of the many eloquent tributes:

> Mind, mind alone, (bear witness, earth and heaven!)
> The living fountains in itself contains
> Of beauteous and sublime: here hand in hand,
> Sit paramount the Graces; here enthroned,
> Celestial Venus, with divinest airs,
> Invites the soul to never-fading joy.

Or perhaps an even greater tribute to the creative power of imagination is that contained in the lyrical strophe of William Collins' *Ode on the Poetical Character*:

Young Fancy thus, to me divinest name,
  To whom, prepared and bathed in Heaven,
  The cest of amplest power is given:
  To few the godlike gift assigns,
  To gird their blessed prophetic loins,
And gaze her visions wild, and feel unmixed her flame!

Certainly related to this faith in imagination is a delight in the mysterious, in the pleasure of sweet sadness that can be found in the best sections of Thomas Warton's *The Pleasures of Melancholy,* in the eerie settings of poems like Robert Blair's *The Grave,* in the deeply felt sorrow of Edward Young's reflections on death expressed in an atmosphere of misty darkness in his celebrated *Night Thoughts.* Lines like the following from *The Pleasures of Melancholy* seem like genuine anticipations of the *weltschmerz* that is characteristic of so much later eighteenth-century literature. One can imagine the lines being spoken by Goethe's Werther or Byron's Childe Harold:

  Let others love the summer evening's smiles,
As listening to some distant waterfall
They mark the blushes of the streaky west:
I choose the pale December's foggy glooms;
Then, when the sullen shades of evening close,
Where through the room a blindly glittering gleam
The dying embers scatter, far remote
From Mirth's mad shouts, that through the lighted roof
Resound with festive echo, let me sit,
Blessed with the lowly cricket's drowsy dirge.
Then let my contemplative thought explore
This fleeting state of things, the vain delights,
The fruitless toils, that still elude our search,
As through the wilderness of life we rove.

Most interesting is a remarkable antiquarianism, which has few, if any, associations with a pedantic interest in the merely ancient. This antiquarianism seems part of a general quest to justify new feelings and attitudes and to find settings and characters appropriate to the quest. Thomas Gray's interest in Norse and Icelandic literature seen in his spectacular *The Bard: A Pindaric Ode* that traces the evolution of English history from the earliest times; Horace Walpole's fascination with the Gothic; Thomas Percy's turning to the wonder of the Middle Ages, especially to the ballad form in his *Reliques of Ancient English Poetry;* William Collins' interest in the primitive in his *Ode on the Popular Superstitions of the Scottish Highlands*—these and many works like them provide ample evidence of a phenomenon that seems to express a certain romantic exuberance within the constraints of classical forms. One of the most popular manifestations of this interest in the past is the Ossian poetry, a creation of the Scottish poet James Macpherson. How powerful is the opening of one of the pieces, *Carthon,* which evokes the spell of ancient warriors in the Scottish Highlands and the faith, bravery, and courage of a remote past:

> A tale of the times of old! The deeds of days
> of other years!
> The murmur of thy streams, O Lora!
> brings back the memory of the past. The
> sound of thy woods, Garmallar, is lovely
> in mine ear. Does thou not behold,
> Malvina, a rock with its head of heath?
> Three aged pines bend from its face; green
> is the narrow plain at its feet;
> there the flower of the mountain grows, and
> shakes its white head in the breeze. The thistle
> is there alone, shedding its ancient beard. Two
> stones, half sunk in the ground, show their
> heads of moss. The deer of the mountain
> avoids the place, for he beholds a dim ghost
> standing there. The mighty lie, O Malvina! in
> the narrow plain of the rock.

The lyrical spirit, whether in Robert Burns's simple delight in rustic life and in the dialect and emotions of his native Scotland—seen in poems like *Ae Fond Kiss, A Red, Red Rose,* or *John Anderson, My Jo*—or in the deeply religious poetry of Isaac Watts and William Cowper, offers still another dimension for study.

What we have said of subject matter can also be said of technique. In an age dominated by the iambic pentameter couplet, blank verse and its accompanying freedom makes a stunning entrance. What better example than in James Thomson's brilliant poem of wonder at the beauties of creation—*The Seasons.* And then there is the remarkable variety of song, ode, and hymn in Collins, Burns, Cowper, and a host of other poets.

In short, the minor poets bring to the student a fuller and more illuminating understanding of the achievement of English Enlightenment literature, and the selections in this section provide an interesting sample.

Suggestions for Further Reading

There is such an abundance of critical writing on the poetry in this section that it is difficult to be selective. Certain general studies continue to be essential: W. J. Bate, *From Classic to Romantic* (1946), and M. H. Abrams, *The Mirror and the Lamp* (1958), describe the literary and critical setting superbly. Other general studies of themes and techniques in the poetry include Hoxie Neale Fairchild, *The Noble Savage* (1928); Kenneth MacLean, *John Locke and English Literature of the Eighteenth Century* (1936); George N. Shuster, *The English Ode from Milton to Keats* (1940); Marjorie Hope Nicolson, *Newton Demands the Muse* (1946); John Arthos, *The Language of Natural Description in Eighteenth-Century Poetry* (1949); James R.

Sutherland, *A Preface to Eighteenth-Century Poetry;* and David Nichol Smith, *Some Observations on Eighteenth-Century Poetry* (1960).

More specialized studies of individual poets can be found in a remarkable collection of essays, *From Sensibility to Romanticism,* eds. Frederick Hilles and Harold Bloom (1965). Another extremely helpful study is Jean Hagstrum, *The Sister Arts: The Tradition of Literary Pictorialism and English Poetry from Dryden to Gray* (1958).

Also recommended are Maurice J. Quinlan, *William Cowper: A Critical Life* (1953); David Daiches, *Robert Burns* (1966); Ralph Cohen, *The Art of Discrimination: Thomson's "The Seasons" and the Art of Criticism* (1964); and David Anderson, *"The Seasons" as Theodicy* (Unpublished Boston College dissertation, 1978); Oliver Sigworth, *William Collins* (1965); and Patricia Spacks, *The Poetry of Vision: Five Eighteenth-Century Poets* (1967).

John Dyer
1699-1757

◆

GRONGAR HILL*

Silent nymph, with curious eye!
Who, the purple evening, lie
On the mountain's lonely van,
Beyond the noise of busy man,
Painting fair the form of things,
While the yellow linnet sings;
Or the tuneful nightingale
Charms the forest with her tale;
Come with all thy various hues,
Come, and aid thy sister Muse;
Now while Phoebus riding high
Gives lustre to the land and sky!
Grongar Hill invites my song,
Draw the landscape bright and strong;
Grongar, in whose mossy cells
Sweetly musing Quiet dwells;
Grongar, in whose silent shade,
For the modest Muses made,
So oft I have, the evening still,
At the fountain of a rill,
Sate upon a flowery bed,
With my hand beneath my head;
While strayed my eyes o'er Towy's flood,
Over mead and over wood,
From house to house, from hill to hill,
Till Contemplation had her fill.
About his checkered sides I wind,
And leave his brooks and meads behind,
And groves, and grottoes where I lay,
And vistas shooting beams of day;
Wide and wider spreads the vale,
As circles on a smooth canal;
The mountains round—unhappy fate,
Sooner or later, of all height—
Withdraw their summits from the skies,
And lessen as the others rise;
Still the prospect wider spreads,
Adds a thousand woods and meads,
Still it widens, widens still,
And sinks the newly-risen hill.
Now I gain the mountain's brow,
What a landscape lies below!
No clouds, no vapours intervene,
But the gay, the open scene
Does the face of Nature show

* Grongar Hill is in Dyer's native Carmarthenshire, in South Wales.

GRONGAR HILL. 3. **van:** summit, top.

23. **Towy:** a town in Merionethshire, Wales.

In all the hues of heaven's bow,
And, swelling to embrace the light,
Spreads around beneath the sight.
Old castles on the cliffs arise,
Proudly towering in the skies!
Rushing from the woods, the spires
Seem from hence ascending fires!
Half his beams Apollo sheds
On the yellow mountain-heads,
Gilds the fleeces of the flocks,
And glitters on the broken rocks!
Below me trees unnumbered rise,
Beautiful in various dyes:
The gloomy pine, the poplar blue,
The yellow beech, the sable yew,
The slender fir that taper grows,
The sturdy oak with broad-spread boughs.
And beyond the purple grove,
Haunt of Phyllis, queen of love!
Gaudy as the opening dawn,
Lies a long and level lawn,
On which a dark hill, steep and high,
Holds and charms the wandering eye!
Deep are his feet in Towy's flood,
His sides are clothed with waving wood,
And ancient towers crown his brow,
That cast an awful look below;
Whose ragged walls the ivy creeps,
And with her arms from falling keeps,
So both a safety from the wind
On mutual dependence find.
'Tis now the raven's bleak abode;
'Tis now the apartment of the toad;
And there the fox securely feeds;
And there the poisonous adder breeds,
Concealed in ruins, moss, and weeds,
While, ever and anon, there falls
Huge heaps of hoary mouldered walls.
Yet Time has seen, that lifts the low,
And level lays the lofty brow,
Has seen this broken pile complete,
Big with the vanity of state;
But transient is the smile of Fate!
A little rule, a little sway,
A sunbeam in a winter's day,
Is all the proud and mighty have
Between the cradle and the grave.
And see the rivers, how they run
Through woods and meads, in shade and sun;
Sometimes swift, sometimes slow,
Wave succeeding wave, they go
A various journey to the deep,
Like human life to endless sleep!
Thus is Nature's vesture wrought,
To instruct our wandering thought;
Thus she dresses green and gay,
To disperse our cares away.
Ever charming, ever new,
When will the landscape tire the view!
The fountain's fall, the river's flow,
The woody valleys warm and low;
The windy summit, wild and high,
Roughly rushing on the sky;
The pleasant seat, the ruined tower,
The naked rock, the shady bower,
The town and village, dome and farm,
Each give each a double charm,
As pearls upon an Ethiop's arm.
See on the mountain's southern side,
Where the prospect opens wide,
Where the evening gilds the tide,
How close and small the hedges lie!
What streaks of meadows cross the eye!
A step methinks may pass the stream,
So little distant dangers seem;
So we mistake the future's face,
Eyed through Hope's deluding glass;
As yon summits soft and fair,
Clad in colours of the air,
Which to those who journey near,
Barren, brown, and rough appear;
Still we tread the same coarse way,
The present's still a cloudy day.
Oh, may I with myself agree,
And never covet what I see,
Content me with an humble shade,
My passions tamed, my wishes laid;
For while our wishes wildly roll,
We banish quiet from the soul;
'Tis thus the busy beat the air,
And misers gather wealth and care.
Now, even now, my joys run high,
As on the mountain turf I lie;
While the wanton Zephyr sings,
And in the vale perfumes his wings;
While the waters murmur deep,
While the shepherd charms his sheep,
While the birds unbounded fly,
And with music fill the sky;
Now, even now, my joys run high.

Be full, ye courts, be great who will;
Search for Peace with all your skill;
Open wide the lofty door;
Seek her on the marble floor;
In vain you search, she is not there;
In vain ye search the domes of Care!
Grass and flowers Quiet treads,
On the meads and mountain-heads,
Along with Pleasure, close allied,
Ever by each other's side:
And often, by the murmuring rill,
Hears the thrush, while all is still,
Within the groves of Grongar Hill.

(1726)

James Thomson
1700-1748

◆

The Seasons

FROM THE PREFACE TO WINTER

I am neither ignorant nor concerned how much one may suffer in the opinion of several persons of great gravity and character by the study and pursuit of poetry.

Although there may seem to be some appearance of reason for the present contempt of it as managed by the most part of our modern writers, yet that any man should seriously declare against that divine art is really amazing. It is declaring against the most charming power of imagination, the most exalting force of thought, the most affecting touch of sentiment—in a word, against the very soul of all learning and politeness. It is affronting the universal taste of mankind, and declaring against what has charmed the listening world from Moses down to Milton. In fine, it is even declaring against the sublimest passages of the inspired writings themselves, and what seems to be the peculiar language of Heaven.

The truth of the case is this: these weak-sighted gentlemen cannot bear the strong light of poetry and the finer and more amusing scene of things it displays. But must those therefore whom Heaven has blessed with the discerning eye shut it to keep them company?

It is pleasant enough, however, to observe frequently in these enemies of poetry an awkward imitation of it. They sometimes have their little brightnesses when the opening glooms will permit. Nay, I have seen their heaviness on some occasions deign to turn friskish and witty, in which they make just such another figure as Æsop's ass when he began to fawn. To complete the absurdity, they would even in their efforts against poetry fain be poetical; like those gentlemen that reason with a great deal of zeal and severity against reason.

That there are frequent and notorious abuses of poetry is as true as that the best things are most liable to that misfortune; but is there no end of that clamorous argument against the use of things from the abuse of them? and yet I hope that no man who has the least sense of shame in him will fall into it after the present sulphureous attacker of the stage.

To insist no further on this head, let Poetry once more be restored to her ancient truth and purity; let her be inspired from Heaven, and in return her incense ascend thither; let her exchange her low, venal, trifling, subjects for such as are fair, useful, and magnificent; and let her execute these so as at once to please, instruct, surprise, and astonish: and then of necessity the most inveterate ignorance and prejudice shall be struck dumb, and poets yet become the delight and wonder of mankind.

But this happy period is not to be expected, till some long-wished, illustrious man of equal power and beneficence rise on the wintry world of letters: one of a genuine and unbounded greatness and generosity of mind; who, far above all the pomp and pride of fortune, scorns the little, addressful flatterer; pierces through the disguised, designing villain; discountenances all the reigning fopperies of a tasteless age; and who, stretching his views into late futurity, has the true interest of virtue, learning, and mankind entirely at heart—a character so nobly desirable that to an honest heart it is almost incredible so few should have the ambition to deserve it.

Nothing can have a better influence towards the revival of poetry than the choosing of great and serious subjects, such as at once amuse the fancy, enlighten the head, and warm the heart. These give a weight and dignity to the poem, nor is the pleasure—I should say rapture—both the writer and the reader feels unwarranted by reason or followed by repentant disgust. To be able to write on a dry, barren theme is looked upon by some as the sign of a happy, fruitful genius:—fruitful indeed! like one of the pendant gardens in Cheapside, watered every morning by the hand of the Alderman himself. And what are we commonly entertained with on these occasions save forced, unaffecting fancies, little, glittering prettinesses, mixed turns of wit and expression, which are as widely different from native poetry as buffoonery is from the perfection of human thinking? A genius fired with the charms of truth and nature is tuned to a sublimer pitch, and scorns to associate with such subjects.

I cannot more emphatically recommend this poetical ambition than by the four following lines from Mr. Hill's poem, called *The Judgment Day*, which is so singular an instance of it:—

For me, suffice it to have taught my Muse,
The tuneful triflings of her tribe to shun;
And raised her warmth such heavenly themes
to choose
As in past ages the best garlands won.

I know no subject more elevating, more amusing, more ready to awake the poetical enthusiasm, the philosophical reflection, and the moral sentiment, than the works of Nature. Where can we meet with such variety, such beauty, such magnificence? All that enlarges and transports the soul? What more inspiring than a calm, wide survey of them? In every dress Nature is greatly charming—whether she puts on the crimson robes of the morning, the strong effulgence of noon, the sober suit of the evening, or the deep sables of blackness and tempest! How gay looks the spring! how glorious the summer! how pleasing the autumn! and how venerable the winter!—But there is no thinking of these things without breaking out into poetry; which is, by the bye, a plain and undeniable argument of their superior excellence.

For this reason the best, both ancient and modern, poets have been passionately fond of retirement and solitude. The wild romantic country was their delight. And they seem never to have been more happy than when, lost in unfrequented fields, far from the little busy world, they were at leisure to meditate, and sing the works of Nature.

The book of Job, that noble and ancient poem, which even strikes so forcibly through a mangling translation, is crowned with a description of the grand works of Nature; and that, too, from the mouth of their Almighty Author.

It was this devotion to the works of Nature that, in his Georgics, inspired the rural Virgil to write so inimitably; and who can forbear joining with him in this declaration of his, which has been the rapture of ages? . . .

Me may the Muses, my supreme delight!
Whose priest I am, smit with immense desire,
Snatch to their care; the starry tracts disclose,
The sun's distress, the labours of the moon;
Whence the earth quakes; and by what force
the deeps
Heave at the rocks, then on themselves reflow;
Why winter suns to plunge in ocean speed;
And what retards the lazy summer night.
But, lest I should these mystic truths attain,
If the cold current freezes round my heart,
The country me, the brooky vales may please
Mid woods and streams unknown.

(1726)

WINTER

THE ARGUMENT

The subject proposed. Address to the Earl of Wilmington. First approach of Winter. According to the natural course of the season, various storms described. Rain. Wind. Snow. The driving of the snows: a man perishing among them; whence reflections on the wants and miseries of human life. The wolves descending from the Alps and Apennines. A winter evening described: as spent by philosophers; by the country people; in the city. Frost. A view of Winter within the polar circle. A thaw. The whole concluding with moral reflections on a future state.

See, Winter comes to rule the varied year
Sullen and sad, with all his rising train—
Vapours, and clouds, and storms. Be these my
theme—
These, that exalt the soul to solemn thought
And heavenly musing. Welcome, kindred glooms!
Cogenial horrors, hail! With frequent foot,
Pleased have I, in my cheerful morn of life,
When nursed by careless solitude I lived
And sung of Nature with unceasing joy,
Pleased have I wandered through your rough
domain;
Trod the pure virgin-snows, myself as pure;
Heard the winds roar, and the big torrent burst;
Or seen the deep-fermenting tempest brewed
In the grim evening sky. Thus passed the time,
Till through the lucid chambers of the south
Looked out the joyous Spring—looked out and
smiled.

To thee, the patron of this first essay,
The Muse, O Wilmington! renews her song.
Since has she rounded the revolving year:
Skimmed the gay Spring; on eagle-pinions
borne,
Attempted through the Summer-blaze to rise;
Then swept o'er Autumn with the shadowy gale;
And now among the wintry clouds again,
Rolled in the doubling storm, she tries to soar,
To swell her note with all the rushing winds,
To suit her sounding cadence to the floods;
As is her theme, her numbers wildly great.
Thrice happy, could she fill thy judging ear
With bold description and with manly thought!
Nor art thou skilled in awful schemes alone,
And how to make a mighty people thrive;
But equal goodness, sound integrity,
A firm, unshaken, uncorrupted soul
Amid a sliding age, and burning strong,
Not vainly blazing, for thy country's weal,
A steady spirit, regularly free—
These, each exalting each, the statesman light
Into the patriot; these, the public hope
And eye to thee converting, bid the Muse
Record what envy dares not flattery call.
Now, when the cheerless empire of the sky
To Capricorn the Centaur-Archer yields,
And fierce Aquarius stains the inverted year—
Hung o'er the farthest verge of heaven, the sun
Scarce spreads o'er ether the dejected day.
Faint are his gleams, and ineffectual shoot
His struggling rays in horizontal lines
Through the thick air; as clothed in cloudy storms,
Weak, wan, and broad, he skirts the southern
sky;
And, soon descending, to the long dark night,
Wide-shading all, the prostrate world resigns.
Nor is the night unwished, while vital heat,
Light, life, and joy the dubious day forsake.
Meantime, in sable cincture, shadows vast,
Deep-tinged and damp, and congregated clouds,
And all the vapoury turbulence of heaven
Involve the face of things. Thus Winter falls.

THE SEASONS. WINTER. **18. Wilmington:** Sir Spencer Compton (1673–1743), Speaker of the House of Commons, made Lord Wilmington in 1730. **30. awful:** awesome. **42–43. Capricorn . . . Aquarius:** On December 21 the sun passes from Sagittarius (the Centaur-Archer) to Capricorn, and then on January 21 to Aquarius.

A heavy gloom oppressive o'er the world,
Through Nature shedding influence malign,
And rouses up the seeds of dark disease.
The soul of man dies in him, loathing life,
And black with more than melancholy views.
The cattle droop, and o'er the furrowed land,
Fresh from the plough, the dun discoloured flocks,
Untended spreading, crop the wholesome root.
Along the woods, along the moorish fens,
Sighs the sad genius of the coming storm;
And up among the loose disjointed cliffs
And fractured mountains wild, the brawling brook
And cave, presageful, send a hollow moan,
Resounding long in listening Fancy's ear.
Then comes the father of the tempest forth,
Wrapped in black glooms. First, joyless rains
obscure
Drive through the mingling skies with vapour foul,
Dash on the mountain's brow, and shake the woods
That grumbling wave below. The unsightly plain
Lies a brown deluge; as the low-bent clouds
Pour flood on flood, yet unexhausted still
Combine, and, deepening into night, shut up
The day's fair face. The wanderers of heaven,
Each to his home, retire, save those that love
To take their pastime in the troubled air,
Or skimming flutter round the dimply pool.
The cattle from the untasted fields return
And ask, with meaning low, their wonted stalls,
Or ruminate in the contiguous shade.
Thither the household feathery people crowd,
The crested cock, with all his female train,
Pensive and dripping; while the cottage-hind
Hangs o'er the enlivening blaze, and taleful
there
Recounts his simple frolic; much he talks,
And much he laughs, nor recks the storm that blows
Without, and rattles on his humble roof.
Wide o'er the brim, with many a torrent swelled,
And the mixed ruin of its banks o'erspread,
At last the roused-up river pours along:
Resistless, roaring, dreadful, down it comes,
From the rude mountain and the mossy wild,
Tumbling through rocks abrupt, and sounding far;
Then o'er the sanded valley floating spreads,
Calm, sluggish, silent; till again, constrained

85. meaning low: meaningful sound. **89. cottage-hind:** a country worker.

Between two meeting hills, it bursts a way
Where rocks and woods o'erhang the turbid stream;
There, gathering triple force, rapid and deep,
It boils and wheels and foams and thunders through.
Nature! great parent! whose unceasing hand
Rolls round the seasons of the changeful year,
How mighty, how majestic are thy works!
With what a pleasing dread they swell the soul,
That sees astonished, and astonished sings!
Ye too, ye winds! that now begin to blow
With boisterous sweep, I raise my voice to you.
Where are your stores, ye powerful beings! say,
Where your aërial magazines reserved
To swell the brooding terrors of the storm?
In what far-distant region of the sky,
Hushed in deep silence, sleep you when 'tis calm?
When from the pallid sky the sun descends,
With many a spot, that o'er his glaring orb
Uncertain wanders, stained; red fiery streaks
Begin to flush around. The reeling clouds
Stagger with dizzy poise, as doubting yet
Which master to obey; while, rising slow,
Blank in the leaden-coloured east, the moon
Wears a wan circle round her blunted horns.
Seen through the turbid fluctuating air,
The stars obtuse emit a shivering ray,
Or frequent seem to shoot athwart the gloom,
And long behind them trail the whitening blaze.
Snatched in short eddies, plays the withered
leaf,
And on the flood the dancing feather floats.
With broadened nostrils to the sky upturned,
The conscious heifer snuffs the stormy gale.
Even as the matron, at her nightly task,
With pensive labour draws the flaxen thread,
The wasted taper and the crackling flame
Foretell the blast. But chief the plumy race,
The tenants of the sky, its changes speak.
Retiring from the downs, where all day long
They picked their scanty fare, a blackening
train
Of clamorous rooks thick-urge their weary flight,
And seek the closing shelter of the grove.
Assiduous in his bower, the wailing owl
Plies his sad song. The cormorant on high
Wheels from the deep and screams along the land.
Loud shrieks the soaring hern, and with wild wing
The circling sea-fowl cleave the flaky clouds.
Ocean, unequal pressed, with broken tide
And blind commotion heaves; while from the shore,
Eat into caverns by the restless wave,
And forest-rustling mountain, comes a voice
That, solemn-sounding, bids the world prepare.
Then issues forth the storm with sudden burst,
And hurls the whole precipitated air
Down in a torrent. On the passive main
Descends the ethereal force, and with strong gust
Turns from its bottom the discoloured deep.
Through the black night that sits immense around,
Lashed into foam, the fierce-conflicting brine
Seems o'er a thousand raging waves to burn.
Meantime the mountain-billows, to the clouds
In dreadful tumult swelled, surge above surge,
Burst into chaos with tremendous roar,
And anchored navies from their stations drive,
Wild as the winds, across the howling waste
Of mighty waters; now the inflated wave
Straining they scale, and now impetuous shoot
Into the secret chambers of the deep,
The wintry Baltic thundering o'er their head.
Emerging thence again, before the breath
Of full-exerted heaven they wing their course,
And dart on distant coasts—if some sharp rock
Or shoal insidious break not their career,
And in loose fragments fling them floating round.
Nor less at land the loosened tempest reigns.
The mountain thunders, and its sturdy sons
Stoop to the bottom of the rocks they shade.
Lone on the midnight steep, and all aghast,
The dark wayfaring stranger breathless toils,
And, often falling, climbs against the blast.
Low waves the rooted forest, vexed, and sheds
What of its tarnished honours yet remain—
Dashed down and scattered by the tearing wind's
Assiduous fury, its gigantic limbs.
Thus struggling through the dissipated grove,
The whirling tempest raves along the plain;
And, on the cottage thatched or lordly roof
Keen-fastening, shakes them to the solid base.
Sleep frighted flies; and round the rocking dome,
For entrance eager, howls the savage blast.
Then too, they say, through all the burdened air
Long groans are heard, shrill sounds, and distant
sighs,
That, uttered by the demon of the night,
Warn the devoted wretch of woe and death.

146. hern: heron.

173. career: movement.

Huge uproar lords it wide. The clouds, commixed
With stars swift-gliding, sweep along the sky.
All Nature reels: till Nature's King, who oft
Amid tempestuous darkness dwells alone,
And on the wings of the careering wind
Walks dreadfully serene, commands a calm;
Then straight air, sea, and earth are hushed at once.
As yet 'tis midnight deep. The weary clouds,
Slow-meeting mingle into solid gloom.
Now, while the drowsy world lies lost in sleep,
Let me associate with the serious Night,
And Contemplation, her sedate compeer;
Let me shake off the intrusive cares of day,
And lay the meddling senses all aside.
Where now, ye lying vanities of life!
Ye ever-tempting, ever-cheating train!
Where are you now? and what is your amount?
Vexation, disappointment, and remorse.
Sad, sickening thought! and yet deluded man,
A scene of crude disjointed visions past,
And broken slumbers, rises still resolved,
With new-flushed hopes, to run the giddy round.
Father of light and life! thou Good Supreme!
O teach me what is good! teach me Thyself!
Save me from folly, vanity, and vice,
From every low pursuit; and feed my soul
With knowledge, conscious peace, and virtue pure—
Sacred, substantial, never-fading bliss!
The keener tempests come, and, fuming dun
From all the livid east or piercing north,
Thick clouds ascend, in whose capacious womb
A vapoury deluge lies, to snow congealed.
Heavy they roll their fleecy world along,
And the sky saddens with the gathered storm.
Through the hushed air the whitening shower descends,
At first thin-wavering, till at last the flakes
Fall broad and wide and fast, dimming the day
With a continual flow. The cherished fields
Put on their winter-robe of purest white.
'Tis brightness all, save where the new snow melts
Along the mazy current. Low the woods
Bow their hoar head; and, ere the languid sun
Faint from the west emits his evening ray,
Earth's universal face, deep-hid and chill,
Is one wild dazzling waste, that buries wide
The works of man. Drooping, the labourer-ox
Stands covered o'er with snow, and then demands
The fruit of all his toil. The fowls of heaven,
Tamed by the cruel season, crowd around
The winnowing store, and claim the little boon
Which Providence assigns them. One alone,
The redbreast, sacred to the household gods,
Wisely regardful of the embroiling sky,
In joyless fields and thorny thickets leaves
His shivering mates, and pays to trusted man
His annual visit. Half afraid, he first
Against the window beats; then brisk alights
On the warm hearth; then, hopping o'er the floor,
Eyes all the smiling family askance,
And pecks, and starts, and wonders where he is—
Till, more familiar grown, the table-crumbs
Attract his slender feet. The foodless wilds
Pour forth their brown inhabitants. The hare,
Though timorous of heart, and hard beset
By death in various forms, dark snares, and dogs,
And more unpitying men, the garden seeks
Urged on by fearless want. The bleating kine
Eye the bleak heaven, and next the glistening earth,
With looks of dumb despair; then, sad-dispersed,
Dig for the withered herb through heaps of snow.
Now, shepherds, to your helpless charge be kind;
Baffle the raging year, and fill their pens
With food at will; lodge them below the storm,
And watch them strict, for, from the bellowing east,
In this dire season, oft the whirlwind's wing
Sweeps up the burden of whole wintry plains
In one wide waft, and o'er the hapless flocks,
Hid in the hollow of two neighbouring hills,
The billowy tempest whelms, till, upward urged,
The valley to a shining mountain swells,
Tipped with a wreath high-curling in the sky.
As thus the snows arise, and, foul and fierce,
All Winter drives along the darkened air,
In his own loose-revolving fields the swain
Disastered stands; sees other hills ascend,
Of unknown joyless brow, and other scenes,
Of horrid prospect, shag the trackless plain;
Nor finds the river nor the forest, hid
Beneath the formless wild, but wanders on
From hill to dale, still more and more astray,
Impatient flouncing through the drifted heaps,

199. careering: fiercely blowing.

244. winnowing store: the grain separated from the chaff during winter. **261. kine:** sheep.

Stung with the thoughts of home—the thoughts of home
Rush on his nerves and call their vigour forth
In many a vain attempt. How sinks his soul!
What black despair, what horror fills his heart,
When, for the dusky spot which fancy feigned
His tufted cottage rising through the snow,
He meets the roughness of the middle waste,
Far from the track and blest abode of man,
While round him night resistless closes fast,
And every tempest, howling o'er his head,
Renders the savage wilderness more wild.
Then throng the busy shapes into his mind
Of covered pits, unfathomably deep,
A dire descent! beyond the power of frost;
Of faithless bogs; of precipices huge,
Smoothed up with snow; and (what is land unknown,
What water) of the still unfrozen spring,
In the loose marsh or solitary lake,
Where the fresh fountain from the bottom boils.
These check his fearful steps; and down he sinks
Beneath the shelter of the shapeless drift,
Thinking o'er all the bitterness of death,
Mixed with the tender anguish nature shoots
Through the wrung bosom of the dying man—
His wife, his children, and his friends unseen.
In vain for him the officious wife prepares
The fire fair-blazing and the vestment warm;
In vain his little children, peeping out
Into the mingling storm, demand their sire
With tears of artless innocence. Alas!
Nor wife nor children more shall he behold,
Nor friends, nor sacred home. On every nerve
The deadly winter seizes, shuts up sense,
And, o'er his inmost vitals creeping cold,
Lays him along the snows a stiffened corse,
Stretched out and bleaching in the northern blast.
  Ah! little think the gay licentious proud,
Whom pleasure, power, and affluence surround—
They who their thoughtless hours in giddy mirth,
And wanton, often cruel, riot waste—
Ah! little think they, while they dance along,
How many feel, this very moment, death
And all the sad variety of pain:
How many sink in the devouring flood,
Or more devouring flame; how many bleed,
By shameful variance betwixt man and man;
How many pine in want, and dungeon glooms,
Shut from the common air and common use
Of their own limbs; how many drink the cup
Of baleful grief, or eat the bitter bread
Of misery; sore pierced by wintry winds,
How many shrink into the sordid hut
Of cheerless poverty; how many shake
With all the fiercer tortures of the mind,
Unbounded passion, madness, guilt, remorse—
Whence, tumbled headlong from the height of life,
They furnish matter for the Tragic Muse;
Even in the vale, where wisdom loves to dwell,
With friendship, peace, and contemplation joined,
How many, racked with honest passions, droop
In deep retired distress; how many stand
Around the death-bed of their dearest friends,
And point the parting anguish! Thought fond man
Of these, and all the thousand nameless ills
That one incessant struggle render life,
One scene of toil, of suffering, and of fate,
Vice in his high career would stand appalled,
And heedless rambling Impulse learn to think;
The conscious heart of Charity would warm,
And her wide wish Benevolence dilate;
The social tear would rise, the social sigh;
And into clear perfection, gradual bliss,
Refining still, the social passions work.
  And here can I forget the generous band
Who, touched with human woe, redressive searched
Into the horrors of the gloomy jail?
Unpitied and unheard where misery moans,
Where sickness pines, where thirst and hunger burn,
And poor misfortune feels the lash of vice;
While in the land of liberty—the land
Whose every street and public meeting glow
With open freedom—little tyrants raged,
Snatched the lean morsel from the starving mouth,
Tore from cold wintry limbs the tattered weed,
Even robbed them of the last of comforts, sleep,
The free-born Briton to the dungeon chained,

311. officious: attentive. **320. corse:** corpse.

348. point: sharpen. **fond:** foolish. **359. generous band:** the Jail Committee that was appointed by Parliament and directed by the great philanthropist James Ogelthorpe. The Committee exposed despicable conditions in debtors' prisons.

Or, as the lust of cruelty prevailed,
At pleasure marked him with inglorious stripes,
And crushed out lives, by secret barbarous ways,
That for their country would have toiled or bled.
O great design! if executed well,
With patient care and wisdom-tempered zeal.
Ye sons of mercy! yet resume the search;
Drag forth the legal monsters into light,
Wrench from their hands Oppression's iron rod,
And bid the cruel feel the pains they give.
Much still untouched remains; in this rank age,
Much is the patriot's weeding hand required.
The toils of law—what dark insidious men
Have cumbrous added to perplex the truth
And lengthen simple justice into trade—
How glorious were the day that saw these broke,
And every man within the reach of right!
By wintry famine roused, from all the tract
Of horrid mountains which the shining Alps
And wavy Apennines and Pyrenees
Branch out stupendous into distant lands,
Cruel as death, and hungry as the grave!
Burning for blood, bony, and gaunt, and grim!
Assembling wolves in raging troops descend;
And, pouring o'er the country, bear along,
Keen as the north wind sweeps the glossy snow.
All is their prize. They fasten on the steed,
Press him to earth, and pierce his mighty heart.
Nor can the bull his awful front defend,
Or shake the murdering savages away.
Rapacious, at the mother's throat they fly,
And tear the screaming infant from her breast.
The godlike face of man avails him naught.
Even Beauty, force divine! at whose bright glance
The generous lion stands in softened gaze,
Here bleeds, a hapless undistinguished prey.
But if, apprised of the severe attack,
The country be shut up, lured by the scent,
On churchyards drear (inhuman to relate!)
The disappointed prowlers fall, and dig
The shrouded body from the grave, o'er which,
Mixed with foul shades and frighted ghosts, they howl.
Among those hilly regions where, embraced
In peaceful vales, the happy Grisons dwell,
Oft, rushing sudden from the loaded cliffs,

384. **toils:** traps. 415. **happy Grisons:** citizens of Grisons, a Swiss canton.

Mountains of snow their gathering terrors roll.
From steep to steep loud thundering down they come,
A wintry waste in dire commotion all;
And herds and flocks and travellers and swains,
And sometimes whole brigades of marching troops,
Or hamlets sleeping in the dead of night,
Are deep beneath the smothering ruin whelmed.
Now, all amid the rigours of the year,
In the wild depth of winter, while without
The ceaseless winds blow ice, be my retreat,
Between the groaning forest and the shore,
Beat by the boundless multitude of waves,
A rural, sheltered, solitary scene,
Where ruddy fire and beaming tapers join
To cheer the gloom. There studious let me sit,
And hold high converse with the mighty dead—
Sages of ancient time, as gods revered,
As gods beneficent, who blessed mankind
With arts and arms, and humanized a world.
Roused at the inspiring thought, I throw aside
The long-lived volume, and deep-musing hail
The sacred shades that slowly rising pass
Before my wondering eyes. First Socrates,
Who, firmly good in a corrupted state,
Against the rage of tyrants single stood,
Invincible! calm reason's holy law,
That voice of God within the attentive mind,
Obeying, fearless or in life or death—
Great moral teacher! wisest of mankind!
Solon the next, who built his commonweal
On equity's wide base; by tender laws
A lively people curbing, yet undamped
Preserving still that quick peculiar fire,
Whence in the laurelled field of finer arts,
And of bold freedom, they unequalled shone,
The pride of smiling Greece and humankind.
Lycurgus then, who bowed beneath the force
Of strictest discipline, severely wise,
All human passions. Following him I see,
As at Thermopylae he glorious fell,
The firm devoted chief who proved by deeds
The hardest lesson which the other taught.

446. **Solon:** the great Athenian lawmaker of the sixth century B.C. noted for his humaneness. 453. **Lycurgus:** the famous Spartan lawmaker of the ninth century B.C. noted for his absolute strictness. 457. **firm devoted chief:** Leonidas of Sparta.

Then Aristides lifts his honest front;
Spotless of heart, to whom the unflattering
voice
Of freedom gave the noblest name of Just;
In pure majestic poverty revered;
Who, even his glory to his country's weal
Submitting, swelled a haughty rival's fame.
Reared by his care, of softer ray appears
Cimon, sweet-souled; whose genius, rising
strong,
Shook off the load of young debauch; abroad
The scourge of Persian pride, at home the friend
Of every worth and every splendid art;
Modest and simple in the pomp of wealth.
Then the last worthies of declining Greece,
Late-called to glory, in unequal times,
Pensive appear. The fair Corinthian boast,
Timoleon, tempered happy, mild, and firm,
Who wept the brother while the tyrant bled;
And, equal to the best, the Theban pair,
Whose virtues, in heroic concord joined,
Their country raised to freedom, empire, fame.
He too, with whom Athenian honour sunk,
And left a mass of sordid lees behind,—
Phocion the Good; in public life severe,
To virtue still inexorably firm;
But when, beneath his low illustrious roof,
Sweet peace and happy wisdom smoothed his
brow,
Not friendship softer was, nor love more kind.
And he, the last of old Lycurgus' sons,
The generous victim to that vain attempt
To save a rotten state—Agis, who saw
Even Sparta's self to servile avarice sunk.
The two Achaian heroes close the train—
Aratus, who a while relumed the soul
Of fondly lingering liberty in Greece;
And he, her darling, as her latest hope,
The gallant Philopoemen, who to arms
Turned the luxurious pomp he could not cure,
Or toiling in his farm, a simple swain,
Or bold and skilful thundering in the field.
Of rougher front, a mighty people come,
A race of heroes! in those virtuous times
Which knew no stain, save that with partial
flame
Their dearest country they too fondly loved.
Her better founder first, the Light of Rome,
Numa, who softened her rapacious sons;
Servius, the king who laid the solid base
On which o'er earth the vast republic spread.
Then the great consuls venerable rise:
The public father who the private quelled,
As on the dread tribunal, sternly sad;
He whom his thankless country could not
lose,
Camillus, only vengeful to her foes;
Fabricius, scorner of all-conquering gold,
And Cincinnatus, awful from the plough;
Thy willing victim, Carthage! bursting loose
From all that pleading Nature could oppose,
From a whole city's tears, by rigid faith
Imperious called, and honour's dire command;

459. Aristides: Athenian politician and general. Although banished in 482 B.C., he returned to aid his rival Themistocles in winning the Battle of Salamis against the Persians. **466. Cimon:** a follower of Aristides and a hero at the Battle of Marathon. **474. Timoleon:** After gallant attempts to dissuade his brother Timophanes from becoming tyrant of Corinth, Timoleon reluctantly consented to his execution. **476. Theban pair:** Pelopidas and Epaminondas, noble youths and close friends, who led Thebes against Sparta in several campaigns. **480. lees:** dregs. **481. Phocion the Good:** brave and virtuous Athenian general and statesman. After arguing for peace with Philip of Macedon, he was condemned to die by hemlock in 317 B.C. **488. Agis:** king of Sparta who sought in vain to restore the laws of Lycurgus and was executed in 240 B.C.

491. Aratus: head of the Achaean League, a union of the states of southern Greece against Macedonia in the third century B.C. **494. Philopoemen:** successor of Aratus, a later leader of the Achaean League, who was killed in 183 B.C. **503. Numa:** second king of Rome, according to legend, who wisely ruled the state founded by Romulus. **504. Servius:** sixth king of Rome, who brought greater democracy. **507. The public father:** Lucius Junius Brutus, who drove the Tarquin foes out of Rome and even condemned his two sons to death when they conspired with the Tarquins. **510. Camillus:** After being banished unjustly, he agreed to return to Rome as Dictator and defeated the Gauls. **511. Fabricius:** notable for his refusal of bribes offered him by the invading King Pyrrhus of Epirus. Fabricius died in poverty. **512. Cincinnatus:** the celebrated leader who returned to his ruling position from his peaceful rural life. **513. Thy willing victim:** Regulus, taken prisoner by Carthage in the first Punic War, returned with a peace mission to Rome. He argued, however, that Rome should continue the war, and, upon returning to Carthage, was executed.

Scipio, the gentle chief, humanely brave,
Who soon the race of spotless glory ran,
And, warm in youth, to the poetic shade
With friendship and philosophy retired;
Tully, whose powerful eloquence a while
Restrained the rapid fate of rushing Rome;
Unconquered Cato, virtuous in extreme;
And thou, unhappy Brutus, kind of heart,
Whose steady arm, by awful virtue urged,
Lifted the Roman steel against thy friend.
Thousands besides the tribute of a verse
Demand, but who can count the stars of heaven?
Who sing their influence on this lower world?
Behold, who yonder comes! in sober state,
Fair, mild, and strong as is a vernal sun:
'Tis Phoebus' self, or else the Mantuan swain!
Great Homer too appears, of daring wing,
Parent of song! and equal by his side,
The British Muse; joined hand in hand they walk,
Darkling, full up the middle steep to fame.
Nor absent are those shades, whose skilful touch
Pathetic drew the impassioned heart, and charmed
Transported Athens with the moral scene;
Nor those who tuneful waked the enchanting lyre.
First of your kind! society divine!
Still visit thus my nights, for you reserved,
And mount my soaring soul to thoughts like yours.
Silence, thou lonely power; the door be thine;
See on the hallowed hour that none intrude,
Save a few chosen friends who sometimes deign
To bless my humble roof with sense refined,
Learning digested well, exalted faith,
Unstudied wit, and humour ever gay.
Or from the Muses' hill will Pope descend,
To raise the sacred hour, to bid it smile,
And with the social spirit warm the heart;
For, though not sweeter his own Homer sings,
Yet is his life the more endearing song.

517. Scipio: Scipio Africanus Minor, after his defeat at Carthage in the Third Punic War, retired to a life of studious leisure. **521. Tully:** Cicero, the great Roman statesman and orator, later killed by the soldiers of Marc Antony. **523. Cato:** Cato the Younger, the great Stoic, who committed suicide rather than submit to Caesar. **524. Brutus:** Marcus Junius Brutus, one of the assassins of Caesar, later committed suicide. **532. Mantuan swain:** Virgil. **535. British Muse:** Milton.

Where art thou, Hammond? thou the darling pride,
The friend and lover of the tuneful throng!
Ah! why, dear youth, in all the blooming prime
Of vernal genius, where, disclosing fast,
Each active worth, each manly virtue lay,
Why wert thou ravished from our hope so soon?
What now avails that noble thirst of fame
Which stung thy fervent breast? that treasured store
Of knowledge, early gained? that eager zeal
To serve thy country, glowing in the band
Of youthful patriots who sustain her name?
What now, alas! that life-diffusing charm
Of sprightly wit? that rapture for the Muse,
That heart of friendship and that soul of joy,
Which bade with softest light thy virtues smile?
Ah! only showed to check our fond pursuits,
And teach our humbled hopes that life is vain!
Thus in some deep retirement would I pass
The winter-glooms with friends of pliant soul,
Or blithe or solemn, as the theme inspired:
With them would search if nature's boundless frame
Was called, late-rising, from the void of night,
Or sprung eternal from the Eternal Mind;
Its life, its laws, it progress, and its end.
Hence larger prospects of the beauteous whole
Would gradual open on our opening minds,
And each diffusive harmony unite
In full perfection to the astonished eye.
Then would we try to scan the moral world,
Which, though to us it seems embroiled, moves on
In higher order, fitted and impelled
By Wisdom's finest hand, and issuing all
In general good. The sage Historic Muse
Should next conduct us through the deeps of time,
Show us how empire grew, declined, and fell
In scattered states; what makes the nations smile,
Improves their soil, and gives them double suns;
And why they pine beneath the brightest skies,
In Nature's richest lap. As thus we talked,
Our hearts would burn within us, would inhale

555. Hammond: James Hammond (1710–1742), a poet-friend of Thomson and a member of the anti-Walpole faction.

That portion of divinity, that ray
Of purest Heaven which lights the public soul
Of patriots and of heroes. But, if doomed
In powerless humble fortune to repress
These ardent risings of the kindling soul,
Then, even superior to ambition, we
Would learn the private virtues—how to glide
Through shades and plains along the smoothest stream
Of rural life; or, snatched away by hope
Through the dim spaces of futurity,
With earnest eye anticipate those scenes
Of happiness and wonder, where the mind,
In endless growth and infinite ascent,
Rises from state to state, and world to world.
But, when with these the serious thought is foiled,
We, shifting for relief, would play the shapes
Of frolic Fancy; and incessant form
Those rapid pictures, that assembled train
Of fleet ideas, never joined before,
Whence lively Wit excites to gay surprise,
Or folly-painting Humour, grave himself,
Calls laughter forth, deep-shaking every nerve.
  Meantime the village rouses up the fire;
While, well attested and as well believed,
Heard solemn, goes the goblin-story round,
Till superstitious horror creeps o'er all.
Or frequent in the sounding hall they wake
The rural gambol. Rustic mirth goes round—
The simple joke that takes the shepherd's heart,
Easily pleased; the long loud laugh sincere;
The kiss, snatched hasty from the sidelong maid
On purpose guardless, or pretending sleep;
The leap, the slap, the haul; and, shook to notes
Of native music, the respondent dance.
Thus jocund fleets with them the winter night.
  The city swarms intense. The public haunt,
Full of each theme and warm with mixed discourse,
Hums indistinct. The sons of riot flow
Down the loose stream of false enchanted joy
To swift destruction. On the rankled soul
The gaming fury falls; and in one gulf
Of total ruin, honour, virtue, peace,
Friends, families, and fortune headlong sink.
Up springs the dance along the lighted dome,
Mixed and evolved a thousand sprightly ways.
The glittering court effuses every pomp;
The circle deepens; beamed from gaudy robes,
Tapers, and sparkling gems, and radiant eyes,
A soft effulgence o'er the palace waves—
While, a gay insect in his summer shine,
The fop, light-fluttering, spreads his mealy wings.
  Dread o'er the scene the ghost of Hamlet stalks;
Othello rages; poor Monimia mourns;
And Belvidera pours her soul in love.
Terror alarms the breast; the comely tear
Steals o'er the cheek; or else the Comic Muse
Holds to the world a picture of itself,
And raises sly the fair impartial laugh.
Sometimes she lifts her strain, and paints the scenes
Of beauteous life—whate'er can deck mankind,
Or charm the heart, in generous Bevil showed.
  O thou whose wisdom, solid yet refined,
Whose patriot virtues, and consummate skill
To touch the finer springs that move the world,
Joined to whate'er the Graces can bestow,
And all Apollo's animating fire,
Give thee with pleasing dignity to shine
At once the guardian, ornament, and joy
Of polished life—permit the rural Muse,
O Chesterfield, to grace with thee her song.
Ere to the shades again she humbly flies,
Indulge her fond ambition, in thy train
(For every Muse has in thy train a place)
To mark thy various full-accomplished mind—
To mark that spirit which with British scorn
Rejects the allurements of corrupted power;
That elegant politeness which excels,
Even in the judgment of presumptuous France,
The boasted manners of her shining court;
That wit, the vivid energy of sense,
The truth of nature, which with Attic point,
And kind well-tempered satire, smoothly keen,
Steals through the soul and without pain corrects.
Or, rising thence with yet a brighter flame,

615. Humour: the older Elizabethan sense of the word suggesting characters revealing some extreme of temperament (e.g., Greed, Lust, Folly). **625. sidelong:** by the side.

647. Monimia: heroine of Thomas Otway's play *The Orphan.* **648. Belvidera:** heroine of Otway's *Venice Preserved.* **655. Bevil:** hero of Richard Steele's *The Conscious Lovers.*

Oh, let me hail thee on some glorious day,
When to the listening senate ardent crowd
Britannia's sons to hear her pleaded cause!
Then, dressed by thee, more amiably fair,
Truth the soft robe of mild persuasion wears;
Thou to assenting reason giv'st again
Her own enlightened thoughts: called from the heart,
The obedient passions on thy voice attend;
And even reluctant party feels a while
Thy gracious power, as through the varied maze
Of eloquence, now smooth, now quick, now strong,
Profound and clear, you roll the copious flood.
 To thy loved haunt return, my happy Muse:
For now, behold! the joyous winter days,
Frosty, succeed; and through the blue serene,
For sight too fine, the ethereal nitre flies,
Killing infectious damps, and the spent air
Storing afresh with elemental life.
Close crowds the shining atmosphere, and binds
Our strengthened bodies in its cold embrace,
Constringent; feeds and animates our blood;
Refines our spirits, through the new-strung nerves
In swifter sallies darting to the brain—
Where sits the soul, intense, collected, cool,
Bright as the skies, and as the season keen.
All nature feels the renovating force
Of Winter—only to the thoughtless eye
In ruin seen. The frost-concocted glebe
Draws in abundant vegetable soul,
And gathers vigour for the coming year;
A stronger glow sits on the lively cheek,
Of ruddy fire; and luculent along
The purer rivers flow; their sullen deeps,
Transparent, open to the shepherd's gaze,
And murmur hoarser at the fixing frost.
 What art thou, Frost? and whence are thy keen stores
Derived, thou secret all-invading power,
Whom even the illusive fluid cannot fly?
Is not thy potent energy, unseen,
Myriads of little salts, or hooked, or shaped
Like double wedges, and diffused immense
Through water, earth, and ether? Hence at eve,
Steamed eager from the red horizon round,
With the fierce rage of Winter deep suffused,
An icy gale, oft shifting, o'er the pool
Breathes a blue film, and in its mid-career
Arrests the bickering stream. The loosened ice,
Let down the flood and half dissolved by day,
Rustles no more; but to the sedgy bank
Fast grows, or gathers round the pointed stone,
A crystal pavement, by the breath of heaven
Cemented firm; till, seized from shore to shore,
The whole imprisoned river growls below.
Loud rings the frozen earth, and hard reflects
A double noise; while, at his evening watch,
The village dog deters the nightly thief;
The heifer lows; the distant waterfall
Swells in the breeze; and with the hasty tread
Of traveller the hollow-sounding plain
Shakes from afar. The full ethereal round,
Infinite worlds disclosing to the view,
Shines out intensely keen, and, all one cope
Of starry glitter, glows from pole to pole.
From pole to pole the rigid influence falls
Through the still night, incessant, heavy, strong,
And seizes nature fast. It freezes on,
Till morn, late-rising o'er the drooping world,
Lifts her pale eye unjoyous. Then appears
The various labour of the silent night:
Prone from the dripping eave and dumb cascade,
Whose idle torrents only seem to roar,
The pendent icicle; the frost-work fair,
Where transient hues and fancied figures rise;
Wide-spouted o'er the hill the frozen brook,
A livid tract, cold-gleaming on the morn;
The forest bent beneath the plumy wave;
And by the frost refined the whiter snow
Incrusted hard, and sounding to the tread
Of early shepherd, as he pensive seeks
His pining flock, or from the mountain top,
Pleased with the slippery surface, swift descends.
 On blithesome frolics bent, the youthful swains,
While every work of man is laid at rest,
Fond o'er the river crowd, in various sport

694. nitre: a supposed nitrous element in the air or in plants. **706. frost-concocted glebe:** frozen soil. **710. luculent:** bright. **714.** Beginning of a section advancing the theory, widely held in Thomson's time, that freezing came from salts in the air. These salts were thought to have such benefits as clearing the air, fertilizing the soil, and warding off infections. **716. illusive fluid:** mercury.

And revelry dissolved; where, mixing glad,
Happiest of all the train; the raptured boy
Lashes the whirling top. Or, where the Rhine
Branched out in many a long canal extends,
From every province swarming, void of care,
Batavia rushes forth; and, as they sweep
On sounding skates a thousand different ways
In circling poise swift as the winds along,
The then gay land is maddened all to joy.
Nor less the northern courts, wide o'er the snow,
Pour a new pomp. Eager, on rapid sleds,
Their vigorous youth in bold contention wheel
The long-resounding course. Meantime, to raise
The manly strife, with highly blooming charms
Flushed by the season, Scandinavia's dames
Or Russia's buxom daughters glow around.
  Pure, quick, and sportful is the wholesome day,
But soon elasped. The horizontal sun
Broad o'er the south hangs at his utmost noon,
And ineffectual strikes the gelid cliff.
His azure gloss the mountain still maintains,
Nor feels the feeble touch. Perhaps the vale
Relents awhile to the reflected ray;
Or from the forest falls the clustered snow,
Myriads of gems, that in the waving gleam
Gay-twinkle as they scatter. Thick around
Thunders the sport of those who with the gun,
And dog impatient bounding at the shot,
Worse than the season desolate the fields,
And, adding to the ruins of the year,
Distress the footed or the feathered game.
  But what is this? Our infant Winter sinks
Divested of his grandeur should our eye
Astonished shoot into the frigid zone,
Where for relentless months continual Night
Holds o'er the glittering waste her starry reign.
There, through the prison of unbounded wilds,
Barred by the hand of Nature from escape,
Wide roams the Russian exile. Naught around
Strikes his sad eye but deserts lost in snow,
And heavy-loaded groves, and solid floods
That stretch athwart the solitary vast
Their icy horrors to the frozen main,
And cheerless towns far distant—never blessed,
Save when its annual course the caravan
Bends to the golden coast of rich Cathay,
With news of humankind. Yet there life glows;
Yet, cherished there, beneath the shining
    waste
The furry nations harbour—tipped with jet,
Fair ermines spotless as the snows they press;
Sables of glossy black; and, dark-embrowned,
Or beauteous freaked with many a mingled hue,
Thousands besides, the costly pride of courts.
There, warm together pressed, the trooping deer
Sleep on the new-fallen snows; and, scarce his head
Raised o'er the heapy wreath, the branching elk
Lies slumbering sullen in the white abyss.
The ruthless hunter wants nor dogs nor toils,
Nor with the dread of sounding bows he drives
The fearful flying race—with ponderous clubs,
As weak against the mountain-heaps they push
Their beating breast in vain, and piteous bray,
He lays them quivering on the ensanguined snows,
And with loud shouts rejoicing bears them home.
There, through the piny forest half-absorpt,
Rough tenant of these shades, the shapeless bear,
With dangling ice all horrid, stalks forlorn;
Slow-paced, and sourer as the storms increase,
He makes his bed beneath the inclement drift,
And, with stern patience, scorning weak complaint,
Hardens his heart against assailing want.
  Wide o'er the spacious regions of the north,
That see Boötes urge his tardy wain,
A boisterous race, by frosty Caurus pierced,
Who little pleasure know and fear no pain,
Prolific swarm. They once relumed the flame
Of lost mankind in polished slavery sunk;
Drove martial horde on horde, with dreadful
    sweep
Resistless rushing o'er the enfeebled south,
And gave the vanquished world another form.
Not such the sons of Lapland: wisely they
Despise the insensate barbarous trade of war;
They ask no more than simple Nature gives;
They love their mountains and enjoy their storms.
No false desires, no pride-created wants,
Disturb the peaceful current of their time,
And through the restless ever-tortured maze
Of pleasure or ambition bid it rage.
Their reindeer form their riches. These their tents,
Their robes, their beds, and all their homely wealth
Supply, their wholesome fare, and cheerful cups.

768. Batavia: Holland. **782. gelid:** frosty. **808. Cathay:** China.

825. ensanguined: bloody. **835. Boötes:** a constellation that moves slowly around the Big Dipper; **wain:** wagon. **836. Caurus:** northwest wind.

Obsequious at their call, the docile tribe
Yield to the sled their necks, and whirl them swift
O'er hill and dale, heaped into one expanse
Of marbled snow, or, far as eye can sweep,
With a blue crust of ice unbounded glazed.
By dancing meteors then, that ceaseless shake
A waving blaze refracted o'er the heavens,
And vivid moons, and stars that keener play
With doubled lustre from the radiant waste,
Even in the depth of polar night they find
A wondrous day—enough to light the chase
Or guide their daring steps to Finland fairs.
Wished Spring returns; and from the hazy south,
While dim Aurora slowly moves before,
The welcome sun, just verging up at first,
By small degrees extends the swelling curve;
Till, seen at last for gay rejoicing months,
Still round and round his spiral course he winds,
And, as he nearly dips his flaming orb,
Wheels up again and re-ascends the sky.
In that glad season, from the lakes and floods,
Where pure Niëmi's fairy mountains rise,
And fringed with roses Tenglio rolls his stream,
They draw the copious fry. With these at eve
They cheerful-loaded to their tents repair,
Where, all day long in useful cares employed,
Their kind unblemished wives the fire prepare.
Thrice happy race! by poverty secured
From legal plunder and rapacious power,
In whom fell interest never yet has sown
The seeds of vice, whose spotless swains ne'er knew
Injurious deed, nor, blasted by the breath
Of faithless love, their blooming daughters woe.
  Still pressing on, beyond Tornea's lake,
And Hecla flaming through a waste of snow,
And farthest Greenland, to the pole itself,
Where, failing gradual, life at length goes out,
The Muse expands her solitary flight;
And, hovering o'er the wild stupendous scene,
Beholds new seas beneath another sky.
Throned in his palace of cerulean ice,
Here Winter holds his unrejoicing court,
And through his airy hall the loud misrule
Of driving tempest is forever heard;
Here the grim tyrant meditates his wrath;
Here arms his winds with all-subduing frost;
Moulds his fierce hail, and treasures up his snows,
With which he now oppresses half the globe.
  Thence winding eastward to the Tartar's coast,
She sweeps the howling margin of the main,
Where, undissolving from the first of time,
Snows swell on snows amazing to the sky;
And icy mountains high on mountains piled
Seem to the shivering sailor from afar,
Shapeless and white, an atmosphere of clouds.
Projected huge and horrid o'er the surge,
Alps frown on Alps; or, rushing hideous down,
As if old Chaos was again returned,
Wide-rend the deep and shake the solid pole.
Ocean itself no longer can resist
The binding fury; but, in all its rage
Of tempest taken by the boundless frost,
Is many a fathom to the bottom chained,
And bid to roar no more—a bleak expanse
Shagged o'er with wavy rocks, cheerless, and void
Of every life, that from the dreary months
Flies conscious southward. Miserable they!
Who, here entangled in the gathering ice,
Take their last look of the descending sun;
While, full of death and fierce with tenfold frost,
The long long night, incumbent o'er their heads,
Falls horrible! Such was the Briton's fate,
As with first prow (what have not Britons dared?)
He for the passage sought, attempted since
So much in vain, and seeming to be shut
By jealous Nature with eternal bars.
In these fell regions, in Arzina caught,
And to the stony deep his idle ship
Immediate sealed, he with his hapless crew,
Each full exerted at his several task,
Froze into statues—to the cordage glued
The sailor, and the pilot to the helm.
  Hard by these shores, where scarce his freezing stream

867. Aurora: goddess of dawn. **875–76. Niëmi:** Thomson refers to Maupertius, *Figure of the Earth* (1738), a land survey in Lapland, as a source for the references in these lines. **887. Tornea's lake:** Tornea's lake is in northern Sweden. **888. Hecla:** the awesome volcano in Iceland. **894. cerulean:** sky-blue.

902. Tartar's coast: Siberia. **925–35. Briton's fate:** a reference to Sir Hugh Willoughby and his ill-fated expedition of 1553 that sought to discover a northeast passage from Europe to India. All hands perished in the hostile elements of Lapland. **930. Arzina:** a harbor in Lapland.

Rolls the wild Oby, live the last of men;
And, half enlivened by the distant sun,
That rears and ripens man as well as plants,
Here human nature wears its rudest form.
Deep from the piercing season sunk in caves,
Here by dull fires and with unjoyous cheer
They waste the tedious gloom: immersed in furs
Doze the gross race—nor sprightly jest nor song
Nor tenderness they know, nor aught of life
Beyond the kindred bears that stalk without—
Till Morn at length, her roses drooping all,
Sheds a long twilight brightening o'er their fields,
And calls the quivered savage to the chase.
  What cannot active government perform,
New-moulding man? Wide-stretching from these shores,
A people savage from remotest time,
A huge neglected empire, one vast mind
By Heaven inspired from Gothic darkness called.
Immortal Peter! first of monarchs! He
His stubborn country tamed,—her rocks, her fens,
Her floods, her seas, her ill-submitting sons;
And, while the fierce barbarian he subdued,
To more exalted soul he raised the man.
Ye shades of ancient heroes, ye who toiled
Through long successive ages to build up
A labouring plan of state, behold at once
The wonder done! behold the matchless prince!
Who left his native throne, where reigned till then
A mighty shadow of unreal power;
Who greatly spurned the slothful pomp of courts;
And, roaming every land, in every port
His sceptre laid aside, with glorious hand
Unwearied plying the mechanic tool,
Gathered the seeds of trade, of useful arts,
Of civil wisdom, and of martial skill.
Charged with the stores of Europe home he goes!
Then cities rise amid the illumined waste;
O'er joyless deserts smiles the rural reign;
Far-distant flood to flood is social joined;
The astonished Euxine hears the Baltic roar;
Proud navies ride on seas that never foamed
With daring keel before; and armies stretch
Each way their dazzling files, repressing here
The frantic Alexander of the north,
And awing there stern Othman's shrinking sons.
Sloth flies the land, and ignorance and vice,
Of old dishonour proud; it glows around,
Taught by the royal hand that roused the whole,
One scene of arts, of arms, of rising trade—
For, what his wisdom planned and power enforced,
More potent still his great example showed.
  Muttering, the winds at eve with blunted point
Blow hollow-blustering from the south. Subdued,
The frost resolves into a trickling thaw.
Spotted the mountains shine; loose sleet descends,
And floods the country round. The rivers swell,
Of bonds impatient. Sudden from the hills,
O'er rocks and woods, in broad brown cataracts,
A thousand snow-fed torrents shoot at once;
And, where they rush, the wide-resounding plain
Is left on slimy waste. Those sullen seas,
That wash the ungenial pole, will rest no more
Beneath the shackles of the mighty north,
But, rousing all their waves, resistless heave.
And hark! the lengthening roar continuous runs
Athwart the rifted deep; at once it bursts,
And piles a thousand mountains to the clouds.
Ill fares the bark, with trembling wretches charged,
That, tossed amid the floating fragments, moors
Beneath the shelter of an icy isle,
While night o'erwhelms the sea, and horror looks
More horrible. Can human force endure
The assembled mischiefs that besiege them round?—
Heart-gnawing hunger, fainting weariness,
The roar of winds and waves, the crush of ice,
Now ceasing, now renewed with louder rage,
And in dire echoes bellowing round the main.
More to embroil the deep, Leviathan
And his unwieldy train in dreadful sport
Tempest the loosened brine; while through the gloom
Far from the bleak inhospitable shore,
Loading the winds, is heard the hungry howl
Of famished monsters, there awaiting wrecks.
Yet Providence, that ever-waking Eye,
Looks down with pity on the feeble toil
Of mortals lost to hope, and lights them safe
Through all this dreary labyrinth of fate.
  'Tis done! Dread Winter spreads his latest glooms,

937. Oby: Ob, the major river in Siberia. **955. Peter:** Peter the Great of Russia. **976. Euxine:** the Black Sea. Peter planned to connect the Black and the Baltic seas. **980. frantic Alexander:** Charles XII of Sweden.

981. Othman's sons: the Turks. **1014. Leviathan:** the great whale.

And reigns tremendous o'er the conquered year.
How dead the vegetable kingdom lies!
How dumb the tuneful! Horror wide extends
His desolate domain. Behold, fond man!
See here thy pictured life; pass some few years,
Thy flowering Spring, thy Summer's ardent strength,
Thy sober Autumn fading into age,
And pale concluding Winter comes at last
And shuts the scene. Ah! whither now are fled
Those dreams of greatness? those unsolid hopes
Of happiness? those longings after fame?
Those restless cares? those busy bustling days?
Those gay-spent festive nights? those veering thoughts,
Lost between good and ill, that shared thy life?
All now are vanished! Virtue sole survives—
Immortal, never-failing friend of man,
His guide to happiness on high. And see!
'Tis come, the glorious morn! the second birth
Of heaven and earth! awakening Nature hears
The new-creating word, and starts to life
In every heightened form, from pain and death
Forever free. The great eternal scheme,
Involving all, and in a perfect whole
Uniting, as the prospect wider spreads,
To reason's eye refined clears up apace,
Ye vainly wise! ye blind presumptuous! now,
Confounded in the dust, adore that Power
And Wisdom—oft arraigned: see now the cause
Why unassuming worth in secret lived
And died neglected; why the good man's share
In life was gall and bitterness of soul;
Why the lone widow and her orphans pined
In starving solitude, while luxury
In palaces lay straining her low thought
To form unreal wants; why heaven-born truth
And moderation fair wore the red marks
Of superstition's scourge; why licensed pain,
That cruel spoiler, that embosomed foe,
Embittered all our bliss. Ye good distressed!
Ye noble few! who here unbending stand
Beneath life's pressure, yet bear up a while,
And what your bounded view, which only saw
A little part, deemed evil, is no more.
The storms of wintry time will quickly pass,
And one unbounded Spring encircle all.

(1726–1746)

Isaac Watts
1674–1748

◆

THE DAY OF JUDGMENT

AN ODE ATTEMPTED IN ENGLISH SAPPHIC*

When the fierce north wind with his airy forces
Rears up the Baltic to a foaming fury,
And the red lightning with a storm of hail comes
Rushing amain down,

How the poor sailors stand amazed and tremble,
While the hoarse thunder, like a bloody trumpet,
Roars a loud onset to the gaping waters,
Quick to devour them!

Such shall the noise be and the wild disorder,
(If things eternal may be like these earthly)
Such the dire terror, when the great Archangel
Shakes the creation,

Tears the strong pillars of the vault of heaven,
Breaks up old marble, the repose of princes;
See the graves open, and the bones arising,
Flames all around 'em!

Hark, the shrill outcries of the guilty wretches!
Lively bright horror and amazing anguish
Stare through their eyelids, while the living worm lies
Gnawing within them.

* A Sapphic is one of several verse forms used by the Greek poetess Sappho (c. 600 B.C.).

Thoughts like old vultures prey upon their heart-
 strings,
And the smart twinges, when the eye beholds the
Lofty Judge frowning, and a flood of vengeance
 Rolling afore him.

Hopeless immortals! how they scream and shiver,
While devils push them to the pit wide-yawning
Hideous and gloomy, to receive them headlong
 Down to the center.

Stop here, my fancy: (all away ye horrid
Doleful ideas); come, arise to Jesus;
How He sits God-like! and the saints around him
 Throned, yet adoring!

Oh may I sit there when he comes triumphant
Dooming the nations! then ascend to glory
While our hosannas all along the passage
 Shout the Redeemer.

(1706)

Edward Young
1683-1765

FROM

The Complaint, or Night Thoughts on Life, Death, and Immortality

NIGHT I

Tired Nature's sweet restorer, balmy Sleep!
He, like the world, his ready visit pays
Where Fortune smiles; the wretched he forsakes;
Swift on his downy pinion flies from woe,
And lights on lids unsullied with a tear.
 From short (as usual) and disturbed repose,
I wake: how happy they who wake no more!
Yet that were vain, if dreams infest the grave.
I wake, emerging from a sea of dreams
Tumultuous; where my wrecked desponding
 thought
From wave to wave of fancied misery
At random drove, her helm of reason lost.
Though now restored, 'tis only change of pain,
(A bitter change!) severer for severe.
The day too short for my distress; and Night,
Even in the zenith of her dark domain,
Is sunshine to the colour of my fate.
 Night, sable goddess! from her ebon throne,
In rayless majesty now stretches forth
Her leaden scepter o'er a slumbering world.
Silence, how dead! and darkness, how profound!
Nor eye nor listening ear an object finds;
Creation sleeps. 'Tis as the general pulse
Of life stood still, and Nature made a pause;
An awful pause! prophetic of her end.
And let her prophecy be soon fulfilled;
Fate! drop the curtain; I can lose no more.
 Silence and Darkness! solemn sisters! twins
From ancient Night, who nurse the tender thought
To reason, and on reason build resolve,
(That column of true majesty in man),
Assist me: I will thank you in the grave;
The grave, your kingdom: there this frame shall fall
A victim sacred to your dreary shrine.
But what are ye?—Thou who didst put to flight
Primeval silence, when the morning stars,
Exulted, shouted o'er the rising ball;
O Thou, whose word from solid darkness struck
That spark, the sun; strike wisdom from my soul;
My soul, which flies to Thee, her trust, her
 treasure,
As misers to their gold, while others rest.
 Through this opaque of nature and of soul,
This double night, transmit one pitying ray,
To lighten and to cheer. Oh, lead my mind,
(A mind that fain would wander from its woe),
Lead it through various scenes of life and death;
And from each scene, the noblest truths inspire.

Nor less inspire my conduct than my song;
Teach my best reason, reason; my best will
Teach rectitude; and fix my firm resolve
Wisdom to wed, and pay her long arrear:
Nor let the phial of thy vengeance, poured
On this devoted head, be poured in vain.
The bell strikes one. We take no note of time
But from its loss. To give it then a tongue
Is wise in man. As if an angel spoke,
I feel the solemn sound. If heard aright,
It is the knell of my departed hours:
Where are they? With the years beyond the flood.
It is the signal that demands dispatch:
How much is to be done? My hopes and fears
Start up alarmed, and o'er life's narrow verge
Look down—on what? a fathomless abyss;
A dread eternity! how surely mine!
And can eternity belong to me,
Poor pensioner on the bounties of an hour?
How poor, how rich, how abject, how august,
How complicate, how wonderful is man!
How passing wonder He who made him such!
Who centered in our make such strange
extremes!
From different natures marvellously mixed,
Connection exquisite of distant worlds!
Distinguished link in being's endless chain!
Midway from nothing to the Deity!
A beam ethereal, sullied and absorpt!
Though sullied and dishonoured, still divine!
Dim miniature of greatness absolute!
An heir of glory! a frail child of dust!
Helpless immortal! insect infinite!
A worm! a god!—I tremble at myself,
And in myself am lost! At home a stranger,
Thought wanders up and down, surprised, aghast,
And wondering at her own: how reason reels!
Oh, what a miracle to man is man,
Triumphantly distressed! what joy, what dread!
Alternately transported and alarmed!
What can preserve my life? or what destroy?
An angel's arm can't snatch me from the grave;
Legions of angels can't confine me there.
'Tis past conjecture; all things rise in proof:
While o'er my limbs sleep's soft dominion spread,
What though my soul fantastic measures trod
O'er fairy fields; or mourned along the gloom
Of pathless woods; or down the craggy steep
Hurled headlong, swam with pain the mantled pool;
Or scaled the cliff, or danced on hollow winds,
With antic shapes, wild natives of the brain?
Her ceaseless flight, though devious, speaks her
nature
Of subtler essence than the trodden clod;
Active, aërial, towering, unconfined,
Unfettered with her gross companion's fall.
Even silent night proclaims my soul immortal;
Even silent night proclaims eternal day.
For human weal, Heaven husbands all events;
Dull sleep instructs, nor sport vain dreams in vain.
Why then their loss deplore, that are not lost?
Why wanders wretched thought their tombs
around,
In infidel distress? Are angels there?
Slumbers, raked up in dust, ethereal fire?
They live! they greatly live a life on earth
Unkindled, unconceived; and from an eye
Of tenderness let heavenly pity fall
On me, more justly numbered with the dead.
This is the desert, this the solitude:
How populous, how vital, is the grave!
This is creation's melancholy vault,
The vale funereal, the sad cypress gloom;
The land of apparitions, empty shades!
All, all on earth is shadow, all beyond
Is substance; the reverse is Folly's creed:
How solid all, where change shall be no more!
This is the bud of being, the dim dawn,
The twilight of our day, the vestibule.
Life's theatre as yet is shut, and Death,
Strong Death, alone can heave the massy bar,
This gross impediment of clay remove,
And makes us embryos of existence free.
From real life, but little more remote
Is he, not yet a candidate for light,
The future embryo, slumbering in his sire.
Embryos we must be, till we burst the shell,
Yon ambient azure shell, and spring to life,
The life of gods, oh transport! and of man.
Yet man, fool man! here buries all his thoughts;
Inters celestial hopes without one sigh.
Prisoner of earth, and pent beneath the moon,
Here pinions all his wishes; winged by Heaven
To fly at infinite; and reach it there,
Where seraphs gather immortality,
On life's fair tree, fast by the throne of God.
What golden joys ambrosial clustering glow

NIGHT THOUGHTS. **52. phial:** a container for holding liquids. **53. devoted:** doomed.

In His full beam, and ripen for the just,
Where momentary ages are no more!
Where time, and pain, and chance, and death
 expire!
And is it in the flight of threescore years,
To push eternity from human thought,
And smother souls immortal in the dust?
A soul immortal, spending all her fires,
Wasting her strength in strenuous idleness,
Thrown into tumult, raptured or alarmed
At aught this scene can threaten or indulge,
Resembles ocean into tempest wrought,
To waft a feather or to drown a fly.
 Where falls this censure? It o'erwhelms myself;
How was my heart incrusted by the world!
Oh, how self-fettered was my groveling soul!
How, like a worm, was I wrapped round and
 round
In silken thought, which reptile Fancy spun,
Till darkened Reason lay quite clouded o'er
With soft conceit of endless comfort here,
Nor yet put forth her wings to reach the skies!
 Night-visions may befriend (as sung above):
Our waking dreams are fatal. How I dreamt
Of things impossible! (Could sleep do more?)
Of joys perpetual in perpetual change!
Of stable pleasures on the tossing wave!
Eternal sunshine in the storms of life!
How richly were my noontide trances hung
With gorgeous tapestries of pictured joys!
Joy behind joy, in endless perspective!
Till at Death's toll, whose restless iron tongue
Calls daily for his millions at a meal,
Starting I woke, and found myself undone.
Where now my frenzy's pompous furniture?
The cobwebbed cottage, with its ragged wall
Of mouldering mud, is royalty to me!
The spider's most attenuated thread
Is cord, is cable, to man's tender tie
On earthly bliss; it breaks at every breeze.
 Oh, ye blest scenes of permanent delight!
Full above measure! lasting beyond bound!
A perpetuity of bliss is bliss.
Could you, so rich in rapture, fear an end,
That ghastly thought would drink up all your joy,
And quite unparadise the realms of light.
Safe are you lodged above these rolling spheres,
The baleful influence of whose giddy dance
Sheds sad vicissitude on all beneath.
Here teems with revolutions every hour;
And rarely for the better; or the best,
More mortal than the common births of Fate.
Each Moment has its sickle, emulous
Of Time's enormous scythe, whose ample sweep
Strikes empires from the root; each Moment plays
His little weapon in the narrower sphere
Of sweet domestic comfort, and cuts down
The fairest bloom of sublunary bliss.
 Bliss! sublunary bliss!—proud words, and vain!
Implicit treason to divine decree!
A bold invasion of the rights of Heaven!
I clasped the phantoms, and I found them air.
Oh, had I weighed it ere my fond embrace!
What darts of agony had missed my heart!
 Death! great proprietor of all! 'tis thine
To tread out empire and to quench the stars.
The sun himself by thy permission shines,
And one day thou shalt pluck him from his sphere.
Amid such mighty plunder, why exhaust
Thy partial quiver on a mark so mean?
Why thy peculiar rancour wreaked on me?
Insatiate archer! could not one suffice?
Thy shaft flew thrice; and thrice my peace was slain;
And thrice, ere thrice yon moon had filled her horn.
O Cynthia! why so pale? dost thou lament
Thy wretched neighbour? Grieve to see thy wheel
Of ceaseless change outwhirled in human life?
How wanes my borrowed bliss! from Fortune's smile
Precarious courtesy! not virtue's sure,
Self-given, solar ray of sound delight.
 In every varied posture, place, and hour,
How widowed every thought of every joy!
Thought, busy thought! too busy for my peace!
Through the dark postern of time long elapsed
Led softly, by the stillness of the night—
Led like a murderer (and such it proves!)
Strays (wretched rover!) o'er the pleasing past;
In quest of wretchedness perversely strays;
And finds all desert now; and meets the ghosts
Of my departed joys; a numerous train!
I rue the riches of my former fate;
Sweet comfort's blasted clusters I lament;
I tremble at the blessings once so dear;
And every pleasure pains me to the heart.
 Yet why complain? or why complain for one?

212. thy shaft . . . thrice: Young had suffered three great losses, most notably the deaths of his wife and stepdaughter. **214. Cynthia:** goddess of the moon. **223. postern:** a private gate or entrance.

Hangs out the sun his lustre but for me,
The single man? Are angels all beside?
I mourn for millions: 'tis the common lot;
In this shape or in that has fate entailed
The mother's throes on all of woman born,
Not more the children, than sure heirs, of
pain.
War, famine, pest, volcano, storm, and fire,
Intestine broils, Oppression with her heart
Wrapped up in triple brass, besiege mankind.
God's image disinherited of day,
Here, plunged in mines, forgets a sun was made.
There, beings deathless as their haughty lord,
Are hammered to the galling oar for life;
And plough the winter's wave, and reap despair.
Some, for hard masters, broken under arms,
In battle lopped away, with half their limbs,
Beg bitter bread through realms their valour saved,
If so the tyrant, or his minion, doom.
Want and incurable disease (fell pair!)
On hopeless multitudes remorseless seize
At once; and make a refuge of the grave.
How groaning hospitals eject their dead!
What numbers groan for sad admission there!
What numbers, once in Fortune's lap high-fed,
Solicit the cold hand of Charity!
To shock us more, solicit it in vain!
Ye silken sons of Pleasure! since in pains
You rue more modish visits, visit here,
And breathe from your debauch: give, and reduce
Surfeit's dominion o'er you; but, so great
Your impudence, you blush at what is right.
Happy! did sorrow seize on such alone.
Not prudence can defend or virtue save;
Disease invades the chastest temperance;
And punishment the guiltless; and alarm
Through thickest shades pursues the fond of
peace.
Man's caution often into danger turns,
And, his guard falling, crushes him to death.
Not Happiness itself makes good her name!
Our very wishes give us not our wish.
How distant oft the thing we doat on most,
From that for which we doat, felicity!
The smoothest course of nature has its pains;
And truest friends, through error, wound our rest.
Without misfortune, what calamities!
And what hostilities, without a foe!
Nor are foes wanting to the best on earth.
But endless is the list of human ills,
And sighs might sooner fail, than cause to sigh.
A part how small of the terraqueous globe
Is tenanted by man! the rest a waste,
Rocks, deserts, frozen seas, and burning sands:
Wild haunts of monsters, poisons, stings, and death.
Such is earth's melancholy map! But, far
More sad! this earth is a true map of man.
So bounded are its haughty lord's delights
To woe's wide empire; where deep troubles toss,
Loud sorrows howl, envenomed passions bite,
Ravenous calamities our vitals seize,
And threatening Fate wide opens to devour.
What then am I, who sorrow for myself?
In age, in infancy, from others' aid
Is all our hope; to teach us to be kind.
That, Nature's first, last lesson to mankind;
The selfish heart deserves the pain it feels;
More generous sorrow, while it sinks, exalts;
And conscious virtue mitigates the pang.
Nor virtue, more than prudence, bids me give
Swoln thought a second channel; who divide,
They weaken too, the torrent of their grief.
Take then, O world! thy much-indebted tear;
How sad a sight is human happiness,
To those whose thought can pierce beyond an hour!
O thou! whate'er thou art, whose heart exults!
Wouldst thou I should congratulate thy fate?
I know thou wouldst; thy pride demands it
from me.
Let thy pride pardon what thy nature needs,
The salutary censure of a friend.
Thou happy wretch! by blindness art thou blessed;
By dotage dandled to perpetual smiles.
Know, smiler! at thy peril art thou pleased;
Thy pleasure is the promise of thy pain.
Misfortune, like a creditor severe,
But rises in demand for her delay;
She makes a scourge of past prosperity,
To sting thee more and double thy distress.
Lorenzo, Fortune makes her court to thee;
Thy fond heart dances, while the siren sings.
Dear is thy welfare; think me not unkind;
I would not damp, but to secure thy joys.

252. minion: servant. **253. fell:** cruel. **264. Surfeit:** excess.

284. terraqueous: consisting of land and water. **314. dandled:** pampered. **321. Lorenzo:** the young ne'er-do-well to whom the poet speaks.

Think not that fear is sacred to the storm;
Stand on thy guard against the smiles of Fate.
Is Heaven tremendous in its frowns? Most sure;
And in its favours formidable too:
Its favours here are trials, not rewards;
A call to duty, not discharge from care;
And should alarm us, full as much as woes;
Awake us to their cause and consequence;
And make us tremble, weighed with our desert;
Awe Nature's tumult and chastise her joys,
Lest while we clasp, we kill them; nay, invert
To worse than simple misery, their charms.
Revolted joys, like foes in civil war,
Like bosom friendships to resentments soured,
With rage envenomed rise against our peace.
Beware what earth calls happiness; beware
All joys, but joys that never can expire.
Who builds on less than an immortal base,
Fond as he seems, condemns his joys to death.
  Mine died with thee, Philander! thy last sight
Dissolved the charm; the disenchanted earth
Lost all her lustre. Where her glittering towers?
Her golden mountains, where? all darkened down
To naked waste; a dreary vale of tears:
The great magician's dead! Thou poor, pale piece
Of outcast earth, in darkness! what a change
From yesterday! Thy darling hope so near
(Long-laboured prize!), oh, how ambition flushed
Thy glowing cheek! ambition truly great,
Of virtuous praise. Death's subtle seed within,
(Sly, treacherous miner!) working in the dark,
Smiled at thy well-concerted scheme, and beckoned
The worm to riot on that rose so red,
Unfaded ere it fell—one moment's prey!
  Man's foresight is conditionally wise;
Lorenzo, wisdom into folly turns
Oft, the first instant its idea fair
To labouring thought is born. How dim our eye!
The present moment terminates our sight;
Clouds, thick as those on doomsday, drown the next;
We penetrate, we prophesy in vain.
Time is dealt out by particles; and each,
Ere mingled with the streaming sands of life,
By fate's inviolable oath is sworn
Deep silence, "Where eternity begins."
  By Nature's law, what may be, may be now;
There's no prerogative in human hours.
In human hearts what bolder thought can rise
Than man's presumption on to-morrow's dawn?
Where is to-morrow? In another world.
For numbers this is certain; the reverse
Is sure to none; and yet on this perhaps,
This peradventure, infamous for lies,
As on a rock of adamant, we build
Our mountain hopes; spin our eternal schemes,
As we the fatal sisters could outspin,
And, big with life's futurities, expire.
  Not even Philander had bespoke his shroud.
Nor had he cause; a warning was denied:
How many fall as sudden, not as safe!
As sudden, though for years admonished home.
Of human ills the last extreme beware—
Beware, Lorenzo! a slow-sudden death.
How dreadful that deliberate surprise!
Be wise to-day; 'tis madness to defer;
Next day the fatal precedent will plead;
Thus on, till wisdom is pushed out of life.
Procrastination is the thief of time;
Year after year it steals, till all are fled,
And to the mercies of a moment leaves
The vast concerns of an eternal scene.
If not so frequent, would not this be strange?
That 'tis so frequent, this is stranger still.
  Of man's miraculous mistakes, this bears
The palm, "That all men are about to live,"
Forever on the brink of being born.
All pay themselves the compliment to think
They one day shall not drivel: and their pride
On this reversion takes up ready praise;
At least, their own; their future selves applauds;
How excellent that life they ne'er will lead!
Time lodged in their own hands is Folly's vails;
That lodged in Fate's, to wisdom they consign;
The thing they can't but purpose, they postpone;
'Tis not in folly, not to scorn a fool;
And scarce in human wisdom to do more.
All promise is poor dilatory man,
And that through every stage: when young, indeed,
In full content we sometimes nobly rest,
Unanxious for ourselves; and only wish,
As duteous sons, our fathers were more wise.

344. Philander: obviously a reference to still a third deceased friend or relative of Young. Philander has not been satisfactorily identified.

402. drivel: speak foolishly; babble. **403. reversion:** anticipation of a future benefit. **406. vails:** gifts.

At thirty man suspects himself a fool;
Knows it at forty, and reforms his plan;
At fifty chides his infamous delay,
Pushes his prudent purpose to resolve;
In all the magnanimity of thought
Resolves, and re-resolves; then dies the same.
And why? Because he thinks himself immortal.
All men think all men mortal, but themselves;
Themselves, when some alarming shock of Fate
Strikes through their wounded hearts the sudden dread;
But their hearts wounded, like the wounded air,
Soon close; where passed the shaft, no trace is found.
As from the wing no scar the sky retains,
The parted wave no furrow from the keel;
So dies in human heart the thought of death.
Even with the tender tear which Nature sheds
O'er those we love, we drop it in their grave.
Can I forget Philander? That were strange!
Oh, my full heart—But should I give it vent,
The longest night, though longer far, would fail,
And the lark listen to my midnight song.
The sprightly lark's shrill matin wakes the morn;
Grief's sharpest thorn hard-pressing on my breast,
I strive, with wakeful melody, to cheer
The sullen gloom, sweet Philomel! like thee,
And call the stars to listen: every star
Is deaf to mine, enamoured of thy lay.
Yet be not vain; there are, who thine excel,
And charm through distant ages: wrapped in shade,
Prisoner of darkness! to the silent hours,
How often I repeat their rage divine,
To lull my griefs, and steal my heart from woe!
I roll their raptures, but not catch their fire.
Dark, though not blind, like thee, Maeonides!
Or, Milton! thee; ah, could I reach your strain!
Or his, who made Maeonides our own,
Man too he sung: immortal man I sing;
Oft bursts my song beyond the bounds of life;
What now but immortality can please?
Oh, had he pressed his theme, pursued the track,
Which opens out of darkness into day!
Oh, had he, mounted on his wing of fire,
Soared where I sink, and sung immortal man!
How had it blessed mankind, and rescued me!

(1742)

437. matin: morning song.

440. Philomel: nightingale. **449. Maeonides:** Homer. **451. his . . . own:** a reference to Alexander Pope, translator of Homer. **452. Man:** Pope's *Essay on Man.*

Robert Blair
1699-1746

◆

FROM
The Grave

The house appointed for all living.
—Job, xxx, 23

Whilst some affect the sun and some the shade,
Some flee the city, some the hermitage,
Their aims as various as the roads they take
In journeying through life—the task be mine
To paint the gloomy horrors of the tomb,
The appointed place of rendezvous, where all
These travellers meet. Thy succours I implore,
Eternal King! whose potent arm sustains
The keys of hell and death. The Grave, dread thing!
Men shiver when thou'rt named; Nature, appalled,
Shakes off her wonted firmness. Ah! how dark
Thy long-extended realms and rueful wastes,
Where naught but silence reigns, and night, dark night,
Dark as was chaos ere the infant sun

Was rolled together, or had tried his beams
Athwart the gloom profound! Thy sickly taper
By glimmering through thy low-browed misty vaults
(Furred round with mouldy damps and ropy slime)
Lets fall a supernumerary horror,
And only serves to make thy night more
irksome.
Well do I know thee by thy trusty yew,
Cheerless, unsocial plant! that loves to dwell
Midst skulls and coffins, epitaphs and worms;
Where light-heeled ghosts and visionary shades,
Beneath the wan cold moon (as fame reports)
Embodied thick, perform their mystic rounds.
No other merriment, dull tree! is thine.
See yonder hallowed fane—the pious work
Of names once famed, now dubious or forgot,
And buried midst the wreck of things which
were;
There lie interred the more illustrious dead.
The wind is up—hark! how it howls! Methinks
Till now I never heard a sound so dreary.
Doors creak, and windows clap, and night's foul
bird,
Rooked in the spire, screams loud; the gloomy
aisles,
Black-plastered, and hung round with shreds of
'scutcheons
And tattered coats of arms, send back the sound
Laden with heavier airs, from the low vaults,
The mansions of the dead. Roused from their
slumbers,
In grim array the grisly spectres rise,
Grin horrible, and obstinately sullen
Pass and repass, hushed as the foot of night.
Again the screech-owl shrieks—ungracious sound!
I'll hear no more; it makes one's blood run chill.
Quite round the pile, a row of reverend elms
(Coeval near with that) all ragged show,
Long lashed by the rude winds; some rift half down
Their branchless trunks, others so thin at top
That scarce two crows could lodge in the same tree.
Strange things, the neighbours say, have happened
here:
Wild shrieks have issued from the hollow tombs;
Dead men have come again, and walked about;
And the great bell has tolled, unrung, untouched.
(Such tales their cheer, at wake or gossiping,
When it draws near to witching time of night.)
Oft in the lone churchyard at night I've seen,
By glimpse of moonshine checkering through the
trees,
The school-boy, with his satchel in his hand,
Whistling aloud to bear his courage up,
And lightly tripping o'er the long flat stones
(With nettles skirted and with moss o'ergrown)
That tell in homely phrase who lie below.
Sudden he starts, and hears, or thinks he hears,
The sound of something purring at his heels;
Full fast he flies, and dares not look behind him,
Till out of breath he overtakes his fellows;
Who gather round, and wonder at the tale
Of horrid apparition, tall and ghastly,
That walks at dead of night, or takes his stand
O'er some new-opened grave, and (strange to
tell!)
Evanishes at crowing of the cock.
The new-made widow too I've sometimes spied,
Sad sight! slow moving o'er the prostrate dead;
Listless she crawls along in doleful black,
Whilst bursts of sorrow gush from either eye,
Fast falling down her now untasted cheek.
Prone on the lowly grave of the dear man
She drops; whilst busy-meddling memory
In barbarous succession musters up
The past endearments of their softer hours,
Tenacious of its theme. Still, still she thinks
She sees him, and indulging the fond thought,
Clings yet more closely to the senseless turf,
Nor heeds the passenger who looks that way.
Invidious Grave—how dost thou rend in sunder
Whom love has knit, and sympathy made one!
A tie more stubborn far than nature's band.
Friendship! mysterious cement of the soul!
Sweetener of life, and solder of society!
I owe thee much. Thou has deserved from
me
Far, far beyond what I can ever pay.
Oft have I proved the labours of thy love,
And the warm efforts of the gentle heart,
Anxious to please. Oh, when my friend and I
In some thick wood have wandered heedless on,
Hid from the vulgar eye, and sat us down
Upon the sloping cowslip-covered bank,
Where the pure limpid stream has slid along
In grateful errors through the underwood,
Sweet-murmuring—methought the shrill-tongued
thrush

THE GRAVE. **19. supernumerary:** extra. **28. fane:** temple. **35. Rooked:** cowering. **36. 'scutcheons:** shields.

Mended his song of love; the sooty blackbird
Mellowed his pipe and softened every note;
The eglantine smelled sweeter, and the rose
Assumed a dye more deep; whilst every flower
Vied with its fellow plant in luxury
Of dress. Oh, then the longest summer's day
Seemed too, too much in haste; still the full heart
Had not imparted half; 'twas happiness
Too exquisite to last! Of joys departed,
Not to return, how painful the remembrance!
Dull Grave! thou spoil'st the dance of youthful blood,
Strik'st out the dimple from the cheek of mirth,
And every smirking feature from the face;
Branding our laughter with the name of madness.
Where are the jesters now? the men of health
Complexionally pleasant? Where the droll,
Whose very look and gesture was a joke
To clapping theatres and shouting crowds,
And made even thick-lipped musing Melancholy
To gather up her face into a smile
Before she was aware? Ah! sullen now,
And dumb as the green turf that covers them!
Where are the mighty thunderbolts of war,
The Roman Cæsars and the Grecian chiefs,
The boast of story? Where the hot-brained youth,
Who the tiara at his pleasure tore
From kings of all the then discovered globe,
And cried, forsooth, because his arm was hampered,
And had not room enough to do its work?
Alas, how slim—dishonourably slim—
And crammed into a space we blush to name!
Proud Royalty! How altered in thy looks!
How blank thy features, and how wan thy hue!
Son of the morning! whither art thou gone?
Where hast thou hid thy many-spangled head,
And the majestic menace of thine eyes,
Felt from afar? Pliant and powerless now;
Like new-born infant wound up in his swathes,
Or victim tumbled flat upon its back,
That throbs beneath the sacrificer's knife;
Mute must thou bear the strife of little tongues,
And coward insults of the base-born crowd,
That grudge a privilege thou never hadst,
But only hoped for in the peaceful grave—
Of being unmolested and alone!
Arabia's gums and odoriferous drugs,
And honours by the heralds duly paid
In mode and form, even to a very scruple;
(Oh cruel irony!) these come too late,
And only mock whom they were meant to honour!
Surely there's not a dungeon-slave that's buried
In the highway, unshrouded and uncoffined,
But lies as soft and sleeps as sound as he.
Sorry preëminence of high descent
Above the vulgar-born, to rot in state!
But see! the well-plumed hearse comes nodding on,
Stately and slow; and properly attended
By the whole sable tribe, that painful watch
The sick man's door, and live upon the dead,
By letting out their persons by the hour
To mimic sorrow, when the heart's not sad.
How rich the trappings, now they're all unfurled
And glittering in the sun! Triumphant entries
Of conquerors, and coronation pomps
In glory scarce exceed. Great gluts of people
Retard the unwieldy show, whilst from the casements
And houses' tops, ranks behind ranks close-wedged
Hang bellying o'er. But tell us, why this waste?
Why this ado in earthing up a carcass
That's fallen into disgrace, and in the nostril
Smells horrible? Ye undertakers! tell us,
Midst all the gorgeous figures you exhibit,
Why is the principal concealed, for which
You make this mighty stir? 'Tis wisely done;
What would offend the eye in a good picture,
The painter casts discreetly into shades.
Proud lineage! now how little thou appearest!
Below the envy of the private man!
Honour, that meddlesome officious ill,
Pursues thee even to death, nor there stops short!
Strange persecution, when the grave itself
Is no protection from rude sufferance!
Absurd! to think to overreach the grave,
And from the wreck of names to rescue ours!
The best-concerted schemes men lay for fame
Die fast away; only themselves die faster.
The far-famed sculptor and the laurelled bard,
Those bold insurancers of deathless fame,
Supply their little feeble aids in vain—
The tapering pyramid, the Egyptian's pride,
And wonder of the world, whose spiky top
Has wounded the thick cloud, and long outlived
The angry shaking of the winter's storm;
Yet, spent at last by the injuries of heaven,
Shattered with age and furrowed o'er with years,

The mystic cone, with hieroglyphics crusted,
Gives way. Oh, lamentable sight! At once
The labour of whole ages lumbers down,
A hideous and misshapen length of ruins!
Sepulchral columns wrestle but in vain
With all-subduing Time; her cankering hand
With calm deliberate malice wasteth them.
Worn on the edge of days, the brass consumes,
The busto moulders, and the deep-cut marble,
Unsteady to the steel, gives up its charge!
Ambition, half convicted of her folly,
Hangs down the head, and reddens at the tale.
Here all the mighty troublers of the earth,
Who swam to sovereign rule through seas of blood,
The oppressive, sturdy, man-destroying villains
Who ravaged kingdoms and laid empires waste
And in a cruel wantonness of power
Thinned states of half their people, and gave up
To want the rest; now, like a storm that's spent,
Lie hushed, and meanly sneak behind thy covert.
Vain thought! to hide them from the general scorn
That haunts and dogs them like an injured ghost
Implacable! Here too the petty tyrant
Of scant domains geographer ne'er noticed,
And, well for neighbouring grounds, of arm as short;
Who fixed his iron talons on the poor,
And gripped them like some lordly beast of prey,
Deaf to the forceful cries of gnawing hunger,
And piteous plaintive voice of misery
(As if a slave was not a shred of nature,
Of the same common nature with his lord)
Now tame and humble, like a child that's whipped,
Shakes hands with dust, and calls the worm his kinsman;
Nor pleads his rank and birthright. Under ground
Precedency's a jest; vassal and lord,
Grossly familiar, side by side consume.
When self-esteem, or others' adulation,
Would cunningly persuade us we were something
Above the common level of our kind,
The Grave gainsays the smooth-complexioned flattery,
And with blunt truth acquaints us what we are.
Beauty! thou pretty plaything! dear deceit!
That steals so softly o'er the stripling's heart,
And gives it a new pulse unknown before!
The Grave discredits thee. Thy charms expunged,
Thy roses faded, and thy lilies soiled,
What hast thou more to boast of? Will thy lovers
Flock round thee now, to gaze and do thee homage?
Methinks I see thee with thy head low laid;
Whilst, surfeited upon thy damask cheek,
The high-fed worm, in lazy volumes rolled,
Riots unscared. For this was all thy caution?
For this thy painful labours at thy glass,
To improve those charms and keep them in repair,
For which the spoiler thanks thee not? Foul feeder!
Coarse fare and carrion please thee full as well,
And leave as keen a relish on the sense.
Look, how the fair one weeps! The conscious tears
Stand thick as dew-drops on the bells of flowers—
Honest effusion! The swoln heart in vain
Works hard to put a gloss on its distress.

. . .

But hold! I've gone too far; too much discovered
My father's nakedness and Nature's shame.
Here let me pause, and drop an honest tear,
One burst of filial duty and condolence,
O'er all those ample deserts Death hath spread,
This chaos of mankind! O great man-eater!
Whose every day is carnival, not sated yet!
Unheard of epicure, without a fellow!
The veriest gluttons do not always cram;
Some intervals of abstinence are sought
To edge the appetite—thou seekest none!
Methinks the countless swarms thou hast devoured,
And thousands that each hour thou gobblest up,
This, less than this, might gorge thee to the full.
But ah! rapacious still, thou gap'st for more;
Like one, whole days defrauded of his meals,
On whom lank Hunger lays her skinny hand,
And whets to keenest eagerness his cravings;
As if diseases, massacres, and poison,
Famine, and war, were not thy caterers!
But know that thou must render up thy dead,
And with high interest too!—They are not thine,
But only in thy keeping for a season,
Till the great promised day of restitution;
When loud diffusive sound from brazen trump
Of strong-lunged cherub shall alarm thy captives,
And rouse the long, long sleepers into life,

204. busto: bust.

Daylight, and liberty.—
Then must thy gates fly open, and reveal
The mines that lay long forming under ground,
In their dark cells immured; but now full ripe,
And pure as silver from the crucible,
That twice has stood the torture of the fire,
And inquisition of the forge. We know
The illustrious Deliverer of mankind,
The Son of God, thee foiled. Him in thy power
Thou couldst not hold; self-vigorous he rose,
And, shaking off thy fetters, soon retook
Those spoils his voluntary yielding lent.
Sure pledge of our releasement from thy thrall—
Twice twenty days he sojourned here on earth,
And showed himself alive to chosen witnesses,
By proofs so strong that the most slow-assenting
Had not a scruple left. This having done,
He mounted up to Heaven. Methinks I see him
Climb the aërial heights, and glide along
Athwart the severing clouds; but the faint eye,
Flung backwards in the chase, soon drops its hold,
Disabled quite, and jaded with pursuing.
Heaven's portals wide expand to let him in,
Nor are his friends shut out; as some great prince
Not for himself alone procures admission,
But for his train; it was his royal will
That where he is there should his followers be.
Death only lies between, a gloomy path,
Made yet more gloomy by our coward fears!
But not untrod, nor tedious; the fatigue
Will soon go off. Besides, there's no by-road
To bliss. Then why, like ill-conditioned children,
Start we at transient hardships in the way
That leads to purer air and softer skies,
And a ne'er-setting sun? Fools that we are!
We wish to be where sweets unwithering bloom,
But straight our wish revoke, and will not go.
So have I seen, upon a summer's even,
Fast by the rivulet's brink, a youngster play:
How wishfully he looks to stem the tide!
This moment resolute, next unresolved;
At last he dips his foot, but as he dips
His fears redouble, and he runs away
From the inoffensive stream, unmindful now
Of all the flowers that paint the further bank,
And smiled so sweet of late.—Thrice welcome Death!
That after many a painful bleeding step
Conducts us to our home, and lands us safe
On the long-wished-for shore. Prodigious change!
Our bane turned to a blessing! Death disarmed
Loses her fellness quite; all thanks to him
Who scourged the venom out! Sure the last end
Of the good man is peace. How calm his exit!
Night-dews fall not more gently to the ground,
Nor weary worn-out winds expire so soft.
Behold him in the evening-tide of life,
A life well spent, whose early care it was
His riper years should not upbraid his green;
But unperceived degrees he wears away,
Yet like the sun seems larger at his setting!
High in his faith and hopes, look how he reaches
After the prize in view, and, like a bird
That's hampered, struggles hard to get away!
Whilst the glad gates of sight are wide expanded
To let new glories in, the first fair fruits
Of the fast-coming harvest. Then—oh then
Each earth-born joy grows vile or disappears,
Shrunk to a thing of naught. Oh, how he longs
To have his passport signed and be dismissed!
'Tis done, and now he's happy! The glad soul
Has not a wish uncrowned. E'en the lag flesh
Rests too in hope of meeting once again
Its better half, never to sunder more.
Nor shall it hope in vain; the time draws on
When not a single spot of burial-earth
Whether on land or in the spacious sea,
But must give back its long-committed dust
Inviolate, and faithfully shall these
Make up the full account; not the least atom
Embezzled or mislaid of the whole tale.
Each soul shall have a body ready-furnished,
And each shall have his own. Hence, ye profane!
Ask not how this can be. Sure the same power
That reared the piece at first, and took it down,
Can re-assemble the loose scattered parts,
And put them as they were. Almighty God
Has done much more, nor is his arm impaired
Through length of days; and what he can he will:
His faithfulness stands bound to see it done.
When the dread trumpet sounds, the slumbering dust,
Not unattentive to the call, shall wake;
And every joint possess its proper place,
With a new elegance of form, unknown

711. fellness: cruelty. **731. lag:** lagging.

To its first state. Nor shall the conscious soul
Mistake its partner; but, amidst the crowd
Singling its other half, into its arms
Shall rush with all the impatience of a man
That's new come home, who having long been absent,
With haste runs over every different room,
In pain to see the whole. Thrice happy meeting!
Nor time nor death shall ever part them more.

'Tis but a night, a long and moonless night,
We make the grave our bed, and then are gone.
Thus at the shut of even, the weary bird
Leaves the wide air, and in some lonely brake
Cowers down and dozes till the dawn of day;
Then claps his well-fledged wings and bears away.

(c. 1730, 1743)

765. brake: a clump of bushes.

Mark Akenside
1721–1770

◆

FROM

The Pleasures of Imagination

ARGUMENT OF THE FIRST BOOK

The subject proposed. Difficulty of treating it poetically. The ideas of the divine mind, the origin of every quality pleasing to the imagination. The natural variety of constitution in the minds of men; with its final cause. The idea of a fine imagination, and the state of the mind in the enjoyment of those pleasures which it affords. All the primary pleasures of the imagination result from the perception of greatness, or wonderfulness, or beauty in objects. The pleasure from greatness, with its final cause. Pleasure from beauty, with its final cause. The connection of beauty with truth and good, applied to the conduct of life. Invitation to the study of moral philosophy. The different degrees of beauty in different species of objects: colour; shape; natural concretes; vegetables; animals; the mind. The sublime, the fair, the wonderful of the mind. The connection of the imagination and the moral faculty. Conclusion.

BOOK THE FIRST

With what attractive charms this goodly frame
Of nature touches the consenting hearts
Of mortal men; and what the pleasing stores
Which beauteous imitation thence derives
To deck the poet's or the painter's toil,
My verse unfolds. Attend, ye gentle powers
Of musical delight! and while I sing
Your gifts, your honours, dance around my strain.
Thou, smiling queen of every tuneful breast,
Indulgent Fancy! from the fruitful banks
Of Avon, whence thy rosy fingers cull
Fresh flowers and dews to sprinkle on the turf
Where Shakespeare lies, be present; and with thee
Let Fiction come, upon her vagrant wings
Wafting ten thousand colours through the air,
Which by the glances of her magic eye
She blends and shifts at will through countless forms,
Her wild creation. Goddess of the lyre,
Which rules the accents of the moving sphere,
Wilt thou, eternal Harmony! descend
And join this festive train? for with thee comes
The guide, the guardian of their lovely sports,
Majestic Truth; and where Truth deigns to come,
Her sister Liberty will not be far.
Be present, all ye Genii who conduct
The wandering footsteps of the youthful bard,
New to your springs and shades; who touch his ear
With finer sounds; who heighten to his eye
The bloom of nature, and before him turn
The gayest, happiest attitude of things.

Oft have the laws of each poetic strain
The critic-verse employed; yet still unsung
Lay this prime subject, though importing most
A poet's name: for fruitless is the attempt,
By dull obedience and by creeping toil
Obscure to conquer the severe ascent
Of high Parnassus. Nature's kindling breath
Must fire the chosen genius; Nature's hand
Must string his nerves, and imp his eagle-wings,
Impatient of the painful steep, to soar
High as the summit; there to breathe at large
Ethereal air, with bards and sages old,
Immortal sons of praise. These flattering scenes,
To this neglected labour court my song;
Yet not unconscious what a doubtful task
To paint the finest features of the mind,
And to most subtile and mysterious things
Give colour, strength, and motion. But the love
Of Nature and the Muses bids explore,
Through secret paths erewhile untrod by man,
The fair poetic region, to detect
Untasted springs, to drink inspiring draughts,
And shade my temples with unfading flowers
Culled from the laureate vale's profound recess,
Where never poet gained a wreath before.

From Heaven my strains begin; from Heaven descends
The flame of genius to the human breast,
And love and beauty, and poetic joy
And inspiration. Ere the radiant sun
Sprang from the east, or 'mid the vault of night
The moon suspended her serener lamp;
Ere mountains, woods, or streams adorned the globe,
Or Wisdom taught the sons of men her lore;
Then lived the Almighty One: then, deep-retired
In his unfathomed essence, viewed the forms,
The forms eternal of created things;
The radiant sun, the moon's nocturnal lamp,
The mountains, woods and streams, the rolling globe,
And Wisdom's mien celestial. From the first
Of days, on them his love divine he fixed,
His admiration: till in time complete,
What he admired and loved, his vital smile
Unfolded into being. Hence the breath
Of life informing each organic frame,
Hence the green earth and wild resounding waves;
Hence light and shade alternate, warmth and cold,
And clear autumnal skies and vernal showers,
And all the fair variety of things.

But not alike to every mortal eye
Is this great scene unveiled. For since the claims
Of social life to different labours urge
The active powers of man, with wise intent
The hand of Nature on peculiar minds
Imprints a different bias, and to each
Decrees its province in the common toil.
To some she taught the fabric of the sphere,
The changeful moon, the circuit of the stars,
The golden zones of heaven; to some she gave
To weigh the moment of eternal things,
Of time and space and fate's unbroken chain,
And will's quick impulse; others by the hand
She led o'er vales and mountains, to explore
What healing virtue swells the tender veins
Of herbs and flowers; or what the beams of morn
Draw forth, distilling from the clifted rind
In balmy tears. But some to higher hopes
Were destined; some within a finer mold
She wrought, and tempered with a purer flame.
To these the Sire Omnipotent unfolds
The world's harmonious volume, there to read
The transcript of himself. On every part
They trace the bright impressions of his hand:
In earth or air, the meadow's purple stores,
The moon's mild radiance, or the virgin's form
Blooming with rosy smiles, they see portrayed
That uncreated beauty which delights
The Mind Supreme. They also feel her charms,
Enamoured; they partake the eternal joy.

For as old Memnon's image, long renowned
By fabling Nilus, to the quivering touch
Of Titan's ray, with each repulsive string
Consenting, sounded through the warbling air
Unbidden strains, even so did Nature's hand
To certain species of external things,
Attune the finer organs of the mind:
So the glad impulse of congenial powers,
Or of sweet sound, or fair proportioned form,
The grace of motion, or the bloom of light,

PLEASURES OF IMAGINATION. **95. clifted rind:** split or cut exterior. **109–11. old Memnon:** a reference to the great statue of the mythical King Memnon in Egypt, a statue which supposedly poured forth sound when struck by the rays of the sun rising.

Thrills through imagination's tender frame,
From nerve to nerve; all naked and alive
They catch the spreading rays; till now the soul
At length discloses every tuneful spring,
To that harmonious movement from without
Responsive. Then the inexpressive strain
Diffuses its enchantment: Fancy dreams
Of sacred fountains and Elysian groves,
And vales of bliss; the intellectual power
Bends from his awful throne a wondering ear,
And smiles; the passions, gently soothed away,
Sink to divine repose, and love and joy
Alone are waking; love and joy, serene
As airs that fan the summer. Oh, attend,
Whoe'er thou art, whom these delights can touch,
Whose candid bosom the refining love
Of Nature warms, oh, listen to my song;
And I will guide thee to her favourite walks,
And teach thy solitude her voice to hear,
And point her loveliest features to thy view.

Know then, whate'er of Nature's pregnant stores,
Whate'er of mimic Art's reflected forms
With love and admiration thus inflame
The powers of Fancy, her delighted sons
To three illustrious orders have referred;
Three sister-graces, whom the painter's hand,
The poet's tongue confesses: the sublime,
The wonderful, the fair. I see them dawn!
I see the radiant visions, where they rise,
More lovely than when Lucifer displays
His beaming forehead through the gates of morn,
To lead the train of Phoebus and the spring.

Say, why was man so eminently raised
Amid the vast creation; why ordained
Through life and death to dart his piercing eye,
With thoughts beyond the limit of his frame;
But that the Omnipotent might send him forth
In sight of mortal and immortal powers,
As on a boundless theatre, to run
The great career of justice; to exalt
His generous aim to all diviner deeds;
To chase each partial purpose from his breast;
And through the mists of passion and of sense,
And through the tossing tide of chance and pain,
To hold his course unfaltering, while the voice
Of truth and virtue, up the steep ascent
Of nature, calls him to his high reward,
The applauding smile of Heaven? Else wherefore burns
In mortal bosoms this unquenchèd hope,
That breathes from day to day sublimer things,
And mocks possession? Wherefore darts the mind,
With such resistless ardour to embrace
Majestic forms; impatient to be free,
Spurning the gross control of wilful might;
Proud of the strong contention of her toils;
Proud to be daring? Who but rather turns
To heaven's broad fire his unconstrainèd view,
Than to the glimmering of a waxen flame?
Who that, from Alpine heights, his labouring eye
Shoots round the wide horizon, to survey
Nilus or Ganges rolling his bright wave
Through mountains, plains, through empires black with shade
And continents of sand; will turn his gaze
To mark the windings of a scanty rill
That murmurs at his feet? The high-born soul
Disdains to rest her heaven-aspiring wing
Beneath its native quarry. Tired of earth
And this diurnal scene, she springs aloft
Through fields of air; pursues the flying storm;
Rides on the volleyed lightning through the heavens;
Or, yoked with whirlwinds and the northern blast,
Sweeps the long tract of day. Then high she soars
The blue profound, and hovering round the sun
Beholds him pouring the redundant stream
Of light; beholds his unrelenting sway
Bend the reluctant planets to absolve
The fated rounds of time. Thence far effused
She darts her swiftness up the long career
Of devious comets; through its burning signs
Exulting measures the perennial wheel
Of nature, and looks back on all the stars,
Whose blended light, as with a milky zone,
Invests the orient. Now amazed she views
The empyreal waste, where happy spirits hold,
Beyond this concave heaven, their calm abode;
And fields of radiance, whose unfading light
Has travelled the profound six thousand years,
Nor yet arrives in sight of mortal things.
Even on the barriers of the world untired
She meditates the eternal depth below;
Till half recoiling, down the headlong steep
She plunges; soon o'erwhelmed and swallowed up

202. empyreal: heavenly.

In that immense of being. There her hopes
Rest at the fated goal. For from the birth
Of mortal man, the Sovereign Maker said
That not in humble nor in brief delight,
Not in the fading echoes of renown,
Power's purple robes, nor Pleasure's flowery lap,
The soul should find enjoyment: but from these
Turning disdainful to an equal good,
Through all the ascent of things enlarge her view,
Till every bound at length should disappear,
And infinite perfection close the scene.

Call now to mind what high capacious powers
Lie folded up in man; how far beyond
The praise of mortals, may the eternal growth
Of nature to perfection half divine
Expand the blooming soul? What pity then
Should sloth's unkindly fogs depress to earth
Her tender blossom; choke the streams of life,
And blast her spring! Far otherwise designed
Almighty wisdom! nature's happy cares
The obedient heart far otherwise incline.
Witness the sprightly joy when aught unknown
Strikes the quick sense, and wakes each active power
To brisker measures: witness the neglect
Of all familiar prospects, though beheld
With transport once; the fond attentive gaze
Of young astonishment; the sober zeal
Of age, commenting on prodigious things.
For such the bounteous providence of Heaven,
In every breast implanting this desire
Of objects new and strange, to urge us on
With unremitted labour to pursue
Those sacred stores that wait the ripening soul
In Truth's exhaustless bosom. What need words
To paint its power? For this the daring youth
Breaks from his weeping mother's anxious arms,
In foreign climes to rove: the pensive sage,
Heedless of sleep or midnight's harmful damp,
Hangs o'er the sickly taper; and untired
The virgin follows, with enchanted step,
The mazes of some wild and wondrous tale,
From morn to eve; unmindful of her form,
Unmindful of the happy dress that stole
The wishes of the youth, when every maid
With envy pined. Hence, finally, by night
The village matron, round the blazing hearth,
Suspends the infant audiences with her tales,
Breathing astonishment! of witching rhymes
And evil spirits; of the death-bed call
Of him who robbed the widow and devoured
The orphan's portion; of unquiet souls
Risen from the grave to ease the heavy guilt
Of deeds in life concealed; of shapes that walk
At dead of night, and clank their chains, and wave
The torch of hell around the murderer's bed.
At every solemn pause the crowd recoils
Gazing each other speechless, and congealed
With shivering sighs: till eager for the event,
Around the beldame all erect they hang,
Each trembling heart with grateful terrors quelled.

But lo! disclosed in all her smiling pomp,
Where Beauty onward moving claims the verse
Her charms inspire: the freely-flowing verse
In thy immortal praise, O form divine,
Smooths her mellifluent stream. Thee, Beauty, thee
The regal dome, and thy enlivening ray
The mossy roofs adore: thou, better sun!
Forever beamest on the enchanted heart
Love and harmonious wonder and delight
Poetic. Brightest progeny of Heaven!
How shall I trace thy features? where select
The roseate hues to emulate thy bloom?
Haste then, my song, through Nature's wide expanse,
Haste then, and gather all her comeliest wealth,
Whate'er bright spoils the florid earth contains,
Whate'er the waters or the liquid air,
To deck thy lovely labour. Wilt thou fly
With laughing Autumn to the Atlantic isles,
And range with him the Hesperian field, and see
Where'er his fingers touch the fruitful grove,
The branches shoot with gold; where'er his step
Marks the glad soil, the tender clusters grow
With purple ripeness, and invest each hill
As with the blushes of an evening sky?
Or wilt thou rather stoop thy vagrant plume,
Where gliding through his daughter's honoured shades,
The smooth Penéus from his glassy flood
Reflects purpureal Tempe's pleasant scene?
Fair Tempe! haunt beloved of sylvan powers,

289. Hesperian: of Hesperus, the evening star. **297–98. Penéus . . . scene:** Penéus is the great river of Thessaly that flows through the vale of Tempe.

Of Nymphs and Fauns; where in the golden age
They played in secret on the shady brink
With ancient Pan: while round their choral steps
Young Hours and genial Gales with constant hand
Showered blossoms, odours, showered ambrosial dews,
And spring's Elysian bloom. Her flowery store
To thee nor Tempe shall refuse; nor watch
Of winged Hydra guard Hesperian fruits
From thy free spoil. Oh bear then, unreproved,
Thy smiling treasures to the green recess
Where young Dione stays. With sweetest airs
Entice her forth to lend her angel form
For Beauty's honoured image. Hither turn
Thy graceful footsteps; hither, gentle maid,
Incline thy polished forehead; let thy eyes
Effuse the mildness of their azure dawn;
And may the fanning breezes waft aside
Thy radiant locks: disclosing, as it bends
With airy softness from the marble neck,
The cheek fair-blooming, and the rosy lip,
Where winning smiles and pleasures sweet as love,
With sanctity and wisdom, tempering blend
Their soft allurement. Then the pleasing force
Of Nature, and her kind parental care
Worthier I'd sing: then all the enamoured youth,
With each admiring virgin, to my lyre
Should throng attentive, while I point on high
Where Beauty's living image, like the morn
That wakes in Zephyr's arms the blushing May,
Moves onward; or as Venus, when she stood
Effulgent on the pearly car, and smiled,
Fresh from the deep, and conscious of her form,
To see the Tritons tune their vocal shells,
And each cerulean sister of the flood
With loud acclaim attend her o'er the waves,
To seek the Idalian bower. Ye smiling band
Of youths and virgins, who through all the maze
Of young desire with rival steps pursue
This charm of beauty; if the pleasing toil
Can yield a moment's respite, hither turn
Your favourable ear, and trust my words.
I do not mean to wake the gloomy form
Of Superstition dressed in Wisdom's garb,
To damp your tender hopes; I do not mean
To bid the jealous thunderer fire the heavens,
Or shapes infernal rend the groaning earth
To fright you from your joys: my cheerful song
With better omens calls you to the field,
Pleased with your generous ardour in the chase,
And warm like you. Then tell me, for ye know,
Does Beauty ever deign to dwell where health
And active use are strangers? Is her charm
Confessed in aught whose most peculiar ends
Are lame and fruitless? Or did Nature mean
This pleasing call the herald of a lie;
To hide the shame of discord and disease,
And catch with fair hypocrisy the heart
Of idle Faith? Oh no! with better cares
The indulgent mother, conscious how infirm
Her offspring tread the paths of good and ill,
By this illustrious image, in each kind
Still most illustrious where the object holds
Its native powers most perfect, she by this
Illumes the headstrong impulse of Desire,
And sanctifies his choice. The generous glebe
Whose bosom smiles with verdure, the clear tract
Of streams delicious to the thirsty soul,
The bloom of nectared fruitage ripe to sense,
And every charm of animated things,
Are only pledges of a state sincere,
The integrity and order of their frame,
When all is well within, and every end
Accomplished. Thus was Beauty sent from Heaven,
The lovely ministress of truth and good
In this dark world: for Truth and Good are one,
And Beauty dwells in them, and they in her,
With like participation. Wherefore then,
O sons of earth! would ye dissolve the tie?
O wherefore, with a rash impetuous aim,
Seek ye those flowery joys with which the hand
Of lavish Fancy paints each flattering scene
Where Beauty seems to dwell, nor once inquire
Where is the sanction of eternal truth,
Or where the seal of undeceitful good,
To save your search from folly! Wanting these,
Lo! Beauty withers in your void embrace,
And with the glittering of an idiot's toy
Did Fancy mock your vows. Nor let the gleam

307. Hydra: the many-headed monster of mythology. Hydra stood watch over the golden apples of the Hesperides. **310. Dione:** consort of Zeus; goddess of the sky. **330. Effulgent:** radiant. **332. Tritons:** sea gods. **333. cerulean:** blue. **335. Idalian bower:** Venus' birth from the foam of the Aegean Sea was associated with the island of Cyprus, where she was worshipped at Idalia.

364. glebe: land.

Of youthful hope that shines upon your hearts
Be chilled or clouded at this awful task,
To learn the lore of undeceitful good
And truth eternal. Though the poisonous charms
Of baleful Superstition guide the feet
Of servile numbers through a dreary way
To their abode, through deserts, thorns, and mire;
And leave the wretched pilgrim all forlorn,
To muse at last amid the ghostly gloom
Of graves, and hoary vaults, and cloistered cells;
To walk with spectres through the midnight shade,
And to the screaming owl's accursed song
Attune the dreadful workings of his heart;
Yet be not ye dismayed. A gentler star
Your lovely search illumines. From the grove
Where Wisdom talked with her Athenian sons,
Could my ambitious hand entwine a wreath
Of Plato's olive with the Mantuan bay,
Then should my powerful verse at once dispel
Those monkish horrors; then in light divine
Disclose the Elysian prospect, where the steps
Of those whom nature charms through blooming walks,
Through fragrant mountains and poetic streams,
Amid the train of sages, heroes, bards,
Led by their winged Genius and the choir
Of laureled science and harmonious art,
Proceed exulting to the eternal shrine,
Where Truth conspicuous with the sister twins,
The undivided partners of her sway,
With Good and Beauty reigns. Oh let not us,
Lulled by luxurious Pleasure's languid strain,
Or crouching to the frowns of bigot Rage,
Oh let us not a moment pause to join
That godlike band. And if the gracious power
Who first awakened my untutored song,
Will to my invocation breathe anew
The tuneful spirit; then through all our paths,
Ne'er shall the sound of this devoted lyre
Be wanting; whether on the rosy mead,
When summer smiles, to warn the melting heart
Of Luxury's allurement; whether firm
Against the torrent and the stubborn hill
To urge bold virtue's unremitted nerve,
And wake the strong divinity of soul
That conquers chance and fate; or whether struck
For sounds of triumph, to proclaim her toils
Upon the lofty summit, round her brow
To twine the wreath of incorruptive praise;
To trace her hallowed light through future worlds,
And bless Heaven's image in the heart of man.

Thus with a faithful aim have we presumed,
Adventurous, to delineate Nature's form;
Whether in vast, majestic pomp arrayed,
Or dressed for pleasing wonder, or serene
In Beauty's rosy smile. It now remains,
Through various being's fair-proportioned scale,
To trace the rising lustre of her charms,
From their first twilight, shining forth at length
To full meridian splendour. Of degree
The least and lowliest, in the effusive warmth
Of colours mingling with a random blaze,
Doth beauty dwell. Then higher in the line
And variation of determined shape,
Where truth's eternal measures mark the bound
Of circle, cube, or sphere. The third ascent
Unites this varied symmetry of parts
With colour's bland allurement; as the pearl
Shines in the concave of its azure bed,
And painted shells indent their speckled wreath.
Then more attractive rise the blooming forms
Through which the breath of Nature has infused
Her genial power to draw with pregnant veins
Nutritious moisture from the bounteous earth,
In fruit and seed prolific: thus the flowers
Their purple honours with the spring resume;
And such the stately tree which autumn bends
With blushing treasures. But more lovely still
Is Nature's charm, where to the full consent
Of complicated members, to the bloom
Of colour, and the vital change of growth,
Life's holy flame and piercing sense are given,
And active motion speaks the tempered soul:
So moves the bird of Juno; so the steed
With rival ardour beats the dusty plain,
And faithful dogs with eager airs of joy
Salute their fellows. Thus doth beauty dwell
There most conspicuous, even in outward shape,
Where dawns the high expression of a mind:
By steps conducting our enraptured search
To the eternal origin, whose power,
Through all the unbounded symmetry of things,
Like rays effulging from the parent sun,
This endless mixture of her charms diffused.
Mind, mind alone, (bear witness, earth and heaven!)
The living fountains in itself contains

470. bird of Juno: the peacock.

Of beauteous and sublime: here hand in hand,
Sit paramount the Graces; here enthroned,
Celestial Venus, with divinest airs,
Invites the soul to never-fading joy.
Look then abroad through nature, to the range
Of planets, suns, and adamantine spheres
Wheeling unshaken through the void immense;
And speak, O man! does this capacious scene
With half that kindling majesty dilate
Thy strong conception, as when Brutus rose
Refulgent from the stroke of Caesar's fate,
Amid the crowd of patriots; and his arm
Aloft extending, like eternal Jove
When guilt brings down the thunder, called aloud
On Tully's name, and shook his crimson steel,
And bade the father of his country, hail?
For lo! the tyrant prostrate on the dust,
And Rome again is free! Is aught so fair
In all the dewy landscapes of the spring,
In the bright eye of Hesper or the morn,
In nature's fairest forms, is aught so fair
As virtuous friendship? as the candid blush
Of him who strives with fortune to be just?
The graceful tear that streams for others' woes?
Or the mild majesty of private life,
Where Peace with ever-blooming olive crowns
The gate; where Honour's liberal hands effuse
Unenvied treasures, and the snowy wings
Of Innocence and Love protect the scene?
Once more search, undismayed, the dark profound
Where nature works in secret; view the beds
Of mineral treasure, and the eternal vault
That bounds the hoary ocean; trace the forms
Of atoms moving with incessant change
Their elemental round; behold the seeds
Of being, and the energy of life
Kindling the mass with ever-active flame:
Then to the secrets of the working mind
Attentive turn; from dim oblivion call
Her fleet, ideal band; and bid them, go!
Break through time's barrier, and o'ertake the hour
That saw the heavens created: then declare
If aught were found in those external scenes
To move thy wonder now. For what are all
The forms which brute, unconscious matter wears,
Greatness of bulk, or symmetry of parts?
Not reaching to the heart, soon feeble grows
The superficial impulse; dull their charms,
And satiate soon, and pall the languid eye.
Not so the moral species, nor the powers
Of genius and design; the ambitious mind
There sees herself; by these congenial forms
Touched and awakened, with intenser act
She bends each nerve, and meditates well-pleased
Her features in the mirror. For of all
The inhabitants of earth, to man alone
Creative Wisdom gave to lift his eye
To truth's eternal measures; then to frame
The sacred laws of action and of will,
Discerning justice from unequal deeds,
And temperance from folly. But beyond
This energy of truth, whose dictates bind
Assenting reason, the benignant sire,
To deck the honoured paths of just and good,
Has added bright imagination's rays:
Where Virtue, rising from the awful depth
Of Truth's mysterious bosom, doth forsake
The unadorned condition of her birth;
And dressed by Fancy in ten thousand hues,
Assumes a various feature, to attract,
With charms responsive to each gazer's eye,
The hearts of men. Amid his rural walk,
The ingenuous youth, whom solitude inspires
With purest wishes, from the pensive shade
Beholds her moving, like a virgin muse
That wakes her lyre to some indulgent theme
Of harmony and wonder: while among
The herd of servile minds, her strenuous form
Indignant flashes on the patriot's eye,
And through the rolls of memory appeals
To ancient honour, or in act serene,
Yet watchful, raises the majestic sword
Of public power, from dark ambition's reach
To guard the sacred volume of the laws.

Genius of ancient Greece! whose faithful steps
Well pleased I follow through the sacred paths
Of nature and of science; nurse divine
Of all heroic deeds and fair desires!
Oh! let the breath of thy extended praise
Inspire my kindling bosom to the height
Of this untempted theme. Nor be my thoughts
Presumptuous counted, if amid the calm
That soothes this vernal evening into smiles,
I steal impatient from the sordid haunts
Of strife and low ambition, to attend
Thy sacred presence in the sylvan shade,

488. adamantine: unbreakable. **493. refulgent:** gleaming. **497. Tully:** Cicero.

By their malignant footsteps ne'er profaned.
Descend, propitious! to my favoured eye;
Such in thy mien, thy warm, exalted air,
As when the Persian tyrant, foiled and stung
With shame and desperation, gnashed his teeth
To see thee rend the pageants of his throne;
And at the lightning of thy lifted spear
Crouched like a slave. Bring all thy martial spoils,
Thy palms, thy laurels, thy triumphal songs,
Thy smiling band of art, thy godlike sires
Of civil wisdom, thy heroic youth
Warm from the schools of glory. Guide my way
Through fair Lyceum's walk, the green retreats
Of Academus, and the thymy vale,
Where oft enchanted with Socratic sounds,
Ilissus pure devolved his tuneful stream
In gentler murmurs. From the blooming store
Of these auspicious fields, may I unblamed
Transplant some living blossoms to adorn
My native clime: while far above the flight
Of fancy's plume aspiring, I unlock
The springs of ancient wisdom! while I join
Thy name, thrice honoured! with the immortal praise
Of nature, while to my compatriot youth
I point the high example of thy sons,
And tune to Attic themes the British lyre.

(1744)

582. Persian tyrant: Xerxes. **591. Lyceum's walk:** Aristotle enjoyed walking in Lyceum, the sacred plot in Athens. **591–92. green . . . Academus:** Plato taught in the vale of Academus, outside of Athens.

594. Ilissus: a river of Attica flowing east and south of Athens.

Joseph Warton
1722–1800

◆

THE ENTHUSIAST: OR, THE LOVER OF NATURE

Ye green-robed Dryads, oft at dusky eve
By wondering shepherds seen, to forests brown,
To unfrequented meads, and pathless wilds,
Lead me from gardens decked with art's vain pomps.
Can gilt alcoves, can marble-mimic gods,
Parterres embroidered, obelisks, and urns
Of high relief; can the long, spreading lake,
Or vista lessening to the sight; can Stowe
With all her Attic fanes, such raptures raise,
As the thrush-haunted copse, where lightly leaps
The fearful fawn the rustling leaves along,
And the brisk squirrel sports from bough to bough,
While from an hollow oak the busy bees
Hum drowsy lullabies? The bards of old,
Fair Nature's friends, sought such retreats, to charm
Sweet Echo with their songs; oft too they met,
In summer evenings, near sequestered bowers,
Or Mountain-Nymph, or Muse, and eager learned
The moral strains she taught to mend mankind.
As to a secret grot Egeria stole
With patriot Numa, and in silent night
Whispered him sacred laws, he listening sat
Rapt with her virtuous voice; old Tiber leaned
Attentive on his urn, and hushed his waves.
  Rich in her weeping country's spoils, Versailles

THE ENTHUSIAST. **1. Dryads:** wood-nymphs. **6. Parterres:** ornamental flower gardens. **8. Stowe:** the estate of Viscount Cobham in Buckinghamshire. **9. fanes:** temples.

20–21. Egeria . . . Numa: The reference here is to the old legend according to which the wood-nymph Egeria gave secret advice to Numa Pompilius, king of Rome. **25. Versailles:** site of the royal palace, near Paris.

May boast a thousand fountains, that can cast
The tortured waters to the distant heavens;
Yet let me choose some pine-topped precipice
Abrupt and shaggy, whence a foamy stream,
Like Anio, tumbling roars; or some bleak heath,
Where straggling stand the mournful juniper,
Or yew-tree scathed; while in clear prospect round,
From the grove's bosom spires emerge, and smoke
In bluish wreaths ascends, ripe harvests wave,
Herds low, and straw-roofed cots appear, and streams
Beneath the sunbeams twinkle. The shrill lark,
That wakes the woodman to his early task,
Or love-sick Philomel, whose luscious lays
Soothe lone night-wanderers, the moaning dove
Pitied by listening milkmaid, far excel
The deep-mouthed viol, the soul-lulling lute,
And battle-breathing trumpet. Artful sounds!
That please not like the choristers of air,
When first they hail th'approach of laughing May.
Creative Titian, can thy vivid strokes,
Or thine, O graceful Raphael, dare to vie
With the rich tints that paint the breathing mead?
The thousand-coloured tulip, violet's bell
Snow-clad and meek, the vermil-tinctured rose,
And golden crocus? Yet with these the maid,
Phillis or Phoebe, at a feast or wake,
Her jetty locks enamels; fairer she,
In innocence and home-spun vestments dressed,
Than if cerulean sapphires at her ears
Shone pendant, or a precious diamond-cross
Heaved gently on her panting bosom white.
Yon Shepherd idly stretched on the rude rock,
Listening to dashing waves, the sea-mew's clang
High-hovering o'er his head, who views beneath
The dolphin dancing o'er the level brine,
Feels more true bliss than the proud admiral,
Amid his vessels bright with burnished gold
And silken streamers, though his lordly nod
Ten thousand war-worn mariners revere.
And great Aeneas gazed with more delight
On the rough mountain shagged with horrid shades,
(Where cloud-compelling Jove, as fancy dreamed,

30. Anio: river in central Italy. **38. Philomel:** the nightingale. **65–77. great Aeneas . . . rest:** The poet here recalls the story from the *Aeneid*, viii, 347–368, in which Virgil visits a primitive settlement built by Evander, a settlement that will eventually become Rome. He stays, to his delight, in Evander's simple cottage.

Descending shook his direful Aegis black)
Than if he entered the high Capitol
On golden columns reared, a conquered world
Contributing to deck its stately head:
More pleased he slept in poor Evander's cot
On shaggy skins, lulled by sweet nightingales,
Than if a Nero, in an age refined,
Beneath a gorgeous canopy had placed
His royal guest, and bade his minstrels sound
Soft slumberous Lydian airs to soothe his rest.
Happy the first of men, ere yet confined
To smoky cities; who in sheltering groves,
Warm caves, and deep-sunk valleys lived and loved,
By cares unwounded; what the sun and showers,
And genial earth untillaged could produce,
They gathered grateful, or the acorn brown,
Or blushing berry; by the liquid lapse
Of murmuring waters called to slake their thirst,
Or with fair Nymphs their sun-brown limbs to bathe;
With Nymphs who fondly clasped their favourite youths,
Unawed by shame, beneath the beechen shade,
Nor wiles nor artificial coyness knew.
Then doors and walls were not; the melting maid
Nor frowns of parents feared nor husband's threats;
Nor had cursed gold their tender hearts allured;
Then beauty was not venal. Injured Love,
O whither, god of raptures, art thou fled?
While Avarice waves his golden wand around,
Abhorred magician, and his costly cup
Prepares with baneful drugs to enchant the souls
Of each low-thoughted fair to wed for gain.
What though unknown to those primeval sires,
The well-arched dome, peopled with breathing forms
By fair Italia's skilful hand, unknown
The shapely column, and the crumbling busts
Of awful ancestors in long descent?
Yet why should man mistaken deem it nobler
To dwell in palaces and high-roofed halls
Than in God's forests, architect supreme!
Say, is the Persian carpet, than the field's
Or meadow's mantle gay, more richly woven;
Or softer to the votaries of ease,

68. Aegis: shield. **77. Lydian:** of Lydia, an ancient country in Asia Minor.

Than bladed grass, perfumed with dew-dropped flowers?
O taste corrupt! that luxury and pomp
In specious names of polished manners veiled,
Should proudly banish Nature's simple charms.
Though the fierce North oft smote with iron whip
Their shivering limbs, though oft the bristly boar
Or hungry lion woke them with their howls,
And scared them from their moss-grown caves to rove,
Houseless and cold in dark, tempestuous nights;
Yet were not myriads in embattled fields
Swept off at once, nor had the raving seas
O'erwhelmed the foundering bark and helpless crew;
In vain the glassy ocean smiled to tempt
The jolly sailor, unsuspecting harm,
For commerce was unknown. Then want and pine
Sunk to the grave their fainting limbs; but us
Excess and endless riot doom to die.
They cropped the poisonous herb unweetingly,
But wiser we spontaneously provide
Rare powerful roots, to quench life's cheerful lamp.
  What are the lays of artful Addison,
Coldly correct, to Shakespeare's warblings wild?
Whom on the winding Avon's willowed banks
Fair fancy found, and bore the smiling babe
To a close cavern: (still the shepherds show
The sacred place, whence with religious awe
They hear, returning from the field at eve,
Strange whisperings of sweet music through the air)
Here, as with honey gathered from the rock,
She fed the little prattler, and with songs
Oft soothed his wondering ears, with deep delight
On her soft lap he sat, and caught the sounds.
  Oft near some crowded city would I walk,
Listening the far-off noises, rattling cars,
Loud shouts of joy, sad shrieks of sorrow, knells
Full slowly tolling, instruments of trade,
Striking mine ears with one deep-swelling hum.
Or wandering near the sea, attend the sounds
Of hollow winds, and ever-beating waves.
Even when wild tempests swallow up the plains,
And Boreas' blasts, big hail, and rains combine
To shake the groves and mountains, would I sit,
Pensively musing on the outrageous crimes
That wake Heaven's vengeance: at such solemn hours,
Demons and goblins through the dark air shriek,
While Hecate with her black-browed sisters nine
Rides o'er the earth, and scatters woes and deaths.
Then, too, they say, in drear Egyptian wilds
The lion and the tiger prowl for prey
With roarings loud! The listening traveler
Starts fear-struck, while the hollow-echoing vaults
Of pyramids increase the deathful sounds.
  But let me never fail in cloudless nights,
When silent Cynthia in her silver car
Through the blue concave slides, when shine the hills,
Twinkle the streams, and woods look tipped with gold,
To seek some level mead, and there invoke
Old Midnight's sister, Contemplation sage,
(Queen of the rugged brow and stern-fixed eye)
To lift my soul above this little earth,
This folly-fettered world; to purge my ears,
That I may hear the rolling planets' song,
And tuneful-turning spheres: If this debarred,
The little fays that dance in neighbouring dales,
Sipping the night-dew, while they laugh and love,
Shall charm me with aërial notes. As thus
I wander musing, lo, what awful forms
Yonder appear! sharp-eyed Philosophy
Clad in dun robes, an eagle on his wrist,
First meets my eye; next virgin Solitude
Serene, who blushes at each gazer's sight;
Then Wisdom's hoary head, with crutch in hand,
Trembling, and bent with age; last Virtue's self
Smiling, in white arrayed, who with her leads
Fair Innocence, that prattles by her side,
A naked boy! Harassed with fear I stop,
I gaze, when Virtue thus—"Whoe'er thou art,
Mortal, by whom I deign to be beheld,
In these my midnight-walks; depart, and say
That henceforth I and my immortal train
Forsake Britannia's isle; who fondly stoops
To Vice, her favourite paramour."—She spoke,

150. Boreas: the north wind.

155. Hecate . . . sisters nine: a goddess who has special powers over sky, earth, and sea. In a more popular conception she is seen as a dark goddess of magic and witchcraft. **163. Cynthia:** moon goddess. **173. fays:** fairies.

And as she turned, her round and rosy neck,
Her flowing train, and long, ambrosial hair,
Breathing rich odours, I enamoured view.
 Oh, who will bear me then to western climes,
(Since Virtue leaves our wretched land) to shades
Yet unpolluted with Iberian swords;
With simple Indian swains, that I may hunt
The boar and tiger through savannahs wild?
There fed on dates and herbs, would I despise
The far-fetched cates of luxury, and hoards
Of narrow-hearted Avarice; nor heed
The distant din of the tumultuous world.
So when rude whirlwinds rouse the roaring main,
Beneath fair Thetis sits, in coral caves,
Serenely gay, nor sinking sailors' cries
Disturb her sportive Nymphs, who round her form
The light fantastic dance, or for her hair
Weave rosy crowns, or with according lutes
Grace the soft warbles of her honeyed voice.

(1744)

199. savannahs: treeless plains.

205. Thetis: a sea-nymph.

William Collins
1721–1759

◆

ODE ON THE POETICAL CHARACTER

STROPHE

As once—if not with light regard
I read aright that gifted bard,
(Him whose school above the rest
His loveliest Elfin queen has blessed)—
One, only one, unrivalled fair,
Might hope the magic girdle wear,
At solemn turney hung on high,
The wish of each love-darting eye;
Lo! to each other nymph in turn applied,
 As if, in air unseen, some hovering hand,
Some chaste and angel friend to virgin fame
 With whispered spell had burst the starting band,
It left unblessed her loathed dishonored side;
 Happier, hopeless fair, if never
 Her baffled hand with vain endeavor
Had touched that fatal zone to her denied!
Young Fancy thus, to me divinest name,
 To whom, prepared and bathed in Heaven,
 The cest of amplest power is given:
 To few the godlike gift assigns,
 To gird their blessed prophetic loins,
And gaze her visions wild, and feel unmixed her flame!

EPODE

The band, as fairy legends say,
Was wove on that creating day,
When He who called with thought to birth
Yon tented sky, this laughing earth,
And dressed with springs, and forests tall,
And poured the main engirting all,
Long by the loved enthusiast wooed,
Himself in some diviner mood,
Retiring, sate with her alone,
And placed her on his sapphire throne,
The whiles, the vaulted shrine around,
Seraphic wires were heard to sound,
Now sublimest triumph swelling,
Now on love and mercy dwelling;
And she, from out the veiling cloud,
Breathed her magic notes aloud:

ODE ON THE POETICAL CHARACTER. **1–6. As once . . . wear:** a reference (not completely accurate) to Spenser's *Faerie Queene* (iv, v). Florimel's girdle could be worn only by a pure woman. Although the girdle belonged to Florimel, only Amoret could wear it.

19. cest: girdle. **34. wires:** metallic strings of a musical instrument.

And thou, thou rich-haired Youth of Morn,
And all thy subject life was born!
The dangerous Passions kept aloof,
Far from the sainted growing woof,
But near it sate ecstatic Wonder,
Listening the deep applauding thunder,
And Truth, in sunny vest arrayed,
By whose the tarsel's eyes were made;
All the shadowy tribes of Mind
In braided dance their murmurs joined,
And all the bright uncounted Powers
Who feed on Heaven's ambrosial flowers.
Where is the bard whose soul can now
Its high presuming hopes avow?
Where he who thinks, with rapture blind,
This hallowed work for him designed?

ANTISTROPHE

High on some cliff, to Heaven up-piled,
Of rude access, of prospect wild,
Where, tangled round the jealous steep,
Strange shades o'erbrow the valley deep,
And holy genii guard the rock,
Its glooms embrown, its springs unlock,
While on its rich ambitious head
An Eden, like his own, lies spread,
I view that oak, the fancied glades among,
By which as Milton lay, his evening ear,
From many a cloud that dropped ethereal dew,
Nigh sphered in Heaven its native strains could
    hear;
On which that ancient trump he reached was hung:
  Thither oft, his glory greeting,
  From Waller's myrtle shades retreating,
With many a vow from Hope's aspiring
    tongue,
My trembling feet his guiding steps pursue;
  In vain—such bliss to one alone,
  Of all the sons of soul was known,
  And Heaven and Fancy, kindred powers,
Have now o'erturned the inspiring bowers,
Or curtained close such scene from every future
    view.

(1746)

39. **rich-haired Youth of Morn:** literally, Apollo; figuratively, the inspired poet. 42. **woof:** woven fabric. 46. **tarsel's:** falcon's. 69. **Waller:** Edmund Waller (1606–1687), here seen as a lesser poet when compared to the greatness of Milton.

ODE ON THE POPULAR SUPERSTITIONS OF THE HIGHLANDS OF SCOTLAND

CONSIDERED AS THE SUBJECT OF POETRY

I

H—, thou return'st from Thames, whose naiads long
  Have seen thee lingering with a fond delay,
  'Mid those soft friends, whose hearts, some
    future day,
Shall melt, perhaps, to hear thy tragic song.
Go, not unmindful of that cordial youth
  Whom, long endeared, thou leav'st by Lavant's
    side;
Together let us wish him lasting truth,
  And joy untainted with his destined bride.
Go! nor regardless, while these numbers boast
  My short-lived bliss, forget my social name;
But think, far off, how, on the southern coast,
  I met thy friendship with an equal flame!
Fresh to that soil thou turn'st, whose every vale
  Shall prompt the poet, and his song demand:
To thee thy copious subjects ne'er shall fail;
  Thou need'st but take the pencil to thy hand,
And paint what all believe who own thy genial land.

II

There must thou wake perforce thy Doric quill;
  'Tis Fancy's land to which thou sett'st thy
    feet;
  Where still, 'tis said, the fairy people meet,
Beneath each birken shade, on mead or hill.
There each trim lass that skims the milky store
  To the swart tribes their creamy bowls allots;
By night they sip it round the cottage door,
  While airy minstrels warble jocund notes.
There every herd by sad experience knows

ODE ON THE POPULAR SUPERSTITIONS. 1. **H—:** John Home (1722–1808), Scottish clergyman and dramatist, author of *Douglas,* a tragedy; **naiads:** river-nymphs. 5–6. **cordial youth . . . side:** the river which runs through Chichester, home of Collins. The "cordial youth" is Thomas Barrow, who introduced Home to Collins. 18. **Doric:** rustic, natural. 21. **birken:** birch. 23. **swart tribes:** a reference to the Brownies of folklore. These creatures helped with the farmwork and, when ignored, often vented their wrath by bringing disease to the animals. 26. **herd:** herdsman.

How, winged with fate, theïr elf-shot arrows fly,
When the sick ewe her summer food foregoes,
Or, stretched on earth, the heart-smit heifers lie.
Such airy beings awe the untutored swain:
Nor thou, though learned, his homelier thoughts neglect;
Let thy sweet Muse the rural faith sustain;
These are the themes of simple, sure effect,
That add new conquests to her boundless reign,
And fill with double force her heart-commanding strain.

III

Even yet preserved, how often mayst thou hear,
Where to the pole the boreal mountains run,
Taught by the father to his listening son,
Strange lays whose power had charmed a Spenser's ear.
At every pause, before thy mind possessed,
Old Runic bards shall seem to rise around,
With uncouth lyres, in many-colored vest,
Their matted hair with boughs fantastic crowned:
Whether thou bidd'st the well-taught hind repeat
The choral dirge that mourns some chieftain brave,
When every shrieking maid her bosom beat,
And strewed with choicest herbs his scented grave;
Or whether, sitting in the shepherd's shiel,
Thou hear'st some sounding tale of war's alarms;
When at the bugle's call, with fire and steel,
The sturdy clans poured forth their bony swarms,
And hostile brothers met, to prove each other's arms.

IV

'Tis thine to sing how, framing hideous spells,
In Sky's lone isle, the gifted wizard seer,
Lodged in the wintry cave with [ ]
Or in the depth of Uist's dark forests dwells:
How they whose sight such dreary dreams engross,
With their own visions oft astonished droop,
When, o'er the watery strath of quaggy moss
They see the gliding ghosts unbodied troop;
Or, if in sports, or on the festive green,
Their [ ] glance some fated youth descry,
Who now perhaps in lusty vigor seen,
And rosy health, shall soon lamented die.
For them the viewless forms of air obey,
Their bidding heed, and at their beck repair:
They know what spirit brews the stormful day,
And, heartless, oft like moody madness stare
To see the phantom train their secret work prepare.

V

[This stanza . . . missing in the manuscript.]

VI

[The first eight lines of this stanza . . . missing in the manuscript.]

What though far off, from some dark dell espied,
His glimmering mazes cheer the excursive sight,
Yet turn, ye wanderers, turn your steps aside,
Nor trust the guidance of that faithless light;
For, watchful, lurking 'mid the unrustling reed,
At those mirk hours the wily monster lies,
And listens oft to hear the passing steed,
And frequent round him rolls his sullen eyes,
If chance his savage wrath may some weak wretch surprise.

VII

Ah, luckless swain, o'er all unblessed indeed!
Whom late bewildered in the dank, dark fen,
Far from his flocks and smoking hamlet then,
To that sad spot [ ]
On him, enraged, the fiend, in angry mood,
Shall never look with pity's kind concern,
But instant, furious, raise the whelming flood
O'er its drowned bank, forbidding all return!
Or, if he meditate his wished escape
To some dim hill, that seems uprising near,
To his faint eye the grim and grisly shape
In all its terrors clad, shall wild appear.

37. boreal: northern. **41. Runic:** ancient Scottish. **48. shiel:** hut. **54. Sky's lone isle:** a reference to the Isle of Skye, one of the Inner Hebrides, off the northwest coast of Scotland. **56. Uist:** The islands of North and South Uist are part of the Outer Hebrides.

59. strath: a wide valley. **96. excursive:** wide-ranging. **100. mirk:** dark.

Meantime the watery surge shall round him rise,
Poured sudden forth from every swelling source!
What now remains but tears and hopeless sighs?
His fear-shook limbs have lost their youthly force,
And down the waves he floats, a pale and breathless corse!

VIII

For him in vain his anxious wife shall wait,
Or wander forth to meet him on his way;
For him in vain at to-fall of the day,
His babes shall linger at the unclosing gate!
Ah, ne'er shall he return! Alone, if night
Her travelled limbs in broken slumbers steep,
With drooping willows dressed, his mournful sprite
Shall visit sad, perchance, her silent sleep;
Then he, perhaps, with moist and watery hand,
Shall fondly seem to press her shuddering cheek,
And with his blue-swoln face before her stand,
And, shivering cold, these piteous accents speak:
"Pursue, dear wife, thy daily toils pursue,
At dawn or dusk, industrious as before;
Nor e'er of me one helpless thought renew,
While I lie weltering on the osiered shore,
Drowned by the kelpie's wrath, nor e'er shall aid thee more!"

IX

Unbounded is thy range; with varied style
Thy Muse may, like those feathery tribes which spring
From their rude rocks, extend her skirting wing
Round the moist marge of each cold Hebrid isle,
To that hoar pile which still its ruins shows;
In whose small vaults a pigmy-folk is found,
Whose bones the delver with his spade upthrows,
And calls them, wondering, from the hallowed ground!

123. to-fall: end. **136. weltering . . . shore:** rolling on the willowed shore. **137. kelpie:** a water spirit. **143–45. small vaults . . . ground:** small bones, possibly of pigmies, were found in a vault on the island of Benbecula. Collins relied heavily on his reading in Martin Martin's *Late Voyage to St. Kilda* (1698) and *Description of the Western Islands of Scotland* (1703, 1716).

Or thither where, beneath the showery West,
The mighty kings of three fair realms are laid;
Once foes, perhaps, together now they rest;
No slaves revere them, and no wars invade:
Yet frequent now, at midnight's solemn hour,
The rifted mounds their yawning cells unfold,
And forth the monarchs stalk with sovereign power,
In pageant robes, and wreathed with sheeny gold,
And on their twilight tombs aërial council hold.

X

But, oh, o'er all, forget not Kilda's race,
On whose bleak rocks, which brave the wasting tides,
Fair Nature's daughter, Virtue, yet abides.
Go! just, as they, their blameless manners trace!
Then to my ear transmit some gentle song.
Of those whose lives are yet sincere and plain,
Their bounded walks the rugged cliffs along,
And all their prospect but the wintry main.
With sparing temperance, at the needful time,
They drain the sainted spring; or, hunger-pressed,
Along the Atlantic rock undreading climb,
And of its eggs despoil the solan's nest.
Thus, blessed in primal innocence, they live
Sufficed and happy with that frugal fare
Which tasteful toil and hourly danger give.
Hard is their shallow soil, and bleak and bare;
Nor ever vernal bee was heard to murmur there!

XI

Nor need'st thou blush that such false themes engage
Thy gentle mind, of fairer stores possessed;
For not alone they touch the village breast,
But filled in elder time, the historic page.
There Shakespeare's self, with every garland crowned,
[ ]
In musing hour his wayward Sisters found,

146–47. thither . . . laid: Early rulers of Scotland, Ireland, and Norway were said to be buried on the island of Iona. **155. Kilda's race:** St. Kilda, outermost island of the Hebrides, and a place of utter simplicity. **164. sainted spring:** St. Kilda's well. **166. solan:** goose.

And with their terrors dressed the magic scene.
  From them he sung, when, 'mid his bold
    design,
Before the Scot, afflicted and aghast,
  The shadowy kings of Banquo's fated line
Through the dark cave in gleamy pageant passed.
  Proceed, nor quit the tales which, simply told,
Could once so well my answering bosom pierce;
  Proceed—in forceful sounds and colors bold
The native legends of thy land rehearse;
To such thy lyre, and suit thy powerful verse.

XII

In scenes like these, which, daring to depart
  From sober truth, are still to nature true,
And call forth fresh delight to Fancy's view,
The heroic muse employed her Tasso's art!
  How have I trembled, when, at Tancred's stroke,
Its gushing blood the gaping cypress poured!
  When each live plant with mortal accents spoke,
And the wild blast upheaved the vanished sword!
  How have I sat, when piped the pensive wind,
To hear his harp by British Fairfax strung!
  Prevailing poet! whose undoubting mind
Believed the magic wonders which he sung!
  Hence at each sound imagination glows!
[ ]
  Hence his warm lay with softest sweetness flows!
Melting its flows, pure, numerous, strong, and clear,
And fills the impassioned heart, and wins the
    harmonious ear!

XIII

All hail, ye scenes that o'er my soul prevail!
Ye [ ] friths and lakes, which, far away,
  Are by smooth Annan filled or pastoral Tay,
Or Don's romantic springs; at distance, hail!
The time shall come, when I, perhaps, may
    tread
  Your lowly glens, o'erhung with spreading broom;
Or, o'er your stretching heaths, by Fancy led;
  [ ]
Then will I dress once more the faded bower,
  Where Jonson sat in Drummond's [ ] shade;
Or crop, from Tiviot's dale, each [ ]
  And mourn, on Yarrow's banks, [ ]
Meantime, ye Powers that on the plains which bore
  The cordial youth, on Lothian's plains, attend!—
Where'er he dwell, on hill or lowly muir,
  To him I lose, your kind protection lend,
And, touched with love like mine, preserve my
    absent friend!

(1749, 1788)

192–96. heroic . . . sword: a reference to Tasso's great epic *Jerusalem Delivered* and to the incident of Tancred and the bloody cypress. **198. To hear . . . strung:** Edward Fairfax translated the *Jerusalem Delivered* in 1600, and the translation was reprinted in 1749.

215. Drummond: The reference here is to Ben Jonson's famous visit to the Scottish poet William Drummond, of Hawthornden, near Edinburgh. Drummond left a celebrated record of their conversations. **216–17. Tiviot . . . Yarrow:** a reference to the Teviot and Yarrow, two famous Scottish rivers celebrated in Border romances and ballads. **219. Lothian's plains:** John Home lived in the County of Lothian, in Scotland. **220. muir:** moor.

Thomas Gray
1716-1771

◆

SONNET

ON THE DEATH OF MR. RICHARD WEST*

In vain to me the smiling mornings shine,
And reddening Phœbus lifts his golden fire;
The birds in vain their amorous descant join,
Or cheerful fields resume their green attire;
These ears, alas! for other notes repine,
A different object do these eyes require;
My lonely anguish melts no heart but mine,
And in my breast the imperfect joys expire.
Yet morning smiles the busy race to cheer,
And new-born pleasure brings to happier men;
The fields to all their wonted tribute bear;
To warm their little loves the birds complain:
I fruitless mourn to him that cannot hear,
And weep the more, because I weep in vain.

(1742, 1775)

ODE ON A DISTANT PROSPECT OF ETON COLLEGE**

Ἄνθρωπος· ἱκανὴ πρόφασις εἰς τὸ δυσ τυχεῖν.***
Menander

Ye distant spires, ye antique towers,
That crown the watery glade,
Where grateful Science still adores
Her Henry's holy Shade;
And ye, that from the stately brow
Of Windsor's heights the expanse below
Of grove, of lawn, of mead survey,
Whose turf, whose shade, whose flowers among
Wanders the hoary Thames along
His silver-winding way:

Ah, happy hills! ah, pleasing shade!
Ah, fields beloved in vain!
Where once my careless childhood strayed,
A stranger yet to pain!
I feel the gales that from ye blow
A momentary bliss bestow,
As, waving fresh their gladsome wing,
My weary soul they seem to soothe,
And, redolent of joy and youth,
To breathe a second spring.

Say, Father Thames, for thou hast seen
Full many a sprightly race
Disporting on thy margent green
The paths of pleasure trace;
Who foremost now delight to cleave
With pliant arm thy glassy wave?
The captive linnet which enthrall?
What idle progeny succeed
To chase the rolling circle's speed,
Or urge the flying ball?

While some on earnest business bent
Their murmuring labors ply
'Gainst graver hours, that bring constraint
To sweeten liberty;
Some bold adventurers disdain
The limits of their little reign,
And unknown regions dare descry;
Still as they run they look behind;
They hear a voice in every wind,
And snatch a fearful joy.

Gay hope is theirs, by fancy fed,
Less pleasing when possessed;
The tear forgot as soon as shed,
The sunshine of the breast;
Theirs buxom health of rosy hue,
Wild wit, invention ever new,

---

* Richard West (1716–1742), poet and friend of Gray. A brilliant scholar, he studied at Oxford, was destined for a career in the law, but died tragically at an early age.

** Eton College, or more properly Eton School, was founded in the fifteenth century by Henry VI, whose statue still stands on the campus. Eton is on the Thames, near Windsor Castle.

*** "I am a man, reason enough for unhappiness."

ODE ON ETON COLLEGE. **23. margent:** shore. **27. linnet:** a songbird.

And lively cheer of vigor born;
The thoughtless day, the easy night,
The spirits pure, the slumbers light,
That fly the approach of morn.

Alas, regardless of their doom,
The little victims play!
No sense have they of ills to come,
Nor care beyond to-day!
Yet see how all around 'em wait
The ministers of human fate,
And black Misfortune's baleful train!
Ah, show them where in ambush stand
To seize their prey the murderous band!
Ah, tell them they are men!

These shall the fury Passions tear,
The vultures of the mind,
Disdainful Anger, pallid Fear,
And Shame that skulks behind;
Or pining Love shall waste their youth,
Or Jealousy with rankling tooth,
That inly gnaws the secret heart,
And Envy wan, and faded Care,
Grim-visaged comfortless Despair,
And Sorrow's piercing dart.

Ambition this shall tempt to rise,
Then whirl the wretch from high,
To bitter Scorn a sacrifice,
And grinning Infamy.
The stings of Falsehood those shall try,
And hard Unkindness' altered eye,
That mocks the tear it forced to flow;
And keen Remorse with blood defiled,
And moody Madness laughing wild
Amid severest woe.

Lo, in the vale of years beneath
A grisly troop are seen,
The painful family of Death,
More hideous than their queen:
This racks the joints, this fires the veins,
That every laboring sinew strains,
Those in the deeper vitals rage;
Lo, Poverty, to fill the band,
That numbs the soul with icy hand,
And slow-consuming Age.

To each his sufferings; all are men,
Condemned alike to groan—
The tender for another's pain,
The unfeeling for his own.
Yet, ah! why should they know their fate,
Since sorrow never comes too late,
And happiness too swiftly flies?
Thought would destroy their paradise.
No more; where ignorance is bliss,
'Tis folly to be wise.

(1742, 1747)

ELEGY WRITTEN IN A COUNTRY CHURCHYARD

The curfew tolls the knell of parting day,
The lowing herd wind slowly o'er the lea,
The ploughman homeward plods his weary way,
And leaves the world to darkness and to me.

Now fades the glimmering landscape on the sight,
And all the air a solemn stillness holds,
Save where the beetle wheels his droning flight,
And drowsy tinklings lull the distant folds;

Save that from yonder ivy-mantled tower
The moping owl does to the moon complain
Of such as, wandering near her secret bower,
Molest her ancient solitary reign.

Beneath those rugged elms, that yew-tree's shade,
Where heaves the turf in many a moldering heap,
Each in his narrow cell forever laid,
The rude forefathers of the hamlet sleep.

The breezy call of incense-breathing morn,
The swallow twittering from the straw-built shed,
The cock's shrill clarion, or the echoing horn,
No more shall rouse them from their lowly bed.

For them no more the blazing hearth shall burn,
Or busy housewife ply her evening care:
No children run to lisp their sire's return,
Or climb his knees the envied kiss to share.

Oft did the harvest to their sickle yield;
Their furrow oft the stubborn glebe has broke;
How jocund did they drive their team afield!
How bowed the woods beneath their sturdy stroke!

Let not Ambition mock their useful toil,
Their homely joys, and destiny obscure;
Nor Grandeur hear with a disdainful smile
The short and simple annals of the poor.

The boast of heraldry, the pomp of power,
And all that beauty, all that wealth e'er gave,
Awaits alike the inevitable hour:
The paths of glory lead but to the grave.

Nor you, ye proud, impute to these the fault,
If Memory o'er their tomb no trophies raise,
Where through the long-drawn aisle and fretted vault
The pealing anthem swells the note of praise.

Can storied urn or animated bust
Back to its mansion call the fleeting breath?
Can Honor's voice provoke the silent dust,
Or Flattery soothe the dull, cold ear of Death?

Perhaps in this neglected spot is laid
Some heart once pregnant with celestial fire;
Hands that the rod of empire might have swayed,
Or waked to ecstasy the living lyre.

But Knowledge to their eyes her ample page,
Rich with the spoils of time, did ne'er unroll;
Chill Penury repressed their noble rage,
And froze the genial current of the soul.

Full many a gem of purest ray serene,
The dark unfathomed caves of ocean bear:
Full many a flower is born to blush unseen,
And waste its sweetness on the desert air.

Some village Hampden, that with dauntless breast
The little tyrant of his fields withstood;
Some mute, inglorious Milton here may rest,
Some Cromwell, guiltless of his country's blood.

The applause of listening senates to command,
The threats of pain and ruin to despise,
To scatter plenty o'er a smiling land,
And read their history in a nation's eyes,

Their lot forbade: nor circumscribed alone
Their growing virtues, but their crimes confined;
Forbade to wade through slaughter to a throne,
And shut the gates of mercy on mankind;

The struggling pangs of conscious truth to hide,
To quench the blushes of ingenuous shame,
Or heap the shrine of Luxury and Pride
With incense kindled at the Muse's flame.

Far from the madding crowd's ignoble strife,
Their sober wishes never learned to stray;
Along the cool, sequestered vale of life
They kept the noiseless tenor of their way.

Yet even these bones from insult to protect,
Some frail memorial still erected nigh,
With uncouth rhymes and shapeless sculpture decked,
Implores the passing tribute of a sigh.

Their name, their years, spelt by the unlettered Muse,
The place of fame and elegy supply;
And many a holy text around she strews,
That teach the rustic moralist to die.

For who, to dumb forgetfulness a prey,
This pleasing anxious being e'er resigned,
Left the warm precincts of the cheerful day,
Nor cast one longing lingering look behind?

On some fond breast the parting soul relies,
Some pious drops the closing eye requires;
E'en from the tomb the voice of Nature cries,
E'en in our ashes live their wonted fires.

For thee who, mindful of the unhonored dead,
Dost in these lines their artless tale relate;
If chance, by lonely contemplation led,
Some kindred spirit shall inquire thy fate,—

Haply some hoary-headed swain may say,
"Oft have we seen him at the peep of dawn
Brushing with hasty steps the dews away,
To meet the sun upon the upland lawn.

"There at the foot of yonder nodding beech
That wreathes its old fantastic roots so high,
His listless length at noontide would he stretch,
And pore upon the brook that babbles by.

"Hard by yon wood, now smiling as in scorn,
Muttering his wayward fancies he would rove;
Now drooping, woeful-wan, like one forlorn,
Or crazed with care, or crossed in hopeless love.

"One morn I missed him on the customed hill,
Along the heath, and near his favorite tree;
Another came; nor yet beside the rill,
Nor up the lawn, nor at the wood was he;

ELEGY WRITTEN IN A COUNTRY CHURCHYARD. **57. Hampden:** John Hampden, famous for his opposition to the ship taxes imposed by Charles I.

"The next, with dirges due, in sad array,
  Slow through the church-way path we saw him borne.
Approach and read (for thou canst read) the lay,
  Graved on the stone beneath yon aged thorn."

THE EPITAPH

Here rests his head upon the lap of earth,
  A youth to Fortune and to Fame unknown;
Fair Science frowned not on his humble birth,
  And Melancholy marked him for her own.

Large was his bounty, and his soul sincere;
  Heaven did a recompense as largely send:
He gave to Misery (all he had), a tear;
  He gained from Heaven ('twas all he wished) a friend.

No farther seek his merits to disclose,
  Or draw his frailties from their dread abode,
(There they alike in trembling hope repose,)
  The bosom of his Father and his God.

(?1742–1750, 1751)

THE PROGRESS OF POESY

A PINDARIC ODE

Φωνᾶντα συνετοῖσιν· ἐς
Δὲ τὸ πᾶν ἑρμηνέων χατίηει.*

Pindar, Olymp. II

I—1

Awake, Aeolian lyre, awake,
And give to rapture all thy trembling strings.
From Helicon's harmonious springs
A thousand rills their mazy progress take;
The laughing flowers that round them blow
Drink life and fragrance as they flow.
Now the rich stream of music winds along,
Deep, majestic, smooth, and strong,
Through verdant vales and Ceres' golden reign;
Now rolling down the steep amain,
Headlong, impetuous, see it pour;
The rocks and nodding groves rebellow to the roar.

I—2

Oh! Sovereign of the willing soul,
Parent of sweet and solemn-breathing airs,
Enchanting shell; the sullen Cares
And frantic Passions hear thy soft control.
On Thracia's hills the Lord of War
Has curbed the fury of his car,
And dropped his thirsty lance at thy command.
Perching on the sceptered hand
Of Jove, thy magic lulls the feathered king,
With ruffled plumes and flagging wing;
Quenched in dark clouds of slumber lie
The terror of his beak, and lightnings of his eye.

I—3

Thee the voice, the dance, obey,
Tempered to thy warbled lay.
O'er Idalia's velvet-green
The rosy-crownèd Loves are seen
On Cytherea's day;
With antic Sports, and blue-eyed Pleasures,
Frisking light in frolic measures;
Now pursuing, now retreating,
Now in circling troops they meet,
To brisk notes in cadence beating
Glance their many-twinkling feet.
Slow melting strains their queen's approach declare;
Where'er she turns the Graces homage pay.
With arms sublime that float upon the air,
In gliding state she wins her easy way;
O'er her warm cheek and rising bosom move
The bloom of young desire and purple light of love.

116: thorn: a plant with thorns.

* "Understandable to the knowing, but requiring explanation for the larger world."

THE PROGRESS OF POESY. **1. Aeolian:** in Greek music, a joyous style. **3. Helicon:** a mountain in southern Greece, regarded as the home of the Muses and the source of poetic inspiration.

9. Ceres: goddess of agriculture. **17. Thracia:** an ancient region in the eastern Balkan peninsula; **Lord of War:** Mars. **21. feathered king:** the eagle, bird of Jove. **27–29. O'er Idalia's . . . day:** The reference is to the birth of Aphrodite, who was born from the Aegean Sea. Aphrodite is often associated with Cyprus, where she was venerated at Idalia, and with Cytherea.

II—1

Man's feeble race what ills await,
Labor, and penury, the racks of pain,
Disease, and sorrow's weeping train,
And death, sad refuge from the storms of fate!
The fond complaint, my song, disprove,
And justify the laws of Jove.
Say, has he given in vain the heavenly Muse?
Night, and all her sickly dews,
Her spectres wan, and birds of boding cry
He gives to range the dreary sky;
Till down the eastern cliffs afar
Hyperion's march they spy, and glittering shafts of war.

II—2

In climes beyond the solar road,
Where shaggy forms o'er ice-built mountains roam,
The Muse has broke the twilight-gloom
To cheer the shivering native's dull abode.
And oft, beneath the odorous shade
Of Chili's boundless forests laid,
She deigns to hear the savage youth repeat
In loose numbers wildly sweet
Their feather-cinctured chiefs and dusky loves.
Her track, where'er the goddess roves,
Glory pursue, and generous shame,
The unconquerable mind, and Freedom's holy flame.

II—3

Woods that wave o'er Delphi's steep,
Isles that crown the Aegean deep,
Fields that cool Ilissus laves,
Or where Maeander's amber waves
In lingering labyrinths creep,
How do your tuneful echoes languish,
Mute, but to the voice of anguish!
Where each old poetic mountain
Inspiration breathed around,
Every shade and hallowed fountain
Murmured deep a solemn sound;
Till the sad Nine in Greece's evil hour
Left their Parnassus for the Latian plains.
Alike they scorn the pomp of tyrant Power,
And coward Vice, that revels in her chains.
When Latium had her lofty spirit lost,
They sought, O Albion! next, thy sea-encircled coast.

III—1

Far from the sun and summer-gale,
In thy green lap was Nature's darling laid,
What time, where lucid Avon strayed,
To him the mighty mother did unveil
Her awful face; the dauntless child
Stretched forth his little arms, and smiled.
"This pencil take," she said, "whose colors clear
Richly paint the vernal year;
Thine too these golden keys, immortal boy!
This can unlock the gates of joy;
Of horror that, and thrilling fears,
Or ope the sacred source of sympathetic tears."

III—2

Nor second he that rode sublime
Upon the seraph-wings of ecstasy,
The secrets of the abyss to spy.
He passed the flaming bounds of place and time;
The living throne, the sapphire-blaze,
Where angels tremble while they gaze,
He saw; but blasted with excess of light,
Closed his eyes in endless night.
Behold where Dryden's less presumptuous car,
Wide o'er the fields of glory bear
Two coursers of ethereal race,
With necks in thunder clothed, and long-resounding pace.

III—3

Hark, his hands the lyre explore!
Bright-eyed Fancy, hovering o'er,
Scatters from her pictured urn
Thoughts that breathe and words that burn.
But ah! 'tis heard no more—
O lyre divine, what daring spirit

53. Hyperion: a blazing sun-god, one of the Titans. **68. Ilissus:** a river flowing through Athens; **laves:** washes.

78. Latian: Roman. **84. Nature's darling:** Shakespeare. **95. second he:** Milton. **112. daring spirit:** a reference to Gray himself.

Wakes thee now? Though he inherit
Nor the pride nor ample pinion
That the Theban Eagle bear,
Sailing with supreme dominion
Through the azure deep of air;
Yet oft before his infant eyes would run
Such forms as glitter in the Muse's ray
With orient hues, unborrowed of the sun;
Yet shall he mount, and keep his distant way
Beyond the limits of a vulgar fate—
Beneath the good how far—but far above the great.

(1754, 1757)

THE BARD*

A PINDARIC ODE

I—1

"Ruin seize thee, ruthless King!
Confusion on thy banners wait,
Though fanned by conquest's crimson wing
They mock the air with idle state.
Helm, nor hauberk's twisted mail,
Nor e'en thy virtues, tyrant, shall avail
To save thy secret soul from nightly fears,
From Cambria's curse, from Cambria's tears!"
Such were the sounds that o'er the crested pride
Of the first Edward scattered wild dismay,
As down the steep of Snowdon's shaggy side
He wound with toilsome march his long array.
Stout Glo'ster stood aghast in speechless trance;
"To arms!" cried Mortimer, and couched his quivering lance.

I—2

On a rock whose haughty brow
Frowns o'er old Conway's foaming flood,
Robed in the sable garb of woe,
With haggard eyes the poet stood
(Loose his beard and hoary hair
Streamed, like a meteor, to the troubled air),
And with a master's hand and prophet's fire
Struck the deep sorrows of his lyre.
"Hark, how each giant oak and desert cave
Sighs to the torrent's awful voice beneath!
O'er thee, O King! their hundred arms they wave,
Revenge on thee in hoarser murmurs breathe;
Vocal no more, since Cambria's fatal day,
To high-born Hoel's harp, or soft Llewellyn's lay.

I—3

"Cold is Cadwallo's tongue,
That hushed the stormy main;
Brave Urien sleeps upon his craggy bed;
Mountains, ye mourn in vain
Modred, whose magic song
Made huge Plinlimmon bow his cloud-topped head.
On dreary Arvon's shore they lie,
Smeared with gore, and ghastly pale;
Far, far aloof the affrighted ravens sail;
The famished eagle screams, and passes by.
Dear lost companions of my tuneful art,
Dear as the light that visits these sad eyes,
Dear as the ruddy drops that warm my heart,
Ye died amidst your dying country's cries—
No more I weep. They do not sleep.
On yonder cliffs, a grisly band,
I see them sit; they linger yet,
Avengers of their native land;
With me in dreadful harmony they join,

115. Theban Eagle: Pindar, the great maker of Greek odes.

* Gray's notebook provides the following summary: "The army of Edward I, as they march through a deep valley, are suddenly stopped by the appearance of a venerable figure seated on the summit of an inaccessible rock, who, with a voice more than human, reproaches the King with all the misery and desolation which he has brought on his country; foretells the misfortunes of the Norman race, and with prophetic spirit declares that all his cruelty shall never extinguish the noble ardor of poetic genius in the island; and that men shall never be wanting to celebrate true virtue and valor in immortal strains, to expose vice and infamous pleasure, and boldly censure tyranny and oppression. His song ended, he precipitates himself from the mountain, and is swallowed up by the river that rolls at its foot."

THE BARD. **5. hauberk:** coat of armor. **8. Cambria:** Wales. **11. Snowdon:** mountain in Wales.

13–14. Glo'ster . . . Mortimer: border lords in the army of Edward. **14. couched:** readied. **16. Conway:** a river in Wales. **18. haggard:** wild. **28. Hoel . . . Llewellyn:** bards. **29–33. Cadwallo . . . Urien . . . Modred:** other historical or mythological bards. **34. Plinlimmon:** a mountain in Wales. **35. Arvon:** Caernarvon, a county in Wales.

And weave with bloody hands the tissue of thy
line.

II—1

" 'Weave the warp, and weave the woof,
The winding-sheet of Edward's race.
Give ample room, and verge enough
The characters of hell to trace.
Mark the year, and mark the night,
When Severn shall re-echo with affright
The shrieks of death through Berkeley's roofs that
ring,
Shrieks of an agonizing king!
She-wolf of France, with unrelenting fangs,
That tear'st the bowels of thy mangled mate,
From thee be born, who o'er thy country hangs,
The scourge of Heaven. What terrors round him
wait!
Amazement in his van, with Flight combined,
And Sorrow's faded form, and Solitude behind.

II—2

" 'Mighty victor, mighty lord,
Low on his funeral couch he lies!
No pitying heart, no eye, afford
A tear to grace his obsequies.
Is the Sable Warrior fled?
Thy son is gone. He rests among the dead.
The swarm that in thy noon-tide beam were born?
Gone to salute the rising morn.
Fair laughs the morn, and soft the zephyr blows,
While proudly riding o'er the azure realm
In gallant trim the gilded vessel goes;
Youth on the prow, and Pleasure at the helm;
Regardless of the sweeping whirlwind's sway,
That, hushed in grim repose, expects his evening
prey.

II—3

" 'Fill high the sparkling bowl,
The rich repast prepare;

55–56. shrieks . . . king: a reference to the murder of Edward II in Berkeley Castle. **57. She-wolf:** Isabel of France, Edward's queen. **63–66. Mighty . . . obsequies:** Edward III, who conquered a large part of France, was abandoned by his children, robbed by his aides and mistress. **67. Sable Warrior:** Edward, the Black Prince, son of Edward III.

Reft of a crown, he yet may share the feast;
Close by the regal chair
Fell Thirst and Famine scowl
A baleful smile upon their baffled guest.
Heard ye the din of battle bray,
Lance to lance, and horse to horse?
Long years of havoc urge their destined course,
And through the kindred squadrons mow their way.
Ye towers of Julius, London's lasting shame,
With many a foul and midnight murder fed,
Revere his consort's faith, his father's fame,
And spare the meek usurper's holy head.
Above, below, the rose of snow,
Twined with her blushing foe, we spread;
The bristled boar in infant-gore
Wallows beneath the thorny shade.
Now, brothers, bending o'er the accursed loom,
Stamp we our vengeance deep, and ratify his doom.

III—1

" 'Edward, lo! to sudden fate
(Weave we the woof: the thread is spun)
Half of thy heart we consecrate.
(The web is wove. The work is done.)'—
Stay, oh stay! nor thus forlorn
Leave me unblessed, unpitied, here to mourn!
In yon bright track that fires the western skies,
They melt, they vanish from my eyes.
But oh! what solemn scenes on Snowdon's height,
Descending slow, their glittering skirts unroll?
Visions of glory, spare my aching sight!
Ye unborn ages, crowd not on my soul!
No more our long-lost Arthur we bewail.
All hail, ye genuine kings, Britannia's issue,
hail!

83. Reference to the Wars of the Roses. **87–88. towers . . . fed:** Henry VI, Edward V, and other members of the royal family were believed to have been murdered in the Tower of London, the oldest part of which was built by Julius Caesar. The lines that follow recount these events. **91–92. Above . . . spread:** a reference to the white and red roses, symbols of York and Lancaster. The roses are joined to represent the marriage of Henry VII of Lancaster to Elizabeth of York. **93. bristled boar:** Richard III, who murdered the two young princes (sons of Edward IV), in the Tower. **99. Half . . . consecrate:** a reference to the death of Eleanor of Castile, Edward's queen, who died shortly after the conquest of Wales.

III—2

"Girt with many a baron bold
Sublime their starry fronts they rear;
And gorgeous dames, and statesman old
In bearded majesty, appear.
In the midst a form divine!
Her eye proclaims her of the Briton line;
Her lion-port, her awe-commanding face,
Attempered sweet to virgin-grace.
What strings symphonious tremble in the air,
What strains of vocal transport round her play!
Hear from the grave, great Taliessin, hear;
They breathe a soul to animate thy clay.
Bright Rapture calls, and soaring, as she sings,
Waves in the eye of Heaven her many-colored wings.

III—3

"The verse adorn again
Fierce War, and faithful Love,
And Truth severe, by fairy Fiction dressed.
In buskined measures move
Pale Grief, and pleasing Pain,
With Horror, tyrant of the throbbing breast.
A voice, as of the cherub-choir,
Gales from blooming Eden bear;
And distant warblings lessen on my ear,
That lost in long futurity expire.
Fond impious man, think'st thou yon sanguine cloud,
Raised by thy breath, has quenched the orb of day?
To-morrow he repairs the golden flood,
And warms the nations with redoubled ray.
Enough for me: with joy I see
The different doom our fates assign.
Be thine despair, and sceptered care;
To triumph, and to die, are mine."
He spoke, and headlong from the mountain's height
Deep in the roaring tide he plunged to endless night.

(1757)

115. form divine: Elizabeth I. **121. Taliessin:** greatest of the bards.

128. buskined measures: the tragedies of Shakespeare. **132. Gales . . . bear:** a reference to Milton's *Paradise Lost*.

Oliver Goldsmith

1730-1774

◆

THE TRAVELLER

OR, A PROSPECT OF SOCIETY

TO THE REV. HENRY GOLDSMITH

Dear Sir,—I am sensible that the friendship between us can acquire no new force from the ceremonies of a Dedication; and perhaps it demands an excuse thus to prefix your name to my attempts, which you decline giving with your own. But as a part of this poem was formerly written to you from Switzerland, the whole can now, with propriety, be only inscribed to you. It will also throw a light upon many parts of it, when the reader understands that it is addressed to a man, who, despising fame and fortune, has retired early to happiness and obscurity, with an income of forty pounds a year.

I now perceive, my dear brother, the wisdom of your humble choice. You have entered upon a sacred office, where the harvest is great and the laborers are but few; while you have left the field of ambition, where the laborers are many and the harvest not worth carrying away. But of all kinds of ambition, what from the refinement of the times, from differing systems of criticism, and from the divisions of party, that which pursues poetical fame is the wildest.

Poetry makes a principal amusement among unpolished nations; but in a country verging to the extremes of refinement, Painting and Music come in for a share. As these offer the feeble mind a less laborious entertainment, they at first rival Poetry, and at length supplant her; they engross all that favor once shown to her, and, though but younger sisters, seize upon the elder's birthright.

Yet, however this art may be neglected by the powerful, it is still in greater danger from the mistaken efforts of the learned to improve it. What criticisms have we not heard of late in favor of blank verse, and Pindaric odes, choruses, anapests, and iambics, alliterative care and happy negligence! Every absurdity has now a champion to defend it; and as he is generally much in the wrong, so he has always much to say—for error is ever talkative.

But there is an enemy to this art still more dangerous—I mean Party. Party entirely distorts the judgment and destroys the taste. When the mind is once infected with this disease, it can only find pleasure in what contributes to increase the distemper. Like the tiger, that seldom desists from pursuing man after having once preyed upon human flesh, the reader who has once gratified his appetite with calumny makes ever after the most agreeable feast upon murdered reputation. Such readers generally admire some half-witted thing, who wants to be thought a bold man, having lost the character of a wise one. Him they dignify with the name of poet; his tawdry lampoons are called satires; his turbulence is said to be force, and his frenzy fire.

What reception a poem may find, which has neither abuse, party, nor blank verse to support it, I cannot tell, nor am I solicitous to know. My aims are right. Without espousing the cause of any party, I have attempted to moderate the rage of all. I have endeavored to show that there may be equal happiness in states that are differently governed from our own; that every state has a particular principle of happiness, and that this principle in each may be carried to a mischievous excess. There are few can judge better than yourself how far these positions are illustrated in this poem.

I am, dear sir, your most affectionate brother,

Oliver Goldsmith.

Remote, unfriended, melancholy, slow,
Or by the lazy Scheldt or wandering Po;
Or onward, where the rude Carinthian boor
Against the houseless stranger shuts the door;
Or where Campania's plain forsaken lies,
A weary waste expanding to the skies;
Where'er I roam, whatever realms to see,
My heart, untravelled, fondly turns to thee,
Still to my brother turns, with ceaseless pain,
And drags at each remove a lengthening
chain.
Eternal blessings crown my earliest friend,
And round his dwelling guardian saints attend;
Blessed by that spot, where cheerful guests retire
To pause from toil and trim their evening fire;
Blessed that abode, where want and pain repair,
And every stranger finds a ready chair;
Blessed be those feasts with simple plenty crowned,
Where all the ruddy family around
Laugh at the jests or pranks that never fail,
Or sigh with pity at some mournful tale,
Or press the bashful stranger to his food,
And learn the luxury of doing good.
But me, not destined such delights to share,
My prime of life in wandering spent, and care,
Impelled with steps unceasing to pursue
Some fleeting good, that mocks me with the view;
That, like the circle bounding earth and skies,
Allures from far, yet, as I follow, flies;
My fortune leads to traverse realms alone,
And find no spot of all the world my own.
Even now, where Alpine solitudes ascend,
I sit me down a pensive hour to spend;
And, placed on high above the storm's career,
Look downward where an hundred realms appear:
Lakes, forests, cities, plains extending wide,
The pomp of kings, the shepherd's humbler pride.
When thus creation's charms around combine,
Amidst the store, should thankless pride repine?
Say, should the philosophic mind disdain
That good which makes each humbler bosom
vain?
Let school-taught pride dissemble all it can,
These little things are great to little man;
And wiser he, whose sympathetic mind
Exults in all the good of all mankind.
Ye glittering towns, with wealth and splendour
crowned,
Ye fields, where summer spreads profusion round,
Ye lakes, whose vessels catch the busy gale,
Ye bending swains, that dress the flowery vale,
For me your tributary stores combine;
Creation's heir, the world—the world is mine!
As some lone miser, visiting his store,
Bends at his treasure, counts, recounts it o'er;
Hoards after hoards his rising raptures fill,
Yet still he sighs, for hoards are wanting still;
Thus to my breast alternate passions rise,

THE TRAVELLER. **2. Scheldt . . . Po:** the first, a river flowing through Holland and Belgium; the second, a major river in Italy. **3. Carinthian:** Carinthia, a mountainous section of Austria. **5. Campania:** the Campagna of Rome.

Pleased with each good that Heaven to man
supplies:
Yet oft a sigh prevails, and sorrows fall,
To see the hoard of human bliss so small;
And oft I wish, amidst the scene, to find
Some spot to real happiness consigned,
Where my worn soul, each wandering hope at rest,
May gather bliss, to see my fellows blessed.
But where to find that happiest spot below,
Who can direct, when all pretend to know?
The shuddering tenant of the frigid zone
Boldly proclaims that happiest spot his own,
Extols the treasures of his stormy seas,
And his long nights of revelry and ease:
The naked negro, panting at the line,
Boasts of his golden sands and palmy wine,
Basks in the glare, or stems the tepid wave,
And thanks his gods for all the good they gave.
Such is the patriot's boast, where'er we roam,
His first, best country ever is at home.
And yet, perhaps, if countries we compare,
And estimate the blessings which they share,
Though patriots flatter, still shall wisdom find
An equal portion dealt to all mankind:
As different good, by Art or Nature given,
To different nations makes their blessings even.
Nature, a mother kind alike to all,
Still grants her bliss at Labor's earnest call;
With food as well the peasant is supplied
On Idra's cliff as Arno's shelvy side;
And though the rocky-crested summits frown,
These rocks by custom turn to beds of down.
From Art more various are the blessings sent;
Wealth, commerce, honor, liberty, content.
Yet these each other's power so strong contest
That either seems destructive of the rest.
Where wealth and freedom reign, contentment fails;
And honor sinks where commerce long prevails.
Hence every state, to one loved blessing prone,
Conforms and models life to that alone.
Each to the favorite happiness attends,
And spurns the plan that aims at other ends:
Till, carried to excess in each domain,
This favorite good begets peculiar pain.
But let us try these truths with closer eyes,
And trace them through the prospect as it
lies;
Here for a while, my proper cares resigned,
Here let me sit in sorrow for mankind;
Like yon neglected shrub, at random cast,
That shades the steep, and sighs at every blast.
Far to the right, where Apennine ascends,
Bright as the summer, Italy extends;
Its uplands sloping deck the mountain's side,
Woods over woods in gay theatric pride;
While oft some temple's moldering tops between
With venerable grandeur mark the scene.
Could Nature's bounty satisfy the breast,
The sons of Italy were surely blessed.
Whatever fruits in different climes are found,
That proudly rise, or humbly court the ground;
Whatever blooms in torrid tracts appear,
Whose bright succession desks the varied year;
Whatever sweets salute the northern sky
With vernal lives, that blossom but to die;
These, here disporting, own the kindred soil,
Nor ask luxuriance from the planter's toil;
While sea-born gales their gelid wings expand
To winnow fragrance round the smiling land.
But small the bliss that sense alone bestows,
And sensual bliss is all the nation knows.
In florid beauty groves and fields appear;
Man seems the only growth that dwindles here.
Contrasted faults through all his manners reign.
Though poor, luxurious; though submissive, vain;
Though grave, yet trifling; zealous, yet untrue;
And even in penance planning sins anew.
All evils here contaminate the mind,
That opulence departed leaves behind;
For wealth was theirs, not far removed the date,
When commerce proudly flourished through the
state.
At her command the palace learned to rise;
Again the long-fallen column sought the skies;
The canvas glowed, beyond even Nature warm,
The pregnant quarry teemed with human form:
Till, more unsteady than the southern gale,
Commerce on other shores displayed her sail;
While naught remained of all that riches gave,
But towns unmanned and lords without a slave,
And late the nation found, with fruitless skill,
Its former strength was but plethoric ill.
Yet, still the loss of wealth is here supplied

84. Idra: a town in Jugoslavia; **Arno:** a river in Tuscany.

105. Apennine: the mountain system extending along the entire length of the Italian peninsula. **144. plethoric:** swollen.

By arts, the splendid wrecks of former pride;
From these the feeble heart and long-fallen mind
An easy compensation seem to find.
Here may be seen, in bloodless pomp arrayed,
The pasteboard triumph and the cavalcade;
Processions formed for piety and love,
A mistress or a saint in every grove.
By sports like these are all their cares beguiled;
The sports of children satisfy the child;
Each nobler aim, repressed by long control,
Now sinks at last, or feebly mans the soul;
While low delights succeeding fast behind,
In happier meanness occupy the mind:
As in those domes where Caesars once bore sway,
Defaced by time, and tottering in decay,
There in the ruin, heedless of the dead,
The shelter-seeking peasant builds his shed;
And, wondering man could want the larger pile,
Exults, and owns his cottage with a smile.
My soul, turn from them; turn we to survey
Where rougher climes a nobler race display,
Where the bleak Swiss their stormy mansions tread,
And force a churlish soil for scanty bread;
No product here the barren hills afford
But man and steel, the soldier and his sword;
No vernal blooms their torpid rocks array,
But winter lingering chills the lap of May;
No zephyr fondly sues the mountain's breast,
But meteors glare, and stormy glooms invest.
Yet still, even here, content can spread a charm,
Redress the clime, and all its rage disarm.
Though poor the peasant's hut, his feasts though small,
He sees his little lot the lot of all;
Sees no contiguous palace rear its head,
To shame the meanness of his humble shed;
No costly lord the sumptuous banquet deal,
To make him loathe his vegetable meal;
But calm, and bred in ignorance and toil,
Each wish contracting, fits him to the soil.
Cheerful at morn, he wakes from short repose,
Breasts the keen air, and carols as he goes;
With patient angle trolls the finny deep,
Or drives his venturous ploughshare to the steep;
Or seeks the den where snow-tracks mark the way,
And drags the struggling savage into day.
At night returning, every labor sped,
He sits him down the monarch of a shed;
Smiles, by his cheerful fire and round surveys
His children's looks, that brighten at the blaze;
While his loved partner, boastful of her hoard,
Displays her cleanly platter on the board;
And haply too some pilgrim, thither led,
With many a tale repays the nightly bed.
Thus every good his native wilds impart
Imprints the patriot passion on his heart;
And even those ills that round his mansion rise,
Enhance the bliss his scanty fund supplies.
Dear is that shed to which his soul conforms,
And dear that hill which lifts him to the storms;
And as a child, when scaring sounds molest,
Clings close and closer to the mother's breast,
So the loud torrent and the whirlwind's roar
But bind him to his native mountains more.
Such are the charms to barren states assigned,
Their wants but few, their wishes all confined;
Yet let them only share the praises due;
If few their wants, their pleasures are but few;
For every want that stimulates the breast
Becomes a source of pleasure when redressed:
Whence from such lands each pleasing science flies,
That first excites desire and then supplies;
Unknown to them, when sensual pleasures cloy,
To fill the languid pause with finer joy;
Unknown those powers that raise the soul to flame,
Catch every nerve and vibrate through the frame;
Their level life is but a smoldering fire,
Unquenched by want, unfanned by strong desire;
Unfit for raptures, or, if raptures cheer,
On some high festival of once a year,
In wild excess the vulgar breast takes fire,
Till, buried in debauch, the bliss expire.
But not their joys alone thus coarsely flow;
Their morals, like their pleasures, are but low;
For, as refinement stops, from sire to son
Unaltered, unimproved, the manners run;
And love's and friendship's finely pointed dart
Fall blunted from each indurated heart.
Some sterner virtues o'er the mountain's breast
May sit, like falcons cowering on the nest;
But all the gentler morals, such as play
Through life's more cultured walks, and charm the way,
These, far dispersed, on timorous pinions fly,

190. savage: beast.

232. indurated: hardened.

To sport and flutter in a kinder sky.
To kinder skies, where gentler manners reign,
I turn; and France displays her bright domain.
Gay, sprightly land of mirth and social ease,
Pleased with thyself, whom all the world can please,
How often have I led thy sportive choir,
With tuneless pipe, beside the murmuring Loire!
Where shading elms along the margin grew,
And freshened from the wave the zephyr flew.
And haply, though my harsh touch, faltering still,
But mocked all tune, and marred the dancer's skill;
Yet would the village praise my wondrous power,
And dance, forgetful of the noontide hour.
Alike all ages: dames of ancient days
Have led their children through the mirthful maze;
And the gay grandsire, skilled in gestic lore,
Has frisked beneath the burden of threescore.
So blessed a life these thoughtless realms display,
Thus idly busy rolls their world away;
Theirs are those arts that mind to mind endear,
For honor forms the social temper here:
Honor, that praise which real merit gains,
Or e'en imaginary worth obtains,
Here passes current; paid from hand to hand,
It shifts in splendid traffic round the land:
From courts to camps, to cottages it strays,
And all are taught an avarice of praise;
They please, are pleased, they give to get esteem,
Till, seeming blessed, they grow to what they seem.
But while this softer art their bliss supplies,
It gives their follies also room to rise;
For praise too dearly loved, or warmly sought,
Enfeebles all internal strength of thought;
And the weak soul, within itself unblessed,
Leans for all pleasure on another's breast.
Hence Ostentation here, with tawdry art,
Pants for the vulgar praise which fools impart;
Here Vanity assume her pert grimace,
And trims her robes of frieze with copper lace;
Here beggar Pride defrauds her daily cheer,
To boast one splendid banquet once a year:
The mind still turns where shifting fashion draws,
Nor weighs the solid worth of self-applause.
To men of other minds my fancy flies,
Embosomed in the deep where Holland lies.
Methinks her patient sons before me stand,
Where the broad ocean leans against the land,
And, sedulous to stop the coming tide,
Lift the tall rampire's artificial pride.
Onward, methinks, and diligently slow,
The firm connected bulwark seems to grow,
Spreads its long arms amidst the watery roar,
Scoops out an empire, and usurps the shore;
While the pent ocean, rising o'er the pile,
Sees an amphibious world beneath him smile:
The slow canal, the yellow-blossomed vale,
The willow-tufted bank, the gliding sail,
The crowded mart, the cultivated plain,
A new creation rescued from his reign.
Thus, while around the wave-subjected soil
Impels the native to repeated toil,
Industrious habits in each bosom reign,
And industry begets a love of grain.
Hence all the good from opulence that springs,
With all those ills superfluous treasure brings,
Are here displayed. Their much-loved wealth imparts
Convenience, plenty, elegance, and arts;
But, view them closer, craft and fraud appear;
Even liberty itself is bartered here.
At gold's superior charms all freedom flies,
The needy sell it, and the rich man buys;
A land of tyrants, and a den of slaves,
Here wretches seek dishonorable graves,
And calmly bent, to servitude conform,
Dull as their lakes that slumber in the storm.
Heavens! how unlike their Belgic sires of old!
Rough, poor, content, ungovernably bold,
War in each breast, and freedom on each brow,
How much unlike the sons of Britain now!
Fired at the sound, my genius spreads her wing,
And flies where Britain courts the western spring;
Where lawns extend that scorn Arcadian pride,
And brighter streams than famed Hydaspes glide;
There all around the gentlest breezes stray,
There gentle music melts on every spray;
Creation's mildest charms are there combined;
Extremes are only in the master's mind.
Stern o'er each bosom Reason holds her state,
With daring aims irregularly great.
Pride in their port, defiance in their eye,
I see the lords of human kind pass by;

253. gestic: dancing. **276. frieze:** a coarse woolen cloth.

286. rampire: dam, rampart. **320. Hydaspes:** the modern Jhelam, a river in India.

Intent on high designs, a thoughtful band,
By forms unfashioned, fresh from Nature's
hand,
Fierce in their native hardiness of soul,
True to imagined right, above control,
While even the peasant boasts these rights to scan,
And learns to venerate himself as man.
Thine, Freedom, thine the blessings pictured here,
Thine are those charms that dazzle and endear;
Too blessed indeed were such without alloy,
But, fostered even by Freedom, ills annoy;
That independence Britons prize too high,
Keeps man from man, and breaks the social
tie;
The self-dependent lordlings stand alone,
All claims that bind and sweeten life unknown.
Here, by the bonds of nature feebly held,
Minds combat minds, repelling and repelled;
Ferments arise, imprisoned factions roar,
Repressed ambition struggles round her shore;
Till overwrought, the general system feels
Its motions stopped, or frenzy fire the wheels.
Nor this the worst. As nature's ties decay,
As duty, love, and honor fail to sway,
Fictitious bonds, the bonds of wealth and law,
Still gather strength, and force unwilling awe.
Hence all obedience bows to these alone,
And talent sinks, and merit weeps unknown;
Till time may come, when, stripped of all her
charms,
The land of scholars and the nurse of arms,
Where noble stems transmit the patriot flame,
Where kings have toiled and poets wrote for fame,
One sink of level avarice shall lie,
And scholars, soldiers, kings, unhonored die.
Yet think not, thus when Freedom's ills I state,
I mean to flatter kings or court the great:
Ye powers of truth, that bid my soul aspire,
Far from my bosom drive the low desire!
And thou, fair Freedom, taught alike to feel
The rabble's rage, and tyrant's angry steel;
Thou transitory flower, alike undone
By proud contempt or favor's fostering sun,
Still may thy blooms the changeful clime endure!
I only would repress them to secure;
For just experience tells, in every soil,
That those who think must govern those that toil;
And all that Freedom's highest aims can reach
Is but to lay proportioned loads on each.
Hence, should one order disproportioned grow,
Its double weight must ruin all below.
Oh, then how blind to all that truth requires,
Who think it freedom when a part aspires!
Calm is my soul, nor apt to rise to arms,
Except when fast-approaching danger warms:
But when contending chiefs blockade the throne,
Contracting regal power to stretch their own;
When I behold a factious band agree
To call it freedom when themselves are free;
Each wanton judge new penal statutes draw,
Laws grind the poor, and rich men rule the law;
The wealth of climes where savage nations roam,
Pillaged from slaves to purchase slaves at home;
Fear, pity, justice, indignation, start,
Tear off reserve, and bare my swelling heart;
Till, half a patriot, half a coward grown,
I fly from petty tyrants to the throne.
Yes, brother, curse with me that baleful hour
When first ambition struck at regal power;
And thus polluting honor in its source,
Gave wealth to sway the mind with double force.
Have we not seen, round Britain's peopled shore,
Her useful sons exchanged for useless ore?
Seen all her triumph but destruction haste,
Like flaring tapers brightening as they waste?
Seen Opulence, her grandeur to maintain,
Lead stern Depopulation in her train,
And over fields where scattered hamlets rose,
In barren solitary, pomp repose?
Have ye not seen, at Pleasure's lordly call,
The smiling, long-frequented village fall?
Beheld the duteous son, the sire decayed,
The modest matron, and the blushing maid,
Forced from their homes, a melancholy train,
To traverse climes beyond the western main;
Where wild Oswego spreads her swamps around,
And Niagara stuns with thundering sound?
Even now, perhaps, as there some pilgrim strays
Through tangled forests and through dangerous
ways,
Where beasts with man divided empire claim,
And the brown Indian marks with murderous aim;
There, while above the giddy tempest flies,
And all around distressful yells arise,
The pensive exile, bending with his woe,
To stop too fearful, and too faint to go,
Casts a long look where England's glories shine,
And bids his bosom sympathize with mine.

411. Oswego: a river in northern New York.

Vain, very vain, my weary search to find
That bliss which only centers in the mind.
Why have I strayed from pleasure and repose,
To seek a good each government bestows?
In every government, though terrors reign,
Though tyrant kings or tyrant laws restrain,
How small, of all that human hearts endure,
That part which laws or kings can cause or
cure!
Still to ourselves in every place consigned,
Our own felicity we make or find;
With secret course which no loud storms annoy,
Glides the smooth current of domestic joy.
The lifted axe, the agonizing wheel,
Luke's iron crown, and Damiens' bed of steel,
To men remote from power but rarely known,
Leave reason, faith, and conscience all our own.

(1764)

THE DESERTED VILLAGE

TO SIR JOSHUA REYNOLDS

Dear Sir,—I can have no expectations in an address of this kind, either to add to your reputation, or to establish my own. You can gain nothing from my admiration, as I am ignorant of that art in which you are said to excel; and I may lose much by the severity of your judgment, as few have a juster taste in poetry than you. Setting interest therefore aside, to which I never paid much attention, I must be indulged at present in following my affections. The only dedication I ever made was to my brother, because I loved him better than most other men. He is since dead. Permit me to inscribe this poëm to you.

How far you may be pleased with the versification and mere mechanical parts of this attempt, I don't pretend to inquire; but I know you will object (and indeed several of our best and wisest friends concur in the opinion) that the depopulation it deplores is nowhere to be seen, and the disorders it laments are only to be found in the poet's own imagination. To this I can scarce make any other answer, than that I sincerely believe what I have written; that I have taken all possible pains in my country excursions, for these four or five years past, to be certain of what I allege; and that all my views and inquiries have led me to believe those miseries real which I here attempt to display. But this is not the place to enter into an inquiry, whether the country be depopulating or not; the discussion would take up much room, and I should prove myself, at best, an indifferent politician, to tire the reader with a long preface, when I want his unfatigued attention to a long poem.

In regretting the depopulation of the country, I inveigh against the increase of our luxuries and here also I expect the shout of modern politicians against me. For twenty or thirty years past it has been the fashion to consider luxury as one of the greatest national advantages, and all the wisdom of antiquity, in that particular, as erroneous. Still, however, I must remain a professed ancient on that head, and continue to think those luxuries prejudicial to states by which so many vices are introduced and so many kingdoms have been undone. Indeed so much has been poured out of late on the other side of the question, that, merely for the sake of novelty and variety, one would sometimes wish to be in the right.

I am, dear sir, your sincere friend, and ardent admirer,

Oliver Goldsmith.

Sweet Auburn! loveliest village of the plain,
Where health and plenty cheered the laboring
swain,
Where smiling spring its earliest visit paid,
And parting summer's lingering blooms delayed;
Dear lovely bowers of innocence and ease,
Seats of my youth, when every sport could please,
How often have I loitered o'er thy green,
Where humble happiness endeared each scene!
How often have I paused on every charm,
The sheltered cot, the cultivated farm,
The never-failing brook, the busy mill,
The decent church that topped the neighboring hill,
The hawthorn bush, with seats beneath the shade,
For talking age and whispering lovers made!
How often have I blessed the coming day,
When toil remitting lent its turn to play,
And all the village train, from labor free,
Led up their sports beneath the spreading tree;
While many a pastime circled in the shade,
The young contending as the old surveyed;
And many a gambol frolicked o'er the ground,

429–38. Except for lines 435–36, this section was written by Samuel Johnson. **436. Luke's iron crown:** George and Luke Dosa led a famous rebellion in Hungary in 1513. For his participation in the uprising, George endured the torture of the hot iron crown. **Damiens' bed of steel:** Damiens tried to assassinate Louis XV in 1757; as a result, he was tortured on an iron bed.

And sleights of art and feats of strength went round;
And still, as each repeated pleasure tired,
Succeeding sports the mirthful hand inspired;
The dancing pair that simply sought renown,
By holding out to tire each other down;
The swain mistrustless of his smutted face,
While secret laughter tittered round the place;
The bashful virgin's sidelong looks of love,
The matron's glance that would those looks
reprove—
These were thy charms, sweet village! sports like
these,
With sweet succession taught even toil to please;
These round thy bowers their cheerful influence
shed;
These were thy charms—but all these charms are
fled.
Sweet smiling village, loveliest of the lawn,
Thy sports are fled and all thy charms withdrawn;
Amidst thy bowers the tyrant's hand is seen,
And desolation saddens all thy green;
One only master grasps the whole domain,
And half a tillage stints thy smiling plain;
No more thy glassy brook reflects the day,
But choked with sedges works its weedy way;
Along thy glades, a solitary guest,
The hollow-sounding bittern guards its nest;
Amidst thy desert walks the lapwing flies,
And tires their echoes with unvaried cries.
Sunk are thy bowers in shapeless ruin all,
And the long grass o'ertops the moldering wall;
And, trembling, shrinking from the spoiler's hand,
Far, far away, thy children leave the land.
Ill fares the land, to hastening ills a prey,
Where wealth accumulates and men decay;
Princes and lords may flourish or may fade;
A breath can make them as a breath has made:
But a bold peasantry, their country's pride,
When once destroyed, can never be supplied.
A time there was, ere England's griefs began,
When every rood of ground maintained its man;
For him light labor spread her wholesome store,
Just gave what life required, but gave no more:
His best companions, innocence and health;
And his best riches, ignorance of wealth.
But times are altered; trade's unfeeling train
Usurp the land, and dispossess the swain;
Along the lawn, where scattered hamlets rose,
Unwieldy wealth and cumbrous pomp repose;
And every want to opulence allied,
And every pang that folly pays to pride.
Those gentle hours that plenty bade to bloom,
Those calm desires that asked but little room,
Those healthful sports that graced the peaceful
scene,
Lived in each look, and brightened all the green—
These, far departing, seek a kinder shore,
And rural mirth and manners are no more.
Sweet Auburn! part of the blissful hour,
Thy glades forlorn confess the tyrant's power.
Here, as I take my solitary rounds
Amidst thy tangling walks and ruined grounds,
And, many a year elapsed, return to view
Where once the cottage stood, the hawthorn
grew,
Remembrance wakes with all her busy train,
Swells at my breast, and turns the past to pain.
In all my wanderings round this world of care,
In all my griefs—and God has given my share—
I still had hopes, my latest hours to crown,
Amidst these humble bowers to lay me down;
To husband out life's taper at the close,
And keep the flame from wasting by repose.
I still had hopes, for pride attends us still,
Amidst the swains to show my book-learned
skill,
Around my fire an evening group to draw,
And tell of all I felt, and all I saw;
And, as a hare whom hounds and horns pursue,
Pants to the place from whence at first she flew,
I still had hopes, my long vexations past,
Here to return—and die at home at last.
O blessed retirement, friend to life's decline,
Retreats from care, that never must be mine,
How happy he who crowns in shades like these
A youth of labor with an age of ease;
Who quits a world where strong temptations try,
And, since 'tis hard to combat, learns to fly!
For him no wretches, born to work and weep,
Explore the mine, or tempt the dangerous deep;
No surly porter stands in guilty state,
To spurn imploring famine from the gate;
But on he moves to meet his latter end,
Angels around befriending virtue's friend;
Bends to the grave with unperceived decay,
While resignation gently slopes the way;
And, all his prospects brightening to the last,

THE DESERTED VILLAGE. **27. mistrustless:** unsuspecting. **58. rood:** rod.

His heaven commences ere the world be past.
Sweet was the sound, when oft at evening's close
Up yonder hill the village murmur rose;
There, as I passed with careless steps and slow,
The mingling notes came softened from below;
The swain responsive as the milkmaid sung,
The sober herd that lowed to meet their young,
The noisy geese that gabbled o'er the pool,
The playful children just let loose from school,
The watch-dog's voice that bayed the whispering wind,
And the loud laugh that spoke the vacant mind—
These all in sweet confusion sought the shade,
And filled each pause the nightingale had made.
But now the sounds of population fail,
No cheerful murmurs fluctuate in the gale,
No busy steps the grass-grown footway tread,
For all the bloomy flush of life is fled;
All but yon widowed, solitary thing,
That feebly bends beside the plashy spring;
She, wretched matron, forced in age, for bread,
To strip the brook with mantling cresses spread,
To pick her wintry fagot from the thorn,
To seek her nightly shed, and weep till morn—
She only left of all the harmless train,
The sad historian of the pensive plain.
Near yonder copse, where once the garden smiled,
And still where many a garden flower grows wild,
There, where a few torn shrubs the place disclose,
The village preacher's modest mansion rose.
A man he was to all the country dear,
And passing rich with forty pounds a year;
Remote from towns he ran his godly race,
Nor e'er had changed, nor wished to change his place;
Unpractised he to fawn, or seek for power,
By doctrines fashioned to the varying hour;
Far other aims his heart had learned to prize,
More skilled to raise the wretched than to rise.
His house was known to all the vagrant train;
He chid their wanderings, but relieved their pain;
The long-remembered beggar was his guest,
Whose beard descending swept his aged breast;
The ruined spendthrift, now no longer proud,
Claimed kindred there, and has his claims allowed;
The broken soldier, kindly bade to stay,
Sat by his fire and talked the night away;
Wept o'er his wounds, or, tales of sorrow done,
Shouldered his crutch and showed how fields were won.
Pleased with his guests, the good man learned to glow,
And quite forgot their vices in their woe;
Careless their merits or their faults to scan,
His pity gave ere charity began.
Thus to relieve the wretched was his pride,
And e'en his failings leaned to virtue's side;
But in his duty prompt at every call,
He watched and wept, he prayed and felt for all:
And, as a bird each fond endearment tries
To tempt its new-fledged offspring to the skies,
He tried each art, reproved each dull delay,
Allured to brighter worlds, and led the way.
Beside the bed where parting life was laid,
And sorrow, guilt, and pain by turns dismayed,
The reverend champion stood. At his control
Despair and anguish fled the struggled soul;
Comfort came down the trembling wretch to raise,
And his last faltering accents whispered praise.
At church, with meek and unaffected grace,
His looks adorned the venerable place;
Truth from his lips prevailed with double sway,
And fools who came to scoff remained to pray.
The service past, around the pious man,
With steady zeal, each honest rustic ran;
Even children followed, with endearing wile,
And plucked his gown, to share the good man's smile.
His ready smile a parent's warmth expressed,
Their welfare pleased him and their cares distressed;
To them his heart, his love, his griefs were given,
But all his serious thoughts had rest in Heaven.
As some tall cliff, that lifts its awful form,
Swells from the vale, and midway leaves the storm,
Though round its breast the rolling clouds are spread,
Eternal sunshine settles on its head.
Beside yon straggling fence that skirts the way,
With blossomed furze unprofitably gay,
There, in his noisy mansion, skilled to rule,
The village master taught his little school.
A man severe he was, and stern to view;

122. vacant: carefree. **132. cresses:** plants.

194. furze: prickly evergreen shrubs.

I knew him well, and every truant knew;
Well had the boding tremblers learned to trace
The day's disasters in his morning face;
Full well they laughed with counterfeited glee
At all his jokes, for many a joke had he;
Full well the busy whisper, circling round,
Conveyed the dismal tidings when he frowned;
Yet he was kind, or, if severe in aught,
The love he bore to learning was in fault;
The village all declared how much he knew;
'Twas certain he could write, and cipher too;
Lands he could measure, terms and tides presage,
And even the story ran that he could gauge:
In arguing, too, the parson owned his skill,
For even though vanquished, he could argue still;
While words of learned length and thundering sound
Amazed the gazing rustics ranged around;
And still they gazed, and still the wonder grew
That one small head could carry all he knew.
But past is all his fame. The very spot
Where many a time he triumphed is forgot.
Near yonder thorn that lifts its head on high,
Where once the sign-post caught the passing eye,
Low lies that house where nut-brown draughts inspired,
Where graybeard mirth and smiling toil retired,
Where village statesmen talked with looks profound,
And news much older than their ale went round.
Imagination fondly stoops to trace
The parlor splendors of that festive place;
The whitewashed wall, the nicely sanded floor,
The varnished clock that clicked behind the door;
The chest contrived a double debt to pay,
A bed by night, a chest of drawers by day;
The pictures placed for ornament and use,
The twelve good rules, the royal game of goose;
The hearth, except when winter chilled the day,
With aspen boughs and flowers and fennel gay;
While broken teacups, wisely kept for show,
Ranged o'er the chimney, glistened in a row.

209. terms: days set aside for payment of rent, dues, etc. **232. twelve . . . goose:** a reference to "King Charles's Twelve Good Rules" (e.g., "Reveal no secrets") hung in printed form in many homes. The "game of goose" was a popular game in which players moved their pieces on a game board, according to the fall of the dice. **234. fennel:** tall herb of the carrot family.

Vain transitory splendors! Could not all
Reprieve the tottering mansion from its fall?
Obscure it sinks, nor shall it more impart
An hour's importance to the poor man's heart;
Thither no more the peasant shall repair
To sweet oblivion of his daily care;
No more the farmer's news, the barber's tale,
No more the woodman's ballad shall prevail;
No more the smith his dusky brow shall clear,
Relax his ponderous strength, and lean to hear;
The host himself no longer shall be found
Careful to see the mantling bliss go round;
Nor the coy maid, half willing to be pressed,
Shall kiss the cup to pass it to the rest.
Yes! let the rich deride, the proud disdain,
These simple blessings of the lowly train;
To me more dear, congenial to my heart,
One native charm, than all the gloss of art;
Spontaneous joys, where nature has its play,
The soul adopts, and owns their first-born sway;
Lightly they frolic o'er the vacant mind,
Unenvied, unmolested, unconfined.
But the long pomp, the midnight masquerade,
With all the freaks of wanton wealth arrayed,—
In these, ere triflers half their wish obtain,
The toiling pleasure sickens into pain;
And e'en while fashion's brightest arts decoy,
The heart distrusting asks if this be joy.
Ye friends to truth, ye statesmen, who survey
The rich man's joys increase, the poor's decay,
'Tis yours to judge how wide the limits stand
Between a splendid and an happy land.
Proud swells the tide with loads of freighted ore,
And shouting Folly hails them from her shore;
Hoards even beyond the miser's wish abound,
And rich men flock from all the world around.
Yet count our gains: this wealth is but a name
That leaves our useful products still the same.
Not so the loss: the man of wealth and pride
Takes up a space that many poor supplied;
Space for his lake, his park's extended bounds,
Space for his horses, equipage, and hounds;
The robe that wraps his limbs in silken sloth
Has robbed the neighboring fields of half their growth;
His seat, where solitary sports are seen,
Indignant spurns the cottage from the green;
Around the world each needful product flies,
For all the luxuries the world supplies;

While thus the land, adorned for pleasure all,
In barren splendor feebly waits the fall.
As some fair female, unadorned and plain,
Secure to please while youth confirms her reign,
Slights every borrowed charm that dress supplies,
Nor shares with art the triumph of her eyes;
But when those charms are past, for charms are frail,
When time advances and when lovers fail,
She then shines forth, solicitous to bless,
In all the glaring impotence of dress:
Thus fares the land, by luxury betrayed,
In nature's simplest charms at first arrayed;
But verging to decline, its splendors rise,
Its vistas strike, its palaces surprise;
While, scourged by famine from the smiling land,
The mournful peasant leads his humble band;
And while he sinks, without one arm to save,
The country blooms—a garden and a grave.
Where then, ah! where shall poverty reside,
To 'scape the pressure of contiguous pride?
If to some common's fenceless limits strayed,
He drives his flock to pick the scanty blade,
Those fenceless fields the sons of wealth divide,
And even the bare-worn common is denied.
If to the city sped—what waits him there?
To see profusion that he must not share;
To see ten thousand baneful arts combined
To pamper luxury, and thin mankind;
To see those joys the sons of pleasure know
Extorted from his fellow-creature's woe.
Here while the courtier glitters in brocade,
There the pale artist plies the sickly trade;
Here while the proud their long-drawn pomps display,
There the black gibbet glooms beside the way;
The dome where Pleasure holds her midnight reign,
Here, richly decked, admits the gorgeous train;
Tumultuous grandeur crowds the blazing square,
The rattling chariots clash, the torches glare.
Sure scenes like these no troubles e'er annoy!
Sure these denote one universal joy!
Are these thy serious thoughts?—Ah, turn thine eyes
Where the poor houseless shivering female lies.
She once, perhaps, in village plenty blessed,
Has wept at tales of innocence distressed;
Her modest looks the cottage might adorn,
Sweet as the primrose peeps beneath the thorn;
Now lost to all—her friends, her virtue fled—
Near her betrayer's door she lays her head,
And, pinched with cold, and shrinking from the shower,
With heavy heart deplores that luckless hour,
When idly first, ambitious of the town,
She left her wheel and robes of country brown.
Do thine, sweet Auburn, thine, the loveliest train—
Do thy fair tribes participate her pain?
E'en now, perhaps, by cold and hunger led,
At proud men's doors they ask a little bread.
Ah, no! To distant climes, a dreary scene,
Where half the convex world intrudes between,
Through torrid tracts with fainting steps they go,
Where wild Altama murmurs to their woe.
Far different there from all that charmed before,
The various terrors of that horrid shore;
Those blazing suns that dart a downward ray,
And fiercely shed intolerable day;
Those matted woods where birds forget to sing,
But silent bats in drowsy clusters cling;
Those poisonous fields with rank luxuriance crowned,
Where the dark scorpion gathers death around;
Where at each step the stranger fears to wake
The rattling terrors of the vengeful snake;
Where crouching tigers wait their hapless prey,
And savage men more murderous still than they;
While oft in whirls the mad tornado flies,
Mingling the ravaged landscape with the skies.
Far different these from every former scene,
The cooling brook, the grassy-vested green,
The breezy covert of the warbling grove,
That only sheltered thefts of harmless love.
Good Heaven! what sorrows gloomed that parting day
That called them from their native walks away;
When the poor exiles, every pleasure past,

316. artist: artisan. **318. gibbet:** gallows.

344. Altama: a reference to the Altamaha River in Georgia, the boundary between the British General Oglethorpe's colony in Georgia and the Spaniards in Florida. This entire section is an interesting example of the picture of America held by an educated Englishman in 1770.

Hung round their bowers, and fondly looked their last,
And took a long farewell, and wished in vain
For seats like these beyond the western main;
And, shuddering still to face the distant deep,
Returned and wept, and still returned to weep.
The good old sire the first prepared to go
To new-found worlds, and wept for others' woe;
But for himself, in conscious virtue brave,
He only wished for worlds beyond the grave.
His lovely daughter, lovelier in her tears,
The fond companion of his helpless years,
Silent went next, neglected of her charms,
And left a lover's for a father's arms.
With louder plaints the mother spoke her woes,
And blessed the cot where every pleasure rose,
And kissed her thoughtless babe with many a tear,
And clasped them close, in sorrow doubly dear;
Whilst her fond husband strove to lend relief
In all the silent manliness of grief.
O Luxury! thou cursed by Heaven's decree,
How ill exchanged are things like these for thee!
How do thy potions, with insidious joy,
Diffuse their pleasures only to destroy!
Kingdoms by thee, to sickly greatness grown,
Boast of a florid vigor not their own:
At every draught more large and large they grow,
A bloated mass of rank, unwieldly woe;
Till, sapped their strength, and every part unsound,
Down, down they sink, and spread a ruin round.
E'en now the devastation is begun,
And half the business of destruction done;
E'en now, methinks, as pondering here I stand,
I see the rural virtues leave the land:
Down where yon anchoring vessel spreads the sail,
That idly waiting flaps with every gale,
Downward they move, a melancholy band,
Pass from the shore, and darken all the strand.
Contented Toil, and hospitable Care,
And kind connubial Tenderness are there;
And Piety with wishes placed above,
And steady Loyalty, and faithful Love.
And thou, sweet Poetry, thou loveliest maid,
Still first to fly where sensual joys invade,
Unfit, in these degenerate times of shame,
To catch the heart, or strike for honest fame;
Dear charming nymph, neglected and decried,
My shame in crowds, my solitary pride;
Thou source of all my bliss and all my woe,
That found'st me poor at first, and keep'st me so;
Thou guide by which the nobler arts excel,
Thou nurse of every virtue, fare thee well!
Farewell! and oh! where'er thy voice be tried,
On Torno's cliffs, or Pambamarca's side,
Whether where equinoctial fervors glow,
Or winter wraps the polar world in snow,
Still let thy voice, prevailing over time,
Redress the rigors of the inclement clime;
Aid slighted truth with thy persuasive train;
Teach erring man to spurn the rage of gain;
Teach him, that states of native strength possessed,
Though very poor, may still be very blessed;
That trade's proud empire hastes to swift decay,
As ocean sweeps the labored mole away;
While self-dependent power can time defy,
As rocks resist the billows and the sky.

(1770)

418. Torno . . . Pambamarca: the river Torno is in northern Sweden. Pambamarca is a mountain in Ecuador. **426–30.** James Boswell attributes these lines to Samuel Johnson.

Thomas Chatterton

1752–1770

◆

AN EXCELENTE BALADE OF CHARITIE

AS WROTEN BIE THE GODE PRIESTE THOMAS ROWLEY, 1464*

In Virgyne the sweltrie sun gan sheene,
And hotte upon the mees did caste his raie;
The apple rodded from its palie greene,
And the mole peare did bende the leafy spraie;
The peede chelandri sunge the livelong daie;
'Twas nowe the pride, the manhode of the yeare,
And eke the grounde was dighte in its mose defte aumere.

The sun was glemeing in the middle of daie,
Deadde still the aire, and eke the welken blue,
When from the sea arist in drear arraie
A hepe of cloudes of sable sullen hue,
The which full fast unto the woodlande drewe,
Hiltring attenes the sunnis fetive face,
And the blacke tempeste swolne and gathered up apace.

Beneath an holme, faste by a pathwaie side,
Which dide unto Seyncte Godwine's convente lede,
A hapless pilgrim moneynge did abide.
Pore in his viewe, ungentle in his weede,
Longe bretful of the miseries of neede,
Where from the hail-stone coulde the almer flie?
He had no housen theere, ne anie convente nie.

Look in his glommed face, his sprighte there scanne;
Howe woe-be-gone, how withered, forwynd, deade!
Haste to thie church-glebe-house, asshrewed manne!
Haste to thie kiste, thie onlie dortoure bedde.
Cale, as the claie whiche will gre on thie hedde,
Is Charitie and Love aminge highe elves;
Knightis and Barons live for pleasure and themselves.

The gatherd storme is rype; the bigge drops falle;
The forswat meadowes smethe, and drenche the raine;
The comyng ghastness do the cattle pall,
And the full flockes are drivynge ore the plaine;
Dashde from the cloudes the waters flott againe;
The welkin opes; the yellow levynne flies;
And the hot fierie smothe in the wide lowings dies.

Liste! now the thunder's rattling clymmynge sound
Cheves slowlie on, and then embollen clangs,
Shakes the hie spyre, and losst, dispended, drown'd,
Still on the gallard eare of terroure hanges;
The windes are up; the lofty elmen swanges:
Again the levynne and the thunder poures,
And the full cloudes are braste attenes in stonen showers.

Spurreynge his palfrie oere the watrie plaine,
The Abbote of Seyncte Godwynes convente came;

* Thomas Rowley, the author, was born at Norton Malreward in Somersetshire, educated at the Convent of St. Kenna at Keynesham, and died at Westbury in Gloucestershire (Chatterton). [Unless otherwise specified, the notes are Chatterton's.]

AN EXCELENTE BALADE OF CHARITIE. 2. **mees:** meads. The sign of the zodiac Virgo extends from August 23 to September 22 [Editor's note]. 3. **rodded:** reddened. 4. **mole:** soft. 5. **peede chelandri:** pied goldfinch. 7. **defte aumere:** ornamental mantle. 9. **welken:** sky. 13. **Hiltring . . . face:** hiding at once the sun's beauteous face. 15. **holme:** oak [Editor's note]. 17. **moneynge:** moaning. 19. **bretful:** filled with. 20. **almer:** beggar.

22. **glommed:** clouded, dejected. 23. **forwynd:** dry, sapless. 24. **church-glebe-house:** grave; **asshrewed:** accursed. 25. **kiste:** coffin; **dortoure:** sleeping room. 26. **Cale:** warm. 30. **forswat:** sun-burnt; **smethe:** smoke; **drenche:** drink. 31. **pall:** frighten. 33. **flott:** fly. 34. **levynne:** lightning. 35. **smothe:** vapor; **lowings:** flames. 36. **clymmynge:** noisy. 37. **cheves:** moves; **embollen:** swollen, strengthened. 39. **gallard:** frightened. 42. **braste:** burst; **stonen:** pelting [Editor's note].

His chapournette was drented with the reine,
And his pencte gyrdle met with mickle shame;
He aynewarde tolde his bederoll at the same;
The storme encreasen, and he drew aside,
With the mist almes-craver neere to the holme to
bide.

His cope was all of Lyncolne clothe so fyne,
With a gold button fasten'd neere his chynne;
His autremete was edged with golden twynne,
And his shoone pyke a loverds mighte have
binne;
Full well it shewn he thoughten coste no sinne:
The trammels of the palfrye pleasde his sighte,
For the horse-millanare his head with roses dighte.

"An almes, sir prieste!" the droppynge pilgrim
saide,
"O! let me waite within your convente dore,
Till the sunne sheneth hie above our heade,
And the loude tempeste of the aire is oer;
Helpless and ould am I alas! and poor;
No house, ne friend, ne moneie in my pouche;
All yatte I call my owne is this my silver crouche."

"Varlet," replyd the Abbatte, "cease your dinne;
This is no season almes and prayers to give;
Mie porter never lets a faitour in;
None touch mie rynge who not in honour live."
And now the sonne with the blacke cloudes did
stryve,
And shettynge on the grounde his glairie raie,
The Abbatte spurrde his steede, and eftsoones
roadde awaie.

Once moe the skie was blacke, the thunder rolde;
Faste reyneynge oer the plaine a prieste was
seen;
Ne dighte full proude, ne buttoned up in golde;
His cope and jape were graie, and eke were
clene;
A Limitoure he was of order scene;
And from the pathwaie side then turned hee,
Where the pore almer laie binethe the holmen tree.

"An almes, sir priest!" the droppynge pilgrim
sayde,
"For sweete Seyncte Marie and your order sake!"
The Limitoure then loosen'd his pouche
threade,
And did thereoute a groate of silver take;
The mister pilgrim dyd for halline shake.
"Here take this silver, it maie eathe thie care;
We are Goddes stewards all, nete of oure owne we
bare.

"But ah! unhailie pilgrim, lerne of me,
Scathe anie give a rentrolle to their Lorde.
Here take my semecope, thou arte bare I see;
Tis thyne; the Seynctes will give me mie
rewarde."
He left the pilgrim, and his waie aborde.
Virgynne and hallie Seyncte, who sitte yn
gloure,
Or give the mittee will, or give the gode man power.

(1777)

45. chapournette: small round hat. **46. pencte:** painted; **mickle:** much [Editor's note]. **47. He . . . bederoll:** He said his beads backwards; he cursed. **49. mist:** poor, needy. **52. autremete:** a loose white robe, worn by priests. **53. And . . . binne:** And his pointed shoes might have been a lord's [Editor's note]. **55. trammels:** shackles. **63. crouche:** cross. **66. faitour:** a beggar, or vagabond.

74. jape: a short surplice. **75. Limitoure:** a friar licensed to beg [Editor's note]. **82. halline:** joy. **83. eathe:** ease. **84. nete:** nought. **85. unhailie:** unhappy. **86. Scathe:** scarcely; **rentrolle:** a large portion of one's fortune [Editor's note]. **88. Seynctes:** Saints [Editor's note]. **91. mittee:** mighty.

William Cowper
1731-1800

FROM

Olney Hymns

PRAISE FOR THE FOUNTAIN OPENED

Zech. xiii. 1

There is a fountain filled with blood
Drawn from Emmanuel's veins;
And sinners, plunged beneath that flood,
Lose all their guilty stains.

The dying thief rejoiced to see
That fountain in his day;
And there have I, as vile as he,
Washed all my sins away.

Dear dying Lamb, thy precious blood
Shall never lose its power;
Till all the ransomed church of God
Be saved, to sin no more.

E'er since, by faith, I saw the stream
Thy flowing wounds supply;
Redeeming love has been my theme,
And shall be till I die.

Then in a nobler sweeter song
I'll sing thy power to save:
When this poor lisping stammering tongue
Lies silent in the grave.

Lord, I believe thou hast prepared
(Unworthy though I be)
For me a blood-bought free reward,
A golden harp for me!

'Tis strung, and tuned, for endless years,
And formed by power divine;
To sound in God the Father's ears,
No other name but thine.

(1779)

OLNEY HYMNS. PRAISE FOR THE FOUNTAIN OPENED. 2. **Emmanuel:** God with us; Jesus.

THE HAPPY CHANGE

How blessed thy creature is, O God,
When with a single eye,
He views the lustre of thy word,
The day-spring from on high!

Through all the storms that veil the skies,
And frown on earthly things,
The Sun of righteousness he eyes,
With healing on his wings.

Struck by that light, the human heart,
A barren soil no more,
Sends the sweet smell of grace abroad,
Where serpents lurked before.

The soul, a dreary province once
Of Satan's dark domain,
Feels a new empire formed within,
And owns a heavenly reign.

The glorious orb, whose golden beams
The fruitful year control,
Since first, obedient to thy word,
He started from the goal;

Has cheered the nations, with the joys
His orient rays impart;
But Jesus, 'tis thy light alone,
Can shine upon the heart.

(1779)

THE SHRUBBERY

WRITTEN IN A TIME OF AFFLICTION

Oh, happy shades—to me unblessed!
Friendly to peace, but not to me!
How ill the scene that offers rest,
And heart that cannot rest, agree!

This glassy stream, that spreading pine,
Those alders quivering to the breeze,
Might soothe a soul less hurt than mine,
And please, if anything could please.

But fixed unalterable care
  Foregoes not what she feels within,
Shows the same sadness everywhere,
  And slights the season and the scene.

For all that pleased in wood or lawn,
  While peace possessed these silent bowers,
Her animating smile withdrawn,
  Has lost its beauties and its powers.

The saint or moralist should tread
  This moss-grown alley, musing, slow;
They seek, like me, the secret shade,
  But not, like me, to nourish woe!

Me fruitful scenes and prospects waste
  Alike admonish not to roam;
These tell me of enjoyments past,
  And those of sorrows yet to come.

(1773, 1782)

*The Castaway**

Obscurest night involved the sky,
  The Atlantic billows roared,
When such a destined wretch as I,
  Washed headlong from on board,
Of friends, of hope, of all bereft,
His floating home forever left.

No braver chief could Albion boast
  Than he with whom he went,
Nor ever ship left Albion's coast,
  With warmer wishes sent.
He loved them both, but both in vain,
Nor him beheld, nor her again.

Not long beneath the whelming brine,
  Expert to swim, he lay;
Nor soon he felt his strength decline,
  Or courage die away;
But waged with death a lasting strife,
Supported by despair of life.

He shouted: nor his friends had failed
  To check the vessel's course,
But so the furious blast prevailed,
  That, pitiless perforce,
They left their outcast mate behind,
And scudded still before the wind.

Some succour yet they could afford;
  And, such as storms allow,
The cask, the coop, the floated cord,
  Delayed not to bestow.
But he (they knew) nor ship, nor shore,
Whate'er they gave, should visit more.

Nor, cruel as it seemed, could he
  Their haste himself condemn,
Aware that flight, in such a sea,
  Alone could rescue them;
Yet bitter felt it still to die
Deserted, and his friends so nigh.

He long survives, who lives an hour
  In ocean, self-upheld;
And so long he, with unspent power,
  His destiny repelled;
And ever, as the minutes flew,
Entreated help, or cried, "Adieu!"

At length, his transient respite past,
  His comrades, who before
Had heard his voice in every blast,
  Could catch the sound no more.
For then, by toil subdued, he drank
The stifling wave, and then he sank.

No poet wept him; but the page
  Of narrative sincere,
That tells his name, his worth, his age,
  Is wet with Anson's tear.
And tears by bards or heroes shed
Alike immortalize the dead.

I therefore purpose not, or dream,
  Descanting on his fate,
To give the melancholy theme

* Based on an actual incident in Richard Walter's *A Voyage Round the World by George Anson* (1748). Cowper recalls a ship rounding Cape Horn, a fierce storm, and the drowning of one of the best men on board.

THE CASTAWAY. **7. No braver chief:** George Anson, leader of the expedition against the Spanish.

24. scudded: drove along. **27. coop:** basket used in fishing. **56. Descanting:** commenting.

A more enduring date;
But misery still delights to trace
Its semblance in another's case.

No voice divine the storm allayed,
No light propitious shone,
When, snatched from all effectual aid,
We perished, each alone;
But I beneath a rougher sea,
And whelmed in deeper gulfs than he.

(1799, 1803)

Robert Burns
1759-1796

◆

THE COTTER'S SATURDAY NIGHT

INSCRIBED TO R. AIKEN, ESQ.*

Let not Ambition mock their useful toil,
Their homely joys and destiny obscure;
Nor grandeur hear, with a disdainful smile,
The short and simple annals of the Poor.

GRAY.

I

My lov'd, my honour'd, much respected friend!
No mercenary bard his homage pays;
With honest pride I scorn each selfish end,
My dearest meed a friend's esteem and praise:
To you I sing, in simple Scottish lays,
The lowly train in life's sequester'd scene;
The native feelings strong, the guileless ways;
What Aiken in a cottage would have been;
Ah! tho' his worth unknown, far happier there,
I ween!

II

November chill blaws loud wi' angry sugh;
The short'ning winter-day is near a close;
The miry beasts retreating frae the pleugh;
The black'ning trains o' craws to their repose:
The toil-worn Cotter frae his labour goes,
This night his weekly moil is at an end,
Collects his spades, his mattocks, and his hoes,
Hoping the morn in ease and rest to spend,
And weary, o'er the moor, his course does hameward
bend.

III

At length his lonely cot appears in view,
Beneath the shelter of an aged tree;
Th' expectant wee things, toddlin, stacher
through
To meet their Dad, wi' flichterin noise an' glee.
His wee bit ingle, blinkin bonnilie,
His clean hearth-stane, his thrifty wifie's smile,
The lisping infant prattling on his knee,
Does a' his weary carking care beguile,
An' makes him quite forget his labour an' his toil.

IV

Belyve the older bairns come drapping in,
At service out, amang the farmers roun';
Some ca' the pleugh, some herd, some tentie
rin
A cannie errand to a neibor town:
Their eldest hope, their Jenny, woman grown,

* Robert Aiken, Solicitor in Ayr, and a famous speaker.

THE COTTER'S SATURDAY NIGHT. **15. moil:** toil. **21. stacher:** totter. **22. flichterin:** fluttering. **23. ingle:** fire. **26. carking:** burdening. **28. Belyve:** later. **30. tentie:** dutifully. **31. cannie:** careful.

In youthfu' bloom, love sparkling in her e'e,
Comes hame, perhaps, to shew a braw new gown,
Or deposite her sair-won penny-fee,
To help her parents dear, if they in hardship be.

V

With joy unfeign'd brothers and sisters meet,
An' each for other's weelfare kindly spiers:
The social hours, swift-wing'd, unnoticed fleet;
Each tells the uncos that he sees or hears;
The parents partial eye their hopeful years;
Anticipation forward points the view.
The mother, wi' her needle an' her sheers,
Gars auld claes look amaist as weel's the new;
The father mixes a' wi' admonition due.

VI

Their master's an' their mistress's command,
The younkers a' are warned to obey;
An' mind their labours wi' an eydent hand,
An' ne'er, tho' out o' sight, to jauk or play;
"An' O! be sure to fear the Lord alway!
An' mind your duty, duly, morn an' night!
Lest in temptation's path ye gang astray,
Implore His counsel and assisting might:
They never sought in vain that sought the Lord aright!"

VII

But hark! a rap comes gently to the door;
Jenny, wha kens the meaning o' the same,
Tells how a neebor lad cam o'er the moor,
To do some errands, and convoy her hame.
The wily mother sees the conscious flame
Sparkle in Jenny's e'e, and flush her cheek;
Wi' heart-struck anxious care, inquires his name,
While Jenny hafflins is afraid to speak;
Weel pleased the mother hears, it's nae wild, worthless rake.

35. sair-won: hard-won. **38. spiers:** inquires. **40. uncos:** wonderful happenings. **44. Gars:** makes; **amaist:** almost. **48. eydent:** careful.

VIII

Wi' kindly welcome, Jenny brings him ben;
A strappin youth; he takes the mother's eye;
Blythe Jenny sees the visit's no ill ta'en;
The father cracks of horses, pleughs, and kye.
The youngster's artless heart o'er flows wi' joy,
But blate and laithfu', scarce can weel behave;
The mother, wi' a woman's wiles, can spy
What makes the youth sae bashfu' an' sae grave;
Weel pleased to think her bairn's respected like the lave.

IX

O happy love! where love like this is found!
O heart-felt raptures! bliss beyond compare!
I've paced much this weary, mortal round,
And sage experience bids me this declare—
"If Heaven a draught of heavenly pleasure spare,
One cordial in this melancholy vale,
'Tis when a youthful, loving, modest pair
In other's arms breathe out the tender tale,
Beneath the milk-white thorn that scents the evening gale."

X

Is there, in human form, that bears a heart—
A wretch! a villain! lost to love and truth!
That can, with studied, sly, ensnaring art,
Betray sweet Jenny's unsuspecting youth?
Curse on his perjur'd arts! dissembling smooth!
Are honour, virtue, conscience, all exiled?
Is there no pity, no relenting ruth,
Points to the parents fondling o'er their child?
Then paints the ruin'd maid, and their distraction wild!

XI

But now the supper crowns their simple board,
The halesome parritch, chief of Scotia's food:
The sope their only hawkie does afford,
That 'yont the hallan snugly chows her cood;

67. kye: cows. **69. blate and laithfu':** shy and reserved. **72. lave:** remainder. **92. Scotia:** Scotland. **93. sope:** food; **hawkie:** cow. **94. hallan:** wall.

The dame brings forth in complimental mood,
To grace the lad, her weel-hained kebbuck, fell,
An' aft he's prest, and aft he ca's it guid;
The frugal wifie, garrulous, will tell
How 'twas a towmond auld, sin' lint was i' the bell.

XII

The cheerfu' supper done, wi' serious face,
They round the ingle form a circle wide;
The sire turns o'er wi' patriarchal grace,
The big ha'-bible, ance his father's pride:
His bonnet reverently is laid aside,
His lyart haffets wearing thin an' bare;
Those strains that once did sweet in Zion glide,
He wales a portion with judicious care;
And "Let us worship God!" he says with solemn air.

XIII

They chant their artless notes in simple guise;
The tune their hearts, by far the noblest aim:
Perhaps Dundee's wild warbling measures rise,
Or plaintive Martyrs, worthy of the name;
Or noble Elgin beets the heavenward flame,
The sweetest far of Scotia's holy lays:
Compared with these, Italian trills are tame;
The tickled ears no heartfelt raptures raise;
Nae unison hae they with our Creator's praise.

XIV

The priest-like father reads the sacred page,
How Abram was the friend of God on high;
Or Moses bade eternal warfare wage
With Amalek's ungracious progeny;
Or how the royal bard did groaning lie
Beneath the stroke of Heaven's avenging ire;
Or Job's pathetic plaint, and wailing cry;
Or rapt Isaiah's wild, seraphic fire;
Or other holy seers that tune the sacred lyre.

96. weel-hained kebbuck, fell: well-preserved, flavorful cheese. **99. towmond:** twelve-month. **105. lyart haffets:** graying sideburns. **107. wales:** chooses. **111. Dundee:** seaport in eastern Scotland. **113. beets:** lights. **121. Amalek:** grandson of Esau.

XV

Perhaps the Christian volume is the theme,
How guiltless blood for guilty man was shed;
How He, who bore in Heaven the second name,
Had not on earth whereon to lay His head:
How His first followers and servants sped;
The precepts sage they wrote to many a land:
How he, who lone in Patmos banishèd,
Saw in the sun a mighty angel stand
And heard great Bab'lon's doom pronounced by Heaven's command.

XVI

Then kneeling down, to Heaven's Eternal King,
The saint, the father, and the husband prays:
Hope "springs exulting on triumphant wing,"
That thus they all shall meet in future days:
There ever bask in uncreated rays,
No more to sigh, or shed the bitter tear,
Together hymning their Creator's praise,
In such society, yet still more dear;
While circling Time moves round in an eternal sphere.

XVII

Compared with this, how poor Religion's pride,
In all the pomp of method and of art,
When men display to congregations wide
Devotion's every grace, except the heart!
The Power, incensed, the pageant will desert,
The pompous strain, the sacerdotal stole;
But haply, in some cottage far apart,
May hear, well pleased, the language of the soul;
And in His Book of Life the inmates poor enrol.

XVIII

Then homeward all take off their several way;
The youngling cottagers retire to rest:
The parent-pair their secret homage pay,
And proffer up to Heaven the warm request,
That He who stills the raven's clamorous nest,

133. he . . . Patmos: St. John saw visions of the Apocalypse on the island of Patmos in the Aegean Sea.

And decks the lily fair in flowery pride,
Would, in the way His wisdom sees the best,
For them and for their little ones provide;
But chiefly, in their hearts with grace divine preside.

XIX

From scenes like these old Scotia's grandeur springs,
That makes her loved at home, revered abroad:
Princes and lords are but the breath of kings,
"An honest man's the noblest work of God":
And certes, in fair virtue's heavenly road,
The cottage leaves the palace far behind;
What is a lordling's pomp! a cumbrous load,
Disguising oft the wretch of human kind,
Studied in arts of hell, in wickedness refin'd!

XX

O Scotia! my dear, my native soil!
For whom my warmest wish to Heaven is sent!
Long may thy hardy sons of rustic toil
Be blest with health, and peace, and sweet content!
And, O! may Heaven their simple lives prevent
From luxury's contagion, weak and vile!
Then, howe'er crowns and coronets be rent,
A virtuous populace may rise the while,
And stand a wall of fire around their much-loved isle.

XXI

O Thou! who poured the patriotic tide
That streamed thro' Wallace's undaunted heart;
Who dared to nobly stem tyrannic pride,
Or nobly die, the second glorious part,
(The patriot's God, peculiarly thou art,
His friend, inspirer, guardian, and reward!)
O never, never, Scotia's realm desert;
But still the patriot, and the patriot-bard,
In bright succession raise, her ornament and guard!

(1785, 1786)

182. **Wallace:** Sir William Wallace (1272?–1305), great Scottish patriot who devoted his life to opposing the English. He was eventually captured and executed in London.

TO A MOUSE

ON TURNING HER UP IN HER NEST WITH THE PLOUGH, NOVEMBER, 1785

Wee, sleekit, cow'rin, tim'rous beastie,
O, what a panic's in thy breastie!
Thou need na start awa sae hasty,
Wi' bickering brattle!
I wad be laith to rin an' chase thee,
Wi' murd'ring pattle!

I'm truly sorry man's dominion
Has broken Nature's social union,
An' justifies that ill opinion
Which makes thee startle
At me, thy poor earth-born companion,
An' fellow-mortal!

I doubt na, whiles, but thou may thieve;
What then? poor beastie, thou maun live!
A daimen icker in a thrave
'S a sma' request:
I'll get a blessin wi' the lave,
And never miss't!

Thy wee bit housie, too, in ruin!
Its silly wa's the win's are strewin!
An' naething, now, to big a new ane,
O' foggage green!
An' bleak December's winds ensuin,
Baith snell an' keen!

Thou saw the fields laid bare and waste,
An' weary winter comin fast,
An' cozie here, beneath the blast,
Thou thought to dwell,
Till crash! the cruel coulter past
Out thro' thy cell.

That wee bit heap o' leaves an' stibble
Has cost thee mony a weary nibble!
Now thou's turn'd out, for a' thy trouble,
But house or hald,
To thole the winter's sleety dribble,
An' cranreuch cauld!

TO A MOUSE. 4. **bickering brattle:** noisy scamper. 6. **murd'ring pattle:** plowstaff. 15. **A . . . thrave:** an occasional ear in twenty-four sheaves. 20. **silly wa's:** feeble walls. 22. **foggage:** grass. 24. **snell:** sharp. 29. **coulter:** the iron blade in front of the plough. 34. **But . . . hald:** without house or home. 35. **thole:** endure. 36. **cranreuch:** hoarfrost.

But, Mousie, thou art no thy lane,
In proving foresight may be vain:
The best laid schemes o' mice an' men
Gang aft a-gley.
An' lea'e us nought but grief an' pain
For promised joy.

Still thou art blest, compared wi' me!
The present only toucheth thee:
But och! I backward cast my e'e
On prospects drear!
An' forward, tho' I canna see,
I guess an' fear!

(1785, 1786)

TO A MOUNTAIN DAISY

ON TURNING ONE DOWN WITH THE PLOUGH, IN APRIL, 1786

Wee modest crimson-tipped flow'r,
Thou'st met me in an evil hour;
For I maun crush amang the stoure
Thy slender stem:
To spare thee now is past my pow'r,
Thou bonnie gem.

Alas! it's no thy neibor sweet,
The bonnie lark, companion meet,
Bending thee 'mang the dewy weet
Wie spreckled breast,
When upward springing, blythe to greet
The purpling east.

Cauld blew the bitter-biting north
Upon thy early humble birth;
Yet cheerfully thou glinted forth
Amid the storm,
Scarce rear'd above the parent-earth
Thy tender form.

The flaunting flow'rs our gardens yield
High shelt'ring woods and wa's maun shield,
But thou, beneath the random bield
O' clod or stane,
Adorns the histie stibble-field,
Unseen, alane.

There, in thy scanty mantle clad,
Thy snawy bosom sun-ward spread,
Thou lifts thy unassuming head
In humble guise;
But now the share uptears thy bed,
And low thou lies!

Such is the fate of artless maid,
Sweet flow'ret of the rural shade,
By love's simplicity betrayed,
And guileless trust,
Till she like thee, all soiled, is laid
Low i' the dust.

Such is the fate of simple bard,
On life's rough ocean luckless starred:
Unskilful he to note the card
Of prudent lore,
Till billows rage, and gales blow hard,
And whelm him o'er!

Such fate to suffering worth is given,
Who long with wants and woes has striven,
By human pride or cunning driven
To mis'ry's brink,
Till wrench'd of ev'ry stay but Heaven,
He, ruin'd, sink!

Ev'n thou who mourn'st the Daisy's fate,
That fate is thine—no distant date;
Stern Ruin's ploughshare drives elate
Full on thy bloom,
Till crushed beneath the furrow's weight
Shall be thy doom!

(1786)

ADDRESS TO THE UNCO GUID, OR THE RIGIDLY RIGHTEOUS

My son, these maxims make a rule,
An' lump them aye thegither:
The rigid righteous is a fool,
The rigid wise anither:
*The cleanest corn that e'er was dight**
May hae some pyles o' caff in;
So ne'er a fellow-creature slight
*For random fits o' daffin.***

SOLOMON (Eccles. vii. 16).

40. a-gley: awry.

TO A MOUNTAIN DAISY. **3. maun:** must; **stoure:** dust. **20. wa's:** walls. **21. bield:** shelter. **23. histie:** dry.

* **dight:** harvested.
** **daffin:** larking.

I

O ye wha are sae guid yoursel,
  Sae pious and sae holy,
Ye've nought to do but mark and tell
  Your neebour's fauts and folly!
Whase life is like a weel-gaun mill,
  Supplied wi' store o' water,
The heaped happer's ebbing still,
  And still the clap plays clatter.

II

Hear me, ye venerable core,
  As counsel for poor mortals,
That frequent pass douce Wisdom's door
  For glaikit Folly's portals;
I, for their thoughtless, careless sakes,
  Would here propone defences,
Their donsie tricks, their black mistakes,
  Their failings and mischances.

III

Ye see your state wi' their's compar'd,
  And shudder at the niffer.
But cast a moment's fair regard,
  What maks the mighty differ;
Discount what scant occasion gave,
  That purity ye pride in,
And (what's aft mair than a' the lave)
  Your better art o' hiding.

IV

Think, when your castigated pulse
  Gies now and then a wallop,
What ragings must his veins convulse,
  That still eternal gallop;
Wi' wind and tide fair i' your tail,
  Right on ye scud your sea-way;
But in the teeth o' baith to sail,
  It maks an unco leeway.

V

See Social life and Glee sit down,
  All joyous and unthinking,
Till, quite transmogrified, they're grown
  Debauchery and Drinking:
O would they stay to calculate
  Th' eternal consequences;
Or your more dreaded hell to state,
  Damnation of expenses!

VI

Ye high, exalted, virtuous Dames,
  Tied up in godly laces,
Before ye gie poor Frailty names,
  Suppose a change o' cases;
A dear lov'd lad, convenience snug,
  A treacherous inclination—
But, let me whisper i' your lug,
  Ye're aiblins nae temptation.

VII

Then gently scan your brother man,
  Still gentler sister woman;
Tho' they may gang a kennin wrang,
  To step aside is human:
One point must still be greatly dark,
  The moving why they do it:
And just as lamely can ye mark
  How far perhaps they rue it.

VIII

Who made the heart, 'tis He alone
  Decidedly can try us;
He knows each chord its various tone,
  Each spring, its various bias:
Then at the balance let's be mute,
  We never can adjust it;
What's done we partly may compute,
  But know not what's resisted.

(1786, 1787)

OF A' THE AIRTS

Of a' the airts the wind can blaw,
  I dearly like the west,
For there the bonie lassie lives,
  The lassie I lo'e best:

ADDRESS TO THE UNCO GUID. **7. happer:** hopper. **8. clap:** clapper. **11. douce:** solemn. **12. glaikit:** silly. **18. niffer:** exchange.

47. lug: ear. **48. aiblins:** possibly, perhaps. **51. kennin:** little.

OF A' THE AIRTS. **1. airts:** directions.

There's wild woods grow, and rivers row,
And mony a hill between;
But day and night my fancy's flight
Is ever wi' my Jean.

I see her in the dewy flowers,
I see her sweet and fair;
I hear her in the tunefu' birds,
I hear her charm the air:
There's not a bonie flower that springs
By fountain, shaw, or green,
There's not a bonie bird that sings,
But minds me o' my Jean.

(1788, 1790)

AFTON WATER

Flow gently, sweet Afton, among thy green braes,
Flow gently, I'll sing thee a song in thy praise;
My Mary's asleep by thy murmuring stream,
Flow gently, sweet Afton, disturb not her dream.

Thou stock-dove whose echo resounds thro' the glen,
Ye wild whistling blackbirds in yon thorny den,
Thou green-crested lapwing, thy screaming forbear,
I charge you disturb not my slumbering fair.

How lofty, sweet Afton, thy neighbouring hills,
Far mark'd with the courses of clear winding rills;
There daily I wander as noon rises high,
My flocks and my Mary's sweet cot in my eye.

How pleasant thy banks and green valleys below,
Where wild in the woodlands the primroses blow;
There oft as mild ev'ning weeps over the lea,
The sweet-scented birk shades my Mary and me.

Thy crystal stream, Afton, how lovely it glides,
And winds by the cot where my Mary resides;
How wanton thy waters her snowy feet lave,
As gathering sweet flow'rets she stems thy clear wave.

Flow gently, sweet Afton, among thy green braes,
Flow gently, sweet river, the theme of my lays;
My Mary's asleep by thy murmuring stream,
Flow gently, sweet Afton, disturb not her dream.

(1789, 1792)

14. **shaw**: thicket.

A RED, RED ROSE

O my luve's like a red, red rose,
That's newly sprung in June:
O my luve's like the melodie
That's sweetly play'd in tune.

As fair art thou, my bonie lass,
So deep in luve am I;
And I will luve thee still, my dear,
Till a' the seas gang dry.

Till a' the seas gang dry, my dear,
And the rocks melt wi' the sun:
And I will luve thee still, my dear,
While the sands o' life shall run.

And fare thee weel, my only luve!
And fare thee weel awhile!
And I will come again, my luve,
Tho' it were ten thousand mile!

(1794, 1796)

FOR A' THAT AND A' THAT

Is there, for honest poverty,
That hangs his head, and a' that;
That coward-slave, we pass him by,
We dare be poor for a' that!
For a' that, and a' that,
Our toils obscure, and a' that,
The rank is but the guinea stamp,
The man's the gowd for a' that.

What though on hamely fare we dine,
Wear hoddin gray, and a' that;
Gie fools their silks, and knaves their wine,
A man's a man for a' that:
For a' that, and a' that,
Their tinsel show, and a' that;
The honest man, tho' e'er sae poor,
Is King o' men for a' that.

Ye see yon birkie, ca'd a lord,
Wha struts, and stares, and a' that;
Tho' hundreds worship at his word,
He's but a coof for a' that:

FOR A' THAT AND A' THAT. 8. **gowd**: gold. 10. **hoddin**: cloth. 17. **birkie**: dandy. 20. **coof**: clod.

For a' that, and a' that:
His riband, star, and a' that,
The man of independent mind,
He looks and laughs at a' that.

A prince can mak a belted knight,
A marquis, duke, and a' that;
But an honest man's aboon his might,
Guid faith he mauna fa' that!
For a' that, and a' that,
Their dignities, and a' that,
The pith o' sense, and pride o' worth,
Are higher rank than a' that.

Then let us pray that come it may,
As come it will for a' that,
That sense and worth, o'er a' the earth,
May bear the gree, and a' that.
For a' that, and a' that,
It's coming yet, for a' that,
That man to man, the warld o'er,
Shall brothers be for a' that.

(1794, 1795)

28. mauna fa': must not claim.

36. gree: prize.

George Crabbe
1754-1832

◆

FROM

The Village

BOOK I

The Subject proposed—Remarks upon Pastoral Poetry—A Tract of Country near the Coast described —An impoverished Borough—Smugglers and their Assistants—Rude Manners of the Inhabitants—Ruinous Effects of a high Tide—The Village Life more generally considered: Evils of it—The youthful Labourer—The old Man: his Soliloquy—The Parish Workhouse: its Inhabitants—The sick Poor: their Apothecary—The dying Pauper—The Village Priest.

The village life, and every care that reigns
O'er youthful peasants and declining swains;
What labour yields, and what, that labour past,
Age, in its hour of languor, finds at last;
What form the real picture of the poor,
Demand a song—the Muse can give no more.
Fled are those times when, in harmonious strains,
The rustic poet praised his native plains:
No shepherds now, in smooth alternate verse,
Their country's beauty or their nymphs' rehearse;
Yet still for these we frame the tender strain,
Still in our lays fond Corydons complain,
And shepherds' boys their amorous pains reveal,
The only pains, alas! they never feel.
On Mincio's banks, in Caesar's bounteous reign,
If Tityrus found the Golden Age again,
Must sleepy bards the flattering dream prolong,
Mechanic echoes of the Mantuan song?
From Truth and Nature shall we widely stray,
Where Virgil, not where Fancy, leads the way?
Yes, thus the Muses sing of happy swains,
Because the Muses never knew their pains:
They boast their peasants' pipes; but peasants now
Resign their pipes and plod behind the plough;
And few, amid the rural tribe, have time
To number syllables and play with rhyme;
Save honest Duck, what son of verse could share
The poet's rapture, and the peasant's care?
Or the great labours of the field degrade,

THE VILLAGE. BOOK I. **27. Duck:** Stephen Duck (1705–1756), the Thresher Poet.

With the new peril of a poorer trade?
From this chief cause these idle praises spring,
That themes so easy few forbear to sing.
For no deep thought the trifling subjects ask;
To sing of shepherds is an easy task.
The happy youth assumes the common strain,
A nymph his mistress, and himself a swain;
With no sad scenes he clouds his tuneful prayer,
But all, to look like her, is painted fair.
I grant indeed that fields and flocks have charms
For him that grazes or for him that farms;
But when amid such pleasing scenes I trace
The poor laborious natives of the place,
And see the midday sun, with fervid ray,
On their bare heads and dewy temples play;
While some, with feebler heads and fainter hearts,
Deplore their fortune, yet sustain their parts,
Then shall I dare these real ills to hide
In tinsel trappings of poetic pride?
No; cast by Fortune on a frowning coast,
Which neither groves nor happy valleys boast;
Where other cares than those the Muse relates,
And other shepherds dwell with other mates;
By such examples taught, I paint the cot,
As Truth will paint it, and as bards will not:
Nor you, ye poor, of lettered scorn complain,
To you the smoothest song is smooth in vain;
O'ercome by labour, and bowed down by time,
Feel you the barren flattery of a rhyme?
Can poets soothe you, when you pine for bread,
By winding myrtles round your ruined shed?
Can their light tales your weighty griefs o'erpower,
Or glad with airy mirth the toilsome hour?
Lo! where the heath, with withering brake grown o'er,
Lends the light turf that warms the neighbouring poor;
From thence a length of burning sand appears,
Where the thin harvest waves its withered ears;
Rank weeds, that every art and care defy,
Reign o'er the land, and rob the blighted rye:
There thistles stretch their prickly arms afar,
And to the ragged infant threaten war;
There poppies, nodding, mock the hope of toil;
There the blue bugloss paints the sterile soil;
Hardy and high, above the slender sheaf,
The slimy mallow waves her silky leaf;
O'er the young shoot the charlock throws a shade,
And clasping tares cling round the sickly blade;
With mingled tints the rocky coasts abound,
And a sad splendour vainly shines around.
So looks the nymph whom wretched arts adorn,
Betrayed by man, then left for man to scorn;
Whose cheek in vain assumes the mimic rose,
While her sad eyes the troubled breast disclose;
Whose outward splendour is but folly's dress,
Exposing most, when most it gilds distress.
Here joyless roam a wild amphibious race,
With sullen woe displayed in every face;
Who, far from civil arts and social fly,
And scowl at strangers with suspicious eye.
Here too the lawless merchant of the main
Draws from his plough the intoxicated swain;
Want only claimed the labour of the day,
But vice now steals his nightly rest away.
Where are the swains, who, daily labour done,
With rural games played down the setting sun;
Who struck with matchless force the bounding ball,
Or made the ponderous quoit obliquely fall;
While some huge Ajax, terrible and strong,
Engaged some artful strippling of the throng,
And fell beneath him, foiled, while far around
Hoarse triumph rose, and rocks returned the sound?
Where now are these?—Beneath yon cliff they stand,
To show the freighted pinnace where to land;
To load the ready steed with guilty haste,
To fly in terror o'er the pathless waste,
Or, when detected in their straggling course,
To foil their foes by cunning or by force;
Or, yielding part (which equal knaves demand),
To gain a lawless passport through the land.
Here, wandering long, amid these frowning fields,
I sought the simple life that Nature yields;
Rapine and Wrong and Fear usurped her place,
And a bold, artful, surly, savage race;
Who, only skilled to take the finny tribe,
The yearly dinner or septennial bribe,
Wait on the shore, and, as the waves run high,
On the tossed vessel bend their eager eye,
Which to their coast directs its venturous way;

72. bugloss: rough weeds. **74. mallow:** a showy flower.

75. charlock: a wild mustard, troublesome in grainfields. **76. tares:** weeds. **96. quoit:** a flat disc of stone or metal thrown as an exercise of skill.

Theirs, or the ocean's, miserable prey.
As on their neighbouring beach yon swallows stand,
And wait for favouring winds to leave the land;
While still for flight the ready wing is spread:
So waited I the favouring hour, and fled—
Fled from these shores where guilt and famine reign,
And cried, "Ah! hapless they who still remain;
Who still remain to hear the ocean roar,
Whose greedy waves devour the lessening shore;
Till some fierce tide, with more imperious sway,
Sweeps the low hut and all it holds away;
When the sad tenant weeps from door to door,
And begs a poor protection from the poor!"
But these are scenes where Nature's niggard hand
Gave a spare portion to the famished land;
Hers is the fault, if here mankind complain
Of fruitless toil and labour spent in vain;
But yet in other scenes more fair in view,
Where Plenty smiles—alas! she smiles for few—
And those who taste not, yet behold her store,
Are as the slaves that dig the golden ore,—
The wealth around them makes them doubly poor.
Or will you deem them amply paid in health,
Labour's fair child, that languishes with wealth?
Go then! and see them rising with the sun,
Through a long course of daily toil to run;
See them beneath the dog-star's raging heat,
When the knees tremble and the temples beat;
Behold them, leaning on their scythes, look o'er
The labour past, and toils to come explore;
See them alternate suns and showers engage,
And hoard up aches and anguish for their age;
Through fens and marshy moors their steps pursue,
When their warm pores imbibe the evening dew;
Then own that labour may as fatal be
To these thy slaves, as thine excess to thee.
Amid this tribe too oft a manly pride
Strives in strong toil the fainting heart to hide;
There may you see the youth of slender frame
Contend with weakness, weariness, and shame;
Yet, urged along, and proudly loth to yield,
He strives to join his fellows of the field.
Till long-contending nature droops at last,
Declining health rejects his poor repast,
His cheerless spouse the coming danger sees,
And mutual murmurs urge the slow disease.
Yet grant them health, 'tis not for us to tell,
Though the head droops not, that the heart is well;
Or will you praise that homely, healthy fare,
Plenteous and plain, that happy peasants share?
Oh! trifle not with wants you cannot feel,
Nor mock the misery of a stinted meal;
Homely, not wholesome, plain, not plenteous, such
As you who praise would never deign to touch.
Ye gentle souls, who dream of rural ease,
Whom the smooth stream and smoother sonnet please;
Go! if the peaceful cot your praises share,
Go look within, and ask if peace be there;
If peace be his—that drooping weary sire,
Or theirs, that offspring round their feeble fire;
Or hers, that matron pale, whose trembling hand
Turns on the wretched hearth the expiring brand!
Nor yet can time itself obtain for these
Life's latest comforts, due respect and ease;
For yonder see that hoary swain, whose age
Can with no cares except his own engage;
Who, propped on that rude staff, looks up to see
The bare arms broken from the withering tree,
On which, a boy, he climbed the loftiest bough,
Then his first joy, but his sad emblem now.
He once was chief in all the rustic trade;
His steady hand the straightest furrow made;
Full many a prize he won, and still is proud
To find the triumphs of his youth allowed;
A transient pleasure sparkles in his eyes,
He hears and smiles, then thinks again and sighs:
For now he journeys to his grave in pain;
The rich disdain him; nay, the poor disdain:
Alternate masters now their slave command,
Urge the weak efforts of his feeble hand,
And, when his age attempts its task in vain,
With ruthless taunts, of lazy poor complain.
Oft may you see him, when he tends the sheep,
His winter charge, beneath the hillock weep;
Oft hear him murmur to the winds that blow
O'er his white locks and bury them in snow,
When, roused by rage and muttering in the morn,

169. stinted: frugal. **179. brand:** a piece of wood that has been burning on the hearth.

He mends the broken hedge with icy thorn:—
"Why do I live, when I desire to be
At once from life and life's long labour free?
Like leaves in spring, the young are blown away,
Without the sorrows of a slow decay;
I, like yon withered leaf, remain behind,
Nipped by the frost and shivering in the wind;
There it abides till younger buds come on,
As I, now all my fellow-swains are gone;
Then, from the rising generation thrust,
It falls, like me, unnoticed to the dust.
"These fruitful fields, these numerous flocks I see,
Are others' gain, but killing cares to me;
To me the children of my youth are lords,
Cool in their looks, but hasty in their words:
Wants of their own demand their care; and who
Feels his own want and succours others too?
A lonely, wretched man, in pain I go,
None need my help, and none relieve my woe;
Then let my bones beneath the turf be laid,
And men forget the wretch they would not aid."
Thus groan the old, till, by disease oppressed,
They taste a final woe and then they rest.
Theirs is yon house that holds the parish-poor,
Whose walls of mud scarce bear the broken door;
There, where the putrid vapours, flagging, play,
And the dull wheel hums doleful through the day;—
There children dwell who know no parents' care;
Parents who know no children's love, dwell there!
Heartbroken matrons on their joyless bed,
Forsaken wives, and mothers never wed;
Dejected widows with unheeded tears,
And crippled age with more than childhood fears;
The lame, the blind, and, far the happiest they!
The moping idiot and the madman gay.
Here too the sick their final doom receive,
Here brought, amid the scenes of grief, to grieve,
Where the loud groans from some sad chamber flow,
Mixed with the clamours of the crowd below;
Here, sorrowing, they each kindred sorrow scan,
And the cold charities of man to man:
Whose laws indeed for ruined age provide,
And strong compulsion plucks the scrap from pride;
But still that scrap is bought with many a sigh,
And pride embitters what it can't deny.
Say ye, oppressed by some fantastic woes,
Some jarring nerve that baffles your repose;
Who press the downy couch, while slaves advance
With timid eye, to read the distant glance;
Who with sad prayers the weary doctor tease,
To name the nameless ever-new disease;
Who with mock patience dire complaints endure,
Which real pain and that alone can cure;
How would ye bear in real pain to lie,
Despised, neglected, left alone to die?
How would ye bear to draw your latest breath,
Where all that's wretched paves the way for death?
Such is that room which one rude beam divides,
And naked rafters form the sloping sides;
Where the vile bands that bind the thatch are seen,
And lath and mud are all that lie between;
Save one dull pane, that, coarsely patched, gives way
To the rude tempest, yet excludes the day:
Here, on a matted flock, with dust o'erspread,
The drooping wretch reclines his languid head;
For him no hand the cordial cup applies,
Or wipes the tear that stagnates in his eyes;
No friends with soft discourse his pain beguile,
Or promise hope till sickness wears a smile.
But soon a loud and hasty summons calls,
Shakes the thin roof, and echoes round the walls;
Anon, a figure enters, quaintly neat,
All pride and business, bustle and conceit;
With looks unaltered by these scenes of woe,
With speed that, entering, speaks his haste to go,
He bids the gazing throng around him fly,
And carries fate and physic in his eye:
A potent quack, long versed in human ills,
Who first insults the victim whom he kills;
Whose murderous hand a drowsy bench protect,
And whose most tender mercy is neglect.
Paid by the parish for attendance here,
He wears contempt upon his sapient sneer;
In haste he seeks the bed where Misery lies,
Impatience marked in his averted eyes;
And, some habitual queries hurried o'er,
Without reply, he rushes on the door:
His drooping patient, long inured to pain,
And long unheeded, knows remonstrance vain;
He ceases now the feeble help to crave
Of man, and silent sinks into the grave.

265. lath: thin, narrow strip of wood. **268. matted flock:** bed made of pieces of cloth. **287. sapient:** knowing (used ironically here).

But ere his death some pious doubts arise,
Some simple fears, which "bold bad" men despise;
Fain would he ask the parish-priest to prove
His title certain to the joys above:
For this he sends the murmuring nurse, who calls
The holy stranger to these dismal walls.
And doth not he, the pious man, appear,
He, "passing rich with forty pounds a year?"
Ah! no; a shepherd of a different stock,
And far unlike him, feeds this little flock:
A jovial youth, who thinks his Sunday's task
As much as God or man can fairly ask;
The rest he gives to loves, and labours light,
To fields the morning, and to feasts the night;
None better skilled the noisy pack to guide,
To urge their chase, to cheer them or to chide;
A sportsman keen, he shoots through half the day,
And, skilled at whist, devotes the night to play:
Then, while such honours bloom around his head,
Shall he sit sadly by the sick man's bed,
To raise the hope he feels not, or with zeal
To combat fears that e'en the pious feel?
Now once again the gloomy scene explore,
Less gloomy now; the bitter hour is o'er,
The man of many sorrows sighs no more.—
Up yonder hill, behold how sadly slow
The bier moves winding from the vale below;
There lie the happy dead, from trouble free,
And the glad parish pays the frugal fee.
No more, O Death! thy victim starts to hear
Churchwarden stern, or kingly overseer;
No more the farmer claims his humble bow,
Thou art his lord, the best of tyrants thou!
Now to the church behold the mourners come,
Sedately torpid and devoutly dumb;
The village children now their games suspend,
To see the bier that bears their ancient friend;
For he was one in all their idle sport,
And like a monarch ruled their little court;
The pliant bow he formed, the flying ball,
The bat, the wicket, were his labours all;
Him now they follow to his grave, and stand
Silent and sad and gazing, hand in hand;
While bending low, their eager eyes explore
The mingled relics of the parish poor.
The bell tolls late, the moping owl flies round,
Fear marks the flight and magnifies the sound;
The busy priest, detained by weightier care,
Defers his duty till the day of prayer;
And, waiting long, the crowd retire distressed,
To think a poor man's bones should lie unblessed.

(1780–1783)

303. See Goldsmith, *The Deserted Village*, l. 142.

A Selection of Critical and Philosophical Prose

Our General Introduction has already suggested the richness and variety of critical and philosophical writing in the English Enlightenment, and the individual introductions to figures like Pope and Johnson have pointed up the major contributions of these writers. Yet these greater figures are part of a larger context—at times traditional and conservative, at other times innovative and futuristic—a context which defies easy description, which looks back to the strictness of Restoration rationalism and forward to Romantic emotionalism. The selections in this section should illuminate that context and suggest some of the variety in the prose literature of the age.

In the late seventeenth and early eighteenth century, a stricter, more dogmatic Neoclassicism dominated thinking and writing—a Neoclassicism that blended the influence of doctrines developed out of ideas long popular in Italy, France, and England with the stern rationalism emerging from philosophers like Descartes, Hobbes, and Locke. On the one hand, a certain traditionalism, oftentimes rooted in second-hand versions of classical theory, placed a strong emphasis on imitating the Ancients and following the rules embodied in their works. (Frequently these rules were formulated from mere observations or suggestions of an Aristotle.) On the other hand, rationalistic philosophy urged the values of probability and judgment in life and art and looked with suspicion on such phenomena as original genius, spontaneity, and imagination. Art, specifically literature, should have a utilitarian function; its most important qualities were moral edification, common sense, and propriety.

One of the most famous early statements of strict Neoclassic criticism can be found in the prefatory epistle to Sir William Davenant's long and tedious epic *Gondibert* (1650), a work dedicated to the philosopher Thomas Hobbes. To Davenant, the poet is not a creator of symbol, a shaper of experience, a man of strong feeling and active imagination. His primary responsibility is to the criterion of verisimilitude, to the truth of fact; he is chiefly a lawgiver, safeguarding manners and morals. Even more important than the epistle, however, was the answer given by Hobbes, whose great work *Leviathan* (1651) was a pioneering force in the evolution of mechanistic, empirical psychology. Acknowledging Davenant's dedication, he proceeded to praise the epic for qualities like health of morality, shape of art, and vigor of expression. Ever a hater of imaginative excess—for him, imagination was "decaying sense"—he regarded art as primarily psychological and rhetorical. In his *Brief on the Art of Rhetoric* (1638) he divides the mind into wit or invention, disposition or judgment, and eloquence that is associated with the ornaments of art. The basic distinction is between wit, the combining and associating faculty, and judgment, the discerning and differentiating power; and this distinction becomes a central one in Augustan criticism. Wit is the inferior faculty, a picture-making process. It is the overseeing power of judgment that tempers wit and brings the true work of art.

John Locke, more sophisticated than Hobbes, nevertheless continues the tradition of empiricism, which stresses the primacy of sensation in the process of knowledge, warns about the power of imagination and association, and yet calls the possibilities of mental activity to the attention of critics and artists, as we shall see shortly. How pointedly he answers his question about the sources of knowledge in his great *Essay Concerning Human Understanding* (1690): "To this I answer, in one word, From experience; in that all our knowledge is founded, and from that it ultimately derives itself. Our observation, employed either about external sensible objects, or about the internal operations of our minds, perceived and reflected upon by ourselves, is that which supplies our understandings with all the materials of thinking. These two are the fountains of knowledge, from whence all the ideas we have, or can naturally have, do spring."

Thomas Rymer is a good example of doctrinaire, unimaginative, practical criticism. A stubborn defender of the truth of fact, he was always suspicious of the flight of the imagination. His *Tragedies of the Last Age Considered* (1678) attacks three plays of Beaumont and Fletcher for violations of common sense and decorum, while his *A Short View of Tragedy* (1693) is most severe on Shakespeare because of what Rymer regards as the improbability of his plots. His celebrated analysis of *Othello* is characterized by observations like the following:

> Othello is made a Venetian general. We see nothing done by him nor related concerning him that comports with the condition of a general, or indeed of a man, unless the killing himself to avoid a death the law was about to inflict upon him. When his jealousy had wrought him up to a resolution of 's taking revenge for the suppos'd injury, he set Iago to the fighting part to kill Cassio, and chuses himself to murder the silly woman his wife, that was like to make no resistance.

> His love and his jealousies are no part of the soldier's character except for comedy.

Interestingly enough—and we have observed the same phenomenon in other areas of Enlightenment thought—even within the strict Neoclassic aesthetic, new forces are at work, often quite unconsciously, as old values are eroded and others developed. A most notable example of such change is the way in which some of the themes of British empirical psychology are turned in new directions. Witness how different interpretations are given to Locke's emphasis on sensation, on the power of association, on the primary qualities that are found objectively in bodies and the secondary qualities that are present because of the activity of the mind. The great essayist Joseph Addison, in so many ways a man of his time in his quest for true wit and refinement in life and literature, stands as a striking example. In his *Spectator* papers on "The Pleasures of the Imagination," he uses Locke as authority for his praise of the delights of sensation, for more romantic qualities like originality and sublimity in art, for those pleasures of the imagination that come not so much from the object but from the mind's interaction with the object. How much he anticipates Burke's ideas on the sublime, as he savors the glories of "an open champaign country, a vast uncultivated desert, of huge heaps of mountains, high rocks and precipices, or a wide expanse of waters, where we are not struck with the novelty or beauty of the sight but with that rude kind of magnificence which appears in many of the stupendous works of nature. Our imagination loves to be filled with an object, or to grasp at anything that is too big for its capacity. We are flung into a pleasing astonishment at such unbounded views, and feel a delightful stillness and amazement in the soul at the apprehension of them." How strong is his praise for the imagination's power to bring new beauties to nature and to convey new secondary pleasures beyond the simple power of sight. "I have," he writes, "here supposed that my reader is acquainted with that great modern discovery which is at present universally acknowledged by all the inquirers into natural philosophy, namely, that light and colors as apprehended by the imagination are only ideas in the mind and not qualities that have any existence in matter. As this is a truth which has been proved incontestably by many modern philosophers and is indeed one of the finest speculations in that science, if the English reader would see the notion explained at large, he may find it in the eighth chapter of the Second Book of Mr. Locke's *Essay on Human Understanding*."

Shaftesbury's emphasis on subjective taste as a judge of beauty, on the power of nature to mold the human spirit, represents still another undercutting of the rationalistic point of view. "No wonder," says Philocles to Theocles in the rhapsodical dialogue of *The Moralists,* "if we are at a loss when we pursue the shadow for the substance. For if we may trust to what our reasoning has taught us, whatever in nature is beautiful or charming is only the faint shadow of that first beauty. So that every real love depending on the mind, and being only the contemplation of beauty either as it really is in itself or as it appears imperfectly in the objects which strike the sense, how can the rational mind rest here or be satisfied with the absurd enjoyment which reaches the sense alone?"

Other theorists point up the search for new sources of aesthetic pleasure, rooted in the subjective and the emotional—among them David Hume on the emotional pleasure of tragedy, Henry Fielding on the comic sense of the ridiculous, Edward Young and William Duff on the originality of true genius, Richard Hurd on the "fine fabling" of the Gothic world. On the level of practical rather than theoretical criticism, it is interesting to observe the setting of new artistic priorities, specifically the reversal of artistic reputations. Joseph Warton, in his monumental *Essay on the Genius and Writings of Pope,* praises the excellence of Pope in the realm of the moral, satiric, and didactic, but does not rank him among the greatest poets. Regarding the "sublime" and "pathetic" as the two genuine sources of great art, he concludes: "I revere the memory of Pope, I respect and honor his abilities, but I do not think him at the head of his profession. In other words, in that species of poetry wherein Pope excelled he is superior to all mankind; and I only say that this species of poetry is not the most excellent one of the art." On the other hand, Thomas Warton, in his *Observations on the "Fairy Queen" of Spenser,* argues for the reevaluation and reestablishment of a poet often treated as antique or crude by Enlightenment critics. Warton, like Hurd, pleads for understanding a work in its historical context, for recognizing that emotional power is a value to be praised. While the *Fairy Queen* may lack "that arrangement and economy which epic severity requires," the great Renaissance epic possesses a quality "which more powerfully attracts us, something which engages the affections, the feelings of the heart, rather than the cold approbation of the head." In a powerful summary statement, he seems to echo Pope's liberalism in the *Essay on Criticism,* indeed even to move beyond it. "If there be any poem whose graces please us because they are situated beyond the reach of art, and where the forces and faculties of creative imagination delight because they are unassisted and unrestrained by those of deliberate judgment, it is this. In reading Spenser, if the critic is not satisfied, yet the reader is transported."

In his noted lectures to the students of the Royal Academy, one of the great figures of the Johnson circle, Sir Joshua Reynolds, reveals the delicate balance of Neoclassic aesthetics. On the one hand, the *Discourses on Art* reveal a fidelity to the mainstream of human experience as well as to the importance of the classical tradition and to the values of decorum and morality. On the other hand, the later lectures, especially, reveal a keen sensitivity to the importance of an art that is original and that can stir the human heart. Reynolds is a stunning example of the depth and breadth of Enlightenment writing. His famous statement in *Discourse XIII* captures a great deal of his spirit: "The great end of all the arts is, to make an impression on the imagination and the feeling. The imitation of nature frequently does this. Sometimes it fails, and something else succeeds. I think therefore the true test of all the arts is not solely whether the production is a true copy of nature, but whether it answers the end of art, which is to produce a pleasing effect upon the mind."

Suggestions for Further Reading

The following represent a small sample of supplementary readings that are useful for those interested in doing further work on the critical and philosophical prose of the

Enlightenment. Scott Elledge, *Eighteenth-Century Critical Essays,* 2 vols. (1961), is a superb collection of major and secondary figures. Oliver Sigworth, *Criticism and Aesthetics, 1660–1800* (1971), although a briefer anthology, presents a useful sample of some of the major work and of minor critical and aesthetic theory that is not readily accessible.

W. J. Bate, *From Classic to Romantic* (1946) and M. H. Abrams, *The Mirror and the Lamp* (1958) describe the critical setting admirably. W. K. Wimsatt and Cleanth Brooks, *Literary Criticism: A Short History* (1957) and René Wellek, *A History of Modern Criticism 1750–1850,* Vol. 1 (1955), have comprehensive sections dealing with Enlightenment criticism.

Also strongly recommended are Samuel Holt Monk, *The Sublime* (1935); Emerson Marks, *The Poetics of Reason: English Neoclassical Criticism* (1968); Howard Anderson and John Shea, eds., *Studies in Criticism and Aesthetics, 1660–1800* (1967).

John Locke
1632-1704

◆

FROM

An Essay Concerning Human Understanding

BOOK I

CHAPTER I

INTRODUCTION

1. *An inquiry into the understanding, pleasant and useful.*—Since it is the understanding that sets man above the rest of sensible beings, and gives him all the advantage and dominion which he has over them, it is certainly a subject, even for its nobleness, worth our labour to inquire into. The understanding, like the eye, whilst it makes us see and perceive all other things, takes no notice of itself; and it requires art and pains to set it at a distance, and make it its own object. But whatever be the difficulties that lie in the way of this inquiry, whatever it be that keeps us so much in the dark to ourselves, sure I am that all the light we can let in upon our own minds, all the acquaintance we can make with our own understandings, will not only be very pleasant, but bring us great advantage in directing our thoughts in the search of other things.

2. *Design.*—This therefore being my purpose, to inquire into the original, certainty, and extent of human knowledge, together with the grounds and degrees of belief, opinion, and assent, I shall not at present meddle with the physical consideration of the mind, or trouble myself to examine wherein its essence consists or by what motions of our spirits, or alterations of our bodies, we come to have any sensation by our organs, or any ideas in our understandings; and whether those ideas do, in their formation, any or all of them, depend on matter or not: these are speculations which, however curious and entertaining, I shall decline, as lying out of my way in the design I am now upon. It shall suffice to my present purpose, to consider the discerning faculties of a man, as they are employed about the objects which they have to do with; and I shall imagine I have not wholly misemployed myself in the thoughts I shall have on this occasion, if, in this historical, plain method, I can give any account of the ways whereby our understandings come to attain those notions of things we have, and can set down any measures of the certainty of our

knowledge, or the grounds of those persuasions which are to be found amongst men, so various, different, and wholly contradictory; and yet asserted somewhere or other with such assurance and confidence, that he that shall take a view of the opinions of mankind, observe their opposition, and at the same time consider the fondness and devotion wherewith they are embraced, the resolution and eagerness wherewith they are maintained, may perhaps have reason to suspect that either there is no such thing as truth at all, or that mankind hath no sufficient means to attain a certain knowledge of it.

3. *Method.*—It is therefore worth while to search out the bounds between opinion and knowledge, and examine by what measures, in things whereof we have no certain knowledge, we ought to regulate our assent, and moderate our persuasions. In order whereunto, I shall pursue this following method:—

First. I shall inquire into the original of those ideas, notions, or whatever else you please to call them, which a man observes, and is conscious to himself he has in his mind; and the ways whereby the understanding comes to be furnished with them.

Secondly. I shall endeavour to show what knowledge the understanding hath by those ideas, and the certainty, evidence, and extent of it.

Thirdly. I shall make some inquiry into the nature and grounds of faith or opinion; whereby I mean, that assent which we give to any proposition as true, of whose truth yet we have no certain knowledge: and here we shall have occasion to examine the reasons and degrees of assent.

4. *Useful to know the extent of our comprehension.*—If by this inquiry into the nature of the understanding, I can discover the powers thereof, how far they reach, to what things they are in any degree proportionate, and where they fail us, I suppose it may be of use to prevail with the busy mind of man to be more cautious in meddling with things exceeding its comprehension, to stop when it is at the utmost extent of its tether, and to sit down in a quiet ignorance of those things which, upon examination, are found to be beyond the reach of our capacities. We should not then, perhaps, be so forward, out of an affectation of an universal knowledge, to raise questions, and perplex ourselves and others with disputes, about things to which our understandings are not suited, and of which we cannot frame in our minds any clear or distinct perceptions, or whereof (as it has, perhaps, too often happened) we have not any notions at all. If we can find out how far the understanding can extend its view, how far it has faculties to attain certainty, and in what cases it can only judge and guess, we may learn to content ourselves with what is attainable by us in this state.

5. *Our capacity suited to our state and concerns.*—For though the comprehension of our understandings comes exceeding short of the vast extent of things, yet we shall have cause enough to magnify the bountiful Author of our being for that proportion and degree of knowledge he has bestowed on us, so far above all the rest of the inhabitants of this our mansion. Men have reason to be well satisfied with what God hath thought fit for them, since he has given them, as St. Peter says, *πάντα πρὸς ζωὴν και εὐσέβειαν*, whatsoever is necessary for the conveniences of life, and information of virtue; and has put within the reach of their discovery, the comfortable provision for this life and the way that leads to a better. How short soever their knowledge may come of an universal or perfect comprehension of whatsoever is, it yet secures their great concernments that they have light enough to lead them to the knowledge of their Maker, and the sight of their own duties. Men may find matter sufficient to busy their heads and employ their hands with variety, delight, and satisfaction, if they will not boldly quarrel with their own constitution, and throw away the blessings their hands are filled with, because they are not big enough to grasp every thing. We shall not have much reason to complain of the narrowness of our minds, if we will but employ them about what may be of use to us; for of that they are very capable: and it will be an unpardonable as well as childish peevishness, if we undervalue the advantages of our knowledge, and neglect to improve it to the ends for which it was given us, because there are some things that are set out of the reach of it. It will be no excuse to an idle and untoward servant, who would not attend his business by candlelight, to plead that he had not broad sunshine. The candle that is set up in us shines bright enough for all our purposes. The discoveries we can make with this ought to satisfy us; and we shall then use our understandings right, when we entertain all objects in that way and proportion that they are suited to

our faculties, and upon those grounds they are capable of being proposed to us; and not peremptorily or intemperately require demonstration, and demand certainty, where probability only is to be had, and which is sufficient to govern all our concernments. If we will disbelieve every thing because we cannot certainly know all things, we shall do much-what as wisely as he who would not use his legs, but sit still and perish because he had no wings to fly.

6. *Knowledge of our capacity a cure of scepticism and idleness.*—When we know our own strength, we shall the better know what to undertake with hopes of success; and when we have well surveyed the powers of our own minds, and made some estimate what we may expect from them, we shall not be inclined either to sit still, and not set our thoughts on work at all, in despair of knowing any thing; nor, on the other side, question every thing, and disclaim all knowledge, because some things are not to be understood. It is of great use to the sailor to know the length of his line, though he cannot with it fathom all the depths of the ocean; it is well he knows that it is long enough to reach the bottom at such places as are necessary to direct his voyage, and caution him against running upon shoals that may ruin him. Our business here is not to know all things, but those which concern our conduct. If we can find out those measures whereby a rational creature, put in that state which man is in in this world, may and ought to govern his opinions and actions depending thereon, we need not be troubled that some other things escape our knowledge.

7. *Occasion of this Essay.*—This was that which gave the first rise to this Essay concerning the Understanding. For I thought that the first step towards satisfying several inquiries the mind of man was very apt to run into, was, to take a survey of our own understandings, examine our own powers, and see to what things they were adapted. Till that was done, I suspected we began at the wrong end, and in vain sought for satisfaction in a quiet and sure possession of truths that most concerned us, whilst we let loose our thoughts into the vast ocean of being; as if all that boundless extent were the natural and undoubted possession of our understandings, wherein there was nothing exempt from its decisions, or that escaped its comprehension. Thus men, extending their inquiries beyond their capacities, and letting their thoughts wander into those depths where they can find no sure footing, it is no wonder that they raise questions and multiply disputes, which, never coming to any clear resolution, are proper only to continue and increase their doubts, and to confirm them at last in perfect scepticism. Whereas, were the capacities of our understandings well considered, the extent of our knowledge once discovered, and the horizon found which sets the bounds between the enlightened and dark parts of things—between what is and what is not comprehensible by us—men would, perhaps with less scruple, acquiesce in the avowed ignorance of the one, and employ their thoughts and discourse with more advantage and satisfaction in the other.

8. *What "idea" stands for.*—Thus much I thought necessary to say concerning the occasion of this inquiry into human understanding. But, before I proceed on to what I have thought on this subject, I must here, in the entrance, beg pardon of my reader for the frequent use of the word "idea" which he will find in the following treatise. It being that term which, I think, serves best to stand for whatsoever is the object of the understanding when a man thinks, I have used it to express whatever is meant by phantasm, notion, species, or whatever it is which the mind can be employed about in thinking; and I could not avoid frequently using it.

I presume it will be easily granted me, that there are such *ideas* in men's minds. Every one is conscious of them in himself; and men's words and actions will satisfy him that they are in others.

Our first inquiry, then, shall be, how they come into the mind.

. . .

BOOK II

CHAPTER I

OF IDEAS IN GENERAL, AND THEIR ORIGINAL

1. *Idea is the object of thinking.*—Every man being conscious to himself, that he thinks, and that which his mind is applied about, whilst thinking, being the ideas that are there, it is past doubt that men have in their mind several ideas, such as are those expressed by the words, "whiteness, hardness,

sweetness, thinking, motion, man, elephant, army, drunkenness," and others: it is in the first place then to be inquired, How he comes by them? I know it is a received doctrine, that men have native ideas and original characters stamped upon their minds in their very first being. This opinion I have at large examined already; and, I suppose, what I have said in the foregoing book will be much more easily admitted, when I have shown whence the understanding may get all the ideas it has, and by what ways and degrees they may come into the mind; for which I shall appeal to every one's own observation and experience.

2. *All ideas come from sensation or reflection.*—Let us then suppose the mind to be, as we say, white paper, void of all characters, without any ideas; how comes it to be furnished? Whence comes it by that vast store, which the busy and boundless fancy of man has painted on it with an almost endless variety? Whence has it all the materials of reason and knowledge? To this I answer, in one word, From experience; in that all our knowledge is founded, and from that it ultimately derives itself. Our observation, employed either about external sensible objects, or about the internal operations of our minds, perceived and reflected on by ourselves, is that which supplies our understandings with all the materials of thinking. These two are the fountains of knowledge, from whence all the ideas we have, or can naturally have, do spring.

3. *The object of sensation one source of ideas.*—First. Our senses, conversant about particular sensible objects, do convey into the mind several distinct perceptions of things, according to those various ways wherein those objects do affect them; and thus we come by those ideas we have of yellow, white, heat, cold, soft, hard, bitter, sweet, and all those which we call sensible qualities; which when I say the senses convey into the mind, I mean, they from external objects convey into the mind what produces there those perceptions. This great source of most of the ideas we have, depending wholly upon our senses, and derived by them to the understanding, I call, "sensation."

4. *The operations of our minds the other source of them.*—Secondly. The other fountain, from which experience furnisheth the understanding with ideas, is the perception of the operations of our own minds within us, as it is employed about the ideas it has got; which operations when the soul comes to reflect on and consider, do furnish the understanding with another set of ideas which could not be had from things without; and such are perception, thinking, doubting, believing, reasoning, knowing, willing, and all the different actings of our own minds; which we, being conscious of, and observing in ourselves, do from these receive into our understandings as distinct ideas, as we do from bodies affecting our senses. This source of ideas every man has wholly in himself; and though it be not sense as having nothing to do with external objects, yet it is very like it, and might properly enough be called "internal sense." But as I call the other "sensation," so I call this "reflection," the ideas it affords being such only as the mind gets by reflecting on its own operations within itself. By reflection, then, in the following part of this discourse, I would be understood to mean that notice which the mind takes of its own operations, and the manner of them, by reason whereof there come to be ideas of these operations in the understanding. These two, I say, viz., external material things as the objects of sensation, and the operations of our own minds within as the objects of reflection, are, to me, the only originals from whence all our ideas take their beginnings. The term "operations" here, I use in a large sense, as comprehending not barely the actions of the mind about its ideas, but some sort of passions arising sometimes from them, such as is the satisfaction or uneasiness arising from any thought.

5. *All our ideas are of the one or the other of these.*—The understanding seems to me not to have the least glimmering of any ideas which it doth not receive from one of these two. External objects furnish the mind with the ideas of sensible qualities, which are all those different perceptions they produce in us; and the mind furnishes the understanding with ideas of its own operations.

These, when we have taken a full survey of them, and their several modes, [combinations, and relations,] we shall find to contain all our whole stock of ideas; and that we have nothing in our minds which did not come in one of these two ways. Let any one examine his own thoughts, and thoroughly search into his understanding, and then let him tell me, whether all the original ideas he has there, are any other than of the objects of his senses, or of the operations of his mind considered as objects of his reflection; and how great a mass of knowledge soever he imagines to be lodged there, he will, upon taking a strict view, see that he has not any idea in his mind but what one of these two have imprinted, though perhaps with infinite variety compounded and enlarged by the understanding, as we shall see hereafter.

6. *Observable in children.*—He that attentively considers the state of a child at his first coming into the world, will have little reason to think him stored with plenty of ideas that are to be the matter of his future knowledge. It is by degrees he comes to be furnished with them; and though the ideas of obvious and familiar qualities imprint themselves before the memory begins to keep a register of time or order, yet it is often so late before some unusual qualities come in the way, that there are few men that cannot recollect the beginning of their acquaintance with them: and, if it were worth while, no doubt a child might be so ordered as to have but a very few even of the ordinary ideas till he were grown up to a man. But all that are born into the world being surrounded with bodies that perpetually and diversely affect them, variety of ideas, whether care be taken about it or not, are imprinted on the minds of children. Light and colours are busy at hand every where when the eye is but open; sounds and some tangible qualities fail not to solicit their proper senses, and force an entrance to the mind; but yet I think it will be granted easily, that if a child were kept in a place where he never saw any other but black and white till he were a man, he would have no more ideas of scarlet or green than he that from his childhood never tasted an oyster or a pine-apple has of those particular relishes.

7. *Men are differently furnished with these according to the different objects they converse with.* —Men then come to be furnished with fewer or more simple ideas from without, according as the objects they converse with afford greater or less variety; and from the operations of their minds within, according as they more or less reflect on them. For, though he that contemplates the operations of his mind cannot but have plain and clear ideas of them; yet, unless he turn his thoughts that way, and considers them attentively, he will no more have clear and distinct ideas of all the operations of his mind, and all that may be observed therein, than he will have all the particular ideas of any landscape, or of the parts and motions of a clock, who will not turn his eyes to it, and with attention heed all the parts of it. The picture or clock may be so placed, that they may come in his way every day; but yet he will have but a confused idea of all the parts they are made of, till he applies himself with attention to consider them each in particular.

8. *Ideas of reflection later, because they need attention.*—And hence we see the reason why it is pretty late before most children get ideas of the operations of their own minds; and some have not any very clear or perfect ideas of the greatest part of them all their lives:—because, though they pass there continually, yet like floating visions, they make not deep impressions enough to leave in the mind, clear, distinct, lasting ideas, till the understanding turns inwards upon itself, reflects on its own operations, and makes them the objects of its own contemplation. Children, when they come first into it, are surrounded with a world of new things, which, by a constant solicitation of their senses, draw the mind constantly to them, forward to take notice of new, and apt to be delighted with the variety of changing objects. Thus the first years are usually employed and diverted in looking abroad. Men's business in them is to acquaint themselves with what is to be found without; and so, growing up in a constant attention to outward sensations, seldom make any considerable reflection on what passes within them till they come to be of riper years; and some scarce ever at all.

9. *The soul begins to have ideas when it begins to perceive.*—To ask, at what time a man has first any ideas, is to ask when he begins to perceive; having ideas, and perception, being the same thing. I know it is an opinion, that the soul always thinks; and that it has the actual perception of ideas in itself constantly, as long as it exists; and that actual thinking is as inseparable from the soul, as actual extension is from the body: which if true, to inquire after the beginning of a man's ideas is the same as to inquire after the beginning of his soul. For by this account, soul and its ideas, as body and its extension, will begin to exist both at the same time.

10. *The soul thinks not always; for this wants proofs.*—But whether the soul be supposed to exist antecedent to, or coeval with, or some time after, the first rudiments or organization, or the begin-

nings of life in the body, I leave to be disputed by those who have better thought of that matter. I confess myself to have one of those dull souls that doth not perceive itself always to contemplate ideas; nor can conceive it any more necessary for the soul always to think, than for the body always to move; the perception of ideas being, as I conceive, to the soul, what motion is to the body: not its essence, but one of its operations; and, therefore, though thinking be supposed never so much the proper action of the soul, yet it is not necessary to suppose that it should be always thinking, always in action: that, perhaps, is the privilege of the infinite Author and Preserver of things, "who never slumbers nor sleeps;" but it is not competent to any finite being, at least not to the soul of man. We know certainly, by experience, that we sometimes think; and thence draw this infallible consequence,—that there is something in us that has a power to think; but whether that substance perpetually thinks, or no, we can be no farther assured than experience informs us. For to say, that actual thinking is essential to the soul and inseparable from it, is to beg what is in question, and not to prove it by reason; which is necessary to be done, if it be not a self-evident proposition. But whether this—that "the soul always thinks," be a self-evident proposition, that everybody assents to on first hearing, I appeal to mankind. [It is doubted whether I thought all last night, or no; the question being about a matter of fact, it is begging it to bring as a proof for it an hypothesis which is the very thing in dispute; by which way one may prove any thing; and it is but supposing that all watches, whilst the balance beats, think, and it is sufficiently proved, and past doubt, that my watch thought all last night. But he that would not deceive himself ought to build his hypothesis on matter of fact, and make it out by sensible experience, and not presume on matter of fact because of his hypothesis; that is, because he supposes it to be so; which way of proving amounts to this,—that I must necessarily think all last night, because another supposes I always think, though I myself cannot perceive that I always do so.

But men in love with their opinions may not only suppose what is in question, but allege wrong matter of fact. How else could any one make it an inference of mine, that a thing is not, because we are not sensible of it in our sleep? I do not say, there is no soul in a man because he is not sensible of it in his sleep; but I do say, he cannot think at any time, waking or sleeping, without being sensible of it. Our being sensible of it is not necessary to any thing but to our thoughts; and to them it is, and to them it will always be, necessary, till we can think without being conscious of it.]

11. *It is not always conscious of it.*—I grant that the soul in a waking man is never without thought, because it is the condition of being awake; but whether sleeping without dreaming be not an affection of the whole man, mind as well as body, may be worth a waking man's consideration; it being hard to conceive that any thing should think and not be conscious of it. If the soul doth think in a sleeping man without being conscious of it, I ask, whether, during such thinking, it has any pleasure or pain, or be capable of happiness or misery? I am sure the man is not, no more than the bed or earth he lies on. For to be happy or miserable without being conscious of it, seems to me utterly inconsistent and impossible. Or if it be possible that the soul can, whilst the body is sleeping, have its thinking, enjoyments, and concerns, its pleasure or pain, apart, which the man is not conscious of, nor partakes in, it is certain that Socrates asleep and Socrates awake is not the same person; but his soul when he sleeps, and Socrates the man, consisting of body and soul, when he is waking, are two persons; since waking Socrates has no knowledge of, or concernment for that happiness or misery of his soul, which it enjoys alone by itself whilst he sleeps, without perceiving any thing of it, no more than he has for the happiness or misery of a man in the Indies, whom he knows not. For if we take wholly away all consciousness of our actions and sensations, especially of pleasure and pain, and the concernment that accompanies it, it will be hard to know wherein to place personal identity.

. . .

CHAPTER II

OF SIMPLE IDEAS

1. *Uncompounded appearances.*—The better to understand the nature, manner, and extent of our knowledge, one thing is carefully to be observed concerning the ideas we have; and that is, that some of them are simple, and some complex.

Though the qualities that affect our senses are, in the things themselves, so united and blended that there is no separation, no distance between them; yet it is plain the ideas they produce in the mind enter by the senses simple and unmixed. For though the sight and touch often take in from the same object, at the same time, different ideas—as a man sees at once motion and colour, the hand feels softness and warmth in the same piece of wax—yet the simple ideas thus united in the same subject are as perfectly distinct as those that come in by different senses; the coldness and hardness which a man feels in a piece of ice being as distinct ideas in the mind as the smell and whiteness of a lily, or as the taste of sugar and smell of a rose; and there is nothing can be plainer to a man than the clear and distinct perception he has of those simple ideas; which, being each in itself uncompounded, contains in it nothing but one uniform appearance or conception in the mind, and is not distinguishable into different ideas.

2. *The mind can neither make nor destroy them.*—These simple ideas, the materials of all our knowledge, are suggested and furnished to the mind only by those two ways above mentioned, viz., sensation and reflection. When the understanding is once stored with these simple ideas, it has the power to repeat, compare, and unite them, even to an almost infinite variety, and so can make at pleasure new complex ideas. But it is not in the power of the most exalted wit or enlarged understanding, by any quickness or variety of thought, to invent or frame one new simple idea in the mind, not taken in by the ways before mentioned; nor can any force of the understanding destroy those that are there: the dominion of man in this little world of his own understanding, being much-what the same as it is in the great world of visible things, wherein his power, however managed by art and skill, reaches no farther than to compound and divide the materials that are made to his hand but can do nothing towards the making the least particle of new matter, or destroying one atom of what is already in being. The same inability will every one find in himself, who shall go about to fashion in his understanding any simple idea not received in by his senses from external objects, or by reflection from the operations of his own mind about them. I would have any one try to fancy any taste which had never affected his palate, or frame the idea of a scent he had never smelt; and when he can do this, I will also conclude, that a blind man hath *ideas* of colours, and a deaf man true, distinct notions of sounds.

3. This is the reason why, though we cannot believe it impossible to God to make a creature with other organs, and more ways to convey into the understanding the notice of corporeal things than those five as they are usually counted, which he has given to man; yet I think it is not possible for any one to imagine any other qualities in bodies, howsoever constituted, whereby they can be taken notice of, besides sounds, tastes, smells, visible and tangible qualities. And had mankind been made with but four senses, the qualities then which are the objects of the fifth sense had been as far from our notice, imagination, and conception, as now any belonging to a sixth, seventh, or eighth sense can possibly be; which, whether yet some other creatures, in some other parts of this vast and stupendous universe, may not have, will be a great presumption to deny. He that will not set himself proudly at the top of all things, but will consider the immensity of this fabric, and the great variety that is to be found in this little and inconsiderable part of it which he has to do with, may be apt to think, that in other mansions of it there may be other and different intelligible beings, of whose faculties he has as little knowledge or apprehension, as a worm shut up in one drawer of a cabinet hath of the senses or understanding of a man; such variety and excellency being suitable to the wisdom and power of the Maker. I have here followed the common opinion of man's having but five senses, though perhaps there may be justly counted more; but either supposition serves equally to my present purpose.

CHAPTER III

OF SIMPLE IDEAS OF SENSE

1. *Division of simple ideas.*—The better to conceive the ideas we receive from sensation, it may not be amiss for us to consider them in reference to the different ways whereby they make their approaches to our minds, and make themselves perceivable by us.

First, then, there are some which come into our minds by one sense only.

Secondly. There are others that convey themselves into the mind by more senses than one.

Thirdly. Others that are had from reflection only.

Fourthly. There are some that make themselves way, and are suggested to the mind, by all the ways of sensation and reflection.

We shall consider them apart under these several heads.

1. There are some ideas which have admittance only through one sense, which is peculiarly adapted to receive them. Thus light and colours, as white, red, yellow, blue, with their several degrees or shades and mixtures, as green, scarlet, purple, sea-green, and the rest, come in only by the eyes; all kinds of noises, sounds, and tones, only by the ears; the several tastes and smells, by the nose and palate. And if these organs, or the nerves which are the conduits to convey them from without to their audience in the brain, the mind's presence-room (as I may so call it), are, any of them, so disordered as not to perform their functions, they have no postern to be admitted by, no other way to bring themselves into view, and be received by the understanding.

The most considerable of those belonging to the touch are heat, and cold, and solidity; all the rest—consisting almost wholly in the sensible configuration, as smooth and rough; or else more or less firm adhesion of the parts, as hard and soft, tough and brittle—are obvious enough.

2. I think it will be needless to enumerate all the particular simple ideas belonging to each sense. Nor indeed is it possible if we would, there being a great many more of them belonging to most of the senses than we have names for. The variety of smells, which are as many almost, if not more, than species of bodies in the world, do most of them want names. *Sweet* and *stinking* commonly serve our turn for these ideas, which in effect is little more than to call them pleasing or displeasing; though the smell of a rose and violet, both sweet, are certainly very distinct ideas. Nor are the different tastes that by our palates we receive ideas of, much better provided with names. *Sweet, bitter, sour, harsh,* and *salt,* are almost all the epithets we have to denominate that numberless variety of relishes which are to be found distinct, not only in almost every sort of creatures, but in the different parts of the same plant, fruit, or animal. The same may be said of colours and sounds. I shall therefore in the account of simple ideas I am here giving, content myself to set down only such as are most material to our present purpose, or are in themselves less apt to be taken notice of, though they are very frequently the ingredients of our complex ideas; amongst which I think I may well account "solidity," which therefore I shall treat of in the next chapter.

. . .

CHAPTER V

OF SIMPLE IDEAS OF DIVERS SENSES

The ideas we get by more than one sense are of space or extension, figure, rest and motion: for these make perceivable impressions both on the eyes and touch; and we can receive and convey into our minds the ideas of the extension, figure, motion, and rest of bodies, both by seeing and feeling. But by having occasion to speak more at large of these in another place, I here only enumerate them.

CHAPTER VI

OF SIMPLE IDEAS OF REFLECTION

1. *Simple ideas of reflection are the operations of the mind about its other ideas.*—The mind, receiving the ideas mentioned in the foregoing chapters from without, when it turns its view inward upon itself, and observes its own actions about those ideas it has, takes from thence other ideas, which are as capable to be the objects of its contemplation as any of those it received from foreign things.

2. *The idea of perception, and idea of willing, we have from reflection.*—The two great and principal actions of the mind, which are most frequently considered, and which are so frequent that every one that pleases may take notice of them in himself, are these two: perception or thinking, and volition or willing. [The power of thinking is called "the understanding," and the power of volition is called "the will"; and these two powers or abilities in the mind are denominated "faculties."] Of some of the modes of these simple ideas of reflection, such as are remembrance, discerning, reasoning, judging, knowledge, faith, &c., I shall have occasion to speak hereafter.

CHAPTER VII

OF SIMPLE IDEAS OF BOTH SENSATION AND REFLECTION

1. *Pleasure and pain.*—There be other simple ideas which convey themselves into the mind by all the ways of sensation and reflection; viz., pleasure or delight, and its opposite, pain or uneasiness; power, existence, unity.

2. Delight or uneasiness, one or other of them, join themselves to almost all our ideas both of sensation and reflection; and there is scarce any affection of our senses from without, any retired thought of our mind within, which is not able to produce in us pleasure or pain. By "pleasure" and "pain," I would be understood to signify whatsoever delights or molests us; whether it arises from the thoughts of our minds, or any thing operating on our bodies. For whether we call it "satisfaction, delight, pleasure, happiness," &c., on the one side; or "uneasiness, trouble, pain, torment, anguish, misery," &c., on the other; they are still but different degrees of the same thing, and belong to the ideas of pleasure and pain, delight or uneasiness; which are the names I shall most commonly use for those two sorts of ideas.

3. The infinite wise Author of our being—having given us the power over several parts of our bodies, to move or keep them at rest as we think fit, and also by the motion of them to move ourselves and other contiguous bodies, in which consist all the actions of our body; having also given a power to our minds, in several instances, to choose amongst its ideas which it will think on, and to pursue the inquiry of this or that subject with consideration and attention—to excite us to these actions of thinking and motion that we are capable of, has been pleased to join to several thoughts and several sensations a perception of *delight*. If this were wholly separated from all our outward sensations and inward thoughts, we should have no reason to prefer one thought or action to another, negligence to attention, or motion to rest: and so we should neither stir our bodies, nor employ our minds; but let our thoughts (if I may so call it) run adrift, without any direction or design; and suffer the ideas of our minds, like unregarded shadows, to make their appearances there as it happened, without attending to them: in which state man, however furnished with the faculties of understanding and will, would be a very idle, unactive creature, and pass his time only in a lazy, lethargic dream. It has therefore pleased our wise Creator to annex to several objects, and to the ideas which we receive from them, as also to several of our thoughts, a concomitant pleasure, and that in several objects to several degrees, that those faculties which he had endowed us with might not remain wholly idle and unemployed by us.

4. *Pain* has the same efficacy and use to set us on work that pleasure has, we being as ready to employ our faculties to avoid that, as to pursue this; only this is worth our consideration—that pain is often produced by the same objects and ideas that produce pleasure in us. This their near conjunction, which makes us often feel pain in the sensations where we expected pleasure, gives us new occasion of admiring the wisdom and goodness of our Maker, who, designing the preservation of our being, has annexed pain to the application of many things to our bodies, to warn us of the harm that they will do, and as advices to withdraw from them. But He, not designing our preservation barely, but the preservation of every part and organ in its perfection, hath in many cases annexed pain to those very ideas which delight us. Thus heat, that is very agreeable to us in one degree, by a little greater increase of it proves no ordinary torment; and the most pleasant of all sensible objects, light itself, if there be too much of it, if increased beyond a due proportion to our eyes, causes a very painful sensation: which is wisely and favourably so ordered by nature, that when any object does by the vehemency of its operation disorder the instruments of sensation, whose structures cannot but be very nice and delicate, we might by the pain be warned to withdraw before the organ be quite put out of order, and so be unfitted for its proper functions for the future. The consideration of those objects that produce it may well persuade us, that this is the end or use of pain: for though great light be insufferable to our eyes, yet the highest degree of darkness does not at all disease them, because that causing no disorderly motion in it, leaves that curious organ unharmed in its natural state. But yet excess of cold as well as heat pains us because it is equally destructive to that temper which is necessary to the preservation of life, and the exercise of the several functions of the body, and which consists in a moderate degree

of warmth, or, if you please, a motion of the insensible parts of our bodies confined within certain bounds.

5. Beyond all this, we may find another reason why God hath scattered up and down several degrees of pleasure and pain in all the things that environ and affect us, and blended them together in all that our thoughts and senses have to do with; that we, finding imperfection, dissatisfaction, and want of complete happiness in all the enjoyments which the creatures can afford us, might be led to seek it in the enjoyment of Him "with whom there is fulness of joy, and at whose right hand are pleasures for evermore."

6. *Pleasure and pain.*—Though what I have here said may not perhaps make the ideas of pleasure and pain clearer to us than our own experience does, which is the only way that we are capable of having them; yet the consideration of the reason why they are annexed to so many other ideas, serving to give us due sentiments of the wisdom and goodness of the Sovereign Disposer of all things, may not be unsuitable to the main end of these inquiries: the knowledge and veneration of Him being the chief end of all our thoughts, and the proper business of all our understandings.

7. *Existence and unity.*—Existence and unity are two other ideas that are suggested to the understanding by every object without, and every idea within. When ideas are in our minds, we consider them as being actually there, as well as we consider things to be actually without us: which is, that they exist, or have existence: and whatever we can consider as one thing, whether a real being or idea, suggests to the understanding the idea of unity.

8. *Power.*—Power also is another of those simple ideas which we receive from sensation and reflection. For, observing in ourselves that we do and can think, and that we can at pleasure move several parts of our bodies which were at rest; the effects also that natural bodies are able to produce in one another occurring every moment to our senses, we both these ways get the idea of power.

9. *Succession.*—Besides these there is another idea, which though suggested by our senses, yet is more constantly offered us by what passes in our minds; and that is the idea of succession. For if we look immediately into ourselves, and reflect on what is observable there, we shall find our ideas always, whilst we are awake or have any thought, passing in train, one going and another coming without intermission.

10. *Simple ideas the materials of all our knowledge.*—These, if they are not all, are at least (as I think) the most considerable of those simple ideas which the mind has, and out of which is made all its other knowledge; all of which it receives only by the two forementioned ways of sensation and reflection.

Nor let any one think these too narrow bounds for the capacious mind of man to expatiate in, which takes its flight farther than the stars, and cannot be confined by the limits of the world; that extends its thoughts often even beyond the utmost expansion of matter, and makes excursions into that incomprehensible inane. I grant all this; but desire any one to assign any simple idea which is not received from one of those inlets before mentioned, or any complex idea not made out of those simple ones. Nor will it be so strange to think these few simple ideas sufficient to employ the quickest thought or largest capacity, and to furnish the materials of all that various knowledge and more various fancies and opinions of all mankind, if we consider how many words may be made out of the various composition of twenty-four letters; or, if, going one step farther, we will but reflect on the variety of combinations may be made with barely one of the above-mentioned ideas, viz., number, whose stock is inexhaustible and truly infinite; and what a large and immense field doth extension alone afford the mathematicians!

CHAPTER VIII

SOME FARTHER CONSIDERATIONS CONCERNING OUR SIMPLE IDEAS OF SENSATION

1. *Positive ideas from privative[1] causes.*—Concerning the simple ideas of sensation it is to be considered, that whatsoever is so constituted in nature as to be able by affecting our senses to cause any perception in the mind, doth thereby produce in the understanding a simple idea; which, whatever be the external cause of it, when it comes to be taken notice of by our discerning faculty, it is by

ESSAY ON HUMAN UNDERSTANDING. 1. **privative:** depriving.

the mind looked on and considered there to be a real positive idea in the understanding, as much as any other whatsoever; though perhaps the cause of it be but a privation in the subject.

2. Thus the ideas of heat and cold, light and darkness, white and black, motion and rest, are equally clear and positive ideas in the mind; though perhaps some of the causes which produce them are barely privations in those subjects from whence our senses derive those ideas. These the understanding, in its view of them, considers all as distinct positive ideas without taking notice of the causes that produce them; which is an inquiry not belonging to the idea as it is in the understanding, but to the nature of the things existing without us. These are two very different things, and carefully to be distinguished; it being one thing to perceive and know the idea of white or black, and quite another to examine what kind of particles they must be, and how ranged in the superficies, to make any object appear white or black.

3. A painter or dyer who never inquired into their causes, hath the ideas of white and black and other colours as clearly, perfectly, and distinctly in his understanding, and perhaps more distinctly than the philosopher who hath busied himself in considering their natures, and thinks he knows how far either of them is in its cause positive or privative; and the idea of black is no less positive in his mind than that of white, however the cause of that colour in the external object may be only a privation.

4. If it were the design of my present undertaking to inquire into the natural causes and manner of perception, I should offer this as a reason why a privative cause might, in some cases at least, produce a positive idea, viz., that all sensation being produced in us only by different degrees and modes of motion in our animal spirits, variously agitated by external objects, the abatement of any former motion must as necessarily produce a new sensation as the variation or increase of it; and so introduce a new idea, which depends only on a different motion of the animal spirits in that organ.

5. But whether this be so or not I will not here determine, but appeal to every one's own experience, whether the shadow of a man, though it consists of nothing but the absence of light (and the more the absence of light is, the more discernible is the shadow), does not, when a man looks on it, cause as clear and positive an idea in his mind as a man himself, though covered over with clear sunshine! And the picture of a shadow is a positive thing. Indeed, we have negative names, [which stand not directly for positive ideas, but for their absence, such as *insipid, silence, nihil,* &c., which words denote positive ideas, *v. g., taste, sound, being,* with a signification of their absence.]

6. *Positive ideas from privative causes.*—And thus one may truly be said to see darkness. For, supposing a hole perfectly dark, from whence no light is reflected, it is certain one may see the figure of it, or it may be painted; or whether the ink I write with make any other idea, is a question. The privative causes I have here assigned of positive ideas are according to the common opinion; but, in truth, it will be hard to determine whether there be really any ideas from a privative cause, till it be determined whether rest be any more a privation than motion.

7. *Ideas in the mind, qualities in bodies.*—To discover the nature of our ideas the better, and to discourse of them intelligibly, it will be convenient to distinguish them, as they are ideas or perceptions in our minds, and as they are modifications of matter in the bodies that cause such perceptions in us; that so we may not think (as perhaps usually is done) that they are exactly the images and resemblances of something inherent in the subject; most of those of sensation being in the mind no more the likeness of something existing without us than the names that stand for them are the likeness of our ideas, which yet upon hearing they are apt to excite in us.

8. Whatsoever the mind perceives in itself, or is the immediate object of perception, thought, or understanding, that I call "idea"; and the power to produce any idea in our mind, I call "quality" of the subject wherein that power is. Thus a snowball having the power to produce in us the idea of white, cold, and round, the powers to produce those ideas in us as they are in the snowball, I call "qualities;" and as they are sensations or perceptions in our understandings, I call them "ideas"; which ideas, if I speak of them sometimes as in the things themselves, I would be understood to mean those qualities in the objects which produce them in us.

9. *Primary qualities.*—Qualities thus considered in bodies are, First, such as are utterly inseparable

from the body, in what estate soever it be; and such as, in all the alterations and changes it suffers, all the force can be used upon it, it constantly keeps; and such as sense constantly finds in every particle of matter which has bulk enough to be perceived, and the mind finds inseparable from every particle of matter, though less than to make itself singly be perceived by our senses: *v. g.*, take a grain of wheat, divide it into two parts, each part has still solidity, extension, figure, and mobility; divide it again, and it retains still the same qualities: and so divide it on till the parts become insensible, they must retain still each of them all those qualities. For, division (which is all that a mill or pestle or any other body does upon another, in reducing it to insensible parts) can never take away either solidity, extension, figure, or mobility from any body, but only makes two or more distinct separate masses of matter of that which was but one before; all which distinct masses, reckoned as so many distinct bodies, after division, make a certain number. These I call *original* or *primary* qualities of body, which I think we may observe to produce simple ideas in us, viz., solidity, extension, figure, motion or rest, and number.

10. *Secondary qualities.*—Secondly. Such qualities, which in truth are nothing in the objects themselves, but powers to produce various sensations in us by their primary qualities, *i. e.*, by the bulk, figure, texture, and motion of their insensible parts, as colours, sounds, tastes, &c., these I call *secondary* qualities. To these might be added a third sort, which are allowed to be barely powers, though they are as much real qualities in the subject as those which I, to comply with the common way of speaking, call qualities, but, for distinction, *secondary* qualities. For, the power in fire to produce a new colour or consistency in wax or clay, by its primary qualities, is as much a quality in fire as the power it has to produce in me a new idea or sensation of warmth or burning, which I felt not before, by the same primary qualities, viz., the bulk, texture, and motion of its insensible parts.

11. *How primary qualities produce their ideas.*—The next thing to be considered is, how bodies produce ideas in us; and that is manifestly by impulse, the only way which we can conceive bodies to operate in.

12. If, then, external objects be not united to our minds when they produce ideas therein, and yet we perceive these original qualities in such of them as singly fall under our senses, it is evident that some motion must be thence continued by our nerves, or animal spirits, by some parts of our bodies, to the brains or the seat of sensation, there to produce in our minds the particular ideas we have of them. And since the extension, figure, number, and motion of bodies of an observable bigness, may be perceived at a distance by the sight, it is evident some singly imperceptible bodies must come from them to the eyes, and thereby convey to the brain some motion which produces these ideas which we have of them in us.

13. *How secondary.*—After the same manner that the ideas of these original qualities are produced in us, we may conceive that the ideas of secondary qualities are also produced, viz., by the operation of insensible particles on our senses. For it being manifest that there are bodies, and good store of bodies, each whereof are so small that we cannot by any of our senses discover either their bulk, figure, or motion (as is evident in the particles of the air and water, and other extremely smaller than those, perhaps as much smaller than the particles of air or water as the particles of air or water are smaller than peas or hailstones): let us suppose at present that the different motions and figures, bulk and number, of such particles, affecting the several organs of our senses, produce in us those different sensations which we have from the colours and smells of bodies, *v. g.*, that a violet, by the impulse of such insensible particles of matter of peculiar figures and bulks, and in different degrees and modifications of their motions, causes the ideas of the blue colour and sweet scent of that flower to be produced in our minds; it being no more impossible to conceive that God should annex such ideas to such motions, with which they have no similitude, than that he should annex the idea of pain to the motion of a piece of steel dividing our flesh, with which the idea hath no resemblance.

14. What I have said concerning colours and smells may be understood also of tastes and sounds, and other the like sensible qualities; which, whatever reality we by mistake attribute to them, are in truth nothing in the objects themselves, but powers to produce various sensations in us, and depend on those primary qualities, viz., bulk, figure, texture, and motion of parts [as I have said].

15. *Ideas of primary qualities are resemblances; of secondary, not.*—From whence I think it is easy to draw this observation, that the ideas of primary qualities of bodies are resemblances of them, and their patterns do really exist in the bodies themselves; but the ideas produced in us by these secondary qualities have no resemblance of them at all. There is nothing like our ideas existing in the bodies themselves. They are, in the bodies we denominate from them, only a power to produce those sensations in us; and what is sweet, blue, or warm in idea, is but the certain bulk, figure, and motion of the insensible parts in the bodies themselves, which we call so.

16. Flame is denominated *hot* and *light;* snow, *white* and *cold;* and manna *white* and *sweet,* from the ideas they produce in us, which qualities are commonly thought to be the same in those bodies that those ideas are in us, the one the perfect resemblance of the other, as they are in a mirror; and it would by most men be judged very extravagant, if one should say otherwise. And yet he that will consider that the same fire that at one distance produces in us the sensation of warmth, does at a nearer approach produce in us the far different sensation of pain, ought to bethink himself what reason he has to say, that this idea of warmth which was produced in him by the fire, is actually in the fire, and his idea of pain which the same fire produced in him the same way is not in the fire. Why is whiteness and coldness in snow and pain not, when it produces the one and the other idea in us, and can do neither but by the bulk, figure, number, and motion of its solid parts?

17. The particular bulk, number, figure, and motion of the parts of fire or snow are really in them, whether any one's senses perceive them or no; and therefore they may be called *real* qualities, because they really exist in those bodies. But light, heat, whiteness, or coldness, are no more really in them than sickness or pain is in manna. Take away the sensation of them; let not the eyes see light or colours, nor the ears hear sounds; let the palate not taste, nor the nose smell; and all colours, tastes, odours, and sounds, as they are such particular ideas, vanish and cease, and are reduced to their causes, *i. e.,* bulk, figure, and motion of parts.

18. A piece of manna of a sensible bulk is able to produce in us the idea of a round or square figure; and, by being removed from one place to another, the idea of motion. This idea of motion represents it as it really is in the manna moving; a circle or square are the same, whether in idea or existence, in the mind or in the manna; and this both motion and figure are really in the manna, whether we take notice of them or no: this every body is ready to agree to. Besides, manna, by the bulk, figure, texture, and motion of its parts, has a power to produce the sensations of sickness, and sometimes of acute pains or gripings, in us. That these ideas of sickness and pain are not in the manna, but effects of its operations on us, and are nowhere when we feel them not; this also every one readily agrees to. And yet men are hardly to be brought to think that sweetness and whiteness are not really in manna, which are but the effects of the operations of manna by the motion, size, and figure of its particles on the eyes and palate; as the pain and sickness caused by manna, are confessedly nothing but the effects of its operations on the stomach and guts by the size, motion, and figure of its insensible parts (for by nothing else can a body operate, as has been proved): as if it could not operate on the eyes and palate, and thereby produce in the mind particular distinct ideas which in itself has not, as well as we allow it can operate on the guts and stomach, and thereby produce distinct ideas which in itself it has not. These ideas being all effects of the operations of manna on several parts of our bodies, by the size, figure, number, and motion of its parts, why those produced by the eyes and palate should rather be thought to be really in the manna than those produced by the stomach and guts: or why the pain and sickness, ideas that are the effects of manna, should be thought to be nowhere when they are not felt: and yet the sweetness and whiteness, effects of the same manna on other parts of the body, by ways equally as unknown, should be thought to exist in the manna, when they are not seen nor tasted would need some reason to explain.

19. *Ideas of primary qualities are resemblances; of secondary, not.*—Let us consider the red and white colours in porphyry; hinder light but from striking on it, and its colours vanish; it no longer produces any such ideas in us. Upon the return of light, it produces these appearances on us again. Can any one think any real alterations are made in the porphyry by the presence or absence of light, and that those ideas of whiteness and redness are really

in porphyry in the light, when it is plain it has no colour in the dark? It has indeed such a configuration of particles, both night and day, as are apt, by the rays of light rebounding from some parts of that hard stone, to produce in us the idea of redness, and from others the idea of whiteness. But whiteness or redness are not in it at any time, but such a texture that hath the power to produce such a sensation in us.

20. Pound an almond, and the clear white colour will be altered into a dirty one, and the sweet taste into an oily one. What real alteration can the beating of the pestle make in any body, but an alteration of the texture of it?

21. Ideas being thus distinguished and understood, we may be able to give an account how the same water, at the same time, may produce the idea of cold by one hand, and of heat by the other; whereas it is impossible that the same water, if those ideas were really in it, should at the same time be hot and cold. For if we imagine warmth as it is in our hands, to be nothing but a certain sort and degree of motion in the minute particles of our nerves or animal spirits, we may understand how it is possible that the same water may at the same time produce the sensation of heat in one hand, and cold in the other; which yet figure never does, that never producing the idea of a square by one hand which has produced the idea of a globe by another. But if the sensation of heat and cold be nothing but the increase or diminution of the motion of the minute parts of our bodies, caused by the corpuscles of any other body, it is easy to be understood that if that motion be greater in one hand than in the other, if a body be applied to the two hands, which has in its minute particles a greater motion than in those of one of the hands, and a less than in those of the other, it will increase the motion of the one hand, and lessen it in the other, and so cause the different sensations of heat and cold that depend thereon.

22. I have, in what just goes before, been engaged in physical inquiries a little farther than perhaps I intended. But it being necessary to make the nature of sensation a little understood, and to make the difference between the qualities in bodies, and the ideas produced by them in the mind, to be distinctly conceived, without which it were impossible to discourse intelligibly of them, I hope I shall be pardoned this little excursion into natural philosophy, it being necessary in our present inquiry to distinguish the primary and real qualities of bodies, which are always in them, (viz., solidity, extension, figure, number, and motion or rest and are sometimes perceived by us, viz., when the bodies they are in are big enough singly to be discerned,) from those secondary and imputed qualities, which are but the powers of several combinations of those primary ones, when they operate without being distinctly discerned; whereby we also may come to know what ideas are, and what are not, resemblances of something really existing in the bodies we denominate from them.

23. *Three sorts of qualities in bodies.*—The qualities then that are in bodies, rightly considered, are of three sorts:

First. The bulk, figure, number, situation, and motion or rest of their solid parts; those are in them, whether we perceive them or not; and when they are of that size that we can discover them, we have by these ideas of the thing as it is in itself, as is plain in artificial things. These I call *primary* qualities.

Secondly. The power that is in any body, by reason of its insensible primary qualities, to operate after a peculiar manner on any of our senses, and thereby produce in us the different ideas of several colours, sounds, smells, tastes, &c. These are usually called *sensible* qualities.

Thirdly. The power that is in any body, by reason of the particular constitution of its primary qualities, to make such a change in the bulk, figure, texture, and motion of another body, as to make it operate on our senses differently from what it did before. Thus the sun has a power to make wax white, and fire, to make lead fluid. [These are usually called "powers."]

The first of these, as has been said, I think may be properly called real, original, or primary qualities, because they are in the things themselves, whether they are perceived or no; and upon their different modifications it is that the secondary qualities depend.

The other two are only powers to act differently upon other things, which powers result from the different modifications of those primary qualities.

24. *The first are resemblances; the second thought resemblances, but are not; the third neither are, nor are thought so.*—But though these two latter sorts of qualities are powers barely, and nothing but

powers, relating to several other bodies, and resulting from the different modifications of the original qualities, yet they are generally otherwise thought of. For the second sort, viz., the powers to produce several ideas in us by our senses, are looked upon as real qualities in the things thus affecting us; but the third sort are called and esteemed barely powers. *V. g.*, the idea of heat or light which we receive by our eyes or touch from the sun, are commonly thought real qualities existing in the sun, and something more than mere powers in it. But when we consider the sun in reference to wax, which it melts or blanches, we look upon the whiteness and softness produced in the wax, not as qualities in the sun, but effects produced by powers in it: whereas, if rightly considered, these qualities of light and warmth, which are perceptions in me when I am warmed or enlightened by the sun, are no otherwise in the sun than the changes made in the wax, when it is blanched or melted, are in the sun. They are all of them equally powers in the sun, depending on its primary qualities, whereby it is able in the one case so to alter the bulk, figure, texture, or motion of some of the insensible parts of my eyes or hands as thereby to produce in me the idea of light or heat, and in the other it is able so to alter the bulk, figure, texture, or motion of the insensible parts of the wax as to make them fit to produce in me the distinct ideas of white and fluid.

25. The reason why the one are ordinarily taken for real qualities, and the other only for bare powers, seems to be because the ideas we have of distinct colours, sounds, &c., containing nothing at all in them of bulk, figure, or motion, we are not apt to think them the effects of these primary qualities which appear not, to our senses, to operate in their production, and with which they have not any apparent congruity, or conceivable connexion. Hence it is that we are so forward to imagine that those ideas are the resemblances of something really existing in the objects themselves, since sensation discovers nothing of bulk, figure, or motion of parts, in their production, nor can reason show how bodies by their bulk, figure, and motion, should produce in the mind the ideas of blue or yellow, &c. But, in the other case, in the operations of bodies changing the qualities one of another, we plainly discover that the quality produced hath commonly no resemblance with any thing in the thing producing it; wherefore we look on it as a bare effect of power. For though, receiving the idea of heat or light from the sun, we are apt to think it is a perception and resemblance of such a quality in the sun, yet when we see wax, or a fair face, receive change of colour from the sun, we cannot imagine that to the perception or resemblance of any thing in the sun, because we find not those different colours in the sun itself: for, our senses being able to observe a likeness or unlikeness of sensible qualities in two different external objects, we forwardly enough conclude the production of any sensible quality in any subject to be an effect of bare power, and not the communication of any quality which was really in the efficient,[2] when we find no such sensible quality in the thing that produced it. But our senses not being able to discover any unlikeness between the idea produced in us and the quality of the object producing it, we are apt to imagine that our ideas are resemblances of something in the objects, and not the effects of certain powers placed in the modification of their primary qualities, with which primary qualities the ideas produced in us have no resemblance.

26. *Secondary qualities twofold: first, immediately perceivable; secondly, mediately perceivable.*—To conclude: Besides those before-mentioned primary qualities in bodies, viz., bulk, figure, extension, number, and motion of their solid parts, all the rest whereby we take notice of bodies and distinguish them one from another, are nothing else but several powers in them depending on those primary qualities, whereby they are fitted, either by immediately operating on our bodies, to produce several different ideas in us; or else by operating on other bodies, so to change their primary qualities as to render them capable of producing ideas in us different from what before they did. The former of these, I think, may be called secondary qualities immediately perceivable; the latter, secondary qualities mediately perceivable.

. . .

CHAPTER XI

OF DISCERNING, AND OTHER OPERATIONS OF THE MIND

1. *No knowledge without discerning.*—Another faculty we may take notice of in our minds, is that

2. efficient: the efficient cause.

of discerning and distinguishing between the several ideas it has. It is not enough to have a confused perception of something in general: unless the mind had a distinct perception of different objects and their qualities, it would be capable of very little knowledge; though the bodies that affect us were as busy about us as they are now, and the mind were continually employed in thinking. On this faculty of distinguishing one thing from another, depends the evidence and certainty of several even very general propositions, which have passed for innate truths; because men, overlooking the true cause why those propositions find universal assent, impute it wholly to native uniform impressions: whereas it in truth depends upon this clear discerning faculty of the mind, whereby it perceives two ideas to be the same or different. But of this more hereafter.

2. *The difference of wit and judgment.*—How much the imperfection of accurately discriminating ideas one from another lies either in the dulness or faults of the organs of sense, or want of acuteness, exercise, or attention in the understanding, or hastiness and precipitancy natural to some tempers, I will not here examine: it suffices to take notice, that this is one of the operations that the mind may reflect on and observe in itself. It is of that consequence to its other knowledge, that so far as this faculty is in itself dull, or not rightly made use of for the distinguishing one thing from another, so far our notions are confused, and our reason, and judgment disturbed or misled. If in having our ideas in the memory ready at hand consists quickness of parts; in this of having them unconfused, and being able nicely to distinguish one thing from another where there is but the least difference, consists in a great measure the exactness of judgment and clearness of reason which is to be observed in one man above another. And hence, perhaps, may be given some reason of that common observation—that men who have a great deal of wit and prompt memories, have not always the clearest judgment or deepest reason. For, wit lying most in the assemblage of ideas, and putting those together with quickness and variety wherein can be found any resemblance or congruity, thereby to make up pleasant pictures and agreeable visions in the fancy; judgment, on the contrary, lies quite on the other side, in separating carefully one from another ideas wherein can be found the least difference, thereby to avoid being misled by similitude and by affinity to take one thing for another. This is a way of proceeding quite contrary to metaphor and allusion, wherein for the most part lies that entertainment and pleasantry of wit which strikes so lively on the fancy, and is therefore so acceptable to all people; because its beauty appears at first sight, and there is required no labour of thought to examine what truth or reason there is in it. The mind, without looking any farther, rests satisfied with the agreeableness of the picture and the gaiety of the fancy; and it is a kind of affront to go about to examine it by the severe rules of truth and good reason; whereby it appears that it consists in something that is not perfectly conformable to them.

(1690)

Joseph Addison
1672–1719

FROM
The Spectator

TRUE WIT

NO. 62, MAY 11, 1711

Scribendi recte sapere est et principium et fons.
—Hor.[1]

Mr. Locke has an admirable reflection upon the difference of wit and judgment whereby he endeavors to show the reason why they are not always the talents of the same person. His words are as follow:

> And hence, perhaps, may be given some reason of that common observation that men who have a great deal of wit and prompt memories have not always the clearest judgments or deepest reason. For wit lying most in the assemblage of ideas, and putting those together with quickness and variety wherein can be found any resemblance or congruity, thereby to make up pleasant pictures and agreeable visions in the fancy; judgment, on the contrary, lies quite on the other side, in separating carefully one from another ideas wherein can be found the least difference, thereby to avoid being misled by similitude, and by affinity to take one thing for another. This is a way of proceeding quite contrary to metaphor and allusion, wherein, for the most part, lies that entertainment and pleasantry of wit which strikes so lively on the fancy, and is therefore so acceptable to all people.[2]

This is, I think, the best and most philosophical account that I have ever met with of wit, which generally, though not always, consists in such a resemblance and congruity of ideas as this author mentions. I shall only add to it by way of explanation, that every resemblance of ideas is not that which we call wit unless it be such a one that gives delight and surprise to the reader. These two properties seem essential to wit, more particularly the last of them. In order, therefore, that the resemblance in the ideas be wit, it is necessary that the ideas should not lie too near one another in the nature of things, for where the likeness is obvious, it gives no surprise. To compare one man's singing to that of another, or to represent the whiteness of any object by that of milk and snow, or the variety of its colors by those of the rainbow, cannot be called wit unless, besides this obvious resemblance, there be some further congruity discovered in the two ideas that is capable of giving the reader some surprise. Thus when a poet tells us the bosom of his mistress is as white as snow, there is no wit in the comparison; but when he adds, with a sigh, that it is as cold too, it then grows into wit. Every reader's memory may supply him with innumerable instances of the same nature. For this reason, the similitudes in heroic poets, who endeavor rather to fill the mind with great conceptions than to divert it with such as are new and surprising, have seldom anything in them that can be called wit. Mr. Locke's account of wit, with this short explanation, comprehends most of the species of wit, as metaphors, similitudes, allegories, enigmas, mottoes, parables, fables, dreams, visions, dramatic writings, burlesque, and all the methods of allusion—as there are many other pieces of wit (how remote soever they may appear at first sight from the foregoing description) which upon examination will be found to agree with it.

As true wit generally consists in this resemblance and congruity of ideas, false wit chiefly consists in the resemblance and congruity sometimes of single letters (as in anagrams, chronograms, lipograms, and acrostics), sometimes of syllables (as in echoes and doggerel rhymes), sometimes of words (as in puns and quibbles), and sometimes of whole sentences or poems cast into the figures of eggs, axes, or altars. Nay, some carry the notion of wit so far as to ascribe it even to external mimicry, and

THE SPECTATOR. NO. 62. **1.** ***Scribendi . . . fons:*** "The source and fountain of writing well is wisdom." See Horace, *Ars Poetica*, l. 309. **2.** See *An Essay Concerning Human Understanding,* II, xi, 2.

to look upon a man as an ingenious person that can resemble the tone, posture, or face of another.

As true wit consists in the resemblance of ideas, and false wit in the resemblance of words, according to the foregoing instances, there is another kind of wit which consists partly in the resemblance of ideas and partly in the resemblance of words, which for distinction's sake I shall call "mixed wit." This kind of wit is that which abounds in Cowley more than in any author that ever wrote. Mr. Waller has likewise a great deal of it. Mr. Dryden is very sparing in it. Milton had a genius much above it. Spenser is in the same class with Milton. The Italians, even in their epic poetry, are full of it. Monsieur Boileau, who formed himself upon the ancient poets, has everywhere rejected it with scorn. If we look after mixed wit among the Greek writers, we shall find it nowhere but in the epigrammatists. There are indeed some strokes of it in the little poem ascribed to Musaeus, which by that, as well as many other marks, betrays itself to be a modern composition. If we look into the Latin writers, we find none of this mixed wit in Virgil, Lucretius, or Catullus; very little in Horace; but a great deal of it in Ovid; and scarce anything else in Martial.

Out of the innumerable branches of mixed wit, I shall choose one instance which may be met with in all the writers of this class. The passion of love in its nature has been thought to resemble fire, for which reason the words *fire* and *flame* are made use of to signify love. The witty poets, therefore, have taken an advantage from the doubtful meaning of the word *fire* to make an infinite number of witticisms. Cowley, observing the cold regard of his mistress's eyes, and at the same time their power of producing love in him, considers them as burning glasses made of ice, and finding himself able to live in the greatest extremities of love, concludes the torrid zone to be habitable. When his mistress has read his letter written in juice of lemon by holding it to the fire, he desires her to read it over a second time by love's flames. When she weeps, he wishes it were inward heat that distilled those drops from the limbeck.[3] When she is absent, he is beyond eighty, that is, thirty degrees nearer the pole than when she is with him. His ambitious love is a fire that naturally mounts upwards; his happy love is the beams of heaven, and his unhappy love flames of hell. When it does not let him sleep, it is a flame that sends up no smoke; when it is opposed by counsel and advice, it is a fire that rages the more by the winds' blowing upon it. Upon the dying of a tree in which he had cut his loves, he observes that his written flames had burnt up and withered the tree. When he resolves to give over his passion, he tells us that one burned like him forever dreads the fire. His heart is an Aetna that, instead of Vulcan's shop, encloses Cupid's forge in it. His endeavoring to drown his love in wine is throwing oil upon the fire. He would insinuate to his mistress that the fire of love, like that of the sun (which produces so many living creatures) should not only warm but beget. Love in another place cooks pleasure at his fire. Sometimes the poet's heart is frozen in every breast, and sometimes scorched in every eye. Sometimes he is drowned in tears and burned in love, like a ship set on fire in the middle of the sea.

The reader may observe in every one of these instances that the poet mixes the qualities of fire with those of love, and in the same sentence speaking of it both as a passion and as real fire, surprises the reader with those seeming resemblances or contradictions that make up all the wit in this kind of writing. Mixed wit, therefore, is a composition of pun and true wit, and is more or less perfect as the resemblance lies in the ideas or in the words. Its foundations are laid partly in falsehood and partly in truth. Reason puts in her claim for one half of it, and extravagance for the other. The only province, therefore, for this kind of wit is epigram, or those little occasional poems that in their own nature are nothing else but a tissue of epigrams. I cannot conclude this head of mixed wit without owning that the admirable poet out of whom I have taken the examples of it had as much true wit as any author that ever writ, and indeed all other talents of an extraordinary genius.

It may be expected, since I am upon this subject, that I should take notice of Mr. Dryden's definition of wit, which, with all the deference that is due to the judgment of so great a man, is not so properly a definition of wit as of good writing in general. Wit, as he defines it, is "a propriety of words and thoughts adapted to the subject." If this be a true definition of wit, I am apt to think that Euclid was the greatest wit that ever set pen to paper: it is certain that never was a greater propriety of words and thoughts adapted to the

3. limbeck: still.

subject than what that author has made use of in his *Elements*. I shall only appeal to my reader if this definition agrees with any notion he has of wit. If it be a true one, I am sure Mr. Dryden was not only a better poet but a greater wit than Mr. Cowley, and Virgil a much more facetious man than either Ovid or Martial.

Bouhours, whom I look upon to be the most penetrating of all the French critics, has taken pains to show that it is impossible for any thought to be beautiful which is not just and has not its foundation in the nature of things; that the basis of all wit is truth; and that no thought can be valuable of which good sense is not the groundwork.[4] Boileau has endeavored to inculcate the same notion in several parts of his writings, both in prose and verse. This is that natural way of writing, that beautiful simplicity, which we so much admire in the compositions of the ancients, and which nobody deviates from but those who want strength of genius to make a thought shine in its own natural beauties. Poets who want this strength of genius to give that majestic simplicity to nature which we so much admire in the works of the ancients are forced to hunt after foreign ornaments and not to let any piece of wit of what kind soever escape them. I look upon these writers as Goths in poetry, who, like those in architecture, not being able to come up to the beautiful simplicity of the old Greeks and Romans, have endeavored to supply its place with all the extravagances of an irregular fancy. Mr. Dryden makes a very handsome observation on Ovid's writing a letter from Dido to Aeneas, in the following words:

> Ovid (says he, speaking of Virgil's fiction of Dido and Aeneas) takes it up after him, even in the same age, and makes an ancient heroine of Virgil's new-created Dido; dictates a letter for her just before her death to the ungrateful fugitive; and, very unluckily for himself, is for measuring a sword with a man so much superior in force to him, on the same subject. I think I may be judge of this, because I have translated both. The famous author of the *Art of Love* has nothing of his own; he borrows all from a greater master in his own profession and, which is worse, improves nothing which he finds. Nature fails him, and being forced to his old shift, he has recourse to witticism. This passes indeed with his soft admirers and gives him the preference to Virgil in their esteem.

Were not I supported by so great an authority as that of Mr. Dryden, I should not venture to observe that the taste of most of our English poets, as well as readers, is extremely Gothic. He quotes Monsieur Segrais[5] for a threefold distinction of the readers of poetry, in the first of which he comprehends the rabble of readers, whom he does not treat as such with regard to their quality, but to their numbers and the coarseness of their taste. His words are as follow:

> Segrais has distinguished the readers of poetry, according to their capacity of judging, into three classes. (He might have said the same of writers too, if he had pleased.) In the lowest form he places those whom he calls *les petits esprits*, such things as are our upper-gallery audience in a play-house, who like nothing but the husk and rind of wit, prefer a quibble, a conceit, an epigram, before solid sense and elegant expression. These are mob-readers. If Virgil and Martial stood for parliament men, we know already who would carry it. But though they make the greatest appearance in the field, and cry the loudest, the best on 't is they are but a sort of French Huguenots, or Dutch boors, brought over in herds, but not naturalized, who have not lands of two pounds per annum in Parnassus, and therefore are not privileged to poll. Their authors are of the same level, fit to represent them on a mountebank's stage, or to be masters of the ceremonies in a bear garden. Yet these are they who have the most admirers. But it often happens, to their mortification, that as their readers improve their stock of sense (as they may by reading better books, and by conversation with men of judgment) they soon forsake them.

I must not dismiss this subject without observing that as Mr. Locke in the passage above-mentioned has discovered the most fruitful source of wit, so there is another of a quite contrary nature to it, which does likewise branch itself out into several kinds. For not only the resemblance but the opposition of ideas does very often produce wit, as I could show in several little points, turns, and antitheses that I may possibly enlarge upon in some future speculation.

4. Dominique Bouhours (1628–1702), French critic, author of *La Manière de bien penser dans les ouvrages d'esprit* (1687), a work later translated as *The Art of Criticism.*

5. Monsieur Segrais: Jean Regnauld de Segrais (1624–1701). Dryden often refers to Segrais' preface to his translation of the *Aeneid.*

DEFECTS IN *PARADISE LOST*

NO. 297, FEBRUARY 9, 1712

Velut si
egregio inspersos reprehendas corpore naevos.

—HOR.[1]

After what I have said in my last Saturday's paper, I shall enter on the subject of this without farther preface, and remark the several defects which appear in the fable, the characters, the sentiments, and the language of Milton's *Paradise Lost,* not doubting but the reader will pardon me if I allege at the same time whatever may be said for the extenuation of such defects. The first imperfection which I shall observe in the fable is that the event of it is unhappy.

The fable of every poem is, according to Aristotle's division, either simple or implex. It is called simple when there is no change of fortune in it, implex when the fortune of the chief actor changes from bad to good, or from good to bad. The implex fable is thought the most perfect—I suppose because it is more proper to stir up the passions of the reader and to surprise him with a greater variety of accidents.

The implex fable is therefore of two kinds: in the first, the chief actor makes his way through a long series of dangers and difficulties till he arrives at honor and prosperity, as we see in the story of Ulysses; in the second, the chief actor in the poem falls from some eminent pitch of honor and prosperity into misery and disgrace. Thus we see Adam and Eve sinking from a state of innocence and happiness into the most abject condition of sin and sorrow.

The most taking[2] tragedies among the ancients were built on this last sort of implex fable, particularly the tragedy of *Oedipus,* which proceeds upon a story, if we may believe Aristotle, the most proper for tragedy that could be invented by the wit of man. I have taken some pains in a former paper to show that this kind of implex fable, wherein the event is unhappy, is more apt to affect an audience than that of the first kind, notwithstanding many excellent pieces among the ancients, as well as most of those which have been written of late years in our own country, are raised upon contrary plans. I must, however, own that I think this kind of fable, which is the most perfect in tragedy, is not so proper for a heroic poem.

Milton seems to have been sensible of this imperfection in his fable, and has therefore endeavored to cure it by several expedients, particularly by the mortification which the great adversary of mankind meets with upon his return to the assembly of infernal spirits, as it is described in a beautiful passage of the Tenth Book, and likewise by the vision wherein Adam at the close of the poem sees his offspring triumphing over his great enemy and himself restored to a happier paradise than that from which he fell.

There is another objection against Milton's fable, which is indeed almost the same with the former, though placed in a different light, namely, that the hero in the *Paradise Lost* is unsuccessful and by no means a match for his enemies. This gave occasion to Mr. Dryden's reflection that the devil was in reality Milton's hero. I think I have obviated this objection in my first paper. The *Paradise Lost* is an epic, or a narrative poem; he that looks for a hero in it searches for that which Milton never intended; but if he will needs fix the name of a hero upon any person in it, it is certainly the Messiah who is the hero, both in the principal action and in the chief episodes. Paganism could not furnish out a real action for a fable greater than that of the *Iliad* or *Aeneid,* and therefore a heathen could not form a higher notion of a poem than one of that kind which they call a heroic. Whether Milton's is not of a sublimer nature I will not presume to determine. It is sufficient that I show there is in the *Paradise Lost* all the greatness of plan, regularity of design, and masterly beauties which we discover in Homer and Virgil.

I must in the next place observe that Milton has interwoven in the texture of his fable some particulars which do not seem to have probability enough for an epic poem, particularly in the actions which he ascribes to Sin and Death, and the picture which he draws of the Limbo of Vanity, with other passages in the Second Book. Such allegories rather savor of the spirit of Spenser and Ariosto than of Homer and Virgil.

In the structure of his poem he has likewise ad-

NO. 297. **1.** ***Velut . . . naevos:*** "Even as if you might criticize moles spread over an attractive body." See Horace, *Serm.,* I, vi, 66. **2. taking:** touching, moving.

mitted of too many digressions. It is finely observed by Aristotle that the author of a heroic poem should seldom speak himself, but throw as much of his work as he can into the mouths of those who are his principal actors. Aristotle has given no reason for this precept, but I presume it is because the mind of the reader is more awed and elevated when he hears Aeneas or Achilles speak than when Virgil or Homer talk in their own persons—besides that assuming the character of an eminent man is apt to fire the imagination and raise the ideas of the author. Tully tells us, mentioning his dialogue *Of Old Age,* in which Cato is the chief speaker, that upon a review of it he was agreeably imposed upon, and fancied that it was Cato, and not he himself, who uttered his thoughts on that subject.[3]

If the reader would be at the pains to see how the story of the *Iliad* and the *Aeneid* is delivered by those persons who act in it, he will be surprised to find how little in either of these poems proceeds from the authors. Milton has, in the general disposition of his fable, very finely observed this great rule, insomuch that there is scarce a third part of it which comes from the poet; the rest is spoken either by Adam and Eve or by some good or evil spirit who is engaged either in their destruction or defense.

From what has been here observed it appears that digressions are by no means to be allowed of in an epic poem. If the poet, even in the ordinary course of his narration, should speak as little as possible, he should certainly never let his narration sleep for the sake of any reflections of his own. I have often observed with a secret admiration that the longest reflection in the *Aeneid* is in that passage of the Tenth Book where Turnus is represented as dressing himself in the spoils of Pallas, whom he had slain. Virgil here lets his fable stand still for the sake of the following remark: "How is the mind of man ignorant of futurity, and unable to bear prosperous fortune with moderation! The time will come when Turnus shall wish that he had left the body of Pallas untouched, and curse the day on which he dressed himself in these spoils." As the great event of the *Aeneid,* and the death of Turnus, whom Aeneas slew because he saw him adorned with the spoils of Pallas, turns upon this incident, Virgil went out of his way to make this reflection upon it, without which so small a circumstance might possibly have slipped out of his reader's memory. Lucan, who was an injudicious poet, lets drop his story very frequently for the sake of unnecessary digressions, or his *diverticula,* as Scaliger calls them.[4] If he gives us an account of the prodigies which preceded the Civil War, he declaims upon the occasion and shows how much happier it would be for man if he did not feel his evil fortune before it comes to pass, and suffer not only by its real weight but by the apprehension of it. Milton's complaint of his blindness, his panegyric on marriage, his reflections on Adam and Eve's going naked, of the angels' eating, and several other passages in his poem are liable to the same exception, though I must confess there is so great a beauty in these very digressions that I would not wish them out of his poem.

I have, in a former paper, spoken of the characters of Milton's *Paradise Lost* and declared my opinion as to the allegorical persons who are introduced in it.

If we look into the sentiments, I think they are sometimes defective under the following heads: first, as there are several of them too much pointed, and some that degenerate even into puns. Of this last kind I am afraid is that in the First Book, where, speaking of the Pigmies, he calls them:

The small Infantry
Warr'd on by Cranes.

Another blemish that appears in some of his thoughts is his frequent allusion to heathen fables, which are not certainly of a piece with the divine subject of which he treats. I do not find fault with these allusions where the poet himself represents them as fabulous, as he does in some places, but where he mentions them as truths and matters of fact. The limits of my paper will not give me leave to be particular in instances of this kind. The reader will easily remark them in his perusal of the poem.

A third fault in his sentiments is an unnecessary ostentation of learning, which likewise occurs very frequently. It is certain that both Homer and Virgil were masters of all the learning of their times, but

3. A reference to Marcus Tullius Cicero. See his *De amicitia,* i, 4.

4. See Lucan's *Pharsalia,* ii, 1.

it shows itself in their works after an indirect and concealed manner. Milton seems ambitious of letting us know, by his excursions on free will and predestination and his many glances upon history, astronomy, geography, and the like, as well as by the terms and phrases he sometimes makes use of, that he was acquainted with the whole circle of arts and sciences.

If, in the last place, we consider the language of this great poet, we must allow what I have hinted in a former paper, that it is often too much labored, and sometimes obscured by old words, transpositions, and foreign idioms. Seneca's objection to the style of a great author, *Riget ejus oratio, nihil in ea placidum, nihil lene,*[5] is what many critics make to Milton. As I cannot wholly refute it, so I have already apologized for it in another paper, to which I may further add that Milton's sentiments and ideas were so wonderfully sublime that it would have been impossible for him to have represented them in their full strength and beauty without having recourse to these foreign assistances. Our language sunk under him and was unequal to the greatness of soul which furnished him with such glorious conceptions.

A second fault in his language is that he often affects a kind of jingle in his words, as in the following passages, and many others:

> That brought into this *World* a *world* of woe.
> . . . Begirt th' Almighty Throne
> *Beseeching* or *besieging* . . .
> Which *tempted* our *attempt* . . .
> At one slight *bound* high overleap'd all *bound.*

I know there are figures for this kind of speech, that some of the greatest ancients have been guilty of it, and that Aristotle himself has given it a place in his *Rhetoric* among the beauties of that art. But as it is in itself poor and trifling, it is, I think, at present universally exploded by all the masters of polite writing.

The last fault which I shall take notice of in Milton's style is the frequent use of what the learned call technical words, or terms of art. It is one of the great beauties of poetry to make hard things intelligible and to deliver what is abstruse of itself in such easy language as may be understood by ordinary readers—besides that the knowledge of a poet should rather seem born with him, or inspired, than drawn from books and systems. I have often wondered how Mr. Dryden could translate a passage out of Virgil after the following manner:

> Tack to the Larboard, and stand off to Sea,
> Veer Star-board Sea and Land.
>
> [*Aeneid,* III, 526]

Milton makes use of *larboard* in the same manner. When he is upon building, he mentions *Doric pillars, pilasters, cornice, frieze, architrave.* When he talks of heavenly bodies, you meet with *ecliptic* and *eccentric,* the *trepidation,* stars dropping from the *zenith,* rays culminating from the *equator.* To which might be added many instances of the like kind in several other arts and sciences.

I shall in my next papers give an account of the many particular beauties in Milton, which would have been too long to insert under those general heads I have already treated of, and with which I intend to conclude this piece of criticism.

THE PLEASURES OF THE IMAGINATION, I

NO. 411, JUNE 21, 1712

The perfection of our sight above our other senses. The pleasures of the imagination arise originally from sight. The pleasures of the imagination divided under two heads. The pleasures of the imagination in some respects equal to those of the understanding. The extent of the pleasures of the imagination. The advantages a man receives from a relish of these pleasures. In what respect they are preferable to those of the understanding.

> *Avia Pieridum peragro loca nullius ante trita solo. Juvat integros accedere fontis atque haurire.*
>
> —LUCR.[1]

5. ***Riget . . . lene:*** "His style is rigid; nothing is easy in it; nothing is smooth." See *Controversia,* VII, iv, 8.

NO. 411. 1. ***Avia . . . haurire:*** "I travel the remote places of the Pierides, never before touched by any man. I rejoice to approach these springs and to drink my fill." See Lucretius, *De Rerum Natura,* i, 926.

Our sight is the most perfect and most delightful of all our senses. It fills the mind with the largest variety of ideas, converses with its objects at the greatest distance, and continues the longest in action without being tired or satiated with its proper enjoyments. The sense of feeling can indeed give us a notion of extension, shape, and all other ideas that enter at the eye, except colors; but at the same time it is very much straitened and confined in its operations to the number, bulk, and distance of its particular objects. Our sight seems designed to supply all these defects, and may be considered as a more delicate and diffusive kind of touch, that spreads itself over an infinite multitude of bodies, comprehends the largest figures, and brings into our reach some of the most remote parts of the universe.

It is this sense which furnishes the imagination with its ideas; so that by the pleasures of the imagination or fancy (which I shall use promiscuously) I here mean such as arise from visible objects, either when we have them actually in our view or when we call up their ideas into our minds by paintings, statues, descriptions, or any the like occasion. We cannot indeed have a single image in the fancy that did not make its first entrance through the sight; but we have the power of retaining, altering, and compounding those images which we have once received into all the varieties of picture and vision that are most agreeable to the imagination, for by this faculty a man in a dungeon is capable of entertaining himself with scenes and landscapes more beautiful than any that can be found in the whole compass of nature.

There are few words in the English language which are employed in a more loose and uncircumscribed sense than those of the fancy and the imagination. I therefore thought it necessary to fix and determine the notion of these two words as I intend to make use of them in the thread of my following speculations, that the reader may conceive rightly what is the subject which I proceed upon. I must therefore desire him to remember that by the pleasures of the imagination I mean only such pleasures as arise originally from sight, and that I divide these pleasures into two kinds: my design being first of all to discourse of those primary pleasures of the imagination which entirely proceed from such objects as are before our eyes; and, in the next place, to speak of those secondary pleasures of the imagination which flow from the ideas of visible objects when the objects are not actually before the eye but are called up into our memories or formed into agreeable visions of things that are either absent or fictitious.

The pleasures of the imagination, taken in their full extent, are not so gross as those of sense nor so refined as those of the understanding. The last are, indeed, more preferable, because they are founded on some new knowledge or improvement in the mind of man; yet it must be confessed that those of the imagination are as great and as transporting as the other. A beautiful prospect delights the soul as much as a demonstration, and a description in Homer has charmed more readers than a chapter in Aristotle. Besides, the pleasures of the imagination have this advantage above those of the understanding, that they are more obvious and more easy to be acquired. It is but opening the eye, and the scene enters. The colors paint themselves on the fancy, with very little attention of thought or application of mind in the beholder. We are struck, we know not how, with the symmetry of anything we see, and immediately assent to the beauty of an object without inquiring into the particular causes and occasions of it.

A man of a polite imagination is let into a great many pleasures that the vulgar are not capable of receiving. He can converse with a picture and find an agreeable companion in a statue. He meets with a secret refreshment in a description and often feels a greater satisfaction in the prospect of fields and meadows than another does in the possession. It gives him, indeed, a kind of property in everything he sees and makes the most rude uncultivated parts of nature administer to his pleasures; so that he looks upon the world, as it were, in another light and discovers in it a multitude of charms that conceal themselves from the generality of mankind.

There are, indeed, but very few who know how to be idle and innocent, or have a relish of any pleasures that are not criminal; every diversion they take is at the expense of some one virtue or another, and their very first step out of business is into vice or folly. A man should endeavor, therefore, to make the sphere of his innocent pleasures as wide as possible, that he may retire into them with safety and find in them such a satisfaction as a wise man would not blush to take. Of this nature are those of the imagination, which do not require such a bent of thought as is necessary to our more serious employments nor, at the same time, suffer the mind to sink into that negligence and remissness which are apt to accompany our more sensual delights, but like a gentle exercise to the faculties awaken them from sloth and idleness without putting them upon any labor or difficulty.

We might here add that the pleasures of the fancy are more conducive to health than those of the understanding, which are worked out by dint of thinking and attended with too violent a labor of the brain. Delightful scenes, whether in nature, painting, or poetry, have a kindly influence on the body as well as the mind, and not only serve to clear and brighten the imagination but are able to disperse grief and melancholy and to set the animal spirits in pleasing and agreeable motions. For this reason Sir Francis Bacon, in his "Essay upon Health," has not thought it improper to prescribe to his reader a poem or a prospect, where he particularly dissuades him from knotty and subtle disquisitions and advises him to pursue studies that fill the mind with splendid and illustrious objects, as histories, fables, and contemplations of nature.

I have in this paper, by way of introduction, settled the notion of those pleasures of the imagination which are the subject of my present undertaking and endeavored, by several considerations, to recommend to my reader the pursuit of those pleasures. I shall, in my next paper, examine the several sources from whence these pleasures are derived.

THE PLEASURES OF THE IMAGINATION, II

NO. 412, JUNE 23, 1712

Three sources of all the pleasures of the imagination, in our survey of outward objects. How what is great pleases the imagination. How what is new pleases the imagination. How what is beautiful in our own species pleases the imagination. How what is beautiful in general pleases the imagination. What other accidental causes may contribute to the heightening of these pleasures.

Divisum sic breve fiet opus.

—MART.[1]

I shall first consider those pleasures of the imagination which arise from the actual view and survey of outward objects. And these, I think, all proceed from the sight of what is great, uncommon, or beautiful. There may, indeed, be something so terrible or offensive that the horror or loathsomeness of an object may overbear the pleasure which results from its greatness, novelty, or beauty; but still there will be such a mixture of delight in the very disgust it gives us as any of these three qualifications are most conspicuous and prevailing.

By greatness I do not only mean the bulk of any single object but the largeness of a whole view considered as one entire piece. Such are the prospects of an open champaign country, a vast uncultivated desert, of huge heaps of mountains, high rocks and precipices, or a wide expanse of waters, where we are not struck with the novelty or beauty of the sight but with that rude kind of magnificence which appears in many of these stupendous works of nature. Our imagination loves to be filled with an object, or to grasp at anything that is too big for its capacity. We are flung into a pleasing astonishment at such unbounded views, and feel a delightful stillness and amazement in the soul at the apprehension of them. The mind of man naturally hates everything that looks like a restraint upon it, and is apt to fancy itself under a sort of confinement when the sight is pent up in a narrow compass and shortened on every side by the neighborhood of walls or mountains. On the contrary, a spacious horizon is an image of liberty, where the eye has room to range abroad, to expatiate at large on the immensity of its views, and to lose itself amidst the variety of objects that offer themselves to its observation. Such wide and undetermined prospects are as pleasing to the fancy as the speculations of eternity or infinitude are to the understanding. But if there be a beauty or uncommonness joined with this grandeur, as in a troubled ocean, a heaven adorned with stars and meteors, or a spacious landscape cut out into rivers, woods, rocks, and mea-

NO. 412. 1. ***Divisum . . . opus:*** "When divided the work thus becomes short." See Martial, *Epigrams,* IV, lxxxii, 8.

dows, the pleasure still grows upon us, as it arises from more than a single principle.

Everything that is new or uncommon raises a pleasure in the imagination because it fills the soul with an agreeable surprise, gratifies its curiosity, and gives it an idea of which it was not before possessed. We are, indeed, so often conversant with one set of objects, and tired out with so many repeated shows of the same things, that whatever is new or uncommon contributes a little to vary human life and to divert our minds for a while with the strangeness of its appearance; it serves us for a kind of refreshment and takes off from that satiety we are apt to complain of in our usual and ordinary entertainments. It is this that bestows charms on a monster and makes even the imperfections of nature please us. It is this that recommends variety, where the mind is every instant called off to something new, and the attention not suffered to dwell too long and waste itself on any particular object. It is this, likewise, that improves what is great or beautiful and makes it afford the mind a double entertainment. Groves, fields, and meadows are at any season of the year pleasant to look upon, but never so much as in the opening of the spring, when they are all new and fresh with their first gloss upon them, and not yet too much accustomed and familiar to the eye. For this reason there is nothing that more enlivens a prospect than rivers, jetteaus,[2] or falls of water, where the scene is perpetually shifting and entertaining the sight every moment with something that is new. We are quickly tired with looking upon hills and valleys, where everything continues fixed and settled in the same place and posture, but find our thoughts a little agitated and relieved at the sight of such objects as are ever in motion and sliding away from beneath the eye of the beholder.

But there is nothing that makes its way more directly to the soul than beauty, which immediately diffuses a secret satisfaction and complacency through the imagination and gives a finishing to anything that is great or uncommon. The very first discovery of it strikes the mind with an inward joy and spreads a cheerfulness and delight through all its faculties. There is not, perhaps, any real beauty or deformity more in one piece of matter than another, because we might have been so made that whatsoever now appears loathsome to us might have shown itself agreeable; but we find by experience that there are several modifications of matter which the mind, without any previous consideration, pronounces at first sight beautiful or deformed. Thus we see that every different species of sensible creatures has its different notions of beauty, and that each of them is most affected with the beauties of its own kind. This is nowhere more remarkable than in birds of the same shape and proportion, where we often see the male determined in his courtship by the single grain or tincture of a feather, and never discovering any charms but in the color of its species.

. . .

There is a second kind of beauty that we find in the several products of art and nature which does not work in the imagination with that warmth and violence as the beauty that appears in our proper species, but is apt, however, to raise in us a secret delight and a kind of fondness for the places or objects in which we discover it. This consists either in the gaiety or variety of colors, in the symmetry and proportion of parts, in the arrangement and disposition of bodies, or in a just mixture and concurrence of all together. Among these several kinds of beauty the eye takes most delight in colors. We nowhere meet with a more glorious or pleasing show in nature than what appears in the heavens at the rising and setting of the sun, which is wholly made up of those different stains of light that show themselves in clouds of a different situation. For this reason we find the poets, who are always addressing themselves to the imagination, borrowing more of their epithets from colors than from any other topic.

As the fancy delights in everything that is great, strange, or beautiful, and is still more pleased the more it finds of these perfections in the same object, so it is capable of receiving a new satisfaction by the assistance of another sense. Thus any continued sound, as the music of birds or a fall of water, awakens every moment the mind of the beholder and makes him more attentive to the several beauties of the place that lie before him. Thus if there arises a fragrancy of smells or perfumes, they

2. jetteaus: ornamental jets of water coming from a fountain or pipe.

heighten the pleasures of the imagination and make even the colors and verdure of the landscape appear more agreeable, for the ideas of both senses recommend each other and are pleasanter together than when they enter the mind separately, as the different colors of a picture, when they are well disposed, set off one another and receive an additional beauty from the advantage of their situation.

THE PLEASURES OF THE IMAGINATION, III

NO. 413, JUNE 24, 1712

Why the necessary cause of our being pleased with what is great, new, or beautiful, unknown. Why the final cause more known and more useful. The final cause of our being pleased with what is great. The final cause of our being pleased with what is new. The final cause of our being pleased with what is beautiful in our own species. The final cause of our being pleased with what is beautiful in general.

Causa latet, vis est notissima.

—OVID.[1]

Though in yesterday's paper we considered how everything that is great, new, or beautiful is apt to affect the imagination with pleasure, we must own that it is impossible for us to assign the necessary cause of this pleasure, because we know neither the nature of an idea nor the substance of a human soul, which might help us to discover the conformity or disagreeableness of the one to the other; and therefore, for want of such a light, all that we can do in speculations of this kind is to reflect on those operations of the soul that are most agreeable, and to range under their proper heads what is pleasing or displeasing to the mind, without being able to trace out the several necessary and efficient causes from whence the pleasure or displeasure arises.

Final causes lie more bare and open to our observation, as there are often a great variety that belong to the same effect; and these, though they are not altogether so satisfactory, are generally more useful than the other, as they give us greater occasion of admiring the goodness and wisdom of the First Contriver.

One of the final causes of our delight in anything that is great may be this. The Supreme Author of our being has so formed the soul of man that nothing but Himself can be its last, adequate, and proper happiness. Because, therefore, a great part of our happiness must arise from the contemplation of His Being, that He might give our souls a just relish of such a contemplation, He has made them naturally delight in the apprehension of what is great or unlimited. Our admiration, which is a very pleasing motion of the mind, immediately arises at the consideration of any object that takes up a great deal of room in the fancy, and by consequence, will improve into the highest pitch of astonishment and devotion when we contemplate His nature, that is neither circumscribed by time nor place, nor to be comprehended by the largest capacity of a created being.

He has annexed a secret pleasure to the idea of anything that is new or uncommon that He might encourage us in the pursuit after knowledge and engage us to search into the wonders of His creation; for every new idea brings such a pleasure along with it as rewards any pains we have taken in its acquisition, and consequently serves as a motive to put us upon fresh discoveries.

He has made everything that is beautiful in our own species pleasant that all creatures might be tempted to multiply their kind and fill the world with inhabitants; for it is very remarkable that wherever nature is crossed in the production of a monster (the result of any unnatural mixture) the breed is incapable of propagating its likeness and of founding a new order of creatures; so that unless all animals were allured by the beauty of their own species, generation would be at an end, and the earth unpeopled.

In the last place, He has made everything that is beautiful in all other objects pleasant, or rather has made so many objects appear beautiful, that He might render the whole creation more gay and delightful. He has given almost everything about us the power of raising an agreeable idea in the

NO. 413. 1. ***Causa . . . notissima:*** "The cause is hidden; the effect is very well known." See *Metamorphoses,* iv, 287.

imagination; so that it is impossible for us to behold His works with coldness or indifference and to survey so many beauties without a secret satisfaction and complacency. Things would make but a poor appearance to the eye if we saw them only in their proper figures and motions. And what reason can we assign for their exciting in us many of those ideas which are different from anything that exists in the objects themselves (for such are light and colors), were it not to add supernumerary ornaments to the universe and make it more agreeable to the imagination? We are everywhere entertained with pleasing shows and apparitions: we discover imaginary glories in the heavens and in the earth and see some of this visionary beauty poured out upon the whole creation; but what a rough unsightly sketch of nature should we be entertained with did all her coloring disappear and the several distinctions of light and shade vanish? In short, our souls are at present delightfully lost and bewildered in a pleasing delusion, and we walk about like the enchanted hero of a romance who sees beautiful castles, woods, and meadows and at the same time hears the warbling of birds and the purling of streams; but upon the finishing of some secret spell, the fantastic scene breaks up, and the disconsolate knight finds himself on a barren heath or in a solitary desert. It is not improbable that something like this may be the state of the soul after its first separation in respect of the images it will receive from matter, though indeed the ideas of colors are so pleasing and beautiful in the imagination that it is possible the soul will not be deprived of them but perhaps find them excited by some other occasional cause, as they are at present by the different impressions of the subtle matter on the organ of sight.

I have here supposed that my reader is acquainted with that great modern discovery which is at present universally acknowledged by all the inquirers into natural philosophy, namely, that light and colors as apprehended by the imagination are only ideas in the mind and not qualities that have any existence in matter. As this is a truth which has been proved incontestably by many modern philosophers and is indeed one of the finest speculations in that science, if the English reader would see the notion explained at large, he may find it in the eighth chapter of the Second Book of Mr. Locke's *Essay on Human Understanding*.

THE PLEASURES OF THE IMAGINATION, VI

NO. 416, JUNE 27, 1712

The secondary pleasures of the imagination. The several sources of these pleasures (statuary, painting, description, and music) compared together. The final cause of our receiving pleasure from these several sources. Of descriptions in particular. The power of words over the imagination. Why one reader more pleased with descriptions than another.

Quatenus hoc simile est oculis, quod mente videmus.

—LUCR.[1]

I at first divided the pleasures of the imagination into such as arise from objects that are actually before our eyes or that once entered in at our eyes and are afterwards called up into the mind, either barely by its own operations or on occasion of something without us, as statues or descriptions. We have already considered the first division and shall, therefore, enter on the other, which, for distinction's sake, I have called the secondary pleasures of the imagination. When I say the ideas we receive from statues, descriptions, or such like occasions are the same that were once actually in our view, it must not be understood that we had once seen the very place, action, or person which are carved or described. It is sufficient that we have seen places, persons, or actions, in general, which bear a resemblance, or at least some remote analogy, with what we find represented—since it is in the power of the imagination, when it is once stocked with particular ideas, to enlarge, compound, and vary them at her own pleasure.

Among the different kinds of representation, statuary is the most natural, and shows us something likest the object that is represented. To make use of a common instance, let one who is born blind take an image in his hands and trace out with his fingers the different furrows and impressions of the chisel,

NO. 416. 1. ***Quatenus . . . videmus:*** "To the extent that what we see in the mind is like what we see with the eyes." See *De Rerum Natura,* IV, 750.

and he will easily conceive how the shape of a man or beast may be represented by it; but should he draw his hand over a picture, where all is smooth and uniform, he would never be able to imagine how the several prominences and depressions of a human body could be shown on a plain piece of canvas, that has in it no unevenness or irregularity. Description runs yet further from the things it represents than painting, for a picture bears a real resemblance to its original which letters and syllables are wholly void of. Colors speak all languages, but words are understood only by such a people or nation. For this reason, though men's necessities quickly put them on finding out speech, writing is probably of a later invention than painting; particularly we are told that in America, when the Spaniards first arrived there, expresses were sent to the Emperor of Mexico in paint, and the news of his country delineated by the strokes of a pencil, which was a more natural way than that of writing, though at the same time much more imperfect, because it is impossible to draw the little connections of speech or to give the picture of a conjunction or an adverb. It would be yet more strange to represent visible objects by sounds that have no ideas annexed to them, and to make something like description in music. Yet it is certain there may be confused, imperfect notions of this nature raised in the imagination by an artificial composition of notes, and we find that great masters in the art are able sometimes to set their hearers in the heat and hurry of a battle, to overcast their minds with melancholy scenes and apprehensions of deaths and funerals, or to lull them into pleasing dreams of groves and Elysiums.

In all these instances this secondary pleasure of the imagination proceeds from that action of the mind which compares the ideas arising from the original objects with the ideas we receive from the statue, picture, description, or sound that represents them. It is impossible for us to give the necessary reason why this operation of the mind is attended with so much pleasure, as I have before observed on the same occasion, but we find a great variety of entertainments derived from this single principle; for it is this that not only gives us a relish of statuary, painting, and description, but makes us delight in all the actions and arts of mimicry. It is this that makes the several kinds of wit pleasant, which consists, as I have formerly shown in the affinity of ideas—and, we may add, it is this also that raises the little satisfaction we sometimes find in the different sorts of false wit, whether it consists in the affinity of letters, as in anagram, acrostic; or of syllables, as in doggerel rhymes, echoes; or of words, as in puns, quibbles; or of a whole sentence or poem to wings and altars. The final cause, probably, of annexing pleasure to this operation of the mind was to quicken and encourage us in our searches after truth, since the distinguishing one thing from another and the right discerning betwixt our ideas depends wholly upon our comparing them together and observing the congruity or disagreement that appears among the several works of nature.

But I shall here confine myself to those pleasures of the imagination which proceed from ideas raised by words, because most of the observations that agree with descriptions are equally applicable to painting and statuary.

Words, when well chosen, have so great a force in them that a description often gives us more lively ideas than the sight of things themselves. The reader finds a scene drawn in stronger colors and painted more to the life in his imagination by the help of words than by an actual survey of the scene which they describe. In this case the poet seems to get the better of nature; he takes, indeed, the landscape after her but gives it more vigorous touches, heightens its beauty, and so enlivens the whole piece that the images which flow from the objects themselves appear weak and faint in comparison of those that come from the expressions. The reason probably may be because in the survey of any object we have only so much of it painted on the imagination as comes in at the eye, but in its description the poet gives us as free a view of it as he pleases and discovers to us several parts that either we did not attend to or that lay out of our sight when we first beheld it. As we look on any object, our idea of it is perhaps made up of two or three simple ideas, but when the poet represents it, he may either give us a more complex idea of it or only raise in us such ideas as are most apt to affect the imagination.

It may be here worth our while to examine how it comes to pass that several readers who are all acquainted with the same language and know the meaning of the words they read should nevertheless have a different relish of the same descriptions. We find one transported with a passage which another runs over with coldness and indifference, or finding the representation extremely natural where another can perceive nothing of likeness and conformity. This different taste must proceed either from the perfection of imagination in one more than in another or from the different ideas that several readers affix to the same words. For to have a true relish and form a right judgment of a description, a man should be born with a good imagination and must have well weighed the force and energy that lie in the several words of a language, so as to be able to distinguish which are most significant and expressive of their proper ideas and what additional strength and beauty they are capable of receiving from conjunction with others. The fancy must be warm to retain the print of those images it hath received from outward objects, and the judgment discerning, to know what expressions are most proper to clothe and adorn them to the best advantage. A man who is deficient in either of these respects, though he may receive the general notion of a description, can never see distinctly all its particular beauties, as a person with a weak sight may have the confused prospect of a place that lies before him without entering into its several parts or discerning the variety of its colors in their full glory and perfection.

THE PLEASURES OF THE IMAGINATION, VIII

NO. 418, JUNE 30, 1712

Why anything that is unpleasant to behold pleases the imagination when well described. Why the imagination receives a more exquisite pleasure from the description of what is great, new, or beautiful. The pleasure still heightened, if what is described raises passion in the mind. Disagreeable passions pleasing when raised by apt descriptions. Why terror and grief are pleasing to the mind when excited by descriptions. A particular advantage the writers in poetry and fiction have to please the imagination. What liberties are allowed them.

Ferat et rubus asper amomum.

—VIRG.[1]

The pleasures of these secondary views of the imagination are of a wider and more universal nature than those it has when joined with sight, for not only what is great, strange, or beautiful but anything that is disagreeable when looked upon pleases us in an apt description. Here, therefore, we must inquire after a new principle of pleasure, which is nothing else but the action of the mind which compares the ideas that arise from words with the ideas that arise from the objects themselves; and why this operation of the mind is attended with so much pleasure we have before considered. For this reason, therefore, the description of a dunghill is pleasing to the imagination if the image be represented to our minds by suitable expressions, though perhaps this may be more properly called the pleasure of the understanding than of the fancy, because we are not so much delighted with the image that is contained in the description as with the aptness of the description to excite the image.

But if the description of what is little, common, or deformed be acceptable to the imagination, the description of what is great, surprising, or beautiful is much more so, because here we are not only delighted with comparing the representation with the original but are highly pleased with the original itself. Most readers, I believe, are more charmed with Milton's description of Paradise than of Hell; they are both perhaps equally perfect in their kind, but in the one the brimstone and sulphur are not so refreshing to the imagination as the beds of flowers and the wilderness of sweets in the other.

There is yet another circumstance which recommends a description more than all the rest, and that is if it represents to us such objects as are apt to raise a secret ferment in the mind of the reader and to work with violence upon his passions. For in this case we are at once warmed and enlightened; so that the pleasure becomes more universal and is several ways qualified to entertain us. Thus, in painting it is pleasant to look on the picture of any face where the resemblance is hit, but the pleasure increases if it be the picture of a face that is beautiful, and is still greater if the beauty be softened with an air of melancholy or sorrow. The two leading passions which the more serious parts of poetry endeavor to stir up in us are terror and pity. And here, by the way, one would wonder how it comes to pass that such passions as are very unpleasant at all other times are very agreeable when excited by

NO. 418. 1. ***Ferat . . . amomum:*** "And the sharp bramble-bush bears spices." See *Eclogues,* iii, 89.

proper descriptions. It is not strange that we should take delight in such passages as are apt to produce hope, joy, admiration, love, or the like emotions in us, because they never rise in the mind without an inward pleasure which attends them. But how comes it to pass that we should take delight in being terrified or dejected by a description, when we find so much uneasiness in the fear or grief which we receive from any other occasion?

If we consider, therefore, the nature of this pleasure, we shall find that it does not arise so properly from the description of what is terrible as from the reflection we make on ourselves at the time of reading it. When we look on such hideous objects, we are not a little pleased to think we are in no danger of them. We consider them at the same time as dreadful and harmless; so that the more frightful appearance they make, the greater is the pleasure we receive from the sense of our own safety. In short, we look upon the terrors of a description with the same curiosity and satisfaction that we survey a dead monster:

> Informe cadaver
> protrahitur. Nequeunt expleri corda tuendo
> terribilis oculos, voltum villosaque saetis
> pectora semiferi atque extinctos faucibus ignis.
>
> —VIRG.[2]

It is for the same reason that we are delighted with the reflecting upon dangers that are past, or in looking on a precipice at a distance which would fill us with a different kind of horror if we saw it hanging over our heads.

In the like manner, when we read of torments, wounds, deaths, and the like dismal accidents, our pleasure does not flow so properly from the grief which such melancholy descriptions give us as from the secret comparison which we make between ourselves and the person who suffers. Such representations teach us to set a just value upon our own condition and make us prize our good fortune which exempts us from the like calamities. This is, however, such a kind of pleasure as we are not capable of receiving when we see a person actually lying under the tortures that we meet with in a description, because in this case the object presses too close upon our senses and bears so hard upon us that it does not give us time or leisure to reflect on ourselves. Our thoughts are so intent upon the miseries of the sufferer that we cannot turn them upon our own happiness; whereas, on the contrary, we consider the misfortunes we read in history or poetry either as past or as fictitious; so that the reflection upon ourselves rises in us insensibly and overbears the sorrow we conceive for the sufferings of the afflicted.

But because the mind of man requires something more perfect in matter than what it finds there and can never meet with any sight in nature which sufficiently answers its highest ideas of pleasantness, or in other words, because the imagination can fancy to itself things more great, strange, or beautiful than the eye ever saw, and is still sensible of some defect in what it has seen—on this account it is the part of a poet to humor the imagination in its own notions by mending and perfecting nature where he describes a reality, and by adding greater beauties than are put together in nature where he describes a fiction.

He is not obliged to attend her in the slow advances which she makes from one season to another or to observe her conduct in the successive production of plants and flowers. He may draw into his description all the beauties of the spring and autumn and make the whole year contribute something to render it the more agreeable. His rose trees, woodbines, and jessamines may flower together, and his beds be covered at the same time with lilies, violets, and amaranths. His toil is not restrained to any particular set of plants, but is proper either for oaks or myrtles, and adapts itself to the products of every climate. Oranges may grow wild in it; myrrh may be met with in every hedge; and if he thinks it proper to have a grove of spices, he can quickly command sun enough to raise it. If all this will not furnish out an agreeable scene, he can make several new species of flowers, with richer scents and higher colors than any that grow in the gardens of nature. His consorts of birds may be as full and harmonious, and his woods as thick and gloomy, as he pleases. He is at no more expense in a long vista than a short one and can as easily throw his cascades from a precipice of half a mile high as from one of

2. **Informe . . . ignis:** "The unformed cadaver is dragged forth. Men cannot satisfy their hearts with beholding the terrible eyes, the face, and the shaggy, bristling breast of the beast, and the quenched fires of his throat." See *Aeneid*, viii, 264.

twenty yards. He has his choice of the winds and can turn the course of his rivers in all the variety of meanders that are most delightful to the reader's imagination. In a word, he has the modeling of nature in his own hands and may give her what charms he pleases, provided he does not reform her too much and run into absurdities by endeavoring to excel.

Thomas Rymer
1641-1713

◆

FROM
Short View of Tragedy

From CHAPTER VII

OTHELLO

From all the tragedies acted on our English stage, *Othello* is said to bear the bell away.[1] The subject is more of a piece, and there is, as it were, some phantom of a fable. The fable is always accounted the soul of tragedy. And it is the fable which is properly the poet's part, because the other three parts of tragedy, to wit, the *characters* are taken from the moral philosopher; the *thoughts,* or sense, from them that teach rhetoric; and the last part, which is the *expression,* we learn from the grammarians.

This fable is drawn from a novel composed in Italian by Giraldi Cinthio, who also was a writer of tragedies, and to that use employed such of his tales as he judged proper for the stage. But with this of the Moor he meddled no farther.

Shakespear alters it from the original in several particulars, but always, unfortunately, for the worse. He bestows a name on his Moor, and styles him the Moor of Venice,—a note of pre-eminence which neither history nor heraldry can allow him. Cinthio, who knew him best, and whose creature he was, calls him simply a *Moor.* We say the Piper of Strasburgh, the Jew of Florence, and, if you please, the Pindar of Wakefield—all upon record, and memorable in their places. But we see no such cause for the Moor's preferment to that dignity. And it is an affront to all chroniclers and antiquaries to top upon 'um a Moor with that mark of renown, who yet had never fallen within the sphere of their cognisance.

Then is the Moor's wife, from a simple citizen in Cinthio, dress'd up with her top knots and rais'd to be *Desdemona,* a Senator's daughter. All this is very strange, and therefore pleases such as reflect not on the improbability. This match might well be without the parents' consent. Old Horace long ago forbad the banns:

> *Sed non ut placidis Coeant immitia, non ut*
> *Serpentes avibus geminentur, tigribus agni.*[2]

THE FABLE

Othello, a Blackmoor Captain, by talking of his prowess and feats of war, makes *Desdemona,* a Senator's daughter, to be in love with him, and to be married to him without her parents' knowledge; and having preferred *Cassio* to be his Lieutenant, a place which his Ensign, *Iago,* sued for, *Iago* in revenge works the Moor into a jealousy that *Cassio* cuckolds him—which he effects by stealing and conveying a certain handkerchief which had at the wedding been by the Moor presented to his bride. Hereupon *Othello* and *Iago* plot the deaths of *Desde-*

SHORT VIEW OF TRAGEDY. **1. bear . . . away:** win the prize.

2. ***Sed . . . agni:*** "But not that beast should mate with tame, or serpents join with birds, or lamb with tigers." See Horace, *Ars Poetica,* ll. 12–13.

mona and *Cassio*. *Othello* murders her, and soon after is convinced of her innocence. And as he is about to be carried to prison in order to be punish'd for the murder, he kills himself.

Whatever rubs or difficulty may stick on the bark, the moral, sure, of this fable is very instructive.

First, this may be a caution to all maidens of quality how, without their parents' consent, they run away with Blackamoors.

Di non si accompagnare con huomo cui la natura & il cielo & il modo della vita disgiunge da noi.——Cinthio.[3]

Secondly, this may be a warning to all good wives that they look well to their linen.

Thirdly, this may be a lesson to husbands that before their jealousy be tragical the proofs may be mathematical.

Cinthio affirms that *She was not overcome by a womanish appetite, but by the virtue of the Moor.* It must be a good-natur'd reader that takes Cinthio's word in this case, tho' in a novel. Shakespear, who is accountable both to the eyes and to the ears, and to convince the very heart of an audience, shews that *Desdemona* was won by hearing Othello talk.

OTHELLO. I spake of most disastrous chances,
Of Moving accidents by flood and field,
Of hair-breadth scapes i' th' imminent deadly breach,
Of being taken by the insolent foe,
And sold to slavery, of my redemption thence,
And portents in my Travels History;
Wherein of Antars vast and Desarts idle,
Rough Quarries, Rocks, and Hills whose heads touch Heaven,
It was my hint to speak,—such was my process;
And of the *Cannibals* that each others eat,
The *Anthropophagi*, and men whose hands
Do grow beneath their shoulders.—
[I, iii, 134–45]

This was the charm, this was the philtre, the love-powder, that took the daughter of this noble Venetian. This was sufficient to make the Blackamoor white, and reconcile all, tho' there had been a cloven foot into the bargain.

A meaner woman might be as soon taken by *Aqua Tetrachymagogon*.[4]

Nodes, cataracts, tumours, chilblains, carnosity, shankers, or any cant in the bill of an High German doctor is as good fustian circumstance, and as likely to charm a senator's daughter. But, it seems, the noble Venetians have an other sense of things. The Doge himself tells us:

DOGE. I think this Tale wou'd win my Daughter too.

Horace tells us:

Intererit Multum———
Colchus an Assyrius, Thebis nutritus an Argis.[5]

Shakespear in this play calls 'em the *supersubtle Venetians*. Yet examine throughout the tragedy, there is nothing in the noble Desdemona that is not below any country chamber-maid with us.

And the account he gives us of their noblemen and senate can only be calculated for the latitude of Gotham.

The character of that state is to employ strangers in their wars: But shall a poet thence fancy that they will set a Negro to be their general, or trust a Moor to defend them against the Turk? With us a Blackamoor might rise to be a trumpeter; but Shakespear would not have him less than a Lieutenant-General. With us a Moor might marry some little drab or small-coal wench; Shakespear would provide him the daughter and heir of some great lord or privy-councellor, and all the town should reckon it a very suitable match. Yet the English are not bred up with that hatred and aversion to the Moors as are the Venetians, who suffer by a perpetual hostility from them,—

Littora littoribus contraria.[6]

Nothing is more odious in Nature than an improbable lie; and certainly never was any play fraught like this of *Othello* with improbabilities.

3. *Di . . . noi:* "Not to marry a man whom nature, and heaven, and state of life separate from us."

4. Tetrachymagogon: *Tatler 240* describes posters bearing the name *Tetrachymagogon*, a physician. These posters drew great mobs and also attracted those who were ill to the extent that they sought out this man for their physician. **5. *Intererit . . . Argis:*** "Much difference will it make—whether a Colchian or an Assyrian, one brought up at Thebes or Argos, be speaking." See Horace, *Ars Poetica*, ll. 114–118. **6. *Littora . . . contraria:*** "Let shore contend with shore." See *Aeneid*, IV, 628.

The *characters* or manners, which are the second part in a tragedy, are not less unnatural and improper than the fable was improbable and absurd.

Othello is made a Venetian general. We see nothing done by him nor related concerning him that comports with the condition of a general, or indeed of a man, unless killing himself to avoid a death the law was about to inflict upon him. When his jealousy had wrought him up to a resolution of's taking revenge for the suppos'd injury, he sets Iago to the fighting part to kill Cassio, and chuses himself to murder the silly woman his wife, that was like to make no resistance.

His love and his jealousie are no part of a soldier's character, unless for comedy.

But what is most intolerable is Iago. He is no Blackamoor soldier, so we may be sure he should be like other soldiers of our acquaintance; yet never in tragedy, nor in comedy, nor in Nature, was a soldier with his character; take it in the author's own words:

EM. Some Eternal Villain,
Some busie and insinuating Rogue,
Some cogging, couzening Slave, to get some
Office. [IV, ii, 130–32]

Horace describes a soldier otherwise:

Impiger, iracundus, inexorabilis, acer.[7]

Shakespear knew his character of Iago was inconsistent. In this very play he pronounces:

If thou dost deliver more or less than Truth,
Thou art no Souldier. [II, iii, 219–20]

This he knew; but to entertain the audience with something new and surprising, against common sense and Nature he would pass upon us a close, dissembling, false, insinuating rascal instead of an open-hearted, frank, plain-dealing soldier, a character constantly worn by them for some thousands of years in the world.

Tiberius Caesar had a poet arraigned for his life, because Agamemnon was brought on the stage by him with a character unbecoming a soldier.

Our ensigns and subalterns, when disgusted by the captain, throw up their commissions, bluster, and are bare-fac'd. Iago, I hope, is not brought on the stage in a red coat. I know not what livery the Venetians wear, but am sure they hold not these conditions to be *alla soldatesca.*

Non sia egli per far la vendetta con insidie, ma con la spada in mano.——Cinthio.[8]

Nor is our poet more discreet in his Desdemona. He had chosen a soldier for his knave, and a Venetian lady is to be the fool.

This senator's daughter runs away to a carrier's inn, the Sagittary, with a blackamoor, is no sooner wedded to him, but the very night she beds him is importuning and teasing him for a young smockfac'd lieutenant, Cassio. And tho' she perceives the Moor jealous of Cassio, yet will she not forbear, but still rings *Cassio, Cassio,* in both his ears.

Roderigo is the cully[9] of Iago, brought in to be murder'd by Iago, that Iago's hands might be the more in blood, and be yet the more abominable villain: who without that was too wicked on all conscience, and had more to answer for than any tragedy or Furies could inflict upon him. So there can be nothing in the characters, either for the profit or to delight an audience.

The third thing to be consider'd is the *thoughts.* But from such characters we need not expect many that are either true, or fine, or noble.

And without these, that is, without sense or meaning, the fourth part of tragedy, which is the *expression,* can hardly deserve to be treated on distinctiy. The verse rumbling in our ears are of good use to help off the action.

In the neighing of an horse, or in the growling of a mastiff, there is a meaning, there is as lively expression, and, may I say, more humanity, than many times in the tragical flights of Shakespear.

Step then amongst the scenes to observe the conduct to this tragedy.

The first we see are Iago and Roderigo, by night in the streets of Venice. After growling a long time together, they resolve to tell Brabantio that his daughter is run away with the Blackamoor. Iago and Roderigo were not of quality to be familiar with Brabantio, nor had any provocation from him to deserve a rude thing at their hands. Brabantio was a noble Venetian, one of the sovereign lords and principal persons in the Government, peer to the most serene Doge, one attended with more

7. ***Impiger . . . acer:*** "Restless, wrathful, ruthless, fierce." See Horace, *Ars Poetica,* l. 121.

8. ***Non . . . mano:*** "He should not seek revenge with tricks, but with the sword in hand." **9. cully:** dupe.

state, ceremony, and punctillio than any English duke or nobleman in the government will pretend to. This misfortune in his daughter is so prodigious, so tender a point, as might puzzle the finest wit of the most supersubtle Venetian to touch upon it, or break the discovery to her father. See then how delicately Shakespear minces the matter:

> ROD. What ho, *Brabantio*, Signior *Brabantio*, ho!
> IAGO. Awake! what ho, *Brabantio!* Thieves, thieves, thieves!
> Look to your House, your Daughter, and your Bags.
> Thieves, thieves!
> Brabantio *at a window*.
> BRA. What is the reason of this terrible summons?
> What is the matter there?
> ROD. Signior, is all your Family within?
> IAGO. Are your Doors lockt?
> BRA. Why, wherefore ask you this?
> IAGO. Sir, you are robb'd; for shame, put on your Gown;
> Your Heart is burst, you have lost half your Soul;
> Even now, very now, an old black Ram
> Is tupping your white Ewe: arise, arise,
> Awake the snorting Citizens with the Bell,
> Or else the Devil will make a Grandsire of you: arise, I say. [I, i, 78–92]

. . .

In former days there wont to be kept at the courts of princes some body in a fool's coat, that in pure simplicity might let slip something which made way for the ill news, and blunted the shock, which otherwise might have come too violent upon the party.

Aristophanes put *Nicias* and *Demosthenes*[10] in the disguise of servants, that they might, without indecency, be drunk; and drunk he must make them that they might without reserve lay open the *arcana* of state, and the knavery of their ministers. . . .

This is address, this is truly satire, where the preparation is such that the thing principally design'd falls in as it only were of course.

But Shakespear shews us another sort of address; his manners of good breeding must not be like the rest of the civil world. Brabantio was not in masquerade, was not *incognito;* Iago well knew his rank and dignity.

> IAGO. The *Magnifico* is much beloved,
> And hath in his effect a voice potential
> As double as the Duke.— [I, ii, 12–14]

But besides the manners to a *Magnifico,* humanity cannot bear that an old gentleman in his misfortune should be insulted over with such a rabble of scoundrel language, when no cause or provocation. Yet thus it is on our stage; this is our school of good manners, and the *speculum vitae.*[11]

But our *Magnifico* is here in the dark, nor are yet his robes on: attend him to the senate house, and there see the difference, see the effects of Purple.

So, by and by, we find the Duke of Venice, with his senators in council, at midnight, upon advice that the Turks, or Ottamites, or both together, were ready in transport ships, put to sea, in order to make a descent upon Cyprus. This is the posture when we see Brabantio and Othello join them. By their conduct and manner of talk, a body must strain hard to fancy the scene at Venice, and not rather in some of our Cinq-ports, where the baily[12] and his fishermen are knocking their heads together on account of some whale, or some terrible broil upon the coast. But to shew them true Venetians, the maritime affairs stick not long on their hand; the public may sink or swim. They will sit up all night to hear a Doctors' Commons, matrimonial cause, and have the merits of the cause at large laid open to 'em, that they may decide it before they stir. What can be pleaded to keep awake their attention so wonderfully?

Never, sure, was form of pleading so tedious and so heavy as this whole scene and midnight entertainment. Take his own words; says the respondent:

> OTH. Most potent, grave, and reverend Signiors,
> My very noble and approv'd good Masters:
> That I have tane away this old mans Daughter,
> It is most true; true, I have Married her;
> The very front and head of my offending
> Hath this extent, no more: rude I am in my speech,
> And little blest with the set phrase of peace;
> For since these Arms of mine had seven years pith,

10. Aristophanes . . . *Demosthenes:* in his play *The Knights.*

11. *speculum vitae:* mirror of life. **12. baily:** chief officer.

Till now some nine Moons wasted, they have us'd
Their dearest action in the Tented Field;
And little of this great World can I speak
More than pertains to Broils and Battail;
And therefore little shall I grace my Cause
In speaking of my self; yet by your gracious patience,
I would a round unravish'd Tale deliver,
Of my whole course of love, what drags, what charms,
What conjuration, and what mighty Magick,
(for such proceedings am I charg'd withal)
I won his Daughter. [I, iii, 76–94]

All this is but preamble to tell the court that he wants words. This was the eloquence which kept them up all night, and drew their attention in the midst of their alarms.

One might rather think the novelty and strangeness of the case prevail'd upon them: no, the senators do not reckon it strange at all. Instead of starting at the prodigy, every one is familiar with Desdemona as he were her own natural father, rejoice in her good fortune, and wish their own several daughters as hopefully married. Should the poet have provided such a husband for an only daughter of any noble peer in England, the Blackamoor must have chang'd his skin to look our House of Lords in the face.

Aeschylus is noted in Aristophanes for letting Niobe be two or three acts on the stage before she speaks.[13] Our noble Venetian, sure, is in the other more unnatural extreme. His words flow in abundance; no butter-queen can be more lavish. Nay, he is for talking of state affairs, too, above anybody:

BRA. Please it your Grace, on to the state Affairs.—
[I, iii, 190]

Yet is this Brabantio sensible of his affliction; before the end of the play his heart breaks, he dies.

BRA. Poor *Desdemona,* I am glad thy Father's dead;
Thy match was mortal to him, and pure grief
Shore his old thread in twain.—
[V, ii, 204–206]

A third part in a tragedy is the *thoughts:* from Venetians, noblemen, and senators we may expect fine thoughts. Here is a trial of skill: for a parting blow, the Duke and Brabantio cap sentences. Where then shall we seek for the thoughts, if we let slip this occasion? Says the Duke:

DUK. Let me speak like your self, and lay a *Sentence*
Which, like a greese or step, may help these lovers
Into your favour.
When remedies are past, the grief is ended
By seeing the worst, which late on hopes depended.
To mourn a mischief that is past and gone
Is the next way to draw more mischief on;
What cannot be preserv'd when Fortune takes,
Patience her injury a Mocker makes.
The rob'd that smiles steals something from a Thief;
He robs himself that spends an hopeless grief.
BRA. So let the Turk of *Cyprus* us beguile;
We lose it not so long as we can smile.
He bears the sentence well, that nothing bears
But the free comfort which from thence he hears;
But he bears both the sentence and the sorrow,
That to pay grief must of poor patience borrow:
These *Sentences,* to Sugar or to Gall,
Begin strong on both sides, are equivocal.
But words are words; I never yet did hear
That the bruis'd Heart was pierced through the Ear.
Beseech you, now to the affairs of State.
[I, iii, 210–220]

How far wou'd the Queen of Sheba have travell'd to hear the wisdom of our noble Venetians? . . .

What provocation or cause of malice our poet might have to libel the most Serene Republic I cannot tell; but certainly there can be no wit in this representation.

(1693)

13. A reference to Aristophanes' play *The Frogs.*

Anthony Ashley Cooper, Third Earl of Shaftesbury
1671–1713

FROM

Characteristics of Men, Manners, Opinions, Times

THE MORALISTS, A PHILOSOPHICAL RHAPSODY

From Part III, Section II

. . .

"It is true," said I (Theocles), "I own it. Your genius, the genius of the place, and the Great Genius have at last prevailed. I shall no longer resist the passion growing in me for things of a natural kind, where neither art nor the conceit or caprice of man has spoiled their genuine order by breaking in upon that primitive state. Even the rude rocks, the mossy caverns, the irregular unwrought grottoes and broken falls of waters, with all the horrid graces of the wilderness itself, as representing nature more, will be the more engaging, and appear with a magnificence beyond the formal mockery of princely gardens. But tell me, I entreat you, how comes it that, excepting a few philosophers of your sort, the only people who are enamored in this way, and seek the woods, the rivers, or seashores, are your poor vulgar lovers?"

"Say not this," replied he, "of lovers only. For is it not the same with poets, and all those other students in nature and the arts which copy after her? In short, is not this the real case of all who are lovers either of the Muses or the Graces?"

"However," said I, "all those who are deep in this romantic way are looked upon, you know, as a people either plainly out of their wits, or overrun with melancholy and enthusiasm. We always endeavor to recall them from these solitary places. And I must own that often when I have found my fancy run this way, I have checked myself, not knowing what it was possessed me, when I was passionately struck with objects of this kind."

"No wonder," replied he, "if we are at a loss when we pursue the shadow for the substance. For if we may trust to what our reasoning has taught us, whatever in nature is beautiful or charming is only the faint shadow of that first beauty. So that every real love depending on the mind, and being only the contemplation of beauty either as it really is in itself or as it appears imperfectly in the objects which strike the sense, how can the rational mind rest here or be satisfied with the absurd enjoyment which reaches the sense alone?"

"From this time forward then," said I, "I shall no more have reason to fear those beauties which strike a sort of melancholy, like the places we have named, or like these solemn groves. No more shall I avoid the moving accents of soft music or fly from the enchanting features of the fairest human face."

"If you are already," replied he, "such a proficient in this new love that you are sure never to admire the representative beauty except for the sake of the original, nor aim at other enjoyment than of the rational kind, you may then be confident." "I am so, and presume accordingly to answer for myself. However, I should not be ill satisfied if you explained yourself a little better as to this mistake of mine you seem to fear." "Would it be any help to tell you that the absurdity lay in seeking the enjoyment elsewhere than in the subject loved?" "The matter, I must confess, is still mysterious." "Imagine then, good Philocles, if being taken with the beauty of the ocean, which you see yonder at a distance, it should come into your head to seek how to command it and, like some mighty admiral, ride master of the sea; would not the fancy be a little absurd?"

"Absurd enough, in conscience. The next thing I should do, it is likely, upon this frenzy, would be to hire some bark and go in nuptial ceremony, Venetian-like, to wed the gulf, which I might call perhaps as properly my own."

"Let who will call it theirs," replied Theocles, "you will own the enjoyment of this kind to be very different from that which should naturally follow from the contemplation of the ocean's beauty. The bridegroom-doge who in his stately bucentaur floats on the bosom of his Thetis has less possession than the poor shepherd who from a hanging rock or point of some high promontory, stretched at his ease, forgets his feeding flocks while he admires her beauty. But to come nearer home and make the question still more familiar. Suppose, my Philocles, that, viewing such a tract of country as this delicious vale we see beneath us, you should, for the enjoyment of the prospect, require the property or possession of the land."

"The covetous fancy," replied I, "would be as absurd altogether as that other ambitious one."

"O Philocles!" said he, "may I bring this yet a little nearer, and will you follow me once more? Suppose that, being charmed as you seem to be with the beauty of those trees under whose shade we rest, you should long for nothing so much as to taste some delicious fruit of theirs; and having obtained of Nature some certain relish by which these acorns or berries of the wood became as palatable as the figs or peaches of the garden, you should afterwards, as oft as you revisited these groves, seek hence the enjoyment of them by satiating yourself in these new delights."

"The fancy of this kind," replied I, "would be sordidly luxurious, and as absurd, in my opinion, as either of the former."

"Can you not then, on this occasion," said he, "call to mind some other forms of a fair kind among us where the admiration of beauty is apt to lead to as irregular a consequence?"

"I feared," said I, "indeed, where this would end, and was apprehensive you would force me at last to think of certain powerful forms in human kind which draw after them a set of eager desires, wishes, and hopes no way suitable, I must confess, to your rational and refined contemplation of beauty. The proportions of this living architecture, as wonderful as they are, inspired nothing of a studious or contemplative kind. The more they are viewed, the further they are from satisfying by mere view. Let that which satisfies be ever so disproportionable an effect, or ever so foreign to its cause, censure it as you please, you must allow, however, that it is natural. So that you, Theocles, for aught I see, are become the accuser of nature by condemning a natural enjoyment."

"Far be it from us both," said he, "to condemn a joy which is from Nature. But when we spoke of the enjoyment of these woods and prospects, we understood by it a far different kind from that of the inferior creatures who, rifling in these places, find here their choicest food. Yet we too live by tasteful food and feel those other joys of sense in common with them. But it was not here, my Philocles, that we had agreed to place our good, nor consequently our enjoyment. We who were rational, and had minds, methought, should place it rather in those minds, which were indeed abused and cheated of their real good when drawn to seek absurdly the enjoyment of it in the objects of sense, and not in those objects they might properly call their own, in which kind, as I remember, we comprehended all which was truly fair, generous, or good."

"So that beauty," said I, "and good with you, Theocles, I perceive, are still one and the same."

"It is so," said he. "And thus are we returned again to the subject of our yesterday's morning conversation. Whether I have made good my promise to you in showing the true good, I know not. But so, doubtless, I should have done with good success had I been able in my poetic ecstasies, or by any other efforts, to have led you into some deep view of Nature and the sovereign genius. We then had proved the force of divine beauty, and formed in ourselves an object capable and worthy of real enjoyment."

"O Theocles!" said I, "well do I remember now the terms in which you engaged me that morning when you bespoke my love of this mysterious beauty. You have indeed made good your part of the condition and may now claim me for a proselyte. If there be any seeming extravagance in the case, I must comfort myself the best I can and consider that all sound love and admiration is enthusiasm: 'The transports of poets, the sublime of orators, the rapture of musicians, the high strains of the virtuosi—all mere enthusiasm! Even learning itself, the love of arts and curiosities, the spirit of travellers and adventurers, gallantry, war, heroism—all, all enthusiasm!' It is enough; I am content to be this new enthusiast in a way unknown to me before."

"And I," replied Theocles, "am content you should call this love of ours enthusiasm, allowing it the privilege of its fellow passions. For is there a fair and plausible enthusiasm, a reasonable ecstasy and transport, allowed to other subjects, such as architecture, painting, music; and shall it be exploded here? Are there senses by which all those other graces and perfections are perceived, and none by which this higher perfection and grace is comprehended? Is it so preposterous to bring that enthusiasm hither and transfer it from those secondary and scanty objects to this original and comprehensive one? Observe how the case stands in all those other subjects of art or science. What difficulty to be in any degree knowing! How long ere a true taste is gained! How many things shocking, how many offensive at first which afterwards are known and acknowledged the highest beauties! For it is not instantly we acquire the sense by which these beauties are discoverable. Labor and pains are required, and time to cultivate a natural genius ever so apt or forward. But who is there once thinks of cultivating this soil, or of improving any sense or faculty which Nature may have given of this kind? And is it a wonder we should be dull then, as we are, confounded and at a loss in these affairs, blind as to this higher scene, these nobler representations? Which way should we come to understand better? Which way be knowing in these beauties? Is study, science, or learning necessary to understand all beauties else? And for the sovereign beauty, is there no skill or science required? In painting there are shades and masterly strokes which the vulgar understand not, but find fault with; in architecture there is the rustic; in music the chromatic kind, and skillful mixture of dissonancies; and is there nothing which answers to this in the whole?"

"I must confess," said I, "I have hitherto been one of those vulgar who could never relish the shades, the rustic, or the dissonancies you talk of. I have never dreamt of such masterpieces in nature. It was my way to censure freely on the first view. But I perceive I am now obliged to go far in the pursuit of beauty, which lies very absconded and deep; and if so, I am well assured that my enjoyments hitherto have been very shallow. I have dwelt, it seems, all this while upon the surface, and enjoyed only a kind of slight superficial beauties, having never gone in search of beauty itself, but of what I fancied such. Like the rest of the unthinking world, I took for granted that what I liked was beautiful and what I rejoiced in was my good. I never scrupled loving what I fancied and aiming only at the enjoyment of what I loved; I never troubled myself with examining what the subjects were, nor ever hesitated about their choice."

"Begin then," said he, "and choose. See what the subjects are, and which you would prefer—which honor with your admiration, love, and esteem. For by these again you will be honored in your turn. Such, Philocles, as is the worth of these companions, such will your worth be found. As there is emptiness or fullness here, so will there be in your enjoyment. See, therefore, where fullness is, and where emptiness. See in what subject resides the chief excellence, where beauty reigns, where it is entire, perfect, absolute; where broken, imperfect, short. View these terrestrial beauties and whatever has the appearance of excellence and is able to attract. See that which either really is or stands as in the room of fair, beautiful, and good. A mass of metal, a tract of land, a number of slaves, a pile of stones, a human body of certain lineaments and proportions—is this the highest of the kind? Is beauty founded then in body only, and not in action, life, or operation?"

"Hold! Hold!" said I, "good Theocles; you take this in too high a key above my reach. If you would have me accompany you, pray lower this strain a little, and talk in a more familiar way."

"Thus then," said he, smiling, "whatever passion you may have for other beauties, I know, good Philocles, you are no such admirer of wealth in any kind as to allow much beauty to it, especially in a rude heap or mass. But in medals, coins, embossed work, statues, and well-fabricated pieces of whatever sort, you can discover beauty and admire the kind." "True," said I, "but not for the metal's sake." "It is not then the metal or matter which is beautiful with you?" "No." "But the art?" "Certainly." "The art then is the beauty?" "Right." "And the art is that which beautifies?" "The same." "So that the beautifying, not the beautified, is the really beautiful?" "It seems so." "For that which is beautified, is beautiful only by the accession of something beautifying, and by the recess or withdrawing of the same, it ceases to be beautiful?" "Be it." "In respect of bodies, therefore, beauty comes and goes?" "So we see." "Nor is the body itself any cause either of its coming or staying?" "None." "So that there is no principle of beauty in body?" "None at all." "For body can noway be the cause of beauty to itself?" "Noway." "Nor govern nor regulate itself?" "Nor yet this." "Nor mean nor intend itself?" "Nor this neither." "Must not that, therefore, which means and intends for it, regulates and orders it, be the principle of beauty to it?" "Of necessity." "And what must that be?" "Mind, I suppose, for what can it be else?"

"Here, then," said he, "is all I would have explained to you before: that the beautiful, the fair, the comely, were never in the matter, but in the art and design; never in body itself, but in the form or forming power. Does not the beautiful form confess this, and speak the beauty of the design whenever it strikes you? What is it but the design which strikes? What is it you admire but mind, or the effect of mind? It is mind alone which forms. All which is void of mind is horrid, and matter formless is deformity itself."

"Of all forms then," said I, "those (according to your scheme) are the most amiable, and in the first order of beauty, which have a power of making other forms themselves. From whence methinks they may be styled the forming forms. So far I can easily concur with you, and gladly give the advantage to the human form above those other beauties of man's formation. The palaces, equipages, and estates shall never in my account be brought in competition with the original living forms of flesh and blood. And for the other, the dead forms of nature, the metals and stones, however precious and dazzling, I am resolved to resist their splendor and make abject things of them, even in their highest pride, when they pretend to set off human beauty, and are officiously brought in aid of the fair."

"Do you not see, then," replied Theocles, "that you have established three degrees or orders of beauty?" "As how?" "Why first, the dead forms, as you properly have called them, which bear a fashion, and are formed, whether by man or Nature, but have no forming power, no action, or intelligence." "Right." "Next, and as the second kind, the forms which form, that is, which have intelligence, action, and operation." "Right still." "Here therefore is double beauty. For here is both the form (the effect of mind) and mind itself. The first kind low and despicable in respect of this other, from whence the dead form receives its luster and force of beauty. For what is a mere body, though a human one, and ever so exactly fashioned, if inward form be wanting, and the mind be monstrous or imperfect, as in an idiot or savage?" "This, too, I can apprehend," said I, "but where is the third order?"

"Have patience," replied he, "and see first whether you have discovered the whole force of this second beauty. How else should you understand the force of love or have the power of enjoyment? Tell me, I beseech you, when first you named these the forming forms, did you think of no other productions of theirs besides the dead kinds, such as the palaces, the coins, the brazen or the marble figures of men? Or did you think of something nearer life?"

"I could easily," said I, "have added that these forms of ours had a virtue of producng other living forms like themselves. But this virtue of theirs, I thought, was from another form above them and could not properly be called their virtue or art, if in reality there was a superior art or something artistlike which guided their hand and made tools of them in this specious work."

"Happily thought," said he; "you have prevented a censure which I hardly imagined you could escape. And here you have unawares discovered that third order of beauty, which forms not only such as we call mere forms but even the forms which form. For we ourselves are notable architects in matter and can show lifeless bodies brought into form and fashioned by our own hands, but that which fashions even minds themselves contains in itself all the beauties fashioned by those minds and is consequently the principle, source, and fountain of all beauty."

"It seems so."

"Therefore whatever beauty appears in our second order of forms, or whatever is derived or produced from thence, all this is eminently, principally, and originally in this last order of supreme and sovereign beauty."

"True."

"Thus architecture, music, and all which is of human invention, resolves itself into this last order."

"Right," said I; "and thus all the enthusiasms of other kinds resolve themselves into ours. The fashionable kinds borrow from us, and are nothing without us. We have undoubtedly the honor of being originals."

"Now, therefore, say again," replied Theocles, "whether are those fabrics of architecture, sculpture, and the rest of that sort the greatest beauties which man forms, or are there greater and better?" "None which I know," replied I. "Think, think again," said he; "and setting aside those productions which just now you excepted against as masterpieces of another hand, think what there are which more immediately proceed from us and may more truly be termed our issue." "I am barren," said I, "for this time; you must be plainer yet, in helping me to conceive." "How can I help you?" replied he. "Would you have me be conscious for you of that which is immediately your own, and is solely in and from yourself?" "You mean my sentiments," said I. "Certainly," replied he, "and together with your sentiments, your resolutions, principles, determinations, actions; whatsoever is handsome and noble in the kind; whatever flows from your good understanding, sense, knowledge, and will; whatever is engendered in your heart, good Philocles, or derives itself from your parent mind, which, unlike to other parents, is never spent or exhausted, but gains strength and vigor by producing. So you, my friend, have proved it, by many a work, not suffering that fertile part to remain idle and unactive. Hence those good parts, which from a natural genius you have raised by due improvement. And here, as I cannot but admire the pregnant genius and parent beauty, so am I satisfied of the offspring, that it is and will be ever beautiful."

I took the compliment, and wished (I told him) the case were really as he imagined, that I might justly merit his esteem and love. My study therefore should be to grow beautiful in his way of beauty, and from this time forward I would do all I could to propagate that lovely race of mental children, happily sprung from such a high enjoyment and from a union with what was fairest and best. "But it is you, Theocles," continued I, "must help my laboring mind and be, as it were, the midwife to those conceptions, which else, I fear, will prove abortive."

"You do well," replied he, "to give me the midwife's part only; for the mind conceiving of itself can only be, as you say, assisted in the birth. Its pregnancy is from its nature. Nor could it ever have been thus impregnated by any other mind than that which formed it at the beginning, and which, as we have already proved, is original to all mental as well as other beauty."

"Do you maintain, then," said I, "that these mental children, the notions and principles of fair, just, and honest, with the rest of these ideas, are innate?"

"Anatomists," said he, "tell us that the eggs, which are principles in body, are innate, being formed already in the foetus before the birth. But when it is, whether before, or at, or after the birth, or at what time after, that either these or other principles, organs of sensation, or sensations themselves are first formed in us is a matter, doubtless, of curious speculation, but of no great importance. The question is whether the principles spoken of are from art or nature. If from nature purely, it is no matter for the time, nor would I contend with you though you should deny life itself to be innate, as imagining it followed rather than preceded the moment of birth. But this I am certain of, that life and the sensations which accompany life, come when they will, are from mere nature, and nothing else. Therefore if you dislike the word *innate,* let us change it, if you will, for *instinct,* and call instinct that which nature teaches, exclusive of art, culture, or discipline."

"Content," said I.

(1709)

SOLILOQUY: OR ADVICE TO THE AUTHOR

From Part III, Section III

. . .

However difficult or desperate it may appear in any artist to endeavor to bring perfection into his work, if he has not at least the idea of perfection to give him aim he will be found very defective and mean in his performance. Though his intention be to please the world, he must nevertheless be, in a manner, *above* it, and fix his eye upon that consummate Grace, that beauty of Nature, and that perfection of numbers, which the rest of mankind, feeling only by the effect whilst ignorant of the cause, term the *Je-ne-sçay-quoy,*[1] the unintelligible, or the I know not what, and suppose to be a kind of charm or enchantment of which the artist himself can give no account.

But here, I find, I am tempted to do what I

CHARACTERISTICS. SOLILOQUY. 1. In modern French: *je ne sais quoi.*

have myself condemned. Hardly can I forbear making some apology for my frequent recourse to the rules of common artists, to the matters of exercise, to the academies of painters, statuaries, and to the rest of the virtuoso-tribe. But in this I am so fully satisfied I have reason on my side, that let custom be ever so strong against me I had rather repair to these inferior schools to search for Truth and Nature than to some other places where higher arts and sciences are professed.

I am persuaded that to be a Virtuoso (so far as befits a Gentleman) is a higher step towards the becoming a man of virtue and good sense, than the being what in this age we call a *Scholar.** For even rude Nature itself, in its primitive simplicity, is a better guide to judgment than improved sophistry and pedantic learning. The *faciunt, næ, intellegendo, ut nihil intellegant*[2] will be ever applied by men of discernment and free thought to such logic, such principles, such forms and rudiments of knowledge as are established in certain schools of literature and science. The case is sufficiently understood even by those who are unwilling to confess the truth of it. Effects betray their causes. And the known turn and figure of those understandings which sprout from Nurseries of this kind give a plain idea of what is judged on this occasion. 'Tis no wonder, if after so wrong a ground of education, there appears to be such need of redress and amendment from that excellent school which we call the World. The mere amusements of gentlemen are found more improving than the profound researches of pedants. And in the management of our youth we are forced to have recourse to the former as an antidote against the genius peculiar to the latter. If the Formalists of this sort were erected into patentees with a sole commission of authorship, we should undoubtedly see such writings in our days as would either wholly wean us from all books in general, or at least from all such as were the product of our own nation under such a subordinate and conforming government.

. . .

One who aspires to the character of a man of breeding and politeness is careful to form his judgment of arts and sciences upon right models of *Perfection.* If he travels to Rome he inquires which are the truest pieces of architecture, the best remains of statues, the best paintings of a Raphael or a Carache. However antiquated, rough, or dismal they may appear to him at first sight, he resolves to view them over and over till he has brought himself to relish them and finds their hidden graces and perfections. He takes particular care to turn his eye from everything which is gaudy, luscious, and of a false taste. Nor is he less careful to turn his ear from every sort of music besides that which is of the best manner, and truest harmony.

'Twere to be wished we had the same regard to a right taste in life and manners. What mortal being once convinced of a difference in *inward* character, and of a preference due to one Kind above another, would not be concerned to make *his own* the best? If Civility and Humanity be a taste; if Brutality, Insolence, Riot be in the same manner a taste; who, if he could reflect, would not chuse to form himself on the amiable and agreeable rather than the odious and perverse model? Who

* It seems indeed somewhat improbable, that according to modern erudition, and as science is now distributed, our ingenious and noble youths should obtain the full advantage of a just and liberal education by uniting the Scholar-part with that of the real Gentlemen and Man of Breeding. Academies for exercises so useful to the public and essential in the formation of a genteel and liberal character are unfortunately neglected. Letters are indeed banished, I know not where, in distant cloisters and unpractised cells, as our Poet has it, confined to the commerce and mean fellowship of bearded boys. The sprightly arts and sciences are severed from *Philosophy,* which consequently must grow dronish, insipid, pedantic, useless, and directly opposite to the real knowledge and practice of the world and mankind. Our youth accordingly seem to have their only chance between two widely different roads, either that of pedantry and school-learning, which lies amidst the dregs and most corrupt part of ancient literature, or that of the fashionable illiterate world, which aims merely at the character of the fine gentleman, and takes up with the foppery of modern languages and foreign wit. The frightful aspect of the former of these roads makes the journey appear desperate and impracticable. Hence that aversion so generally conceived against a *learned character,* wrong turned and hideously set out under such difficulties and in such seeming labyrinths and mysterious forms. As if a Homer or a Xenophon, imperfectly learnt in raw years, might not afterwards, in a riper age, be studied as well in a capital city and amidst the world as at a college or country-town.

2. ***faciunt . . . intellegant:*** "Do they not reveal by too much learning that they know nothing." See Terence's *Andria,* "Prologue," l. 17.

would not endeavor to force Nature as well in this respect as in what relates to a taste or judgment in other arts and sciences? For in each place the force on Nature is used only for its redress. If a natural good taste be not already formed in us, why should not we endeavor to form it and become *natural?*

> "I like! I fancy! I admire! How? By accident: or as I please. No. But I learn to fancy, to admire, to please as the subjects themselves are deserving and can bear me out. Otherwise, I like at this hour but dislike the next. I shall be weary of my pursuit, and, upon experience, find little pleasure in the main if my choice and judgment in it be from no other rule than that single one, *because I please*. Grotesque and monstrous figures often please. Cruel spectacles and barbarities are also found to please, and, in some tempers, to please beyond all other subjects. But is this pleasure right? And shall I follow it if it presents? Not strive with it, or endeavor to prevent its growth or prevalency in my temper?—How stands the case in a more soft and flattering kind of pleasure?—Effeminancy pleases me. The Indian figures, the Japan-work, the enamel strike my eye. The luscious colours and glossy paint gain upon my fancy. A French or Flemish style is highly liked by me at first sight, and I pursue my liking. But what ensues?—Do I not forever forfeit my good relish? How is it possible I should thus come to taste the beauties of an Italian master, or of a hand happily formed on Nature and the Ancients? 'Tis not by wantonness and humour that I shall attain my end, and arrive at the enjoyment I propose. The Art itself is severe: the rules rigid. And if I expect the knowledge should come to me by accident or in play, I shall be grosly deluded and prove myself, at best, a mock-virtuoso, or mere pedant of the kind."

Here therefore we have once again exhibited our moral science, in the same method and manner of soliloquy as above. To this correction of humour and formation of a taste, our reading, if it be of the right sort, must principally contribute. Whatever company we keep, or however polite and agreeable their characters may be with whom we converse or correspond, if the authors we read are of another kind we shall find our palate strangely turned their way. We are the unhappier in this respect for being scholars if our studies be ill chosen. Nor can I, for this reason, think it proper to call a man well-read who reads many authors, since he must of necessity have more ill models, than good, and be more stuffed with bombast, ill fancy, and wry thought than filled with solid sense and just imagination.

But notwithstanding this hazard of our taste from a multiplicity of reading, we are not, it seems, the least scrupulous in our choice of subject. We read whatever comes next us. What was first put into our hand when we were young serves us afterwards for serious study and wise research when we are old. We are many of us, indeed, so grave as to continue this exercise of youth through our remaining life.

. . .

One would imagine that our philosophical writers, who pretend to treat of morals, should far out-do mere poets in recommending virtue and representing what was fair and amiable in human actions. One would imagine that if they turned their eye towards remote countries (of which they affect so much to speak) they should search for that simplicity of manners and innocence of behaviour which has been often known among mere savages ere they were corrupted by our commerce and, by sad example, instructed in all kinds of treachery and inhumanity. 'Twould be of advantage to us to hear the causes of this strange corruption in ourselves, and be made to consider of our deviation from Nature and from that just purity of manners which might be expected, especially from a people so assisted and enlightened by Religion. For who would not naturally expect more justice, fidelity, temperance, and honesty from Christians than from Mahometans or mere pagans? But so far are our modern moralists from condemning any unnatural vices or corrupt manners, whether in our own or foreign climates, that they would have Vice itself appear as natural as Virtue, and from the worst examples, would represent to us, "That all actions are naturally indifferent; that they have no note or character of good or ill in themselves; but are distinguished by mere fashion, law, or arbitrary decree." Wonderful philosophy! raised from the dregs of an illiterate, mean kind which was ever despised among the great Ancients and rejected by all men of action or sound erudition; but, in these ages, imperfectly copied from the original, and, with much disadvantage, imitated and assumed in common both by devout and indevout attempters in the moral kind.

Should a writer upon music, addressing himself to the students and lovers of the art, declare to them, "That the measure or rule of harmony was caprice or will, humour or fashion," 'tis not very likely he should be heard with great attention or treated with real gravity. For harmony is harmony by Nature, let men judge ever so ridiculously of music. So is symmetry and proportion founded still in Nature, let men's fancy prove ever so barbarous, or their fashions ever so Gothic in their architecture, sculpture, or whatever other designing art. 'Tis the same case where Life and Manners are concerned. Virtue has the same fixed standard. The same numbers, harmony, and proportion will have place in morals, and are discoverable in the characters and affections of mankind, in which are laid the just foundations of an art and science superior to every other of human practice and comprehension.

This, I suppose therefore, is highly necessary that a writer should comprehend. For things are stubborn, and will not be as we fancy them or as the fashion varies, but as they stand in Nature. Now whether the writer be poet, philosopher, or of whatever kind, he is in truth no other than *a copyist after Nature.* His style may be differently suited to the different times he lives in, or to the different humour of his age or nation; his manner, his dress, his colouring may vary. But if his drawing be uncorrect, or his design contrary to Nature, his piece will be found ridiculous when it comes thoroughly to be examined. For Nature will not be mocked. The prepossession against her can never be very lasting. Her decrees and instincts are powerful and her sentiments in-bred. She has a strong party abroad, and as strong a one within ourselves: and when any slight is put upon her she can soon turn the reproach, and make large reprisals on the taste and judgment of her antagonists.

Whatever philosopher, critic, or author is convinced of this prerogative of Nature will easily be persuaded to apply himself to the great work of reforming his Taste, which he will have reason to suspect if he be not such a one as has deliberately endeavored to frame it by the just Standard of Nature. Whether this be his case he will easily discover by appealing to his memory. For custom and fashion are powerful seducers, and he must of necessity have fought hard against these to have attained that justness of taste which is required in one who pretends to follow Nature. But if no such conflict can be called to mind, 'tis a certain token that the party has his taste very little different from the vulgar. And on this account he should instantly betake himself to the wholesome practice recommended in this treatise. He should set afoot the powerfullest faculties of his mind, and assemble the best forces of his wit and judgment, in order to make a formal descent on the Territories of the Heart: resolving to decline no combat, nor hearken to any terms till he had pierced into its inmost provinces and reached the seat of Empire. No treaties should amuse him, no advantages lead him aside. All other speculations should be suspended, all other mysteries resigned till this necessary campaign was made and these inward conflicts learnt, by which he would be able to gain at least some tolerable insight into *himself*, and knowledge of *his own natural Principles.*

(1711)

Joseph Warton
1722-1800

FROM

An Essay on the Genius and Writings of Pope

TO THE REVEREND DR. YOUNG, RECTOR OF WELWYN, IN HERTFORDSHIRE

Dear Sir,

Permit me to break into your retirement, the residence of virtue and literature, and to trouble you with a few reflections on the merits and real character of an admired author and on other collateral subjects of criticism that will naturally arise in the course of such an inquiry. No love of singularity, no affectation of paradoxical opinions, gave rise to the following work. I revere the memory of Pope, I respect and honor his abilities, but I do not think him at the head of his profession. In other words, in that species of poetry wherein Pope excelled he is superior to all mankind; and I only say that this species of poetry is not the most excellent one of the art.

We do not, it should seem, sufficiently attend to the difference there is betwixt a man of wit, a man of sense, and a true poet. Donne and Swift were undoubtedly men of wit and men of sense, but what traces have they left of pure poetry? It is remarkable that Dryden says of Donne, "He was the greatest wit, though not the greatest poet, of this nation." Fontenelle and La Motte[1] are entitled to the former character, but what can they urge to gain the latter? Which of these characters is the most valuable and useful is entirely out of the question. All I plead for is to have their several provinces kept distinct from each other and to impress on the reader that a clear head and acute understanding are not sufficient alone to make a poet; that the most solid observations on human life expressed with the utmost elegance and brevity are morality, and not poetry; that the *Epistles* of Boileau in rhyme are no more poetical than the *Characters* of La Bruyère in prose; and that it is a creative and glowing *imagination, acer spiritus ac vis,*[2] and that alone, that can stamp a writer with this exalted and very uncommon character which so few possess and of which so few can properly judge.

For one person who can adequately relish and enjoy a work of imagination, twenty are to be found who can taste and judge of observations on familiar life and the manners of the age. The satires of Ariosto are more read than the *Orlando Furioso,* or even Dante. Are there so many cordial admirers of Spenser and Milton as of *Hudibras,* if we strike out of the number of these supposed admirers those who appear such out of fashion and not of feeling? Swift's "Rhapsody on Poetry" is far more popular than Akenside's noble "Ode to Lord Huntingdon." The epistles on the characters of men and women and your sprightly satires, my good friend, are more frequently perused and quoted than "L'Allegro" and "Il Penseroso" of Milton. Had you written only these satires, you would, indeed, have gained the title of a man of wit and a man of sense, but, I am confident, would not insist on being denominated a poet merely on their account.

Non satis est puris versum perscribere verbis.[3]

It is amazing this matter should ever have been mistaken, when Horace has taken particular and repeated pains to settle and adjust the opinion in question. He has more than once disclaimed all right and title to the name of poet on the score of his ethic and satiric pieces.

GENIUS AND WRITINGS OF POPE. **1. Fontenelle . . . La Motte:** Bernard le Bovier de Fontenelle (1659–1757), literary critic, took the side of the Moderns in the perennial debate over the superiority of the Ancients to the Moderns. Antoine Houdar de la Motte (1672–1731), French poet and critic, was another participant in the debate.

2. See Horace, *Serm.*, I, iv, 46. **3. Non . . . verbis:** "It is not enough to write a line of plain words." See Horace, *Serm.*, I, iv, 54.

Neque enim concludere versum
dixeris esse satis.[4]

[These] are lines often repeated, but whose meaning is not extended and weighed as it ought to be. Nothing can be more judicious than the method he prescribes of trying whether any composition be essentially poetical or not, which is to drop entirely the measures and numbers and transpose and invert the order of the words, and in this unadorned manner to peruse the passage. If there be really in it a true poetical spirit, all your inversions and transpositions will not disguise and extinguish it, but it will retain its luster like a diamond unset and thrown back into the rubbish of the mine. Let us make a little experiment on the following well-known lines:

> Yes, you despise the man that is confined to books, who rails at humankind from his study, though what he learns he speaks, and may perhaps advance some general maxims or may be right by chance. The coxcomb bird, so grave and so talkative, that cries whore, knave, and cuckold from his cage, though he rightly call many a passenger, you hold him no philosopher. And yet, such is the fate of all extremes, men may be read too much, as well as books. We grow more partial, for the sake of the observer, to observations which we ourselves make; less so to written wisdom, because another's. Maxims are drawn from notions, and those from guess.[5]

What shall we say of this passage? Why, that it is most excellent sense, but just as poetical as the "Qui fit Maecenas" of the author who recommends this method of trial. Take ten lines of the *Iliad, Paradise Lost,* or even of the *Georgics* of Virgil, and see whether, by any process of critical chemistry, you can lower and reduce them to the tameness of prose. You will find that they will appear like Ulysses in his disguise of rags, still a hero, though lodged in the cottage of the herdsman Eumaeus.

The sublime and the pathetic are the two chief nerves of all genuine poesy. What is there transcendently sublime or pathetic in Pope? In his works there is, indeed, *nihil inane, nihil arcessitum; puro tamen fonti quam magno flumini proprior,* as the excellent Quintilian remarks of Lysias.[6] And because I am, perhaps, unwilling to speak out in plain English, I will adopt the following passage of Voltaire, which in my opinion as exactly characterizes Pope as it does his model Boileau, for whom it was originally designed:

> Incapable peut-être du sublime qui élève l'âme, et du sentiment qui l'attendrit, mais fait pour éclairer ceux à qui la nature accorda l'un et l'autre, laborieux, sévère, précis, pur, harmonieux, il devint, enfin, le poète de la raison.[7]

Our English poets may, I think, be disposed in four different classes and degrees. In the first class I would place only three sublime and pathetic poets: Spenser, Shakespeare, Milton. In the second class should be ranked such as possessed the true poetical genius in a more moderate degree, but who had noble talents for moral, ethical, and panegyrical poesy. At the head of these are Dryden, Prior, Addison, Cowley, Waller, Garth, Fenton, Gay, Denham, Parnell. In the third class may be placed men of wit, of elegant taste, and lively fancy in describing familiar life, though not the higher scenes of poetry. Here may be numbered Butler, Swift, Rochester, Donne, Dorset, Oldham. In the fourth class the mere versifiers, however smooth and mellifluous some of them may be thought, should be disposed. Such as Pitt, Sandys, Fairfax, Broome, Buckingham, Lansdowne. This enumeration is not intended as a complete catalogue of writers, and in their proper order, but only to mark out briefly the different species of our celebrated authors. In which of these classes Pope deserves to be placed the following work is intended to determine.

I am, Dear Sir,
Your affectionate
And faithful servant

4. Neque . . . satis: "For you would not say it was enough to finish a verse." See Horace, *Serm.,* I, iv, 40. **5.** Pope, *Moral Essays,* I, 1–14.

6. *nihil . . . proprior:* "Nothing foolish or far-fetched. Nevertheless, I would compare him to a pure spring rather than a great river." See Quintilian, *Institutes,* X, i, 78. **7. Incapable . . . raison:** "Incapable perhaps of the sublimity which elevates the soul, and of the sentiment which soothes it, but capable of illuminating those to whom nature grants both the one and the other, laborious, correct, precise, pure, harmonious, he becomes, finally, the poet of reason." See *Discours à sa réception à l'Académie Française.*

From SECTION IX, OF THE *ESSAY ON MAN*

If it be a true observation that for a poet to write happily and well he must have seen and felt what he describes and must draw from living models alone, and if modern times from their luxury and refinement afford not manners that will bear to be described, it will then follow that those species of poetry bid fairest to succeed at present which treat of things, not men; which deliver doctrines, not display events. Of this sort is didactic and descriptive poetry. Accordingly, the moderns have produced many excellent pieces of this kind. We may mention the *Syphilis* of Fracastorius, the *Silkworms* and *Chess* of Vida, the *Ambra* of Politian, the *Agriculture* of Alamanni, the *Art of Poetry* of Boileau, the *Gardens* of Rapin, the *Cyder* of Philips, the *Chase* of Somerville, the *Pleasures of Imagination,* the *Art of Preserving Health,* the *Fleece,* the *Religion* of Racine the Younger, the elegant Latin poem of Browne on the immortality of the soul, the Latin poems of Stay and Boscovick, and the philosophical poem before us, to which, if we may judge from some beautiful fragments, we might have added Gray's didactic poem on education and government, had he lived to finish it; and the *English Garden* of Mr. Mason must not be omitted.

The *Essay on Man* is as close a piece of argument, admitting its principles, as perhaps can be found in verse. Pope informs us in his first preface "that he chose his epistolary way of writing, notwithstanding his subject was high and of dignity, because of its being mixed with argument which of its nature approacheth to prose." He has not wandered into any useless digressions, has employed no fictions, no tale or story, and has relied chiefly on the poetry of his style for the purpose of interesting his readers. His style is concise and figurative, forcible and elegant. He has many metaphors and images artfully interspersed in the driest passages, which stood most in need of such ornaments. Nevertheless, there are too many lines in this performance plain and prosaic. The meaner the subject is of a preceptive poem, the more striking appears the art of the poet. It is even of use, perhaps, to choose a low subject. In this respect Virgil had the advantage over Lucretius. The latter, with all his vigor and sublimity of genius, could hardly satisfy and come up to the grandeur of his theme. Pope labors under the same difficulty. If any beauty in this essay be uncommonly transcendent and peculiar, it is brevity of diction which, in a few instances, and those pardonable, has occasioned obscurity. It is hardly to be imagined how much sense, how much thinking, how much observation on human life is condensed together in a small compass. He was so accustomed to confine his thoughts in rhyme that he tells us he could express them more shortly this way than in prose itself. On its first publication Pope did not own it, and it was given by the public to Lord Paget, Dr. Young, Dr. Desaguliers,[8] and others. Even Swift seems to have been deceived. There is a remarkable passage in one of his letters:

> I confess I did never imagine you were so deep in morals or that so many new and excellent rules could be produced so advantageously and agreeably in that science from any one head. I confess in some places I was forced to read twice. I believe I told you before what the Duke of D— said to me on that occasion, how a judge here, who knows you, told him that on the first reading those essays he was much pleased but found some lines a little dark; on the second most of them cleared up and his pleasure increased; on the third he had no doubt remaining and then he admired the whole.

The subject of this essay is a vindication of providence in which the poet proposes to prove that of all possible systems, infinite wisdom has formed the best; that in such a system, coherence, union, subordination are necessary; and if so, that appearances of evil, both moral and natural, are also necessary and unavoidable; that the seeming defects and blemishes in the universe conspire to its general beauty; that as all parts in an animal are not eyes and as in a city, comedy, or picture, all ranks, characters, and colors are not equal or alike, even so, excesses and contrary qualities contribute to the proportion and harmony of the universal system; that it is not strange that we should not be able to discover perfection and order in every instance, because in an infinity of things mutually relative a mind which sees not infinitely can see nothing fully. This doctrine was inculcated by Plato and the Stoics, but more amply and particularly by the later Platonists, and by Antoninus and Simplicius. In

8. **Lord Paget . . . Desaguliers:** Paget wrote an *Essay on Human Life* in 1834. Desaguliers was a fellow of the Royal Society and a lecturer on scientific matters.

illustrating his subject Pope has been much more deeply indebted to the *Theodicée* of Leibnitz, to Archbishop King's *Origin of Evil,* and to the *Moralists* of Lord Shaftesbury, than to the philosophers above mentioned. The late Lord Bathurst repeatedly assured me that he had read the whole scheme of the *Essay on Man* in the handwriting of Bolingbroke and drawn up a series of propositions which Pope was to versify and illustrate, in doing which, our poet, it must be confessed, left several passages so expressed as to be favorable to fatalism and necessity, notwithstanding all the pains that can be taken and the turns that can be given to those passages to place them on the side of religion and make them coincide with the fundamental doctrines of revelation.

Awake, my St. John! leave all meaner things
To low ambition, and the pride of Kings.
Let us (since life can little more supply
Than just to look about us and to die)
Expatiate free o'er all this scene of Man;
A mighty maze! but not without a plan.

This opening is awful and commands the attention of the reader. The word *awake* has peculiar force and obliquely alludes to his noble friend's leaving his political for philosophical pursuits. May I venture to observe that the metaphors in the succeeding lines, drawn from the field sports of setting and shooting, seem below the dignity of the subject, especially,

Eye Nature's walks, shoot Folly as it flies,
And catch the Manners living as they rise.

But vindicate the ways of God to Man.

This line is taken from Milton:

And justify the ways of God to man [*sic*].

Pope seems to have hinted by this allusion to the *Paradise Lost* that he intended his poem for a defense of providence as well as Milton, but he took a very different method in pursuing that end and imagined that the goodness and justice of the Deity might be defended *without* having recourse to the doctrine of a future state and of the depraved state of man.

. . .

The lamb thy riot dooms to bleed today,
Had he thy Reason would he skip and play?
Pleas'd to the last he crops the flow'ry food,
And licks the hand just rais'd to shed his blood.
[I, 81]

The tenderness of this striking image, and particularly the circumstance in the last line, has an artful effect in alleviating the dryness in the argumentative parts of the essay and interesting the reader.

The soul uneasy, and confin'd from home,
Rests and expatiates in a life to come.
[I, 97]

In former editions it used to be printed *at home,* but this expression seeming to exclude a future existence (as to speak the plain truth it was intended to do) it was altered to *from home,* not only with great injury to the harmony of the line, but also to the reasoning of the context.

Lo, the poor Indian! whose untutor'd mind
Sees God in clouds, or hears him in the wind;
His soul proud Science never taught to stray
Far as the solar walk, or milky way;
Yet simple Nature to his hope has giv'n,
Behind the cloud-topt hill, an humbler heav'n;
Some safer world in depth of woods embrac'd,
Some happier island in the wat'ry waste,
Where slaves once more their native land
behold,
No fiends torment, no Christians thirst for gold.
To Be, contents his natural desire,
He asks no Angel's wing, no Seraph's fire;
But thinks, admitted to that equal sky,
His faithful dog shall bear him company.
[I, 99]

Pope has indulged himself in but few digressions in this piece; this is one of the most poetical. Representations of undisguised nature and artless innocence always amuse and delight. The simple notions which uncivilized nations entertain of a future state are many of them beautifully romantic and some of the best subjects for poetry. It has been questioned whether the circumstance of the dog, although striking at the first view, is introduced with propriety, as it is known that this animal is not a native of America. The notion of seeing God in clouds and hearing him in the wind cannot be enough applauded.

From burning suns when livid deaths descend,
When earthquakes swallow, or when tempests
sweep
Towns to one grave, whole nations to the deep?
[I, 142]

I quote these lines as an example of energy of style and of Pope's manner of compressing together many images without confusion and without superfluous epithets. Substantives and verbs are the sinews of language.

. . .

All are but parts of one stupendous whole,
Whose body Nature is, and God the soul;
That chang'd thro' all, and yet in all the same;
Great in the earth as in th' aethereal frame;
Warms in the sun, refreshes in the breeze,
Glows in the stars, and blossoms in the trees;
Lives thro' all life, extends thro' all extent,
Spreads undivided, operates unspent;
Breathes in our soul, informs our mortal part,
As full, as perfect, in a hair as heart;
As full, as perfect, in vile Man that mourns,
As the rapt Seraph, that adores and burns:
To him on high, no low, no great, no small;
He fills, he bounds, connects, and equals all!
[I, 267]

Whilst I am transcribing this exalted description of the omnipresence of the Deity, I feel myself almost tempted to retract an assertion in the beginning of this work that there is nothing transcendently sublime in Pope. These lines have all the energy and harmony that can be given to rhyme.

. . .

Who taught the nations of the field and wood
To shun their poison and to choose their food?
Prescient, the tides or tempests to withstand,
Build on the wave, or arch beneath the sand?
[III, 99]

This passage is highly finished; such objects are more suited to the nature of poetry than abstract ideas. Every verb and epithet has here a descriptive force. We find more imagery from these lines to the end of the epistle than in any other parts of this essay. The origin of the connections in social life, the account of the state of nature, the rise and effects of superstition and tyranny, and the restoration of true religion and just government, all these ought to be mentioned as passages that deserve high applause, nay as some of the most exalted pieces of English poetry.

. . .

A better would you fix?
Then give Humility a coach and six.
[IV, 169]

Worth makes the man, and want of it, the fellow,
The rest is all but leather or prunella.
[IV, 203]

Not one looks backward, onward still he goes,
Yet ne'er looks forward further than his nose.
[IV, 223]

To sigh for ribands if thou art so silly,
Mark how they grace Lord Umbra, or Sir Billy.
[IV, 277]

In a work of so serious and severe a cast, in a work of reasoning, in a work of theology designed to explain the most interesting subject that can employ the mind of man, surely such strokes of levity, of satire, of ridicule, however poignant and witty, are ill placed and disgusting, are violations of that propriety which Pope in general so strictly observed.

(1756, 1782)

Thomas Warton
1728-1790

◆

FROM

Observations on the Fairy Queen

SECTION I, OF THE PLAN AND CONDUCT OF THE *FAIRY QUEEN*

When the works of Homer and Aristotle began to be restored and studied in Italy, when the genuine and uncorrupted sources of ancient poetry and ancient criticism were opened, and every species of literature at last emerged from the depths of Gothic ignorance and barbarity, it might have been expected that, instead of the romantic manner of poetical composition introduced and established by the Provençal bards, a new and more legitimate taste of writing would have succeeded. With these advantages it was reasonable to conclude that unnatural events, the machinations of imaginary beings, and adventures entertaining only as they were improbable would have given place to justness of thought and design, and to that decorum which nature dictated and which the example and the precept of antiquity had authorized. But it was a long time before such a change was effected. We find Ariosto, many years after the revival of letters, rejecting truth for magic, and preferring the ridiculous and incoherent excursions of Boiardo to the propriety and uniformity of the Grecian and Roman models. Nor did the restoration of ancient learning produce any effectual or immediate improvement in the state of criticism. Beni, one of the most celebrated critics of the sixteenth century, was still so infatuated with a fondness for the old Provençal vein that he ventured to write a regular dissertation in which he compares Ariosto with Homer.*

* *Comparizione di T. Tasso con Amero e Virgilio, insieme con la difesa dell'Ariosto paragonato ad Omero.* [Warton's note.]

Trissino, who flourished a few years after Ariosto, had taste and boldness enough to publish an epic poem, written in professed imitation of the *Iliad.*** But this attempt met with little regard or applause for the reason on which its real merit was founded. It was rejected as an insipid and uninteresting performance, having few devils or enchantments to recommend it. To Trissino succeeded Tasso, who in his *Gierusaleme Liberata* took the ancients for his guides, but was still too sensible of the popular prejudice in favor of ideal beings and romantic adventures to neglect or omit them entirely. He had studied and acknowledged the beauties of classical purity. Yet he still kept his first and favorite acquaintance, the old Provençal poets, in his eyes, like his own Rinaldo, who after he had gazed on the diamond shield of truth, and with seeming resolution was actually departing from Armida and her enchanted gardens, could not help looking back upon them with some remains of fondness. Nor did Tasso's poem, though composed in some measure on a regular plan, give its author, among the Italians at least, any greater share of esteem and reputation on that account. Ariosto, with all his extravagancies, was still preferred. The superiority of the *Orlando Furioso* was at length established by a formal decree of the Academicians della Crusca, who amongst other literary debates held a solemn court of inquiry concerning the merit of both poems.

Such was the prevailing taste when Spenser projected the *Fairy Queen*, a poem which, according to the practice of Ariosto, was to consist of allegories, enchantments, and romantic expeditions, conducted by knights, giants, magicians, and fictitious beings. It may be urged that Spenser made an unfortunate choice and discovered but little judgment in adopting Ariosto for his example rather than Tasso, who had so evidently exceeded his rival, at least in conduct and decorum. But our author

** *L'Italia Liberata de Soti,* 1524. It is in blank verse, which the author would have introduced instead of the terza rima of Dante, or the ottava of Boccace. [Warton's note.]

naturally followed the poem which was most celebrated and popular. For although the French critics universally gave the preference to Tasso, yet in Italy the partisans on the side of Ariosto were by far the most powerful, and consequently in England; for Italy in the age of Queen Elizabeth gave laws to our island in all matters of taste, as France has done ever since. At the same time it may be supposed that of the two Ariosto was Spenser's favorite, and that he was naturally biased to prefer that plan which would admit the most extensive range for his unlimited imagination. What was Spenser's particular plan in consequence of this choice, and how it was conducted, I now proceed to examine.

The poet supposes that the *Fairy Queen*, according to an established annual custom, held a magnificent feast which continued twelve days, on each of which, respectively, twelve several complaints are presented before her. Accordingly, in order to redress the injuries which were the occasion of these several complaints, she dispatches, with proper commissions, twelve different knights, each of which, in the particular adventure allotted to him, proves an example of some particular virtue, as of holiness, temperance, justice, chastity; and has one complete book assigned to him, of which he is the hero. But besides these twelve knights, severally exemplifying twelve moral virtues, the poet has constituted one principal knight or general hero, viz., Prince Arthur. This personage represents magnificence, a virtue which is supposed to be the perfection of all the rest. He moreover assists in every book, and the end of his actions is to discover and win Gloriana, or Glory. In a word, in this character the poet professes to portray "the image of a brave knight perfected in the twelve private moral virtues."

It is evident that our author in establishing one hero who, seeking and attaining one grand end, which is Gloriana, should exemplify one grand character—or a brave knight perfected in the twelve private moral virtues—copied the cast and construction of the ancient epic. But sensible as he was of the importance and expediency of the unity of the hero and of his design, he does not, in the meantime, seem convinced of the necessity of that unity of action by the means of which such a design should be properly accomplished. At least, he has not followed the method practiced by Homer and Virgil in conducting their respective heroes to the proposed end.

It may be asked with great propriety how does Arthur execute the grand, simple, and ultimate design intended by the poet? It may be answered, with some degree of plausibility, that by lending his respective assistance to each of the twelve knights who patronize the twelve virtues, in his allotted defense of each, Arthur approaches still nearer and nearer to Glory, till at last he gains a complete possession. But surely to assist is not a sufficient service. This secondary merit is inadequate to the reward. The poet ought to have made this "brave knight" the leading adventurer. Arthur should have been the principal agent in vindicating the cause of holiness, temperance, and the rest. If our hero had thus, in his own person, exerted himself in the protection of the twelve virtues, he might have been deservedly styled the perfect pattern of all, and consequently would have succeeded in the task assigned, the attainment of Glory. At present he is only a subordinate or accessory character. The difficulties and obstacles which we expect him to surmount in order to accomplish his final achievement are removed by others. It is not he who subdues the dragon, in the First Book, or quells the magician Busirane, in the Third. These are the victories of St. George and of Britomart. On the whole, the twelve knights do too much for Arthur to do anything, or at least, so much as may be reasonably required from the promised plan of the poet. While we are attending to the design of the hero of the book, we forget that of the hero of the poem. Dryden remarks, "We must do Spenser that justice to observe that magnanimity (magnificence), which is the true character of Prince Arthur, shines throughout the whole poem and succors the rest when they are in distress." If the magnanimity of Arthur did, in reality, thus shine in every part of the poem with a superior and steady luster, our author would fairly stand acquitted. At present it bursts forth but seldom, in obscure and interrupted flashes. "To succor the rest when they are in distress"[1] is, as I have hinted, a circumstance of too little importance in the character of this universal champion. It is a service to be performed in the cause of the hero of the epic poem by some dependent or inferior chief, the business of a Gyas or a Cloanthus.

On the whole, we may observe that Spenser's

OBSERVATIONS ON THE "FAIRY QUEEN." 1. See *Aeneid*, vi, 727.

adventures, separately taken as the subject of each single book, have not always a mutual dependence upon each other and consequently do not properly contribute to constitute one legitimate poem. Hughes, not considering this, has advanced a remark in commendation of Spenser's critical conduct which is indeed one of the most blameable parts of it. "If we consider the First Book as an entire work of itself, we shall find it to be no irregular contrivance. There is one principal action, which is completed in the twelfth canto, and the several incidents are proper, as they tend either to obstruct or promote it."

As the heroic poem is required to be one whole, compounded of many various parts, relative and dependent, it is expedient that not one of those parts should be so regularly contrived, and so completely finished, as to become a whole of itself. For the mind, being once satisfied in arriving at the consummation of an orderly series of events, acquiesces in that satisfaction. Our attention and curiosity are in the midst diverted from pursuing, with due vigor, the final and general catastrophe. But while each part is left incomplete, if separated from the rest, the mind, still eager to gratify its expectations, is irresistibly and imperceptibly drawn from part to part till it receives a full and ultimate satisfaction from the accomplishment of one great event, which all those parts, following and illustrating each other, contributed to produce.

Our author was probably aware that by constituting twelve several adventures for twelve several heroes the want of a general connection would often appear. On this account, as I presume, he sometimes resumes and finishes in some distant book a tale formerly begun and left imperfect. But as numberless interruptions necessarily intervene, this proceeding often occasions infinite perplexity to the reader. And it seems to be for the same reason that after one of the twelve knights has achieved the adventure of his proper book, the poet introduces him in the next book acting perhaps in an inferior sphere and degraded to some less dangerous exploit. But this conduct is highly inartificial, for it destroys that repose which the mind feels after having accompanied a hero through manifold struggles and various distresses to success and victory. Besides, when we perceive him entering upon any less illustrious attempt, our former admiration is in some measure diminished. Having seen him complete some memorable conquest, we become interested in his honor, and are jealous concerning his future reputation. To attempt, and even to achieve, some petty posterior enterprise is to derogate from his dignity and to sully the transcendent luster of his former victories.

Spenser perhaps would have embarrassed himself and the reader less had he made every book one entire detached poem of twelve cantos, without any reference to the rest. Thus he would have written twelve different books, in each of which he might have completed the pattern of a particular virtue in twelve knights respectively. At present he has remarkably failed, in endeavoring to represent all the virtues exemplified in one. The poet might either have established twelve knights without an Arthur, or an Arthur without twelve knights. Upon supposition that Spenser was resolved to characterize the twelve moral virtues, the former plan perhaps would have been best; the latter is defective as it necessarily wants simplicity. It is an action consisting of twelve actions, all equally great and unconnected between themselves, and not compounded of one uninterrupted and coherent chain of incidents tending to the accomplishment of one design.

I have before remarked that Spenser intended to express the character of a hero perfected in the twelve moral virtues by representing him as assisting in the service of all till at last he becomes possessed of all. This plan, however injudicious, he certainly was obliged to observe. But in the Third Book, which is styled the Legend of Chastity, Prince Arthur does not so much as lend his assistance in the vindication of that virtue. He appears, indeed, but not as an agent, or even an auxiliary, in the adventure of the book.

Yet it must be confessed that there is something artificial in the poet's manner of varying from historical precision. This conduct is rationally illustrated by himself. According to this plan, the reader would have been agreeably surprised in the last book when he came to discover that the series of adventures which he had just seen completed were undertaken at the command of the Fairy Queen and that the knights had severally set forward to the execution of them from her annual birthday festival. But Spenser, in most of the books, has injudiciously forestalled the first of these particulars, which certainly should have been concealed till the last book, not only that a needless repetition of the same thing might be prevented, but that an opportunity might be secured of striking the reader's mind with a circumstance new and unexpected.

But notwithstanding the plan and conduct of Spenser in the poem before us is highly exceptionable, yet we may venture to pronounce that the scholar has more merit than his master in this respect, and that the *Fairy Queen* is not so confused and irregular as the *Orlando Furioso*. There is indeed no general unity which prevails in the former: but, if we consider every book, or adventure, as a separate poem, we shall meet with so many distinct, however imperfect, unities, by which an attentive reader is less bewildered than in the maze of indigestion and incoherence of which the latter totally consists, where we seek in vain either for partial or universal integrity.

> Ut nec pes nec caput uni
> reddatur formae.[2]

Ariosto has his admirers, and most deservedly. Yet every classical, every reasonable critic must acknowledge that the poet's conception in celebrating the madness, or, in other words, describing the irrational acts, of a hero, implies extravagance and absurdity. Orlando does not make his appearance till the Eighth Book, where he is placed in a situation not perfectly heroic. He is discovered to us in bed, desiring to sleep. His ultimate design is to find Angelica, but his pursuit of her is broken off in the Thirtieth Book, after which there are sixteen books in none of which Angelica has the least share. Other heroes are likewise engaged in the same pursuit. After reading the first stanza, we are inclined to think that the subject of the poem is the expedition of the Moors into France, under the emperor Agramante, to fight against Charlemagne; but this business is the most insignificant and inconsiderable part of it. Many of the heroes perform exploits equal, if not superior, to those of Orlando, particularly Ruggiero, who closes the poem with a grand and important achievement, the conquest and death of Rodomont. But this event is not the completion of a story carried on principally and perpetually through the work.

This spirited Italian passes from one incident to another, and from region to region, with such incredible expedition and rapidity that one would think he was mounted upon his winged steed Ippogrifo. Within the compass of ten stanzas he is in England and the Hesperides, in the earth and the moon. He begins the history of a knight in Europe and suddenly breaks it off to resume the unfinished catastrophe of another in Asia. The reader's imagination is distracted and his attention harassed, amidst the multiplicity of tales, in the relation of which the poet is at the same instant equally engaged. To remedy this inconvenience, the compassionate expositors have affixed in some of the editions marginal hints, informing the bewildered reader in what book and stanza the poet intends to recommence an interrupted episode. This expedient reminds us of the awkward artifice practiced by the first painters. However, it has proved the means of giving Ariosto's admirers a clear comprehension of his stories, which otherwise they could not have obtained without much difficulty. This poet is seldom read a second time in order—that is, by passing from the First Canto to the Second, and from the Second to the rest in succession—[but] by thus pursuing, without any regard to the proper course of the books and stanzas, the different tales, which, though all somewhere finished, yet are at present so mutually complicated that the incidents of one are perpetually clashing with those of another. The judicious Abbé Dubos observes happily enough that "Homer is a geometrician in comparison of Ariosto."[3] His miscellaneous contents cannot be better expressed than by the two first verses of his exordium:

> Le Donni, i Cavallìer, l'Arme, gli Amori,
> Le Cortegie, le' audaci Imprese, io canto.[4]

But it is absurd to think of judging either Ariosto or Spenser by precepts which they did not attend to. We who live in the days of writing by rule are apt to try every composition by those laws which we have been taught to think the sole criterion of excellence. Critical taste is universally diffused, and we require the same order and design which every modern performance is expected to have in poems where they never were regarded or intended. Spen-

2. Ut . . . formae: "Neither foot nor head can be assigned to a single form." See Horace, *Ars Poetica*, l. 8.

3. See his *Réflexions critiques sur la poésie et sur la peinture* (1719), I, xxxiv. **4. Le Donni . . . canto:** "Of ladies, knights, arms, love's pleasures; of courtesies, of bold feats I sing."

ser (and the same may be said of Ariosto) did not live in an age of planning. His poetry is the careless exuberance of a warm imagination and a strong sensibility. It was his business to engage the fancy and to interest the attention by bold and striking images, in the formation and the disposition of which little labor or art was applied. The various and the marvellous were the chief sources of delight. Hence we find our author ransacking alike the regions of reality and romance, of truth and fiction, to find the proper decorations and furniture for his fairy structure. Born in such an age, Spenser wrote rapidly from his own feelings, which at the same time were naturally noble. Exactness in his poem would have been like the cornice which a painter introduced in the grotto of Calypso. Spenser's beauties are like the flowers in Paradise.

> Which not nice Art
> In Beds and curious Knots, but Nature boon
> Pour'd forth profuse on Hill and Dale and Plain,
> Both where the morning Sun first warmly smote
> The open field, and where the unpierc't shade
> Imbrown'd the noontide Bow'rs.
> [*Paradise Lost*, IV, 241]

If the *Fairy Queen* be destitute of that arrangement and economy which epic severity requires, yet we scarcely regret the loss of these while their place is so amply supplied by something which more powerfully attracts us, something which engages the affections, the feelings of the heart, rather than the cold approbation of the head. If there be any poem whose graces please because they are situated beyond the reach of art, and where the force and faculties of creative imagination delight because they are unassisted and unrestrained by those of deliberate judgment, it is this. In reading Spenser, if the critic is not satisfied, yet the reader is transported.

SECTION X, OF SPENSER'S ALLEGORICAL CHARACTER

In reading the works of a poet who lived in a remote age, it is necessary that we should look back upon the customs and manners which prevailed in that age. We should endeavor to place ourselves in the writer's situation and circumstances. Hence we shall become better enabled to discover how his turn of thinking and manner of composing were influenced by familiar appearances and established objects which are utterly different from those with which we are at present surrounded. For want of this caution too many readers view the knights and damsels, the tournaments and enchantments, of Spenser, with modern eyes, never considering that the encounters of chivalry subsisted in our author's age; that romances were then most eagerly and universally studied; and that consequently Spenser, from the fashion of the times, was induced to undertake a recital of chivalrous achievements and to become, in short, a *romantic* poet.

Spenser in this respect copied real manners no less than Homer. A sensible historian observes that "Homer copied true natural manners, which, however rough and uncultivated, will always form an agreeable and interesting picture. But the pencil of the English poet (Spenser) was employed in drawing the affectations, and conceits, and fopperies of chivalry." [5] This, however, was nothing more than an imitation of real life, as much, at least, as the plain descriptions in Homer, which corresponded to the simplicity of manners then subsisting in Greece. Spenser, in the address of the *Shepherd's Calendar* to Sir Philip Sidney, couples his patron's learning with his skill in chivalry, a topic of panegyric which would sound very odd in a modern dedication, especially before a set of pastorals. "To the noble and virtuous gentleman, most worthy of all titles, both of Learning and *Chivalry*, Master Philip Sydney."

> Go little book; thyself present,
> As child whose parent is unkent,[6]
> To him that is the president
> Of nobleness and *Chivalry*.

. . .

In the reign of Henry VIII classical literature began to be received and studied in England, and the writings of the ancients were cultivated with true taste and erudition by Sir Thomas More, Colet, Ascham, Leland, Cheke, and other illustrious rivals in polished composition. Erasmus was entertained and patronized by the king and nobility; and the Greek language, that inestimable repository of genuine elegance and sublimity, was taught and ad-

5. See David Hume, *History of England Under the House of Tudor* (1759), II, 739. **6. unkent:** unknown.

mired. In this age flourished John Skelton, who, notwithstanding the great and new lights with which he was surrounded, contributed nothing to what his ancestors had left him, nor do I perceive that his versification is in any degree more refined than that of one of his immediate predecessors, Hawes. Indeed, one would hardly suspect that he wrote in the same age with his elegant contemporaries Surrey and Wyatt. His best pieces are written in the allegorical manner, and are his [*Garland*] *of Laurel,* and *Bouge of Court.* But the genius of Skelton seems little better qualified for picturesque than satirical poetry. In the one he wants invention, grace, and dignity; in the other, wit and good manners.

I should be guilty of injustice to a nation which amid a variety of disadvantages has kept a constant pace with England in the progress of literature if I neglected to mention in this general review two Scottish poets who flourished about this period. Sir David Lindsay and Sir William Dunbar, the former of which in his *Dream,* and other pieces, and the latter in his "Golden Terge," or "Shield," appear to have been animated with the noblest spirit of allegoric fiction.

Soon afterwards appeared a series of poems entitled *The Mirror of Magistrates,* formed upon a dramatic plan, and capable of admitting some of the most affecting pathetical strokes. But these pieces, however honored with the commendation of Sidney, seem to be little better than a biographical detail. There is one poem indeed, among the rest, which exhibits a group of imaginary personages so beautifully drawn that in all probability they contributed to direct, at least to stimulate, Spenser's imagination in the construction of the like representations. Thus much may be truly said, that Sackville's Induction approaches nearer to the *Fairy Queen* in the richness of allegoric description than any previous or succeeding poem.

After the *Fairy Queen,* allegory began to decline, and by degrees gave place to a species of poetry whose images were of the metaphysical and abstracted kind. This fashion evidently took its rise from the predominant studies of the times, in which the disquisitions of school divinity and the perplexed subtilities of philosophic disputation became the principal pursuits of the learned.

Then Una Fair gan drop her princely mien.

James I is contemptuously called a pedantic monarch. But surely nothing could be more serviceable to the interests of learning at its infancy than this supposed foible. "To stick the doctor's chair into the throne" was to patronize the literature of the times. In a more enlightened age, the same attention to letters and love of scholars might have produced proportionable effects on sciences of real utility. This cast of mind in the King, however indulged in some cases to an ostentatious affectation, was at least innocent.

Allegory, notwithstanding, unexpectedly rekindled some faint sparks of its native splendor in *The Purple Island* of Fletcher, with whom it almost as soon disappeared, when a poetry succeeded in which imagination gave way to correctness, sublimity of description to delicacy of sentiment, and majestic imagery to conceit and epigram. Poets began now to be more attentive to words than to things and objects. The nicer beauties of happy expression were preferred to the daring strokes of great conception. Satire, that bane of the sublime, was imported from France. The muses were debauched at court, and polite life and familiar manners became their only themes. The simple dignity of Milton was either entirely neglected or mistaken for bombast and insipidity by the refined readers of the dissolute age, whose taste and morals were equally vitiated.

(1754)

Edward Young

1683-1765

◆

From CONJECTURES ON ORIGINAL COMPOSITION

Imitations are of two kinds: one of nature, one of authors. The first we call originals, and confine the term imitation to the second. I shall not enter into the curious inquiry of what is, or is not, strictly speaking, original, content with what all must allow, that some compositions are more so than others; and the more they are so, I say, the better. Originals are, and ought to be, great favourites, for they are great benefactors; they extend the republic of letters, and add a new province to its dominion. Imitators only give us a sort of duplicates of what we had, possibly much better, before; increasing the mere drug of books, while all that makes them valuable, knowledge and genius, are at a stand. The pen of an original writer, like Armida's[1] wand, out of a barren waste calls a blooming spring. Out of that blooming spring an imitator is a transplanter of laurels, which sometimes die on removal, always languish in a foreign soil.

But suppose an imitator to be most excellent (and such there are), yet still he but nobly builds on another's foundation; his debt is, at least, equal to his glory; which, therefore, on the balance, cannot be very great. On the contrary, an original, though but indifferent (its originality being set aside), yet has something to boast; it is something to say with him in *Horace, Meo sum Pauper in aere;*[2] and to share ambition with no less than Caesar, who declared he had rather be the first in a village than the second at Rome.

Still farther: an imitator shares his crown, if he has one, with the chosen object of his imitation; an original enjoys an undivided applause. An original may be said to be of a vegetable nature; it rises spontaneously from the vital root of genius; it grows, it is not made. Imitations are often a sort of manufacture wrought up by those mechanics, art and labour, out of pre-existent materials not their own. . . .

But why are originals so few? not because the writer's harvest is over, the great reapers of antiquity having left nothing to be gleaned after them; nor because the human mind's teeming time is past, or because it is incapable of putting forth unprecedented births; but because illustrious examples engross, prejudice, and intimidate. They engross our attention, and so prevent a due inspection of ourselves; they prejudice our judgement in favour of their abilities, and so lessen the sense of our own; and they intimidate us with the splendour of their renown, and thus under diffidence bury our strength. Nature's impossibilities, and those of diffidence lie wide asunder.

Let it not be suspected, that I would weakly insinuate anything in favour of the moderns, as compared with ancient authors; no, I am lamenting their great inferiority. But I think it is no necessary inferiority; that it is not from divine destination, but from some cause far beneath the moon: I think that human souls, through all periods, are equal; that due care and exertion would set us nearer our immortal predecessors than we are at present; and he who questions and confutes this, will show abilities not a little tending toward a proof of that equality which he denies.

After all, the first ancients had no merit in being originals: they could not be imitators. Modern writers have a choice to make; and therefore have a merit in their power. They may soar in the regions of liberty, or move in the soft fetters of easy imitation; and imitation has as many plausible reasons to urge, as pleasure had to offer to Hercules. Hercules made the choice of an hero, and so became immortal.

Yet let not assertors of classic excellence imagine, that I deny the tribute it so well deserves. He that admires not ancient authors, betrays a secret he would conceal, and tells the world that he does not understand them. Let us be as far from neglecting, as from copying, their admirable compositions: sacred be their rights, and inviolable their fame. Let our understanding feed on theirs; they afford the

CONJECTURES. **1. Armida:** the enchantress in Tasso's *Jerusalem Delivered.* **2. *Meo . . . aere:*** "I am poor in my wealth." See Horace, *Epistles,* II, ii, 12.

noblest nourishment; but let them nourish, not annihilate, our own. When we read, let our imagination kindle at their charms; when we write, let our judgement shut them out of our thoughts; treat even Homer himself as his royal admirer was treated by the cynic; bid him stand aside, nor shade our composition from the beams of our own genius; for nothing original can rise, nothing immortal can ripen, in any other sun.

Must we then, you say, not imitate ancient authors? Imitate them by all means; but imitate aright. He that imitates the divine *Iliad* does not imitate Homer; but he who takes the same method, which Homer took, for arriving at a capacity of accomplishing a work so great. Tread in his steps to the sole fountain of immortality; drink where he drank, at the true Helicon, that is, at the breast of Nature: imitate; but imitate not the composition, but the man. For may not this paradox pass into a maxim? viz. "The less we copy the renowned ancients, we shall resemble them the more."

But possibly you may reply, that you must either imitate Homer, or depart from Nature. Not so: for suppose you were to change place, in time, with Homer; then, if you write naturally, you might as well charge Homer with an imitation of you. Can you be said to imitate Homer for writing so, as you would have written, if Homer had never been? As far as a regard to Nature, and sound sense, will permit a departure from your great predecessors; so far, ambitiously, depart from them; the farther from them in similitude, the nearer are you to them in excellence; you rise by it into an original; become a noble collateral, not an humble descendant from them. Let us build our compositions with the spirit, and in the taste, of the ancients; but not with their materials: thus will they resemble the structures of Pericles at Athens, which Plutarch commends for having had an air of antiquity as soon as they were built. All eminence, and distinction, lies out of the beaten road; excursion and deviation are necessary to find it; and the more remote your path from the highway, the more reputable; if, like poor Gulliver (of whom anon), you fall not into a ditch, in your way to glory.

What glory to come near, what glory to reach, what glory (presumptuous thought!) to surpass our predecessors! And is that then in Nature absolutely impossible? Or is it not, rather, contrary to Nature to fail in it? Nature herself sets the ladder, all wanting is our ambition to climb. For by the bounty of Nature we are as strong as our predecessors; and by the favour of time (which is but another round in Nature's scale) we stand on higher ground. As to the first, were they more than men? Or are we less? Are not our minds cast in the same mould with those before the flood? . . . It is by a sort of noble contagion, from a general familiarity with their writings, and not by any particular sordid theft, that we can be the better for those who went before us.

(1759)

David Hume

1711–1776

◆

FROM

Four Dissertations

OF TRAGEDY

It seems an unaccountable pleasure which the spectators of a well-written tragedy receive from sorrow, terror, anxiety, and other passions that are in themselves disagreeable and uneasy. The more they are touched and affected, the more are they delighted with the spectacle; and as soon as the uneasy passions cease to operate, the piece is at an end. One scene of full joy and contentment and security is the utmost that any composition of this kind can bear, and it is sure always to be the concluding one. If in the texture of the piece there be interwoven any scenes of satisfaction, they afford only faint gleams of pleasure, which are thrown in by way of variety, and in order to plunge the actors into deeper distress by means of that contrast and disappointment. The whole art of the poet is employed in rousing and supporting the compassion and indignation, the anxiety and resentment, of his audience. They are pleased in proportion as they are afflicted, and never are so happy as when they employ tears, sobs, and cries to give vent to their sorrow and relieve their heart, swollen with the tenderest sympathy and compassion.

The few critics who have had some tincture of philosophy have remarked this singular phenomenon and have endeavored to account for it.

L'Abbé Dubos, in his reflections on poetry and painting,[1] asserts that nothing is in general so disagreeable to the mind as the languid, listless state of indolence into which it falls upon the removal of all passion and occupation. To get rid of this painful situation, it seeks every amusement and pursuit—business, gaming, shows, executions—whatever will rouse the passions and take its attention from itself. No matter what the passion is, let it be disagreeable, afflicting, melancholy, disordered, it is still better than that insipid languor which arises from perfect tranquillity and repose.

It is impossible not to admit this account as being, at least in part, satisfactory. You may observe when there are several tables of gaming that all the company run to those where the deepest play is, even though they find not there the best players. The view, or at least imagination, of high passions arising from great loss or gain affects the spectator by sympathy, gives him some touches of the same passions, and serves him for a momentary entertainment. It makes the time pass the easier with him, and is some relief to that oppression under which men commonly labor when left entirely to their own thoughts and meditations.

We find that common liars always magnify in their narrations all kinds of danger, pain, distress, sickness, deaths, murders, and cruelties; as well as joy, beauty, mirth, and magnificence. It is an absurd secret which they have for pleasing their company, fixing their attention, and attaching them to such marvellous relations, by the passions and emotions which they excite.

There is, however, a difficulty in applying to the present subject in its full extent this solution, however ingenious and satisfactory it may appear. It is certain that the same object of distress which pleases in a tragedy, were it really set before us, would give the most unfeigned uneasiness, though it be then the most effectual cure to languor and indolence. Monsieur Fontenelle seems to have been sensible of this difficulty, and accordingly attempts another solution of the phenomenon, at least makes some addition to the theory above mentioned:

> Pleasure and pain, says he, which are two sentiments so different in themselves, differ not so much in their cause. From the instance of tickling it appears that the movement of pleasure pushed a little too far becomes pain, and that the movement of pain a little moderated becomes pleasure. Hence it proceeds that there is such a thing as a sorrow, soft and agreeable;

FOUR DISSERTATIONS. TRAGEDY. 1. A reference to the *Réflexions critiques sur la poésie et sur la peinture* (1719) by Jean-Baptiste Dubos (1670–1742).

> it is a pain weakened and diminished. The heart likes naturally to be moved and affected. Melancholy objects suit it, and even disastrous and sorrowful, provided they are softened by some circumstance. It is certain that on the theater the representation has always the effect of reality; yet it has not altogether that effect. However we may be hurried away by the spectacle, whatever dominion the senses and imagination may usurp over the reason, there still lurks at the bottom a certain idea of falsehood in the whole of what we see. This idea, though weak and disguised, suffices to diminish the pain which we suffer from the misfortunes of those whom we love and to reduce that affliction to such a pitch as converts it into a pleasure. We weep for the misfortune of a hero to whom we are attached. In the same instant we comfort ourselves by reflecting that it is nothing but a fiction. And it is precisely that mixture of sentiments which composes an agreeable sorrow, and tears that delight us. But as that affliction which is caused by exterior and sensible objects is stronger than the consolation which arises from an internal reflection, they are the effects and symptoms of sorrow that ought to predominate in the composition. (*Réflexions sur la poétique,* xxxvi)

This solution seems just and convincing, but perhaps it wants still some new addition in order to make it answer fully the phenomenon which we here examine. All the passions excited by eloquence are agreeable in the highest degree, as well as those which are moved by painting and the theater. The epilogues of Cicero are, on this account chiefly, the delight of every reader of taste, and it is difficult to read some of them without the deepest sympathy and sorrow. His merit as an orator no doubt depends much on his success in this particular. When he had raised tears in his judges and all his audience, they were then the most highly delighted, and expressed the greatest satisfaction with the pleader. The pathetic description of the butchery made by Verres of the Sicilian captains[2] is a masterpiece of this kind, but I believe none will affirm that the being present at a melancholy scene of that nature would afford any entertainment. Neither is the sorrow here softened by fiction, for the audience were convinced of the reality of every circumstance. What is it, then, which in this case raises a pleasure from the bosom of uneasiness, so to speak, and a pleasure which still retains all the features and outward symptoms of distress and sorrow?

I answer: This extraordinary effect proceeds from that very eloquence with which the melancholy scene is represented. The genius required to paint objects in a lively manner, the art employed in collecting all the pathetic circumstances, the judgment displayed in disposing them—the exercise, I say, of these noble talents, together with the force of expression and beauty of oratorial numbers, diffuse the highest satisfaction on the audience and excite the most delightful movements. By this means the uneasiness of the melancholy passions is not only overpowered and effaced by something stronger of an opposite kind but the whole impulse of those passions is converted into pleasure and swells the delight which the eloquence raises in us. The same force of oratory employed on an uninteresting subject would not please half so much, or rather would appear altogether ridiculous; and the mind, being left in absolute calmness and indifference, would relish none of those beauties of imagination or expression which, if joined to passion, give it such exquisite entertainment. The impulse or vehemence arising from sorrow, compassion, indignation receives a new direction from the sentiments of beauty. The latter, being the predominant motion, seize the whole mind and convert the former into themselves, at least tincture them so strongly as totally to alter their nature. And the soul, being at the same time roused by passion and charmed by eloquence, feels on the whole a strong movement which is altogether delightful.

The same principle takes place in tragedy—with this addition, that tragedy is an imitation; and imitation is always of itself agreeable. This circumstance serves still farther to smooth the motions of passion and convert the whole feeling into one uniform and strong enjoyment. Objects of the greatest terror and distress please in painting, and please more than the most beautiful objects that appear calm and indifferent. The affection, rousing the mind, excites a large stock of spirit and vehemence, which is all transformed into pleasure by the force of the prevailing movement. It is thus the fiction of tragedy softens the passion, by an infusion of a new feeling, not merely by weakening or diminishing the sorrow. You may by degrees weaken a real sorrow till it totally disappears; yet in none of its

2. In C. Verrem, II, v, 118.

gradations will it ever give pleasure except, perhaps, by accident, to a man sunk under lethargic indolence whom it rouses from that languid state.

To confirm this theory, it will be sufficient to produce other instances where the subordinate movement is converted into the predominant, and gives force to it, though of a different and even sometimes though of a contrary nature.

Novelty naturally rouses the mind and attracts our attention, and the movements which it causes are always converted into any passion belonging to the object, and join their force to it. Whether an event excite joy or sorrow, pride or shame, anger or good will, it is sure to produce a stronger affection when new or unusual. And though novelty of itself be agreeable, it fortifies the painful as well as agreeable passions.

Had you any intention to move a person extremely by the narration of any event, the best method of increasing its effect would be artfully to delay informing him of it, and first to excite his curiosity and impatience before you let him into the secret. This is the artifice practiced by Iago in the famous scene of Shakespeare, and every spectator is sensible that Othello's jealousy acquires additional force from his preceding impatience and that the subordinate passion is here readily transformed into the predominant one.

Difficulties increase passions of every kind, and by rousing our attention and exciting our active powers, they produce an emotion which nourishes the prevailing affection.

Parents commonly love that child most whose sickly, infirm frame of body has occasioned them the greatest pains, trouble, and anxiety in rearing him. The agreeable sentiment of affection here acquires force from sentiments of uneasiness.

Nothing endears so much a friend as sorrow for his death. The pleasure of his company has not so powerful an influence.

Jealousy is a painful passion; yet without some share of it, the agreeable affection of love has difficulty to subsist in its full force and violence. Absence is also a great source of complaint among lovers, and gives them the greatest uneasiness, yet nothing is more favorable to their mutual passion than short intervals of that kind. And if long intervals often prove fatal, it is only because through time men are accustomed to them, and they cease to give uneasiness. Jealousy and absence in love compose the *dolce peccante*[3] of the Italians, which they suppose so essential to all pleasure.

There is a fine observation of the elder Pliny, which illustrates the principle here insisted on.

> It is very remarkable, says he, that the last works of celebrated artists, which they left imperfect, are always the most prized, such as the *Iris* of Aristides, the *Tyndarides* of Nicomachus, the *Medea* of Timomachus, and the *Venus* of Apelles. These are valued even above their finished productions. The broken lineaments of the piece, and the half-formed idea of the painter, are carefully studied; and our very grief for that curious hand, which had been stopped by death, is an additional increase to our pleasure. [*Nat. hist.* xxxv. 40]

These instances (and many more might be collected) are sufficient to afford us some insight into the analogy of nature, and to show us that the pleasure which poets, orators, and musicians give us by exciting grief, sorrow, indignation, compassion, is not so extraordinary or paradoxical as it may at first sight appear. The force of imagination, the energy of expression, the power of numbers, the charms of imitation—all these are naturally, of themselves, delightful to the mind. And when the object presented lays also hold of some affection, the pleasure still rises upon us by the conversion of this subordinate movement into that which is predominant. The passion, though perhaps naturally, and when excited by the simple appearance of a real object, it may be painful, yet is so smoothed and softened and mollified when raised by the finer arts that it affords the highest entertainment.

To confirm this reasoning, we may observe that if the movements of the imagination be not predominant above those of the passion, a contrary effect follows, and the former, being now subordinate, is converted into the latter, and still farther increases the pain and affliction of the sufferer.

Who could ever think of it as a good expedient for comforting an afflicted parent to exaggerate, with all the force of elocution, the irreparable loss which he has met with by the death of a favorite child? The more power of imagination and expression you here employ, the more you increase his despair and affliction.

The shame, confusion, and terror of Verres, no doubt, rose in proportion to the noble eloquence

3. **dolce peccante:** sweet sinning.

and vehemence of Cicero; so also did his pain and uneasiness. These former passions were too strong for the pleasure arising from the beauties of elocution, and operated, though from the same principle, yet in a contrary manner, to the sympathy, compassion, and indignation of the audience.

Lord Clarendon, when he approaches towards the catastrophe of the royal party, supposes that his narration must then become infinitely disagreeable; and he hurries over the king's death without giving us one circumstance of it.[4] He considers it as too horrid a scene to be contemplated with any satisfaction, or even without the utmost pain and aversion. He himself, as well as the readers of that age, were too deeply concerned in the events, and felt a pain from subjects which a historian and a reader of another age would regard as the most pathetic and most interesting, and by consequence, the most agreeable.

An action represented in tragedy may be too bloody and atrocious. It may excite such movements of horror as will not soften into pleasure, and the greatest energy of expression bestowed on descriptions of that nature serves only to augment our uneasiness. Such is that action represented in the *Ambitious Stepmother*,[5] where a venerable old man, raised to the height of fury and despair, rushes against a pillar, and striking his head upon it, besmears it all over with mingled brains and gore. The English theater abounds too much with such shocking images.

Even the common sentiments of compassion require to be softened by some agreeable affection in order to give a thorough satisfaction to the audience. The mere suffering of plaintive virtue under the triumphant tyranny and oppression of vice forms a disagreeable spectacle, and is carefully avoided by all masters of the drama. In order to dismiss the audience with entire satisfaction and contentment, the virtue must either convert itself into a noble, courageous despair, or the vice receive its proper punishment.

Most painters appear in this light to have been very unhappy in their subjects. As they wrought much for churches and convents, they have chiefly represented such horrible subjects as crucifixions and martyrdoms, where nothing appears but tortures, wounds, executions, and passive suffering, without any action or affection. When they turned their pencil from this ghastly mythology, they had commonly recourse to Ovid, whose fictions, though passionate and agreeable, are scarcely natural or probable enough for painting.

The same inversion of that principle which is here insisted on displays itself in common life, as in the effects of oratory and poetry. Raise so the subordinate passion that it becomes the predominant, it swallows up that affection which it before nourished and increased. Too much jealousy extinguishes love. Too much difficulty renders us indifferent. Too much sickness and infirmity disgusts a selfish and unkind parent.

What so disagreeable as the dismal, gloomy, disastrous stories with which melancholy people entertain their companions? The uneasy passion being there raised alone, unaccompanied with any spirit, genius, or eloquence, conveys a pure uneasiness, and is attended with nothing that can soften it into pleasure or satisfaction.

(1757)

OF THE STANDARD OF TASTE

The great variety of taste, as well as of opinion, which prevails in the world is too obvious not to have fallen under everyone's observation. Men of the most confined knowledge are able to remark a difference of taste in the narrow circle of their acquaintance, even where the persons have been educated under the same government and have early imbibed the same prejudices. But those who can enlarge their view to contemplate distant nations and remote ages are still more surprised at the great inconsistence and contrariety. We are apt to call barbarous whatever departs widely from our own taste and apprehension, but soon find the epithet of reproach retorted on us. And the highest arrogance and self-conceit is at last startled on observing an equal assurance on all sides, and scruples amidst such a contest of sentiment to pronounce positively in its own favor.

As this variety of taste is obvious to the most careless inquirer, so will it be found, on examination, to be still greater in reality than in appear-

4. A reference to Clarendon's great *History of the Rebellion and Civil Wars in England Begun in the Year 1641* (1702–1704), Book XI. 5. *Ambitious Stepmother:* the play by Nicholas Rowe.

ance. The sentiments of men often differ with regard to beauty and deformity of all kinds, even while their general discourse is the same. There are certain terms in every language which import blame, and others praise; and all men who use the same tongue must agree in their application of them. Every voice is united in applauding elegance, propriety, simplicity, spirit in writing; and in blaming fustian, affectation, coldness, and a false brilliancy. But when critics come to particulars, this seeming unanimity vanishes, and it is found that they had affixed a very different meaning to their expressions. In all matters of opinion and science, the case is opposite. The difference among men is there oftener found to lie in generals than in particulars, and to be less in reality than in appearance. An explanation of the terms commonly ends the controversy, and the disputants are surprised to find that they had been quarreling, while at bottom they agreed in their judgment.

Those who found morality on sentiment more than on reason are inclined to comprehend ethics under the former observation, and to maintain that in all questions which regard conduct and manners the difference among men is really greater than at first sight it appears. It is indeed obvious that writers of all nations and all ages concur in applauding justice, humanity, magnanimity, prudence, veracity; and in blaming the opposite qualities. Even poets and other authors whose compositions are chiefly calculated to please the imagination are yet found, from Homer down to Fénelon, to inculcate the same moral precepts, and to bestow their applause and blame on the same virtues and vices. This great unanimity is usually ascribed to the influence of plain reason, which in all these cases maintains similar sentiments in all men and prevents those controversies to which the abstract sciences are so much exposed. So far as the unanimity is real, this account may be admitted as satisfactory. But we must also allow that some part of the seeming harmony in morals may be accounted for from the very nature of language. The word *Virtue*, with its equivalent in every tongue, implies praise; as that of *vice* does blame. And no one, without the most obvious and grossest impropriety, could affix reproach to a term which in general acceptation is understood in a good sense, or bestow applause where the idiom requires disapprobation. Homer's general precepts, where he delivers any such, will never be controverted; but it is obvious that when he draws particular pictures of manners and represents heroism in Achilles and prudence in Ulysses, he intermixes a much greater degree of ferocity in the former and of cunning and fraud in the latter than Fénelon would admit of. The sage Ulysses in the Greek poet seems to delight in lies and fictions and often employs them without any necessity or even advantage. But his more scrupulous son, in the French epic writer, exposes himself to the most imminent perils rather than depart from the most exact line of truth and veracity.

The admirers and followers of the *Alcoran* insist on the excellent moral precepts interspersed throughout that wild and absurd performance. But it is to be supposed that the Arabic words which correspond to the English *equity, justice, temperance, meekness, charity,* were such as, from the constant use of that tongue, must always be taken in a good sense; and it would have argued the greatest ignorance, not of morals, but of language, to have mentioned them with any epithets besides those of applause and approbation. But would we know whether the pretended prophet had really attained a just sentiment of morals? Let us attend to his narration, and we shall soon find that he bestows praise on such instances of treachery, inhumanity, cruelty, revenge, bigotry as are utterly incompatible with civilized society. No steady rule of right seems there to be attended to, and every action is blamed or praised so far only as it is beneficial or hurtful to the true believers.

The merit of delivering true general precepts in ethics is indeed very small. Whoever recommends any moral virtues really does no more than is implied in the terms themselves. That people who invented the word *charity* and used it in a good sense inculcated more clearly and much more efficaciously the precept "be charitable" than any pretended legislator or prophet who should insert such a maxim in his writings. Of all expressions, those which together with their other meaning imply a degree either of blame or approbation are the least liable to be perverted or mistaken.

It is natural for us to seek a "standard of taste," a rule by which the various sentiments of men may be reconciled, at least a decision afforded, confirming one sentiment and condemning another.

There is a species of philosophy which cuts off all hopes of success in such an attempt and represents the impossibility of ever attaining any standard of taste. The difference, it is said, is very wide between judgment and sentiment. All sentiment is right, because sentiment has a reference to nothing beyond itself, and is always real wherever a man is conscious of it. But all determinations of the understanding are not right, because they have a reference to something beyond themselves, to wit, real matter of fact, and are not always conformable to that standard. Among a thousand different opinions which different men may entertain of the same subject, there is one, and but one, that is just and true; and the only difficulty is to fix and ascertain it. On the contrary, a thousand different sentiments excited by the same object are all right, because no sentiment represents what is really in the object. It only marks a certain conformity or relation between the object and the organs or faculties of the mind; and if that conformity did not really exist, the sentiment could never possibly have being. Beauty is no quality in things themselves. It exists merely in the mind which contemplates them, and each mind perceives a different beauty. One person may even perceive deformity where another is sensible of beauty, and every individual ought to acquiesce in his own sentiment without pretending to regulate those of others. To seek the real beauty or real deformity is as fruitless an inquiry as to pretend to ascertain the real sweet or real bitter. According to the disposition of the organs, the same object may be both sweet and bitter, and the proverb has justly determined it to be fruitless to dispute concerning tastes. It is very natural, and even quite necessary, to extend this axiom to mental as well as bodily taste, and thus common sense, which is so often at variance with philosophy, especially with the sceptical kind, is found, in one instance at least, to agree in pronouncing the same decision.

But though this axiom by passing into a proverb seems to have attained the sanction of common sense, there is certainly a species of common sense which opposes it, at least serves to modify and restrain it. Whoever would assert an equality of genius and elegance between Ogilby and Milton, or Bunyan and Addison, would be thought to defend no less an extravagance than if he had maintained a molehill to be as high as Teneriffe, or a pond as extensive as the ocean. Though there may be found persons who give the preference to the former authors, no one pays attention to such a taste, and we pronounce, without scruple, the sentiment of these pretended critics to be absurd and ridiculous. The principle of the natural equality of tastes is then totally forgot, and while we admit it on some occasions, where the objects seem near an equality, it appears an extravagant paradox, or rather a palpable absurdity, where objects so disporportioned are compared together.

It is evident that none of the rules of composition are fixed by reasonings *a priori*, or can be esteemed abstract conclusions of the understanding, from comparing those habitudes and relations of ideas which are eternal and immutable. Their foundation is the same with that of all the practical sciences, experience; nor are they anything but general observations concerning what has been universally found to please in all countries and in all ages. Many of the beauties of poetry, and even of eloquence, are founded on falsehood and fiction, on hyperboles, metaphors, and an abuse or perversion of terms from their natural meaning. To check the sallies of the imagination and to reduce every expression to geometrical truth and exactness would be the most contrary to the laws of criticism, because it would produce a work which by universal experience has been found the most insipid and disagreeable. But though poetry can never submit to exact truth, it must be confined by rules of art, discovered to the author either by genius or observation. If some negligent or irregular writers have pleased, they have not pleased by their transgressions of rule or order, but in spite of these transgressions. They have possessed other beauties, which were conformable to just criticism, and the force of these beauties has been able to overpower censure, and give the mind a satisfaction superior to the disgust arising from the blemishes. Ariosto pleases, but not by his monstrous and improbable fictions, by his bizarre mixture of the serious and comic styles, by the want of coherence in his stories, or by the continual interruptions of his narration. He charms by the force and clearness of his expression, by the readiness and variety of his inventions, and by his natural pictures of the passions, especially those of the gay and amorous kind. And however his faults may diminish our satisfaction, they are not able entirely to destroy it.

Did our pleasure really arise from those parts of his poem which we denominate faults, this would be no objection to criticism in general. It would only be an objection to those particular rules of criticism which would establish such circumstances to be faults and would represent them as universally blameable. If they are found to please, they cannot be faults, let the pleasure which they produce be ever so unexpected and unaccountable.

But though all the general rules of art are founded only on experience and on the observation of the common sentiments of human nature, we must not imagine that on every occasion the feelings of men will be conformable to these rules. Those finer emotions of the mind are of a very tender and delicate nature, and require the concurrence of many favorable circumstances to make them play with facility and exactness according to their general and established principles. The least exterior hindrance to such small springs or the least internal disorder disturbs their motion and confounds the operation of the whole machine. When we would make an experiment of this nature and would try the force of any beauty or deformity, we must choose with care a proper time and place and bring the fancy to a suitable situation and disposition. A perfect serenity of mind, a recollection of thought, a due attention to the object, if any of these circumstances be wanting, our experiment will be fallacious, and we shall be unable to judge of the catholic and universal beauty. The relation which nature has placed between the form and the sentiment will at least be more obscure, and it will require greater accuracy to trace and discern it. We shall be able to ascertain its influence not so much from the operation of each particular beauty as from the durable admiration which attends those works that have survived all the caprices of mode and fashion, all the mistakes of ignorance and envy.

The same Homer who pleased at Athens and Rome two thousand years ago is still admired at Paris and at London. All the changes of climate, government, religion, and language have not been able to obscure his glory. Authority or prejudice may give a temporary vogue to a bad poet or orator, but his reputation will never be durable or general. When his compositions are examined by posterity or by foreigners, the enchantment is dissipated, and his faults appear in their true colors. On the contrary, a real genius, the longer his works endure, and the more wide they are spread, the more sincere is the admiration which he meets with. Envy and jealousy have too much place in a narrow circle, and even familiar acquaintance with his person may diminish the applause due to his performances. But when these obstructions are removed, the beauties which are naturally fitted to excite agreeable sentiments immediately display their energy; and while the world endures, they maintain their authority over the minds of men.

It appears, then, that amidst all the variety and caprice of taste there are certain general principles of approbation or blame whose influence a careful eye may trace in all operations of the mind. Some particular forms or qualities from the original structure of the internal fabric are calculated to please, and others to displease, and if they fail of their effect in any particular instance, it is from some apparent defect or imperfection in the organ. A man in a fever would not insist on his palate as able to decide concerning flavors; nor would one affected with the jaundice pretend to give a verdict with regard to colors. In each creature there is a sound and a defective state, and the former alone can be supposed to afford us a true standard of taste and sentiment. If in the sound state of the organ there be an entire or a considerable uniformity of sentiment among men, we may thence derive an idea of the perfect beauty, in like manner as the appearance of objects in daylight to the eye of a man in health is denominated their true and real color, even while color is allowed to be merely a phantasm of the senses.

Many and frequent are the defects in the internal organs which prevent or weaken the influence of those general principles on which depends our sentiment of beauty or deformity. Though some objects by the structure of the mind be naturally calculated to give pleasure, it is not to be expected that in every individual the pleasure will be equally felt. Particular incidents and situations occur which either throw a false light on the objects or hinder the true from conveying to the imagination the proper sentiment and perception.

One obvious cause why many feel not the proper sentiment of beauty is the want of that delicacy of imagination which is requisite to convey a sensibility of those finer emotions. This delicacy everyone pretends to. Everyone talks of it, and would reduce every kind of taste or sentiment to its standard. But as our intention in this essay is to mingle some light of the understanding with the feelings of sentiment, it will be proper to give a more accurate definition of delicacy than has hitherto been attempted. And not to draw our philosophy from too profound a source, we shall have recourse to a noted story in *Don Quixote*.

It is with good reason, says Sancho to the squire with the great nose, that I pretend to have a judgment in wine: this is a quality hereditary in our family. Two of my kinsmen were once called to give their opinion of a hogshead which was supposed to be excellent, being old and of a good vintage. One of them tastes it, considers it, and after mature reflection pronounces the wine to be good, were it not for a small taste of leather which he perceived in it. The other, after using the same precautions, gives also his verdict in favor of the wine, but with the reserve of a taste of iron which he could easily distinguish. You cannot imagine how much they were both ridiculed for their judgment. But who laughed in the end? On emptying the hogshead, there was found at the bottom an old key with a leathern thong tied to it.

The great resemblance between mental and bodily taste will easily teach us to apply this story. Though it be certain that beauty and deformity, more than sweet and bitter, are not qualities in objects, but belong entirely to the sentiment, internal or external, it must be allowed that there are certain qualities in objects which are fitted by nature to produce those particular feelings. Now as these qualities may be found in a small degree, or may be mixed and confounded with each other, it often happens that the taste is not affected with such minute qualities, or is not able to distinguish all the particular flavors amidst the disorder in which they are presented. Where the organs are so fine as to allow nothing to escape them, and at the same time so exact as to perceive every ingredient in the composition, this we call delicacy of taste, whether we employ these terms in the literal or metaphorical sense. Here then the general rules of beauty are of use, being drawn from established models and from the observation of what pleases or displeases when presented singly and in a high degree. And if the same qualities, in a continued composition and in a smaller degree, affect not the organs with a sensible delight or uneasiness, we exclude the person from all pretensions to this delicacy. To produce these general rules or avowed patterns of composition is like finding the key with the leathern thong, which justified the verdict of Sancho's kinsmen and confounded those pretended judges who had condemned them. Though the hogshead had never been emptied, the taste of the one was still equally delicate, and that of the other equally dull and languid. But it would have been more difficult to have proved the superiority of the former, to the conviction of every bystander. In like manner, though the beauties of writing had never been methodized or reduced to general principles, though no excellent models had ever been acknowledged, the different degrees of taste would still have subsisted, and the judgment of one man been preferable to that of another; but it would not have been so easy to silence the bad critic, who might always insist upon his particular sentiment and refuse to submit to his antagonist. But when we show him an avowed principle of art, when we illustrate this principle by examples whose operation, from his own particular taste, he acknowledges to be conformable to the principle, when we prove that the same principle may be applied to the present case, where he did not perceive or feel its influence, he must conclude, upon the whole, that the fault lies in himself, and that he wants the delicacy which is requisite to make him sensible of every beauty and every blemish, in any composition or discourse.

It is acknowledged to be the perfection of every sense or faculty to perceive with exactness its most minute objects and allow nothing to escape its notice and observation. The smaller the objects are which become sensible to the eye, the finer is that organ, and the more elaborate its make and composition. A good palate is not tried by strong flavors, but by a mixture of small ingredients, where we are still sensible of each part, notwithstanding its minuteness and its confusion with the rest. In like manner, a quick and acute perception of beauty and deformity must be the perfection of our mental taste, nor can a man be satisfied with himself while he suspects that any excellence or blemish in a discourse has passed him unobserved. In this case, the perfection of the man and the perfection of the sense or feeling are found to be united. A very delicate palate on many occasions may be a great inconvenience both to a man himself and to his friends, but a delicate taste of wit or beauty must always be a desirable quality, because it is the source of all the finest and most innocent enjoyments of which human nature is susceptible. In this decision the sentiments of all mankind are agreed. Wherever you can ascertain a delicacy of taste, it is sure to meet with approbation, and the best way of ascertaining it is to appeal to those models and principles which have been established by the uniform consent and experience of nations and ages.

But though there be naturally a wide difference in point of delicacy between one person and another, nothing tends further to increase and improve this talent than practice in a particular art, and the frequent survey or contemplation of a particular species of beauty. When objects of any kind are first presented to the eye or imagination, the sentiment which attends them is obscure and confused, and the mind is, in a great measure, incapable of pronouncing concerning their merits or defects. The taste cannot perceive the several excellencies of the performance, much less distinguish the particular character of each excellency and ascertain its quality and degree. If it pronounce the whole in general to be beautiful or deformed, it is the utmost that can be expected, and even this judgment a person so unpracticed will be apt to deliver with great hesitation and reserve. But allow him to acquire experience in those objects, his feeling becomes more exact and nice. He not only perceives the beauties and defects of each part but marks the distinguishing species of each quality and assigns it suitable praise or blame. A clear and distinct sentiment attends him through the whole survey of the objects, and he discerns that very degree and kind of approbation or displeasure which each part is naturally fitted to produce. The mist dissipates which seemed formerly to hang over the object. The organ acquires greater perfection in its operations and can pronounce, without danger of mistake, concerning the merits of every performance. In a word, the same address and dexterity which practice gives to the execution of any work is also acquired by the same means, in the judging of it.

So advantageous is practice to the discernment of beauty that before we can give judgment on any work of importance it will even be requisite that that very individual performance be more than once perused by us and be surveyed in different lights with attention and deliberation. There is a flutter or hurry of thought which attends the first perusal of any piece and which confounds the genuine sentiment of beauty. The relation of the parts is not discerned. The true characters of style are little distinguished. The several perfections and defects seem wrapped up in a species of confusion, and present themselves indistinctly to the imagination. Not to mention that there is a species of beauty which, as it is florid and superficial, pleases at first, but being found incompatible with a just expression either of reason or passion, soon palls upon the taste and is then rejected with disdain, at least rated at a much lower value.

It is impossible to continue in the practice of contemplating any order of beauty without being frequently obliged to form comparisons between the several species and degrees of excellence, and estimating their proportion to each other. A man who has had no opportunity of comparing the different kinds of beauty is indeed totally unqualified to pronounce an opinion with regard to any object presented to him. By comparison alone we fix the epithets of praise or blame and learn how to assign the due degree of each. The coarsest daubing contains a certain luster of colors and exactness of imitation, which are so far beauties, and would affect the mind of a peasant or Indian with the highest admiration. The most vulgar ballads are not entirely destitute of harmony or nature, and none but a person familiarized to superior beauties would pronounce their numbers harsh, or narration uninteresting. A great inferiority of beauty gives pain to a person conversant in the highest excellence of the kind, and is for that reason pronounced a deformity, as the most finished object with which we are acquainted is naturally supposed to have reached the pinnacle of perfection and to be entitled to the highest applause. One accustomed to see and examine and weigh the several performances admired in different ages and nations can alone rate the merits of a work exhibited to his view and assign its proper rank among the productions of genius.

But to enable a critic the more fully to execute this undertaking, he must preserve his mind free from all prejudice and allow nothing to enter into his consideration but the very object which is submitted to his examination. We may observe that every work of art, in order to produce its due effect on the mind, must be surveyed in a certain point of view, and cannot be fully relished by persons whose situation, real or imaginary, is not conformable to that which is required by the performance. An orator addresses himself to a particular audience, and must have a regard to their particular genius, interests, opinions, passions, and prejudices; otherwise he hopes in vain to govern their resolutions and inflame their affections. Should they even have entertained some prepossessions against him, however unreasonable, he must not overlook this disadvantage but, before he enters upon the subject, must endeavor to conciliate their affection and acquire their good graces. A critic of a different age or nation who should peruse this discourse must have all these circumstances in his eye and must place himself in the same situation as the audience, in order to form a true judgment of the oration. In like manner, when any work is addressed to the public, though I should have a friendship or enmity with the author, I must depart from this situation, and considering myself as a man in general, forget, if possible, my individual being and my peculiar circumstances. A person influenced by prejudice complies not with this condition, but obstinately maintains his natural position without placing himself in that point of view which the performance supposes. If the work be addressed to persons of a different age or nation, he makes no allowance for their peculiar views and prejudices, but full of the manners of his own age and country, rashly condemns what seemed admirable in the eyes of those for whom alone the discourse was calculated. If the work be executed for the public, he never sufficiently enlarges his comprehension or forgets his interest as a friend or enemy, as a rival or commentator. By this means, his sentiments are perverted; nor have the same beauties and blemishes the same influence upon him as if he had imposed a proper violence on his imagination and had forgotten himself for a moment. So far his taste evidently departs from the true standard, and of consequence loses all credit and authority.

It is well known that in all questions submitted to the understanding, prejudice is destructive of sound judgment and perverts all operations of the intellectual faculties. It is no less contrary to good taste, nor has it less influence to corrupt our sentiment of beauty. It belongs to good sense to check its influence in both cases, and in this respect, as well as in many others, reason, if not an essential part of taste, is at least requisite to the operations of this latter faculty. In all the nobler productions of genius there is a mutual relation and correspondence of parts, nor can either the beauties or blemishes be perceived by him whose thought is not capacious enough to comprehend all those parts and compare them with each other in order to perceive the consistence and uniformity of the whole. Every work of art has also a certain end or purpose for which it is calculated, and is to be deemed more or less perfect as it is more or less fitted to attain this end. The object of eloquence is to persuade, of history to instruct, of poetry to please by means of the passions and the imagination. These ends we must carry constantly in our view when we peruse any performance, and we must be able to judge how far the means employed are adapted to their respective purposes. Besides, every kind of composition, even the most poetical, is nothing but a chain of propositions and reasonings—not always, indeed, the justest and most exact, but still plausible and specious, however disguised by the coloring of the imagination. The persons introduced in tragedy and epic poetry must be represented as reasoning and thinking and concluding and acting suitably to their character and circumstances; and without judgment, as well as taste and invention, a poet can never hope to succeed in so delicate an undertaking. Not to mention that the same excellence of faculties which contributes to the improvement of reason, the same clearness of conception, the same exactness of distinction, the same vivacity of apprehension, are essential to the operations of true taste, and are its infallible concomitants. It seldom or never happens that a man of sense who has experience in any art cannot judge of its beauty; and it is no less rare to meet with a man who has a just taste without a sound understanding.

Thus, though the principles of taste be universal, and nearly, if not entirely, the same in all men, yet few are qualified to give judgment on any work of art, or establish their own sentiment as the standard of beauty. The organs of internal sensation are seldom so perfect as to allow the general principles their full play, and produce a feeling correspondent to those principles. They either labor under some defect, or are vitiated by some disorder, and by that means excite a sentiment which may be pronounced erroneous. When the critic has no delicacy, he judges without any distinction, and is only affected by the grosser and more palpable qualities of the object; the finer touches pass unnoticed and disregarded. Where he is not aided by practice, his verdict is attended with confusion and hesitation. Where no comparison has been employed, the most frivolous beauties, such as rather merit the name of defects, are the object of his admiration. Where he lies under the influence of prejudice, all his natural sentiments are perverted. Where good sense is wanting, he is not qualified to discern the beauties of design and reasoning, which are the highest and most excellent. Under some or other of these imperfections, the generality of men labor, and hence a true judge in the finer arts is observed, even during the most polished ages, to be so rare a character. Strong sense, united to delicate sentiment, improved by practice, perfected by comparison, and cleared of all prejudice, can alone entitle critics to this valuable character; and the joint verdict of such, wherever they are to be found, is the true standard of taste and beauty.

But where are such critics to be found? By what marks are they to be known? How distinguish them from pretenders? These questions are embarrassing, and seem to throw us back into the same uncertainty from which, during the course of this essay, we have endeavored to extricate ourselves.

But if we consider the matter aright, these are questions of fact, not of sentiment. Whether any particular person be endowed with good sense and a delicate imagination, free from prejudice, may often be the subject of dispute, and be liable to great discussion and inquiry; but that such a character is valuable and estimable will be agreed in by all mankind. Where these doubts occur, men can do no more than in other disputable questions which are submitted to the understanding: They must produce the best arguments that their invention suggests to them; they must acknowledge a true and decisive standard to exist somewhere, to wit, real existence and matter of fact; and they must have indulgence to such as differ from them in their appeals to this standard. It is sufficient for our present purpose if we have proved that the taste of all individuals is not upon an equal footing and that some men in general, however difficult to be particularly pitched upon, will be acknowledged by universal sentiment to have a preference above others.

But in reality the difficulty of finding, even in particulars, the standard of taste is not so great as it is represented. Though in speculation we may readily avow a certain criterion in science and deny it in sentiment, the matter is found in practice to be much more hard to ascertain in the former case than in the latter. Theories of abstract philosophy, systems of profound theology, have prevailed during one age. In a successive period these have been universally exploded; their absurdity has been detected; other theories and systems have supplied their place, which again gave place to their successors. And nothing has been experienced more liable to the revolutions of chance and fashion than these pretended decisions of science. The case is not the same with the beauties of eloquence and poetry. Just expressions of passion and nature are sure, after a little time, to gain public applause, which they maintain for ever. Aristotle and Plato and Epicurus and Descartes may successively yield to each other, but Terence and Virgil maintain a universal, undisputed empire over the minds of men. The abstract philosophy of Cicero has lost its credit; the vehemence of his oratory is still the object of our admiration.

Though men of delicate taste be rare, they are easily to be distinguished in society by the soundness of their understanding and the superiority of their faculties above the rest of mankind. The ascendant which they acquire gives a prevalence to that lively approbation with which they receive any productions of genius, and renders it generally predominant. Many men when left to themselves have but a faint and dubious perception of beauty who yet are capable of relishing any fine stroke which is pointed out to them. Every convert to the admiration of the real poet or orator is the cause of some new conversion. And though prejudices may prevail for a time, they never unite in celebrating any rival to the true genius, but yield at last to the force of nature and just sentiment. Thus, though a civilized nation may easily be mistaken in the choice of their admired philosopher, they never have been found long to err in their affection for a favorite epic or tragic author.

But notwithstanding all our endeavors to fix a standard of taste and reconcile the discordant apprehensions of men, there still remain two sources of variation which are not sufficient indeed to confound all the boundaries of beauty and deformity, but will often serve to produce a difference in the degrees of our approbation or blame. The one is the different humors of particular men, the other, the particular manners and opinions of our age and country. The general principles of taste are uniform in human nature; where men vary in their judgments, some defect or perversion in the faculties may commonly be remarked, proceeding either from prejudice, from want of practice, or want of delicacy, and there is just reason for approving one taste and condemning another. But where there is such a diversity in the internal frame or external situation as is entirely blameless on both sides, and leaves no room to give one the preference above the other, in that case a certain degree of diversity in judgment is unavoidable, and we seek in vain for a standard by which we can reconcile the contrary sentiments.

A young man whose passions are warm will be more sensibly touched with amorous and tender images than a man more advanced in years who takes pleasure in wise, philosophical reflections concerning the conduct of life and moderation of the passions. At twenty Ovid may be the favorite author, Horace at forty, and perhaps Tacitus at fifty. Vainly would we, in such cases, endeavor to enter into the sentiments of others, and divest ourselves of those propensities which are natural to us. We choose our favorite author as we do our friend, from a conformity of humor and disposition. Mirth or passion, sentiment or reflection, whichever of these most predominates in our temper, it gives us a peculiar sympathy with the writer who resembles us.

One person is more pleased with the sublime; another with the tender; a third with raillery. One has a strong sensibility to blemishes, and is extremely studious of correctness; another has a more lively feeling of beauties, and pardons twenty absurdities and defects for one elevated or pathetic stroke. The ear of this man is entirely turned towards conciseness and energy; that man is delighted with a copious, rich, and harmonious expression. Simplicity is affected by one; ornament by another. Comedy, tragedy, satire, odes, have each its partisans, who prefer that particular species of writing to all others. It is plainly an error in a critic to confine his approbation to one species or style of writing and condemn all the rest. But it is almost impossible not to feel a predilection for that which suits our particular turn and disposition. Such preferences are innocent and unavoidable and can never reasonably be the object of dispute, because there is no standard by which they can be decided.

For a like reason we are more pleased, in the course of our reading, with pictures and characters that resemble objects which are found in our own age or country than with those which describe a different set of customs. It is not without some effort that we reconcile ourselves to the simplicity of ancient manners and behold princesses carrying water from the spring, and kings and heroes dressing their own victuals. We may allow in general that the representation of such manners is no fault in the author nor deformity in the piece; but we are not so sensibly touched with them. For this reason, comedy is not easily transferred from one age or nation to another. A Frenchman or Englishman is not pleased with the *Andria* of Terence, or *Clitia* of Machiavelli, where the fine lady upon whom all the play turns never once appears to the spectators, but is always kept behind the scenes, suitably to the reserved humor of the ancient Greeks and modern Italians. A man of learning and reflection can make allowance for these peculiarities of manners, but a common audience can never divest themselves so far of their usual ideas and sentiments as to relish pictures which nowise resemble them.

But here there occurs a reflection which may, perhaps, be useful in examining the celebrated controversy concerning ancient and modern learning, where we often find the one side excusing any seeming absurdity in the ancients from the manners of the age, and the other refusing to admit this excuse, or at least admitting it only as an apology for the author, not for the performance. In my opinion, the proper boundaries in this subject have seldom been fixed between the contending parties. Where any innocent peculiarities of manners are represented, such as those above mentioned, they ought certainly to be admitted, and a man who is shocked with them gives an evident proof of false delicacy and refinement. The poet's "monument more durable than brass" must fall to the ground like common brick or clay, were men to make no allowance for the continual revolutions of manners and customs, and would admit of nothing but what was suitable to the prevailing fashion. Must we throw aside the pictures of our ancestors because of their ruffs and farthingales? But where the ideas of morality and decency alter from one age to another, and where vicious manners are described without being marked with the proper characters of blame and disapprobation, this must be allowed to disfigure the poem, and to be a real deformity. I cannot, nor is it proper I should, enter into such sentiments; and however I may excuse the poet on account of the manners of his age, I never can relish the composition. The want of humanity and of decency, so conspicuous in the characters drawn by several of the ancient poets, even sometimes by Homer and the Greek tragedians, diminishes considerably the merit of their noble performances and gives modern authors an advantage over them. We are not interested in the fortunes and sentiments of such rough heroes; we are displeased to find the limits of vice and virtue so much confounded; and whatever indulgence we may give to the writer on account of his prejudices, we cannot prevail on ourselves to enter into his sentiments, or bear an affection to characters which we plainly discover to be blamable.

The case is not the same with moral principles as with speculative opinions of any kind. These are in continual flux and revolution. The son embraces a different system from the father. Nay, there scarcely is any man who can boast of great constancy and uniformity in this particular. Whatever speculative errors may be found in the polite writings of any age or country, they detract but little from the value of those compositions. There needs but a certain turn of thought or imagination to make us enter into all the opinions which then prevailed and relish the sentiments or conclusions derived from them. But a very violent effort is requisite to change our judgment of manners and excite sentiments of approbation or blame, love or hatred, different from those to which the mind from long custom has been familiarized. And where a man is confident of the rectitude of that moral standard by which he judges, he is justly jealous of it, and will not pervert the sentiments of his heart for a moment in complaisance to any writer whatsoever.

Of all speculative errors those which regard religion are the most excusable in compositions of genius; nor is it ever permitted to judge of the civility or wisdom of any people, or even of single persons, by the grossness or refinement of their theological principles. The same good sense that directs men in the ordinary occurrences of life is not hearkened to in religious matters, which are supposed to be placed altogether above the cognizance of human reason. On this account, all the absurdities of the pagan system of theology must be overlooked by every critic who would pretend to form a just notion of ancient poetry; and our posterity, in their turn, must have the same indulgence to their forefathers. No religious principles can ever be imputed as a fault to any poet while they remain merely principles and take not such strong possession of his heart as to lay him under the imputation of bigotry or superstition. Where that happens, they confound the sentiments of morality and alter the natural boundaries of vice and virtue. They are therefore eternal blemishes according to the principle above mentioned; nor are the prejudices and false opinions of the age sufficient to justify them.

It is essential to the Roman Catholic religion to inspire a violent hatred of every other worship and to represent all pagans, Mohammedans, and heretics as the objects of divine wrath and vengeance. Such sentiments, though they are in reality very blamable, are considered as virtues by the zealots of that communion and are represented in their tragedies and epic poems as a kind of divine heroism. This bigotry has disfigured two very fine tragedies of the French theater, *Polyeucte* and *Athalie*, where an intemperate zeal for particular modes of worship is set off with all the pomp imaginable, and forms the predominant character of the heroes. "What is this," says the sublime Joad to Josabet, finding her in discourse with Mathan, the priest of Baal, "Does the daughter of David speak to this traitor? Are you not afraid lest the earth should open and pour forth flames to devour you both? Or, lest these holy walls should fall and crush you together? What is his purpose? Why comes that enemy of God hither to poison the air which we breathe with his horrid presence?" Such sentiments are received with great applause on the theater of

Paris; but at London the spectators would be full as much pleased to hear Achilles tell Agamemnon that he was a dog in his forehead and a deer in his heart, or Jupiter threaten Juno with a sound drubbing if she will not be quiet.

Religious principles are also a blemish in any polite composition when they rise up to superstition and intrude themselves into every sentiment, however remote from any connection with religion. It is no excuse for the poet that the customs of his country had burdened life with so many religious ceremonies and observances that no part of it was exempt from that yoke. It must forever be ridiculous in Petrarch to compare his mistress, Laura, to Jesus Christ. Nor is it less ridiculous in that agreeable libertine, Boccaccio, very seriously to give thanks to God Almighty and the ladies, for their assistance in defending him against his enemies.

(1757)

Richard Hurd

1720-1808

◆

FROM

Letters on Chivalry and Romance

LETTER XII

The wonders of chivalry were still in the memory of men, were still existing, in some measure, in real life, when Chaucer undertook to expose the barbarous relaters of them.

This ridicule, we may suppose, hastened the fall both of chivalry and romance. At least from that time the spirit of both declined very fast, and at length fell in such discredit that when now Spenser arose, and with a genius singularly fitted to immortalize the land of faery, he met with every difficulty and disadvantage to obstruct his design.

The age would no longer bear the naked letter of these amusing stories, and the poet was so sensible of the misfortune that we find him apologizing for it on a hundred occasions. But apologies, in such circumstances, rarely do any good. Perhaps they only served to betray the weakness of the poet's cause, and to confirm the prejudices of his reader. However, he did more than this. He gave an air of mystery to his subject, and pretended that his stories of knights and giants were but the cover to abundance of profound wisdom.

In short, to keep off the eyes of the profane from prying too nearly into his subject, he threw about it the mist of allegory: he moralized his song, and the virtues and vices lay hid under his warriors and enchanters—a contrivance which he had learned indeed from his Italian masters, for Tasso had condescended to allegorize his own work, and the commentators of Ariosto had even converted the extravagances of the *Orlando Furioso* into moral lessons.

And this, it must be owned, was a sober attempt in comparison of some projects that were made about the same time to serve the cause of the old, and now expiring, romances. For it is to be observed, that the idolizers of these romances did by them what the votaries of Homer had done by him. As the times improved and would less bear his strange tales, they *moralized* what they could, and turned the rest into mysteries of natural science. And as this last contrivance was principally designed to cover the monstrous stories of the pagan gods, so it served the lovers of romance to palliate the no less monstrous stories of magic and enchantments. . . .

But to return to Spenser, who, as we have seen, had no better way to take in his distress than to hide his faery fancies under the mystic cover of moral allegory. The only favourable circumstance that attended him (and this no doubt encouraged, if it did not produce, his untimely project) was that he was somewhat befriended in these fictions, even when interpreted according to the letter, by the romantic spirit of his age, much countenanced, and for a time brought into fresh credit, by the romantic Elizabeth. Her inclination for the fancies of chivalry is well known, and obsequious wits and courtiers would not be wanting to feed and flatter it. In short, tilts and tournaments were in vogue: the *Arcadia,* and the *Faery Queen* were written.

With these helps the new spirit of chivalry made a shift to support itself for a time, when reason was but dawning, as we may say, and just about to gain the ascendant over the portentous spectres of the imagination. Its growing splendour, in the end, put them all to flight, and allowed them no quarter even amongst the poets. So that Milton, as fond as we have seen he was of the Gothic fictions, durst only admit them on the bye, and in the way of simile and illustration only.

And this, no doubt, was the main reason of his relinquishing his long-projected design of Prince Arthur, at last, for that of the *Paradise Lost,* where, instead of giants and magicians, he had angels and devils to supply him with the marvellous with greater probability. Yet, though he dropped the tales, he still kept to the allegories of Spenser. And even this liberty was thought too much, as appears from the censure passed on his Sin and Death by the severer critics.

Thus at length the magic of the old romances was perfectly dissolved. They began with reflecting an image indeed of the feudal manners, but an image magnified and distorted by unskilful designers. Common sense being offended with these perversions of truth and nature (still accounted the more monstrous, as the ancient manners they pretended to copy after were now disused, and of most men forgotten), the next step was to have recourse to *allegories.* Under this disguise they walked the world a while, the excellence of the moral and the ingenuity of the contrivance making some amends, and being accepted as a sort of apology for the absurdity of the literal story.

Under this form the tales of faery kept their ground, and even made their fortune at court, where they became, for two or three reigns, the ordinary entertainment of our princes. But reason, in the end (assisted, however, by party and religious prejudices), drove them off the scene, and would endure these lying wonders neither in their own proper shape nor as masked in figures.

Henceforth, the taste of wit and poetry took a new turn, and Fancy, that had wantoned it so long in the world of fiction, was now constrained, against her will, to ally herself with strict truth if she would gain admittance into reasonable company.

What we have gotten by this revolution, you will say, is a great deal of good sense. What we have lost is a world of fine fabling, the illusion of which is so grateful to the *charmed spirit* that, in spite of philosophy and fashion, *Faery* Spenser still ranks highest among the poets; I mean with all those who are either come of that house, or have any kindness for it.

Earth-born critics, my friend, may blaspheme,

"But all the GODS are ravish'd with delight
Of his celestial Song, and music's wondrous
might."

(1762)

William Duff
1732-1815

FROM

An Essay on Original Genius

AND ITS VARIOUS MODES OF EXERTION . . . PARTICULARLY IN POETRY

A glowing ardor of imagination is indeed (if we may be permitted the expression) the very soul of poetry. It is the principal source of inspiration, and the poet who is possessed of it, like the Delphian priestess, is animated with a kind of divine fury. The intenseness and vigour of his sensations produce the enthusiasm of imagination which, as it were, hurries the mind out of itself, and which is vented in warm and vehement description, exciting in every susceptible breast the same emotions that were felt by the author himself. It is this *enthusiasm* which gives life and strength to poetical representations, renders them striking imitations of nature, and thereby produces that inchanting delight which genuine poetry is calculated to inspire. Without this animating principle all poetical and rhetorical compositions are spiritless and languid, like those bodies that are drained of their vital juices: they are therefore read with indifference or insipidity; the harmony of the numbers, if harmonious, may tickle the ear, but being destitute of nerves, that is of passion and sentiment, they can never affect the heart.

Thus we have pointed out and illustrated the most distinguishing ingredients of *original genius* in poetry; we shall conclude the present section with inquiring into the first and most natural exertions of genius in this divine art.

We may venture then to lay it down as a position highly probable, that the first essays of original genius will be in *allegories, visions,* or the creation of ideal beings of one kind or another. There is no kind of invention in which there is fuller scope afforded to the exercise of imagination than in that of *allegory,* which has this advantage over most other fables, that in it the author is by no means restricted to such an exact probability as is required in those fables that instruct us by a representation of actions which, though not real, must always, however, be such as might have happened. Let it be observed, that we are here speaking of allegory in its utmost latitude. We are not ignorant that there is a species of it which, like the Epic fable, attempts to instruct by the invention of a series of incidents strictly probable. Such are the beautiful and striking allegories contained in different parts of the Sacred Writings. But there is another kind of allegorical fable in which there is very little regard shewn to probability. Its object also is instruction, though it does not endeavour to instruct by real or probable actions; but wrapt in a veil of exaggerated, yet delicate and apposite fiction, is studious at once to delight the imagination and to impress some important maxim upon the mind. Of this kind is the *Fairy Queen* of Spenser. As in this species of allegory we neither expect what is true nor what is like the truth, so we read such fabulous compositions partly for the sake of the morals they contain, but principally for the sake of gratifying that curiosity, so deeply implanted in the human mind, of becoming acquainted with new and marvellous events. We are in this case in a great measure upon our guard against the delusions of fancy, are highly pleased with the narrative, though we do not allow it to impose upon us so far as to obtain our credit. Yet such is the power of ingenious fiction over our minds that we are not only captivated and interested by a relation of surprising incidents, though very improbable, but, during the time of the relation at least, we forget that they are fictitious, and almost fancy them to be real. This deceit, however, lasts no longer than the perusal, in which we are too much agitated to reflect on the probability or improbability of the events related; but when that is over the inchantment vanishes in the cool moment of deliberation, and, being left at leisure to think and reason, we never admit as true what is not strictly probable.

As we are treating of allegorical fables, it may not be amiss to observe, with regard to the kind last mentioned in particular, that the liberties indulged to it, though prodigiously various and extensive, are not however without certain restrictions. Thus, though we do not require probability in the general contexture of the fable, justness of manners must be preserved in this, as well as in the other species of fabulous composition; the incidents must be suitable to the characters to which they are accommodated; those incidents must likewise clearly point out or imply the moral they are intended to illustrate; and they must, in order to captivate the imagination, be new and surprising at the same time that they are to be perfectly consistent with each other. It is evident, however, that these slight restraints prove no real impediment to the natural impulse and excursions of *Genius,* but that they serve rather to point and regulate its course. It is likewise equally evident that this last mentioned species of allegory presents a noble field for the display of a rich and luxuriant imagination, and that to excel in it requires the utmost fertility of invention, since every masterly composition of this kind must be the mere creation of the poet's fancy.

We observed likewise that *original genius* will naturally discover itself in *visions.* This is a species of fiction to succeed in which with applause requires as much poetic inspiration as any other species of composition whatever. That enthusiasm of imagination, which we considered as an essential characteristic of original genius, is indispensibly necessary to the enraptured Bard who would make his readers feel those impetuous transports of passion which occupy and actuate his own mind. He must himself be wrought up to a high pitch of extasy if he expects to throw us into it. Indeed, it is the peculiar felicity of an original author to feel in the most exquisite degree every emotion, and to see every scene he describes. By the vigorous effort of a creative imagination he calls shadowy substances and unreal objects into existence. They are present to his view, and glide, like spectres, in silent, sullen majesty before his astonished and intranced sight. In reading the description of such apparitions we partake of the author's emotion; the blood runs chill in our veins, and our hair stiffens with horror.

It would far exceed the bounds prescribed to this Essay to point out all the particular tracks which an original genius will strike out in the extensive sphere of imagination, as those paths are so various and devious. In the meantime we may observe, that as the hand of Nature hath stamped different minds with a different kind and degree of originality, giving each a particular bent to one certain object or pursuit, original authors will pursue the track marked out by Nature, by faithfully following which they can alone hope for immortality to their writings and reputation. Thus while one writer, obeying the impulse of his genius, displays the exuberance of his fancy in the beautiful and surprising fictions of allegory, another discovers the fertility and extent of his imagination, as well as the justness of his judgment, in the conduct of the epic or dramatic fable, in which he raises our admiration, our terror, or our pity, as occasion may require.

Upon the whole, we need not hesitate to affirm that original genius will probably discover itself either in allegories, visions, or in the creation of ideal figures of one kind or another. The probability that it will do so is derived from that innate tendency to fiction which distinguishes such a genius, and from the natural bias of fiction to run in this particular channel: for the imagination of a poet, whose genius is truly original, finding no objects in the visible creation sufficiently marvellous and new, or which can give full scope to the exercise of its powers, naturally bursts into the ideal world in quest of more surprising and wonderful scenes, which it explores with insatiable curiosity, as well as with exquisite pleasure; and depending in its excursion wholly on its own strength, its success in this province of fiction will be proportionable to the plastic power of which it is possessed. In case, however, the position just advanced should appear problematical to some, we shall confirm it by arguments drawn from experience, which will serve to shew that *original poetic genius* hath in fact exerted its powers in the manner above specified.*

* Longinus considers introducing visions into composition, and supporting them with propriety, as one of the boldest efforts either of rhetorical or poetic genius. He observes, that they contribute much to the grandeur, to the splendor, and to the efficacy of an oration in particular. . . . He observes [further] that there is a difference betwixt visions adapted to rhetoric, and such as are adapted to poetry; but that they both concur in producing a violent commotion of mind. [See Longinus, *On the Sublime,* Section 15. Editor's note.]

In proof of this assertion, we might adduce the whole system of heathen mythology. What are all the fabulous and allegorical relations of antiquity concerning the nature, generation, powers and offices of the pagan deities, but the inventions of men of genius? Poets and priests were unquestionably the original authors of all the theological systems of the Gentile world. A ray, ultimately derived from divine revelation, did sometimes indeed burst through the cloud of human error, but was soon obscured, if not smothered, by the superstitions of men; and oral tradition, that fallacious guide, was buried under a mass of absurdity and folly. Though the heathen theology must be confessed to be the disgrace and degradation of human reason, yet it must also be acknowledged to be a remarkable proof of the creative power of human imagination; and at the same time that we condemn it as a religious creed, we must admire it as a system of ingenious fiction. The Greek theology was of all other systems the most ingenious. What a strange but fanciful account may we collect from those ancient authors, Homer and Hesiod, of the nature and employment of the numerous deities which Greece acknowledged? We find the celestial divinities, Jupiter and Juno, Minerva and Venus, Mars and Apollo, sometimes quaffing nectar in their golden cups and reposing themselves in indolent tranquility, served by Hebe, and attended by Mercury, the swift-winged messenger of the Gods: at other times we see them mixing among the Trojan and Grecian hosts, taking part in mortal quarrels as partiality or favour dictated, inspiring the army whose cause they embraced with their counsel and aiding it by their power, driving on or stemming the tide of battle and alternately hastening and retarding the decrees of fate.

. . .

From this general and imperfect view of the Greek mythology, it is evident that original genius did in ancient Greece always discover itself in allegorical fiction, or in the creation of ideal figures of one kind or another; in inventing and adding new fables to the received systems of mythology, or in altering and improving those that had been already invented. The immense and multifarious system of the Greek theology was a work of many centuries, and rose gradually to that height in which it now appears. Some additions were daily made to it by the poets and men of lively imagination till that huge pile of superstition was completed which, in its ruins, exhibits so striking a monument of human ingenuity and folly. If, after what has been alleged, any one should question whether the fabulous theology now considered be an effect or indication of *original genius,* we would only desire him to suppose the mythology of Homer annihilated. What a blank would such annihilation make in the divine *Iliad*! Destitute of its celestial machinery, would it not be in a great measure an inanimate mass? It would at least lose much of that variety, dignity and grandeur which we admire in it at present, and much of that pleasing and surprising fiction which gives such exquisite delight to the imagination.

It would be easy to confirm the position we have laid down, that *original genius* always discovers itself in allegories, visions, or the invention of ideal characters, by examples drawn from the Eastern and the Egyptian mythology, which was so full of fable and hieroglyphical emblems; but we shall waive the consideration of these as superfluous after what hath been already urged, and conclude this part of our subject with observing that the Eastern manner of writing is, and hath ever been, characterised by a remarkable boldness of sentiment and expression, by the most rhetorical and poetical figures of speech; and that many of the compositions of the Eastern nations abound with allegories, visions and dreams, of which we have several admirable examples in the sacred writings.

SECTION V

That Original Poetic Genius will in general be displayed in its utmost Vigour in the Early and Uncultivated Periods of Society which are peculiarly favorable to it. And that It will seldom appear in a very high Degree in Cultivated Life.

Having pointed out the exertions of *original genius* in the different arts, and particularly in poetry, we shall now consider the period of society most favourable to the display of originality of genius in the last mentioned art; and this period we affirm to be the earliest and least cultivated.

To assert that this divine art, to an excellence in which the highest efforts of human genius are requisite, should attain its utmost perfection in the infancy of society, when mankind are only emerging from a state of ignorance and barbarity, will appear a paradox to some, though it is an unquestionable truth; and a closer attention will convince us that it is agreeable to reason as well as confirmed by experience.

While arts and sciences are in their first rude and imperfect state, there is great scope afforded for the exertions of Genius. Much is to be observed; much is to be discovered and invented. Imagination, however, in general exerts itself with more success in the arts than in the sciences, in the former of which its success is more rapid than in the latter. Active as this faculty is in its operations, its discoveries in science are for the most part attained by slow and gradual steps. They are the effect of long and severe investigation, and receive their highest improvement in the most civilized state of society. On the other hand the efforts of imagination, in poetry at least, are impetuous, and attain their utmost perfection at once, even in the rudest form of social life. This art does not require long and sedulous application to confer originality and excellence on its productions: its earliest unlaboured essays generally possess both in the highest degree. The reasons why they do so will be assigned immediately. In the meantime we may observe, as a circumstance deserving our attention, that this is by no means the case with the other arts, but is peculiar to poetry alone. Painting, eloquence, music, and architecture attain their highest improvement by the repeated efforts of ingenious artists, as well as the sciences by the reiterated researches and experiments of philosophers, though, as we have already observed, imagination operates with greater rapidity in the improvement of the former than in that of the latter; but still it operates gradually in the improvement of both. There never arose an eminent painter, orator, musician, architect, or philosopher in any age completely self-taught, without being indebted to his predecessors in the art or science he professed. Should it be objected that the art of painting was revived, and brought to the utmost perfection to which it ever arrived in modern times, in one single age, that of Leo the Tenth,[1] we answer that the Italian masters, though they had none of the ancient paintings to serve them as models, had however some admirable remains both of the Grecian and Roman statuary, which, by heightening their ideas of excellence in its sister art and kindling their ambition, contributed greatly to the perfection of their works. Arts and sciences indeed generally rise and fall together; but, excepting poetry alone, they rise and fall by just, though not always by equal degrees: sometimes advancing with quicker progress to the summit of excellence, sometimes declining from it by slower steps in proportion to the different degrees of genius and application with which they are cultivated, considered in connection with those external causes which promote or obstruct their improvement. It is very remarkable, however, that in the earliest and most uncultivated periods of society poetry is by one great effort of nature, in one age, and by one individual, brought to the highest perfection to which human genius is capable of advancing it, not only when the other arts and sciences are in a languishing state, but when they do not so much as exist. Thus Homer wrote his *Iliad* and *Odyssey* when there was not a single picture to be seen in Greece; and Ossian[2] composed *Fingal* and *Temora* when none of the arts, whether liberal or mechanical, were known in his country. This is a curious phenomenon; let us endeavor to account for it.

The first reason we shall assign of *original poetic genius* being most remarkably displayed in an early and uncultivated period of society arises from the antiquity of the period itself, and from the appearance of novelty in the objects which Genius contemplates. A poet or real genius, who lives in a distant uncultivated age, possesses great and peculiar advantages for original composition by the mere antiquity of the period in which he lives. He

AN ESSAY ON ORIGINAL GENIUS. **1.** Leo the Tenth (1475–1521), second son of Lorenzo de'Medici, the Magnificent, was Pope from 1513–1521. **2. Ossian:** a reference to James Macpherson (1736–1796), the Scottish poet who produced the epics *Fingal* and *Temora* in 1762 and 1763. He claimed these poems to be translations from the Gaelic of a poet named Ossian, but Johnson and others challenged his credibility, and most of the works came to be regarded as his own.

is perhaps the first poet who hath arisen in this infant state of society, by which means he enjoys the undivided empire of Imagination without a rival. The mines of Fancy not having been opened before his time are left to be digged by him, and the treasures they contain become his own by a right derived from the first discovery. The whole system of nature and the whole region of fiction yet unexplored by others is subjected to his survey, from which he culls those rich spoils which adorn his compositions and render them original. It may be said indeed, in answer to this, and it is true, that the stores of nature are inexhaustible by human imagination, and that her face is ever various and ever new; but it may be replied that some of her stores are more readily found than others, being less hid from the eye of Fancy, and some of her features more easily hit, because more strongly marked. The first good poet, therefore, professing those unrifled treasures, and contemplating these unsullied features, could not fail to present us with a draught so striking as to deserve the name of a complete *original*. We may further observe that the objects with which he is surrounded have an appearance of novelty which, in a more cultivated period, they in a great measure lose, but which, in that we are speaking of, excites an attention, curiosity and surprise highly favourable to the exertion of genius, and somewhat resembling that which Milton attributes to our first ancestor:

> Straight toward Heaven my wond'ring eyes I
> turn'd,
> And gaz'd a while the ample sky.
> *Paradise Lost*, Book viii, line 257.
>
> About me round I saw
> Hill, dale, and shady woods, and sunny plains,
> And liquid lapse[3] of murmuring streams.
> Line 261.

Such a person looks round him with wonder; every object is new to him and has the power to affect him with surprise and pleasure; and as he is not familiarised by previous description to the scenes he contemplates, these strike upon his mind with their full force; and the imagination, astonished and enraptured with the survey of the vast, the wild, and the beautiful in nature, conveyed through the medium of sense, spontaneously expresses its vivid ideas in bold and glowing metaphors, in sublime, animated, and picturesque description. Even a poet of ordinary genius will in such a state of society present us with some original ideas in his composition. For nature, lying open to his view in all its extent and variety, in contemplating this unbounded field so small a part of which hath been yet occupied by others, he can hardly fail to select some distinguishing objects which have escaped the notice of the vulgar, and which described in poetry may stamp upon it a degree of originality.

We may add that the productions of the early ages, when they present to us scenes of nature and a state of life we are little acquainted with, and which are very different from those that now subsist, will to us appear original, though they may not be really such if the true originals are lost of which the works that yet remain are only copies or imitations. Thus the Comedies of Terence are valued because the originals of Menander, which the Roman poet imitated, excepting a few fragments, are lost. Could the works of the latter be recovered, those of the former would lose much of their reputation. Thus far the superiority of poetic genius in those early ages is accidental, and therefore no way meritorious. It is the effect of a particular situation. It is the consequence of antiquity.

The next reason we shall give why original poetic genius appears in its utmost perfection in the first periods of social life is the simplicity and uniformity of manners peculiar to such periods.

Manners have a much greater effect on the exertions of poetic genius than is commonly imagined. The simple manners which prevail among most nations in the infancy of society are peculiarly favourable to such exertions. In this primitive state of nature, when mankind begin to unite in society, the manners, sentiments, and passions are (if we may use the expression) perfectly *original*. They are the dictates of nature, unmixed and undisguised: they are therefore more easily comprehended and described. The poet in describing his own feelings describes also the feelings of others; for in such a state of society these are similar and uniform in all. Their tastes, dispositions, and manners are thrown into the same mould and generally formed upon one and the same model. Artless and tender loves, generous friendships, and warlike exploits compose the history of this uncultivated period, and the poet who relates these, feeling the

3. lapse: flow of water.

inspiration of his subject, is himself animated with all the ardor of the *Lover*, the *Friend*, and the *Hero*. Hence, as his sensations are warm and vivid, his sentiments will become passionate or sublime as the occasion may require, his descriptions energetic, his stile bold, elevated, and metaphorical, and the whole, being the effusion of a glowing fancy and an impassioned heart, will be perfectly natural and *original*. Thus far, then, an early and uncultivated state of society, in which the manners, sentiments and passions run in the uniform current above-mentioned (as they do in most infant societies) appears favourable to the display of original poetic genius.

A third cause of this quality's being remarkably exerted in an early period of society is the leisure and tranquillity of uncultivated life, together with the innocent pleasures which generally attend it.

Genius naturally shoots forth in the simplicity and tranquillity of uncultivated life. The undisturbed peace and the innocent rural pleasures of this primeval state are, if we may so express it, congenial to its nature. A poet of true genius delights to contemplate and describe those primitive scenes which recall to our remembrance the fabulous era of the golden age. Happily exempted from that tormenting ambition and those vexatious desires which trouble the current of modern life, he wanders with a serene, contented heart through walks and groves consecrated to the Muses; or, indulging a sublime, pensive, and sweetly-soothing melancholy, strays with a slow and solemn step through the unfrequented desert, along the naked beach, or the bleak and barren heath. In such a situation every theme is a source of inspiration, whether he describes the beauties of nature, which he surveys with transport, or the peaceful innocence of those happy times which are so wonderfully soothing and pleasing to the imagination. His descriptions, therefore, will be perfectly vivid and original, because they are the transcript of his own feelings. Such a situation as that we have above represented is particularly favourable to a pastoral poet, and is very similar to that enjoyed by Theocritus,[4] which no doubt had a happy influence on his compositions, and it is a situation highly propitious to the efforts of every species of poetic genius.

4. **Theocritus:** Theocritus was a Greek pastoral poet of the third century B.C.

Perhaps we may be thought to refine too much on this point, and it may be questioned whether such tranquillity and innocence as we have above supposed have ever existed in any state of society. To this we may answer, that though the traditionary or even historical accounts of the early ages are not much to be depended on, yet those ancient original poems which we have in our hands give us reason to think that a certain innocence of manners, accompanied with that tranquillity which is its consequence, prevailed among those people whom we are not ashamed to call barbarous in a much higher degree than in more modern and cultivated periods.

The last cause we shall assign why original poetic genius appears in its utmost perfection in the uncultivated ages of society is its exemption from the rules and restraints of criticism, and its want of that knowledge which is acquired from books. When we consider learning and critical knowledge as unfavourable to original poetry we hope we shall not be accused of pleading the cause of ignorance, rusticity, and barbarism any more than, when we speak of the happy influence of the simple, uncultivated periods of society on the productions of the above-mentioned art, we shall be supposed to prefer those rude and artless ages to a highly civilized state of life. The effects of literature and criticism in the improvement of all the sciences and all the arts (excepting poetry alone), and the advantages of a state of civilization in augmenting and refining the pleasures of social life, are too obvious to require to be pointed out. We are at present only concerned to examine the effects of learning and critical knowledge on original poetry, the want of which we affirm to be one of the principal causes of this art being carried to its highest perfection in the first uncultivated periods of human society.

Let us inquire into the effects of these upon the mind of a poet possessed of a high degree of original genius. By an acquaintance with that literature which is derived from books, it will be granted, he may attain the knowledge of a great variety of events, and see human nature in a great variety of forms. By collecting the observations and experience of past ages, by superadding his own, and by reasoning justly from acknowledged principles, he may, no doubt, acquire more accurate and extensive ideas of the works of Nature and Art, and may likewise be thereby qualified to inrich the sciences with new discoveries as well as most of the arts with new inventions and improvements. In his own art only he can never become an original author by such means, nor, strictly speaking, so much as acquire the materials by the use of which he may justly attain this character: for the ideas derived from books, that is, from the ideas of others, can by no process of poetical chymistry confer perfect originality. Those ideas which are the intire creation of the mind, or are the result of the poet's own observations and immediately drawn from nature, are the only original ones in the proper sense. A poet who adopts images, who culls out incidents he has met with in the writings of other authors, and who imitates characters which have been portrayed by other poets, or perhaps by historians, cannot surely with any propriety be considered as an *Original,* though he may at the same time discover considerable powers of imagination in adapting those images and incidents, as well as transforming and molding these characters to the general design of his poem. In order to become a poet perfectly original (of whom only it must be remembered we are here treating) he must, if he should attempt Epic poetry, invent images, incidents, and characters: tradition may indeed supply him with the groundworks of the poem, as it did Homer, but the superstructure must be altogether his own. In executing such a work, what aid can a truly original poet receive from books? If he borrows aid from the performances of others, he is no longer a complete *Original.* To maintain this character throughout he must rely on his own fund: his own plastic imagination must supply him with every thing.

But such intire originality very rarely happens, especially in a modern age. Many of the most splendid images of poetry have been already exhibited, many of the most striking characters in human life have been delineated, and many of the most beautiful objects of nature, and such as are most obvious, have been described by preceding bards. It will be very difficult, therefore, for their successors to select objects which the eye of Fancy hath never explored, and none but a genius uncommonly original can hope to accomplish it.

There are very different degrees of originality in poetry, and several eminent geniuses in this art, possessing a very considerable share of originality themselves, have, however, been contented to imitate the great Father of Epic Poetry in one circumstance or another, partly perhaps through a consciousness of their being unable to produce any thing of a different kind equal to his compositions, partly through a natural tendency to imitate the excellencies they admired in a model rendered venerable by the concurrent testimonies of all ages in his favour, and partly through the real difficulty of attaining complete originality in the province of the *Epopœa*[5] after him. Thus Virgil copied many of the episodes and images of the Mæonian Bard; Tasso imitated some of this character, as well as adopted a part of his imagery; and even the divine Milton condescended, in a very few instances indeed, to imitate this prince of ancient poets in cases where his own genius, left to its native energy and uninfluenced by an acquaintance with the writings of Homer, would have enabled him to equal the Greek poet. An instance of this kind occurs in the end of the fourth book of *Paradise Lost,* where Milton informs us that Satan, while he was preparing for a dreadful combat with his antagonist, fled away upon observing that one of the scales which were suspended from heaven kicked the beam, thereby presaging to him an unfortunate issue of the encounter. By this cool expedient, which was suggested by that passage of Homer in which Jupiter is supposed to weigh the fates of Hector and Achilles in his golden balance, Milton has prevented the consequences of this horrid fray, sacrificed a real excellence to a frivolous imitation, and very much disappointed the eager expectations of the reader. The poet's own genius, had he been unacquainted with the *Iliad,* would naturally have led him to describe those mighty combatants engaged in dreadful fight; but a propensity to the imitation of so eminent an author repressed the native ardor of his own imagination. This single instance is sufficient to shew us the effect of literature on the mind of a poet of original genius, whose exertions it probably will in some instances suppress but cannot in any instance assist. On the other hand, a poet living in the more early periods of society, having few or no preceding bards for his models, is in very little hazard of being betrayed into imitation, which in a modern age it is so difficult to avoid; but, giving full scope to the bent of

5. *Epopœa:* epic poetry.

his genius, he is enabled, if he is possessed of a high degree of this quality, to produce a work completely original. From this train of reasoning it appears that the literature which is acquired from books, especially from the works of preceding bards, is unfavourable to originality in poetry, and that poets who live in the first periods of society, who are destitute of the means of learning, and consequently are exempted from the possibility of imitation, enjoy peculiar advantages for original composition.

. . .

The candid reader will observe that the question we have been examining is not whether critical learning be upon the whole really useful to an author of genius so as to render his works more perfect and accurate, but what its particular effect will be upon the productions of a genius truly original. We are far from intending to disregard or censure those rules "for writing well," which have been established by sound judgment and an exact discernment of the various species of composition, an attempt that would be equally weak and vain. On the contrary, we profess a reverence for those laws of writing which good sense and the corresponding voice of ages have pronounced important, and we consider them as what ought never to be violated; though with respect to others of a more trivial nature, however binding they may be upon ordinary authors, we can look upon them in no other light than as the frivolous fetters of original genius, to which it has submitted through fear, always improperly, and sometimes ridiculously, but which it may boldly shake off at pleasure, at least whenever it finds them suppressing its exertion, or whenever it can reach an uncommon excellence by its emancipation.

Upon the whole, from the reasons above assigned, it seems evident, that the *early uncultivated* ages of society are most favourable to the display of original genius in poetry; whence it is natural to expect that in such ages the greatest Originals in this art will always arise. Unhappily for us, this point does not admit of proof from an induction of many particulars, for very few original poems of those nations among whom they might have been expected have descended through the vicissitudes and revolutions of so many ages to our times. Most of the monuments of genius, as well as the works of art, have perished in the general wreck of empire, and we can only conjecture the merit of such as are lost from that of the small number of those which remain. While the works of Homer and Ossian, however, are in our hands, these, without any other examples, will be sufficient to establish the truth of the first part of our assertion, that in the early periods of society original poetic genius will in general be exerted in its utmost vigour. Let us now proceed to shew the truth of the second part of it, which was that this quality will seldom appear in a very high degree in cultivated life, and let us assign the reasons of it.

Shakespeare is the only modern author, (whose times, by the way, compared with the present are not very modern) whom, in point of originality, we can venture to compare with those eminent ancient poets above-mentioned. In sublimity of genius indeed, Milton is inferior to neither of them; but it cannot be pretended that he was so complete an Original as the one or the other, since he was indebted to the sacred writings for several important incidents, and for many sublime sentiments to be met with in *Paradise Lost*, not to mention what was formerly observed, that in a few passages he imitated the great *Father of Poetry*. With respect to Shakespeare therefore, admitting him to be a modern author, he is at any rate but a single exception; though indeed his genius was so strangely irregular and so different from that of every other mortal, *Cui nihil simile aut secundum*,[6] that no argument can be drawn from such an example to invalidate our position, since he would probably have discovered the same great and eccentric genius, which we so much admire at present, in any age or country whatever. External causes, though they have great influence on common minds, would have had very little on such a one as Shakespeare's. Let it be confessed, however, in justice to our own age, that if it hath not produced such perfect Originals as those above-mentioned, which perhaps may be partly imputed to the influence of causes peculiar to the present period and state of society, yet it hath produced several elegant, and some exalted geniuses in poetry who are distinguished also by a very considerable degree of originality, and such as is rarely to be met with in a modern age. The

6. ***Cui . . . secundum:*** "Nothing equal to or even second to him." See Horace, *Carmina,* I, xii, 18.

names of Young, Gray, Ogilvie, Collins, Akenside, and Mason, as they do honour to the present age, will probably be transmitted with reputation to posterity. But since it must be universally allowed that such intire originality as we have shown to be competent to an uncultivated period hath never yet appeared in modern times, excepting in the single instance above-mentioned, it may be worth the while to inquire into the causes why it so seldom appears, or can be expected to appear, in cultivated life.

If we have successfully investigated the causes why original poetic genius is most remarkably displayed in the uncultivated state of society, we shall probably discover that the chief causes of its being rarely found in the same degree in more civilized ages are the opposites of the former. Thus the first cause we assigned of this quality's being exerted in a higher degree in the earlier periods of social life was deduced from the antiquity of those periods, and the small progress of cultivation in them. One reason, therefore, why it will so seldom appear in a later period must be the disadvantage of living so long after the field of Fancy hath been preoccupied by the more ancient bards. We have already allowed that a truly original poet will strike out a path for himself, but it must likewise be allowed that to do so after his illustrious predecessors will at least be more difficult. To what hath been above advanced on this head we shall here only add a single observation, that should any modern poet with justice claim an equality of merit with the renowned Ancients in point of originality, he would, considering the disadvantages he must labour under, be intitled to a still superior share of reputation. In the meantime we may reasonably infer that the difference in the period of society above-mentioned will always prove unfavourable to the originality of a modern poet, and may be considered as one cause why this quality rarely appears in a very high degree in polished life.

. . .

Having considered the effect of these accomplishments upon the mind of an original poet at great length in the former part of this section, we shall conclude with a remark which will exhibit in one view the substance of what hath been more fully discussed in the preceding pages. It is, that though the progress of Literature, Criticism, and Civilization have contributed to unfold the powers and extend the empire of Reason, have taught men to think more justly as well as to express their sentiments with more precision, have had the happiest influence on the arts and sciences in general (since by communicating the discoveries, inventions, and observations of preceding ages they have facilitated the way to future inventions and discoveries, and have been highly conducive to their improvement), yet the art of original poetry, to an excellence in which the wild exuberance and plastic force of Genius are the only requisites, hath suffered, instead of having gained, from the influence of the above-mentioned causes, and will, for the most part, be displayed in its utmost perfection in the early and uncultivated periods of social life.

(1767)

Sir Joshua Reynolds
1723–1792

◆

FROM

Discourses on Art

From DISCOURSE VI*

The travellers into the East tell us that when the ignorant inhabitants of those countries are asked concerning the ruins of stately edifices yet remaining amongst them, the melancholy monuments of their former grandeur and long-lost science, they always answer that they were built by magicians. The untaught mind finds a vast gulf between its own powers, and those works of complicated art, which it is utterly unable to fathom; and it supposes that such a void can be passed only by supernatural powers.

And, as for artists themselves, it is by no means their interest to undeceive such judges, however conscious they may be of the very natural means by which their extraordinary powers were acquired; though our art, being intrinsically imitative, rejects this idea of inspiration, more perhaps than any other.

It is to avoid this plain confession of truth, as it should seem, that this imitation of masters, indeed almost all imitation, which implies a more regular and progressive method of attaining the ends of painting, has ever been particularly inveighed against with great keenness, both by ancient and modern writers.

To derive all from native power, to owe nothing to another, is the praise which men who do not much think on what they are saying bestow sometimes upon others, and sometimes on themselves; and their imaginary dignity is naturally heightened by a supercilious censure of the low, the barren, the grovelling, the servile imitator. It would be no wonder if a student, frightened by these terrific and disgraceful epithets with which the poor imitators are so often loaded, should let fall his pencil in mere despair (conscious as he must be how much he has been indebted to the labours of others, how little, how very little of his art was born with him); and consider it as hopeless to set about acquiring by the imitation of any human master what he is taught to suppose is matter of inspiration from heaven.

Some allowance must be made for what is said in the gaiety of rhetoric. We cannot suppose that anyone can really mean to exclude all imitation of others. A position so wild would scarce deserve a serious answer; for it is apparent, if we were forbid to make use of the advantages which our predecessors afford us, the art would be always to begin, and consequently remain always in its infant state; and it is a common observation that no art was ever invented and carried to perfection at the same time. . . .

What we now call genius begins, not where rules, abstractedly taken, end; but where known vulgar and trite rules have no longer any place. It must of necessity be that even works of genius, like every other effect, as they must have their cause, must likewise have their rules; it cannot be by chance that excellences are produced with any constancy or any certainty, for this is not the nature of chance; but the rules by which men of extraordinary parts, and such as are called men of genius, work, are either such as they discover by their own peculiar observations, or of such a nice texture as not easily to admit being expressed in words; especially as artists are not very frequently skilful in that mode of communicating ideas. Unsubstantial, however, as these rules may seem, and difficult as it may be to convey them in writing, they are still seen and felt in the mind of the artist; and he works from them with as much certainty as if they were embodied, as I may say, upon paper. It is true, these refined principles cannot be always made palpable, like the more gross rules of art; yet it does not follow, but that the mind may be put in such a train that it shall perceive, by a kind of scientific sense, that propriety, which words, particularly words of unpractised

* Delivered in 1774.

writers, such as we are, can but very feebly suggest.

Invention is one of the great marks of genius; but if we consult experience, we shall find that it is by being conversant with the inventions of others that we learn to invent; as by reading the thoughts of others we learn to think.

Whoever has so far formed his taste as to be able to relish and feel the beauties of the great masters has gone a great way in his study; for, merely from a consciousness of this relish of the right, the mind swells with an inward pride, and is almost as powerfully affected as if it had itself produced what it admires. Our hearts, frequently warmed in this manner by the contact of those whom we wish to resemble, will undoubtedly catch something of their own way of thinking; and we shall receive in our own bosoms some radiation at least of their fire and splendour. That disposition, which is so strong in children, still continues with us, of catching involuntarily the general air and manner of those with whom we are most conversant; with this difference only, that a young mind is naturally pliable and imitative; but in a more advanced state it grows rigid, and must be warmed and softened before it will receive a deep impression.

From these considerations, which a little of your own reflection will carry a great way further, it appears, of what great consequence it is that our minds should be habituated to the contemplation of excellence; and that, far from being contented to make such habits the discipline of our youth only, we should, to the last moment of our lives, continue a settled intercourse with all the true examples of grandeur. Their inventions are not only the food of our infancy, but the substance which supplies the fullest maturity of our vigour.

The mind is but a barren soil; a soil which is soon exhausted, and will produce no crop, or only one, unless it be continually fertilised and enriched with foreign matter.

When we have had continually before us the great works of art to impregnate our minds with kindred ideas, we are then, and not till then, fit to produce something of the same species. We behold all about us with the eyes of those penetrating observers whose works we contemplate; and our minds, accustomed to think the thoughts of the noblest and brightest intellects, are prepared for the discovery and selection of all that is great and noble in nature. The greatest natural genius cannot subsist on its own stock: he who resolves never to ransack any mind but his own will be soon reduced, from mere barrenness, to the poorest of all imitations; he will be obliged to imitate himself, and to repeat what he has before often repeated. When we know the subject designed by such men, it will never be difficult to guess what kind of work is to be produced.

It is vain for painters or poets to endeavour to invent without materials on which the mind may work, and from which invention must orginate. Nothing can come of nothing.

Homer is supposed to be possessed of all the learning of his time; and we are certain that Michael Angelo and Raffaelle were equally possessed of all the knowledge in the art which had been discovered in the works of their predecessors.

A mind enriched by an assemblage of all the treasures of ancient and modern art will be more elevated and fruitful in resources, in proportion to the number of ideas which have been carefully collected and thoroughly digested. There can be no doubt but that he who has the most materials has the greatest means of invention; and if he has not the power of using them, it must proceed from a feebleness of intellect, or from the confused manner in which those collections have been laid up in his mind.

The addition of other men's judgment is so far from weakening our own, as is the opinion of many, that it will fashion and consolidate those ideas of excellence which lay in embryo, feeble, ill-shaped, and confused, but which are finished and put in order by the authority and practice of those whose works may be said to have been consecrated by having stood the test of ages. . . .

DISCOURSE XIII

DELIVERED TO THE STUDENTS OF THE ROYAL ACADEMY, ON THE DISTRIBUTION OF THE PRIZES, DECEMBER 11, 1786

Art not merely Imitation, but under the Direction of the Imagination. In what Manner Poetry, Painting, Acting, Gardening, and Architecture depart from Nature.

Gentlemen,

To discover beauties, or to point out faults, in the works of celebrated masters, and to compare the conduct of one artist with another, is certainly no mean or inconsiderable part of criticism; but this is still no more than to know the art through the artist. This test of investigation must have two capital defects; it must be narrow, and it must be uncertain. To enlarge the boundaries of the art of painting, as well as to fix its principles, it will be necessary, that *that* art and *those* principles should be considered in their correspondence with the principles of the other arts which, like this, address themselves primarily and principally to the imagination. When those connected and kindred principles are brought together to be compared, another comparison will grow out of this; that is, the comparison of them all with those of human nature, from whence arts derive the materials upon which they are to produce their effects.

When this comparison of art with art, and of all arts with the nature of man, is once made with success, our guiding lines are as well ascertained and established, as they can be in matters of this description.

This, as it is the highest style of criticism, is at the same time the soundest; for it refers to the eternal and immutable nature of things.

You are not to imagine that I mean to open to you at large, or to recommend to your research, the whole of this vast field of science. It is certainly much above my faculties to reach it; and though it may not be above yours to comprehend it fully, if it were fully and properly brought before you, yet perhaps the most perfect criticism requires habits of speculation and abstraction, not very consistent with the employment which ought to occupy and the habits of mind which ought to prevail in a practical artist. I only point out to you these things, that when you do criticise (as all who work on a plan will criticise more or less), your criticism may be built on the foundation of true principles; and that though you may not always travel a great way, the way that you do travel may be the right road.

I observe, as a fundamental ground, common to all the arts with which we have any concern in this discourse, that they address themselves only to two faculties of the mind, its imagination and its sensibility.

All theories which attempt to direct or to control the art, upon any principles falsely called rational, which we form to ourselves upon a supposition of what ought in reason to be the end or means of art, independent of the known first effect produced by objects on the imagination, must be false and delusive. For though it may appear bold to say it, the imagination is here the residence of truth. If the imagination be affected, the conclusion is fairly drawn; if it be not affected, the reasoning is erroneous, because the end is not obtained; the effect itself being the test, and the only test, of the truth and efficacy of the means.

There is in the commerce of life, as in art, a sagacity which is far from being contradictory to right reason, and is superior to any occasional exercise of that faculty; which supersedes it; and does not wait for the slow progress of deduction, but goes at once, by what appears a kind of intuition, to the conclusion. A man endowed with this faculty feels and acknowledges the truth, though it is not always in his power, perhaps, to give a reason for it; because he cannot recollect and bring before him all the materials that gave birth to his opinion; for very many and very intricate considerations may unite to form the principle, even of small and minute parts, involved in, or dependent on, a great system of things: though these in process of time are forgotten, the right impression still remains fixed in his mind.

This impression is the result of the accumulated experience of our whole life, and has been collected, we do not always know how, or when. But this mass of collective observation, however acquired, ought to prevail over that reason, which, however powerfully exerted on any particular occasion, will probably comprehend but a partial view of the subject; and our conduct in life as well as in the arts is, or ought to be, generally governed by this habitual reason: it is our happiness that we are enabled to draw on such funds. If we were obliged to enter into a theoretical deliberation on every occasion, before we act, life would be at a stand, and art would be impracticable.

It appears to me, therefore, that our first thoughts, that is, the effect which anything produces on our minds, on its first appearance, is never to be forgotten; and it demands for that reason, because it is the first, to be laid up with care. If this be not done, the artist may happen to impose on himself by partial reasoning; by a cold consideration of those animated thoughts which proceed, not perhaps from caprice or rashness (as he may afterwards conceit), but from the fulness of his mind, enriched with the copious stores of all the various inventions which he had ever seen, or had ever passed in his mind. These ideas are infused into his design, without any conscious effort; but if he be not on his guard, he may reconsider and correct them, till the whole matter is reduced to a commonplace invention.

This is sometimes the effect of what I mean to caution you against; that is to say, an unfounded distrust of the imagination and feeling, in favour of narrow, partial, confined, argumentative theories; and of principles that seem to apply to the design in hand; without considering those general impressions on the fancy in which real principles of *sound reason,* and of much more weight and importance, are involved, and, as it were, lie hid, under the appearance of a sort of vulgar sentiment.

Reason, without doubt, must ultimately determine everything; at this minute it is required to inform us when that very reason is to give way to feeling.

Though I have often spoken of that mean conception of our art which confines it to mere imitation, I must add, that it may be narrowed to such a mere matter of experiment, as to exclude from it the application of science, which alone gives dignity and compass to any art. But to find proper foundations for science is neither to narrow nor to vulgarise it; and this is sufficiently exemplified in the success of experimental philosophy. It is the false system of reasoning, grounded on a partial view of things, against which I would most earnestly guard you. And I do it rather, because those narrow theories, so coincident with the poorest and most miserable practice, and which are adopted to give it countenance, have not had their origin in the poorest minds, but in the mistakes, or possibly in the mistaken interpretations, of great and commanding authorities. We are not therefore in this case misled by feeling, but by false speculation.

When such a man as Plato speaks of painting as only an imitative art, and that our pleasure proceeds from observing and acknowledging the truth of the imitation, I think he misleads us by a partial theory. It is in this poor, partial, and so far false view of the art, that Cardinal Bembo[1] has chosen to distinguish even Raffaelle himself, whom our enthusiasm honours with the name of Divine. The same sentiment is adopted by Pope in his epitaph on Sir Godfrey Kneller;[2] and he turns the panegyric solely on imitation, as it is a sort of deception.

I shall not think my time misemployed, if by any means I may contribute to confirm your opinion of what ought to be the object of your pursuit; because, though the best critics must always have exploded this strange idea, yet I know that there is a disposition towards a perpetual recurrence to it, on account of its simplicity and superficial plausibility. For this reason I shall beg leave to lay before you a few thoughts on this subject; to throw out some hints that may lead your minds to an opinion (which I take to be the truth), that painting is not only to be considered as an imitation, operating by deception, but that it is, and ought to be, in many points of view, and strictly speaking, no imitation at all of external nature. Perhaps it ought to be as far removed from the vulgar idea of imitation, as the refined civilised state in which we live, is removed from a gross state of nature; and those who have not cultivated their imaginations, which the majority of mankind certainly have not, may be said, in regard to arts, to continue in this state of nature. Such men will always prefer imitation to that excellence which is addressed to another faculty that they do not possess; but these are not the persons to whom a painter is to look, any more than a judge of morals and manners ought to refer controverted points upon those subjects to the opinions of people taken from the banks of the Ohio, or from New Holland.

It is the lowest style only of arts, whether of painting, poetry, or music, that may be said, in the vulgar sense, to be naturally pleasing. The higher

DISCOURSES ON ART. DISCOURSE XIII. **1. Cardinal Bembo:** Pietro Bembo (1470–1547), Italian humanist, Cardinal of the Roman Catholic Church. Bembo, a famous Italian critic, had a strongly classical orientation. **2. Sir Godfrey Kneller:** Gottfried Kneller (1646–1723), portrait painter of German birth, who succeeded Van Dyck as official portrait painter of the Court in London.

efforts of those arts, we know by experience, do not affect minds wholly uncultivated. This refined taste is the consequence of education and habit; we are born only with a capacity of entertaining this refinement, as we are born with a disposition to receive and obey all the rules and regulations of society; and so far it may be said to be natural to us, and no further.

What has been said, may show the artist how necessary it is, when he looks about him for the advice and criticism of his friends, to make some distinction of the character, taste, experience, and observation in this art of those from whom it is received. An ignorant uneducated man may, like Apelles's critic,[3] be a competent judge of the truth of the representation of a sandal; or to go somewhat higher, like Molière's old woman, may decide upon what is nature, in regard to comic humour; but a critic in the higher style of art ought to possess the same refined taste, which directed the artist in his work.

To illustrate this principle by a comparison with other arts, I shall now produce some instances to show, that they, as well as our own art, renounce the narrow idea of nature, and the narrow theories derived from that mistaken principle, and apply to that reason only which informs us not what imitation is,—a natural representation of a given object, —but what it is natural for the imagination to be delighted with. And perhaps there is no better way of acquiring this knowledge, than by this kind of analogy: each art will corroborate and mutually reflect the truth on the other. Such a kind of juxtaposition may likewise have this use, that whilst the artist is amusing himself in the contemplation of other arts, he may habitually transfer the principles of those arts to that which he professes; which ought to be always present in his mind, and to which everything is to be referred.

So far is art from being derived from, or having any immediate intercourse with, particular nature as its model, that there are many arts that set out with a professed deviation from it.

This is certainly not so exactly true in regard to painting and sculpture. Our elements are laid in gross common nature,—an exact imitation of what is before us: but when we advance to the higher state, we consider this power of imitation, though first in the order of acquisition, as by no means the highest in the scale of perfection.

Poetry addresses itself to the same faculties and the same dispositions as painting, though by different means. The object of both is to accommodate itself to all the natural propensities and inclinations of the mind. The very existence of poetry depends on the licence it assumes of deviating from actual nature, in order to gratify natural propensities by other means, which are found by experience full as capable of affording such gratification. It sets out with a language in the highest degree artificial, a construction of measured words, such as never is, nor ever was used by man. Let this measure be what it may, whether hexameter or any other metre used in Latin or Greek—or rhyme, or blank verse varied with pauses and accents, in modern languages,—they are all equally removed from nature, and equally a violation of common speech. When this artificial mode has been established as the vehicle of sentiment, there is another principle in the human mind, to which the work must be referred, which still renders it more artificial, carries it still further from common nature, and deviates only to render it more perfect. That principle is the sense of congruity, coherence, and consistency, which is a real existing principle in man; and it must be gratified. Therefore having once adopted a style and a measure not found in common discourse, it is required that the sentiments also should be in the same proportion elevated above common nature, from the necessity of there being an agreement of the parts among themselves, that one uniform whole may be produced.

To correspond therefore with this general system of deviation from nature, the manner in which poetry is offered to the ear, the tone in which it is recited, should be as far removed from the tone of conversation, as the words of which that poetry is composed. This naturally suggests the idea of modulating the voice by art, which I suppose may be considered as accomplished to the highest degree of excellence in the recitative of the Italian Opera; as we may conjecture it was in the chorus that attended the ancient drama. And though the most violent passions, the highest distress, even death itself, are expressed in singing or recitative,

3. **Apelles's critic:** Apelles, fourth century B.C. Greek painter, and one of the most famous artists of antiquity. The reference here is to the story of the shoemaker who criticized a slipper in Apelles' Venus.

I would not admit as sound criticism the condemnation of such exhibitions on account of their being unnatural.

If it is natural for our senses, and our imaginations, to be delighted with singing, with instrumental music, with poetry, and with graceful action, taken separately (none of them being in the vulgar sense natural, even in that separate state); it is conformable to experience, and therefore agreeable to reason as connected with and referred to experience, that we should also be delighted with this union of music, poetry, and graceful action, joined to every circumstance of pomp and magnificence calculated to strike the senses of the spectator. Shall reason stand in the way, and tell us that we ought not to like what we know we do like, and prevent us from feeling the full effect of this complicated exertion of art? This is what I would understand by poets and painters being allowed to dare everything; for what can be more daring, than accomplishing the purpose and end of art, by a complication of means, none of which have their archetypes in actual nature?

So far therefore is servile imitation from being necessary, that whatever is familiar, or in any way reminds us of what we see and hear every day, perhaps does not belong to the higher provinces of art, either in poetry or painting. The mind is to be transported, as Shakspeare expresses it, *beyond the ignorant present* to ages past. Another and a higher order of beings is supposed; and to those beings everything which is introduced into the work must correspond. Of this conduct, under these circumstances, the Roman and Florentine schools afford sufficient examples. Their style by this means is raised and elevated above all others; and by the same means the compass of art itself is enlarged.

We often see grave and great subjects attempted by artists of another school; who, though excellent in the lower class of art, proceeding on the principles which regulate that class, and not recollecting, or not knowing, that they were to address themselves to another faculty of the mind, have become perfectly ridiculous.

The picture which I have at present in my thoughts is a sacrifice of Iphigenia, painted by Jan Steen,[4] a painter of whom I have formerly had occasion to speak with the highest approbation; and even in this picture, the subject of which is by no means adapted to his genius, there is nature and expression; but it is such expression, and the countenances are so familiar, and consequently so vulgar, and the whole accompanied with such finery of silks and velvets, that one would be almost tempted to doubt, whether the artist did not purposely intend to burlesque his subject.

Instances of the same kind we frequently see in poetry. Parts of Hobbes's translation of Homer are remembered and repeated merely for the familiarity and meanness of their phraseology, so ill corresponding with the ideas which ought to have been expressed, and, as I conceive, with the style of the original.

We may proceed in the same manner through the comparatively inferior branches of art. There are in works of that class, the same distinction of a higher and a lower style; and they take their rank and degree in proportion as the artist departs more, or less, from common nature, and makes it an object of his attention to strike the imagination of the spectator by ways belonging especially to art,—unobserved and untaught out of the school of its practice.

If our judgments are to be directed by narrow, vulgar, untaught, or rather ill-taught reason, we must prefer a portrait by Denner or any other high finisher, to those of Titian or Vandyck; and a landscape of Vanderheyden to those of Titian or Rubens; for they are certainly more exact representations of nature.

If we suppose a view of nature represented with all the truth of the *camera obscura,* and the same scene represented by a great artist, how little and mean will the one appear in comparison of the other, where no superiority is supposed from the choice of the subject. The scene shall be the same, the difference only will be in the manner in which it is presented to the eye. With what additional superiority then will the same artist appear when he has the power of selecting his materials, as well as elevating his style? Like Nicolas Poussin,[5] he transports us to the environs of ancient Rome, with all the objects which a literary education makes so precious and interesting to man: or, like Sebas-

4. Jan Steen: Dutch painter (1626–1679), noted for his portrayal of the social life of his time.

5. Nicolas Poussin: noted French painter (1594–1665).

tian Bourdon,[6] he leads us to the dark antiquity of the Pyramids of Egypt; or, like Claude Lorrain,[7] he conducts us to the tranquillity of arcadian scenes and fairyland.

Like the history-painter, a painter of landscapes in this style and with this conduct sends the imagination back into antiquity; and, like the poet, he makes the elements sympathise with his subject; whether the clouds roll in volumes, like those of Titian or Salvator Rosa,[8] or, like those of Claude, are gilded with the setting sun; whether the mountains have sudden and bold projections, or are gently sloped; whether the branches of his trees shoot out abruptly in right angles from their trunks, or follow each other with only a gentle inclination. All these circumstances contribute to the general character of the work, whether it be of the elegant, or of the more sublime kind. If we add to this the powerful materials of lightness and darkness, over which the artist has complete dominion, to vary and dispose them as he pleases; to diminish, or increase them, as will best suit his purpose, and correspond to the general idea of his work; a landscape thus conducted, under the influence of a poetical mind, will have the same superiority over the more ordinary and common views, as Milton's *Allegro* and *Penseroso* have over a cold prosaic narration or description; and such a picture would make a more forcible impression on the mind than the real scenes, were they presented before us.

If we look abroad to other arts, we may observe the same distinction, the same division into two classes; each of them acting under the influence of two different principles, in which the one follows nature, the other varies it, and sometimes departs from it.

The theatre, which is said *to hold the mirror up to nature,* comprehends both those sides. The lower kind of comedy or farce, like the inferior style of painting, the more naturally it is represented, the better; but the higher appears to me to aim no more at imitation, so far as it belongs to anything like deception, or to expect that the spectators should think that the events there represented are really passing before them, than Raffaelle in his cartoons, or Poussin in his sacraments, expected it to be believed, even for a moment, that what they exhibited were real figures.

For want of this distinction, the world is filled with false criticism. Raffaelle is praised for naturalness and deception, which he certainly has not accomplished, and as certainly never intended; and our late great actor, Garrick, has been as ignorantly praised by his friend Fielding; who doubtless imagined he had hit upon an ingenious device, by introducing in one of his novels (otherwise a work of the highest merit) an ignorant man, mistaking Garrick's representation of a scene in Hamlet for reality. A very little reflection will convince us, that there is not one circumstance in the whole scene that is of the nature of deception. The merit and excellence of Shakspeare, and of Garrick, when they were engaged in such scenes, is of a different and much higher kind. But what adds to the falsity of this intended compliment is that the best stage-representation appears even more unnatural to a person of such a character, who is supposed never to have seen a play before, than it does to those who have had a habit of allowing for those necessary deviations from nature which the art requires.

In theatric representation, great allowances must always be made for the place in which the exhibition is represented; for the surrounding company, the lighted candles, the scenes visibly shifted in your sight, and the language of blank verse, so different from common English; which merely as English must appear surprising in the mouths of Hamlet, and all the court and natives of Denmark. These allowances are made; but their being made puts an end to all manner of deception: and further, we know that the more low, illiterate, and vulgar any person is, the less he will be disposed to make these allowances, and of course to be deceived by any imitation; the things in which the trespass against nature and common probability is made in favour of the theatre being quite within the sphere of such uninformed men.

Though I have no intention of entering into all the circumstances of unnaturalness in theatrical representations, I must observe, that even the expression of violent passion is not always the most

6. **Sebastian Bourdon:** French painter (1616–1671), noted for his large historical and religious paintings. 7. **Claude Lorrain:** French landscape painter (1600–1682). 8. **Salvator Rosa:** a versatile Italian artist (1615–1673), of the Neopolitan School, noted for his landscape and historical scenes, and as a portrait painter.

excellent in proportion as it is the most natural; so great terror and such disagreeable sensations may be communicated to the audience, that the balance may be destroyed by which pleasure is preserved, and holds its predominance in the mind: violent distortion of action, harsh screamings of the voice, however great the occasion, or however natural on such occasion, are therefore not admissible in the theatric art. Many of these allowed deviations from nature arise from the necessity which there is, that everything should be raised and enlarged beyond its natural state; that the full effect may come home to the spectator, which otherwise would be lost in the comparatively extensive space of the theatre. Hence the deliberate and stately step, the studied grace of action, which seems to enlarge the dimensions of the actor, and alone to fill the stage. All this unnaturalness, though right and proper in its place, would appear affected and ridiculous in a private room; *quid enim deformius, quam scenam in vitam transferre?*[9]

And here I must observe, and I believe it may be considered as a general rule, that no art can be engrafted with success on another art. For though they all profess the same origin, and to proceed from the same stock, yet each has its own peculiar modes both of imitating nature, and of deviating from it, each for the accomplishment of its own particular purpose. These deviations, more especially, will not bear transplantation to another soil.

If a painter should endeavour to copy the theatrical pomp and parade of dress and attitude, instead of that simplicity, which is not a greater beauty in life than it is in painting, we should condemn such pictures, as painted in the meanest style.

So also gardening, as far as gardening is an art, or entitled to that appellation, is a deviation from nature; for if the true taste consists, as many hold, in banishing every appearance of art, or any traces of the footsteps of man, it would then be no longer a garden. Even though we define it "Nature to advantage dress'd," and in some sense is such, and much more beautiful and commodious for the recreation of man; it is, however, when so dressed, no longer a subject for the pencil of a landscape-painter, as all landscape-painters know, who love to have recourse to nature herself, and to dress her according to the principles of their own art; which are far different from those of gardening, even when conducted according to the most approved principles; and such as a landscape-painter himself would adopt in the disposition of his own grounds, for his own private satisfaction.

I have brought together as many instances as appear necessary to make out the several points which I wished to suggest to your consideration in this discourse, that your own thoughts may lead you further in the use that may be made of the analogy of the arts, and of the restraint which a full understanding of the diversity of many of their principles ought to impose on the employment of that analogy.

The great end of all those arts is, to make an impression on the imagination and the feeling. The imitation of nature frequently does this. Sometimes it fails, and something else succeeds. I think therefore the true test of all the arts is not solely whether the production is a true copy of nature, but whether it answers the end of art, which is to produce a pleasing effect upon the mind.

It remains only to speak a few words of architecture, which does not come under the denomination of an imitative art. It applies itself, like music (and I believe we may add poetry), directly to the imagination, without the intervention of any kind of imitation.

There is in architecture, as in painting, an inferior branch of art, in which the imagination appears to have no concern. It does not, however, acquire the name of a polite and liberal art, from its usefulness, or administering to our wants or necessities, but from some higher principle: we are sure that in the hands of a man of genius it is capable of inspiring sentiment, and of filling the mind with great and sublime ideas.

It may be worth the attention of artists to consider what materials are in their hands, that may contribute to this end; and whether this art has it not in its power to address itself to the imagination with effect, by more ways than are generally employed by architects.

To pass over the effect produced by that general symmetry and proportion, by which the eye

9. ***quid . . . transferre:*** "For what is more distorted than transferring stage presentation into life?"

is delighted, as the ear is with music, architecture certainly possesses many principles in common with poetry and painting. Among those which may be reckoned as the first is that of affecting the imagination by means of association of ideas. Thus, for instance, as we have naturally a veneration for antiquity, whatever building brings to our remembrance ancient customs and manners, such as the castles of the barons of ancient chivalry, is sure to give this delight. Hence it is that *towers and battlements*[10] are so often selected by the painter and the poet, to make a part of the composition of their ideal landscape; and it is from hence in a great degree, that in the buildings of Vanbrugh, who was a poet as well as an architect, there is a greater display of imagination than we shall find perhaps in any other, and this is the ground of the effect we feel in many of his works, notwithstanding the faults with which many of them are justly charged. For this purpose, Vanbrugh appears to have had recourse to some of the principles of the Gothic architecture; which, though not so ancient as the Grecian, is more so to our imagination, with which the artist is more concerned than with absolute truth.

The barbaric splendour of those Asiatic buildings, which are now publishing by a member of this Academy, may possibly, in the same manner, furnish an architect, not with models to copy, but with hints of composition and general effect, which would not otherwise have occurred.

It is, I know, a delicate and hazardous thing (and as such I have already pointed it out), to carry the principles of one art to another, or even to reconcile in one object the various modes of the same art, when they proceed on different principles. The sound rules of the Grecian architecture are not to be lightly sacrificed. A deviation from them, or even an addition to them, is like a deviation or addition to, or from, the rules of other arts, —fit only for a great master, who is thoroughly conversant in the nature of man, as well as all combinations in his own art.

It may not be amiss for the architect to take advantage *sometimes* of that to which I am sure the painter ought always to have his eyes open, mean the use of accidents; to follow when they lead, and to improve them, rather than always to trust to a regular plan. It often happens that additions have been made to houses, at various times, for use or pleasure. As such buildings depart from regularity, they now and then acquire something of scenery by this accident, which I should think might not unsuccessfully be adopted by an architect, in an original plan, if it does not too much interfere with convenience. Variety and intricacy is a beauty and excellence in every other of the arts which address the imagination; and why not in architecture?

The forms and turnings of the streets of London, and other old towns, are produced by accident, without any original plan or design; but they are not always the less pleasant to the walker or spectator, on that account. On the contrary, if the city had been built on the regular plan of Sir Christopher Wren, the effect might have been, as we know it is in some new parts of the town, rather unpleasing; the uniformity might have produced weariness, and a slight degree of disgust.

I can pretend to no skill in the detail of architecture. I judge now of the art, merely as a painter. When I speak of Vanbrugh, I mean to speak of him in the language of our art. To speak then of Vanbrugh in the language of a painter, he had originality of invention, he understood light and shadow, and had great skill in composition. To support his principal object he produced his second and third groups or masses; he perfectly understood in his art what is the most difficult in ours, the conduct of the background, by which the design and invention is set off to the greatest advantage. What the background is in painting, in architecture is the real ground on which the building is erected; and no architect took greater care than he that his work should not appear crude and hard: that is, it did not abruptly start out of the ground without expectation or preparation.

This is a tribute which a painter owes to an architect who composed like a painter; and was defrauded of the due reward of his merit by the wits of his time, who did not understand the principles of composition of poetry better than he; and who knew little or nothing of what he understood perfectly, the general ruling principles of architecture

10. ***towers and battlements:*** see Milton, *L'Allegro*: "Towers and battlements it sees / Bosom'd high in tufted trees."

and painting. His fate was that of the great Perrault;[11] both were the objects of the petulant sarcasms of factious men of letters; and both have left some of the fairest ornaments which to this day decorate their several countries; the façade of the Louvre, Blenheim, and Castle Howard.

Upon the whole, it seems to me, that the object and intention of all the arts is to supply the natural imperfection of things, and often to gratify the mind by realising and embodying what never existed but in the imagination.

It is allowed on all hands, that facts and events, however they may bind the historian, have no dominion over the poet or the painter. With us, history is made to bend and conform to this great idea of art. And why? Because these arts, in their highest province, are not addressed to the gross senses, but to the desires of the mind, to that spark of divinity which we have within, impatient of being circumscribed and pent up by the world which is about us. Just so much as our art has of this, just so much of dignity, I had almost said of divinity, it exhibits; and those of our artists who possessed this mark of distinction in the highest degree acquired from thence the glorious appellation of Divine.

(1794)

11. **Claude Perrault:** famous French architect (1613–1688). His greatest achievement is the east façade of the Louvre, known as the Colonnade.

Selected Modern Critical Essays

W. J. Bate

THE CLASSIC AND NEO-CLASSIC PREMISES

Conceptions of the nature and purpose of art closely parallel man's conceptions of himself and of his destiny. For art, in one of its primary functions, is the interpreter of values, and aesthetic criticism, when it rises above mere technical analysis, attempts to grasp and estimate these values in order to judge the worth of the interpretation. The period which is often called the European Enlightenment—a period which extends roughly from the middle of the seventeenth century through the close of the eighteenth—is in this sense the transitional meeting-ground between two dominant epochs of modern thinking.

The earlier portion of the Enlightenment marks the final subsiding of the European Renaissance: it comprises the consolidation and in some respects the extreme development of the value it inherited. Concluding as it did a Renaissance of extraordinary intellectual activity, it possessed ready at hand a body of conceptions which had been widely urged in philosophical and scientific writing and brilliantly exemplified in all the arts. Much of its inheritance consisted of a collective system of values to which—because of the lack of any more specific or generally accepted term—the broad and chameleon-like word "humanism" has often been applied. The word may be easily disputed. But whatever term we apply to it, this general outlook or system of values is one which largely permeated

---

Reprinted by permission of the publishers from *From Classic to Romantic: Premises of Taste in Eighteenth-Century England* by Walter Jackson Bate, Cambridge, Mass.: Harvard University Press, Copyright, 1946 by the President and Fellows of Harvard College; renewed © 1974 by Walter Jackson Bate.

classical thought, and also received some qualification and re-direction by Christian elements in the later Middle Ages and the Renaissance. Though indefinite and even vague in a few of its exterior ramifications, it was always unified in its fundamental purpose and approach: it viewed man's intellectual and moral nature as ideally the same, and it assumed as its goal the evolution of the total man in accordance with that view. It especially emphasized man's ethical "reason" as his own distinctive nature, and as the means of gaining insight into the ideal and of comprehending the standard or end which this ideal comprises. Humanism, as it is used in this special sense, is almost another word for classicism itself. Similarly, the codification of some of the means and premises which Renaissance humanism postulated for the attainment or portrayal of this standard, the carrying to an extreme conclusion of others, and the inevitable counteractions to which this codification gave rise, may, in a general sense, be said to comprise neoclassicism as an historical phenomenon. And within these codifications and reactions the various neo-classic conceptions of taste largely reside.

I

On a journey through France with the Thrales, Dr. Johnson, while the scenery was being admired, impatiently retorted: "A blade of grass is always a blade of grass, whether in one country or another. . . . Men and women are my subjects of inquiry; let us see how these differ from those we have left behind." The statement is reminiscent of that made by Socrates to Phaedrus, as the two reclined on the bank of the Ilyssus: "I am a lover of knowledge; and the men who dwell in the city are my teachers, and not the trees or the country." Such sentiments would have elicited at least some agreement from any classicist, even a less sternly ethical one than was Socrates or Johnson. The absence or the depreciation of the landscape in Greek and Roman art is no historical accident: whether the classical artist sought to portray physical or moral beauty, his attention was directed to its existence and its ideal potentiality in the human being. Similarly, to Michelangelo and Raphael, and to the enormous group of artists which pivots about them, the landscape was of merely complementary interest. As late as 1719 the Abbé du Bos could write, with reasonable representativeness:

> The finest landskip, were it even Titian's or Caraccio's, does not affect us. . . . The most knowing painters have been so thoroughly convinced of this truth, that it is rare to find any *mere* landskips of theirs without an intermixture of figures. They have therefore thought proper to people them, as it were, by introducing into their pieces a subject composed of several personages, whereof the action might be capable of moving, and consequently of engaging us.[1]

The classical direction of art to human actions and potentialities mirrors the traditional humanistic stress upon moral knowledge and cultivation rather than upon the scientific investigation of the external world. The classical moralist, without being narrowly dogmatic, might still dissent from the view of a recent scientist who took issue with Terence's statement, *Homo sum, humani nil a me alienum puto*—"I am a man, and consider nothing that is human to be foreign to me"—and who thought it should be altered to read: "I am a space-time event, and I deem nothing that is a space-time event to be foreign to me." "Our business here," said Locke, humanistic even in his empiricism, "is not to know all things, but those which concern our conduct." A fair number of early eighteenth-century satires, of which that in *Gulliver's Travels* on the Academy of Lagado is the preëminent example, rest upon this conviction. The activities with which the Academy was occupied—extracting sunbeams out of cucumbers, condensing air into a tangible substance, making gunpowder from ice, attempting to plot the date of the sun's eventual extinction—are instanced by Swift to signify an amoral tendency to be "curious and conceited in matters where we have least concern, and for which we are least adapted either by study or nature." Gulliver's Houyhnhnm master, in the fourth voyage, found it strange that "a creature pretending to *Reason*" should devote himself much to "natural philosophy"; and he concluded that, if mankind were not destroyed through the growing horror of war, such an indiscriminate devotion would only "multiply our original wants," and then lead us "to spend our whole lives in vain endeavours to supply them by our own inventions."

To Dr. Johnson, again, only the study of man's ideals and conduct deserves to be called "intercourse with intellectual nature":

> The knowledge of external nature, and the sciences which that knowledge requires or includes, are not the great or frequent business of the human mind. Whether we provide for action or conversation, . . . the first requisite is the religious and moral knowledge of right and wrong; the next is an acquaintance with the history of mankind, and with those examples which may be said to embody truth, and prove by events the reasonableness of opinions. . . . We are perpetually moralists, but we are geometricians only by chance. Our intercourse with intellectual nature is necessary; our speculations upon matter are voluntary, and at leisure.[2]

Consequently, as Johnson elsewhere stated, "He who thinks reasonably must think morally." To the classicist, indeed, any rational evaluation of the beautiful was, in the widest implication of the word, a moral one, which simultaneously transcended and gauged or controlled the worth of strictly aesthetic feelings or reactions; nor would the classicist have taken very seriously Poe's attack on those who attempt "to reconcile the obstinate oils and waters of Poetry and Truth."

With such a direction and aim assumed for art, the classical and Renaissance conception of the poet as a teacher of moral excellence was a logical conclusion. "For what ought we to admire the poet?" asked Aristophanes; and his answer was "because the poet makes better men." The good can be conceived and then taught only by the good; and the insistence of Cicero, Quintilian, and others that the orator must first of all be a good man was repeatedly applied to the poet in Renaissance and eighteenth-century criticism. Again, since his concern is man, the poet must be versed in the customs and manners of men, not as they are found under local and temporary conditions, but as they mirror the immutable principles and aspirations of human beings throughout history. The constancy of the basic working of human nature is stressed in most early eighteenth-century writing. A characteristic contention is an article in the *British Magazine* (1760) which has as its subject the "similitude of genius" in Horace, Boileau, and Pope as indicative of "that ingenious observation of Plutarch, that Nature delights in reproducing the same characters." Or, similarly, Richard Hurd, in his "Discourse on Poetical Imitation," defends apparent imitation of earlier works on the basis that both the passions and manners are "constant in their effects," and successive writers must necessarily deal with much the same situations.

The profit gained from history is ethical in that it furnishes aid in estimating what is general and what is merely accidental. "History's chief use," said Hume, "is only to discover the constant and universal principles of human nature." In the *Tour to the Hebrides,* Boswell records Monboddo as stating: "The history of manners is the most valuable. I never set a high value on any other history":

> Johnson. "Nor I; and therefore I esteem biography, as giving us what comes near to ourselves. . . ." Boswell. "But in the course of general history, we find manners. In wars, we see the dispositions of people, their degrees of humanity, and other particulars." Johnson. "Yes; but then you must take all the facts to get this, and it is but a little you get." Monboddo. "And it is that little which makes history valuable." [3]

The long and hearty duration of classical antiquity's experience with society, and the brilliant interpretation which it evolved, made both the history of its experience and the study of its verdicts of primary value to the artist's comprehension of man's ideal and general nature; and the authority of antiquity, as a consequence, was continually upheld. John Dennis censured Pope's failure to state more precisely from what the ideal of man's nature is to be taken; and he added that Horace had not merely told his readers that the principal source of good writing is moral learning, but had "pointed to the very Books where they might find that moral Philosophy"—that is, the works of Plato.

The prevalence of didactic art in the late seventeenth and early eighteenth centuries, and the frequent employment in criticism of purely didactic values, are a somewhat extreme development of this premise. Aristotle had stated that the subject of poetry, though necessarily ethical in purpose, was less the exposition of moral theory than the revelation of "the manners of men"; and Renaissance critics, as in Scaliger's admonition that "the poet teaches character through *actions,*" generally reiterated this distinction. Joseph Trapp, lecturing at Oxford early in the eighteenth century, stressed the ethical end of poetry as illustrative and not as didactically explanatory; and a similar emphasis is not uncommon in other English critics of the day. But in practice, and somewhat in precept, the late seventeenth century increasingly inclined towards the didactic direction which Roman poetry, proceeding from an ethical standpoint, had also taken. The unhesitating adoption of the verse-essay by Boileau, Pope, and a plentiful number of other writers is symptomatic of the evolution; and the same may be said to some extent of the pronounced contemporary rise of verse-satire, which, Dryden maintained, "is of the nature of moral philosophy, as being instructive." The famous attack on the *Immorality and Profaneness of the English Stage* (1698) by Jeremy Collier, who regarded criticism as irresponsible and even harmful if it did not put into practice the moral considerations it extolled, was only a vigorous application of the precepts of Boileau, Rapin, Dacier, and indeed the bulk of Renaissance and eighteenth-century critics. Scaliger, although Aristotle had thought differently, had emphasized the necessity of portraying, in the drama, the reward of virtue and the punishment of vice; D'Aubignac and others considered this "the most indispensable rule of dramatic poetry"; and the occasional critical premium throughout the eighteenth century on "poetic justice"—which was given its name by Thomas Rymer, and which had as many opponents as it had adherents—exemplifies an extreme development and subsequent petrification of the broad humanistic conception of the poet's ethical function.

II

Arising from the classical assumption that man's reason and his moral nature are one is the belief that character can be justly formed and guided only by a genuine insight into the universal, and by the rational grasp of the decorum, measure, and standard which characterize the ideal. The portrayal of the universal in art—the exhibition, in other words, of the general in the particular, of the one in the many—can achieve permanent success only if the particulars employed are reasonably common to the experience of cultivated mankind throughout successive generations. Indeed, the most pervasive single tendency of almost all classicism may be defined, as Mr. Santayana has said, by the phrase "the idealization of the familiar." The achievement of this goal may utilize various means; but they are in all cases related directly to man, and are based upon man's common intellectual, aesthetic, and moral experience and interest. The representation of familiar examples of character; the embodiment of the ideal potentialities of the human figure, as in classical and Renaissance sculpture; the illustration of the working of primary and elementary feelings and passions, divorced from situations peculiar only to a specific locality or time; the delineation of the progress and objective significance of those climactic occurrences of destiny, especially death, which are common to all, and of the manner in which human reactions to such occurrences most fully and nobly reveal themselves; and, above all, the expression in such types, postures, attitudes, exertions, or passions, of those laws and indeed heroic ideals which are manifested and held by the most exemplary in all ages and places:—the employment, depiction, and idealization of these form the province and purpose of classical art.

A corollary of this dedication to the elementary and primary had always been, in classical thought, an emphasis on clarity of expression. To the ancient rhetoricians, such as Cicero and Quintilian, one of the first requisites of art had been lucidity and immediacy of communication. And the widespread preoccupation of Restoration and early eighteenth-century British critics with simplicity of style, the attacks on complicated metaphor by such writers as Thomas Sprat, John Eachard, and Lord Lansdowne, the stress on the employment of an idiom and of stylistic devices which, from long sanction and use, had become intimately and prevalently known, the growing disfavor with which "metaphysical" verse was viewed, the common attitude towards poetry as a branch of rhetoric, the painstaking attempt by later critics to outline concretely the means by which clarity of diction, metaphor, and sentence-structure might be attained—often accompanied by appeal to the authority of classical rhetoricians—such tendencies, though they reveal other intentions as well, are a neo-classic reassertion of the importance of the familiar as far as stylistic values are concerned.

"*Truth* in poetry," said Hurd, paraphrasing Horace, "means such an expression as conforms to the general nature of things: *falsehood*, that which, however suitable to the particular instance in view, doth yet not correspond to such *general nature*." And the classical aesthetic values of unity, simplicity, and the natural and harmonious adaptation of parts to the whole are founded upon a confidence in the truth and grandeur of ordered generality. They may be said to stand opposed, for example, to the romantic cherishing of the surprise in variety, the wonder and mystery in contemplating the strange and occasionally the grotesque, which attend upon an indiscriminate amusement and transitory delight in the particular.

This emphasis on the stripping of all that is extraneous and accidental in the portrayal of the familiar is not to be confused, of course, with the intention of "naturalism." To the classicist, "naturalism," especially in its more extreme form, could be only a partial view of phenomena. Its essentially empirical standpoint, that is, would display a disregard of those fundamental realities which only the ideal can signify and declare; and, to take but one instance, the classicist postulated as a general rule that the writing of tragedy could have little success without a judicious selection of the characters portrayed. The feelings and thoughts of the character can be participated in and can be said to have significance only in proportion as the character himself is capable of feeling and thinking. Oedipus, Antigone, Prometheus, and Lear are tragic characters; Wordsworth's Betty Foy, "the idiot mother of the idiot boy," or Harry Gill, who is continually cold and whose "teeth chatter, chatter still," are hapless enough beings, but they have hardly the significance of Hamlet. "How shall our attention," said the Abbé du Bos, "be engaged by a picture representing a peasant driving a couple of beasts along the highway?" Such a picture "may possibly amuse us some few moments, and may even draw from us an applause of the artist's abilities in imitating, but can never raise any emotion or concern." Painters of genuine insight do not picture

> a man going along the highroad, or . . . a woman carrying fruit to market; they commonly present us with figures that *think*, in order to make us think; they paint men hurried with passions, to the end that ours may also be raised, and our attention fixed by this very agitation.[4]

The naturalistic writer, it is true, attempts to approach the norm, and to discard the adventitious; but at least the more extreme naturalist may be said, in a sense, to assume the lowest as the norm, and to view whatever is better as an unexpected if happy gain or as helpful to "progress"; while the classicist conceives the highest as the norm, and regards whatever falls below, not as "natural," but as corruption. The difference resides in the interpretation of "nature." To the naturalist, nature is inevitably what he empirically judges as reality, in which any human idealization discovered is not inherent or actual but either something superimposed, something simply displayed as a psychological reaction of human beings under given circumstances, or at best something useful or desirable for the social, scientific, and humanitarian betterment of mankind. The various shades of meaning in the use of the word "nature" in English neo-classic thought have been sufficiently traced, especially by Mr. Lovejoy, and need not be recapitulated here. It is sufficient to state that in general the classical conception of nature, from the Greeks to almost the middle of the eighteenth century, is that central idea and form which the particular struggles to attain; and when Aristotle defined poetry as an "imitation of nature," he did not mean the indiscriminate copying of any individual, but rather the selective imitation of what is general and representative in man. Dennis condemned Pope for not defining "nature" in as unmistakably plain detail as Horace, who

> makes it as clear as the Sun, what it is to follow Nature in giving us a draught of human Life, and of the manners of Men, and that is, not to draw after particular Men, who are but Copies and imperfect Copies of the great universal Pattern; but to consult that innate Original, and that universal Idea, which the Creator has fix'd in the minds of ev'ry reasonable Creature.[5]

"What is natural," said Grotius, "we must judge by those in whom nature is *least* corrupt"; and those who serve as concrete if not wholly ideal standards for the natural are "those who are most civilized." The conception of "nature" as the ultimate standard, as the essential meaning and final aim of life, underlies the classical conviction that the end of art is the revelation to man and the rational, ethical inculcation in him of that ideal perfection of which, in a degree varying according to his own character, he as a particular is only a faulty image.

III

In its devotion to the rationally conceived ideal, classicism is opposed not only to the naturalistic but to any other conception of art which can be designated as personal or local—to the conception of art, in other words, as sheer emotional experience for its own sake, as intellectual amusement, or as propaganda. It views the mere stimulation of emotional excitement and the unschooled liberation of impulses as at best a temporary narcotic, the awakening from which inevitably brings in its train—as some later aspects of European romanticism were perhaps to illustrate—a dichotomy of mind and feeling, and a dissatisfaction based not so much on intellectual conviction and criticism as on mere insecurity of feeling.

Given the universal character of its ethical standpoint, classicism draws a marked distinction between centrality and diversity, between man's unified rational grasp of his ideal nature, and his peripheral and independent development, as a particular, of the impulses and reactions which comprise what is occasionally called his personality. Indeed, classicism assumes that only through the former can genuine individual fulfillment be found. For it regards man's feelings as by themselves helpless, blind, and eminently susceptible to dictation of some sort. They are not, that is, free to determine themselves, but are inevitably led by something else: they are subject to whatever is in closest or most vital proximity to them—whether it be a rationally determined end which is vividly and firmly held in the mind, or whether, if this end be lacking, it be merely whatever external environment chance may offer. It is in this respect that Dr. Johnson could state, with complete practicality: "Whatever withdraws us from the power of our senses, whatever makes the past, the distant, or the future predominate over the present, advances us in the dignity of thinking beings." True individual freedom accrues in the channeling of man's responses towards an end which reason conceives to transcend the local and temporary; its opposite exists when such a formative and determining conception is lacking, and habit is established through chance, fashion, local custom, or individual caprice.

Classicism does not subscribe, therefore, to the belief that man's feelings and responses are themselves inherently good—a belief which was to underlie at least some romantic assumptions towards the close of the eighteenth century. And just as art itself is inadequate when it is conditioned largely by the customs and opinions of a transitory society, or when its primary purpose is to serve either as an emotional narcotic or as an esoteric exercise of ingenuity; similarly, in the role of the artist as propagandist, as an indulger in subjective sensibility, or as the mere craftsman, there is much that fails to attain and indeed obstructs what, in the classical sense, a man should be.

To rest a determination of values upon the feelings, the floating inclinations, or the varying empirically-held opinions of particular individuality is to rest it upon the most fluid of foundations. For the abandonment of the centrally ideal by empirical relativism not only results in a conflict of predilections from man to man, but, as Irving Babbitt so frequently insisted, in conflict and change within even the same man. Its probable consequence, of which European art and thought of the past century contain frequent instances, may be typified by D. H. Lawrence's rather confused assertion: "I am many men. . . . Who are you? How many selves have you? And which of these selves do you want to be?"; and the classicist might question whether an even more ultimate conclusion was not exemplified in a recent poem which begins with the declaration "I am four monkeys," and concludes with the question "How many monkeys are you?" Against the fluidity and relativism of either personal or else local and fashionable predilection, classicism places universal "nature" as that centripetal and "just standard" which, said Pope, is "at once the source, and end, and test of art," and which also comprises, in its broad ethical character, "the source, and end, and test" of all that may be called the ideal of man.

"Besides the purging of the passions," said Thomas Rymer, poetry infuses order and justness of comprehension into the mind simply by its reflection, in the form and outline of its own structure, of "that constant order, that harmony and beauty of Providence." [6] For the very nature of the universal, in its transcendence and control over the accidental and specific, exemplifies order and harmony; and the living exhibition of order and the persuasive infiltration of it into man's moral and mental character are both a vital aspect of the means by which art simultaneously "delights and teaches," and also an end for which it performs these functions. It is ethical in furnishing both the process and the aim.

With the same assumption, the notable classical discussions, such as that in Plato's *Republic,* of the fundamental importance of music in the ethical inculcation of order, measure, and harmony, are occasionally repeated and applied with historical pertinence in neo-classic criticism. Characteristic is a book by the opponent of Shaftesbury, John Brown, one of the purposes of which is to illustrate that, in past cultures, "As every change of Manners influenced their Music, so by a reciprocal Action, every Considerable Change of Music influenced their Manners." When music had attained in Greece a sufficiently high development in order and universality of form, it was rightly esteemed, said Brown, as

> a *necessary Accomplishment:* And an Ignorance of this Art was regarded as a capital Defect. Of this we have an Instance, even in Themistocles himself, who was upbraided with his Ignorance of Music. The whole country of *Cynaethe* laboured under a parallel Reproach: And all the enormous *Crimes* committed there, were attributed by the neighbouring States to the *Neglect* of *Music.*—What wonder? For according to the Delineation here given of ancient Greek Music, their ignorance implied a general Deficiency in the three great articles of a social Education, *Religion, Morals,* and *Polity.*[7]

The classical doctrine of exemplifying order in art often finds a humanistically Christian expression in eighteenth-century criticism as it had even more frequently in the Renaissance. "The great Design of Arts," Dennis maintained, "is to restore the Decays that happen'd to human Nature by the Fall, by restoring Order"; and "if the end of Poetry," he added, "be to instruct and reform the World, that is, to bring Mankind from Irregularity, Extravagance, and Confusion, to Rule and Order, how this should be done by a thing that is in itself irregular and extravagant, is difficult to be conceiv'd." [8] Poetry, as Aristotle had pointed out, possesses a more general truth than does history, and presents, in its selection and form, a model or imitation of more valid pertinence. And the representation of order being an aesthetic end, it must, as Charles Gildon said, "have certain Means of attaining that End, which are the *Rules* of *Art.*"

IV

The primary rule may perhaps be defined as *decorum.* In Aristotelian and indeed most classical use of the term, decorum consists in the simultaneous "preservation and ennobling of the type"—in a faithful adherence to a probability of manners and language in the dramatic character and, at the same time, in a deepening of the import of this probability by disclosing its connection, not merely with temporary or social law, but with that which reason conceives as universal and ideal. Decorum, especially in neo-classic thought, was occasionally developed to certain conclusions and conventions which were perhaps as contradictory to the general rule of decorum as any other excess would be. Thus, the insistence on the unity and probability of a character's actions found a somewhat extreme ramification in the theory of the "ruling passion," which was perhaps more widespread in neo-classic precept, if not practice, than in the Renaissance. Yet the theory of the "ruling passion" was hardly universal; and the moderate issue which Dryden took with it was by no means unique:

> A character, or that which distinguishes one man from all others, cannot be supposed to consist of one particular virtue, or vice, or passion only; but 'tis a composition of qualities which are not contrary to one another in the same person; thus, the same man may be liberal and valiant, but not liberal and covetous . . . yet it is still to be observed, that the virtue, vice, or passion, ought to be shown in every man, as predominant over all the rest.[9]

A similar rather confined application of the rule of decorum was frequently made in respect to rank or condition: even Dryden, for example, states that "when a poet has given the dignity of a king to one of his persons, in all his actions and speeches that person must discover majesty, magnanimity, and jealousy of power, because these are suitable to the general manners of a king"; and similar assertions are a commonplace throughout eighteenth-century European criticism. Still, such an application—though rather absurd, as Johnson pointed out, when measured against a broader interpretation of decorum—cannot appear as an extreme aberration when one recalls that many of the social distinctions of classical and Renaissance life had, in a sense, something of an intellectual justification in that underlying conception of "degree" and order which the aesthetic principles of classicism and neo-classicism also reflect.

The rule and order of decorum are of special importance in the total formation and unraveling of the outline or plot of action in dramatic or epic poetry. "The manners, in a poem," said Dryden, "are understood to be those inclinations, whether natural or acquired, which move and carry us to actions, good, bad, or indifferent . . . ; or which incline the persons to such or such actions." If several inclinations or actions, for example, have a common source in their past, they are immanent in that past; and again, since that source is perpetuated, as it were, in the subsequent inclinations or actions to which it gives rise, those resulting phenomena have a degree of immanence in each other.

With its goal of rendering vital the probability and ideal meaning which compose decorum, art seeks to declare the unity of this immanence; it attempts, in other words, to descry and exhibit the order and law disclosed in the interweaving of past, present, and future, of event and inclination, of action and ideal. It was earlier stated that, in the classical conception, the very nature of unity or order presupposes for its delineation an ordered approach, an approach, in fact, which necessitates *rule*. "If the rules be well considered," Dryden quotes from Rapin, "we shall find them to be made only to reduce Nature into method, to trace her step by step, and not to suffer the least mark to escape us: 'tis only by these, that probability . . . is maintained, which is the soul of poetry." [10] The interplay of action, motive, and event in the *Iliad*, as might be expected, is summarized and extolled with special frequency, and usually with the purpose of illustrating, as Gildon says, that "this productive Chain of Incidents, in the *Iliad*, could not be formed without admirable Art and Design; and consequently, by such Rules as no Man since has ever been able to alter for the better." The often unfavorable attitude in neo-classic criticism towards many of the more exuberant romances of the Renaissance was largely conditioned by the importance attributed to a simple but closely interwoven unity of action. The ordered construction of the *Iliad*, for example, presents a strong contrast with the lack of it in such a poem as Spenser's *Faerie Queene*, which D'Avenant regarded as a dream "such as Poets and Painters, by being overstudious, may have in the beginning of Feavers," and which even neo-classic admirers of Spenser, like John Hughes, thought hopelessly "distracting" in its "want of Unity."

Among the dramatic rules formulated as subordinate and contributory to the broad governing rule of decorum, the most preëminent, and later the most controversial, were the famous "unities." It is characteristic of the empiricism which he accelerated, and which a century later gave support to the frequent romantic concern with the individual particular, that Thomas Hobbes should have considered the design and plot of a poem as less important than the language; and it is equally characteristic that Dryden should have censured him for doing so:

> Mr. Hobbes, in the preface to his own bald translation of the *Iliad* (studying poetry as he did mathematics, when it was too late) . . . begins the praise of Homer where he should have ended it. He tells us that the first beauty of an epic poem consists in diction; that is, in the choice of words, and harmony of numbers. Now the words are the colouring of the work, which, in the order of nature, is last to be considered. The design, the disposition, manners, and the thoughts, are all before it.[11]

It is the "*Fable* or *Plot*," states Rymer, "which all conclude to be the *Soul* of a *Tragedy;* which, with the *Ancients*, is always found to be a *reasonable Soul;* but *with us*, for the most part, a *brutish*. . . ." [12] "The most beautiful colors laid on without proportion," Aristotle had said, "will not give as much pleasure as the chalk outline of a portrait." The neo-classic doctrine of the "unities," which are frequently compared with "proportion" in painting, constitutes a rather exaggerated offshoot and codification of the classical emphasis on the order and probability of interrelation in the total structure of plot or outline.

Aristotle had mentioned the importance of a "unity of action"—a coherence and order, as a single whole, of events and conclusion. As for the unities of "place" and of "time," he said nothing at all about the former; and, about the latter, he merely observed that, in Greek poetry, the length of time elapsing in the action of dramatic tragedy differs from that of the epic: "For tragedy endeavors, as far as possible, to confine itself to a single revolution of the sun, or but slightly to exceed this limit; whereas the action of the epic has no limit of time." Aristotle's tentative statement about the customary practice of Greek tragedy was hardened into a rule in the first half of the sixteenth century by the Italian critic Giraldi Cintio: within another two or three generations, the restriction to a single day of the time of action in the drama had become a prevalent rule of decorum; and some critics, like Minturno, basing their deduction on the time covered in the *Iliad* and the *Aeneid,* attempted to restrict the action of the epic to a year.

Similarly, in the latter half of the sixteenth century, another Italian, Castelvetro, formulated the rule of the "unity of place" on the ground that, since its action takes place before our eyes, the drama would lose all verisimilitude, all probability, if a change of place were made in the course of it. Castelvetro became so enamored of the unities of time and place, and perhaps also of the prospect of the ingenuity which would be necessary to satisfy them, that he considered the one unity upon which Aristotle had insisted—the unity of action—as quite secondary, and as merely a convenient means of helping to fulfill the requirements of the other two! Within a hundred years after Castelvetro, the unity of place, like that of time, had achieved as much vogue and as much ingenuity of application as even he could have desired. But by the middle of the eighteenth century, these two unities were taken with less seriousness than is sometimes supposed; and Johnson was not alone in regarding them as giving "more trouble to the poet, than pleasure to the auditor," and in considering a drama that observed them "as an elaborate curiosity, as the product of superfluous and ostentatious art, by which is shewn rather, what is possible, than what is necessary."

V

It is the inherent order and proportion of the whole which comprises, in Pope's words, "the naked nature, and the living grace":

'Tis not the lip, or eye, we beauty call,
But the joint force and full result of all.

Aristotle's emphasis on plot rather than on the portrayal of particular characters—his insistence, in other words, that man be revealed through the instrumentality of ordered actions rather than that events be shown through the medium of the feelings and identities of particular men—may be said to illustrate the classical conviction that poetry should seek less to arouse and give voice to the personal associations and feelings of the observer than to guide them, and to impose upon them a finished ideal. The representation of the human being in classical sculpture or painting has a similar end: it does not, by the portrayal of individual "expression" in its model, seek to evoke images from past experiences and thus appeal to the affections and associations of the beholder, but rather, by an imitation of the ideal, to form and control those affections and associations. Such a purpose is ethical in the very broadest sense of the word: for the classical attempt to embody, in plot, design, rhythm, or visual proportion, an "imitation" of the fundamental order and decorum of the universal is not to be viewed as "abstraction" but rather as "integration" and completion; it aspires to present an ideal end and a finished totality which the distinctive "expression" of the model, as a particular, cannot give.

Individual portraiture in painting or sculpture, for example, necessarily diverts art from the whole to only a specific performance and to an incomplete disclosure of one's personal identity. Classical sculpture, on the other hand, does not essay very often the piecemeal and miscellaneous expression of isolated actions, or of such single facets of individual character as would necessarily result from the representation of a given act, position, or facial feature. It endeavors, rather, to picture, in the light of an ideal, the total capacity of the human figure, and to endow it with that completeness which would have originally been formed and determined only by multifarious and rounded activities. It seeks to offer a concluded and integrated synthesis of all ideal human aspects, which, since they cannot be articulated in single performances without the exclusion of some of them and the loss of completeness and unison, are presented, as it were, potentially rather than kinetically, and as in perpetual readiness rather than in active execution.

Xenophon records Socrates as saying that "It is the business of the sculptor to represent in bodily form the energies of the spirit." The spirit, the ideal, is neither a means nor a reaction: it is an end, a fruition. It signifies the *ethos* or "character" —which is eternal and changeless—rather than the *pathos* or "feeling," which is passing and in flux. And from the revelation of the potentialities of this fruition, of this changeless *ethos,* and from the subduing and disciplining of these potentialities to the consonance and decorum of the ideal, arise the inherent finality, the repose and serenity, which are the properties of classical sculpture, architecture, and writing. "We are lovers of beauty," said Pericles of the Athenians, but of beauty "in its *frugal* forms." Similarly, music deserves to be specified as integrated rather than abstract when it becomes classical: when, disregarding appeal to subjective mood or transitory fashion, it weaves a disciplined structure from simple chords and melodies, and, combining with freedom and spontaneity a rational decorum of selection and design, renders audible and definite the potentialities of that proportion and form which alone may be said to constitute the universal in music.

Beneath the classical conception of the ideal and of the essential order, rule, and harmony which characterize it, is, of course, a general conviction of the absoluteness of divine law. The humanistic watchword for the knowledge of this law, as Mr. Bush's lectures on humanism have shown,[13] is *sapientia,* which Cicero defined as the knowledge of "the bonds of union between divinity and man and the relations of man to man." It had been the invaluable contribution of the Greek Sophists to illustrate that the material world, without exception, is characterized by continual flux; and as eighteenth and nineteenth-century empiricism itself, pursuing its logical evolution, was at length to conclude, the forces which dominate or issue from the material world are equally changing. To the "humanist," therefore,—in the sense in which the word has been used in this chapter—the law to which man by his intrinsic nature is subjected is not to be confused with the forces, intelligible or unintelligible, which appear to operate in the phenomenal and animal world, or with such compulsions or necessities as appear to play upon the individual man when he is considered as an atom in social dynamics. Indeed, the humanistic contention is that man possesses an end of his own; that his distinctive privilege consists in his ability to conceive the character of this ideal end; and that for man to be "natural" does not mean for him to live in accordance with what he judges the phenomenal world to be—as both romantic primitivism and empirical science were, in their varying ways, to encourage him to do—but rather to manifest the absolute and centrally unified "nature," the joint ethical and rational fruition, which is at once his obligation and prerogative to fulfill. For the grasping of the nature of this ideal, and for comprehending its ethical import, Renaissance humanistic thought, in the main, had assumed three means, the complete employment of any one of which necessarily involved the employment of the others.

The philosophical conception of the universal was given its original formulation, of course, by Plato; and from the specific issues raised by him, almost all the extensions, re-applications, and contradictions of the theory of universals take their distinctive direction. The history of European philosophy, Mr. Whitehead has said, is "a series of footnotes to Plato." Certainly, since the delineation of most arguments proving the existence and character of the ideal is essentially a recapitulation of the bulk of classical thought, humanistic writers of the Renaissance continually emphasized the importance of classical authority. Even in such a figure as Montaigne, "the vagabondage and egotism," as one critic has said, "are more or less superficial. What we find under the surface is a fairly firm conviction, based on the Greek, and especially the Latin, classics, as to what the true man should be." Again, the humanistic conception of what comprises "natural law"—the law, order, and character, that is to say, of the universal—was strongly interwoven with Christian elements: in this sense, it continues, of course, a widespread tendency of medieval thought; and the complete indebtedness of Grotius to Aquinas and the Spanish Thomists, as Mr. Chroust has shown, is an outstanding example.

Lastly, and like classicism itself, Renaissance humanism placed its confidence in that faculty which alone distinguishes man from lower creation, and which may be designated as "reason." The belief that, with the removal of "reason," not man but only animal is left may seem obvious to the point of being banal; yet the neglect or actual discarding of this commonplace was to plunge European philosophy, by the close of the eighteenth century, into a disunity which was without parallel in its entire history, and from which it has shown no genuine sign of emergence.

> I affirm [said Erasmus], that, as the instinct of the dog is to hunt, of the bird to fly, of the horse to gallop, so the natural bent of man is to philosophy and right and conduct. . . . What is the proper nature of man? Surely it is to live the life of reason, for reason is the peculiar prerogative of man.[14]

From the moral exercise of this faculty, aided by classical authority and religious purpose, insight into the universal may be attained; and the grasp of the absolute standard which that insight affords is, for the humanist, the sure and indeed the only means of estimating the simultaneously real, beautiful, and good, and of evaluating the material reflection of these universals in both human ethics and art.

To know the ideally good with genuine conviction is to insure the fulfillment of it in judgment and act. Humanism, from Plato through the Renaissance, in general subscribes to the contention that what may be called the "will" is dependent upon the "reason," and is determined by it. To know the good is to do it: not to do it arises from a misapprehension of precisely what the good is; it may arise, for example, from the belief that another course of action is preferable or at least more pleasant for oneself—a belief which implies an ignorant confusion of the good with pleasure. The prevalence and strength of this ethical principle in later medieval and Renaissance thought may be illustrated by the fact that the word "dunce" was coined in honor of the extreme followers of Duns Scotus, whose philosophy of "voluntarism" maintained that the will is not dependent at all upon the reason. In the opinion of many of the opponents of Scotus, to say that the will was independent of a rational guide was not, in the final analysis, to maintain that the will was "free": it was rather to admit as an ultimate conclusion that the will is so completely determined by the chain of fluctuating forces and circumstances in the material world that ethical judgment of motives is impossible. Indeed, the will is free only *through* its dependence on the intellect. Because the will follows the intellectual conviction of what is good —and such a conviction implies not an acquiescent half-conception but a firm and vital grasp of the good—all evaluation and all ethical action which proceeds from that evaluation are, in the traditional phrase, *sub ratione boni.*

VI

The exercise of reason, therefore, and the proper use by it of experience, of classical philosophy, and of humanistic studies in general, result in forming the temper and tone of character, the standard of judgment, purposes, and conduct, and the subsequent abidance by that standard, which together constitute the fulfillment of man's "nature." Thus Erasmus could insist that "Nature hath endued man with knowledge of liberal sciences and a fervent desire of knowledge: which thing as it doth most specially withdraw man's wit from all beastly wildness, so hath it a special grace *to get and knit together love and friendship.*"[15]

Such a fulfillment of his ideal "nature" will not suffer a man to incline towards whatever would deprive him of the companionship of the noble and the rationally good in art or conduct. He carries within him his own standard not as a dogma to which to adhere in letter, but as a living intuition; indeed Plato and Aristotle would not have understood the divorce between reason and intuition which seventeenth-century mathematical rationalism was to encourage and European romanticism was generally to accept.

The man who possesses this insight, at once rational and moral, is to be considered, Aristotle had maintained, as the arbiter in all questions of aesthetic taste and of ethics. With Renaissance humanists, and especially with those neo-classic critics, such as Dennis, who are relatively close to the humanistic spirit, this contention is increasingly applied with historical pertinence as well: rational determination of the absolute and ideally good in taste and morality is to be facilitated and made more authoritative by the study of the preferences and the conduct of the best in all ages, and especially in classical antiquity.

Some indication was earlier given of the more radical ramifications in Renaissance and neo-classic criticism of the classical and humanistic principles of decorum, of proportion, and of the ethical purpose of the poet. Similarly, from the humanistic emphasis upon reason as man's distinctive faculty and as his means of contact with the universe, there arise in the Renaissance and culminate in neo-classicism an optimism, based on a confidence in the order of the universe and in man's ability to conceive and abide by that order, and also, with an accompanying trust that only "method" is needed to arrive at and reflect that order, a widespread interest in method itself. "From heavenly harmony," wrote Dryden, "this universal frame began"; and as reason underlies the law and order of nature, human reason is an extension and mirroring of that universal harmony. "Nature," said Dennis, paraphrasing D'Aubignac, is "that Rule and Order and Harmony which we find in the visible Creation," while "Reason is the very same throughout the invisible Creation. For Reason is Order and the Result of Order." [16] Not to conceive and act aright is simply a failure to perceive, by rational means, the nature of order: "nothing can be irregular either in our Conceptions or our Actions, any further than it swerves from Rule, that is, from Reason." [17] Consequently, as Pope stated,

All Nature is but art, unknown to thee;
All chance, direction, which thou canst not see;
All discord, harmony not understood;
All partial evil, universal good.

Renaissance humanism had been characterized by faith based upon reason. The eighteenth century, Mr. Whitehead has said, is "an age of reason based upon faith"—"a faith in the order of nature," of the universal frame.[18] The statement is especially an adequate definition of the movement which was known as Deism, and which was peculiarly indicative of a prevailing temper of the Enlightenment. It is true not only of such thoroughgoing rationalists as Samuel Clarke, John Toland, or Matthew Tindal, who strove to make their blueprints of the universe "reasonably" and even mathematically demonstrable. Its reflection is strong even in the "moral sense" deists such as Shaftesbury and his prolific following: characteristic are the very names of such Shaftesburyan poems as Henry Brooke's *Universal Beauty* (1728–1735), John Gilbert Cooper's *The Power of Harmony* (1745), James Harris's *Concord* (1751), and a bevy of other poems with such titles as *Order* or *Design and Beauty*. It is significant that the English neo-classic figures who most strenuously combat this easy optimism—Swift, Bishop Butler, and Johnson—are men who are at once distinguished by an intense religious conviction and by a genuinely classical conception of the problem of evil inherent in the empirical world.

Accompanying the optimistic generalization that the "rules" which reason discovers are "nature methodized," was an essentially unclassical interest in "method" itself. The exemplification of this interest may be generally described as twofold. It is shown in a somewhat excessive and increasingly academic investigation of the rules which should comprise method, and in an attempt to apply them, whether in aesthetics, morality, or theology, with almost mathematical precision. A further manifestation, above all in British empiricism, was a growing attention to the nature of the reasoning and "methodizing" faculty itself—a tendency which, by the middle of the eighteenth century, was to culminate in a marked skepticism about both reason and method, and was therefore to furnish an argumentative basis for romanticism. Many of the varying English neo-classic conceptions of what constitutes aesthetic judgment, except where they are directly classical in origin, may be said to have been largely determined by the paths which the investigation of "method" pursued. In addition, an inevitable antagonism to this excessive methodizing became increasingly marked, with a resulting emphasis upon feeling; but this emphasis was to receive small philosophical support until its mighty ally, British psychological empiricism, abandoned "reason" for subjective "sentiment."

NOTES

1. *Critical Reflections on Poetry, Painting, and Music* (tr. Thomas Nugent, 1748), I, 44.
2. *Life of Milton, Works* (1820), IX, 91.
3. (Edd. Pottle and Bennett, 1936), p. 55.
4. *Reflections*, I, 42, 44–45.
5. *Reflections upon a Late Rhapsody Called an Essay upon Criticism* (1711), p. 31.
6. *The Tragedies of the Last Age, Considered and Examined by the Practice of the Ancients and by the Common Sense of All Ages* (1678), p. 140.

7. *Dissertation on the Rise, Union, and Power, the Progressions, Separations, and Corruptions of Poetry and Music* (1763), pp. 126–127.

8. *Grounds of Criticism in Poetry* (1704), chap. ii.

9. *Preface to Troilus and Cressida, Essays* (ed. Ker, 1926), I, 215.

10. *Preface to Troilus and Cressida, Essays,* I, 213.

11. Preface to the *Fables, Essays,* II, 252.

12. *Tragedies of the Last Age,* p. 4.

13. *The Renaissance and English Humanism* (Toronto: 1939), chap. ii.

14. *De Pueris Instituendis,* in *Erasmus Concerning the Aim and Method of Education* (ed. Woodward, Cambridge, 1904), p. 190.

15. *Against War* (ed. Einstein, Boston: 1907), pp. 8–9.

16. *Advancement and Reformation of Modern Poetry* (1701), pp. [14–15].

17. *Grounds of Criticism in Poetry* (1704), p. 5.

18. *Science and the Modern World* (1925), p. 83.

B. H. Bronson

WHEN WAS NEOCLASSICISM?

Chambers, in his provocative book *The History of Taste,* pointed out that when the greatest monuments of classic art—the Parthenon, the Athena Parthenos, and other glories of Periclean Athens—came into being, no appreciation of these masterpieces was expressed in writing. No literary evidence survives to show that the aesthetic consciousness of that golden day had reached a level more sophisticated than that of admiring "gold-and-glitter." [1] Art, to be sure, had value, but it was prized for irrelevant reasons, reasons potentially inimical to a free development of the artistic impulse. The reasons were moral, idealistic, or civil: concerned, that is, with useful instruction, or regulative norms, or polity. Art was always to serve some ulterior, public purpose. The artist was of little account or interest in himself but the impersonal object in view was important. Thus the name of Ictinus, and his part in designing the Parthenon, were only of local and immediate concern and were soon forgotten. Pericles could propose divesting the Athena Parthenos of her gold, should the city need the money. The vandalism of such an act he ignores, as he ignores the name of the sculptor, Phidias, his friend. But piety, he allows, would of course require restitution to the goddess. Likewise Herodotus, a world traveler exactly contemporary, estimates the weight of the gold he has seen and carefully inquired about, in famous temples and statues, but says nothing about the aesthetic properties—unless mere size be such—of the works he describes. Thus, for instance: "there was in this temple the figure of a man, twelve cubits high, entirely of solid gold." Or again, Thucydides, on any question of beauty, is equally noncommittal.

Plato, we remember, judges art as the excellence of a *copy* thrice removed from the original, and justifies it only so far as it instructs. Aristotle, in the *Poetics,* also bases the arts on imitation, and our pleasure in them in recognition—that is, of the object represented, whether actual, probable, or ideal ("such as it was or is, such as it is supposed, or such as it ought to be").[2] Led by the Sophists, eventually we approach an art appreciation loosened from the tether of pedagogy and religion, and flowing toward the Hellenistic Renaissance and the consequent Alexandrian efflorescence of patron, collector, connoisseur, antiquary, and dilettante—*id genus omne.* In due course, Rome abandons her earlier puritanic asceticism, is drawn into the Hellenistic current, and imbibes culture and corruption from the vanquished. By the time of Augustus, Rome has little more to learn, though the

From *Studies in Criticism and Aesthetics, 1660–1800,* edited by H. P. Anderson and J. S. Shea (University of Minnesota Press, 1967). Reprinted by permission of the author.

process continues "as streams roll down, enlarging as they flow."

Classicism, then, as a conscious theory of art, as doctrine defensible and defended, was, in the ancient world, Hellenistic, not Hellenic. May we not proceed to hazard the generalization that there can hardly be such a phenomenon as a primary, original classicism? For by the time we meet conscious formulations of aesthetic principle, it is always Neoclassicism that we confront. The doctrinal motivation is always traditional, invoking established norms, and to these the artist's individuality is subservient. Subservient, but not servile nor suppressed by them—rather, inspired—for the attitude is one of worshipful acceptance. Tradition is Law, in fullest realization of which lies the artist's supreme satisfaction. When this frame of mind has become self-conscious and deliberate, with allegiance acknowledged, we are in the presence of Neoclassicism.

Thus, the Augustan classicism of the first century B.C. was an integral part of the Hellenistic cultural renaissance: it was a neoclassical movement, consciously recreative of older and purer models. Terence remembered Menander, Catullus, Sappho, Vergil, Homer and Theocritus. Similarly, of course, the Italian Renaissance is a gradual recovery of the values and ideals of antiquity. Brunelleschi, Alberti, Vignola, Palladio, Lomazzo were neoclassicists in the fullest sense, votaries of ancient order and system, profound students of the Vitruvian precepts. In the following century, the learned genius of Poussin, the encyclopedic labors of Junius, and the poetical treatise of Dufresnoy led to the crystallization of the classical code by the French Academy, establishing the example of the Ancients as "one clear, unchanging, universal light." Under these auspices, English Neoclassicism is launched; and here begins *our* more particular field of inquiry.

The elder of us were bred up in the critical conviction that the eighteenth century was one century we needn't worry about: we knew precisely where it stood, and what it stood for. It was fixed in its appointed place, and there it would always be when we cared to look again. We understood its values, and they bored us. The interesting thing was to see how the human spirit struggled out of that straitjacket into new life. As students of English literature, we knew that its tenets had reached their probably ultimate exemplification in the work of Pope, and that what followed in his track was only feebler and more arid imitation, while the buds of fresh romantic promise were beginning here and there to peep out timidly. That this view, or something like it, is still current is suggested by a front-page article on Christopher Smart in the *Times Literary Supplement*, entitled "Lucky Kit?" "To us," we read, "Smart seems one of the first rebels against the rational behaviour and rationalist thought which have come down like a bad debt from his century to ours." [3] One might have thought that a statute of limitation could ere now have been invoked in such a case.

However the debt may lie, certain it is that that century no longer looks so placid as formerly, whether because we have done more reading, or because events of recent decades have affected our eyesight, or because the newer telescopic lenses have altered the range of visibility and brought things into sharper focus. More seems to have been going on formerly than we had suspected. The painstaking and systematic research of our minute topographers has left seemingly few corners of the eighteenth-century terrain unscrutinized. The net result of this turning over of all such reading as was never read—well, hardly ever—has been to reveal a region of the most baffling complexity and self-contradiction, in which can be found almost anything we choose to seek. Wherever we pause, we are bewildered by the diversity that surrounds us: not alone in the conflict of opinion but shot through the very texture of every considerable author's or artist's work. Of even the chief spokesmen this is probably true. Pope is no exception. The difficulty of making a consistent pattern of Johnson's thinking is notorious. Yet when we look at the authoritative surveys of critical historians, such is not the impression we receive. Their momentum bears us stoutly forward, and at any point they tell us where we are, how many miles we have traveled, how far we have still to go. Best safety lies perhaps in maintaining our speed; but there might be something deceptive in this sense of undeniable progress: "The rough road then, returning in a round, / Mock'd our impatient steps, for all was fairy ground."

All the authoritative guides tell us—and we believe them, do we not?—that the road sets out from "Neoclassicism" and in due course arrives at "Romanticism," taking roughly a century to cover the distance. As we trace it, the landscape visibly alters: it grows less cultivated, more picturesque, wilder. The vegetation is ranker, the hills are higher and more precipitous; the road begins to wind, first in graceful curves (the "line of beauty"); then, adapting itself to the ruggeder country, skirting torrents overhung with jagged rock and blasted old trees, becomes ever more irregular and full of surprises. The wayfarer is at first likely to be struck with solemn awe; later, he finds himself almost breathless and gasping with fearful joy; and at last, in self-surrender, now with streaming eyes, now with shouts of apolaustic abandon, identifies himself with the spirit of what he beholds—or rather, perhaps, identifies what he beholds with his own exalted and pathetic state.

But we have been snatched aloft on the wings of metaphor. Let us decline from the resulting oversimplification and try to regain our composure. And first, returning to Neoclassicism, let us acknowledge that, if regarded as a distinct phase of Art, separate in time and visible effects, in England it never really existed. Or, if it ever took palpable shape, that was only in the pages of certain bloodless theorists, whose formulations, when themselves regarded as efforts of the imagination or works of art, are the sole extant examples of its wholehearted enforcement. Conceptually, it exists as a theoretical terminus that was not and could not be reached in practice, a *reductio ad absurdum* of valid and defensible ideals.

We observed that Classicism, wherever it achieves self-consciousness, in works of art or in underlying doctrine, is always retrospective and therefore essentially neoclassical. Now we have declared that in actual fact a truly neoclassical work of art, as the term is usually employed, was never created in England. The solution of this apparent contradiction is that for practical purposes the troublesome term Neoclassicism is otiose and expendable. It pretends to a distinction without a difference, for the difference is only in degree, not in kind; while the instances of it are hypothetical. The simple term Classicism, then, with occasional inflections, will answer all our needs, and the tautological *neo-* may be dismissed unlamented.

We know pretty clearly what we mean by Classicism, and therefore need not be overelaborate in definition. Briefly to recapitulate: Man, being endowed with ratiocination, has as his birthright the key to proper conduct. What he does ought to be in conformity with the best use of the faculty that so far as he can tell distinguishes him from all other living things. If he so employs it, he may arrive at reasonable inferences about his relation to the universe, and his limitations; about his responsibilities and obligations to himself and to society—"Placed on this isthmus of a middle state." He ought thereby to be led to the recognition of those ideals of truth, morality, order, harmony, which he shares with his fellow man.

In Art, the classical ideals follow from these premises. All the arts—the nobler ones especially—imitate nature, in the sense that they search for a norm, or an ideal, that shall perfectly fulfill and express the natural capabilities or potentialities of the entities, or class of entities, represented: not for the worse but for the essentially typical, or for the better. Analysis has ranked the categories and genres from high to low, has differentiated their characteristic excellences and shown their special objectives. It has noted the appeal of simplicity, the charm of variety within perspicuous unity, the desirability of balance and proportion. And it has discerned a large number of proprieties great and small which can be drawn up and codified at will under the general head of Decorum. The latter are what provide the Dick Minims with their chief exercise and they are, to be sure, the readiest subjects for discussion and debate.

From the ancient classical world we have by a miracle of good fortune inherited a body of literature in many kinds, a large amount of sculpture and sufficient remains of architecture to serve as enduring models of such shining merit that they can hardly be surpassed. They establish the moral and rationally ideal bases of art, teach virtue, and provide inexhaustible illustration of aesthetic beauty and truth . . . So much may suffice by way of summary.

Whatever date may be chosen to mark the beginning of the new age of classicism, in England the emotional state of the last decades of the seventeenth century, like the political situation, is in equilibrium highly precarious. Everywhere the dominant impression is one of instability and insecurity, of which the Stuarts in their brilliant undependability are almost the paradigm. A music characteristically of poignant, nostalgic sweetness, frequent change of tempo, brevity of movement. An architecture eclectic and experimental in its major examples, inclining to the theatrical and grandiloquent. A poetry incapable of broad definition, containing Milton, Butler, Marvell, the pyrrhonism of Rochester, the sweep of Dryden: in over-all summary uncommitted and capable of anything from the sublime to the obscene. Classic control is an ideal then but seldom exemplified and, in a society standing in need of the strong purgatives of Swift's satire, most often perceptible only through a screen of negative images. On the heels of the brittle artificiality of Restoration comedy, and subsiding from the stratosphere of Dryden's heroic drama, the tumultuous rant of Nat Lee, the passionate distresses of Southerne, and the pathos of Otway, the last decade of the century sees the rise of sentimental comedy and the stage is committed to the new era with irresistible parting tenderness, tears of welcome, abundance of fine feeling and flown phrasing. " 'Tis well an old age is out, And time to begin a new." The air is heavy with *un*restrained emotion. John Dennis, the foremost dramatic critic of the new decade, and no contemptible judge when all is said, puts Otway next to Euripides for "a Faculty in touching the softer Passion" [4]—a rating which will be repeated when, much later, Joseph Warton exalts him among "sublime and pathetic poets." [5]

Sublimity is constantly in the thought of Dennis and his contemporaries, made vividly aware of Longinus by Boileau. With consequent editions, translations, and commentaries arriving post with post, Longinus in the front of the eighteenth century is a name to conjure with, in the defense of irregular genius and unbounded Nature. The critics invoke him with a fervor not often accorded the tame Quintilian, who "the justest rules and clearest method joined." The six lines devoted to Longinus in that handbook of Augustan orthodoxy, Pope's *Essay*, are a timely corrective of too rigid notions of that school:

> Thee, bold Longinus! all the Nine inspire,
> And bless their Critic with a Poet's *Fire*.
> An *ardent* Judge, who *zealous* in his trust,
> With *warmth* gives sentence, yet is always just;
> Whose own example strengthens all his laws;
> And is himself that great Sublime he draws.
> (ll. 675–80)

Pegasus spurns the common track, takes a nearer way, and all his end at once attains. Here Pope cites an interesting analogy:

> In prospects [i.e., natural scenery] thus,
> some objects please our eyes,
> Which out of nature's common order rise,
> The shapeless rock, or hanging precipice.
> Great Wits sometimes may gloriously offend,
> And rise to faults *true* Critics dare not mend.
> (ll. 156–60) [6]

A quarter of a century earlier, Dennis, crossing the Alps, called Longinus to mind. Walking, he says, "upon the very brink . . . of Destruction," he was moved to introspection:

> . . . all this produc'd . . . in me . . . a delightful Horrour, a terrible Joy, and at the same time, that I was infinitely pleas'd, I trembled . . . Then we may well say of her [Nature] what some affirm of great Wits, that her careless, irregular and boldest Strokes are most admirable. For the Alpes are works which she seems to have design'd, and executed too in Fury. Yet she moves us less, where she studies to please us more.[7]

This passage, penned in the very year when Pope was born, and published in 1693, must surely have lain in the poet's mind, to produce the same comparison between "great wits" and wild Nature at the opportune moment. But the coincidence failed to sweeten the personal relations of the two men.

Along with frank emotional outbursts, preoccupation with the appearance of Nature is one of the traditional signals, as all know who gladly teach and all who docilely learn, of the rising tide of Romanticism. Yet here at the outset of the century, in the very Citadel of the Rules, we observe these full-fledged extravagancies. Loving description of a gentler Nature fills early pages of Pope, in the 1704 half of *Windsor Forest*, in the *Pastorals* —recall the extremes of empathetic trees and blushing flowers: these springing under the footfall of beauty, those crowding into a shade. Pathetic tenderness, heightening to overwhelming passion, suffuses the *Elegy* and the amazing *Eloisa to Abelard.* And later, of course, praise of Nature and of God in Nature finds supreme expression in the first Epistle of the *Essay on Man*. Already, however, by the date of the latter, Thomson had published the most extended paean to Nature in all her moods that his century, or probably any century, was to see in verse. But, as we shall increasingly observe, it is significant of a trend that, as the years passed, Thomson tried to intellectualize his spontaneous overflow of powerful emotion by injecting more and more sociological, philosophic, politico-economic, and other filler: "untuning the sky," to borrow a phrase from an elder poet, by cerebration.

During these same decades external Nature was receiving tribute in other art forms as well as in poetry. By this time, a great tonal poet, Handel, had written work that both in quantity and quality sets him high among those artists of all time who have made Nature an important part of their subject matter. I do not speak metaphorically but with literal truth. To illustrate, an example may be cited, convenient because brief and universally familiar, though all but unrecognized in such a connection. In the opera *Serse,* there is an aria mistakenly called the "Largo from *Xerxes*," or more popularly, "Handel's Largo." As we know, Handel was a dramatic composer, which means that his creative imagination went hand in hand with textual idea. This is not to say that the process of translating consisted of choosing particular notes to represent named objects—though, in its place, he did not disdain particular imitation of that kind. His genius, however, lay in finding musical equivalents for moods, emotions, scenes coming to him in verbal form. Thus, in the aria mentioned, he is calling up the musical image of a tree: a tree which has grown with the seasons, in the favoring sun and air, and has put forth spreading branches that provide a cool, rustling delight in which to respire and be thankful, "Annihilating all that's made / To a green thought in a green shade." The verbal statement is perfectly explicit about this:

> *Recitative:* Fair, soft, leafy branches of my belovèd sycamore, for you may fate shine brightly. Let thunder, lightning, and storm never outrage your precious peace, nor desecrate you with violence.
>
> *Larghetto* (not *Largo*): Never gave tree a dearer, sweeter, more lovely shade. (Ombra mai fù di vegetabile cara ed amabile soave più.)

The world, of course, has taken that larghetto to its heart for a talisman against mischance in all weathers. But when we return to the stated literal meaning, could (we ask) that total experience, sensuous, sensible, spiritual, be more satisfyingly evoked?

Nature in Handel's music is a topic large enough for extended study. *L'Allegro ed Il Penseroso,* for example, contains abundant responses, from the obvious sound effects of the chirping cricket, the fluting bird song, the ringing round of the merry bells, and the "bellman's drowsy charm," to the subtle impressionism of the "whisp'ring winds soon lull[ing] asleep" in a D minor cadence hushed with twilight, and the rising moon evoked by a voice-line that climbs slowly for an octave and a half. Our total sense of the work, to quote Winton Dean, "is not a matter of pictorial embellishment, but of a creative sympathy transfusing the entire score, a sympathy with English life and the English scene which is perhaps the profoundest tribute Handel ever paid to the land of his adoption." [8] But on the larger subject of Handel's intense susceptibility to nature's more permanent features, Dean declares, with a just disregard of irrelevant temporal considerations: "There is something Wordsworthian in Handel's view of nature, and a strong element of Hellenic pantheism; a consciousness of the immanence of some superhuman power, aloof yet omnipresent, is often combined with a sense of mystery and awe." [9]

To understand Handel's music as description inevitably requires a little concentrated study. Our contemporary notions of the true and proper functions of music are so opposite to the traditions out of which his art grew that at first it seems almost belittling to suggest that he intended his compositions to be understood so literally. But it will not do to ignore the fact, or to laugh off the theory behind it as the midsummer madness of an era now happily outgrown. The problems of imitation in the arts are basic to all classical theory and practice. It is especially important for us to realize that the kind of imitation involved in Handel's work is not a mere invitation to free subjective reverie on the listener's part, the uncontrolled Träumerei, beginning anywhere, to which the latter-day concertgoer is all too prone. If we wish to converse in this tongue, we must learn it. Simply to follow it at all, we have to know its scope and purpose.

The musicians of that period believed that music could and should be a kind of sound-language, precise in the expression of ideas, emotional states, conceptions. But they always started from verbal language, and built an accompanying system of tonal equivalents. Motion swift or slow, rough or even, unbroken or interrupted, was easy enough, given the verbal clue; so too were onomatopoetic concepts, ideas of sound or sound-producing agents, water, wind, animal noises—as exemplified, for instance, in Vivaldi's *Seasons*. Place relations like high or low, near or far, found ready musical equivalents—again if words confirmed them. Handel's contemporary and boyhood friend, Johann Mattheson, who developed this language with extreme elaboration (1739), made a useful classification.[10] He divided the "figures" or *loci topici* into two sorts, *loci notationis* and *loci descriptionis*. The first were the abstract technical devices of music, like inversion, repetition, imitation in its compositional sense. The second were the devices with nonmusical implication, emblematic in meaning, allegorical, metaphorical, of pictorial similitude. In practice, of course, the two kinds were mutually collaborative and consubstantial. The metaphysical and ethical significance of Music had not yet faded from memory. Music had once been next to Divinity in importance because on earth it was the image of celestial order, harmony, and proportion: the Higher mathematics, in fact, with a capital H. It *must* therefore have intellectual meaning, and there ought to be no unbridgeable gap between the physical and metaphysical in music. To give it ideational significance and coherency was not merely right but almost an obligation. As Bukofzer admirably stated the case: "Music reached out from the audible into the inaudible world; it extended without a break from the world of the senses into that of the mind and intellect . . . Audible form and inaudible order were not mutually exclusive or opposed concepts . . . but complementary aspects of one and the same experience: the unity of sensual and intellectual understanding."[11] *Die Affektenlehre*, then, was not the quaint, Shandean aberration it is commonly reported to be. It strove to bring a little more of the unknown within the bounds of the knowable; to introduce evidences of order at the frontiers of rational experience. It became absurd only when it was pushed to extremes—as happened also to rules vainly imposed on other forms of aesthetic expression.

One of its benefits was to describe and objectify emotions in such a way that our private feelings could be shared—identified, experienced, and made generally available in a recognizable musical shape. This, I take it, is the impulse behind all allegory. The process of personifying the passions in *descriptio*, by means of rhythm, tonality, modes, and keys with an established significance, renders music continually allegorical and thereby intellectually viable. This is the rationale of Handel's music, and, basically, it embodies a profoundly classical ideal. Let us not be intimidated by the term Baroque, which in music is a neologism of perhaps mainly negative utility. So universal a man as Handel will not be contained in a narrow room, and we must be wary of trying to impound him. But one thing is certain: it is not for being a revolutionary that he was exalted in his own century. Nor, on the contrary, when in the days of Mannheim and Vienna the classical forms of that great musical age were reaching perfection, was it for being reactionary that Handel's towering genius was arriving at full recognition. From the middle of the century on, whatever school was in the ascendant in England, his fame never ceased.

To emphasize Handel's firm classic alignment is not to do him any injustice. Apart from external nature, the themes that seldom fail to strike fire in his imagination, from *Acis and Galatea* and *Esther* to the very end, were drawn from two sources, the Old Testament and Greek myth. His chief formal innovation lay in the use he made in the oratorios—but not the operas—of the chorus, where his debt is to Greek tragedy via Racine's imitative handling of it. In him appears a similar deployment of choral participation on two levels: that is, both within and above the dramatic action. The chorus concentrates the issues and sums them up; and they rise in and out of that involvement and not as a moral tag superimposed from without. This important insight I owe again to Winton Dean. "With Handel," Dean declares, "as with the Greeks, the force of such pronouncements varies in proportion with their dramatic motivation. The central themes of *Saul*, *Belshazzar*, *Hercules*, and *Jephtha*, round which the whole plot revolves, are envy, *hubris*, sexual jealousy, and submission to destiny—all favorite subjects of the Greeks—and it is no accident that those works are conspicuous both for the grandeur of their choruses and for the overriding unity of their style. Handel in this temper reminds us again and again of Aeschylus."[12]

Without leaving problems of imitation, and still pursuing the classical ideals, we may shift now to the subject of landscape gardening, wherein the mid-century is seen to have defined its sympathies and characterized itself in especially typical fashion. Not the least characteristic fact here is the confluence of contradictory impulses that blur the purpose and direction of changes taking place. Are we watching the gradual repossession of England by Nature with the approach of the Romantic Age, or is the motivation behind this movement quite another thing? Which, it may be asked, is the more romantic, in the deepest sense, the appeal to the eye or the appeal to the mind which "creates, transcending these, / Far other worlds and other seas?"

Several kinds of imitation are involved here, of which we may distinguish two or three in what may have been the order of their emergence. Under the guidance of Sir William Temple, who led away from the stiff, geometrical garden patterns in vogue at the end of the seventeenth century, with their radiating or parallel straight walks, clipped hedges, trees shaped in balls, cones, pyramids symmetrically balanced, the century opened with a strong impulse toward the "Sharawadgi," the supposed sophistication of oriental irregularity. Pevsner has shown the political overtones of English "liberty" in this movement. Shaftesbury's declared approbation of the "horrid graces of the wilderness" indicates British restiveness under too strict control, and also reflects anti-Gallic sentiment in opposition to the rule of Lenôtre.[13] The English Constitution was a *natural* growth, was it not?

This tendency soon broadened and blended with Augustan ideas of classical attitudes toward Nature. The great Roman poets were all poets of nature, assuming the pastoral frame of mind, reveling in country philosophizing, cultivating the natural delights of their rural retreats. The mood was inherited from the Hellenistic development of natural parks and gardens, associated with the Muses and philosophical discussion, and carried on in the Sicilian pastoral tradition and its Alexandrian sequel. Country life in the sumptuous villas of the later Roman nobles, statesmen, generals, not to mention emperors, had much of what the English landed gentry emulated in their great estates; and similar attitudes toward the natural scene seem to have been generated in both worlds.

Even before William Kent came the experiments of Vanbrugh and Bridgman at Castle Howard, Blenheim, and Stowe in romantic gardening. H. F. Clark observes:

> The triumph of the irregular occurred during the rise of Palladianism in architecture. Both were derived from classical sources filtered through the work of Italian Renaissance scholarship . . . Irregular gardens were as classical and correct as the buildings of the Burlington group . . . [Sir Henry Wotton's precept that] "as fabrics should be regular, so gardens should be irregular," was a truth which classical authority was found to have practiced . . . [This, it was asserted] was "the method laid down by Virgil in his second *Georgic*." Addison, whose vogue as a leader of taste was enormous, brought the weight of his authority to the side of change by claiming that his own taste was Pindaric, that in his garden it was difficult to distinguish between the garden and the wilderness.[14]

Chiswick Park, begun after Burlington's first visit to Italy, was one of the first of the new irregular gardens, in which, it appears, Pope himself had a hand along with Bridgman. Kent continued it, and Pope theorized the work in his Epistle to Burlington.

Nothing is clearer than that these designers painted primarily to the mind's eye, and aimed at presenting to the observer temporal vistas. "What an advantage," exclaims Shenstone,

> must some Italian seats derive from the circumstance of being situate on ground mentioned in the classicks! And, even in England, wherever a park or garden happens to have been the scene of any event in history, one would surely avail one's self of that circumstance, to make it more interesting to the imagination. Mottoes should allude to it, columns, &c. record it; verses moralize upon it.[15]

Like the poets with their bejeweled incrustations of literary quotation, they enriched the scene by setting up as many echoes as possible, by every variety of associational device that might stimulate the imagination and excite emotion. Urns and obelisks, statues and temples evoked the classical nostalgia on three levels: through the recollection of actual classical scenes; through such scenes idealized in the idyllic canvases of Poussin and Claude; and by recalling images and sentiments from the ancient poets with whose work so much of their literary experience was impregnated. This art, then, was an imitative art not only in a pictorial sense but also in its close kinship to literature.

The art of music and the art of gardening are alike in the fact that specific meaning in both must be introduced from another medium. Music, we have seen, expresses ideas by developing a metaphorical language that must depend on verbal assistance for correct interpretation of any but the most rudimentary conceptions. But modes and keys acquire independent meaning from repetitional use; and conventional rhythms, meters, and musical figures will convey an accepted sense without the help of intermediaries. Obviously, we must have been tutored in order to understand: it is not enough to be sensitive to musical impressions. Similarly, now, gardening developed its own *Affektenlehre.* The language of flowers has always been a very arbitrary one that had to be memorized; but the toughness and durability of oaks, the dark foliage of yews, the cadent habit of willows, have supplied an obvious symbolism that by association is generally known and acknowledged.

It may be that in some parts of the Orient the language of vegetation has been pursued to such a degree of cerebral sophistication that complex ideas can be formulated by its means alone. If so, it would of course presume in the recipients equal study, knowledge of conventions, and fastidious discrimination in their use. Among the English, poets have been the earliest interpreters and moralizers of natural phenomena. Topographical poetry was already in vogue by the time the landscape artists began to elaborate the extrasensory content of nature in their pictorial compositions. "So," writes Dyer in "Grongar Hill,"

> So we mistake the future's face,
> Ey'd thro' hope's deluding glass,
> As yon summits soft and fair,
> Clad in colours of the air,
> Which, to those who journey near,
> Barren, brown, and rough appear . . .
> Thus is nature's vesture wrought
> To instruct our wand'ring thought.
> (ll. 121–26, 99–100)

The landscape designers determined to make equally certain, by the employment of adventitious means, by architecture, sculpture, inscriptional mottoes, artful scenic punctuation,[16] and control of point of view, that the significance of their statements should be rightly understood. Indeed, it sometimes seems as though they resent the pulse of life and would fix the scene in a single moment of time, like the garden in Chaucer's dream, where the sun was always temperate and never set, and change of seasons was unknown. "To see one's urns, obelisks, and waterfalls laid open," Shenstone reflects, "the nakedness of our beloved mistresses, the Naiads and the Dryads, exposed by that ruffian Winter to universal observation: is a severity scarcely to be supported by the help of blazing hearths, chearful companions, and a bottle of the most grateful burgundy." [17]

But, as the decades passed, purposes were clarified, subtler meaning was directed to a wider "literate" public, and taste altered. Imitation grew more sophisticated and in a sense more philosophical. The classical idea of what nature herself intended in an imperfect realization of purpose in any given local effort, struggling with intractable elements, became the overriding concern. The genius of place held the secret, and it was the duty of the artist to consult this genius and liberate it into perfect expression. The art, however, lay in ridding it of local idiosyncrasy and domestic encumbrances, which were like bad personal habits, the uncouth awkwardness of village speech, dress, or manners. It was a generalized, ideal beauty that was sought, the perfect classical statement that did not imply stereotyped repetition or dull platitude but became a fresh and living realization of universal truth. "Great thoughts," Johnson said, "are always general."

To reconstitute the face of nature in this way was to compose three-dimensional paintings not from devotion to the charms of nature but according to an intellectual conception as classical as the modeling of antique sculpture. Truth to an ideal beauty, essentialized from a myriad of imperfectly beautiful particulars, was the object here as there: to be real but not realistic, natural but not naturalistic—"the artifice of eternity," the mind's embodiment. "Objects," Shenstone wrote, "should indeed be less calculated to strike the immediate eye, than the judgment or well-formed imagination." To be sure, there are natural proprieties, rules derived from Nature's own practice, "discovered, not devised." "The eye should always look rather down upon water." "The side-trees in vistas should be so circumstanced as to afford a probability that they grew by nature." "Hedges, appearing as such, are universally bad." "All trees" (that is, species of them) "have a character analogous to that of men . . . A large, branching, aged oak is perhaps the most venerable of all inanimate objects." [18]

It must be apparent, then, that what we have

been tracing is not the development of a more and more romantic love of an external Nature uncontaminated by the hand of man; but rather a more and more subtly refined Art, working with natural phenomena as its plastic elements, on the same classical principles that had been operative in literary art, sculpture, architecture, and were now coming to new and vigorous life in English painting, and, soon after, in the classical revival in France. How, then, is it permissible to use this art of landscape gardening as proof of the continual progress toward Romanticism? Brown's notorious "capabilities" were basically a classical theory—a point too seldom acknowledged.

So far as concerns the cult of the Picturesque, it may be fair to say that it is the belated psychologizing stepchild of the much earlier cult of irregularity, via the theories of Burke at the mid-century and concerned to rationalize, not to retreat into, wilderness. It set up "savage" Rosa, who had not lacked earlier admirers—note Walpole's outburst, going over the Alps with Gray in 1739: "Precipices, mountains, torrents, wolves, rumblings, Salvator Rosa!" [19]—on a higher pedestal than Claude, partly in conscious protest against a late classicism that it felt had become too pure. The asymmetry of the older Baroque tradition, continued on the Continent in the Rococo, no doubt also helped to familiarize sensitive spirits with these "Gothic" tastes.

The connection between the landscape gardener's and the painter's point of view was patent to all. Shenstone pronounced: "Landskip [which he distinguishes from 'prospects,' or distant views] should contain variety enough to form a picture upon canvas; and this is no bad test, as I think the landskip painter is the gardiner's best designer. The eye requires a sort of balance here; but not so as to encroach upon probable nature." [20] But there was as yet no school of English landscape painters to provide models, and of course Shenstone was looking toward Italy. Not until the seventh decade, when Richard Wilson translated the English scene into classical terms, was the need supplied. Hitherto, no painter of the English natural scene had appeared who could hold a candle to Claude or the Poussins. And, in fact, when we look for classicism of any sort among *early* eighteenth-century British painters, it is very hard to find. The sequence of names, Holbein, Van Dyck, Lely, Kneller, covers in symbolic outline much of the earlier history of British art. Against this long tradition of foreign lawgivers, and the current snobbery of the Connoisseurs, Hogarth fought with every weapon he could find or invent. He managed to loosen the soil for a British planting. He was no traditionalist and neither by precept nor practice did his influence tell in the direction of Classicism. It was not, however, ancient art he was tilting against but snobbery and pseudo-connoisseurs.[21] But neither would anyone be likely to attach a Romantic label to him. Although he was a theorist, he was by temperament an improviser more interested in facts than in formulas. His masterpieces, e.g., Captain Coram's portrait, his Mrs. Salter, the sketches of the Shrimp Girl, and his Servants, do not set up for "ideal nature," though the Coram has been called one of the great original landmarks of British portraiture.

Ellis Waterhouse dates the beginning of the classical age in British painting precisely at 1760, with the accession of George III and the first public exhibition of the newly incorporated Society of Artists.[22] To this exhibition Reynolds contributed his "Duchess of Hamilton as Venus." The following year Hogarth sent his ill-starred "Sigismonda"; in 1764, Benjamin West entered his first classical history picture. But matters were already getting out of hand because the rules were so permissive that anything sent in was eligible to be shown—even paper cutouts; and the Academy was inaugurated in 1768 to introduce some needful measures to control rights of entry.

Thenceforward, after the establishment of the Royal Academy, throughout Reynolds's presidency, in spite of shortcomings and backslidings, the principles of the Grand Style predominated. During the decade of the seventies, Reynolds made his most determined effort to emulate the old Renaissance masters. This was also the time of his greatest influence. From the late seventies through the early eighties, Barry was doing his big work ("Progress of Human Culture") for the Royal Society of Arts, the logical fulfillment, if not the triumph, of the doctrine. The history picture, in full panoply and classical costume, stood up for the main, and West, with crown patronage, Gavin Hamilton, Copley, Opie, Northcote, and Reynolds as well, strove to realize the ideal. But other winds were blowing, and the mesmerism of Raphael and Michelangelo lost compulsion with the passing years. By 1790, the history piece had been, if not declassicized, then refurbished in modern guise, and "ideal nature" in the Grand Style, though still a noble ideal, no longer compelled assent—at least in England.

Nonetheless, with the presidential addresses of Reynolds, we are given the *first* great *literary* statement of the classical ideal in painting. Professor Bate goes even further, declaring that "Reynolds' *Discourses* comprise perhaps the most representative single embodiment in English of eighteenth-century aesthetic principles." [23] The *Discourses* were delivered over a very long span—from January 1769 to December 1790—and were first published complete in 1794. They had a cumulative power; and it is beyond contradiction that eighteenth-century classical *doctrine* reaches its climactic formulations in the last decades of the age.

As for Reynolds's own enormous achievement on canvas, it is very difficult to confine. "Damn him," exclaimed Gainsborough in grudging acknowledgment, "how various he is!" At the end of his life, Reynolds simply and regretfully confessed that Michelangelo's example had been too lofty for imitation: "I have taken another course, one more suited to my abilities, and to the taste of the times in which I live." [24] Nevertheless, this clear and uplifted spirit, this "very great man," as Johnson justly called him, did incontrovertibly succeed, without violating the bond of individual portraiture, in typifying and idealizing for all time a class, a portion of society, a way of life, in dozens of his numberless subjects. In the abundant best of his canvases, we seem to have been shown, not merely so many named personages, but a great deal of the age in which they lived. In a subtle way, he reconciled the individual portrait to the generalized, ideal history piece, a marriage most fully exemplified in his monumental *Family of the Duke of Marlborough,* but demonstrated as well in many of his more informal works.

If there were stirrings against the classical teaching of Reynolds in the art of painting, the doctrine was hardly questioned when applied to sculpture. Reynolds devoted his Tenth Discourse to this subject. In it he rebukes all attempts to include elements of the picturesque, or such pictorial effects as flying drapery or wind-swept hair, or contrasts of light and shade, or imbalance, as a child against a full-size figure, or a stooping figure as companion to an upright one. The delight of sculpture, he declares, is an intellectual delight in the contemplation of perfect beauty, in which the physical pleasure has little part. This art only partly represents nature. "Sculpture," Reynolds pronounces, "is formal, regular, and austere; disdains all familiar objects, as incompatible with its dignity, and is an enemy to every species of affectation. . . . In short, whatever partakes of fancy or caprice, or goes under the denomination of Picturesque . . . is incompatible with that sobriety and gravity which is peculiarly the characteristic of this art." [25]

It is plain that the work of the previous generation of sculptors, even the great Roubillac in his funerary monuments, would not have been approved by Reynolds, because their work was semi-dramatic, and aimed to make a theatrical statement. But the new members of the Royal Academy, Nollekens, Flaxman, Banks, and Bacon, received the doctrine *con amore.* Nollekens persisted, after his years in Rome, in modeling even Johnson without benefit of wig, evoking (it is said) Johnson's growling protest: "Though a man may for convenience wear a cap in his own chamber, he ought not [in a bust] to look as if he had taken physic." Flaxman's work is filled with the distillation of eighteenth-century ideas of "the just designs of Greece." [26] He worked in Rome 1787–1790. Bacon's statue of Johnson, in St. Paul's, in toga and cropped head, perfectly fulfills Reynolds's notion of "ideal nature." Indeed, Katherine Esdaile, the historian of British sculpture, is filled with indignation at the lamentable triumph achieved by classicism over the native tradition of good homely realism. It is certain that in this art, if naturalism means the tendency toward Romantic individualism, the last two decades of the eighteenth century were a palpable retrogression from its arrival.

A kindred spirit is visible in architecture. The Burlingtonian tradition, carried past 1750 by Isaac Ware, James Paine, and Sir Robert Taylor, was reinvigorated, reoriented, and archaeologized, in part through the excitement over Pompeii at the mid-century, and by investigation all the way from Paestum, Sicily, Athens, as far eastward as Palmyra. The fifties were a decade of strenuous field work by both English and French in Greek and Roman antiquities. Soufflot and Leroy, the Comte de Caylus, Stuart and Revett, William Chambers, Winckelmann, Clérisseau, were some of the best known, and Piranesi, who published three sets of Roman engravings by 1754—not to mention the official volumes on Herculaneum beginning to appear in 1757. Robert Adam's first tour lasted from 1753 to 1758. He filled notebook after notebook with archaeological studies. His brother James followed his example in 1760. James Stuart's and Nicholas Revett's *Antiquities of Athens,* published in 1762, was based on their investigations of the previous decade. Lord Anson's London house, in the Greek style, was the first conspicuous result. Between the two stricter modes, the Palladian and Athenian, falls the revolutionary Adam work, more various, freer, but classical in inspiration, and enormously successful, influential, and fashionable. Fiske Kimball, in fact, our most painstaking authority on the Rococo, credits Adam's vogue with being responsible for the demise of that style even in France, its originator.[27] Sir William Chambers likewise throws his weight solidly behind the classical tradition (apart from sowing his wild oats in Chinese gardens); so did the Woods of Bath; and even James Wyatt, although flirting occasionally with the Gothic, began and continued throughout his career with classically designed buildings. Fashions in architecture are not easily overturned. But the Adam brothers were thoroughgoing, and did really change the look of things. And their regulation, of course, affected all the interior appointments, from carpet to ceiling, wall decoration, furniture, and lighting. Wedgwood, who belongs to the same decades, with his Etruscan and classical pottery adorned with charming antique luting modeled by Flaxman, fitted in beautifully here. Moreover, thanks to the practical improvements of Caslon in type-founding, and the fanatical perfectionism of Baskerville in the middle decades, fine printing was moving on a parallel course. Along with the extreme beauty and refinement of his Roman type, Baskerville was learning how to manipulate the white space on his page, until his Latin titles sprang out three-dimensional, like antique urns and pedestals standing in the open air, bearing classical inscriptions. His example was not lost on his immediate successors, and in the hands of the Foulis brothers, of Bensley, and Bulmer—with the aid of such designers as Wilson, Fry, the Martins, and Figgins—printing became more classically splendid right to the end of the century. It would be hard to conceive of any piece of furniture more thoroughly at home in the library of an Adam house than some of the magnificent quartos and folios that were published in the years when those great houses were built or remodeled: Syon, Osterly, Kedleston, Kenwood, Luton Hoo, Mellerstain, Newby Hall, and many another. Appropriately, some of the most sumptuous volumes were works of the line of architects already named, Burlingtonians and Classicists both: Campbell's *Vitruvius Britannicus,* Burlington's *Fabbriche Antiche,* Chambers's *Treatise,* Stuart's and Revett's *Antiquities of Athens,* Robert Adam's *Ruins of Diocletian's Palace* and the Adam brothers's *Works in Architecture* are only a few of the most distinguished. They had, moreover, an international circulation and international influence.

If, in summarizing our impressions of the latter decades of the century we recall that Goldsmith then showed in his two great essays in decasyllabic couplets how freshly the Augustan music could be reembodied in the hands of a master of that tradition; if we add to Reynolds's *Discourses* Johnson's *Lives of the Poets* (1779–1781): we shall be in no danger of attributing to Classicism an early demise. If we set beside these masterpieces Gibbon's magnificent elegiac monument to ancient Rome (1776–1787), a supreme embodiment of the Augustan spirit—an epic, as Lewis Curtis demonstrates, reared to celebrate Wisdom and Moral Virtue guiding Power, and warning against surrender;[28] and if, moreover, we remember Burke's nobly conservative defense of the principle of continuity and tradition: we shall not imagine that the Classical Age dwindled or died from anemia and decay. Classicism is a faith, and, being a faith, therefore never fully realized but demanding constant effort from its devotees to attain the values it essentially embodies: the humane ideals of rational truth, moral virtue, order, and beauty expressive of these goods. The community of artists and thinkers with whom we are here concerned, whatever their individual variance, ardently professed and diligently sustained these convictions in art and in life. Burke's *Letter to a Noble Lord* (1796) is not the least splendid expression of that spirit, and George Sherburn's sentence upon it is finely appropriate: "The echo from Virgil may serve to remind us that Burke's art came from the ancients, and that with the figured and fervent mood of his last works eighteenth-century prose goes out in a blaze of noble artifice." [29]

In studying the past, we have grown so habituated to our progressive way of anticipating the future in its earliest premonitory signs that we seldom allow a moment's reflection to the oversimplification and really gross distortion of the historical truth of any actual moment of the past which this practice entails. To the people who are living in it, the present seldom looks like the future. Very few have the leisure for prophecy—except of calamity—or the power of disinterested observation and detachment. The present is always a confused muddle of conflicting values and doubtful issues, and the battle never ceases.

Much earlier, I quoted a dubious couplet: "The rough road then, returning in a round, / Mock'd our impatient steps, for all was fairy ground." It would not be surprising if no one recognized the lines, which intrinsically are hardly memorable. They are part of Johnson's crafty demonstration that in Pope's celebrated onomatopoetic description of the labors of Sisyphus—

> With many a weary step, and many a groan,
> Up a high hill he heaves a huge round stone;
> The huge round stone, resulting with a bound,
> Thunders impetuous down, and smoaks along
>   the ground.

—"the mind governs the ear and the sounds are estimated by their meaning." [30] They do not make very good sense; but I intended to impose on them a kind of symbolic sense, to suggest that the looks of the road and the speed of the passage were highly subjective matters, largely dependent upon—or at least radically affected by—the purpose and preoccupations of the passenger. I have wished in this paper to spend an hour looking at the eighteenth century as if it were a spatial rather than a temporal panorama. For a while I was tempted to take as my title, "From Romantic to Classic," thinking thereby to point the moral in a ready and easy way. The pretty paradox seemed to provide a sort of compass or a means of escape from the bewildering complexities wherein I was stumbling. And indeed it was a help, though insufficient, by its inherent magnetic property of lifting by attraction one sort of matter from the indiscriminate mass.

But, in the end, it had to be rejected because the truth is that, as historians, we are not obliged to travel the road either in one direction or in the other. Both ends of the panorama are equally open to our elevated, timeless vision. A topographical map does not itself move: it lies open to inspection. It is not like Rabelais's Island of Odes, "où les chemins cheminent, comme animaux." Its roads, on the contrary, stay exactly where they are laid down.

It is worthwhile, I think, and corrective of the distortions arising from our obsession with interpretation *ex post facto,* to try to look at an Age in the richness of its complexities and contradictions. If we did not know—or if we could awhile forget—that the Age of Romanticism followed on the heels of the Age of Enlightenment, should we not quite naturally be seeing the eighteenth century in quite another than the customary view: as in fact a period when the spirit of Classicism steadily *refined* its values, grew increasingly *assured* in its declaration of them, and never knew better their true and vital meaning and importance than when on the verge of losing them?

> This thou perceiv'st, which makes thy love
>   more strong,
> To love that well which thou must leave ere
>   long.

Hence, I have been concerned to call to mind the emotional ferment, the resistance to rule, the communion with external nature, all those signs and signals of "Romanticism" that complicate the *opening* of the Age of Reason; next, the irregular and disconcertingly rhythmless horizon line where at unpredictable intervals the different arts thrust up their temporal peaks; and, toward the close of the century, the passion for order, the lofty vision of a timeless beauty, the powerful affirmations of faith in man's ability to define and by strenuous effort to approximate it by the rational use of his human endowment, his shared inheritance, native and natural: the persistent and lasting devotion to the Classical Ideal.

NOTES

1. Frank P. Chambers, *The History of Taste* (New York, 1932), pp. 273ff.
2. *Poetics* 1460b 10.

3. *Times Literary Supplement,* December 29, 1961, p. 921.

4. "Remarks upon Mr. Pope's Translation of Homer" (1717), *Critical Works,* ed. Edward Niles Hooker (Baltimore, 1943), II, 121.

5. Joseph Warton, *An Essay on the Genius and Writings of Pope* (London, 1756), I, dedication. Otway was demoted in later editions.

6. Ed. Warburton, 1744. Earlier editions place the last couplet at ll. 152–53; Warburton returned to that order in 1764.

7. *Miscellanies in Verse and Prose* (1693), ed. Edward Niles Hooker, II, 380–81.

8. Winton Dean, *Handel's Dramatic Oratorios and Masques* (London and New York, 1959), p. 320.

9. *Ibid.*, p. 63.

10. Johann Mattheson, *Der volkommene Capellmeister* (Hamburg, 1739).

11. Manfred Bukofzer, *Music in the Baroque Era* (New York, 1947), p. 369.

12. Dean, *Handel's Dramatic Oratorios and Masques,* p. 41.

13. Nikolaus Pevsner, "The Genesis of the Picturesque," *The Architectural Review,* November 1944; also the same author's *The Englishness of English Art* (London, 1956), p. 156.

14. H. F. Clark, *The English Landscape Garden* (London, 1948), pp. 12–13.

15. William Shenstone, "Unconnected Thoughts on Gardening" in *Works* (1768 ed.) II, 113.

16. The neat word is A. R. Humphreys's in *William Shenstone* (Cambridge, 1937), p. 100.

17. Shenstone, "Unconnected Thoughts," II, 121.

18. *Ibid., passim.*

19. Horace Walpole to Richard West, September 28, 1739.

20. Shenstone, "Unconnected Thoughts," II, 115.

21. J. T. A. Burke, "Classical Aspect of Hogarth's Theory of Art" in *England and the Mediterranean Tradition* (Oxford, 1945).

22. Ellis K. Waterhouse, *Painting in Britain, 1530–1790,* Pelican History of Art (Baltimore, 1953), p. 157.

23. Walter Jackson Bate, *From Classic to Romantic* (Cambridge, Massachusetts, 1946), Chapter III, §6, p. 79.

24. Conclusion of the Fifteenth Discourse, December 10, 1790.

25. Conclusion of the Tenth Discourse, December 11, 1780.

26. An offshoot of this impulse is to be observed in the sudden flood of Homeric illustration after 1750, reaching its classical climax about 1790. See Dora Wiebenson, "Subjects from Homer's Iliad in Neoclassical Art," *Art Bulletin,* XLVI (March 1964), 23–37.

27. Fiske Kimball, *The Creation of the Rococo* (Philadelphia, 1943), pp. 207ff.

28. "Gibbon's Paradise Lost" in *The Age of Johnson: Essays Presented to Chauncey Brewster Tinker,* ed. F. W. Hilles (New Haven, 1949), pp. 73ff.

29. George Sherburn, "The Restoration and Eighteenth Century" in *A Literary History of England,* ed. Albert Baugh (New York, 1948), p. 1094.

30. Johnson, Life of Pope, paragraph 332 (*Lives of the Poets,* ed. G. Birkbeck Hill [Oxford, 1905], III, 231).

Geoffrey Tillotson

"NATURE" AND CORRECTNESS IN THE POETRY OF POPE

Seldom has the *fiat* of an older poet fallen on more attentive ears than Walsh's on Pope's. Pope told Spence that

> About fifteen [i.e. 1703 or thereabouts], I got acquainted with Mr. Walsh. He used to encourage me much, and used to tell me, that there was one way left of excelling: for though we had several great poets, we never had any one great poet that was correct; and he desired me to make that my study and aim.[1]

On the face of it this advice appears suited to a prose writer rather than to a poet. But for Pope and his contemporaries the word *correctness* had the full colour of novelty. The meaning Walsh gave it was little older than Pope himself. According to the *O.E.D.* the word had been first used in its new sense by Dryden in the Prologue to *Aurengzebe* (1676):

> What Verse can do, he has perform'd in this,
> Which he presumes the most correct of his.

Spence gives Walsh's statement a narrow interpretation:

> This, I suppose, first led Mr. Pope to turn his lines over and over again so often, which he continued to do till the last; and did it with surprising facility.

Spence considers the anecdote to refer simply to versification, and no doubt this is what Walsh principally intended. In Dryden the word had had this connotation. Correctness, however, had, or came to have, a more comprehensive meaning for Pope.

I

There were elements in this wider connotation which inevitably had more impressiveness for Pope and his contemporaries than for any later age, but much of what Pope understood by correctness has permanent validity since, in forming his principles, he took over nothing that he did not find reasonable. For Pope correctness was the newest term in that Aristotelian body of doctrines which had grown to such firm proportions in the work of sixteenth- and seventeenth-century critics. Correctness freshened the inevitable homage to Aristotle, gave the poet's orthodoxy the self-respect of an original contribution, the zest of not being entirely like his predecessors. Aristotle had considered poetry as an imitation. But the poet, he had counselled, must not simply copy what he finds before him. His art must help nature to realize the perfection, the grand simplicity,[2] which she is aiming at but is always being accidentally prevented from realizing. The poet must discover the balked intentions of nature and so vicariously free her. He must allow nature freedom to become Nature. He will do this by removing all the accidentals, by seeking the common ground in the mind of all men (or of all men who can be thought of as having minds) and by erecting his poem on that:

> First follow Nature, and your judgment frame
> By her just standard, which is still the same:
> Unerring NATURE, still divinely bright,
> One clear, unchang'd, and universal light,
> Life, force, and beauty, must to all impart,
> At once the source, and end, and test of Art.[3]

But, not unduly, the Renaissance critics felt nervous about how this selection and idealization should be accomplished. It was part of a natural humility before the newly discovered or newly valued treasures of antiquity:

> with reference to what model or standard were they to select in arriving at their ideal imitation? If they selected with reference to an image of perfection in the mind, they invited the reader or beholder likewise to look within in estimating the justness of the imitation. But to do this would for the neo-classicist be to lose himself in the vaguely subjective; it would be to set up an inner rather than an outer norm, the one thing above all he was trying to avoid.

From *On the Poetry of Pope* by Geoffrey Tillotson (1938), pp. 1–42. Reprinted by permission of Oxford University Press.

> Why not get around the whole difficulty, and at the same time show proper humility, by foregoing the attempt to imitate Nature directly, and imitating rather those great writers in whom the voice of universal tradition tells us we find her idealized image? Little need to go directly to nature, says Scaliger, when we have in Virgil a second nature. The writer does not need to chase an elusive image of perfection in his own mind, but merely to copy Virgil; and the reader is also saved the trouble of looking within, and has merely to compare Virgil with the copy.[4]

The ancients had "followed Nature" and so a later poet with Nature as his aim would be wise to imitate them: if he followed the ancient way of following Nature, his own imitation of Nature would be more likely to turn out satisfactory both for his own age and for later ages. Virgil, indeed, had worked on the same principle. He had found that to imitate Homer was the same thing as to imitate nature:

> Nature and Homer were, he found, the same.[5]

If Virgil had imitated Homer, to imitate either Virgil or Homer seemed theoretically the same thing. In reality the two things were very different. Pope said as much in conversation with Spence:

> In speaking of comparisons upon an absurd and unnatural footing, he mentioned Virgil and Homer; Corneille and Racine; the little ivory statue of Polycletes and the Colossus.—Magis pares quam similes? [asks Spence]. "Ay, that's it in one word." [6]

To imitate not Homer but Virgil was more congenial to the Renaissance poet, since the dominating element in the Renaissance was Latin. In English poetry it is the poets of Rome who have most say till the purer glory of Athens is discovered more fully in the mid-eighteenth century and has its effect on the poetry of Collins, Keats, and Shelley. When put beside Virgil, Homer seemed too primitive for an age already enchanting itself with the gilded profusion of the baroque. Dryden, for instance, considers it a pity that Homer lived too early to benefit by the Latin poets' discovery of the "turn." And so *Haec omnia quae imiteris, habes apud alteram naturam, id est Virgilium.*[7] For Berkeley, the young Pope is "one who knows so well how to write like the old Latin poets." [8]

The allegiance to the original and secondary ideas of imitation meant allegiance to certain correct literary forms, and Pope is often found writing in these forms. As a boy he had written a tragedy, stealing plentifully from the *Iliad.* An early epic, with Alcander, Prince of Rhodes, as hero, was written and destroyed. His published work begins, as Virgil's had begun, with *Pastorals.* "My next work, after my Epic," he told Spence, "was my Pastorals; so that I did exactly what Virgil says of himself [in his sixth Eclogue]." [9] After the *Pastorals* come translations from Ovid and Statius, the mock epic, *Rape of the Lock,* and the *Dunciad,* the full-length translations of Homer, the Horatian essays and epistles. In the *Elegy to the Memory of an Unfortunate Lady* Pope writes a Roman elegy and *Eloisa to Abelard* is in the manner of the *Heroides.* Pope's allegiance to antiquity must not, however, be exaggerated. Pope, at bottom, is himself. He was not the man to place a pedantic interpretation on his correctness, his imitation. He imitates not only Romans but Chaucer, Donne, and several smaller English poets. He feels himself as free as the scarcely correct Dryden to angle where he chooses, and in many ways considers himself to be carrying on Dryden's work. He seeks and praises power, spiritedness, colour, whether in men or writings. He honours the brother of his friend Arbuthnot in these terms:

> The spirit of Philanthropy, so long dead to our world, is revived in him: he is a philosopher all of fire; so warmly, nay so wildly in the right, that he forces all others about him to be so too, and draws them into his own Vortex. . . .[10]

The "fire" of the great poets has never been more brilliantly defined than in Pope's *Preface* to his own fiery *Iliad*:

> that unequal'd Fire and Rapture, which is so forcible in *Homer,* that no Man of a true Poetical Spirit is Master of himself while he reads him. What he writes is of the most animated Nature imaginable; every thing moves, every thing lives, and is put in Action. . . . Exact Disposition, just Thought, correct Elocution, polish'd Numbers, may have been found in a thousand; but this Poetical *Fire,* this *Vivida vis animi,* in a very few. Even in Works where all those are imperfect or neglected, this can over-power Criticism, and make us admire even while we dis-approve. Nay, where this appears, tho' attended with Absurdities, it

> brightens all the Rubbish about it, 'till we see nothing but its own Splendor. This *Fire* is discern'd in *Virgil*, but discern'd as thro' a Glass, reflected, and more shining than warm, but every where equal and constant: In *Lucan* and *Statius*, it bursts out in sudden, short, and interrupted Flashes: In *Milton*, it glows like a Furnace kept up to an uncommon Fierceness by the Force of Art: In *Shakespear*, it strikes before we are aware, like an accidental Fire from Heaven: But in *Homer*, and in him only, it burns every where clearly, and every where irresistibly.[11]

One of Pope's terms of commendation is the newly invented "romantic," and he plans poems which were to have been very wild.[12] For all his Palladian principles he can remark, in a ramshackle old country house, "one vast arch'd window beautifully darken'd with divers scutcheons of painted glass: one shining pane in particular bears date 1286." [13] In a letter to Addison he records how "strangely divided" his mind is between "losing [his] whole comprehension in the boundless space of Creation" and "groveling . . . in the very centre of nonsense . . . this little instant of our life . . . (as Shakespear finely words it) is rounded with a sleep." [14] He has a sense of the darkness which surrounds all human systems:

> The highest gratification we receive here [on earth] from company is Mirth, which at the best is but a fluttering unquiet motion, that beats about the breast for a few moments, and after leaves it void and empty. . . . What we here call science and study, are little better: the greater number of arts to which we apply ourselves are mere groping in the dark. . . .[15]

He writes, and helps to write, indecent poetry and prose which offends the serious ideal of correctness, but rightly insists, when the authorship becomes known, that there is a distinction between work and play.[16]

The *Essay on Criticism* shows him abhorring the "correctly cold," shows him ready to "snatch a grace beyond the reach of art." [17] He believes, then and always, that

> Some beauties yet no Precepts can declare,
> For there's a happiness as well as care. . . .[18]

And although this idea had occurred to earlier critics, Pope believes it with the force of his whole mind. He takes over the classic items in his creed with his eyes well open. He has his own intuitions about poetry and he knows that they must have first say:

> The great secret how to write well, is to know thoroughly what one writes about, and not to be affected . . . to write naturally,[19]

and

> Arts are taken from nature; and after a thousand vain efforts for improvements, are best when they return to their first simplicity.[20]

Wordsworth or anybody might have said the same thing. Indeed, there is little to fear for an author who borrows his rules for writing from the critics but whose standards for taking or rejecting are so right. Pope knew his own powers. He impressed so expert a judge as Dr. Johnson that "it was [his] felicity to rate himself at his real value." [21] Aristotle and his interpreters (often wrong-headed) counted for less with the better poets of the seventeenth and eighteenth centuries than with the less good. The poets who were too pettily concerned with keeping to the "rules" were those who were incapable of writing so as to "tear [the] heart" with pity and terror—the catharsis which Aristotle had made the end of all those means he had observed to be employed in the drama known to him. The phrase just quoted is from the passage in the *Epistle to Augustus* in which Pope considers it necessary to state explicitly what the business of the dramatic poet is.[22] The better poets followed their instincts even though they put up a fashionable show of conforming. They would have expressed themselves with little essential difference even if Aristotle had never written, much less been interpreted and misinterpreted. It was not so much the critics, for instance, who governed the shaping of *Paradise Lost*, but Milton who had read Homer, Virgil, and Dante. The fine autobiographical openings of four of the twelve books could be condemned by reference to Aristotle's writing, though of course it is very doubtful if Aristotle himself would have condemned them. Pope writes in classic kinds when he does so write, not because of critics but because of poets, and not simply because of poets but because of his own genius. If Virgil, Ovid, and Horace had never written, Pope would have been virtually what he was, though he might not so easily have found out what he was. Although epic and tragedy were theoretically the ideal goals of all great poets, Pope has nothing to show in either kind. He recognized that his genius lay elsewhere. He burns all traces of his youthful indiscretion in attempting them, using excerpts from them later as illustrations for the *Peri Bathous*.[23] Later in life he plans a blank verse epic on Brutus but, like Dryden's projected epic on King Arthur, it does not get written—to the satisfaction of Joseph Warton and to the relief of Dr. Johnson.[24] He translates Homer, but does not scruple, any more than Dryden did, to make an original poem of the translation. And although he imitates frequently, he is always writing what he must. He had always too much wildness, sensitiveness, "happy valiancy" about him as a poet to be dispirited by having taken correctness for his aim. He merited from the start Dr. Johnson's magnificent tribute, a paean which does not lose sight of its subject:

> . . . good sense alone is a sedate and quiescent quality, which manages its possessions well, but does not increase them; it collects few materials for its own operations, and preserves safety, but never gains supremacy. Pope had likewise genius; a mind active, ambitious, and adventurous, always investigating, always aspiring; in its widest searches still longing to go forward, in its highest flights still wishing to be higher; always imagining something greater than it knows, always endeavouring more than it can do.[25]

Pope is himself. He is also of his own time. But he is nevertheless half a Roman poët. His profoundest kinship is with Virgil. After Virgil came Ovid and Horace. Pope feels as they felt. He feels sometimes also as their successors—Statius and Lucan—felt. (To the end he persisted in ranking Statius next to Virgil among the Roman poets.)[26] These Romans deepen his melancholy, his tenderness. They help him in his search for what may be accounted beautiful and for the substance of the good life, as he saw that the statues of the ancients had helped Jervas to his "beautiful and noble ideas." [27] The Roman poets deepen his mood and strengthen his sense of what is worthy. They help him to form his critical standards of poetry. George Moore considered that the work of Jane Austen would have been thoroughly intelligible to Virgil and his fellows:

> if the great dead were to reawaken, the Austen wine might be offered to Virgil, Catullus, Horace, Longus, Apuleius and Petronius Arbiter without fear that they would run to the window to puke, making wry faces.[28]

The same can be said of Pope. Indeed, he may be considered as working with something like that criterion in view. His work satisfies his own standards of Nature.

II

This may be seen clearly in his erotic poems. His master for these poems is not Donne; his masters are Ovid and the poets of the Silver Age whose sense of pathos softened so many rugged places in their epics. In the Horatian *Essay on Criticism* Pope had dealt severely with the metaphysical poets and their "glitt'ring thoughts struck out in ev'ry line," their "glaring chaos and wild heap of wit," since

> True wit is Nature to advantage dress'd,
> What oft was thought, but ne'er so well express'd.[29]

Horace opened his *Ars Poetica* by laughing at a picture which mixed together several incongruous objects—his test of bad art is always the social one of whether or not it prompts scornful laughter. Pope might dally with such a style himself, but only for his own amusement or that of his friend:

> If I knew how to entertain you thro' the rest of this paper, it should be spotted and diversified with conceits all over; you should be put out of breath with laughter at each sentence, and pause at each period, to look back over how much wit you have pass'd. . . .[30]

Pope's views on the metaphysical style are those of Dryden and are, later, those of Dr. Johnson. In congratulating the Earl of Dorset on his love poems, Dryden had shown up Donne as academic rather than amorous:

> He affects the metaphysics, not only in his satires, but in his amorous verses, where nature only should reign; and perplexes the minds of the fair sex with nice speculations of philosophy, when he should engage their hearts, and entertain them with the softness of love.[31]

Pope's position had been stated at length and with spirit and perception by his friend Walsh in the preface to the anonymous *Letters and Poems,*

Amorous and Gallant (1692). The passage is worth quoting at length:[32]

> Those who are conversant with the Writings of the Antients, will observe a great difference between what they, and the Moderns have publish'd upon this Subject [love]. The occasions upon which the Poems of the former are written, are such as happen to every Man almost that is in Love; and the Thoughts such, as are natural for every Man in love to think. The Moderns on the other hand have sought out for Occasions, that none meet with, but themselves; and fill their Verses with thoughts that are surprizing and glittering, but not tender, passionate, or natural to a Man in Love.
>
> To judge which of these two are in the right; we ought to consider the end that People propose in writing Love-Verses: And that I take not to be the getting Fame or Admiration from the World, but the obtaining the Love of their Mistress;[33] and the best way I conceive to make her love you, is to convince her that you love her. Now this certainly is not to be done by forc'd Conceits, far-fetch'd Similes, and shining Points; but by a true and lively Representation of the Pains and Thoughts attending such a Passion.
>
> *Si vis me flere, dolendum est:*
> *Primum ipsi tibi, tunc tua me infortunia laedent.*
>
> I would as soon believe a Widow in great grief for her Husband, because I saw her dance a *Corant* about his Coffin, as believe a Man in Love with his Mistress for his writing such Verses, as some great Modern Wits have done upon theirs.
>
> I am satisfied that *Catullus, Tibullus, Propertius,* and *Ovid,* were in love with their Mistresses, while they upbraid them, quarrel with them, threaten them, and forswear them; but I confess I cannot believe *Petrarch* in Love with his, when he writes conceits upon her Name, her Gloves, and the place of her Birth. I know it is natural for a Lover, in Transports of Jealousie, to treat his Mistress with all the Violence imaginable; but I cannot think it natural for a Man, who is much in Love, to amuse himself with such Trifles as the other. I am pleas'd with *Tibullus,* when he says, he could live in a Desart with his Mistress, where never any Humane Foot-steps[34] appear'd, because, I doubt not but he really thinks what he says; but I confess I can hardly forbear laughing when *Petrarch* tells us, he could live without any other sustenance than his Mistresses Looks. . . .

He tries to be scrupulously fair to seventeenth-century poets:

> There are no Modern Writers, perhaps, who have succeeded better in Love-Verses than the *English*. . . . Never was there a more copious Fancy or greater reach of Wit, than what appears in Dr. *Donne;* nothing can be more gallant or gentile than the Poems of Mr. Waller; nothing more gay or sprightly than those of Sir *John Suckling;* and nothing fuller of Variety and Learning than Mr. *Cowley*'s.

And yet what he most wants to see in a love poem is lacking:

> However, it may be observ'd, that among all these, that Softness, Tenderness, and Violence of Passion, which the Ancients thought most proper for Love-Verses, is wanting. . . .[35]

Pope attempts in *Eloisa to Abelard* to supply the lack, and writes the best Heroic Epistle since Ovid.

III

The contemporary esteem for ancient poetry led to a narrowing of the range of the emotions considered appropriate for display in poetry. In the equable light of the Roman poets, enthusiasm and rapture seemed the crackling of thorns under a pot. The emotions of serious poems, it was held, should not, like those of Donne's lyrics, be the emotions of a young man uttered seemingly in the very moments of passion. They should be more steady, more permanent, emotions which Virgil could have sympathized with and understood. More than any other English poets, Dryden, Pope, Johnson, and Gray voice the emotion of a weighty serious melancholy, varying in its degree and quality, of course, from poet to poet and from poem to poem. Pope in particular attains those moods in which pity is found trembling like a frightened dove or in which it moves over the mind like a slow dumb wave, a bulge of deep water. Spence and Martha Blount tell how Pope would weep over tender passages in the poets—and one must remember that weeping had not yet become a fashion.[36] In his own poetry of this kind, the mood is preserved from sentimentality by the technical control, which is the evidence of a moral control. The versification never lets it sag. Pope may even seem to be smiling at the gilded facets of the words—it was part of the good breeding of the age to attend to the sparkles of filtered light in the deepest shadow. His voice may scarcely be discerned to tremble; the reader guesses at the weight of the emotions while he watches the unfolding screen of syllables. *The Elegy to the Memory of an Unfortunate Lady* is one instance, or the *Epistle to Robert, Earl of Oxford,* or lines such as these:

> Blest be the *Great!* for those they take away,
> And those they left me; for they left me GAY;
> Left me to see neglected Genius bloom,
> Neglected die, and tell it on his tomb:
> Of all thy blameless life the sole return
> My Verse, and QUEENSB'RY weeping o'er thy
> urn! [37]

Pope's melancholy is perhaps the deepest of all the many layers in the satire.

IV

To follow Nature meant to provide "the general" rather than "the particular." This provision is made in all Pope's work. His satires, of course, are brilliant with particulars since they are out to show the age its very "form and pressure," but Pope in these poems maintains the general in his attitude, in the processes of the thought, in the mind behind the detail. Pope differs in this from Donne. Donne extends the bounds of his readers' experience, Pope makes his readers realize the quality of what they have already experienced:

> Pope springs eternal in the human breast,
> What oft was thought but ne'er so well express'd.[38]

No man until Donne wrote saw lovers' absence as like a pair of compasses. Absence for Eloisa provokes no discoveries of this individual kind. Pope does provide discoveries for the reader but they are discoveries made among the materials in his memory; an example is the famous lines on Vice:

> Vice is a monster of so frightful mien,
> As, to be hated, needs but to be seen;
> Yet seen too oft, familiar with her face,
> We first endure, then pity, then embrace.[39]

Dr. Johnson's words on Gray's *Elegy* could apply as well to Pope:

> The *Church-yard* abounds with images which find a mirrour in every mind, and with sentiments to which every bosom returns an echo. The four stanzas beginning "Yet even these bones" are to me original: I have never seen the notions in any other place; yet he that reads them here persuades himself that he has always felt them.[40]

Like Gray, Pope gives final utterance to what oft was thought and, besides this, enlarges the reader's realization of material which has lain in his mind "unthought," embryonic or unvalued. He was still following Nature, that is, tracking her down.

V

For most of the poets of the earlier eighteenth century Nature had a strictly human connotation. But man lived his life partly at least in a world of "rocks and stones and trees" as well as in the world of himself and other men, and so this Nature included whatever of external nature was found relevant to man. Wordsworth, of course, mixed the human and the external in other proportions and, according to his tenets, Pope was deficient in allusions to this external nature. He withheld from Pope the title of great poet principally because of that deficiency.[41] In a letter to Dyce of 12 January 1829, Wordsworth wrote:

> These three writers, Thomson, Collins, and Dyer, had more poetic imagination than any of their contemporaries, unless we reckon Chatterton as of that age. I do not name Pope, for he stands alone, as a man most highly gifted; but unluckily he took the plain when the heights were within his reach.

It is clear from this grouping that Wordsworth is thinking mainly of the poetic imagination as it is active in descriptions of external nature. He is reverting to the position he took up in 1815, in the *Essay, Supplementary to the Preface* [of the *Lyrical Ballads*]:

> Now, it is remarkable that, excepting the nocturnal *Reverie of Lady Winchelsea,* and a passage or two in the *Windsor Forest* of Pope, the poetry of the period intervening between the publication of the *Paradise Lost* and the *Seasons* does not contain a single new image of external nature.

These words are meant to provoke feeling rather than to provide strict truth. There had, of course, been plentiful exceptions to Wordsworth's dictum —Dryden, for instance, and Pope himself outside *Windsor Forest.* (Tennyson noted that "Pope here and there has a real insight into Nature, for example about the spider, which

> Feels at each thread and lives along the line.')[42]

And there had also been John Philips, Parnell, Gay, and minor poets such as Purney and William Diaper. But a great bulk of evidence remains to favour Wordsworth's view. Copious description of external nature was never very near to the heart of Dryden and Pope, Young, and the rest. On the other hand, in whatever ways the poets of the early nineteenth century differed from one another, they all found in external nature a great deal of their material.

Wordsworth regarded the poet as a "man speaking to men." By this he meant something like deep calling to deep, an angel speaking to fellow angels. But that call and speech would have seemed mad to the Augustans since what it was trying to communicate transcended the ordinary established limits of man's mind, transcended Nature. Man was not an angel. Living his life among men, he had not enough use for sunsets, celandines, yew-trees, cuckoos, eagles, to warrant the long contemplations on them which Wordsworth wished to share with him. At most such things could be little more than decorations. Wordsworth, as a poet, was not a man speaking to men so much as a visionary trying to open a neglected door in the human mind, a door that the eighteenth century tended to keep closed so as to avoid the draughts. For Dryden, Pope, Young, and Johnson, the poet was a man speaking to the other members of a civilized society who resembled the poet in all but poetic gifts. Pope considered that his more intellectual poems were addressed to a small group. He tells Caryll, for instance, that he does not expect a second edition of the *Essay on Criticism* (the first edition numbered a thousand copies) since "not One Gentleman in threescore even of a Liberall Education can understand" it.[43] But Pope's audience was usually larger than that—the *Rape of the Lock* in its second form sold to the extent of three thousand copies in four days.[44] Pope's audience was limited only by the barrier of a "Liberall Education." And that audience had been prepared for him by preceding poets and writers who had contributed particular elements in that liberal education—by Waller and Dryden, by the authors of the *Miscellanies* and, not least, by Congreve and Wycherley. Whereas, to some extent, Wordsworth had to create his audience, Pope found an audience waiting for what he could give. This addressing of the civilized man meant a special area of subject matter for poetry. For Pope and the rest, the proper study of mankind is man, that is, the permanent core of human nature which remains independent of all extravagance, local, physical, intellectual or religious. Whatever else they spoke of, it was with man as stated reference. Man was the centre, however wide the circle described by his stretched compass. But it was not often that man was found stretching his compass very much farther than the "town," than the society of his fellows. The part played by external nature in the mind of civilized man is always relatively a small part, and this necessary restriction of interest gets mirrored in the poetry he is inspiring. There is therefore more of society in eighteenth-century poetry than of trees and "lonely hills."

The poets of the late seventeenth and early eighteenth centuries saw and valued the large freedom of landscape, though Dryden, like most men, found that his eye could only find continuous rest on what was green in it.[45] That large freedom they saw and valued but had little cause to use. The limb of the human compass was seldom wheeled widely enough to include it. If the compass did include it and it got into poetry, its powerfulness often shrank because of the correctness of the couplets which these poets were finding so perfect for their strictly human material. This shrinkage, however, is never found in Pope's descriptions. In his mature work a landscape will often be allotted only a single couplet, sometimes two. But the space of those twenty syllables has the appearance of infinity. There is no other poet who habitually catches so much in a small glass. The *Dunciad*, for instance, provides the following:

> Lo! where Maeotis sleeps, and hardly flows
> The freezing Tanais thro' a waste of snows[46]

> To Isles of fragrance, lily-silver'd vales,
> Diffusing languor in the panting gales . . .[47]

> So clouds, replenish'd from some bog below,
> Mount in dark volumes, and descend in snow.[48]

> As to soft gales top-heavy pines bow low
> Their heads, and lift them as they cease to
> blow[49]

> See, round the Poles where keener spangles shine,
> Where spices smoke beneath the burning Line.[50]

Or there is the line:

> The sick'ning stars fade off th'ethereal plain.[51]

When poets like Thomson, Young, Dyer, and to a less extent John Philips, wanted to describe landscape or skyscape more often than their fellows, they were wise to break away from the couplet into blank verse. In any case they could not have used the couplet as Pope used it. Pope was never tempted to break away from the couplet for any major work because he could make it do all that he wanted.

Pope is under no delusions about the splendour and beauty of the world. He lived almost all his young life in the country. He is a country poet for Gay:

> You, who the Sweets of Rural Life have known,
> Despise th'ungrateful Hurry of the Town . . .[52]

and Berkeley, who has just thanked Pope for the *Rape of the Lock*, sees him also as a country poet, though with a field which could be expanded:

> Green fields and groves, flowery meadows and purling streams are no where in such perfection as in England: but if you would know lightsome days, warm suns, and blue skies, you must come to Italy: and to enable a man to describe rocks and precipices, it is absolutely necessary that he pass the Alps.[53]

Even when he went to live at Twickenham, he was still virtually living in the country. His eye was sharp. He had begun as early as 1713 to take lessons in painting from Jervas, and painting still further sharpened his eyes. "I begin," he tells Gay, "to discover beauties that were till now imperceptible to me" and though he amusingly instances the "corner of an eye," the "turn of a nose or ear, the smallest degree of light and shade on a cheek, or in a dimple," the quality of the phrasing shows that there is more than amorousness behind it.[54] There is much important evidence in the letters and in Spence's *Anecdotes* of the completeness of Pope's aesthetic sense. He notes, for instance, that small black and white landscape drawings can give no idea of "beautiful country," since they deprive it "of the light and lustre of nature." [55] Writing to Jervas he says, "I hope the Spring will restore you to us, and with you all the beauties and colours of nature." [56] These phrases are memorable and an apposite illustration of W. P. Ker's remark:

> . . . do not the advocates of the romantic revival, and the return to Nature, sometimes speak as if no one in the eighteenth century had ever looked from a height over open country, as if the daedal earth had been treated for the time somehow like Giotto's portrait of Dante in the Bargello at Florence, its green, white and red made decent and uncompromising with a coat of chocolate? [57]

We find Pope mentioning "a solitary walk by moonshine." [58] Or there is this extended description two years later:

> I came from Stonor . . . to Oxford the same night. Nothing could have more of that Melancholy which once us'd to please me, than that days journey: For after having passd thro' my favorite Woods in the forest, with a thousand Reveries of past pleasures; I rid over hanging hills, whose tops were edgd with groves, & whose feet water'd with winding rivers, listening to the falls of Cataracts below, & the murmuring of winds above. The gloomy Verdure of Stonor succeeded to these, & then the Shades of the Evening overtook me, the Moon rose in the clearest Sky I ever saw, by whose solemn light I pac'd on slowly, without company, or any interruption, to the range of my thoughts. About a mile before I reachd Oxford, all the Night bells toll'd, in different notes; the Clocks of every College answered one another; & told me, some in a deeper, some in a softer voice, that it was eleven a clock. . . .[59]

Torbay "is a paradise," and "summer . . . a kind of heaven, when we wander in a paradisaical scene among groves and gardens. . . ." [60] Autumn, "the decay of the year," is

> the best time . . . for a painter; there is more variety of colours in the leaves, the prospects begin to open, thro' the thinner woods, over the valleys; and thro' the high canopies of trees to the higher arch of heaven: the dews of the morning impearl every thorn, and scatter diamonds on the verdant mantle of the earth; the frosts are fresh and wholesome: what would you have? the Moon shines too, tho' not for Lovers these cold nights, but for Astronomers.[61]

This should be placed alongside Dr. Johnson's defence of the "general" against the numbering of "the different shades in the verdure of the forest."[62] Pope sees landscape often, though not always, as a painter, but the point is that he is excited by it and interested in observing different effects. This element in his work—in both the prose and the poetry—has been neglected by other critics than Wordsworth. It is absurd, of course, that any poet worth the name should be thought of as blind to external nature and I should perhaps apologize for demonstrating the obvious.

Spence records two *obiter dicta* of Pope which are of primary importance:

> That Idea of the Picturesque, from the swan just gilded with the sun amidst the shade of a tree over the water [*on the Thames*].
>
> A tree is a nobler object than a prince in his coronation robes.—Education leads us from the admiration of beauty in natural objects, to the admiration of artificial (or customary) excellence.—I don't doubt but that a thorough-bred lady might admire the stars, *because* they twinkle like so many candles at a birth-night.[63]

There are frequent descriptions of swans in English poetry—Spenser's stanza of linked syntax long drawn out in the *Prothalamion,* many small references in Keats, Wordsworth's

> The swan on still St. Mary's Lake
> Floats double, swan and shadow,[64]

Yeats's Leda poem[65]—but it does not seem that any poet has had Pope's luck or has troubled to look at a swan often enough to find it, rare almost as the phoenix, at a perfect moment. In the second passage Pope is found deploring the effects of the education which makes a thorough-bred lady invert the relative values of stars and indoor lighting. It was with this for theme that Wordsworth wrote the Lucy poem, "Three years she grew. . . ." Pope is under no delusion about the beauty and splendour of external nature. He knows but has usually no reason for stating. As objects of beauty he prefers trees to coronation robes, stars to candelabra, but he has no description of a tree to put beside that of Belinda's exquisite petticoat; and the star to which he gave most attention was the fictitious Ovidian one, the translated lock of Belinda. The court decoration—

> Bare the mean Heart that lurks beneath a
> *Star*—[66]

was of more value to his poetry than Hesperus, though its vanity strikes him as the more wretched because of the purity of Hesperus. Even in the superb line

> The sick'ning stars fade off th'ethereal plain[67]

Pope is not thinking of an actual night, but of the night in the mind of man when a curtain of intellectual darkness is being let fall. He is never for a moment forgetting that man is his theme, and, since civilized man spends the dark hours mostly under a roof, it is sentimental to consider that stars have, in the sum of life, more value for him than indoor lighting.

Pope's theme becomes more and more that of man in society. Perhaps by 1717 he was coming to see that moral and satiric writing was his true bent. In devoting himself to it more and more exclusively, he had the ancient authority which he coveted:

> [The Ancients] constantly apply'd themselves not only to that art, but to that single branch of an art, to which their talent was most powerfully bent. . . .[68]

Pope's growing knowledge of his powers must have been strengthened when the independent and vigorous Atterbury is so rapt with the "Verses on Mr. Addison" that he writes:

> Since you now therefore know where your real strength lies, I hope you will not suffer that talent to lie unemploy'd. . . .[69]

This limiting of subject excluded automatically the frequent allusion to trees and mountains. But civilized man must not be held deficient in sense of beauty because he did not seek to exercise it among mountains. Indeed, if the truth must be told, it may well have been the sharpness of that sense which decreed the abstention. If he excluded external nature from a large share of his attention, he was continuously aware, simply because of his civilization, of the works of man's hands. And, since this was the eighteenth century, that work was, almost automatically, beautiful in itself. Up to the nineteenth century, the product of, say, the silversmith was required to be beautiful. It was regarded at its proper worth, as embodying the aspiration, the schooled judgment of form and purpose, the skill, of one who was to metal something not unlike what the sonneteer was to words. The delight in the work of man's hands had been particularly strong at the Renaissance, when humanistic values stood high. It was included in Hamlet's paean on man: "how infinite in faculty." For the Elizabethans a term of high commendation is "very artificial." [70] This delight in the products of manual art lasts well into the eighteenth century and finds its most perfect expression in Pope. It seems astonishing after the Chinese and Japanese, the Indians, the Persians, the Greeks and Romans, even after the clumsy fiery Elizabethans, that the work of man's hands in stone and metal should ever have missed receiving its full honour. Yet the Romantics seem to have preferred any accidental assemblage of "natural objects"—even if the result of what the insurance companies would call an "act of God"—to the art of man. Among them it was Keats alone who gave art its full due. His acknowledgement was the most handsome he could pay, since his aesthetic theory reached its most exalted expression in the *Ode to a Grecian Urn.* Wordsworth offers no exception. When he found that earth had not anything to show more fair than Westminster at early morning, he was still virtually among his Lakes—the architecture was only an abnormally small and still item in a sky-and-waterscape. And in the same way architecture counts for little in *Tintern Abbey.* In the main the Romantic poets' ideal of beauty was provided by untouched external nature, and Keats is usually among them. Their sense of beauty is independent of a sense of form. Wordsworth seeks "a something far more deeply interfused" among the bleak, magnificent or placid phenomena of the Lakes. Shelley is all for light and wind, Keats for colour and luxurious substance. But they seldom see how the materials provided by the earth can attain a perfection of form, and even of symbol, in the work of man's hands. Pope gives as much (or more) attention to considering such man-made beauty as to describing untouched external nature, and it is the exquisiteness of his sense of the possibilities of this kind of beauty that provokes some of his best descriptive satire. To step from his own deliberated house and garden—"All gardening is landscape painting" [71]—into the enormous pomp of Timon's proved intolerable. We know from Pope's statements to Spence that he required form from anything before he could pronounce it beautiful. From the tangle of materials out of which he made the descriptions in *Windsor Forest,* Pope selects only what he can place together in formal relationship—one landscape he found already half formalized for him by being isolated and inverted in reflecting water. But for Timon or his architectural deputy, form was attainable without deliberation, without the observance of the aesthetic properties. The elements of a proper and beautiful social arrangement may be discovered in the silver ceremonial at Hampton Court:

For lo! the board with cups and spoons is crown'd,
The berries crackle, and the mill turns round;
On shining Altars of Japan they raise
The silver lamp; the fiery spirits blaze:
From silver spouts the grateful liquors glide,
While China's earth receives the smoking tide. [72]

But Timon's coarse numerical bid for grandeur is excruciating:

Greatness, with Timon, dwells in such a draught
As brings all Brobdignag before your thought.
To compass this, his building is a Town,
His pond an Ocean, his parterre a Down:
Who but must laugh, the Master when he sees,
A puny insect, shiv'ring at a breeze!
Lo, what huge heaps of littleness around!
The whole, a labour'd Quarry above ground;
Two Cupids squirt before; a Lake behind
Improves the keenness of the Northern wind.
His Gardens next your admiration call,
On ev'ry side you look, behold the Wall!
No pleasing Intricacies intervene,
No artful wildness to perplex the scene;
Grove nods at grove, each Alley has a brother,
And half the platform just reflects the other.
The suff'ring eye inverted Nature sees,
Trees cut to Statues, Statues thick as trees;
With here a Fountain, never to be play'd;
And there a Summer-house, that knows no shade;
Here Amphitrite sails thro' myrtle bow'rs;
There Gladiators fight, or die, in flow'rs;
Un-water'd see the drooping sea-horse mourn,
And swallows roost in Nilus' dusty Urn. [73]

Pope's sense of beauty was more practical than that of Wordsworth. Not that Wordsworth's was impractical—a sunrise could certainly minister to a mind diseased or, if not that, to a mind unclean. But there are few whom life allows the opportunities for such a catharsis and meantime the mind remains smutted. There is more chance of the day's salvation if the cleansing comes from a stone urn in a garden, a carved portico or even the very cups and spoons: especially so, since such things are worthy of their contact with the various light of Wordsworth's skies. The proportion of external nature in the theme of Pope's poetry is, more nearly than that in the poetry of most nineteenth century poets, the proportion in the life of normal human beings. The poet of Nature is too near the still sad, or the lively, music of humanity to be a nature-poet.

VI

"The life of a Wit is a warfare upon earth," wrote Pope in the preface to his collected *Works* of 1717.[74] It was in this long warfare that Pope would seem to have lost sight of his correct standards.

As a man Pope does not come up at all points to the ideal which readers elect for great authors. As early as 1712, Caryll had referred punningly to his "Popish tricks,"[75] and a man who is found once in clever subterfuge has all his actions suspected. In passing judgment on Pope's character, the nineteenth century went to the two extremes. At one extreme stands Byron. His mother's attitude to his lameness may have helped to sharpen his moral sympathy with Pope—his literary sympathy, of course, needed no sharpening. Byron will always receive the amazed gratitude of the "friends of Pope" for his angry allusion to him as "the most *faultless* of Poets, and almost of men."[76] To balance this half a century later is the maniacal denigration of the Rev. Whitwell Elwin. Scholarship, which partly means the getting at historical truth in minute particulars, may in time free Pope from much that has been laid to his charge, and form grounds for judging the rest. Scholarship is, indeed, already doing this. Professor Sherburn's *Early Career* has already shown that it is ridiculous to believe the worst of Pope. Mr. Norman Ault's researches in the canon of Pope's writings are incidentally contributing to the same conclusion. And in 1930, four years before Professor Sherburn's book, Miss Sitwell had already hit upon the reasonable attitude to Pope's character, mainly by the exercise of a vivid intuitive sympathy.

In judging the nature of Pope's personal satire one has to remember that it does not stand alone, that it exists in a thick context of abuse. Pope is not sharp, cruel, nasty and his fellow satirists gentle and clean. They are all as sharp, cruel, and nasty as they can be. And all of them, including Pope, write as well as they can, that is, make as much of their material as possible. Pope and the others always use against a man as much as they can find—truth or rumour about his person, character, history, habits. As an object of such abuse, Pope was exceptionally vulnerable. Never indeed has a satirist provided in his own person more obvious targets. Any urchin could, and probably did, ridicule his dwarfish, twisted body since, at that time, cripples still seemed comic, and even

> Swift expires a driv'ler and a show.[77]

With all this against him it is remarkable that Pope became a satirist at all. It would have been much safer to have gone on writing stanzas on solitude, pastorals, lines on universal Nature. With all the obvious odds against him, he entered the warfare of the wits. Not enough has been made of his courage.

His enemies, of course, made the most of his physique. A fair instance of their manner would be Dennis's *Remarks on Mr. Pope's Rape of the Lock* (1728) which deliberately sets out to be temperate in abuse. Throughout this pamphlet Pope is referred to by phrases such as "the Folly, the Pride, and the Petulancy of that little Gentleman *A. P—E,*" "the little facetious Gentleman," "the only foul-mouth'd Fellow in *England,*" "a little conceited incorrigible Creature, that like the Frog in the Fable, swells and is angry because he is not allow'd to be as great as the Ox," "this little Creature, who is as diminutive an Author as he is an Animal," "a little Monster." Pope must not be condemned because, like Swift, he uses the contemporary weapons.

It is worth noting that he makes the most of the faces of his victims. The lines on Dennis in the *Essay on Criticism* fix on his facial expression:

> But *Appius* reddens at each word you speak,
> And stares, tremendous, with a threat'ning eye,
> Like some fierce Tyrant in old tapestry.[78]

And there are the "earnest eyes, and round unthinking face" of Sir Plume.[79] Pope's own face was of course the only unimpeachable item in his appearance.

Pope is sometimes found making the first attack, sometimes he was attacked first. Mr. Ault has made the plausible suggestion[80] that, since the lines on Appius are seemingly based on personal observation, Pope and Dennis may have met and, at that meeting, Pope may have been angered, or even snubbed, by Dennis. Dennis, that is, may have attacked him first. Certainly Pope sometimes attacked first. Ned Ward, for example, who had always respected Pope,[81] found himself pilloried over again in the *Dunciad*. But this treatment of Ward points criticism to adopt a different standard. In Pope's eye, a man, otherwise inoffensive, might offend through his badness as a writer. For Pope, a bad author was to literature what a fool or a knave was to life. The *Dunciad* attacks the denizens of Grub Street not as men first of all but as authors. The poem, strictly speaking, was not personal in origin. It was part of the programme of the Scriblerus Club, the society formed by Arbuthnot, Swift, Parnell, Gay, and Pope to expose bad writing and pedantry.[82] It is the cruellest satire of its age only because Pope is the best writer.

But satire is not the only ingredient in Pope's satires. Pope always constructs as well as destroys. He always makes clear his moral position, and does not stop till he has filled the eye with the spectacle of virtue. Whatever people may think of his private character—and of this there have been and are very few who are qualified to have an opinion—that character as it is revealed positively in the poetry is almost wholly admirable. Pope's sense of correctness (to put it no higher than that) would have made it impossible that it should not be so. Even if the reader considers that the torture of Pope's satire is often too exquisite to have come from a great human moralist, he must admit that satire of this kind is not the only satire in Pope, and that satire of this or any other kind is not the only moral poetry in Pope:

> Hence Satire rose, that just the medium hit,
> And heals with Morals what it hurts with
> Wit.[83]

The vicious or foolish characters are tortured, but the vice or folly is always measured against a proper, a "correct" scale of human values, against a scale which Pope is always ready to state, to state precisely, and, as in the exciting fourth Epistle of the *Essay on Man*, to state at length. Indeed, no other English poet (or letter-writer) puts and answers the question how to live with such sensitive and noble concern. The tone of this poetry (and this prose) must convince the reader that he is in the presence of one whose sense of virtue is as alert as the trembling, vivid eye one notes in his portraits.

Keats speaks of the "snail-horn perception of beauty." And Pope's perception of moral beauty, of moral depravity, and of all the subtleties componded between them is a perception similarly tender. This is a quality rare indeed among satiric writers, and probably unique. There is certainly no other poet who combines the capacity exemplified in the character of Atticus with that exemplified, for instance, in Clarissa's speech opening Canto V of the *Rape of the Lock* or in any of the verses to Martha Blount:

> But, Madam, if the fates withstand, and you
> Are destin'd Hymen's willing Victim too;
> Trust not too much your now resistless charms,
> Those, Age or Sickness, soon or late disarms:
> Good humour only teaches charms to last,
> Still makes new conquests, and maintains the
> past;
> Love, rais'd on Beauty, will like that decay,
> Our hearts may bear its slender chain a day;
> As flow'ry bands in wantonness are worn,
> A morning's pleasure, and at ev'ning torn;
> This binds in ties more easy, yet more strong,
> The willing heart, and only holds it long.[84]

These poems are the most Virgilian poems of friendship in the language. And Pope's letters seem more concerned with friendship than with any other subject. He writes them usually "in all friendly laziness." [85] He tells Swift:

> Now as I love you better than most I have ever met with in the world, and esteem you too the more, the longer I have compared you with the rest of the world; so inevitably I write to you more negligently, that is, more openly, and what all but such as love one another will call writing worse.[86]

Friendship was powerful indeed if it could make one write negligently who, like Ovid, had been born with literary finger tips. And turning back to the poetry, Pope is not simply the poet of Atossa or the references to Lady Mary Wortley Montagu. If Sporus and Chartres are hated, Swift, Gay, Arbuthnot, Berkeley and Allen, are praised. If the *Dunciad* freezes the grimace on the face of Dullness it is because of Pope's regard for the "bright countenance"[87] of intelligence. It is the conclusion of the *Dunciad* which most truly represents Pope's position, however much he has enjoyed the slime of the poetic games. Even by such simple tests his work is often noble. And in the most biting satiric analyses, pity may be as active as detestation. The character of Atticus hangs on a condition:

> Peace to all such! but were there One whose fires
> True Genius kindles, and fair Fame inspires....

If there were such a one, who but must laugh—

> Who would not weep, if ATTICUS were he?

(And one must remember that Atticus does not represent the only verdict passed on Addison. There was also this, in commendation:

> ... (excuse some Courtly stains)
> No whiter page than Addison remains.
> He, from the taste obscene reclaims our youth,
> And sets the Passions on the side of Truth,
> Forms the soft bosom with the gentlest art,
> And pours each human Virtue in the heart.[88])

William Cleland is not far from the truth when, in a letter to Gay, he defends the Essay "Of Taste" (*Moral Essays* IV) and uses the words "modest Epistle" and "how tenderly these Follies are treated."[89] These qualities of tenderness and friendship were properly esteemed by one person at least in the nineteenth century. Hazlitt records how, in a dialogue with Ayrton, Lamb (who could read Pope "over and over for ever") spoke particularly of Pope's compliments. His examples concluded with the "list of his early friends" from the *Epistle to Arbuthnot*. Lamb recited "with a slight hectic on his cheek and his eye glistening":

> But why then publish? *Granville* the polite,
> And knowing *Walsh*, would tell me I could write;
> Well-natur'd *Garth* inflam'd with early praise;
> And *Congreve* lov'd, and *Swift* endur'd my lays;
> The courtly *Talbot, Somers, Sheffield* read;
> Ev'n mitred *Rochester* would nod the head,
> And *St. John*'s self (great *Dryden*'s friends before)
> With open arms receiv'd one Poet more.
> Happy my studies, when by these approv'd!
> Happier their author, when by these belov'd!
> From these the world will judge of men and books,
> Not from the *Burnets, Oldmixons,* and *Cookes*.[90]

"Here his voice totally failed him, and throwing down the book, he said 'Do you think I would not wish to have been friends with such a man as this?' "[91]

If such is the emotional response to a list of Pope's early friends, what can be said of that to the close of the *Epilogue to the Satires*?

> Ask you what Provocation I have had?
> The strong Antipathy of Good to Bad.
> When Truth or Virtue an Affront endures,
> Th' Affront is mine, my friend, and should be yours.
> Mine as a Foe profess'd to false Pretence,
> Who think a Coxcomb's Honour like his Sense;
> Mine, as a Friend to ev'ry worthy mind;
> And mine as Man, who feel for all mankind.

His friend interrupts with:

> You're strangely proud.

and Pope replies:

> So proud, I am no Slave:
> So impudent, I own myself no Knave:
> So odd, my Country's Ruin makes me grave.
> Yes, I am proud; I must be proud to see
> Men not afraid of God, afraid of me:
> Safe from the Bar, the Pulpit, and the Throne,
> Yet touch'd and sham'd by Ridicule alone.
> O sacred weapon! left for Truth's defence,
> Sole Dread of Folly, Vice and Insolence!
> To all but Heav'n-directed hands deny'd,
> The Muse may give thee, but the Gods must guide:
> Rev'rent I touch thee! but with honest zeal,
> To rouse the Watchmen of the public Weal;
> To Virtue's work provoke the tardy Hall,
> And goad the Prelate slumb'ring in his Stall.
> Ye tinsel Insects! whom a Court maintains,
> That count your Beauties only by your Stains,
> Spin all your Cobwebs o'er the Eye of Day!
> The Muse's wing shall brush you all away:
> All his Grace preaches, all his Lordship sings,
> All that makes Saints of Queens, and Gods of Kings,—
> All, all but Truth drops dead-born from the Press,
> Like the last Gazette, or the last Address.[92]

Despite everything that the eighteenth and nineteenth century found to dislike in Pope, one is left with a sense of this reverence for the sacredness of his weapon. Along with the torture there is all the poetry in praise of virtue, and, which is strange, the poetry of the praise is as magnificent as that of the detestation.

More than any other author Pope can create in the reader that brimming fullness of mood in face of what he shows as precious in human life, a mood both autumnal and vernal, solemn yet fertile, melancholy and exalted. His imitation of the ancients led him to nothing more rare than this Virgilian fount of wisdom and tenderness. It is significant that the words "language of his heart" come twice in his poetry, that Bolingbroke is praised for causing him to

> turn . . . the tuneful art
> From sounds to things, from fancy to the heart.[93]

The language of his heart was one that he spoke without taint of sentimentality. When he speaks it, one is reminded of the similar experience afforded by Mozart's slow movements, since in him, too, an exquisite regard for surface gives a masking decency and humility to the full emotions; and, moreover, in Mozart there is often a strictly ticking accompaniment to the "emotional" melody which finds its counterpart in the precision of Pope's versification. We see the chastened survivor of the tumult rather than the sufferer. It is a sadder and wiser spirit which is remembering. The reader is reverent, too. Hazlitt, the profoundest critic of the *Rape of the Lock* did not know whether to laugh or to weep over the poem. When Pope speaks seriously in his own person, there is nothing in his language of what Keats called the egotistical sublime. It is un-Miltonic in its quietness. To withdraw in pride, to dwell apart like a star, would have offended the ideal of "correctness." When he did withdraw, it was into final silence and unhappiness. The note appended to the *Epilogue:*

> This was the last poem of the kind printed by our author, with a resolution to publish no more; but to enter thus, in the most plain and solemn manner he could, a sort of PROTEST against that insuperable corruption and depravity of manners, which he had been so unhappy as to live to see. Could he have hoped to have amended any, he had continued those attacks; but bad men were grown so shameless and so powerful, that Ridicule was become as unsafe as it was ineffectual. The Poem raised him, as he knew it would, some enemies; but he had reason to be satisfied with the approbation of good men, and the testimony of his own conscience.

There is no reason to consider these noble sentences as hypocritical. They represent a solemn moment for the eighteenth century, the closing down in long-deferred disillusion of a great critical intelligence, the most vigilant and subtle discriminator of intention and conduct in the whole gamut of our literature.

NOTES

1. J. Spence, *Anecdotes*, ed. S. W. Singer (1820), 280.

2. A phrase adapted from Gray's letter to West, 16 Nov. 1739: "I own I have not, as yet, any where met with those grand and simple works of Art, that are to amaze one, and whose sight one is to be the better for . . ."

3. *Ess. on Crit.*, 68 ff.

4. Irving Babbitt, *The New Laokoon* (1910), 11–13.

5. *Ess. on Crit.*, 135.

6. Spence, *Anecdotes*, 9.

7. Scaliger, *Poetics*, III, IV.

8. Letter to Pope, 1 May 1714. Printed by Pope in his *Letters*.

9. Spence, *Anecdotes*, 278.

10. Letter to Digby, 1 Sept. 1722. My citations from Pope's correspondence are mainly drawn from the letters which he himself printed. I have taken them on their face value as Pope printed them since I believe this value to represent the truth—or one of several truths—though not always the fact. The text followed is that of Warburton's edition of 1753, which he considered the most correct.

11. Preface to *Iliad*, 1715, (folio ed.), B 1^v-$B2^v$.

12. See p. 43 [Tillotson, *On the Poetry of Pope* (1938)].

13. Letter to the Duke of Buckingham probably from Stanton Harcourt, 1718.

14. 14 Dec. 1713.

15. Letter to Edward Blount, 10 Feb. 1715–16.

16. Letter to Swift, 16 Feb. 1732–3.

17. *Ess. on Crit.* 240 and 153.

18. Id. 141–2.

19. Spence, *Anecdotes*, 291.

20. Id. 11–12.

21. *Lives of the Poets,* ed. G. Birkbeck Hill, iii, 89.

22. lines 340 ff.

23. See Spence, 276–8, and G. Sherburn's *Early Career of Pope,* 84, note 3.

24. *Essay on the Genius and Writings of Pope,* ed. 1806, i. 275–6; *Lives of the Poets,* ed. G. Birkbeck Hill, iii. 188. Pope's plan for the poem exists in Brit. Mus. MS. Egerton 1950, fol. 4 ff. Eight lines survive intact and were printed (imperfectly) by Snyder, *Journal of English and Germanic Philology,* xviii. 583, from fol. 6ʳ of the same MS. Apparently they form the opening of the poem:

> The Patient Chief, who lab'ring long, arrivd
> On Britains [Coast *deleted*] Shore [*written above with a dash preceding*] and brought with fav'ring Gods
> Arts Arms & Honour to her Ancient Sons:
> Daughter of Memory! [instructive Muse *deleted*] from [elder *deleted*] Time [*last three words written above*]
> Recall; and me, wᵗʰ Britains Glory fird,
> Me, far from meaner Care or meaner Song,
> Snatch to thy Holy Hill of spotless Bay,
> My Countrys Poet, to record her Fame.

The three remaining lines are mutilated, the paper being torn across.

25. *Lives of the Poets,* ed. G. Birkbeck Hill, iii, 217.

26. See Spence, *Anecdotes,* 274 and 279.

27. Letter to Jervas, 29 Nov. 1716.

28. *Avowals,* ed. 1924, 35.

29. lines 290–8.

30. Letter to Digby, 31 Mar. 1718.

31. "Discourse concerning the Original and Progress of Satire," *Essays,* ed. Ker, ii. 19.

32. Charles Gildon quotes it in his Epistle Dedicatory to David Crauford's *Ovidius Britannicus* (1703). Dr. Johnson considered the preface "very judicious" (*Lives,* ed. G. Birkbeck Hill, i. 330).

33. This is, of course, a naïve explanation, but the love poet certainly wants the world (including his mistress) to think that this is his aim. Drayton's sonnets, for instance, were criticized by Drummond for showing love for his Muse rather than for his mistress.

34. Corrected from "Foost-steps."

35. Sig. A3ʳ–A5ʳ.

36. Spence, 260.

37. *Epistle to Arbuthnot,* 255 ff.

38. I owe this witticism to my brother Mr. Arthur Tillotson.

39. *Ess. on Man,* ii, 217 ff.

40. *Lives,* ed. G. Birkbeck Hill, iii, 441–2.

41. I take Wordsworth as representative. His statements on Pope belong to that early nineteenth-century controversy on Pope's status as poet. The controversy is a muddle of vituperation, pedantry, and vital aesthetics, and represents the nearest thing English literature can show to a battle of poetic principles such as that which waged round Victor Hugo. Though Pope is the stated subject, the real question at issue is the nature of the true poet. The history of the controversy has been set out by J. J. van Rennes in his *Bowles, Byron and the Pope-Controversy* (1927). Joseph Warton, Johnson, and De Quincey—in the *Encyclopædia Britannica* (1837)—also contributed notably to the subject.

42. *Alfred Lord Tennyson A Memoir by his Son* (1897), ii, 286. The line quoted is *Essay on Man,* i, 218.

43. Letter of 19 July 1711.

44. Letter to Caryll, 12 March 1714.

45. Cf. Mason, *English Garden* (1772), i, 422–3:

> For green is to the eye, what to the ear
> Is harmony, or to the smell the rose.

46. iii, 87–8.

47. iv, 303–4.

48. ii, 363–4.

49. ii, 391–2.

50. iii, 69–70.

51. iv, 636.

52. *Rural Sports,* 1713, ll. 1–2. And cf. *To Bernard Lintott,* 1712, 80–3.

53. Letter of 1 May 1714, from Leghorn.

54. Letter of 23 Aug. 1713.

55. Letter to Caryll, 5 Dec. 1712.

56. 29 Nov. 1716.

57. *The Eighteenth Century* (*Collected Essays,* i, 78).

58. Letter to Edward Blount, 10 Feb. 1715–16.

59. Letter to the Misses Blount, probably 1717: quoted by Sherburn, *Early Career of Pope,* 213.

60. Letters to Edward Blount, 27 June 1723, and 13 Sept. 1725.

61. Letter to Digby, 10 Oct. 1723.

62. *Rasselas*, chap. x.
63. p. 11.
64. *Yarrow Unvisited.*
65. *Leda and the Swan.*
66. *Im. of Hor.* Sat. II, i. To Mr. Fortescue, 108.
67. *Dunciad*, iv, 636.
68. Preface to *Works* 1717.
69. Letter of 26 Feb. 1721.
70. See, for example, the descriptions of pageants in Nichols's *Progresses.* In the passage on coronation robes quoted above the word has still its root meaning.
71. Spence, 144.
72. *Rape of the Lock*, iii, 105 ff.
73. *Mor. Ess.*, iv. *Of the Use of Riches.* To Burlington, 103 ff.
74. Sig. a 15.
75. Replied to by Pope in his letter to Caryll of 21 Dec. 1712.
76. In a letter to Murray, 4 Nov. 1820. *Letters and Journals*, ed. R. E. Prothero (1901), v, 109.
77. Johnson, *Vanity of Human Wishes*, 316.
78. 585 ff.
79. *Rape of the Lock*, iv, 125.
80. *Prose Works of Alexander Pope* (1936), i, xiii.
81. I am indebted for this fact to Miss L. Herron.
82. The best account of the origin and aim of the *Dunciad* is Professor R. K. Root's Introduction to his facsimile of the *Dunciad Variorum.*
83. *Im. of Hor.* Ep. II, i. To Augustus, 261–2.
84. *Epistle to Miss Blount, with the Works of Voiture*, 57 ff.
85. Letter to Jervas, 14 Nov. 1716.
86. Letter to Swift, 28 Nov. 1729.
87. Milton's phrase concerning truth in the autobiographical preface to Book II of *The Reason of Church Government.*
88. *Im. of Horace.* Ep. II, i. To Augustus, 215 ff.
89. 16 Dec. 1731. It does not matter for the present purpose whether or not Pope wrote this letter for him, or supervised it.
90. 135 ff.
91. *Of Persons One Would Wish to Have Seen*, Works, ed. P. P. Howe, xvii, 128.
92. *Dialogue* ii, 197 ff.
93. *Ep. to Arbuthnot*, 399, *Im. of Hor.* Ep. II, i. To Augustus, 78, and *Essay on Man*, iv, 391–2.

Cleanth Brooks

THE CASE OF MISS ARABELLA FERMOR

Aldous Huxley's lovers, "quietly sweating, palm to palm," may be conveniently taken to mark the nadir of Petrarchianism. The mistress is no longer a goddess—not even by courtesy. She is a congeries of biological processes and her too evident mortality is proclaimed at every pore. But if we seem to reach, with Huxley's lines, the end of something, it is well to see what it is that has come to an end. It is not the end of a naïve illusion.

The Elizabethans, even those who were immersed in the best tradition of Petrarchianism, did not have to wait upon the advent of modern science to find out that women perspired. They were thoroughly aware that woman was a biological organism, but their recognition of this fact did not prevent them from asserting, on occasion, that she was a goddess, nevertheless. John Donne, for instance, frequently has it both ways: indeed, some of the difficulty which the modern reader has with his poems may reside in the fact that he sometimes

From *The Well-Wrought Urn: Studies in the Structure of Poetry* (New York: Harcourt, Brace and World, Inc., 1947), pp. 80–104. Reprinted by permission of the author.

has it both ways in the same poem. What is relevant to our purposes here is not the occurrence of a line like "Such are the sweat drops of my Mistres breast" in one of the satiric "elegies," but the occurrence of lines like

Our hands were firmely cimented
With a fast balme, which thence did spring

in a poem like "The Ecstasy"! The passage quoted, one may argue, glances at the very phenomenon which Huxley so amiably describes; but Donne has transmuted it into something else.

But if Donne could have it both ways, most of us, in this latter day, cannot. We are disciplined in the tradition of either-or, and lack the mental agility—to say nothing of the maturity of attitude—which would allow us to indulge in the finer distinctions and the more subtle reservations permitted by the tradition of both-and. Flesh *or* spirit, merely a doxy or purely a goddess (or alternately, one and then the other), is more easily managed in our poetry, and probably, for that matter, in our private lives. But the greater poems of our tradition are more ambitious in this matter: as a consequence, they come perhaps nearer the truth than we do with our ordinary hand-to-mouth insights. In saying this, however, one need by no means confine himself to the poetry of Donne. If we are not too much blinded by our doctrine of either-or, we shall be able to see that there are many poems in the English tradition which demonstrate a thorough awareness of the problem and which manage, at their appropriate levels, the same kinds of synthesis of attitudes which we associate characteristically with Donne.

Take Pope's *Rape of the Lock,* for instance. Is Belinda a goddess, or is she merely a frivolous tease? Pope himself was, we may be sure, thoroughly aware of the problem. His friend Swift penetrated the secrets of the lady's dressing room with what results we know. Belinda's dressing table, of course, is bathed in a very different atmosphere; yet it may be significant that Pope is willing to allow us to observe his heroine at her dressing table at all. The poet definitely means to give us scenes from the greenroom, and views from the wings, as well as a presentation "in character" on the lighted stage.

Pope, of course, did not write *The Rape of the Lock* because he was obsessed with the problem of Belinda's divinity. He shows, indeed, that he was interested in a great many things: in various kinds of social satire, in a playful treatment of the epic manner, in deflating some of the more vapid clichés that filled the love poetry of the period, and in a dozen other things. But we are familiar with Pope's interest in the mock-epic as we are not familiar with his interest in the problem of woman as goddess; and moreover, the rather lurid conventional picture of Pope as the "wicked wasp of Twickenham"—the particular variant of the either-or theory as applied to Pope—encourages us to take the poem as a dainty but rather obvious satire. There is some justification, therefore, for emphasizing aspects of the poem which have received little attention in the past, and perhaps for neglecting other aspects of the poem which critics have already treated in luminous detail.

One further point should be made: if Pope in this account of the poem turns out to be something of a symbolist poet, and perhaps even something of what we call, in our clumsy phrase, a "metaphysical poet" as well, we need not be alarmed. It matters very little whether or not we twist some of the categories which the literary historian jealously (and perhaps properly) guards. It matters a great deal that we understand Pope's poem in its full richness and complexity. It would be an amusing irony (and one not wholly undeserved) if we retorted upon Pope some of the brittleness and inelasticity which we feel that Pope was inclined to impose upon the more fluid and illogical poetry which preceded him. But the real victims of the maneuver, if it blinded us to his poem, would be ourselves.

Pope's own friends were sometimes guilty of oversimplifying and reducing his poem by trying to make it accord with a narrow and pedantic logic. For example, Bishop Warburton, Pope's friend and editor, finds an error in the famous passage in which Belinda and her maid are represented as priestesses invoking the goddess of beauty. Warburton feels forced to comment as follows: "There is a small inaccuracy in these lines. He first makes his Heroine the chief Priestess, then the Goddess herself." The lines in question run as follows:

First, rob'd in White, the Nymph intent adores
With Head uncover'd, the *Cosmetic* Pow'rs.

A heav'nly Image in the Glass appears,
To that she bends, to that her Eyes she
rears. . . .

It is true that Pope goes on to imply that Belinda is the chief priestess (by calling her maid the "inferior Priestess"), and that, a few lines later, he has the maid deck the goddess (Belinda) "with the glitt'ring Spoil." But surely Warburton ought not to have missed the point: Belinda, in worshiping at the shrine of beauty, quite naturally worships herself. Whose else is the "heav'nly Image" which appears in the mirror to which she raises her eyes? The violation of logic involved is intended and is thoroughly justified. Belinda *is* a goddess, but she puts on her divinity at her dressing table; and, such is the paradox of beauty-worship, she can be both the sincere devotee and the divinity herself. We shall certainly require more sensitive instruments than Bishop Warburton's logic if we are to become aware of some of the nicest effects in the poem.

But to continue with the dressing-table scene:

The Fair each moment rises in her Charms,
Repairs her Smiles, awakens ev'ry Grace,
And calls forth all the Wonders of her Face;
Sees by Degrees a purer Blush arise,
And keener Lightnings quicken in her Eyes.

It is the experience which the cosmetic advertisers take at a level of dead seriousness, and obviously Pope is amused to have it taken seriously. And yet, is there not more here than the obvious humor? Belinda is, after all, an artist, and who should be more sympathetic with the problems of the conscious artist than Pope himself? In our own time, William Butler Yeats, a less finicky poet than Pope, could address a "young beauty" as "dear fellow artist."

In particular, consider the "purer Blush." Why purer? One must not laugh too easily at the purity of the blush which Belinda is engaged in painting upon her face. After all, may we not regard it as a blush "recollected in tranquillity," and therefore a more ideal blush than the spontaneous actual blush which shame or hauteur on an actual occasion might bring? If we merely read "purer" as ironic for its opposite, "impurer"—that is, unspontaneous and therefore unmaidenly—we shall miss not only the more delightful aspects of the humor, but we shall miss also Pope's concern for the real problem. Which is, after all, the more maidenly blush? That will depend, obviously, upon what one considers the essential nature of maidens to be; and Belinda, we ought to be reminded, is not the less real nor the less feminine because she fails to resemble Whittier's robust heroine, Maude Muller.

One is tempted to insist upon these ambiguities and complexities of attitude, not with any idea of overturning the orthodox reading of Pope's irony, but rather to make sure that we do not conceive it to be more brittle and thin than it actually is. This fact, at least, should be plain: regardless of what we may make of the "purer Blush," it is true that Belinda's dressing table does glow with a special radiance and charm, and that Pope, though amused by the vanity which it represents, is at the same time thoroughly alive to a beauty which it actually possesses.

There is a further reason for feeling that we shall not err in taking the niceties of Pope's descriptions quite seriously. One notices that even the metaphors by which Pope characterizes Belinda are not casual bits of decoration, used for a moment, and then forgotten. They run throughout the poem as if they were motifs. For instance, at her dressing table Belinda is not only a priestess of "the Sacred Rites of Pride," but she is also compared to a warrior arming for the fray. Later in the poem she is the warrior once more at the card table in her conquest of the two "adventrous Knights"; and again, at the end of the poem, she emerges as the heroic conqueror in the epic encounter of the beaux and belles.

To take another example, Belinda, early in the poem, is compared to the sun. Pope suggests that the sun recognizes in Belinda a rival, and fears her:

Sol thro' white Curtains shot a tim'rous Ray,
And op'd those Eyes that must eclipse the Day.

But the sun's fear of Belinda has not been introduced merely in order to give the poet an opportunity to mock at the polite cliché. The sun comparison appears again at the beginning of Canto II:

Not with more Glories, in th' Etherial Plain,
The Sun first rises o'er the purpled Main,
Than issuing forth, the Rival of his Beams
Lanch'd on the Bosom of the silver *Thames*.

Belinda is like the sun, not only because of her bright eyes, and not only because she dominates her special world ("But ev'ry Eye was fix'd on her alone"). She is like the sun in another regard:

> Bright as the Sun, her Eyes the Gazers strike,
> And, like the Sun, they shine on all alike.

Is this general munificence on the part of Belinda a fault or a virtue? Is she shallow and flirtatious, giving her favors freely to all; or, does she distribute her largesse impartially like a great prince? Or, is she simply the well-bred belle who knows that she cannot play favorites if she wishes to be popular? The sun comparison is able to carry all these meanings, and therefore goes past any momentary jest. Granting that it may be overingenious to argue that Belinda in Canto IV (the gloomy Cave of Spleen) represents the sun in eclipse, still the sun comparison does appear once more in the poem, and quite explicitly. As the poem closes, Pope addresses Belinda thus:

> When those fair Suns shall sett, as sett they
> must,
> And all those Tresses shall be laid in Dust;
> *This Lock*, the Muse shall consecrate to Fame,
> And mid'st the stars inscribe *Belinda*'s Name!

Here, one notices that the poet, if he is forced to concede that Belinda's eyes are only metaphorical suns after all, still promises that the ravished lock shall have a celestial eternity, adding, like the planet Venus, "new Glory to the shining Sphere!" And here Pope, we may be sure, is not merely playful in his metaphor. Belinda's name has been inscribed in the only heaven in which a poet would care to inscribe it. If the skeptic still has any doubts about Pope's taking Belinda very seriously, there should be no difficulty in convincing him that Pope took his own work very seriously indeed.

We began by raising the question of Belinda's status as a goddess. It ought to be quite clear that Pope's attitude toward Belinda is not exhausted in laughing away her claims to divinity. The attitude is much more complicated than that. Belinda's charm is not viewed uncritically, but the charm is real: it can survive the poet's knowledge of how much art and artifice have gone into making up the charm. The attitude is not wholly unrelated to that of Mirabell toward Millamant in Congreve's *The Way of the World*. Mirabell knows that his mistress has her faults, but as he philosophically remarks: ". . . I like her with all her faults; nay, like her for her faults. Her follies are so natural, or so artful, that they become her. . . . she once used me with that insolence, that in revenge I took her to pieces, sifted her, and separated her failings: I studied 'em, and got 'em by rote. . . . They are now grown as familiar to me as my own frailties; and in all probability, in a little time longer, I shall like 'em as well." The relation of author to creation can be more philosophical still: and though Pope's attitude toward his heroine has a large element of amused patronage in it, I find no contempt. Rather, Pope finds Belinda charming, and expects us to feel her charm.

To pursue the matter of attitude further still, what, after all, is Pope's attitude toward the iridescent little myth of the sylphs which he has provided to symbolize the polite conventions which govern the conduct of maidens? We miss the whole point if we dismiss the sylphs as merely "supernatural machinery." In general, we may say that the myth represents a qualification of the poet's prevailingly naturalistic interpretation. More specifically, it represents his attempt to do justice to the intricacies of the feminine mind. For, in spite of Pope's amusement at the irrationality of that mind, Pope acknowledges its beauty and its power.

In making this acknowledgement, he is a good realist—a better realist, indeed, than he appears when he tries to parade the fashionable ideas of the Age of Reason as in his "Essay on Man." He is good enough realist to know that although men in their "Learned Pride" may say that it is Honor which protects the chastity of maids, actually it is nothing of the sort: the belles are not kept chaste by any mere abstraction. It is the sylphs, the sylphs with their interest in fashion notes and their knowledge of the feminine heart:

> With varying Vanities, from ev'ry Part,
> They shift the moving Toyshop of their Heart;
> Where Wigs with Wigs, with Sword-knots
> Sword-knots strive,
> Beaus banish Beaus, and Coaches Coaches
> drive.

Yet the myth of the sylphs is no mere decoration to this essentially cynical generalization. The sylphs do represent the supernatural, though the supernatural reduced, of course, to its flimsiest proportions. The poet has been very careful here. Even Belinda is not made to take their existence too seriously. As for the poet, he very modestly recuses himself from rendering any judgment at all by ranging himself on the side of "Learned Pride":

Some secret Truths from Learned Pride
 conceal'd,
To Maids alone and Children are reveal'd:
What tho' no Credit doubting Wits may give?
The Fair and Innocent shall still believe.

In the old wives' tale or the child's fairy story may lurk an item of truth, after all. Consider the passage carefully.

"Fair" and "Innocent" balance "Maids" and "Children." Yet they act further to color the whole passage. Is "fair" used merely as a synonym for "maids"—e.g., as in "the fair"? Or, is it that beauty is easily flattered? The doctrine which Ariel urges Belinda to accept is certainly flattering: "Hear and believe! thy own Importance know / . . . unnumber'd Spirits round thee fly. . . ." Is "innocent" to be taken to mean "guiltless," or does it mean "naïve," perhaps even "credulous"? And how do "fair" and "innocent" influence each other? Do the fair believe in the sylphs because they are still children? (Ariel, one remembers, begins by saying: "If e'er one Vision touch'd thy *infant* Thought . . .") Pope is here exploiting that whole complex of associations which surround "innocence" and connect it on the one hand with more than worldly wisdom and, on the other, with simple gullibility.

Pope, as we now know, was clearly unjust in suggesting that Addison's advice against adding the machinery of the sylphs was prompted by any desire to prevent the improvement of the poem. Addison's caution was "safe" and natural under the circumstances. But we can better understand Pope's pique if we come to understand how important the machinery was to become in the final version of the poem. For it is Pope's treatment of the sylphs which allows him to develop, with the most delicate modulation, his whole attitude toward Belinda and the special world which she graces. It is precisely the poet's handling of the supernatural—the level at which he is willing to entertain it—the amused qualifications which he demands of it—that makes it possible for him to state his attitude with full complexity.

The sylphs are, as Ariel himself suggests, "honor," though honor rendered concrete and as it actually functions, not honor as a dry abstraction. The sylphs' concern for good taste allows little range for critical perspective or a sense of proportion. To Ariel it will really be a dire disaster whether it is her honor or her new brocade that Belinda stains. To stain her honor will certainly constitute a breach of good taste—whatever else it may be—and that for Ariel is enough. Indeed, it is enough for the rather artificial world of manners with which Pope is concerned.

The myth of the sylphs is, thus, of the utmost utility to Pope: it allows him to show his awareness of the absurdities of a point of view which, nevertheless, is charming, delightful, and filled with a real poetry. Most important of all, the myth allows him to suggest that the charm, in part at least, springs from the very absurdity. The two elements can hardly be separated in Belinda; in her guardian, Ariel, they cannot be separated at all.

In this connection, it is well to raise specifically the question of Pope's attitude toward the "rape" itself. We certainly underestimate the poem if we rest complacently in the view that Pope is merely laughing at a tempest in a teapot. There is such laughter, to be sure, and late in the poem, Pope expresses his own judgment of the situation, employing Clarissa as his mouthpiece. But the tempest, ridiculous though it is when seen in perspective, is a real enough tempest and related to very real issues. Indeed, Pope is able to reduce the incident to its true importance, precisely because he recognizes clearly its hidden significance. And nowhere is Pope more careful to take into account all the many sides of the situation than just here in the loss of the lock itself.

For one thing, Pope is entirely too clear-sighted to allow that the charming Belinda is merely the innocent victim of a rude assault. Why has she cherished the lock at all? In part at least, "to the Destruction of Mankind," though mankind, of course, in keeping with the convention, wishes so to be destroyed. Pope suggests that the Baron may even be the victim rather than the aggressor—it is a moot question whether he has seized the lock or been ensnared by it. Pope does this very skillfully, but with great emphasis:

Love in these Labyrinths his Slaves detains,
And mighty Hearts are held in slender Chains.
With hairy Springes we the Birds betray,
Slight Lines of Hair surprize the Finny Prey,
Fair Tresses Man's Imperial Race insnare,
And Beauty draws us with a single Hair.

Indeed, at the end of the poem, the poet addresses his heroine not as victim but as a "murderer":

> For, after all the Murders of your Eye,
> When, after Millions slain, your self shall
> die. . . .

After all, does not Belinda want the Baron (and young men in general) to covet the lock? She certainly does not want to retain possession of the lock forever. The poet naturally sympathizes with Belinda's pique at the way in which the Baron obtains the lock. He must, in the war of the sexes, coax her into letting him have it. Force is clearly unfair, though blandishment is fair. If she is an able warrior, she will consent to the young man's taking the lock, though the lock still attached to her head—and on the proper terms, honorable marriage. If she is a weak opponent, she will yield the lock, and herself, without any stipulation of terms, and will thus become a ruined maid indeed. Pope has absolutely no illusions about what the game is, and is certainly not to be shocked by any naturalistic interpretation of the elaborate and courtly conventions under which Belinda fulfills her natural function of finding a mate.

On the other hand, this is not at all to say that Pope is anxious to do away with the courtly conventions as a pious fraud. He is not the romantic anarchist who would abolish all conventions because they are artificial. The conventions not only have a regularizing function: they have their own charm. Like the rules of the card game in which Belinda triumphs, they may at points be arbitrary; but they make the game possible, and with it, the poetry and pageantry involved in it, in which Pope very clearly delights.

The card game itself, of course, is another symbol of the war of the sexes. Belinda must defeat the men; she must avoid that debacle in which

> The *Knave of Diamonds* tries his wily Arts,
> And wins (oh shameful Chance!) the *Queen of*
> *Hearts.*

She must certainly avoid at every cost becoming a ruined maid. In the game as played, there is a moment in which she is "Just in the Jaws of Ruin, and *Codille,*" and gets a thrill of delicious excitement at being in so precarious a position.

If the reader objects that the last comment suggests a too obviously sexual interpretation of the card game, one must hasten to point out that a pervasive sexual symbolism informs, not only the description of the card game, but almost everything else in the poem, though here, again, our tradition of either-or may cause us to miss what Pope is doing. We are not forced to take the poem as either sly, bawdy *or* as delightful fantasy. But if we are to see what Pope actually makes of his problem, we shall have to be alive to the sexual implications which are in the poem.

They are perfectly evident—even in the title itself; and the poem begins with an address to the Muse in which the sexual implications are underscored:

> Say what strange Motive, Goddess! cou'd
> compel
> A well-bred Lord t'assault a gentle *Belle*?
> Oh say what stranger Cause, yet unexplor'd,
> Cou'd make a gentle *Belle* reject a *Lord*?

True, we can take *assault* and *reject* in their more general meanings, not in their specific Latin senses, but the specific meanings are there just beneath the surface. Indeed, it is hard to believe, on the evidence of the poem as a whole, that Pope would have been in the least surprised by Sir James Frazer's later commentaries on the ubiquity of hair as a fertility symbol. In the same way, one finds it hard to believe, after some of the material in the "Cave of Spleen" section ("And Maids turn'd Bottels, call aloud for Corks"), that Pope would have been too much startled by the theories of Sigmund Freud.

The sexual implications become quite specific after the "rape" has occurred. Thalestris, in inciting Belinda to take action against the Baron, cries:

> Gods! shall the Ravisher display your Hair,
> While the Fops envy, and the Ladies stare!

Even if we take *ravisher* in its most general sense, still the sexual symbolism lurks just behind Thalestris' words. Else why should honor be involved as it is? Why should the Baron desire the lock, and why should Belinda object so violently, not as to an act of simple rudeness, but to losing "honor" and becoming a "degraded Toast"? The sexual element is involved at least to the extent that Belinda feels that she cannot afford to suffer the Baron, without protest, to take such a "liberty."

But a deeper sexual importance is symbolized by

the whole incident. Belinda's anguished exclamation—

> Oh hadst thou, Cruel! been content to seize
> Hairs less in sight, or any Hairs but these!

carries on, unconsciously, the sexual suggestion. The lines indicate, primarily, of course, Belinda's exasperation at the ruining of her coiffure. The principal ironic effect, therefore, is one of bathos: her angry concern for the prominence of the lock deflates a little her protests about honor. (Something of the bathos carries over to the sexual parallel: it is hinted, perhaps, that the worst thing about a real rape for the belle would be that it could not be concealed.) But though Belinda's vehemence gives rise to these ironies, the exclamation itself is dramatically appropriate; and Belinda would doubtless have blushed to have her emphasis on "any" interpreted literally and rudely. In her anger, she is obviously unconscious of the *faux pas.* But the fops whose admiring and envious comments on the exposed trophy Thalestris can predict —"Already hear the horrid things they say"— would be thoroughly alive to the unconscious *double entendre.* Pope's friend, Matthew Prior, wrote a naughty poem in which the same *double entendre* occurs. Pope himself, we may be sure, was perfectly aware of it.

In commenting on Pope's attitude toward the rape, we have suggested by implication his attitude toward chastity. Chastity is one of Belinda's most becoming garments. It gives her her retinue of airy guardians. As a proper maiden, she will keep from staining it just as she will keep from staining her new brocade. Its very fragility is part of its charm, and Pope becomes something of a symbolist poet in suggesting this. Three times in the poem he refers to the breaking of a frail china jar, once in connection with the loss of chastity, twice in connection with the loss of "honor" suffered by Belinda in the "rape" of the lock:

> Whether the Nymph shall break *Diana's* Law,
> Or some frail *China* Jar receive a Flaw. . . .
>
> Or when rich *China* Vessels, fal'n from high,
> In glittring Dust and painted Fragments lie!
>
> Thrice from my trembling hands the *Patch-box* fell;
> The tott'ring *China* shook without a Wind. . . .

Pope does not say, but he suggests, that chastity is, like the fine porcelain, something brittle, precious, useless, and easily broken. In the same way, he has hinted that honor (for which the sylphs, in part, stand) is something pretty, airy, fluid, and not really believed in. The devoted sylph who interposes his "body" between the lock and the closing shears is clipped in two, but honor suffers little damage:

> Fate urg'd the Sheers, and cut the *Sylph* in twain,
> (But Airy Substance soon unites again).

It would be easy here to turn Pope into a cynic; but to try to do this is to miss the point. Pope does not hold chastity to be of no account. He definitely expects Belinda to be chaste; but, as a good humanist, he evidently regards virginity as essentially a negative virtue, and its possession, a temporary state. He is very far from associating it with any magic virtue as Milton does in his *Comus.* The only magic which he will allow it is a kind of charm—a *je-ne-sais-quoi* such as the sylphs possess.

Actually, we probably distort Pope's views by putting the question in terms which require an explicit judgment at all. Pope accepts in the poem the necessity for the belle to be chaste just as he accepts the necessity for her to be gracious and attractive. But in accepting this, he is thoroughly alive to the cant frequently talked about woman's honor, and most of all, he is ironically, though quietly, resolute in putting first things first. This, I take it, is the whole point of Clarissa's speech. When Clarissa says:

> Since painted, or not painted, all shall fade,
> And she who scorns a Man, must die a Maid,

we need not assume with Leslie Stephen that Pope is expressing a smug masculine superiority, with the implication that, for a woman, spinsterhood is the worst of all possible ills. (There is actually no reason for supposing that Pope thought it so.) The real point is that, for Belinda, perpetual spinsterhood *is* the worst of all possible ills. In her own terms, it would be a disaster to retain her locks forever—locks turned to gray, though still curled with a pathetic hopefulness, unclaimed and unpossessed by any man. Belinda does not want *that;* and it is thus a violation of good sense to lose sight of the fact that the cherished lock is finally only a means to an end—one weapon to be used by the warrior in the battle, and not the strongest weapon at that.

Clarissa is, of course, promptly called a prude, and the battle begins at once in perfect disregard of the "good sense" that she has spoken. Pope is too fine an artist to have it happen otherwise. Belinda *has* been sorely vexed—and she, moreover, remains charming, even as an Amazon. After all, what the poet has said earlier is sincerely meant:

> If to her share some Female Errors fall,
> Look on her Face, and you'll forget 'em all.

Though Pope obviously agrees with Clarissa, he is neither surprised nor particularly displeased with his heroine for flying in the face of Clarissa's advice.

The battle of the sexes which ensues parodies at some points the combat in the great epic which Milton fashioned on the rape of the apple. But the absurdity of a battle in which the contestants cannot be killed is a flaw in Milton's great poem, whereas Pope turns it to beautiful account in his. In *Paradise Lost,* the great archangels single each other out for combat in the best Homeric style. But when Michael's sword cleaves the side of Lucifer, the most that Milton can do with the incident is to observe that Lucifer feels pain, for his premises force him to hurry on to admit that

> . . . th'Ethereal substance clos'd
> Not long divisible. . . .

Lucifer is soon back in the fight, completely hale and formidable as ever. We have already seen how delightfully Pope converts this cabbage into a rose in the incident in which the sylph, in a desperate defense of the lock, is clipped in two by the shears.

The absurdity of a war fought by invulnerable opponents gives an air of unreality to the whole of Milton's episode. There is a bickering over rules. Satan and his followers cheat by inventing gunpowder. The hosts under Michael retort by throwing the celestial hills at the enemy; and the Almighty, to put a stop to the shameful rumpus, has the Son throw the troublemakers out. But if the fight were really serious, a fight to the death, why does the heavenly host not throw the hills in the first place? Or, why does not the Almighty cast out the rebels without waiting for the three days of inconclusive fighting to elapse? The prevailing atmosphere of a game—a game played by good little boys and by unmannerly little ruffians, a game presided over by the stern schoolmaster, haunts the whole episode. The advantage is wholly with Pope here. By frankly recognizing that the contest between his beaux and belles is a game, he makes for his basic intention.

The suspicion that Pope in this episode is glancing at Milton is corroborated somewhat by Pope's general use of his celestial machinery. The supernatural guardians in *The Rape of the Lock* are made much of, but their effectiveness is hardly commensurate with their zeal. The affinities of the poem on this point are again with *Paradise Lost,* not with the *Iliad.* In Milton's poem, the angels are carefully stationed to guard Adam and Eve in their earthly home, but their protection proves, in the event, to be singularly ineffectual. They cannot prevent Satan from finding his way to the earth; and though they soar over the Garden, their "radiant Files, / Daz'ling the Moon," they never strike a blow. Even when they discover Satan, and prepare to engage him in combat, God, at the last moment, prevents the fight. Indeed, for all their numbers and for all their dazzling splendor, they succeed in determining events not at all. They can merely, in the case of Raphael, give the human pair advice and warning. Milton, though he loved to call their resonant names, and evidently tried to provide them with a realistic function, was apparently so fearful lest he divert attention from Adam's own freely made decision that he succeeds in giving them nothing to do.

If this limitation constitutes another ironical defect, perhaps, in Milton's great epic, it fits Pope's purposes beautifully. For, as we have seen, Pope's supernatural machinery is as airy as gossamer, and the fact that Ariel can do no more than Raphael, advise and warn—for all his display of zeal—makes again for Pope's basic intention. The issues in Pope's poem are matters of taste, matters of "good sense," and the sylphs do not violate the human limitations of this world which Pope has elected to describe and in terms of which judgments are to be made. Matters of morality—still less, the ultimate sanctions of morality—are never raised.

One more of the numerous parallels between *The Rape of the Lock* and *Paradise Lost* ought to be mentioned here, even though it may well be one of which Pope was unconscious. After the Fall has taken place, Michael is sent to prepare Adam for his expulsion from the happy garden. The damage has been done, the apple has been plucked and eaten, the human pair must prepare to go out into the "real" world, the "fallen" world of our ordinary human experience. Yet, Michael promises that Adam can create within his own breast "A Paradise . . . happier farr." Clarissa's advice to Belinda makes the same point. For better or worse, the lock has been lost. That fact must be accepted. In suggesting Belinda's best course under the circumstances, Clarissa raises quite explicitly Belinda's status as a divinity:

> Say, why are Beauties prais'd and honour'd
> most . . .
> Why Angels call'd, and Angel-like ador'd?

The divine element cannot reside in mere beauty alone, painted cheeks, bright eyes, curled locks. All human beauty is tainted with mortality: true "angelhood" resides in a quality of mind, and therefore can survive the loss of mere mortal beauty —can survive the loss of the lock, even the destruction of its beauty by the shears of time. The general parallel between the two speeches is almost complete. Belinda's true divinity, like Adam's happier paradise, is to be found within her. Pope, like Milton, can thus rationalize the matter in terms which allow him to dismiss the supernatural machinery and yet maintain the presence of a qualified supernatural in the midst of a stern and rational world in which no longer one may expect "God or Angel Guest / With Man, as with his Friend, familiar us'd / To sit indulgent"—an altered world in which Belinda will expect no more intimate communications from Ariel, and where she, like Adam and Eve, must rely on an inner virtue for advice and protection.

Indeed, one is tempted to complete the parallel by suggesting that Belinda is, at this point, like Adam, being prepared to leave her happy garden world of innocence and maidenly delight for a harsher world, the world of human society as it is and with the poetic illusions removed.

To return to the battle between the beaux and belles: here Pope beautifully unifies the various motifs of the poem. The real nature of the conventions of polite society, the heroic pretensions of that society as mirrored in the epic, the flattering clichés which society conventionally employs—all come in for a genial ragging. Indeed, the clichés of the ardent lover become the focal point of concentration. For the clichés, if they make the contention absurd and pompous, do indicate, by coming alive on another level, the true, if unconscious, nature of the struggle.

> No common Weapons in their Hands are
> found,
> Like Gods they fight, nor dread a mortal
> Wound.

"Like Gods they fight" should mean, in the epic framework, "with superhuman energy and valor." And "nor dread a mortal Wound" logically completes "Like Gods they fight"—until a yet sterner logic asserts itself and deflates the epic pomp. A fight in which the opponents cannot be killed is only a sham fight. Yet, this second meaning is very rich after all, and draws "Like Gods they fight" into its own orbit of meanings: there may be an extra zest in the fighting because it *is* an elaborate game. One can make godlike gestures because one has the invulnerability of a god. The contest is godlike, after all, because it is raised above the dust and turmoil of real issues. Like an elaborate dance, it symbolizes real issues but can find room for a grace and poetry which in a more earnest struggle are lost.

I have said earlier that Pope, by recognizing the real issues involved, is able to render his mock-epic battle meaningful. For the beaux of Hampton Court, though in truth they do not need to dread a mortal wound, can, and are prepared to die. We must remember that "to die" had at this period, as one of its submeanings, to experience the consummation of the sexual act. Pope's invulnerable beaux rush bravely forward to achieve such a death; for the war of the sexes, when fought seriously and to the death, ends in such an act.

The elegant battleground resounds with the cries of those who die "in *Metaphor*, and . . . in *Song*." In some cases, little more is implied than a teasing of the popular clichés about bearing a "living Death," or being burnt alive in Cupid's flames. But few will question the sexual implications of "die" in the passage in which Belinda overcomes the Baron:

> Nor fear'd the Chief th'unequal Fight to try,
> Who sought no more than on his Foe to
> die. . . .
> "Boast not my Fall" (he cry'd) "insulting Foe!
> Thou by some other shalt be laid as low. . . ."

The point is not that Pope is here leering at bawdy meanings. In the full context of the poem, they are not bawdy at all—or, perhaps we put the matter more accurately if we say that Pope's *total* attitude, as reflected in the poem, is able to absorb and digest into itself the incidental bawdy of which Pope's friends, and obviously Pope himself, were conscious. The crucial point is that Pope's interpretation of Belinda's divinity does not need to flinch from bawdy interpretations. The further meanings suggested by the naughty *double entendres* are not merely snickering jibes which contradict the surface meaning: rather those further meanings constitute the qualifying background against which Belinda's divinity is asserted. Pope's testimony to Belinda's charm is not glib; it is not thin and one-sided. It is qualified by, though not destroyed by, a recognition of all the factors involved—even of those factors which seem superficially to negate it. The touch is light, to be sure; but the poem is not flimsy, not mere froth. The tone is ironical, but the irony is not that of a narrow and acerb satire; rather it is an irony which accords with a wise recognition of the total situation. The "form" of the poem is, therefore, much more than the precise regard for a set of rules and conventions mechanically apprehended. It is, finally, the delicate balance and reconciliation of a host of partial interpretations and attitudes.

It was observed earlier that Pope is able to reduce the "rape" to its true insignificance because he recognizes, as his characters do not, its real significance. Pope knows that the rape has in it more of compliment than of insult, though he naturally hardly expects Belinda to interpret it thus. He does not question her indignation, but he does suggest that it is, perhaps, a more complex response than Belinda realizes. Pope knows too how artificial the social conventions really are and he is thoroughly cognizant of the economic and biological necessities which underlie them—which the conventions sometimes seem to mask and sometimes to adorn. He is therefore not forced to choose between regarding them as either a hypocritical disguise or as a poetic and graceful adornment. Knowing their true nature, he can view this outrage of the conventions with a wise and amused tolerance, and can set it in its proper perspective.

Here the functional aspect of Pope's choice of the epic framework becomes plain. The detachment, the amused patronage, the note of aloof and impartial judgment—all demand that the incident be viewed with a large measure of aesthetic distance. Whatever incidental fun Pope may have had with the epic conventions, his choice of the mock-epic fits beautifully his general problem of scaling down the rape to its proper insignificance. The scene is reduced and the characters become small and manageable figures whose actions can always be plotted against a larger background.

How large that background is has not always been noticed. Belinda's world is plainly a charming, artificial world; but Pope is not afraid to let in a glimpse of the real world which lies all about it:

> Mean while declining from the Noon of Day,
> The Sun obliquely shoots his burning Ray;
> The hungry Judges soon the Sentence sign,
> And Wretches hang that Jury-men may Dine;
> The Merchant from th'*Exchange* returns in
>   Peace,
> And the long Labours of the *Toilette* cease—
> *Belinda* now . . .

It is a world in which business goes on and criminals are hanged for all that Belinda is preparing to sit down to omber. This momentary glimpse of the world of serious affairs, of the world of business and law, of the world of casualness and cruelty, is not introduced merely to shrivel the high concerns of polite society into ironical insignificance, though its effect, of course, is to mock at the seriousness with which the world of fashion takes its affairs. Nor is the ironical clash which is introduced by the passage uncalculated and unintentional: it is not that Pope himself is unconsciously callous—without sympathy for the "wretches." The truth is that Pope's own perspective is so scaled, his totality of view so honest, that he can afford to embellish his little drama as lovingly as he likes without for a moment losing sight of its final triviality. A lesser poet would either have feared to introduce an echo of the "real" world lest the effect prove to be too discordant, or would have insisted on the discord and moralized, too heavily and bitterly, the contrast between the gay and the serious. Pope's tact is perfect. The passage is an instance of the complexity of tone which the poem possesses.

Maynard Mack

"WIT AND POETRY AND POPE": SOME OBSERVATIONS ON HIS IMAGERY

The point of departure of this essay is the current and useful description of Pope's kind of poetry as a poetry of statement.[1] One advantage of this description is that it is general enough to apply to other poetry as well. It asks us to bear in mind—what the temper of our present sensibility often disposes us to forget—that all poetry is in some sense poetry of statement; that without statement neither the Metaphysical kind of poem, witty, intellectual, and definitive, nor the Romantic kind, fluid and as it were infinitive (to mention only two) could be articulated at all; and accordingly, that the project of discrimination we are engaged on here is one of degree and not of kind.

Still, the real merit of the phrase is that it can apply specifically to Pope: it can set the problem. On the one hand, Pope writes a poetry with striking prose affinities. It has the Augustan virtues of perspicuity and ease which, whatever their status in poetry, are among the distinguishing attributes of prose discourse. It utilizes the denotative emphasis of Augustan diction, its precision and conciseness; the logical emphasis inherent in couplet rhetoric, its parallelism and antithesis. And it honours a whole body of reticences, reserves, restraints, exemplified perhaps best in the term "correctness," which tend to subdue and generalize its feeling and its wit. On the other hand, every reader of Pope is conscious of a host of qualities that look the other way. There is the kind of thing that Mr. Eliot is apparently glancing at when he says of Dryden's poetry that it states "immensely." [2] Or Mr. Tillotson, when he remarks in Pope a "composite activity," "a combination of simultaneous effects." [3] Or what Mr. Leavis and Mr. Wimsatt have pointed to in saying that Pope reconciles correctness with a subtle complexity, offsets and complicates the abstract logical patterns of his verse with counter patterns which are alogical, poetic.[4]

Facing this duality in its leading poet, the eighteenth century (if I may over-simplify to make the point) was usually able to read the terms as "poetry is statement" and dismiss the problem: "If Pope be not a poet, where is poetry to be found?" [5] The nineteenth century tended to re-aline the terms in an antithesis, "poetry or statement," and rested its case by denying Pope a poet's name: "Dryden and Pope are not classics of our poetry, they are classics of our prose." [6] Our own present rephrasing, in which the antithesis becomes a paradox, seems to me an improvement. It enables us to take account of both extremes; to see that if Johnson was right in his evaluation of Pope's success, Arnold was right in his perception of some of the conditions out of which the success was made. By the same token, it enables us to situate the distinctive character of Pope's achievement—and hence of the critical problem he presents—in a very special kind of reconciliation between qualities of poetry and prose, a reconciliation managed even after the maximum concessions have been made to prose.

In this essay I want to discuss some of the aspects of this reconciliation that affect Pope's imagery. We regard imagery to-day, especially metaphor, as the most essential of the means by which language achieves poetic character, whether we choose to designate this character in its totality as "iconic," "alogical," "opaque," "complex," or by any other of our present set of honorific terms. If we are right in this assumption about metaphor, it implies that a poetry of statement will be signalized not by the absence of metaphorical effects but by their use in such a way that they do not disturb a logical surface of statement. And this, I think, is true in the case of Pope. In response to the sensi-

From *Pope and his Contemporaries*, edited by James L. Clifford and Louis A. Landa (1949), pp. 20–40. Reprinted by permission of Oxford University Press.

bility of his time (and doubtless his own sensibility, too), Pope seems to me to have evolved an amazing variety of ways of obtaining the interest, richness, or tensions of metaphor while preserving, at any rate in appearance, those prose-like simplicities without which (as he probably agreed with Swift) "no human Performance can arrive to any great Perfection." [7] My purpose here is therefore to indicate some of the general principles that govern the effect of metaphor in Pope's poetry and then proceed to several of his characteristic methods of obtaining the benefits of metaphor without being, in any of the ordinary senses, strikingly metaphoric.

Probably the best place to begin an examination of this kind is with a passage from Pope's *Elegy on the Death of an Unfortunate Lady,* which has often been cited as evidence of his belonging to the Metaphysical "line of wit":

> Most souls, 'tis true, but peep out once an age,
> Dull sullen pris'ners in the body's cage:
> Dim lights of life that burn a length of years,
> Useless, unseen, as lamps in sepulchres;
> Like Eastern kings a lazy state they keep,
> And close confin'd to their own palace sleep.[8]

The general affinities of these lines with Metaphysical poetry certainly need no emphasis, and the opening metaphor, at least, can be traced back through Dryden's

> imprison'd in so sweet a cage
> A soul might well be pleas'd to pass an age[9]

to Donne's

> She, whose faire body no such prison was
> But that a Soule might well be pleas'd to passe
> An age in her.[10]

Since we are looking for differences, however, we must not fail to notice that Pope rarely uses these extensive collocations of witty and ingenious images, and that when he does, it is almost always to establish something that his poems intend to disvalue—here a death-in-life theme, contrasting with a life-in-death theme built up around the lady. In consequence, only certain areas in Pope's poetry show the type of imagery that most Metaphysical poems tend to show throughout, with the result that the centre of gravity in his poetry often passes to other kinds of complication. It passes, for example, to such powerful counterpointings of tone and meaning as are obtained in the *Unfortunate Lady* by modulating from lines like those quoted to those beginning "Yet shall thy grave with rising flow'rs be drest." [11] The contrast in theme and feeling that these lines offer to those above is one that Donne would have elected to obtain through a conjunction of brilliant images. Pope obtains it—not only here, but habitually in his poems—through a conjunction of styles. The implied comparison usually possesses the richness and suggestiveness of a metaphor, but is not, in any strict sense, metaphorical.

We must notice also in the passage quoted that the images, witty and to some extent ingenious as they are, stem from comparisons that are at bottom traditional and familiar—the soul as prisoner, lamp, monarch, the body as cage, sepulchre, palace. This is Pope's normal practice. Except in comic poetry like the *Dunciad* (where, again, it is partly a matter of disvaluing) he rarely stresses heterogeneity in the objects he brings together. For this reason he has little occasion to expand or amplify his comparisons in the manner we associate with Donne. It has not been often enough remarked, I think, that the "extended" Metaphysical image is a simple consequence of the Metaphysical discovery of "occult resemblances in things apparently unlike." That is to say, if one sets about comparing lovers to compasses at all, or the world to a beheaded man,[12] one is bound to specify in some detail the nature of the resemblances that make the image relevant; the value of the image is, as it were, generated in the process of constructing it. But it is also spent there. If such images seem wittier than any other kind because they display their wit at length, they also have less power in reserve. There is nothing in Donne's compass image, handsome as it is, to tempt the imagination to keep on unfolding it beyond the point at which the poet leaves it. On the other hand, Donne's gold-leaf image in the same poem has this power. It has it because it is powerfully compressed, and it can be powerfully compressed because it does not have to generate all its own potential: it is nourished at the source by normal and traditional associations. Pope's images, as suggested above, rely heavily on such associations. They take the ordinary established relationships of, say, singing and breath and soul, flesh and oblivion and marble, sepulchre and decay, finger and flute, parent and child, body and beauty, and with a delicate readjustment, freshen and fortify their implications:

Oft as the mounting larks their notes prepare
They fall, and leave their little lives in air.

Tho' cold like you, unmov'd and silent grown,
I have not yet forgot myself to stone.

See the sad waste of all-devouring years,
How Rome her own sad sepulchre appears.

Such were the notes thy once-lov'd poet sung,
Till death untimely stopp'd his tuneful
tongue.[13]

Me, let the tender Office long engage
To rock the Cradle of reposing Age.

Still round and round the ghosts of beauty
glide,

And haunt the places where their honour
died.[14]

Finally, we must notice that the closed couplet exercises on images a peculiarly muting or subordinating influence. When we look at Dryden's lines quoted earlier, we see that, though he has taken over in large part the very words of Donne, the image in his verse has somehow become submerged. The reason, I think, is partly that Donne has sprawled the image across a weak rhyme which calls no attention to itself, whereas Dryden has suspended it within a strong rhyme which has a meaning of its own—which suggests, in fact, a correspondence between the soul's envelopment in body and its envelopment in time. Partly, also, that the movement of Donne's lines (and this is customary in his couplet poetry) exists simply to carry the image on its back; its pattern, in so far as it has any, is determined by and coextensive with the image. Dryden's couplet, on the other hand, being closed, has an assertive pattern of its own. The coiling and uncoiling rhythmical effect that comes from alternation of inverted with normal word order works with the movement of meaning to emphasize the logical stages of the soul's acceptance ("so sweet a cage"; "might well be pleas'd"; "pleased to pass an age") and the climactic stage is affirmed by rhyme. The closed couplet, in other words, tends to subdue images by putting them into competition with other forms of complication.

This point can be illustrated equally well from Pope. In the lines from the *Unfortunate Lady,* certainly the wittiest and boldest image is that in the third couplet. Yet here again the interest of the comparison has to compete with other interests—the strong rhyme, the parallelism, the humorously inverted syntax in both lines, which by withholding the completion of the sense units as long as possible keeps rather a lazy state itself.[15] Or take a passage in which Pope is developing one of Donne's images. This is Donne:

Now
The ladies come; As Pirates, which doe know
That there came weak ships fraught with
Cutchannel
The men board them.[16]

This is Pope:

Painted for sight, and essenc'd for the smell,
Like Frigates fraught with Spice and
Cochine'l,
Sail in the Ladies: How each Pyrate eyes
So weak a Vessel, and so rich a Prize!
Top-gallant he, and she in all her Trim,
He boarding her, she striking sail to him.[17]

Donne is not at his best in this case, and Pope has the advantage of maturing Donne's idea at length—about as much at length as he was ever inclined to go. Still, leaving all that aside, one can see, I think, that Pope's figure, in spite of its richer elaborations, is not the primary and exclusive focus of attention that Donne's is. Donne's, as in our earlier instance, is the sole occupant of the verse rhetoric which presents it; Pope's is jostled for *Lebensraum* by many other contenders. There is, first, the drama of the ladies' arrival, which the verse itself is at some pains to enact in the first two and a half lines. Then there is the confrontation of forces in line 3, and the double assessment of the booty in line 4, both again rhetorically enacted. Finally, in line 5 comes a brilliant chiastic *rapprochement* of male and female in their bedizenment, to be followed in line 6 by an extension and also a qualification of this *rapprochement* with respect to sex (both parties are interested in the amorous duel, but their functions differ), the former carried by the metrical parallel, the latter by the antithesis in the sense. All these effects grow out of the potentialities of couplet rhetoric, not out of the image; and though they may co-operate with imagery, as here, they have a life of their own which tends to mute it.[18]

So far we have been discussing orthodox kinds of imagery in Pope's poetry, together with some of the modifications to which this imagery is subjected. It is time to turn now to some of his more reticent modes of imaging, which achieve metaphorical effect without using what it is customary to regard as metaphor. The first of these may be studied in his proper names.

Pope's names warrant an essay in themselves. With the possible exception of Milton, no poet has woven so many so happily into verse. And this is not simply because, as Pope said of himself,

> Whoe'er offends, at some unlucky Time,
> Slides into Verse, and hitches in a Rhyme,[19]

but because Pope saw, like Milton, the qualitative elements (including in Pope's case the humorous qualities) that could be extracted from proper names. For an effect of romance, sonority, and exoticism akin to Milton's, though much mitigated by the couplet, any passages of his translation of Homer's catalogue of ships will do:

> The Paphlagonians Pylaemenes rules,
> Where rich Henetia breeds her savage Mules,
> Where Erythinus' rising Clifts are seen,
> Thy Groves of Box, Cytorus! ever green;
> And where Aegyalus and Cromna lie,
> And lofty Sesamus invades the Sky;
> And where Parthenius, roll'd thro' Banks of Flow'rs,
> Reflects her bord'ring Palaces and Bow'rs.[20]

For a combination of romance and humour, this passage:

> First he relates, how sinking to the chin,
> Smit with his mien, the Mud-nymphs suck'd him in:
> How young Lutetia, softer than the down,
> Nigrina black, and Merdamante brown,
> Vy'd for his love in jetty bow'rs below,
> As Hylas fair was ravish'd long ago.[21]

And for pure humour:

> 'Twas chatt'ring, grinning, mouthing, jabb'ring all,
> And Noise and Norton, Brangling and Breval,
> Dennis and Dissonance, and captious Art,
> And Snip-snap short, and Interruption smart,
> And Demonstration thin, and Theses thick,
> And Major, Minor, and Conclusion quick.[22]

It will be observed in all these passages that as the names slide into verse they tend to take on a metaphorical colouring. Those in the first and third passages are of real places and persons, but the poetry does not require, any more than Milton's, that we identify them closely. Instead they become vehicles of an aura of associations clinging to epic warriors before Troy, or else of the vulgarity of a disputatious literature, which swallows up writers as Noise, Brangling, Dissonance swallow up Norton, Breval, and Dennis. Pope is a master of this metaphorical play with names. Sometimes the names he uses are quasi-metaphorical to begin with, like those he has invented in the Lutetia passage above. Or like those which allude—Adonis, Atossa, Shylock, Balaam, Timon, Sporus. Or those which have an allegorical cast—Uxorio, Worldly, Sir Morgan, Sir Visto, Patritio, Papillia, Hippia. Or those which personify—Avarice, Profusion, Billingsgate, Sophistry, Mathesis. Pope's habit with these classes of names is to interlayer them among his real objects and real persons, so that there results an additional and peculiarly suggestive kind of metaphorical play between concrete and abstract: allegorical Sir Morgan astride his cheese;[23] allusive Adonis driving to St. James's a whole herd of swine;[24] or personified Morality, Chicane, Casuistry, and Dulness suddenly brought into incongruous union with a judge named Page:

> Morality, by her false Guardians drawn,
> Chicane in Furs, and Casuistry in Lawn,
> Gasps, as they straiten at each end the cord,
> And dies, when Dulness gives her Page the word.[25]

Unquestionably, however, Pope's best metaphorical effects with names were obtained from specific ones, as in the lines on Dennis and Dissonance above. Did a certain duchess show an indiscriminate appetite for men? How better image it than with a nice derangement of proper names, opened with a particularly felicitous "what":

> What has not fired her bosom or her brain?
> Caesar and Tall-boy, Charles, and Charlemagne.[26]

Did the vein of poetry in contemporary versifiers hardly weigh up to a gramme? Then doubtless it was an age when

> nine such Poets made a Tate.[27]

Why was philosophy at Oxford so backward, so ponderous? Because the Oxford logicians came riding whip and spur, through thin and thick,

> On German Crousaz and Dutch Burgersdyck.[28]

Or, since the current drama was slavishly derivative, why not let the patchwork image be projected partly with syntax and partly with names—a roll-call of stately ones, a tumbling huddle of risible ones:

A past, vamp'd, future, old reviv'd, new piece,
Twixt Plautus, Fletcher, Shakespeare, and Corneille
Can make a Cibber, Tibbald, or Ozell.[29]

A second restrained mode of imaging in Pope's poetry is the allusion. Not simply the kind of descriptive allusion to persons, places, events, and characters that all poets make continual use of, and of which I shall say nothing here, but a kind that is specifically evaluative, constructing its image by setting beside some present object or situation not so much another object or situation as another dimension, a different sphere—frequently for the purpose of diminishing what is present, but often, too, for the purpose of enlarging or elevating it. Familiar examples of the first use are the correspondence of Sporus to Satan in one of his more degrading disguises—"at the Ear of *Eve*, familiar Toad";[30] or (more humorously) of Cibber to Satan, on his exalted throne, at the opening of *Dunciad*, ii. A less familiar example is the witty correspondence suggested in *Dunciad*, iv between the dunces irresistibly drawn into the gravitational field of Dulness—

by sure Attraction led
And strong impulsive gravity of Head—[31]

and the feeling Sin has in Milton's poem, after the Fall, of being pulled toward earth by "sympathy, or some connatural force,"

Powerful at greatest distance to unite
With secret amity things of like kind. . . .
Nor can I miss the way, so strongly drawn
By this new-felt attraction and instinct.[32]

As for the second use, the *Essay on Man* begins with a particularly fine example, in the "garden tempting with forbidden fruit";[33] while *Windsor Forest* both begins and ends with one; the groves of Eden, which establish the central symbol of the poem; and the dove of Noah, also described as the dove of grace and peace, which throws around Pope's vision of England as she comes out of her continental wars all the seventeenth-century religious associations of covenant, happy rescue, and divine mission.[34]

This evaluative kind of metaphor in Pope, whether diminishing or enlarging, is usually religious, and often very powerfully so. Here are some instances in the lighter hues (I limit myself to instances that I think have not been recorded by Pope's editors):

And Heav'n is won by violence of song.[35]
And Zeal for that great House which eats him up.[36]
Blest be the *Great!* for those they take away.[37]
And instant, fancy feels th' imputed sense.[38]

These colours are darker:

Each does but hate his neighbour as himself.[39]
What Lady's Face is not a whited Wall? [40]

And this, though light in tone, carries a scathing indictment of the perversion of religious values in a money culture. Since it admirably illustrates the way allusion can construct a cogent metaphor without intruding on a casual surface and is, in fact, one of the most scarifying passages Pope ever wrote, I quote it in full:

On some, a *Priest* succinct in Amice white,
Attends, *all flesh is nothing in his Sight!*
Beeves, at his touch, at once to jelly *turn*,
And the huge Boar is shrunk into an *Urn:*
The board with specious *miracles* he loads,
Turns Hares to Larks, and Pigeons into Toads.
Another (for in all what one can shine?)
Explains the Seve and Verdeur of the *Vine.*
What cannot copious *Sacrifice attone?*
Thy Treufles, Perigord! thy Hams, Bayonne!
With French *Libation*, and Italian Strain
Wash Bladen *white*, and *expiate* Hays's stain.
Knight lifts the head, for what are crowds undone
To *three essential* Partridges *in one.*[41]

There are two other modes of imagery of which Pope is fond, modes that the concision of the closed couplet encourages and almost insists on, though no other writer of the couplet has perfected them to a like extent. These are pun and juxtaposition. Juxtaposition operates in Pope's poetry in several ways. One of them, as has lately been pointed out,[42] is through zeugma, which the economy of this verse form often calls for and which can itself be modulated either into metaphor—"Or stain her Honour, or her new Brocade," or into pun—"And sometimes Counsel take—and sometimes *Tea.*" [43] (In either case, the effect is ultimately metaphorical, a correspondence being suggested between Belinda's attitudes to chastity and brocade, or between Queen Anne's, and her society's, to politics and tea.)

My own concern, however, is not with zeugma, but with the metaphorical effects that can arise from simple juxtaposition. For example, from a list of items *seriatim,* with one inharmonious term:

> Puffs, Powders, Patches, Bibles, Billet-doux.[44]

Or from a simple parallel inside the line:

> Dried Butterflies, and Tomes of Casuistry.[45]

Or from a similar parallel inside the couplet:

> Now Lapdogs give themselves the rowzing Shake,
> And sleepless Lovers, just at Twelve, awake.[46]

This is a very versatile device. In the *Rape of the Lock,* from which the above examples are taken, Pope uses it to mirror in his lines and couplets the disarray of values in the society he describes, the confounding of antithetical objects like lapdogs and lovers, bibles and *billets-doux.* On the other hand, in the *Essay on Man,* this same device, redirected by the context, can be made to mirror the "equalizing" view of antithetical objects taken by the eye of God or by the god-like magnanimous man:

> A hero perish, or a sparrow fall.[47]
> As toys and empires, for a god-like mind.[48]

It is also a very sensitive device. The potential metaphor that every juxtaposition tends to carry in suspension requires only the slightest jostling to precipitate it out. Sometimes a well-placed alliteration will do it:

> The Mind, in Metaphysics at a Loss,
> May wander in a wilderness of Moss.[49]

Sometimes an inter-animation of words, as here between the "smooth" eunuch and the "eas'd" sea:

> Where, eas'd of Fleets, the Adriatic main
> Wafts the smooth Eunuch and enamour'd Swain.[50]

And sometimes a set of puns, as in this example, fusing the biologist with the object of his study:

> The most recluse, discreetly open'd, find
> Congenial matter in the Cockle-kind.[51]

Pun, of course, brings before us Pope's most prolific source of imagery in his comic and satiric poetry—which is to say, in the bulk of his work. His puns in other poems—*Windsor Forest, Eloisa,* the *Essay on Man,* the *Essay on Criticism*—are deeply buried and always reticent. But in the satires and the *Dunciad,* particularly the latter, he spends them openly and recklessly, with superb effect. They cease to be in these poems ordinary puns, like those we find in Metaphysical poetry, where, because of the conceit, pun has a lesser job to do; they become instead Metaphysical conceits themselves, yoking together violently, as Mr. Leavis has noticed,[52] the most heterogeneous ideas. Moreover, when they are used together with ordinary images, the real metaphorical power is likely to be lodged in them. Thus the following figures are not especially bold themselves, but the puns inside them open out like peacocks' tails:

> Ye tinsel Insects! whom a Court maintains,
> That counts your Beauties only by your *Stains.*

> On others Int'rest her gay liv'ry flings,
> Int'rest that waves on *Party-colour'd* wings.

> At length Corruption, like a gen'ral flood,
> (So long by watchful ministers withstood)
> Shall deluge all; and Av'rice, creeping on,
> Spread like a *low-born* mist, and blot the sun.[53]

Here, then, are four classes of metaphorical effect in Pope's poetry, all of them obtained outside the normal channels of overt simile and metaphor. One of them, juxtaposition (its collateral descendant, zeugma, would make a second), stems from the structure of the closed couplet itself. Two more, allusion and pun, are encouraged to a large extent by its fixed and narrow room. And none of them, it is important to notice, calls attention to itself as metaphorical. Between them, nevertheless, without violating at all the prose conventions of the Augustan mode, they do a good deal of the work that we today associate with the extended metaphor and conceit.

The devices of complication touched on in the preceding sections pertain primarily to local texture: the line and couplet. I want to add to these, in conclusion, three patterns that are more pervasive; that help supply the kind of unity in Pope's poems which he is popularly not supposed to have. Actually, there is a wide variety of such patterns. There are the characteristics of the dramatic speaker of every poem, who shifts his style, manner, and quality of feeling considerably from poem to poem, as anyone will see who will compare carefully the *Essay on Criticism* with the *Essay on Man*, or the *Epistle to Dr. Arbuthnot* with that to Augustus. There is the character of the interlocutor in the poems that have dialogue, by no means a man of straw. There is the implicit theme, usually announced in a word or phrase toward the outset of the poem, and while seldom developed in recurrent imagery, as in Shakespeare, almost always developed in recurrent references and situations. There is also, often, a kind of pattern of words that reticulates through a poem, enmeshing a larger and larger field of associations—for instance, words meaning light in the *Essay on Criticism,* or the word "head" (and, of course, all terms for darkness) in the *Dunciad.* And there are a great many more such unifying agents.

The three that I shall examine briefly here are irony, the portrait, and mock-heroic. Pope's irony, fully analysed, would require a book. The point about it that is most relevant to our present topic is that it is a mode of complication closely resembling metaphor. At its most refined, in fact, as in Swift's *Modest Proposal* or Pope's praise of George II in the *Epistle to Augustus,* it asks us to lay together not two, but three different perspectives on reality. First, the surface, and second, the intended meanings, these two corresponding roughly to vehicle and tenor in a metaphor; and then, third—to use again the Pope and Swift examples—the kind of propositions that English projectors were *usually* making about Ireland, or the poets about George II. Pervasive irony of this type—of which there is a good deal in Pope—tends to resist the presence of bold imagery, for two reasons. In the first place, because it consists already in a mutual translation, to and fro, between one kind of complex whole with all its particularities clinging to it (what is said), and a different complex whole with all its revised particularities (what is meant); a translation that profuse or striking imagery only clutters and impedes. And in the second place, because the success of the medium depends on adopting the attitudes, motives, and so far as possible even the terms of a very conventional point of view. If one is going to write an ironic love song "in the modern taste," one almost has to refer to "Cupid's purple pinions" [54]; or if a panegyric on George II, to the usual terms for kingly prowess:

> Your Country, chief, in Arms abroad defend.[55]

To find a more striking phrase would destroy the subtlety of the ironic comment (i.e., its resemblance to what a Cibber might have said); and would, of course, too, destroy the mutual translation between the arms of battle and those of Madame Walmoden.

To all this, in the *Epistle to Augustus,* is added the further layer of metaphor that results from Pope's imitation of what Horace had written about *his* Caesar. Nor is this layer confined alone to the poems which are imitations. The Roman background, it has been well observed, is a kind of universal Augustan metaphor or "myth." [56] It lies behind Pope's work, and much of Swift's and Fielding's, like a charged magnetic field, a reservoir of attitudes whose energy can be released into their own creations at a touch. Not through the Horatian or Virgilian or Ovidian tags; these are only its minor aspect; but through the imposed standard of a mighty and civilized tradition in arts, morals, government. At the same time, conveniently, it is a standard that can be used two ways: for a paradigm of the great and good now lost in the corruptions of the present, as in the comparison of George II with Augustus Caesar; or for the head-waters of a stream down which still flow the stable and continuing classic values:

> You show us Rome was glorious, not profuse.
> The world's just wonder, and ev'n thine, O
> Rome!
> Who would not weep, if Atticus were he! [57]

This last example brings us to Pope's portraits. These, again, have the complicating characteristics of metaphors, without drawing attention to themselves as such. They are often erroneously called "illustrations," as if their content were exhausted in being identified with some abstraction implied or stated by the poem. But what abstractions will exhaust the characters of Atticus, Sporus, Atossa, Balaam, and a score of others? To instance from one of the simplest portraits, so that it may be quoted entire, here is Narcissa:

> "Odious! in woollen! 'twould a saint provoke!"
> (Were the last words that poor Narcissa
> spoke):
> "No, let a charming chintz, and Brussels lace
> Wrap my cold limbs, and shade my lifeless
> face:

One would not, sure, look frightful when one's
dead:
And—Betty—give this cheek a little red." [58]

This, to the extent that it illustrates anything, illustrates the poem's prose argument that our ruling passion continues to our last breath. But as a metaphor it explores, not without considerable profundity, through the character of one type of woman, the character of the human predicament itself. Here we have, as her name implies, the foolish self-lover; but also—in a wider, more inevitable, and uncensorable sense—the self-lover who inhabits each of us by virtue of our mortal situation, the very principle of identity refusing to be erased. Here, too, we have the foolish concern for appearances, vastly magnified by the incongruity of its occasion; but also the fundamental human clutching at the familiar and the known. And embracing it all is the central paradox of human feelings about death and life. Cold limbs don't need wrapping (the conjunction of terms itself suggests that death can be apprehended but not comprehended), nor dead faces shading; and yet, as our own death rituals show, somehow they do. The levels of feeling and experience startled into activity in this short passage can hardly be more than pointed at in the clumsiness of paraphrase. The irony of words like "saint," the ambiguities of "charming" and "shade," the tremendous compression in "frightful," of "the anguish of the marrow, The ague of the skeleton," accumulate as one contemplates them.

All of Pope's portraits have at least the complexity of this one, and all are equally metaphorical in effect. If they do not call attention to themselves as metaphors, it is probably because in them the vehicle has largely absorbed the tenor; for metaphors in general seem to take on prominence according as both the tenor and the vehicle (viz., lovers as well as compasses) are insisted on at once. In any case, they behave like metaphors in Pope's poems, usually assuming, in addition to their functions locally, an important unifying role. Sometimes they define the entire structure of a poem, as in *Moral Essays*, ii, where they develop the easy-going aphorism of the opening—"Most women have no characters at all"—into a mature interpretation of what personality is. Sometimes they supply the central symbols, as with Timon in *Moral Essays*, iv, "Vice" in Dialogue ii of the *Epilogue to the Satires*, or the Man of Ross and Balaam in *Moral Essays*, iii. Likewise, in *Arbuthnot*, Atticus and Sporus appear at just the crucial phrases in the argument and knit up, as it were, the two essential ganglia in the sinews of the drama that the poem acts out between the poet and his adversaries. They give us, successively, the poet analytical and judicial, who can recognize the virtues of his opponents ("Blest with each Talent and each Art to please"), whose deliberation is such that he can even mirror in his language—its subjunctives, its antitheses, the way it hangs the portrait over an individual without identifying it with him—the tentative, insinuating, never-wholly-committed hollow man who is Atticus; and then the poet roused and righteous, no longer judicial but executive, touching with Ithuriel's spear the invader in the garden, spitting from his mouth (with a concentration of sibilants and labials) the withered apple-seed. Both portraits are essential to the drama that unifies the poem.

The great pervasive metaphor of Augustan literature, however, including Pope's poetry, is the metaphor of tone: the mock-heroic. It is very closely allied, of course, to the classical or Roman myth touched on earlier and is, like that, a reservoir of strength. By its means, without the use of overt imagery at all, opposite and discordant qualities may be locked together in "a balance or reconcilement of sameness with difference, of the general with the concrete, the idea with the image, the individual with the representative, the sense of novelty and freshness with old and familiar objects"—the mock-heroic seems made on purpose to fit this definition of Coleridge's of the power of imagination. For a literature of decorums like the Augustan, it was a metaphor with every sort of value. It could be used in the large, as in *Joseph Andrews, Tom Jones,* the *Beggar's Opera,* the *Rape of the Lock,* the *Dunciad,* or in the small—the passage, the line. It could be set in motion by a passing allusion, not necessarily to the classics:

Calm Temperance, whose blessings those
partake,
Who hunger, and who thirst, for scribling sake;

by a word:

Glad chains, warm furs, broad banners, and
broad faces;

even by a cadence:

And the fresh vomit run for ever green.[59]

Moreover, it was a way of getting the local, the ephemeral, the pressure of life as it was lived, into poetry, and yet distancing it in amber:

That live-long wig, which Gorgon's self might own,
Eternal buckle takes in Parian stone.[60]

It was also a way of qualifying an attitude, of genuinely "heroicizing" a Man of Ross, a parson Adams, a School-mistress, yet undercutting them with a more inclusive attitude:

Rise, *honest* Muse! and sing the Man of Ross.[61]

Above all—and this, I think, was its supreme advantage for Pope—it was a metaphor that could be made to look two ways. If the heroic genre and the heroic episodes lurking behind the *Rape of the Lock* diminish many of the values of this society, they also partially throw their weight behind some others. Clarissa's speech is an excellent case in point.[62] Her words represent a sad shrinkage from the epic views of Glaucus which reverberate behind them, views involving real heroism and (to adapt Mr. Eliot's phrase) the awful daring of a real surrender. Still, the effect of the contrast is not wholly minimizing. Clarissa's vision of life, worldly as it is when seen against the heroic standard, surpasses the others in the poem and points, even if obliquely, to the tragic conflict between the human lot and the human will that is common to life at every level.

This flexibility of the mock-heroic metaphor is seen in its greatest perfection in the *Dunciad.* There are, indeed, three thicknesses of metaphor in this poem: an overall metaphor, in which the poem as a whole serves as vehicle for a tenor which is the decline of literary and human values generally; a network of local metaphor, in which this poem is especially prolific; and in between, the specifically mock-heroic metaphor which springs from holding the tone and often the circumstances of heroic poetry against the triviality of the dunces and their activities. But what is striking about this metaphor in the *Dunciad,* and indicative of its flexibility, is that it is applied quite differently from the way it is applied in the *Rape of the Lock.* There, the epic mode as vehicle either depresses the values of the actors, as with Belinda, or somewhat supports them, as with Clarissa. Here, on the contrary, one of the two lines of development (the comic) grows from allowing the actors to depress and degrade the heroic mode, its dignity and beauty. Again and again Pope builds up in the poem effects of striking epic richness, only to let them be broken down, disfigured, stained—as the word "vomit" stains the lovely movement and suggestion of the epic line quoted above. Thus the diving and other games in Book II disfigure the idea of noble emulation and suggest the befoulment of heroic values through the befoulment of the words and activities in which these values are recorded. Thus the fop's Grand Tour in IV mutilates a classical and Renaissance ideal (cf. also Virgil's Aeneas, to whose destined wanderings toward Rome the fop's are likened) of wisdom ripened by commerce with men and cities. Indeed, the lines of the whole passage are balanced between the ideal and the fop's perversions of it:

A dauntless infant! never scar'd with God.
Europe he saw, and Europe saw him too.
Judicious drank, and greatly daring dined;

or between related ideals and what has happened to them:

To happy Convents, bosomed deep in Vines,
Where slumber Abbots, purple as their Wines.

or between epic resonances, the epic names, and the sorry facts:

To where the Seine, obsequious as she runs,
Pours at great Bourbon's feet her silken sons.[63]

This is one line of development in the *Dunciad.* The other is its converse: the epic vehicle is gradually made throughout the poem to enlarge and give a status of serious menace to all this ludicrous activity. Here the epic circumstance of a presiding goddess proved invaluable. Partly ludicrous herself, she could also become the locus of inexhaustible negation behind the movements of her trivial puppets; her force could be associated humorously, but also seriously, with the powerful names of Chaos, Night, Anti-Christ, and with perversions of favourite order symbols like the sun, monarchy, and gravitation. Here, too, the epic backgrounds as supplied by Milton could be drawn in. Mr. C. S. Lewis has remarked of *Paradise Lost* that "only those will fully understand it who see that it might have been a comic poem."[64] The *Dunciad* is one realization of that might-have-been. Over and above the flow of Miltonic echoes and allusions, or the structural resemblances like Cibber's (or Theobald's) Pisgah-vision based on Adam's, or the clustered names of dunces like those of Milton's devils, thick as the leaves that strew bad books in Grubstreet—the *Dunciad* is a version of Milton's theme in being the story of an uncreating Logos. As the poem progresses, our sense of this increases through the calling in of more and more powerful associations by the epic vehicle. The activities of the dunces and of Dulness are more and more equated with religious anti-values, culminating in the passage on the Eucharist quoted earlier. The metaphor of the coronation of the king-dunce moves always closer to and then flows into the metaphor of the Day of the Lord, the descent of the anti-Messiah, the uncreating Word. Meantime, symbols which have formerly been ludicrous—insects, for instance, or sleep—are given by this expansion in the epic vehicle a more sombre cast. The dunces thicken and become less individual, more anonymous, expressive of blind inertia—bees in swarm, or locusts blackening the land. Sleep becomes tied up with its baser physical manifestations, with drunkenness, with deception, with ignorance, with neglect of obligation, and finally with death. This is the sleep which *is* death, we realize, a *Narrendämmerung*, the twilight of the moral will. And yet, because of the ambivalence of the mock-heroic metaphor, Pope can keep to the end the tension between all these creatures as comic and ridiculous, and their destructive potentiality in being so. Certainly two of the finest puns in any poetry are those with which he continues to exploit this tension at the very end of the poem, when Dulness finally *yawns* and Nature *nods*.

The purpose of this essay has been to supply a few, a very few, of the materials that are requisite for giving the phrase "poetry of statement" specific content. I have tried to suggest that Pope is poetic, but not in the way that the Metaphysicals are poetic, even where he is most like them; that if the prominent metaphor is the distinctive item in their practice, this has been replaced in Pope's poetry partly by devices of greater compression, like allusion and pun, partly by devices that are more distributive, like irony and mock-heroic, and of course by a multitude of other elements—the net effect of all these being to submerge the multiplicities of poetic language just beneath the singleness of prose. Twenty-five years ago it would have been equally important to say that Pope is not poetic as the Romantics are poetic, for in this century there has always been a tendency to subsume him as far as possible under the reigning orthodoxy. It is true that in certain areas Pope's poetry faintly resembles that of the Romantics; in certain others, that of the line of wit. But the task of criticism for the future, when we are likely to be paying more and more attention to Pope as our own poetry moves in the direction suggested by Mr. Auden, and by Mr. Eliot in his *Quartets*, is not with Pope as a pre-Romantic or a post-Metaphysical, but as an Augustan poet whose peculiar accomplishment, however we may choose to rate it on the ultimate scale of values, was the successful fusion of some of the most antithetical features of verse and prose.

NOTES

1. The phrase probably owes its present currency to Mr. Mark Van Doren's use of it in his study of *The Poetry of John Dryden* (1920; republished in 1931 and 1946).

2. T. S. Eliot, "John Dryden," 1922 (*Selected Essays*, 1932, p. 273).

3. G. Tillotson, *On the Poetry of Pope* (1938), pp. 156, 141. Cf. also his *Essays in Criticism* (1942), p. 103.

4. F. R. Leavis, *Revaluation* (1936), p. 71; W. K. Wimsatt, "Rhetoric and Poems: The Example of Pope" (in *English Institute Essays, 1948*, published by the Columbia University Press, 1949).

5. Johnson, "Life of Pope" (*Lives of the Poets*, ed. G. B. Hill, iii, 251).

6. Arnold, "The Study of Poetry," *Essays in Criticism, Second Series* (*Wks.*, 1903, iv, 31).

7. *A Letter to a Young Clergyman*, 1721 (*Wks.*, ed. Herbert Davis, ix, 68).

8. Ll. 17–22. This passage is cited for its metaphysical character by Middleton Murry, *Countries of the Mind* (1922), p. 86; and F. R. Leavis, op. cit., pp. 70 ff.

9. *To the Duchess of Ormond*, ll. 118–19.

10. *The Second Anniversary,* ll. 221–3.

11. Ll. 63 ff.

12. For the second instance, see *The Second Anniversary,* ll. 9 ff.

13. This example illustrates particularly well the way in which an unbroken logical surface can cushion and absorb a powerful or even violent image. If we were to paraphrase the image, we should have to say something like: "Death took up the instrument of Parnell's music, and fingering (stopping) it in his own (untimely) tempo, brought the music to a premature (untimely) stop." Yet the effect of the normal logical meaning of "stopp'd" is to carry us smoothly across the opposites that are being yoked here.

14. The quotations are from *Windsor Forest,* ll. 133–4; *Eloisa to Abelard,* ll. 23–4; *To Mr. Addison,* ll. 1–2; *To Robert, Earl of Oxford,* ll. 1–2; *Epistle to Dr. Arbuthnot,* ll. 408–9; and *Moral Essays,* ii, 241–2.

15. This effect is easily verified by rearranging the words in normal order.

16. *Satyre IV,* ll. 187–90.

17. *The Fourth Satire of Dr. John Donne, Versifyed,* ll. 226–31.

18. See also on this point, with respect to Dryden, M. W. Prior, *The Language of Tragedy* (1947), p. 169.

19. *Imit. of Hor., Sat. II,* i, ll. 77–8.

20. *Iliad,* ii, 1034 ff.

21. *Dunciad* (1743), ii, 331–6.

22. Ibid. 237–42.

23. *Moral Essays,* iii, 61.

24. *Moral Essays,* iii, 73–4.

25. *Dunciad* (1743), iv, 27–30.

26. *Moral Essays,* ii, 78.

27. *Epistle to Dr. Arbuthnot,* l. 190.

28. *Dunciad* (1743), iv, 198.

29. Ibid. i, 284–6.

30. *Epistle to Dr. Arbuthnot,* l. 319.

31. Ll. 75–6.

32. Bk. x, ll. 244 ff.

33. Ep. i, 8.

34. Ll. 8 and 429–30.

35. *Imit. of Hor., Ep. II.* i, l. 240. Cf. Matt. xi, 12.

36. *Moral Essays,* iii, 208. Cf. Ps. lxix, 9.

37. *Epistle to Dr. Arbuthnot,* l. 225. Cf. Job i, 21.

38. *Dunciad,* ii, 200. Cf. the theological sense of "imputed."

39. *Moral Essays,* iii, 108. Cf. Matt. xxii, 39. I have noticed this allusion elsewhere (*College English* [1946], vii, 269).

40. *The Fourth Satire of Dr. John Donne, Versifyed,* l. 151. Cf. Matt. xxiii, 27. (The allusion is Pope's addition.)

41. *Dunciad* (1743), iv, 549–62. (Italics mine.)

42. In Mr. Wimsatt's essay cited above, p. 21, n. 1. Cf. also Austin Warren, "The Mask of Pope" (*Rage for Order,* 1948, p. 45).

43. *Rape of the Lock,* ii, 107, iii, 8.

44. Ibid. i, 138.

45. Ibid. v, 122. A particularly graceful comparison in its suggestion of a common animation, brilliance, delicacy of movement, and perishableness in the worlds of ethics and Lepidoptera.

46. Ibid. i, 15–16.

47. Ep. i, 88.

48. Ep. iv, 180.

49. *Dunciad* (1743), iv, 449–50.

50. Ibid. 309–10.

51. *Dunciad* (1743), iv, 447–8.

52. Op. cit., p. 99.

53. From *Epil. to the Sats.,* Dial. ii, 220–1; *Dunciad* (1743), iv, 537–8; and *Moral Essays,* iii, 135–8. (Italics mine.)

54. Cf. Swift's *A Love Song, in the Modern Taste,* st. 1.

55. *Imit. of Hor., Ep. II,* i, l. 3.

56. Cf. J. C. Maxwell, "Demigods and Pickpockets," *Scrutiny,* xi (1942–3), 34 ff.

57. From *Moral Essays,* iv, 23; *Essay on Criticism,* l. 248; *Epistle to Dr. Arbuthnot,* l. 214.

58. *Moral Essays,* i, 246–51.

59. From *Dunciad* (1743), i, 49–50, 88; ii, 156.

60. *Moral Essays,* iii, 294–5.

61. Ibid. 250. (Italics mine.) The blend of irony and praise is carefully maintained throughout the passage.

62. Canto v, ll. 9 ff.

63. *Dunciad* (1743), iv, 284 ff.

64. *A Preface to Paradise Lost* (1942), p. 93.

Louis I. Bredvold

THE GLOOM OF THE TORY SATIRISTS

Gloom, in all its varieties, is distasteful, and we are always pleased to have remedies for it, and even excuses for avoiding it. Dr. Johnson, who wrestled manfully with his own painful melancholia, once counselled Lucy Porter that it is useless and foolish, and perhaps sinful, to be gloomy. This is the language of good sense. But Dr. Johnson would have been the first to admit that this good sense is a standard of but limited application to great literature, certainly to the gloom of satire. It is hardly the final word on the great denunciations of mankind by Hamlet and King Lear. But it has too often been accepted as the final word on the satire of Pope and Swift. They have been charged with the sin of excessive gloom, of bitterness so extreme that it becomes unwholesome malignancy. Readers who will respond wholeheartedly to other satire hesitate before the work of these men, on guard against the moral perversity they are sure they will find there. That a dark, almost impervious gloom enveloped them is undeniable. But it may be well to inquire into the question whether it is so unwholesome. Gloom may have a variety of causes and take a variety of forms, and some of them are certainly free from the spiritual darkness which could be called sin.

Our judgement of Swift and Pope, and our insight into them as well, depend not a little on our preserving proportion, on our recognition of their normal human qualities, and on our restraint in playing up sensational elements. The charitableness of both men, for instance, has been acknowledged with more perplexity than sympathetic understanding.[1] Even Leslie Stephen, as he was trying to present Pope sympathetically, could write: "There is no particular merit in loving a mother" (a painful remark, not to be matched elsewhere in biography; it could have appeared only in a life of Pope), "but few biographies give a more striking proof that the loving discharge of a common duty may give a charm to a whole character. It is melancholy to add that we often have to appeal to this part of his story, to assure ourselves that Pope was really deserving of some affection." [2] Such an admission that some human qualities, at once heavily discounted, may be discovered in a venomous creature lays bare the whole mental process of denigration in a passage which its author probably did not intend to be harsh.

It would seem, too, that too much has been made of the impairing influence on Swift and Pope of their "crazy constitutions," as if their satire were a phase of their medical history. There has grown up around them a kind of cult of the satiric genius as a tortured mind inhabiting a tortured body. Pope's deformity and weakness seem to add an appropriate grotesqueness to a sinister character. Swift's final insanity, which, so far as modern medical authorities can determine, was most likely the last stage of a life-long disease of the inner ear and which was therefore unrelated to his satire either as cause or effect, is raised to a more than medical significance as the fitting conclusion of the career of a bitter satirist, the awful disintegration of a great mad genius in self-devouring rage. And his remark that he would die like the tree, first at the top, is repeated with all the solemnity of an oracular doom in Greek tragedy, whereas common sense tells us that, within the limits of Swift's medical knowledge, it could only have been the apprehension of a sufferer from chronic headaches. Had Swift not lived beyond the scriptural age of three score and ten, his biographies would not have been overcharged with these dramatic themes of premonition and fate. We should still have had the "mad parson," but we might have had fewer intimations that his satire verges on madness, in quite another sense.

As for the diseases of the mind, the heaviest charge against Pope and Swift is a negativeness of spirit which depresses the worth and dignity of human life. But pessimism is a concept so vague and broad that it often leads to erroneous infer-

From *Pope and His Contemporaries*, edited by James L. Clifford and Louis A. Landa (1949), pp. 1–19. Reprinted by permission of Oxford University Press.

ences and interpretations. The Tory satirists, the group gathered about Pope and Swift, did not suffer from philosophical or religious pessimism, or from anything that can be called *Weltschmerz*. There is no spiritual *malaise* in them; their gloom is not an enervating apathy. They seem generally to have had firm faith in the ultimate right order of things, and we must avoid carrying back to them such more recent philosophies of despair as are familiar in our post-Schopenhauer era. We do not even find in them that melancholy brooding over the destiny of man which in their century oppressed Johnson and Gray. The Christian resignation of Johnson to a world in which there is little to be enjoyed and much to be endured would have fitted well with their satire—as it did with Johnson's—but it is not an attitude characteristic of Swift or Pope. Nor were they steeped, as Gray was, in the melancholy wisdom of the Greeks, which in its sobriety and humility was so nearly allied to the sadness of Johnson. Gray's *Ode on a Distant Prospect of Eton College* with its motto from Menander, and his *Hymn to Adversity* with a similar motto from Aeschylus, all admonish us that an enduring heart is the gift the gods have fittingly bestowed on the sons of men.

Such views of human fate touch issues above and beyond the reach of satire, and it was not any such cosmic gloom which hung over the Tory satirists, but a mundane darkness conjured up by human folly and knavery. The satirists were much more attentive to the problems of the world of men than to ultimate questions of philosophy and religion. Even Pope's *Essay on Man* (radiating optimism, not gloom), which seems to have come as a surprise to Swift ("I confess I did never imagine you were so deep in morals"),[3] and Bolingbroke's philosophical excursions, were speculations of a kind not common among them, and certainly did not constitute any bond of union. Prior rebuked the system-building pretensions of the human reason in both *Alma* and *Solomon*. Swift habitually ridiculed those philosophers who deal in cosmic explanations, and in *A Tale of a Tub* (Section ix) attributed their "innovations" to madness. The learning of the Brobdingnagians "is very defective," reports Gulliver, "consisting only in morality, history, poetry, and mathematics, wherein they must be allowed to excel. But the last of these is wholly applied to what may be useful in life, to the improvement of agriculture, and all mechanical arts; so that among us it would be little esteemed. And as to ideas, entities, abstractions, and transcendentals, I could never drive the least conception into their heads." Stella, indeed, "understood the Platonic and Epicurean philosophy, and judged very well of the defects of the latter," as Swift recorded in his memoir of her, and her programme of studies, we may be sure, reflected the intellectual character of her friend and tutor, who never in his writings alluded to Socrates or Plato except with respect. But we know that Swift valued the Socratic dialogues, not for any "abstractions and transcendentals," but for their ethical and political wisdom. Gulliver's master among the Houyhnhnms laughed "that a creature pretending to reason should value itself upon the knowledge of other people's conjectures, and in things where that knowledge, if it were certain, could be of no use. Wherein he agreed entirely with the sentiments of Socrates, as Plato delivers them; which I mention as the highest honour I can do that prince of philosophers." Moral and political wisdom occupies a level a little lower than metaphysics, and doubtless a little lower also than the greatest poetry. But Swift's genius moved in this middle flight, and here his massive common sense and his satiric gift had their full opportunity. The moment we try to read more into Swift than he read in Socrates, we misinterpret him. In one of his greatest passages he praised credulity as "a more peaceful possession of the mind than curiosity," and laid down the proposition "that wisdom, which converses about the surface," is therefore preferable "to that pretended philosophy, which enters into the depth of things, and then comes gravely back with information and discoveries, that in the inside they are good for nothing."[4] Anyone who has had experience in reading this passage with modern young people can testify that it is more often than not taken as the language of philosophical nihilism. But Swift was not thinking in metaphysical terms about appearance and reality. He was letting his irony play over the repugnance some people feel for satire, for "the art of exposing weak sides, and publishing infirmities." It was in "most corporeal beings," that is, human beings, such as the flayed woman and the stripped carcass of the beau, that "the outside hath been infinitely preferable to the in." The "serene, peaceful state, of being a fool among knaves" is a moral condition which we may choose, but for which we must ourselves accept the responsibility.

In this exposure of the insides of human nature, in stripping the human carcass, the satirists were united, but again only on the level of practical common sense; they were observers, not spinners of theory. They naturally ignored the cynical materialistic psychology of Hobbes and Mandeville, which was completely alien to their spirit. But it is significant that they could not agree even on the system of La Rochefoucauld. When Pope wrote Swift in October 1725 that he was busy with "a set of maxims in opposition to all Rochefoucauld's principles," he drew from Swift the celebrated confession that La Rochefoucauld "is my favourite, because I found my whole character in him. However I will read him again, because it is possible I may have since undergone some alterations." [5] Bolingbroke promptly dissociated himself from "the founder of your sect, that noble original whom you think it so great an honour to resemble." [6] From Gay and Arbuthnot we have no comment on the matter. Swift therefore stands alone among these men as a professed disciple of the author of the *Maxims.*

But we must not take this profession too literally, as Professor Quintana has already warned us.[7] The famous system of reducing every virtue to a form of disguised selfishness, though far from being the whole of the *Maxims,* is nevertheless their conspicuous and distinguishing feature. With a finesse far beyond the capacity of either Hobbes or Mandeville, whose systems at some points paralleled his, La Rochefoucauld exposed certain kinds of deception which human nature practises on itself. He applied his method with brilliant virtuosity, but it must be admitted that his commentary on human nature is rather specialized and iterative. One can learn and practise the trick of it. To turn from the *Maxims* to the works of Swift is like passing from a narrow room into the great world. Swift also probed the deceitfulness of the human heart, but his *art de connaître les hommes* is not reducible to rule or system. In both originality of thought and fertility of wit Swift was the greater man, and the philosophy of the *Maxims* could have filled only one corner of his capacious mind. When Swift remarks that "complainers never succeed at Court, though railers do," [8] we note his characteristic qualities in the brief pronouncement; the startling, amusingly cynical paradox mellows, as we linger over it, into an utterance of shrewdness and practical wisdom.

Swift habitually wrote with the purpose of imparting wisdom, and his satire is therefore quite different in tone and temper from that of La Rochefoucauld. The latter composed his observations in the period after his retirement from active life, when he could assume the vantage of a seigniorial detachment; he played the roles of spectator, psychologist, and stylist. For the author of the *Maxims* a fault in mankind was something to be disdainfully indicated and wittily exposed; but for Swift it was also something to be judged, castigated, and corrected. Swift wrote, not from a position of detachment, but in the stream of events. Aside from his *bagatelles,* he was normally a publicist, a man of action, by every instinct a manager of affairs. From his retreat at Letcombe in the fateful month of July 1714 he truly described himself to Arbuthnot: "I could never let people run mad without telling and warning them sufficiently." His whole biography is a continuous record of his attempts to patch up differences, guide the choice of policies, abolish abuses, manage the presentation of new political and ecclesiastical measures, and in general serve as counsellor to anyone and everyone with whom business or friendship brought him into contact. His interest in history, which Professor Nichol Smith has noted,[9] is another aspect of his eminently practical cast of mind. His satire is so largely occasional and journalistic because of this innate urge for action, and it can be fully understood only as a part of the history of his time.

As these practical urges of Swift's nature differentiate his satire on the one hand from the amused detachment of La Rochefoucauld, so on the other they distinguish it from the depressive melancholy that feeds on stagnant brooding. The satire of Swift, even at its bitterest, never depends for its intensity on any sense of frustration; it has the force of intellectual statement—often mock-scientific in tone—and has the effect of arousing in the reader, by means of the *vis comica* and indignation, a will to action which is sympathetic with Swift's own character. Even the darkest page of

Swift leaves us with this feeling of soundness at the core, with a firm conviction of our moral competence and responsibility. It is the expression of a bitter but not a sick mind, and has the invigorating power of a call to action.

This firm grip on actualities is characteristic also of the satire of the other members of Swift's brotherhood, Arbuthnot, Gay, and Pope. They were as ready as Swift, whose genius towered among them, to aline themselves in political struggles, even though political parties were still thought undesirable in principle. A political party—that is, the party one was opposed to—was a faction seeking to disrupt the national unity. To give up one's neutrality and become a party man, even with the right party, was in a sense a sacrifice of moral position and justifiable only because the nation was in danger. In an age when each party maintained that it was the voice of the nation and the other was a faction, it was natural that imputations of political and moral turpitude should be freely exchanged in the controversy on the real issues. Friendships across the political line were chilled by suspicion and could be maintained only by cautious and magnanimous demeanour on both sides. Hence the peculiarly bitter asperities of both Whig and Tory satirists and their tendency to resort to the lampoon, the popular weapon of all parties in all the controversies of the age, literary as well as political. Hence also the practical intent of so much of the Tory satire. For better as well as for worse, the Tory satirists were in the mêlée, not above it, and they wrote with the conviction that they were dealing battle-blows to save from extinction the virtue and glory of England.

Wit and politics drew them together before the end of Queen Anne's reign into a literary collaboration symbolized by the Scriblerus Club, which diverted itself by ridiculing pedantry rather than political iniquity. But the inclusion in this brotherhood of Oxford and Bolingbroke indicates that the Tory complexion of the group was as openly professed as the Whiggism of Button's Coffee House. Arbuthnot, the universally beloved physician to the Queen, had already ventured into Tory journalism and thus discovered that vein of satire which "lay like a Mine in the Earth, which the Owner for a long time never knew of." [10] In a companionship so intimate and so congenial it is difficult to divine what each individual contributed to the other; but in the free give and take many a suggestion thrown out by one man in a convivial hour was later developed by another into a major literary work. Henceforth the members of the Scriblerus Club constituted a defensive and offensive alliance; they freely exchanged confidences; they distrusted the same men and the same measures; above all they were agreed on the unreliability of the nature of that animal called man.

The sincerity of their professions was immediately put to the severest test by the disintegration of the ministry of Oxford and Bolingbroke. In the sequence of events leading up to the final catastrophe they had an opportunity to observe how precariously the welfare of the whole nation, present and future, depended on traits of human character. In bitterness they had to admit to themselves and to one another that England was, from their point of view, being betrayed by their own friends, Oxford and Bolingbroke, not to mention the indecisive poor sick queen. Swift indicated publicly his own forecast of the disaster that was coming by withdrawing early in the summer to Letcombe, whence he refused angrily all solicitations to return to the scene where the drama was playing itself out. He was "weary to death of Courts and Ministers and business and politics. . . . I shall say no more but that I care not to live in storms when I can no longer do service in the ship and am able to get out of it." [11] He was, however, busy writing something that he thought would "vex" the great ministers; it was the pamphlet, *Some Free Thoughts upon the Present State of Affairs*, in which he set forth how, with other policies, and more wisdom, and less foolish dissension among the ministers, the "present state of affairs" might have been far different. "It may serve for a great lesson of humiliation to mankind," Swift was writing in the rectory at Letcombe, "to behold the habits and passions of men otherwise highly accomplished, triumphing over interest, friendship, honour, and their own personal safety, as well as that of their country, and probably of a most gracious princess, who hath entrusted it to them." [12] Such were the reflections Swift intended to publish to the nation as the crisis was approaching. The pamphlet was a castigating sermon to his friends, the Tory ministers, who had been measured by the moral test and found wanting. They had also failed by the test of common sense, from first to last so important in the eyes of Swift; their "mystical manner of proceeding" baffled and galled him:

> I have been frequently assured by great ministers, that politics were nothing but common sense; which, as it was the only thing they spoke, so it was the only thing they could have wished I should not believe. God hath given the bulk of mankind a capacity to understand reason when it is fairly offered; and by reason they would easily be governed, if it were left to their choice. Those princes in all ages who were most distinguished for their mysterious skill in government, found by the event, that they had ill consulted their own quiet, or the ease and happiness of their people.[13]

Swift's bitter anger at Oxford and Bolingbroke in 1714 reappeared years later as the contempt of the King of Brobdingnag for "all *mystery, refinement,* and *intrigue,* either in a prince or a minister." The lovable Arbuthnot was, if anything, more severe even than Swift:

> I have an opportunity calmly and philosophically to consider that treasure of vileness and baseness, that I always believed to be in the heart of man; and to behold them exert their insolence and baseness; every new instance, instead of surprising and grieving me, as it does some of my friends, really diverts me, and in a manner improves my theory.[14]

That is a satirist's view of human nature, but Swift and Arbuthnot were not at this time engaging in satire; they were assessing in all seriousness the moral meaning of the Tory collapse. Their intellectual honesty and resolute clear-sightedness in this episode vouches for their integrity when they turn to satire.

In spite of these strains the personal friendships between wits and ministers held fast, not least perhaps because of the candour and sincerity in which Swift set an example. "In your public capacity," Swift told Oxford, "you have often angered me to the heart, but, as a private man, never." [15] The threats of danger which for a time hung over Oxford, Bolingbroke, Ormond, and Prior naturally only strengthened the loyalties of the whole group. However, defeated and dispersed as they were, they hardly ventured into politics for a dozen years. Swift won a heartening victory in the early twenties with his *Drapier's Letters,* but it was only towards 1726, when Swift first dared to return to London, carrying with him the completed manuscript of *Gulliver's Travels,* that the survivors of the Scriblerus Club (Oxford and Parnell and Prior had died) resumed their old intimacy and gathered their forces for their great campaign. Bolingbroke had returned from France and rejoined Pope. Letters to and from Swift became more frequent and in 1725 contained suggestions that he might risk a visit to England. On 15 October Pope expressed a hope that "you are coming towards us, and that you incline more and more to your old friends in proportion as you draw nearer to them; in short that you are getting into our vortex." Two days later Arbuthnot added his plea: "I cannot help imagining some of our old club met together like mariners after a storm." It was as mariners after a storm that they met again the following summer.

But new storms had been brewing, and, with their sense of solidarity renewed, they were soon to be engaged in a prolonged satirical crusade against the degeneracy of the times. Even their ridicule of pendantry, dullness, and bad taste now assumed a larger social significance, as related to their general attack on moral and political corruption. Dr. Johnson, whose misfortune it was never to understand Swift, thought they were all guilty of self-righteousness:

> From the letters that pass between him [Swift] and Pope it might be inferred that they, with Arbuthnot and Gay, had engrossed all the understanding and virtue of mankind, that their merits filled the world; or that there was no hope of more. They shew the age involved in darkness, and shade the picture with sullen emulation.[16]

The satirist is perforce a judge, and he is nothing unless he can speak with the voice of righteousness. The darkness of his gloom is the measure of the depth of his indignation, and a sense of isolation is inevitable in his calling. Johnson had himself in his younger days joined forces with the Tories against the corruption of the Walpole era, and his satire in *London* is as gloomy and scornful as any. The warm friendship and mutual confidence which Pope and Swift and their friends so constantly reaffirmed in their letters was the obverse of their common bitterness over the decay of the nation. It is possible to agree in substance with the somewhat sentimental comment of Richter, with which Birkbeck Hill annotated the passage just quoted from Johnson:

> Have not many others felt themselves, like me, warmed and encouraged by the touching quiet love of these manly hearts, which, though cold, cutting, and sharp to the outer world, yet laboured and throbbed in their common inner world warmly and tenderly for one another?[17]

Good satire may be withering, it may be dark anger, it may be painfully bitter; but it cannot be great satire without having at its core a moral idealism expressing itself in righteous indignation. The *saeva indignatio* which Swift suffered from is radically different in quality from a morbid *Schadenfreude*. Once that distinction is admitted we have the essential justification for our pleasure in satire, as well as an understanding of the fellow feeling with which the satirists sustained one another.

In the declining moral tone of England under Walpole they now professed to see the extinction of the best elements of English life. Under the circumstances it was inevitable that they should turn their satire on the political situation. The leaders of the Opposition to Walpole and the Court were mostly veteran Tories, old friends of Swift and Pope, and there was Bolingbroke operating without much disguise in the background. The satirists had a score to settle with the Whigs in general, but Walpole provided them with special opportunities for the exercise of their talent, which they were not backward to improve. John Gay was able, by adding some political touches to his ballad operas, to raise an ominous political storm, accompanied by a minor social disturbance at Court; the inoffensive Gay, as Arbuthnot wrote Swift, became "one of the obstructions to the peace of Europe," and "if he should travel about the country he would have hecatombs of roasted oxen sacrificed to him." Swift, from Dublin, congratulated Gay on "the felicity of thriving by the displeasure of Courts and Ministers."[18] The political strains and tensions of the time became increasingly apparent in the life and work of Pope, now entering upon the period of his greatest poetic achievement. It was therefore only to be expected that, in spite of his professed resolution to avoid party, he should find that his satire involved him in attacks on the corruption emanating from high places. In the final *Dunciad* the celebration of the Greater Mysteries of the Goddess of Dullness is opened by a wizard who represents the Court influence and who is therefore assumed to stand for Walpole himself:

> With that, a Wizard old his Cup extends;
> Which whoso tastes, forgets his former friends,
> Sire, Ancestors, Himself. One casts his eyes
> Up to a Star, and like Endymion dies:
> A Feather, shooting from another's head,
> Extracts his brain; and Principle is fled;
> Lost is his God, his Country, every thing:
> And nothing left but Homage to a King!
> The vulgar herd turn off to roll with Hogs,
> To run with Horses, or to hunt with Dogs;
> But, sad example! never to escape
> Their Infamy, still keep the human shape.[19]

The Mysteries which are thus happily initiated under the highest auspices lead directly to the final triumph of Chaos and Universal Darkness in those concluding lines which Dr. Johnson always praised as noble, and which bring to a climax and conclusion the satirical career of Pope in all its aspects. After that pronouncement of doom there was nothing more to be said.

But Pope and his friends, apostles of disenchantment, were by no means alone in their apprehensions for England. Walpole enjoys a bad preeminence among English statesmen for drawing upon himself the hostility of writers of all parties and shades of party, men representing the best elements in the nation. Poets and satirists alike show the age involved in darkness. The old Tories associated amicably with the younger Whigs, the Boy Patriots. By 1735 Pope was on the friendliest terms with the future Earl of Chatham, whose letters and speeches at this time abounded with such expressions as "this gloomy scene" and "this disgraced country." This was the age that we know from Hogarth's pictures, from Fielding's political farces and *Jonathan Wild*. The literature of protest was copious, and Warton's list of some of the notable contributions will indicate its great variety of source and nature:

> About this time a great spirit of liberty was prevalent. All the men of wit and genius joined in increasing it. Glover wrote his *Leonidas*; Nugent his *Odes to Mankind* and *to Mr. Pulteney*; King his *Miltonis Epistola* and *Templum Libertatis*; Thomson his *Brittania*, his *Liberty*, and his *Agamemnon*; Mallet his *Mustapha*;

> Brooke his *Gustavus Vasa*; Pope his *Imitations* and these two *Dialogues* [the *Epilogue to the Satires*]; and Johnson his *London*.[20]

In his poem Johnson described the metropolis of those "degenerate days" in these terms:

> Here let those reign, whom pensions can incite
> To vote a patriot black, a courtier white;
> Explain their country's dear-bought rights
> away,
> And plead for pirates in the face of day;
> With slavish tenets taint our poison'd youth,
> And lend a lie the confidence of truth.[21]

This gloomy theme of the decadence of England continued to occupy English writers as long as English politics remained in the doldrums, even after Walpole was gone. The sentimentalists echoed its phrases, especially in their eulogies of the life of primitive man; Joseph Warton, in *The Enthusiast* (1744), wished to escape to a life among the simple Indian swains of the New World, "since Virtue leaves our wretched land." John Brown summed up the whole case thoroughly and elaborately when he published in 1757 his famous *Estimate of the Manners and Principles of the Times*. The "ruling character" of the times he asserted to be "a vain, luxurious, and selfish effeminacy." He laid the blame impartially at the door of every portion of the public; but the political significance of his indictment is evident from his characterization of Walpole "in these few words, that while he seemed to *strengthen* the *Superstructure*, he *weakened* the *Foundations* of our Constitution." [22]

But Brown's sensational book, after being the town talk for a season, lapsed thereafter into an obscurity from which even modern scholars have been reluctant to rescue it. It happened to come out in the very year when Pitt began the great administration which was to win England glorious victories abroad and restore her morale at home. The grim predictions of Brown were made to seem spectral and unreal by the splendours of Pitt's leadership, and therefore, as Lecky long ago pointed out, it is difficult even for us to do full justice to the *Estimate*.[23] The Tory satirists of course suffered a similar loss of credit. When Dr. Johnson in his old age was writing the *Lives of the Poets* he had only words of disparagement for the "long course of opposition to Sir Robert Walpole," the opposition to which he had in 1739 contributed *Marmor Norfolciense*, but which he now said "had filled the nation with clamours for liberty, of which no man felt the want, and with care for liberty, which was not in danger." [24] About the same time Joseph Warton expressed a similar judgement in his commentary on Pope's two *Dialogues* of 1738:

> The satire in these pieces is of the strongest kind; sometimes, direct and declamatory, at others, ironical and oblique. It must be owned to be carried to excess. Our country is represented as totally ruined, and overwhelmed with dissipation, depravity, and corruption. Yet this very country, so emasculated and debased by every species of folly and wickedness, in about twenty years afterwards, carried its triumphs over all its enemies, through all the quarters of the world, and astonished the most distant nations with a display of uncommon efforts, abilities, and virtues. So vain and groundless are the prognostications of poets, as well as politicians.[25]

It was the fate of all the literature of the Opposition to Walpole to appear excessive as it receded into the past. All the Cassandra prophecies of doom, the bitter diatribes of the satirists, the patriotic appeals of the poets, even the jeremiads of Pitt himself, faded into historical documents. Henceforth, to recapture their original appeal, and even to understand what they contributed to the regenerative forces aroused by Pitt, has required the exercise of the historical imagination.

On the whole, these historical considerations seem favourable to the satirists and a justification of their indignation. Literal accuracy is not, of course, to be expected in satire, which, like caricature, presents a truth by means of a distortion. In satire, as in any art which aims to imitate nature under ideal conditions, the general ideas and qualities of mind of the artist command our real attention and determine our response. The mass of contemporaneous references in the work of the Tory satirists, with the subsidiary question of their faithfulness to fact, must not be allowed to obscure the permanent values enveloped in the tissue of particulars. The satire of this group, taken as a whole, reflects the general views of life held by all its members. They were not content with attacking moral and political corruption merely on the superficial level of fashions or manners or passing social conditions. They would not "sodder and patch up the flaws and imperfections of nature." Basically, they were opposed to the sect, to be met with in all ages, which holds that the evil in the world is not in men, but between them. They probed for its origin in the recesses of human nature; they cut into the flesh. All their allusions to particular individuals provide so many case-histories of the baseness of man. Their work remains for all ages a painful discipline in self-examination and humiliation.

In this disillusionment, as in their politics, the satirists were old-fashioned. When they are viewed against the setting of the history of literature and thought of the whole eighteenth century, they appear as survivors of a dying era. Even as they were at work, they were challenged by what seemed a more modern spirit, a more sympathetic and comforting way of looking at human nature. The "softness of the heart," Steele intimated in his preface to *The Conscious Lovers* (1723), is a greater merit than the "hardness of the head." In the early years of the century this spirit flourished in Whig literary circles, very obvious in Steele, more subtly pervasive in Addison. As the century progressed it gradually prevailed everywhere; in spite of the declared opposition of Fielding and Johnson and Burke, the "new sensibility" dominated in poetry, drama, and fiction. The same change was going on in France and the rest of Europe. La Rochefoucauld was replaced by Vauvenargues; Rousseau attacked Molière and drenched Europe in sentiment. Towards the end of the century the doctrine of the essential goodness of man became the basic tenet of the French revolutionary philosophers, and of William Godwin, who believed that nature never made a dunce. In our own time it serves as the indispensable assumption of those schools of political thought which attribute the evils of our human condition exclusively to environment, absolve human nature from all fault, and, as a logical consequence, outlaw genetics as an "anti-social science." In the present day the Tory satirists appear as old-fashioned, and to young readers as novel, as the doctrine of original sin.

The new literature of sentiment in the eighteenth century had, of course, its merits, especially as an influence in the reformation of manners, and Addison's work was highly praised for this reason by both Gay and Pope.[26] But ever since the eighteenth century the custom has obtained of pointing the praise of these merits by adding some disparagement of Pope and Swift. Joseph Warton quoted with approval James Harris, nephew and disciple of Shaftesbury: "Whoever has been reading this unnatural Filth," Harris wrote, referring to the fourth book of *Gulliver's Travels,* "let him turn for a moment to a *Spectator* of Addison, and observe the Philanthropy of that Classical writer." [27] As no one writer is adequate to all the needs of literature or life, it may be equally appropriate to recommend the satirists as a complement and correction to the literature of philanthropy.

Mandeville, a tavern character whose malice sharpened his wit, was especially qualified to expose the weaknesses of what he disliked. He disliked the *Characteristics* of the third Earl of Shaftesbury, which presented a system of ethics not only contrary to his own, but, he maintained, contrary to the teachings of "the generality of moralists and philosophers" up to that time. Shaftesbury, he said,

> imagines that men without any trouble or violence upon themselves may be naturally virtuous. He seems to require and expect goodness in his species, as we do a sweet taste in grapes and China oranges, of which, if any of them are sour, we boldly pronounce that they are not come to that perfection their nature is capable of. . . . His notions I confess are generous and refined; they are a high compliment to human-kind, and capable by the help of a little enthusiasm of inspiring us with the most noble sentiments concerning the dignity of our exalted nature. What a pity it is that they are not true! [28]

Mandeville likewise turned his sarcasm on Steele:

> When the incomparable Sir Richard Steele, in the usual elegance of his easy style, dwells on the praises of his sublime species, and with all the embellishments of rhetoric sets forth the excellency of human nature, it is impossible not to be charmed with his happy turns of thought, and the politeness of his expresions. But tho' I have been often moved by the force of his eloquence, and ready to swallow the ingenious sophistry with pleasure, yet I could never be so serious, but reflecting on his artful encomiums I thought on the tricks made use of by the women that would teach children to be mannerly.[29]

These criticisms of Shaftesbury and Steele stem from Mandeville's materialistic system, but they have a value of their own as shrewd observations. Dr. Johnson, who of course abhorred any materialistic system, could say late in his life: "I read Mandeville forty, or, I believe, fifty years ago. He did not puzzle me; he opened my eyes into real life very much."

All readers have, like Mandeville, been charmed by the gentleness and easy indulgence which grace the *Tatler* and the *Spectator* even in their satiric moods. But complacency is an extremely vulnerable attitude. At the end of a paper recommending the art of dancing as "a great improvement, as well as embellishment to the theatre," Steele observes, with perhaps a touch of humour, that "delicacy in pleasure is the first step people of condition take in reformation from vice." [30] A jolly way of doing the best one can with people of condition, but on second thought a most incautious remark on the part of one who professed to abhor cynicism, and most undiscriminating coming from a moral reformer. Burke, in a famous passage, said that "vice itself lost half its evil, by losing all its grossness"; but he avoided saying that vice in this way lost its viciousness and changed into virtue. Addison charmed his friends, but he was apparently not a laughing man. He agreed with Hobbes that laughter "is nothing else but sudden Glory arising from some sudden Conception of some Eminency in our selves, by Comparison with the Infirmity of others, or with our own formerly"; that is, laughter arises from the passion of derision and is reprehensible.[31] It is therefore not surprising that Addison "always preferred Chearfulness to Mirth."

> The latter I consider as an act, the former as a Habit of the Mind. Mirth is short and transient, Chearfulness fix'd and permanent. Those are often raised into the greatest Transports of Mirth, who are subject to the greatest Depressions of Melancholy: On the contrary, Chearfulness, tho' it does not give the Mind such an exquisite Gladness, prevents us from falling into any depths of Sorrow.[32]

In unperturbable serenity Addison concluded that "there are but two things which, in my Opinion, can reasonably deprive us of this Chearfulness of Heart," namely, Guilt and Atheism. Admitting that Addison does himself some injustice in this paper, granting that a perverse generation, perhaps of Tory fox-hunters, might really drive him at times to what Mark Twain called a state of mind bordering on impatience, the reader cannot but remark how perfectly this celebration of cheerfulness betrays Addison's limitations, his complacency, his lack of penetration. This is, indeed, the "serene, peaceful state, of being a fool among knaves." There is an abysmal division between men of this cast of mind and the satirists. When Thomas Tickell, Addison's friend and biographer, had newly arrived in Dublin as under-secretary and had established himself on a friendly footing with Swift, he ventured to inquire regarding the manuscript of an "imaginary treatise" of which he had heard. But Swift declined to favour him, saying that *Gulliver's Travels* would not please Tickell, "chiefly because they wholly disagree with your notions of persons and things." [33]

Through all the ages there has been this opposition of the tough-minded and the tender-minded—William James's classification of philosophies and philosophers. In the eighteenth century it was the tender-minded who were gaining in popularity and were controlling the new literary modes. They were the party of the moderns, and until recently they have prescribed the tone of most of the criticism of the satirists. But the tough-minded also, in their way, have a claim to the title of friend of man. They warn against the illusions which not only end in bitterness but corrupt the heart in the process. They provide a discipline in looking steadily at the stark truth. In September 1725, shortly before Swift penned the famous letter to Pope about the philosophy of *Gulliver's Travels*, he was busy assisting and advising the mercurial Thomas Sheridan, who was in trouble over a politically imprudent sermon and had been removed from the Viceroy's list of chaplains. Swift interceded with Tickell, to whom he explained that Sheridan, "as he is a creature without cunning, so he hath not overmuch advertency." To the naïve Sheridan himself he gave this advice: "You should think and deal with every man as a villain, without calling him so, or flying from him, or valuing him less. This is an old true lesson." [34] There appears the paradox of Swift's misanthropy, and perhaps it is the paradox also of Pope's portrait of Atticus, where, to use the words of Wotton, "grief is forced to laugh against her will." For all his perspicacity into the nature of "that animal called man," Swift heartily loved individuals, and did not value them less because he had to speak to them with candour.

The tough-minded have always produced realistic literature, sometimes certainly very unpleasant.

The Tory satirists shared the temper and ideals of the great French classical writers of the age of Louis XIV, who also aimed to anatomize man with complete honesty, to portray man in his true colours and lineaments. "Rien n'est beau que le vrai," said Boileau, their literary dictator. This very general dictum meant, among other things, that all extravagance and sentimentality, all credulous softening of the harsh truth, were to be shunned as offensive weakness. This is what the French call *le naturalisme classique*. The same spirit pervades the work of the Tory satirists—the pastorals, fables, and ballad operas of Gay, the poems, histories, and polemics of Swift, the political satires of Arbuthnot, the ethic and satiric poems of Pope. The gloom of these men is not an indulgence in lyrical melancholia, but the astringent and penetrating observation of the realist. That is why the tough-minded literature they left behind has recommended itself to generations of English-speaking readers. The popular appropriation of the figure of John Bull as representative of the English character is a tribute, not only to the genius of Arbuthnot, but in a larger way also to the spirit of the *naturalisme classique* of the whole group. If the Tory satirists are rightly called pessimists, their pessimism is of a variety both tonic and exhilarating.

NOTES

1. The need for correction in Swift's case is thoroughly shown by Louis A. Landa in an article on "Jonathan Swift and Charity," in the *Journal of English and Germanic Philology*, xliv (1945), 337–50.
2. *Alexander Pope* (1908), p. 100.
3. Swift to Pope, 1 Nov. 1734.
4. *A Tale of a Tub*, section lx.
5. Swift to Pope, 26 Nov. 1725.
6. Bolingbroke to Swift, 14 Dec. 1725.
7. *The Mind and Art of Jonathan Swift* (1936), pp. 159–62 and 301–2.
8. Swift to Pope, 29 Sept. 1725.
9. *Letters of Swift to Ford* (1935), Introduction, pp. xxxi ff.
10. Swift to Arbuthnot, 25 July 1714.
11. Swift to Archdeacon Walls, 11 June 1714.
12. Swift, *Prose Works*, ed. Temple Scott, v, 405.
13. Ibid., 396.
14. Arbuthnot to Swift, 12 Aug. 1714.
15. Swift to Oxford, 3 July 1714. Swift was equally frank to Bolingbroke in his letter of 7 Aug.
16. *Lives of the Poets*, ed. Birkbeck Hill, iii, 61.
17. Ibid., 62, note 1.
18. Swift to Gay, 20 Nov. 1729.
19. *Dunciad*, iv, 517–28.
20. Quoted by Birkbeck Hill in Johnson's *Lives of the Poets*, iii, 179, note 6.
21. *London*, 51–6.
22. *Estimate* (1757), p. 115.
23. Lecky, *History of England in the Eighteenth Century* (1892), ii, 91.
24. *Lives of the Poets*, ed. Hill, iii, 289.
25. *Essay on Pope* (1782), ii, 357. Warton adds a note: "We cannot ascribe these successes, as M. de Voltaire does, to the effects of *Brown's Estimate*."
26. Gay, *The Present State of Wit* (1711), quoted in Lewis Melville, *Life and Letters of John Gay* (1921), pp. 11–14; Pope, *Epistle to Augustus*, 215–20.
27. Warton, *Essay on Pope* (1782), ii, 344–5.
28. *Fable of the Bees*, ed. F. B. Kaye (1924), i, 323.
29. Ibid. i, 52–3.
30. *Spectator*, 370.
31. Ibid., 47.
32. Ibid., 381.
33. Swift to Tickell, 7 July 1726.
34. Swift to Sheridan, 11 Sept. 1725.

John M. Bullitt

SATIRIC DETACHMENT IN JONATHAN SWIFT: INVECTIVE, DIMINUTION, IRONY

INVECTIVE

The author-reader relationship is nowhere a more delicate and sensitive affair than in satire. For the success of satire depends very much upon the author's ability to involve his readers on his side of a moral issue—to make them share his condemnation. In order to achieve and then maintain this subtle relationship, the satirist must allow himself neither to relax into an uncritical and laughing amusement nor to lose his temper. There is abundant evidence to show that Swift could delight in comedy for its own sake, as, for example, in his punning mock Latin poem, "A Love Song":

Apud in is almi des ire,
Mimis tres I ne ve re qui re.
Alo veri findit a gestis,
His miseri ne ver at restis.[1]

But Swift's general tendency of mind was to vent his deep, bitter, and disillusioned anger against the proud fraud of human effort. Perhaps the ultimate difference between the satire of Swift and that of most of his contemporaries—both in England and France—is that Swift really cared. However, revealed intensity of feeling, as Swift recognized early in his writing career, is incompatible with the comic spirit; and both consciously and perhaps unconsciously—with a self-protective need—he developed a variety of techniques which dissociated himself, and consequently his feelings, from any direct vis-à-vis relationship with his object. In satire, as much as and perhaps more than in any other literary genre, an apparent *detachment* from too intense a personal involvement is the necessary precondition to greatness.

It is useful to remember that Dryden in his *Discourse Concerning the Original and Progress of Satire* accepts the "general signification of the word," satire, to be an "invective," or a "reflection, as we use that word in the worst sense; or, as the French call it, more properly, *médisance*." Whether good or bad, general or particular, true or false, savage or humorous, prosaic or poetic—any literary attack upon the vice or folly of men and manners may be contained under the general word satire. This general definition implies, of course, no evaluation of the different kinds of satire. Dryden supplies this qualitative distinction when he insists that "the best and finest manner of satire" appears in "laughing a fool out of countenance." The laughter of good satire arises from that "fine raillery" which attacks its object from the flank with wit and technical skill, rather than crudely and brutally from the front. Dryden summarizes this distinction in saying:

> . . . there is still a vast difference betwixt the slovenly butchering of a man, and the fineness of a stroke that separates the head from the body, and leaves it standing in its place. A man may be capable, as Jack Ketch's wife said of his servant, of a plain piece of work, a bare hanging; but to make a malefactor die sweetly, was only belonging to her husband.[2]

Here Dryden suggests an important and fundamental distinction between the direct criticism of invective and the fine stroke of ridicule. If all satire is criticism, then invective, at its lowest level of "butchery," is merely that criticism in which the author vilifies an object directly and openly without recourse to wit and with no attempt to arouse the comic spirit. It is a frontal attack, and its abuse is not mingled with sufficient wit or technical ingenuity to evoke any response lighter than the "vehement emotions" of anger and rage. The substance of this kind of satire is outright denunciation. It not only proceeds from the conviction that the object is evil, hateful, and probably dangerous, but it also expresses this belief overtly in vilification and vituperation. Its tendency, therefore, is towards the expression of an emotional extreme: it tends to magnify and exaggerate the viciousness of the object and it finds its vocabulary in the lexicon of hyperbole and billingsgate.

When Saint Paul castigated the Gentiles, he expressed himself in the direct abuse of invective, damning a whole people as sinners

> . . . filled with all unrighteousness, fornication, wickedness, covetousness, maliciousness; full of envy, murder, debate, deceit, malignity; whisperers, backbiters, haters of God, despiteful, proud, boasters, inventors of evil things, disobedient to parents, without understanding, covenantbreakers, without natural affection, implacable, unmerciful:[3]

This powerful catalogue of vices exemplifies (if considered as satire) the limitations of invective when a writer directly communicates his anger through a series of exact verbal equivalents of the object attacked. Indeed, the passage is a "plain piece of work, a bare hanging." The technique itself is a kind of *amplification,* that traditional figure of rhetoric which, as Thomas Wilson defined it, "consisteth in heaping and enlarging of those places, which serve for confirmation of a matter."[4] As invective, this passage expresses Paul's rage with painful clarity; as ridicule, however, which is not content with self-expression but aims to *persuade and direct the reader's own responses against the criticized object,* the passage is less successful. The relation between the author and the object of attack is, in this case, so intense and monocular, and expressed with so much direct anger, that the reader tends to *withdraw* his sympathy from Paul and to conclude, perhaps, that the abuse is a feverish exaggeration. "Anger does not beget anger," David Worcester has observed; when we see a man in a furious passion, instead of feeling *with* him we are likely to protect ourselves from sharing his painful emotion by laughing *at* him—even to the point of ridiculing him as a "lobster-faced baboon in a fit."[5]

An antipodal contrast to this passage may be found in Rabelais: "The cake-bakers . . . did injure them most outrageously," Rabelais tells us,

> . . . calling them prating gablers, lickorous gluttons, freckled bittors, mangy rascals, shite-a-bed scoundrels, drunken roysters, sly knaves, drowsy loiterers, slap-sauce fellows, slabberdegullion druggels, lubbardly louts, cousening foxes, ruffian rogues, paltry customers, sycophant varlets . . . (Book I, Chap. 25)

and so on for half a page. This abusive catalogue is also an invective, but its effect upon the reader is to stimulate neither anger nor withdrawal, but laughter. The reason seems to be that the technique of exaggeration is here contrived to be amusing in itself. Moreover, not only is the author himself *detached* from any real anger, but the anger of the cake-bakers, too, is without real virulence. It is not the emotion of Rabelais or the bakers which affects the reader; it is the remarkable variety and exaggerated exuberance with which it is expressed. As in the passage I have just cited from the Bible, this Rabelaisian invective diverts the reader's attention from the object attacked, but in this case to the technique of its expression. Similarly, too, this direct abuse is unsuccessful satire, although for somewhat different reasons. Not only is the satiric object here obscure (do we contemn the cake-bakers' vulgar invective or sympathize with the cake-bakers' contempt for Gargantua's party?); but, unlike that in the Bible, the seeming content of criticism is not *criticism* at all. At least the reader recognizes that most of the bakers' anger is harmlessly expended in verbosity; where there is such a plethora of metaphor, and where the words have so slight an accuracy of denotation, the content of criticism is overshadowed by the humour of wordplay. In short, whereas Paul's invective nullifies itself in its excessive contempt, that of the cake-bakers spends itself in a humour almost devoid of criticism.

Of the Rabelaisian kind of direct invective, which sports playfully with words, there seems to be remarkably little in Swift's prose satire. Occasionally, however, Swift's strongly developed sense of play found release in subordinating satiric criticism to his delight in sheer verbal ingenuity. In *A Tale of a Tub,* for instance, he describes Peter's Bulls in terms which are reminiscent of the extravagant gusto of the cake-bakers: ". . . they would *Roar,* and *Spit,* and *Belch,* and *Piss,* and *Fart,* and *Snivel* out *Fire,* and keep a perpetual *Coyl,* till you flung them a Bit of *Gold*" (p. 112). Although the description has considerable satiric direction, the piling up of these Anglo-Saxon and vulgar monosyllables gives an exuberance and gaiety to the satire which takes the edge off Swift's latent savage intensity. Perhaps an even better example of the comic technique taking precedence over the satiric content may be seen in the catalogue of medical remedies which a Laputan projector offered as cures for politicians:

> This doctor therefore proposed . . before the members sat, [to] administer to each of them lenitives, aperitives, abstersives, corrosives, restringents, palliatives, laxatives, cephalalgics, icterics, apophlegmatics, acoustics, as their several cases required; and according as these medicines should operate, repeat, alter, or omit them at the next meeting.[6]

Unlike the Rabelaisian abuse of the cake-bakers, there is no doubt here about Swift's satiric intention both to ridicule politicians and the jargon of the physician's trade. But seen in its effect upon the reader, this catalogue of medical terms stimulates through its very exaggeration our laughter as much as our contempt. A similar Rabelaisian sporting with words informs Swift's satiric thrust at contemporary poets: "... for although we have not one masterly poet, yet we abound with wardens and beadles, having a multitude of poetasters, poetitoes, parcel-poets, poet-apes and philo-poets, ..."[7] These passage share with much of the humour of Rabelais a preponderance of the sense of comedy over the sense of direct satire.

If Swift rarely relaxed into Rabelais' easy chair, he almost never donned the hair shirt of an angry Saint Paul—not because he felt less intensely but because he organized his anger into an artful rhetoric. When Swift employs invective, he generally includes some sly indirection of technique which relieves and interrupts the pattern of his contempt. In such cases, the readers' emotions are, for a moment, intellectualized, and this temporary relief allies us with Swift and makes possible a coalescence of contempt and laughter. Even in the final voyage of *Gulliver's Travels,* which is as savage an indictment of humanity as has ever been written, Gulliver's most violent diatribe against his own society is not without an element of technical indirection:

> I wanted no fence against fraud or oppression; here was neither physician to destroy my body, nor lawyer to ruin my fortune; no informer to watch my words and actions, or forge accusations against me for hire: here were no gibers, censurers, backbiters, pickpockets, highwaymen, housebreakers, attorneys, bawds, buffoons, gamesters, politicians, wits, splenetics, tedious talkers, controvertists, ravishers, murderers, robbers, virtuosos; no leaders or followers of party and faction; no encouragers to vice, by seducement or examples; no dungeon, axes, gibbets, whipping-posts, or pillories; no cheating shopkeepers or mechanics; no pride, vanity, or affectation; no fops, bullies, drunkards, strolling whores, or poxes; no ranting, lewd, expensive wives; no stupid, proud pedants; no importunate, overbearing, quarrelsome, noisy, roaring, empty, conceited, swearing companions; no scoundrels, raised from the dust for the sake of their vices, or nobility thrown into it on account of their virtues; no *lords, fiddlers, judges, or dancing-masters.*[8]

Even if we make Gulliver a surrogate for Swift (an identification not entirely plausible), we see at once that he is able, in spite of the intensity of his feelings, to conclude his invective with a witticism which immediately detaches him from mere violence: "No lords, fiddlers, judges, or dancing-masters." What makes invective poor as satire is the excess of expressed feelings; what rescues this passage from the overheated venom of mere abuse is the "economy," to use Freud's word, of its final witty juxtaposition. Gulliver had his eye not only on his hated England, but also on the technical virtuosity with which he could express his contempt. The reader is able to sympathize with Gulliver and to join with him in his equation of lords and judges with fiddlers and dancing-masters.

DIMINUTION

The witty juxtaposition and, by inference, equation of dignified with admittedly undignified professions reflect a tendency fundamental to all satire: professions and actions to which custom has allowed authority and importance are, in Kenneth Burke's phrase, "converted downwards."[9] The mixed catalogue is a convenient device by which to show this tendency at work. Swift's *A Serious and Useful Scheme to Make an Hospital for Incurables* contains nearly fifteen pages of listed "incurables." Although we are never unaware of Swift's misanthropic intention to damn mankind in general, we are also continually surprised out of anger by the wit of the juxtapositions. For example, when Swift lists those incurables who "lie for their interest," he includes in one list "fishmongers, flatterers, pimps, lawyers, fortune-hunters, and fortune-tellers." Similarly, Swift herds together such incurables as "attorneys, solicitors, pettifoggers, scriveners, usurers, hackney-clerks, pickpockets, pawn-brokers, jailors, and justices of the peace," as well as "hounds, horses, whores, sharpers, surgeons, tailors, pimps, masquerades, or architects." [10] This device is an important one among the almost infinite variety of techniques used in *A Tale of a Tub* to degrade professions in general: Swift mixes "Eves-droppers, Physicians, Mid-wives, small Politicians, Friends fallen out, Repeating Poets, Lovers Happy or in Despair, Bawds, Privy-Counsellours, Pages, Parasites and Buffoons"; he joins in a single list "*Parliament-, Coffee-, Play-, Bawdy-houses*"; and "*Beaux, Fiddlers, Poets,* and *Politicians*" [11] are huddled together in an uneasy equality. In all these catalogues the element of witty surprise is strong enough to startle the mind from the sense of total contempt and, although the critical content is manifestly present, it coalesces with the reader's recognition of the technique itself.

Now, in any angry invective against specific abuses or general actions, we may sense fear as well as scorn. If the object attacked is great enough or dangerous enough to be feared, it may often acquire a compelling attractiveness, possibly even a certain magnificence. The most prominent example is that of Satan in *Paradise Lost*. The very scope and dimension of the evil he represents could, in the eighteenth century, be felt as "sublime." Blake was not alone in feeling that perhaps Milton himself was of Satan's party. One may, indeed, "first endure, then pity, then embrace" a monster as fearful as Satan; both his evil and his punishment exist on so cosmic a level as to arouse our respect. The effectiveness of the satirist, however, must be measured by the extent to which he is able to arouse contempt unmixed with any such incipient admiration. Joseph Conrad's sense of the dimly perceived evil lying behind the appearances of life led him in at least one story, *The Heart of Darkness,* to distinguish sharply between the cosmic evil of an ultimate horror and what he called the "flabby devil" of man's ordinary vice. Between the grandeur of Milton's Satan and the mere vulgarity of Conrad's "flabby devil" has fallen the shadow of satiric diminution. If Satan inspires us with a secret pity and terror, Conrad's "papier-mâché Mephistopheles" is not worth the powder to blow him up.

This technique of rendering devils flabby is a common literary device which was discussed in rhetorical handbooks under the Greek title, *meiosis,* meaning, literally, "belittling" or "diminution." [12] Diminution may be described briefly as the use of any "ugly or homely images" which are intended to diminish the dignity of an object. In a sense, of course, nearly all satire might be included within this broad definition. But a more specific meaning is suggested when we recall Puttenham's description of it as the "disabler," a figure useful to express "derision and for a kind of contempt." Specifically, then, diminution is any kind of speech which tends, either by the force of low or vulgar imagery, or by other suggestion, to depress an object below its usually accepted status. Diminution may be accomplished in a variety of ways. A similarity may be drawn between an object and one which is universally acknowledged to be inferior; the comparison results, of course, in the primary object absorbing the contemptibility of the secondary object. Diminution may also be effected by dwelling upon certain physical characteristics of a person and then, by synechdoche, equating the whole object with that one part. Diminution may be expressed in innumerable other forms; it may appear as direct abuse, irony, litotes, and so on. The following paragraphs touch primarily on some types of diminution which Swift used in direct satire.

One of Swift's most expert devices of direct diminution was the attribution of *failure and impotence* to an opponent. In Puttenham's sense, this was to "disable" an opponent by showing him to be not dangerous but merely offensive and disgusting. This kind of attack appeals to no logic of argument; it is aimed solely at degradation through contrasting an opponent's attempt to be powerful with his actual failure. Sometimes he joins the idea of failure with a comparison to an animal which may offend our senses, but is too weak to inspire our terror. A characteristic example of this kind of direct diminution is seen in Swift's attack upon Tindal's "The Rights of the Christian Church . . .":

> But still there is the same flatness of thought and style; the same weak advances toward wit and raillery. . . . And, lastly, the same rapid venom sprinkled over the whole; which, like the dying impotent bite of a trodden benumbed snake, may be nauseous and offensive, but cannot be very dangerous.[13]

The passage arouses no loud laughter, but the author's seeming detachment from anger and his skillful deflating of Tindal's pretensions create a sense of the ridiculous without the admixture of stronger emotions. Similar diminution through the use of debasing imagery, joined with the content of impotence and failure, is developed indirectly throughout *A Tale of a Tub*. A remarkable illustration of Swift's use of direct diminution in that work, is found in the passage:

> May their own Dullness, or that of their Party, be no Discouragement for the Authors to proceed; but let them remember, it is with *Wits* as with *Razors,* which are never so apt to *cut* those they are employ'd on, as when they have *lost their Edge*. Besides, those whose Teeth are too rotten to bite, are best of all others, qualified to revenge that Defect with their Breath (p. 49).

By debasing metaphors Swift shows his critics to be dangerous only in their dullness, and then shows this to be no real danger at all but, rather, something merely shameful and unpleasant. A sexual analogy may well underlie the basic humour of the device —the analogy involving sexual incapacity. And Swift often arouses an amused contempt by the indirect equation between a man's intellectual failures and his sexual life. Alexander Pope, whose own variety of satiric methods includes many in common with Swift, availed himself of the disgraceful connotations of sexual incapacity when, in the familiar Sporus passage, in the *Epistle to Dr. Arbuthnot*, he characterized Lord Hervey's rhetoric as "florid impotence" (l. 317). Impotence of any sort is a possible subject of ridicule, and Swift makes frequent use of it.

A more direct, less subtle method of diminution is attained through comparisons with lower animals. Swift was alert to any method of arousing contempt, and he often appealed to the associations with human vice traditionally acquired by many lower animals. A few examples here are sufficient to illustrate his use in direct abuse of what we may call "bestial diminution." In the passage quoted above, the satiric effect of Swift's disdain for Tindal's wit depends in part upon the graphic image of "the dying impotent bite of a trodden benumbed *snake*." Swift here gives a local habitation and a name to Tindal's weakness of thought. The abusive ideas which, in the abusive catalogue, remain simply as abstractions, are here attached to a concrete image. Death, impotence, and insensitivity lose their abstract generality when thus associated with a creature to which the mind brings already existing attitudes of disgust. Accordingly, this bestial comparison gives a compression to Swift's contempt which is absent in more general abuse. This compression is similarly attained in Swift's direct satire (which follows a series of indirect and ironical attacks) upon the "True Criticks" in *A Tale of a Tub*:

> The *True Criticks* are known by their Talent of swarming about the noblest Writers, to which they are carried meerly by Instinct, as a Rat to the best Cheese, or a Wasp to the fairest Fruit. . . . A *True Critick*, in the Perusal of a Book, is like a *Dog* at a Feast, whose Thoughts and Stomach are wholly set upon what the Guests *fling away*, and consequently is apt to *Snarl* most, when there are the fewest Bones (pp. 103–104).

Not only do the series of comparisons degrade the critic, they also serve to place his ignominy in sharp contrast with the nobility of the works criticized. It is evident that this device may be among the easiest possible in satire; even the abusive catalogue, when it is performed through amplification, requires some breadth of vocabulary. But all that is necessary to simple bestial diminution is the recognition that certain animals have absorbed different human and unpleasant associations. Swift's use of this device, however, is rarely overworked and when it appears it comes as a shock. Moreover, Swift often complicates the device by setting up a contrast between animals which have pleasant, and those which have unpleasant, associations. In a sense, this use of bestial comparisons becomes almost allegorical with each animal standing for a specific quality. An example of an extremely effective and surprising contrast is found in Drapier's question: "It is no loss of honour to submit to the lion, but who, with the figure of a man, can think with patience of being devoured alive by a rat?" [14] Much of this effect results, also, from opposing the passive idea of "submission" to the lion and the activity of "being devoured alive" by the rat.

Invective, when coupled with an un-Rabelaisian sincerity, may declare outrage, but as a method of satire, of making men uncomfortable in their vices, it fails in almost direct proportion to the honesty of its expression. It fails to communicate that artistic *control* which is so essential to literary craftsmanship, because, without it, the outraged moralist will fail to arouse belief. Diminution, on the other hand, is the very heart of satire. It can, of course, be so direct and vituperative that, in the process of reducing an object to what is disgusting and loathsome, it loses the control and guidance of its literary purpose. But when diminution is effected by a skillful and organized artistic effort, when wit is employed to relieve the naked intensity of indignation, satire approaches its neoclassic aims. Swift recognized, however, that diminution, no matter how witty, could never be completely transmitted by direct attack. And it was partly to preserve his own personal detachment and partly to increase the distance between himself, as moralist, and his audience, that Swift developed the techniques of irony with an unrivaled brilliance.

IRONY

Irony has accumulated so many meanings in its long history that the word justifies Otto Ribbeck's description of it as *proteusartig*. How many shapes it has assumed is suggested when we recall the distinctions, to name only a few, that have been drawn among Socratic irony, dramatic irony, Romantic irony, irony of understatement; irony has been studied as a rhetorical device and has been extended to include a whole mode of behaviour. It is certain, however, that the first great ironist was Socrates, although, as G. G. Sedgewick reminds us in *Of Irony, Especially in Drama*, the term "eiron" was first applied to Socrates as a term of abuse—meaning something like "sly-foxery," tinged, perhaps, with connotations of "low-bred." The most influential definition of the word appeared in Aristotle's *Nichomachean Ethics* where for the first time irony was associated with "understatement." Aristotle, in describing the honesty of "truthful man" places it as a mean between *alazoneia*, the boastful man's tendency to exaggerate, and *eironeia*, the "mock-modest" man's tendency to understate the truth. Using Socrates as his example, Aristotle somewhat uneasily praises the ironist as being "more attractive" than the braggart because understaters "speak not for gain but to avoid parade." As Sedgewick emphasizes, however, Aristotle's idea of the Socratic *eironeia* meant more than a mere rhetorical device of understatement: "In the *Ethics*, *eironeia* is a pervasive mode of behaviour, a constant pretence of self-depression—of which understatement is only one manifestation."[15] The very essence of the word, whether considered as a rhetorical trope (along with synechdoche, metonomy, and hyperbole) or as a whole way of life, is dissimulation: the ironist appears to say or to be one thing while making it apparent to his audience that he means or is something quite different.

It was as a technique of satiric utterance that Swift seems to have viewed irony which, he said in his *Verses on the Death of Dr. Swift*, "I was born to introduce, / Refin'd it first, and shew'd its Use" (ll. 57–58). The "use" of irony lies preeminently in its capacity to create the appearance of the satirist's emotional detachment. When Aristotle discusses irony in his *Rhetoric*, he notes that the "ironical man jokes to amuse himself," (1419b) and it is in this spirit that Swift writes in defense of his own ironic *"laughing with a few friends in a corner."*[16] As we have seen, the limitations of invective lie in its display of an excess of concern —the reader may distrust violence in a moralist and the person attacked may congratulate himself on his own importance. On the other hand, ironic laughter from the corner is, perhaps, the most effective form of diminution at the satirist's disposal. By disdaining to exert himself directly against an opponent, the ironist preserves a status of superiority to what he attacks and invites the reader to join him (and his coterie of select and privileged souls) on the mountaintop of truth.

PRAISE-BLAME INVERSION

The first use of the word "irony" in English appeared in 1502 when, as the *New English Dictionary* tells us, Wynken de Worde spoke of "yronye of grammar, by the whyche a man sayth one and gyveth to understande the contrarye." In *The Arte of English Poesie* (1589), Puttenham called irony a "dry-mocke," and, by the end of the eighteenth century, it was taken for granted that irony fused both dissimulation and mockery. Accordingly, Bailey's *Dictionary* (6th ed., 1733) defined the word as "a Figure in *Rhetorick*, by which we speak contrary to what we think, by Way of Derision or Mockery to him we argue or talk with." Now, the satirist is concerned with both evaluating the world and communicating these judgments to his readers. The simplest form of satiric irony, by which the satirist can "speak contrary to what he thinks," is through the *inversion* of these judgments: the satirist pretends *to praise what he means to condemn* or he pretends *to condemn what he means to praise.* It is of this inversion that Quintilian speaks when he says *laudis adsimulatione detrahere et vituperationis laudare.*

In *A Tale of a Tub* Swift first displayed his remarkable talent as a mock eulogist. Indeed, the whole tale is ironically organized as a panegyric upon the moderns, written by a modern and for the moderns. The reader is introduced to the panegyrical intention of the essay at the very outset when he reads the list of titles, written by the same "author," which will be "speedily published." These include the extremes of both a *Panegyrick upon the World* and a *Panegyrical Essay upon the Number Three.* In a masterful account of the reasons why the former treatise had not yet appeared in print, Swift in the "Preface" gives a further twist of diminution to his inverted praise: ". . . I am so entirely satisfied with the whole present Procedure of human Things, that I have been for some Years preparing Materials towards *A Panegyrick upon the World;* to which I intend to add a Second Part, entituled, *A Modest Defence of the Proceedings of the Rabble in all Ages.* Both these I had Thought to publish by way of Appendix to the following Treatise; but finding my Common-Place-Book fill much slower than I had reason to suspect, I have chosen to defer them to another occasion" (pp. 53–54).[17] This encomiastic intention, however, is not thwarted in other matters and he pursues his joyful praise of the moderns throughout the remainder of the tale.

Swift's ironic tendency to exaggerate praise into a paean of indirect damnation can be illustrated in almost every satire he ever wrote. How easily and naturally he adopted the indirection of ironic eulogy may be seen in his marginalia, written in longhand on his own copy of Dr. Gibbs's translation of fifteen psalms of David; the comments were evidently intended not for publication but simply for Swift's own private amusement. In the midst of other remarks which specifically ridicule or parody Gibbs's logic, diction, rhymes and so on, Swift includes encomiums upon the poetry: "Admirably reasoned and connected!" he exclaims over one stanza which says that if God is angered by his foes then those are happy who have confidence in Him; to Gibbs's line that men should "with *fear* / His joyful praise proclaim," Swift gives his bland approval: "Very proper to make a joyful proclamation with fear"; Swift lauds another foolish idea with the praises: "A good principle!"; and to the lines,

> O Lord, how glorious are the ways
> Of Thy good Providence!
> Thou, Lord, Whose blessed Name I praise,
> True justice dost dispense,

Swift notes in the margin: "Do not these verses end very sublimely?"[18] The irony of this praise is at once apparent. Not only are the comments imbedded among other remarks more directly contemptuous and slighting, but the praise sends our eye to the text of Gibbs's version, and Swift is confident that the text will damn itself. The device, then, provides one more kind of detachment in which the values of an object are presented in such a way that they seem to ridicule themselves, and Swift can eliminate the personal element of his own critical intervention.

A device so simple and obvious might be expected to dull itself with repetition, but Swift avails himself of a variety of other techniques with which to diversify the basic pattern of inverted eulogy. Two passages drawn from *A Letter to the Bishop of St. Asaph* will serve as example. The Bishop, William Fleetwood, who was a favourite of Queen Anne, was also a Whig in politics and an advocate of Low Church principles in religion. He published four of his sermons with a preface attacking Harley's Tory administration, and the Whigs of the Kit-Cat Club inserted the preface as a party pamphlet in the *Spectator.* In his *Letter* answering the preface, Swift characteristically denies any need for praising Fleetwood: "Nor need I run riot in encomium and panegyric," he says to the Bishop, "since you can perform that part so much better for yourself." Nevertheless, the *Letter* is a riot of praise for the Bishop, his ideas, and even his prose style:

> Here, your lordship rises, if possible above yourself: Never was such strength of thought,

> such beauty of expression, so happily joined together. Heavens! Such force, such energy in each pregnant word! Such fire, such fervour, in each glowing line! One would think your lordship was animated with the same spirit with which our hero fought. Who can read, unmoved, these following strokes of oratory? "Such was the fame, such was the reputation . . ." &c. O! the irresistible charm of the word "such!" Well, since Erasmus wrote a treaty in praise of Folly, and my Lord Rochester an excellent poem upon Nothing, I am resolved to employ the "Spectator," or some of his fraternity, (dealers in words) to write an encomium upon Such.[19]

This is "gay contempt" at its very best. The contrast and incongruity between the exaggerated praise and the foolishly diminutive word "such" tends to reduce the word below even its usual status. From something innocuous, the word has been "converted downward" to something contemptible through mere excess and exaggeration. Moreover, the whole passage is a parody of the very fault it satirizes; Swift's own use of "such" as a means to exaggerate praise turns the passage into dramatic irony: the reader (audience) is detached from the satirist's position and perceives for himself that the appearance of vigor created by the word "such" is in fact the merest verbiage. The level of ironic detachment created by this dramatic representation of the folly which Swift is attacking is paralleled by another level of conscious ambiguity. The praise of Fleetwood's rising "if possible above yourself" contains not only a logical impossibility in the physical world, but all the suppressed connotations which Swift brought to the idea of soaring above matter and good sense. In addition, there is an immediate ambiguity in Swift's identifying the happy junction of Fleetwood's thought and expression; the parody of the latter reflects by association upon the former. And the word "unmoved" is charged with the *double-entendre* of our being "moved" either to praise or to laughter by those "strokes of oratory."

Swift's cleverness in mingling ambiguity with exaggerated praise may be even more clearly illustrated in another passage from this vigorous and comic satire. Instead of focusing upon details of diction or rhetorical devices (Swift had also praised the "expressive dash," or aposiopesis, through which this "consumate orator" showed that his "very silence is thus eloquent"), Swift praises the essay as a whole:

> I cannot but observe with infinite delight, that the reasons your lordship gives for reprinting those immortal pieces, are urged with that strength and force, which is peculiar to your lordship's writings, and is such, as all who have any regard for truth, or relish for good writing, must admire, though none can sufficiently commend. In a word, the preface is equal to the sermons, less than that ought not, and more can not, be said of it.[20]

Swift creates the impression of praise with very few words which state approbation. The only standard of reference he supplies is the rest of Fleetwood's writings; the preface is said to reflect that "peculiar" strength and force which mark all his works, and the concluding sentence with its distinction between "can not" and "ought not" is loaded with the possibility of two meanings. And even the commendatory words are chosen with care for their suggestive implications; whether Swift takes "infinite delight" (he cannot be "unmoved") in the excellence of these writings or in their *absurdity* is equally possible, and whether Swift's "admiration" is directed towards Fleetwood's truth and good style or towards his departure from them is likewise left to the reader to determine. The ambiguity of "admire" is even more sharply seen when we recall the pejorative connotations of the word in the early eighteenth century. The pieces could be equally "immortal" as monuments of stupidity as of wisdom, and the phrase "none can sufficiently commend" might well mean that no commendation is possible where there is no excellence.

The converse of this ironical technique is, of course, *to condemn what we mean to praise*. A characteristic example is to be found in Swift's defense of Carteret, who was among the very few men sent from England to govern Ireland for whom Swift had any respect. Carteret became the Lord Lieutenant of Ireland, and it was to him that Swift made the famous remark: "What, in God's name, do you do here? Get back to your own country, and send us our boobies again." Even in praise Swift was oblique and the remark recalls his practice in his letters of couching his highest compliments in terms of abuse. When a number of Whigs led by one Richard Tighe attempted to discredit Carteret on the grounds that he had favoured

Tories, Swift jumped to the defense and wrote *A Vindication of his Excellency the Lord C—t.* Swift introduces his essay with an elaborate presentation of Carteret's "faults." Well educated at Oxford, Carteret "could never wipe off the stain, nor wash out the tincture of his University acquirements and dispositions," Swift laments. He then proceeds to particularize upon these grievous faults:

> To this another misfortune was added; that it pleased God to endow him with great natural talents, memory, judgment, comprehension, eloquence, and wit. And, to finish the work, all these were fortified even in his youth, with the advantages received by such employments as are best fitted both to exercise and polish the gifts of nature and education. . . . I cannot omit another weak side in his Excellency, for it is known, and can be proved upon him, that Greek and Latin books might be found every day in his dressing-room, if it were carefully searched. . . . I have it from good hands, that when his Excellency is at dinner with one or two scholars at his elbows, he grows a most unsupportable, and unintelligible companion to all the fine gentlemen around the table.[21]

Thus Swift "freely acknowledges" the "failings" of Carteret and succeeds in constructing by indirection a positive portrait of the idealized educated gentleman and man of affairs.

This dissimulation of moral attitude is the method underlying most of Swift's irony and it is readily seen to be a technique of the practiced orator. That is, the speaker addresses his audience directly but varies his discourse by appearing to say one thing when in reality he is communicating the contrary. Shakespeare provides us with a classic expression of the effectiveness of this venerable technique in Antony's praise of Brutus as "an honourable man." But Swift, although profoundly influenced, as I will emphasize later, by the classical tradition of rhetoric, extended his irony far beyond the potentialities of spoken oratory. His irony achieves its most compelling power when "dissimulation" ceases to be the technique of an advocate and becomes instead subordinated to a more complex artistic intention. That is, at its best, Swift's irony becomes *dramatic;* the disparity between appearance and reality no longer exists as a device of the speaker but is itself embodied in an objective situation. Swift's tendency away from invective and towards a more fully developed artistic detachment completes itself in dramatic characterization.

IRONIC MASKS

In the above examples of simulated panegyric, Swift's own voice is heard directly only in his marginalia on Dr. Gibbs's paraphrase of the psalms. But in the other essays, he has developed a *fictitious author* who acts as a vehicle for the irony. The full title, for example, of the eulogy on Fleetwood reads: *A Letter of Thanks from my Lord W . . . n to the Lord Bp. of S. Asaph in the Name of the Kit-Cat Club* and the piece is signed by "the greatest (next yourself) of your lordship's admirers, Wharton."[22] Not only must the reader convert seeming praise into actual condemnation, but he also perceives that the supposed author, Wharton, dramatizes a new dimension of satiric attack. As Maynard Mack has observed, "an assumed identity, a *persona,* a mask," was a "specialty of the Augustan Age," and although it is not "fatal" to identify Wordsworth with the "speaker" of the "Ode on Intimations of Immortality," in Augustan satire "this identification is very often fatal."[23] When, in the *Dunciad,* Pope apostrophized Swift by "Whatever title please thine ear / Dean, Drapier, Bickerstaff, or Gulliver" (Bk. I, ll. 19–20) he listed in a pentameter line's narrow room but a small fraction of Swift's assumed identities. Included among these *personae* are Simon Wagstaff, the Examiner, Gregory Misorarum, Sieur de Baudrier, Ebenezer Elliston, Thomas Hope, "A Person of Quality," "A Friend of the Author," and a host of anonymous projectors, politicians, freethinkers, atheists, and Grub Street hacks. Obviously, Swift had a practical reason for concealing himself behind many of these assumed identities: the penalties for sedition were severe and Swift's pamphlets were more than once condemned as both libelous and seditious. In 1714, a reward of £300 was offered for the discovery of the author of *The Publick Spirit of the Whigs,* and in 1724 a similar reward was posted for the disclosure of M. B. Drapier's identity as author of *A Letter to the Whole People of Ireland*—although, in the latter case, Swift's identity was generally known and his safety lay in the strength of an aroused public opinion directed against Wood's patent and in favour of Swift as the saviour of Ireland. Far more important, however, than these practical and political reasons for concealing his identity was the more fundamental reason that Swift could partially conceal behind ironic masks the intensity of his personal involvement—and thereby, of course, at the same time energize his readers into a greater intensity of imaginative awareness than would be possible with a more direct approach.

Amidst the variety of fictitious authors presented by Swift, we may distinguish two major kinds of *personae*. The first, and least complex kind, is the mask of what we may call "the detached observer." This mask is similar to that of the typical Augustan figure, the Spectator, and in Swift's writing differs mainly in the variety of its guises. In such essays as Swift's *A Letter to a Young Gentleman Lately enter'd into Holy Orders,* and *Of the Education of Ladies,* as well as in his contributions to *The Examiner,* we perceive him assuming the role of a speaker who, though not Swift himself, nonetheless expresses with only slight dissimulation Swift's own moral attitudes. In *A Letter to a Young Gentleman,* for example, he offers genuine and thoughtful advice on the learning, rhetoric, and rationality proper to a pulpit orator. He writes, however, not as the Dean of St. Patrick's, but as "A Person of Quality"—his initialed signature is "A.B."—and he delivers his advice from the point of view of a well-informed and intelligent layman whose opinion reflects that of "the generality of mankind" and of those "who are hearers" and not preachers.[24] By appearing as an objective and disinterested commentator on the more frequent abuses in the pulpit, Swift creates an atmosphere of veracity and his arguments convince because they avoid the "enthusiasm" of special pleading.

There is probably no science which seems to be more detached from human emotions than is mathematics. And although abstract Cartesian rationalism was a constant thorn in Swift's side, he himself made frequent and effective use of the *impersonality* of arithmetic. There is a distinct difference in effect between saying "all men are fools" and saying "after careful count, I find that thirty-nine out of forty men are fools." The distinction is less in the actual proportion—which is within one man of being the same—than in the pretended detachment of the author, who claims to have made an actual computation and who presents only the objective statistics of his observation. Swift habitually used this device of computation in sustaining his role of detached observer, as may be seen in *A Project for the Advancement of Religion* where he solemnly attempts to prove that the wickedness of the age is not merely a "form of speech" but is an "undoubted truth":

> For, first; to deliver nothing but plain matter of fact without exaggeration or satire; I suppose it will be granted, that *hardly one in a hundred* among our people of quality or gentry, appears to act by any principle of religion. . . . Then, it is observed abroad, that no race of mortals hath so little sense of religion, as the English soldiers; to confirm which, I have been often told by great officers in the army, that . . . they *could not recollect three of their profession,* who seemed to regard or believe one syllable of the Gospel.[25]

The tone of this whole passage is one of unbiased calm. The objectivity is produced partly by the computation itself and partly by the denial of exaggeration, the appeal to what readily "will be granted." As to computation itself, part of its effect lies in Swift's use of negatives: "hardly one in a hundred" and "could not recollect three." Swift suggests that the numbers are the absolute maximum and that, in fact, if his personal opinion were consulted, he would put them much lower. In the fragmentary essay, *Of the Education of Ladies,* Swift enters into a long and brilliantly effective computation of the numbers of educated younger brothers of the gentry:

> Of this kind, I reckon, by *a favourable computation, there may possibly be found, by a strict search* among the nobility and gentry throughout England, about five hundred. Among those of all other callings or trades, who are able to maintain a son at the university, about treble that number. The sons of clergymen bred to learning with any success, must . . . be very inconsiderable . . . I shall therefore count them to be not above fourscore. But, *to avoid fractions,* I shall suppose there may possibly be a round number of two thousand male human creatures in England (including Wales), who have a tolerable share of reading and good sense. I include in this list all persons of superior abilities, or great genius, or true judgment and taste, or of profound literature, who, I am confident, we may reckon to be *at least* five-and-twenty.

Thus, Swift supposes that out of fifteen thousand families "one in thirty" may be tolerably educated; but he then fears the censure that this number is too high, and "upon cooler thoughts, to avoid all cavils," he reduces his computation to one thousand. The enumeration helps to detach Swift from his own emotional contempt for the general ignorance of the English gentleman. The atmosphere of detachment and objectivity which gives to the passage its humourous flavor is created by Swift's care in avoiding any personal assessment of his own. "There may possibly be found, by a strict search," not only suggests that the figures could be arrived at by any objective statistician but that these figures are an absolute maximum. Similarly, the phrase, "at least," which Swift often used to connote the minimum number possible is here used with an ironic twist; the number is so low that to think of it as a possible minimum is to feel again the almost complete absence of learning. Finally, the effect of this cool appraisal of the numerical deficiency of learning is increased by Swift's ironic fear that others will think him too generous, and his "cooler thought" makes him halve the number.[26]

The dissimulated urbanity and objectivity of this kind of irony brings us to Swift's most complex masks. When writing in the guise of a detached observer, Swift may be said to be dramatizing himself, in the sense that he appears to be more dispassionate than in fact he really is—a disparity he manages to communicate with great subtlety and ingenuity. This distinction between the appearance and the reality of Swift's expression may be carried one step further. Instead of dramatizing himself as an observer meticulously and often ingenuously noting the folly of mankind, he dramatizes this folly in action. That is, Swift relinquishes his role as commentator and his satire becomes an *imitation*, in the classic sense, of what he means to condemn. In short, Swift's most powerful satires exemplify *dramatic irony* and appeal to an intellectualized concept of irony more profound than mere rhetorical dissimulation.

A succinct definition of dramatic irony has been given by Sedgewick, who calls it "the sense of contradiction felt by spectators of a drama who see a character acting in ignorance of his condition." In irony of this kind, it is a situation and the character's part in that situation which create irony. The character enjoys the felicitous "possession of being well deceived" by appearances while remaining blissfully ignorant of the reality of the situation; at the same time, the spectator apprehends both the appearance and the reality and knows how the actor ought to be responding. In Swift's satire, the character's "ignorance" is generally of a particular kind: he is ignorant of the correct evaluation of his own moral nature. Accordingly, Gulliver's reflections on the discrepancy between man's real nature and man's false evaluation of himself may be taken as the foundation of Swift's own perception of ironic contradiction:

> I am not in the least provoked at the sight of a lawyer, a pickpocket, a colonel, a fool, a lord, a gamester, a politician, a whore-master, a physician, an evidence, a suborner, an attorney, a traitor, or the like; this is all according to the due course of things: but when I behold a lump of deformity, and diseases both in body and mind, smitten with *pride*, it immediately breaks all the measures of my patience; neither shall I be ever able to comprehend how such an animal and such a vice could tally together.[27]

Not merely ignorance of self, but ignorance aggravated by an assertive, confident, and pretentious complacency—this is the basic ironic "situation" in Swift's satire. In dramatizing this situation, in creating *personae* who embody and illustrate the ironic contradiction between what *seems* to them and what, as the reader knows, actually *is*, Swift mastered a form of satiric art which has been well described by Ricardo Quintana as "situational satire." In dramatic irony, Swift eliminates himself as a critical interpreter of man's action and permits the "self-developing irony of the situation"[28] to speak for itself directly to the reader. No satirist has developed a technique more moving or persuasive than this one.

Just how powerful an instrument of satire Swift's ironic masks can be is demonstrated in *A Modest Proposal*. What gives to this short essay its unique horror is not the proposal itself, which might well have been crudely disgusting, but the character of the "author." For the fictitious author, Swift's mask, is a perfect example of a character "acting in ignorance of his condition." He is, in Maynard Mack's phrase, "intoxicated with his own good intentions";[29] his sensibility to the "deplorable state of the kingdom" reflects his own estimate of himself as a humane, benevolent, and pious man whose deepest feelings of pity and patriotic duty have been aroused by the misery he sees around him. The projector is not consciously malevolent and it is his unconscious and involuntary revelation of brutality which creates the terrifying ironic contradiction. For this author exhibits an inhumanity which has become so habitual that it operates unseen as a norm of value. He is not concerned with the encumbrance of poor people who are old and sick, because, he tells us hopefully, "it is very well known, that they are every day dying, and rotting, by cold, and famine, and filth, and vermin, as fast as can be reasonably expected." The discrepancy between humanitarian sentiment and actual brutality is objectified in the unconscious assumption of the projector that men and women are indistinguishable from brute beasts. A child is described as "just dropt from its dam," and the proposer computes the number of "carcasses" which would be taken by Dublin alone. This tendency to *dehumanize* man and to view him as no more than an economic "saleable commodity" is furthered by the projector's careful statistical analysis of the population and the exact computation of income derivable from the sale of young and succulent children. The crowning revelation to the reader of the author's self-delusion is the final statement that "I have not the least personal interest" in the proposal because "I have no children by which I can propose to get a single penny; the youngest being nine years old and my wife past child bearing." An economist to the end, the author remains oblivious to what is evidently the cause of his disinterestedness: the total absence of any personal involvement in the realities of misery.[30]

If the "author" of *A Modest Proposal* is immodestly deluded in himself, Swift's most complex mask, the character of Lemuel Gulliver, is the victim of an even greater complacency. For in *Gulliver's Travels* Swift fulfills the promise, made over twenty years earlier by the "modern" author of *A Tale of a Tub,* to write a *Panegyrick upon the World,* and Gulliver becomes the most frustrated eulogist in literature. The intricate and shifting patterns of irony which complicate the first three voyages of the travels depend essentially upon the inversion of blame and praise. Gulliver condemns as "very defective" what the reader recognizes to be Swift's idealized educational system of the Brobdingnagians, and Gulliver disdains as a form of madness the activities in the Academy of Lagado of the "political projectors" who

> were proposing schemes for persuading monarchs to choose favourites upon the score of their wisdom, capacity and virtue; of teaching ministers to consult the public good; of rewarding merit, great abilities, eminent services; of instructing princes to know their true interest by placing it on the same foundation with that of their people; of choosing for employments persons qualified to exercise them; with many other wild impossible chimaeras, that never entered before into the heart of man to conceive, and confirmed in me the old observation, that there is nothing so extravagant and irrational which some philosophers have not maintained for truth.[31]

But it is as a panegyrist of his own country that Gulliver most characteristically reveals himself. The most accurate description of Gulliver's fundamental nature is that given by Swift who called his hero a "prostitute flatterer" and a man "whose chief study is to extenuate the vices, and magnify the virtues, of mankind, and perpetually dins our ears with the praises of his country in the midst of corruption . . ."[32] In "A Voyage to Brobdingnag," the king of that gigantic people arrived at unflattering conclusions about the human world, basing his deductions upon Gulliver's own description of England. To these contemning observations, Gulliver answers with chauvinistic fervour:

> And thus he continued on, while my colour came and went several times, with indignation to hear our noble country, the mistress of arts and arms, the scourge of France, the arbitress of Europe, the seat of virtue, piety, honour, and truth, the pride and envy of the world, so contemptuously treated.[33]

Somewhat later, when he resumed his talks with the emperor, Gulliver was granted another opportunity to eulogize his nation, and he

> wished for the tongue of Demosthenes or Cicero, that might have enabled me to celebrate the praise of my own dear native country in a style equal to its merits and felicity (p. 130).

He proceeds to deliver what the emperor calls "a most admirable panegyric" upon England. He praises the "illustrious body called the House of Peers," notes the "extraordinary care always taken of their education in arts and arms," and describes them as

> champions always ready for the defence of their prince and country, by their valour, con-

> duct and fidelity. That these were the ornament and bulwark of the kingdom, worthy followers of their most renowned ancestors, whose honour had been the reward of their virtue, from which their posterity were never once known to degenerate (p. 131).

Gulliver eulogizes the bishops whom he calls the "wisest counsellors" and "deservedly distinguished by the sanctity of their lives and the depth of their erudition." The House of Commons is praised for being composed of men selected "for their great abilities and love of their country, to represent the wisdom of the whole nation." But the Brobdingnagian emperor is undeceived and proceeds to inspect beyond the surface of this eulogistic cant; by inquiry he quickly determines that the excellence of England lies no deeper than Gulliver's praise and that, in reality, the English are a "pernicious race of little odious vermin" (p. 136). Through Gulliver's exaggerated praise, Swift accomplishes two ends. He relieves the emotional tension which would result from the direct and unironic attack of the emperor; he also is able to dramatize, without his personal intervention, the incongruity which he felt existed between the ideal state of government and the appearance. The spectator who first perceives the incongruity is, of course, the emperor, and we identify ourselves (as did Swift) with his final judgment. But in the last voyage Gulliver's eulogistic spirit survives, strangely enough, even the bitter lesson he learned among the Houyhnhnms; and after a long and direct attack (Gulliver makes it himself) against mankind's colonizing customs, he denies that he meant to include England within the compass of his criticism. He goes even further and praises his country as

> an example to the whole world for their wisdom, care, and justice in planting colonies; their liberal endowments for the advancement of religion and learning; their choice of devout and able pastors to propagate Christianity; their caution in stocking their provinces with people of sober lives and conversations from this the mother kingdom; their strict regard to the distribution of justice, in supplying the civil administration through all their colonies with officers of the greatest abilities, utter strangers to corruption; and to crown all, by sending the most vigilant and virtuous governors, who have no other views than the happiness of the people over whom they preside, and the honour of the King their master (pp. 305–306).

Unlike the projector of *A Modest Proposal,* who remains ignorant of himself to the very end, Gulliver in the fourth voyage discovers at last that his felicity has resulted from his self-deception. An ironic situation loses its irony with the advent of self-knowledge; and when that knowledge is a terrifying insight into evil and is accompanied by all the bitterness of a profound disillusionment, irony passes the threshold of tragedy. The tragic overtones of earlier voyages were relieved by the reader's perception of the ridiculous contradiction between Gulliver's complacency and man's actual worth. But with Gulliver's new insight into things as they are, the contradiction evaporates and we are brought face to face with one man's despairing vision of his own limitations. In the process of this final awakening, the mask of Gulliver slips and it is hard not to hear the voice of Swift himself and not to find in the dramatized tragedy of Gulliver the personal tragedy of Swift's own exasperated awareness. Some recent criticism has attempted to show that, contrary to more traditional interpretations, Swift in no way identified himself with Gulliver and that, in the fourth voyage, Gulliver is "at a still greater remove than in earlier books from Swift the narrator." [34] According to this point of view, the Houyhnhnms do not represent Swift's ideal of reason but a false ideal of a cold and abstract rationality which Gulliver foolishly attempts to emulate as the highest good;[35] similarly, Gulliver's identification of man with the Yahoos is said to reflect an opposite extreme of misanthropy which Swift also intended to ridicule. This provocative critical idea is summarized in Professor Mack's observation: "Though Gulliver makes the error of identifying himself and other human beings completely with the Yahoos, we and Swift do not. Nor do we take the ideal life for man, as Gulliver does, to be the tepid rationality of the horses . . . For the truth, as we are meant to realize, is that man is neither irrational physicality like the Yahoos nor passionless rationality like the Houyhnhnms . . . but *animal rationis capax.*" [36] This is a valuable interpretation and serves as a useful reminder that Swift does not idealize Gulliver's isolation from mankind regardless of individual excellence. Nevertheless, we must also remain aware that "A Voyage to the Houyhnhnms" is not a cool analysis of a philosophic problem—a dispassionate study of the dualism in man's nature. For it is rather the culmination and climax of an attack on man's *pride* in deceiving himself into the belief that he is rational and virtuous when, in reality, he has not developed his reason, and his virtue is merely appearance. In other words, the focus of the last voyage is not upon a description of the dualism of man's nature, but upon the disparity between what man is and what Gulliver had thought man to be. Accordingly, Swift avails himself of the most extreme symbols with which to startle and shock his reader out of complacency; and as Gulliver's self-revelation increases, as he becomes aware of his own deluded evaluation of mankind, his devastating disgust with the hypocrisy and self-delusion of his own species is uttered in the voice of his creator. To read *Gulliver's Travels* as a treatise on human psychology is to miss entirely the intensity of Swift's anger and despair at the disparity, so lately discovered by Gulliver, between man's opinion of himself and the reality of man's limitations.

Through his irony and especially his ironic masks, Swift achieved a high degree of artistic detachment. But what gives the explosive power to this irony is the reader's recognition that Swift's seeming detachment is the artifice of a creative mind controlling, forming, and channeling the most intense personal involvement. Swift's detachment, that is to say, is not the product of any withdrawal from responsibility. Swift has no connection with any romantic view of the artist as a vagrant whose art expresses his desire to burst conventions and soar unfettered over circumstance. Nor has Swift any kinship with that romantic writer described by Santayana as a "solipsistic poet, proud of his every mood, and sure only of his present sensations." Swift's satire testifies repeatedly to his attempt to subject the intensity of his "present sensations" to the discipline of an artistic form with a social purpose. But his feelings always lurk somewhere just below the surface of his irony, and the effort of will he seems to manifest in controlling these emotions intensifies the reader's own awareness of Swift's real and profound *attachment* to life. Without the discipline of a highly developed artistic conscience Swift's satire would have expressed his true *saeva indignatio* "in Timon's manner"—as Gulliver finally does; through irony, however, and the technique of dramatizing his deepest convictions in objective equivalents, Swift's satire attains that aesthetic beauty which, in Coleridge's phrase, derives from the "union of the shapely and the vital."

NOTES

1. *The Poems of Jonathan Swift* (ed. Harold Williams, 1937), III, 1039.

2. *The Poetical Works of John Dryden* (ed. G. R. Noyes, Cambridge Edition, 1908), p. 313.

3. Romans 1:29–31.

4. *Arte of Rhetorique* (ed. G. H. Mair, 1909), p. 115.

5. *The Art of Satire* (1940), pp. 17–18.

6. *Gulliver's Travels* in *Works*, VIII, 196.

7. *A Letter of Advice to a Young Poet* in *Works*, XI, 111.

8. *Works*, VIII, 287–288.

9. *Attitudes Towards History* (1937), I, 53–54.

10. *Works*, VII, 288, 290, 295, 299.

11. Pp. 108 (I omit the bracket after "Physicians"), 79, 179.

12. Decorum in the Renaissance use of *meiosis* has been ably treated by Rosamunde Tuve in *Elizabethan and Metaphysical Imagery* (Chicago, 1947), pp. 196 ff.

13. *Remarks upon a Book Intituled "The Rights of the Christian Church, &c."* in *Works*, III, 83. Similarly, Swift speaks of Tindal's treatise as being "... wholly devoid of wit or learning, under the most violent and weak endeavours and pretences to both" (p. 87), and he denies Tindal the satisfaction of believing he has, through his attacks, done any "mischief to religion": for then Tindal "will reply in triumph, that this was his design; and I am loth to mortify him, by asserting he hath done none at all" (p. 88). A similar point of departure is taken by Swift against Wharton: "He seems to be but an ill dissembler and an ill liar, though they are the two talents he most practices, and most values himself upon. The ends he has gained by lying, appear to be more owing to the frequency than the art of them; his lies being sometimes detected in an hour, often in a day, and always in a week." *A Short Character of His Excellency, Thomas Earl of Wharton, Lord Lieutenant of Ireland* in *Works*, V, 9. In a different manner but with similar effect, Swift mentions the author of

one political pamphlet as a man who "... Takes upon him the three characters of a despiser, a threatener and a railer; and succeeds so well in the two last, that it has made him miscarry in the first." *Some Remarks upon a Pamphlet, Entitl'd A letter to the Seven Lords of the Committee Appointed to Examine Gregg* in *Works*, V, 34. Thus Swift reduces the author to impotency in the one quality which could be dangerous to Swift's own self-esteem. The same pattern is followed in *A Tale of a Tub* when Swift describes Wotton's *Reflections* as "made up of half Invective, and half Annotation. In the latter of which he has generally succeeded well enough" (p. 11).

14. *Works*, VI, 39. See Swift's observation: "... the church appeareth to me like the sick old lion in the fable, who, after having his person outraged by the bull, the elephant, the horse, and the bear, took nothing so much to heart as to find himself at last insulted by the spurn of an ass." *Remarks upon a Book* in *Works*, III, 87.

15. *Of Irony, Especially in Drama* (Toronto, 1948), p. 7.

16. "The Intelligencer, Numb. 111," *Works*, IX, 318; my italics.

17. As the Examiner, Swift's notebook filled somewhat more quickly, but his subject matter had changed: "I have likewise in my cabinet certain quires of paper filled with facts of corruption, mismanagement, cowardice, treachery, avarice, ambition, and the like, with an alphabetical table, to save trouble." "The Examiner, Numb. 29," *Works*, IX, 182.

18. *Swift's Remarks on Dr. Gibbs's Paraphrase of the Psalms* in *Works*, IV, 235, 237, 240.

19. *Works*, V, 265, 266.

20. *Ibid.*, pp. 264, 267, 268.

21. *Works*, VII, 232–233.

22. *Works*, V, 268.

23. *The Augustans* (ed. Maynard Mack, 1950; Vol. V of *English Masterpieces: An Anthology of Imaginative Literature from Chaucer to T. S. Eliot*, ed. Maynard Mack), p. 11.

24. *Works*, III, 207.

25. *Works*, III, 29.

26. *Works*, XI, 63–64; my italics. Other characteristic illustrations of Swift's elaborate computation of statistics may be found in: *The Swearer's-Bank* in *Works*, VII, 41–46, *A Vindication of His Excellency, the Lord C—t* in *ibid.*, pp. 246–249, *A Proposal for an Act of Parliament, to Pay off the Debt of the Nation, without Taxing the Subject* in *ibid.*, pp. 253–258, *A Serious and Useful Scheme, to Make an Hospital for Incurables* in *ibid.*, pp. 296–298. Much of the verisimilitude in *Gulliver's Travels* depends upon statistical detail: see, for example, *Works*, VIII, 20, 22, 25, 26, 31, 32, 40, 88, 94, 97, 114–117.

27. *Works*, VIII, 307.

28. "Situational Satire: A Commentary on the Method of Swift," *University of Toronto Quarterly*, XVII (January 1948), 135.

29. *The Augustans*, p. 12.

30. *Works*, VII, 207, 208, 209, 212, 214, 216. Cf. Swift's *Answer to the Craftsman* for an almost equally powerful use of dehumanizing statistics; Swift ironically supports the license granted to the king of France to export from Ireland "some thousand bodies of healthy, young, living men, to supply his Irish regiments," and Swift demonstrates "by computing the maintenance of a tall, hungry Irishman, in food and clothes, to be only at five pounds a head, here will be thirty thousand pounds per annum saved clear to the nation." *Works*, VII, 220, 221.

31. *Works*, VIII, 195.

32. Letter to Mrs. Howard (Nov. 27, 1726), *The Correspondence of Jonathan Swift, D.D.* (ed. F. Elrington Ball, 1910–14), III, 366.

33. *Works*, VIII, 109.

34. *Gulliver's Travels* (ed. Robert B. Heilman, Modern Library College Edition, 1950), p. xiv.

35. See Kathleen M. Williams, "Gulliver's Voyage to the Houyhnhnms," *ELH, XVIII* (December 1951), 275–286.

36. *The Augustans*, pp. 15–16.

Robert Voitle

THE BASES OF MORALITY IN SAMUEL JOHNSON

Johnson's practical ethic is so unsystematic that only a fool would expect to find an elaborate, regular theory underlying it. Yet it is justifiable to inquire into what Johnson means by *good* when he tells us, for instance, that self-knowledge is good, or by *duty,* when he declares that beneficence is our duty. Johnson's failure to arrange his moral notions into complex patterns does not rule out the possibility that he may have done some thinking on the fundamental problems of ethics in an orderly or, at least, consistent manner.

It may well be that the immediate source of his practical statements is some muddied and turbulent fountain of anxieties and other drives—for some time now it has been the fashion to depict Johnson as the most eminently irrational product of an age which is still celebrated, rightly or wrongly, as an era of calm and practical good sense. Even if this is the case, we must investigate these impulses—while avoiding the temptation to perform any new psychological analyses—because whatever proportions of reason, emotion, and instinct are responsible for his moral fervor, it is obvious that Johnson's practical moralizing springs directly from convictions so powerful that no discussion of him as a moralist can be complete unless they are considered.

Only one of Johnson's essays is of much help in devising an orderly approach to his unsystematic moral convictions, the review of Soame Jenyns's *Free Enquiry into the Nature and Origin of Evil.* Johnson's comments on Jenyns's attempt to classify ethical theories are particularly useful to us, and they carry all the more weight because he never bestows praise on Jenyns freely. Johnson begins by saying that

> the first pages of the fourth letter are such, as incline me both to hope and wish that I shall find nothing to blame in the succeeding part. He offers a criterion of action, on account of virtue and vice, for which I have often contended, and which must be embraced by all who are willing to know, why they act, or why they forbear to give any reason of their conduct to themselves or others.

And then he reprints these pages in full. The heart of Jenyns's argument is contained in this passage:

> They who extol the truth, beauty, and harmony of virtue, exclusive of its consequences, deal but in pompous nonsense; and they, who would persuade us, that good and evil are things indifferent, depending wholly on the will of God, do but confound the nature of things, as well as all our notions of God himself, by representing him capable of willing contradictions. . . . It is the consequences, therefore, of all human actions that must stamp their value. So far as the general practice of any action tends to produce good, and introduce happiness into the world, so far may we pronounce it virtuous; so much evil as it occasions, such is the degree of vice it contains.[1]

In other words, an action is morally commendable not because it proceeds from a beautifully virtuous character, or because it is produced by obedience to some edict, but on account of its results. Morality can be regarded as principally a matter of virtue, of duty, or of consequences; and the last of these is the true criterion. To this Johnson responds eloquently, "Si sic omnia dixisset!" and proceeds to add a lengthy proviso on the dangers of seeking to penetrate remote consequences, which qualifies Jenyns's thesis but slightly.

Of course, it would be putting too much stress on a single statement to accept as definitive Johnson's rejections of the two approaches to morality, and then proceed to analyze the third, which he accepts—consequences as criterion. But perhaps the three criteria can be used to provide a framework, as points of reference, in analyzing the convictions which underlie Johnson's practical moralizing.

An interesting aspect of this classification which Johnson endorses so enthusiastically is its resem-

---

blance to that devised by the late Professor John Laird of Aberdeen, one of the most stimulating writers on British empiricism, in his *Enquiry into Moral Notions* (1935). Laird felt that all moral notions can ultimately be referred to one or another of three terms—virtue, duty, or benefit—and that these terms are irreducible. According to Laird, the same ultimate criteria underlie systematic ethical philosophies which Jenyns and Johnson see as governing more popular and less abstruse moral thought.

David Hume, for example, often propounds an ethic of virtue, despite his utilitarian bent.

> 'Tis evident, that when we praise any actions, we regard only the motives that produced them, and consider the actions as signs or indications of certain principles in the mind and temper. The external performance has no merit. We must look within to find the moral quality.

But these "principles" are elements of character not principles of duty, for *"no action can be virtuous, or morally good, unless there be in human nature some motive to produce it, distinct from the sense of its morality."* [2]

In what is essentially a reply to Hume, Immanuel Kant comes as close as anyone ever has to a pure ethic of duty. Notice how he depreciates the role of temperament or character in his interpretation of the text "Thou shalt love thy neighbor as thyself":

> Love, as an affection, cannot be commanded, but beneficence for duty's sake may; even though we are not impelled to it by any inclination—nay, are even repelled by a natural and unconquerable aversion. This is *practical* love, and not *pathological*—a love which is seated in the will, and not in the propensions of sense—in principles of action and not tender sympathy; and it is this love alone which can be commanded.[3]

He goes on to dismiss the ethic of benefit just as peremptorily as he did that of virtue, when he states "that the purposes which we may have in view in our action or their effects regarded as ends and springs of the will, cannot give to actions any unconditional or moral worth."

Opposed to both of these fundamental attitudes is the moralist who stresses benefit, a figure who has become familiar enough since Johnson's day that no example need be cited. He concerns himself with actions and results, and he insists that it is the end achieved which governs the morality of an action, not the character from which it proceeds or the sense of duty behind it.

Of course, no one of these three criteria need predominate; a moralist may stress first one and then another, even though most tend to emphasize just one. To return to the practical level, consider the most popular devotional work of eighteenth-century England, William Law's *A Serious Call to a Devout and Holy Life*. In an apparent attempt to consider all phases of religious morality, Law organized the book so that virtue, duty, and benefit are each taken up separately. The first four chapters deal with the "virtues" and "tempers" of Christians, and in them Law insists that men must possess "the *intention* to please God in all their actions." In the fifth chapter the text changes abruptly from "the intention to please God," to the absolute necessity for obedience to divine will: "Our blessed Saviour has plainly turn'd our thoughts this way, by making this petition a constant part of all our prayers, *Thy will be done on earth, as it is in heaven.*" Throughout the following chapters the terms of a duty ethic constantly recur—"law," "rule," "command," "duty," "obligation." We cannot expect Law to give benefit equal status with Christian virtue and obedience to duty, but the last three chapters before he turns from morality to formal devotion are given over to "shewing how great devotion fills our lives with the greatest peace and happiness that can be enjoy'd in this life" and that lack of devotion will produce misery and disquiet.

Such a balanced point of view is uncommon among popular moralists of Johnson's time, especially is it rare in purely secular writers. That increasing emphasis on the emotions which we have already discussed, results in what is predominantly an ethic of virtue. Strictly speaking, virtue is a quality which inheres in the individual moral agent, and it is of this sort of criterion which Johnson's contemporaries are stressing at the expense of all other considerations when they center their attentions on benevolent emotions, when they assume that if individuals are goodhearted, worthy actions and beneficial results will follow automatically.

In Chapter II, I made the obvious suggestion that the growing emphasis on emotion in morals is related to the change in the concept of the rational faculty and that Johnson is antagonistic toward sentimental morality because he is devoted to the ideals of freedom and responsibility which were bound up with the traditional humanistic notion that the reason is supreme in ethics. Another factor in the rise of sentimental morality is the growing optimism regarding human nature. To base morality on good affections one must feel sure that either man's emotions are naturally good, or that good ones can be easily planted or nurtured in the human breast. Here, too, is an aspect of sentimental morality bound to arouse opposition in the pessimistic Johnson.

To choose an extreme example of this optimism, it is easy to imagine how Johnson must have reacted on that day when he was trapped in a stagecoach with nothing to read but Laurence Sterne's *Sermons*, if he got as far as the seventh one, where Yorick tells his readers that if they observe a typical young man, as yet untouched by the disillusioning world, they

> will find that one of the first and leading propensities of his nature is that, which discovers itself in the desire of society, and the spontaneous love towards those of his kind. . . . Agreeably to this, observe how warmly, how heartily he enters into friendships,—how disinterested, and unsuspicious in the choice of them,—how generous and open in his professions!—how sincere and honest in making them good!—When his friend is in distress,—what lengths he will go,—what hazards he will bring upon himself,—what embarrassment upon his affairs to extricate and serve him! [4]

In other words, the only thing wrong with human nature and emotions is that the world corrupts them.

No one today is likely to think of Sterne as a moralist, even when he speaks from the pulpit, but on such optimistic estimates of humanity as his was based the cult of feeling—what might be termed a pseudo-ethic of virtue—which sanctioned the pleasurable pastime of emoting for emotion's sake, on the pretext that emotion is all that matters in morality and that good emotions are so efficacious that actions and their results need not be regarded at all.

Oliver Goldsmith, to choose another example, professes to hate feelers as intensely as Johnson does, yet in his attack on sentimentalism he is trying to purify the springs of behavior, to cultivate those seeds of benevolence which according to his own more favorable estimate are planted in the human character. The benevolent affections are to be exercised disinterestedly for good ends, not for the sake of pleasure or applause. Therefore, Goldsmith's paragon of virtue, the Man in Black who appears in "The Citizen of the World," is the antithesis of a feeler. He affects misanthropy in order to conceal "virtues which others take such pains to display," while within, he positively seethes with benevolent emotions, and at the sight of distress "his heart is dilated with the most unbounded love," "his cheek glows with compassion," his looks soften with pity. According to Goldsmith, the sentimentalist is wrong not because he exaggerates the importance of benevolent emotions but because he perverts them.

Even Henry Fielding, who is opposite to Sterne in so many respects, shares with him the contemporary disposition to make morals principally a matter of character and emotion.[5] With Goldsmith, he insists that the only reliable test of good nature is good works. Unlike him, and unlike Sterne, Fielding is not sanguine in his attitude toward the raw stuff of human nature. Man is often dominated by his passions, sometimes, Fielding suggests, by a ruling passion, and, as Booth discovers, the prospect of Divine rewards and punishment is necessary to make men behave. Yet because he conceives of goodness in terms of good nature, Fielding's is no less an ethic of virtue than the sentimentalists', and, as with them, it is optimism which distinguishes him from Johnson, his faith that once benevolent emotions are established in an individual's breast, they become a strong-flowing and steady spring of good actions.

Johnson's pessimism prevents him from accepting even that mild form of sentimental morality preached by Henry Fielding. Johnson doubts the efficacy of good intentions, he suspects human motives, and he feels that "the depravity of mankind is so easily discoverable, that nothing but the desert or the cell can exclude it from notice." [6] As might be expected, many people were shocked by these sentiments. Their reactions range all the way from the relatively mild protests of Mrs. Chapone and of Lady MacLeod, who, when she asked if no man were naturally good, got the reply, "No madam, no more than a wolf," to William Mudford's vituperative comments on the *Rambler:*

> What a depraved picture of human nature is this! In what a world of infamy and guilt do we

> exist! Where shall we seek for friendship where all are false; where shall we repose our griefs where none are virtuous? Alas! How may the most exalted intellect be corrupted by a pernicious indulgence of rancorous prejudices? [7]

It is true that Johnson became somewhat more optimistic as he grew older, but this is chiefly because he tempered his expectations and became more tolerant of human failings.

Perhaps it is this pessimism which provokes the occasional critic to call Johnson a Calvinist. The accusation is unfair, as we saw in Chapter II, yet excusable, because often Johnson seems to feel that man has no more freedom than the bare minimum necessary to make moral struggle worthwhile. Beneficence, the cardinal virtue, is acquired, not innate, for "naturally a child seizes directly what it sees, and thinks of pleasing itself only. By degrees, it is taught to please others, and to prefer others; and that this will ultimately produce the greatest happiness." [8] Nor is complacence ever in order once the lessons of morality have been learned: "to contend with the predominance of successive passions, to be endangered first by one affection, and then by another, is the condition upon which we are to pass our time." [9]

If Laird is correct in his assumption that no moralist can completely disregard any one of the three criteria—virtue, duty, or benefit—we should expect Johnson to concern himself with virtue part of the time, and, of course, this is the case. He is even willing to grant that "we have a certain degree of feeling to prompt us to do good," but adds, "more than that, Providence does not intend." [10] And, like all practical moralists, Johnson is very much concerned with developing virtuous traits of character among his readers. In fact, he believes that happiness is to a large extent dependent upon the formation of proper habits of mind. But virtue or good character is to Johnson's way of thinking instrumental and never complete in itself. Although character is quite important practically, the moral quality of an action does not ultimately depend on the goodness or badness, the virtue or vice, of the one who performs it.

Illustrative of Johnson's feelings about the relationship of the springs of a given action to its morality are his remarks on motive and intent. Some of these comments are very typical of the time. For instance, on the day when Boswell first visited him in his chambers, Johnson declared that

> the morality of an action depends on the motive from which we act. If I fling half a crown to a beggar with intention to break his head, and he picks it up and buys victuals with it, the physical effect is good; but with respect to me, the action is very wrong. [11]

And many years later he remarked in a similar vein that "if a profuse man, who does not value his money, and gives a large sum to a whore, gives half as much, or an equally large sum to relieve a friend, it cannot be esteemed as virtue." [12]

Sometimes Johnson's statements reflect his age's insistence that disinterested benevolence is the only source of true charity. In his most effective sermon on charity, the fourth, he warns his listeners that Divine favor cannot be won by that sort of beneficence which is prompted by a desire for applause or for some other personal gratification. Nor can beneficence be wholly a matter of doing one's duty either. It is commanded that we be just to our fellow-beings, but the rule

> is not equally determinate and absolute, with respect to offices of kindness, and acts of liberality, because liberality and kindness, absolutely determined, would lose their nature; for how could we be called tender, or charitable, for giving that which we are absolutely forbidden to withhold? [13]

Good intentions may be necessary if the doer of a beneficial action is to gain any merit by it, but they do not excuse an act which turns out to be harmful. In this conviction Johnson runs counter to the spirit of eighteenth-century popular morality, which he accurately characterizes when he notes that "there is no topick more the favourite of the present age, than the innocence of errour accompanied with sincerity." [14]

In this remark one can discern Johnson's dogged and practical empiricism, which is as much a barrier to his acceptance of any ethic based principally on character or virtue, as his pessimism regarding human nature. It is comparatively easy to determine whether an action conforms to some principle of duty or whether the proximate results are good, but frequently it is very difficult to ascertain the true motive behind it. Even the actor may not know what his motive is, and if he does, he may not be willing to admit it to himself or to others. If too much stress is put upon virtuous motives, the morality of an action cannot be verified in a quarter where objective comparison is possible; instead it must be determined in the confused shadowland of impulse, appetite, and emotion. It was not just prejudice which caused Johnson to react so violently when Boswell remarked, with what may have been mock innocence, that he believed Rousseau meant well:

> Sir, that will not do. We cannot prove any man's intention to be bad. You may shoot a man through the head, and say you intended to miss him; but the Judge will order you to be hanged. An alledged want of intention, when evil is committed, will not be allowed in a court of justice.[15]

Johnson concedes that good motives are a necessary condition if any action is to confer merit on the one who performs it, but he insists that they can never in themselves be a sufficient condition for terming any action good.

The moral life is a life of constant activity. It is this belief that most decisively sets Johnson apart from those moralists who emphasize character and virtue. We have already seen many examples of his insistence that morality is not primarily a matter of being something, or even of becoming something, but of doing. Witness, his disdain for escapists and recluses. The cloisterer may be of spotless virtue; he may be wise and know all things, but a truly good man he cannot be, because a good man strives. "It cannot be allowed, that flight is victory; or that he fills his place in creation laudably, who does no ill, *only* because he does *nothing*." [16] Or, as Thomas Nettleton, a contemporary moralist, pungently phrased it, "the religious recluse hopes to merit heaven by being good for nothing on earth."

Activity is so tightly and uniformly woven into the texture of Johnson's moral notions that by examining the motives behind his insistence on it and selecting those which he seems to regard as most urgent, it should be possible to discover his basic moral convictions. Or, to put it in terms of the criteria which he himself thought of as characterizing the different approaches to morals, it should be possible to find out whether Johnson thinks men should act because it is their duty to do so, or, whether as he claims in his review of Jenyns's *Enquiry*, for the sake of the resulting benefits. And if consequences are the criterion, we should be able to determine the nature of these ultimate benefits or ends.

Sometimes the activity which Johnson recommends in his moral essays is merely instrumental or prudential. It consists of what he calls in the twelfth Sermon "actions of necessity," which involve no moral choice. On one level, his poem "The Ant" deals with this motive to action:

> How long shall sloth usurp thy useless hours,
> Dissolve thy vigour, and enchain thy powers?
> While artful shades thy downy couch enclose,
> And soft solicitation courts repose,
> Amidst the drousy charms of dull delight,
> Year chases year, with unremitted flight,
> Till want, now following fraudulent and slow,
> Shall spring to seize thee like an ambush'd foe.[17]

More often there are ethical issues involved. In the first place, he feels so strongly that idleness is the mother of vice, that on occasion he is willing to recommend almost any sort of activity, no matter how frivolous, in preference to it. In defense of a company of virtuosos, he says that "whatever busies the mind without corrupting it, has at least this use, that it rescues the day from idleness, and he that is never idle will not often be vicious." [18] And even mild dissipation is preferable to some of the passions which idleness breeds:

> As Idleness is apt to give opportunities for the Cultivation of that Sensibility which is always blunted by Employment, so says he it nurses all evil and prurient Passions; and it is upon this Principle that Mr. Johnson recommends Dissipation to those who are but poorly supplied with intellectual Entertainment.[19]

Behind these traditional comments is Johnson's belief that "the old peripatetick principle, that *Nature abhors a vacuum,* may be properly applied to the intellect, which will embrace anything, however absurd or criminal, rather than be wholly without an object." [20] According to Mrs. Thrale he constantly referred to this notion:

> The vacuity of Life had at some early Period in his Life perhaps so struck upon the Mind of Mr. Johnson, that it became by repeated Impression his favourite hypothesis. . . . all was done to fill up the Time upon his Principle. One Man for example was profligate, followed

> the Girls or the Gaming Table,—why Life *must* be filled up Madam, & the Man was capable of nothing less Sensual.[21]

The thought of this boredom, this vacuity of life which always must be filled up, often was in itself more appalling to Johnson than some of the vices bred by it. Here we may seem to wander for a moment from the moral doctrines to approach closer to the man himself, but there is no need to apologize, because naturally the distinction between the two will grow more tenuous as we deal more with basic convictions. Of course, there is some danger in assuming, as scholars do occasionally, that Johnson's moral writings are actually essays in self-criticism, that he is usually prescribing for his own maladies. Although Johnson knows the human heart and mind so well only because he sees himself with such disquieting clarity, it seems prudent to assume that as a moralist he has objective control of both his personae and his topics, and that the choice of topics is dictated by his notion of what it is in his readers which most needs correction.

Yet, when his biographers repeatedly point out a specific weakness in his character it is safe to assume that he has his own predicament in mind when he prescribes for the weakness. The letter of Dick Linger in *Idler* No. 21 is certainly such an instance; here Johnson describes the balance of opposing forces which results in the dreary equilibrium of boredom and apathy:

> Those only will sympathize with my complaint, whose imagination is active, and resolution weak, whose desires are ardent, and whose choice is delicate; who cannot satisfy themselves with standing still, and yet cannot find a motive to direct their course.

This dead calm is so unbearable that men will risk their lives to break free from it. Johnson feels that those soldiers who desire war most "are neither prompted by malevolence nor patriotism; they neither pant for laurels, nor delight in blood; but long to be delivered from the tyranny of idleness, and restored to the dignity of active beings." [22] And it is hard to disagree with him.

Johnson's insomnia served to intensify the particular dilemma which his own indolence bred. There are perhaps less than twenty references to his sleeplessness available to us, but those comments which have survived disclose that the intensity of his malady was all out of proportion to the number of allusions to it. We know, for instance, that next to the anniversary of his wife's death, March 28th, the date to which Johnson's memory most often turned during his last decade was August 30, 1773, when he had enjoyed such a remarkable sleep at Fort Augustus in the Highlands. Six years before this memorable occasion, on an evening when he feels he will be able to rest, he prays hopefully in his *Prayers and Meditations* that "perhaps this may be such a sudden relief as I once had by a good night's rest in Fetter Lane." This means that he clearly recalls a night of sleep which he enjoyed, at the very least, eighteen years before.

Johnson's insomnia may have been more severe than that experienced by most men, but his symptoms are familiar enough. He is perturbed at night and irresolute and listless by day, so that he can work only "by sudden snatches." An especially active imagination such as Johnson's adds to the tortures of insomnia, for in bed the wits remain keen, and vivid images flit through the mind at an astonishing speed. Connections never before perceived become as clear as if they had always been known. In a sense, the insomniac is most creative when he suffers most. Yet the visions can be terrible, and, if they are not, the victim becomes depressed anyhow when he tries to make use of them, because the remarkable fabrics dissolve away as rapidly as they appeared, leaving their creator enervated and apathetic after the briefest spurt of real activity.

Bate is certainly correct in relating Johnson's insomnia to his fear of death, but it is one of those paradoxes so typical of human nature that on a purely conscious level, Johnson actually fears not going to sleep, the most corrosive of all the anxieties which afflict the insomniac.[23] In 1772 Johnson writes to John Taylor that he has lost command of his own attention,

> Of this power which is of the highest importance to the tranquillity of life, I have for some time past been so much exhausted, that I do not go into a company towards night in which I forsee anything disagreeable, nor enquire after any thing to which I am not indifferent, lest something, which I know to be nothing, should fasten upon my imagination, and hinder me from sleep.[24]

Not just some special anxiety, but almost any concern can dilate to become the thief of his repose. And so Johnson was ensnared by a malady insidiously circular in its workings: Anxiety or the physical discomfort he suffered for most of his life keeps him awake. When day comes he is indolent because of fatigue and accomplishes nothing, and this in turn arouses guilt and the fear that the experience will be repeated. If, by chance, he is able to fall asleep toward morning and "is tempted to repair the deficiencies of the night," the time lost while he dawdles in bed also breeds guilty anxieties, which do their work the next night. Thus, the disease feeds upon itself, making Johnson increasingly subject to a vacuity and indolence from which he is progressively less and less capable of escaping.

As W. B. C. Watkins aptly put it, "the Castle of Indolence is merely a way-station to the Cave of Despair." There are innumerable conjectures as to the causes and nature of Johnson's melancholy;[25] however, for our purposes his own account in "The Vision of Theodore, Hermit of Teneriffe" (1748) is sufficient to show why he considered action the best therapy:

> There were others . . . who retreated from the heat and tumult of the way, not to the bowers of Intemperance, but to the maze of Indolence. . . . They wandered on from one double of the labyrinth to another with the chains of Habit hanging secretly upon them, till, as they advanced, the flowers grew paler, and the scents fainter; they proceeded in their dreary march without pleasure in their progress, yet without the power to return; and had this aggravation above all others, that they were criminal but not delighted. The drunkard . . . laughed over his wine; the ambitious man triumphed in the miscarriage of his rival; but the captives of Indolence had neither superiority nor merriment. Discontent lowered in their looks, and sadness hovered round their shades; yet they crawled on reluctant and gloomy, till they arrived at the depth of the recess, varied only with poppies and night-shade, where the dominion of Indolence terminates, and the hopeless wanderer is delivered up to Melancholy; the chains of Habit are rivetted for ever; and Melancholy, having tortured her prisoner for a time, consigns him at last to the cruelty of Despair.[26]

There may be some question regarding what it was that Johnson found at the end of the dreary march, but there is none concerning the intensity with which he dreaded what was waiting there or what measures he proposed for avoiding it.

Fortunately, few of us are so severely afflicted with melancholy as Johnson was, and his prescription for driving off the black dog will be but intermittently useful to most men. And even in Johnson's case, the usefulness of activity as a preventive for melancholy does not fully explain why he recommended it so strongly. Prudence may dictate acting, idleness may breed vice, despair may be wrong and certainly it is painful, but none of these circumstances accounts for the intensity of the guilty anguish which Johnson felt whenever he reflected upon his past indolence.

In *The Achievement of Samuel Johnson,* W. J. Bate demonstrates that Johnson assigns to activity still another therapeutic function more profound in its implications and universally relevant. It is a means to a generally healthful mind, and to human fulfillment—"the developing and completing of human nature." Bate focuses on the peculiar dilemma which confronts man because of the way imagination and desire interact to produce hope. As Mary Lascelles describes the situation in her essay "Rasselas Reconsidered,"

> man, forbidden to despair, is bound for disappointment: he is forever dissatisfied because he must seek the satisfaction proper to his nature elsewhere, but what he is, here, forever hinders this search. Thus he becomes an inveterate gambler with hope.[27]

This is so, Bate says, because "in the very activity or process of wishing, there are inherent liabilities that are able to undercut the wish itself—the liabilities that the 'capacity of the imagination' is always so 'much larger than actual enjoyment,' and that nevertheless it tends to simplify, to fix on a specific object." These objects are unstable, but even if they were not, our ability to enjoy them would be.[28]

This phenomenon involves what I described in Chapter I in rather graceless terms as future psychological hedonism. Johnson repeatedly asserts his conviction that man never is, but is always to be, blessed: "that man is never happy for the present is so true, that all his relief from unhappiness is only forgetting himself for a little while. Life is a progress from want to want, not from enjoyment to enjoyment." [29] However, there is a paradox involved, which is expressed in Thomas Campbell's couplet:

> Thus, with delight, we linger to survey
> The promised joys of life's unmeasured way.

Semantically want cannot be enjoyment, but it is delight or pleasure and, thus, want, not enjoyment provides most of the happiness we are allotted in the present state. Rasselas is being quite logical when he exclaims "I have already enjoyed too much; give me something to desire," for, "attainment is followed by neglect, and possession by disgust," but hope, the product of desire and imagination, is ever green.

Future psychological hedonism is not what the eighteenth century would consider a moral principle; it merely describes the working of the mind. Therefore, controlling this particular process is more a matter of prudence than morality. Most of our happiness may come from desiring, but so does much of our pain, as we learn from episode after episode in *Rasselas*. Johnson says in one of his letters that "hope is itself a species of happiness, & perhaps the chief happiness which this World affords, but like all other pleasures immoderately enjoyed, the excesses of hope must be expiated by pain, & expectations improperly indulged must end in disappointment." [30]

Nevertheless, Bate feels that Johnson considers this continual activity of desiring to be morally formative under the proper circumstances. If it is turned inward, it will operate destructively and isolate the individual, but when the process is turned outward, and active links of sympathy and understanding with what is outside are formed, the individual will grow and profit. We "project ourselves forward—into our future condition . . . and bend our efforts to secure it," only if we are "able to turn outside our present sensations in another way, and lose the sense of our 'personal identity' in some *other* object," only if we have not isolated ourselves.[31]

Bate's interpretation of Johnson does involve a serious problem. Mere growing outward is not development, because process is not inherently beneficial. Cancer is a process. Presumably the individual will profit through trial and error, but life is too short for most men to lift themselves very high by this means. There must be some shaping end toward which the organism strives, or there must be some implicit pattern or potency which the organism fulfills, such as that of the oak in the acorn. Unless there is a formative element involved, Johnson's concept depends on the end-in-view and necessarily suffers from that same defect which consigned the principal American contribution to ethics, Pragmatism, to the philosophical rag bag.

This question is especially pertinent where Johnson is concerned, because despite his sloth he has more than his share of that Dionysian impulse which we all possess, the urge to act, not in order to attain anything, but simply to be doing.

> To strive with difficulties, and to conquer them, is the highest human felicity; the next is, to strive, and to deserve to conquer: but he whose life has passed without a contest, and who can boast neither success nor merit, can survey himself only as a useless filler of existence; and if he is content with his own character, must owe his satisfaction to insensibility.[32]

The term *useless* applied to the idler suggests that Johnson has some sort of overriding purpose in mind here; yet what he is celebrating is activity itself, pure striving, not desire and enjoyment of some immediate end, not movement toward some ultimate end, not development or self-realization. This impulse to activity is almost never pure; on the other hand, more frequently than we realize, ends are contrived to satisfy its urgings. The purer it becomes, the more ethical problems it creates—this is our concern with it. Some formidable metaphysical arguments can be erected upon the hypothesis of flux, but for the moralist's creations it affords a slippery and insecure foundation.

Bate answers the question as to what it is which gives form and direction to this growth by pointing to Johnson's deep longing for the stability of truth. This is the shaping end toward which the organism strives. He remarks that human development

> involves not the rejection but the use of primary human capacities—an active "concord and harmony," as Plato said, "of definite and particular pleasures and appetites." Furthermore, almost all of these pleasures or appetites have within themselves a *potential* yearning—perhaps too blind to be called desire—to reassure themselves and to work toward reality. As Johnson said, the "heart naturally loves truth"—it wants, at least, the security which truth alone can give.[33]

It is possible to quarrel about some details of this ethic of self-realization. If, for instance, one accepts the proposition that Johnson's theory of knowledge is largely derived from Locke, Bate's thesis presents some formidable epistemological difficulties. But it is unquestionably true that Johnson regards the fulfillment of man's potentialities as one of the ultimate ends of morality. No one could witness his repeated insistence that social beings must strive to live up to their capabilities and the lacerating guilt he felt when he thought he was wasting his own powers and not grant this.

I think that the importance of the principle of self-realization in Johnson's moral thinking can be confirmed by considering what he has to say about the nature of happiness. Although happiness may as a will-o-the-wisp delude man into an unending chase through bewildering and often treacherous bogs, Johnson never does deny that it is something real and substantial, a good of the highest order. The fault lies not in the goal but in the manner men quest after it and, especially, in their ignorance of its true nature.

Practical moralists are often vague when they come to describe the nature of ultimate goods, but Johnson's readers could hardly plead this excuse with respect to happiness, for he speaks explicitly concerning its various qualities, even though he offers no neat and concise definition. Happiness should not, for instance, be confused with mere pleasure. The latter which Johnson defines as immediate "gratification of the mind or senses," is certainly a good, but he so hedges it about with restrictions that it can serve as a very limited end, at best. It is true that we naturally seek pleasure and that it is imprudent or foolish to spurn pleasure when it may be enjoyed without guilt. Johnson became more and more convinced as he grew older that "when pleasure can be had it is fit to catch it: Every hour takes away part of the things that please us, and perhaps part of our disposition to be pleased." [34] On the other hand, many pleasures are directly evil and some it is imprudent to enjoy. Throughout his more sober essays Johnson admonishes his readers that they often will be called on to make the traditional choice of Hercules, between virtue and pleasure.[35] And frequently he consoles them with the sentiment that in Heaven "pleasure and virtue will be perfectly consistent."

The superiority of happiness derives from a number of characteristics. In the first place, despite the *Dictionary*, Johnson commonly thinks of happiness as rational or mental, as opposed to pleasure, which he conceives of as more sensuous—sometimes wholly sensuous, as when in the course of what is a rather calm argument with Boswell he says "When we talk of pleasure, we mean sensual pleasure. . . . Philosophers tell you, that pleasure is *contrary* to happiness. Gross men prefer animal pleasure." [36] Secondly, unlike pleasures, happiness is usually complex; it "consists in the multiplicity of agreeable consciousness." Because he believes happiness to be complex, Johnson agrees with Locke and contradicts Hume in maintaining that it cannot be the subject of any simple calculus, "Sir, that all who are happy, are equally happy, is not true. A peasant and a philosopher may be equally *satisfied*, but not equally *happy*. . . . A peasant has not capacity for having equal happiness with a philosopher." And these differences in the human capacity for happiness are qualitative as well as quantitative, for "our Maker, who, though he gave us such varieties of temper and such difference of powers, yet designed us all for happiness, undoubtedly intended that we should obtain that happiness by different means." [37]

Johnson's concept of happiness has its dynamic aspects, too. As we have seen, it is not a passive state of placid contentment. "Life affords no higher pleasure than that of surmounting difficulties, passing from one step to another, forming new wishes, and seeing them gratified." Rather than the satisfaction of specific desires, often it is the process itself which gives happiness, the satisfaction of having striven well, whether all our objectives are attained or not. Legitimate self-esteem plays an important role, which is the reason why it is so difficult to remain idle and happy.[38]

Something more than simple activity is involved in this dynamic concept of happiness. For one so pessimistic regarding human motives and human fortunes Johnson upon occasion is remarkably sanguine about the possibility of human progress, collective and individual. He is thinking of moral progress, however. Something can be done about slavery, for instance, because from his point of view the problem is moral, not sociological or economic. Johnson's most judicious statement of this faith in reformation which all moralists must possess is in the last *Adventurer* where he takes stock of what he has accomplished, and comes to the conclusion that "the progress of reformation is gradual and silent, as the evening shadows." And three years later, to Soame Jenyns's doubts that man was created perfect, Johnson replied that "the perfection which man once had, may be so easily conceived, that, without any unusual strain of imagination, we can figure its revival." [39] This perfection is depicted in the sixth Sermon, where Johnson writes of his

Utopia, a society in which all are happy because all are virtuous.

Utopia will never come, and any progress toward it must be painfully slow, yet the notion of perfection, or, rather, perfecting, is an essential part of Johnson's concept of happiness. When this and all the other tendencies we have noted are taken into account—that happiness is a complex and dynamic phenomenon involving the exercise of man's highest capabilities as well as his less exalted modes of experience—it appears likely that had Johnson given us a formal definition of happiness, it would be much like the one by Bishop Hooker which he chose as an example for the *Dictionary:*

> Happiness is that estate whereby we attain, so far as possibly may be attained, the full possession of that which simply for itself is to be desired, and containeth in it after an eminent sort the contentation of our desires, the highest degree of all our perfection.

Or it would be like that of Cumberland, with which he was also familiar:

> I am to advertise the Reader, that by *their Happiness* I here mean their true and intire Happiness; which comprehends all the attainable Perfections both of Mind and Body. . . . Likewise by *those Actions which are suppos'd to be the Means of this Happiness,* I understand, principally, the intire Series of Actions thro' the whole course of Life, which may promote that End.[40]

Thus, a consideration of what Johnson has to say about the nature of happiness tends to confirm Bate's thesis that the legitimate goal of the activity which Johnson constantly insists upon is self-realization; but it also raises a rather vexing question—just whose happiness is involved? Bate's apparent purpose is to present those phases of Johnson's wisdom which because of their persisting, universal relevance are the most useful to the modern reader. This purpose his book fulfills admirably. An eighteenth-century reader, however, perhaps because the altruism which so thoroughly permeates our social, political, economic, and moral presuppositions—no matter how rarely it is translated into action—was in his day just winning acceptance, would be curious about the possibility of conflict between the interests of the individual moral agent and the happiness of others. Of course, in the process of turning outward, which Bate sees as essential to the perfecting of the psychological organism, the individual would presumably grow less attentive to his own happiness and more to that of others, but at best this is merely using altruism therapeutically, as a device to benefit oneself. At worst, it is possible to imagine a person perfecting himself—in Bate's terms, achieving a healthy mind—to a considerable degree, without regarding the interests of others, or even at the expense of others. This, as it should be evident from the discussion of his practical ethic, Johnson would regard as vicious.

The eighteenth-century Englishman, made increasingly aware of this dilemma because of the rise of the altruistic spirit, tried to resolve it by proving that self-love and social are really the same. Sometimes, for example, he appealed to the hedonistic impulse: if the greatest of all pleasures is doing good for others, it follows that one best fulfills his obligation to himself by assuming that he has one to the rest of mankind. Johnson was not above pointing out these extra dividends when he sought to persuade his readers to beneficence, but it is obvious that he regarded them merely as inducements, essentially vicarious and but occasionally effective.

In the first place, he says over and over that real beneficence must proceed from principles not feelings. Anyone who bases his beneficence on pleasurable emotion is likely to end as he began, in merely feeling, rather than doing. Secondly, Johnson was positively distrustful of the pleasures of benevolence, so much so that in his personal charity he seems to have sought to counterbalance them by courting ingratitude and unpleasantness.

Another argument, on a higher level, one which Johnson did esteem, derives from the paradoxical nature of the pursuit for happiness. We learn from *Rasselas* that the more strenuously a man pursues happiness the less likely he is to capture it, yet, although happiness is attainable, neither will it come to him who stands and waits. This dilemma, Johnson had resolved ten years before in *The Vanity of Human Wishes.* If one devotes all his energies to striving for virtue, the mind makes the happiness it does not find. However, Johnson was here adapting a classic precept of the pagan moralists of antiquity to a Christian context. *Happiness* comes for a large part in that "happier state" referred to at the end of *The Vanity of Human Wishes.* Johnson had too much common sense to suggest, as some did, that pursuing of virtue rather than pleasure will guarantee temporal happiness.

The age's favorite argument for reconciling self-love and social is that first systematically propounded by Cumberland and which in Johnson's thinking takes the form which I have called altruistic utilitarianism. The utilitarian process is obviously inefficient; no specific individual can be sure that his efforts add anything to the general happiness or that the efforts of others will render him happy. But if we accept Johnson's premises that, at best, the political and economic organism can provide only minimal goods—those things without which happiness is impossible—beneficence is certainly the most prudent course for him who seeks his own happiness. It is the way which most directly *tends* toward his happiness in a world where very few expectations are certain of fulfillment.

However, as we have seen in Chapter V, Johnson pushes altruism beyond the point where it can result in any possible benefit for the individual moral agent. If the largest effective social unit is the state and the principle of utility does not function beyond its limits, what practical advantage can he offer his readers to persuade them that they must "love all men"? His concern for the natives of Abyssinia or the Indians of Canada is explained by his own universal compassion, but we cannot account in this way for recurring phrases such as "the great republic of mankind," "the universal league of social beings," and "the great law of mutual benevolence." Clearly, the happiness of others involves values which cannot be completely translated into terms of one's own happiness. In Johnson's moral thought the happiness of others is an end in itself.

We may conclude, then, that although Johnson exhibits a concern with good intentions which is normal to his day and shares with most moralists a faith in the importance of the development of proper habits and sound character, he disagrees with those contemporaries who make morality principally a matter of virtuous character. He does not regard morality as mainly consisting in being good-hearted or in *being* anything, because above all morality to him means *doing*. The chief goals of the activity so fundamental to his moral thinking are the happiness of the agent, which involves self-realization, and the happiness of others.

NOTES

1. *Works,* VI, 66–68.

2. *A Treatise of Human Nature,* ed. L. A. Selby-Bigge (Oxford, 1888), pp. 477, 479. These examples are cited by Laird.

3. *Fundamental Principles of the Metaphysics of Morals,* trans. Thomas K. Abbott (Chicago, 1949), p. 17.

4. Laurence Sterne, *The Sermons of Mr. Yorick* (New York, 1904), I, 117–118.

5. A concise and perceptive summary of Fielding's moral notions is given by George Sherburn in his "Fielding's Social Outlook," *PQ,* XXXV (1956), 1–23.

6. *Works,* III, 322 (*Rambler* No. 175).

7. *A Critical Enquiry into the Moral Writings of Dr. Samuel Johnson* (1802), p. 24.

8. *Life,* V, 211 (*Journal of a Tour to the Hebrides*).

9. *Works,* III, 219 (*Rambler* No. 151).

10. *Life,* II, 94. See also *Works,* IX, 322 (Sermon IV).

11. *Life,* I, 397–398.

12. *Life,* III, 195.

13. *Works,* II, 381–382 (*Rambler* No. 81).

14. *Works,* IX, 354 (Sermon VII).

15. *Life,* II, 12.

16. *Works,* IX, 313 (Sermon III).

17. *Poems,* 151–152.

18. *Works,* III, 333 (*Rambler* No. 178).

19. *Thraliana,* I, 180.

20. *Works,* II, 402.

21. *Thraliana,* I, 179. See also I, 254.

22. *Works,* IV, 210, 211.

23. *The Achievement of Samuel Johnson* (New York, 1955), p. 160.

24. *Letters,* I, 281.

25. The most satisfying discussion is still that of W. B. C. Watkins in his *Perilous Balance* (Princeton, 1939).

26. *Works,* IX, 174–175.

27. *Essays and Studies,* New Series, IV (1951), 45.

28. *The Achievement of Samuel Johnson,* pp. 81–82.

29. *Life,* III, 53.

30. *Letters,* I, 137.

31. *The Achievement of Samuel Johnson,* pp. 139–140.

32. *Works,* IV, 108–109 (*Adventurer* No. 111).

33. *The Achievement of Samuel Johnson,* p. 140.

34. *Letters,* II, 198.

35. See the frontispiece to the *Preceptor* for a pictorial representation of this very common eighteenth-century theme.

36. *Life,* III, 246. See also *Rasselas,* p. 15.

37. *Life,* II, 9; *Works,* IV, 127 (*Adventurer* No. 126). A similar statement is made by Locke in a quotation used by Johnson under *happiness* in the *Dictionary.*

38. One of the most effective arguments from the point of view described in this paragraph is to be found in *Adventurer* No. 111.

39. *Works,* VI, 73.

40. *The Laws of Nature,* p. 269. Maxwell is sometimes awkward, but his is truer to the original than the other English translations.

W. J. Bate

THE LITERARY CRITICISM OF SAMUEL JOHNSON: HUMANISM AND CLASSICAL REALISM

If Johnson's criticism rests on any one principle more than another it is on the classical conviction that the aim of art—as indeed of all humanistic pursuits—is the mental and moral enlargement of man, and that art attains this end through a moving and imaginative presentation of truth. In justifying Shakespeare's intermingling of tragic and comic scenes, Johnson stated that "there is always an appeal open from criticism to nature." Despite his acute and informed interest in the technical problems of literature, his primary concern was with its ultimate end and function, and, as a true classicist, he evaluated the means to the degree that they furthered that end. For Johnson, the knowledge to be desired is the knowledge of what principles, qualities, or values are most universal or persisting. It is the objective knowledge of what he called "*general* nature." The more universal and far-reaching the truth desired or conveyed by art, the closer art comes to fulfilling its primary aim. Moreover, "nothing can please many, and please long, but just representations of general nature." The poet, as "the interpreter of Nature," must therefore try to "divest himself of the prejudices of his age and country," and attempt to grasp and disclose general truths, "which will always be the same." With this point of view in mind, one sees that most of Johnson's adverse criticism is directed against whatever distorts "general nature" or abandons it in order to concentrate on isolated details, cater to temporary fashions, or satisfy arbitrary "rules" of art. In opposing this last tendency, Johnson overturned extreme neoclassic dogma, not on romantic, but on broadly classical grounds.

From *Criticism: The Major Texts* by Walter Jackson Bate,

2

Of the innumerable "novels and romances that wit or idleness, vanity or indigence, have pushed into the world, there are very few of which the end cannot be conjectured from the beginning." Far from demanding more real imagination, improbable fiction requires the author to do little more, as Johnson said, than to gain a moderate "fluency of language" and then "retire to his closet, let loose his invention, and heat his mind with incredibilities." Johnson also viewed askance in the drama the growing obsession which made of romantic love the "universal agent . . . by whose power all good and evil is distributed, and every action quickened or retarded." By such false emphasis, "probability is violated" and "life is misrepresented." It is significant to Johnson that romantic love has little place in the dramas of Shakespeare, "who caught his ideas from the living world." Similarly, like the great neoclassic realist, Jonathan Swift, Johnson despised pastoral poetry: "an intelligent reader acquainted with the scenes of real life sickens at the mention of the *crook*, the *pipe*, the *sheep*, and the *kids*," which can please only "barbarians in the dawn of literature, and children in the dawn of life." This dislike of the pastoral as a genre should be borne in mind in reading Johnson's famous remarks on Milton's *Lycidas*. Though his bias does not justify, it helps at least to explain his approach.

Truth to life, then, is the first criterion. But this does not mean for Johnson a naturalistic concentration on particular details. The excessive use of what we now call "local color," the interest in unique and individual traits of character, the portraying of transitory, local fashions and manners, in whatever level of society, will in the future give a work little more than documentary interest; though it "easily finds readers," it also "quickly loses them." The Puritans satirized in Butler's *Hudibras* have only historical importance. Homer, on the other hand, survives because his "positions are general . . . with very little dependence on local or temporary customs." In Shakespeare, who is probably without equal as a poet of "general nature," the characters are "not modified by the customs of particular places, unpractised by the rest of the world . . . or by the accidents of transient fashions or temporary opinions: they are the genuine progeny of common humanity, such as the world will always supply . . ." The aim of the poet, in other words, is not to "number the streaks of the tulip." Hence Johnson's strictures on detailed particularity of style, by which the "grandeur of generality," he felt, was lost. One example is his attitude toward the specific metaphors and images in the more extreme "metaphysical" poets. Despite his respect for the learning and original thinking of these poets, Johnson believed that, because of their "laboured particularities," the mind of the reader "is turned more upon . . . that from which the illustration is drawn, than that to which it is applied," and that so "analytic" a style fails effectively to exhibit the wide "prospects of nature, or the scenes of life." Another example is Johnson's opposition to "pedantry" in style—the use of out-of-the-way references, or deliberate "imitations" of past writers—as in Milton's Latin idiom, or Shakespeare's more ostentatious allusions in some of the longer set speeches, or the specialized knowledge assumed for reading Pope's *Imitations of Horace*. Johnson particularly censured imitations, such as those of Spenser that were common in the eighteenth century. They may show industry and please the learned by unexpected parallels. However, they "appeal not to reason or passion," but to "accidental" memory: "An imitation of Spenser is nothing to a reader, however acute, by whom Spenser has never been perused."

3

In the eighteenth-century approach to "imitations" of authors, one may at once see the two diverse sides of neoclassicism: the more self-conscious and restricted side, based on authority and past models, that leads to the writing of "imitations"; and the broader side that rejects them by placing truth to "general nature," and the direct appeal to "reason or passion," as the first requirement of art. Johnson, more than any other neoclassic critic, either in England or the Continent, exemplifies the latter, broader side. In a general sense, he admitted that some imitation of earlier writers is unavoidable. Especially in the great works of antiquity, the approach to the general characteristics of nature has been tested by the repeated judgment of centuries. The writer, therefore, may profit from studying the principles and aims of these works. But to copy the specific and external qualities of earlier writing is to "tread a beaten walk." In this respect, "no man ever yet became great by imitation." We may again remember the maxim of Edward Young: he that imitates the *Iliad* is not imitating Homer. And in reading Young's *Conjectures on Original Composition*, Johnson was surprised to find Young "receive as novelties" what Johnson himself "thought very common thoughts."

An even greater neglect of "general nature" is the arbitrary codifying of "rules" such as we find in Thomas Rymer or in "the minute and slender criticism of Voltaire." Indeed, one of the most notable achievements of Johnson is that, by broadly applying the principle of "general nature," he repudiated, on rational and classical grounds, many of the external neoclassic rules. "It ought," he said in *Rambler,* No. 156, "to be the first endeavour of a writer to distinguish nature from custom; or that which is established because it is right, from that which is right only because it is established." Self-authorized critics, "out of various means by which the same end [the compact and truthful presenting of nature] may be attained, selected such as happened to occur to their own reflexion," and then arbitrarily tried to give them "the certainty and stability of science." Hence Johnson, in his great *Preface to Shakespeare,* justifies Shakespeare's neglect of three major neoclassic "rules" by bringing to bear a more open-minded and flexible conception of decorum, based directly on nature itself. In wishing, for example, to stress the general "type" rather than the particular individual, neoclassic theory had interpreted its belief in keeping "decorum of type" to apply to what Coleridge would call the "exterior" rather than the "interior" character of a man. Thus Dennis and Rymer, said Johnson, in reacting to Shakespeare's characters "think his Romans not sufficiently Roman; and Voltaire censures his kings as not completely royal." Shakespeare preserves the "essential character" of the type. But his types are more pervasive than the mere classes and the external and changeable "drapery" of local customs that Rymer and Voltaire have in mind; in Johnson's words, "a poet overlooks the casual distinction of country and condition, as a painter, satisfied with the figure, neglects the drapery."

Again, in answering the neoclassic charges against Shakespeare's use of both tragic and comic elements in the same play, Johnson undercuts such complaints by returning to the central classical premise: "the end of poetry is to instruct by pleasing," to enlarge our conception of nature, to infiltrate knowledge into our awareness through a process of pleasing. The "mingled drama," therefore, is easily justified both by its closeness to nature and by the obvious pleasure it has given. Finally, Johnson sweeps aside the traditional arguments for the "unities" of time and place as a means of verisimilitude in a searching and common-sense analysis of "dramatic illusion." We are often told that the drama will not seem real if the scene keeps changing, and if the time supposedly covered by the action is much longer than the two or three hours that we sit in the theater. But the spectator does not believe he is actually at Alexandria to begin with, and therefore is not surprised or incredulous at finding himself later in Rome. As for time, the imagination can as easily conceive "a lapse of years . . . as a passage of hours." No more heed of time and place need be given by the spectator of a play "than by the reader of a narrative, before whom may pass in an hour the life of a hero, or the revolutions of an empire." It is significant in this respect that what to a noted French writer should seem revolutionary and "romantic" was, to the conservative English classicist, Johnson, simply common sense. For, as W. P. Ker pointed out, Stendhal, in his *Racine et Shakespeare* (1822), translated Johnson's remarks on the unities and appropriated them as a romantic manifesto.

4

Johnson's reassertion of classical aims is therefore broadly positive and affirmative. Hence it is not easy to account for the nineteenth-century belief that his criticism was usually negative and carping, and that he was a rigid advocate of extreme neoclassic standards of "correctness." For the only "rules" that we find Johnson occasionally stressing are the classical and in some cases neoclassic rules concerning diction, metaphor, and versification. Even these, more often than not, he applies flexibly and with common sense; and the ideal he has in mind is an intellectually active and alertly effective use of language. The *Life of Gray* contains several examples. In Gray's playful "Ode on the Death of a Favourite Cat," the cat, looking for goldfish, falls into the tub and is drowned. Johnson points out the irrelevance of the conclusion, "all that glisters" is not "gold." If, says Johnson, "*what glistered* had been *gold,* the cat would not have gone into the water; and, if she had, would not less have been drowned." By some nineteenth-century writers Johnson would here be dismissed as "unimaginative" and too literal. Twentieth-century critics, however, would be quick to agree that the poem is structually weak, and that the conclusion does not organically develop from the body of the poem. In such a work as the *Life of Gray,* therefore, Johnson should not be regarded as vaguely opposing what we now call "romanticism." Rather, he anticipated such present-day critics as T. S.

Eliot in feeling the poverty of "wit" and intellectual energy in the poetry of his own day and in decrying the substitution of stock devices, employed in the belief, as Johnson said, that "not to write prose is certainly to write poetry." He also doubted, as did Eliot later, the value of Milton's influence on minor poets, particularly in their blank verse. Speaking of Thomas Warton, for example, he made up a parody ending, "Wearing out life's evening gray"; *"Gray evening,"* added Johnson, "is common enough; but *evening gray* he'd think fine."

Moreover, Johnson was still a critic in the original sense—a sense that includes evaluating and judging. Where some nineteenth-century English writers eulogized Shakespeare and Milton indiscriminately, and considered Johnson insensitive for not doing likewise, he did not hesitate, in evaluating the work of these poets, to point out what he believed to be its lacks or faults as well as its merits. If, for example, some of the conclusions of Shakespeare's plays seem weak or sudden, as in *Henry V* and *All's Well That Ends Well,* Johnson did not scruple to say as much, and to add, as in the case of *All's Well,* "Of all this Shakespeare could not be ignorant, but Shakespeare wanted to conclude his play." Similarly, Johnson openly noted what he considered faults of style that resulted from Shakespeare's rapid writing. But in such instances, as Sir Walter Raleigh has said, he was "not attacking Shakespeare; he is assuming his greatness, and helping to define it . . ." Again, if Johnson irritated admirers of Milton by his comments on *Lycidas* and by saying of *Paradise Lost* that no one "ever wished it longer," it should be remembered that he offers the first great critique of *Paradise Lost* and that he concludes his *Life of Milton* by stating, of this "wonderful performance," that it "is not the greatest of heroic poems, only because it is not the first" —that is, only because it had Homer before it as an original model.

Even at the present time it is too quickly assumed that, in the *Life of Cowley,* Johnson is merely presenting the classical charge against the "metaphysical" poets. In a sense he is doing that. He points out what he considers to be their weaknesses when they are judged against the highest standards of poetry. But he also suggests the basis on which they can be defended or justified. And he does this so effectively that recent exponents of the "metaphysical" style often build upon his premises, and even use his terminology as a starting point: the *"discordia concors;* a combination of dissimilar images, or discovery of occult resemblances in things apparently unlike." It should be noted that Johnson, in the *Life of Cowley,* attempted to broaden again the idea of "wit," which —as in Pope's definition, "What oft was thought, but ne'er so well expressed,"—had become "reduced," Johnson felt, "from strength of thought to happiness of language." To write in the "metaphysical" style—and this was high praise from Johnson—"it was at least necessary to read and think." The variety of "wit" that he found in the "metaphysical" poets, moreover, was one that he described as "more rigorously and philosophically considered." If Johnson presented the classical charge against the "metaphysical" poets, he also offered at least the basis for the classical defense of them. He did not, it is true, view them as ideal models. His concern was to see them, in a balanced way, for what they were, and, at a time when they were almost forgotten, to find a critical framework for them, and to discover a basis on which they could be understood and evaluated.

5

It was manifest to Johnson, that in order to grasp general reality and portray it in the form of art, the first requirement is "reason." But by "reason" he meant a far more complete activity of mind than mere deductive abstraction. He would not have agreed with the extreme neoclassic rationalists that sheer method and abstract logic are the main key to anything except the particular sciences built specifically upon them. For Johnson, who was very English in his empirical-mindedness, firmly believed in the value of concrete experience. On the other hand, he felt that every effort should be made to widen this experience by drawing upon that of others. Moreover, "to judge rightly of the present, we must oppose it to the past; for all judgment is comparative . . ." Hence the importance of studying the practical experiences of the past as shown in the history of manners, judgments, tastes, and values. Special attention should be given to those that have persisted beyond a particular age or locality, for what the majority of intelligent and discriminating people persist in valuing over different periods of time can greatly assist us toward a flexible standard for judging what will continue to appeal. It is on this basis that Johnson begins the *Preface to Shakespeare* with the statement that "to works not raised upon principles demonstrative and scientific, but appealing wholly to observation and experience, no other test can be applied than length of duration and continuance of esteem."

But, according to Johnson, this full exertion of mind, directed by reason and the intelligent use of experience, must also include emotion and the imagination. Among the primary subjects of the poet, none is more important than human nature itself and its motivating passions. The poet, needless to say, can hardly understand and portray human passion without being himself susceptible to it. Moreover, if the "end of poetry is to instruct *by pleasing*," poetry must tap human feeling in order to relate it to insight. Johnson's only qualification was that *mere* emotion, by itself, was not a trustworthy guide, and that emotion is of value only to the degree that it is fed and informed by reason and knowledge. His attitude toward the function of the imagination was similar. It is frequently said that Johnson "distrusted" the imagination, but what he distrusted was the use of the imagination as a practical, moral guide. For him the term still meant "image-making," not the entire play of mind that Coleridge, for example, meant by the word. Hence Johnson rightly took it for granted that mere unguided "image-making," left to itself, can lead to any end, including nightmares and insanity. Johnson's distrust of imagination and emotion as exclusive moral guides was increased by his fear of his own vivid imagination and strong feelings. Much of his life was devoted to a courageous struggle against what he called "that hunger of imagination which preys incessantly upon life." On the other hand, he also took it for granted that imagination is necessary in art. The more of it one has, the better, provided it be informed and "regulated" by knowledge. Since imagination and feeling tend to follow whatever is before them—an object, a remembered image, an association, a fear or hope—it is the task of reason to make sure that what they follow is not the result of mere whim, accident, or local custom and chance environment.

The aim, in short, is to cleave to the rational conception of what is true with such vigor and firmness that this conception will then arouse, lead, and channel the feelings and the imagination toward it. This broad classical conviction is as far from the narrow, anti-imaginative bias of extreme neoclassicism as it is from the loose, watery emotionalism of the extreme romantic. And the conviction gains force as Johnson applied it, because his own life may be described as an energetic effort to realize, deeply and emotionally, the truths that his reason perceived. He was not entirely successful, of course, nor did the temper or character of his own period offer much encouragement. "Lonely in his life," as T. S. Eliot has said, "Johnson seems . . . still more lonely in his intellectual and moral significance." Yet both as a critic and as a moralist, Johnson never lost sight of what is centrally important. The outstanding characteristic of his writing, therefore, is its *sanity;* and it is a sanity that is all the stronger and more genuine because it is a rational attitude to which Johnson clung, with a powerful exertion of will, in self-preservation against his own emotionally turbulent nature. In the mind and the literary achievement of Johnson, the classical tradition, at least as an unbroken continuity, finally comes to its close. But in doing so, it rises once again to a living and pervasive applicability to literature and human life.

Paul Fussell

THE FACTS OF WRITING AND THE JOHNSONIAN SENSES OF LITERATURE

If we are to understand everything that Johnson's literary performance has to tell us, we must pause for a moment here to consider some of the facts of writing. Like "the facts of life," they may seem at first glance a little startling; but also like those other facts, once we're in on the secret we wonder how we could have been so innocent before.

What constitutes literature? Simply this: the decision of an audience that a piece of writing is "literary." An act of what observers will consent to consider literature can take place only when an individual talent engages and, as it were, fills in the shape of a pre-existing form that a particular audience is willing to regard as belonging to the world of literature. This is the only reason why lecture notes, say, no matter how brilliantly conceived and finely executed, are not regarded as literary. This is the only reason why an "outline" is conceived to be pre-literary rather than literary: no matter how much genuine literary distinction it can show (unity, coherence, emphasis, precision of texture), it can never be a work of literature simply because its form is *infra dig.* The same is true of letters to the editor, notes to the milkman, theatrical program-notes, the discourses on phonograph-record sleeves, and the inscriptions authors are pleased to write in presentation copies of their books. William Faulkner's Nobel Prize utterance was widely regarded as literary by some people because it took the form of a genre—the short oration or "address," as in *The Gettysburg Address*—to which such people consent to attach literary value. If it had appeared as a letter to the editor, its value would have been seriously diminished.

To perceive that Joyce's *Ulysses* belongs to the genre "novel," most people would have to have in hand more than a single section. Considered by itself, the language of the Sirens episode is so *outré* that, as Stuart Gilbert reports, "when it was sent by the author from Switzerland to England during the First World War, the Censor held it up, suspecting that it was written in some secret code. Two English writers (it is said) examined the work and came to the conclusion that it was not 'code' but literature of some eccentric kind."[1] And in the opposite way, a detective play currently popular in London works and finally delights only because the audience makes the assumption that a theatrical program is what it appears to be, that it has always the same degree of validity and trustworthiness as genre. It is an assumption about the conventional status of a written document that provides the spring for the play. And as John Sparrow reminds us, a problem we solve only by knowing about genre is this: how do we in fact distinguish between an "inscription" in a public place that is designed to be merely a notice ("George Washington lived here") and one that asks us to attend to its literary quality ("Their Name Liveth Forevermore")?[2]

Like other sorts of public notices, what literature is at any historical moment depends wholly on conventions which appear and depart, wax and wane, fructify or deaden. The making of literature is a matter of the engagement of a vulnerable self with a fairly rigid coded medium so tough that it bends and alters only under the most rigorous pressure, pressure which only the rarest spirits among writers can exert. The idea of the "coded medium" is a modern way of conceiving of a relatively fixed literary genre. *This coded medium comes inevitably from outside the writer*: otherwise it fails to transmit signals recognizable to the observer. Which is another way of saying what Northrop Frye has said: "The *forms* of literature can no more exist outside literature than the forms of sonata and fugue and rondo can exist outside music."[3] The medium is a public property which is not inside the writer.

When a young person today decides that he must perform in the role of writer, his eye fixed on all the romantic emoluments which modern folklore attaches to that role, the first thing he does —most often without realizing it—is to settle on a genre which will satisfy both his sense of social appropriateness and his audience's presumed sense of what literature is. Nine times out of ten he will select either the short or the long autobiographical fiction as the most suitable arena for the exercise and exhibition of his own powers: the archetype he imitates is Joyce's *A Portrait of the Artist as a Young Man.* The tenth time he will select the short, intense, quasi-confessional lyric poem: here Baudelaire as refracted in early Eliot is likely to be the model. The literary beginner of our own time has in effect these two essential choices only, although as his literary career proceeds a third genre may offer itself: the Absurd play, or Camp melodrama, stiff with the residue of Expressionism and Dada. It takes a mature and experienced sensibility which has long since passed through these stages to do what Norman Mailer has done, to appropriate a genre not considered literary—the news story, the "report," the eyewitness account—and make it serve literary purposes. But most writers are not mature and experienced, and it is thus largely within the three genres I have indicated—autobiographical fiction, confessional lyric, and Absurd play—that the contemporary so-called "creative" imagination harbors,

feeding
A little life with dried tubers.

Add to these three genres the last recourses of the middle-aged literary intelligence in exhaustion —the review, the critical essay, and the critical book—and you have what amounts to a complete catalog of the forms within which it is possible today to imagine serious literary purpose showing itself. The point we will find emerging is ironic: for all its illusion of a new freedom and amplitude, modern writing actually takes place in a vastly shrunken, impoverished, and dis-peopled genre world, even if it is a world where the genres are as rigid as they always have been. To begin a literary career today with, say, a poetic satire, or a long narrative poem, or a sermon, or a straightfaced ironic essay, or a travel book would be to begin no literary career at all. These would be taken as exercises in either high antiquarianism or low journalism, never as exhibitions of "creativity." The fact is that no matter what one's ambitions of freedom, one writes essentially what other people are writing. The fact is that genuine creativity shows itself not in the invention of forms or modes but in the accuracy with which distinct public forms of all kinds are recognized and the appropriateness with which they are exploited.

This is why I want to offer Johnson as a prime example of "the writer." His own life of writing took place in the midst of a heady profusion and variety of genres. Indeed, to think of what an open, "free" literary world would be like, a world where the available forms are almost numberless and infinitely variegated, is to imagine oneself in something like Johnson's literary circumstances. During his long career he exercised himself, often anonymously, in more of the various literary "kinds" than perhaps any other writer has ever done. Consider: he worked in tragedy, biography, the periodical essay, the oriental tale, the travel book, the political tract, the critical essay, and the book review; in the oration, the sermon, the letter, the prayer, the dedication, the preface, the legal brief, and the petition to royalty; in the poetic satire, the Horatian ode, the elegy, the theatrical prologue and epilogue, the song, the Anacreontic lyric, the epigram, and the epitaph. He was a master even of the advertisement, the political handbill, and the medical prescription. Few friends who needed anything written were ever turned away, so long as what they wanted was in a genre in which Johnson felt comfortable. The only consequential contemporary categories to which he never turned his hand were the novel, stage comedy, the Pindaric ode, and the pastoral. He felt no attraction to the first two, he distrusted the third, and he scorned the last. The novel carried implications of sexual looseness, stage comedy implications of sheer levity: knowing himself intimately, he could not imagine himself as the author of either. The Pindaric ode he distrusted as a vehicle likely to unleash at least the appearance of passion, which, given his make-up, was all too likely to surface anyhow. And working in pastoral would mean allying oneself to the tradition of *Lycidas,* which might imply that one was willing to mingle Christian conclusions with pagan images, thus suggesting, perhaps, that they were of approximately equal validity and use.

If it is true that he could not write everything, it

is also true that no other writer of his time wrote in so many forms. One reason he was able to do this is that he was working before the widespread belief that writing is necessarily a self-expressive act verging on confession. By scrutinizing his intercourse with genres we can thus recover, I think, something like an orthodox literary sense of the relation between a writer's individual uniqueness and the objective sameness that characterizes the world of genres. And as I focus from time to time on Johnson's way with genres, I am going to be suggesting that his way is really the way of all writers, despite their often colorful statements to the contrary.

In his own time Johnson's reputation was firmly that of a writer. It was only later, after the dramaturgy of Boswell and Macaulay, that he turned into the folklore image which still prevents an open access to the writings. With the air of enunciating a commonplace, the author of Johnson's obituary in the *Gentleman's Magazine* called him "the pride of English literature"; Thomas Tyers testified that "he was born for nothing but to write"; and three years after his death George Horne, Bishop of Norwich, observed: "The little stories of his oddities and infirmities in common life will, after a while, be overlooked and forgotten; but his writings will live forever, still more and more studied and admired." But when Boswell and Macaulay had finished with him, he was turned into a combination of Mr. Punch, John Bull, and a sort of Lord North of criticism, with overtones of creepy, half-sane religious superstition and brutal literary "prejudices." As Donald Greene has acutely perceived, the arch-snob James Boswell colored the image of the actual Johnson and offered it as a totem of reaction, "Toryism," and sentimental Jacobitism, largely as a buttress for his own insecure sense of personal sufficiency. What Boswell required was that Johnson seem to validate a world in which a Laird of Auchinleck would have a necessary, rightful place. Hence his worshipful terms for Johnson, terms which have done so much both to frighten readers from his works and to make them misread what they encounter there. To Boswell he is "that literary monarch," "the mighty sage," "the great intellectual light," and, of course, "my illustrious friend."

Macaulay's denigration of Johnson—like Boswell's encomiums, ironically—has had the effect of relieving most people from any obligation to consult the writings. As Macaulay says:

> His conversation appears to have been quite equal to his writings in matter, and far superior to them in manner. . . . As soon as he took his pen in his hand to write for the public, his style became systematically vicious. . . . When he wrote for publication, he did his sentences out of English into Johnsonese. . . . His whole code of criticism rested on pure assumption. . . . The characteristic peculiarity of his intellect was the union of great powers with low prejudices.[4]

These canards sent abroad by Macaulay—largely, we now see, for Whig political purposes—still operate powerfully as critical home truths. Michael Joyce, whom no one could convict of a want of essential intelligence, can write in 1955:

> The truth is that no man has reached such high eminence in the world of English letters with so little *specific* talent for literature as Johnson. . . . At its best his writing is as masterly as his talk, but it was curiously uneven: he never achieved that complete control of his medium which is the hallmark of the finished artist. . . .[5]

And even the enlightened Mona Wilson, editor of the Nonesuch *Johnson,* feels obliged to recommend him this way:

> He is often dull: unless you know him [she has in mind Boswell's *Life*] much of his writing is dead as well as dull.

But by way of palliation she goes on:

> Many of his pages were written for bread [notice the assumption that the best writing is necessarily and self-evidently free expression freely undertaken], many in sorrow and despair, all of them in the torture of a melancholy which he may hold off for a time but never dispels.

After this virtual equation of literary value with the self-expression of cheerful materials, she concludes:

> It would be a weary if not impossible task to read the whole of Johnson's writing without the support of a personal sympathy.[6]

J. W. M. Thompson feels plenty of that personal sympathy, but even he returns to the old theme: "One needs, of course, a sense of duty to read through all the 208 *Ramblers* from start to finish today."[7]

Persuaded by the testimony of such witnesses, it is little wonder that readers today turn from the writings to embrace a fictive substitute named "Dr." Johnson and to support a quasi-religious cult which detaches him almost entirely from literary theory and shifts him over (I almost wrote Him) into personal and Anglican folklore. Sometimes the folklore veneration approaches actual canonization, with Lichfield serving as the Fatima of the cult. There today at the Birthplace, guided by the curator (a young Chinese devotee from Hong Kong), the faithful are invited to venerate such relics as "Dr. Johnson's silver bib-holder" and "the saucer which was used every morning by Dr. Johnson, on which his breakfast roll was placed."

Venerators and close readers—the two establish the polarities of the Johnsonian "double tradition" noticed by Bertrand Bronson:[8] the tradition, on the one hand, of "Doctor Johnson," the folklore *domine* and Tory projected in Boswell's *Life,* and the tradition, on the other hand, of Samuel Johnson, writer, poet, critic, and foremost literary intelligence of his day. Even if we are sophisticated well above bib-holders and saucers, the way we read him will seem to depend in large part on which of the two traditions has had the greater effect on us. Donald Greene observes:

> It is apparent that there has . . . existed a "double tradition" of Johnson the writer—two quite contradictory ways of reading the words on a Johnsonian page. The one sees it as exuberant with concrete and vivid imagery; the other finds only a drear waste of "abstraction" and inflated, pompous verbosity. The one sees Johnson the critic as highly concerned to promote the use of effective imagery as an indispensable quality of the highest poetry; the other finds him suspicious, even fearful of it.[9]

Learning to read Johnson requires first a look at what literature seemed to him to be.

Imlac declares to Rasselas: "Inconsistencies cannot both be right; but, imputed to man, they may both be true." Johnson was always hospitable to inconsistencies so long as they constituted an honest registration of empirical actuality. The honesty is what matters. Boswell was fascinated with Johnson's massive inconsistencies, and it is the theme of those inconsistencies that provides him with his fully-orchestrated conclusion to the *Life of Johnson,* a book which is really a series of variations on Boswell's point that "Man is, in general, made up of contradictory qualities." Johnson's tendency toward inconsistency is perhaps most clearly apparent in his unremitting condemnation of moral backsliding on principle ("Never accustom your mind to mingle virtue and vice") which accompanies—to Boswell's frequent astonishment—a genuine fellow-feeling with actual backsliders like Richard Savage, Topham Beauclerk, Henry Thrale, and Boswell himself. As Bronson has said, "Philosophy was too narrow a room for his humanity: he could not look upon a metaphysical system, no matter how pretty the structure, as a desirable exchange for the rich irrelevancies and contradictions by which men live."[10]

Johnson's sense of literature derives from a central contradiction that we would not be surprised to meet if we had not simplified him out of all recognition. This contradiction is one between the social sense that literature is a mere rhetorical artifice akin to legal advocacy, and the religious sense that for the literarily gifted the production of literature and the living of the life of writing are very like a Christian sacrament. The opposition is between a cunning knowingness and an almost unbelievable innocence. The important thing is that both senses are fully developed in Johnson and that both senses are likely to operate at almost the same time. We should explore first the side of this polarity where literature appears as a social, argumentative, and (merely) affective function.

The impact of the law and of lawyers upon Johnson's literary sensibility has never been emphasized enough. His boyish introduction to learning took place in the legal atmosphere of the Lichfield Grammar School, proud of its record of producing lawyers and justices. A boy attending such a school would never have been allowed to forget what he was there for. As an adult he selected London lodgings very near the Inns of Court, and the bulk of his middle-class friends were lawyers. It is no accident that his two main biographers, Boswell and Sir John Hawkins, were lawyer and judge respectively: as legally trained professionals, both were drawn to a mind which so ably could conceive of literature in terms they too could understand, namely, as quasi-legal argument. At the age of thirty-two Johnson spent three whole years writing legal argument as he unlawfully—the contradiction is pleasant and instructive—wrote for *The Gentleman's Magazine* the accounts of the parliamentary debates. We remember the very many times Boswell solicited his advice on specific cases and points of law, and we remember the many brilliant legal briefs Johnson wrote for Boswell as a result. His experience of the law was both theoretical and practical. William Bowles reports: "At one period of his life he used to frequent the office of a Justice of the Peace, under the idea that much of real life is to be learned at such places."[11]

But his deepest immersion in the legal occurred late in his fifties. The great jurist Sir William Blackstone had vacated the Vinerian chair at Oxford. One of Johnson's friends, Judge Robert Chambers, was elected in 1766 to succeed Blackstone in the professorship. Chambers was only twenty-nine, and he was neither a gifted writer nor an impressive legal intelligence. For the next two years Johnson secretly assisted him by quietly writing the Vinerian law lectures for him. The sixty lectures comprise some 1,600 pages. Johnson's seriousness about all this, his sense that even though he may be embarking on a rhetorical enterprise not too different from a literary fraud substantial public benefits may emerge, can perhaps be inferred from a prayer "Before the Study of Law," which he recorded in 1765, a year before he knew he would be writing for Chambers:

> Almighty God, the giver of wisdom, without whose help resolutions are vain, without whose blessing study is ineffectual, enable me, if it be thy will, to attain such knowledge as may qualify me to direct the doubtful, and instruct the ignorant, to prevent wrongs, and terminate contentions; and grant that I may use that knowledge which I shall attain to thy glory and my own salvation, for Jesus Christ's sake. Amen.

It was only his premature departure from Oxford, enforced by poverty, that kept him from the systematic professional training that would have made him a lawyer instead of a writer. There is no doubt that he would have preferred the law. At one point we find him scribbling in some rough notes what we would call a rationalization of the life of writing compared with the life of legal advocacy:

> If write well, not less innocent or laudable than prescribing—pleading—judging. . . . If ill, fails with less hazard to the public than others. The prescriber—pleader—judge hurt others.[12]

But despite such attempts to persuade himself that he had done just as well to become a writer, he never stilled in himself the old legal fervor. When he was almost seventy, Sir William Scott said to him: "What a pity it is, Sir, that you did not follow the profession of the law. You might have been Lord Chancellor of Great Britain, and attained to the dignity of the Peerage. . . ." Boswell continues his report of the incident: "Johnson, upon this, seemed much agitated; and in an angry tone exclaimed, 'Why will you vex me by suggesting this, when it is too late?' " We can appreciate the weight of Johnson's contribution to Anglo-Saxon jurisprudence in the Chambers lectures by remembering that he was competing with Blackstone, whose Vinerian lectures became his *Commentaries on the Laws of England.*

It would be a mistake to imagine that in his leanings toward the law Johnson is behaving very idiosyncratically. He is only one among countless eighteenth-century writers who were bred to the law only to deviate into literature. Indeed, this was a convention of behavior almost as inviolable in the eighteenth century as the current convention that a respectable lyric poet must teach in a college and that a Beat poet must not. All this legal study and attendance at the Inns of Court by bright young men throughout the eighteenth century could not help stimulate a bent for argument and rhetoric, as well as a feeling that carefully uttered things—poems, for example—must be carefully uttered in a way that one has been taught. All this legal consciousness could not help stimulate skill in the management of images and ideas less for their own delightful sake than as elements in a process of advocacy. From this proximity of the law to literature stems the very eighteenth-century idea that the act of literature is necessarily an act of argument, that the writer, even when he assumes the role of poet, is most comparable to a barrister arguing a case. Like the barrister, the poet is skilled more in selecting and arranging objective points with an eye to their impact on the audience, a jury of readers, than in exposing his personal singularity or unlocking his heart in public. What the advocate actually thinks about the case in hand is irrelevant: what he says about it publicly determines his failure or success.

From this legal, rhetorical, and effective conception of writing emerge many of Johnson's most impressive literary perceptions. When in his legal mood he is deeply suspicious of any conception of literature which would—naïvely and preposterously, in his view—associate the literary act with the impulse toward uncoded self-expression. One of the most delightful moments in the *Life of Pope,* for example, is his dogged refusal to admit that the private, personal letter is anything but a formal and objective literary genre whose conventions are such that, given the depravity of human nature, almost anything *but* the actual truth about the writer can be disclosed in it. "Of [Pope's] social qualities," he writes,

> if an estimate be made from his letters, an opinion too favorable cannot easily be formed; they exhibit a perpetual and unclouded effulgence of general benevolence and particular fondness.

But actually, he continues,

> Very few can boast of hearts which they dare lay open to themselves, and of which, by whatever accident exposed, they do not shun a distinct and continued view; and certainly what we hide from ourselves we do not show to our friends.

The conclusion is inescapable: the personal letter is exactly the *least* sincere and natural of all the genres:

> There is, indeed, no transaction which offers stronger temptations to fallacy and sophistication than epistolary intercourse.

Which is to say that, paradoxically, there is no literary kind, not even the pastoral or the epitaph or the masque, whose conventions and rhetorical environment remove it further from "nature" or the artless than the personal letter. So much for appearances.

Again, writing to Mrs. Thrale in 1777, Johnson takes pains to explode the common myth that a genre like the letter, because it uses the conventions of sincerity and openness, is thus a vehicle of genuine self-disclosure. With the sort of sardonic irony possible only to those whose sense of genre is exquisitely developed, he tells Mrs. Thrale:

> In a man's letters, you know, Madam, his soul lies naked; his letters are only the mirror of his breast; whatever passes within him is shown undisguised in its natural process. Nothing is inverted, nothing distorted. You see systems in their elements, you discover actions in their motives.

And he goes on to stigmatize this plausible proposition as a "great truth sounded by the knowing to the ignorant, and so echoed by the ignorant to the knowing." Is he thinking perhaps of Henry Fielding, who had written in his Preface to Sarah Fielding's *Familiar Letters on David Simple* (1747):

> Those writings which are called letters may be divided into four classes. Under the first class may be ranged those letters, as well ancient as modern, which have been written by men who have filled up the principal characters on the stage of life upon great and memorable occasions. These have been always esteemed as the most valuable parts of history, as they are not only the most authentic memorials of facts, but as they serve greatly to illustrate the true character of the writer, and do in a manner introduce the person himself to our acquaintance.

Cant, Johnson would say. The Bishop of St. Asaph is another who has not thought about the matter enough. He once said to Johnson that "it appeared from Horace's writings that he was a cheerful, contented man. JOHNSON. 'We have no reason to believe that, my Lord. Are we to think Pope was happy, because he says so in his writings? We see in his writings what he wished the state of his mind to appear.' "

But the letter is only one of the genres whose operation makes "self-expression" either a ridiculous image or a dangerous and ultimately self-destructive illusion. The poem is another. As Johnson observes in the *Life of Pope,* "Poets do not always express their own thoughts." He illustrates this principle in the *Life of Thomson*:

> Savage, who lived much with Thomson, once told me he heard a lady remarking that she could gather from his works three parts of his character, that he was "a great lover, a great swimmer, and rigorously abstinent"; but, said Savage, he knows not any love but that of the sex; he was perhaps never in cold water in his life; and he indulges himself in all the luxury that comes within his reach.

Again, Johnson instructs Lord Monboddo, who, like Thomson's "lady," also entertains simplistic and sentimental notions about literary composition:

> It does not always follow . . . that a man who has written a good poem on an art has prac-

> ticed it. Philip Miller told me that in [John] Philips' *Cider: A Poem* all the precepts were just, and indeed better than in books written for the purpose of instructing, yet Philips had never made cider.

Clearly "making" books is an operation by itself.

What all this shows is that Johnson fully understands that the relation between poet and poem is not the relation between penitent and confessor: it is rather the relation between barrister and client. Regardless of his personal adhesions, the barrister is to collect, arrange, and express appropriately—which means convincingly—all the materials he can find which favor his client's position. As Johnson puts it when talking about the epitaph as a genre,

> The writer of an epitaph is not to be considered as saying nothing but what is strictly true. Allowance must be made for some degree of exaggerated praise. In lapidary inscriptions a man is not upon oath.

Nor is he any more "upon oath" in his temporary engagement with any other genre. No friend of idleness, Johnson at least would understand what Blake is getting at with "soft deceit" in

> Soft deceit and idleness,
> These are beauty's sweetest dress.

A good way to get a feeling for Johnson's rhetorical and legal sense of literature is to attend closely to the recorded activity of his mind on one given day of his life. The day I choose is Sunday, August 15, 1773: he and Boswell are starting to tour the Hebrides, and on August 15 they are in Edinburgh. Boswell spends the day introducing his "illustrious friend" to various Scottish intellectuals, and during the long day the talk weaves in and out of numerous topics. But it returns constantly to two: the law and literature. In the morning, as Boswell reports,

> We talked of the practice of the law. Sir William Forbes said he thought an honest lawyer should never undertake a cause [case] which he was satisfied was not a just one. "Sir," said Mr. Johnson, "a lawyer has no business with the justice or injustice of the cause which he undertakes. . . . The justice or injustice of the cause is to be decided by the judge. . . . Lawyers [like poets, we may observe] are a class of the community who, by study and experience, have acquired the art and power of arranging evidence and of applying to the points at issue what the law has settled."

To this Boswell listens admiringly, and he comments: "This was sound practical doctrine, and rationally repressed a too-refined scrupulosity of conscience."

After this conversation in the morning, Johnson and his Scottish admirers attend a sermon, thus undergoing another experience of literature employed in the service less of "sincerity" than of advocacy. The sermon over, conversation turns to James Beattie's *Essay on Truth* (1770), an attack on the skepticism of Hume, and now Johnson chooses to image the philosophic dialogue between Beattie and Hume as adversary proceedings. As he says: "Treating your adversary with respect is giving him an advantage to which he is not entitled. The greatest part of men cannot judge of reasoning, and are impressed by character; so that if you allow your adversary a respectable character, they will think that though you differ from him, you may be in the wrong."

Johnson next receives the historian William Robertson, who arrives after dinner for wine and conversation. The talk turns now to matters of eloquence and literature, and yet the legal theme persists as a sort of ground bass. Edmund Burke, says Johnson, in his literary character has "great variety of knowledge, store of imagery, copiousness of language." According to Boswell's account of the conversation, just forty seconds later Johnson is moved to say that "he believed Burke was intended for the law, but either had not money enough to follow it or had not diligence enough." This leads to talk about general powers of mind. As Boswell reports,

> Robertson said one had more judgment, another more imagination. JOHNSON. "No, Sir; it is only one man has more mind than another. He may direct it differently; he may by accident see the success of one kind of study and take a desire to excel in it. I am persuaded that had Sir Isaac Newton applied to poetry, he would have made a very fine epic poem. I could as easily apply to law as to tragic poetry." BOSWELL. "Yet, Sir, you *did* apply to tragic poetry, not to law." JOHNSON. "Because, Sir, I had not money to study law."

Of this virtual equation of advocacy with the arts of epic and tragedy—notice the suggestive word *made*—Jean Hagstrum has rightly said:

> In this lively interchange of opinion Johnson denies any special position to literature and

> removes from it the mystification that has often surrounded it. He relates it to the law, to mathematics, and to other coördinate disciplines. The assumption is that literature . . . is an austere and rigorous mental pursuit.[13]

This long day of conversation associating law, eloquence, intellectual characteristics, the choice of careers, epic, and tragedy ends with Johnson's memorable expression of good-natured contempt for Garrick's flamboyant style in tragic acting. It is a remark emphasizing artistic awareness and control that suitably brings this day to a close. Boswell says, "When I asked him, 'Would not you, Sir, start as Mr. Garrick does if you saw a ghost?' he answered, 'I hope not. If I did, I should frighten the ghost.' "

Making the proper *effect* on the audience is thus what literature is for. Johnson's concern about the affective operations of works of art regardless of the personal intention or actual state of mind of those who "make" them is reflected even in his nonliterary moments. Fanny Burney reports a conversation between Johnson and Henry Thrale on the not very momentous matter of Johnson's ambition to buy for his fireplace a jack, that is, a conspicuous clockwork engine for turning a roasting spit mechanically:

> JOHNSON. "I have some thoughts (with a profound gravity) of buying a jack, because I think a jack is some credit to a house."
> MR. THRALE. "Well, but you'll have a spit too?"
> JOHNSON. "No, Sir, no; that would be superfluous; for we shall never use it; if a jack is seen, a spit will be presumed!"

We could hardly find a more memorable formula for Johnson's shrewd rhetorical sense of literature: "If a jack is seen, a spit will be presumed." Which is to say that if emotion in a poem is seen, a common reader will naturally presume a cause of emotion in the writer of the poem, and that is all to the good. But a more sophisticated reader will know that actually there is no necessary cause of emotion in the writer: what is "in" him at the moment of writing is simply a mastery of techniques for imposing an illusion by the known means appropriate to the genre in which he is working. Actual emotion would be "superfluous," an encumbrance and a waste of time.

This acute awareness of necessary artifice constitutes one of the poles of Johnson's sense of literature. We must now consider the other pole, which we will find him embracing no less seriously. Our text now is his *Life of Milton,* especially the passage embodying the well-known denigration of *Lycidas.* And when considering Johnson on *Lycidas,* we must remember that his depreciation of that poem occurs within a context of critical praise of Milton's epic achievement so lavish and enthusiastic that it seems hardly to belong to the familiar Johnson at all. He concludes the *Life of Milton* and his appraisal of *Paradise Lost* in these terms: "[*Paradise Lost*] is not the greatest of heroic poems, only because it is not the first." That is, it is second only to the *Iliad*: it is superior to all others, including the *Odyssey,* the *Aeneid,* and the epics of the Italian Renaissance. This is a remarkable flux of enthusiasm from Johnson, the man who was constantly reminding his friends that nothing damaged an object or person so severely as excessive praise. We should always be mindful of this warm conclusion of the *Life of Milton* when we encounter his earlier scorn for Milton's republicanism, his "Turkish contempt of females," and his performance in pastoral elegy.

Johnson begins his critical scrutiny of *Lycidas* this way:

> One of the poems on which much praise has been bestowed ["much praise" of anything always triggers Johnson's skeptical contrariness] is *Lycidas,* of which the diction is harsh, the rhymes uncertain, and the numbers unpleasing.

So far Johnson's critical action has taken place well within the boundaries ordained by his sense of literature as rhetoric. Milton's language in *Lycidas* is too rare and remote ("harsh") to operate upon the normal reader. The rhymes occur unpredictably, with the result that the reader, naturally expecting rhyming at established, predictable intervals, is frustrated as he reads. And the versification likewise distresses the reader accustomed to the milder metrical surprises customary in Augustan poetry. Johnson maintains his affective focus through the next sentence:

> What beauty there is we must therefore seek in the sentiments and images.

We notice that Johnson's eye is still on that part of the process of literary transmission where rhetoric presides; that is, on the relation, necessarily social as well as artistic, between speaker and audience.

But with the next sentence everything changes. We are suddenly whisked out of the world of rhetoric altogether and thrust into quite another critical atmosphere. Sophistication suddenly yields to what must strike us as an almost unbelievable naïveté. For now Johnson attacks on the premise that a poem ought to embody the actual personal emotion of its contriver, presumably—and this is always an embarrassment to theories of self-expression—at the exact moment when the composition was begun:

> [*Lycidas*] is not to be considered as the effusion of real passion; for passion runs not after remote allusions and obscure opinions.

Having shifted the critical focus without warning, he goes on now to talk not about the effect of the work on the apprehender but about a totally different subject, the authenticity of the "passion" which, we are asked to assume with Johnson, gave rise to the poetic artifact in the first place:

> Passion plucks no berries from the myrtle and ivy, nor calls upon Arethuse and Mincius, nor tells of "rough satyrs and fauns with cloven heel."

What Johnson assumes here—and in a way which he would be quick to reprehend when in his "rhetorical" mood—is that actual passion was actually felt by the maker of the poem, and that this undeniable passion has leaked away or been invalidated by having been encoded injudiciously. Assuming that actual grief ought really to be present in the writer—that is, that the man and the poet are identical—he goes on to assert: "Where there is leisure for fiction there is little grief."

The premises underlying such formulations are close to the premises of Method acting, and in his rhetorical moments Johnson is quite ready to equate the actor with the writer or rhetor. When he is in his rhetorical posture he naturally feels nothing but disdain for the assumptions made by the eighteenth-century equivalent of the Method actor. As Boswell writes:

> Johnson . . . had thought more upon the subject of acting than might be generally supposed. Talking of it one day to Mr. [John Philip] Kemble, he said, "Are you, Sir, one of those enthusiasts who believe yourself transformed into the very character you represent?" Upon Mr. Kemble's answering that he never felt so strong a persuasion himself: "To be sure not, Sir (said Johnson); the thing is impossible. And if Garrick really believed himself to be that monster Richard the Third, he deserved to be hanged every time he performed it."

But what Johnson demands of the Milton of *Lycidas* is very like what he condemns in theatrical "enthusiasts"; he really expects Milton on this occasion to have behaved like a Method actor, to have felt real grief and to have embodied it in some presumably non-literary code.

On another, more important, occasion, Johnson likewise indicates that he will have no truck with the assumptions ultimately underlying theories of literary "sincerity." The occasion is the *Preface to Shakespeare,* where he advances hard-headed empirical arguments against the unities of time and place in the drama:

> The truth is that the spectators are always in their senses, and know, from the first act to the last, that the stage is only a stage, and that the players are only players. They come to hear a certain number of lines recited with just gesture and elegant modulation. . . . Where is the absurdity of allowing that space to represent first Athens, and then Sicily, which was always known to be neither Sicily nor Athens, but a modern theater?

But what he requires of *Lycidas* is that it cease being a poem, that is, a confessed theater of artifice, and become instead an actual utterance of instinctive grief, like a cry or a sob. In his other mood, he knows, of course, much better than this: when, for example, he wants to lament the death of Dr. Robert Levet, he betakes himself to the artificial mechanisms of stanza form and poetic diction, and he uses a meter deriving from previous poems rather than from the pulses of his heart. Likewise in his Prayers, where he stays as close as he can to convention so that he will have something meaningful to say. But with *Lycidas* he chooses to forget that a poem is only a poem, and that by definition the poet is a contriver of effects, not an experiencer of emotion. He chooses to forget that the reader of a poem, very like the spectator in the theater, comes to the poem to be given "a certain number of lines" contrived "with just gesture and elegant modulation."

After his inquiry into the validity of the grief felt by the man Milton before or perhaps during the composition of *Lycidas* (or maybe even during one of its revisions—which one?), an inquiry which strikes us as so un-shrewd as to embarrass any critic, he proceeds, oscillating now between his polar senses of literature as self-expression and actual record, on the one hand, and, on the other, of literature as rhetoric and necessary artifice:

> In this poem, there is no nature, for there is no truth.

This means two things at once: it means that considered as an act of self-expression the poem is too grossly a lie because we know that the grief it pretends to register was not felt by the author; and at the same time it means that the poem, considered as a piece of rhetoric, employs a code which strikes the reader as too "remote" from the artistically familiar to stimulate a conventional, and thus a literary or even "stock," response. Johnson's statement means these two things at once, but the simultaneousness of the meanings does not make them any more compatible. And he continues:

> There is no art, for there is nothing new.

He has now stepped wholly back into the critical world of rhetorical analysis, deploring the exhaustion of a genre. It is his powerful sense of the exhaustion of the genre of pastoral elegy that urges him to his next lively, perpetually delightful statement:

> Its form is that of a pastoral, easy, vulgar, and therefore disgusting; whatever images it can supply are long ago exhausted——

But as he goes on, he swings toward the other pole, momentarily abandoning objective questions of genre-exhaustion to probe again the matter of sincerity:

> ——and its inherent improbability always forces dissatisfaction on the mind.

The antithetic critical emphases, now on rhetoric, now on sincerity, interweave as Johnson proceeds, but we feel that what the interweaving produces is not of one texture: it is rather like a fabric made by weaving together the inorganic and the organic, steel filaments with silk:

> When Cowley tells of Hervey that they studied together, it is easy *to suppose* how much *he must miss* the companion of his labors and the partner of his discoveries; but what image of tenderness *can be excited by* these lines!
>
> We drove afield, and both together heard
> What time the grey fly winds her sultry horn,
> Batt'ning our flocks with the fresh dews of night.
>
> *We know that they never drove afield, and that they had no flocks to batten;* and though it be allowed that *the representation* may be allegorical, the true meaning is so uncertain and remote that *it is never sought* because *it cannot be known* when it is found [my emphases].

After another paragraph devoted to condemning "mythological imagery, such as a college easily supplies," Johnson implicitly discloses what has been troubling him all along: the poem, taken either as "expression" or artifact, can easily embolden impiety because it mingles pagan with Christian myth as if they are of equal efficacy:

> This poem has yet a grosser fault. With these trifling fictions [that is, "the puerilities of obsolete mythology"] are mingled the most awful and sacred truths, such as ought never to be polluted with such irreverent combinations. The shepherd . . . is now a feeder of sheep, and afterwards an ecclesiastical pastor, a superintendent of a Christian flock. Such equivocations are always unskillful; but here they are indecent, and at least approach to impiety, of which, however, I believe the writer not to have been conscious.

Of course Milton was not conscious of any risk of impiety in the way Johnson was, for Johnson was beleaguered by Freethinkers and aware that he did not have much company in his defense of the shaky Christian fortress against the assaults of critics like Voltaire and Hume. His sensitivity to the tiniest literary threats to orthodoxy is acute. In *Rambler* 140 he censures Milton's reference in *Samson Agonistes* to the patently fictive phoenix as if it were as real as the rest of his materials. And in *Rambler* 168 his objection to the "low" word *dunnest* in *Macbeth* I, v, 48–52 ("an epithet now seldom heard but in the stable") arises not from linguistic snobbery but from the fact that the word occurs only two lines before the word *heaven* used as a metaphor for God: its proximity thus might be thought to lower or trivialize a religious image associated with the obligations of conscience.

We see, then, that it is Johnson's sense of the subtle moral and theological damage *Lycidas* may do *to the reader* that provides the spring for the whole critique. In perceiving that his care is ultimately for the reader, we may say that what finally wins out is his sense that literature is primarily rhetoric. But this sense wins out only after a very dubious battle with a contradictory conception of what writing is.

Any lingering superstition that Johnson can be meaningfully described as, in some way, a "neo-classic" critic ("With him it is all white or black, right or wrong: there exists only one standard, which is the classical, that can win the approval of Samuel Johnson the Dictator"—L. Archer-Hind, 1925)[14] will be evaporated by a close scrutiny of his remarks on *Lycidas*, a poem in which "there is no art, for there is nothing new." It is precisely the neo-classic element in the poem that disgusts him.

To turn to the *Life of Prior* is to see clearly that Johnson is not a neo-classicist but an empiricist. And here again we experience his oscillations between the poles established by the rhetorical and the self-expressive conceptions of writing. He begins the critical part of the *Life of Prior* by stressing Prior's skill in rhetoric, his willingness to exercise himself in a variety of known styles, not all of which, obviously, can "naturally" be his "own," in the sense that a person is conceived to have one style in which he expresses himself most "sincerely." "Prior," Johnson says,

> has written with great variety, and his variety has made him popular. He has tried all styles, from the grotesque to the solemn, and has not so failed in any as to incur derision or disgrace.

After thus registering Prior's easy intercourse with a whole world of objective styles, and registering it with a high consciousness of the social contexts of rhetoric ("derision or disgrace"), Johnson focuses on Prior's performance within the various genres. And now of Prior's love poems he astonishes us by saying:

> In his amorous effusions he is less happy [than in his Tales]; for they are not dictated by nature or by passion, and have neither gallantry nor tenderness.

Surely what he is saying is that these love poems fail of the illusions of gallantry and tenderness *because* they are not dictated by actual or natural passion. As he points out, the artistic result of this deplorable insincerity is a plethora of neo-classical Venuses and Cupids, darts and quivers, all of which, he says, "is surely despicable." And, he continues, "even when [Prior] tries to act the lover without the help of gods or goddesses, his thoughts are unaffecting or remote." We are to deduce that the thoughts are unaffecting or remote because they issue from a convention rather than a unique, genuine personal occasion. Boswell reports: "Mrs. Thrale disputed with him on the merit of Prior. He attacked him powerfully; said he wrote of love like a man who had never felt it: his love verses were college verses." In the *Life of Hammond* Johnson puts the point a little differently, but no less clearly: "He that courts his mistress with Roman imagery deserves to lose her; for she may with good reason suspect his sincerity." Again, in the *Life of Cowley*, he argues that Petrarch's love poems are more valid than Cowley's because Petrarch was really a lover. As he says, "He that professes love ought to feel its power." Here his assumptions about literary sincerity are like those in the *Life of Waller*, where he takes Waller to task for writing panegyrics alike to Charles I, Cromwell, and Charles II in their seasons. It is impossible, says Johnson, to witness behavior like this "without some contempt and indignation."

But while he is implying that certain kinds of writing must be sincere to be valid, he is implying at the same time that there are certain poetic forms in which it is difficult for communication to take place. As we have seen, neo-classic pastoral is one such form. Another is the neo-classic love poem. A third is the religious lyric. Like the love song, it deals with a matter too elemental—or too embarrassing—to be embodied in poetry. As Johnson says in the *Life of Waller*:

> Contemplative piety, or the intercourse between God and the human soul, cannot be poetical. Man, admitted to implore the mercy of his Creator, and plead the merits of his Redeemer, is already in a higher state than poetry can confer.

Which is to say that literature is only literature after all. As Maurice Quinlan has perceived, "His general dislike of religious poetry . . . was based on his belief that verse was a too artful and therefore not a sincere means of addressing or praising the Deity."[15] But even here, where Johnson is finding certain poetic forms or rhetorical stances impossible, he is really focusing on the nature of the *passion* which presumably underlies and determines them. That the passion is genuine, even sacred, and not affected for purposes of artistic illusion he has no doubts.

These, then, are the poles defining the Johnsonian senses of literature. On the one hand, literature is akin to legal argument and implies a similar objective process: a canvass of received formulations and devices which will work—that is, persuade—because they are familiar. On the other hand, literature is what happens when genuine self-expression occurs: it emanates from a motive which shuns the familiar in favor of the unique, the "authentic." It could be argued, I suppose, that Johnson's relation to these poles is something like a coherent suspension (the word *tension* would come in nicely) rather than the contradictory oscillation I have suggested. But the trouble with such a view is that it would risk imposing a system (or, in Johnson's own skeptical term, a "scheme") on a literary sensibility which, for all its appearance of judiciousness, is really madly irrational, unsystematic, impulsive, and untidy. As a critic adrift without the neo-classic certainties, Johnson could be said to have been mad all his life, or at least not sober. Dr. Richard Brocklesby gives an acute interpretation of his predicament:

> His religion . . . made his extraordinary talents of mind continually at war with each other, so that in his later days his philosophy seemed to draw his mind one way, and his religion biassed him to the contrary. . . .[16]

This warfare seems to be the cause as it is the analogue of the battle between his two senses of literature—between the "philosophic," indeed worldly, sense that literature ought to be rhetorical, i.e., effective; and the ultimately religious sense that it ought to be, before all else, honest.

Of Johnson's conversation Oliver Goldsmith once said: "There is no arguing with Johnson; for when his pistol misses fire, he knocks you down with the butt end of it." The two Johnsonian senses of literature seem to me as far apart as the business end and the butt end of the pistol. His theory of literature can be said to achieve unity only in the sense that the mind busy at either pole applies to its tasks the same energy and raciness, brings to its inconsistent, pragmatic, empirical but nonetheless urgent business the same quality of honesty. It is an honesty which refuses to report contradictions as elements in a coherent system. "Inconsistencies cannot both be right; but, imputed to man, they may both be true."

And why shouldn't Johnson be inconsistent? He had no notion that two hundred years after his time he would be an "object of study." He is engaged in a day-by-day struggle to be plausible, intelligent, and faithful to the pressure of the moment, and the schemes and systems of a reason-worshiping world—especially those systems the future has devised for making literature a teachable, memorizable subject—are irrelevant to his activity. Perhaps they are irrelevant to ours.

NOTES

1. *James Joyce's Ulysses* (London, 1930; reprinted [Peregrine Books] 1963), p. 213, n. 1.
2. *Visible Words: A Study of Inscriptions in and as Books and Works of Art* (Cambridge, 1969), p. 2.
3. *Anatomy of Criticism* (Princeton, 1957), p. 97.
4. Review of John Wilson Croker's edition of Boswell's *Life of Johnson* in the *Edinburgh Review*, September, 1831. I have altered the order of Macaulay's strictures.
5. *Samuel Johnson* (London, 1955), p. vii.
6. *Johnson: Prose and Poetry* (London, 1957), p. 9.
7. *Spectator*, February 14, 1970, p. 210.
8. "The Double Tradition of Dr. Johnson," *ELH: A Journal of English Literary History*, XVIII (June, 1951), pp. 90–106.
9. " 'Pictures to the Mind': Johnson and Imagery," in *Johnson, Boswell, and Their Circle: Essays Presented to Lawrence Fitzroy Powell* (Oxford, 1965), p. 156.
10. *Johnson Agonistes and Other Essays* (Cambridge, 1946), p. 8.
11. Marshall Waingrow, ed., *The Correspondence and Other Papers of James Boswell relating to the Making of the Life of Johnson* (New York, 1969), p. 249.
12. E. L. McAdam, Jr., *Dr. Johnson and the English Law* (Syracuse, 1951), pp. 162–63.
13. *Samuel Johnson's Literary Criticism* (Minneapolis, 1952), p. 48.

14. Introduction to Johnson's *Lives of the Poets* (Everyman edition, 2 vols.: London, 1925), p. ix. Reprinted unchanged in 1946.

15. *Samuel Johnson: A Layman's Faith* (Madison, 1964), p. 196.

16. Waingrow, ed., *Correspondence*, p. 31.

Gerald W. Chapman

THE ORGANIC PREMISE IN BURKE'S THOUGHT

Burke means many things to many men. His prelacy in conservatism is commonly recognized; yet, as Harold Laski says, Burke also gives "deep comfort to men of liberal temper." [1] He is neoclassic, but also romantic; he is a nationalistic citizen of the world and a Tory Whig, a throwback to the seventeenth century and a seminal thinker for the nineteenth, an Irishman who reveals much that is best in the English mind, a busy-buzzing M.P. whom at least three respectable judges—Hazlitt, Arnold, and Leslie Stephen—have called the greatest prose writer in English literature. He is one of those great amphibious Englishmen, not quite liberal, not quite conservative, poetically open in his thinking, broadly practical in his poetry, whose diffuse and many-mansioned thought seems always implicit with a coherent and synthetic system which, however, is never achieved. Laski, after a cautious sizing-up from an opposing camp, pronounced Burke the greatest figure in the history of English politics, and sensed in his writings the latent but obscure presence of "a system which, even in its unfinished implications, is hardly less gigantic than that of Hobbes or Bentham." [2] Observing that Burke's emphasis on expediency is not, to his mind, a real "release from metaphysical inquiry," Laski went on to suggest "that what was needed in Burke's philosophy was the clear avowal of the metaphysic it implied." [3] One might like to agree, and to announce that at last, after a century and a half of mellowing, the metaphysical system is ready to be avowed, that one can drag it out of obscurity into the limelight and the applause of the world. But no. Pin Burke down at one point, and he dances away at another, in what Hazlitt called admiringly, his "circumgyrations." His thought is a master-solvent of antinomies—metaphysics and common sense, poetry and practicality, liberalism and conservatism, neoclassicism and romanticism, Christianity and pragmatism, to name but a few. Every digging after "Burke's system" to date has come up with a something bleached of the full meaning and value of the context—"Burke's sense." One is reminded of nothing so much as the affectionate frustration of a modern interpreter of Hooker:

> He is both a Humanist and a Protestant, both a Thomist and an Augustinian, both a rationalist and a traditionalist; he believed both in authority and freedom, both in consent and obligation, both in law and sovereignty, both in uniformity and toleration, both in Church and State, both in human nature and in the Fall.[4]

Something there seems to be about the characteristically English mind which is a living paradox. Possibly, somewhere in the depths of Burke's "experienced benignity" may have lain, or may lie, a system. To ignore a latent coherency and rational dependence in his *ad hoc* propositions is surely to miss a principal feature in his thought and a source of his quality. But the possibility of abstracting a

Reprinted by permission of the publishers from *Edmund Burke: The Practical Imagination* by Gerald W. Chapman, Cambridge, Mass.: Harvard University Press, system is small. One may suspect that dying in 1897, or in 1997, Burke would have bequeathed the same character of splendidly unfinished thought, and that for future as for present readers he will remain a living paradox.

More than any other single figure, he typifies the union, in his own thinking, of what are perhaps the two greatest achievements of English culture to date—its literary imagination, and its success in practical politics.

Certain specific drifts of his thought are, of course, evident. Burke is a key—if not the first great—exemplar of the *geschictlichen Sinn* in one of its forms—a mode of imaginative sensibility to the past, and to the present as continuous with the past, which has added a new dimension to human experience. It has not gone unappreciated. Coleridge perceived, and learned from Burke's historical sense. The strange and passionate Novalis remarked of the *Reflections*: "Burke has written a revolutionary book against the Revolution." [5] Later in the century Lord Acton, then only twenty-four, perceived the amazing subtlety and novelty of Burke's penetration of history even in the youthful *Essay Towards an Abridgement of English History*, which Burke turned off at twenty-eight. As there is very little doubt, he said, that "Burke was our greatest statesman," so if he had persisted, he "would have been the first of our historians." Acton admired Burke's freedom from pedantry, capacity for scholarship, vigor of experience—and his intelligent appreciation of the medieval:

> Several generations of men were still to follow, who were to derive their knowledge of the Middle Ages from the Introduction to Robertson's *Charles V*, to study ecclesiastical history in the pages of Gibbon, and to admire Hume as the prince of historians. At the age of thirty [*sic*], Burke proved himself superior to that system of prejudice and ignorance which was then universal, and which is not yet completely dissipated.[6]

Burke had the imagination to seize a contemplative order of history which was imperfectly conscious, obscurely felt, in the cultural life of his period, and which the life of his period sorely required. Clinging to his theory that romanticism and the recovery of medieval sympathies among Protestants were intimately related, Acton concluded, in a note near the end of his life: "History issues from the Romantic School. Piecing together what the Rev[olution] snapped. It hails from Burke, as Education from Helvetius, or Emancipation from the Quakers." [7] Accepting Acton's view, Herbert Butterfield could state as late as 1955 that Burke—instead of Sir Walter Scott—"exerted the presiding influence over the historical movement of the nineteenth century." [8] Certainly one cannot turn to Burke from the cunning succinctness of Hume, or the erudite analyses and massive ironic portraiture of Gibbon, without sensing that one is present somehow in a new world—superficially familiar, yet at bottom strangely altered and intense.

Burke is hardly a romantic medievalist, however. To understand his thought with reference to political developments in early nineteenth-century Germany, where his influence was enormous, is almost inevitably to short-change its neoclassic, eighteenth-century, practical, and characteristically English, spirit. Conservative followers in Germany—his friend Brandes, Rehburg and Möser—admired Burke's sense of living in history, and what appeared to them his aristocratic responsibility and attack upon natural law; romantic organicists—Novalis, Adam Müller, and Stein—abstracted from him an idealization of the medieval state to accommodate their own admiration of the ancient Holy Roman Empire. The common denominator of all, as of the publicist Gentz, was that they used Burke's name, example, and ideas to express their hatred of the French Revolution. Much of the dust raised by these men has settled upon Burke's reputation and obscured his full quality. As Reinhold Aris justly remarks: "When Burke praised the age of chivalry he was using a historic flourish to strengthen his position, but he would have been horrified at the idea that someone would use his arguments in order to revive feudalism." [9] In spirit, Burke is really more comparable with the half-romanticist, half-classicist Goethe, who called himself a "moderate liberal"—one who "tries, with the means at his command, to do as much good as ever he can, but is cautious of wishing to destroy immediately by fire and sword faults which are often inevitable. He endeavours by intelligent progress gradually to suppress public wrongs, without simultaneously spoiling just as much that is good by taking violent measures. He contents himself, in this always imperfect world, with what is good, until time and circumstances favour the attainment of something better."[10]

Burke approaches politics in a hardheaded and present-minded fashion, as well as with that quality of imagination which might be called romantic and historical; he turns upon hard fact, wherever it is to be met, a contemplative subtlety and concrete appreciativeness. He is committed to a *practical* approach to politics, and those features in his thought which link with the romantic and the medieval rise, as it were, as by-products of other and, one may think, equally significant features—his old-fashioned love of liberty, his classical discipline; his humanitarianism; his prosaic duties as an M.P.; his lawyer's respect for process, negotiation, and specific reason; his confidence that the natural law persists; his play of satire and concern for decorum; his confidence in common sense. As G. M. Young observes, classical criticism of every kind is "a form of public service," whose interest is not "to expatiate on the result, but to show how it was brought about, because by studying that you may be able to produce something like the same result yourself."[11] It asks "how to do it." Confronted with a novel occasion, Burke searches its texture of necessities, its correlation of component factors, for the course of action latently most effective, and for the "principles" or fruitful generalities which may be applied in future occasions to produce, or avoid, like effects, or which at least increase one's intelligence of probabilities. Hence his emphasis upon "common sense." Unwilling to jump with each fashionable evolution of opinion, Burke suspends commitment until the rear dimensions of experience and old partiality, various, multiform, and intricate, are brought up to be compared critically and, if possible, reconciled. He applies new knowledge wherever it throws a clear light, but would apply it in moderation—that is, intelligently—with due regard to its ascertained limits within the context of the familiar and the past. He tries not to be one of those whose accurate and logical reasonings bring them up against an impasse, or who, being too exquisite in their conjectures of the future, can only bring to the gross emergences of actuality an immense surprise. Common sense, restrained by the actual, is often blind to hypothetical goods and obstinate within the familiar, but it is also capable of great delicacy of adjustment to novel occasions. Unburdened with the vanity of hypostatized systems, it is more natively responsive to main events. It is the particular stage of intelligence in which the relation of imagined probabilities to a factual situation is clearly descried. There is much truth in Laski's conclusion that Burke "is destined doubtless to live rather as the author of some maxims that few statesmen will dare to forget than as the creator of a system";[12] he will live by the example of his moral elevation and by the perpetual relevance of his thought "in that middle ground between the facts and speculation [where] his supremacy is unapproached."[13] A man in politics, Burke said, must seek "the exactest detail of circumstances, guided by the surest general principles that are necessary to direct experiment and inquiry, in order again from those details to elicit principles, firm and luminous general principles, to direct a practical legislative proceeding."[14]

Even at those moments when, one feels, the vast seething stability of the organic commonwealth looms hauntingly in his imagination, Burke is less interested in painting his fancy of it, or in spinning a theory about it, than in deciding how, in all common sense, one had best behave, and in keeping his generalizations "useful" or "expedient." He is intent upon abstracting *axioms of practical method,* whose spirit W. E. H. Lecky has caught in so brilliant an epitome that one can do no better than to quote him at length:

> Government is obliged to discharge the most various functions, to aim at many distinct and sometimes inconsistent ends. It is the trustee and the guardian of the multifarious, complicated, fluctuating, and often conflicting interests of a highly composite and artificial society. The principle that tends towards one set of advantages impairs another. The remedies which apply to one set of dangers would, if not partially counteracted, produce another. The institutions which are admirably adapted to protect one class of interests, may be detrimental to another. It is only by constant adjustments, by checks and counterchecks, by various contrivances adapted to various needs, by compromises between competing interests, by continual modifications applied to changing circumstances, that a system is slowly formed which corresponds to the requirements and conditions of the country, discharges the greatest number of useful functions, and favours in their due proportion and degree the greatest number of distinct and often diverging inter-

> ests. The comparative prominence of different interests, tendencies, and dangers, must continually occupy the legislator, and he will often have to provide limitations and obstacles to the very tendency which he wishes to make the strongest in his legislation.[15]

Furthermore, though in his attacks upon "metapoliticians," upon natural rights, *raison*, and conventional contract theory, Burke seems, at times, as German romanticists thought, to desert natural law for a philosophy of organic process, yet the fact remains that every effort to draw his implicit assumptions into an organic focus sooner or later, after every partial success, will confront the obstinate and opaque presence of Nature.[16] View it from what perspective you will, Nature will not yield, will not take its place in the system. At point after point, Burke's magnificent intellect pushes beyond and shatters that Nature which had become a platitude of the salon, and that Nature which only named a comfortable emotion and was idolized either as a set of propositions or as a mythic image. One thinks of his grasp of American character and growth; his awareness of the mutual relatedness and interpenetrative correspondence of elements in the empire, in the constitution, in the "commonwealth" of Europe; his reaching out into the uniqueness of Indian life; his watching, horrified, the "unfolding of the Germ of Jacobinism." [17] Time after time, guided as it were by some intuitive navigation, his thinking breaks upon the mystery of organic process. Yet only to retract on other occasions. When all is said, an older idea of nature remains essential in his thought, a clear and distinct concept of "law" accessible to reason, including that "eternal, immutable law in which will and reason are the same." [18] His search for practical principles, for example, implies belief in a human nature more or less recurrent within actual political occasions, no matter how cautious he is about predicting the limits of its possibilities.

The whole tradition of English empiricism (not to mention Christian humanism) lies behind him; and in many ways, what was happening to English empiricism, generally speaking, explains the status of Nature in his thought.

Bacon, to take a representative figure, is an example of English empiricism in a dramatic early stage. His imagination is still active about first principles, still charged with grateful vision and jealous of its purity. He is busied with originating new strategy to solve the age-old conflicts of permanence and change. Bacon is dedicated to changing the world by learning the "causes," the limitations of possibility, of change in nature. His metaphysics pushes him constantly into the realm of hard fact and practical suggestion, but always in behalf of the larger aim—the "interpretation" of nature. The Nature that emerges in his thinking is significant of things to come in the way that the child is father of the man. A vision of things melts into subtle crevices of the mind and silently motivates thinking. Visions are causes in history. The Nature which Bacon isolates for thought, however exquisitely subtle and beautiful its movements, amounts in the end to a uniform texture of causes, fixed in a static eternity of relation. True, "in nature nothing really exists beside individual bodies," but within *the acts and changes* of individual bodies there is a "latent process" which is "perfectly continuous" though invisible in its causal texture, and this causal texture "embraces the unity of nature in substances the most unlike." [19] Thus, the causal texture (rational unity) of concrete change is the true object of philosophy, and hence the name "rational empiricism." Rational empiricism is the faith that all concrete particulars are generated by interlocking principles which, though very intricate and obscure, can nevertheless be inferred from their "effects." The empiricist always watches concrete "effects," discriminates abstract relations or connections among them, in hopes thereafter to direct his knowledge to the discovery, generation, or control of new "effects." This is true, for example, of Newton, who in the *Opticks* fatefully labels the up-and-down method "analysis" and "synthesis":

> By this way of analysis we may proceed from compounds to ingredients, and from motions to the forces producing them; and in general, from effects to their causes, and from particular causes to more general ones, till the argument end in the most general. This is the method of analysis: and the synthesis consists in assuming the causes discovered, and established as principles, and by them explaining the phenomena proceeding from them.[20]

But later empiricists, turning their thought to politics, art, morals, history, and psychology, wade into unsuspected deeps of metaphysical darkness, from which, generally speaking, English empiricism only begins to emerge, in its theoretical foundations, in the twentieth century (for example, in the works of Whitehead and Russell). For it is the paradox of rational empiricism, fully illustrated in Bacon's own arguments, that in shuttling back and forth between fact and law, selecting facts to form laws and forming laws to explain facts, it tends to complete itself in systems of greater and greater abstraction from the very "experience" it pronounces solely real. Later inheritors of empiricism, like Burke, faced the obstinate paradox that the more empirical they became the less rational, and the more rational the less empirical. They came to experience more than they could rationally account for. Thus they wrestled with insistent dualisms of permanence and change, unity and multeity, generality and particularity, abstraction and circumstance, ideality and fact. Facts had penumbras and fringe areas of meaning that defied classification and experimental rule, and unfolded vistas of startling complexity and nuance. One thinks of Montesquieu's idea of "spirit"; of Burke's response to the "great contexture of the mysterious whole"; of Sir Joshua Reynolds' trying to decide what "Idea" was; of Lord Kames' being haunted by "relations":

> Cause and effect, contiguity in time or in place, high and low, prior and posterior, resemblance, contrast, and a thousand other relations connect things together without end. Not a single thing appears solitary and altogether devoid of connection: the only difference is, that some are intimately connected, some more slightly, some near, some at a distance.[21]

One may also remember that Kames goes on puzzling until he describes a work of art as like an "organic system" in which it is required that "its parts be orderly arranged and mutually connected, bearing each of them a relation to the whole, some more intimate, some less, according to their destination."[22]

Partly from this love quarrel of the rational and empirical faculties, whose marriage Bacon sang with such hope, something indeed like "organicism" is born. The texture of enduring causes too subtle for sense and *a priori* reason is a haunting certainty which must somehow be reconciled with fleeting fact and value. The practical empiricist, like Burke, discovers his need for a self-legislated restraint of reason in order to continue "empirical." He resists the threat of mental inflation; he stops the dangerous spiral of his thinking, so as not to break his moorings in experience and perish in the thin air of conceptual abstraction. Thus, though he may not escape believing in a universal order of causes, he shies from it with reverent caution. He is committed to the theory of a strict, overarching rational order, but also to an exploration of actual existence for its latent and emergent circumstances. Nature yields something to History, and the chain of causes is submerged in the chain of events. He may grow resentful of other empiricists, trenchant intellects who cling fast to rational systems, to "metaphysics," without staying open to the nuances of actuality and practice which have a vital bearing on the case at hand. He becomes suspicious of their "reason," though he may learn from it, and cultivates in himself an imaginative sagacity which, turning outward upon current or past events, and being nourished by his general power of experiencing, searches for "practical" principles—which, "feeling the effect" (a constant motif in Burke), then grasps discrete circumstances into a unity expressive of latent particular relations.

In this reaction from the Nature of mechanico-materialism and its "philosophy of death,"[23] as Coleridge called it, Burke indeed approximated thinking of an "organic" character. A host of conditioning ideas like *continuity, the virtual, permanence* and *change, spirit, coalescence, interrelation,* and *vital character* threw open vistas of perception in his experience and suggested to him frequently that reality is like *this* and not like *that.* For example, it occurred to him as early as 1774, in the quiet of his notes, that the "real character" of the English parliament derived from its reconciliation of permanence and change, past and present: from the perpetuity of its actualization within novelties of the historical process.

> Nothing is more beautiful in the theory of parliaments than that principle of renovation, and union of permanence and change, that are happily mixed in their constitution:—that in all our changes we are never either wholly old or wholly new:—that there are enough of the old to preserve unbroken the traditionary chain of the maxims and policy of our ancestors, and the law and custom of parliament; and enough of the new to invigorate us and bring us to our true character, by being taken fresh from

> the mass of the people; and the whole, though mostly composed of the old members, have, notwithstanding, a new character, and may have the advantage of change without the imputation of inconstancy.[24]

The idea of *the organic* is implicit insofar as the term implies a recognition that reality presents itself as a fabric of actualizing possibilities requiring the human mind to make endless reconciliations of possession and emergence, each emergent as it is assimilated, modifying the whole tenor of the possessed, by an endless feeling attention to incursions of novelty, like showers of meteoric light within the atmosphere of the familiar. No example could seem clearer. Yet this reconciliation of permanence and change in English institutions Burke called "the pattern of nature." [25] The importance of this perpetual confrontation of tradition, law, or custom, with change, was that the more changes it withstood or negotiated, without loss of its essentials (principles, fundamentals), the more likely that its principles correspond with Nature, to which an empirical appeal is always open. Burke's organicism, therefore, is not thoroughgoing or exclusive; natural law is still a regulative notion; one has to do with an "organicism," so to speak, evolved and sustained on strictly empirical premises; one confronts another antinomy reconciled in practice when it might appear irreconcilable to logic.

Wherever one turns, the story is the same. There seems hardly a trend of Burke's thinking for which there is no countertrend almost equally essential, locked up in the mystery of his quality and not to be shaken out. Patterns of meaning break toward system, then stop, or fall away; ideas familiar enough at one point appear elsewhere suffused with uniqueness, in flickering degrees of intensity and in fresh relations; what is dark or tentative at one point is clarified at another, but rarely completed. Burke's organicism is a premise for experience, not a systematic philosophy of the kind which soared into fashion during the nineteenth century, after his death; it has affinities with Hooker instead of with Hegel, with Wordsworth instead of with Novalis, or in this century with Whitehead instead of, say, with Heidegger. It is practical and imaginatively open, and must be experienced many-sidedly as a spirit of his thought within *ad hoc* occasions.

One must search his particular judgments, then, not for a system, but for a characteristic activity, of which they are *ad hoc* expressions. The unity in Burke's thought would seem to lie in the character of his intelligence as it operates upon the life of his time. It is a mode of imaginative practicality which has appeared in English culture within many very different and often cross theoretical positions—a peculiar fusion of poetic conception and literary brilliance, ethical awareness and religious reverence, preference for concrete inquiry and compromise, common sense and sense of duty, and what Fox called a "reverse of selfishness." Burke was at once, for his time, its exemplar, and in some measure, by rendering it conscious, its creator.

NOTES

Since there exists no modern standard edition of Burke, I have used the one which I found most convenient: The Works of the Right Honourable Edmund Burke, *Bohn's British Classics, 8 vols. (London, 1854), cited hereafter by volume and page numbers only.*

1. Harold J. Laski, *Political Thought in England from Locke to Bentham* (London, 1944), p. 172.
2. *Ibid.*, pp. 213–214.
3. *Ibid.*, pp. 206–207.
4. Christopher Morris, *Political Thought in England: Tyndale to Hooker* (London, 1953), p. 197.
5. Reinhold Aris, *History of Political Thought in Germany from 1789 to 1815* (London, 1936), p. 270.
6. *The Rambler*, April 1858, quoted in *Essays on Church and State*, ed. Douglas Woodruff (London, 1952), pp. 455–456. Acton probably valued the many passages which suggest an organic grasp of history. For one example among many, it occurred to Burke as early as 1757 that Roman *municipia*, provinces, and colonies in early Britain, though "dissimilar parts," were however, "far from being discordant": "[They] united to make a firm and compact body, the motion of any member of which could only serve to confirm and establish the whole; and when time was given to this structure to coalesce and settle, it was found impossible to break any part of it from the empire.

"By degrees the several parts blended and softened into one another" (VI, 220).

7. Add. 5437, Acton Papers, Cambridge Univ. Library, quoted in Herbert Butterfield, *Man on His Past: the Study of the History of Historical Scholarship*, Wiles Lecture (Cambridge, Eng., 1955), p. 70. Cf. Alfred Cobban, *Edmund Burke and the Revolt Against the Eighteenth Century: A Study of the Political and Social Thinking of Burke, Wordsworth, Coleridge, and Southey* (London, 1929), pp. 258–268. However, on such grounds, one may fix responsibility for "romanticism" upon developments in the general culture of England as well as upon Burke.

Professor Wellek, watching it guide *The Rise of Literary History* (Chapel Hill, 1941), defines the "historical sense" as "a recognition of the individuality in its historical setting and an appreciation of the historical process into which individualities fit" (p. 48). In aesthetics, theory of language, and history of literature, he finds it characterized by a shift towards an irrational or emotionalistic psychology, the genetic approach working from origins, and the concept of internal, necessary evolution emergent from biological analogies (p. 94). Such "historism," according to Professor Wellek's later *A History of Modern Criticism* (New Haven, 1955), began in England, but (reaching an "impasse" by the end of the century) was taken over, deepened, and refined by German thinkers who better grasped its philosophical problems and potentialities, and in turn worked out modern organicism. The difficulty with his brilliant analysis is that it underplays national differences; it tends to assume the organic is the organic, wherever you find it; but his abstracted likeness conceals a gulf of practical assumption beneath. For example, each pole of an analogy has specific content, and what is implied by the use of an organic analogy depends very much upon the content, which is often national; what is meant by a "national mind," for example, is in good part determined by how one is accustomed to think of the human mind in fact. Burke warned ("Policy of the Allies," III, 456) against losing one's sense of the concrete in the rarefied air of abstract constructs: "our guides, the historians, who are to give us their true interpretation, are . . . often fonder of system than of truth."

The historical sense in England seems to have been a cultural diffusion, something like an aspect of national character very long in forming, not a professional code or a school of thought like history *en philosophe*. The oversimplification of national character is a pitfall for historians of ideas. For example, Cobban, who also paid a passing notice to the philosophic implications of biological analogies, with side glances at German thought, attributed Burke's concept of "growth" in the state to "the influence of Leibnitz's principle, only at the present day being challenged in the sciences, that Nature never makes jumps and nothing happens all at once. With Burke the idea penetrates to political thought" (*Revolt Against the Eighteenth Century*, p. 91). Yet in truth, the *feeling* for continuity and growth in the English commonwealth and "slow change, analogous in its gradualness and unconsciousness to the processes of vegetable nature, or better still to the mutations and conservation of heredity," reached expression in England well before Leibnitz was born—for example, among Elizabethan and Jacobean antiquaries. Butterfield, in *The Englishman and His History* (Cambridge, Eng., 1945) shows how far back the historical sense goes. He quotes from Spelman's *Of the Ancient Government of England*:

"To tell the Government of *England* under the old *Saxon* laws, seemeth a *Utopia* to us present; strange and uncouth; yet can there be no period assign'd, wherein either the frame of those laws was abolished or this of ours entertained; but as Day and Night creep insensibly, one upon the other, so also hath this Alteration grown upon us insensibly, every age altering something, and no age seeing more than what themselves are Actors in, nor thinking it to have been otherwise than as themselves discover it by the present" (Butterfield, p. 36).

Burke, who used and praised Spelman in his youthful abridgment of English history, (I, 414) also borrowed the idea, the phrasing, and the striking day-night image in "Thoughts on the Cause of the Present Discontents" (I, 7–8, 22). A few decades later, Coke was feeling something similar; and even using an "organic" metaphor: "Interroge pristinam generationem (for out of old fields must come the new corn) and diligently search out the judgements of our forefathers: and that for divers reasons . . . we are but of yesterday (and therefore had need of the wisdome of those that were before us) and had been ignorant (if we had not received light and knowledge from our forefathers) and our daies upon the earth are but as a shadow in respect of the old and auncient daies and times past, wherein the lawes have been by the wisdom of the most excellent men, in many successions of ages, by long and continuall experience (the triall of right and truth) fined and refined, which no one man (being of so short a time) albeit hee had in his head the wisdome of all the men in the world, in any one age could never have effected or attained unto" (Butterfield, p. 50).

Whatever the hap of ideas derived from it, a historical sense has continued a lively part of English culture *mutatis mutandis* from early times down to the present moment—for example, in the criticism of T. S. Eliot—and it very much interested Burke to clarify it and keep it alive for his own day. Not before Burke, however, did the historical sense rise to such brilliantly self-conscious expression as specifically part of the national character; perhaps Acton's remark has a virtual truth.

8. Butterfield, *Man on His Past*, p. 18. The list of great or near-great historians whose thought was shaped by Burke is astonishingly long—for example, Macaulay, Savigny, Guizot, Niebuhr, De Tocqueville, Lecky, Stephen.

9. Aris, *Thought in Germany*, p. 309.

10. *Ibid.*, p. 187.

11. *Last Essays* (London, 1950), pp. 107–108.

12. Laski, *Locke to Bentham*, p. 213.

13. *Ibid.*, p. 174.

14. "Thoughts on Scarcity," V, 87.

15. W. E. H. Lecky, *A History of England in the Eighteenth Century* (New York, 1882), III, 228.

16. The number of critics who associate Burke with "the organic" is legion; but very few try to explain what they mean by it. Understandably. "The organic," as it circulates in free usage, is a house of many mansions, a dark house with dark rooms, each with obscure passageways into all the others: one can walk from room to room, straining to see, and never know precisely where one is—except that one is inside a house. C. E. Vaughan is an exception: "Burke," *Studies in the History of Political Philosophy Before and After Rousseau*, ed. A. G. Little (Manchester, 1925), II, 26 ff. He finds in Burke "the whole theory of the State as an organism." Cf. Augustine Birrell, *Obiter Dicta*, 2nd Series (New York, 1887), pp. 188–190; Edward Dowden, *French Revolution and English Literature* (New York, 1897), p. 95; Ivor Brown, *English Political Theory*, 2nd edn. revised (London, 1929), pp. 71, 76; Sir Leslie Stephen, *History of English Thought in the Eighteenth Century*, 3rd edn. (New York, 1949), II, 230; F. J. C. Hearnshaw, "Edmund Burke," *The Social and Political Ideas of Some Representative Thinkers of the Revolutionary Era* (London, 1931), pp. 96–97; Lecky, *England in the Eighteenth Century*, pp. 224, 236. For dissenting or qualifying opinions, see Cobban, *Revolt Against the Eighteenth Century*, pp. 89–93; Lois Whitney, *Primitivism and the Idea of Progress in English Popular Literature of the Eighteenth Century* (Baltimore, 1934), pp. 200–201; Irving Babbitt, "Burke and the Moral Imagination," *Democracy and Leadership* (Cambridge, Mass., 1924), pp. 100–101.

17. Burke to Windham, Oct. 1793, *Correspondence of Edmund Burke and William Windham with Other Illustrative Letters from the Windham Papers in the British Museum*, ed. J. P. Gilson, Roxburghe Club (Cambridge, Eng., 1910), p. 72. Cf. p. 90.

18. "Reflections," II, 366.

19. *Novum Organum*, Bk. II, aphorisms ii–vi.

20. Quoted in E. A. Burtt, *The Metaphysical Foundations of Modern Physical Science* (New York, 1932), p. 221.

21. Henry Home (Lord Kames), *Elements of Criticism*, ed. and rev. J. R. Boyd (New York, 1866), p. 31.

22. *Ibid.*, p. 35. Burke apparently looked upon Kames's work as continuous with his own. When Malone, in 1789, suggested that Burke revise and enlarge *The Sublime and the Beautiful*, in the light of thirty years' experience, Burke answered that the train of his thinking had moved away from aesthetics—"such speculations"—and that, though the subject was new when he wrote, Lord Kames and others had "gone over the same ground" more recently. See James Prior, *Life of the Right Honourable Edmund Burke*, 5th edn. (London, 1854), p. 47; and Donald Cross Bryant, *Edmund Burke and His Literary Friends*, Washington University Studies, New Series, Language and Literature, No. 9 (December, 1939), p. 234. Kames's using the phrase "organic system" is notable. Most English thinkers at different periods who have been attracted to the organic premise, or interested in it—for example, Hobbes, Coleridge, Whitehead—are unable to accept all the implications that can be

made to flow from it without qualification. The "mechanical" is made to persist alongside. Whitehead, for example, described the metaphysical doctrine in *Science and the Modern World* (New York, 1925) as "the theory of organic mechanism" (ch. 5). Similarly, the "artificial animal" of the *Leviathan* is hardly more than emblematic; such hints of organicism as are present are rendered thoroughly mechanical by Hobbes's view of nature and man. Coleridge, though he hates anything smacking of the "mechanical," is not really an exception. His lifelong ambition to reconcile Plato and Aristotle in an indigenously English system amounts to little more, in one light, than his inability to rest in the notions taken in from contemporary German thought (Platonic, organic), his brilliantly felt and obscurely achieved ambition to make them jibe with the commonsensical, practical, and traditionary (Anglican, Aristotelian, and "mechanical-empirical").

23. Quoted in Basil Willey, "Thought," *The Character of England*, ed. Ernest Barker (Oxford, 1947), p. 335.

24. Notes for Speech on Amendment on the Address, Nov. 30, 1774, *Correspondence of the Right Honourable Edmund Burke*, ed. Charles William, Earl Fitzwilliam, and Sir Richard Bourke [1844], Rivington edn. (London, 1852), II, 415–416.

25. "Reflections" II, 307. On the persistence of Nature in his thought, see Willey, *The Eighteenth Century Background: Studies on the Idea of Nature in the Thought of the Period* (London, 1940), pp. 240–252, esp. 243–245.

Burke, like Kames, simply refuses to give up the idea of Nature as a fixed objective harmony in things, always the same; and yet one confronts the paradox that in seeking to conform his thinking with Nature, he turns to History. To follow the "nature" of a case apparently means to Burke to keep in view at one time as many operative factors as the evidence of the case admits or unfolds; at any given moment to allow diverse, and often conflicting factors to express their actuality within the case at hand, with a view to their reconciliation. By such a method, looking backward and forward, without pre-judged design, but holding to what one achieves stage after stage with a kind of prejudice, holding the achieved in stable suspension, acknowledging its first claim, its contingent option—by such a method, one is committed to the progressive definition of a *character* (a concrete "nature") and as new or unconsidered factors are encountered and reconciled, and old factors die out of relevance, of a *character* which sometimes may be said to "grow" in the complexity of its characterization, sometimes merely continues in the essence of what it was.

John L. Mahoney

ADDISON AND AKENSIDE: THE IMPACT OF PSYCHOLOGICAL CRITICISM ON EARLY ENGLISH ROMANTIC POETRY

The empirical psychology of John Locke was undoubtedly one of the dominating influences on later eighteenth-century English thought. Indeed, it would be safe to assert that the ideas of Locke's *Essay Concerning Human Understanding*, at least in their more general aspects, were familiar to the greater body of educated Englishmen during the century. The very tenor of his writings was bound to have a marked influence on a poet like Mark Akenside who, as can be seen in his poetry, was constantly interested in new methods of expression and new bases for his observations and feelings, and who to a greater extent than most poets of his

From the *British Journal of Aesthetics*, 6 (1966), 365–74. Reprinted by permission.

age revealed in his work those undercurrents of thought which were leading to a radically different kind of poetry. Modern scholarship affords ample evidence that Akenside employed Lockean ideas. The real problem, however, is how the ideas of Locke came to be employed by Akenside, since there is no direct evidence that he had read the actual writings of Locke; and his poetry, although embodying many of the doctrines of the philosopher, is notably lacking in the exact Lockean terminology. It is precisely this factor which leads one to the suspicion that Akenside became familiar with Locke's psychology chiefly through the critical writings of Joseph Addison. In his series of essays on the pleasures of the imagination in the *Spectator* which Akenside, by his own statement,[1] had read, Addison interpreted and, as it were, popularized many of Locke's ideas, particularly those ideas concerning the position of the imaginative faculty in the process of knowledge.

With this fact as a background the influence of Addison can be rather clearly traced in Akenside's poetry with its deeper probing into the powers of imagination, its emphasis on the superiority of the senses to the reasoning faculty, its appeal to taste as the final arbiter of excellence, and many other themes which are typical of later Romantic poetry. More important than the often frigid, non-melodious verse of Akenside is the fact that his poetry is a definite sign of the operation of the mechanistic psychology of the century on changing theories of imagination. In a sense Addison is part of the movement in English aesthetic theory, extending roughly from Hobbes through Alison, which sought to explain and evaluate literature on psychological rather than traditional or systematic grounds. It was a movement which concentrated less on the work of art itself but was concerned rather with such problems as why a work of art pleases and what are the particular qualities of the pleasure it gives. In considering Addison's *Spectator* papers on the imagination Clarence D. Thorpe contends that "whatever its imperfections, Addison's treatise carried weight, enough apparently to furnish decisive impetus to a movement that was completely to discredit the merely formalistic parts of neoclassicism and was to result in a new aesthetic for England. . . . It is no small thing surely that looking back now we are able to see that nearly all of the outstanding characteristics of the new empirical pragmatic criticism as it evolved in the eighteenth century were in one way or another anticipated by Addison." [2]

One of the most notable elements in the poetry of Akenside is the glorification of the imagination and of all forms of sense knowledge. It is at the root of the greater part of his poetry. To him the powers of imagination were unlimited and capable of providing all the pleasures necessary for full enjoyment of life. Indeed, sensation was the final basis of knowledge itself. Akenside's ultimate indebtedness was to Locke, but his immediate debt was to Addison, as can be seen not only in the ideas expressed in his poetry but in some cases even in the wording itself. In the first sentence of the Design of *The Pleasures of Imagination*, Akenside states his theme when he writes: "There are certain powers in human nature which seem to hold a middle ground between the organs of bodily sense and the faculties of moral perception. They have been call'd by a very general name, The Powers of Imagination"—a statement which is a reflection in both idea and language of Addison's contention that the pleasures of imagination "are not so gross as those of sense, nor so refined as those of understanding." [3] Addison's full exposition is seen in his contention that:

> The pleasures of the imagination, taken in the full extent, are not so gross as those of sense, nor so refined as those of understanding. The last are indeed more preferable, because they are founded on some new knowledge or improvement in the mind of man; yet it must be confessed that those of the imagination are as great and as transporting as the other. A beautiful prospect delights the soul as much as a demonstration; and a description in Homer has charmed more readers than a chapter in Aristotle. Besides, the pleasures of the imagination have this advantage over those of the understanding, that they are more obvious and easier to be acquired; it is but opening the eye, and the scene enters: the colours paint themselves on the fancy, with very little attention of thought or application of the mind of the beholder.[4]

Mark Akenside followed a similar pattern in his argument. Although he did not deny the value of the intellect, he stressed the superiority of the imagination and the ease with which the pleasures of the imagination may be acquired. Just as in the passage from Addison, the emphasis is on the "eye" and on the brightness of the imagination as opposed to the mysteries of the intellect:

For of all
The inhabitants of earth, to man alone
Creative Wisdom gave to lift his eye
To Truth's eternal measures; thence to frame
The sacred laws of action and of will,
Discerning justice from unequal deeds,
And temperance from folly. But beyond
This energy of Truth, whose dictates bind
Assenting Reason, the benignant Sire,
To deck the honour'd paths of just and good,
Has added bright Imagination's rays:
Where Virtue, rising from the awful depth
Of Truth's mysterious bosom, doth forsake
The unadourn'd condition of her birth;
And dress'd by Fancy in ten thousand hues,
Assumes a various feature, to attract,
With charms responsive to each gazer's eye,
The hearts of men.[5]

The sense of sight is the greatest of the senses, for it is the ultimate source of knowledge and the necessary requisite for enjoying the pleasures of imagination. Hence the poetry of Akenside emphasizes visual imagery to a much greater extent than imagery appealing to the other senses. He gives his own reasons when he writes:

Or shall I mention, where cœlestial truth
Her awful light discloses, to bestow
A more majestic pomp on beauty's frame?
For man loves knowledge, and the beams of truth
More welcome touch the understanding's eye,
Than all the blandishments of sound his ear,
Than all of taste his tongue.[6]

In this respect Akenside is very close to Addison's explanation that "our sight is the most perfect and most delightful of all our senses: it fills the mind with the largest variety of ideas, converses with its objects at the greatest distance, and continues the longest in action without being tired or satiated with its proper enjoyments." [7] In this stressing of the senses, and of sight in particular, one can observe one of the essential features of the empirical theory of knowledge. Many literary men of the early eighteenth century had too often retreated into the quiet realm of introspection where mind is supreme; they had too long neglected a world of light, colour and beauty.

The increasing attention of the later eighteenth century to the sense of sight gradually developed into an interest in all the senses, their processes and their inter-relationships. Addison stressed particularly the Lockean idea that all the senses act in harmony while subordinated to the sense of sight. His notion that imagination, delighting in the perceptions of one sense, is "capable of receiving a new satisfaction by the assistance of another sense" [8] is closely paralleled by Akenside's description of the increased delights in the sweets of one sense because of the concurrence of other senses. In illustrating the perfect working together of all the senses toward the final result in the act of perception, Addison wrote:

> As the fancy delights in everything that is great, strange or beautiful, and is still more pleased the more it finds of these perfections in the same objects, so it is capable of finding new satisfaction by the assistance of another sense. Thus any continued sound, as the music of birds, or a fall of water awakens every moment the mind of the beholder, and makes him more attentive to the several beauties of the place that lie before him. Thus if there arises a fragrancy of smells or perfumes, they heighten the pleasure of the imagination, and make even the colours and verdure of the landscape appear more agreeable; for the ideas of the senses recommend each other, and are pleasanter together than when they enter the mind separately.[9]

Akenside, ever the philosophic poet and ever the eclectic, versified this same idea of the harmony of the senses in several places in *The Pleasures of Imagination.* It is striking to observe in Akenside an attention to the "waves with sweeter music" and the "fragrance of the rose," features which had also attracted Addison in the passage where he refers to the beauty of sound in a "fall of water" and to the "fragrancy of smells."

The sweets of sense,
Do they not often with kind accession flow,
To raise harmonious Fancy's native charm?
So while we taste the fragrance of the rose
Glows not her blush the fairer? While we view
Amid the noontide walk a limpid rill
Gush through the trickling herbage, to the thirst
Of summer yielding the delicious draught
Of cool refreshment; o'er the mossy brink
Shines not the surface clearer, and the waves
With sweeter music as they flow? [10]

Another feature of Addison's treatment of the imagination which was of particular interest to Akenside, and which formed an essential part of his poetry, was his foundation of all knowledge on sensation and imagination. To Addison, as to Locke, the mind at birth was like white paper untouched by any impressions, and all knowledge made its entrance through the sense of sight. In the vein of Locke's empiricism he explicitly stated that knowledge has no further basis than ideas of sensation. These sensations are immediate, direct and clear, and after they have been passively received by the senses they are lodged in the imagination. There is no process of abstraction; the intellectual faculty does not educe those qualities which are predicable of the many and then construct the universal idea. Hence for Addison as a critic the imagination and imagery assumed positions of major importance in the consideration of the work of art. In his own words:

> We cannot indeed have a single image in the fancy that did not make its first entrance through the sight; but we have the power of retaining, altering, and compounding those images, which we have once received, into all the varieties of picture and vision that are most agreeable to the imagination; for by this faculty a man in a dungeon is capable of entertaining himself with scenes and landscapes more beautiful than can be found in the whole compass of nature.[11]

Likewise to Mark Akenside imagination was primarily a power of observation, and consequently a faculty of physical rather than intellectual experience. Following Addison's exposition which has just been quoted, he shows a mind closely dependent on the world of sensible objects for its ideas. A comparison of the following lines from *The Pleasures of Imagination* with the preceding passage from Addison will reveal a notable similarity in meaning between the words "retaining," "altering," "compounding" and "varieties" in the essay and "compares," "blends," "ranges" and "varies" in the poem. Akenside proceeded thus in his exposition of how the sensible objects of nature are operated on by the imagination:

> Thus at length
> Endow'd with all that nature can bestow,
> The child of Fancy oft in silence bends
> With conscious pride. From them he oft resolves
> To frame he knows not what excelling things
> And win he knows not what sublime regard
> Of praise and wonder.
>
> . . .
>
> Anon ten thousand shapes,
> Like spectres trooping to the wizard's call
> Flit swift before him.
>
> . . .
>
> With fixt gaze
> He marks the rising phantoms. Now compares
> Their different forms; now blends them, now divides,
> Enlarges, and extenuates by turns;
> Opposes, ranges in fantastic bands,
> And infinitely varies.[12]

It is fairly safe to assert that in the latter half of the eighteenth century poetry began to swing to the other end of the philosophic pendulum, from a poetry governed in large part by form with less insistence on feeling and emotion to one possessed of an invigorating conception of nature, of strong sentiment and of sensuous beauty. Despite the fact that moralizing and emphasis on conventional form and structures are still present to a certain extent in their poetry, Akenside and many of his associates were describing the sea, the sky and the mountains with a vigour and a beauty that were definitely not in the Neo-Classic tradition. In many of the passages which have been examined thus far naturalistic descriptions have become the most important sections of the poem, while the interest has shifted from the city to the country as the best exemplar of the beauties described. Addison had written that greatness, novelty and beauty were the chief sources of delight to the imagination. In discussing the quality of greatness he wrote of

> . . . the prospects of an open champaign country, a vast uncultivated desert, of huge heaps of mountains, high rocks and precipices, or a wide expanse of waters, where we are not struck with the novelty of beauty of the sight, but with that rude kind of magnificence. . . . Our imagination loves to be filled with an object, or to grasp at anything that is too big for its capacity. We are flung into a pleasing astonishment at such unbounded views, and feel a delightful stillness and amazement in the soul at the apprehension of them.[13]

Akenside, who adopted the Addisonian categories of greatness, novelty and beauty as the chief stimuli of the imagination, followed Addison's description of the quality of greatness as he wrote:

> Who that, from Alpine heights, his labouring eye
> Shoots round the wide horizon, to survey,

> Nilus or Ganges rolling his bright wave
> Through mountains, plains, through empires black with shade,
> And continents of sand, will turn his gaze
> To mark the windings of a scanty rill
> That murmurs at his feet? The high-born soul
> Disdains to rest her heaven-aspiring wing
> Beneath its native quarry. Tired of earth
> And this diurnal scene, she springs aloft
> Through fields of air, pursues the flying storm,
> Rides on the vollied lightning through the heavens,
> Or, yoked with whirlwinds in the northern blast.
> Sweeps the long tract of day.[14]

As a poet Akenside was particularly interested in Locke's theory of primary and secondary qualities as interpreted by Addison because it attributed to the individual not only the ability to understand external nature but, in his own lesser way, even to create it. To summarize the theory briefly, in bodies there are primary qualities of which a body cannot be deprived, such as solidity, extension, figure and mobility; and there are secondary qualities, such as colours, sounds and tastes, which in truth are nothing in the objects themselves but powers to produce sensations in us by means of their primary qualities. In *The Spectator* Addison stated this theory and its source directly:

> I have here supposed that my reader is acquainted with that great modern discovery, which is at present universally acknowledged by all inquirers into natural philosophy, namely, that light and colours, as apprehended by the imagination, are only ideas in the mind and not qualities that have any existence in matter . . . if the English reader would see the notion expanded at large, he may find it in the eighth chapter of the second book of Mr. Locke's Essay on Human Understanding.[15]

The theory is developed much more fully in another section. Speaking of God, Addison said:

> In the last place, he has made everything that is beautiful in all other objects appear more beautiful, that he might render the whole Creation more gay and delightful. He has given everything about us the power of raising an agreeable idea in the imagination. . . . Things would make but a poor appearance to the eye if we saw them only in their proper figures and motions. And what can we assign for their exciting in us many of those ideas which are different from anything that exists in the objects themselves (for such are light and colours) were it not to add supernumerary ornaments to the universe and make it more agreeable to the imagination? We are everywhere entertained with pleasing shows and apparitions, we discover imaginary glories in the heavens and in the earth, and see some of the visionary beauty poured out over the whole creation.[16]

The significance of such a theory for poets and poetry is seen in Akenside's expression of it in *The Pleasures of Imagination,* in which he was clearly indebted to Addison not only for the main ideas of the theory but even for much of the terminology employed. The close relation of the wording in Addison and Akenside is remarkable. Akenside also argued that primary qualities belong to nature, while secondary qualities come from the mind of man. In reality God has given poets and all men the power to find in nature more than actually exists there. Men have creative powers which may be used to enhance the beauties of nature. Speaking of external nature and its relation to the minds of men, he proceeded thus:

> Wherefore then her form
> So exquisitely fair? her breath perfum'd
> With such ethereal sweetness? whence her voice
> The impassion'd soul? and whence the robes of light
> Which thus invest her with more lively pomp
> Than Fancy can describe? Whence but from Thee,
> O source divine of ever-flowing love
> And thy unmeasur'd goodness? Not content
> With every food of life to nourish men,
> By kind illusions of the wondering sense,
> Thou mak'st all Nature beauty to his eye,
> Or music to his ear.[17]

In examining more closely the relationship of the last two passages one notes that both present a question as to the source of the secondary qualities of matter, "ideas which are different from anything that exists in the objects themselves." Addison is concerned with secondary qualities such as colours; Akenside is concerned with shape, smell, sound and colours. Both contend that God has given men these powers, and their phrasing is noticeably similar. Addison writes that "he has made everything that is beautiful in all other objects appear beautiful, that he might render the whole Creation more gay and delightful." In similar fashion Akenside writes: "Thou mak'st all Nature beauty to his eye / Or music to his ear." To Addison the secondary qualities are "pleasing shows and apparitions"; to Akenside they are "kind illusions." The similarity of ideas and expressions in this and many other passages leads one to the conclusion that Akenside was in large measure influenced by Addison in framing his poem *The Pleasures of Imagination.*

Probably the most interesting of all the influences of Addison's psychological criticism on Akenside and on early Romantic poetry was his interpretation of Locke's theory of the association of ideas. Akenside would be particularly interested in such a theory because of the uses to which it could be put in his poetry. According to this theory, widely discussed in the seventeenth and eighteenth centuries, ideas which are apparently unrelated gain a particular relation in the minds of some men so that they are always associated, and when one enters the imagination, all its related ideas appear with it. Hence a poet employing this theory might use one idea and call up an entire scene in the imagination of his reader. Addison's expression of the association of ideas proceeds in the following manner:

> We may observe, that any single circumstances of what we have formerly seen often raises up a whole scene of imagery, and awakens numberless ideas that before slept in the imagination; such a particular smell or colour is able to fill the mind, on a sudden, with the picture of the fields or gardens where we first met with it and to bring up into view all the variety of images that once attended it. Our imagination takes the hint, and leads unexpectedly into cities or theatres, plains or meadows.[18]

The same notion of the chance combination of ideas and the power of one idea to summon up all its associates is clearly exemplified in Akenside's lines:

> For when the different images of things
> By chance combin'd, have struck th' attentive
> soul
> With deeper impulse, or connected long,
> Have drawn her frequent eye; howe'er distinct
> Th' external scenes, yet oft the ideas gain
> From that conjunction an external tie,
> And sympathy unbroken. Let the mind
> Recall one partner of the various league,
> Immediate, lo! the firm confederates rise.[19]

This brief survey reveals how deeply Mark Akenside was influenced by Addison's essays, specifically by those which were popularizations of Locke's psychology. Far more important than Akenside himself, however, is the fact that operating under this influence he seems to be typical of a growing attitude fostered in large part by Addison's psychological criticism. In Akenside and later poets the emphasis gradually began to shift from the rather objective view of poetry held in the early part of the century to a subjective view which attributed new and more exciting powers to man himself. The imagination slowly came to the forefront, and its supremacy in the scheme of things was generally held to be a fact. As a result, poets often became aware that nature was something to which they could respond without accusations of juvenility. Instead of viewing nature from a distance poets gradually began to feel a greater nearness to, even a unity with, nature. Akenside, despite his lack of great artistic talent, is in a sense typical of the new ideas and changes in poetry and aesthetics. In this entire scheme Joseph Addison and the psychological approach to criticism played a vital role.

NOTES

1. Mark Akenside, *The Pleasures of Imagination.* "*The Design.*" All citations to Akenside in my text are to *The Poetical Works of Mark Akenside*, ed. Charles Cowden Clarke (Edinburgh: William P. Nimmo, 1868).

2. Clarence D. Thorpe, "Addison's Contributions to Criticism," *The Seventeenth Century* (Stanford University Press, 1951), p. 324.

3. *The Spectator*, 411.

4. *The Spectator*, 411.

5. Mark Akenside, *The Pleasures of Imagination*, I, 537–54.

6. *The Pleasures of Imagination*, II, 97–103.

7. *The Spectator*, 411.

8. *The Spectator*, 412.

9. *The Spectator*, 412.

10. *The Pleasures of Imagination*, II, 73–83.

11. *The Spectator*, 411.

12. *The Pleasures of Imagination*, III, 373–95.

13. *The Spectator*, 412.

14. *The Pleasures of Imagination*, I, 177–90.

15. *The Spectator*, 413.

16. *The Spectator*, 413.

17. *The Pleasures of Imagination*, III, 481–93.

18. *The Spectator*, 417.

19. *The Pleasures of Imagination*, III, 313–20.

Patricia M. Spacks

VISION AND MEANING IN EIGHTEENTH-CENTURY POETRY

AN INTRODUCTION TO THE PROBLEM

The work of all five poets considered in this study is extremely uneven. In the case of Christopher Smart, a romantic explanation is tempting: he wrote great poetry when liberated by madness from the restriction of contemporary convention, weaker verse when constrained by the established forms of his time. Yet this account is by no means fully satisfactory when one recalls, for example, the expert manipulation of "poetic diction" in *A Song to David;* and no explanation of even equivalent accuracy readily presents itself for Thomson, Collins, Gray and Cowper.

Whatever the causes of the great inequality of accomplishment these poets display, one of its effects has surely been to encourage critical underestimation of their capacities. The reader who remembers *The Task* or *The Seasons* as a tedious experience is unlikely to be aware of the superb passages such poems contain. An experience of Gray's extreme artifice may make it difficult to catch his note of plangency; Collins's weaker personifications may merge in the mind with Joyce Kilmer's, making it difficult to perceive the visionary energy of his best ones. To reveal the sources of both artistic strength and weakness in these five poets of sensibility, I have chosen to study them in the light of the critical theory and the poetic conventions of their time and with reference to the expectations of the modern close reader. These poets offer a complex set of aesthetic problems, solutions, partial solutions and failures which may be analyzed by concentrating on the meaning in their work of the visual and the visionary.

Samuel Johnson's *Dictionary* (1755) offers four definitions of *vision,* two having to do with perception of the visible, two with more complicated sorts of "seeing."

1. Sight; the faculty of seeing.
2. The act of seeing.
3. A supernatural appearance; a spectre; a phantom.
4. A dream; something shown in a dream. A dream happens to a sleeping, a vision may happen to a waking man. A dream is supposed natural, a vision miraculous; but they are confounded.

The last two definitions describe modes of perceptual expansion: perception of the ordinarily invisible (the supernatural) or the construction of new appearances which may be supposed miraculous, but may also be, like dreams, products of the imagination. *Visionary,* in Johnson's account of it, means, "Imaginary; not real; perceived by the imagination only."

These two notions of vision, as a power for perceiving reality or for expanding it, are both of vital importance to eighteenth-century poetry. The century's critics and poets alike believed that visual imagery was essential to effective poetry.[1] Ernest Tuveson has suggested the similarity between the poetic and the philosophic preoccupation with the imagery of sight: "From the nature of the mind as described by Locke, we could expect a new poetry to be highly visual in nature, for the faculty of sight came to monopolize the analysis of intellectual activity. Since ideas are images, since even complex ideas are multiple pictures, and since understanding itself is a form of perception, the visual and the intellectual would tend to become amalgamated."[2] Distinct visual imagery was almost a defining characteristic of successful poetry in most genres.

But what is the precise nature of "distinct visual imagery"? When Thomson and Cowper describe the same phenomena in roughly similar vocabularies, their descriptions are strikingly different. Here are two accounts of a snowfall, one first included in the second edition of "Winter" (1726; but quoted here in its slightly altered final form), the other from *The Task,* almost sixty years later:

> Through the hushed air the whitening shower
> descends.

Reprinted by permission of the publishers from *The Poetry of Vision: Five Eighteenth-Century Poets* by Patricia Meyer Spacks, Cambridge, Mass.: Harvard University Press,

At first thin-wavering; till at last the flakes
Fall broad and wide and fast, dimming the day
With a continual flow. The cherished fields
Put on their winter-robe of purest white.
'Tis brightness all; save where the new snow
melts
Along the mazy current. Low the woods
Bow their hoar head; and, ere the languid sun
Faint from the west emits his evening ray,
Earth's universal face, deep-hid and chill,
Is one wild dazzling waste, that buries wide
The works of man.
("Winter," ll. 229–240)

Tomorrow brings a change, a total change!
Which even now, though silently perform'd,
And slowly, and by most unfelt, the face
Of universal nature undergoes.
Fast falls a fleecy show'r: the downy flakes,
Descending, and with never-ceasing lapse,
Softly alighting upon all below,
Assimilate all objects. Earth receives
Gladly the thick'ning mantle; and the green
And tender blade, that fear'd the chilling blast,
Escapes unhurt beneath so warm a veil.
(*The Task,* IV, 322–332)

Thomson's description is far more specific than Cowper's. His scene is concretely imagined: fields, river, woods; Cowper, on the other hand, describes the snow as covering generalized "earth" or even more generalized "universal nature." Thomson wishes us to "see" the process by which the snowfall gains in intensity; and he calls our attention to various modes of contrast: between the "dimming" effect of falling snow and the "brightness" of the snow fallen; similarly, between the dimness of "the languid sun" and the dazzle of the snow on which it shines. There is contrast, too, in the snow's function as adornment for the fields and as burden for the woods; visual contrast between the snow's whiteness and the blackness of its melting on the water; the contrast of paradox in "dazzling waste," with its implication of beauty in desolation.

Cowper considers contrast of a larger and simpler sort. Before the storm description, several lines (311–321) stress the variations in color perceptible in the scene before it is enveloped by snow. The significant contrast is between variety and uniformity; consequently, the emphasis of the account of the actual snowfall is necessarily on its singleness of effect. This snow does not vary its rate of fall; "never-ceasing," inexorable, it simply covers all. There is no need to specify what it envelops; the point is that it "assimilate[s] *all* objects."

Cowper, unlike Thomson, here deals directly with feeling, both sensuous and emotional. Initially, we learn that the snowfall is "by most unfelt." By the end of the passage, we know that earth receives her mantle "gladly," and that snow protects "the green / and tender blade" which has "feared" the winter's blasts. Feeling is asserted to reside in nature rather than in man, although the reader must feel as well: the "total change" described commands his wonder. The coming of the snow testifies to the benevolence of the natural order; we imagine the "face" of an abstract "universal nature" instead of contemplating the concrete (although of course very general) "universal face" of earth. Thomson's pattern of contrasts and of kinships between the human and natural world (implied by his reference to "cherished fields" and to "the works of man" as well as by his figurative language) is more intricate than Cowper's; and the difference in the patterns, the meanings, which interest the two poets determines the differences in their visual presentations of a natural event.

In their general import, the two descriptions exemplify significant facts about the poets although these selections are by no means fully characteristic. It would be easy to find examples in which Cowper is far more specific than Thomson; such examples are probably more abundant than their opposites. Yet Thomson tends to concern himself with certain sorts of *meaning* (particularly about relations between the human and non-human aspects of nature); Cowper is interested in aesthetic patternings and in certain kinds of *feeling.* For him meaning often derives from feeling; for Thomson the process is usually reversed.

Poetic descriptions must be controlled by poetic purpose; for this reason, to analyze the significance of visual imagery, or its nature, becomes in practice a complex problem. For the modern critic, two large issues seem particularly vital: what exactly is the nature of the "poetry of vision" in the eighteenth century; and to what purposes was the reliance on imagery turned?

The century's criticism elaborately explored the first of these questions. As Meyer Abrams has demonstrated,[3] the notion that poetry, like the other arts, was essentially imitative, offering a reflection of the real world, remained dominant throughout the eighteenth century. If the function of the poet was to imitate, to offer a "speaking picture," one test of his achievement might be the accuracy with which he rendered the world around him. The better the poet, the more exact his reproduction of external reality. "Description is the great test of a Poet's imagination," Hugh Blair pronounced; "and always distinguishes an original from a second-rate Genius." [4] His contemporary Richard Hurd, on the other hand, asserted flatly that "the poet has a world of his own, where experience has less to do, than consistent imagination," that poets, "lyars by profession," do not expect to have their lies believed, but demand imaginative participation from their readers: "a legend, a tale, a tradition, a rumour, a superstition; in short, any thing is enough to be the basis of their air-form'd *visions*." [5]

The diametrically opposed views of poetry implied by these quotations define the poles of eighteenth-century critical theory. It may be safely said that virtually all literary critics and rhetoricians agreed on the fundamental importance of imagery to poetry—although Edmund Burke had serious doubts whether it functioned as most critics supposed, to create images in the mind of the reader. But about the nature of the good poetic image there were divergent views. Many critics assumed that the mark of the good image is its precise, accurate, vivid rendering of actuality.[6] They were pleased to find the accuracy of the naturalist or of the close observer of human nature made part of verse; they admired Thomson for the quality of his recorded observation. The vision they valued was almost scientific in its precision; they might praise a poet by saying that he showed the reader nature as if through a microscope.

Some, on the other hand, valued Hurd's "air-form'd *visions*" far more highly than any rendition of actuality. Although they might agree that precision and vividness of imagery were admirable, they would define the poetic gift as the power to bring such precision and vividness to the creation of compelling fictions. To them images could seem the very *substance* of poetry, not its decoration; they might admire Collins. And they could even—like Hurd—suggest an actual divorce between the world of the poet and that of normal human experience.

Both these views are stated or implied by critics writing throughout the century, all of whom admired the "visual" in poetry, many of whom felt that the "visual" included a great deal. A single critic might praise accuracy in the rendition of images and extravagance in their conception. The vision which records actuality and the visions which can hardly be distinguished from dreams alike provided material for the images which were widely agreed to be a distinguishing mark of poetry. As early as 1757, Robert Andrews rejected the distinction between kinds of images, explaining that the mere existence of images was far more important than their nature, and that imagery is improperly called "one constituent of Poetry . . . ; for it is rather its essence, its soul and body: so that the more or less any composition has of it, it has the more or less of Poetry." [7]

Ideas about the value of different kinds of imagery reflected psychological as well as aesthetic theory. John Locke's description of perception, which of course stresses the importance of the visual, also emphasizes that only a few primary qualities actually reside in the perceived object; the more numerous secondary qualities, such as color, are products of the perceiver's mind.[8] Physical vision, then, cannot offer a precise picture of objective reality; poetic records of that vision are one degree farther removed from reality. Memory and selection have intervened even before the translation of sense impression into language; no matter how "objective" the poet, how concerned to convey the actual appearance of an object, he must offer in his images an impression of his own imaginative processes. So the kind of poetic vision which perceives and describes a tree and the kind which perceives and describes a centaur, or a figure of Revenge, are at opposite ends of a single continuum: the difference between them is one of degree of imaginative activity—more importantly than of kind.

The poet, then, must necessarily alter actuality in his very attempts to render it. But to what extent are his alterations valuable in themselves? For Locke, the specifically poetic resource of "wit" ("lying most in the assemblage of ideas, and putting them together with quickness and variety, wherein can be found any resemblance or congruity, thereby to make up pleasant pictures and agreeable visions in the fancy") was inferior in value to "judgment," the discriminating power which separates ideas on the basis of even the most minute difference, in order "to avoid being misled by similitude." The procedures of judgment, Locke points out, are quite opposed to "metaphor and allusion; wherein for the most part lies that entertainment and pleasantry of wit, which strikes so lively on the fancy, and therefore is so acceptable to all people, because its beauty appears at first sight, and there is required no labour of thought to examine what truth or reason there is in it."[9] Although the "agreeable visions" that wit produces combine ideas gained from experience, they bear little essential relation to actuality; figurative language should be scorned because the reader's response to it, instantaneous and nonintellectual, is likely to mislead him.

But the Lockean psychology did not necessarily imply Locke's value judgments. Joseph Addison quoted approvingly the entire passage from Locke on wit, judgment and metaphor,[10] but his own emphasis in dealing with such matters was far less dominated by the assumption that intellectual activity is the most significant mode of human endeavor.[11] Indeed, he suggested that the poet's deviations from actuality are not only inevitable but valuable, that the poet's selectivity or heightening is vital to the achieved aesthetic effect.[12] It is an easy step from this view to the notion of the poet as maker, his achievements analogous to God's, and Addison took that step, thus placing himself in a long and eloquent critical tradition.[13] The talent of affecting the imagination, he wrote, "has something in it like creation; it bestows a kind of existence, and draws up to the reader's view several objects which are not to be found in being. It makes additions to nature, and gives a greater variety to God's works."[14] Earlier, he had supplied a longer statement of the same arguments:

> But because the mind of man requires something more perfect in matter, than what it finds there, and can never meet with any sight in Nature which sufficiently answers its highest ideas of pleasantness; or, in other words, because the imagination can fancy to itself things more great, strange, or beautiful, than the eye ever saw, and is still sensible of some defect in what it has seen; on this account it is the part of the poet to humour the imagination in its own notions, by mending and perfecting Nature where he describes a reality, and by adding greater beauties than are put together in Nature, where he describes a fiction.[15]

According to Addison's own statement, all pleasures of the imagination are based on the sight; no image can be created which does not originate in the physical faculty of vision. But here he points out explicitly the limitations of the eye in comparison with the creative imagination, which can produce visions "more great, strange, or beautiful than the eye ever saw." If the power of sight is in one sense the poet's most important resource, it can also be his limitation if he fails to go beyond it. The poet must, Addison clearly states, exceed verisimilitude even when he describes reality; he must also be willing to deal in fictions.

The progression of ideas which led Addison to his exalted sense of the poet's function was highly characteristic of his contemporaries and even of much later eighteenth-century critics. A mass of the century's literary criticism appears to rest on the assumption that poetic excellence in the creation of images consists in the accuracy with which the external world is reproduced, but such a view was formulated most often in some limited context of concentration on a particular poet, a specific rhetorical device, a special sort of imagery. Critics who concerned themselves with broader aesthetic issues more characteristically echoed Addison in expressing their awareness that the best poet was not the photographer—to use a modern metaphor—but the creative painter. "The mind of man possesses a sort of creative power of its own," wrote Burke,[16] and the fact was widely recognized. William Duff's *Essay on Original Genius* (1767) declares, "That Imagination is the quality of all others most essentially requisite to the existence of Genius, will universally be acknowledged,"[17] before offering a detailed account of the activities of imagination. The power of the poet's imagination, Duff explains, is directly associated with the intensity of his feeling, yet poetic images are finally self-justifying, through their beauty, their variety, or their wonder; they prove the presence of imagination and nothing more is required of them.[18] The most impassioned defences of imagination in the eighteenth century tend to resolve themselves in this way. Although they may explore the processes through which images are created—concluding, characteristically, that the poet's emotions are the vital source of his fictions[19]—they most frequently demand of an image only that it vividly exist. Yet one may also note some tendency to assume that the most "creative" images, the ones based on imaginative visions far removed from actuality, must be the best.

The eighteenth-century emphasis on the value of imagery—whatever, precisely, *imagery* might mean—seems in some ways singularly modern: our own era has its exponents of image-making as the supreme poetic skill. "It is better to present one Image in a lifetime than to produce voluminous works," wrote Ezra Pound.[20] "Imagist" poetry, to be sure, is radically different from that of Thomson and Gray, contemporaries admired by the earlier glorifiers of imagery. The discursive elements in the work of the eighteenth-century poets seem now at least as conspicuous as the images, which can no longer excite rapturous praise. Something in the structure and texture of much eighteenth-century verse obscures the vividness and clarity of imagery which it may actually possess; if the value placed on imagery accords with certain modern theories, the *use* made of it bears little relation to twentieth-century theory or practice.

This brings us back to the second fundamental critical problem about the eighteenth-century poetry of vision, a question never fully raised by eighteenth-century critics: to what purposes was the reliance on imagery turned? The question was not asked, clearly, because in general terms its answer was assumed: imagery was instrumental in fulfilling the functions of poetry, to please and to instruct. Perhaps the most eloquent statement of this general view comes from Thomas Sprat, who provides a strong defense of "the Ornaments of speaking" in the very act of rejecting them. He explains the original function of such ornaments: "to describe *Goodness, Honesty, Obedience*; in larger, fairer, and more moving Images: to represent *Truth*, cloth'd with Bodies; and to bring *Knowledge* back again to our very senses, from whence it was at first deriv'd to our understandings." [21] Now, however, Sprat continues, language, like men, is grown corrupt, and figurative language no longer serves its proper purpose; for this reason it must be abandoned. Fénelon, on the other hand, with a similar conviction of "the Degeneracy of human Nature," believes that imagery provides the only feasible means for keeping a reader's attention on abstract truth.[22] The end of poetry was agreed to be moral instruction; imagery provided a method for achieving this end.

This large and vague assumption about the place of imagery, however, is hardly adequate to explain its various functions in the actual poetry of the eighteenth century, or its various sorts of success and failure. In 1817, some appropriate questions about function were finally asked—fully answered, rather, without being asked. Samuel Taylor Coleridge, in *Biographia Literaria*, wrote, that images, however beautiful or accurate, "do not of themselves characterize the poet. They become proofs of original genius only as far as they are modified by a predominant passion; or by associated thoughts or images awakened by that passion; or when they have the effect of reducing multitude to unity, or succession to an instant; or lastly, when a human and intellectual life is transferred to them from the poet's own spirit." [23]

In an obvious sense, Coleridge's remarks seem a logical development of ideas articulated from the mid-eighteenth century on, not a departure from them. Bishop Lowth and William Duff had both recognized the connection between the poet's passions and the nature of the images he creates. Yet the shift of emphasis in Coleridge's view exemplifies a real imaginative leap. There is a vast gap between the idea that interesting images are the product of passion and the idea that they are interesting *only as far as* they manifest passion or otherwise reveal the poet's mental and emotional processes. The specific functions here accorded to imagery are all aspects of the poet's self-revelation; the new specificity about the meaning of images is part of a new interest in the individual poet and the way in which his essential being is exposed by his utterance. It is, in short, a single manifestation of the general shift Professor Abrams has documented from the imitative to the expressive theory of poetry.

Yet it would be a mistake to assume the poetry waited upon criticism before becoming, in fact, "expressive." When one examines the poetry of the eighteenth century, after its opening two decades, that poetry which Coleridge, on the whole, patronized or actively scorned, it seems surprising that the view Coleridge articulated had to wait so long to find statement: it is implied by a good deal of the verse written between 1726 and 1800, which manipulates imagery in elaborate ways to express emotion or to stimulate "associated thoughts" or to sum up and emblemize multiplicity or to convey the "spirit" of its author. Nor does this paraphrase of Coleridge fully sum up the variety of purposes for which imagery was actually employed, the ways in which it was used. Of course poetic practice is characteristically in advance of theory. Wordsworth, Coleridge, Pound or Wallace Stevens may define, explain and justify his own experimentation, but less theoretically oriented poets have frequently created a quiet revolution long before the critics realized it had taken place. The eighteenth century was, in some respects, a period of such revolution; its nature, and its relation to contemporary critical theory, are well worth examining.

We know a good deal already about the language of eighteenth-century poetry. It has long been recognized that the poets of the 1700's did not, after all, rely solely on an artificial diction which they suddenly discarded in 1798. Pope's varied vocabulary has been analyzed and admired, his use of classic rhetorical devices examined; the philosophical implications of periphrasis have been explored; we know about the rhetoric of the heroic couplet; we have statistical records of the proportions of nouns, verbs and adjectives and of the most frequently used words in the major poetry of the age. But the "sublime" poets, the poets of sensibility, have been less thoroughly examined than their predecessors in the "line of wit," and many questions about poetic language in use remain yet unanswered. What is the relation between critical theory and poetic practice in regard to imagery? "Judgment begets the strength and structure, and Fancy begets the ornaments of a Poem," wrote Thomas Hobbes, in 1650.[24] A hundred years later, "fancy" had assumed a far more important place in critical theory; but what was its place in the actual writing of poetry? Why, when rhetorical theory insisted so emphatically on the poetic value of conciseness, was the actual poetry determinedly diffuse? (One recalls Dr. Johnson's account of reading aloud only every other line of *The Seasons,* to the admiration of the listeners.) To what extent could the poetic language of the eighteenth century be individualized? Such questions can only be answered by close examination of the century's poetry, in conjunction with its theory.

As subjects for such examination Thomson, Collins, Gray, Smart and Cowper seem obvious choices. All wrote the poetry of sensibility; although all except Collins made at least brief excursions into satire, their main poetic achievement is verse of feeling and description. They span three-quarters of the century, from 1726 (when "Winter," the first part of *The Seasons,* was published) to 1799, when Cowper wrote "The Castaway." All rely heavily on visual imagery of one sort or another: cursory examination of their work suggests that Thomson and Cowper depend more on recorded visions of reality; Collins and Smart are "visionary" in a fashion which may take them far from actuality; Gray occupies a middle position, employing both kinds of vision. Through analysis of these poets' work, and of the theoretical commentary which surrounded it, we may hope to discover a good deal of what, precisely, comprised the "visual" in eighteenth-century poetry; how vision was expressed and used; how adequate the poetic resources of the period were to its poetic aims.

NOTES

1. For treatment of various aspects of the connection between sight and aesthetic theory, see M. H. Abrams, *The Mirror and the Lamp: Romantic Theory and the Critical Tradition* (New York: Norton, 1958); Jean Hagstrum, *The Sister Arts: The Tradition of Literary Pictorialism and English Poetry from Dryden to Gray* (Chicago: University of Chicago Press, 1958); Kenneth MacLean, *John Locke and English Literature of the Eighteenth Century* (New Haven: Yale University Press, 1936); Gordon McKenzie, *Critical Responsiveness: A Study of the Psychological Current in Later Eighteenth-Century Criticism* (Berkeley: University of California Press, 1949); Ernest Lee Tuveson, *The Imagination As a Means of Grace: Locke and the Aesthetics of Romanticism* (Berkeley: University of California Press, 1960); A. S. P. Woodhouse, "The Poetry of Collins Reconsidered," *From Sensibility to Romanticism,* ed. F. W. Hilles and Harold Bloom (New York: Oxford University Press, 1965), pp. 93–137. Marjorie Nicolson, in *Newton Demands the Muse* (Princeton: Princeton University Press, 1946), documents the importance for poetry of Newton's theories of vision. In the light of the work that has been done already, I shall suggest only sketchily the extent of the various critical utterances about sight as it relates to poetic theory and practice.

2. Tuveson, *Imagination As a Means of Grace,* pp. 72–73.

3. In Abrams, *The Mirror and the Lamp,* passim.

4. Blair adds that the inferior sort of writer is

vague in his descriptions: "we apprehend the object described very indistinctly. Whereas, a true Poet makes us imagine that we see it before our eyes; he catches the distinguishing features; he gives it the colours of life and reality; he places it in such a light, that a Painter could copy after him." Both quotations come from *Lectures on Rhetoric and Belles Lettres*, 2 vols. (Dublin, 1783), II, 371.

5. Richard Hurd, *Letters on Chivalry and Romance, with the Third Elizabethan Dialogue*, ed. Edith J. Morley (London: Henry Frowde, 1911), p. 138; pp. 135–136.

6. For Joseph Warton's statement of this view see pp. 14–15 of Spacks, *The Poetry of Vision*.

7. Robert Andrews, "A Hint to British Poets," *Eidyllia* (Edinburgh, 1757), p. 4; quoted by Ralph Cohen, *The Art of Discrimination: Thomson's* The Seasons *and the Language of Criticism* (Berkeley: University of California Press, 1964), p. 164.

8. "There is nothing like our ideas existing in the bodies themselves. They are, in the bodies we denominate from them, only a power to produce those sensations in us." *An Essay Concerning Human Understanding*, ed. Alexander Campbell Fraser, 2 vols. (Oxford, 1894), I, 173.

9. Ibid., I, 203.

10. *Spectator* #62 (11 May 1711); *The Spectator*, with introduction and notes by George A. Aitken, 8 vols. (London, 1898), I, 320.

11. "Our sight is the most perfect and most delightful of all our senses. . . . It is this sense which furnishes the imagination with its ideas; so that by the pleasures of the imagination or fancy (which I shall use promiscuously) I here mean such as arise from visible objects, either when we have them actually in our view, or when we call up their ideas into our minds. . . . We cannot indeed have a single image in the fancy that did not make its first entrance through the sight; but we have the power of retaining, altering and compounding those images which we have once received into all the varieties of picture and vision that are most agreeable to the imagination." *Spectator* #411 (21 June 1712); VI, 72–73. Although Addison here closely paraphrases Locke, he does not directly compare the pleasures of the imagination to those of the judgment, so does not suggest that they are inferior. The *value* of close imaginative approximations of actuality, as opposed to the more fantastic creations of the fancy, yet remained to be discussed.

12. "Words, when well chosen, have so great a force in them, that a description often gives us more lively ideas than the sight of things themselves. . . . As we look on any object our idea of it is, perhaps, made up of two or three simple ideas; but when the poet represents it, he may either give us a more complex idea of it, or only raise in us such ideas as are most apt to affect the imagination." *Spectator* #416 (27 June 1712); VI, 100–101.

13. The view that the poet was an almost divine creator was current in the sixteenth century. George Puttenham's comparison of the poet to God is well-known: "A Poet is as much to say as a maker . . . Such as (by way of resemblance and reuerently) we may say of God: who without any truell to his diuine imagination, made all the world of nought, nor also by any paterne or mould as the Platonicks with their Idees do phantastically suppose. Euen so the very Poet makes and contriues out of his owne braine both the verse and matter of his poeme, and not by any foreine copie or example." Puttenham goes on to point out that the poet may also be justly termed an imitator, "because he can expresse the true and liuely of euery thing is set before him, and which he taketh in hand to describe," but there is no doubt which of his functions is more important. See *The Art of English Poesie* (London, 1589), p. 1. J. C. Scaliger makes a similar point, emphasizing the superiority of poetry to those arts which involve merely accurate representation. Poetry, he says, is all-inclusive, "excelling those other arts, that while they . . . represent things just as they are, in some sense like a speaking picture, the poet depicts quite another sort of nature, and a variety of fortunes; in fact, by so doing, he transforms himself almost into a second deity." See Marvin T. Herrick, "The Place of Rhetoric in Poetic Theory," *The Quarterly Journal of Speech*, XXXIV (1948), 5. Francis Bacon points out that the special function of poetry is to remake the world closer to the heart's desire: "POESIE is a part of Learning in measure of words for the most part restrained: but in all other points extremely licensed: and doth truly referre to the Imagination: which beeing not tyed to the Lawes of Matter; may at pleasure ioyne that which Nature hath seuered: & seuer that which Nature hath ioyned. . . . The vse of this FAINED HISTORIE, hath beene to giue some shadowe of satisfaction to the minde of Man in those points,

wherein the Nature of things doth denie it, the world being in proportion inferiour to the soule: by reason whereof there is agreeable to the spirit of Man, a more ample Greatnesse, a more exact Goodnesse; and a more absolute varietie than can bee found in the Nature of things." See *Of the Proficience and Aduancement of Learning, Diuine and Humane* (London, 1605), Bk. II, fol. 17v.

These sixteenth- and seventeenth-century statements rest on the assumption that the "enlarging" vision, creator of a sort of super-reality more closely related to the supernatural than to the natural, is vital poetic equipment; the vision which simply provides a record of reality is, from this point of view, far less significant. Such assumptions did not disappear in the eighteenth century, although they might coexist with apparently contradictory ones. Professor Abrams explains how the idea of pleasure as the proper purpose of poetry involved awareness of the need to go beyond imitation. The result was that figurative language achieved great importance as a poetic device. "Certain kinds of deviation from literal language came to be treated, not as ornaments, or veiled reflections of truth, but as instances of the poetic creation of another world, peopled with its own manner of non-empirical beings." *Mirror and the Lamp*, p. 288.

14. *Spectator* #421 (3 July 1712); VI, 122.

15. *Spectator* #418 (30 June 1712); VI, 110.

16. Edmund Burke, "Introduction on Taste," *A Philosophical Enquiry into the Origin of Our Ideas of the Sublime and Beautiful*, ed. J. T. Boulton (London: Routledge and Kegan Paul, 1958), p. 16.

17. William Duff, *An Essay on Original Genius* (London, 1767), p. 6.

18. Later Duff defines explicitly the role of the *poet's* imagination: "A Poet . . . who is possessed of original Genius, feels in the strongest manner every impression made upon the mind, by the influence of external objects on the sense, or by reflection on those ideas which are treasured up in the repository of the memory, and is consequently qualified to express the vivacity and strength of his own feelings. If we suppose a person endued with this quality to describe real objects and scenes, such as are either immediately present to his senses, or recent in his remembrance; he will paint them in such vivid colours, and with so many picturesque circumstances, as to convey the same lively and fervid ideas to the mind of the Reader, which possessed and filled the imagination of the Author. If we suppose him to describe unreal objects or scenes, such as exist not in nature, but may be supposed to exist, he will present to us a succession of them equally various and wonderful, the mere creation of his own fancy; and by the strength of his representation, will give to an illusion all the force and efficacy of a reality." Pp. 159–160.

19. Bishop Lowth, for example, points out that the poet who is moved by an experience or an appearance necessarily transforms it in describing it. "The mind, with whatever passion it be agitated, remains fixed upon the object that excited it; and while it is earnest to display it, is not satisfied with a plain and exact description; but adopts one agreeable to its own sensations, splendid or gloomy, jocund or unpleasant. For the passions are naturally inclined to amplification; they wonderfully magnify and exaggerate whatever dwells upon the mind, and labour to express it in animated, bold, and magnificent terms." Robert Lowth, *Lectures on the Sacred Poetry of the Hebrews*, tr. G. Gregory, 2 vols. (London, 1787), I, 309. (First published, in Latin, 1753).

20. "A Retrospect," *Literary Essays of Ezra Pound*, ed. T. S. Eliot (London: Faber and Faber, 1954), p. 4.

21. Thomas Sprat, *The History of the Royal-Society of London, for the Improving of Natural Knowledge* (London, 1667), p. 112.

22. "Ever since the Fall of ADAM, Men's Thoughts have been so low and grovelling, that they are unattentive to moral Truths; and can scarce conceive any thing but what affects their Senses. In this consists the Degeneracy of human Nature. People grow soon weary of Contemplation: Intellectual Ideas do not strike their Imagination: so that we must use sensible and familiar Images to support their Attention, and convey abstracted Truths to their Minds." François de Salignac de la Mothe Fénelon, *Dialogues Concerning Eloquence*, tr. William Stevenson (London, 1722), p. 80. John Dennis offered a slightly different justification for poetic emphasis on visual imagery, maintaining that the sense of sight "is a sence that the Poet ought chiefly to entertain; because it contributes more than any other to the exciting of strong Passion." *The Advancement and Reformation of Modern Poetry* (London, 1701), p. 186.

23. Samuel Taylor Coleridge, *Biographia Liter-*

aria; or Biographical Sketches of My Literary Life and Opinions, 2 vols. (London, 1817), 17–18.

24. Hobbes's Answer to Davenant's Preface to "Gondibert," *Critical Essays of the Seventeenth Century,* ed. J. E. Spingarn, 3 vols. (Oxford: Oxford University Press, 1908–09), II, 59.

Oliver F. Sigworth

AN INTRODUCTION TO ENGLISH AESTHETICS AND CRITICISM, 1660–1800

Everyone now recognizes that we cannot look at literary criticism during the eighteenth century as a smoothly flowing neoclassic river rudely interrupted about midcourse by the tumultuous rapids of romanticism. Even in Dryden's criticism appear eddies which seem to forecast Wordsworth, and the "Preface" to the *Lyrical Ballads* reads at some points more like Samuel Johnson than Samuel Coleridge. The complications of the passage from late seventeenth- to early nineteenth-century criticism do not encourage brevity of exposition, nor do they facilitate lucidity. What is brief may be lucid yet misleading; what is both lucid and accurate can hardly be brief in telling the story. The reader must therefore be warned that the tale is not so simple as I make it seem, that every statement needs qualification, and that, on the whole, it is best to read the texts themselves.

Since any discussion of the criticism of the period 1660 to 1800 is inevitably saddled with the term "neoclassicism," it is as well to begin with an effort to determine what that term, as applied to criticism and nothing else, may mean. As used in the history of criticism in English the term is not a very happy one, for it implies that about 1660, when Charles II and his court came over from France, there was a sharp break with what all literary historians agree to call the English renaissance, and that thereafter criticism wandered, stultified, in dry and cold deserts until rescued by Wordsworth and Coleridge with the warm, life-giving waters of romanticism. Whether it was a rescue or not may be debated, but if it was a rescue it was not from any critical doctrines suddenly introduced or from a *critical* temper in any way new in 1660.

This is not the occasion to review the history of literary criticism in England from the beginnings to 1660, but we must recognize that such critical documents as exist before our period are generally what we can only call "neoclassic"—that is, they look back to the literary ideas of Plato, Aristotle, Cicero, Quintilian, and Horace, but they look back to these doctrines through the spyglass of Italian and French criticism of the sixteenth century. They are renaissance critical documents; but the renaissance itself was, after all, a revival of the classical ideal, at least as far as criticism is concerned, and no matter how exuberant English poetry of the sixteenth century was, when educated men talked about poetry they talked in "neoclassic" terms. Sidney's treatise is a case in point, a methodical and delightfully written exposition of the ideas received in the best literary society; even his famous remark about the old song of Percy and Douglas which so moved his heart concludes, in the best neoclassic tone, "what would it worke trymmed in the gorgeous eloquence of *Pindar*?"—a matter of regret, obviously, that "some blinde Crouder" had not sufficiently studied the classics. It is probably a pity that Ben Jonson never wrote a full-blown art of poetry, for there, judging from *Timber,* we would have seen neoclassicism as full-fledged as in Dryden, though probably somewhat less adaptable.

"Neoclassic" criticism, then, is renaissance criti-

From *Criticism and Aesthetics 1660–1800,* Essays collected and edited by Oliver F. Sigworth.

cism, and from the standpoint of the history of criticism, the early eighteenth century is the last phase of the renaissance. To the classic canon, however, one extremely important addition must be noted in the rediscovery of Longinus, whose *On the Sublime,* though available since 1554, was not much heeded on the Continent until Boileau's translation of 1674, after which it swept France and especially England like a winter tempest. One could argue that the Longinian storm heralded the spring of romanticism, and it may be necessary to do so, but the fact is also that his precepts (which, it must be emphasized, are rhetorical and have in themselves nothing to do with that "natural sublime" so beloved of the later eighteenth century) were quickly accommodated to the existing body of criticism, giving it added range but not yet disturbing the calm center.

The calm center of renaissance, or neoclassic, criticism looked at literature in a way quite foreign to the romantic, or modern, sensibility. At its basis was the conception of genre, of literary works existing as species in an absolute sense. The reality of a literary work and the means by which it imitated the "clear, unchanged, and universal light" of "nature" was a function of its partaking of the species which it singly represented. Just as we think of the "catness" of a cat as a function of the fact that it is representative of the feline species, so to renaissance critics the "tragicness" of a tragedy was a function of its relation to the Aristotelian norms as supplemented by Vida, Castelvetro, and others. There was considerable argument about the nature of the genres, and in favor of extending their scope or of establishing new ones, but the conception of genre as a basis for criticism was not seriously challenged.

For confirmation of this view one need again look no further than Sidney. After the few preliminary words by Sprat about language, the present collection begins with the Earl of Mulgrave's "Essay," modeled ultimately of course on Horace though directly on Boileau, a summary of conventional renaissance poetics with which Sidney would have been quite in accord. Mulgrave is clearly familiar, whether at first or second hand does not matter, with sixteenth- and seventeenth-century Continental criticism and with critical traditions extending back ultimately to the Ancients. He is telling us what every cultivated man believed, though sometimes, as with Dryden, diffidently. What the cultivated man believed was that when a poet sat down to write he might indeed look in his heart and might indeed be inspired by a divine afflatus, for the idea that neoclassic precepts required only rigid adherence to "rules" cannot be supported by any document known to me. Even Aristotle had at one point equated the poet and the madman, and Scaliger in the mid-sixteenth century had spoken of the poet transforming himself "almost into a second Deity, fashioning images of things that are not, as well as images more beautiful than life of those things which are." What we now call "imagination" or "inspiration" was never discounted, but such inspiration emerged *in form* as a tragedy, or comedy, or ode, pastoral, elegy, satire, or epistle; if the inspiration were really divine, it might emerge as a *poem,* that is, an epic, which Dryden, voicing the standard doctrine, called "undoubtedly the greatest work which the soul of man is capable to perform." That Fielding had to write of the novel in terms of epic and history is explained by this fact; there existed neither a critical tradition into which the novel could fit, nor a vocabulary with which to describe it. The fact may also indicate at least one reason why the novel as a form did not flower until after neoclassic criticism as we are speaking of it had begun to lose its power.

Each genre had its own rules, its own (to use the proper term) *decorum,* which extended not only to matters of form and structure—matters which we still vaguely understand—but also to verse and diction. Nobody in the eighteenth century understood the precepts of decorum or observed them so diligently as Pope, and in the works of no other poet in English is there to be found a wider variety or more precise use of the various poetic dictions. In his use of couplet form and diction in relation to the poetic species he was assaying, Pope attempted and achieved the "correctness" which William Walsh, the mentor of his youth, told him was the attribute of no earlier poet in English. It is, aside from the very conception itself of genre, the eighteenth-century critics' conception of diction which most sets them apart from us. The fact that the greatest critic of the century, Samuel Johnson, still propounded the precepts relating to diction while no longer much interesting himself in questions of genre shows not only the pervasiveness of the idea, but shows also that the idea did, in fact, outlive its time, for during the latter part of Johnson's life criticism was becoming "modern."

It is, of course, a ridiculous oversimplification to speak of only two strains of criticism during any period as complex as the one we are considering. Something, however, did happen which leads us from the genre criticism of Mulgrave to the *aesthetics* of the later century (esthetics: a term which I shall use to mean the discussion of art in terms of feeling), and we can discuss the ideas to which this change may be attributed as a second strain of criticism during the eighteenth century. The term "esthetics," in fact, was invented during the 1750s, though it was invented by Baumgarten in Germany and did not appear in English (as "the science which treats of sensuous perception") until about 1800. The first use of the word in its modern philosophical sense—a sense to which I do not limit myself—is not recorded by the *Oxford English Dictionary* until 1832. The term was newly invented, but the possibility of discussing art in terms of its affective qualities was embryonic as early as Addison, and we would certainly need to look behind Addison to the third Earl of Shaftesbury's emphasis on sensibility and taste were we to attempt a history of the idea. We can, then, in fact we probably should, speak of Burke's *Philosophical Enquiry into the Origin of Our Ideas of the Sublime and the Beautiful* (1757) as a treatise on esthetics rather than as criticism. It is not even out of place to consider Addison's essays on the imagination in the same large context of esthetics.

In the *Spectator* papers on *Paradise Lost* (1712) Addison is practicing renaissance criticism. He discusses the poem from the standpoint of the rules for the epic (and finds it not wanting), and methodically pursues the prescribed course in examining the fable, characters, sentiments, and language, pointing out the faults under these headings, and then proceeding for twelve papers to discuss the "beauties." In his eleven essays of the same year on the "Pleasures of the Imagination," however, Addison is venturing into esthetics in the special sense in which I use the term. The emphasis is on the pleasure which natural objects as well as literary imitation of them may provide, rather than on generic form as a basis for judgment. The emphasis is not for that reason alone entirely remote from the best neoclassic doctrine, for the pseudo-Horatian dictum was, we must recall, "instruct *and delight*," and basic to Addison's criticism is the idea that it is the duty of the poet to generalize, that is, to imitate that unchanging nature which all men at all times know. We look back at least as far as Ronsard and Scaliger, just as we look ahead to Samuel Johnson, when we read:

> But because the mind of man requires something more perfect in matter, than what it finds there, and can never meet with any sight in nature which sufficiently answers its highest ideas of pleasantness; or, in other words, because the imagination can fancy to itself things more great, strange, or beautiful, than the eye ever saw, and is still sensible of some defect in what it has seen; on this account it is the part of a poet to humour the imagination in its own notions, by mending and perfecting nature where he describes a reality, and by adding greater beauties than are put together in nature, where he describes a fiction. (No. 418)

This is "imitation" in the truest sense of the complicated word so beloved of neoclassic critics; it is imitation in this sense that leads naturally to the investigation of the peculiar human qualities, possessed by some authors but not others, pursued in the numerous discussions of "genius." The genius is the man who has the ability to imitate truly and to transform himself "almost into a second deity" and mend and perfect nature, to see nature—the "nature of things"—as it really is behind the imperfect manifestations evident to our senses. The genius, then, is naturally one prone to the "great thoughts" which are the *sine qua non* of the noble rhetoric Longinus discussed in *On the Sublime*. The fact of his genius, of his capacity to see the eternal in nature, inspires the noble rhetoric; the great thoughts in noble rhetoric stir our feelings, and the imagination (still in the limited Addisonian sense of the image-making ability of the mind) is stimulated to see a higher reality.

It was not long before the rhetorical part of the progression of *great thoughts* : *rhetoric* : *feeling* took a secondary position or dropped out of sight. Nothing could stir great thoughts like great objects in nature (note the changing definition of that word!), therefore nothing could stir our feelings so profoundly as these great objects. Burke's *Philosophical Enquiry* is the crossroads. We have arrived at the "natural sublime," which the great genius was most able to imitate simply because he was most susceptible to great thoughts; but note that whereas in Longinus the author supplied the rhetoric which stimulated these profound feelings, in the new dispensation the feelings are stirred directly by the objects themselves, and the progression becomes *great objects* : *great thoughts* : *feeling* : *poetry*. From this position we do not have far to go to reach that "sense sublime / Of something far more deeply interfused" in nature which inspired Wordsworth, and before long we need only nature, not even great objects: "For me the meanest flower that blows can give / Thoughts that do often lie too deep for tears." We have, indeed, *esthetics,* for there becomes no way to discuss art (if one is discussing it from this standpoint) except in terms of feeling. The genres and the decorums associated with them become irrelevant.

Such seems to me the major movement of criticism during the eighteenth century, but there are so many byways, so many interruptions and deflections in the path which I have made seem all too plain, that to introduce any one of them without introducing them all would lead only to confusion and to the extending of this introduction to intolerable length. Neoclassicism, in the sense that men continued to resort to the Ancients for instruction and delight, persisted to the end of the century, as it persists today; in the truest sense of the word Burke was a neoclassicist, yet it was Burke who produced the most "romantic" esthetic document of the century. What we must keep in mind is that neoclassicism and romanticism are not polar. They are, rather, cultural constants. The change which I have described, great as it appears, was, finally, a change of emphasis.

Index of Authors, Titles, and First Lines[*]

---

[*] Authors' names are in **boldface** type; titles in *italics;* and first lines in roman.

1 2 3 4 5 6 7 8 9 10